PrincetonReview.com

P9-DCM-857
3 7901 00487 506 4

371. 9047 KRA ---- DEM
Kravets, Marybeth.
The K & W guide to colleges for students with learning differences

THE K&W GUIDE TO COLLEGES

FOR STUDENTS WITH LEARNING DIFFERENCES

15TH EDITION

MARYBETH KRAVETS, MA

AND IMY F. WAX, MS

JASPER COUNTY PUBLIC LIBRARY
DeMotte Branch
DeMotte, Indiana 46310-0016

Penguin Random House

The Princeton Review
110 East 42nd Street, 7th Floor
New York, NY 10017
Email: editorialsupport@review.com

©2021 by Kravets, Wax & Associates, Inc., and The Princeton Review, Inc.

Published in the United States by Penguin Random House LLC, New York, and in Canada by Random House of Canada, a division of Penguin Random House Ltd., Toronto.

Terms of Service: The Princeton Review Online Companion Tools ("Student Tools") for retail books are available for only the two most recent editions of that book. Student Tools may be activated only once per eligible book purchased for a total of 24 months of access. Activation of Student Tools more than once per book is in direct violation of these Terms of Service and may result in discontinuation of access to Student Tools Services.

ISBN: 978-0-525-57030-1
ISSN: 1934-4775

The Princeton Review is not affiliated with Princeton University.

If there are any important late-breaking developments, changes, or corrections to the materials in this book, we will post that information online in the Student Tools. Register your book and check your Student Tools to see if there are any updates posted there.

Editors: Aaron Riccio and Anna Goodlett
Production Editor: Liz Dacey
Production Artist: Deborah Weber
Printed in the United States of America.

10 9 8 7 6 5 4 3 2 1

15th Edition

Editorial
Rob Franek, Editor-in-Chief
David Soto, Director of Content Development
Stephen Koch, Survey Manager
Deborah Weber, Director of Production
Gabriel Berlin, Production Design Manager
Selena Coppock, Director of Editorial
Aaron Riccio, Senior Editor
Meave Shelton, Senior Editor
Christopher Chimera, Editor
Anna Goodlett, Editor
Eleanor Green, Editor
Orion McBean, Editor
Patricia Murphy, Editorial Assistant

Penguin Random House Publishing Team
Tom Russell, VP, Publisher
Alison Stoltzfus, Publishing Director
Amanda Yee, Associate Managing Editor
Ellen Reed, Production Manager
Suzanne Lee, Designer

From the Authors of The K&W Guide......

It's hard to believe that so many years have gone by since Marybeth and I were talking in her office at the high school. I had come in to see what she had in her files and approached her with questions. We discovered that we had a mutual desire to understand what college options were available for students with learning differences. Our children have grown. My children, with learning differences and Attention Deficit Disorder, have moved forward and found success in their lives as adults. Yet each time we update our edition of the K&W Guide, I remember my concerns about how to figure out where would be the best college environment. I wondered if there would be the right type of support for their specific learning challenges.

Both Marybeth and I were working with students who had a diagnosis, she as the college counselor at our local high school, myself as a psychotherapist in private practice. Colleges have come a long way since the day we tried to interest a publisher in our book and were told, "There is no audience for this type of resource book." Students are more informed about their learning issues and parents are more educated about how to understand their children's learning style. Colleges have so many different types and levels of support that it's become more important than ever to be able to distinguish what is and isn't necessary for the college student.

This book was created to help students feel confident about what they can expect from a college and for parents and professionals to be able to understand if the college is truly a "good match." It's very difficult for any parent to see their student as they are today and not for whom they hope they will be one day. It's very important that when looking for a college and a college support program that the parent takes a step back, looks at the child in front of them and recognizes what they need in the immediate, not years from the time they enter college.

It's much easier today, many editions later, for Marybeth and me to feel confident and comfortable approaching colleges and requesting detailed information. At one time there were only a select few. Today students have a large group from which to pick. But pick carefully. Look at courses required to enter, and courses required to graduate. Keep in mind that getting in is the first hurdle, staying in is the true challenge. We are so appreciative of Penguin Random House and The Princeton Review for their continued confidence and support in guaranteeing that we as authors of the K&W Guide are given the opportunity to write our book to serve a very deserving population of amazing learners. The K&W Guide is created by us with a great deal of passion and hope that families will feel they have an excellent resource to provide guidance and that their students will feel confident that there is a dream to dream.

Marybeth Kravets and Imy Wax
Co-authors of the *K&W Guide*

Dedication & Acknowledgments

This book is a labor of love. It is written to help individuals throughout the world who have been identified as having Attention Deficit Hyperactivity Disorder, Autism Spectrum Disorder or any other Learning Difference and who are seeking the right match and fit for life after high school. The KW Guide is an educational tool for all of the families, professionals, and friends who know someone who has a learning difference or other learning issues.

Our gratitude to the families of Marybeth Kravets and Imy Wax for their patience and support in this continued endeavor: Wendy, Steve, Allison, Connor, Isabel, Cooper, Mark, Sara, David, Robbie, Bennett, Cathy (in loving memory), Dan, Andrea, BJ, Matthew, Leia, Maise, Blue, Dr. Jack, Howard, Lisa, Bill, Niaya, Ellis, Gary, Tamar, Jordan, Eli, Debrah, Greg, Jamie, Joe, Benji, Goldie, Sadie, and Judy. To all of the colleges who provide services and programs to promote the educational endeavors and dreams of students with learning differences or Attention Deficit Hyperactivity Disorder or are on the Autism Spectrum.

We would also like to thank all of the contributors in the *K&W Guide* who share their thoughts and experiences with learning differences and Attention Deficit Hyperactivity Disorder. Our appreciation to Dr. Miriam Pike, Head of School for Wolcott College Prep High School, Chicago, Illinois and Stephanie Gordon for their professional guidance, and to our amazing research team, Linda Jamrozy, Emily Jann, Wendy Perlin and Carol Sharp for their support in our endeavor. Finally, we want thank The Princeton Review and Penguin Random House for their continued confidence in the publication of the K&W Guide to Colleges for Students with Learning Differences.

Contents

Get More **(Free)** Content at **PrincetonReview.com/cracking**

As easy as 1•2•3

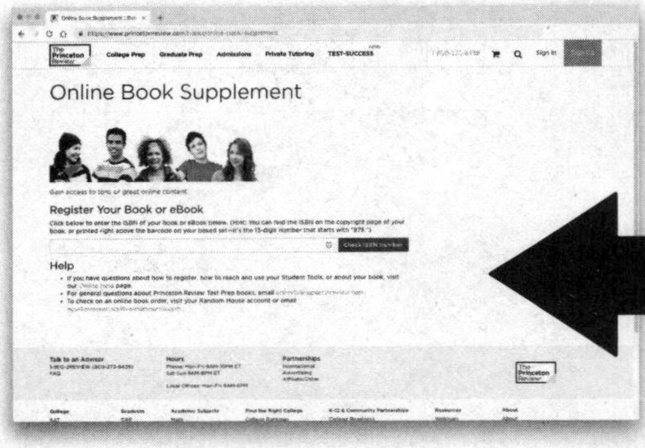

1 Go to PrincetonReview.com/cracking and enter the following ISBN for your book:
9780525570301

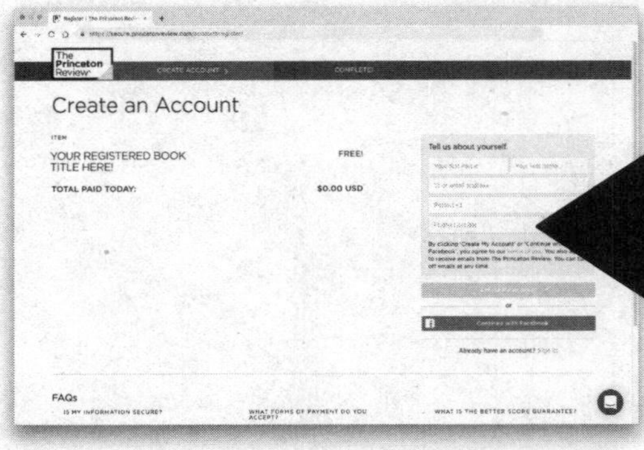

2 Answer a few simple questions to set up an exclusive Princeton Review account. *(If you already have one, you can just log in.)*

3 Enjoy access to your **FREE** content!

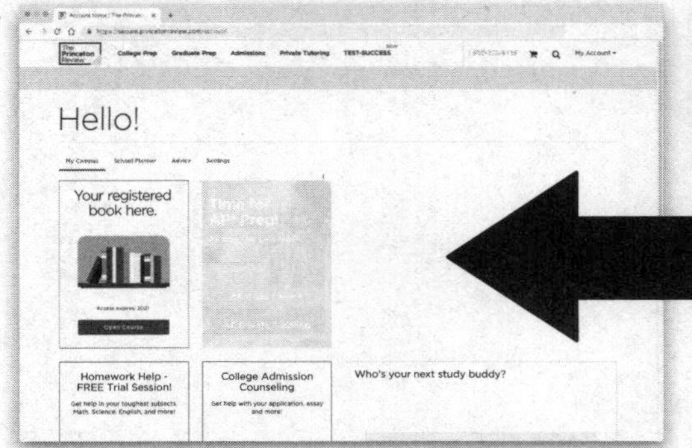

Once you've registered, you can...

- Take a full-length practice SAT
- Take a full-length practice ACT
- Access additional online resources, such as the Quick Contact Reference List, tips on getting ready (including a college interview preparation form), and an index of schools by support level
- Use our searchable rankings from *The Best 386 Colleges* to find out more information about your dream school
- Get valuable advice about applying to college
- Check for late-breaking updates or corrections to this edition

Need to report a potential **content** issue?

Contact **EditorialSupport@review.com**
and include:

- full title of the book
- ISBN
- page number

Need to report a **technical** issue?

Contact **TPRStudentTech@review.com**
and provide:

- your full name
- email address used to register the book
- full book title and ISBN
- Operating system (Mac/PC) and browser (Firefox, Safari, etc.)

Foreword

Supporting Neurodiverse Learners

by Dr. Arlene Tan

I am honored to have been given this opportunity to write the foreword for the 15th edition of the *K&W Guide to Colleges for Students with Learning Differences*. I spent about 20 years immersed in neuropsychological research, seeking to learn brain-behavior connections. My research interests evolved from developmental psychology, language and cognition, to models of recovery in traumatic brain injury. In the last 10 years as the Director of the Achieve Program at Southern Illinois University, it has been my privilege to work with college students who experience learning differently and help them develop strategies to adapt to learning independently.

Using a neuropsychological approach, I have sought to assist students in rediscovering themselves, to peel away the labels of their childhood diagnoses, and to help them better understand their strengths, styles, inherent weaknesses, and in particular, their habits and routines. I try to help students develop practical strategies to adapt to the rigors, expectations, and requirements of university curriculum as they move from a structured system of instruction, guidance, and extensive support, to a life of independent learning and self-sufficiency. Additionally, I have tried to help students become more familiar with the standards and expectations of college to help them better understand the type of support they may need, to raise their awareness and to work proactively. Most importantly, I try to impress on students that success in college is very much determined by their personal dedication to structure, consistency, and accountability.

Digital Age of Education

In recent years, higher education has been undergoing a significant transformation in how information is delivered. Now students entering college directly out of high school are expected to learn more, learn fast, and learn independently. For most, traditional lectures have been replaced by video content. Traditional textbooks are replaced by online articles and readings. Homework is assigned, completed, and submitted via websites and graded automatically. Interactions and connection with experienced faculty and professors who become mentors and who inspire learning are greatly reduced.

Nonetheless, with all the advancements in technology, the current understanding and delivery of accommodations for academic needs has never been better. Thanks to online content delivery, assistive technology is woven into the fabric of our daily lives. These days, videos, audio playback, text to speech, captioning, dictation, and voice commands are common conveniences, not accommodations. YouTube videos, discussion posts, blogs, and e-texts are gradually replacing traditional assessment methods: term papers, pop-quizzes, unit tests, and final exams.

These new teaching and learning methods support multi-approach, flexible, and hybrid learning that reach a wider audience of students with increased efficiency. Clearly, digital content delivery, technologically-based teaching, and independent learning are becoming the status quo. Digital education places a much higher responsibility of the learning process on the student. It greatly reduces the impact of the teacher and creates significant barriers to the connection between a teacher and student. This inhibits the teacher from ever knowing who the student is as a person and how the student learns.

The Burden of Self-Directed Learning

These new innovative and high-tech models of content delivery have the basic assumption that students are motivated self-directed learners and critical thinkers who, as digital natives, can navigate course expectations with minimal support, while managing their own time and priorities. Unfortunately, we find that students, particularly first-years, struggle to meet these expectations, having come from a high school experience that imposes rigid structure and directive instructional methods.

Moreover, self-directed learning online places a significant cognitive load on students' processing abilities, especially those who already experience challenges in comprehension, processing, attention, memory, reading, writing, and executive function. Often, these students experience frustration with mistakes in understanding instructions, confusing deadlines, and inability to comprehend digital content. When these students are not able to personally connect with their teacher, their frustrations can quickly lead to feeling overwhelmed, and put them at risk for stress, anxiety, and even depression.

Additionally, most young college students tend to reach out for help only when they find themselves in need of help. For many, asking for help is difficult. Sadly, few of these students truly understand how quickly they can fall behind, and by the time they realize it and try to seek help, they find it may be too late in the semester to salvage their grades.

Essential Considerations for Support in College

Self-directed learning, as required by the current direction in which higher education is moving, demands immense self-discipline and intrinsic motivation. It also requires the student to have good cognitive, language, and processing skills. Most essentially, students must have good executive function abilities to self-manage, plan, reflect, and critically evaluate. Students who experience learning differently or whose neuropsychological profile may be atypical, are often at a disadvantage in these circumstances and may benefit from additional support.

The K&W Guide to Colleges for Students with Learning Differences provides up-to-date information for the many programs available in colleges and universities across the United States. Each of these programs have their unique institutional missions, program objectives, operational directions, and services but are all vested in supporting and helping students. Being aware of the demands of college curriculum and honestly assessing the level of support the student may require are important factors in selecting the right fit of support and services in college. It is imperative that students now understand that it is their individual responsibility to establish some level of structure and be the primary party responsible for maintaining a close connection with the resource or support program at their school. This is a change from elementary and high school where time and classes are structured, and teachers actively seek out the student to provide support.

I have been privileged to celebrate the success of college students for many years. While there are many factors that contribute to these positive results, there are three key strategies.

Establish Structure: It is important to have structured time, like the 8-8-8 model of 8 hours of work, 8 hours of play, and 8 hours of sleep. College is a full-time job, and a typical workday, like a typical day in high school, is 8 hours long. Thus, the 8 hours of a college workday should comprise class time, homework time, and study time.

Access Support: Know where to go for support before any academic issues arise. Be sure to have documentation on file where accommodations and services are approved. Know what the procedure is to notify professors of any accommodations that are needed.

Be a self-advocate: Take personal responsibility. This is an interactive process that involves continued communication with all stakeholders. Open communication enables the student to receive timely and solution-based support. Continue to develop the mindset, skills and habits necessary for success.

College is a big step into independence, and it is critical to know how to structure your day, understand your challenges, and be willing to seek the appropriate assistance. Best of luck on this exciting journey.

Arlene A. Tan, Ph.D., has been the director of the Achieve Program (achieve.siu.edu) at Southern Illinois University in Carbondale, Illinois since 2010 and has spent over two decades immersed in neuropsychological research. She can be reached at 618-453-6135.

Introduction

Thoughts From . . . a Parent of a Student With Learning Challenges

When we began the process of exploring college options for our daughter, we had no idea what was involved in the process, let alone how best to support her as a student with learning differences.

What we came to understand was that like most things, it's a matter of preparation and care at the beginning. The first task was finding a professional educational consultant with the expertise that the co-author of this book, Marybeth Kravets, brings to the discussion. It had an immediate, calming effect on us all. And the second—equally important—was her sharing with us the book you're holding in your hands.

Finding the right college for our daughter was about identifying what was important for her, in terms of both available support and the social-cultural environment. This book—and the voluminous amount of knowledge its co-authors have—provided our daughter and our family with an inordinately helpful set of tools. The details herein helped us not only understand the critical differences in the levels of support afforded by different institutions. It helped us match those support levels with the things our daughter felt passionate about in academics and extracurricular activities. That made filtering through an extraordinary amount of information not only possible, but relatively easy. Above all else, this book made it clear where to focus.

Armed with that focus, and an exceptional amount of hard work, our daughter was accepted at every school to which she applied, including her first choice, the University of Denver.

We are so grateful for the book and hope you find it as helpful and focusing as we did.

Joel Grossman, CTO at Legacy.com, Chicago, Illinois
Amy Schiffman, President & CEO, Evolve Giving Group, Chicago, Illinois

Thoughts From . . . a Disability Attorney

10 Things College Students with Disabilities Need to Know About their Rights

by Matt Cohen

1. What schools are covered by the disability laws? Section 504 applies to all colleges and universities that receive federal financial assistance. The Americans with Disabilities Act applies to all colleges and universities unless they're religiously controlled. The IDEA (the special education law) does not apply to colleges and universities at all.

2. Can colleges and universities ask you about your medical conditions or disabilities in your admissions application? No. You may choose to disclose that you have a disability if you wish to, but you cannot be required to disclose your disability prior to admission.

3. Is it a good idea for me to disclose that I have a disability on my application? There is no right or wrong answer to this question. Some students decide it will be helpful to their application to disclose their disability and perhaps write about it. Others feel it may dispose the school to reject them.

4. Is it the responsibility of the college to determine if I have a disability and require accommodations after I have been accepted? No. Unlike public elementary and secondary schools, colleges and universities are not responsible for discovering if a student has a disability. The burden is on the student to self-disclose that they have a disability and are seeking accommodations. This is done by notifying the college disability services office. Sometimes students decide not to seek accommodations because they are embarrassed or feel they don't need them, then seek help when they are experiencing academic or disciplinary problems. It is generally more difficult to get help and to obtain the protection of the law if students wait until they are in trouble to disclose their disability and seek help.

5. Who is entitled to accommodations? A person is entitled to reasonable accommodations if they meet a number of criteria. First, the person must have an impairment that substantially limits a major life activity, such as physical, emotional, learning, reading, concentrating, thinking, and communicating. The college must broadly interpret the meaning of disability. Second, the person must meet the general qualifications for participation in the program or activity that they are applying for, either with or without accommodations. Third, they must establish that they: a) have a physical, emotional or learning, impairment, b) need specific accommodations, and c) that these accommodations are "reasonable."

6. What if my disability is controlled by medication or other measures that allow me to function normally? Schools are not allowed to use the effect of mitigating measures as a basis to deny eligibility.

7. What am I entitled to if I have a disability? You may not be entitled to the same level of services in college that you may have been eligible for in elementary and secondary school. You are only entitled to "reasonable accommodations," as long as they are not unduly burdensome and do not result in a fundamental alteration of the college's programs. These can include accommodations like extended time on deadlines and tests, preferential seating, access to

lecture notes, or use of assistive technology to allow the student to more easily complete the work. Colleges must engage in an interactive process with the student in determining if a requested accommodation is reasonable. The reasonable accommodations requirement also applies to campus housing. Campus housing accommodations may include being issued a single dorm room at the same cost as having a roommate and the ability to have an emotional support animal in campus housing. It also applies to the academic and recreational spaces on campus.

8. If I had an IEP or 504 Plan in high school, am I automatically entitled to accommodations in college? No. An IEP is terminated when a student graduates from high school and colleges use a 504 Plan to provide accommodations. The college has a right to review your clinical documentation and history of prior support. Prior eligibility does not automatically mean you will be eligible in college, but it does help to support the need for ongoing accommodations.

9. Does the absence of eligibility for an IEP or 504 Plan in high school disqualify me from receiving accommodations in college? No. It may make it harder to obtain the eligibility for accommodations, but not impossible. You will need to provide current clinical documentation of the disability along with an explanation of why the disability was not diagnosed and/or accommodated previously. Generally, you will need to provide recent testing that documents the presence of your disability, especially if you have learning disabilities, ADHD, or other disabilities that may change in their impact over time.

10. What can I do if the school denies that I have a disability or refuses my request for a specific accommodation? If that happens, you have the right to file a grievance or appeal within the college and you can also file a complaint with the U.S. Department of Education Office for Civil Rights or the U.S. Department of Justice Civil Rights Division, Disability Rights Unit.

Matt Cohen is the founder of Matt Cohen and Associates, a Chicago based disability rights law firm, and has almost 40 years of experience advocating on behalf of people with disabilities. Matt can be reached at 866-787-9270 or mdcspedlaw@gmail.com. His website is www.mattcohenandassociates.com.

General Guidelines for Documentation of a Learning Disability

1. A comprehensive psychoeducational or neuropsychological evaluation that provides a diagnosis of a learning disability must be submitted. The report should indicate the current status and impact of the learning disability in an academic setting. If another diagnosis is applicable (e.g., ADHD, mood disorder), it should be stated.

2. The evaluation must be conducted by a professional who is certified/licensed in the area of learning disabilities, such as a clinical or educational psychologist, school psychologist, and neuropsychologist or learning disabilities specialist. The evaluator's name, title, and professional credentials and affiliation should be provided.

3. The evaluation must be based on a comprehensive assessment battery:

   Aptitude: Average broad cognitive functioning must be demonstrated on an individually administered intelligence test, preferably administered during high school or beyond, such as the WAIS, WISC, Woodcock-Johnson Cognitive Battery, and Kaufman Adolescent and Adult Intelligence Test. Subtest scores, regular and scaled, should be listed.

   Academic Achievement: A comprehensive academic achievement battery, such as the WJ and WIAT, should document achievement deficits relative to potential. The battery should include current levels of academic functioning in relevant areas, such as reading, oral and written language, and mathematics. Standard scores and percentiles for administered subtests should be stated. Specific achievement tests can also be included, such as the Nelson-Denny Reading Test and Test of Written Language (TOWL), as well as informal measures (e.g., informal reading inventories and writing samples).

   Information Processing: Specific areas of information processing (e.g., short- and long-term memory, auditory and visual perception/processing, executive functioning) should be assessed.

   Social-Emotional Assessment: To rule out a primary emotional basis for learning difficulties and provide information needed to establish appropriate services, a social-emotional assessment (using formal assessment instruments and/or clinical interview) should be conducted.

   Clinical Summary: A diagnostic summary should present a diagnosis of a specific learning disability; provide impressions of the testing situation; interpret the testing data; and indicate how patterns in the student's cognitive ability, achievement, and information processing reflect the presence of a learning disability. Recommendations should be provided for specific accommodations based on disability-related deficits. For students just graduating high school, an evaluation reflecting current levels of academic skills should have been administered while in high school; for students who have been out of school for a number of years, documentation will be considered on a case-by-case basis. Additional documents that do not constitute sufficient documentation, but that may be submitted in addition to a psychological, psychoeducational or neuropsychological evaluation include an individualized education plan (IEP), a 504 plan, and/or an educational assessment.

General Guidelines for Documentation of Attention Deficit Hyperactivity Disorder (ADHD)

Students requesting accommodations and services on the basis of an Attention Deficit Hyperactivity Disorder (ADHD) are required to submit documentation that establishes a disability and supports the need for the accommodations recommended and requested.

1. A *qualified* professional must conduct the evaluation. Those who conduct the assessment, make the diagnosis of ADHD, detail symptoms, provide relevant history, determine functional limitations, and provide recommendations for accommodation must be licensed mental health professionals. Primary care or general practice physicians are not considered qualified to complete an ADHD evaluation.

2. Documentation must be current (typically within three years). The provision of accommodations is based upon an assessment of the current impact of the student's disability on learning in the college setting.

3. Documentation *must* be comprehensive. Requirements for any diagnostic report are:

   - A medical or clinical diagnosis of ADHD based on DSM criteria
   - Assessment/testing profile and interpretation of the assessment instruments used that supports the diagnosis. Acceptable measures include objective measures of attention and discrimination or valid and reliable observer or self-report, such as the following:
     - Conner's Continuous Performance Task (CPT)
     - Test of Variables of Attention (TOVA)
     - Behavioral Assessment System for Children
     - Conner's Adult ADHD Rating Scale (CAARS)
     - CAARS-L; the long version of the self-report form
     - CARRS-O; the observer form
     - Brown Attention Deficit Disorder Scale
   - A clear description of the functional limitations in the educational setting, specifying the major life activities that are affected to a substantial degree because of the disability
   - Relevant history, including developmental, family, medical, psychosocial, pharmacological, educational and employment (ADHD is by definition first exhibited in childhood, so the assessment should include historical information establishing symptoms of ADHD throughout childhood, adolescence, and into adulthood)
   - A description of the specific symptoms manifesting themselves at the present time that may affect the student's academic performance
   - Medications the student is currently taking, as well as a description of any limitations that may persist even with medication

General Guidelines for Documentation of Autism Spectrum Disorder

A. Persistent deficits in social communication and social interaction across multiple contexts, as manifested by the following, currently or by history:

1. Deficits in social-emotional reciprocity, such as abnormal social approach and failure of normal back-and-forth conversation; reduced sharing of interests, emotions, or affect; and failure to initiate or respond to social interactions.
2. Deficits in nonverbal communicative behaviors used for social interaction, such as poorly integrated verbal and nonverbal communication; abnormalities in eye contact and body language or deficits in understanding and use of gestures; and a total lack of facial expressions and nonverbal communication.
3. Deficits in developing, maintaining, and understanding relationships, such as difficulty adjusting behavior to suit various social contexts; difficulty in sharing imaginative play or in making friends; and absence of interest in peers.

Specify current severity:

Severity is based on social communication impairments and restricted, repetitive patterns of behavior.

B. Restricted, repetitive patterns of behavior, interests, or activities, as manifested by at least two of the following, currently or by history (examples are illustrative, not exhaustive; see text):

1. Stereotyped or repetitive motor movements, use of objects, or speech (e.g., simple motor stereotypes, lining up toys or flipping objects, echolalia, idiosyncratic phrases).
2. Insistence on sameness, inflexible adherence to routines, or ritualized patterns of verbal or nonverbal behavior (e.g., extreme distress at small changes, difficulties with transitions, rigid thinking patterns, greeting rituals, need to take same route or eat same food every day).
3. Highly restricted, fixated interests that are abnormal in intensity or focus (e.g., strong attachment to or preoccupation with unusual objects, excessively circumscribed or perseverative interests).
4. Hyper- or hyporeactivity to sensory input or unusual interest in sensory aspects of the environment (e.g., apparent indifference to pain/temperature, adverse response to specific sounds or textures, excessive smelling or touching of objects, visual fascination with lights or movement).

Specify current severity:

Severity is based on social communication impairments and restricted, repetitive patterns of behavior.

C. Symptoms must be present in the early developmental period (but may not become fully manifest until social demands exceed limited capacities or may be masked by learned strategies in later life).

D. Symptoms cause clinically significant impairment in social, occupational, or other important areas of current functioning.

E. These disturbances are not better explained by intellectual disability (intellectual developmental disorder) or global developmental delay. Intellectual disability and Autism Spectrum Disorder frequently co-occur; to make comorbid diagnoses of Autism Spectrum Disorder and intellectual disability, social communication should be below that expected for general developmental level.

Note: Individuals with a well-established DSM diagnosis of autistic disorder, Asperger's disorder, or pervasive developmental disorder not otherwise specified should be given the diagnosis of Autism Spectrum Disorder. Individuals who have marked deficits in social communication, but whose symptoms do not otherwise meet criteria for Autism Spectrum Disorder, should be evaluated for social (pragmatic) communication disorder.

Specify if:

- With or without accompanying intellectual impairment
- With or without accompanying language impairment
- Associated with a known medical or genetic condition or environmental factor
- Associated with another neurodevelopmental, mental, or behavioral disorder
- With catatonia (refer to the criteria for catatonia associated with another mental disorder)

How to Use This Guide

The *K&W Guide to Colleges for Students with Learning Differences* includes information on colleges and universities that offer services to students with learning differences such as specific learning disabilities, Attention Deficit Hyperactivity Disorder or Asperger Syndrome Disorder.

Learning Disability (LD): A learning disability is a neurological condition that interferes with an individual's ability to store, process, or produce information.

Attention Deficit Hyperactive Disorder (ADHD): A learning disability in which affected individuals generally have challenges paying attention or concentrating. They can't seem to follow directions and are easily bored or frustrated with tasks. They also tend to move constantly and are impulsive, not stopping to think before they act. These behaviors are generally common in children, but they occur more often than usual and are more severe in a child with ADHD.

Autism Spectrum Disorder (ASD): A group of developmental disabilities that can cause significant social, communication and behavioral challenges.

No two colleges are identical in the programs or services they provide, but there are some similarities. For the purpose of this guide, the services and programs at the various colleges have been grouped into three categories.

Structured Programs (SP)

Colleges with Structured Programs offer the most comprehensive services for students with learning disabilities. The director and/or staff are certified in learning disabilities or related areas. The director is actively involved in the admission decision and, often, the criteria for admission may be more flexible than general admission requirements. Services are highly structured, and students are involved in developing plans to meet their particular learning styles and needs. Often students in Structured Programs sign a contract agreeing to actively participate in the program. There is usually an additional fee for the enhanced services. Students who have participated in a Structured Program or Structured Services in high school such as the Learning Disabilities Resource Program, individualized or modified coursework, tutorial assistance, academic monitoring, note-takers, test accommodations, or skill classes might benefit from exploring colleges with Structured Programs or Coordinated Services.

Coordinated Services (CS)

Coordinated Services differ from Structured Programs in that the services are not as comprehensive. These services are provided by at least one certified learning disability specialist. The staff is knowledgeable and trained to provide assistance to students to develop strategies for their individual needs. The director of the program or services may be involved in the admission decision, be in a position to offer recommendations to the admissions office on the potential success of the applicant, or to assist the students with an appeal if denied admission to the college. Receiving these services generally requires specific documentation of the learning disability—students are encouraged to self-identify prior to entry. Students voluntarily request accommodations or services in the Coordinated Services category, and there may be specific skills courses or remedial classes available or required for students with learning disabilities who are admitted probationally or conditionally. High school students who may have enrolled in some modified or remedial courses, utilized test accommodations, or required tutorial assistance, but who typically requested services only as needed, might benefit from exploring colleges with Coordinated Services or Services.

Services (S)

Services are the least comprehensive of the three categories. Colleges offering Services generally are complying with the federal mandate requiring reasonable accommodations to all students with appropriate and current documentation. These colleges routinely require documentation of the disability in order for the students with LD/ADHD to receive accommodations. Staff and faculty actively support the students by providing basic services to meet the needs of the students. Services are requested on a voluntarily basis, and there may be some limitations as to what is reasonable and the degree of services available. Sometimes, just the small size of the student body allows for the necessary personal attention to help students with learning disabilities succeed in college. High school students who require minimum accommodations, but who would find comfort in knowing that services are available, knowing who the contact person is, and knowing that this person is sensitive to students with learning disabilities, might benefit from exploring colleges providing Services or Coordinated Services.

Categories Used to Describe the Programs and Services at Colleges and Universities

The K&W Guide to Colleges for Students with Learning Differences includes information on colleges and universities that offer services to students with learning differences such as specific learning disabilities, Attention Deficit Hyperactivity Disorder or Asperger Syndrome Disorder.

Each college in the book is covered on two pages and is arranged alphabetically by state. The first page of each spread begins with pertinent **PROGRAMS/SERVICES FOR STUDENTS WITH LEARNING DIFFERENCES** that describe the learning disability program or services. This is followed by an **ADMISSIONS** section that details special procedures and requirements for enrollment, and then an **Additional Information** portion that outlines specific information about services offered. At the bottom of the first page, **ADMISSIONS INFO FOR STUDENTS WITH LEARNING DIFFERENCES** emphasizes what documentation is required and where it needs to be submitted.

On the second page, you'll see both a map and a tab that pinpoint which state the school is located it, and what cities are in the immediate area. You'll also get **GENERAL ADMISSIONS** information, and a list of **FINANCIAL AID** and **CAMPUS LIFE** offerings. Note, too, that in the **ACCOMMODATIONS OR SERVICES** section, that schools determine services *individually*. Finally, in the grey sidebars on both pages, you'll find relevant facts and figures about:

- the **CAMPUS** environment
  - Rural (in or near a rural community, population under 5,000)
  - Village (in or near a small town, population 5,000–24,999)
  - Town (in or near a large town, population 25,000–74,999)
  - City (in the metropolitan area of a small/medium city, population 75,000–299,999)
  - Metropolis (in the metropolitan area of a major city, population 300,000+)
- the **STUDENT** demographics
- the **FINANCIAL FACTS** on tuition costs
- **GENERAL ADMISSION** application fees and registration dates, and common ACT/SAT score ranges
- a sense of class sizes in **ACADEMICS**
- the various **ACCOMMODATIONS** offered
- and whether waivers are allowed in **COLLEGE GRADUATION REQUIREMENTS**

The authors have made a conscientious effort to provide the most current information possible. However, names, costs, dates, policies, and other information are always subject to change, and colleges of particular interest or importance to the reader should be contacted directly for verification of the data. This is especially true in the wake of COVID-19, where many schools that normally require test scores to be submitted have chosen to temporarily become test optional, or to make other alterations to their standard admission policies. If a school has temporary testing changes, those are listed in the "SAT/ACT Required" field, but you should always check with the school to make sure there have not been any additional changes.

School Profiles

Auburn University at Montgomery

P.O. Box 244023, Montgomery, AL 36124-4023 • Admissions: 334-244-3615 • Fax: 334-244-3795 **Support: S**

CAMPUS	
Type of school	Public
Environment	City
STUDENTS	
Undergrad enrollment	4,435
% male/female	36/64
% from out of state	6
% frosh live on campus	45
FINANCIAL FACTS	
Annual in-state tuition	$7,992
Annual out-of-state tuition	$17,952
Room and board	$10,296
Required fees	$868
GENERAL ADMISSIONS INFO	
Application fee	$0
Regular application deadline	8/1
Nonfall registration	Yes
Range SAT EBRW	485–560
Range SAT Math	470–550
Range ACT Composite	19–23
ACADEMICS	
Student/faculty ratio	16:1
% students returning for sophomore year	66
Most classes have 20–29 students.	

Programs/Services for Students with Learning Differences

AUM and the Center for Disability Services assists in the implementation of special accommodations in academic and campus life activities. It is the mission of AUM to make educational opportunities available to everyone. The Center for Disability Services (CDS) provides academic support services to students with disabilities. By providing opportunities for enhancing educational, technological, vocational and self-advocacy skills, CDS helps individuals with disabilities to become more self-reliant, self-motivated, and more successful citizens of the community. Students with a documented disability simply register with CDS prior to the beginning of each semester that they are enrolled at AUM. Students needing accommodation may contact the center regarding documentation guidelines and services.

Admissions

To be fully admitted applicants must have a 3.0 GPA without ACT or SAT or 18 ACT or 940 SAT score and 2.3 GPA. Regular applicants who do not meet admission criteria are considered for the Bridge Program with no special application. If applying as a Bridge student the GPA can be between 2.3–2.99 without test scores, otherwise a minimum 17 ACT or 820 SAT score and 2.3 GPA is required. ACT or SAT scores are optional and if submitted, AUM will superscore. Even if a student does not fully meet all the requirements for admission to Auburn Montgomery, the student still may find a home through the Bridge Program. This program is designed for students who meet specific academic criteria in order to enroll in courses designed to prepare them for full admission.

Additional Information

The Bridge program provides qualified students with extra academic support for one semester prior to gaining full admission to AUM. During the Bridge semester, students will be enrolled in courses designed specifically for bridging the gap to a continued and successful college career. Bridge courses consist of a University Success course, as well as a Math and/or English course. Throughout the semester, faculty and staff on the Bridge team will assist students by implementing skill-building exercises for success in college. The Bridge program is designed to help familiarize students with campus resources, while showing students how to thrive at AUM.

ADMISSIONS INFO FOR STUDENTS WITH LEARNING DIFFERENCES

Phone: 334-244-3631 • Fax: 334-244-3907 • Email: tmassey2@aum.edu

SAT/ACT required: No
Interview required: No
Essay required: No
Additional application required: Contract after admission
Documentation submitted to: Center for Disability Services

Special Ed. HS course work accepted: Yes
Separate application required for Programs/Services: No
Documentation required for:
LD: Psychoeducational based on DSM standards, to include IQ and achievement standard test scores.
ADHD: Psychoeducational based on DSM standards, to include IQ and achievement and behavioral checklist scores.
ASD: Neuropsychological and/or Psychoeducational evaluation based on DSM standards.

Auburn University at Montgomery

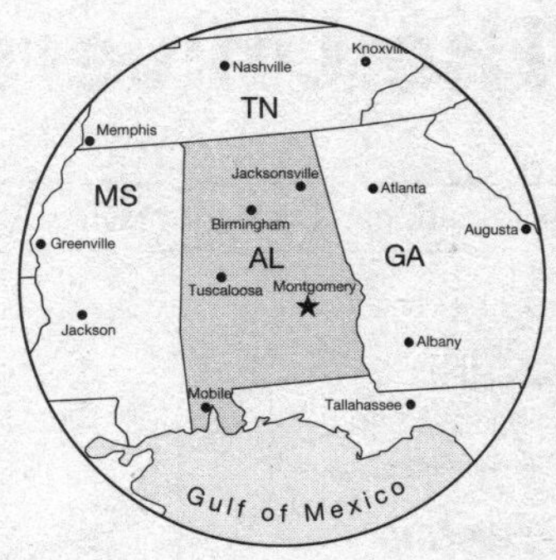

Alabama

General Admissions

Very important factors include: rigor of secondary school record, academic GPA, standardized test scores. High school diploma is required and GED is accepted. *Academic units recommended:* 3 English, 3 math, 2 science, 2 science labs, 2 foreign language, 2 social studies, 2 history, 2 academic electives. Institution is test optional for entering fall 2021. Check admissions website for updates.

Accommodations or Services

Accommodations are decided upon an individual basis after a thorough review of appropriate, current documentation. The accommodations requests must be supported through the documentation provided and must be logically linked to the current impact of the condition on academic functioning.

Financial Aid

Students should submit: FAFSA. *Need-based scholarships/grants offered:* College/university scholarship or grant aid from institutional funds; Federal Pell; Private scholarships; SEOG; State scholarships/grants. *Loan aid offered:* Direct PLUS loans; Direct Subsidized Stafford Loans; Direct Unsubsidized Stafford Loans. Federal Work-Study Program available. Institutional employment available.

Campus Life

Activities: Campus Ministries; Choral groups; Dance; Drama/theater; International Student Organization; Literary magazine; Musical theater; Student government; Student newspaper. **Organizations:** 52 registered organizations, 12 honor societies, 6 religious organizations, 3 fraternities, 6 sororities. **Athletics (Intercollegiate):** *Men:* baseball, basketball, cheerleading, soccer, tennis. *Women:* basketball, cheerleading, soccer, softball, tennis.

ACCOMMODATIONS	
Allowed in exams:	
Calculators	Yes
Dictionary	Yes
Computer	Yes
Spell-checker	Yes
Extended test time	Yes
Scribe	Yes
Proctors	Yes
Oral exams	Yes
Note-takers	Yes
Support services for students with:	
LD	Yes
ADHD	Yes
ASD	Yes
Distraction-reduced environment	Yes
Recording of lecture allowed	Yes
Reading technology	Yes
Audio books	Yes
Other assistive technology	Yes
Priority registration	Yes
Added costs of services:	
For LD	No
For ADHD	No
For ASD	No
LD specialists	No
ADHD & ASD coaching	Yes
ASD specialists	No
Professional tutors	No
Peer tutors	Yes
Max. hours/week for services	Varies
How professors are notified of student approved accommodations	Student

COLLEGE GRADUATION REQUIREMENTS	
Course waivers allowed	No
Course substitutions allowed	Yes
In what courses: Math	

The University of Alabama in Huntsville

301 Sparkman Drive, Huntsville, AL 35899 • Admissions: 256-824-2773 • Fax: 256-824-4539 **Support: S**

CAMPUS

Type of school	Public
Environment	City

STUDENTS

Undergrad enrollment	7,785
% male/female	58/42
% from out of state	20
% frosh live on campus	66

FINANCIAL FACTS

Annual in-state tuition	$9,730
Annual out-of-state tuition	$22,126
Room and board	$10,400
Required fees	$1,392

GENERAL ADMISSIONS INFO

Application fee	$30
Regular application deadline	Rolling
Nonfall registration accepted	Yes
Admission may be deferred	Yes
Range SAT EBRW	470–570
Range SAT Math	510–720
Range ACT Composite	25–31

ACADEMICS

Student/faculty ratio	18:1
% students returning for sophomore year	83

Most classes have 20–29 students.

Programs/Services for Students with Learning Differences

The Office of Student Development Services offers a variety of services and accommodations to assist students with disabilities in eliminating barriers they encounter in pursuing higher education. The office's main objective is to provide access to academic, social, cultural, recreational, and housing opportunities at the university. A student is considered registered with Disability Support Services (DSS) when they have completed all application paperwork, their intake/registration paperwork has been approved, and they have had an interview with a 504 Coordinator. The services offered through this office encourage students to achieve and maintain autonomy.

Admissions

Each applicant is evaluated based on individual merit and demonstrated success in a rigorous academic environment. High school coursework, grade point average, and ACT/SAT scores are weighed heavily; however, these criteria do not constitute the entire foundation for an admission decision. An applicant with a grade point average of 2.9 and a composite score of 20 on the ACT or an equivalent SAT score, for example, is considered a strong candidate for admission. UAH does not require letters of recommendation or an essay for admission consideration. There is no special LD admission process. If a student becomes subject to academic suspension, the suspension is for a minimum of one term, and the student must petition the Admissions Committee for approval to reenroll.

Additional Information

The Academic Coaching Program helps UAH students improve their performance in and out of class by offering sessions on study skills, organization skills, and management strategies. Academic coaches can help students learn how to prioritize and manage their time, set clear and relevant goals, and utilize strategies that reflect their learning preferences. The Peer Assisted Study Sessions (PASS) Program offers regularly scheduled review sessions led by PASS leaders who have previously taken the course and been trained to tutor.

ADMISSIONS INFO FOR STUDENTS WITH LEARNING DIFFERENCES

Phone: 256-824-1997 • Fax: 256-824-5655 • Email: dssproctor@uah.edu

SAT/ACT required: Yes
Interview required: No
Essay required: No
Additional application required: No
Documentation submitted to: Disability Support Services

Special Ed. HS course work accepted: Yes
Separate application required for Programs/Services: Yes
Documentation required for:
LD: Psychoeducational evaluation
ADHD: Psychoeducational evaluation
ASD: Psychoeducational evaluation

The University of Alabama in Huntsville

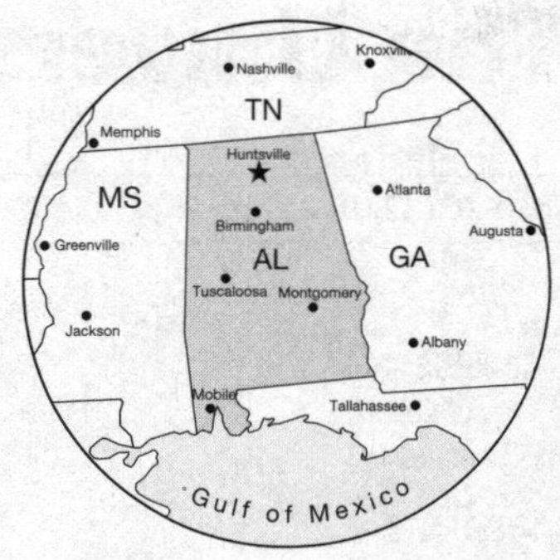

General Admissions

Very important factors considered include: academic GPA, standardized test scores. *Other factors considered include:* level of applicant's interest. *Freshman admission requirements:* High school diploma is required and GED is accepted. *Academic units required:* 4 English, 3 math, 3 science, 4 social studies, 6 academic electives. *Academic units recommended:* 4 English, 4 math, 4 science, 2 science labs, 2 foreign language, 4 social studies, 6 academic electives. Requires applicants to submit either the SAT or ACT.

Accommodations or Services

Accommodations are decided upon an individual basis after a thorough review of appropriate, current documentation. The accommodations requests must be supported through the documentation provided and must be logically linked to the current impact of the condition on academic functioning. A letter of accommodation (LOA) is sent to students by email and students must have the LOA signed by the professor. The student is responsible for getting the LOA back to the Disability Support Services.

Financial Aid

Students should submit: FAFSA. Applicants will be notified of awards on a rolling basis beginning 4/1. The Princeton Review suggests that all financial aid forms be submitted as soon as possible after October 1. *Need-based scholarships/grants offered:* College/university scholarship or grant aid from institutional funds; Federal Nursing Scholarships; Federal Pell; Private scholarships; SEOG; State scholarships/grants. *Loan aid offered:* Direct PLUS loans; Direct Subsidized Stafford Loans; Direct Unsubsidized Stafford Loans. Federal Work-Study Program available. Institutional employment available.

Campus Life

Activities: Campus Ministries; Choral groups; Concert band; Dance; Drama/theater; International Student Organization; Jazz band; Model UN; Music ensembles; Musical theater; Opera; Pep band; Student government; Student newspaper. **Organizations:** 52 registered organizations, 24 honor societies, 5 religious organizations. 7 fraternities, 4 sororities. **Athletics (Intercollegiate):** *Men:* baseball, basketball, cheerleading, cross-country, ice hockey, soccer, tennis, track/field (outdoor), track/field (indoor). *Women:* basketball, cheerleading, cross-country, soccer, softball, tennis, track/field (outdoor), track/field (indoor), volleyball. On-Campus Highlights: Charger Union, University Fitness Center, Charger Village, Central Campus Residence Hall, Shelby Center.

ACCOMMODATIONS

Allowed in exams:	
Calculators	Yes
Dictionary	Yes
Computer	Yes
Spell-checker	Yes
Extended test time	Yes
Scribe	Yes
Proctors	Yes
Oral exams	Yes
Note-takers	Yes
Support services for students with:	
LD	Yes
ADHD	Yes
ASD	Yes
Distraction-reduced environment	Yes
Recording of lecture allowed	Yes
Reading technology	Yes
Audio books	No
Other assistive technology	Yes
Priority registration	Yes
Added costs of services:	
For LD	No
For ADHD	No
For ASD	No
LD specialists	No
ADHD & ASD coaching	Yes
ASD specialists	No
Professional tutors	No
Peer tutors	No
Max. hours/week for services	Unlimited
How professors are notified of student approved accommodations	Student and Director

COLLEGE GRADUATION REQUIREMENTS

Course waivers allowed	Yes
In what courses: Individual case-by-case decisions	
Course substitutions allowed	Yes
In what courses: Individual case-by-case decisions	

The University of Alabama—Tuscaloosa

Box 870132, Tuscaloosa, AL 35487-0132 • Admissions: 205-348-5666 • Fax: 205-348-9046 **Support: S**

CAMPUS

Type of school	Public
Environment	City

STUDENTS

Undergrad enrollment	31,900
% male/female	45/55
% from out of state	61
% frosh live on campus	95

FINANCIAL FACTS

Annual in-state tuition	$10,780
Annual out-of-state tuition	$30,250
Room and board	$10,836
Required fees	$0

GENERAL ADMISSIONS INFO

Application fee	$40
Regular application deadline	Rolling
Nonfall registration	Yes
Admission may be deferred	Yes
Range SAT EBRW	550–660
Range SAT Math	530–680
Range ACT Composite	23–31

ACADEMICS

Student/faculty ratio	20:1
% students returning for sophomore year	87

Most classes have 20–29 students.

Programs/Services for Students with Learning Differences

Students with disabilities can access services and accommodations through the Office of Disability Services. The ODS provides individualized academic accommodations and support services and encourages students to be self-advocates in seeking support. Students need to provide appropriate documentation to be eligible for accommodations and services. Additionally, students must formally request to meet with ODS and then, once approved, the student must meet with each professor to present the official letter of accommodations and to determine how each professor will implement the appropriate accommodations.

Admissions

All students must meet regular entrance requirements. An ACT and/or SAT is required. (A writing score is not required but can be reviewed if a student does not meet regular admissions standards as set forth by the ACT/SAT and GPA requirements.) An applicant with a 2.9 GPA and 20 ACT or SAT equivalent is considered a strong candidate for admission. U of A looks for 4 years English, 4 years social sciences, 3 years math, 3 years natural sciences, 1 unit of foreign language, and 4 units of other academic courses in fine arts, computer literacy, mathematics, natural sciences, and foreign language. Students who exceed the minimum number of units in math, natural sciences, or foreign language will be given additional consideration. An interview with the Office of Disability Services is recommended. Applicants who are denied admission to the University may appeal the admission decision if they have academic achievements, personal achievements, or special circumstances that were not considered when the admissions decision was made. The deans of the university may, upon appeal, waive or modify conditions of admission for individual freshman and transfer applicants.

Additional Information

The Capstone Center for Student Success (CCSS) provides a network of support services including tutorial assistance, supplemental instruction, academic peer mentoring, study skills workshops, and academic coaching and advising. The Crimson Edge is a two-semester program that helps students manage the transition to a university academic environment. Students in this category are not on probation but are limited to 15 credit hours during their first semester and must enroll in an academic support class.

ADMISSIONS INFO FOR STUDENTS WITH LEARNING DIFFERENCES

Phone: 205-348-4285 • Fax: 205-348-0804 • Email: vanessa.goepel@ua.edu

SAT/ACT required: Yes
Interview required: No
Essay required: No
Additional application required: Yes
Documentation submitted to: Office of Disability Services

Special Ed. HS course work accepted: Yes
Separate application required for Programs/Services: Yes
Documentation required for:
LD: Psychoeducational evaluation
ADHD: Psychoeducational evaluation
ASD: Psychoeducational evaluation

The University of Alabama—Tuscaloosa

Alabama

General Admissions

Very important factors include: rigor of secondary school record, academic GPA, standardized test scores. *Important factors include:* class rank. *Other factors include:* application essay, recommendation(s), interview, extracurricular activities, talent/ability, character/personal qualities, first generation, alumni/ae relation, volunteer work, work experience. High school diploma is required and GED is accepted. *Academic units required:* 4 English, 3 math, 3 science, 2 science labs, 1 foreign language, 4 social studies, 5 academic electives. *Academic units recommended:* 4 English, 3 math, 3 science, 2 science labs, 2 foreign language, 4 social studies, 5 academic electives. Requires applicants to submit either the SAT or ACT.

Accommodations or Services

Accommodations are decided upon an individual basis after a thorough review of appropriate, current documentation. The accommodations requests must be supported through the documentation provided and must be logically linked to the current impact of the condition on academic functioning.

Financial Aid

Students should submit: FAFSA; Application for Academic Scholarships. *Need-based scholarships/grants offered:* College/university scholarship or grant aid from institutional funds; Federal Nursing Scholarships; Federal Pell; Private scholarships; SEOG; State scholarships/grants. *Loan aid offered:* Direct PLUS loans; Direct Subsidized Stafford Loans; Direct Unsubsidized Stafford Loans. Institutional employment available.

Campus Life

Activities: Campus Ministries; Choral groups; Concert band; Dance; Drama/theater; International Student Organization; Jazz band; Literary magazine; Marching band; Model UN; Music ensembles; Musical theater; Opera; Pep band; Radio station; Student government; Student newspaper; Student-run film society; Symphony orchestra; Television station. **Organizations:** 583 registered organizations, 44 honor societies, 73 religious organizations, 43 fraternities, 24 sororities. **Athletics (Intercollegiate):** *Men:* baseball, basketball, cross-country, diving, football, golf, swimming, tennis, track/field (outdoor), track/field (indoor). *Women:* basketball, crew/rowing, cross-country, diving, golf, gymnastics, soccer, softball, swimming, tennis, track/field (outdoor), track/field (indoor), volleyball.

ACCOMMODATIONS

Allowed in exams:	
Calculators	Yes
Dictionary	Yes
Computer	Yes
Spell-checker	Yes
Extended test time	Yes
Scribe	Yes
Proctors	Yes
Oral exams	Yes
Note-takers	Yes
Support services for students with:	
LD	Yes
ADHD	Yes
ASD	Yes
Distraction-reduced environment	Yes
Recording of lecture allowed	Yes
Reading technology	Yes
Audio books	Yes
Other assistive technology	Yes
Priority registration	Yes
Added costs of services:	
For LD	No
For ADHD	No
For ASD	No
LD specialists	No
ADHD & ASD coaching	Yes
ASD specialists	Yes
Professional tutors	Yes
Peer tutors	Yes
Max. hours/week for services	Varies
How professors are notified of student approved accommodations	Student

COLLEGE GRADUATION REQUIREMENTS

Course waivers allowed	No
Course substitutions allowed	Yes
In what courses: Case by case basis	

University of Alaska Anchorage

3211 Providence Drive, Anchorage, AK 99508-8046 • Admissions: 907-786-1480 • Fax: 907-786-4888 **Support: S**

CAMPUS

Type of school	Public
Environment	City

STUDENTS

Undergrad enrollment	9,261
% male/female	42/58
% from out of state	7

FINANCIAL FACTS

Annual in-state tuition	$5,616
Annual out-of-state tuition	$19,200
Room and board	$9,868
Required fees	$1,398

GENERAL ADMISSIONS INFO

Application fee	$0
Regular application deadline	7/15
Nonfall registration	Yes
Admission may be deferred	Yes
Range SAT EBRW	520–620
Range SAT Math	500–600
Range ACT Composite	17–24

ACADEMICS

Student/faculty ratio	11:1
% students returning for sophomore year	66

Most classes have 10–19 students.

Programs/Services for Students with Learning Differences

The University of Alaska—Anchorage provides equal opportunities for students who have disabilities. Academic support services are available to students with learning disabilities. Staff trained to work with students with disabilities coordinate these services. To allow time for service coordination, students are encouraged to contact the Disability Support Services (DSS) office several weeks before the beginning of each semester. Ongoing communication with the staff throughout the semester is encouraged.

Admissions

All students must meet the same admission requirements. Standardized tests (ACT/SAT) are not used for admission but are used for placement in math and writing courses. The minimum GPA for admission is 2.5. However, applicants with 2.0–2.5 GPA can be admitted to certain programs with academic advising as a requirement. Admission to specific programs of study may have specific course work or testing criteria that all students will have to meet. Individuals with learning disabilities are admitted via the standard admissions procedures that apply to all students submitting applications for formal admission. Students with documentation of a learning disability are eligible to receive support services once they are enrolled in the university. LD students who self-disclose during the admission process are referred to DSS for information about services and accommodations.

Additional Information

The Academic Coach Center helps students develop academic skills. It is offered in individual sessions with a peer coach or in group workshops led by peer coaches, staff, and faculty. Coaching coordinates with tutoring, advising and mentoring and compliments the classroom-based instructional experience. There is no separate tutoring for students with learning disabilities. The Learning Commons provides tutorial help for all students through reading, writing, math, language, communication, and science labs. With appropriate documentation, students with LD or ADHD may have access to accommodations such as testing modifications, distraction-free testing environments, scribes, proctors, note-takers, calculators, dictionaries, and computers in exams, and access to assistive technology.

ADMISSIONS INFO FOR STUDENTS WITH LEARNING DIFFERENCES

Phone: 907-786-4530 • Fax: 907-786-4531 • Email: uaa_dss@alaska.edu

SAT/ACT required: No
Interview required: No
Essay required: No
Additional application required: No
Documentation submitted to: Disability Support Services

Special Ed. HS course work accepted: Yes
Separate application required for Programs/Services: No
Documentation required for:
LD: Psychoeducational evaluation
ADHD: Psychoeducational evaluation
ASD: Psychoeducational evaluation

University of Alaska Anchorage

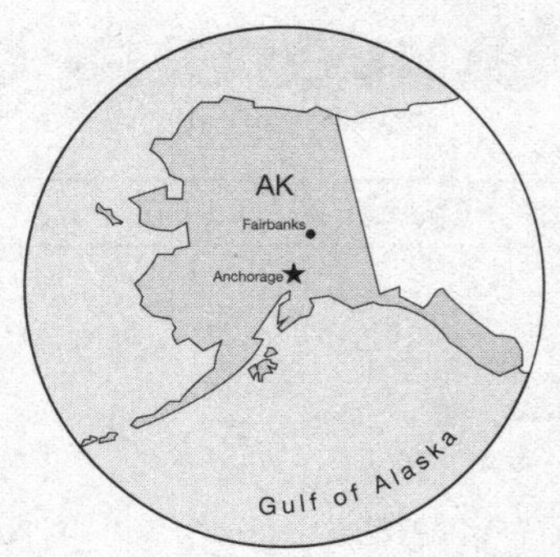

General Admissions

Very important factors include: rigor of secondary school record. *Other factors include:* class rank, standardized test scores, talent/ability. High school diploma is required and GED is accepted. Standardized test scores are not used in the admission decision; however, they are used for math and writing course level placement.

Accommodations or Services

Accommodations are decided upon an individual basis after a thorough review of appropriate, current documentation. The accommodations requests must be supported through the documentation provided and must be logically linked to the current impact of the condition on academic functioning.

Financial Aid

Students should submit: FAFSA. Applicants will be notified of awards on a rolling basis beginning 2/1. *Need-based scholarships/grants offered:* College/university scholarship or grant aid from institutional funds; Federal Pell; Private scholarships; SEOG; State scholarships/grants. *Loan aid offered:* Federal Work-Study Program available. Institutional employment available.

Campus Life

Activities: Campus Ministries; Choral groups; Dance; Drama/theater; International Student Organization; Jazz band; Literary magazine; Model UN; Music ensembles; Musical theater; Opera; Radio station; Student government; Student newspaper; Student-run film society. **Organizations:** 70 registered organizations, 5 honor societies, 5 religious organizations, 1 fraternity, 2 sororities. **Athletics (Intercollegiate):** *Men:* basketball, cross-country, ice hockey, skiing (downhill/alpine), skiing (Nordic/cross-country). *Women:* basketball, cross-country, gymnastics, skiing (downhill/alpine), skiing (Nordic/cross-country), volleyball.

ACCOMMODATIONS

Allowed in exams:	
Calculators	Yes
Dictionary	Yes
Computer	Yes
Spell-checker	Yes
Extended test time	Yes
Scribe	Yes
Proctors	Yes
Oral exams	Yes
Note-takers	Yes
Support services for students with:	
LD	Yes
ADHD	Yes
ASD	Yes
Distraction-reduced environment	Yes
Recording of lecture allowed	Yes
Reading technology	Yes
Audio books	No
Other assistive technology	Yes
Priority registration	Yes
Added costs of services:	
For LD	No
For ADHD	No
For ASD	No
LD specialists	No
ADHD & ASD coaching	No
ASD specialists	No
Professional tutors	No
Peer tutors	Yes
Max. hours/week for services	Unlimited
How professors are notified of student approved accommodations	By student initiated letters sent through Disability Support

COLLEGE GRADUATION REQUIREMENTS

Course waivers allowed	Yes
In what courses: Individual case-by-case basis	
Course substitutions allowed	Yes
In what courses: Individual case-by-case basis	

Alaska

University of Alaska Fairbanks

1731 Chandalar Drive, Fairbanks, AK 99775-7480 • Admissions: 907-474-7500 • Fax: 907-474-5379 **Support: S**

CAMPUS

Type of school	Public
Environment	City

STUDENTS

Undergrad enrollment	6,284
% male/female	40/60
% from out of state	15

FINANCIAL FACTS

Annual in-state tuition	$8,868
Annual out-of-state tuition	$26,538
Room and board	$10,540
Required fees	$1,500

GENERAL ADMISSIONS INFO

Application fee	$50
Regular application deadline	6/15
Nonfall registration	Yes

Admission may be deferred.

Range SAT EBRW	520–650
Range SAT Math	500–630
Range ACT Composite	17–25

ACADEMICS

Student/faculty ratio	8:1
% students returning for sophomore year	73

Most classes have 10–19 students.

Programs/Services for Students with Learning Differences

The University of Alaska is committed to providing equal opportunity to students with disabilities. The purpose of Disability Services (DS) is to provide equal access to higher education for students with disabilities. Disability Services strives to ensure universal access to classes, course work, housing, programs and activities. UAF has designated Disability Services to determine reasonable accommodations for students with disabilities.

Admissions

To enter as a freshman for a baccalaureate degree there are two options: 1) high school diplomas, 2.5 in core courses and GPA 3.0 and no cut-off on ACT/SAT; 2) high school diploma, 2.5 in core courses, a minimum 2.5 GPA and ACT 18 or SAT 970. Core curriculum 4 years English, 3 years math, 3 years social sciences, and 3 years natural or physical sciences. Foreign languages are recommended. Students can be provisionally accepted if they make up course deficiencies with a C or better in each of the developmental or university courses and complete nine credits of general degree requirements with a C or better.

Additional Information

The Student Development and Learning Center provides tutoring, individual instruction in basic skills and counseling, career-planning services, and assessment testing. The Developmental Writing & Reading Lab supports students with developmental writing and reading classes, including help with all developmental writing and reading assignments. The Center for Student Rights and Responsibilities (CSRR) supports student-centered programs and services to help students achieve personal, educational, and social goals. CSRR encourages students to be successful in all aspects of their lives.

ADMISSIONS INFO FOR STUDENTS WITH LEARNING DIFFERENCES

Phone: 907-474-5655 • Fax: 907-474-5688 • Email: mcmatthews@alaska.edu

SAT/ACT required: Yes (Test optional for 2021)
Interview required: No
Essay required: No
Additional application required: No
Documentation submitted to: Disability Services

Special Ed. HS course work accepted: Yes
Separate application required for Programs/Services: No
Documentation required for:
LD: Psychoeducational evaluation
ADHD: Psychoeducational evaluation
ASD: Psychoeducational evaluation

University of Alaska Fairbanks

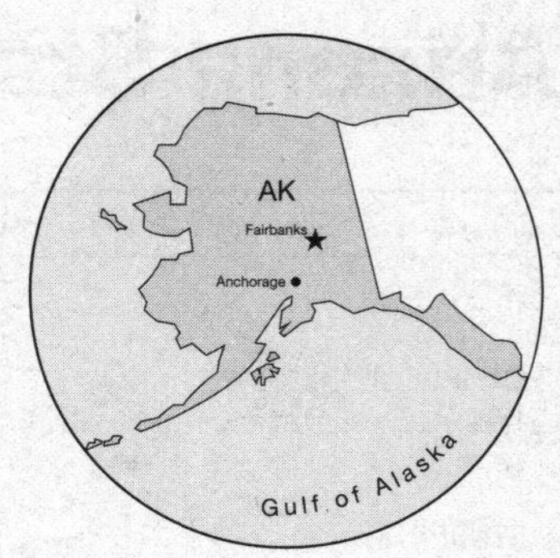

General Admissions

Very important factors include: academic GPA. High school diploma is required, and GED is not accepted. *Academic units required:* 4 English, 3 math, 3 science, 1 science lab, 3 social studies. *Academic units recommended:* 2 foreign language. If applying to UAF for the Academic Year 2020–21 or 2021–22, ACT and SAT scores will be waived.

Accommodations or Services

Accommodations are decided upon an individual basis after a thorough review of appropriate, current documentation. The accommodations requests must be supported through the documentation provided and must be logically linked to the current impact of the condition on academic functioning.

Financial Aid

Students should submit: FAFSA; Institution's own financial aid form Applicants will be notified of awards on a rolling basis beginning 2/15. *Need-based scholarships/grants offered:* College/university scholarship or grant aid from institutional funds; Federal Pell; Private scholarships; SEOG; State scholarships/grants. *Loan aid offered:* Direct PLUS loans; Direct Subsidized Stafford Loans; Direct Unsubsidized Stafford Loans; State Loans. Federal Work-Study Program available. Institutional employment available.

Campus Life

Activities: Campus Ministries; Choral groups; Dance; Drama/theater; International Student Organization; Jazz band; Literary magazine; Model UN; Music ensembles; Radio station; Student government; Student newspaper; Symphony orchestra. **Organizations:** 134 registered organizations, 7 honor societies, 7 religious organizations, 1 fraternity, 1 sorority. **Athletics (Intercollegiate):** *Men:* basketball, cross-country, ice hockey, riflery, skiing (Nordic/cross-country). *Women:* basketball, cross-country, riflery, skiing (Nordic/cross-country), volleyball.

ACCOMMODATIONS

Allowed in exams:	
Calculators	Yes
Dictionary	Yes
Computer	Yes
Spell-checker	Yes
Extended test time	Yes
Scribe	Yes
Proctors	Yes
Oral exams	Yes
Note-takers	Yes
Support services for students with:	
LD	Yes
ADHD	Yes
ASD	Yes
Distraction-reduced environment	Yes
Recording of lecture allowed	Yes
Reading technology	Yes
Audio books	No
Other assistive technology	Yes
Priority registration	Yes
Added costs of services:	
For LD	No
For ADHD	No
For ASD	No
LD specialists	No
ADHD & ASD coaching	No
ASD specialists	No
Professional tutors	No
Peer tutors	No
Max. hours/week for services	Varies
How professors are notified of student approved accommodations	Student

COLLEGE GRADUATION REQUIREMENTS

Course waivers allowed	No
Course substitutions allowed	Yes

Arizona State University

Admissions Services Applicant Processing, Tempe, AZ 85287-1004 • Admissions: 480-965-7788 • Fax: 480-965-3610 **Support: CS**

CAMPUS

Type of school	Public
Environment	Metropolis

STUDENTS

Undergrad enrollment	44,038
% male/female	55/45
% from out of state	27
% frosh live on campus	76

FINANCIAL FACTS

Annual in-state tuition	$10,710
Annual out-of-state tuition	$28,800
Room and board	$13,164
Required fees	$628

GENERAL ADMISSIONS INFO

Application fee	$50
Regular application deadline	Rolling
Nonfall registration	Yes
Admission may be deferred	Yes
Range SAT EBRW	560–670
Range SAT Math	560–690
Range ACT Composite	22–28

ACADEMICS

Student/faculty ratio	19:1
% students returning for sophomore year	88

Programs/Services for Students with Learning Differences

The Disability Resource Center provides services to qualified students with disabilities on all ASU campuses. For convenience, students will find offices located at the Downtown, Polytechnic, Tempe, and West locations. The staff recommends and implements reasonable and effective accommodations and services with appropriate student documentation. Students are provided with self-advocacy training and may be referred, for example, to the Student Success Centers or Writing Centers.

Admissions

All students are required to meet the same admissions requirements for the university. For general admission students should have 4 years English, 4 years math, 3 years science, 2 years social science, 2 years foreign language, and 1 year fine arts. Applicants must meet one of the following: rank in the top 25% of their class or have a 3.0 GPA, 22 ACT, or 1040 SAT (24 ACT or 1110 SAT for nonresidents). Applicants who do not meet these standards will be evaluated through an Individual Review process.

Additional Information

There are seven Disability Access Consultants who are available to work with the students. Approximately 1,600 students are registered and about 25% of those students have documented learning disabilities. Two of the Access consultants work with students on the spectrum and will meet with the students regularly for informal coaching. They assist the students with choosing classes with professors that will be a good fit. There is a semester long class the students are encouraged to sign up for to help teach socialization. Informal coaching is provided only if requested and the goal would be to engage this coaching only for the short term. If students need more coaching, they may be referred to the Trio Program.

ADMISSIONS INFO FOR STUDENTS WITH LEARNING DIFFERENCES

Phone: 480-965-1234 • Fax: 480-965-0441 • Email: drc@asu.edu

SAT/ACT required: No
Interview required: No
Essay required: No
Additional application required: No
Documentation submitted to: Disability Resource Center

Special Ed. HS course work accepted: Yes
Separate application required for Programs/Services: No
Documentation required for:

LD: The DRC will accept diagnoses of a Learning Disability that is based on comprehensive, age-appropriate, psychoeducational evaluations that demonstrate current functional limitations of the disability.
ADHD: The DRC will accept diagnoses of ADHD that is based on comprehensive, age-appropriate, psychoeducational evaluations that demonstrate current functional limitations of the disability.
ASD: The DRC will accept diagnoses of an Autism Spectrum Disorder that is based on comprehensive, age-appropriate, psychoeducational evaluations that demonstrate current functional limitations of the disability.

Arizona State University

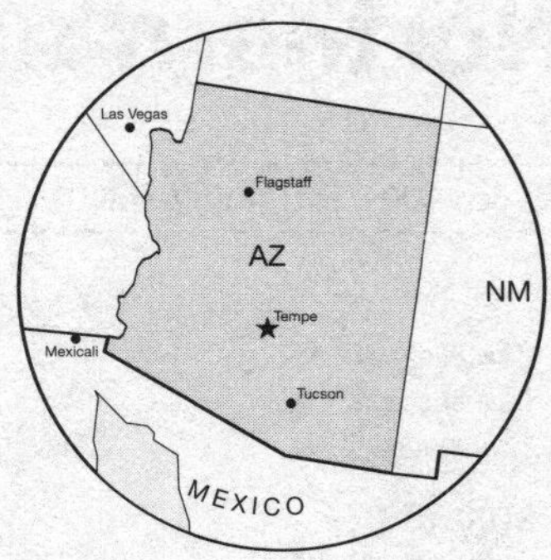

General Admissions

Very important factors include: class rank, academic GPA, standardized test scores. *Important factors include:* rigor of secondary school record. *Other factors include:* state residency. High school diploma is required and GED is accepted. *Academic units required:* 4 English, 4 math, 3 science, 3 science labs, 2 foreign language, 1 social studies, 1 history, 1 unit from above areas or other academic areas. ACT or SAT scores are not required for admission, but may be submitted for merit scholarship consideration and ASU course placement. They are also required for some majors.

Accommodations or Services

Accommodations are decided upon an individual basis after a thorough review of appropriate, current documentation. The accommodations requests must be supported through the documentation provided and must be logically linked to the current impact of the condition on academic functioning.

Financial Aid

Students should submit: FAFSA. *Need-based scholarships/grants offered:* College/university scholarship or grant aid from institutional funds; Federal Pell; Private scholarships; SEOG; State scholarships/grants; United Negro College Fund. *Loan aid offered:* Direct PLUS loans; Direct Subsidized Stafford Loans; Direct Unsubsidized Stafford Loans. Federal Work-Study Program available. Institutional employment available.

Campus Life

Activities: Campus Ministries; Choral groups; Concert band; Dance; Drama/theater; International Student Organization; Jazz band; Literary magazine; Marching band; Model UN; Music ensembles; Musical theater; Opera; Student government; Student newspaper; Student-run film society; Symphony orchestra. **Organizations:** 847 registered organizations, 19 honor societies, 69 religious organizations, 42 fraternities, 33 sororities. **Athletics (Intercollegiate):** *Men:* baseball, basketball, cross-country, diving, football, golf, swimming, track/field (outdoor), wrestling. *Women:* basketball, cross-country, diving, golf, gymnastics, soccer, softball, swimming, tennis, track/field (outdoor), volleyball, water polo.

ACCOMMODATIONS

Allowed in exams:	
Calculators	Yes
Dictionary	Yes
Computer	Yes
Spell-checker	Yes
Extended test time	Yes
Scribe	Yes
Proctors	Yes
Oral exams	Yes
Note-takers	Yes
Support services for students with:	
LD	Yes
ADHD	Yes
ASD	Yes
Distraction-reduced environment	Yes
Recording of lecture allowed	Yes
Reading technology	Yes
Audio books	Yes
Other assistive technology	Yes
Priority registration	Yes
Added costs of services:	
For LD	No
For ADHD	No
For ASD	No
LD specialists	Yes
ADHD & ASD coaching	Yes
ASD specialists	No
Professional tutors	No
Peer tutors	Yes
Max. hours/week for services	Varies
How professors are notified of student approved accommodations	Student and Disability Office

COLLEGE GRADUATION REQUIREMENTS

Course waivers allowed	No
Course substitutions allowed	Yes

In what courses: Case by case basis

Arizona

Northern Arizona University

PO Box 4084, Flagstaff, AZ 86011-4084 • Admissions: 928-523-5511 • Fax: 928-523-6023 **Support: CS**

CAMPUS

Type of school	Public
Environment	Town

STUDENTS

Undergrad enrollment	26,135
% male/female	38/62
% from out of state	31
% frosh live on campus	89

FINANCIAL FACTS

Annual in-state tuition	$10,650
Annual out-of-state tuition	$25,270
Room and board	$10,534
Required fees	$1,246

GENERAL ADMISSIONS INFO

Application fee	$25
Regular application deadline	8/1
Nonfall registration	Yes
Admission may be deferred	Yes
Range SAT EBRW	520–620
Range SAT Math	520–610
Range ACT Composite	19–25

ACADEMICS

Student/faculty ratio	19:1
% students returning for sophomore year	78

Most classes have 20–29 students.

Programs/Services for Students with Learning Differences

Disability Resources provides services and accommodations to all NAU students with appropriate accommodations. Students must self-identify, and it could take several weeks to be approved for services. Therefore, students are encouraged to register early. Any information students can provide prior to meeting with the DR would be very beneficial in setting up accommodations before the semester begins.

Admissions

To be a qualified individual with a disability, students must meet our academic and technical standards required for admission. General admission requirements for unconditional admission include: 4 years of English, 4 years of math; 2 years of social science with 1 year being American history; 2–3 years of science lab with additional requirements; 1 year of fine arts; and 2 years of a foreign language. (Students may be admitted conditionally with course deficiencies, but not in both math and science.) In-state residents should have a 2.5 GPA, be in the top 50 percent of their high school class (a 3.0 GPA or being in the upper 25 percent of their graduating class is required for non-residents), or earn an SAT combined score of 930 (1010 for non-residents) or an ACT score of 22 (24 for non-residents). Conditional admissions is possible with a 2.5–2.99 GPA or being in the top 50 percent of their graduating class and strong ACT/SAT scores. Exceptional admission may be offered to 10 percent of the new freshmen applicants or transfer applicants. If applicants submit the ACT or SAT the Writing section is not required.

Additional Information

Every student has individual needs and will be evaluated based on documentation and appropriate accommodations. Through the Academic Success Center, a learning specialist meets one-on-one to help students with learning strategies and the development of an individualized plan for success. Students can receive help with time management, test-taking skills, reading comprehension, note-taking, critical thinking, and motivation. Students can access free tutoring from peer academic coaches. Additionally, academic workshops are offered throughout the semester.

ADMISSIONS INFO FOR STUDENTS WITH LEARNING DIFFERENCES

Phone: 928-523-8773 • Fax: 928-523-8747 • Email: DR@nau.edu

SAT/ACT required: No
Interview required: No
Essay required: No
Additional application required: Yes
Documentation submitted to: Disability Resources

Special Ed. HS course work accepted: Yes
Separate application required for Programs/Services: Yes
Documentation required for:
- **LD:** In order to evaluate accommodation and service requests, Disability Resources will need information about how your disability is likely to impact a student at Northern Arizona University.
- **ADHD:** Psychoeducational evaluation
- **ASD:** Psychoeducational evaluation

Northern Arizona University

General Admissions

Very important factors include: academic GPA. *Important factors include:* rigor of secondary school record, standardized test scores. *Other factors include:* class rank. High school diploma is required and GED is accepted. *Academic units required:* 4 English, 4 math, 3 science, 3 science labs, 2 foreign language, 1 social studies, 1 history, 1 unit from above areas or other academic areas. SAT/ACT considered only when minimum GPA and/or class rank is not met.

Accommodations or Services

Accommodations are decided upon an individual basis after a thorough review of appropriate, current documentation. The accommodations requests must be supported through the documentation provided and must be logically linked to the current impact of the condition on academic functioning.

Financial Aid

Students should submit: FAFSA. *Need-based scholarships/grants offered:* College/university scholarship or grant aid from institutional funds; Federal Nursing Scholarships; Federal Pell; Private scholarships; SEOG; State scholarships/grants. *Loan aid offered:* Direct PLUS loans; Direct Subsidized Stafford Loans; Direct Unsubsidized Stafford Loans. Federal Work-Study Program available. Institutional employment available.

Campus Life

Activities: Campus Ministries; Choral groups; Concert band; Dance; Drama/theater; International Student Organization; Jazz band; Literary magazine; Marching band; Model UN; Music ensembles; Musical theater; Opera; Pep band; Radio station; Student government; Student newspaper; Student-run film society; Symphony orchestra; Television station. **Organizations:** 386 registered organizations, 23 honor societies, 23 religious organizations, 16 fraternities, 15 sororities. **Athletics (Intercollegiate):** *Men:* basketball, cheerleading, cross-country, football, tennis, track/field (outdoor). *Women:* basketball, cheerleading, cross-country, diving, golf, soccer, swimming, tennis, track/field (outdoor), volleyball.

Las Vegas
Flagstaff
AZ
NM
Phoenix
Mexicali
Tucson
MEXICO

ACCOMMODATIONS

Allowed in exams:	
Calculators	Yes
Dictionary	Yes
Computer	Yes
Spell-checker	Yes
Extended test time	Yes
Scribe	Yes
Proctors	Yes
Oral exams	Yes
Note-takers	Yes
Support services for students with:	
LD	Yes
ADHD	Yes
ASD	Yes
Distraction-reduced environment	Yes
Recording of lecture allowed	Yes
Reading technology	Yes
Audio books	Yes
Other assistive technology	Yes
Priority registration	Yes
Added costs of services:	
For LD	No
For ADHD	No
For ASD	No
LD specialists	Yes
ADHD & ASD coaching	Yes
ASD specialists	Yes
Professional tutors	No
Peer tutors	Yes
Max. hours/week for services	Varies
How professors are notified of student approved accommodations	Student

COLLEGE GRADUATION REQUIREMENTS

Course waivers allowed	No
Course substitutions allowed	Yes
In what courses: Case by case basis	

University of Arizona

PO Box 210073, Tucson, AZ 85721-0073 • Admissions: 520-621-3237 • Fax: 520-621-9799 **Support: SP**

CAMPUS

Type of school	Public
Environment	Metropolis

STUDENTS

Undergrad enrollment	34,591
% male/female	46/54
% from out of state	39
% frosh live on campus	76

FINANCIAL FACTS

Annual in-state tuition	$11,299
Annual out-of-state tuition	$35,326
Room and board	$13,050
Required fees	$1,412

GENERAL ADMISSIONS INFO

Application fee	$50
Regular application deadline	5/1
Nonfall registration	Yes
Range SAT EBRW	560–670
Range SAT Math	550–690
Range ACT Composite	21–29

ACADEMICS

Student/faculty ratio	15:1
% students returning for sophomore year	83

Most classes have 10–19 students.

Programs/Services for Students with Learning Differences

The Disability Resource Center (DRC) provides accommodations and services to students with appropriate documentation. Every student is reviewed individually to determine if additional information is necessary to support accommodation requests. The Strategic Alternative Learning Technique Program (SALT) is a fee-for-service, structured support program for students with learning disabilities, ADHD or ASD.

Admissions

Students must submit a general application to the University and a SALT application. Students may check the box on the general application indicating they are interested in SALT. Students are admitted to the University and then reviewed by SALT. General admission criteria include: 4 English, 4 math, 3 science, 2 social studies, 2 foreign language, 1 fine art. Deficiencies can be made up in English with ACT sub score of 21, Math ACT sub score 24 and science ACT sub score 20. Most applicants are admissible with required courses and either 24 ACT (22 ACT resident) or SAT 1110 (SAT 1040 resident) or top ¼ of the class. SALT application should be submitted early in the process. All SALT applicants should answer 3 essay questions: 1) Why are you applying to SALT and how do you plan to use the services; 2) Describe a difficult situation you have encountered in your life, and tell how you handled the situation; 3) Tell about your strengths, skills and talents. Students can submit documentation of a disability to Admissions and to SALT or answer SALT question #4 which asks for a description of academic challenges and the support services used to manage those challenges.

Additional Information

The SALT program provides comprehensive support to UA students with learning and attention challenges. There are yearly fees for participating in the SALT program. The SALT program includes: 1) Tutoring; 2) Strategic Learning Specialists who point people to campus resources, design Individualized Learning Plans, teach strategies to help improve academics, and monitor academic progress; 3) Educational Technology; and 4) Life and ADHD Coaching.

ADMISSIONS INFO FOR STUDENTS WITH LEARNING DIFFERENCES

Fax: 520-621-9423 • Email: drc-info@email.arizona.edu

SAT/ACT required: No
Interview required: No
Essay required: Yes for SALT
Additional application required: Yes for SALT
Documentation submitted to: Disability Services and SALT

Special Ed. HS course work accepted: Yes
Separate application required for Programs/Services: Yes
Documentation required for:
LD: Psychoeducational evaluation
ADHD: Psychoeducational evaluation
ASD: Psychoeducational evaluation

University of Arizona

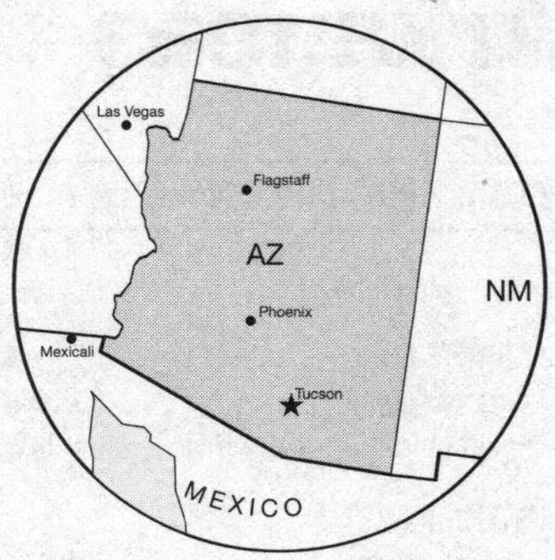

General Admissions

Very important factors include: rigor of secondary school record, academic GPA. *Important factors include:* standardized test scores, extracurricular activities, talent/ability, character/personal qualities, level of applicant's interest. *Other factors include:* class rank, application essay, recommendation(s), volunteer work, work experience. High school diploma is required and GED is accepted. *Academic units required:* 4 English, 4 math, 3 science, 3 science labs, 2 foreign language, 2 social studies, 1 visual/performing arts. *Academic units recommended:* 4 English, 4 math, 3 science, 3 science labs, 2 foreign language, 2 social studies, 1 visual/performing arts. Submitting your official SAT/ACT scores is optional for admissions consideration. However, they are required for consideration for merit scholarships, admission to the UA Honors College, the College of Fine Arts, the College of Nursing, the College of Architecture, Planning and Landscape Architecture, and College of Engineering.

Accommodations or Services

Accommodations are decided upon an individual basis after a thorough review of appropriate, current documentation. The accommodations requests must be supported through the documentation provided and must be logically linked to the current impact of the condition on academic functioning.

Financial Aid

Students should submit: FAFSA; Institution's own financial aid form. *Need-based scholarships/grants offered:* College/university scholarship or grant aid from institutional funds; Federal Pell; Private scholarships; SEOG; State scholarships/grants. *Loan aid offered:* Direct PLUS loans; Direct Subsidized Stafford Loans; Direct Unsubsidized Stafford Loans. Federal Work-Study Program available. Institutional employment available.

Campus Life

Activities: Campus Ministries; Choral groups; Concert band; Dance; Drama/theater; International Student Organization; Jazz band; Literary magazine; Marching band; Model UN; Music ensembles; Musical theater; Opera; Pep band; Radio station; Student government; Student newspaper; Symphony orchestra; Television station; Yearbook. **Organizations:** 920 registered organizations, 49 honor societies, 69 religious organizations, 25 fraternities, 24 sororities. **Athletics (Intercollegiate):** *Men:* baseball, basketball, cross-country, diving, football, golf, swimming, tennis, track/field (outdoor). *Women:* basketball, cross-country, diving, golf, gymnastics, soccer, softball, swimming, tennis, track/field (outdoor), track/field (indoor), volleyball.

ACCOMMODATIONS

Allowed in exams:	
Calculators	Yes
Dictionary	Yes
Computer	Yes
Spell-checker	Yes
Extended test time	Yes
Scribe	Yes
Proctors	Yes
Oral exams	Yes
Note-takers	Yes
Support services for students with:	
LD	Yes
ADHD	Yes
ASD	Yes
Distraction-reduced environment	Yes
Recording of lecture allowed	Yes
Reading technology	Yes
Audio books	Yes
Other assistive technology	Yes
Priority registration	No
Added costs of services:	
For LD	Yes for SALT
For ADHD	Yes for SALT
For ASD	Yes for SALT
LD specialists	Yes
ADHD & ASD coaching	Yes
ASD specialists	Yes
Professional tutors	Yes
Peer tutors	Yes
Max. hours/week for services	Varies
How professors are notified of student approved accommodations	Student and DR

COLLEGE GRADUATION REQUIREMENTS

Course waivers allowed	No
Course substitutions allowed	Yes
In what courses: Varies	

Arizona

Arkansas State University

PO Box 600, State University, Jonesboro, AR 72467 • Admissions: 870-972-3024 • Fax: 870-972-3406 **Support: S**

CAMPUS

Type of school	Public
Environment	Town

STUDENTS

Undergrad enrollment	8,928
% male/female	40/60
% from out of state	13
% frosh live on campus	74

FINANCIAL FACTS

Annual in-state tuition	$8,900
Annual out-of-state tuition	$15,960
Room and board	$9,672
Required fees	$2,826

GENERAL ADMISSIONS INFO

Application fee	$30
Regular application deadline	1st Class Day
Nonfall registration	Yes
Range SAT EBRW	510–610
Range SAT Math	500–610
Range ACT Composite	21–27

ACADEMICS

Student/faculty ratio	16:1
% students returning for sophomore year	73

Most classes have 20–29 students.

Programs/Services for Students with Learning Differences

Arkansas State Disability Services' provides students with disabilities access to resources. Although A-State does not offer a specialized curriculum for persons with disabilities, A-State does offer a variety of support services to students with appropriate documentation.

Admissions

Unconditional admission requires a high school GPA of 2.75 and either a minimum ACT composite score of 21 or SAT score of 990 on the Reading and Math. To be considered for conditional admission to Arkansas State University, an applicant must meet the following requirements of a high school GPA of 2.3 and a minimum ACT of 19 or SAT score of 910–989. All incoming freshmen with an ACT of 28 (or higher) and a high school GPA of 3.5 (or higher) will be formally admitted to the Honors College, for which there is no separate application.

Additional Information

The Learning Commons offers free drop-in, peer one-on-one, and small group tutoring. Peer or graduate student assistants lead learning groups to students enrolled in some classes that might be considered high risk. Academic Success Coaches who are graduate assistants help students create a study plan for a particular course, assist with study skills or developing a time management plan. Every fall term, students are required to make an appointment to meet with their Disability Services Counselor to review and request their accommodations. In the spring they update the request online.

ADMISSIONS INFO FOR STUDENTS WITH LEARNING DIFFERENCES

Phone: 870-972-3664 • Fax: 870-972-3351 • Email: jrmason@astate.edu

SAT/ACT required: Yes
Interview required: No
Essay required: No
Additional application required: Yes
Documentation submitted to: Disability Services

Special Ed. HS course work accepted: Yes
Separate application required for Programs/Services: Yes
Documentation required for:
LD: Psychoeducational evaluation
ADHD: Psychoeducational evaluation
ASD: Psychoeducational evaluation

Arkansas State University

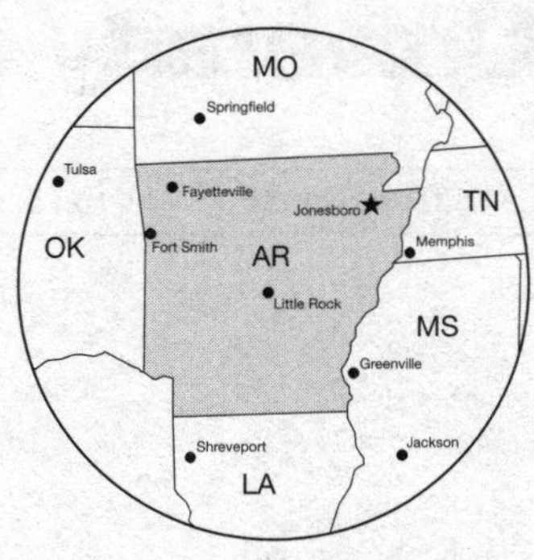

General Admissions

Very important factors include: rigor of secondary school record, standardized test scores, academic GPA. *Important factors include:* class rank. *Other factors include:* recommendation(s), talent/ability. High school diploma is required and GED is accepted. *Academic units required:* 4 English, 4 math, 3 science, 3 science labs, 1 social studies, 2 history. *Academic units recommended:* 2 foreign language. An official ACT score or comparable SAT or ASSET is required. The minimum ACT composite score is 21.

Accommodations or Services

Accommodations are decided upon an individual basis after a thorough review of appropriate, current documentation. The accommodations requests must be supported through the documentation provided and must be logically linked to the current impact of the condition on academic functioning.

Financial Aid

Students should submit: FAFSA, Institution's own financial aid form. *Need-based scholarships/grants offered:* College/university scholarship or grant aid from institutional funds; Federal Pell; Private scholarships; SEOG; State scholarships/grants. *Loan aid offered:* Direct PLUS loans; Direct Subsidized Stafford Loans; Direct Unsubsidized Stafford Loans. Federal Work-Study Program available. Institutional employment available.

Campus Life

Activities: Campus Ministries; Choral groups; Concert band; Dance; Drama/theater; International Student Organization; Jazz band; Marching band; Model UN; Music ensembles; Musical theater; Opera; Pep band; Radio station; Student government; Student newspaper; Symphony orchestra; Television station; Yearbook. **Organizations:** 175 registered organizations, 10 honor societies, 25 religious organizations, 13 fraternities, 7 sororities. **Athletics (Intercollegiate):** *Men:* baseball, basketball, cross-country, football, golf, track/field (outdoor), track/field (indoor). *Women:* basketball, cross-country, golf, soccer, tennis, track/field (outdoor), track/field (indoor), volleyball.

ACCOMMODATIONS

Allowed in exams:	
Calculators	Yes
Dictionary	Yes
Computer	Yes
Spell-checker	Yes
Extended test time	Yes
Scribe	Yes
Proctors	Yes
Oral exams	Yes
Note-takers	Yes
Support services for students with:	
LD	Yes
ADHD	Yes
ASD	Yes
Distraction-reduced environment	Yes
Recording of lecture allowed	Yes
Reading technology	Yes
Audio books	Yes
Other assistive technology	Yes
Priority registration	Yes
Added costs of services:	
For LD	No
For ADHD	No
For ASD	No
LD specialists	No
ADHD & ASD coaching	Yes
ASD specialists	No
Professional tutors	No
Peer tutors	Yes
Max. hours/week for services	7
How professors are notified of student approved accommodations	Student and Disability Office

COLLEGE GRADUATION REQUIREMENTS

Course waivers allowed: Yes
In what courses: Accommodations for physical education requirement.

Course substitutions allowed: Yes
In what courses: Accommodations for physical education requirement.

Arkansas

University of Arkansas

232 Silas H. Hunt Hall, Fayetteville, AR 72701 • Admissions: 479-575-5346 • Fax: 479-575-7515 **Support: S**

CAMPUS

Type of school	Public
Environment	City

STUDENTS

Undergrad enrollment	22,757
% male/female	46/54
% from out of state	46
% frosh live on campus	91

FINANCIAL FACTS

Annual in-state tuition	$7,384
Annual out-of-state tuition	$23,422
Room and board	$11,020
Required fees	$1,746

GENERAL ADMISSIONS INFO

Application fee	$40
Regular application deadline	8/1
Nonfall registration	Yes
Range SAT EBRW	570–650
Range SAT Math	550–650
Range ACT Composite	23–30

ACADEMICS

Student/faculty ratio	18:1
% students returning for sophomore year	84

Most classes have 10–19 students.

Programs/Services for Students with Learning Differences

The philosophy of the Center for Educational Access is to provide an environment in which students are encouraged to develop independence and the ability to self-advocate and to gain a knowledge of resources on campus. Provision of reasonable accommodations is determined individually, based on the nature of the student's disability.

Admissions

Applicants to the university for the school years 2020–2021 or 2021–2022 are not required to submit ACT or SAT. However, students may submit test scores if they would like them to be used in the admission process. There are two options for undergraduate applicants. Option 1 requires 16 core courses with at least a 2.5 GPA and a cumulative GPA of 3.0. Option 2 requires a 2.5 in the 16 core courses and a 2.5 GPA with an ACT of 18+ or SAT of 970+, although this ACT/SAT requirement is waived for 2020–2022.

Additional Information

The Center for Educational Access offers reasonable accommodations to students with appropriate documentation. The EMPOWER Program on campus offers a four-year, non-degree college experience program for students with cognitive disabilities that incorporates functional academics, independent living, employment, social/leisure skills, and health/wellness skills in a public university setting with the goal of producing self-sufficient young adults. The University of Arkansas program is offered for students who demonstrate the ability to safely live independently, sustain employment, and socially integrate during their enrollment. The program progresses with an emphasis on workplace experience, community integration, and independent living with transitionally reduced supports. Students who successfully complete the program will receive a certificate of program completion.

ADMISSIONS INFO FOR STUDENTS WITH LEARNING DIFFERENCES

Fax: 479-575-7445 • Email: ada@uark.edu

SAT/ACT required: No
Interview required: No
Essay required: No
Additional application required: Yes
Documentation submitted to: Center for Educational Access

Special Ed. HS course work accepted: Yes
Separate application required for Programs/Services: Yes
Documentation required for:
LD: Psychoeducational evaluation
ADHD: Psychoeducational evaluation
ASD: Psychoeducational evaluation

University of Arkansas

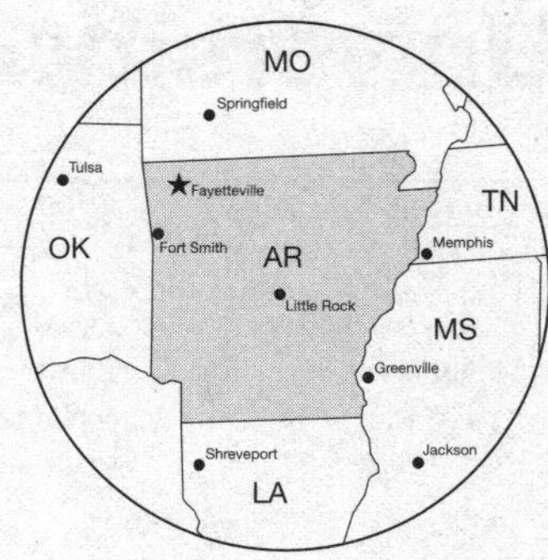

General Admissions

Very important factors include: academic GPA, standardized test scores. *Other factors include:* rigor of secondary school record, class rank, application essay, recommendation(s), extracurricular activities, talent/ability, character/personal qualities, first generation, alumni/ae relation, geographical residence, state residency, volunteer work, work experience. High school diploma is required and GED is accepted. *Academic units required:* 4 English, 4 math, 3 science, 1 science lab, 1 social studies, 2 history, 2 academic electives. *Academic units recommended:* 4 English, 4 math, 3 science, 1 science lab, 2 foreign language, 1 social studies, 2 history, 2 academic electives. Applicants with a 3.2 high school GPA or higher (on a standard 4.0 scale) will be reviewed for admission to the University without a qualifying test score, but must submit ACT, SAT, or Next Generation Accuplacer scores for placement and enrollment purposes. Policy as of August 2020.

Accommodations or Services

Accommodations are decided upon an individual basis after a thorough review of appropriate, current documentation. The accommodations requests must be supported through the documentation provided and must be logically linked to the current impact of the condition on academic functioning.

Financial Aid

Students should submit: FAFSA. Applicants will be notified of awards on a rolling basis beginning 3/1. *Need-based scholarships/grants offered:* College/university scholarship or grant aid from institutional funds; Federal Pell; Private scholarships; SEOG; State scholarships/grants. *Loan aid offered:* Direct PLUS loans; Direct Subsidized Stafford Loans; Direct Unsubsidized Stafford Loans. Federal Work-Study Program available. Institutional employment available.

Campus Life

Activities: Campus Ministries; Choral groups; Concert band; Dance; Drama/theater; International Student Organization; Jazz band; Marching band; Model UN; Music ensembles; Musical theater; Opera; Pep band; Radio station; Student government; Student newspaper; Symphony orchestra; Television station; Yearbook. **Organizations:** 443 registered organizations, 47 honor societies, 19 fraternities, 15 sororities. **Athletics (Intercollegiate):** *Men:* baseball, basketball, cross-country, football, golf, tennis, track/field (outdoor), track/field (indoor). *Women:* basketball, cross-country, diving, golf, gymnastics, soccer, softball, swimming, tennis, track/field (outdoor), track/field (indoor), volleyball.

ACCOMMODATIONS

Allowed in exams:	
Calculators	Yes
Dictionary	Yes
Computer	Yes
Spell-checker	Yes
Extended test time	Yes
Scribe	Yes
Proctors	Yes
Oral exams	Yes
Note-takers	Yes
Support services for students with:	
LD	Yes
ADHD	Yes
ASD	Yes
Distraction-reduced environment	Yes
Recording of lecture allowed	Yes
Reading technology	Yes
Audio books	Yes
Other assistive technology	Yes
Priority registration	Yes
Added costs of services:	
For LD	No
For ADHD	No
For ASD	Yes
LD specialists	No
ADHD & ASD coaching	No
ASD specialists	Yes
Professional tutors	No
Peer tutors	Yes
Max. hours/week for services	Varies
How professors are notified of student approved accommodations	Student

COLLEGE GRADUATION REQUIREMENTS

Course waivers allowed	No
Course substitutions allowed	Yes
In what courses: Case by case basis	

University of the Ozarks

415 N College Avenue, Clarksville, AR 72830 • Admissions: 479-979-1227 **Support: SP**

CAMPUS

Type of school	Private (nonprofit)
Environment	Village

STUDENTS

Undergrad enrollment	812
% male/female	49/51
% from out of state	40
% frosh live on campus	86

FINANCIAL FACTS

Annual tuition	$26,792
Room and board	$7,600
Required fees	$1,000

GENERAL ADMISSIONS INFO

Application fee	$0
Regular application deadline	rolling
Nonfall registration	Yes

Admission may be deferred.

Range SAT EBRW	450–510
Range SAT Math	420–540
Range ACT Composite	18–23

ACADEMICS

Student/faculty ratio	15:1

Programs/Services for Students with Learning Differences

The University of the Ozarks established the Jones Learning Center, a comprehensive program for students with learning disabilities, in 1971. Students with documented disabilities are totally integrated into campus life in both curricular and extra-curricular activities. The service model that is used is one that includes an academic support coordinator that the student meets with daily who is responsible for the individualized planning and implementation of the student's program of study, helps the student with executive functioning skills, acts as a secondary advisor, and monitors the student's progress. Students receive help in understanding their learning styles, utilizing their strengths, circumventing deficits, building skills, and becoming independent learners.

Admissions

The standard admission criteria to U of Ozarks reviews the high school transcript and the results on the ACT or SAT. Typically applicants will have a 2.0 GPA and 18 ACT. There is also a Test Optional Admission where no ACT or SAT is required. Students applying Test Optional need to submit a letter of recommendation, an essay, an interview with the admission committee, a resume plus one of the additional requirements including community service, extracurricular activities or personal or group achievements. If a student who is applying to the Jones Learning Center (JLC) meets the general admissions criteria and also has a specific learning disability, AD/HD or ASD, he/she is also admitted to the JLC. If the student does not meet the general admissions criteria, the director will closely review the file and any additional information provided and make a decision about admission. Motivation and work ethic are key factors in the admission decision.

Additional Information

The JLC provides a structured comprehensive support program to students with LD, ADHD, or ASD and other learning differences. Trained staff helps students acquire and apply social thinking and independent learning skills. JLC helps students transition during freshman year through individual and group consultations, academic support, strategies in studying and organization, and social programming. The JLC is designed for capable students who may need additional residential support during freshman year. This is a fee-based program.

ADMISSIONS INFO FOR STUDENTS WITH LEARNING DIFFERENCES

Phone: 479-979-1439 • Fax: 479-979-1477 • Email: chigh@ozarks.edu

SAT/ACT required: No
Interview required: Yes if applying Test Optional
Essay required: Yes if applying Test Optional
Additional application required: Yes
Documentation submitted to: JLC

Special Ed. HS course work accepted: Yes
Separate application required for Programs/Services: Yes
Documentation required for:
- **LD:** Psychoeducational evaluation
- **ADHD:** Psychoeducational evaluation
- **ASD:** Psychoeducational evaluation

University of the Ozarks

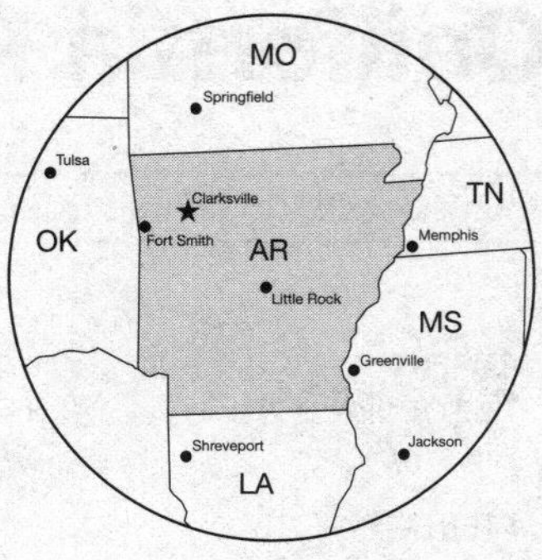

General Admissions

Very important factors include: standardized test scores, application essay, recommendations interview, extracurricular activities, character/personal qualities, volunteer work, work experience, level of applicant's interest. *Important factors include:* Rigor of secondary school record, talent/ability, first generation, Alumni/ae relation. *Other factors include:* state residency. High school diploma is required and GED is accepted. *Academic units required:* 4 English, 4 math, 3 science, 2 science labs, 2 foreign language, 1 social studies, 2 history. Prospective students applying to Ozarks are no longer required to submit ACT or SAT scores as part of the admission process. Applicants who decide to apply test-optional will receive full consideration for admission, without penalty.

Accommodations or Services

Accommodations are decided upon an individual basis after a thorough review of appropriate, current documentation. The accommodations requests must be supported through the documentation provided and must be logically linked to the current impact of the condition on academic functioning.

Financial Aid

Students should submit: FAFSA. Applicants will be notified of awards on or about 3/25. *Need-based scholarships/grants offered:* College/university scholarship or grant aid from institutional funds; Federal Nursing Scholarships; Federal Pell; Private scholarships; SEOG; State scholarships/ grants; United Negro College Fund. *Loan aid offered:* Federal Work-Study Program available. Institutional employment available.

Campus Life

Activities: Campus Ministries; Choral groups; Drama/theater; International Student Organization; Literary magazine; Music ensembles; Radio station; Student government; Student-run film society; Television station; Yearbook. **Organizations:** 40 registered organizations, 6 honor societies, 7 religious organizations. **Athletics (Intercollegiate):** *Men:* baseball, basketball, cheerleading, cross-country, soccer, tennis. *Women:* basketball, cheerleading, cross-country, soccer, softball, tennis.

ACCOMMODATIONS

Allowed in exams:	
Calculators	Yes
Dictionary	No
Computer	Yes
Spell-checker	Yes
Extended test time	Yes
Scribe	Yes
Proctors	Yes
Oral exams	Yes
Note-takers	Yes
Support services for students with:	
LD	Yes for JLC
ADHD	Yes for JLC
ASD	Yes for JLC
Distraction-reduced environment	Yes
Recording of lecture allowed	Yes
Reading technology	Yes
Audio books	Yes
Other assistive technology	Yes
Priority registration	Yes
Added costs of services:	
For LD	Yes
For ADHD	Yes
For ASD	Yes
LD specialists	Yes
ADHD & ASD coaching	Yes
ASD specialists	Yes
Professional tutors	Yes
Peer tutors	Yes
Max. hours/week for services	Varies
How professors are notified of student approved accommodations	Student and Disability Resources

COLLEGE GRADUATION REQUIREMENTS

Course waivers allowed	No
Course substitutions allowed	Yes
In what courses: Case by case basis	

California Polytechnic State University

Admissions Office, San Luis Obispo, CA 93407-0031 • Admissions: 805-756-2311 • Fax: 805-756-5400 **Support: S**

CAMPUS	
Type of school	Public
Environment	Town
STUDENTS	
Undergrad enrollment	20,401
% male/female	52/48
% from out of state	7
% frosh live on campus	100
FINANCIAL FACTS	
Annual in-state tuition	$10,071
Annual out-of-state tuition	$23,760
Room and board	$15,705
Required fees	$4,206
GENERAL ADMISSIONS INFO	
Application fee	$55
Regular application deadline	11/ 3
Nonfall registration	No
Range SAT EBRW	620–700
Range SAT Math	620–740
Range ACT Composite	26–32
ACADEMICS	
Student/faculty ratio	18:1
% students returning for sophomore year	94

Most classes have 20–29 students.

Programs/Services for Students with Learning Differences

The goal of the Disability Resource Center is to help students with learning disabilities use their learning strengths. The DRC interacts with students and faculty and provides a newsletter and open house to keep the university population aware of what is available through the DRC. Incoming students are encouraged to meet with college advisors, in conjunction with DRC staff, to receive assistance in the planning of class schedules. This allows for the selection of appropriate classes to fit particular needs and personal goals. Students are responsible for requesting accommodations and services and must provide a written, comprehensive psychological and/or medical evaluation verifying the diagnosis. The Cal Poly Student Learning Outcomes model promotes student personal growth and the development of self-advocacy for full inclusion of qualified students with verified disabilities. The promotion of student self-reliance and responsibility are necessary adjuncts to educational development.

Admissions

Admission is competitive in all majors. Students must declare a major when applying. Cal Poly comprehensively reviews all applications for students who have strong academic records and are active in and outside the classroom. ACT or SAT will not be used in the admission review for 2021 applicants and will be reviewed for admission decisions on future applicants. Students are evaluated by the cognitive and non-cognitive variables under the faculty-mandated MultiCriteria Admission (MCA) process. Admissions considers intended program of study (the major to which the application is made); college prep courses; GPA in college-preparatory courses; extracurricular activities and work experience; coursework with a grade of C or better.

Additional Information

Incoming students who want accommodations must contact the DRC for assistance. Each student who contacts the DRC is assigned to work with an Access Specialist who is knowledgeable in the student's area of impairment. The assigned Access Specialist will determine what appropriate accommodations should be made available to the student. Supportive services may include alternative format materials, assistive listening devices, note taking, taped textbooks, test accommodations, tutorial services, and writing assistance. The Academic Skills Center (ASC) offers a variety of academic enrichment programs consisting of Supplemental Workshops and Study Session in addition to online study strategies available 24 hours a day.

ADMISSIONS INFO FOR STUDENTS WITH LEARNING DIFFERENCES

Phone: 805-756-1395 • Fax: 805-756-5451 • Email: drc@calpoly.edu

SAT/ACT required: Yes (Test blind for 2021)
Interview required: No
Essay required: No
Additional application required: No
Documentation submitted to: Disability Resource Center

Special Ed. HS course work accepted: No
Separate application required for Programs/Services: No
Documentation required for:
LD: Psychoeducational evaluation
ADHD: Psychoeducational evaluation
ASD: Psychoeducational evaluation

California Polytechnic State University

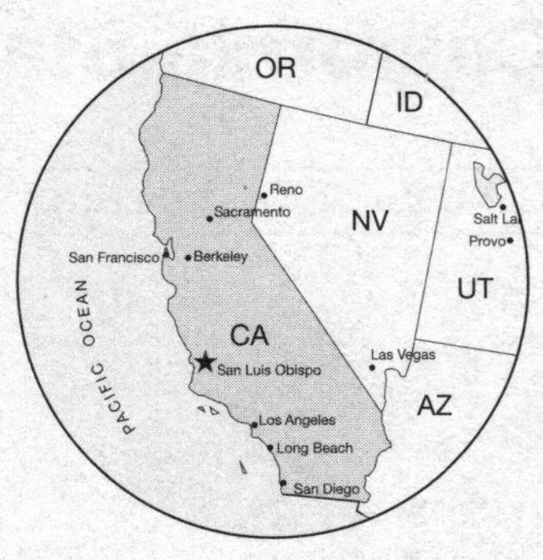

General Admissions

Very important factors include: rigor of secondary school record, academic GPA, and standardized tests are optional. *Other factors include:* extracurricular activities, talent/ability, first generation, geographical residence, volunteer work, work experience. High school diploma is required and GED is accepted. *Academic units required:* 4 English, 3 math, 2 science, 2 science labs, 2 foreign language, 1 social studies, 1 history, 1 academic elective, 1 visual/performing arts. *Academic units recommended:* 4 English, 4 math, 4 science, 2 science labs, 4 foreign language, 1 social studies, 1 history, 1 academic elective, 2 visual/performing arts. Test scores for Fall 2021 admission decisions will NOT be considered. Please consult CalPoly's admissions website for updates.

Accommodations or Services

Accommodations are decided upon an individual basis after a thorough review of appropriate, current documentation. The accommodations requests must be supported through the documentation provided and must be logically linked to the current impact of the condition on academic functioning.

Financial Aid

Students should submit: FAFSA. *Need-based scholarships/grants offered:* College/university scholarship or grant aid from institutional funds; Federal Pell; Private scholarships; SEOG; State scholarships/grants. *Loan aid offered:* Direct PLUS loans; Direct Subsidized Stafford Loans; Direct Unsubsidized Stafford Loans. Federal Work-Study Program available. Institutional employment available.

Campus Life

Activities: Campus Ministries; Choral groups; Concert band; Dance; Drama/theater; International Student Organization; Jazz band; Literary magazine; Marching band; Model UN; Music ensembles; Musical theater; Opera; Pep band; Radio station; Student government; Student newspaper; Student-run film society; Symphony orchestra; Television station. **Organizations:** 386 registered organizations, 20 honor societies, 19 religious organizations, 19 fraternities, 16 sororities. **Athletics (Intercollegiate):** *Men:* baseball, basketball, cross-country, football, golf, soccer, swimming, tennis, track/field (outdoor), wrestling. *Women:* basketball, cross-country, golf, soccer, softball, swimming, tennis, track/field (outdoor), track/field (indoor), volleyball.

ACCOMMODATIONS

Allowed in exams:	
Calculators	Yes
Dictionary	Yes
Computer	Yes
Spell-checker	Yes
Extended test time	Yes
Scribe	Yes
Proctors	Yes
Oral exams	Yes
Note-takers	Yes
Support services for students with:	
LD	Yes
ADHD	Yes
ASD	Yes
Distraction-reduced environment	Yes
Recording of lecture allowed	Yes
Reading technology	Yes
Audio books	Yes
Other assistive technology	Yes
Priority registration	Yes
Added costs of services:	
For LD	No
For ADHD	No
For ASD	No
LD specialists	No
ADHD & ASD coaching	No
ASD specialists	No
Professional tutors	No
Peer tutors	No
Max. hours/week for services	No
How professors are notified of student approved accommodations	Student

COLLEGE GRADUATION REQUIREMENTS

Course waivers allowed	No
Course substitutions allowed	Yes
In what courses: Case by case basis	

California

California State Polytechnic University, Pomona

3801 W Temple Ave., Pomona, CA 91768 • Admissions: 909-869-5299 • Fax: 909-869-4529 **Support: CS**

CAMPUS	
Type of school	Public
Environment	City
STUDENTS	
Undergrad enrollment	26,368
% male/female	53/47
% from out of state	2
% frosh live on campus	44
FINANCIAL FACTS	
Annual in-state tuition	$5,742
Annual out-of-state tuition	$17,622
Room and board	$15,791
Required fees	$1,654
GENERAL ADMISSIONS INFO	
Application fee	$70
Regular application deadline	11/3
Nonfall registration	No
Range SAT EBRW	500–620
Range SAT Math	510–650
Range ACT Composite	19–27
ACADEMICS	
Student/faculty ratio	24:1
% students returning for sophomore year	89
Most classes have 30–39 students.	

Programs/Services for Students with Learning Differences

The Disability Resource Center (DRC) uses an integrated online system for students to access their accommodation. Although the DRC's primary focus is accommodative services, the DRC also provides individualized guidance to students to address their disability-related, academic, ad psychosocial barriers. The DRC's dual focus on both accommodations and supplemental advising allows the DRC student to be able to be successful at the University.

Admissions

Students must meet the university's regular entrance requirements, including C or better in the subject requirements of 4 years of English, 3 years of math, 1 year of U.S. history, 2 years of science lab, 2 years of a foreign language, 1 year of visual or performing arts, and 3 years of academic electives and a qualifiable eligibility index based on high school GPA. ACT or SAT scores will not be used in the admission review for 2021 applicants and will be reviewed for admission decisions on future applicants. Applicants with LD are encouraged to complete college prep courses. However, if students are unable to fulfill a specific course requirement because of a learning disability, alternative college-prep courses may be substituted. Substitutions may be granted, although course substitutions could limit access to some majors. Students are encouraged to self-disclose a learning disability if it would help to explain lower grades. Students who self-disclose are reviewed by DSS, which provides a recommendation to admissions.

Additional Information

Executive Functioning Skills Coaching is an 8-week program that helps students overcome executive functioning challenges such as time management, self-regulation, initiating assignments, and prioritizing. Executive Engagement Coaching is a program that focuses on student self-awareness, self-advocacy, behavior self-regulation and goal setting. Students work with coaches to develop study habits and identify strengths. Additionally, the DRC autism specialist with Counseling and Psychological Services leads a social skill coaching group for students who are anxious and would benefit from peer connections. This is a 10-week program that focuses mainly on how to make and keep friends and manage conflicts. Peer Advocating for Student Success (PASS) provides peer mentors to meet with students and give them a safe place to explore challenges.

ADMISSIONS INFO FOR STUDENTS WITH LEARNING DIFFERENCES

Phone: 909-869-3333 • Fax: 909-869-3271 • Email: drc@cpp.edu

SAT/ACT required: Yes (Test blind for 2021)
Interview required: No
Essay required: No
Additional application required: No
Documentation submitted to: Disability Resource Center

Special Ed. HS course work accepted: No
Separate application required for Programs/Services: No
Documentation required for:
LD: Psychoeducational evaluation
ADHD: Psychoeducational evaluation
ASD: Psychoeducational evaluation

California State Polytechnic University, Pomona

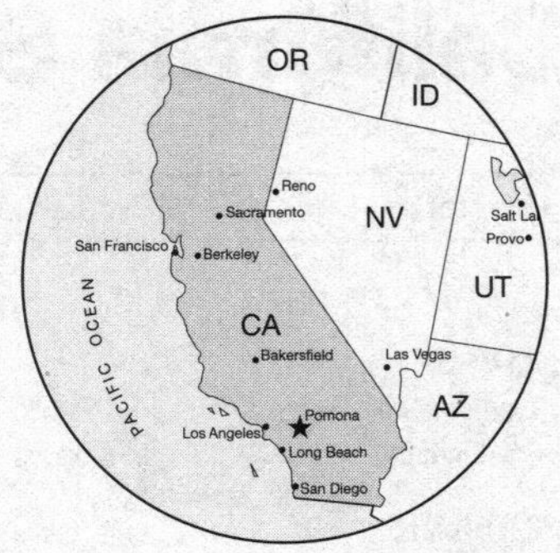

General Admissions

Very important factors include: rigor of secondary school record, and academic GPA. Cal Poly is Test Optional. High school diploma is required and GED is accepted. *Academic units required:* 4 English, 3 math, 2 science, 2 science labs, 2 foreign language, 1 social studies, 1 history, 1 academic elective, 1 visual/performing arts. *Academic units recommended:* 4 math. The California State University (CSU) will temporarily suspend the use of ACT/SAT examinations in determining admission eligibility for all CSU campuses for the 2021–2022 academic year. This temporary change of admission eligibility applies only for the Fall 2021 admission cycle.

Accommodations or Services

Accommodations are decided upon an individual basis after a thorough review of appropriate, current documentation. The accommodations requests must be supported through the documentation provided and must be logically linked to the current impact of the condition on academic functioning.

Financial Aid

Students should submit: Institution's own financial aid form. *Need-based scholarships/grants offered:* College/university scholarship or grant aid from institutional funds; Federal Pell; Private scholarships; SEOG; State scholarships/grants. *Loan aid offered:* Direct PLUS loans; Direct Subsidized Stafford Loans; Direct Unsubsidized Stafford Loans. Federal Work-Study Program available. Institutional employment available.

Campus Life

Activities: Campus Ministries; Choral groups; Concert band; Dance; Drama/theater; International Student Organization; Jazz band; Literary magazine; Model UN; Music ensembles; Musical theater; Opera; Pep band; Student government; Student newspaper; Symphony orchestra; Yearbook. **Organizations:** 429 registered organizations, 36 honor societies, 13 religious organizations, 10 fraternities, 6 sororities. **Athletics (Intercollegiate):** *Men:* baseball, basketball, cheerleading, cross-country, soccer, tennis, track/field (outdoor). *Women:* basketball, cheerleading, cross-country, soccer, tennis, track/field (outdoor), volleyball.

ACCOMMODATIONS

Allowed in exams:	
Calculators	Yes
Dictionary	Yes
Computer	Yes
Spell-checker	Yes
Extended test time	Yes
Scribe	Yes
Proctors	Yes
Oral exams	Yes
Note-takers	Yes
Support services for students with:	
LD	Yes
ADHD	Yes
ASD	Yes
Distraction-reduced environment	Yes
Recording of lecture allowed	Yes
Reading technology	Yes
Audio books	No
Other assistive technology	Yes
Priority registration	Yes
Added costs of services:	
For LD	No
For ADHD	No
For ASD	No
LD specialists	Yes
ADHD & ASD coaching	Yes
ASD specialists	Yes
Professional tutors	No
Peer tutors	Yes
Max. hours/week for services	Varies
How professors are notified of student approved accommodations	Student and Disability Office

COLLEGE GRADUATION REQUIREMENTS

Course waivers allowed	No
Course substitutions allowed	Yes
In what courses: Case by case basis	

California State University, Fresno

5150 North Maple Ave. M/S JA 57, Fresno, CA 93740-8026 • Admissions: 559-278-2261 • Fax: 559-278-4812 **Support: CS**

CAMPUS

Type of school	Public
Environment	Metropolis

STUDENTS

Undergrad enrollment	18,784
% male/female	43/57
% from out of state	<1
% frosh live on campus	22

FINANCIAL FACTS

Annual in-state tuition	$6,927
Annual out-of-state tuition	$16,431
Room and board	$16,788
Required fees	$1,181

GENERAL ADMISSIONS INFO

Application fee	$55
Regular application deadline	11/3
Nonfall registration	Yes
Range SAT EBRW	400–510
Range SAT Math	410–530
Range ACT Composite	16–22

ACADEMICS

Student/faculty ratio	22:1
% students returning for sophomore year	86

Most classes have 20–29 students.

Programs/Services for Students with Learning Differences

There are a wide range of services provided by Services for Students with Disabilities (SSD). Services are determined on a case-by-case basis and the goal is to meet reasonable accommodations for students with appropriate documentation.

Admissions

Students are admitted based on specific courses and their GPA after 9th grade. Students must have at least a C in 4 English, 3 math, 2 social science, 2 science and 2 foreign language classes. The foreign language requirement may be waived in rare cases when supported by the testing data supporting a relevant learning disability. The ACT or SAT will not be used in the admission review for 2021 applicants and will be reviewed for admission decisions on future applicants. Other factors such as impaction and residency status are also considered in the admission decision and admission to the university depends on the capacity of the major that the student has indicated on the application for admission. Once a student submits an application, he or she cannot request to change the major they have listed during the review process. Once admitted, the student is registered for courses based on the choice of major that was identified in the application for admission. The student's mandatory orientation, advising, and registration are all be based on the choice of major. Applicants can be considered for an alternate major if there is capacity for new student enrollment in the alternate major.

Additional Information

Students meet with a Disability Management Specialist to determine appropriate accommodations. SSD provides note-taking support services designed to supplement a student's learning process by having a note-taker record the important information delivered in a lecture environment. These services do not replace the requirement for students to attend class. For students with a diagnosis of ASD there is a Mentoring and Peer Support program (MAPS) offered through SSD.

ADMISSIONS INFO FOR STUDENTS WITH LEARNING DIFFERENCES

Phone: 559-278-2811 • Fax: 559-278-4214 • Email: ssdstaff@csufresno.edu

SAT/ACT required: Yes (Test blind for 2021)
Interview required: Yes
Essay required: Yes
Additional application required: No
Documentation submitted to: Disabled Student Services

Special Ed. HS course work accepted: No
Separate application required for Programs/Services: No
Documentation required for:
LD: Psychoeducational evaluation
ADHD: Psychoeducational evaluation
ASD: Psychoeducational evaluation

California State University, Fresno

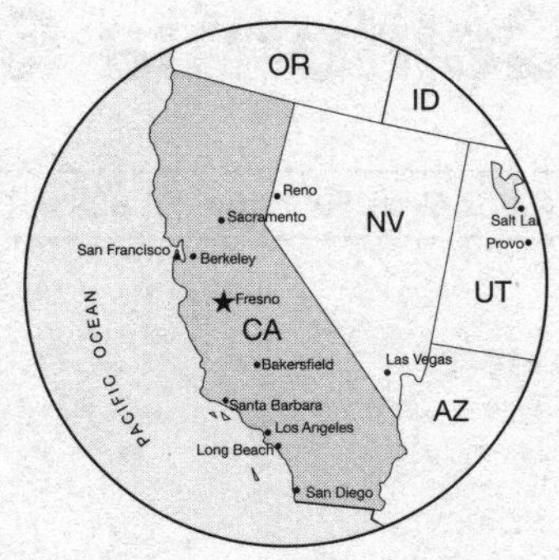

General Admissions

Very important factors include: rigor of secondary school record, and academic GPA. Standardized test scores of ACT or SAT are Optional. High school diploma is required and GED is accepted. *Academic units required:* 4 English, 3 math, 1 science, 1 science lab, 2 foreign language, 1 social studies, 1 history, 1 academic elective, 1 visual/performing arts.

Accommodations or Services

Accommodations are decided upon an individual basis after a thorough review of appropriate, current documentation. The accommodations requests must be supported through the documentation provided and must be logically linked to the current impact of the condition on academic functioning.

Financial Aid

Students should submit: FAFSA. Applicants will be notified of awards on a rolling basis beginning 3/1. *Need-based scholarships/grants offered:* College/university scholarship or grant aid from institutional funds; Federal Pell; Private scholarships; SEOG; State scholarships/grants. *Loan aid offered:* Direct PLUS loans; Direct Subsidized Stafford Loans; Direct Unsubsidized Stafford Loans. Federal Work-Study Program available. Institutional employment available.

Campus Life

Activities: Choral groups; Concert band; Dance; Drama/theater; International Student Organization; Jazz band; Marching band; Music ensembles; Musical theater; Radio station; Student government; Student newspaper; Symphony orchestra; Television station; Yearbook. **Organizations:** 250 registered organizations, 21 honor societies, 11 religious organizations, 19 fraternities, 13 sororities. **Athletics (Intercollegiate):** *Men:* baseball, basketball, cheerleading, cross-country, football, golf, tennis, track/field (outdoor). *Women:* basketball, cheerleading, cross-country, diving, equestrian sports, golf, lacrosse, light weight football, soccer, softball, swimming, tennis, track/field (outdoor), volleyball.

ACCOMMODATIONS

Allowed in exams:	
Calculators	Yes
Dictionary	Yes
Computer	Yes
Spell-checker	Yes
Extended test time	Yes
Scribe	Yes
Proctors	Yes
Oral exams	Yes
Note-takers	Yes
Support services for students with:	
LD	Yes
ADHD	Yes
ASD	Yes
Distraction-reduced environment	Yes
Recording of lecture allowed	Yes
Reading technology	Yes
Audio books	Yes
Other assistive technology	Yes
Priority registration	Yes
Added costs of services:	
For LD	No
For ADHD	No
For ASD	No
LD specialists	Yes
ADHD & ASD coaching	Yes
ASD specialists	Yes
Professional tutors	Yes
Peer tutors	Yes
Max. hours/week for services	Varies
How professors are notified of student approved accommodations	Student

COLLEGE GRADUATION REQUIREMENTS

Course waivers allowed	No
Course substitutions allowed	No

California State University, Fullerton

P.O.Box 6900, Fullerton, CA 92834-6900 • Admissions: 657-278-7788 • Fax: 657-278-7699 **Support: CS**

CAMPUS

Type of school	Public
Environment	City

STUDENTS

Undergrad enrollment	34,921
% male/female	43/57
% from out of state	1
% frosh live on campus	27

FINANCIAL FACTS

Annual in-state tuition	$6,927
Annual out-of-state tuition	$16,431
Room and board	$16,788
Required fees	$1,181

GENERAL ADMISSIONS INFO

Application fee	$70
Regular application deadline	11/3
Nonfall registration	Yes
Range SAT EBRW	510–600
Range SAT Math	520–600
Range ACT Composite	19–24

ACADEMICS

Student/faculty ratio	25:1
% students returning for sophomore year	89

Most classes have 20–29 students.

Programs/Services for Students with Learning Differences

The Office of Disability Support Services provides Counselors to help plan a CSUF experience to meet a student's individual needs. The program is designed to increase retention and graduation rates for underrepresented students. Students are encouraged to fulfill their academic and career potential by participating in an exceptional support environment. Each participant is teamed with an academic counselor for one-on-one mentoring and advisement. The emphasis is on providing students with personal attention and access to support services that include academic advisement; tutoring (referrals for individual and group tutoring including review sessions in select courses and development of study group); cocurricular events; peer mentoring for first-time freshmen; workshops and study-skills courses in reading, writing, math and other subjects, as well as time management; counseling; and an introduction to campus resources.

Admissions

Students are admitted based on specific courses and GPA from 10th and 11th grade. Students must have at least a C in 4 English, 3 math, 2 social science, 2 science and 2 foreign language classes. The foreign language requirement may be waived in rare cases when supported by testing data that supports a relevant learning disability. The ACT or SAT will not be used in the admission review for 2021 applicants and will be reviewed for admission decisions on future applicants. Other factors such as impacted majors and residency status are also considered in the admission decision. Admission depends on the capacity of the major that the student has indicated on the application for admission. Once students submit an application they cannot request to change the major they have listed on the application. Once admitted the student is registered for courses based on the choice of major that was identified in the application for admission.

Additional Information

Peer mentors are available to work individually or in groups with students. Note-takers are recruited from classes in which the SSS student is enrolled. Student Academic Services provides activities and services to promote the development of the whole student, academically, intellectually, and socially. The goal of the Student Academic Services is to improve the retention at CSUF toward graduation.

ADMISSIONS INFO FOR STUDENTS WITH LEARNING DIFFERENCES

Phone: 657-278-3112 • Fax: 657-278-2408 • Email: lpalmerton@fullerton.edu

SAT/ACT required: Yes (Test blind for 2021)
Interview required: No
Essay required: No
Additional application required: No
Documentation submitted to: Disabled Student Services

Special Ed. HS course work accepted: No
Separate application required for Programs/Services: No
Documentation required for:
LD: Psychoeducational evaluation
ADHD: Psychoeducational evaluation
ASD: Psychoeducational evaluation

California State University, Fullerton

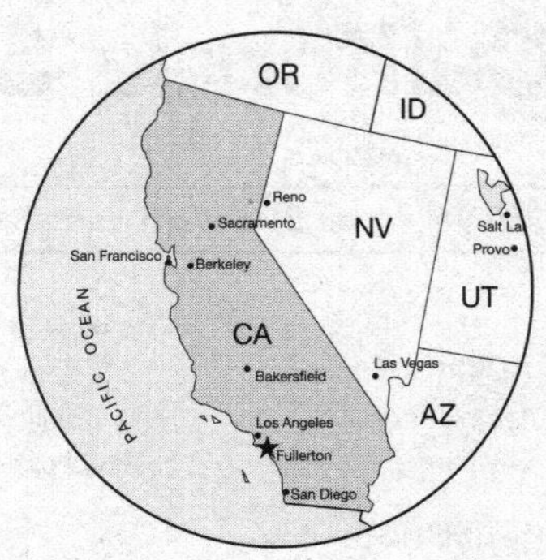

General Admissions

Very important factors include: academic GPA, geographical residence, state residency. High school diploma is required and GED is accepted. *Academic units required:* 4 English, 3 math, 2 science, 2 science labs, 2 foreign language, 1 social studies, 1 history, 1 academic elective, 1 visual/performing arts. *Academic units recommended:* 4 English, 3 math, 2 science, 2 science labs, 3 foreign language, 1 social studies, 1 history, 1 academic elective, 1 visual/performing arts.

Accommodations or Services

Accommodations are decided upon an individual basis after a thorough review of appropriate, current documentation. The accommodations requests must be supported through the documentation provided and must be logically linked to the current impact of the condition on academic functioning.

Financial Aid

Students should submit: FAFSA. *Need-based scholarships/grants offered:* College/university scholarship or grant aid from institutional funds; Federal Pell; Private scholarships; SEOG; State scholarships/grants. *Loan aid offered:* Direct PLUS loans; Direct Subsidized Stafford Loans; Direct Unsubsidized Stafford Loans. Federal Work-Study Program available. Institutional employment available.

Campus Life

Activities: Choral groups; Concert band; Dance; Drama/theater; International Student Organization; Jazz band; Model UN; Music ensembles; Musical theater; Radio station; Student government; Student newspaper; Symphony orchestra. **Organizations:** 374 registered organizations, 17 honor societies, 29 religious organizations, 14 fraternities, 11 sororities. **Athletics (Intercollegiate):** *Men:* baseball, basketball, cross-country, fencing, soccer, track/field (outdoor), wrestling. *Women:* basketball, cross-country, fencing, gymnastics, soccer, softball, tennis, track/field (outdoor), volleyball.

ACCOMMODATIONS

Allowed in exams:	
Calculators	Yes
Dictionary	Yes
Computer	Yes
Spell-checker	Yes
Extended test time	Yes
Scribe	Yes
Proctors	Yes
Oral exams	Yes
Note-takers	Yes
Support services for students with:	
LD	Yes
ADHD	Yes
ASD	Yes
Distraction-reduced environment	Yes
Recording of lecture allowed	Yes
Reading technology	Yes
Audio books	Yes
Other assistive technology	Yes
Priority registration	Yes
Added costs of services:	
For LD	No
For ADHD	No
For ASD	No
LD specialists	Yes
ADHD & ASD coaching	No
ASD specialists	No
Professional tutors	No
Peer tutors	Yes
Max. hours/week for services	Varies
How professors are notified of student approved accommodations	Student

COLLEGE GRADUATION REQUIREMENTS

Course waivers allowed	No
Course substitutions allowed	No

California State University, Long Beach

1250 Bellflower Boulevard, Long Beach, CA 90840 • Admissions: 562-985-5471 • Fax: 562-985-4973 **Support: CS**

CAMPUS

Type of school	Public
Environment	Metropolis

STUDENTS

Undergrad enrollment	32,079
% male/female	44/56
% from out of state	1
% frosh live on campus	36

FINANCIAL FACTS

Annual in-state tuition	$6,846
Annual out-of-state tuition	$17,142
Room and board	$13,938
Required fees	$1,108

GENERAL ADMISSIONS INFO

Application fee	$0
Regular application deadline	11/3
Nonfall registration	Yes
Range SAT EBRW	460–570
Range SAT Math	470–600
Range ACT Composite	19-24

ACADEMICS

Student/faculty ratio	24:1
% students returning for sophomore year	91

Most classes have 20–29 students.

Programs/Services for Students with Learning Differences

The Bob Murphy Access Center helps students with disabilities at California State University, Long Beach. The Stephen Benson Program is a part of the Bob Murphy Access Center and supports students with learning disabilities.

Admissions

The Special Admission process is a means by which applicants who may not meet the California State University Long Beach (CSULB) admission requirements due to a disability but who are "otherwise qualified" may request special consideration for admission. The Bob Murphy Access Center facilitates this process by consulting with Enrollment Services while providing additional information about each applicant's special circumstances. It is the committee's function to evaluate disability documentation using guidelines established by the California State University (CSU) system. All applicants are reviewed on a case-by-case basis. Neither the ACT nor SAT will be used in the admission review for 2021 applicants but will be reviewed for admission decisions on future applicants.

Additional Information

The LIFE Project (Learning Independence for Empowerment) is for students with an Autism Spectrum Disorder. During the LIFE Project meetings, students get support with social interactions, time management, and self-governing abilities. The program promotes independence and autonomy through social interactions, coaching and role-play. There is no fee for students to participate in this LIFE project through BMAC. The Stephen Benson program provides counseling for clarification of issues related to learning disabilities, makes recommendations for accommodations, and fosters self-advocacy in students.

ADMISSIONS INFO FOR STUDENTS WITH LEARNING DIFFERENCES

Phone: 562-985-4430 • Fax: 562-985-4529 • Email: dss@csulb.edu

SAT/ACT required: Yes (Test blind for 2021)
Interview required: No
Essay required: Yes
Additional application required: No
Documentation submitted to: Bob Murphy Access Center

Special Ed. HS course work accepted: Yes
Separate application required for Programs/Services: No
Documentation required for:
LD: Psychoeducational evaluation
ADHD: Psychoeducational evaluation
ASD: Psychoeducational evaluation

California State University, Long Beach

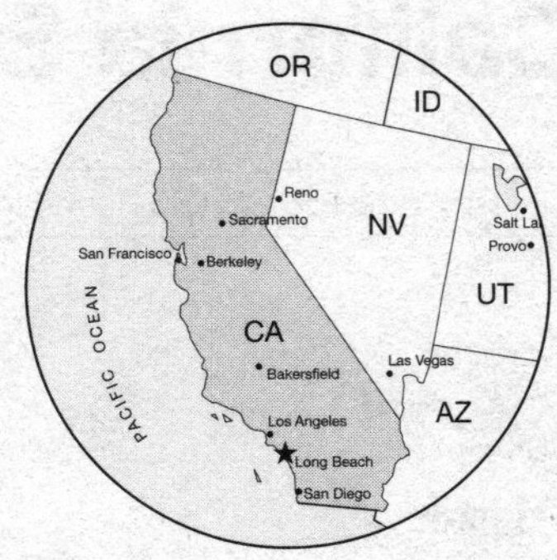

General Admissions

Very important factors include: academic GPA, standardized test scores, geographical residence, state residency. *Important factors include:* talent/ability. *Other factors include:* rigor of secondary school record, application essay, recommendation(s), extracurricular activities, character/personal qualities, volunteer work, work experience. High school diploma is required and GED is accepted. *Academic units required:* 4 English, 3 math, 2 science, 2 science labs, 2 foreign language, 1 social studies, 1 history, 1 academic elective, 1 unit from above areas or other academic areas.

Accommodations or Services

Accommodations are decided upon an individual basis after a thorough review of appropriate, current documentation. The accommodations requests must be supported through the documentation provided and must be logically linked to the current impact of the condition on academic functioning.

Financial Aid

Students should submit: Business/Farm Supplement; CSS/Financial Aid PROFILE; FAFSA; Noncustodial PROFILE. Applicants will be notified of awards on or about 4/1. *Need-based scholarships/grants offered:* College/university scholarship or grant aid from institutional funds; Federal Pell; Private scholarships; SEOG; State scholarships/grants. *Loan aid offered:* Direct PLUS loans; Direct Subsidized Stafford Loans; Direct Unsubsidized Stafford Loans. Federal Work-Study Program available. Institutional employment available.

Campus Life

Activities: Choral groups; Concert band; Dance; Drama/theater; Jazz band; Literary magazine; Music ensembles; Musical theater; Opera; Radio station; Student government; Student newspaper; Student-run film society; Symphony orchestra; Television station; Yearbook. **Organizations:** 300 registered organizations, 25 honor societies, 20 religious organizations, 16 fraternities, 15 sororities. **Athletics (Intercollegiate):** *Men:* baseball, basketball, cross-country, golf, track/field (outdoor), volleyball, water polo. *Women:* basketball, cross-country, golf, soccer, softball, tennis, track/field (outdoor), volleyball, water polo.

ACCOMMODATIONS

Allowed in exams:	
Calculators	Yes
Dictionary	Yes
Computer	Yes
Spell-checker	Yes
Extended test time	Yes
Scribe	Yes
Proctors	Yes
Oral exams	Yes
Note-takers	Yes
Support services for students with:	
LD	Yes
ADHD	Yes
ASD	Yes
Distraction-reduced environment	Yes
Recording of lecture allowed	Yes
Reading technology	Yes
Audio books	Yes
Other assistive technology	Yes
Priority registration	Yes
Added costs of services:	
For LD	No
For ADHD	No
For ASD	No
LD specialists	Yes
ADHD & ASD coaching	Yes
ASD specialists	Yes
Professional tutors	No
Peer tutors	Yes
Max. hours/week for services	Varies
How professors are notified of student approved accommodations	Student

COLLEGE GRADUATION REQUIREMENTS

Course waivers allowed	Varies
In what courses: Case by case basis	
Course substitutions allowed	Yes
In what courses: Case by case basis	

California State University, Northridge

Admissions and Records, CSU Northridge, Northridge, CA 91330-8207 • Admissions: 818-677-3700 • Fax: 818-677-3766 **Support: CS**

CAMPUS	
Type of school	Public
Environment	City
STUDENTS	
Undergrad enrollment	34,633
% male/female	45/55
% from out of state	3
% frosh live on campus	1
FINANCIAL FACTS	
Annual in-state tuition	$7,012
Annual out-of-state tuition	$18,892
Room and board	$11,662
Required fees	$635
GENERAL ADMISSIONS INFO	
Application fee	$70
Regular application deadline	11/30
Nonfall registration	Yes
Range SAT EBRW	460–570
Range SAT Math	450–560
Range ACT Composite	16–22
ACADEMICS	
Student/faculty ratio	27:1
% students returning for sophomore year	78

Programs/Services for Students with Learning Differences

Disability Resources and Educational Services (DRES) assists students with disabilities in reaching their full potential. The program offers a comprehensive and well-coordinated system of educational support services that allow students to be judged on the basis of their ability rather than disability. In order to accommodate different needs DRES has developed an individualized learning plan called "journey to success" to provide support to students during their transition into college. This support continues with mentoring and advising. Students must register with DRES to be eligible.

Admissions

There is no special admission process for students with learning disabilities. However, if a student applies to the university and is rejected, they may appeal the decision. Students must get a C or better in: 4 years English, 3 years math, 1 year history, 1 year science, 2 years foreign language, 1 year visual/performing arts, and 3 years of electives. Neither the ACT nor SAT will be used in the admission review for 2021 applicants but will be reviewed for admission decisions on future applicants. California residents receive priority whenever admission space is limited.

Additional Information

In addition to the Journey to Success, the DRES offers the Thriving and Achieving Program (TAP) that supports the academic, personal and career success of students with disabilities. Academic coaches support students in TAP through peer mentoring and strategic tutoring. Connection Points offers group seminars for students to meet and interact.

ADMISSIONS INFO FOR STUDENTS WITH LEARNING DIFFERENCES

Phone: 818-677-2684 • Fax: 818-677-4932 • Email: dres@csun.edu

SAT/ACT required: Yes (Test blind for 2021)
Interview required: Yes
Essay required: No
Additional application required: No
Documentation submitted to: Disability Resources and Educational Services

Special Ed. HS course work accepted: Yes
Separate application required for Programs/Services: No
Documentation required for:
LD: Psychoeducational evaluation
ADHD: Psychoeducational evaluation
ASD: Psychoeducational evaluation

California State University, Northridge

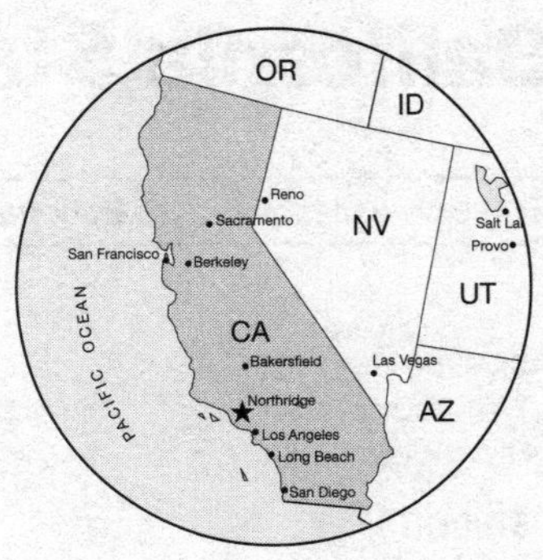

General Admissions

Very important factors include: standardized test scores. High school diploma is required and GED is accepted. *Academic units required:* 4 English, 3 math, 1 science, 2 science labs, 2 foreign language, 2 history, 1 academic elective, 1 unit from above areas or other academic areas.

Accommodations or Services

Accommodations are decided upon an individual basis after a thorough review of appropriate, current documentation. The accommodations requests must be supported through the documentation provided and must be logically linked to the current impact of the condition on academic functioning.

Financial Aid

Students should submit: FAFSA. Applicants will be notified of awards on a rolling basis beginning 3/15. *Need-based scholarships/grants offered:* College/university scholarship or grant aid from institutional funds; Federal Nursing Scholarships; Federal Pell; Private scholarships; SEOG; State scholarships/grants. *Loan aid offered:* Federal Work-Study Program available. Institutional employment available.

Campus Life

Activities: Choral groups; Concert band; Dance; Drama/theater; International Student Organization; Jazz band; Literary magazine; Marching band; Music ensembles; Musical theater; Radio station; Student government; Student newspaper; Yearbook. **Organizations:** 323 registered organizations, 15 honor societies, 17 religious organizations, 24 fraternities, 12 sororities. **Athletics (Intercollegiate):** *Men:* baseball, basketball, cross-country, diving, football, golf, soccer, swimming, track/field (outdoor), track/field (indoor), volleyball. *Women:* basketball, cross-country, diving, football, golf, soccer, softball, swimming, tennis, track/field (outdoor), track/field (indoor), volleyball.

ACCOMMODATIONS

Allowed in exams:	
Calculators	Yes
Dictionary	Yes
Computer	Yes
Spell-checker	Yes
Extended test time	Yes
Scribe	Yes
Proctors	Yes
Oral exams	Yes
Note-takers	Yes
Support services for students with:	
LD	Yes
ADHD	Yes
ASD	Yes
Distraction-reduced environment	Yes
Recording of lecture allowed	Yes
Reading technology	Yes
Audio books	Yes
Other assistive technology	Yes
Priority registration	Yes
Added costs of services:	
For LD	No
For ADHD	No
For ASD	No
LD specialists	Yes
ADHD & ASD coaching	No
ASD specialists	No
Professional tutors	No
Peer tutors	Yes
Max. hours/week for services	2
How professors are notified of student approved accommodations	Student

COLLEGE GRADUATION REQUIREMENTS

Course waivers allowed	No
Course substitutions allowed	No

California State University, San Bernardino

5500 University Parkway, San Bernardino, CA 92407-2397 • Admissions: 909-537-5188 • Fax: 909-537-7034 **Support: CS**

CAMPUS

Type of school	Public
Environment	City

STUDENTS

Undergrad enrollment	18,114
% male/female	39/61
% from out of state	<1
% frosh live on campus	14

FINANCIAL FACTS

Annual in-state tuition	$6,660
Annual out-of-state tuition	$18,000
Room and board	$13,435
Required fees	$1,254

GENERAL ADMISSIONS INFO

Application fee	$55
Regular application deadline	12/4
Nonfall registration	Yes
Range SAT EBRW	460–550
Range SAT Math	450–540
Range ACT Composite	15–19

ACADEMICS

Student/faculty ratio	28:1
% students returning for sophomore year	86

Most classes have 20–29 students.

Programs/Services for Students with Learning Differences

Services to Students with Disabilities (SSD) assures each student an opportunity to experience equity in education. Once a student has completed an assessment the staff helps the student to develop compensatory methods for handling assignments and classroom projects. Careful attention is paid to helping the student acquire learning skills and formulating and implementing specific strategies for notetaking and management of written materials. Recommendations are designed for each student as a result of a psychometric assessment, personal interview, and academic requirements. The emphasis of the plan is to assist the students with a learning disability in finding techniques to deal with it in college and the future.

Admissions

Entrance requires a minimum 15-unit pattern of courses for admission as a first-time freshman. Each unit is equal to a year of study in a subject area. A grade of C (GPA 2.0) or better is required for each course used to meet any subject requirement. Neither the ACT nor SAT will be used in the admission review for 2021 applicants but will be reviewed for admission decisions on future applicants. California residents are given priority in the admission process wherever space is limited.

Additional Information

Services and accommodations for students with appropriate documentation could include the following: the use of calculators, dictionaries, computers, or spellchecker during exams; extended time on tests; distraction-free testing environments; oral exams; notetakers; proctors; scribes; tape recorders in class; books on tape; assisting technology; and priority registration. Specific services include assessment counseling and testing accommodations. Students on academic probation have two quarters to raise their GPA to a 2.0.

ADMISSIONS INFO FOR STUDENTS WITH LEARNING DIFFERENCES

Phone: 909-537-5238 • Fax: 909-537-7090 • Email: SSD@csusb.edu

SAT/ACT required: Yes (Test blind for 2021)
Interview required: No
Essay required: No
Additional application required: Yes
Documentation submitted to: SSD

Special Ed. HS course work accepted: Yes
Separate application required for Programs/Services: Yes
Documentation required for:
LD: Psychoeducational evaluation
ADHD: Psychoeducational evaluation
ASD: Psychoeducational evaluation

California State University, San Bernardino

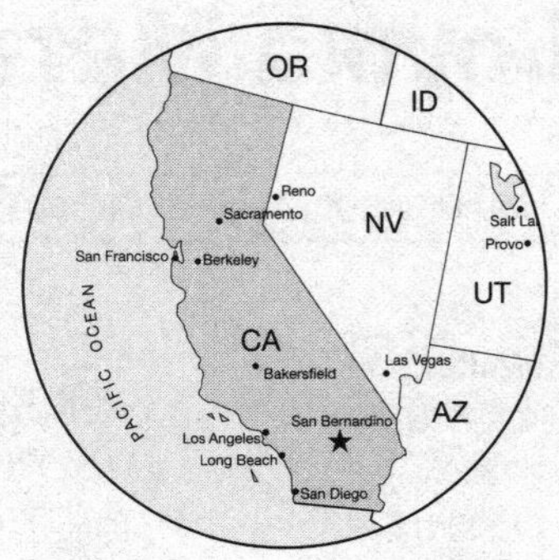

General Admissions

Very important factors include: academic GPA, standardized test scores. *Important factors include:* geographical residence. High school diploma is required and GED is accepted. *Academic units required:* 4 English, 3 math, 2 science, 2 science labs, 2 foreign language, 1 social studies, 1 history, 1 academic elective, 1 visual/performing arts.

Accommodations or Services

Accommodations are decided upon an individual basis after a thorough review of appropriate, current documentation. The accommodations requests must be supported through the documentation provided and must be logically linked to the current impact of the condition on academic functioning.

Financial Aid

Students should submit: FAFSA; Institution's own financial aid form. Applicants will be notified of awards on a rolling basis beginning 3/1. *Need-based scholarships/grants offered:* College/university scholarship or grant aid from institutional funds; Federal Pell; Private scholarships; SEOG; State scholarships/grants. *Loan aid offered:* Direct PLUS loans; Direct Subsidized Stafford Loans; Direct Unsubsidized Stafford Loans. Federal Work-Study Program available. Institutional employment available.

Campus Life

Activities: Campus Ministries; Choral groups; Concert band; Dance; Drama/theater; International Student Organization; Jazz band; Model UN; Music ensembles; Musical theater; Radio station; Student government; Student newspaper; Television station. **Organizations:** 100 registered organizations, 6 honor societies. **Athletics (Intercollegiate):** *Men:* baseball, basketball, golf, soccer, swimming, water polo. *Women:* basketball, cross-country, soccer, softball, swimming, tennis, volleyball, water polo.

ACCOMMODATIONS

Allowed in exams:	
Calculators	Yes
Dictionary	Yes
Computer	Yes
Spell-checker	Yes
Extended test time	Yes
Scribe	Yes
Proctors	Yes
Oral exams	Yes
Note-takers	Yes
Support services for students with:	
LD	Yes
ADHD	Yes
ASD	Yes
Distraction-reduced environment	Yes
Recording of lecture allowed	Yes
Reading technology	Yes
Audio books	Yes
Other assistive technology	Yes
Priority registration	Yes
Added costs of services:	
For LD	No
For ADHD	No
For ASD	No
LD specialists	Yes
ADHD & ASD coaching	No
ASD specialists	No
Professional tutors	No
Peer tutors	Yes
Max. hours/week for services	Varies
How professors are notified of student approved accommodations	Student and Disability Office

COLLEGE GRADUATION REQUIREMENTS

Course waivers allowed	No
Course substitutions allowed	No

Loyola Marymount University

1 LMU Drive, Los Angeles, CA 90045-2659 • Admissions: 310-338-2750 **Support: CS**

CAMPUS

Type of school	Private (nonprofit)
Environment	Town

STUDENTS

Undergrad enrollment	6,638
% male/female	45/55
% from out of state	33
% frosh live on campus	94

FINANCIAL FACTS

Annual Tuition	$52,402
Room and board	$15,550

GENERAL ADMISSIONS INFO

Application fee	$60
Regular application deadline	1/15
Nonfall registration	Yes
Admission may be deferred	Yes
Range SAT EBRW	620–700
Range SAT Math	610–710
Range ACT Composite	27–31

ACADEMICS

Student/faculty ratio	10:1
% students returning for sophomore year	89

Most classes have 10–19 students.

Programs/Services for Students with Learning Differences

The Office of Disability Support Services (DSS) provides specialized assistance and resources to students with disabilities. Students may choose whether to disclose a disability. A student with a disability will not receive accommodations unless he or she requests them and follows the University's procedures for obtaining those services. Students must also be able to meet the minimal standards of both the University and the particular school, program, service or activity to which admission is sought.

Admissions

There is no special admissions process for students with disabilities. LMU does not engage in any affirmative action programs for students with disabilities. The admission decision will be based upon the student's grade point average, strength of curriculum, the application essay, letters of recommendation, and extracurricular activities. Enrolled students have an average GPA of 3.8. Students are encouraged to have completed 4 years English, 3 years social sciences, 3 years foreign language, 3 years math (4 years for engineering and science), 2 years science, and 1 year elective. LMU is test optional for 2021 and will revisit this policy for future applicants.

Additional Information

The Academic Resource Center offers course-specific tutoring, study skills programs (which include learning time management, overcoming test anxiety, conquering math word problems, mastering the textbook, preparing for exams, and studying efficiently), and other academic support programs with fulltime professional staff members. Specific accommodations for LD students with appropriate documentation could include: priority registration, notetakers, readers, transcribers, alternate testing conditions, taped books, and advocacy.

ADMISSIONS INFO FOR STUDENTS WITH LEARNING DIFFERENCES

Phone: 310-338-4216 • Fax: 310-338-5344 • Email: dsslmu@lmu.edu

SAT/ACT required: Yes (Test optional for 2021)
Interview required: No
Essay required: Yes
Additional application required: No
Documentation submitted to: Disability Support Services

Special Ed. HS course work accepted: No
Separate application required for Programs/Services: No
Documentation required for:
LD: Psychoeducational evaluation
ADHD: Psychoeducational evaluation
ASD: Psychoeducational evaluation

Loyola Marymount University

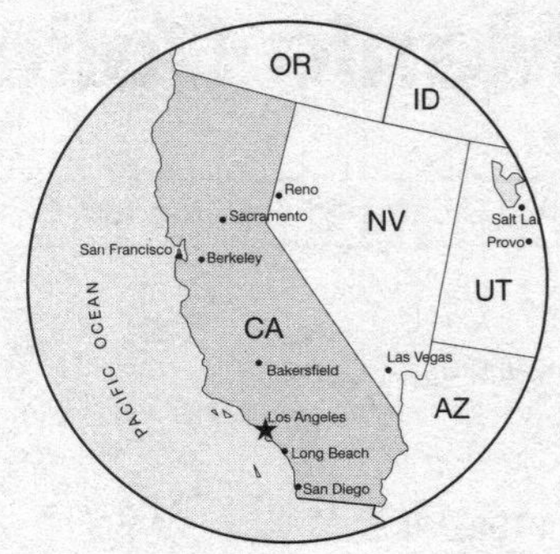

General Admissions

Very important factors include: academic GPA. *Important factors include:* rigor of secondary school record, application essay, standardized test scores, talent/ability, character/personal qualities. *Other factors include:* class rank, recommendation(s), extracurricular activities, first generation, alumni/ae relation, volunteer work, work experience. High school diploma is required and GED is accepted. *Academic units recommended:* 4 English, 3 math, 2 science, 2 science labs, 3 foreign language, 3 social studies, 1 academic elective.

Accommodations or Services

Accommodations are decided upon an individual basis after a thorough review of appropriate, current documentation. The accommodations requests must be supported through the documentation provided and must be logically linked to the current impact of the condition on academic functioning.

Financial Aid

Students should submit: FAFSA. *Need-based scholarships/grants offered:* College/university scholarship or grant aid from institutional funds; Federal Pell; Private scholarships; SEOG; State scholarships/grants. *Loan aid offered:* Direct PLUS loans; Direct Subsidized Stafford Loans; Direct Unsubsidized Stafford Loans. Federal Work-Study Program available. Institutional employment available.

Campus Life

Activities: Campus Ministries; Choral groups; Dance; Drama/theater; International Student Organization; Literary magazine; Model UN; Music ensembles; Opera; Radio station; Student government; Student newspaper; Student-run film society; Television station; Yearbook. **Organizations:** 185 registered organizations, 23 honor societies, 9 religious organizations, 11 fraternities, 12 sororities. **Athletics (Intercollegiate):** *Men:* baseball, basketball, crew/rowing, cross-country, golf, soccer, tennis, water polo. *Women:* basketball, crew/rowing, cross-country, soccer, softball, swimming, tennis, volleyball, water polo.

ACCOMMODATIONS

Allowed in exams:	
Calculators	Yes
Dictionary	Yes
Computer	Yes
Spell-checker	Yes
Extended test time	Yes
Scribe	Yes
Proctors	Yes
Oral exams	Yes
Note-takers	Yes
Support services for students with:	
LD	Yes
ADHD	Yes
ASD	Yes
Distraction-reduced environment	Yes
Recording of lecture allowed	Yes
Reading technology	Yes
Audio books	Yes
Other assistive technology	Yes
Priority registration	Yes
Added costs of services:	
For LD	No
For ADHD	No
For ASD	No
LD specialists	Yes
ADHD & ASD coaching	No
ASD specialists	No
Professional tutors	No
Peer tutors	Yes
Max. hours/week for services	1 each subject
How professors are notified of student approved accommodations	Student

COLLEGE GRADUATION REQUIREMENTS

Course waivers allowed	No
Course substitutions allowed	No

California

Menlo College

1000 El Camino Real, Atherton, CA 94027 • Admissions: 650-543-3753 • Fax: 650-543-4103 **Support: S**

CAMPUS	
Type of school	Private (nonprofit)
Environment	Town
STUDENTS	
Undergrad enrollment	894
% male/female	55/45
% from out of state	27
FINANCIAL FACTS	
Annual tuition	$45,050
Room and board	$15,900
Required fees	$810
GENERAL ADMISSIONS INFO	
Application fee	$40
Regular application deadline	1/15
Nonfall registration	Yes
Admission may be deferred	Yes
ACADEMICS	
% students returning for sophomore year	74
Most classes have 20–29 students.	

Programs/Services for Students with Learning Differences

The Gullard Family Academic Success Center (ASC) welcomes all students including those with learning, psychological, and attention challenges. In its new configuration with the Bowman Library, now the Learning Community Commons, services have broadened to include library staff and resources. Students who present proper documentation of a disability may qualify for accommodations. All students are welcome to utilize the services of the Academic Success Center. Students may drop in to the Academic Success Center for assistance at any time during normal hours.

Admissions

Students are admitted to Menlo College on their own merits, without regard to disability. If students choose to self-disclose their learning challenges, they are encouraged to meet with the Academic Success Center in advance of their arrival to arrange for early set-up of accommodations. Menlo values the individual strengths and diversity that students bring to Menlo, so we choose not to follow a specific formula when making our admission decisions. Each applicant is reviewed individually, and the acceptance decisions are based on many factors including the strength of your course curriculum, the school you attend(ed), and your grades. In addition, Menlo considers extracurricular activities, community involvement, employment, and leadership roles. Menlo College is most interested in the quality of students' activities, rather than the quantity. One supplemental essay is required regarding reasons for seeking a college education.

Additional Information

The Academic Success Center provides a "one-stop" center for information and resources that are key to academic and career success. The services include: advising, advocacy, assistive technology, note takers, books on tape, tutoring lab and writing center, testing and tutoring, documentation analysis and faculty liaison for Students with Disabilities. The Academic Success Center will help students improve test performance, obtain or update their Degree Check Sheet(s), understand why they may attend class regularly, but feel like they're missing important points or having trouble completing tests in the allotted time, feel like they don't have enough time to get everything done, not sure how to take notes, need a tutor or study group, or want information on meeting with your academic advisor. The tutoring center is staffed by peer tutors.

ADMISSIONS INFO FOR STUDENTS WITH LEARNING DIFFERENCES

Phone: 650-543-3720 • Fax: 650-543-4120 • Email: disabilityservices@menlo.edu

SAT/ACT required: No
Interview required: No
Essay required: Yes
Additional application required: No
Documentation submitted to: Disability Services

Special Ed. HS course work accepted: Yes
Separate application required for Programs/Services: No
Documentation required for:
LD: Psychoeducational evaluation
ADHD: Psychoeducational evaluation
ASD: Psychoeducational evaluation or psychiatrist or physician's report

Menlo College

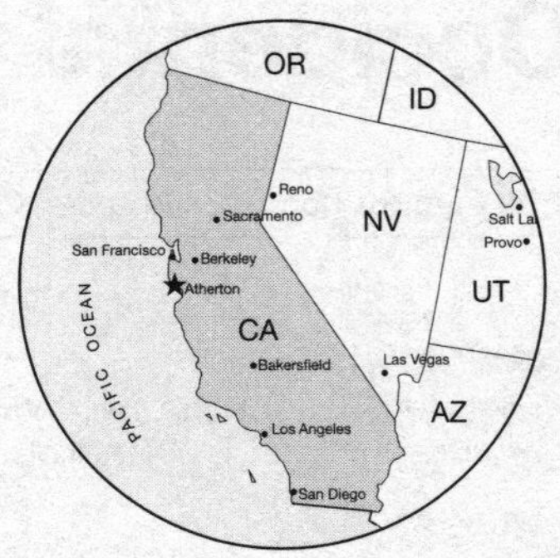

General Admissions

Very important factors include: rigor of secondary school record, academic GPA, standardized test scores. *Important factors include:* class rank, application essay, recommendation(s), character/personal qualities, volunteer work. *Other factors include:* interview, alumni/ae relation, work experience, level of applicant's interest. High school diploma is required and GED is accepted. *Academic units recommended:* 4 English, 3 math, 3 science, 2 foreign language, 3 social studies.

Accommodations or Services

Accommodations are decided upon an individual basis after a thorough review of appropriate, current documentation. The accommodations requests must be supported through the documentation provided and must be logically linked to the current impact of the condition on academic functioning.

Financial Aid

Students should submit: FAFSA. *Need-based scholarships/grants offered:* College/university scholarship or grant aid from institutional funds; Federal Pell; SEOG; State scholarships/grants. *Loan aid offered:* Direct PLUS loans; Direct Subsidized Stafford Loans; Direct Unsubsidized Stafford Loans. Federal Work-Study Program available. Institutional employment available.

Campus Life

Activities: Dance; International Student Organization; Student government; Student newspaper; Student-run film society. **Organizations:** 38 registered organizations, 3 honor societies. **Athletics (Intercollegiate):** *Men:* baseball, basketball, cross-country, football, golf, soccer, wrestling. *Women:* basketball, cross-country, soccer, softball, volleyball, wrestling.

ACCOMMODATIONS

Allowed in exams:	
Calculators	Yes
Dictionary	Yes
Computer	Yes
Spell-checker	Yes
Extended test time	Yes
Scribe	Yes
Proctors	Yes
Oral exams	Yes
Note-takers	Yes
Support services for students with:	
LD	Yes
ADHD	Yes
ASD	Yes
Distraction-reduced environment	Yes
Recording of lecture allowed	Yes
Reading technology	Yes
Audio books	Yes
Other assistive technology	Yes
Priority registration	No
Added costs of services:	
For LD	No
For ADHD	No
For ASD	No
LD specialists	No
ADHD & ASD coaching	No
ASD specialists	No
Professional tutors	Yes
Peer tutors	Yes
Max. hours/week for services	As needed
How professors are notified of student approved accommodations	Student and Disability Office

COLLEGE GRADUATION REQUIREMENTS

Course waivers allowed	Yes
In what courses: Foreign language and math (for some majors)	
Course substitutions allowed	Yes
In what courses: Foreign language and math (for some majors)	

California

Occidental College

1600 Campus Road, Los Angeles, CA 90041-3314 • Admissions: 800-825-5262 • Fax: 323-341-4875 **Support: S**

CAMPUS

Type of school	Private (nonprofit)
Environment	Metropolis

STUDENTS

Undergrad enrollment	2,066
% male/female	42/58
% from out of state	59
% frosh live on campus	100

FINANCIAL FACTS

Annual tuition	$55,980
Room and board	$16,600
Required fees	$596

GENERAL ADMISSIONS INFO

Application fee	$65
Regular application deadline	1/1
Nonfall registration	No

Admission may be deferred.

Range SAT EBRW	650–730
Range SAT Math	650–750
Range ACT Composite	28–32

ACADEMICS

Student/faculty ratio	9.5:1
% students returning for sophomore year	93

Most classes have 10–19 students.

Programs/Services for Students with Learning Differences

The Office of Disability Services is committed to enhancing students' academic development and independence. The goal is to create a supportive community that promotes awareness, sensitivity and understanding of students with disabilities. Documentation must be provided to access accommodations and are determined on a case-by-case basis.

Admissions

Occidental utilizes a comprehensive review process when considering students for admission. The college values academic performance, extracurricular achievement and personal attributes when evaluating first-year and transfer applications. In the review of an academic record, Occidental places the most emphasis on course rigor and classroom performance. Occidental is test optional and does not require students to submit either the ACT or SAT. Interviews are not required but are highly recommended and are offered virtually.

Additional Information

Students with documented learning disabilities meet with staff in the Disability Services Office to determine eligibility for accommodations and services. Typical accommodations if appropriate include: extended testing time, use of computer or assistive technology, reduced distraction testing environment, use of a calculator or spell checker, notetaker/recorder during lectures, or reduced course load. There are many opportunities for support for all students at Occidental. The Scientific Scholars Achievement Program is student-led and promotes community building between students and faculty. The Academic Mastery Program provides workshops to promote excellence in science and math and the Center for Digital Liberal Arts provides technical support to students.

ADMISSIONS INFO FOR STUDENTS WITH LEARNING DIFFERENCES

Phone: 323-259-2969 • Fax: 323-341-4927 • Email: accessibility@oxy.edu

SAT/ACT required: Yes (Test optional for 2021)
Interview required: Recommended
Essay required: Yes
Additional application required: No
Documentation submitted to: Disability Services

Special Ed. HS course work accepted: Yes
Separate application required for Programs/Services: Yes
Documentation required for:
- **LD:** Psychoeducational evaluation/assessment
- **ADHD:** Psychoeducational evaluation/assessment
- **ASD:** Psychoeducational evaluation/assessment

Occidental College

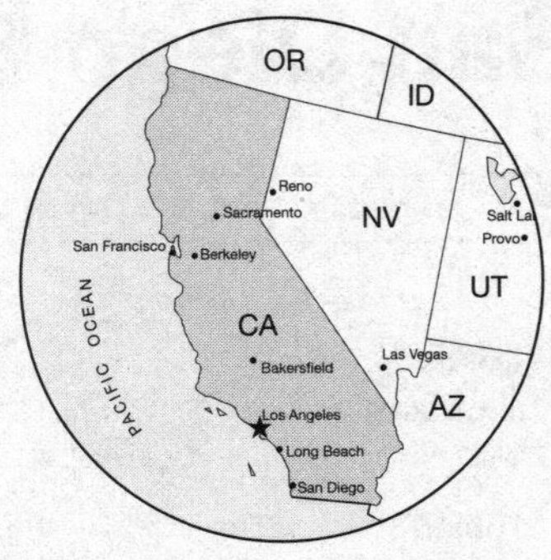

General Admissions

Very important factors include: rigor of secondary school record, academic GPA, application essay. *Important factors include:* class rank, standardized test scores, recommendation(s), extracurricular activities, character/ personal qualities, volunteer work. *Other factors include:* interview, talent/ ability, first generation, alumni/ae relation, geographical residence, racial/ ethnic status, level of applicant's interest. High school diploma is required and GED is accepted. *Academic units recommended:* 4 English, 4 math, 3 science, 3 foreign language, 3 social studies.

Accommodations or Services

Accommodations are decided upon an individual basis after a thorough review of appropriate, current documentation. The accommodations requests must be supported through the documentation provided and must be logically linked to the current impact of the condition on academic functioning.

Financial Aid

Students should submit: CSS/Financial Aid PROFILE; FAFSA; Noncustodial PROFILE; State aid form. *Need-based scholarships/grants offered:* College/ university scholarship or grant aid from institutional funds; Federal Pell; Private scholarships; SEOG; State scholarships/grants. *Loan aid offered:* Direct PLUS loans; Direct Subsidized Stafford Loans; Direct Unsubsidized Stafford Loans. Federal Work-Study Program available. Institutional employment available.

Campus Life

Activities: Campus Ministries; Choral groups; Concert band; Dance; Drama/theater; International Student Organization; Jazz band; Literary magazine; Music ensembles; Musical theater; Radio station; Student government; Student newspaper; Student-run film society; Symphony orchestra; Yearbook. **Organizations:** 117 registered organizations, 8 honor societies, 9 religious organizations, 2 fraternities, 4 sororities. **Athletics (Intercollegiate):** *Men:* baseball, basketball, cross-country, diving, football, golf, soccer, swimming, tennis, track/field (outdoor), water polo. *Women:* basketball, cross-country, diving, golf, lacrosse, soccer, softball, swimming, tennis, track/field (outdoor), volleyball, water polo.

ACCOMMODATIONS

Allowed in exams:	
Calculators	Yes
Dictionary	Yes
Computer	Yes
Spell-checker	Yes
Extended test time	Yes
Scribe	Yes
Proctors	Yes
Oral exams	Yes
Note-takers	Yes
Support services for students with:	
LD	Yes
ADHD	Yes
ASD	Yes
Distraction-reduced environment	Yes
Recording of lecture allowed	Yes
Reading technology	Yes
Audio books	Yes
Other assistive technology	Yes
Priority registration	Yes
Added costs of services:	
For LD	No
For ADHD	No
For ASD	No
LD specialists	No
ADHD & ASD coaching	Yes
ASD specialists	No
Professional tutors	No
Peer tutors	Yes
Max. hours/week for services	Varies
How professors are notified of student approved accommodations	Student

COLLEGE GRADUATION REQUIREMENTS

Course waivers allowed	No
In what courses: No waiver, but can substitute Foreign Language, Math	
Course substitutions allowed	Yes
In what courses: Case by case basis	

California

San Diego State University

5500 Campanile Drive, San Diego, CA 92182-7455 • Admissions: 619-594-6336 **Support: CS**

CAMPUS

Type of school	Public
Environment	Metropolis

STUDENTS

Undergrad enrollment	30,612
% male/female	45/55
% from out of state	11
% frosh live on campus	71

FINANCIAL FACTS

Annual in-state tuition	$7,720
Annual out-of-state tuition	$19,600
Room and board	$18,531

GENERAL ADMISSIONS INFO

Application fee	$70
Regular application deadline	11/3
Nonfall registration	Yes
Range SAT EBRW	560–650
Range SAT Math	550–670
Range ACT Composite	22–29

ACADEMICS

Student/faculty ratio	25:1
% students returning for sophomore year	89

Most classes have 20–29 students.

Programs/Services for Students with Learning Differences

The Student Ability Success Center (SASC) at San Diego State University offers support and accommodations to students with documented disabilities. To further this mission, SASC is committed to the following: minimizing academic barriers, promoting self-advocacy, and working collaboratively with SDSU faculty, staff, and the campus community to increase disability awareness.

Admissions

All applicants must meet the admission criteria for California State University and San Diego State University. Students must elect a major during the application process. All majors are very competitive, and there are more applicants than there are spaces. Applicants are ranked within each major, rather than overall. The popularity of majors changes every year based on the applicant pool. Admission is major-specific, which means applicants cannot change the major during the application process. Specific majors will have additional requirements that must be met for admission to the major and the university such as dance, music, nursing and theater performance. Students who are denied admission may appeal to have their application reviewed by submitting a letter of appeal that details extenuating circumstances that impacted their academic record. It is, however, unlikely that a decision will be reversed.

Additional Information

Students are encouraged to get volunteer note-takers from among other students enrolled in the class. Limited tutoring is available based on documented functional limitations related to subject matter. Tutoring, when authorized, is available at no charge. Students with learning disabilities may request permission to tape a lecture. Students with documented disabilities may utilize classroom test accommodations at the Calpulli Center test facility. This may include extended test time, readers, writers, tests in alternative format, or a quiet testing environment. Students will also need permission from the professor to use a calculator, dictionary, computer, or spellchecker in exams. High Tech Center is an assistive technology center available to students with disabilities.

ADMISSIONS INFO FOR STUDENTS WITH LEARNING DIFFERENCES

Phone: 619-594-6473 • Fax: 619-594-4315 • Email: earos@sdsu.edu

SAT/ACT required: Yes (Test blind for 2021)
Interview required: No
Essay required: No
Additional application required: Yes
Documentation submitted to: SASC

Special Ed. HS course work accepted: Yes
Separate application required for Programs/Services: Yes
Documentation required for:
LD: Psychoeducational evaluation
ADHD: Psychoeducational evaluation
ASD: Psychoeducational evaluation

San Diego State University

General Admissions

Very important factors include: rigor of secondary school record, academic GPA, standardized test scores. *Important factors include:* geographical residence, state residency. High school diploma is required and GED is accepted. *Academic units required:* 4 English, 3 math, 2 science, 2 science labs, 2 foreign language, 1 social studies, 1 history, 1 academic elective, 1 visual/performing arts. *Academic units recommended:* 4 math.

Accommodations or Services

Accommodations are decided upon an individual basis after a thorough review of appropriate, current documentation. The accommodations requests must be supported through the documentation provided and must be logically linked to the current impact of the condition on academic functioning.

Financial Aid

Students should submit: Business/Farm Supplement; CSS/Financial Aid PROFILE; FAFSA; Noncustodial PROFILE. Applicants will be notified of awards on a rolling basis beginning 12/15. *Need-based scholarships/grants offered:* College/university scholarship or grant aid from institutional funds; Federal Pell; Private scholarships; SEOG; State scholarships/grants. *Loan aid offered:* Direct PLUS loans; Direct Subsidized Stafford Loans; Direct Unsubsidized Stafford Loans. Federal Work-Study Program available. Institutional employment available.

Campus Life

Activities: Campus Ministries; Choral groups; Concert band; Dance; Drama/theater; International Student Organization; Jazz band; Literary magazine; Marching band; Music ensembles; Musical theater; Opera; Pep band; Radio station; Student government; Student newspaper; Student-run film society; Symphony orchestra; Television station. **Organizations:** 385 registered organizations, 27 honor societies, 17 religious organizations, 22 fraternities, 22 sororities. **Athletics (Intercollegiate):** *Men:* baseball, basketball, football, golf, soccer, tennis. *Women:* basketball, crew/rowing, cross-country, diving, golf, soccer, softball, swimming, tennis, track/field (outdoor), track/field (indoor), volleyball, water polo.

ACCOMMODATIONS

Allowed in exams:	
Calculators	Yes
Dictionary	Yes
Computer	Yes
Spell-checker	Yes
Extended test time	Yes
Scribe	Yes
Proctors	Yes
Oral exams	Yes
Note-takers	Yes
Support services for students with:	
LD	Yes
ADHD	Yes
ASD	Yes
Distraction-reduced environment	Yes
Recording of lecture allowed	Yes
Reading technology	Yes
Audio books	Yes
Other assistive technology	Yes
Priority registration	Yes
Added costs of services:	
For LD	No
For ADHD	No
For ASD	No
LD specialists	Yes
ADHD & ASD coaching	No
ASD specialists	No
Professional tutors	Yes
Peer tutors	Yes
Max. hours/week for services	Varies
How professors are notified of student approved accommodations	Student

COLLEGE GRADUATION REQUIREMENTS

Course waivers allowed	No
Course substitutions allowed	Yes
In what courses: Case by case basis	

San Francisco State University

1600 Holloway Avenue, San Francisco, CA 93132 • Admissions: 415-338-6486 • Fax: 415-338-3880 **Support: CS**

CAMPUS	
Type of school	Public
Environment	Metropolis
STUDENTS	
Undergrad enrollment	25,917
% male/female	45/55
% from out of state	1
% frosh live on campus	60
FINANCIAL FACTS	
Annual in-state tuition	$5,742
Annual out-of-state tuition	$17,622
Room and board	$15,201
Required fees	$1,694
GENERAL ADMISSIONS INFO	
Application fee	$70
Regular application deadline	11/30
Nonfall registration	Yes
Range SAT EBRW	470–580
Range SAT Math	470–570
Range ACT Composite	17–22
ACADEMICS	
Student/faculty ratio	22:1
% students returning for sophomore year	79
Most classes have 20–29 students.	

Programs/Services for Students with Learning Differences

The Disability Program and Resource Center (DPRC) is available to promote and provide equal access to the classroom and campus-related activities. A full range of support services is provided so that students may define and achieve personal autonomy at SFSU. The staff is sensitive to the diversity of disabilities, including those only recently recognized as disabilities requiring reasonable accommodations. Confidential support services are available. All students registered with DPRC are eligible for disability management advising. This consists of helping students access services from DPRC; manage DPRC services and school in general; problem-solve conflicts/ concerns that are disability-related with individuals, programs, and services on campus; and understand "reasonable accommodation" under the law.

Admissions

All freshman applicants are encouraged to complete 15 units of college prep subjects. If a student is admissible but has not completed specific course requirements as the result of a learning disability, the student can appeal to admissions. The appeal should include documentation that supports the disability and explains why the student was unable to complete specific requirements. The university is test optional and does not require the submission of the ACT or SAT. Out-of-state applicants must meet a higher admission standard than in-state applicants.

Additional Information

Students with disabilities may seek a course substitution for graduation requirements by consulting with the Disability Programs and Resource Center. Course substitutions may limit later enrollment in certain majors. The DPRC offers a drop-in center with available tutorial services. The DPRC can also arrange for test accommodations and note-takers and will advocate for the student. The staff is very involved and offers comprehensive services through a team approach. There are no developmental courses offered at the university. However, there are skills classes. Students with documented LD may request assistance in locating tutors. Other services may include registration assistance, campus orientation, note-takers, readers, test-taking assistance, tutoring, disability-related counseling, and referral information.

ADMISSIONS INFO FOR STUDENTS WITH LEARNING DIFFERENCES

Phone: 415-338-2472 • Fax: 415-338-1041 • Email: dprc@sfsu.edu

SAT/ACT required: Yes (Test blind for 2021)
Interview required: Yes
Essay required: Yes
Additional application required: No
Documentation submitted to: Disability Programs and Resource Center

Special Ed. HS course work accepted: Yes
Separate application required for Programs/Services: No
Documentation required for:
LD: Psychoeducational evaluation
ADHD: Psychoeducational evaluation
ASD: Psychoeducational evaluation

San Francisco State University

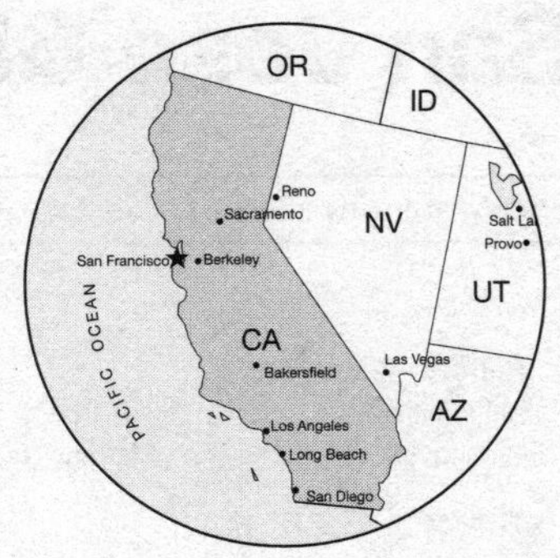

General Admissions

Very important factors include: rigor of secondary school record, academic GPA, but ACT or SAT score is not required. *Important factors include:* state residency. *Other factors include:* geographical residence. High school diploma is required and GED is accepted. *Academic units required:* 4 English, 3 math, 2 science, 2 science labs, 2 foreign language, 1 social studies, 1 history, 1 academic elective, 1 visual/performing arts. *Academic units recommended:* 4 English, 4 math, 2 science, 2 science labs, 2 foreign language, 1 social studies, 1 history, 1 academic elective, 1 visual/performing arts.

Accommodations or Services

Accommodations are decided upon an individual basis after a thorough review of appropriate, current documentation. The accommodations requests must be supported through the documentation provided and must be logically linked to the current impact of the condition on academic functioning.

Financial Aid

Students should submit: FAFSA. Applicants will be notified of awards on or about 4/1. *Need-based scholarships/grants offered:* College/university scholarship or grant aid from institutional funds; Federal Pell; Private scholarships; SEOG; State scholarships/grants. *Loan aid offered:* Direct PLUS loans; Direct Subsidized Stafford Loans; Direct Unsubsidized Stafford Loans. Federal Work-Study Program available. Institutional employment available.

Campus Life

Activities: Choral groups; Concert band; Dance; Drama/theater; International Student Organization; Jazz band; Literary magazine; Marching band; Music ensembles; Musical theater; Opera; Radio station; Student government; Student newspaper; Student-run film society; Symphony orchestra; Television station. **Organizations:** 127 registered organizations, 8 honor societies, 14 religious organizations, 12 fraternities, 18 sororities. **Athletics (Intercollegiate):** *Men:* baseball, basketball, cross-country, soccer, wrestling. *Women:* basketball, cross-country, soccer, softball, track/field (outdoor), track/field (indoor), volleyball.

ACCOMMODATIONS

Allowed in exams:	
Calculators	Yes
Dictionary	Yes
Computer	Yes
Spell-checker	Yes
Extended test time	Yes
Scribe	Yes
Proctors	Yes
Oral exams	No
Note-takers	Yes
Support services for students with:	
LD	Yes
ADHD	Yes
ASD	Yes
Distraction-reduced environment	Yes
Recording of lecture allowed	Yes
Reading technology	Yes
Audio books	Yes
Other assistive technology	Yes
Priority registration	Yes
Added costs of services:	
For LD	No
For ADHD	No
For ASD	No
LD specialists	Yes
ADHD & ASD coaching	No
ASD specialists	No
Professional tutors	Yes
Peer tutors	Yes
Max. hours/week for services	Varies
How professors are notified of student approved accommodations	Student

COLLEGE GRADUATION REQUIREMENTS

Course waivers allowed	Yes
In what courses: Case by case basis	
Course substitutions allowed	Yes
In what courses: Case by case basis	

San Jose State University

One Washington Square, San Jose, CA 95192-0016 • Admissions: 408-283-7500 • Fax: 408-924-2050 **Support: CS**

CAMPUS

Type of school	Public
Environment	Metropolis

STUDENTS

Undergrad enrollment	27,895
% male/female	50/50
% from out of state	1
% frosh live on campus	56

FINANCIAL FACTS

Annual in-state tuition	$5,742
Annual out-of-state tuition	$15,246
Room and board	$16,248
Required fees	$2,110

GENERAL ADMISSIONS INFO

Application fee	$70
Regular application deadline	11/30
Nonfall registration	Yes
Range SAT EBRW	510–620
Range SAT Math	520–640
Range ACT Composite	18–27

ACADEMICS

Student/faculty ratio	27:1
% students returning for sophomore year	87

Most classes have 20–29 students.

Programs/Services for Students with Learning Differences

The Accessible Education Center provides services and accommodations to students with documented disabilities. The AEC promotes independence and academic excellence by applying universal design concepts. AEC will help students manage resources, advocate on behalf of students, and ensure access to the curriculum for students with disabilities.

Admissions

Freshman applicants must first meet the CSU eligibility requirements for admission. Applicants need to have a C or better in 2 years history, 3 years mathematics, 2 years lab science, 4 years English, 2 years language other than English, and one year of visual and performing arts plus 1 additional elective. Meeting minimum admission requirements does not guarantee admission as admission is competitive and many majors are impacted. San José State gives preference to local applicants from the Santa Clara County. SJSU is test optional and students are not required to submit an ACT or SAT. Admission to majors varies and applicants are encouraged to pick their major and alternate major very carefully. Applicants cannot change their major during the application process once the application has been submitted.

Additional Information

Students meet with an AEC professional counselor to review documentation and implement reasonable and appropriate academic accommodations. The Interactive Process is a collaborative process with the student and the AEC professional. Students will receive academic advising with selecting courses, meeting university graduation requirements, and academic petitions if needed.

ADMISSIONS INFO FOR STUDENTS WITH LEARNING DIFFERENCES

Phone: 408-924-6000 • Fax: 408-924-5999 • Email: aec-info@sjsu.edu

SAT/ACT required: Yes (Test blind for 2021)
Interview required: No
Essay required: No
Additional application required: No
Documentation submitted to: AEC

Special Ed. HS course work accepted: Yes
Separate application required for Programs/Services: No
Documentation required for:
LD: Psychoeducational evaluation
ADHD: Psychoeducational evaluation
ASD: Psychoeducational evaluation identifying the diagnosis of autism

San Jose State University

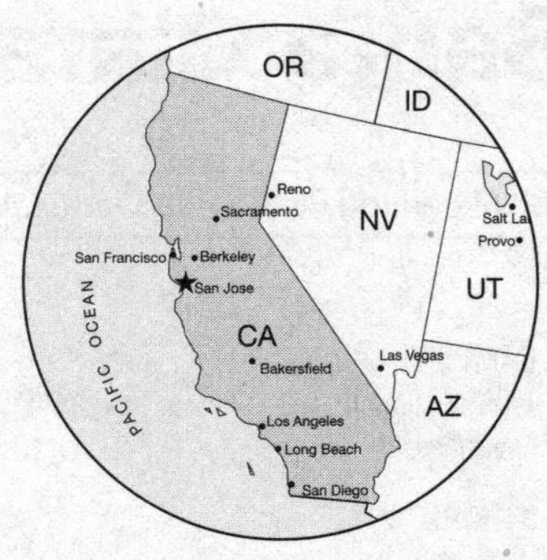

General Admissions

Very important factors include: rigor of secondary school record, academic GPA, standardized test scores. *Important factors include:* geographical residence, state residency. High school diploma is required and GED is accepted. *Academic units required:* 4 English, 3 math, 2 science, 2 science labs, 2 foreign language, 1 social studies, 1 history, 1 academic elective, 1 visual/performing arts. *Academic units recommended:* 4 math, 3 science, 3 science labs.

Accommodations or Services

Accommodations are decided upon an individual basis after a thorough review of appropriate, current documentation. The accommodations requests must be supported through the documentation provided and must be logically linked to the current impact of the condition on academic functioning.

Financial Aid

Students should submit: FAFSA; Institution's own financial aid form. Applicants will be notified of awards on or about 7/15. *Need-based scholarships/grants offered:* College/university scholarship or grant aid from institutional funds; Federal Pell; Private scholarships; SEOG; State scholarships/grants. *Loan aid offered:* Direct PLUS loans; Direct Subsidized Stafford Loans; Direct Unsubsidized Stafford Loans. Federal Work-Study Program available. Institutional employment available.

Campus Life

Activities: Campus Ministries; Choral groups; Concert band; Dance; Drama/theater; International Student Organization; Jazz band; Literary magazine; Marching band; Model UN; Music ensembles; Opera; Pep band; Radio station; Student government; Student newspaper; Student-run film society; Symphony orchestra. **Organizations:** 450 registered organizations, 13 honor societies, 20 religious organizations, 26 fraternities, 19 sororities. **Athletics (Intercollegiate):** *Men:* baseball, basketball, cheerleading, cross-country, diving, football, golf, soccer, softball, swimming, volleyball, water polo. *Women:* basketball, cheerleading, cross-country, diving, golf, gymnastics, soccer, softball, swimming, tennis, volleyball, water polo.

ACCOMMODATIONS

Allowed in exams:	
Calculators	Yes
Dictionary	Yes
Computer	Yes
Spell-checker	Yes
Extended test time	Yes
Scribe	Yes
Proctors	Yes
Oral exams	Yes
Note-takers	Yes
Support services for students with:	
LD	Yes
ADHD	Yes
ASD	Yes
Distraction-reduced environment	Yes
Recording of lecture allowed	Yes
Reading technology	Yes
Audio books	Yes
Other assistive technology	Yes
Priority registration	Yes
Added costs of services:	
For LD	No
For ADHD	No
For ASD	No
LD specialists	Yes
ADHD & ASD coaching	No
ASD specialists	No
Professional tutors	No
Peer tutors	Yes
Max. hours/week for services	Varies
How professors are notified of student approved accommodations	Student

COLLEGE GRADUATION REQUIREMENTS

Course waivers allowed	No
Course substitutions allowed	Yes
In what courses: Case by case basis	

Santa Clara University

500 El Camino Real, Santa Clara, CA 95053 • Admissions: 408-554-4700 • Fax: 408-554-5255 **Support: S**

CAMPUS

Type of school	Private (nonprofit)
Environment	City

STUDENTS

Undergrad enrollment	5,676
% male/female	50/50
% from out of state	42
% frosh live on campus	96

FINANCIAL FACTS

Annual Tuition	$54,987
Room and board	$15,972
Required fees	$642

GENERAL ADMISSIONS INFO

Application fee	$60
Regular application deadline	1/7
Nonfall registration	No

Admission may be deferred.

Range SAT EBRW	630–700
Range SAT Math	650–740
Range ACT Composite	28–32

ACADEMICS

Student/faculty ratio	10:1
% students returning for sophomore year	94

Most classes have 10–19 students.

Programs/Services for Students with Learning Differences

The primary mission of the Office of Accessible Education (OAE) is to enhance academic progress, promote social involvement, and build bridges connecting students to university services. OAE is a resource area within the Drahmann Center that helps to ensure equal access to all academic and programmatic activities for students with disabilities. Academic Support Services assists in teaching students effective self-advocacy skills under the student development model. Students must submit proper documentation to obtain services.

Admissions

Students should meet the minimum high school course requirements: History and Social Science: 3 years, English: 4 years, mathematics: 3 years required; 4 years recommended lab science: 2 years required; 3 years recommended, language other than English: 2 years required; 3 years recommended; 4 years preferred, visual and performing arts: 1 year recommended. Applicants select one of the academic schools/colleges: the College of Arts and Sciences, the Leavey School of Business, or the School of Engineering. While the selectivity between schools and programs does not vary greatly, academic readiness for the program of interest will be gauged based on a student's expressed interest. Santa Clara University adopted a two-year "test optional" policy beginning with Fall 2021 first-year applicants. Scores on the SAT or ACT are not required for students applying to Santa Clara University nor will they be disadvantaged for doing so in the admission process.

Additional Information

OAE staff meets individually with students. Some of the academic accommodations provided include notetaking, library assistance, and test accommodations. Other support services include priority registration; tutoring or academic counseling: and workshops on legal issues and self-advocacy. CONVERT is a self-service, computer-automated document conversion tool that allows students to convert documents into a variety of alternative formats. Notetaking services are provided to eliminate the competitive disadvantage under which the students with disabilities function.

ADMISSIONS INFO FOR STUDENTS WITH LEARNING DIFFERENCES

Phone: 408-554-4109 • Email: oae@scu.edu

SAT/ACT required: Yes (Test optional for 2021)
Interview required: No
Essay required: No
Additional application required: Yes
Documentation submitted to: OAE

Special Ed. HS course work accepted: Yes
Separate application required for Programs/Services: Yes
Documentation required for:
- **LD:** Psychoeducational evaluation
- **ADHD:** Psychoeducational evaluation
- **ASD:** Psychoeducational evaluation

Santa Clara University

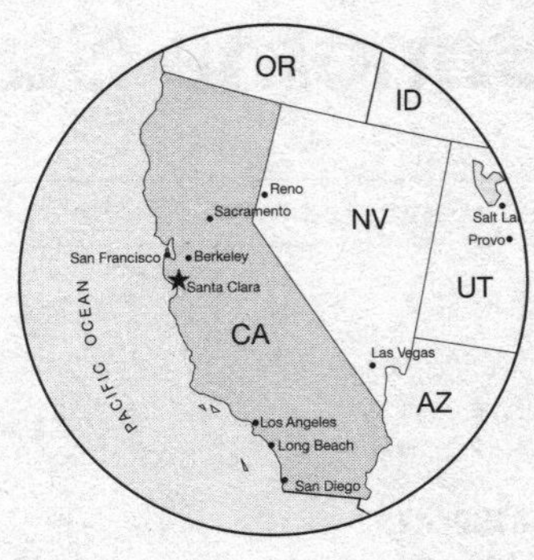

General Admissions

Very important factors include: rigor of secondary school record, academic GPA, application essay. *Important factors include:* class rank, standardized test scores, recommendation(s), extracurricular activities, talent/ability, character/personal qualities, first generation, alumni/ae relation. *Other factors include:* geographical residence, state residency, religious affiliation/commitment, work experience, level of applicant's interest. High school diploma is required and GED is accepted. *Academic units required:* 4 English, 3 math, 2 science, 2 foreign language, 3 social studies. *Academic units recommended:* 4 English, 4 math, 3 science, 3 foreign language, 3 social studies, 1 visual/performing arts. ACT/SAT optional.

Accommodations or Services

Accommodations are decided upon an individual basis after a thorough review of appropriate, current documentation. The accommodations requests must be supported through the documentation provided and must be logically linked to the current impact of the condition on academic functioning.

Financial Aid

Students should submit: CSS/Financial Aid PROFILE; FAFSA. *Need-based scholarships/grants offered:* College/university scholarship or grant aid from institutional funds; Federal Pell; Private scholarships; SEOG; State scholarships/grants. *Loan aid offered:* Direct PLUS loans; Direct Subsidized Stafford Loans; Direct Unsubsidized Stafford Loans. Federal Work-Study Program available. Institutional employment available.

Campus Life

Activities: Campus Ministries; Choral groups; Concert band; Dance; Drama/theater; International Student Organization; Jazz band; Literary magazine; Model UN; Music ensembles; Musical theater; Opera; Pep band; Radio station; Student government; Student newspaper; Student-run film society; Symphony orchestra; Yearbook. **Organizations:** 160 registered organizations, 28 honor societies, 11 religious organizations. **Athletics (Intercollegiate):** *Men:* baseball, basketball, crew/rowing, cross-country, golf, soccer, tennis, track/field (outdoor), water polo. *Women:* basketball, crew/rowing, cross-country, golf, soccer, softball, tennis, track/field (outdoor), volleyball, water polo.

ACCOMMODATIONS

Allowed in exams:	
Calculators	Yes
Dictionary	Yes
Computer	Yes
Spell-checker	Yes
Extended test time	Yes
Scribe	Yes
Proctors	Yes
Oral exams	Yes
Note-takers	Yes
Support services for students with:	
LD	Yes
ADHD	Yes
ASD	Yes
Distraction-reduced environment	Yes
Recording of lecture allowed	Yes
Reading technology	Yes
Audio books	Yes
Other assistive technology	Yes
Priority registration	Yes
Added costs of services:	
For LD	No
For ADHD	No
For ASD	No
LD specialists	No
ADHD & ASD coaching	No
ASD specialists	No
Professional tutors	No
Peer tutors	Yes
Max. hours/week for services	Varies
How professors are notified of student approved accommodations	Student and OAE

COLLEGE GRADUATION REQUIREMENTS

Course waivers allowed	Yes
In what courses: Math & Foreign Language	
Course substitutions allowed	Yes
In what courses: Math & Foreign Language	

California

Sonoma State University

1801 East Cotati Avenue, Rohnert Park, CA 94928 • Admissions: 707-664-2778 • Fax: 707-664-2060 **Support: S**

CAMPUS

Type of school	Public
Environment	Town

STUDENTS

Undergrad enrollment	8,143
% male/female	38/62
% from out of state	1
% frosh live on campus	86

FINANCIAL FACTS

Annual in-state tuition	$7,952
Annual out-of-state tuition	$19,832
Room and board	$14,282

GENERAL ADMISSIONS INFO

Application fee	$70
Regular application deadline	12/15
Nonfall registration	Yes
Range SAT EBRW	490–590
Range SAT Math	480–580
Range ACT Composite	17–23

ACADEMICS

Student/faculty ratio	23:1
% students returning for sophomore year	78

Most classes have 20–29 students.

Programs/Services for Students with Learning Differences

Disability Services for Students (DSS) ensures that people with disabilities receive equal access to higher education. DSS helps students develop self-determination and independence. DSS will review requests for services and accommodations through factors such as the documentation from professionals specializing in the area of the student's diagnosed disability, the student's functional limitations, and the student's input and accommodation history in regard to particular needs and limitations. DSS works with the student and relevant faculty and staff through an interactive process designed to achieve an accommodation that meets the needs of all parties.

Admissions

Applicants must meet the course requirements with a C or better in 2 years history/social science, 4 years English, 3 years math (4 recommended), 2 years lab science, 2 years foreign language, 1 year visual and performing arts, and 1 year elective. Students are encouraged to enroll in a senior year English course and quantitative math course. ACT/SAT are optional for 2021 and will be reviewed for future applicants. California residents will be evaluated with a 2.0–2.49 GPA. Non-residents may be eligible for evaluation with a 3.0 GPA or higher and required courses.

Additional Information

The Learning and Academic Resource Center (LARC) houses several academic support services including the Writing Center, the Tutorial Program, and Supplemental Instruction. The Supplemental Instruction Program (SI) is peer-led and helps students with academic subjects. Study sessions are led by trained SI Leaders who have mastered the course content. Writing Intensive Curriculum Courses are provided to help students with writing across the curriculum and for the Written English Proficiency Test (WEPT).

ADMISSIONS INFO FOR STUDENTS WITH LEARNING DIFFERENCES

Phone: 707-664-2677 • Fax: 707-664-3330 • Email: disability.services@sonoma.edu

SAT/ACT required: Yes (Test blind for 2021)
Interview required: No
Essay required: No
Additional application required: No
Documentation submitted to: Disability Services

Special Ed. HS course work accepted: No
Separate application required for Programs/Services: No
Documentation required for:
LD: Psychoeducational evaluation
ADHD: Psychoeducational evaluation
ASD: Psychoeducational evaluation

Sonoma State University

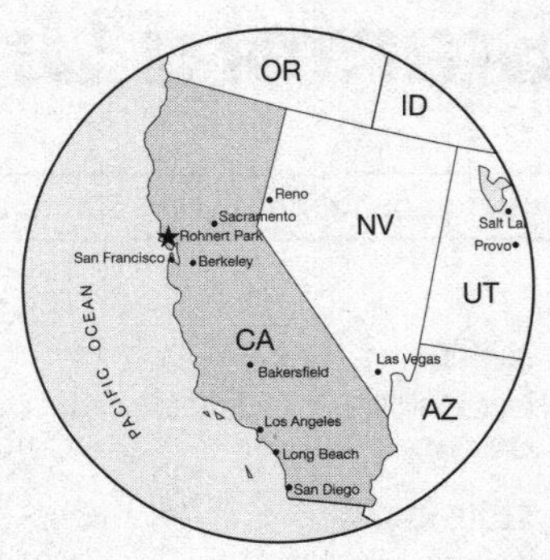

General Admissions

Very important factors include: academic GPA, standardized test scores. *Other factors include:* geographical residence. High school diploma is required and GED is accepted. *Academic units required:* 4 English, 3 math, 2 science, 1 science lab, 2 foreign language, 2 history, 1 academic elective, 1 visual/performing arts, 1 unit from above areas or other academic areas.

Accommodations or Services

Accommodations are decided upon an individual basis after a thorough review of appropriate, current documentation. The accommodations requests must be supported through the documentation provided and must be logically linked to the current impact of the condition on academic functioning.

Financial Aid

Students should submit: FAFSA. *Need-based scholarships/grants offered:* College/university scholarship or grant aid from institutional funds; Federal Pell; Private scholarships; SEOG; State scholarships/grants; United Negro College Fund. *Loan aid offered:* Direct PLUS loans; Direct Subsidized Stafford Loans; Direct Unsubsidized Stafford Loans. Federal Work-Study Program available. Institutional employment available.

Campus Life

Activities: Choral groups; Dance; Drama/theater; Jazz band; Literary magazine; Music ensembles; Musical theater; Opera; Pep band; Radio station; Student government; Student newspaper; Symphony orchestra. **Organizations:** 109 registered organizations, 2 honor societies, 4 religious organizations, 8 fraternities, 10 sororities. **Athletics (Intercollegiate):** *Men:* baseball, basketball, soccer, tennis. *Women:* basketball, cross-country, soccer, softball, tennis, track/field (outdoor), volleyball.

ACCOMMODATIONS

Allowed in exams:	
Calculators	Yes
Dictionary	Yes
Computer	Yes
Spell-checker	Yes
Extended test time	Yes
Scribe	Yes
Proctors	Yes
Oral exams	Yes
Note-takers	Yes
Support services for students with:	
LD	Yes
ADHD	Yes
ASD	Yes
Distraction-reduced environment	Yes
Recording of lecture allowed	Yes
Reading technology	Yes
Audio books	Yes
Other assistive technology	Yes
Priority registration	Yes
Added costs of services:	
For LD	No
For ADHD	No
For ASD	No
LD specialists	No
ADHD & ASD coaching	No
ASD specialists	No
Professional tutors	No
Peer tutors	Yes
Max. hours/week for services	Varies
How professors are notified of student approved accommodations	Student

COLLEGE GRADUATION REQUIREMENTS

Course waivers allowed	No
Course substitutions allowed	Yes
In what courses: Case by case basis	

California

Stanford University

Undergraduate Admission, Stanford, CA 94305-6106 • Admissions: 650-723-2091 • Fax: 650-723-6050 **Support: S**

CAMPUS

Type of school	Private (nonprofit)
Environment	City

STUDENTS

Undergrad enrollment	6,994
% male/female	50/50
% from out of state	61
% frosh live on campus	100

FINANCIAL FACTS

Annual tuition	$55,473
Room and board	$17,255
Required fees	$696

GENERAL ADMISSIONS INFO

Application fee	$90
Regular application deadline	1/2
Nonfall registration	No

Admission may be deferred. Yes

Range SAT EBRW	700–770
Range SAT Math	740–800
Range ACT Composite	32–35

ACADEMICS

Student/faculty ratio	5:1
% students returning for sophomore year	99

Most classes have 10–19 students.

Programs/Services for Students with Learning Differences

Stanford University has an institutional commitment to providing equal educational opportunities for qualified students with disabilities. Stanford University has a strong commitment to maintaining a diverse and stimulating academic community, representing a broad spectrum of talents and experiences. Students with disabilities, actively participating in the various aspects of life at Stanford, are an essential part of that diversity.

Admissions

Applicants apply to the university in general and not to a particular college or major. Applicants must submit either the ACT or SAT and can self-report the highest scores in the testing section of either the Common Application or Coalition Application. If a student is admitted and accepts the offer, then the student must submit the ACT or SAT score to the university. Stanford has a Restrictive Early Action option which is non-binding. However, the applicant cannot apply to any other private or public college or university with a binding decision. Interviews are optional. Stanford is highly selective.

Additional Information

The Office of Accessible Education at Stanford is committed to helping students take full advantage of all the educational opportunities at Stanford. A student with a documented disability may request a modification of certain generally applicable requirements. The Center for Teaching and Learning provides all Stanford students with academic skills resources. Academic coaches provide a "personal trainer" who observes a student's strategies and techniques, suggests changes to the student's approach, and provides encouragement as a way to implement new ways of learning. Academic coaches hold advanced degrees. Peer Learning Consultants are undergraduate and graduate students who help other students develop effective learning strategies. Learning consultants offer one-on-one academic coaching, workshops, consultations, and academic programming to address a variety of academic skills. Quiet study spaces are available. Language Conversation Partners (LCPs) support students in improving their speaking skills and are designed to help students meet the oral proficiency objectives of a language course. Students must be enrolled in a course at the Stanford Language Center to use the LCPs. Subject tutors are available in many other courses. The Schwab Learning Center teaches students to understand their own individual learning history and strengths and provides strategies to optimize potential.

ADMISSIONS INFO FOR STUDENTS WITH LEARNING DIFFERENCES

Phone: 650-723-1066 • Email: oae-contactus@stanford.edu

SAT/ACT required: Yes (Test optional for 2021)
Interview required: No
Essay required: Yes
Additional application required: No
Documentation submitted to: Office of Accessible Education

Special Ed. HS course work accepted: Yes
Separate application required for Programs/Services: No
Documentation required for:
LD: Psychoeducational evaluation
ADHD: Psychoeducational evaluation
ASD: Psychoeducational evaluation

Stanford University

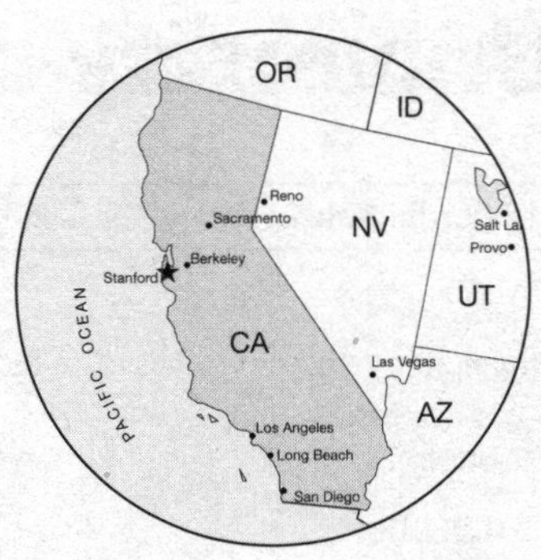

General Admissions

Very important factors include: rigor of secondary school record, class rank, academic GPA, application essay, standardized test scores, recommendation(s), extracurricular activities, talent/ability, character/personal qualities. *Other factors include:* interview, first generation, alumni/ae relation, geographical residence, racial/ethnic status, volunteer work, work experience. High school diploma is required and GED is accepted. *Academic units recommended:* 4 English, 4 math, 3 science, 3 science labs, 3 foreign language, 3 social studies.

Accommodations or Services

Accommodations are decided upon an individual basis after a thorough review of appropriate, current documentation. The accommodations requests must be supported through the documentation provided and must be logically linked to the current impact of the condition on academic functioning.

Financial Aid

Students should submit: CSS/Financial Aid PROFILE; FAFSA; Noncustodial PROFILE. *Need-based scholarships/grants offered:* College/university scholarship or grant aid from institutional funds; Federal Pell; Private scholarships; SEOG; State scholarships/grants. *Loan aid offered:* Direct PLUS loans; Direct Subsidized Stafford Loans; Direct Unsubsidized Stafford Loans. Federal Work-Study Program available. Institutional employment available.

Campus Life

Activities: Campus Ministries; Choral groups; Concert band; Dance; Drama/theater; International Student Organization; Jazz band; Literary magazine; Marching band; Model UN; Music ensembles; Musical theater; Opera; Pep band; Radio station; Student government; Student newspaper; Student-run film society; Symphony orchestra; Television station; Yearbook. **Organizations:** 600 registered organizations, 35 religious organizations, 16 fraternities, 14 sororities. **Athletics (Intercollegiate):** *Men:* baseball, basketball, crew/rowing, cross-country, diving, fencing, football, golf, gymnastics, sailing, soccer, swimming, tennis, track/field (outdoor), volleyball, water polo, wrestling. *Women:* basketball, crew/rowing, cross-country, diving, fencing, field hockey, golf, gymnastics, lacrosse, sailing, soccer, softball, squash, swimming, synchronized swimming, tennis, track/field (outdoor), volleyball, water polo.

ACCOMMODATIONS

Allowed in exams:	
Calculators	Yes
Dictionary	Yes
Computer	Yes
Spell-checker	Yes
Extended test time	Yes
Scribe	Yes
Proctors	No
Oral exams	No
Note-takers	Yes
Support services for students with:	
LD	Yes
ADHD	Yes
ASD	Yes
Distraction-reduced environment	Yes
Recording of lecture allowed	Yes
Reading technology	Yes
Audio books	Yes
Other assistive technology	Yes
Priority registration	No
Added costs of services:	
For LD	No
For ADHD	No
For ASD	No
LD specialists	No
ADHD & ASD coaching	No
ASD specialists	No
Professional tutors	Yes
Peer tutors	Yes
Max. hours/week for services	Varies
How professors are notified of student approved accommodations	Student

COLLEGE GRADUATION REQUIREMENTS

Course waivers allowed	No
Course substitutions allowed	Yes

In what courses: Case by case basis

California

University of California—Berkeley

110 Sproul Hall, Berkeley, CA 94720-5800 • Admissions: 510-642-6000 **Support: CS**

CAMPUS	
Type of school	Public
Environment	City
STUDENTS	
Undergrad enrollment	30,602
% male/female	47/53
% from out of state	16
% frosh live on campus	96
FINANCIAL FACTS	
Annual in-state tuition	$11,442
Annual out-of-state tuition	$41,196
Room and board	$19,620
Required fees	$3,073
GENERAL ADMISSIONS INFO	
Application fee	$70
Regular application deadline	11/3
Nonfall registration	Yes
Range SAT EBRW	640–740
Range SAT Math	660–790
Range ACT Composite	28–34
ACADEMICS	
Student/faculty ratio	20:1
% students returning for sophomore year	97
Most classes have 10–19 students.	

Programs/Services for Students with Learning Differences

The Disabled Student Program (DSP) works to sustain a supportive environment that provides appropriate and necessary disability-related accommodations, enables students to demonstrate their knowledge and skills, facilitates students' success in academic pursuits, and promotes independence. DSP's services assist students as they develop their skills and the qualities needed to meet their educational, personal, and professional goals.

Admissions

Applicants to UC Berkeley must meet very selective criteria. The university is test optional and ACT or SAT scores are not required but can be submitted. There is an Augmented Review process which provides additional review for a select group of applicants who are near the general admission requirements but present an incomplete picture of their qualifications or show extraordinary circumstances that invite further review. These applicants could have a special talent, or the application may not explain a major disadvantage. Applicants referred for the Augmented Review process must demonstrate levels of academic preparation and personal qualities that indicate the potential to succeed in college. Only 15% of applicants can be referred to the Augmented Review process. These applicants may submit one or more of the following supplemental items: 1) a questionnaire that requires narrative responses about accomplishments, circumstances, and home or school environment; 2) 7th semester grades or most recent grades; 3) up to 2 letters of recommendation that focus on cognitive and psycho-social abilities. Letters of recommendation can only be submitted by applicants selected for Augmented Review, applicants considered for admission by exception, and/or applicants given a special review. The admission process is carefully monitored for non-standard admissions practices and/or ancillary processes feeding into the admissions process, such as recommendations for admission from athletics and other departments to protect the admission process.

Additional Information

Academic coaching and consultations on strategic learning and studying practices are available in the Student Learning Center. The Student Learning Center employs professional, as well as, peer tutors. The Learning Center also provides a Summer Bridge Program that serves a globally diverse community of entering undergraduates in an academic program. The DSP provides academic accommodations; consulting with instructors about accommodations; academic strategies and study skills; academic advising, adaptive technology, and support groups for students with LD/ADHD.

ADMISSIONS INFO FOR STUDENTS WITH LEARNING DIFFERENCES

Phone: 510-642-0518 • Fax: 510-643-9686

SAT/ACT required: Yes (Test blind through 2022)
Interview required: No
Essay required: Yes
Additional application required: No
Documentation submitted to: Disabled Student Program

Special Ed. HS course work accepted: Yes
Separate application required for Programs/Services: No
Documentation required for:
LD: Psychoeducational evaluation
ADHD: Psychoeducational evaluation
ASD: Psychoeducational evaluation

University of California— Berkeley

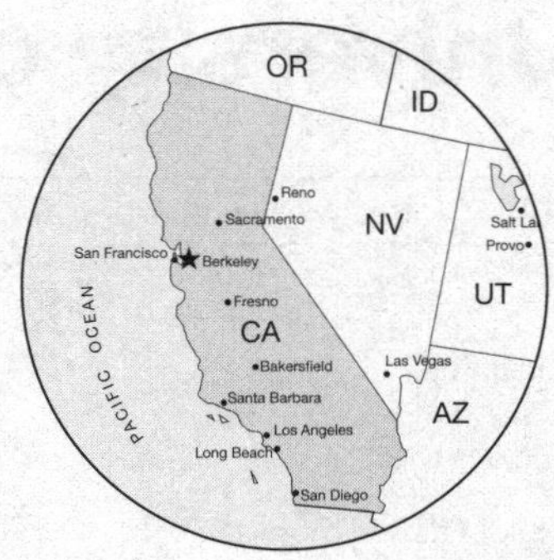

General Admissions

Very important factors include: rigor of secondary school record, academic GPA, application essay, standardized test scores. *Important factors include:* extracurricular activities, character/personal qualities. *Other factors include:* recommendation(s), first generation, state residency. High school diploma is required and GED is accepted. *Academic units required:* 4 English, 3 math, 2 science, 2 science labs, 2 foreign language, 2 history, 1 academic elective, 1 visual/performing arts. *Academic units recommended:* 4 English, 4 math, 3 science, 3 science labs, 3 foreign language, 2 history, 1 academic elective, 1 visual/performing arts.

Accommodations or Services

Accommodations are decided upon an individual basis after a thorough review of appropriate, current documentation. The accommodations requests must be supported through the documentation provided and must be logically linked to the current impact of the condition on academic functioning.

Financial Aid

Students should submit: FAFSA; Institution's own financial aid form; State aid form. Applicants will be notified of awards on a rolling basis beginning 12/1. *Need-based scholarships/grants offered:* College/university scholarship or grant aid from institutional funds; Federal Pell; Private scholarships; SEOG; State scholarships/grants. *Loan aid offered:* Direct PLUS loans; Direct Subsidized Stafford Loans; Direct Unsubsidized Stafford Loans. Federal Work-Study Program available. Institutional employment available.

Campus Life

Activities: Campus Ministries; Choral groups; Concert band; Dance; Drama/theater; International Student Organization; Jazz band; Literary magazine; Marching band; Model UN; Music ensembles; Musical theater; Pep band; Radio station; Student government; Student newspaper; Student-run film society; Symphony orchestra; Television station; Yearbook. **Organizations:** 300 registered organizations, 6 honor societies, 28 religious organizations, 38 fraternities, 19 sororities. **Athletics (Intercollegiate):** *Men:* baseball, basketball, crew/rowing, cross-country, diving, football, golf, gymnastics, rugby, sailing, soccer, swimming, tennis, track/field (outdoor), water polo. *Women:* basketball, crew/rowing, cross-country, diving, field hockey, golf, gymnastics, lacrosse, sailing, soccer, softball, swimming, tennis, track/field (outdoor), volleyball, water polo.

ACCOMMODATIONS

Allowed in exams:	
Calculators	Yes
Dictionary	Yes
Computer	Yes
Spell-checker	Yes
Extended test time	Yes
Scribe	Yes
Proctors	Yes
Oral exams	No
Note-takers	Yes
Support services for students with:	
LD	Yes
ADHD	Yes
ASD	Yes
Distraction-reduced environment	Yes
Recording of lecture allowed	Yes
Reading technology	Yes
Audio books	Yes
Other assistive technology	Yes
Priority registration	Yes
Added costs of services:	
For LD	No
For ADHD	No
For ASD	No
LD specialists	Yes
ADHD & ASD coaching	No
ASD specialists	No
Professional tutors	No
Peer tutors	Some individual tutoring is available through the TRIO grant.
Max. hours/week for services	Varies
How professors are notified of student approved accommodations	Student

COLLEGE GRADUATION REQUIREMENTS

Course waivers allowed	Yes
In what courses: Math waivers are considered on a case-by-case basis.	
Course substitutions allowed	Yes
In what courses: Math waivers are considered on a case-by-case basis.	

University of California—Los Angeles

1147 Murphy Hall, Los Angeles, CA 90095-1436 • Admissions: 310-825-3101 • Fax: 310-206-1206 **Support: CS**

CAMPUS

Type of school	Public
Environment	Metropolis

STUDENTS

Undergrad enrollment	31,441
% male/female	42/58
% from out of state	13
% frosh live on campus	98

FINANCIAL FACTS

Annual in-state tuition	$11,994
Annual out-of-state tuition	$43,188
Room and board	$16,104
Required fees	$1,838

GENERAL ADMISSIONS INFO

Application fee	$70
Regular application deadline	11/3
Nonfall registration	No
Range SAT EBRW	640–740
Range SAT Math	640–790
Range ACT Composite	27–34

ACADEMICS

Student/faculty ratio	18:1
% students returning for sophomore year	96

Most classes have 10–19 students.

Programs/Services for Students with Learning Differences

The Center for Accessible Education (CAE) provides academic accommodations and support services for regularly enrolled, matriculating students with documented permanent and temporary disabilities. UCLA complies with state, federal, and university guidelines that mandate full access for students with disabilities, including learning disabilities. Students with other documented types of learning disabilities, including attention deficit hyperactive disorder and traumatic brain injury, are also served by CAE.

Admissions

There are no special admissions criteria for students with learning disabilities. For students applying for admission in 2021 and 2022, the ACT or SAT is optional. Students will not be penalized in the admissions review process for not submitting ACT/SAT scores. Additionally, for students who opt to submit the ACT or SAT, the Writing sections of either test are not required. The GPA from the 10th and 11th grade are used for admission. Applicants must complete 11 of the 15 required courses by the start of senior year. These courses include 2 years of history/social science, 4 years English, 3 years math (4 recommended), 2 years lab science (3 recommended), 2 years foreign language (3 years recommended), and 1 year of a single year-long approved visual and performing arts course, and 1 additional year of an elective. UCLA is extremely competitive in admissions and receives more applications than it can admit. Non-residents must meet higher admission standards than residents of the state of California.

Additional Information

Pathway at UCLA Extension is a sequential program for students with intellectual and other developmental disabilities, offering a blend of educational, social, and vocational experiences, taught and supervised by experienced instructors sensitive to the individual needs of students. Pathway students attend classes and participate with UCLA students in social, recreational, and cultural activities. The students develop lifelong learning skills, experience internships that support future career options, develop self-advocacy skills and independence through community activities, learn social skills and have the opportunities to assess their own individual needs and self-enrichment.

ADMISSIONS INFO FOR STUDENTS WITH LEARNING DIFFERENCES

Phone: 310-825-1501 • Fax: 310-825-9656

SAT/ACT required: No
Interview required: No
Essay required: Yes
Additional application required: No
Documentation submitted to: Center for Accessible Education

Special Ed. HS course work accepted: Yes
Separate application required for Programs/Services: No
Documentation required for:
LD: Psychoeducational evaluation
ADHD: Psychoeducational evaluation
ASD: Psychoeducational evaluation

University of California—Los Angeles

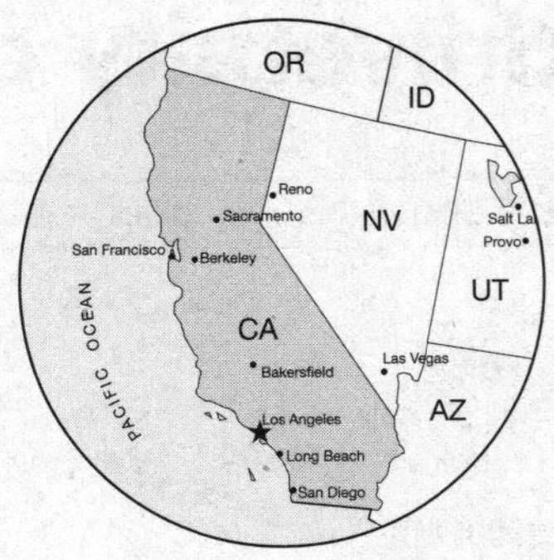

General Admissions

Very important factors include: rigor of secondary school record, academic GPA, application essay, standardized test scores. *Important factors include:* extracurricular activities, talent/ability, character/personal qualities. *Other factors include:* first generation, geographical residence, state residency. High school diploma is required and GED is accepted. *Academic units required:* 4 English, 3 math, 2 science, 2 science labs, 2 foreign language, 2 history, 1 academic elective, 1 visual/performing arts. *Academic units recommended:* 4 English, 4 math, 3 science, 3 science labs, 3 foreign language, 2 history, 1 academic elective, 1 visual/performing arts.

Accommodations or Services

Accommodations are decided upon an individual basis after a thorough review of appropriate, current documentation. The accommodations requests must be supported through the documentation provided and must be logically linked to the current impact of the condition on academic functioning.

Financial Aid

Students should submit: FAFSA; State aid form. Applicants will be notified of awards on a rolling basis beginning 3/1. *Need-based scholarships/grants offered:* College/university scholarship or grant aid from institutional funds; Federal Pell; Private scholarships; SEOG; State scholarships/grants. *Loan aid offered:* Direct PLUS loans; Direct Subsidized Stafford Loans; Direct Unsubsidized Stafford Loans. Federal Work-Study Program available. Institutional employment available.

Campus Life

Activities: Campus Ministries; Choral groups; Concert band; Dance; Drama/theater; International Student Organization; Jazz band; Literary magazine; Marching band; Model UN; Music ensembles; Musical theater; Opera; Pep band; Radio station; Student government; Student newspaper; Student-run film society; Symphony orchestra; Television station; Yearbook. **Organizations:** 850 registered organizations, 21 honor societies, 35 fraternities, 35 sororities. **Athletics (Intercollegiate):** *Men:* baseball, basketball, cross-country, football, golf, soccer, tennis, track/field (outdoor), track/field (indoor), volleyball, water polo. *Women:* basketball, crew/rowing, cross-country, diving, golf, gymnastics, soccer, softball, swimming, tennis, track/field (outdoor), track/field (indoor), volleyball, water polo.

ACCOMMODATIONS

Allowed in exams:	
Calculators	Yes
Dictionary	Yes
Computer	Yes
Spell-checker	Yes
Extended test time	Yes
Scribe	Yes
Proctors	Yes
Oral exams	No
Note-takers	Yes
Support services for students with:	
LD	Yes
ADHD	Yes
ASD	Yes
Distraction-reduced environment	Yes
Recording of lecture allowed	Yes
Reading technology	Yes
Audio books	No
Other assistive technology	Yes
Priority registration	Yes
Added costs of services:	
For LD	No
For ADHD	No
For ASD	No
LD specialists	Yes
ADHD & ASD coaching	No
ASD specialists	No
Professional tutors	No
Peer tutors	Yes
Max. hours/week for services	Unlimited
How professors are notified of student approved accommodations	Student and Disability Office

COLLEGE GRADUATION REQUIREMENTS

Course waivers allowed	No
Course substitutions allowed	Yes
In what courses: Case by case basis	

California

University of California—San Diego

9500 Gilman Drive, La Jolla, CA 92093-0021 • Admissions: 858-534-4831 • Fax: 858-534-5723 **Support: CS**

CAMPUS

Type of school	Public
Environment	Metropolis

STUDENTS

Undergrad enrollment	30,645
% male/female	50/50
% from out of state	7
% frosh live on campus	90

FINANCIAL FACTS

Annual in-state tuition	$11,442
Annual out-of-state tuition	$41,196
Room and board	$14,821
Required fees	$2,728

GENERAL ADMISSIONS INFO

Application fee	$125
Regular application deadline	11/3
Nonfall registration	No
Range SAT EBRW	610–710
Range SAT Math	620–780
Range ACT Composite	24–33

ACADEMICS

Student/faculty ratio	19:1
% students returning for sophomore year	93

Most classes have 10–19 students.

Programs/Services for Students with Learning Differences

The Office for Students with Disabilities (OSD) at UC San Diego works with students with documented disabilities, reviewing documentation and determines reasonable accommodations. OSD recognizes the unique challenges that some students with disabilities face, as disability impacts all areas of life.

Admissions

There is no special admissions process for students with learning disabilities. All applicants must meet the same admission criteria. Students must satisfy subject, GPA, and examination requirements. 15 units of high school courses must be completed to fulfill the subject requirements. At least 7 of those 15 units must be taken in the last 2 years of high school and a grade of C or greater must be earned: History (2 years), English (4 years), Math (3 years, although 4 years are recommended), Lab science (2 years, although 3 years are recommended), Language other than English (2 years although 3 years are recommended), Visual and Performing Arts (1 year), College Prep Electives (1 year). Students need to earn a minimum GPA based on "a-g" courses taken in the 10th and 11th grades. The ACT or SAT is optional for students applying for 2021 or 2022 and will be evaluated for future applicants.

Additional Information

Tutoring in most subjects is offered at all colleges and usually at no fee. The Writing Hub supports student writers through one-on-one writing consultations. Students get feedback on writing projects during the writing process. The Office of Academic Support & Instructional Services (OASIS) provides free tutoring, workshops, mentoring and counseling to all students. At the Teaching + Learning Commons, students get support for academic courses, subjects, and projects through group settings or one-on-one assistance, in person or online. In the Academic Achievement Hub learning strategists are available to work with students. The Summer Bridge Program is open to first-year, first-time UC San Diego admitted students. Attending the 8-week free Bridge program, students take courses for credit and are assigned a mentor.

ADMISSIONS INFO FOR STUDENTS WITH LEARNING DIFFERENCES

Phone: 858-534-4382 • Fax: 858-534-4650 • Email: jboval@ucsd.edu

SAT/ACT required: No
Interview required: No
Essay required: Yes
Additional application required: No
Documentation submitted to: OSD

Special Ed. HS course work accepted: Yes
Separate application required for Programs/Services: No
Documentation required for:
- **LD:** Psychoeducational evaluation
- **ADHD:** Psychoeducational evaluation
- **ASD:** Psychoeducational evaluation

University of California—San Diego

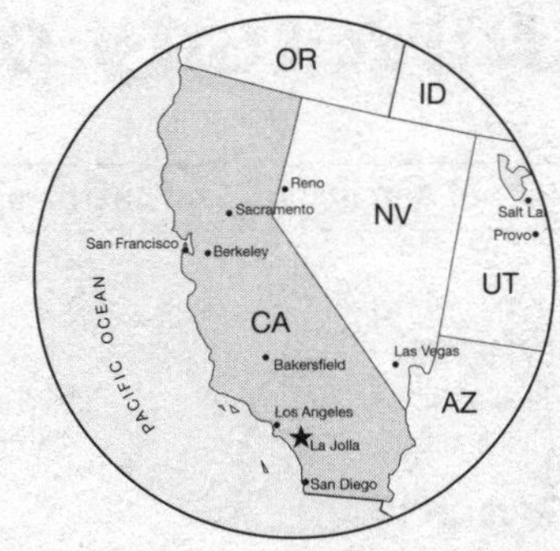

General Admissions

Very important factors include: rigor of secondary school record, academic GPA, application essay, standardized test scores. *Important factors include:* extracurricular activities, talent/ability, character/personal qualities, state residency, volunteer work. *Other factors include:* first generation, geographical residence, work experience. High school diploma is required and GED is accepted. *Academic units required:* 4 English, 3 math, 2 science, 2 science labs, 2 foreign language, 2 history, 1 academic elective, 1 visual/performing arts. *Academic units recommended:* 4 English, 4 math, 3 science, 3 science labs, 3 foreign language, 2 history, 1 academic elective, 1 visual/performing arts.

Accommodations or Services

Accommodations are decided upon an individual basis after a thorough review of appropriate, current documentation. The accommodations requests must be supported through the documentation provided and must be logically linked to the current impact of the condition on academic functioning.

Financial Aid

Students should submit: . Need-based scholarships/grants offered: College/university scholarship or grant aid from institutional funds; Federal Pell; Private scholarships; SEOG; State scholarships/grants. *Loan aid offered:* Direct PLUS loans; Direct Subsidized Stafford Loans; Direct Unsubsidized Stafford Loans. Federal Work-Study Program available. Institutional employment available.

Campus Life

Activities: Campus Ministries; Choral groups; Concert band; Dance; Drama/theater; International Student Organization; Jazz band; Literary magazine; Marching band; Model UN; Music ensembles; Musical theater; Opera; Pep band; Radio station; Student government; Student newspaper; Student-run film society; Symphony orchestra; Television station; Yearbook. **Organizations:** 531 registered organizations, 4 honor societies, 36 religious organizations, 16 fraternities, 12 sororities. **Athletics (Intercollegiate):** *Men:* baseball, basketball, crew/rowing, cross-country, diving, fencing, golf, soccer, swimming, tennis, track/field (outdoor), volleyball, water polo. *Women:* basketball, crew/rowing, cross-country, diving, fencing, soccer, softball, swimming, tennis, track/field (outdoor), volleyball, water polo.

ACCOMMODATIONS

Allowed in exams:	
Calculators	Yes
Dictionary	Yes
Computer	Yes
Spell-checker	Yes
Extended test time	Yes
Scribe	Yes
Proctors	Yes
Oral exams	Yes
Note-takers	Yes
Support services for students with:	
LD	Yes
ADHD	Yes
ASD	Yes
Distraction-reduced environment	Yes
Recording of lecture allowed	Yes
Reading technology	Yes
Audio books	Yes
Other assistive technology	Yes
Priority registration	Yes
Added costs of services:	
For LD	No
For ADHD	No
For ASD	No
LD specialists	Yes
ADHD & ASD coaching	Yes
ASD specialists	No
Professional tutors	Yes
Peer tutors	Yes
Max. hours/week for services	Varies
How professors are notified of student approved accommodations	Student

COLLEGE GRADUATION REQUIREMENTS

Course waivers allowed	No
Course substitutions allowed	No

University of California—Santa Barbara

Office of Admissions, Santa Barbara, CA 93106-2014 • Admissions: 805-893-2881 • Fax: 805-893-2676 **Support: CS**

CAMPUS

Type of school	Public
Environment	City

STUDENTS

Undergrad enrollment	23,349
% male/female	45/55
% from out of state	6
% frosh live on campus	92

FINANCIAL FACTS

Annual in-state tuition	$11,442
Annual out-of-state tuition	$41,196
Room and board	$15,389
Required fees	$2,949

GENERAL ADMISSIONS INFO

Application fee	$70
Regular application deadline	11/30
Nonfall registration	No
Range SAT EBRW	620–720
Range SAT Math	620–770
Range ACT Composite	25–33

ACADEMICS

Student/faculty ratio	17:1
% students returning for sophomore year	92

Most classes have 20–29 students.

Programs/Services for Students with Learning Differences

The Disabled Student Program (DSP) is a department within the Division of Student Affairs that provides support to students with temporary and permanent disabilities, assures equal access to all educational and academic programs, and fosters student independence. The DSP office serves as a liaison regarding issues and regulations related to students with disabilities. DSP provides reasonable accommodations based on individual needs supported by appropriate documentation and will not compromise the academic integrity of the student's academic program.

Admissions

All students must meet the university requirements for admissions. Students may self-disclose their disability in their personal statement. Each essay is reviewed by three readers who assign a score to the application. The university seeks high achieving students who have made the most of their circumstances and are involved in a variety of activities. California students applying as first year must have a minimum 3.0 weighted GPA in 10th and 11th grade classes and be enrolled in college prep classes. UCSB is Test Optional and ACT or SAT scores are not required for admission. Once students with disabilities are admitted to the university, they may apply to the Disabled Students Program.

Additional Information

Students with disabilities submit an online application for academic accommodations to DSP. Documentation of incoming students for the fall quarter is reviewed by the Documentation Review Committee beginning the third week of June each year. Students receive an email regarding their DSP status. Students are invited to a fall DSP orientation program and meet with their disabilities specialist. Non-remedial drop in, group and individualized tutoring, as well as study skills workshops, are offered through the campus tutoring center, Campus Learning Assistance Services (CLAS), for all university students.

ADMISSIONS INFO FOR STUDENTS WITH LEARNING DIFFERENCES

Phone: 805-893-2668 • Fax: 805-893-7127 • Email: gary.white@sa.ucsb.edu

SAT/ACT required: Yes (Test blind through 2022)
Interview required: No
Essay required: Yes
Additional application required: No
Documentation submitted to: The Disabled Students Program

Special Ed. HS course work accepted: Yes
Separate application required for Programs/Services: No
Documentation required for:
LD: Psychoeducational evaluation
ADHD: Psychoeducational evaluation
ASD: Psychoeducational evaluation

University of California—Santa Barbara

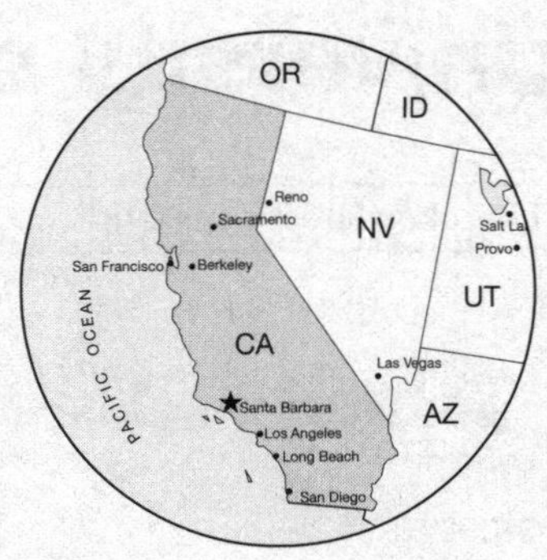

General Admissions

Very important factors include: academic GPA, application essay, standardized test scores. *Important factors include:* rigor of secondary school record. *Other factors include:* extracurricular activities, talent/ability, character/personal qualities, first generation, geographical residence, state residency, volunteer work, work experience. High school diploma is required and GED is accepted. *Academic units required:* 4 English, 3 math, 2 science, 2 science labs, 2 foreign language, 2 history, 1 academic elective, 1 visual/performing arts. *Academic units recommended:* 4 English, 4 math, 3 science, 3 science labs, 3 foreign language, 2 history, 1 academic elective, 1 visual/performing arts.

Accommodations or Services

Accommodations are decided upon an individual basis after a thorough review of appropriate, current documentation. The accommodations requests must be supported through the documentation provided and must be logically linked to the current impact of the condition on academic functioning.

Financial Aid

Students should submit: FAFSA. *Need-based scholarships/grants offered:* College/university scholarship or grant aid from institutional funds; Federal Pell; SEOG; State scholarships/grants. *Loan aid offered:* Direct PLUS loans; Direct Subsidized Stafford Loans; Direct Unsubsidized Stafford Loans. Federal Work-Study Program available. Institutional employment available.

Campus Life

Activities: Campus Ministries; Choral groups; Concert band; Dance; Drama/theater; International Student Organization; Jazz band; Literary magazine; Model UN; Music ensembles; Musical theater; Opera; Pep band; Radio station; Student government; Student newspaper; Student-run film society; Symphony orchestra; Television station; Yearbook. **Organizations:** 404 registered organizations, 13 honor societies, 16 religious organizations, 12 fraternities, 20 sororities. **Athletics (Intercollegiate):** *Men:* baseball, basketball, cross-country, diving, golf, gymnastics, soccer, swimming, tennis, track/field (outdoor), volleyball, water polo. *Women:* basketball, cross-country, diving, gymnastics, soccer, softball, swimming, tennis, track/field (outdoor), volleyball, water polo.

ACCOMMODATIONS

Allowed in exams:	
Calculators	Yes
Dictionary	Yes
Computer	Yes
Spell-checker	Yes
Extended test time	Yes
Scribe	Yes
Proctors	Yes
Oral exams	Yes
Note-takers	Yes
Support services for students with:	
LD	Yes
ADHD	Yes
ASD	Yes
Distraction-reduced environment	Yes
Recording of lecture allowed	Yes
Reading technology	Yes
Audio books	Yes
Other assistive technology	Yes
Priority registration	Yes
Added costs of services:	
For LD	No
For ADHD	No
For ASD	No
LD specialists	Yes
ADHD & ASD coaching	No
ASD specialists	No
Professional tutors	No
Peer tutors	Yes
Max. hours/week for services	No
How professors are notified of student approved accommodations	Student and Disability Office

COLLEGE GRADUATION REQUIREMENTS

Course waivers allowed	No
Course substitutions allowed	No

University of San Francisco

2130 Fulton Street, San Francisco, CA 94117 • Admissions: 415-422-6563 • Fax: 415-422-2217 **Support: CS**

CAMPUS

Type of school	Private (nonprofit)
Environment	Metropolis

STUDENTS

Undergrad enrollment	6,510
% male/female	38/62
% from out of state	33
% frosh live on campus	86

FINANCIAL FACTS

Annual tuition	$51,930
Room and board	$15,990
Required fees	$552

GENERAL ADMISSIONS INFO

Application fee	$70
Regular application deadline	1/15
Nonfall registration	Yes

Admission may be deferred.

Range SAT EBRW	570–660
Range SAT Math	560–670
Range ACT Composite	22–29

ACADEMICS

Student/faculty ratio	13:1
% students returning for sophomore year	85

Most classes have 10–19 students.

Programs/Services for Students with Learning Differences

The mission of Student Disability Services (SDS) is to support students with disabilities services and accommodations based on appropriate documentation. SDS ensures that students have access to student life and receive educational support and services to guide their academic and personal success. SDS arranges accommodations on an individual basis during the intake/eligibility process.

Admissions

All applicants must meet the same general admission requirements. The average GPA is 3.5. USF is test optional and ACT/SAT is not required for admission. For applicants who submit scores the mid-50% SAT is 1130–1310 and the mid-50% ACT is 22–29. USF is a Jesuit university that welcomes students of all faith or no faith. The essay prompt asks applicants to speak to how they see themselves becoming part of the Jesuit mission. Course requirements include 4 years English, 3 years math (engineering applicants must have taken pre-calculus), 3 years social science, 2 lab science (nursing requires chemistry and either physics or biology, and 2 years of foreign language.

Additional Information

USF provides pre-admission counseling and new student orientation. Students need to register with SDS using an online application and submit documentation. Students can use a Verification of Disability Form while they are gathering documentation. Every student will meet with a Disability Specialist to have a conversation about their experience and discuss appropriate accommodations and academic adjustments. Students have access to priority registration and can access academic guidance. This process can take up to 10 days and students are encouraged to engage with SDS in advance of the start of the school year.

ADMISSIONS INFO FOR STUDENTS WITH LEARNING DIFFERENCES

Phone: 415-422-2613 • Fax: 415-422-5906 • Email: sds@usfca.edu

SAT/ACT required: No
Interview required: No
Essay required: Yes for general admission
Additional application required: Yes
Documentation submitted to: SDS

Special Ed. HS course work accepted: Yes
Separate application required for Programs/Services: Yes
Documentation required for:
LD: Psychoeducational evaluation
ADHD: Psychoeducational evaluation
ASD: Psychoeducational evaluation

University of San Francisco

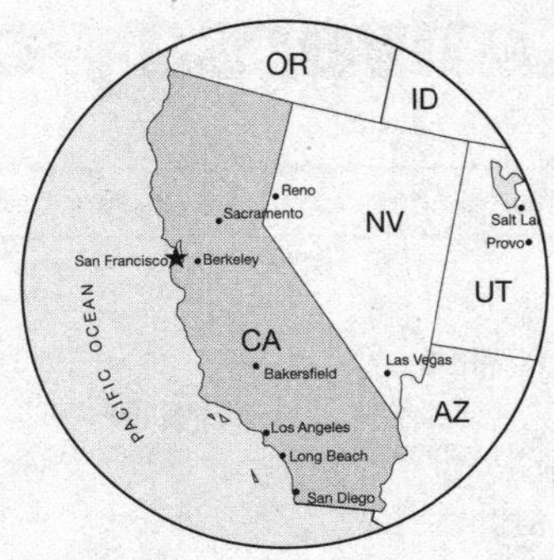

General Admissions

Very important factors include: rigor of secondary school record, academic GPA. *Important factors include:* application essay, character/personal qualities, volunteer work. *Other factors include:* class rank, standardized test scores, recommendation(s), interview, extracurricular activities, talent/ability, first generation, alumni/ae relation, racial/ethnic status, work experience, level of applicant's interest. High school diploma is required and GED is accepted. *Academic units required:* 4 English, 3 math, 2 science, 2 science labs, 2 foreign language, 3 social studies, 6 academic electives.

Accommodations or Services

Accommodations are decided upon an individual basis after a thorough review of appropriate, current documentation. The accommodations requests must be supported through the documentation provided and must be logically linked to the current impact of the condition on academic functioning.

Financial Aid

Students should submit: FAFSA; State aid form. *Need-based scholarships/grants offered:* College/university scholarship or grant aid from institutional funds; Federal Pell; Private scholarships; SEOG; State scholarships/grants. *Loan aid offered:* Direct PLUS loans; Direct Subsidized Stafford Loans; Direct Unsubsidized Stafford Loans. Federal Work-Study Program available. Institutional employment available.

Campus Life

Activities: Campus Ministries; Choral groups; Dance; Drama/theater; International Student Organization; Jazz band; Literary magazine; Marching band; Music ensembles; Musical theater; Pep band; Radio station; Student government; Student newspaper; Television station; Yearbook. **Organizations:** 149 registered organizations, 7 honor societies, 3 religious organizations, 4 fraternities, 6 sororities. **Athletics (Intercollegiate):** *Men:* baseball, basketball, cross-country, golf, riflery, soccer, tennis, track/field (outdoor). *Women:* basketball, cross-country, golf, riflery, soccer, tennis, track/field (outdoor), volleyball.

ACCOMMODATIONS

Allowed in exams:	
Calculators	Yes
Dictionary	Yes
Computer	Yes
Spell-checker	Yes
Extended test time	Yes
Scribe	Yes
Proctors	Yes
Oral exams	Yes
Note-takers	Yes
Support services for students with:	
LD	Yes
ADHD	Yes
ASD	Yes
Distraction-reduced environment	Yes
Recording of lecture allowed	Yes
Reading technology	Yes
Audio books	Yes
Other assistive technology	Yes
Priority registration	Yes
Added costs of services:	
For LD	No
For ADHD	No
For ASD	No
LD specialists	Yes
ADHD & ASD coaching	Yes
ASD specialists	No
Professional tutors	Yes
Peer tutors	Yes
Max. hours/week for services	Varies
How professors are notified of student approved accommodations	Student and Disability Office

COLLEGE GRADUATION REQUIREMENTS

Course waivers allowed	No
Course substitutions allowed	Yes

In what courses: For those students who are eligible substitutions may be available for foreign language and/or math.

California

University of Southern California

Office of Admission (University Park Campus), Los Angeles, CA 90089-0911 • Admissions: 213-740-1111 • Fax: 213-821-0200 **Support: CS**

CAMPUS

Type of school	Private (nonprofit)
Environment	Metropolis

STUDENTS

Undergrad enrollment	19,908
% male/female	48/52
% from out of state	35
% frosh live on campus	98

FINANCIAL FACTS

Annual tuition	$59,260
Room and board	$15,437
Required fees	$1,015

GENERAL ADMISSIONS INFO

Application fee	$85
Regular application deadline	1/15
Nonfall registration	Yes

Admission may be deferred.

Range SAT EBRW	670–740
Range SAT Math	690–790
Range ACT Composite	31–34

ACADEMICS

Student/faculty ratio	8:1
% students returning for sophomore year	96

Most classes have 10–19 students.

Programs/Services for Students with Learning Differences

Disability Services and Programs offers a comprehensive support program. DSP serves the USC community ensuring equal access, removing obstacles, and advocating for students with disabilities to increase education and awareness. DSP employs specialists with advanced degrees in fields relevant to disability services for higher education. This team offers expertise to students, faculty, staff, and other campus partners. Students registered with DSP are assigned to a specific DSP Specialist, who serves as the student's specific point of contact.

Admissions

There are no special admissions for students with learning disabilities. There are no specific course requirements for admission. However, students typically admitted have pursued the most rigorous program available to them in all of the academic areas. USC looks carefully at courses taken for an intended college major. There is no formula to being admitted. USC looks at potential, motivation, grit, and each student's passion about learning and future involvement in research. Some majors do require a portfolio or an audition, and faculty from these programs provide feedback to the admission committee. Applicants can be considered for a second-choice major or could be admitted "undecided/undeclared."

Additional Information

The services provided are modifications that are determined to be appropriate for students with LD. During the first 3 weeks of each semester, students are seen on a walk-in basis by the staff at DSP. Students need documentation supporting the request for accommodations. Support most often involves one-on-one attention for academic planning, scheduling, organization, and methods of compensation. Students are offered standing appointments with learning assistants and subject tutors. Course accommodations could include taping of lectures, note-taking, extended time for tests, use of word processor, proofreader, limiting scheduling of consecutive exams, and advocacy. Other services include support groups, counseling, and coaching.

ADMISSIONS INFO FOR STUDENTS WITH LEARNING DIFFERENCES

Phone: 213-740-0776 • Email: kortschakcenter@usc.edu

SAT/ACT required: Yes (Optional 2021)
Interview required: No
Essay required: Yes
Additional application required: No
Documentation submitted to: Disability Services and Programs

Special Ed. HS course work accepted: Yes
Separate application required for Programs/Services: No
Documentation required for:
LD: Psychoeducational evaluation
ADHD: Psychoeducational evaluation
ASD: Psychoeducational evaluation

University of Southern California

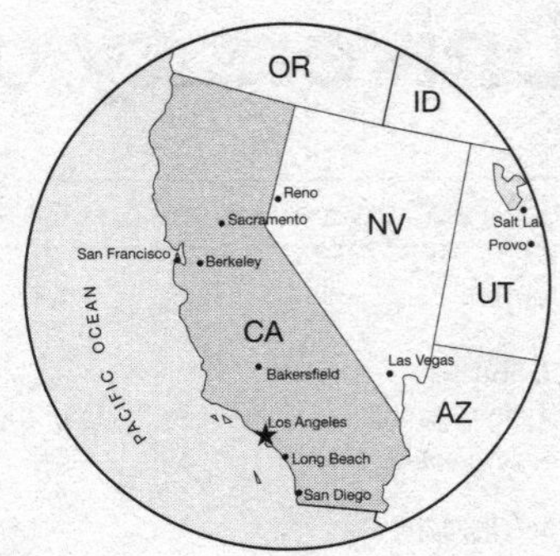

General Admissions

Very important factors include: rigor of secondary school record, academic GPA, application essay, standardized test scores, recommendation(s). *Important factors include:* extracurricular activities, talent/ability, character/personal qualities. *Other factors include:* first generation, alumni/ae relation, racial/ethnic status, volunteer work, work experience. High school diploma is required and GED is not accepted. *Academic units required:* 4 English, 3 math, 2 science, 2 science labs, 2 foreign language, 2 social studies, 3 academic electives. *Academic units recommended:* 4 English, 4 math, 3 science, 3 science labs, 3 foreign language, 3 social studies, 3 academic electives.

Accommodations or Services

Accommodations are decided upon an individual basis after a thorough review of appropriate, current documentation. The accommodations requests must be supported through the documentation provided and must be logically linked to the current impact of the condition on academic functioning.

Financial Aid

Students should submit: FAFSA. Applicants will be notified of awards on a rolling basis beginning 2/1. *Need-based scholarships/grants offered:* College/university scholarship or grant aid from institutional funds; Federal Pell; Private scholarships; SEOG; State scholarships/grants. *Loan aid offered:* Direct PLUS loans; Direct Subsidized Stafford Loans; Direct Unsubsidized Stafford Loans. Federal Work-Study Program available. Institutional employment available.

Campus Life

Activities: Campus Ministries; Choral groups; Concert band; Dance; Drama/theater; International Student Organization; Jazz band; Literary magazine; Marching band; Model UN; Music ensembles; Musical theater; Opera; Pep band; Radio station; Student government; Student newspaper; Student-run film society; Symphony orchestra; Television station; Yearbook. **Organizations:** 850 registered organizations, 46 honor societies, 87 religious organizations, 32 fraternities, 26 sororities. **Athletics (Intercollegiate):** *Men:* baseball, basketball, diving, football, golf, swimming, tennis, track/field (outdoor), volleyball, water polo. *Women:* basketball, crew/rowing, cross-country, diving, golf, soccer, swimming, tennis, track/field (outdoor), volleyball, water polo.

ACCOMMODATIONS

Allowed in exams:	
Calculators	Yes
Dictionary	Yes
Computer	Yes
Spell-checker	Yes
Extended test time	Yes
Scribe	Yes
Proctors	Yes
Oral exams	Yes
Note-takers	Yes
Support services for students with:	
LD	Yes
ADHD	Yes
ASD	Yes
Distraction-reduced environment	Yes
Recording of lecture allowed	Yes
Reading technology	Yes
Audio books	Yes
Other assistive technology	Yes
Priority registration	Yes
Added costs of services:	
For LD	No
For ADHD	No
For ASD	No
LD specialists	Yes
ADHD & ASD coaching	Yes
ASD specialists	No
Professional tutors	Yes
Peer tutors	Yes
Max. hours/week for services	Varies
How professors are notified of student approved accommodations	Student

COLLEGE GRADUATION REQUIREMENTS

Course waivers allowed	No
Course substitutions allowed	No

University of the Pacific

3601 Pacific Avenue, Stockton, CA 95211 • Admissions: 209-946-2211 • Fax: 209-946-4213 **Support: CS**

CAMPUS

Type of school	Private (nonprofit)
Environment	City

STUDENTS

Undergrad enrollment	3,640
% male/female	48/52
% from out of state	8
% frosh live on campus	75

FINANCIAL FACTS

Annual tuition	$48,904
Room and board	$13,740
Required fees	$684

GENERAL ADMISSIONS INFO

Application fee	$0
Regular application deadline	1/15
Nonfall registration	Yes

Admission may be deferred.

Range SAT EBRW	550–660
Range SAT Math	570–700
Range ACT Composite	23–31

ACADEMICS

Student/faculty ratio	14:1
% students returning for sophomore year	83

Most classes have 10–19 students.

Programs/Services for Students with Learning Differences

There is no special program for students with learning disabilities. Services for Students with Disabilities (SSD) provides accommodations for all students with documented disabilities. Documentation for LD must include psychoeducational evaluations from a professional. The documentation for ADHD must be from a medical doctor. Students register for services after admission by contacting SSD. The ultimate goal is for the student to earn a degree that is unmodified and unflagged. Faculty and staff are dedicated to providing students with learning disabilities all reasonable accommodations so that they may enjoy academic success.

Admissions

UOP welcomes students with learning disabilities. However, all applicants must meet the same admission criteria. UOP is test optional and does not require applicants to submit their ACT or SAT. University courses are open to anyone during Summer Sessions. However, students taking summer courses should not assume that participation in Pacific Summer will lead to admission for enrollment in the regular academic year.

Additional Information

All admitted students are eligible for LD services with the appropriate assessment documentation. Academic Support Services offers services to improve learning opportunities for students with LD and are provided within reasonable limits. These services could include diagnostic assessment, accommodations for academic needs, electronic books and alternate formatting, readers, tutorials for academic courses, and referrals to appropriate resources. Skills courses for credit are available in reading, study skills, writing, and math. Services and accommodations are available for undergraduate and graduate students.

ADMISSIONS INFO FOR STUDENTS WITH LEARNING DIFFERENCES

Phone: 209-946-3221 • Fax: 209-946-2278 • Email: dnuss@pacific.edu

SAT/ACT required: No
Interview required: No
Essay required: Yes
Additional application required: No
Documentation submitted to: SSD

Special Ed. HS course work accepted: Yes
Separate application required for Programs/Services: No
Documentation required for:
LD: Psychoeducational evaluation
ADHD: Psychoeducational evaluation
ASD: Psychoeducational evaluation

University of the Pacific

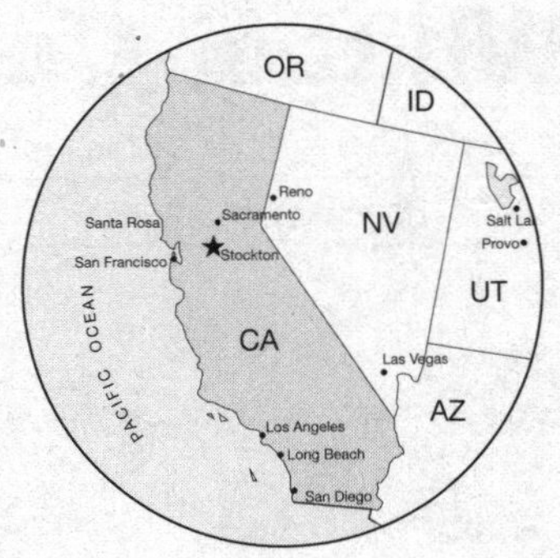

General Admissions

Very important factors include: rigor of secondary school record. *Important factors include:* academic GPA, standardized test scores, extracurricular activities, first generation. *Other factors include:* class rank, application essay, recommendation(s), talent/ability, character/personal qualities, alumni/ae relation, geographical residence, racial/ethnic status, volunteer work, work experience. High school diploma is required and GED is accepted. *Academic units recommended:* 4 English, 4 math, 3 science labs, 2 foreign language, 2 social studies, 1 history, 1 academic elective, 1 visual/performing arts.

Accommodations or Services

Accommodations are decided upon an individual basis after a thorough review of appropriate, current documentation. The accommodations requests must be supported through the documentation provided and must be logically linked to the current impact of the condition on academic functioning.

Financial Aid

Students should submit: FAFSA. Applicants will be notified of awards on a rolling basis beginning 12/31. *Need-based scholarships/grants offered:* College/university scholarship or grant aid from institutional funds; Federal Pell; Private scholarships; SEOG; State scholarships/grants. *Loan aid offered:* Direct PLUS loans; Direct Subsidized Stafford Loans; Direct Unsubsidized Stafford Loans.

Campus Life

Activities: Campus Ministries; Choral groups; Concert band; Dance; Drama/theater; International Student Organization; Jazz band; Literary magazine; Model UN; Music ensembles; Musical theater; Opera; Pep band; Radio station; Student government; Student newspaper; Student-run film society; Yearbook. **Organizations:** 100 registered organizations, 14 honor societies, 10 religious organizations, 8 fraternities, 7 sororities. **Athletics (Intercollegiate):** *Men:* baseball, basketball, golf, swimming, tennis, volleyball, water polo. *Women:* basketball, cross-country, field hockey, soccer, softball, swimming, tennis, volleyball, water polo.

ACCOMMODATIONS

Allowed in exams:	
Calculators	Yes
Dictionary	Yes
Computer	Yes
Spell-checker	Yes
Extended test time	Yes
Scribe	Yes
Proctors	Yes
Oral exams	Yes
Note-takers	Yes
Support services for students with:	
LD	Yes
ADHD	Yes
ASD	Yes
Distraction-reduced environment	Yes
Recording of lecture allowed	Yes
Reading technology	Yes
Audio books	Yes
Other assistive technology	Yes
Priority registration	Yes
Added costs of services:	
For LD	No
For ADHD	No
For ASD	No
LD specialists	Yes
ADHD & ASD coaching	Yes
ASD specialists	Yes
Professional tutors	Yes
Peer tutors	Yes
Max. hours/week for services	Varies
How professors are notified of student approved accommodations	Director

COLLEGE GRADUATION REQUIREMENTS

Course waivers allowed	No
Course substitutions allowed	Yes
In what courses: Case by case basis	

Whittier College

13406 E. Philadelphia Street, Whittier, CA 90608 • Admissions: 562-907-4238 • Fax: 562-907-4870 **Support: CS**

CAMPUS

Type of school	Private (nonprofit)
Environment	City

STUDENTS

Undergrad enrollment	1,776
% male/female	44/56
% from out of state	19
% frosh live on campus	68

FINANCIAL FACTS

Annual tuition	$48,924
Room and board	$14,438
Required fees	$590

GENERAL ADMISSIONS INFO

Application fee	$0
Regular application deadline	2/1
Nonfall registration	Yes
Admission may be deferred	Yes
Range SAT EBRW	530–620
Range SAT Math	510–600
Range ACT Composite	20–26

ACADEMICS

Student/faculty ratio	12:1
% students returning for sophomore year	79

Most classes have 10–19 students.

Programs/Services for Students with Learning Differences

The director of The Office of Disability Services provides assistance to students with documented disabilities. Accommodation requests are made through the director's office. Students with disabilities must make their needs known to the director of Disability Services to receive accommodations. To arrange for services, students must self-disclose the disability and make an individual appointment to discuss their accommodation requests with the director. Learning Support Services offers additional services: peer tutoring, workshops on study skills, and basic English and math skills assistance. These services are provided at no cost.

Admissions

There is no special admissions process for students with disabilities. All applicants are expected to meet the same admission criteria. Whittier is test optional and ACT/SAT scores are not required. However, students who apply as test optional with a GPA under 3.0 could be required to provide test scores to be considered for admission. Students that apply as Test-Optional that have a Whittier Admission GPA under a 3.0 could be required to provide standardized test scores in order to be considered for admission. The Whittier Admission GPA is a 9–11 grade, a weighted GPA that includes all academic classes.

Additional Information

Through the Office of Disability Services students have access to Supportive Education Services (SES)/Case Management Services. These services offer individualized services to students with ADHD/ADD and Autism Spectrum Disorders/Pervasive Developmental Disorders. The central goal is to help students learn coping strategies to address symptoms such as problems with concentration, memory issues, test anxiety and support with organization. The use of calculators, dictionaries, computers, or spell checkers in exams would be considered on a case-by-case basis, depending on appropriate documentation and student needs. Students with appropriate documentation will have access to note-takers, readers, extended exam times, alternative exam locations, proctors, scribes, oral exams, assistive technology books on tape, and priority registration. All students have access to a Math Lab, a Writing Center, a Learning Lab, and Academic Counseling.

ADMISSIONS INFO FOR STUDENTS WITH LEARNING DIFFERENCES

Phone: 562-907-4825 • Fax: 562-907-4827

SAT/ACT required: No
Interview required: No
Essay required: Yes
Additional application required: No
Documentation submitted to: Office of Disability Services

Special Ed. HS course work accepted: Yes
Separate application required for Programs/Services: No
Documentation required for:
LD: Psychoeducational evaluation
ADHD: Psychoeducational evaluation
ASD: Psychoeducational evaluation

Whittier College

General Admissions

Very important factors include: rigor of secondary school record, academic GPA, application essay, recommendation(s), character/personal qualities. *Important factors include:* interview, extracurricular activities, talent/ability. *Other factors include:* class rank, standardized test scores, first generation, alumni/ae relation, geographical residence, state residency, racial/ethnic status, work experience. High school diploma is required and GED is accepted. *Academic units required:* 3 English, 2 math, 1 science, 1 science lab, 2 foreign language, 1 social studies. *Academic units recommended:* 4 English, 3 math, 2 science, 3 foreign language, 2 social studies.

Accommodations or Services

Accommodations are decided upon an individual basis after a thorough review of appropriate, current documentation. The accommodations requests must be supported through the documentation provided and must be logically linked to the current impact of the condition on academic functioning.

Financial Aid

Students should submit: FAFSA. Applicants will be notified of awards on a rolling basis beginning 2/15. *Need-based scholarships/grants offered:* College/university scholarship or grant aid from institutional funds; Federal Pell; Private scholarships; SEOG; State scholarships/grants. *Loan aid offered:* Direct PLUS loans; Direct Subsidized Stafford Loans; Direct Unsubsidized Stafford Loans. Federal Work-Study Program available.

Campus Life

Activities: Campus Ministries; Choral groups; Dance; Drama/theater; International Student Organization; Jazz band; Literary magazine; Model UN; Music ensembles; Radio station; Student government; Student newspaper; Student-run film society; Television station; Yearbook. **Organizations:** 60 registered organizations, 17 honor societies, 6 religious organizations, 4 fraternities, 5 sororities. **Athletics (Intercollegiate):** *Men:* baseball, basketball, cross-country, diving, football, golf, lacrosse, soccer, swimming, tennis, track/field (outdoor), water polo. *Women:* basketball, cross-country, diving, lacrosse, soccer, softball, swimming, tennis, track/field (outdoor), volleyball, water polo.

ACCOMMODATIONS

Allowed in exams:	
Calculators	Yes
Dictionary	Yes
Computer	Yes
Spell-checker	Yes
Extended test time	Yes
Scribe	Yes
Proctors	Yes
Oral exams	No
Note-takers	Yes
Support services for students with:	
LD	Yes
ADHD	Yes
ASD	Yes
Distraction-reduced environment	Yes
Recording of lecture allowed	Yes
Reading technology	Yes
Audio books	Yes
Other assistive technology	Yes
Priority registration	Yes
Added costs of services:	
For LD	No
For ADHD	No
For ASD	No
LD specialists	Yes
ADHD & ASD coaching	Yes
ASD specialists	Yes
Professional tutors	No
Peer tutors	Yes
Max. hours/week for services	Unlimited
How professors are notified of student approved accommodations	Student and Disability Office

COLLEGE GRADUATION REQUIREMENTS

Course waivers allowed — Yes

In what courses: Foreign Language, Math

Course substitutions allowed — Yes

In what courses: Foreign Language, Math

California

Colorado State University—Pueblo

2200 Bonforte Boulevard, Pueblo, CO 81001 • Admissions: 719-549-2461 • Fax: 719-549-2419 **Support: S**

CAMPUS

Type of school	Public
Environment	City

STUDENTS

Undergrad enrollment	4,385
% male/female	46/54
% from out of state	14
% frosh live on campus	49

FINANCIAL FACTS

Annual in-state tuition	$10,664
Annual out-of-state tuition	$18,862
Room and board	$10,930

GENERAL ADMISSIONS INFO

Application fee	$25
Regular application deadline	8/1
Nonfall registration	Yes

Admission may be deferred.

Range SAT EBRW	460–570
Range SAT Math	460–550
Range ACT Composite	18–24

ACADEMICS

Student/faculty ratio	14:1
% students returning for sophomore year	68

Most classes have 10–19 students.

Programs/Services for Students with Learning Differences

The Mission of the Disability Resource and Support Center at Colorado State University—Pueblo provides reasonable academic accommodations and support, designed to students with documented disabilities.

Admissions

Colorado State University—Pueblo's admission process is reasonable and fair and the goal is to provide access to a 4-year college degree to any student who is academically prepared. CSU Pueblo admission committee evaluates student preparation, including ACT/SAT score, high school GPA, and academic rigor. Most students with a 2.0 GPA are considered for admission. Applicants are encouraged to complete 4 years of English, 3 years of math, 3 years of science, 3 years of social studies (including one year of U.S. History), 2 years of a foreign language, and 2 years of academic electives. Applicants who do not meet admission standards are encouraged to submit personal statements explaining their circumstances and to show academic progress throughout high school.

Additional Information

The Center for Academic Enrichment (CAE) provides programs and services designed to promote student achievement. The staff focuses on enrollment, retention, and the academic experience of students to guide them toward independence. Skills classes are offered in note-taking strategies, study skills, and textbook reading strategies. The request for the use of a dictionary, computer, or spellchecker during exams will depend on the student's documented needs and permission from the professor. Students with specific needs are encouraged to provide documentation that specifically identifies the disability and the accommodations needed. Tutoring is available through Student and Academic Services. The Academic Improvement Program helps students who are on GPA alerts or academic probation develop an Academic Improvement Plan to promote success. The Writing Room offers one-on-one writing assistance.

ADMISSIONS INFO FOR STUDENTS WITH LEARNING DIFFERENCES

Phone: 719-549-2648 • Email: DRO@csupueblo.edu

SAT/ACT required: Yes (Test optional for 2021)
Interview required: No
Essay required: No
Additional application required: No
Documentation submitted to: Disability Resource and Support Center

Special Ed. HS course work accepted: Yes
Separate application required for Programs/Services: No
Documentation required for:
LD: Psychoeducational evaluation
ADHD: Psychoeducational evaluation
ASD: Psychoeducational evaluation

Colorado State University—Pueblo

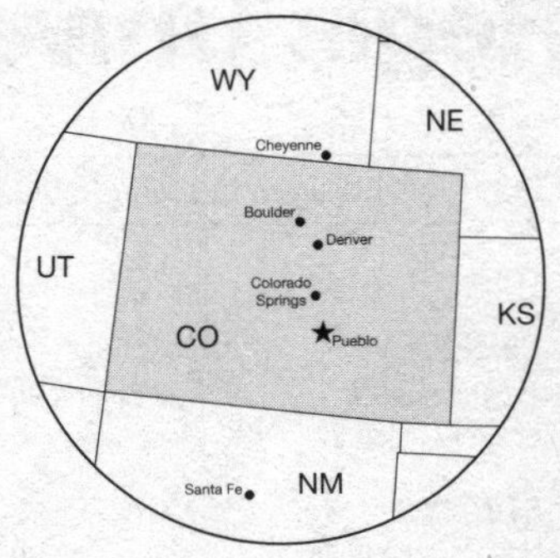

Colorado

General Admissions

Very important factors include: rigor of secondary school record, academic GPA, standardized test scores. *Important factors include:* class rank. *Other factors include:* application essay, recommendation(s), interview, talent/ability, character/personal qualities, volunteer work, work experience, level of applicant's interest. High school diploma is required and GED is accepted. *Academic units required:* 4 English, 3 math, 3 science, 2 science labs, 2 foreign language, 2 social studies, 1 history. *Academic units recommended:* 4 English, 3 math, 3 science, 2 science labs, 2 foreign language, 2 social studies, 1 history.

Accommodations or Services

Accommodations are decided upon an individual basis after a thorough review of appropriate, current documentation. The accommodations requests must be supported through the documentation provided and must be logically linked to the current impact of the condition on academic functioning.

Financial Aid

Students should submit: FAFSA; State aid form. Applicants will be notified of awards on a rolling basis beginning 12/1. *Need-based scholarships/grants offered:* College/university scholarship or grant aid from institutional funds; Federal Pell; Private scholarships; SEOG; State scholarships/grants.

Campus Life

Activities: Choral groups; Concert band; Dance; Jazz band; Literary magazine; Music ensembles; Pep band; Student government; Student newspaper; Symphony orchestra; Television station. **Organizations:** 24 registered organizations, 6 honor societies, 4 religious organizations, 2 fraternities, 1 sorority. **Athletics (Intercollegiate):** *Men:* baseball, basketball, golf, soccer, tennis. *Women:* basketball, cross-country, golf, soccer, softball, tennis, volleyball.

ACCOMMODATIONS

Allowed in exams:	
Calculators	Yes
Dictionary	Yes
Computer	Yes
Spell-checker	Yes
Extended test time	Yes
Scribe	Yes
Proctors	Yes
Oral exams	Yes
Note-takers	Yes
Support services for students with:	
LD	Yes
ADHD	Yes
ASD	Yes
Distraction-reduced environment	Yes
Recording of lecture allowed	Yes
Reading technology	Yes
Audio books	Yes
Other assistive technology	Yes
Priority registration	Yes
Added costs of services:	
For LD	No
For ADHD	No
For ASD	No
LD specialists	No
ADHD & ASD coaching	No
ASD specialists	No
Professional tutors	No
Peer tutors	Yes
Max. hours/week for services	As needed
How professors are notified of student approved accommodations	Student

COLLEGE GRADUATION REQUIREMENTS

Course waivers allowed	No
Course substitutions allowed	Yes
In what courses: Case by case basis	

Regis University

3333 Regis Boulevard, Denver, CO 80221-1099 • Admissions: 303-458-4900 • Fax: 303-964-5534 **Support: S**

CAMPUS

Type of school	Private (nonprofit)
Environment	Metropolis

STUDENTS

Undergrad enrollment	3,500
% male/female	39/61
% from out of state	42

FINANCIAL FACTS

Annual tuition	$38,208
Room and board	$12,460
Required fees	$350

GENERAL ADMISSIONS INFO

Application fee	$0
Regular application deadline	4/15
Nonfall registration	Yes

Admission may be deferred.

Range SAT EBRW	520–630
Range SAT Math	510–610
Range ACT Composite	21–27

ACADEMICS

% students returning for sophomore year	84

Most classes have 10–19 students.

Programs/Services for Students with Learning Differences

Student Disability and University Testing provides support to students with disabilities. The application process is designed to help all students navigate the process of registering with SDS/UT. Students requesting reasonable accommodations must complete an application, submit documentation of a disabling condition, and participate in an intake appointment. It is strongly recommended that students complete the application as early as possible.

Admissions

There is no special admission for students with learning disabilities. Interviews are not required. Regis is test optional and ACT/SAT scores are not required for admission. Students need to show sufficient evidence of motivation and ability to succeed in college, even though they may not have the required GPA. Recommendations and extracurricular activities will be considered. Students can be admitted on probation. Students will need a 2.0 GPA to return the second semester if admitted on probation.

Additional Information

SDS/UT does not offer tutoring services specifically for students with disabilities. Instead, Regis offers all students resources to support their academic success. The Writing Center, Tutoring Services, and Academic Success Workshops are located in the Learning Commons. These services support writing in many subjects through one-to-one and group sessions. Students are responsible for requesting accommodations by completing an application, submitting documentation of a disabling condition, and participating in an intake appointment. Students are encouraged to complete the application as early as possible. Students request academic accommodations each semester. Approved academic accommodations become active after students make a request with SDS/UT.

ADMISSIONS INFO FOR STUDENTS WITH LEARNING DIFFERENCES

Phone: 303-458-4941 • Fax: 303-964-6595 • Email: disability@regis.edu

SAT/ACT required: No
Interview required: No
Essay required: No
Additional application required: No
Documentation submitted to: Student Disability and University Testing

Special Ed. HS course work accepted: Yes
Separate application required for Programs/Services: No
Documentation required for:
LD: Psychoeducational evaluation
ADHD: Psychoeducational evaluation
ASD: Psychoeducational evaluation

Regis University

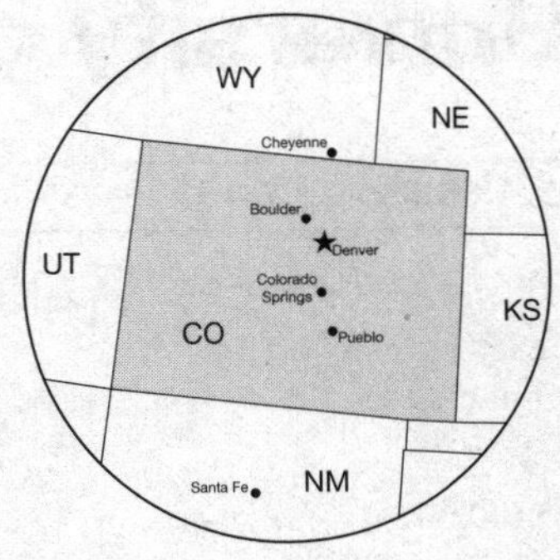

Colorado

General Admissions

Very important factors include: rigor of secondary school record, academic GPA, standardized test scores, character/personal qualities. *Important factors include:* application essay, *Other factors include:* class rank, recommendation(s), interview, extracurricular activities, talent/ability, first generation, alumni/ae relation, racial/ethnic status, volunteer work, work experience, level of applicant's interest. High school diploma is required and GED is accepted. *Academic units recommended:* 4 English, 3 math, 2 science, 1 science lab, 2 foreign language, 2 social studies, 1 academic elective.

Accommodations or Services

Accommodations are decided upon an individual basis after a thorough review of appropriate, current documentation. The accommodations requests must be supported through the documentation provided and must be logically linked to the current impact of the condition on academic functioning.

Financial Aid

Students should submit: FAFSA. *Need-based scholarships/grants offered:* College/university scholarship or grant aid from institutional funds; Federal Pell; Private scholarships; SEOG; State scholarships/grants. *Loan aid offered:* Direct PLUS loans; Direct Subsidized Stafford Loans; Direct Unsubsidized Stafford Loans. Federal Work-Study Program available. Institutional employment available.

Campus Life

Activities: Campus Ministries; Choral groups; Concert band; Dance; Drama/theater; International Student Organization; Jazz band; Literary magazine; Music ensembles; Musical theater; Radio station; Student government; Student newspaper; Yearbook. **Athletics (Intercollegiate):** *Men:* baseball, basketball, cross-country, golf, soccer. *Women:* basketball, cross-country, lacrosse, soccer, softball, volleyball.

ACCOMMODATIONS

Allowed in exams:	
Calculators	Yes
Dictionary	Yes
Computer	Yes
Spell-checker	Yes
Extended test time	Yes
Scribe	Yes
Proctors	Yes
Oral exams	Yes
Note-takers	Yes
Support services for students with:	
LD	Yes
ADHD	Yes
ASD	Yes
Distraction-reduced environment	Yes
Recording of lecture allowed	Yes
Reading technology	Yes
Audio books	Yes
Other assistive technology	Yes
Priority registration	Yes
Added costs of services:	
For LD	No
For ADHD	No
For ASD	No
LD specialists	No
ADHD & ASD coaching	No
ASD specialists	No
Professional tutors	No
Peer tutors	Yes
Max. hours/week for services	Varies
How professors are notified of student approved accommodations	Student

COLLEGE GRADUATION REQUIREMENTS

Course waivers allowed	Yes

In what courses: All students must take three hours of math. Foreign culture courses are substituted for foreign language if the documentation verifies a disability.

Course substitutions allowed	Yes

In what courses: All students must take three hours of math. Foreign culture courses are substituted for foreign language if the documentation verifies a disability.

University of Colorado Boulder

552 UCB, Boulder, CO 80309-0552 • Admissions: 303-492-6301 • Fax: 303-735-2501 **Support: CS**

CAMPUS

Type of school	Public
Environment	City

STUDENTS

Undergrad enrollment	30,673
% male/female	55/45
% from out of state	42
% frosh live on campus	94

FINANCIAL FACTS

Annual in-state tuition	$10,728
Annual out-of-state tuition	$36,546
Room and board	$14,778
Required fees	$1,772

GENERAL ADMISSIONS INFO

Application fee	$50
Regular application deadline	1/15
Nonfall registration	Yes

Admission may be deferred.

Range SAT EBRW	580–670
Range SAT Math	560–690
Range ACT Composite	25–31

ACADEMICS

Student/faculty ratio	18:1
% students returning for sophomore year	87

Most classes have 10–19 students.

Programs/Services for Students with Learning Differences

Disability Services ensures that students with disabilities are provided appropriate support and accommodations. The University of Colorado Boulder believes that students with disabilities are an important group that adds diversity to the university community. Students are encouraged to engage in their own academic and personal learning and use the resources provided by the university.

Admissions

An applicant's learning disability is not considered in an admission decision. All applicants are required to meet the Minimum Academic Preparation Standards (MAPS), including 4 years of English, 4 years of math, 3 years of natural science, 3 years of social science (including geography), 3 years of a foreign language, and 1 year of an elective; fine and performing arts are encouraged. Courses taken before 9th grade are accepted as long as the documentation provided shows that the courses were completed. American Sign Language is a qualified substitute for a foreign language. Successfully completing 2 years of a foreign language will satisfy the foreign language requirement regardless of whether the courses were taken before the 9th grade. Students with deficiencies may be admitted to the university provided they meet the other admission standards of test scores, rank in class (if provided), and GPA. The university does not give extra weight to honors, AP courses, or IB curricula. However, the admissions committee does consider the number of courses taken in honors, AP, or IB when calculating a GPA.

Additional Information

Students must meet with Disability Services to discuss support services and accommodations that are appropriate. Strategy development is offered in study skills, reading, test performance, stress reduction, time management, and writing skills. There is a "Flexibility with Attendance and Assignment Deadlines Plan (Flex Plan)," which is an accommodation that implements a reasonable modification to attendance and assignment deadlines for courses. Faculty are required to complete and submit this plan to Disability Services when requested. The Alternate Format Production and Access Center (AFPAC) is for students who have an accommodation to use an alternate format for class materials. Students must be registered with Disability Services and approved to receive this accommodation in order to take advantage of this service. Tutors are available for all university students in labs; tutors are also provided for students with disabilities.

ADMISSIONS INFO FOR STUDENTS WITH LEARNING DIFFERENCES

Phone: 303-492-8671 • Fax: 303-492-5601 • Email: dsinfo@colorado.edu

SAT/ACT required: Yes (Test optional for 2021)
Interview required: No
Essay required: Yes
Additional application required: Yes
Documentation submitted to: Disability Services

Special Ed. HS course work accepted: Yes
Separate application required for Programs/Services: Yes
Documentation required for:
- **LD:** Psychoeducational evaluation
- **ADHD:** Psychoeducational evaluation
- **ASD:** Psychoeducational evaluation

University of Colorado Boulder

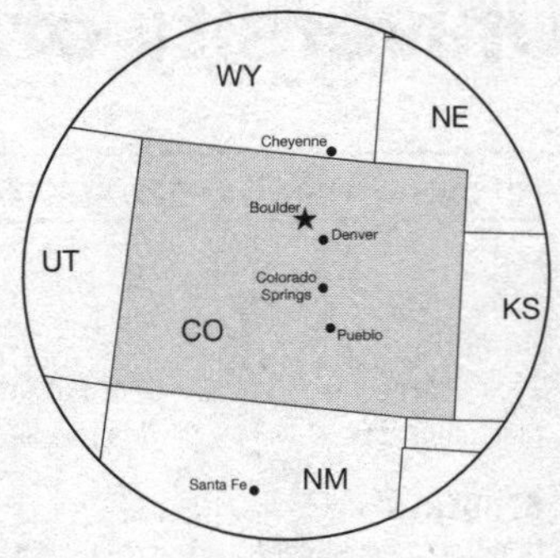

Colorado

General Admissions

Very important factors include: rigor of secondary school record, academic GPA, standardized test scores. *Important factors include:* application essay, recommendation(s), extracurricular activities, talent/ability, character/personal qualities, first generation. *Other factors include:* class rank, alumni/ae relation, geographical residence, state residency, racial/ethnic status, volunteer work, work experience. High school diploma is required and GED is accepted. *Academic units required:* 4 English, 4 math, 3 science, 2 science labs, 3 foreign language, 3 social studies, 1 history, 1 unit from above areas or other academic areas.

Accommodations or Services

Accommodations are decided upon an individual basis after a thorough review of appropriate, current documentation. The accommodations requests must be supported through the documentation provided and must be logically linked to the current impact of the condition on academic functioning.

Financial Aid

Students should submit: FAFSA. *Need-based scholarships/grants offered:* College/university scholarship or grant aid from institutional funds; Federal Pell; Private scholarships; SEOG; State scholarships/grants. *Loan aid offered:* Direct PLUS loans; Direct Subsidized Stafford Loans; Direct Unsubsidized Stafford Loans. Federal Work-Study Program available. Institutional employment available.

Campus Life

Activities: Campus Ministries; Choral groups; Concert band; Dance; Drama/theater; International Student Organization; Jazz band; Literary magazine; Marching band; Model UN; Music ensembles; Musical theater; Opera; Pep band; Radio station; Student government; Student newspaper; Student-run film society; Symphony orchestra. **Organizations:** 576 registered organizations, 32 honor societies, 30 religious organizations, 31 fraternities, 18 sororities. **Athletics (Intercollegiate):** *Men:* basketball, cross-country, football, golf, skiing (downhill/alpine), skiing (Nordic/cross-country), track/field (outdoor), track/field (indoor). *Women:* basketball, cross-country, golf, skiing (downhill/alpine), skiing (Nordic/cross-country), soccer, tennis, track/field (outdoor), track/field (indoor), volleyball.

ACCOMMODATIONS

Allowed in exams:	
Calculators	Yes
Dictionary	Yes
Computer	Yes
Spell-checker	Yes
Extended test time	Yes
Scribe	Yes
Proctors	Yes
Oral exams	Yes
Note-takers	Yes
Support services for students with:	
LD	Yes
ADHD	Yes
ASD	Yes
Distraction-reduced environment	Yes
Recording of lecture allowed	Yes
Reading technology	Yes
Audio books	Yes
Other assistive technology	Yes
Priority registration	No
Added costs of services:	
For LD	No
For ADHD	No
For ASD	No
LD specialists	Yes
ADHD & ASD coaching	No
ASD specialists	No
Professional tutors	No
Peer tutors	Yes
Max. hours/week for services	Varies
How professors are notified of student approved accommodations	Student

COLLEGE GRADUATION REQUIREMENTS

Course waivers allowed	No
Course substitutions allowed	No

University of Colorado at Colorado Springs

1420 Austin Bluffs Parkway, Colorado Springs, CO 80918 • Admissions: 719-255-3084 **Support: CS**

CAMPUS

Type of school	Public
Environment	Metropolis

STUDENTS

Undergrad enrollment	10,196
% male/female	48/52
% from out of state	13
% frosh live on campus	57

FINANCIAL FACTS

Annual in-state tuition	$8,539
Annual out-of-state tuition	$20,635
Room and board	$18,917

GENERAL ADMISSIONS INFO

Application fee	$50
Regular application deadline	5/1
Nonfall registration	Yes

Admission may be deferred.

Range SAT EBRW	510–620
Range SAT Math	510–610
Range ACT Composite	21–26

ACADEMICS

Student/faculty ratio	17:1
% students returning for sophomore year	70

Most classes have 10–19 students.

Programs/Services for Students with Learning Differences

The mission of Disability Services ensures that students with disabilities receive reasonable accommodations and services to participate fully in the academic environment. The Office of Inclusive Services offers a program and support for students with intellectual disabilities.

Admissions

There is not a special admission process for students with disabilities. 75% of admitted students have a 3.0 or higher GPA and have a minimum ACT score of 20 or higher, or a minimum SAT score of 1070 or higher. Applicants who do not meet the 3.0 GPA and/or test scores are still encouraged to apply to UCCS. These students will be reviewed under special circumstances and their applications, essays, and letters of recommendations will be reviewed by the admissions committee. Essays should explain grades, any life events that might have affected academic performance, goals, and any information that strengthens the application. Students are encouraged to submit two letters of recommendation. Students applying for nursing, business, or engineering who do not meet the general admission criteria will be considered for admission to the College of Letters, Arts and Sciences until they meet the professional college requirements.

Additional Information

The Office of Inclusive Services at UCCS provides students with intellectual disabilities the necessary supports to allow them to access academic, career and social activities on campus. Services are provided by trained mentors, student volunteers, and faculty to meet the learning needs and career goals for these students. Students earn a nationally recognized certificate, take a few courses in their field of interest, participate in internships, are involved in campus activities and develop a plan to their career. Admission decisions are based on the student's learning needs and motivation to attend college; the ability of the Office of Inclusive Services to meet the needs of the student; the ability of the student to be independent enough to navigate between classes and other activities; the potential of the student to be successful in achieving set goals; and a family/guardian commitment to support the student's goals.

ADMISSIONS INFO FOR STUDENTS WITH LEARNING DIFFERENCES

Phone: 719-255-3354 • Fax: 719-255-3195 • Email: dservice@uccs.edu

SAT/ACT required: Yes (Test optional for 2021)
Interview required: No
Essay required: No
Additional application required: No
Documentation submitted to: Disability Services or Office of Inclusive Services

Special Ed. HS course work accepted: Yes
Separate application required for Programs/Services: Yes
Documentation required for:
LD: Psychoeducational evaluation
ADHD: Psychoeducational evaluation
ASD: Psychoeducational evaluation

University of Colorado at Colorado Springs

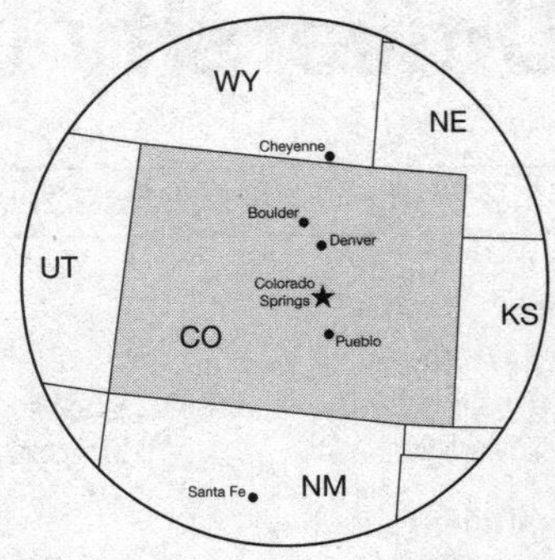

Colorado

General Admissions

Very important factors include: rigor of secondary school record, class rank, academic GPA, standardized test scores. *Other factors include:* application essay, recommendation(s). High school diploma is required and GED is accepted. *Academic units required:* 4 English, 4 math, 3 science, 2 science labs, 1 foreign language, 3 social studies, 1 history, 2 academic electives. *Academic units recommended:* 4 English, 4 math, 3 science, 2 science labs, 1 foreign language, 3 social studies, 1 history, 2 academic electives.

Accommodations or Services

Accommodations are decided upon an individual basis after a thorough review of appropriate, current documentation. The accommodations requests must be supported through the documentation provided and must be logically linked to the current impact of the condition on academic functioning.

Financial Aid

Students should submit: FAFSA; State aid form. Applicants will be notified of awards on a rolling basis beginning 3/1. *Need-based scholarships/grants offered:* College/university scholarship or grant aid from institutional funds; Federal Pell; Private scholarships; SEOG; State scholarships/grants. *Loan aid offered:* Direct PLUS loans; Direct Subsidized Stafford Loans; Direct Unsubsidized Stafford Loans.

Campus Life

Activities: Choral groups; Dance; Drama/theater; International Student Organization; Literary magazine; Pep band; Radio station; Student government; Student newspaper; Television station. **Organizations:** 55 registered organizations, 4 honor societies, 7 religious organizations, 1 sorority. **Athletics (Intercollegiate):** *Men:* basketball, cross-country, golf, soccer, tennis, track/field (outdoor). *Women:* basketball, cross-country, softball, tennis, track/field (outdoor), volleyball.

ACCOMMODATIONS

Allowed in exams:	
Calculators	Yes
Dictionary	Yes
Computer	Yes
Spell-checker	Yes
Extended test time	Yes
Scribe	Yes
Proctors	Yes
Oral exams	Yes
Note-takers	No
Support services for students with:	
LD	Yes
ADHD	Yes
ASD	Yes
Distraction-reduced environment	Yes
Recording of lecture allowed	Yes
Reading technology	Yes
Audio books	Yes
Other assistive technology	Yes
Priority registration	No
Added costs of services:	
For LD	No
For ADHD	No
For ASD	No
LD specialists	Yes
ADHD & ASD coaching	No
ASD specialists	Yes
Professional tutors	No
Peer tutors	Yes
Max. hours/week for services	Varies
How professors are notified of student approved accommodations	Student

COLLEGE GRADUATION REQUIREMENTS

Course waivers allowed	No
Course substitutions allowed	Yes
In what courses: Case by case basis	

University of Denver

Office of Admission, Denver, CO 80208 • Admissions: 303-871-2036 • Fax: 303-871-3301 **Support: SP**

CAMPUS

Type of school	Private (nonprofit)
Environment	Metropolis

STUDENTS

Undergrad enrollment	5,755
% male/female	46/54
% from out of state	63
% frosh live on campus	94

FINANCIAL FACTS

Annual tuition	$52,596
Room and board	$15,056
Required fees	$1,179

GENERAL ADMISSIONS INFO

Application fee	$65
Regular application deadline	1/15
Nonfall registration	Yes

Admission may be deferred.

Range SAT EBRW	590–670
Range SAT Math	580–680
Range ACT Composite	26–31

ACADEMICS

Student/faculty ratio	12:1
% students returning for sophomore year	86

Most classes have 10–19 students.

Programs/Services for Students with Learning Differences

The Disability Services Program (DSP) provides students with disabilities an equal opportunity to participate academically and socially at the university. Accommodations are provided at no cost to any student who presents the appropriate documentation. The Learning Effectiveness Program (LEP) provides individualized support for neuro diverse learners with learning disabilities, ADHD, or students on the autism spectrum or students who have a history of learning differences. There is an additional fee for students enrolled in the LEP Program. The four cornerstones include self-awareness, self-advocacy, accountability, and self-determination.

Admissions

Admission to the university is distinct from enrollment in the LEP. All potential DU candidates must submit a general admissions application, essay, recommendations, activity sheet, and high school transcript. DU is test optional and ACT/SAT scores are not required for admission to the university. Students applying to LEP must be accepted by DU and submit a separate application to the LEP as well as provide documentation of LD/ADHD through recent diagnostic tests. Strengths, weaknesses, maturity level, ability to handle frustration, and feelings about limitations should also be included in documentation sent to the LEP. A campus visit and interview with LEP is recommended after submission of all documentation and testing. In general admissions, DU looks for students who have challenged themselves academically and recommends 4 years English, 3–4 years math, 3–4 years social studies, 3–4 years science, and 3–4 foreign languages. Extracurricular activities are important as are the teacher/counselor recommendations. DU is test optional and an ACT/SAT score is not required for admission but can be submitted if an applicant feels it is beneficial. There is no disadvantage to not submitting the ACT/SAT. DU reviews the essay, GPA, courses, and recommendations and evaluates trends in grades, academic rigor, activities, leadership, and volunteerism.

Additional Information

LEP services are only available to students who are enrolled in the LEP program. The LEP is fee-for-service and provides services beyond the mandated accommodations provided under Section 504. The director in the LEP is an LD specialist and staff members are professionally trained. Students have weekly meetings with their case manager. **The Journey to Empowerment Through Transition (JETT) Experience** is a comprehensive transition experience for students enrolled in the Learning Effectiveness Program (LEP) that provides them with the skills for navigating change prior to the start of college.

ADMISSIONS INFO FOR STUDENTS WITH LEARNING DIFFERENCES

Phone: 303-871-3241 • Email: dsp@du.edu

SAT/ACT required: No
Interview required: No
Essay required: Yes
Additional application required: Yes
Documentation submitted to: Disability Services and LEP

Special Ed. HS course work accepted: Yes
Separate application required for Programs/Services: Yes
Documentation required for:
LD: Psychoeducational evaluation
ADHD: Psychoeducational evaluation
ASD: Psychoeducational evaluation

University of Denver

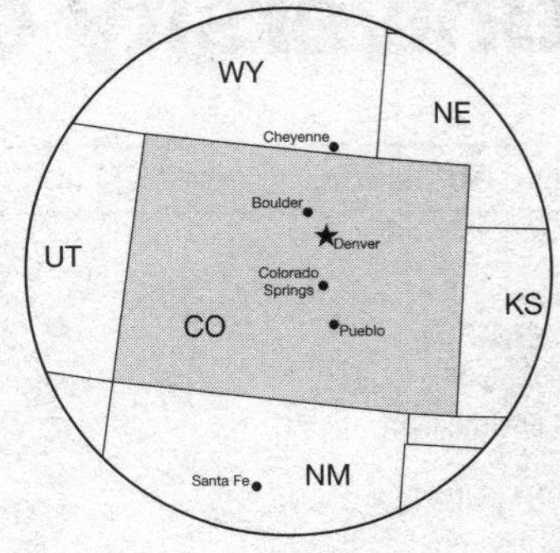

General Admissions

Very important factors include: rigor of secondary school record, academic GPA, standardized test scores. *Important factors include:* application essay, recommendation(s), extracurricular activities, talent/ability, character/ personal qualities. *Other factors include:* first generation, alumni/ae relation, geographical residence, racial/ethnic status, volunteer work, work experience, level of applicant's interest. High school diploma is required and GED is accepted. *Academic units recommended:* 4 English, 4 math, 4 science, 2 science labs, 4 foreign language, 4 social studies.

Accommodations or Services

Accommodations are decided upon an individual basis after a thorough review of appropriate, current documentation. The accommodations requests must be supported through the documentation provided and must be logically linked to the current impact of the condition on academic functioning.

Financial Aid

Students should submit: FAFSA. Applicants will be notified of awards on a rolling basis beginning 3/1. *Need-based scholarships/grants offered:* College/ university scholarship or grant aid from institutional funds; Federal Pell; Private scholarships; SEOG; State scholarships/grants. *Loan aid offered:* Direct PLUS loans; Direct Subsidized Stafford Loans; Direct Unsubsidized Stafford Loans. Federal Work-Study Program available. Institutional employment available.

Campus Life

Activities: Campus Ministries; Choral groups; Concert band; Dance; Drama/theater; International Student Organization; Jazz band; Literary magazine; Marching band; Model UN; Music ensembles; Musical theater; Opera; Pep band; Radio station; Student government; Student newspaper; Student-run film society; Symphony orchestra. **Organizations: Athletics (Intercollegiate):** *Men:* basketball, diving, golf, ice hockey, lacrosse, skiing (downhill/alpine), skiing (Nordic/cross-country), soccer, swimming, tennis. *Women:* basketball, diving, golf, gymnastics, lacrosse, skiing (downhill/ alpine), skiing (Nordic/cross-country), soccer, swimming, tennis, volleyball.

ACCOMMODATIONS

Allowed in exams:	
Calculators	Yes
Dictionary	Yes
Computer	Yes
Spell-checker	Yes
Extended test time	Yes
Scribe	Yes
Proctors	Yes
Oral exams	Yes
Note-takers	Yes
Support services for students with:	
LD	Yes
ADHD	Yes
ASD	Yes
Distraction-reduced environment	Yes
Recording of lecture allowed	Yes
Reading technology	Yes
Audio books	Yes
Other assistive technology	Yes
Priority registration	Yes
Added costs of services:	
For LD	Yes
For ADHD	Yes
For ASD	Yes
LD specialists	Yes
ADHD & ASD coaching	No
ASD specialists	Yes
Professional tutors	Yes
Peer tutors	Yes
Max. hours/week for services	80
How professors are notified of student approved accommodations	Student

COLLEGE GRADUATION REQUIREMENTS

Course waivers allowed	No
Course substitutions allowed	Yes

In what courses: Case by case basis

University of Northern Colorado

UNC Admissions, Greeley, CO 80639 • Admissions: 970-351-2881 • Fax: 970-351-2984 **Support: S**

CAMPUS

Type of school	Public
Environment	City

STUDENTS

Undergrad enrollment	8,446
% male/female	33/67
% from out of state	14
% frosh live on campus	85

FINANCIAL FACTS

Annual in-state tuition	$10,424
Annual out-of-state tuition	$22,496
Room and board	$11,684

GENERAL ADMISSIONS INFO

Application fee	$50
Regular application deadline	8/1
Nonfall registration	Yes

Admission may be deferred.

Range SAT EBRW	490–610
Range SAT Math	480–590
Range ACT Composite	19–26

ACADEMICS

Student/faculty ratio	17:1
% students returning for sophomore year	72

Most classes have 20–29 students.

Programs/Services for Students with Learning Differences

The Disability Resource Center (DRC) Office recognizes a disability as a valued aspect of diversity and guarantees students with disabilities with access to the University of Northern Colorado community as a matter of equity and inclusion. The office provides the university with resources, education, and direct services to design a more welcoming and inclusive environment. The Disability Resource Center (DRC) offers services to students and faculty. Students meet collaboratively with DRC staff to determine what accommodations are appropriate. Students must provide documentation that supports their need for accommodations.

Admissions

There is no special admission process for students with learning disabilities. All students with disabilities are admitted to UNC under the standard admission requirements of the university. Applicants are expected to have a minimum 2.5 GPA. ACT or SAT is required, but the writing section is not. The mid 50% of the applicants have 3.0–3.8 GPA, 19–25 ACT, 1020–1030 SAT. Most applicants have 4 years English, 4 years math, 3 years natural science, 3 years social science, 1 year foreign language and 2 years electives. Applicants to Theater Arts, Dance and Music must submit additional materials. The School of Art and Design does not require any additional portfolio, but students are welcome to submit one if desired.

Additional Information

Services include learning strategies, organizational skills, and advocacy skills; reader program; test accommodations; assistance in arranging for note-takers; and assistive technology, including voice synthesizers, screen readers, screen enlargers, scanners, voice-recognition computer systems, large monitors, and word processing with spellchecker. Workshops are offered in student skills, organizational skills, study strategies, and time management. These workshops are electives and are not for credit.

ADMISSIONS INFO FOR STUDENTS WITH LEARNING DIFFERENCES

Phone: 970-351-2289 • Fax: 970-351-4166 • Email: DRC@unco.edu

SAT/ACT required: Yes (Test optional for 2021)
Interview required: No
Essay required: No
Additional application required: No
Documentation submitted to: Disability Support Services (DSS)

Special Ed. HS course work accepted: Yes
Separate application required for Programs/Services: No
Documentation required for:
LD: Psychoeducational evaluation
ADHD: Psychoeducational evaluation
ASD: Psychoeducational evaluation

University of Northern Colorado

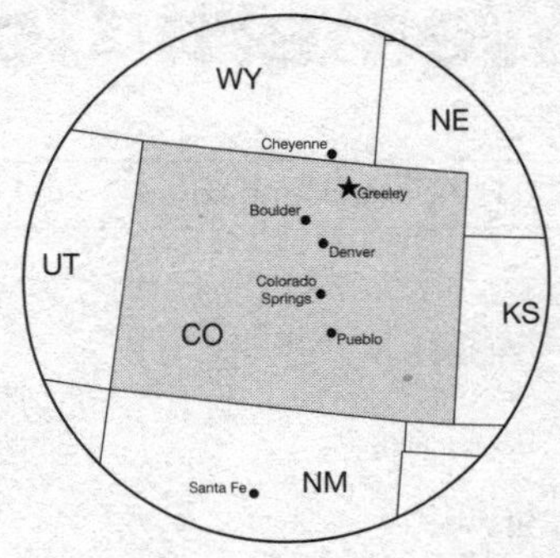

General Admissions

Very important factors include: class rank, academic GPA, standardized test scores. *Other factors include:* rigor of secondary school record, interview, extracurricular activities, talent/ability, character/personal qualities, first generation, alumni/ae relation, geographical residence, state residency, volunteer work, work experience, level of applicant's interest. High school diploma is required and GED is accepted. *Academic units recommended:* 4 English, 4 math, 3 science, 2 science labs, 1 foreign language, 2 social studies, 1 history, 2 academic electives.

Accommodations or Services

Accommodations are decided upon an individual basis after a thorough review of appropriate, current documentation. The accommodations requests must be supported through the documentation provided and must be logically linked to the current impact of the condition on academic functioning.

Financial Aid

Students should submit: FAFSA. *Need-based scholarships/grants offered:* College/university scholarship or grant aid from institutional funds; Federal Pell; Private scholarships; SEOG; State scholarships/grants. *Loan aid offered:* Direct PLUS loans; Direct Subsidized Stafford Loans; Direct Unsubsidized Stafford Loans. Federal Work-Study Program available. Institutional employment available.

Campus Life

Activities: Campus Ministries; Choral groups; Concert band; Dance; Drama/theater; International Student Organization; Jazz band; Literary magazine; Marching band; Music ensembles; Musical theater; Opera; Student government; Student newspaper; Student-run film society; Symphony orchestra; Television station. **Organizations:** 154 registered organizations, 34 honor societies, 14 religious organizations, 10 fraternities, 13 sororities. **Athletics (Intercollegiate):** *Men:* baseball, basketball, football, golf, tennis, track/field (outdoor), wrestling. *Women:* basketball, cross-country, diving, golf, soccer, softball, swimming, tennis, track/field (outdoor), volleyball.

ACCOMMODATIONS

Allowed in exams:	
Calculators	Yes
Dictionary	Yes
Computer	Yes
Spell-checker	Yes
Extended test time	Yes
Scribe	Yes
Proctors	Yes
Oral exams	Yes
Note-takers	Yes
Support services for students with:	
LD	Yes
ADHD	Yes
ASD	Yes
Distraction-reduced environment	Yes
Recording of lecture allowed	Yes
Reading technology	Yes
Audio books	Yes
Other assistive technology	Yes
Priority registration	Yes
Added costs of services:	
For LD	No
For ADHD	No
For ASD	No
LD specialists	No
ADHD & ASD coaching	No
ASD specialists	No
Professional tutors	No
Peer tutors	Yes
Max. hours/week for services	Varies
How professors are notified of student approved accommodations	Student and Disability Office

COLLEGE GRADUATION REQUIREMENTS

Course waivers allowed	No
Course substitutions allowed	No

Western Colorado University

600 N. Adams, Gunnison, CO 81231 • Admissions: 970-943-2119 • Fax: 970-943-2363 **Support: S**

CAMPUS

Type of school	Public
Environment	Rural

STUDENTS

Undergrad enrollment	3,073
% male/female	53/47
% from out of state	25
% frosh live on campus	95

FINANCIAL FACTS

Annual in-state tuition	$6,816
Annual out-of-state tuition	$18,600
Room and board	$9,874
Required fees	$3,829

GENERAL ADMISSIONS INFO

Application fee	$30
Regular application deadline	3/1
Nonfall registration	Yes
Range SAT EBRW	500–610
Range SAT Math	500–590
Range ACT Composite	20–26

ACADEMICS

Student/faculty ratio	18:1
% students returning for sophomore year	65

Most classes have 10–19 students.

Programs/Services for Students with Learning Differences

Disability Services, located in Western's Academic Resource Center, coordinates support services for all qualified students with disabilities. The program offers a variety of resources and accommodations to assist students as they pursue their academic and career goals. While providing a supportive environment, we encourage students to develop independence and take responsibility for their academic experiences. Personal consultation and workshops are available to help students improve learning, problem-solving, and self-advocacy skills.

Admissions

Admission to Western depends on academic performance and background, standardized test scores, and personal attributes. In addition to general admissions requirements, Western State recommends a personal essay and recommendations from teachers, counselors, or others who know the student's academic ability. The college tries to admit those students who have demonstrated their ability to succeed. The mid 50% GPA is 3.0–3.8 and the mid 50% ACT is 20–25 or SAT 1025–1200. However, Western Colorado University is test optional and ACT or SAT score is not required for admission. Western requires 4 years of English, 4 years of mathematics, 3 years of natural science, 3 years of social science, 1 year of foreign language, and 2 years of electives. If students feel that they need to provide additional information, they can submit an essay on why they are applying to Western, or a personal statement to explain specific information, letters of recommendation, or a resume. Other factors used in the admission decision include an upward trend in grades, potential for success in college, leadership roles, volunteerism, and any situations that had an impact on the student during high school. However, academic preparation is key to admission.

Additional Information

Once registered with Disability Services, students will be scheduled for an intake session with staff to review policies, procedures, resources, and accommodations. Some of the services used by students include test accommodations, taped textbooks, readers, scribes, notetakers, and assistance with academic advising and course registration. Individual learning skills assistance is available through appointments and workshops. The staff works with students to help them develop effective learning skills and study strategies in areas such as reading, memory, test taking, note-taking, organization, and time management. The Academic Resource Center is available to help students develop an understanding of their individual learning styles and utilize the Academic Resource Center's resources.

ADMISSIONS INFO FOR STUDENTS WITH LEARNING DIFFERENCES

Phone: 970-943-7056 • Fax: 970-943-3409

SAT/ACT required: Yes (Test optional for 2021)
Interview required: No
Essay required: No
Additional application required: No
Documentation submitted to: Disability Services

Special Ed. HS course work accepted: Yes
Separate application required for Programs/Services: No
Documentation required for:
LD: Psychoeducational evaluation
ADHD: Psychoeducational evaluation
ASD: Psychoeducational evaluation

Western Colorado University

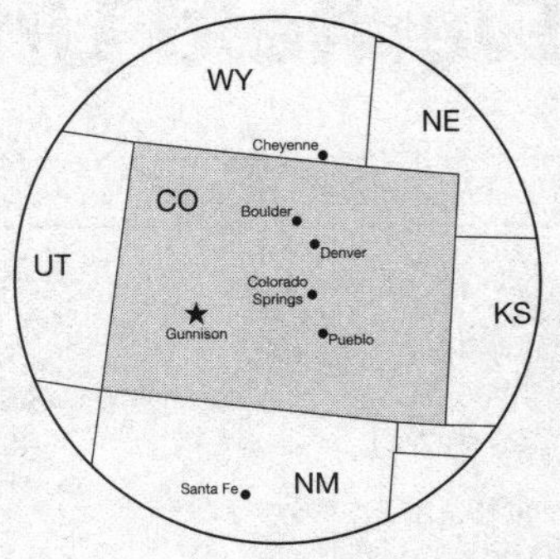

Colorado

General Admissions

Very important factors include: rigor of secondary school record, class rank, academic GPA, standardized test scores. *Important factors include:* application essay, recommendation(s). *Other factors include:* interview, extracurricular activities, talent/ability, character/personal qualities, first generation, alumni/ae relation, volunteer work, work experience. High school diploma is required and GED is accepted.

Accommodations or Services

Accommodations are decided upon an individual basis after a thorough review of appropriate, current documentation. The accommodations requests must be supported through the documentation provided and must be logically linked to the current impact of the condition on academic functioning.

Financial Aid

Students should submit: FAFSA. *Need-based scholarships/grants offered:* College/university scholarship or grant aid from institutional funds; Federal Pell; Private scholarships; SEOG; State scholarships/grants. *Loan aid offered:* Direct PLUS loans; Direct Subsidized Stafford Loans; Direct Unsubsidized Stafford Loans. Federal Work-Study Program available. Institutional employment available.

Campus Life

Activities: Campus Ministries; Choral groups; Concert band; Dance; Drama/theater; International Student Organization; Jazz band; Literary magazine; Music ensembles; Pep band; Radio station; Student government; Student newspaper; Symphony orchestra; Television station. **Organizations:** 60 registered organizations, 8 honor societies, 5 religious organizations. **Athletics (Intercollegiate):** *Men:* basketball, cross-country, football, track/field (outdoor), track/field (indoor), wrestling. *Women:* basketball, cross-country, track/field (outdoor), track/field (indoor), volleyball.

ACCOMMODATIONS

Allowed in exams:	
Calculators	Yes
Dictionary	No
Computer	Yes
Spell-checker	Yes
Extended test time	Yes
Scribe	Yes
Proctors	Yes
Oral exams	Yes
Note-takers	Yes
Support services for students with:	
LD	Yes
ADHD	Yes
ASD	Yes
Distraction-reduced environment	Yes
Recording of lecture allowed	Yes
Reading technology	Yes
Audio books	Yes
Other assistive technology	Yes
Priority registration	Yes
Added costs of services:	
For LD	No
For ADHD	No
For ASD	No
LD specialists	No
ADHD & ASD coaching	No
ASD specialists	No
Professional tutors	No
Peer tutors	Yes
Max. hours/week for services	Varies
How professors are notified of student approved accommodations	Student

COLLEGE GRADUATION REQUIREMENTS

Course waivers allowed	No
Course substitutions allowed	No

Fairfield University

1073 North Benson Road, Fairfield, CT 06824 • Admissions: 203-254-4100 • Fax: 203-254-4199 **Support: S**

CAMPUS

Type of school	Private (nonprofit)
Environment	Town

STUDENTS

Undergrad enrollment	4,250
% male/female	41/59
% from out of state	73
% frosh live on campus	95

FINANCIAL FACTS

Annual tuition	$50,550
Room and board	$15,610
Required fees	$770

GENERAL ADMISSIONS INFO

Application fee	$60
Regular application deadline	1/15
Nonfall registration	Yes

Admission may be deferred.

Range SAT EBRW	610–670
Range SAT Math	600–680
Range ACT Composite	26–30

ACADEMICS

Student/faculty ratio	12:1
% students returning for sophomore year	90

Most classes have 20–29 students.

Programs/Services for Students with Learning Differences

The Office of Accessibility provides reasonable accommodations to students with disabilities who provide appropriate documentation. Students are responsible for providing letters of accommodations to each professor. Fairfield University is a Jesuit institution and prides itself in the personal interest professors take in their students to understand their strengths and weaknesses.

Admissions

There are no differences in the admission criteria for students with learning differences. Fairfield University is test optional. Applicants who elect not to submit test scores are encouraged to schedule an interview. The admission committee reviews academic achievement and extracurricular activities. As a Jesuit university, it is important for applicants to embrace the mission and vision of the college. Applicants typically have earned A– to B+ grades in a college prep curriculum.

Additional Information

The Office of Academic Support and Retention provides individual and group services to increase academic success. Through this office, students can access several resources such as a tutoring center, math center, and writing center all staffed by peer tutors. When students request an accommodation with a test or exam, the professor must complete an Exam Agreement confirming that the student has requested to take an exam in the OOA exam room. Students need to make this Exam Request for every exam they need to take with OOA.

ADMISSIONS INFO FOR STUDENTS WITH LEARNING DIFFERENCES

Phone: 203-254-4081 • Fax: 203-254-4314 • Email: OOA@fairfield.edu

SAT/ACT required: No
Interview required: Recommended
Essay required: No
Additional application required: No
Documentation submitted to: Office of Accessibility

Special Ed. HS course work accepted: No
Separate application required for Programs/Services: No
Documentation required for:
LD: Psychoeducational evaluation
ADHD: Psychoeducational evaluation
ASD: Psychoeducational evaluation

Fairfield University

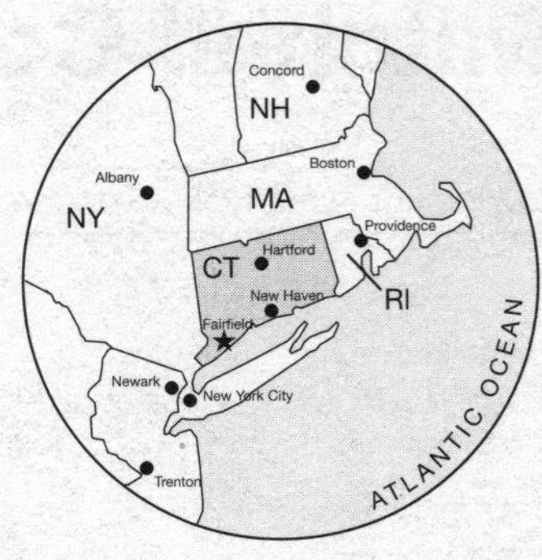

General Admissions

Very important factors include: rigor of secondary school record, academic GPA, application essay, recommendation(s). *Important factors include:* interview, extracurricular activities, talent/ability, character/personal qualities, first generation, volunteer work. *Other factors include:* class rank, standardized test scores, alumni/ae relation, geographical residence, racial/ ethnic status. High school diploma is required and GED is accepted. *Academic units required:* 4 English, 3 math, 3 science, 2 science labs, 2 foreign language, 2 social studies, 2 history. *Academic units recommended:* 4 English, 4 math, 4 science, 4 foreign language, 2 social studies, 2 history.

Accommodations or Services

Accommodations are decided upon an individual basis after a thorough review of appropriate, current documentation. The accommodations requests must be supported through the documentation provided and must be logically linked to the current impact of the condition on academic functioning.

Financial Aid

Students should submit: Business/Farm Supplement; CSS/Financial Aid PROFILE; FAFSA; Noncustodial PROFILE. *Need-based scholarships/grants offered:* College/university scholarship or grant aid from institutional funds; Federal Pell; Private scholarships; SEOG; State scholarships/grants. *Loan aid offered:* Direct PLUS loans; Direct Subsidized Stafford Loans; Direct Unsubsidized Stafford Loans. Federal Work-Study Program available. Institutional employment available.

Campus Life

Activities: Campus Ministries; Choral groups; Concert band; Dance; Drama/theater; International Student Organization; Jazz band; Literary magazine; Model UN; Music ensembles; Musical theater; Pep band; Radio station; Student government; Student newspaper; Student-run film society; Symphony orchestra; Television station; Yearbook. **Organizations:** 112 registered organizations, 21 honor societies, 24 religious organizations. **Athletics (Intercollegiate):** *Men:* baseball, basketball, crew/rowing, cross-country, diving, golf, lacrosse, soccer, swimming, tennis. *Women:* basketball, crew/rowing, cross-country, diving, field hockey, golf, lacrosse, soccer, softball, swimming, tennis, volleyball.

Connecticut

ACCOMMODATIONS

Allowed in exams:	
Calculators	Yes
Dictionary	No
Computer	Yes
Spell-checker	Yes
Extended test time	Yes
Scribe	Yes
Proctors	Yes
Oral exams	Yes
Note-takers	Yes
Support services for students with:	
LD	No
ADHD	No
ASD	No
Distraction-reduced environment	Yes
Recording of lecture allowed	Yes
Reading technology	Yes
Audio books	Yes
Other assistive technology	Yes
Priority registration	Yes
Added costs of services:	
For LD	No
For ADHD	No
For ASD	No
LD specialists	No
ADHD & ASD coaching	No
ASD specialists	No
Professional tutors	No
Peer tutors	Yes
Max. hours/week for services	4
How professors are notified of student approved accommodations	Student

COLLEGE GRADUATION REQUIREMENTS

Course waivers allowed: Yes
In what courses: foreign language and math

Course substitutions allowed: Yes
In what courses: foreign language and math

Mitchell College

437 Pequot Avenue, New London, CT 06320 • Admissions: 860-701-5011 • Fax: 860-444-1209 **Support: SP**

CAMPUS

Type of school	Private (nonprofit)
Environment	Town

STUDENTS

Undergrad enrollment	642
% male/female	56/44
% from out of state	35
% frosh live on campus	82

FINANCIAL FACTS

Annual tuition	$32,960
Room and board	$13,906
Required fees	$2,112

GENERAL ADMISSIONS INFO

Regular application deadline	Rolling
Nonfall registration	Yes

Admission may be deferred.

ACADEMICS

% students returning for sophomore year	63

Most classes have 10–19 students.

Programs/Services for Students with Learning Differences

Mitchell College is dedicated to providing a student-centered, supportive learning environment that addresses the educational needs of all students, including those with disabilities. The Bentsen Learning Center offers academic and other supports through three tiers of academic support. Level 1, Comprehensive Strategic Learning, has students working with a learning specialist three times a week and using an individual learning support program designed based on strengths, weaknesses, and student goals. In Level 2, Enhanced Strategic Learning, students have less direct involvement or assistance and meet twice a week individually or in small groups. Level 3, Transitional Strategic Learning, is only for returning students who can apply a variety of learning strategies on their own but may still benefit from limited support and one weekly meeting with a learning specialist. Federally mandated services and accommodations are provided through the Accessibility Services.

Admissions

Applicants can use the Common Application or the Unique Minds Fast Application to apply to Mitchell College or to the Thames Academy, a transition-year program. Mitchell College is test-optional and does not require the ACT or SAT for admission. Applicants can also apply to the Mystic Program, a support program for admitted students.

Additional Information

The Thames Academy is a transition program that is fully integrated into the Mitchell College campus. It is a fee-based program offering a year of academic preparation that students take between the end of their high school education and the start of their college studies. Unlike traditional post-grad programs at prep schools, Thames Academy at Mitchell College provides college-level courses for credit. Located on Mitchell College Campus, the Academy provides a structured residential program within a collegiate environment and co-curricular interaction with two- and four-year students. Mitchell College also offers the Mystic Program which is for students who are admitted to the college but who would benefit from unique skills building opportunities during freshman year. The Mystic Program concentrates on five core competencies including self-awareness, decision making, relationship skills, social awareness, and self-management. This is a fee-based program in addition to the general tuition for the college.

ADMISSIONS INFO FOR STUDENTS WITH LEARNING DIFFERENCES

Phone: 860-701-5145 • Fax: 860-701-5090 • Email: admissions@mitchell.edu

SAT/ACT required: No
Interview required: Yes
Essay required: Yes
Additional application required: Yes for Bensten and Thames
Documentation submitted to: Accessibility Services, Bentsen, or Thames

Special Ed. HS course work accepted: Yes
Separate application required for Programs/Services: Yes
Documentation required for:
LD: Psychoeducational evaluation
ADHD: Psychoeducational evaluation
ASD: Psychoeducational evaluation

Mitchell College

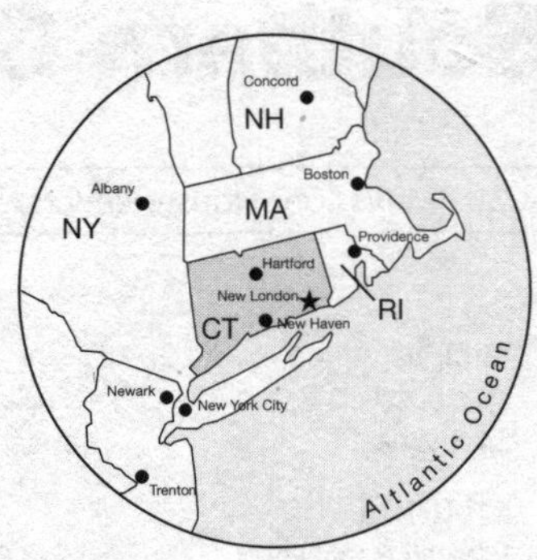

General Admissions

Very important factors include: academic GPA, interview. *Important factors include:* rigor of secondary school record, application essay, recommendation(s), extracurricular activities, character/personal qualities, volunteer work. *Other factors include:* standardized test scores, talent/ability, alumni/ae relation, work experience. High school diploma is required and GED is accepted. *Academic units recommended:* 4 English, 3 math, 3 science, 2 social studies, 2 history, 2 academic electives.

Accommodations or Services

Accommodations are decided upon an individual basis after a thorough review of appropriate, current documentation. The accommodations requests must be supported through the documentation provided and must be logically linked to the current impact of the condition on academic functioning.

Financial Aid

Students should submit: FAFSA. *Need-based scholarships/grants offered:* College/university scholarship or grant aid from institutional funds; Federal Pell; Private scholarships; SEOG; State scholarships/grants. *Loan aid offered:* Direct PLUS loans; Direct Subsidized Stafford Loans; Direct Unsubsidized Stafford Loans. Federal Work-Study Program available. Institutional employment available.

Campus Life

Activities: Dance; Drama/theater; Radio station; Student government. **Organizations:** 30 registered organizations, 8 honor societies. **Athletics (Intercollegiate):** *Men:* baseball, basketball, cross-country, golf, lacrosse, soccer, tennis. *Women:* basketball, cross-country, golf, soccer, softball, tennis, volleyball.

ACCOMMODATIONS

Allowed in exams:	
Calculators	Yes
Dictionary	Yes
Computer	Yes
Spell-checker	Yes
Extended test time	Yes
Scribe	Yes
Proctors	Yes
Oral exams	Yes
Note-takers	Yes
Support services for students with:	
LD	Yes
ADHD	Yes
ASD	Yes
Distraction-reduced environment	Yes
Recording of lecture allowed	Yes
Reading technology	Yes
Audio books	Yes
Other assistive technology	Yes
Priority registration	Yes
Added costs of services:	
For LD	Yes
For ADHD	Yes
For ASD	Yes
LD specialists	Yes
ADHD & ASD coaching	Yes
ASD specialists	No
Professional tutors	Yes
Peer tutors	No
Max. hours/week for services	4
How professors are notified of student approved accommodations	Student

COLLEGE GRADUATION REQUIREMENTS

Course waivers allowed	No
Course substitutions allowed	Yes
In what courses: Case by case basis	

Connecticut

Southern Connecticut State University

SCSU-Admissions House, New Haven, CT 06515-1202 • Admissions: 203-392-5644 • Fax: 203-392-5727 **Support: CS**

CAMPUS

Type of school	Public
Environment	Village

STUDENTS

Undergrad enrollment	7,962
% male/female	39/61
% from out of state	5
% frosh live on campus	62

FINANCIAL FACTS

Annual in-state tuition	\$6,162
Annual out-of-state tuition	\$18,436
Room and board	\$8,832
Required fees	\$5,640

GENERAL ADMISSIONS INFO

Application fee	\$50
Regular application deadline	4/1
Nonfall registration	Yes

Admission may be deferred.

Range SAT EBRW	470–560
Range SAT Math	440–530
Range ACT Composite	16–25

ACADEMICS

Student/faculty ratio	13:1
% students returning for sophomore year	73

Most classes have 20–29 students.

Programs/Services for Students with Learning Differences

The mission of the DRC (Disability Resource Center) is to ensure educational equity for students with disabilities. The DRC assists students in arranging for individualized accommodations and support services. The DRC provides assistance with developing compensatory strategies such as time management, study skills, and identifying strengths and weaknesses. The DRC also helps with course selection, promotion of self-determination in areas of self-advocacy, goal setting, and career development.

Admissions

There is no special admissions process for students with learning disabilities. All applicants must meet the same criteria. Course requirements include 4 years of English, 3 years of math, 2 years of science, 2 years of a foreign language (recommended), 2 years of social studies, and 2 years of history. The average GPA is a 3.0. The mid 50% range for SAT is 980–1180 and ACT 18–21.

Additional Information

The DRC supports Outreach Unlimited, which is a student organization primarily made up of students with disabilities. DRC Specialists offer weekly appointments of a first come first serve basis. Academic Success Coaching includes professional and peer coaches to help students create action plans for effective study strategies. PALS is a non-remedial approach to provide students with additional academic support. PALS is a program that places trained peers into certain courses and then these peers facilitate study sessions and collaborative activities to encourage peer-to-peer interaction. The DRC also offers a free semester-long workshop called Raise. Professional and peer mentors meet with students one hour a week to encourage students to be motivated and refocus. The Center on Excellence on Autism Spectrum Disorders serves the college community and other members of the community. The college students have access to the DRC, Academic Success Center, Counseling and the Center for Educational and Assistive Technology.

ADMISSIONS INFO FOR STUDENTS WITH LEARNING DIFFERENCES

Phone: 203-392-6828 • Fax: 203-392-6829 • Email: DRC@southernct.edu

SAT/ACT required: No
Interview required: No
Essay required: No
Additional application required: No
Documentation submitted to: Disability Resource Center

Special Ed. HS course work accepted: Yes
Separate application required for Programs/Services: No
Documentation required for:
LD: Psychoeducational evaluation
ADHD: Psychoeducational evaluation
ASD: Psychoeducational evaluation

Southern Connecticut State University

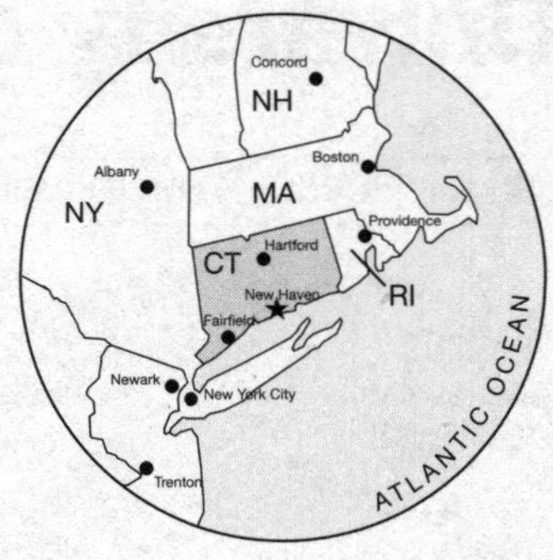

General Admissions

Very important factors include: rigor of secondary school record, academic GPA. *Important factors include:* class rank, application essay, standardized test scores, recommendation(s). *Other factors include:* extracurricular activities, talent/ability, character/personal qualities, first generation, volunteer work, work experience. High school diploma is required and GED is accepted. *Academic units required:* 4 English, 3 math, 2 science, 1 science lab, 2 foreign language, 2 social studies, 2 history. *Academic units recommended:* 4 English, 4 math, 3 science, 4 foreign language, 3 social studies, 3 history.

Accommodations or Services

Accommodations are decided upon an individual basis after a thorough review of appropriate, current documentation. The accommodations requests must be supported through the documentation provided and must be logically linked to the current impact of the condition on academic functioning.

Financial Aid

Students should submit: FAFSA; Institution's own financial aid form. *Need-based scholarships/grants offered:* College/university scholarship or grant aid from institutional funds; Federal Pell; SEOG; State scholarships/grants. *Loan aid offered:* Federal Work-Study Program available. Institutional employment available.

Campus Life

Activities: Campus Ministries; Choral groups; Dance; Drama/theater; International Student Organization; Literary magazine; Music ensembles; Musical theater; Pep band; Radio station; Student government; Student newspaper; Television station; Yearbook. **Organizations:** 63 registered organizations, 12 honor societies, 4 religious organizations, 5 fraternities, 6 sororities. **Athletics (Intercollegiate):** *Men:* baseball, basketball, cross-country, football, golf, gymnastics, ice hockey, rugby, soccer, softball, swimming, track/field (outdoor), track/field (indoor), volleyball, wrestling. *Women:* basketball, cheerleading, cross-country, field hockey, golf, gymnastics, rugby, soccer, softball, swimming, track/field (outdoor), track/field (indoor), volleyball.

ACCOMMODATIONS

Allowed in exams:	
Calculators	Yes
Dictionary	Yes
Computer	Yes
Spell-checker	Yes
Extended test time	Yes
Scribe	Yes
Proctors	Yes
Oral exams	Yes
Note-takers	Yes
Support services for students with:	
LD	Yes
ADHD	Yes
ASD	Yes
Distraction-reduced environment	Yes
Recording of lecture allowed	Yes
Reading technology	Yes
Audio books	Yes
Other assistive technology	Yes
Priority registration	Yes
Added costs of services:	
For LD	No
For ADHD	No
For ASD	No
LD specialists	Yes
ADHD & ASD coaching	Yes
ASD specialists	Yes
Professional tutors	Yes
Peer tutors	Yes
Max. hours/week for services	Varies
How professors are notified of student approved accommodations	Student

COLLEGE GRADUATION REQUIREMENTS

Course waivers allowed	No
Course substitutions allowed	Yes
In what courses: Foreign Language	

Connecticut

University of Connecticut

2131 Hillside Road, Storrs, CT 06268-3088 • Admissions: 860-486-3137 • Fax: 860-486-1476 **Support: CS**

CAMPUS

Type of school	Public
Environment	Town

STUDENTS

Undergrad enrollment	18,847
% male/female	49/51
% from out of state	19
% frosh live on campus	96

FINANCIAL FACTS

Annual in-state tuition	$14,406
Annual out-of-state tuition	$37,074
Room and board	$13,258
Required fees	$3,428

GENERAL ADMISSIONS INFO

Application fee	$80
Regular application deadline	1/15
Nonfall registration	Yes

Admission may be deferred.

Range SAT EBRW	590–680
Range SAT Math	600–710
Range ACT Composite	26–32

ACADEMICS

Student/faculty ratio	16:1
% students returning for sophomore year	94

Most classes have 10–19 students.

Programs/Services for Students with Learning Differences

The Center for Students with Disabilities engages in an individualized process with each student to determine reasonable and appropriate accommodations. In addition to accommodations, the center also offers an enhanced fee-for-service program, referred to as Beyond Access, which provides students with an opportunity to work one-on-one with a trained strategy instructor. Beyond Access helps students identify strengths and challenges. It also guides students to increase awareness of strategies, skills, and technologies to use in and out of the classroom, so as to encourage active networking and communication and to help students become successful self-advocates.

Admissions

There is no separate application or application process for students with LD. Students must meet regular admissions requirements for admissions into UConn. Courses required for admission include 4 years English, 3 years math, 2 years social studies (including U.S. history), 2 years foreign language (English speakers must take two years of the same foreign language and non-English speakers can use English to meet the foreign language requirement. Foreign language taken in middle school is accepted but it must be continued into high school.), 2 years lab science, 3 years electives. The School of Engineering and School of Nursing requires chemistry and physics. U Conn is test optional and there is no disadvantage for applicants who do not submit the ACT or SAT. Two letters of recommendation are optional but are highly encouraged.

Additional Information

Students enrolled in Beyond Access work closely with a trained Strategy Instructor (SI) to design and customize their program based on their individual goals and learning profile. Students in Beyond Access work on developing social and life skills along with strategies to handle stress, reading, writing, math, memory, focus, and planning for a future career. This program goes above and beyond mandated federal requirements, and there is a fee to participate in the various Tracks. In Track III students can receive 3 hours of support each week ($3,600 per semester); Track II provides two hours of support per week ($2,700 per semester); Flex Track I offers 1 ½ hours per week ($2,200 per semester); and Track I is one hour per week ($1,800 per semester). Track I, Flex I, and Tracks II and III are offered every summer.

ADMISSIONS INFO FOR STUDENTS WITH LEARNING DIFFERENCES

Phone: 860-486-2020 • Email: csd@uconn.edu

SAT/ACT required: Yes (Test optional through 2023)
Interview required: Recommended
Essay required: Yes
Additional application required: Yes for Beyond Access
Documentation submitted to: CSD

Special Ed. HS course work accepted: Yes
Separate application required for Programs/Services: Yes for Beyond Access
Documentation required for:
LD: Psychoeducational evaluation
ADHD: Psychoeducational evaluation
ASD: Psychoeducational evaluation

University of Connecticut

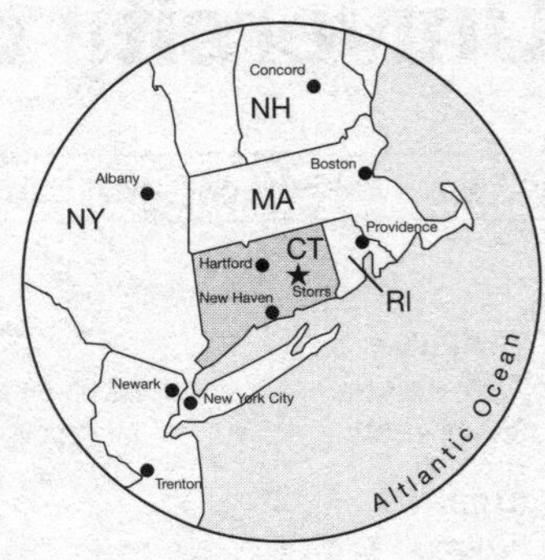

General Admissions

Very important factors include: rigor of secondary school record, class rank, academic GPA, standardized test scores. *Important factors include:* application essay, recommendation(s), extracurricular activities, talent/ability, character/personal qualities, first generation. *Other factors include:* alumni/ae relation, geographical residence, state residency, racial/ethnic status, work experience, level of applicant's interest. High school diploma is required and GED is accepted. *Academic units required:* 4 English, 3 math, 2 science, 2 science labs, 2 foreign language, 2 social studies, 3 academic electives. *Academic units recommended:* 3 foreign language.

Accommodations or Services

Accommodations are decided upon an individual basis after a thorough review of appropriate, current documentation. The accommodations requests must be supported through the documentation provided and must be logically linked to the current impact of the condition on academic functioning.

Financial Aid

Students should submit: FAFSA. Applicants will be notified of awards on a rolling basis beginning 3/1. *Need-based scholarships/grants offered:* College/university scholarship or grant aid from institutional funds; Federal Pell; Private scholarships; SEOG; State scholarships/grants. *Loan aid offered:* Direct PLUS loans; Direct Subsidized Stafford Loans; Direct Unsubsidized Stafford Loans. Federal Work-Study Program available. Institutional employment available.

Campus Life

Activities: Campus Ministries; Choral groups; Concert band; Dance; Drama/theater; International Student Organization; Jazz band; Literary magazine; Marching band; Model UN; Music ensembles; Musical theater; Opera; Pep band; Radio station; Student government; Student newspaper; Student-run film society; Symphony orchestra; Television station; Yearbook. **Organizations:** 765 registered organizations, 23 honor societies, 30 religious organizations, 23 fraternities, 13 sororities. **Athletics (Intercollegiate):** *Men:* baseball, basketball, cross-country, diving, football, golf, ice hockey, soccer, swimming, tennis, track/field (outdoor), track/field (indoor). *Women:* basketball, crew/rowing, cross-country, diving, field hockey, ice hockey, lacrosse, soccer, softball, swimming, tennis, track/field (outdoor), track/field (indoor), volleyball.

ACCOMMODATIONS

Allowed in exams:	
Calculators	Yes
Dictionary	Yes
Computer	Yes
Spell-checker	Yes
Extended test time	Yes
Scribe	Yes
Proctors	Yes
Oral exams	Yes
Note-takers	Yes
Support services for students with:	
LD	Yes
ADHD	Yes
ASD	Yes
Distraction-reduced environment	Yes
Recording of lecture allowed	Yes
Reading technology	Yes
Audio books	Yes
Other assistive technology	Yes
Priority registration	Yes
Added costs of services:	
For LD	Yes for Beyond Access
For ADHD	Yes for Beyond Access
For ASD	Yes for Beyond Access
LD specialists	Yes
ADHD & ASD coaching	No
ASD specialists	No
Professional tutors	Yes
Peer tutors	Yes
Max. hours/week for services	1–3
How professors are notified of student approved accommodations	Student and Disability Office

COLLEGE GRADUATION REQUIREMENTS

Course waivers allowed	No
Course substitutions allowed	Yes
In what courses: Case by case basis	

Connecticut

University of Hartford

200 Bloomfield Avenue, West Hartford, CT 06117 • Admissions: 860-768-4296 • Fax: 860-768-4961 **Support: CS**

CAMPUS

Type of school	Private (nonprofit)
Environment	Metropolis

STUDENTS

Undergrad enrollment	4,793
% male/female	48/52
% from out of state	56
% frosh live on campus	82

FINANCIAL FACTS

Annual tuition	$40,490
Room and board	$13,200
Required fees	$3,070

GENERAL ADMISSIONS INFO

Application fee	$35
Regular application deadline	2/15
Nonfall registration	Yes

Admission may be deferred.

Range SAT EBRW	520–620
Range SAT Math	510–610
Range ACT Composite	22–27

ACADEMICS

Student/faculty ratio	9:1
% students returning for sophomore year	75

Most classes have 10–19 students.

Programs/Services for Students with Learning Differences

The Access-Ability Services is designed to meet the unique educational needs of students with documented disabilities such as learning disabilities, AD/HD, and Autism Spectrum Disorder. The aim is to help students learn how to manage their challenges by promoting self-advocacy and independence in a supportive environment.

Admissions

Students with learning disabilities do not apply to the Access-Ability Services, but do apply directly to one of the nine schools and colleges within the university. If admitted, students with learning disabilities may then elect to receive the support services offered. The Admissions committee pays particular attention to the student's individual talents and aspirations, especially as they relate to programs available at the university. Some borderline applicants may be admitted as a summer admission. Course requirements include 4 years English, 2 years math, 2 years science, 2 years social studies, plus electives. Substitutions are allowed on rare occasions and depend on disability and major. One of the options during the application process, students can apply to Hillyer College, which provides the first two years of a four-year undergraduate degree. Students who enter the U of Hartford in Hillyer College are part of the University of Hartford from the beginning through the dual admission program.

Additional Information

Hillyer College students have access to a challenging curriculum in small classes with faculty mentoring. Accessibility Services gives students access to professional academic coaches. First year students may meet once per week for 30–45 minutes, and sophomores may meet biweekly based on availability of appointments. Upperclassmen may access "Drop-In" appointments. Academic Coaches may work with students on topics including: adjusting to college, time management, organization, stress management, note taking and test preparation, and self-advocacy.

ADMISSIONS INFO FOR STUDENTS WITH LEARNING DIFFERENCES

Phone: 860-768-4312 • Fax: 860-768-4183

SAT/ACT required: No
Interview required: No
Essay required: Yes
Additional application required: No
Documentation submitted to: Access-Ability Services

Special Ed. HS course work accepted: Yes
Separate application required for Programs/Services: No
Documentation required for:
LD: Psychoeducational evaluation
ADHD: Psychoeducational evaluation
ASD: Psychoeducational evaluation

University of Hartford

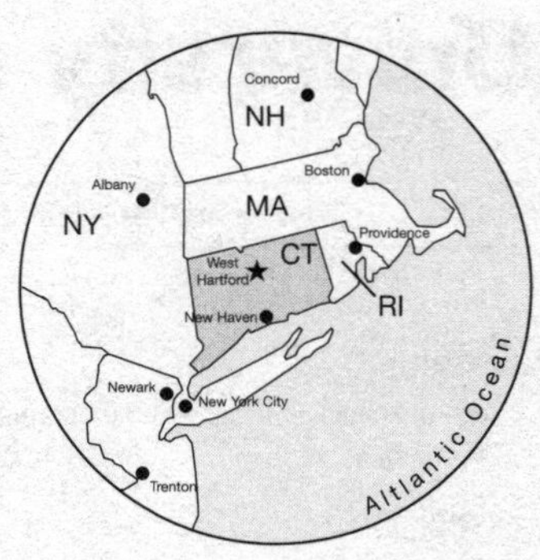

General Admissions

Very important factors include: rigor of secondary school record. *Important factors include:* class rank, academic GPA. *Other factors include:* application essay, recommendation(s), interview, extracurricular activities, talent/ability, character/personal qualities. High school diploma is required, and GED is accepted. *Academic units required:* 4 English, 2 math, 2 science, 2 social studies, 2 history, 4 academic electives. *Academic units recommended:* 3 math, 3 science, 2 foreign language.

Accommodations or Services

Accommodations are decided upon an individual basis after a thorough review of appropriate, current documentation. The accommodations requests must be supported through the documentation provided and must be logically linked to the current impact of the condition on academic functioning.

Financial Aid

Students should submit: FAFSA; Institution's own financial aid form. Applicants will be notified of awards on a rolling basis beginning 4/1. *Need-based scholarships/grants offered:* College/university scholarship or grant aid from institutional funds; Federal Pell; Private scholarships; SEOG; State scholarships/grants. *Loan aid offered:* Direct PLUS loans; Direct Subsidized Stafford Loans; Direct Unsubsidized Stafford Loans.

Campus Life

Activities: Campus Ministries; Choral groups; Concert band; Dance; Drama/theater; International Student Organization; Jazz band; Literary magazine; Music ensembles; Musical theater; Opera; Pep band; Radio station; Student government; Student newspaper; Student-run film society; Symphony orchestra; Television station; Yearbook. **Organizations:** 93 registered organizations, 22 honor societies, 7 religious organizations, 16 fraternities, 14 sororities. **Athletics (Intercollegiate):** *Men:* baseball, basketball, cross-country, golf, lacrosse, soccer, tennis, track/field (outdoor), track/field (indoor). *Women:* basketball, cross-country, golf, soccer, softball, tennis, track/field (outdoor), track/field (indoor), volleyball.

ACCOMMODATIONS

Allowed in exams:	
Calculators	Yes
Dictionary	Yes
Computer	Yes
Spell-checker	Yes
Extended test time	Yes
Scribe	Yes
Proctors	Yes
Oral exams	Yes
Note-takers	Yes
Support services for students with:	
LD	Yes
ADHD	Yes
ASD	Yes
Distraction-reduced environment	Yes
Recording of lecture allowed	Yes
Reading technology	Yes
Audio books	Yes
Other assistive technology	Yes
Priority registration	Yes
Added costs of services:	
For LD	No
For ADHD	No
For ASD	No
LD specialists	Yes
ADHD & ASD coaching	No
ASD specialists	No
Professional tutors	No
Peer tutors	Yes
Max. hours/week for services	Varies
How professors are notified of student approved accommodations	Student and Disability Office

COLLEGE GRADUATION REQUIREMENTS

Course waivers allowed	Yes
In what courses: Math and Foreign Language	
Course substitutions allowed	Yes
In what courses: Math and Foreign Language	

Connecticut

University of New Haven

300 Boston Post Road, West Haven, CT 06516 • Admissions: 203-932-7000 • Fax: 203-931-6093 **Support: S**

CAMPUS

Type of school	Private (nonprofit)
Environment	Town

STUDENTS

Undergrad enrollment	4,863
% male/female	44/56
% from out of state	57
% frosh live on campus	84

FINANCIAL FACTS

Annual tuition	$41,654
Room and board	$17,374

GENERAL ADMISSIONS INFO

Application fee	$50
Regular application deadline	Rolling
Nonfall registration	Yes
Range SAT EBRW	520–620
Range SAT Math	510–600
Range ACT Composite	21–27

ACADEMICS

Student/faculty ratio	16:1
% students returning for sophomore year	77

Most classes have 10–19 students.

Programs/Services for Students with Learning Differences

The primary responsibility of Accessibility Resources Center (ARC) is to provide services and support that promote access educational programs and services for students with disabilities. Students must self-identify and submit documentation of a disability and the need for accommodations. Students must follow the policies and procedures for seeking accommodations. Staff members act as advocates, liaisons, planners, and troubleshooters. However, the staff encourages students to be independent.

Admissions

The University of New Haven is test optional for all applicants except those applying to major in Forensic Science or applying to the Honors College. Each applicant is assigned a personal admission counselor to provide assistance during the application process. If applicants are using the Common Application, they will be required to answer the general essay prompt. Applicants who are applying Early Decision must have an interview. Foreign language is not required for admission. Students with learning disabilities may self-disclose if they feel that it would positively affect the admissions decision. Students admitted as a conditional admit are limited to four classes for the first semester.

Additional Information

The Center for Learning Resources (CLR) offers free tutoring for all students, including students with disabilities. These tutors are available more that 60 hours a week and can help students in more than 30 different subject areas. The Center for Student Success helps students to become familiar with resources on campus and to support their efforts toward graduation. ARC provides services that include the coordination of classroom accommodations, such as extended time for exams; use of a tape recorder, calculator, and note-takers. The Office of Academic Services presents free workshops on improving study skills, such as getting organized, textbook and lecture note-taking techniques, and test preparation and strategies.

ADMISSIONS INFO FOR STUDENTS WITH LEARNING DIFFERENCES

Phone: 203-932-7331 • Fax: 203-931-6082 • Email: LCopneyOkeke@newhaven.edu

SAT/ACT required: No
Interview required: No
Essay required: No
Additional application required: No
Documentation submitted to: Accessibility Resources Center

Special Ed. HS course work accepted: Yes
Separate application required for Programs/Services: No
Documentation required for:
LD: Psychoeducational evaluation
ADHD: Psychoeducational evaluation
ASD: Psychoeducational evaluation

University of New Haven

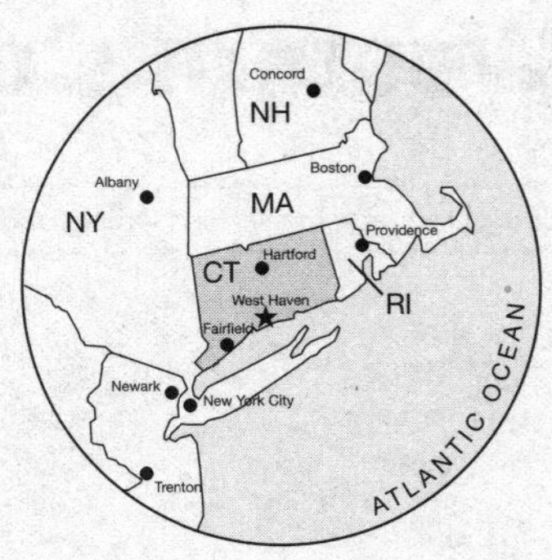

General Admissions

Very important factors include: academic GPA. *Important factors include:* application essay, recommendation(s). *Other factors include:* rigor of secondary school record, standardized test scores, interview, extracurricular activities, character/personal qualities, volunteer work, work experience, level of applicant's interest. High school diploma is required and GED is accepted. *Academic units recommended:* 4 English, 3 math, 3 science, 2 science labs, 2 foreign language, 3 social studies.

Accommodations or Services

Accommodations are decided upon an individual basis after a thorough review of appropriate, current documentation. The accommodations requests must be supported through the documentation provided and must be logically linked to the current impact of the condition on academic functioning.

Financial Aid

Students should submit: FAFSA; Institution's own financial aid form. Applicants will be notified of awards on a rolling basis beginning 3/3. *Need-based scholarships/grants offered:* College/university scholarship or grant aid from institutional funds; Federal Pell; Private scholarships; SEOG; State scholarships/grants. *Loan aid offered:* Direct PLUS loans; Direct Subsidized Stafford Loans; Direct Unsubsidized Stafford Loans. Federal Work-Study Program available. Institutional employment available.

Campus Life

Activities: Campus Ministries; Dance; Drama/theater; International Student Organization; Marching band; Model UN; Music ensembles; Pep band; Radio station; Student government; Student newspaper; Television station; Yearbook. **Organizations:** 165 registered organizations. **Athletics (Intercollegiate):** *Men:* baseball, basketball, cross-country, golf, lacrosse, soccer, track/field (outdoor), track/field (indoor), volleyball. *Women:* basketball, cheerleading, cross-country, lacrosse, soccer, softball, tennis, volleyball.

ACCOMMODATIONS

Allowed in exams:	
Calculators	Yes
Dictionary	Yes
Computer	Yes
Spell-checker	Yes
Extended test time	Yes
Scribe	Yes
Proctors	Yes
Oral exams	No
Note-takers	Yes
Support services for students with:	
LD	Yes
ADHD	Yes
ASD	Yes
Distraction-reduced environment	Yes
Recording of lecture allowed	Yes
Reading technology	Yes
Audio books	Yes
Other assistive technology	Yes
Priority registration	No
Added costs of services:	
For LD	No
For ADHD	No
For ASD	No
LD specialists	No
ADHD & ASD coaching	No
ASD specialists	No
Professional tutors	No
Peer tutors	Yes
Max. hours/week for services	Unlimited
How professors are notified of student approved accommodations	Student

COLLEGE GRADUATION REQUIREMENTS

Course waivers allowed	No
Course substitutions allowed	Yes

In what courses: Case by case basis

Western Connecticut State University

Undergraduate Admissions Office, Danbury, CT 06810-6855 • Admissions: 203-837-9000 • Fax: 203-837-8338 **Support: CS**

CAMPUS

Type of school	Public
Environment	City

STUDENTS

Undergrad enrollment	4,982
% male/female	47/53
% from out of state	26
% frosh live on campus	47

FINANCIAL FACTS

Annual in-state tuition	$11,781
Annual out-of-state tuition	$25,185
Room and board	$11,937

GENERAL ADMISSIONS INFO

Application fee	$50
Regular application deadline	4/1
Nonfall registration	Yes

Admission may be deferred.

Range SAT EBRW	520–620
Range SAT Math	500–600
Range ACT Composite	20–25

ACADEMICS

Student/faculty ratio	12:1
% students returning for sophomore year	74

Most classes have 20–29 students.

Programs/Services for Students with Learning Differences

AccessAbility Services (AAS) provides accommodations and support services to undergraduate and graduate students with documented disabilities. Accommodations are designed to level the playing field while maintaining the integrity of academic programs. Each student who requests accommodations from AAS is considered on a case-by-case basis. The goal is to provide reasonable accommodations and services while supporting each student in developing the skills necessary to be independent learners. Under the umbrella of Student Affairs, AAS collaborates with all departments within the university. AAS is proactive in providing institutional planning to ensure that the university meets the diverse needs of students.

Admissions

Western Connecticut State University is test optional for students with 3.0 GPA. Applicants not submitting ACT or SAT must state why they are applying test optional and respond to the question "Where do you see yourself in four years, and what are three goals you would like to accomplish as an undergraduate?" Applicants must also submit a resume of activities and/or two letters of recommendations. Students who apply without the ACT or SAT will be required to take placement tests prior to enrolling in classes and will not be eligible for merit scholarships. Students who submit test scores should have 21 ACT or higher or 1080 SAT or higher. Students should have a 3.0 GPA and have 4 years of English, 3 years math, 2 years social sciences, 2 years lab science, and 2–3 years foreign language (recommended). Nursing applicants may need higher requirements and music applicants are required to have an audition.

Additional Information

Services include priority registration, tutoring, testing accommodations, and advocacy and counseling. The university does not offer any skills classes. Academic Coaching and Educational Support (ACES) offers one-on-one academic coaching to students on a first-come, first-serve basis in the areas of time management, organization, study preparation, stress management, and academic strategies. Students are encouraged to schedule weekly or biweekly meeting at the beginning of the semester as space is limited.

ADMISSIONS INFO FOR STUDENTS WITH LEARNING DIFFERENCES

Phone: 203-837-3235 • Fax: 203-837-8225 • Email: morele@wcsu.edu

SAT/ACT required: No
Interview required: No
Essay required: Yes if test optional
Additional application required: No
Documentation submitted to: Access/Ability Services

Special Ed. HS course work accepted: Yes
Separate application required for Programs/Services: No
Documentation required for:
LD: Psychoeducational evaluation
ADHD: Psychoeducational evaluation
ASD: Psychoeducational evaluation

Western Connecticut State University

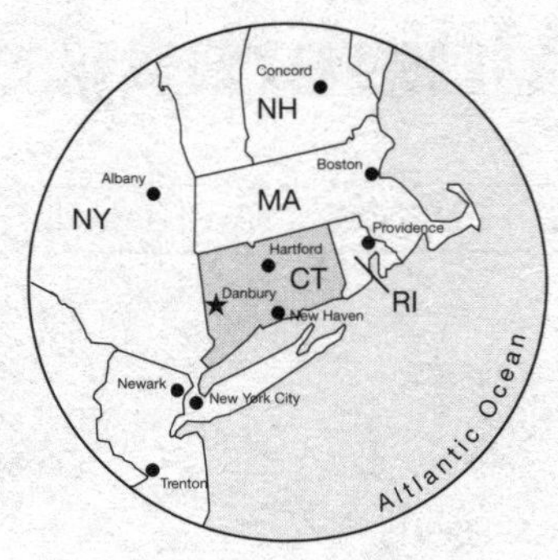

General Admissions

Very important factors include: rigor of secondary school record, standardized test scores, talent/ability. *Important factors include:* class rank, academic GPA, extracurricular activities. *Other factors include:* application essay, recommendation(s), interview, character/personal qualities, alumni/ae relation, state residency, racial/ethnic status, volunteer work, work experience. High school diploma is required and GED is accepted. *Academic units required:* 4 English, 3 math, 2 science, 2 science labs, 2 foreign language, 1 social studies, 1 history.

Accommodations or Services

Accommodations are decided upon an individual basis after a thorough review of appropriate, current documentation. The accommodations requests must be supported through the documentation provided and must be logically linked to the current impact of the condition on academic functioning.

Financial Aid

Students should submit: FAFSA. *Need-based scholarships/grants offered:* College/university scholarship or grant aid from institutional funds; Federal Pell; Private scholarships; SEOG; State scholarships/grants. *Loan aid offered:* Direct PLUS loans; Direct Subsidized Stafford Loans; Direct Unsubsidized Stafford Loans. Federal Work-Study Program available. Institutional employment available.

Campus Life

Activities: Campus Ministries; Choral groups; Concert band; Dance; Drama/theater; International Student Organization; Jazz band; Literary magazine; Music ensembles; Musical theater; Opera; Pep band; Radio station; Student government; Student newspaper; Symphony orchestra. **Organizations:** 79 registered organizations, 8 honor societies, 3 religious organizations, 3 fraternities, 4 sororities. **Athletics (Intercollegiate):** *Men:* baseball, basketball, football, lacrosse, soccer, tennis. *Women:* basketball, field hockey, lacrosse, soccer, softball, swimming, tennis, volleyball.

ACCOMMODATIONS

Allowed in exams:	
Calculators	Yes
Dictionary	Yes
Computer	Yes
Spell-checker	Yes
Extended test time	Yes
Scribe	Yes
Proctors	Yes
Oral exams	Yes
Note-takers	Yes
Support services for students with:	
LD	Yes
ADHD	Yes
ASD	Yes
Distraction-reduced environment	Yes
Recording of lecture allowed	Yes
Reading technology	Yes
Audio books	Yes
Other assistive technology	Yes
Priority registration	Yes
Added costs of services:	
For LD	No
For ADHD	No
For ASD	No
LD specialists	Yes
ADHD & ASD coaching	No
ASD specialists	No
Professional tutors	Yes
Peer tutors	Yes
Max. hours/week for services	Varies
How professors are notified of student approved accommodations	Student and Disability Office

COLLEGE GRADUATION REQUIREMENTS

Course waivers allowed — Yes
In what courses: As required depending on the student's ability

Course substitutions allowed — Yes
In what courses: As required depending on the student's ability

Connecticut

University of Delaware

210 South College Ave., Newark, DE 19716 • Admissions: 302-831-8123 • Fax: 302-831-6905 **Support: SP**

CAMPUS

Type of school	Public
Environment	Town

STUDENTS

Undergrad enrollment	18,766
% male/female	42/58
% from out of state	62
% frosh live on campus	92

FINANCIAL FACTS

Annual in-state tuition	$12,730
Annual out-of-state tuition	$34,160
Room and board	$13,472
Required fees	$1,920

GENERAL ADMISSIONS INFO

Application fee	$75
Regular application deadline	1/15
Nonfall registration	Yes

Admission may be deferred.

Range SAT EBRW	590–670
Range SAT Math	580–690
Range ACT Composite	24–30

ACADEMICS

Student/faculty ratio	12:1
% students returning for sophomore year	91

Most classes have 20–29 students.

Programs/Services for Students with Learning Differences

Eligibility for reasonable accommodations is determined on a case-by-case basis upon receipt of appropriate documentation in order to determine that a disability exists and results in a functional limitation. Requested accommodations must be supported by the documentation and be logically linked to the current impact of the disability. Accommodations are provided in order to provide equal access to university course work, activities, and programs. Accommodations may not interfere with or alter the essential skills of course curriculum.

Admissions

Applicants are typically admitted to their first choice major if admitted to the university. Applicants should only list a second major if there is active interest. Courses required include 4 English, 3 math, 3 science, 4 social studies, 2 foreign language, and 2 electives. Foreign language taken prior to 9th grade is not counted. Once students with disabilities accept the offer of admission, they should self-disclose the disability to the Office of Disability Support Services (DSS).

Additional Information

Career and Life Studies Certificate (CLSC) is a two-year, residential certificate program at the University of Delaware for students with intellectual disabilities (ID). CLSC provides academic, career and independent living support. CLSC students take classes, participate in internships, or work and participate in campus life. Applicants are reviewed by admissions, must meet federal eligibility requirements, and have goals that fit for CLSC. Eligible and qualified applicants are invited for an on-campus interview and given the opportunity to observe a class. Each year, 12 students are admitted to the program. The Spectrum Scholars Program is for students with a documented diagnosis of ASD who have been offered full-time, freshman admission. Students admitted to this competitive cohort participate in coaching, mentoring, and in their academic programs. Preference will be given to students majoring in Computer & Information Sciences and Electrical & Computer Sciences.

ADMISSIONS INFO FOR STUDENTS WITH LEARNING DIFFERENCES

Phone: 302-831-4643 • Fax: 302-831-3261 • Email: dssoffice@udel.edu

SAT/ACT required: Yes (Test optional for 2021)
Interview required: No
Essay required: Yes
Additional application required: No
Documentation submitted to: Disability Support Services

Special Ed. HS course work accepted: Yes
Separate application required for Programs/Services: Yes
Documentation required for:
LD: Psychoeducational evaluation
ADHD: Psychoeducational evaluation
ASD: Psychoeducational evaluation

University of Delaware

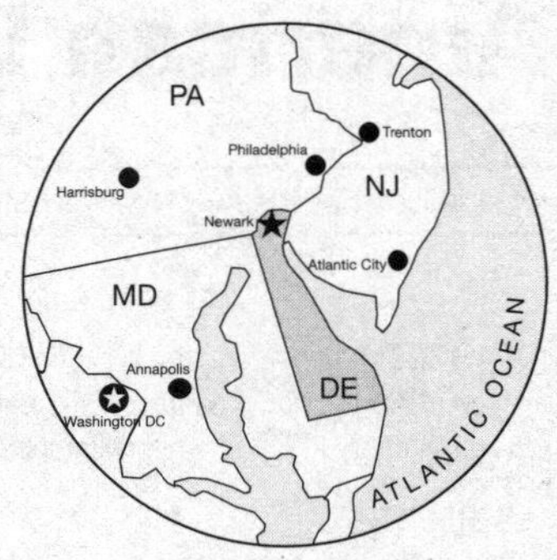

General Admissions

Very important factors include: rigor of secondary school record, academic GPA, state residency. *Important factors include:* application essay, standardized test scores (optional for 2021), recommendation(s), extracurricular activities, talent/ability, character/personal qualities, volunteer work, work experience. *Other factors include:* class rank, interview, first generation, alumni/ae relation, geographical residence, racial/ethnic status, level of applicant's interest. *Freshman admission requirements:* High school diploma is required and GED is accepted. *Academic units required:* 4 English, 3 math, 3 science, 2 science labs, 2 foreign language, 2 social studies, 2 history, 2 academic electives. *Academic units recommended:* 4 English, 4 math, 4 science, 3 science labs, 4 foreign language, 2 social studies, 2 history, 2 academic electives.

Accommodations or Services

Accommodations are decided upon an individual basis after a thorough review of appropriate, current documentation. The accommodations requests must be supported through the documentation provided and must be logically linked to the current impact of the condition on academic functioning.

Financial Aid

Students should submit: FAFSA; State aid form. Applicants will be notified of awards on a rolling basis beginning 4/15. *Need-based scholarships/grants offered:* College/university scholarship or grant aid from institutional funds; Federal Pell; Private scholarships; SEOG; State scholarships/grants. *Loan aid offered:* Direct PLUS loans; Direct Subsidized Stafford Loans; Direct Unsubsidized Stafford Loans. Federal Work-Study Program available. Institutional employment available.

Campus Life

Activities: Campus Ministries; Choral groups; Concert band; Dance; Drama/theater; International Student Organization; Jazz band; Literary magazine; Marching band; Model UN; Music ensembles; Musical theater; Opera; Pep band; Radio station; Student government; Student newspaper; Student-run film society; Symphony orchestra; Television station. **Organizations:** 350 registered organizations, 16 honor societies, 20 religious organizations, 24 fraternities, 19 sororities. **Athletics (Intercollegiate):** *Men:* baseball, basketball, cross-country, diving, football, golf, lacrosse, soccer, swimming, tennis, track/field (outdoor). *Women:* basketball, crew/rowing, cross-country, diving, field hockey, lacrosse, soccer, softball, swimming, tennis, track/field (outdoor), track/field (indoor), volleyball.

ACCOMMODATIONS

Allowed in exams:	
Calculators	Yes
Dictionary	No
Computer	Yes
Spell-checker	Yes
Extended test time	Yes
Scribe	Yes
Proctors	Yes
Oral exams	No
Note-takers	Yes
Support services for students with:	
LD	Yes
ADHD	Yes
ASD	Yes
Distraction-reduced environment	Yes
Recording of lecture allowed	Yes
Reading technology	Yes
Audio books	Yes
Other assistive technology	Yes
Priority registration	Yes
Added costs of services:	
For LD	No
For ADHD	No
For ASD	No
LD specialists	Yes
ADHD & ASD coaching	Yes
ASD specialists	No
Professional tutors	No
Peer tutors	Yes
Max. hours/week for services	Varies
How professors are notified of student approved accommodations	Student and DSS

COLLEGE GRADUATION REQUIREMENTS

Course waivers allowed	No
Course substitutions allowed	Yes
In what courses: Case by case basis	

Delaware

American University

4400 Massachusetts Ave. NW, Washington, DC 20016-8001 • Admissions: 202-885-6000 • Fax: 202-885-1025 **Support: SP**

CAMPUS

Type of school	Private (nonprofit)
Environment	Metropolis

STUDENTS

Undergrad enrollment	7,659
% male/female	38/62
% from out of state	80

FINANCIAL FACTS

Annual tuition	$50,542
Room and board	$14,980
Required fees	$819

GENERAL ADMISSIONS INFO

Application fee	$75
Regular application deadline	1/15
Nonfall registration	Yes

Admission may be deferred.

Range SAT EBRW	620–700
Range SAT Math	590–690
Range ACT Composite	27–31

ACADEMICS

Student/faculty ratio	12:1
% students returning for sophomore year	87

Most classes have 10–19 students.

Programs/Services for Students with Learning Differences

The Academic Support Center (ASC) provides extensive support for students with documented learning disabilities and ADHD. Any student whose documentation meets university guidelines can access approved accommodations, work with a learning specialist, meet with the assistive technology specialist, use the Writing Lab, request peer tutors, and take advantage of group workshops. The Learning Services Program (LSP), within the ASC, is a mainstream freshman transition program offering additional support for students who apply to the program with learning disabilities that impact writing. There is a one-time fee for this program, and students must apply at the time they apply to the university. Disability services continue to be available until graduation.

Admissions

Students with LD must be admitted to the university and then to the Learning Services Program. Students who wish to have program staff consult with the Admissions Office about their LD during the admissions process must submit a supplemental application to the Learning Services Program that requires documentation of the LD. Students should indicate interest in the program on their application. Special education courses taken in high school may be accepted if they meet the criteria for the Carnegie Units. The academic credentials of successful applicants with LD fall within the range of regular admissions criteria: the mean GPA is around 3.2 with an ACT ranging from 27–31 and SAT from 1210–1390. American Sign Language is an acceptable substitution for foreign language. The admission decision is made by a special Admissions Committee and is based on the high school record, recommendations, and all pertinent diagnostic reports.

Additional Information

All students work with an academic advisor in their school or college; students in the Learning Services Program have an advisor who consults on their learning disability. Students in the program meet weekly with a learning specialist for individual sessions that help them further develop college-level reading, writing, and study strategies—and with a writing tutor. Peer tutors assist with course content tutoring. Accommodations are based on diagnostic testing. Students are held to the same academic standards as all students but may meet these standards through nontraditional means.

ADMISSIONS INFO FOR STUDENTS WITH LEARNING DIFFERENCES

Phone: 202-885-3360 • Fax: 202-885-1042 • Email: asac@american.edu

SAT/ACT required: No
Interview required: No
Essay required: Yes
Additional application required: Yes
Documentation submitted to: Learning Services Program

Special Ed. HS course work accepted: Yes
Separate application required for Programs/Services: Yes
Documentation required for:
- **LD:** Psychoeducational evaluation
- **ADHD:** Psychoeducational evaluation
- **ASD:** Psychoeducational evaluation

American University

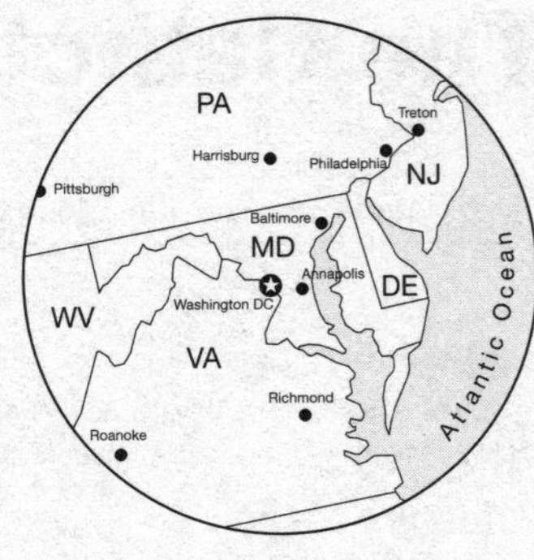

General Admissions

Very important factors include: rigor of secondary school record, academic GPA, level of applicant's interest. *Important factors include:* application essay, recommendation(s), extracurricular activities, talent/ability, character/personal qualities, volunteer work. *Other factors include:* standardized test scores, first generation, alumni/ae relation, geographical residence, racial/ethnic status, work experience. *Freshman admission requirements:* High school diploma is required and GED is accepted. *Academic units required:* 4 English, 3 math, 3 science, 2 science labs, 2 foreign language, 2 social studies, 3 academic electives. *Academic units recommended:* 4 English, 4 math, 4 science, 3 foreign language, 4 social studies, 4 academic electives.

Accommodations or Services

Accommodations are decided upon an individual basis after a thorough review of appropriate, current documentation. The accommodations requests must be supported through the documentation provided and must be logically linked to the current impact of the condition on academic functioning.

Financial Aid

Students should submit: CSS/Financial Aid PROFILE; FAFSA. *Need-based scholarships/grants offered:* College/university scholarship or grant aid from institutional funds; Federal Pell; Private scholarships; SEOG. *Loan aid offered:* Direct PLUS loans; Direct Subsidized Stafford Loans; Direct Unsubsidized Stafford Loans. Federal Work-Study Program available. Institutional employment available.

Campus Life

Activities: Campus Ministries; Choral groups; Concert band; Dance; Drama/theater; International Student Organization; Jazz band; Literary magazine; Model UN; Music ensembles; Musical theater; Opera; Pep band; Radio station; Student government; Student newspaper; Student-run film society; Symphony orchestra; Television station; Yearbook. **Organizations:** 200 registered organizations, 12 honor societies, 17 religious organizations. **Athletics (Intercollegiate):** *Men:* basketball, cross-country, diving, soccer, swimming, track/field (outdoor), track/field (indoor), wrestling. *Women:* basketball, cross-country, diving, field hockey, lacrosse, soccer, swimming, track/field (outdoor), track/field (indoor), volleyball.

ACCOMMODATIONS

Allowed in exams:	
Calculators	Yes
Dictionary	Yes
Computer	Yes
Spell-checker	Yes
Extended test time	Yes
Scribe	Yes
Proctors	Yes
Oral exams	Yes
Note-takers	Yes
Support services for students with:	
LD	Yes
ADHD	Yes
ASD	Yes
Distraction-reduced environment	Yes
Recording of lecture allowed	Yes
Reading technology	Yes
Audio books	Yes
Other assistive technology	Yes
Priority registration	Yes
Added costs of services:	
For LD	Yes
For ADHD	Yes
For ASD	Yes
LD specialists	Yes
ADHD & ASD coaching	Yes
ASD specialists	No
Professional tutors	No
Peer tutors	Yes
Max. hours/week for services	Varies
How professors are notified of student approved accommodations	Student

COLLEGE GRADUATION REQUIREMENTS

Course waivers allowed	No
Course substitutions allowed	No

District of Columbia

The Catholic University of America

Office of Undergraduate Admissions, Washington, DC 20064 • Admissions: 202-319-5305 • Fax: 202-319-6533 **Support: CS**

CAMPUS

Type of school	Private (nonprofit)
Environment	Metropolis

STUDENTS

Undergrad enrollment	3,237
% male/female	45/55
% from out of state	96
% frosh live on campus	92

FINANCIAL FACTS

Annual tuition	$48,600
Room and board	$15,820
Required fees	$816

GENERAL ADMISSIONS INFO

Application fee	$0
Regular application deadline	1/15
Nonfall registration	Yes

Admission may be deferred.

Range SAT EBRW	580–670
Range SAT Math	550–660
Range ACT Composite	24–29

ACADEMICS

Student/faculty ratio	10:1
% students returning for sophomore year	88

Most classes have 10–19 students.

Programs/Services for Students with Learning Differences

The Catholic University of America provides programs and services designed to support and encourage the integration of students with disabilities into the mainstream of the University community. The Office of Disability Support Services (DSS) assists in creating an accessible University community where students with disabilities have an equal opportunity to fully participate in all aspects of the educational environment. The program cooperates through partnerships with students, faculty, and staff to promote students' independence and to ensure recognition of their abilities, not disabilities. Staff is available to answer questions concerning accommodations and services available and to provide information about and give referrals to admissions, registration, financial aid, and other services within the university. The 248 model was designed for incoming students' transition to college life. Students meet one-to-one with a learning specialist in a semi-structured format during the first semester to help them develop skills that lead to college success. The meetings address questions about accommodation utilization, ensure that students are on track for success, and determine if other supports are needed.

Admissions

Documentation of your disability should not be sent with your application. Prospective students with disabilities are encouraged to write an additional personal statement. Once enrolled at the university, students with a learning disability that impairs the ability to acquire a foreign language may apply to substitute for the graduation language requirement.

Additional Information

Once students have been admitted, they should contact DSS and request an Intake Packet. DSS will review the application and documentation and determine accommodations and services. Students must complete a request form each semester to obtain an accommodation letter to give to professors. The Learning Specialist is available to meet one-on-one with students who are registered with DSS. The Learning Specialist helps students improve their learning.

ADMISSIONS INFO FOR STUDENTS WITH LEARNING DIFFERENCES

Phone: 202-319-5211 • Fax: 202-319-5126 • Email: CUA-DSS@cua.edu

SAT/ACT required: Yes (Test blind for 2021)
Interview required: No
Essay required: Recommended
Additional application required: Yes
Documentation submitted to: Disability Support Services

Special Ed. HS course work accepted: Yes
Separate application required for Programs/Services: Yes
Documentation required for:
LD: Psychoeducational evaluation
ADHD: Psychoeducational evaluation
ASD: Psychoeducational evaluation

The Catholic University of America

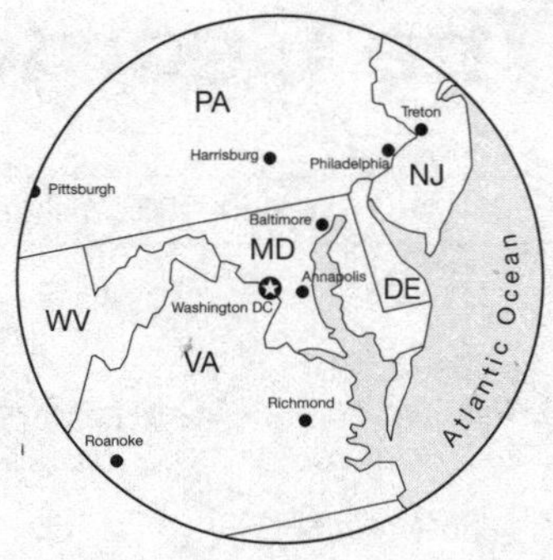

General Admissions

Very important factors include: rigor of secondary school record, academic GPA, character/personal qualities. *Important factors include:* application essay, recommendation(s), extracurricular activities, first generation. *Other factors include:* class rank, standardized test scores, interview, talent/ability, alumni/ae relation, geographical residence, racial/ethnic status, volunteer work, work experience, level of applicant's interest. High school diploma is required and GED is accepted. *Academic units recommended:* 4 English, 4 math, 3 science, 2 science labs, 3 foreign language, 4 social studies.

Accommodations or Services

Accommodations are decided upon an individual basis after a thorough review of appropriate, current documentation. The accommodations requests must be supported through the documentation provided and must be logically linked to the current impact of the condition on academic functioning.

Financial Aid

Students should submit: CSS/Financial Aid PROFILE; FAFSA; Noncustodial PROFILE. *Need-based scholarships/grants offered:* College/university scholarship or grant aid from institutional funds; Federal Pell; Private scholarships; SEOG; State scholarships/grants. *Loan aid offered:* Direct PLUS loans; Direct Subsidized Stafford Loans; Direct Unsubsidized Stafford Loans. Federal Work-Study Program available. Institutional employment available.

Campus Life

Activities: Campus Ministries; Choral groups; Concert band; Dance; Drama/theater; International Student Organization; Jazz band; Literary magazine; Model UN; Music ensembles; Musical theater; Opera; Radio station; Student government; Student newspaper; Student-run film society; Symphony orchestra. **Organizations:** 109 registered organizations, 16 honor societies, 10 religious organizations, 1 fraternity, 1 sorority. **Athletics (Intercollegiate):** *Men:* baseball, basketball, cross-country, football, lacrosse, soccer, swimming, tennis, track/field (outdoor), track/field (indoor). *Women:* basketball, cross-country, field hockey, lacrosse, soccer, softball, swimming, tennis, track/field (outdoor), track/field (indoor), volleyball.

ACCOMMODATIONS

Allowed in exams:	
Calculators	Yes
Dictionary	No
Computer	Yes
Spell-checker	Yes
Extended test time	Yes
Scribe	Yes
Proctors	Yes
Oral exams	No
Note-takers	Yes
Support services for students with:	
LD	Yes
ADHD	Yes
ASD	Yes
Distraction-reduced environment	Yes
Recording of lecture allowed	Yes
Reading technology	Yes
Audio books	Yes
Other assistive technology	Yes
Priority registration	Yes
Added costs of services:	
For LD	No
For ADHD	No
For ASD	No
LD specialists	Yes
ADHD & ASD coaching	Yes
ASD specialists	No
Professional tutors	No
Peer tutors	Yes
Max. hours/week for services	Varies
How professors are notified of student approved accommodations	Student

COLLEGE GRADUATION REQUIREMENTS

Course waivers allowed	No
Course substitutions allowed	Yes

In what courses: Foreign Language and Math

The George Washington University

800 21st St NW Suite 100, Washington, DC 20052 • Admissions: 202-994-6040 • Fax: 202-994-0325 **Support: CS**

CAMPUS

Type of school	Private (nonprofit)
Environment	Metropolis

STUDENTS

Undergrad enrollment	12,484
% male/female	38/62
% from out of state	96
% frosh live on campus	97

FINANCIAL FACTS

Annual tuition	$58,550
Room and board	$14,711
Required fees	$90

GENERAL ADMISSIONS INFO

Application fee	$80
Regular application deadline	1/1
Nonfall registration	Yes

Admission may be deferred.

Range SAT EBRW	630–720
Range SAT Math	650–750
Range ACT Composite	29–33

ACADEMICS

Student/faculty ratio	13:1
% students returning for sophomore year	92

Most classes have 10–19 students.

Programs/Services for Students with Learning Differences

Disability Support Services (DSS) provides support to learning disabled students so that they can participate fully in university life, derive the greatest benefit from their educational experiences, and achieve maximum personal success. Students with LD/ADHD are served through DSS. The staff is committed to providing student-centered services that meet the individual needs of each student. The ultimate goal of DSS is to assist students with disabilities as they gain knowledge to recognize strengths, accommodate differences, and become strong self-advocates. Staff are available to discuss issues such as course load, learning strategies, academic accommodations, and petitions for course waivers or substitutions. DSS offers individual assistance in addressing needs not provided through routine services.

Admissions

GW is test-optional, meaning students applying for freshman or transfer admission are not required to submit standardized test scores (SAT or ACT), except in the following select circumstances: Applicants applying to the accelerated Seven-Year B.A./M.D. Program; Applicants who are homeschooled or who attend an online high school; Applicants who attend secondary schools that provide only narrative evaluations rather than some form of grading scale; Recruited NCAA Division I athletes. GW takes a holistic approach to the application review process, and has no minimum GPA or SAT/ACT requirements for admission. However, admission to GW is competitive and admitted students are typically strong academic students in their high school graduating class.

Additional Information

To be eligible, a student must provide to DSS documentation that substantiates the need for such services in compliance with Section 504 of the Rehabilitation Act and the Americans with Disabilities Act (ADA). Services provided without charge to students may include registration assistance, reading services, assistive technology, learning specialist services, notetaking assistance, test accommodations, and referrals. DSS does not provide content tutoring, although it is available on a fee basis from other campus resources.

ADMISSIONS INFO FOR STUDENTS WITH LEARNING DIFFERENCES

Phone: 202-994-8250 • Fax: 202-994-7610 • Email: dss@gwu.edu

SAT/ACT required: No
Interview required: No
Essay required: Yes
Additional application required: No
Documentation submitted to: Disability Support Services

Special Ed. HS course work accepted: Yes
Separate application required for Programs/Services: No
Documentation required for:
LD: Psychoeducational evaluation
ADHD: Psychoeducational evaluation
ASD: Psychoeducational evaluation

The George Washington University

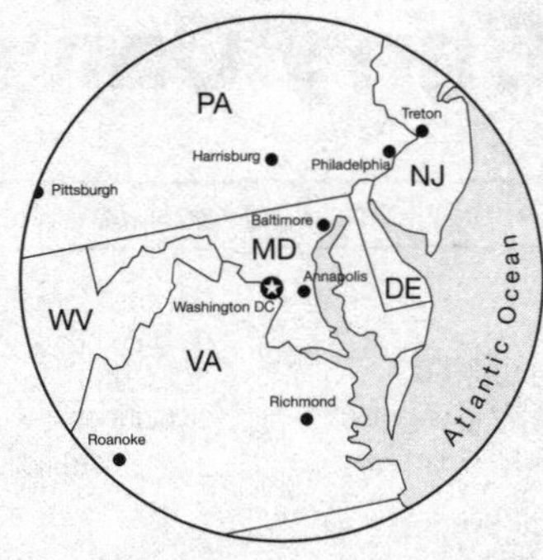

General Admissions

Very important factors include: rigor of secondary school record, academic GPA. *Important factors include:* application essay, recommendation(s), extracurricular activities, talent/ability, volunteer work. *Other factors include:* standardized test scores, character/personal qualities, first generation, alumni/ae relation, geographical residence, racial/ethnic status, work experience, level of applicant's interest. *Freshman admission requirements:* High school diploma is required and GED is accepted. *Academic units required:* 4 English, 2 math, 2 science, 1 science lab, 2 foreign language, 2 social studies. *Academic units recommended:* 4 English, 4 math, 4 science, 4 foreign language, 4 social studies.

Accommodations or Services

Accommodations are decided upon an individual basis after a thorough review of appropriate, current documentation. The accommodations requests must be supported through the documentation provided and must be logically linked to the current impact of the condition on academic functioning.

Financial Aid

Students should submit: CSS/Financial Aid PROFILE; FAFSA; Noncustodial PROFILE. *Need-based scholarships/grants offered:* College/university scholarship or grant aid from institutional funds; Federal Pell; SEOG; State scholarships/grants. *Loan aid offered:* Direct PLUS loans; Direct Subsidized Stafford Loans; Direct Unsubsidized Stafford Loans. Federal Work-Study Program available. Institutional employment available.

Campus Life

Activities: Choral groups; Concert band; Dance; Drama/theater; International Student Organization; Jazz band; Literary magazine; Marching band; Model UN; Music ensembles; Musical theater; Pep band; Radio station; Student government; Student newspaper; Student-run film society; Symphony orchestra; Television station; Yearbook. **Organizations:** 220 registered organizations, 3 honor societies, 5 religious organizations, 12 fraternities, 9 sororities. **Athletics (Intercollegiate):** *Men:* baseball, basketball, crew/rowing, cross-country, diving, fencing, golf, rugby, soccer, squash, swimming, tennis, water polo. *Women:* basketball, crew/rowing, cross-country, fencing, gymnastics, soccer, swimming, tennis, volleyball.

ACCOMMODATIONS

Allowed in exams:	
Calculators	Yes
Dictionary	Yes
Computer	Yes
Spell-checker	Yes
Extended test time	Yes
Scribe	Yes
Proctors	Yes
Oral exams	Yes
Note-takers	Yes
Support services for students with:	
LD	Yes
ADHD	Yes
ASD	Yes
Distraction-reduced environment	Yes
Recording of lecture allowed	Yes
Reading technology	Yes
Audio books	Yes
Other assistive technology	Yes
Priority registration	Yes
Added costs of services:	
For LD	No
For ADHD	No
For ASD	No
LD specialists	Yes
ADHD & ASD coaching	No
ASD specialists	No
Professional tutors	No
Peer tutors	No
Max. hours/week for services	Varies
How professors are notified of student approved accommodations	Student

COLLEGE GRADUATION REQUIREMENTS

Course waivers allowed	Yes
In what courses: Case-by-case basis	
Course substitutions allowed	Yes
In what courses: Case-by-case basis	

District of Columbia

Barry University

11300 NE 2nd Avenue, Miami Shores, FL 33161-6695 • Admissions: 305-899-3100 • Fax: 305-899-2971 **Support: SP**

CAMPUS

Type of school	Private (nonprofit)
Environment	Metropolis

STUDENTS

Undergrad enrollment	3,747
% male/female	37/63
% from out of state	39
% frosh live on campus	70

FINANCIAL FACTS

Annual tuition	$30,600
Room and board	$11,506

GENERAL ADMISSIONS INFO

Application fee	$0
Regular application deadline	Rolling
Nonfall registration	Yes

Admission may be deferred.

Range SAT EBRW	480–550
Range SAT Math	450–530
Range ACT Composite	17–21

ACADEMICS

Student/faculty ratio	10:1
% students returning for sophomore year	65

Most classes have 10–19 students.

Programs/Services for Students with Learning Differences

Barry University offers a fee-for-service support program for students with LD. The Center for Advanced Learning (CAL) Program is a comprehensive, intensive, structured, and individualized approach to assisting students with LD throughout their college careers. It is designed to move students gradually toward increasing self-direction in academic, personal, and career activities. This program affirms Barry University's commitment to expand college opportunities to students with LD and provide the specialized services that can enhance college success. CAL program objectives: all students have a right to fair and accessible education regardless of their challenges and learning differences; with the right level of support, students can succeed; to provide individualized and specialized tutoring, mentoring, and advising services by compassionate, experienced professional staff; and a dedication to helping our students achieve their educational goals.

Admissions

Students with learning disabilities/ADHD must meet the regular admission criteria for the university, which includes 2.0 GPA, ACT of 17 or above or SAT of 960 or above, and 4 years of English, 3–4 years of math, 3 years of natural science, and 3–4 years of social science. There is a process of individual review by learning disability professionals for those students who have a diagnosed disability and who do not meet the general admission criteria. These students must provide appropriate and current LD/ADHD documentation and be interviewed by the Director of the CAL Program. Students admitted are expected to meet all requirements established for them and those of the specific university program in which they enroll.

Additional Information

The CAL Program includes a full range of professionally managed and intensive support services that includes the following: review of diagnostic information allowing for development of a personalized educational plan; individual and small-group subject-area tutoring; instruction in learning and study strategies; academic advising; assistance in developing interpersonal skills; individual and small-group personal, academic, and career counseling; assistance in obtaining study aids and training in the use of assistive technology; computer access; special test administration services; and advocacy with faculty. Additionally, all students have access to a math lab, reading and writing centers, and selected educational seminars. All instructional staff hold advanced degrees in their area of specialization, no peer tutors are used.

ADMISSIONS INFO FOR STUDENTS WITH LEARNING DIFFERENCES

Phone: 305 899-3488 • Fax: 305-899-3056 • Email: lvillegas@barry.edu

SAT/ACT required: No
Interview required: No
Essay required: No
Additional application required: No
Documentation submitted to: Center for Advanced Learning

Special Ed. HS course work accepted: Yes
Separate application required for Programs/Services: No
Documentation required for:
LD: Psychoeducational evaluation
ADHD: Psychoeducational evaluation
ASD: Psychoeducational evaluation

Barry University

General Admissions

Very important factors include: academic GPA, standardized test scores. *Important factors include:* talent/ability, character/personal qualities. *Other factors include:* rigor of secondary school record, class rank, recommendation(s), extracurricular activities, first generation, volunteer work, level of applicant's interest. High school diploma is required and GED is accepted. *Academic units recommended:* 4 English, 3 math, 3 science, 3 social studies.

Accommodations or Services

Accommodations are decided upon an individual basis after a thorough review of appropriate, current documentation. The accommodations requests must be supported through the documentation provided and must be logically linked to the current impact of the condition on academic functioning.

Financial Aid

Students should submit: FAFSA. *Need-based scholarships/grants offered:* College/university scholarship or grant aid from institutional funds; Federal Nursing Scholarships; Federal Pell; Private scholarships; SEOG; State scholarships/grants. *Loan aid offered:* Direct PLUS loans; Direct Subsidized Stafford Loans; Direct Unsubsidized Stafford Loans. Federal Work-Study Program available. Institutional employment available.

Campus Life

Activities: Campus Ministries; Dance; Drama/theater; International Student Organization; Literary magazine; Music ensembles; Musical theater; Opera; Radio station; Student government; Student newspaper; Television station; Yearbook. **Organizations:** 58 registered organizations, 20 honor societies, 1 religious organization, 2 fraternities, 2 sororities. **Athletics (Intercollegiate):** *Men:* baseball, basketball, golf, soccer, tennis. *Women:* basketball, crew/rowing, golf, soccer, softball, tennis, volleyball.

ACCOMMODATIONS

Allowed in exams:	
Calculators	Yes
Dictionary	Yes
Computer	Yes
Spell-checker	Yes
Extended test time	Yes
Scribe	Yes
Proctors	Yes
Oral exams	Yes
Note-takers	Yes
Support services for students with:	
LD	Yes
ADHD	Yes
ASD	Yes
Distraction-reduced environment	Yes
Recording of lecture allowed	Yes
Reading technology	Yes
Audio books	Yes
Other assistive technology	Yes
Priority registration	No
Added costs of services:	
For LD	Yes
For ADHD	Yes
For ASD	Yes
LD specialists	Yes
ADHD & ASD coaching	Yes
ASD specialists	No
Professional tutors	Yes
Peer tutors	No
Max. hours/week for services	Unlimited
How professors are notified of student approved accommodations	Student and Disability Office

COLLEGE GRADUATION REQUIREMENTS

Course waivers allowed	No
Course substitutions allowed	Yes
In what courses: Case by case basis	

Beacon College

105 E. Main Street, Leesburg, FL 34748 • Admissions: 352-638-9731 • Fax: 352-787-0721 **Support: SP**

CAMPUS

Type of school	Private (nonprofit)
Environment	Village

STUDENTS

Undergrad enrollment	416
% male/female	63/37
% from out of state	69
% frosh live on campus	99

FINANCIAL FACTS

Annual tuition	$42,600
Room and board	$12,816

GENERAL ADMISSIONS INFO

Application fee	$50
Regular application deadline	8/1
Nonfall registration	Yes

ACADEMICS

Student/faculty ratio	10:1
% students returning for sophomore year	71

Most classes have 12–16 students.

Programs/Services for Students with Learning Differences

Beacon College was founded to award bachelor degrees to students with learning disabilities, ADHD and other learning differences. The College is committed to student success, offering academic and personal support services that help each student achieve his or her goals. The four-year graduation rate far surpasses the national average for students with learning disabilities, proving the effectiveness of the teaching model founded at the College. Every Beacon student leaves the College with stronger critical thinking skills and, due to a strong four-year Career Development program, professional skills designed to help each student understand his or her specific skill set and goals. Career Development courses, along with professional internships, help insure each student embarks on the appropriate career path after leaving Beacon. The fact that 83.3% of graduating students either obtain a job or continue in their education after leaving Beacon demonstrates the success of this program.

Admissions

In order to be considered for admissions to Beacon College, an applicant must submit: a completed application, nonrefundable $50.00 application fee, and psychoeducational evaluation (completed within three years) that documents a learning disability, or AD/HD. The evaluation must include a complete WAIS with sub-test scores and assessments in reading and math. Official high school transcripts showing successful completion of a standard high school diploma or GED is also required. Beacon College does not place heavy emphasis on SAT/ACT scores. Interviews are preferred and provide a better understanding of the applicant.

Additional Information

The cornerstone of educational support services at Beacon College is our Academic Mentoring Program. In order to foster success, each student receives one-to-one academic mentoring services, which are designed to enhance academic performance and develop skills for lifelong learning. The Field Placement Program allows students to complete supervised hours in the workplace to enhance their resumes and further their employment skills. The Cultural Studies Abroad Program gives students the opportunity to experience the life, history, culture, cuisine, architecture, music, and literature of exotic places. During the past ten years, students and professors have traveled to Italy, Greece, France, Spain, Australia, Russia, Sweden, Austria, England, and Ireland.

ADMISSIONS INFO FOR STUDENTS WITH LEARNING DIFFERENCES

Phone: 855-220-5376 • Fax: 352-787-0796 • Email: admissions@beaconcollege.edu

SAT/ACT required: No
Interview required: No
Essay required: No
Additional application required: No
Documentation submitted to: Admissions

Special Ed. HS course work accepted: Yes
Separate application required for Programs/Services: No
Documentation required
- **LD:** Psychoeducational evaluation
- **ADHD:** Psychoeducational evaluation
- **ASD:** Psychoeducational evaluation

Beacon College

General Admissions

Very important factors include: recommendation(s). *Important factors include:* rigor of secondary school record, application essay, standardized test scores, talent/ability, character/personal qualities. *Other factors include:* class rank, academic GPA, interview, extracurricular activities, volunteer work, work experience. High school diploma is required and GED is accepted. *Academic units required:* 4 English, 1 math, 1 science, 1 social studies, 2 history, 3 academic electives.

Accommodations or Services

Accommodations are decided upon an individual basis after a thorough review of appropriate, current documentation. The accommodations requests must be supported through the documentation provided and must be logically linked to the current impact of the condition on academic functioning.

Financial Aid

Students should submit: FAFSA. Applicants will be notified of awards on a rolling basis beginning 2/1. *Need-based scholarships/grants offered:* College/university scholarship or grant aid from institutional funds; Federal Pell; Private scholarships; SEOG; State scholarships/grants. *Loan aid offered:* Direct PLUS loans; Direct Subsidized Stafford Loans; Direct Unsubsidized Stafford Loans. Federal Work-Study Program available.

Campus Life

Activities: Choral groups; Drama/theater; Literary magazine; Student government; Student newspaper; Yearbook. **Organizations:** 13 registered organizations, 1 honor society, 1 fraternity, 1 sorority.

ACCOMMODATIONS

Allowed in exams:	
Calculators	Yes
Dictionary	Yes
Computer	Yes
Spell-checker	Yes
Extended test time	Yes
Scribe	Yes
Proctors	Yes
Oral exams	Yes
Note-takers	Yes
Support services for students with:	
LD	Yes
ADHD	Yes
ASD	Yes
Distraction-reduced environment	Yes
Recording of lecture allowed	Yes
Reading technology	Yes
Audio books	Yes
Other assistive technology	Yes
Priority registration	Yes
Added costs of services:	
For LD	No
For ADHD	No
For ASD	No
LD specialists	Yes
ADHD & ASD coaching	Yes
ASD specialists	Yes
Professional tutors	Yes
Peer tutors	Yes
Max. hours/week for services	Varies
How professors are notified of student approved accommodations	Student and Disability Office

COLLEGE GRADUATION REQUIREMENTS

Course waivers allowed	Yes
In what courses: Math	
Course substitutions allowed	Yes
In what courses: Math	

Florida

Eckerd College

4200 54th Avenue South, St. Petersburg, FL 33711 • Admissions: 727-864-8331 • Fax: 727-866-2304 **Support: S**

CAMPUS	
Type of school	Private (nonprofit)
Environment	City
STUDENTS	
Undergrad enrollment	1,989
% male/female	33/67
% from out of state	79
% frosh live on campus	98
FINANCIAL FACTS	
Annual tuition	$47,044
Room and board	$13,492
Required fees	$660
GENERAL ADMISSIONS INFO	
Application fee	$40
Regular application deadline	Rolling
Nonfall registration	Yes
Admission may be deferred.	
Range SAT EBRW	560–650
Range SAT Math	530–630
Range ACT Composite	23–29
ACADEMICS	
Student/faculty ratio	12:1
% students returning for sophomore year	81
Most classes have 20–29 students.	

Programs/Services for Students with Learning Differences

Eckerd provides students equal access to facilities, programs and services of the College. We support students with documented disabilities and provide a "level playing field" so that all students have the opportunity to succeed. Eckerd College is committed to providing support services that enable students with disabilities to participate in, and benefit from, all College programs and activities. Eckerd College has placed the Office of Accessibility in the Center for Academic Excellence.

Admissions

Grades are important and so are personal merits. Eckerd seeks applicants who have taken high school courses that are demanding and rigorous. Most students have taken honors, accelerated, advanced placement, dual enrollment, and/or international baccalaureate courses. We also look for solid grades in tough courses. The average GPA for an entering freshman is 3.5 and most students come from the top 20% of their high school classes. Courses required are 4 years English, 3 years math, 3 years sciences, 3 years history or social science, and 2 years foreign language. More weight is given to courses and grades than SAT or ACT scores, if provided. For applicants seeking admission in Fall 2021 and Fall 2022, we will not require SAT or ACT scores for consideration. Applicants should demonstrate leadership accomplishments in school, community, or church and should have a commitment to community service.

Additional Information

The John M. Bevan Center for Academic Excellence (BCAE) offers students resources and opportunities to achieve academic excellence. Peer mentoring creates community among new students and fosters development of academic skills. Academic coaching, workshops on study skills and time management, and tutoring to support student learning.

ADMISSIONS INFO FOR STUDENTS WITH LEARNING DIFFERENCES

Phone: 727-864-7723 • Fax: 727-866-2304 • Email: accessibility@eckerd.edu

SAT/ACT required: Yes (Test optional through 2022)
Interview required: No
Essay required: Yes
Additional application required: No
Documentation submitted to: Office of Accessibility

Special Ed. HS course work accepted: Yes
Separate application required for Programs/Services: No
Documentation required for:
LD: Psychoeducational evaluation
ADHD: Psychoeducational evaluation
ASD: Psychoeducational evaluation

Eckerd College

General Admissions

Very important factors include: rigor of secondary school record, academic GPA. *Important factors include:* application essay, standardized test scores, recommendation(s), interview, extracurricular activities, talent/ability, character/personal qualities, volunteer work. *Other factors include:* class rank, first generation, alumni/ae relation. *Freshman admission requirements:* High school diploma is required and GED is accepted. *Academic units recommended:* 4 English, 3 math, 3 science, 2 science labs, 2 foreign language, 2 social studies, 1 history, 3 academic electives.

Accommodations or Services

Accommodations are decided upon an individual basis after a thorough review of appropriate, current documentation. The accommodations requests must be supported through the documentation provided and must be logically linked to the current impact of the condition on academic functioning.

Financial Aid

Students should submit: FAFSA. *Need-based scholarships/grants offered:* College/university scholarship or grant aid from institutional funds; Federal Pell; SEOG; State scholarships/grants. *Loan aid offered:* Direct PLUS loans; Direct Subsidized Stafford Loans; Direct Unsubsidized Stafford Loans. Federal Work-Study Program available. Institutional employment available.

Campus Life

Activities: Campus Ministries; Choral groups; Concert band; Dance; Drama/theater; International Student Organization; Literary magazine; Music ensembles; Radio station; Student government; Student newspaper. **Organizations:** 117 registered organizations, 8 honor societies, 5 religious organizations. **Athletics (Intercollegiate):** *Men:* baseball, basketball, golf, sailing, soccer, tennis. *Women:* basketball, golf, sailing, soccer, softball, tennis, volleyball.

ACCOMMODATIONS

Allowed in exams:	
Calculators	Yes
Dictionary	Yes
Computer	Yes
Spell-checker	Yes
Extended test time	Yes
Scribe	Yes
Proctors	Yes
Oral exams	Yes
Note-takers	Yes
Support services for students with:	
LD	Yes
ADHD	Yes
ASD	Yes
Distraction-reduced environment	Yes
Recording of lecture allowed	Yes
Reading technology	Yes
Audio books	Yes
Other assistive technology	Yes
Priority registration	Yes
Added costs of services:	
For LD	No
For ADHD	No
For ASD	No
LD specialists	No
ADHD & ASD coaching	No
ASD specialists	No
Professional tutors	No
Peer tutors	Yes
Max. hours/week for services	Varies
How professors are notified of student approved accommodations	Student

COLLEGE GRADUATION REQUIREMENTS

Course waivers allowed	No
Course substitutions allowed	No

Flagler College

74 King Street St., Augustine, FL 32085-1027 • Admissions: 904-819-6220 • Fax: 904-819-6466 **Support: S**

CAMPUS

Type of school	Private (nonprofit)
Environment	Village

STUDENTS

Undergrad enrollment	2,862
% male/female	32/68
% from out of state	59
% frosh live on campus	95

FINANCIAL FACTS

Annual tuition	$19,940
Room and board	$12,540
Required fees	$100

GENERAL ADMISSIONS INFO

Application fee	$50
Regular application deadline	3/1
Nonfall registration	Yes

Admission may be deferred.

Range SAT EBRW	530–630
Range SAT Math	500–580
Range ACT Composite	21–26

ACADEMICS

Student/faculty ratio	16:1
% students returning for sophomore year	72

Most classes have 10–19 students.

Programs/Services for Students with Learning Differences

The Disability Resource Center provides academic accommodations, support services, and assistive technology in coordination with Flagler College's mission of high-quality education in a caring and supportive environment. The vision of this unit is to aid in the development of self-advocating and competent students and to help students with disabilities through the provisions of academic accommodations, personalized learning strategies, and the prudent management of support services and assistive technology. The proper documentation qualifies students for any relevant accommodations under Section 504 of the Rehabilitation Act of 1973 and the Americans with Disabilities Act (ADA).

Admissions

Flagler College is test optional so ACT/SAT scores are not required. Applicants can use the Common Application or the Flagler College Application. The essay prompts are different in each of these applications. The average GPA is about 3.5. Flagler College allows applicants to self-report their grades and courses. Students requiring accommodations to complete the admission application procedures should contact the Office of Services for Students with Disabilities. However, no disclosure need be made unless accommodations are needed, although students can disclose a learning disability in the application if a student feels this would better describe a challenge. Students, upon admission to Flagler College, have the opportunity to declare a disability and to request academic accommodations.

Additional Information

The Disability Resource Center is available to provide learning strategies and time-management advice as well as reasonable modifications and academic adjustments if the student avails themselves of the service. Otherwise, the student is expected to be responsible to manage their own assignments. The Academic Success Lab helps students with effective test-taking skills, content reading, time management, speaking, and listening strategies. Help with critical thinking skills and memorization techniques are also available.

ADMISSIONS INFO FOR STUDENTS WITH LEARNING DIFFERENCES

Phone: 904 819-6460 • Email: ppownall@flagler.edu

SAT/ACT required: No
Interview required: No
Essay required: Yes
Additional application required: No
Documentation submitted to: Disability Resource Center

Special Ed. HS course work accepted: Yes
Separate application required for Programs/Services: No
Documentation required for:
LD: Psychoeducational evaluation
ADHD: Psychoeducational evaluation
ASD: Psychoeducational evaluation

Flagler College

General Admissions

Very important factors include: academic GPA, standardized test scores. *Important factors include:* rigor of secondary school record, application essay, recommendation(s), first generation, geographical residence. *Other factors include:* extracurricular activities, character/personal qualities, alumni/ae relation, volunteer work, work experience, level of applicant's interest. *Freshman admission requirements:* High school diploma is required and GED is accepted. *Academic units recommended:* 4 English, 4 math, 3 science, 1 science lab, 2 foreign language, 1 social studies, 3 history.

Accommodations or Services

Accommodations are decided upon an individual basis after a thorough review of appropriate, current documentation. The accommodations requests must be supported through the documentation provided and must be logically linked to the current impact of the condition on academic functioning.

Financial Aid

Students should submit: FAFSA; State aid form. *Need-based scholarships/grants offered:* College/university scholarship or grant aid from institutional funds; Federal Pell; Private scholarships; SEOG; State scholarships/grants. *Loan aid offered:* Direct PLUS loans; Direct Subsidized Stafford Loans; Direct Unsubsidized Stafford Loans. Federal Work-Study Program available. Institutional employment available.

Campus Life

Activities: Campus Ministries; Choral groups; Dance; Drama/theater; International Student Organization; Literary magazine; Model UN; Musical theater; Radio station; Student government; Student newspaper; Student-run film society. **Organizations:** 49 registered organizations, 13 honor societies, 7 religious organizations. **Athletics (Intercollegiate):** *Men:* baseball, basketball, cross-country, golf, soccer, tennis. *Women:* basketball, cross-country, golf, soccer, softball, tennis, volleyball.

ACCOMMODATIONS

Allowed in exams:	
Calculators	Yes
Dictionary	Yes
Computer	Yes
Spell-checker	Yes
Extended test time	Yes
Scribe	Yes
Proctors	Yes
Oral exams	Yes
Note-takers	Yes
Support services for students with:	
LD	Yes
ADHD	Yes
ASD	Yes
Distraction-reduced environment	Yes
Recording of lecture allowed	Yes
Reading technology	Yes
Audio books	Yes
Other assistive technology	Yes
Priority registration	Yes
Added costs of services:	
For LD	No
For ADHD	No
For ASD	No
LD specialists	No
ADHD & ASD coaching	Yes
ASD specialists	No
Professional tutors	No
Peer tutors	Yes
Max. hours/week for services	12
How professors are notified of student approved accommodations	Student

COLLEGE GRADUATION REQUIREMENTS

Course waivers allowed	No
Course substitutions allowed	Yes
In what courses: Case-by-case basis	

Florida

Florida A&M University

Room 204, Tallahassee, FL 32307-3200 • Admissions: 850-599-3796 • Fax: 850-599-3069 **Support: CS**

CAMPUS	
Type of school	Public
Environment	City
STUDENTS	
Undergrad enrollment	7,818
% male/female	35/65
% from out of state	15
FINANCIAL FACTS	
Annual in-state tuition	$5,645
Annual out-of-state tuition	$17,585
Room and board	$10,986
Required fees	$140
GENERAL ADMISSIONS INFO	
Application fee	$30
Regular application deadline	5/1
Nonfall registration	Yes
Range SAT EBRW	530–590
Range SAT Math	500–570
Range ACT Composite	19–23
ACADEMICS	
Student/faculty ratio	15:1
% students returning for sophomore year	80
Most classes have 20–29 students.	

Programs/Services for Students with Learning Differences

The Center for Disability Access and Resources (CeDAR) at Florida A&M University provides comprehensive services and accommodations to FAMU students with disabilities. As an advocate for students with disabilities, CeDAR collaborates with faculty, staff, and community partners to provide accommodations for the unique needs of students both in and out of the classroom. The mission is to provide enriching support programs, services, and reasonable accommodations. CeDAR hopes to foster a sense of empowerment in students with disabilities by educating them about their legal rights and responsibilities so that they can make informed choices, be critical thinkers, and self advocates. The goal is to ensure students with disabilities have access to the same programs, opportunities, and activities available to all FAMU students. The team works to celebrate and reward the unique backgrounds, viewpoints, skills, and talents of all CeDAR students.

Admissions

CeDAR helps applicants who do not meet standard admission criteria to be admitted to FAMU under alternate criteria when appropriate based on the applicant's disability. Students are reviewed under alternate criteria. In implementing this procedure, the CeDAR shall not compromise academic or admission standards in any way. Students requesting an alternate review must request this review in writing and provide documentation certifying the existence of a disability; and verifying functional limitations imposed. These applicants are forwarded to CeDAR by admissions and a review confirms that the applicant's disability necessitates using alternate criteria. CeDAR will make a recommendation to admissions.

Additional Information

The CeDAR offers a six-week summer transition program (CSSI; required attendance for some incoming students with a disability who request special admissions consideration) to students who will be graduating or have graduated from high school. This program provides students a chance to focus on remediation of skill deficits, technology, and researching their area of disability. There are no fees for services provided. Enrollment in the CeDAR ART Program comes with a recommendation for provisional admission to the university for the preceding summer term. Enrollees are required to attend and successfully complete the College Study Skills Institute (CSSI) held during the summer before a final recommendation for continued enrollment will be offered. The CeDAR ART Program is a two-year commitment to the institution as a stipulation for a student's continued enrollment at FAMU.

ADMISSIONS INFO FOR STUDENTS WITH LEARNING DIFFERENCES

Phone: 850-599-3180 • Fax: 850-561-2513 • Email: cedar@famu.edu

SAT/ACT required: Yes
Interview required: No
Essay required: Yes
Additional application required: No
Documentation submitted to: Center for Disability Access and Resources

Special Ed. HS course work accepted: Yes
Separate application required for Programs/Services: Yes
Documentation required for:
LD: Psychoeducational evaluation
ADHD: Psychoeducational evaluation
ASD: Psychoeducational evaluation

Florida A&M University

General Admissions

Very important factors include: rigor of secondary school record, academic GPA, application essay, standardized test scores, recommendation(s), first generation. *Important factors include:* extracurricular activities, talent/ability, character/personal qualities, state residency. *Other factors include:* alumni/ae relation, volunteer work, work experience. *Freshman admission requirements:* High school diploma is required and GED is accepted. *Academic units required:* 4 English, 4 math, 3 science, 2 science labs, 2 foreign language, 3 social studies, 2 academic electives.

Accommodations or Services

Accommodations are decided upon an individual basis after a thorough review of appropriate, current documentation. The accommodations requests must be supported through the documentation provided and must be logically linked to the current impact of the condition on academic functioning.

Financial Aid

Students should submit: FAFSA. Applicants will be notified of awards on a rolling basis beginning 3/1. *Need-based scholarships/grants offered:* College/university scholarship or grant aid from institutional funds; Federal Pell; Private scholarships; SEOG; State scholarships/grants; United Negro College Fund. *Loan aid offered:* Direct PLUS loans; Direct Subsidized Stafford Loans; Direct Unsubsidized Stafford Loans. Federal Work-Study Program available. Institutional employment available.

Campus Life

Activities: Campus Ministries; Choral groups; Concert band; Dance; Drama/theater; International Student Organization; Jazz band; Literary magazine; Marching band; Music ensembles; Musical theater; Pep band; Radio station; Student government; Student newspaper; Symphony orchestra; Television station; Yearbook. **Organizations:** 169 registered organizations, 9 honor societies, 5 religious organizations, 5 fraternities, 3 sororities. **Athletics (Intercollegiate):** *Men:* baseball, basketball, cheerleading, cross-country, football, golf, swimming, tennis, track/field (outdoor), track/field (indoor). *Women:* basketball, bowling, cheerleading, cross-country, golf, softball, swimming, tennis, track/field (outdoor), track/field (indoor), volleyball.

ACCOMMODATIONS

Allowed in exams:	
Calculators	Yes
Dictionary	Yes
Computer	Yes
Spell-checker	Yes
Extended test time	Yes
Scribe	Yes
Proctors	Yes
Oral exams	Yes
Note-takers	Yes
Support services for students with:	
LD	Yes
ADHD	Yes
ASD	Yes
Distraction-reduced environment	Yes
Recording of lecture allowed	Yes
Reading technology	Yes
Audio books	Yes
Other assistive technology	No
Priority registration	No
Added costs of services:	
For LD	No
For ADHD	No
For ASD	No
LD specialists	Yes
ADHD & ASD coaching	No
ASD specialists	No
Professional tutors	Yes
Peer tutors	Yes
Max. hours/week for services	Varies
How professors are notified of student approved accommodations	Student

COLLEGE GRADUATION REQUIREMENTS

Course waivers allowed	Yes
In what courses: Depending on the course and program of study	
Course substitutions allowed	Yes
In what courses: Depending on the course and program of study	

Florida Atlantic University

777 Glades Road, Boca Raton, FL 33431-0991 • Admissions: 561-297-3040 • Fax: 561-297-2758 **Support: CS**

CAMPUS

Type of school	Public
Environment	City

STUDENTS

Undergrad enrollment	24,842
% male/female	43/57
% from out of state	6
% frosh live on campus	58

FINANCIAL FACTS

Annual in-state tuition	$6,099
Annual out-of-state tuition	$21,655
Room and board	$12,030

GENERAL ADMISSIONS INFO

Application fee	$30
Regular application deadline	5/1
Nonfall registration	Yes

Admission may be deferred.

Range SAT EBRW	550–630
Range SAT Math	530–610
Range ACT Composite	22–26

ACADEMICS

Student/faculty ratio	21:1
% students returning for sophomore year	82

Most classes have 20–29 students.

Programs/Services for Students with Learning Differences

Student Accessibility Services (SAS) provides comprehensive academic support services including advocacy, academic accommodations, Assistive Technology equipment/software training, Assistive Technology Computer Lab, Learning Strategies training, and an active student organization. SAS has offices across three of FAU's campuses—Boca Raton, Davie, and Jupiter; however, accessibility services are available for students attending any of the six FAU campuses.

Admissions

FSU has minimum scores and GPA for automatic admission: 3.3 GPA and ACT of 22 or SAT equivalent. The mid 50% GPA is 3.8–4.5 and ACT 23–27 or SAT 1110–1240. No essay is required unless applying to the Honors College. Course required include 4 English, 4 math, 3 natural sciences, 3 social sciences, 2 foreign language and 2 electives. Some colleges require additional courses including an audition for music majors. There is no special application process for students with LD/ADHD/ASD.

Additional Information

The FAU Academy for Community Inclusion is a college program for high school graduates who have been diagnosed with intellectual and developmental disabilities. The program allows students to earn certificates in supported employment, supported community access, and supported community living. These certificates are offered in an inclusive college environment on the FAU Jupiter campus. The program allows students to participate in college activities, clubs, organizations, that are available to all FAU students.

ADMISSIONS INFO FOR STUDENTS WITH LEARNING DIFFERENCES

Phone: 561-297-3880 • Fax: 561-297-2184 • Email: glyew@health.fau.edu

SAT/ACT required: Yes
Interview required: No
Essay required: No
Additional application required: No
Documentation submitted to: Student Accessibility Services

Special Ed. HS course work accepted: Yes
Separate application required for Programs/Services: No
Documentation required for:
LD: Psychoeducational evaluation
ADHD: Psychoeducational or neuropsychoeducational evaluation
ASD: Psychoeducational evaluation

Florida Atlantic University

General Admissions

Very important factors include: academic GPA, standardized test scores. *Important factors include:* rigor of secondary school record, class rank. *Other factors include:* application essay, recommendation(s), extracurricular activities, talent/ability, character/personal qualities, first generation, alumni/ae relation, volunteer work, level of applicant's interest. *Freshman admission requirements:* High school diploma is required and GED is accepted. *Academic units required:* 4 English, 4 math, 3 science, 2 science labs, 2 foreign language, 3 social studies, 3 academic electives. *Academic units recommended:* 4 English, 4 math, 3 science, 2 science labs, 2 foreign language, 3 social studies, 3 academic electives.

Accommodations or Services

Accommodations are decided upon an individual basis after a thorough review of appropriate, current documentation. The accommodations requests must be supported through the documentation provided and must be logically linked to the current impact of the condition on academic functioning.

Financial Aid

Students should submit: FAFSA; Institution's own financial aid form. Applicants will be notified of awards on a rolling basis beginning 3/1. *Need-based scholarships/grants offered:* College/university scholarship or grant aid from institutional funds; Federal Nursing Scholarships; Federal Pell; Private scholarships; SEOG; State scholarships/grants. *Loan aid offered:* Direct PLUS loans; Direct Subsidized Stafford Loans; Direct Unsubsidized Stafford Loans. Federal Work-Study Program available. Institutional employment available.

Campus Life

Activities: Campus Ministries; Choral groups; Concert band; Dance; Drama/theater; International Student Organization; Jazz band; Literary magazine; Marching band; Model UN; Music ensembles; Musical theater; Opera; Pep band; Radio station; Student government; Student newspaper; Student-run film society; Symphony orchestra; Television station. **Organizations:** 300 registered organizations, 11 honor societies, 6 religious organizations, 16 fraternities, 12 sororities. **Athletics (Intercollegiate):** *Men:* baseball, basketball, cheerleading, cross-country, diving, football, golf, soccer, swimming, tennis. *Women:* basketball, cheerleading, cross-country, diving, golf, soccer, softball, swimming, tennis, track/field (outdoor), volleyball.

ACCOMMODATIONS

Allowed in exams:	
Calculators	Yes
Dictionary	Yes
Computer	Yes
Spell-checker	Yes
Extended test time	Yes
Scribe	Yes
Proctors	Yes
Oral exams	Yes
Note-takers	Yes
Support services for students with:	
LD	Yes
ADHD	Yes
ASD	Yes
Distraction-reduced environment	Yes
Recording of lecture allowed	Yes
Reading technology	Yes
Audio books	Yes
Other assistive technology	No
Priority registration	No
Added costs of services:	
For LD	No
For ADHD	No
For ASD	No
LD specialists	Yes
ADHD & ASD coaching	No
ASD specialists	No
Professional tutors	No
Peer tutors	Yes
Max. hours/week for services	Varies
How professors are notified of student approved accommodations	Student

COLLEGE GRADUATION REQUIREMENTS

Course waivers allowed	Yes
In what courses: Varies	
Course substitutions allowed	Yes
In what courses: Math and Foreign Language	

Florida

Florida State University

PO Box 3062400, Tallahassee, FL 32306-2400 • Admissions: 850-644-6200 • Fax: 850-644-0197 **Support: S**

CAMPUS

Type of school	Public
Environment	City

STUDENTS

Undergrad enrollment	32,649
% male/female	43/57
% from out of state	11
% frosh live on campus	76

FINANCIAL FACTS

Annual in-state tuition	$5,666
Annual out-of-state tuition	$18,796
Room and board	$11,088

GENERAL ADMISSIONS INFO

Application fee	$30
Regular application deadline	3/1
Nonfall registration	Yes
Range SAT EBRW	610–670
Range SAT Math	590–670
Range ACT Composite	26–30

ACADEMICS

Student/faculty ratio	21:1
% students returning for sophomore year	93

Most classes have 10–19 students.

Programs/Services for Students with Learning Differences

The Office of Accessibility Services (OAS) was established to serve as an advocate for Florida State students with disabilities and ensure that reasonable accommodations are provided. Florida State University is committed to providing a quality education to all qualified students and does not discriminate on the basis of race, creed, color, sex, religion, national origin, age, disability, genetic information, veterans' status, marital status, sexual orientation, gender identity, gender expression, or any other legally protected group status. Through the provision of academic accommodations, testing support, assistive technologies, coaching, and a space for students to feel part of the FSU community the OAS creates an environment of success.

Admissions

The academic profile of the middle 50 percent of first years has an ACT composite of 26–30 and 1200–1340 SAT. In addition to the academic profile, a variety of other factors are also considered in the review process. These include the written essay, the rigor and quality of courses and curriculum, grade trends, class rank, strength of senior schedule in academic subjects, math level in the senior year, and number of years in a sequential foreign language.

Additional Information

Students who choose to disclose their disability to receive accommodations must complete a Request for Services form provided by the OAS. For an LD, documentation must be current. Staff members assist students in exploring their needs and determining the necessary services and accommodations. Academic accommodations include alternate text formats, alternative testing location, extended time, reader and/or scribe, and in-class note-takers. Staff members meet individually with students with LD/ADHD. Services include teaching study skills, memory enhancement techniques, organizational skills, test-taking strategies, stress management techniques, ways to structure tutoring for best results, and skills for negotiating accommodations with instructors. The Student Disability Union (SDU) acts as a support group for students with disabilities.

ADMISSIONS INFO FOR STUDENTS WITH LEARNING DIFFERENCES

Phone: 850-644-9566 • Fax: 850-645-1852 • Email: oas@fsu.edu

SAT/ACT required: Yes
Interview required: No
Essay required: Yes
Additional application required: No
Documentation submitted to: Office of Accessibility Services

Special Ed. HS course work accepted: Yes
Separate application required for Programs/Services: No
Documentation required for:
LD: Psychoeducational evaluation
ADHD: Psychoeducational evaluation
ASD: Psychoeducational evaluation

Florida State University

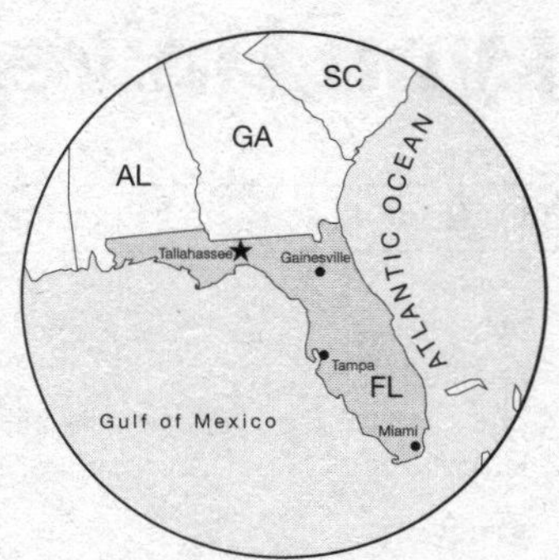

General Admissions

Very important factors include: rigor of secondary school record. *Important factors include:* academic GPA, standardized test scores, talent/ability, state residency. *Other factors include:* class rank, application essay, extracurricular activities, character/personal qualities, first generation, geographical residence, volunteer work, work experience. High school diploma is required and GED is accepted. *Academic units required:* 4 English, 4 math, 3 science, 2 science labs, 2 foreign language, 1 social studies, 2 history, 3 academic electives. *Academic units recommended:* 4 English, 4 math, 4 science, 2 science labs, 4 foreign language, 2 social studies, 2 history, 3 academic electives.

Accommodations or Services

Accommodations are decided upon an individual basis after a thorough review of appropriate, current documentation. The accommodations requests must be supported through the documentation provided and must be logically linked to the current impact of the condition on academic functioning.

Financial Aid

Students should submit: FAFSA; Institution's own financial aid form. Applicants will be notified of awards on a rolling basis beginning 2/15. *Need-based scholarships/grants offered:* College/university scholarship or grant aid from institutional funds; Federal Pell; Private scholarships; SEOG; State scholarships/grants; United Negro College Fund. *Loan aid offered:* Direct PLUS loans; Direct Subsidized Stafford Loans; Direct Unsubsidized Stafford Loans. Federal Work-Study Program available. Institutional employment available.

Campus Life

Activities: Campus Ministries; Choral groups; Concert band; Dance; Drama/theater; International Student Organization; Jazz band; Literary magazine; Marching band; Model UN; Music ensembles; Musical theater; Opera; Pep band; Radio station; Student government; Student newspaper; Student-run film society; Symphony orchestra; Television station; Yearbook. **Organizations:** 763 registered organizations, 63 honor societies, 56 religious organizations, 23 fraternities, 24 sororities. **Athletics (Intercollegiate):** *Men:* baseball, basketball, cheerleading, cross-country, diving, football, golf, swimming, tennis, track/field (outdoor), track/field (indoor). *Women:* basketball, cheerleading, cross-country, diving, golf, soccer, softball, swimming, tennis, track/field (outdoor), track/field (indoor), volleyball.

ACCOMMODATIONS

Allowed in exams:	
Calculators	Yes
Dictionary	Yes
Computer	Yes
Spell-checker	Yes
Extended test time	Yes
Scribe	Yes
Proctors	Yes
Oral exams	Yes
Note-takers	Yes
Support services for students with:	
LD	Yes
ADHD	Yes
ASD	Yes
Distraction-reduced environment	Yes
Recording of lecture allowed	Yes
Reading technology	Yes
Audio books	Yes
Other assistive technology	Yes
Priority registration	Yes
Added costs of services:	
For LD	No
For ADHD	No
For ASD	No
LD specialists	No
ADHD & ASD coaching	No
ASD specialists	Yes
Professional tutors	No
Peer tutors	Yes
Max. hours/week for services	Varies
How professors are notified of student approved accommodations	Student

COLLEGE GRADUATION REQUIREMENTS

Course waivers allowed	No
Course substitutions allowed	Yes

In what courses: Case-by-case basis

Lynn University

3601 North Military Trail, Boca Raton, FL 33431-5598 • Admissions: 561-237-7900 • Fax: 561-237-7100 **Support: SP**

CAMPUS	
Type of school	Private (nonprofit)
Environment	City
STUDENTS	
Undergrad enrollment	2,401
% male/female	50/50
% from out of state	45
% frosh live on campus	81
FINANCIAL FACTS	
Annual tuition	$37,600
Room and board	$12,470
Required fees	$2,250
GENERAL ADMISSIONS INFO	
Application fee	No
Regular application deadline	8/1
Nonfall registration	Yes
Admission may be deferred.	
Range SAT EBRW	462–516
Range SAT Math	428–494
Range ACT Composite	19–21
ACADEMICS	
Student/faculty ratio	18:1
% students returning for sophomore year	71
Most classes have 20–29 students.	

Programs/Services for Students with Learning Differences

The goal at Lynn University is to empower independent learners. Our academic support program, IAL (Institute for Achievement and Learning) provides cohesive academic support primarily to students with learning disabilities. Students with ADHD, ASD, and mental health diagnoses find participation in this fee-based program useful as well. Standard documentation is required for students requesting ADA accommodations.

Admissions

Student diagnoses are not part of our Admissions process. Students interact with ADA or IAL after acceptance into the university. Students should submit the general application to Lynn University. Admissions criteria are dependent on the level of services required. Students who are not applying to the Institute for Achievement and Learning should be able to demonstrate that they have taken rigorous high school courses. Some students may be admitted provisionally after submitting official information. Typically, these students have an ACT of 18 or lower or an SAT of 850 or lower and 2.5 GPA, although Lynn is test optional.

Additional Information

Features of the IAL (Institute for Achievement and Learning) program include: individual and group tutoring; study strategy sessions to enhance study and organizational skills; test anxiety sessions; faculty progress reports; extended time exams and alternative testing procedures; academic coaching and schedule planning; selected core courses offered through IAL trained faculty who teach students in a multimodality style in order to meet students' individual needs; communicative intervention with faculty and thematic instruction. The program uses a diagnostic coaching model to address behavioral issues such as organization skills, prioritizing of assignments and daily activities, strategies for procrastination, time management skills, coping with impulsivity, strategies to aid with focus and attention in and out of the classroom and study skills. Students should apply to Lynn University through the admission department. When filling out their application, if they are seeking additional support services, they should check the box stating they "would like to be considered for additional academic support."

ADMISSIONS INFO FOR STUDENTS WITH LEARNING DIFFERENCES

Phone: (561) 237-7000 • Fax: (561) 237-7107 • Email: admission@lynn.edu

SAT/ACT required: No
Interview required: No
Essay required: Yes
Additional application required: No
Documentation submitted to: Institute for Achievement and Learning

Special Ed. HS course work accepted: Yes
Separate application required for Programs/Services: No
Documentation required for:
LD: Psychoeducational evaluation
ADHD: Neuropsychological testing or psychological educational testing
ASD: Neuropsychological testing or psychological educational evaluation

Lynn University

General Admissions

Very important factors include: rigor of secondary school record, academic GPA, application essay. *Important factors include:* class rank, standardized test scores, recommendation(s), interview, extracurricular activities, character/personal qualities, volunteer work, work experience. *Other factors include:* level of applicant's interest. High school diploma is required and GED is accepted. *Academic units recommended:* 4 English, 4 math, 4 science, 2 social studies, 2 history.

Accommodations or Services

Accommodations are decided upon an individual basis after a thorough review of appropriate, current documentation. The accommodations requests must be supported through the documentation provided and must be logically linked to the current impact of the condition on academic functioning.

Financial Aid

Students should submit: FAFSA. *Need-based scholarships/grants offered:* College/university scholarship or grant aid from institutional funds; Federal Pell; Private scholarships; SEOG; State scholarships/grants. *Loan aid offered:* Direct PLUS loans; Direct Subsidized Stafford Loans; Direct Unsubsidized Stafford Loans. Federal Work-Study Program available. Institutional employment available.

Campus Life

Activities: Campus Ministries; Dance; Drama/theater; International Student Organization; Literary magazine; Model UN; Music ensembles; Musical theater; Radio station; Student government; Student newspaper; Student-run film society; Symphony orchestra; Television station. **Organizations:** 33 registered organizations, 2 honor societies, 3 religious organizations, 3 fraternities, 2 sororities. **Athletics (Intercollegiate):** *Men:* baseball, basketball, golf, soccer, tennis. *Women:* basketball, golf, soccer, softball, tennis, volleyball.

ACCOMMODATIONS

Allowed in exams:	
Calculators	Yes
Dictionary	No
Computer	Yes
Spell-checker	Yes
Extended test time	Yes
Scribe	Yes
Proctors	Yes
Oral exams	No
Note-takers	Yes
Support services for students with:	
LD	Yes
ADHD	Yes
ASD	Yes
Distraction-reduced environment	Yes
Recording of lecture allowed	Yes
Reading technology	Yes
Audio books	Yes
Other assistive technology	Yes
Priority registration	No
Added costs of services:	
For LD	Yes
For ADHD	Yes
For ASD	Yes
LD specialists	Yes
ADHD & ASD coaching	Yes
ASD specialists	Yes
Professional tutors	Yes
Peer tutors	No
Max. hours/week for services	45
How professors are notified of student approved accommodations	Student

COLLEGE GRADUATION REQUIREMENTS

Course waivers allowed	No
Course substitutions allowed	No

New College of Florida

5800 Bay Shore Road, Sarasota, FL 34243-2109 • Admissions: 941-487-5000 • Fax: 941-487-5001 **Support: S**

CAMPUS

Type of school	Public
Environment	Town

STUDENTS

Undergrad enrollment	702
% male/female	37/63
% from out of state	17
% frosh live on campus	93

FINANCIAL FACTS

Annual in-state tuition	$6,916
Annual out-of-state tuition	$29,944
Room and board	$9,529

GENERAL ADMISSIONS INFO

Application fee	$30
Regular application deadline	4/15
Nonfall registration	No

Admission may be deferred.

Range SAT EBRW	620–700
Range SAT Math	560–660
Range ACT Composite	25–31

ACADEMICS

Student/faculty ratio	7:1
% students returning for sophomore year	86

Most classes have 10–19 students.

Programs/Services for Students with Learning Differences

Currently registered New College students can apply for disability services through the Office of Student Affairs. It is the mission of Student Disability Services (SDS) to create and maintain an environment on the New College campus that recognizes and supports students with disabilities by assuring them equal access to all educational opportunities. SDS offers a range of services to students including reasonable accommodations, referrals to campus and community services, advocacy, and auxiliary aids. These services are designed to support the students' participation in all programs and activities offered at New College. Services are individually designed and based on the specific needs of each student as identified and documented by SDS. In order to be eligible for disability related services, students are required to register and provide documentation of their disability through the SDS. If special accommodations are necessary, the student will be assisted in the development and implementation of the plan. The process is intended to coordinate efforts with faculty members and college staff while maintaining privacy for the student.

Admissions

The College will grant reasonable substitution or modification of any admission requirement based on evidence submitted by the applicant and through consultation with the College's Disabilities Services Coordinator, that the failure of the applicant to meet the requirement is due to his or her disability, and does not constitute a fundamental alteration in the nature of the College's academic program. ACT/SAT can be self-reported. Factors used in admission are: level of difficulty of course work, grades, essay, SAT or ACT scores, letter of recommendation, and activities. Accepted students generally have a mid-50% weighted GPA 3.71-4.31, SAT 1200–1360 or ACT 25–30. Course requirements include: 4 English, 4 math, 3 science, 3 social science, 2 foreign language, and 2 additional academic electives.

Additional Information

Testing Accommodations include extended time for exams (1.5 to 2x normal time allowed); alternate location/decreased distraction for exams; ability to request alternate exam date or time; use of computer for exams; and a reader for exam. Classroom accommodations could include: notetaking services; enlarged course material; permission to record lectures; computer in class to take notes; assistive listening devices; speech-to-text service; and textbooks in alternate format. Student Success Coaches are trained peer

ADMISSIONS INFO FOR STUDENTS WITH LEARNING DIFFERENCES

Phone: 941-487-4496 • Fax: 941-487-4517 • Email: disabilityservices@ncf.edu

SAT/ACT required: Yes
Interview required: No
Essay required: No
Additional application required: No
Documentation submitted to: Student Disability Services

Special Ed. HS course work accepted: Yes
Separate application required for Programs/Services: No
Documentation required for:
LD: Psychoeducational evaluation
ADHD: Psychoeducational evaluation
ASD: Psychoeducational evaluation

New College of Florida

coaches who meet with students one-on-one or in group study sessions. Coaches work with students on a variety of topics including faculty relationships, focus management, goal setting, learning style, note-taking, organization, prioritization, project management, reading comprehension, student skills, stress management, test taking, and time management.

General Admissions

Very important factors include: rigor of secondary school record, academic GPA, application essay. *Important factors include:* class rank, standardized test scores, recommendation(s), extracurricular activities, character/personal qualities. *Other factors include:* talent/ability, first generation, alumni/ae relation, geographical residence, state residency. High school diploma is required and GED is accepted. *Academic units required:* 4 English, 4 math, 3 science, 2 science labs, 2 foreign language, 3 social studies, 2 academic electives. *Academic units recommended:* 4 English, 4 math, 4 science, 2 science labs, 4 foreign language, 4 social studies, 4 academic electives.

Accommodations or Services

Accommodations are decided upon an individual basis after a thorough review of appropriate, current documentation. The accommodations requests must be supported through the documentation provided and must be logically linked to the current impact of the condition on academic functioning.

Financial Aid

Students should submit: FAFSA. *Need-based scholarships/grants offered:* College/university scholarship or grant aid from institutional funds; Federal Pell; Private scholarships; SEOG; State scholarships/grants. *Loan aid offered:* Direct PLUS loans; Direct Subsidized Stafford Loans; Direct Unsubsidized Stafford Loans. Federal Work-Study Program available. Institutional employment available.

Campus Life

Activities: Campus Ministries; Choral groups; Dance; Drama/theater; International Student Organization; Jazz band; Literary magazine; Music ensembles; Musical theater; Radio station; Student government; Student newspaper; Student-run film society. **Organizations:** 53 registered organizations, 1 honor society, 3 religious organizations. **Athletics (Intercollegiate):** *Men:* sailing. *Women:* sailing.

ACCOMMODATIONS

Allowed in exams:	
Calculators	Yes
Dictionary	Yes
Computer	Yes
Spell-checker	Yes
Extended test time	Yes
Scribe	Yes
Proctors	Yes
Oral exams	Yes
Note-takers	Yes
Support services for students with:	
LD	Yes
ADHD	Yes
ASD	Yes
Distraction-reduced environment	Yes
Recording of lecture allowed	Yes
Reading technology	Yes
Audio books	Yes
Other assistive technology	Yes
Priority registration	Yes
Added costs of services:	
For LD	No
For ADHD	No
For ASD	No
LD specialists	No
ADHD & ASD coaching	Yes
ASD specialists	No
Professional tutors	No
Peer tutors	Yes Coaches
Max. hours/week for services	Varies
How professors are notified of student approved accommodations	Both

COLLEGE GRADUATION REQUIREMENTS

Course waivers allowed	No
Course substitutions allowed	No

Stetson University

421 N. Woodland Blvd., DeLand, FL 32723 • Admissions: 386-822-7100 • Fax: 386-822-7112 **Support: S**

CAMPUS

Type of school	Private (nonprofit)
Environment	Town

STUDENTS

Undergrad enrollment	3,135
% male/female	43/57
% from out of state	25
% frosh live on campus	83

FINANCIAL FACTS

Annual tuition	$49,140
Room and board	$14,640
Required fees	$360

GENERAL ADMISSIONS INFO

Application fee	$50
Regular application deadline	3/1
Nonfall registration	Yes

Admission may be deferred.

Range SAT EBRW	570–660
Range SAT Math	540–640
Range ACT Composite	22–29

ACADEMICS

Student/faculty ratio	13:1
% students returning for sophomore year	77

Most classes have 10–19 students.

Programs/Services for Students with Learning Differences

Academic Success works to ensure equal access to the learning opportunities offered at Stetson University for all students. This is accomplished through reasonable accommodations for the classroom, as well as education for the campus community around principles of universal design and inclusion. For students interested in establishing accommodations, there are two pieces of documentation needed. The first is an Accommodations Profile where a student can share their prior academic experience, including strengths as a student and the barriers encountered in the learning environment. The second is supporting documentation.

Admissions

All students go through the standard admissions process. Average GPA is 3.8. ACT/SAT is optional. Courses required include: English 4 years, mathematics 3 years, science 3 years, foreign language 2 years, social studies 2 years.

Additional Information

There is a three-step process to establish accommodations. Students complete an Accommodations Profile that provides students with a chance to share their personal academic experience including strengths as a student, barriers encountered in the learning environment, and previous accommodations. Students provide supporting documentation and each student meets with a staff member to discuss and establish appropriate accommodations for their time at Stetson University. In addition to ensuring access for students, Academic Success also offers a number of resources focused on supporting a student's success. We offer tutoring in a number of courses across disciplines to help student's develop the content knowledge to be successful in their courses. We also offer success coaching to enhance overall academic skills including time management, note taking, active reading, test preparation, and test taking strategies.

ADMISSIONS INFO FOR STUDENTS WITH LEARNING DIFFERENCES

Phone: 386-822-7127 • Fax: 386-822-7322 • Email: asc@stetson.edu

SAT/ACT required: No
Interview required: No
Essay required: Recommended
Additional application required: No
Documentation submitted to: Academic Success

Special Ed. HS course work accepted: Yes
Separate application required for Programs/Services: No
Documentation required for:
LD: Psychoeducational evaluation
ADHD: Psychoeducational evaluation
ASD: Psychoeducational evaluation

Stetson University

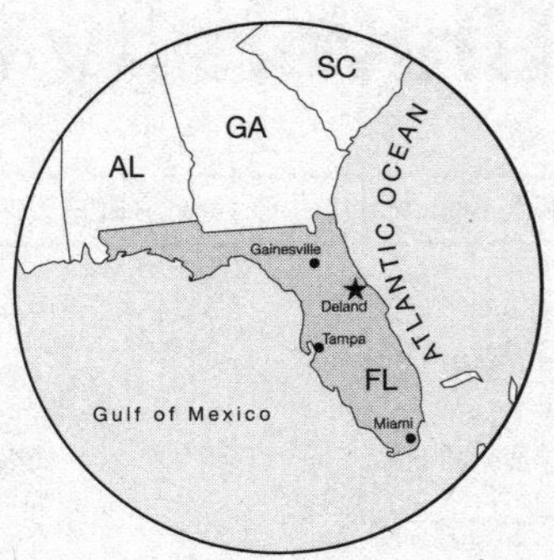

General Admissions

Very important factors include: rigor of secondary school record, academic GPA. *Important factors include:* class rank, application essay, standardized test scores, recommendation(s), interview, extracurricular activities, talent/ability, character/personal qualities. *Other factors include:* alumni/ae relation, geographical residence, state residency, racial/ethnic status. High school diploma is required and GED is accepted. *Academic units required:* 4 English, 3 math, 3 science, 2 foreign language, 2 social studies.

Accommodations or Services

Accommodations are decided upon an individual basis after a thorough review of appropriate, current documentation. The accommodations requests must be supported through the documentation provided and must be logically linked to the current impact of the condition on academic functioning.

Financial Aid

Students should submit: FAFSA. *Need-based scholarships/grants offered:* College/university scholarship or grant aid from institutional funds; Federal Pell; Private scholarships; SEOG; State scholarships/grants. *Loan aid offered:* Direct PLUS loans; Direct Subsidized Stafford Loans; Direct Unsubsidized Stafford Loans. Federal Work-Study Program available. Institutional employment available.

Campus Life

Activities: Campus Ministries; Choral groups; Concert band; Dance; Drama/theater; International Student Organization; Jazz band; Literary magazine; Marching band; Music ensembles; Musical theater; Opera; Pep band; Radio station; Student government; Student newspaper; Student-run film society; Symphony orchestra. **Organizations:** 114 registered organizations, 17 honor societies, 11 religious organizations, 9 fraternities, 6 sororities. **Athletics (Intercollegiate):** *Men:* baseball, basketball, crew/rowing, cross-country, golf, soccer, tennis. *Women:* basketball, crew/rowing, cross-country, golf, soccer, softball, tennis, volleyball.

ACCOMMODATIONS

Allowed in exams:	
Calculators	Yes
Dictionary	Yes
Computer	Yes
Spell-checker	Yes
Extended test time	Yes
Scribe	Yes
Proctors	Yes
Oral exams	No
Note-takers	Yes
Support services for students with:	
LD	Yes
ADHD	Yes
ASD	Yes
Distraction-reduced environment	Yes
Recording of lecture allowed	Yes
Reading technology	Yes
Audio books	Yes
Other assistive technology	Yes
Priority registration	Yes
Added costs of services:	
For LD	No
For ADHD	No
For ASD	No
LD specialists	No
ADHD & ASD coaching	Yes
ASD specialists	No
Professional tutors	No
Peer tutors	Yes
Max. hours/week for services	Varies
How professors are notified of student approved accommodations	Director

COLLEGE GRADUATION REQUIREMENTS

Course waivers allowed	No
Course substitutions allowed	Yes
In what courses: Case by case basis	

University of Central Florida

P.O. Box 160111, Orlando, FL 32816-0111 • Admissions: 407-823-3000 • Fax: 407-823-5625 **Support: CS**

CAMPUS

Type of school	Public
Environment	City

STUDENTS

Undergrad enrollment	58,998
% male/female	45/55
% from out of state	7
% frosh live on campus	71

FINANCIAL FACTS

Annual in-state tuition	$5,954
Annual out-of-state tuition	$20,980
Room and board	$10,300

GENERAL ADMISSIONS INFO

Application fee	$30
Regular application deadline	May 1
Nonfall registration	Yes
Range SAT EBRW	590–670
Range SAT Math	580–670
Range ACT Composite	25–30

ACADEMICS

Student/faculty ratio	30:1
% students returning for sophomore year	92

Most classes have 20–29 students.

Programs/Services for Students with Learning Differences

Students can access Learning Skills Specialists through the Student Academic Resource Center (SARC). Consultation services are one-on-one and provided free of charge. Students have the opportunity to meet with a specialist to assess study skills, understand learning styles, and learn new strategies for effective learning at the college level. Student Accessibility Services provides information and individualized services consistent with the student's documented disability. To be eligible for disability-related services, individuals must have a documented disability as defined by applicable federal and state laws. Individuals seeking services are required to provide recent documentation from an appropriate health-care provider or professional. Separate from Student Accessibility Services is the Center for Autism and Related Disabilities (CARD) at University of Central Florida. CARD provides individualized, direct consultative assistance to individuals with ASD in Central Florida and their families, and support and social groups for teens and adults with ASD.

Admissions

Admission to the University of Central is the same for all students, including standardized test scores, academic GPA and core academic units. Students with disabilities who have not taken a foreign language in high school must submit, along with appropriate documentation, a letter from a school official verifying that not taking a foreign language was an accommodation for the disability. If a student needs special admission consideration based on a disability, the student should send the requested appropriate documentation to the Undergraduate Admissions Office. Satisfying minimum requirements does not guarantee admission to UCF since preference will be given to those students whose credentials indicate the greatest promise of academic success.

Additional Information

The Student Accessibility Services provides information and individualized services consistent with the student's documented disability. The Student Accessibility Service program provides high-quality academic support programs, including tutoring and supplemental instruction, retention programs, academic advising programs, and various other academic programs and services. The Math Lab provides tutoring for students enrolled in mathematics courses. The University Writing Center (UWC) provides free writing support to all undergraduates and graduates at the University of Central Florida.

ADMISSIONS INFO FOR STUDENTS WITH LEARNING DIFFERENCES

Phone: 407-823-2371 • Fax: 407-823-2372 • Email: sas@ucf.edu

SAT/ACT required: Yes
Interview required: Yes
Essay required: Yes
Additional application required: No
Documentation submitted to: Student Accessibility Services

Special Ed. HS course work accepted: Yes
Separate application required for Programs/Services: No
Documentation required for:
LD: Psychoeducational evaluation
ADHD: Psychoeducational evaluation
ASD: Psychoeducational evaluation

University of Central Florida

General Admissions

Very important factors include: rigor of secondary school record, academic GPA, standardized test scores. *Important factors include:* application essay, *Other factors include:* class rank, extracurricular activities, talent/ability, character/personal qualities, first generation, alumni/ae relation, geographical residence, state residency, volunteer work, work experience, level of applicant's interest. High school diploma is required and GED is accepted. *Academic units required:* 4 English, 4 math, 3 science, 2 science labs, 2 foreign language, 3 social studies, 2 academic electives.

Accommodations or Services

Accommodations are decided upon an individual basis after a thorough review of appropriate, current documentation. The accommodations requests must be supported through the documentation provided and must be logically linked to the current impact of the condition on academic functioning.

Financial Aid

Students should submit: FAFSA. Applicants will be notified of awards on a rolling basis beginning 4/1. *Need-based scholarships/grants offered:* College/university scholarship or grant aid from institutional funds; Federal Pell; Private scholarships; SEOG; State scholarships/grants. *Loan aid offered:* Direct PLUS loans; Direct Subsidized Stafford Loans; Direct Unsubsidized Stafford Loans. Federal Work-Study Program available. Institutional employment available.

Campus Life

Activities: Campus Ministries; Choral groups; Concert band; Dance; Drama/theater; International Student Organization; Jazz band; Literary magazine; Marching band; Model UN; Music ensembles; Musical theater; Pep band; Radio station; Student government; Student-run film society; Symphony orchestra; Television station. **Organizations:** 612 registered organizations, 34 honor societies, 45 religious organizations, 21 fraternities, 20 sororities. **Athletics (Intercollegiate):** *Men:* baseball, basketball, cheerleading, cross-country, football, golf, soccer, tennis. *Women:* basketball, cheerleading, crew/rowing, cross-country, golf, soccer, softball, tennis, track/field (outdoor), track/field (indoor), volleyball.

ACCOMMODATIONS

Allowed in exams:	
Calculators	Yes
Dictionary	Yes
Computer	Yes
Spell-checker	Yes
Extended test time	Yes
Scribe	Yes
Proctors	Yes
Oral exams	No
Note-takers	Yes
Support services for students with:	
LD	Yes
ADHD	Yes
ASD	Yes
Distraction-reduced environment	Yes
Recording of lecture allowed	Yes
Reading technology	Yes
Audio books	Yes
Other assistive technology	Yes
Priority registration	Yes
Added costs of services: No	
For LD	No
For ADHD	No
For ASD	No
LD specialists	Yes
ADHD & ASD coaching	Yes
ASD specialists	No
Professional tutors	Yes
Peer tutors	Yes
Max. hours/week for services	Varies
How professors are notified of student approved accommodations	Director

COLLEGE GRADUATION REQUIREMENTS

Course waivers allowed	No
Course substitutions allowed	Yes
In what courses: Case-by-case basis	

University of Florida

201 Criser Hall, Gainesville, FL 32611-4000 • Admissions: 352-392-1365 • Fax: 352-392-2115 **Support: CS**

CAMPUS

Type of school	Public
Environment	City

STUDENTS

Undergrad enrollment	34,523
% male/female	44/56
% from out of state	8
% frosh live on campus	83

FINANCIAL FACTS

Annual in-state tuition	$6,381
Annual out-of-state tuition	$28,658
Room and board	$10,220

GENERAL ADMISSIONS INFO

Application fee	$30
Regular application deadline	3/1
Range SAT EBRW	650–720
Range SAT Math	660–750
Range ACT Composite	28–33

ACADEMICS

Student/faculty ratio	17:1
% students returning for sophomore year	97

Programs/Services for Students with Learning Differences

The Disability Resource Center (DRC) celebrates disability identity as a valued aspect of diversity. We champion a universally accessible community that supports the holistic advancement of individuals with disabilities.

Admissions

Applicants with learning disabilities apply to the University under the same guidelines as all other students. However, applicants with any disability can request special consideration because of disability. Few students are admitted purely on academic merit. While the potential for academic success is a primary consideration, UF's comprehensive holistic application review also considers personal essays, academic awards, extracurricular activities, family background and home community. All information in the applicant's file, academic and nonacademic, is considered in relation to the size and strength of the applicant pool. Mid 50% have a 4.4–4.6 weighted GPA and 30–33 ACT or 1320–1460 SAT. Pathway to Campus Enrollment (PaCE) provides the opportunity for the university to enroll more freshmen. It combines online and residential learning, and is an official form of enrollment. These students will start their degree online and then transition to campus to complete studies.

Additional Information

The Dean of Students Office sponsors "Preview," a mandatory registration and orientation program. The DRC offers First Year Florida–Disability Resource Center Edition, for first year Gators with disabilities to learn about resources on campus for health and well-being, social and emotional engagement, and academic success. The DRC offers several student groups that are open for all DRC students. Groups are held on a weekly, biweekly, or monthly basis, depending on the group.

ADMISSIONS INFO FOR STUDENTS WITH LEARNING DIFFERENCES

Phone: 352-392-8565 • Fax: 352-392-8570 • Email: GerardoA@ufsa.ufl.edu

SAT/ACT required: Yes
Interview required: No
Essay required: Yes
Additional application required: Yes
Documentation submitted to: DRC

Special Ed. HS course work accepted: Yes
Separate application required for Programs/Services: Yes
Documentation required for:
LD: Psychoeducational evaluation
ADHD: Psychoeducational evaluation
ASD: Psychoeducational evaluation

University of Florida

General Admissions

Very important factors include: rigor of secondary school record, academic GPA, application essay, extracurricular activities, talent/ability, character/personal qualities, volunteer work. *Important factors include:* standardized test scores, first generation. *Other factors include:* class rank, geographical residence, state residency, level of applicant's interest. High school diploma is required and GED is accepted. *Academic units required:* 4 English, 4 math, 3 science, 2 science labs, 2 foreign language, 3 social studies.

Accommodations or Services

Accommodations are decided upon an individual basis after a thorough review of appropriate, current documentation. The accommodations requests must be supported through the documentation provided and must be logically linked to the current impact of the condition on academic functioning.

Financial Aid

Students should submit: FAFSA. Applicants will be notified of awards on a rolling basis beginning 2/15. *Need-based scholarships/grants offered:* College/university scholarship or grant aid from institutional funds; Federal Pell; Private scholarships; SEOG; State scholarships/grants; United Negro College Fund. *Loan aid offered:* Direct PLUS loans; Direct Subsidized Stafford Loans; Direct Unsubsidized Stafford Loans. Federal Work-Study Program available. Institutional employment available.

Campus Life

Activities: Campus Ministries; Choral groups; Concert band; Dance; Drama/theater; International Student Organization; Jazz band; Literary magazine; Marching band; Model UN; Music ensembles; Musical theater; Opera; Pep band; Radio station; Student government; Student newspaper; Student-run film society; Symphony orchestra; Television station; Yearbook. **Organizations:** 925 registered organizations, 25 honor societies, 46 religious organizations, 36 fraternities, 28 sororities. **Athletics (Intercollegiate):** *Men:* baseball, basketball, cross-country, diving, football, golf, swimming, tennis, track/field (outdoor), track/field (indoor). *Women:* basketball, cross-country, diving, golf, gymnastics, lacrosse, soccer, softball, swimming, tennis, track/field (outdoor), track/field (indoor), volleyball.

ACCOMMODATIONS

Allowed in exams:	
Calculators	Yes
Dictionary	Yes
Computer	Yes
Spell-checker	Yes
Extended test time	Yes
Scribe	Yes
Proctors	Yes
Oral exams	Yes
Note-takers	Yes
Support services for students with:	
LD	Yes
ADHD	Yes
ASD	Yes
Distraction-reduced environment	Yes
Recording of lecture allowed	Yes
Reading technology	Yes
Audio books	Yes
Other assistive technology	Yes
Priority registration	Yes
Added costs of services:	
For LD	No
For ADHD	No
For ASD	No
LD specialists	Yes
ADHD & ASD coaching	Yes
ASD specialists	No
Professional tutors	No
Peer tutors	Yes
Max. hours/week for services	Varies
How professors are notified of student approved accommodations	Student

COLLEGE GRADUATION REQUIREMENTS

Course waivers allowed	No
Course substitutions allowed	Yes
In what courses: Math and Foreign Language	

University of Tampa

401 West Kennedy Boulevard, Tampa, FL 33606-1490 • Admissions: 813-253-6211 • Fax: 813-258-7398 **Support: S**

CAMPUS

Type of school	Private (nonprofit)
Environment	Metropolis

STUDENTS

Undergrad enrollment	8,685
% male/female	42/58
% from out of state	69
% frosh live on campus	95

FINANCIAL FACTS

Annual tuition	$28,802
Room and board	$11,526
Required fees	$2,082

GENERAL ADMISSIONS INFO

Application fee	$40
Regular application deadline	3/1
Nonfall registration	Yes

Admission may be deferred.

Range SAT EBRW	550–630
Range SAT Math	550–620
Range ACT Composite	23–28

ACADEMICS

Student/faculty ratio	17:1
% students returning for sophomore year	78

Most classes have 20–29 students.

Programs/Services for Students with Learning Differences

The University of Tampa supports the efforts and welfare of all of its students including the provision of reasonable accommodations to eligible students. Academic Excellence Programs and Student Disability Services are committed to the principles and practices of universal design and provide student with disabilities needed accommodations to equalize their access to the educational experience.

Admissions

All applicants must meet the same general admission requirements. There is no special application process for students with learning disabilities. The university is test optional for 2021 and spring 2022 and will review this policy in the future. Some majors (such as athletic training, education, nursing, music, performing arts and theater) require an additional application, portfolio, or audition.

Additional Information

The Academic Success Center provides students with the tools they need to succeed academically through the following programs: Academic Coaching, Academic Skills Course, Academic Excellence Program, Academic Tutoring, Students Overcoming Academic Roadblocks (SOAR), Strengths-Based Education Program, and the Saunders Writing Center. Academic Coaching has two types of options: drop-in sessions for immediate assistance and structure-coaching sessions that are designed for students to meet with an academic coach four times a semester.

ADMISSIONS INFO FOR STUDENTS WITH LEARNING DIFFERENCES

Phone: 813-257-3266 • Email: disability.services@ut.edu

SAT/ACT required: Yes (Test optional through 2022)
Interview required: No
Essay required: Yes
Additional application required: No
Documentation submitted to: Student Disability Services

Special Ed. HS course work accepted: Yes
Separate application required for Programs/Services: No
Documentation required for:
LD: Psychoeducational evaluation
ADHD: Psychoeducational evaluation
ASD: Psychoeducational evaluation

University of Tampa

General Admissions

Very important factors include: rigor of secondary school record, academic GPA, standardized test scores. *Important factors include:* application essay, recommendation(s), talent/ability. *Other factors include:* class rank, interview, extracurricular activities, character/personal qualities, first generation, alumni/ae relation, volunteer work, work experience, level of applicant's interest. High school diploma is required and GED is accepted. *Academic units required:* 4 English, 3 math, 3 science, 2 science labs, 2 foreign language, 3 social studies, 3 academic electives.

Accommodations or Services

Accommodations are decided upon an individual basis after a thorough review of appropriate, current documentation. The accommodations requests must be supported through the documentation provided and must be logically linked to the current impact of the condition on academic functioning.

Financial Aid

Students should submit: FAFSA. Applicants will be notified of awards on a rolling basis beginning 3/15. *Need-based scholarships/grants offered:* College/university scholarship or grant aid from institutional funds; Federal Nursing Scholarships; Federal Pell; Private scholarships; SEOG; State scholarships/grants. *Loan aid offered:* Direct PLUS loans; Direct Subsidized Stafford Loans; Direct Unsubsidized Stafford Loans. Federal Work-Study Program available. Institutional employment available.

Campus Life

Activities: Campus Ministries; Choral groups; Concert band; Dance; Drama/theater; International Student Organization; Jazz band; Literary magazine; Model UN; Music ensembles; Musical theater; Pep band; Radio station; Student government; Student newspaper; Student-run film society; Symphony orchestra; Television station; Yearbook. **Organizations:** 267 registered organizations, 15 honor societies, 7 religious organizations, 15 fraternities, 12 sororities. **Athletics (Intercollegiate):** *Men:* baseball, basketball, cross-country, golf, soccer, swimming. *Women:* basketball, crew/rowing, cross-country, soccer, softball, swimming, tennis, volleyball.

ACCOMMODATIONS

Allowed in exams:	
Calculators	Yes
Dictionary	Yes
Computer	Yes
Spell-checker	Yes
Extended test time	Yes
Scribe	Yes
Proctors	Yes
Oral exams	Yes
Note-takers	Yes
Support services for students with:	
LD	Yes
ADHD	Yes
ASD	Yes
Distraction-reduced environment	Yes
Recording of lecture allowed	Yes
Reading technology	Yes
Audio books	Yes
Other assistive technology	Yes
Priority registration	No
Added costs of services:	
For LD	No
For ADHD	No
For ASD	No
LD specialists	No
ADHD & ASD coaching	No
ASD specialists	No
Professional tutors	No
Peer tutors	Yes
Max. hours/week for services	Varies
How professors are notified of student approved accommodations	Both

COLLEGE GRADUATION REQUIREMENTS

Course waivers allowed	Yes
In what courses: Math	
Course substitutions allowed	Yes
In what courses: Math	

University of West Florida

11000 University Parkway, Pensacola, FL 32514-5750 • Admissions: 850-474-2230 • Fax: 850-474-3360 **Support: CS**

CAMPUS

Type of school	Public
Environment	City

STUDENTS

Undergrad enrollment	9,531
% male/female	43/57
% from out of state	11
% frosh live on campus	54

FINANCIAL FACTS

Annual in-state tuition	$4,319
Annual out-of-state tuition	$16,587
Room and board	$11,268
Required fees	$2,041

GENERAL ADMISSIONS INFO

Application fee	$30
Regular application deadline	6/30
Nonfall registration	Yes

Admission may be deferred.

Range SAT EBRW	540–620
Range SAT Math	520–610
Range ACT Composite	22–27

ACADEMICS

Student/faculty ratio	20:1
% students returning for sophomore year	82

Most classes have 20–29 students.

Programs/Services for Students with Learning Differences

The Argos for Autism Program (AAP) is a service offered by Student Accessibility Resources that provides academic, social, life skills, and career planning to UWF students with autism. Service options for Argo students include Accessibility Coaching, Academic Coaching, and an AAP Professional Bridge Program that helps juniors and seniors prepare for the transition to career after college. AAP hosts an early arrival program for students identified as having ASD to provide them with the tools for success as they transition to the university setting. There is a nominal fee for this 2-day program.

Admissions

Applicants with learning disabilities apply to the University under the same guidelines as all other students. Applicants are reviewed holistically, including test scores, rigor of academics, GPA, essay, letters of recommendation, extra-curricular activities, and volunteerism.

Additional Information

Academic Coaching provides one-on-one sessions led by student staff trained to help students develop the necessary skills to become successful and self-directed lifelong learners. Coaching provides academic skill-building in areas such as time management, note taking, study skills, test prep, and goal setting. Students will learn effective techniques for academic success by developing learning and personal management strategies. Additional tutoring and learning services are offered through the Center for Academic Success.

ADMISSIONS INFO FOR STUDENTS WITH LEARNING DIFFERENCES

Phone: 850-474-2387 • Email: sar@uwf.edu

SAT/ACT required: Yes
Interview required: No
Essay required: No
Additional application required: No
Documentation submitted to: Student Accessibility Resources

Special Ed. HS course work accepted: Yes
Separate application required for Programs/Services: For AAP
Documentation required for:
LD: Psychoeducational or neuropsychological evaluation
ADHD: Psychoeducational or neuropsychological evaluation
ASD: Psychoeducational or neuropsychological evaluation

University of West Florida

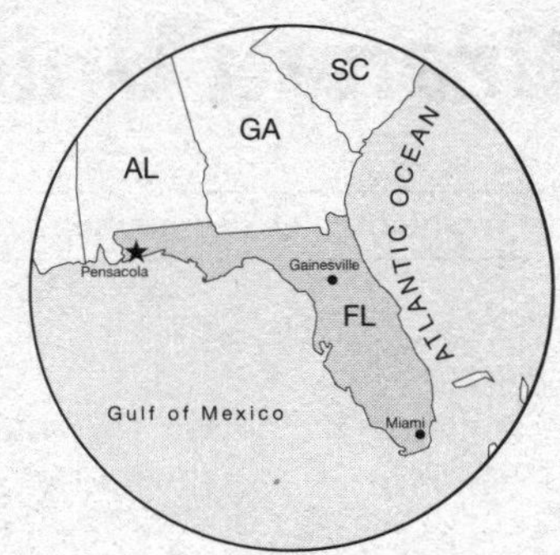

General Admissions

Very important factors include: rigor of secondary school record, academic GPA, standardized test scores. *Other factors include:* application essay, recommendation(s), extracurricular activities, talent/ability, character/ personal qualities, first generation, alumni/ae relation, geographical residence, state residency, volunteer work, work experience. High school diploma is required and GED is accepted. *Academic units required:* 4 English, 3 math, 3 science, 2 science labs, 2 foreign language, 3 social studies, 4 academic electives.

Accommodations or Services

Accommodations are decided upon an individual basis after a thorough review of appropriate, current documentation. The accommodations requests must be supported through the documentation provided and must be logically linked to the current impact of the condition on academic functioning.

Financial Aid

Students should submit: CSS/Financial Aid PROFILE; FAFSA; Noncustodial PROFILE. Applicants will be notified of awards on or about 4/1. *Need-based scholarships/grants offered:* College/university scholarship or grant aid from institutional funds; Federal Pell; Private scholarships; SEOG; State scholarships/grants. *Loan aid offered:* Direct PLUS loans; Direct Subsidized Stafford Loans; Direct Unsubsidized Stafford Loans. Federal Work-Study Program available. Institutional employment available.

Campus Life

Activities: Campus Ministries; Choral groups; Concert band; Dance; Drama/ theater; International Student Organization; Jazz band; Music ensembles; Musical theater; Pep band; Radio station; Student government; Student newspaper; Symphony orchestra; Television station. **Organizations:** 154 registered organizations, 7 honor societies, 10 religious organizations, 9 fraternities, 7 sororities. **Athletics (Intercollegiate):** *Men:* baseball, basketball, cross-country, golf, soccer, tennis. *Women:* basketball, cross-country, golf, soccer, softball, tennis, volleyball.

ACCOMMODATIONS

Allowed in exams:	
Calculators	Yes
Dictionary	No
Computer	Yes
Spell-checker	No
Extended test time	Yes
Scribe	Yes
Proctors	Yes
Oral exams	No
Note-takers	Yes
Support services for students with:	
LD	Yes
ADHD	Yes
ASD	Yes
Distraction-reduced environment	Yes
Recording of lecture allowed	Yes
Reading technology	Yes
Audio books	Yes
Other assistive technology	Yes
Priority registration	Yes
Added costs of services:	
For LD	No
For ADHD	No
For ASD	Yes
LD specialists	No
ADHD & ASD coaching	Yes
ASD specialists	Yes
Professional tutors	No
Peer tutors	Yes
Max. hours/week for services	Varies
How professors are notified of student approved accommodations	Students

COLLEGE GRADUATION REQUIREMENTS

Course waivers allowed	Yes
In what courses: Case-by-case basis	
Course substitutions allowed	Yes
In what courses: Case-by-case basis	

Florida

Brenau University

500 Washington St SE, Gainesville, GA 30501 • Admissions: 770-534-6100 • Fax: 770-538-4306 **Support: CS**

CAMPUS

Type of school	Private (nonprofit)
Environment	Town

STUDENTS

Undergrad enrollment	1,671
% male/female	9/91
% from out of state	5
% frosh live on campus	50

FINANCIAL FACTS

Annual tuition	$29,370
Room and board	$12,500
Required fees	$1,714

GENERAL ADMISSIONS INFO

Application fee	$0
Regular application deadline	Rolling
Nonfall registration	Yes

Admission may be deferred.

Range SAT EBRW	460–560
Range SAT Math	440–550
Range ACT Composite	16–23

ACADEMICS

Student/faculty ratio	9:1
% students returning for sophomore year	55

Most classes have 10–19 students.

Programs/Services for Students with Learning Differences

Brenau University strives to embrace a culture of inclusion and diversity and values all kinds of minds and learning styles. It seeks to support students who have learning differences and disabilities by going above and beyond federal requirements with free professional tutoring, professional counseling, academic coaching, as well as accommodations. Small class sizes and the smaller, safe campus with free city bus access for students is an ideal environment for many learners who have learning disabilities.

Admissions

There is no special admissions process for students with disabilities; it is general admission. However, students who have disabilities may find it beneficial that no minimum ACT or SAT score is required. Students who disclose a disability to Admissions will be put in touch with the Learning Center for a tour or meeting with the director. However, the student may choose to not disclose to Admissions staff and instead call the Learning Center directly to schedule a tour or meeting and all information will be held confidential and not revealed to Admissions.

Additional Information

The Learning Center sponsors study skills and test-taking workshops each semester. It's also a resource for students with learning disabilities, such as Attention Deficit Disorder. Learning Center students can register early and receive regular academic advising from the Director of the program. Study skills and computer skills courses are offered for credit. At all service levels students may take tests in an extended-time format where oral assistance is available. Learning Center students begin tutoring with professional tutors during the first week of the term and contract to regularly attend tutoring sessions throughout the semester. All LC students may receive one free hour of educational support per week in addition to scheduled tutoring. Students may be tutored in one to four academic classes per semester.

ADMISSIONS INFO FOR STUDENTS WITH LEARNING DIFFERENCES

Phone: 770-534-6133 • Fax: 770-297-5883 • Email: jloggins@brenau.edu

SAT/ACT required: No
Interview required: No
Essay required: No
Additional application required: No
Documentation submitted to: Learning Center

Special Ed. HS course work accepted: Yes
Separate application required for Programs/Services: No
Documentation required for:
LD: Psychoeducational evaluation
ADHD: Psychoeducational evaluation
ASD: Psychoeducational evaluation

Brenau University

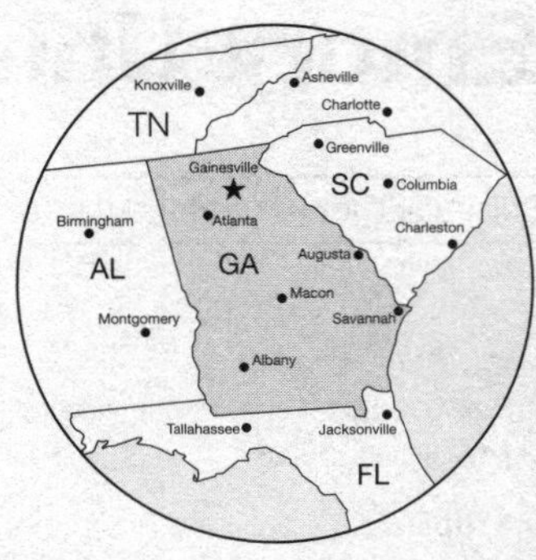

Georgia

General Admissions

Very important factors include: academic GPA. *Important factors include:* rigor of secondary school record. *Other factors include:* class rank, application essay, standardized test scores, recommendation(s), interview, extracurricular activities, talent/ability, character/personal qualities, first generation, alumni/ae relation, volunteer work, work experience. High school diploma is required and GED is accepted. *Academic units required:* 4 English, 4 math, 3 science, 2 foreign language, 3 social studies.

Accommodations or Services

Accommodations are decided upon an individual basis after a thorough review of appropriate, current documentation. The accommodations requests must be supported through the documentation provided and must be logically linked to the current impact of the condition on academic functioning.

Financial Aid

Students should submit: FAFSA. Applicants will be notified of awards on a rolling basis beginning 3/1. *Need-based scholarships/grants offered:* College/university scholarship or grant aid from institutional funds; Federal Pell; Private scholarships; SEOG; State scholarships/grants. *Loan aid offered:* Direct PLUS loans; Direct Subsidized Stafford Loans; Direct Unsubsidized Stafford Loans. Federal Work-Study Program available. Institutional employment available.

Campus Life

Activities: Campus Ministries; Choral groups; Concert band; Dance; Drama/theater; International Student Organization; Jazz band; Literary magazine; Music ensembles; Musical theater; Opera; Pep band; Radio station; Student government; Student newspaper; Yearbook. **Organizations:** 46 registered organizations, 20 honor societies, 2 religious organizations, 8 sororities. **Athletics (Intercollegiate):** *Women:* basketball, cross-country, soccer, softball, swimming, tennis, volleyball.

ACCOMMODATIONS

Allowed in exams:	
Calculators	Yes
Dictionary	Yes
Computer	Yes
Spell-checker	Yes
Extended test time	Yes
Scribe	Yes
Proctors	Yes
Oral exams	Yes
Note-takers	No
Support services for students with:	
LD	Yes
ADHD	Yes
ASD	Yes
Distraction-reduced environment	Yes
Recording of lecture allowed	Yes
Reading technology	Yes
Audio books	Yes
Other assistive technology	Yes
Priority registration	Yes
Added costs of services:	
For LD	No
For ADHD	No
For ASD	No
LD specialists	Yes
ADHD & ASD coaching	Yes
ASD specialists	Yes
Professional tutors	Yes
Peer tutors	Yes
Max. hours/week for services	Varies
How professors are notified of student approved accommodations	Both

COLLEGE GRADUATION REQUIREMENTS

Course waivers allowed	No
Course substitutions allowed	Yes
In what courses: Case-by-case basis	

Emory University

Boiseuillet Jones Center, Atlanta, GA 30322 • Admissions: 404-727-6036 • Fax: 404-727-4303 **Support: S**

CAMPUS	
Type of school	Private (nonprofit)
Environment	City
STUDENTS	
Undergrad enrollment	7,023
% male/female	40/60
% from out of state	80
% frosh live on campus	100
FINANCIAL FACTS	
Annual tuition	$53,070
Room and board	$14,972
Required fees	$734
GENERAL ADMISSIONS INFO	
Application fee	$75
Regular application deadline	1/1
Nonfall registration	No
Admission may be deferred.	
Range SAT EBRW	670–740
Range SAT Math	690–790
Range ACT Composite	31–34
ACADEMICS	
Student/faculty ratio	9:1
% students returning for sophomore year	95
Most classes have 10–19 students.	

Programs/Services for Students with Learning Differences

The Department of Accessibility Services is committed to advancing an accessible and "barrier-free" environment for its students, faculty, staff, patients, guests, and visitors by ensuring that the principles of access, equity, inclusion, and learning are applied and realized. Learning specialists are available to assist students in developing skills and strategies to define learning goals and individualized plans to reach a student's academic potential.

Admissions

Admissions is the same for all students. Teacher and/or counselor recommendations may be weighted more heavily in the admissions process. All applicants are evaluated individually and admitted based on potential for success. All first-year freshman applicants to Emory University are required to submit scores from either the SAT or the ACT, but while these scores are important, they are not the deciding factors. Strong grades in rigorous courses may cause the committee to overlook below average standardized test scores, but high board scores will never make up for an applicant's weak course selection or grades.

Additional Information

The needs of students with learning disabilities are met through academic accommodations and a variety of support services. Tutoring is offered by Emory College in most subjects on a one-on-one basis or in small groups. DAS staff provides information for students about how to access specific accommodation needs once they have accepted and begun their academic work.

ADMISSIONS INFO FOR STUDENTS WITH LEARNING DIFFERENCES

Phone: 404-727-9877 • Fax: 404-727-1126 • Email: accessibility@emory.edu

SAT/ACT required: Yes (Test optional for 2021)
Interview required: No
Essay required: No
Additional application required: No
Documentation submitted to: Department of Accessibility Services

Special Ed. HS course work accepted: Yes
Separate application required for Programs/Services: No
Documentation required for:
LD: Psychoeducational evaluation
ADHD: Psychoeducational evaluation
ASD: Psychoeducational evaluation

Emory University

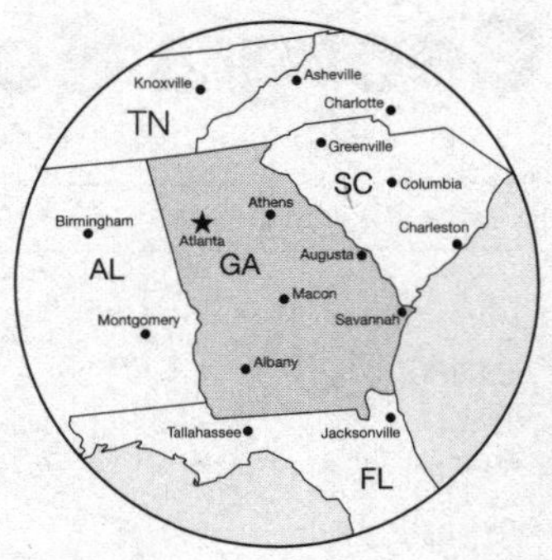

Georgia

General Admissions

Very important factors include: rigor of secondary school record, academic GPA, recommendation(s), extracurricular activities, talent/ability, character/personal qualities. *Important factors include:* application essay, standardized test scores. *Other factors include:* class rank, interview, first generation, alumni/ae relation, geographical residence, state residency, racial/ethnic status, work experience. High school diploma is required and GED is not accepted. *Academic units recommended:* 4 English, 4 math, 4 science, 2 science labs, 4 foreign language, 2 social studies, 2 history, 1 computer science, 1 visual/performing arts.

Accommodations or Services

Accommodations are decided upon an individual basis after a thorough review of appropriate, current documentation. The accommodations requests must be supported through the documentation provided and must be logically linked to the current impact of the condition on academic functioning.

Financial Aid

Students should submit: CSS/Financial Aid PROFILE; FAFSA; Noncustodial PROFILE. *Need-based scholarships/grants offered:* College/university scholarship or grant aid from institutional funds; Federal Pell; Private scholarships; SEOG; State scholarships/grants. *Loan aid offered:* Direct PLUS loans; Direct Subsidized Stafford Loans; Direct Unsubsidized Stafford Loans. Federal Work-Study Program available. Institutional employment available.

Campus Life

Activities: Campus Ministries; Choral groups; Concert band; Dance; Drama/theater; International Student Organization; Jazz band; Literary magazine; Model UN; Music ensembles; Musical theater; Opera; Radio station; Student government; Student newspaper; Student-run film society; Symphony orchestra; Television station. **Organizations:** 161 registered organizations, 28 honor societies, 26 religious organizations, 17 fraternities, 12 sororities. **Athletics (Intercollegiate):** *Men:* baseball, basketball, cross-country, diving, golf, soccer, swimming, tennis, track/field (outdoor). *Women:* basketball, cross-country, diving, soccer, softball, swimming, tennis, track/field (outdoor), volleyball.

ACCOMMODATIONS

Allowed in exams:	
Calculators	Yes
Dictionary	Yes
Computer	Yes
Spell-checker	Yes
Extended test time	Yes
Scribe	Yes
Proctors	Yes
Oral exams	Yes
Note-takers	No
Support services for students with:	
LD	Yes
ADHD	Yes
ASD	Yes
Distraction-reduced environment	Yes
Recording of lecture allowed	Yes
Reading technology	Yes
Audio books	Yes
Other assistive technology	Yes
Priority registration	Yes
Added costs of services:	
For LD	No
For ADHD	No
For ASD	No
LD specialists	No
ADHD & ASD coaching	No
ASD specialists	No
Professional tutors	No
Peer tutors	Yes
Max. hours/week for services	2
How professors are notified of student approved accommodations	Student

COLLEGE GRADUATION REQUIREMENTS

Course waivers allowed	No
Course substitutions allowed	No

Georgia Southern University

P.O. Box 8024, Statesboro, GA 30460 • Admissions: 912-478-5391 • Fax: 912-478-7240 **Support: S**

CAMPUS

Type of school	Public
Environment	Town

STUDENTS

Undergrad enrollment	22,715
% male/female	44/56
% from out of state	7
% frosh live on campus	81

FINANCIAL FACTS

Annual in-state tuition	$5,464
Annual out-of-state tuition	$19,282
Room and board	$10,070
Required fees	$2,092

GENERAL ADMISSIONS INFO

Application fee	$30
Regular application deadline	5/1
Nonfall registration	Yes

Admission may be deferred.

Range SAT EBRW	540–610
Range SAT Math	510–590
Range ACT Composite	20–25

ACADEMICS

Student/faculty ratio	20:1
% students returning for sophomore year	78

Most classes have 20–29 students.

Programs/Services for Students with Learning Differences

Georgia Southern University offers a variety of services specifically tailored to afford students with learning disabilities an equal opportunity for success. These services are in addition to those provided to all students and to the access provided by campus facilities. Opportunities available through the Student Accessibility Resource Center, include special registration, which allows students to complete the course registration process without going through the standard procedure, and academic/personal assistance for students who are having difficulty with passing a class and need help with time management, note-taking skills, study strategies, and self-confidence. The university has a support group designed to help students with disabilities deal with personal and academic problems related to their disability

Admissions

There is no special admission procedure for students with LD. All applicants must meet the same minimum requirements of 2.5 GPA and 20 ACT or 1030 SAT. The Office of Admissions can admit new freshmen to the Liberty Campus as long as they have earned a high school diploma. However, if students are admitted without meeting the admission criteria listed above for the Statesboro and Liberty Campuses, they must complete thirty or more credit hours with a cumulative 2.0+ GPA and make up and Required High School Curriculum deficiencies before transitioning from Liberty to another Georgia Southern campus.

Additional Information

The Academic Success Center offers a variety of tutoring and workshop services. However, the professional staff members of the Student Accessibility Resource Center are available to meet with students individually to help ensure their specific needs/goals are being addressed.

ADMISSIONS INFO FOR STUDENTS WITH LEARNING DIFFERENCES

Phone: 912-478-1566 • Fax: 912-478-1419 • Email: sarcboro@georgiasouthern.edu

SAT/ACT required: No (depending on GPA)
Interview required: No
Essay required: No
Additional application required: No
Documentation submitted to: Student Accessibility Resource Center

Special Ed. HS course work accepted: Yes
Separate application required for Programs/Services: No
Documentation required for:
LD: Psychoeducational evaluation
ADHD: Psychoeducational evaluation
ASD: Psychoeducational evaluation

Georgia Southern University

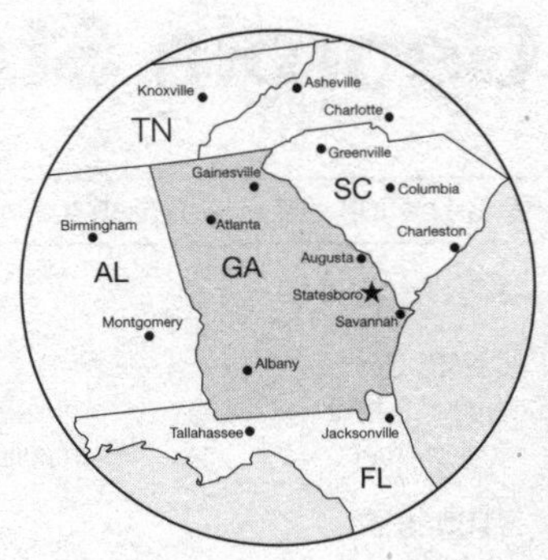

General Admissions

Very important factors include: rigor of secondary school record, academic GPA, standardized test scores. *Other factors include:* class rank. High school diploma is required and GED is not accepted. *Academic units required:* 4 English, 4 math, 4 science, 2 science labs, 2 foreign language, 3 social studies.

Accommodations or Services

Accommodations are decided upon an individual basis after a thorough review of appropriate, current documentation. The accommodations requests must be supported through the documentation provided and must be logically linked to the current impact of the condition on academic functioning.

Financial Aid

Students should submit: FAFSA. *Need-based scholarships/grants offered:* College/university scholarship or grant aid from institutional funds; Federal Pell; Private scholarships; SEOG; State scholarships/grants. *Loan aid offered:* Direct PLUS loans; Direct Subsidized Stafford Loans; Direct Unsubsidized Stafford Loans. Federal Work-Study Program available. Institutional employment available.

Campus Life

Activities: Campus Ministries; Choral groups; Concert band; Dance; Drama/theater; International Student Organization; Jazz band; Literary magazine; Marching band; Music ensembles; Musical theater; Opera; Radio station; Student government; Student newspaper; Student-run film society; Symphony orchestra. **Organizations:** 280 registered organizations, 17 honor societies, 24 religious organizations, 48 fraternities, 12 sororities. **Athletics (Intercollegiate):** *Men:* baseball, basketball, cheerleading, football, golf, soccer, tennis. *Women:* basketball, cheerleading, cross-country, diving, soccer, softball, swimming, tennis, track/field (outdoor), volleyball.

ACCOMMODATIONS

Allowed in exams:	
Calculators	Yes
Dictionary	Yes
Computer	Yes
Spell-checker	Yes
Extended test time	Yes
Scribe	No
Proctors	Yes
Oral exams	Yes
Note-takers	Yes
Support services for students with:	
LD	Yes
ADHD	Yes
ASD	No
Distraction-reduced environment	Yes
Recording of lecture allowed	Yes
Reading technology	Yes
Audio books	Yes
Other assistive technology	Yes
Priority registration	Yes
Added costs of services:	
For LD	No
For ADHD	No
For ASD	No
LD specialists	No
ADHD & ASD coaching	Yes
ASD specialists	No
Professional tutors	No
Peer tutors	Yes
Max. hours/week for services	Varies
How professors are notified of student approved accommodations	Student

COLLEGE GRADUATION REQUIREMENTS

Course waivers allowed	Yes
In what courses: Foreign language and math	
Course substitutions allowed	Yes
In what courses: Foreign language and math	

Georgia State University

PO Box 4009, Atlanta, GA 30302-4009 • Admissions: 404-413-2500 • Fax: 404-413-2002 **Support: CS**

CAMPUS

Type of school	Public
Environment	Metropolis

STUDENTS

Undergrad enrollment	27,296
% male/female	41/59
% from out of state	5
% frosh live on campus	58

FINANCIAL FACTS

Annual in-state tuition	$8,948
Annual out-of-state tuition	$27,986
Room and board	$13,800
Required fees	$2,128

GENERAL ADMISSIONS INFO

Application fee	$60
Regular application deadline	6/1
Nonfall registration	Yes

Admission may be deferred.

Range SAT EBRW	970–1150
Range SAT Math	500–590
Range ACT Composite	20–26

ACADEMICS

Student/faculty ratio	26:1
% students returning for sophomore year	80

Most classes have 20–29 students.

Programs/Services for Students with Learning Differences

Georgia State University is committed to helping each student, including those students with disabilities; realize his or her full potential. This commitment is fulfilled through the provision of reasonable accommodations to ensure equitable access to its programs and services for all qualified students with disabilities. In general, the university will provide accommodations for students with disabilities on an individualized and flexible basis. It is the student's responsibility to seek available assistance and make his or her needs known. All students are encouraged to contact the Access and Accommodations Center and/or Student Support Services in the early stages of their college planning. The pre-admission services include information regarding admission requirements and academic support services. Students should register with both services before classes begin. This will assure that appropriate services are in place prior to the first day of classes.

Admissions

Students with LD must meet the same admission criteria as all other applicants. The university uses a predicted GPA of 2.1 for admission to a degree program or a GPA of 1.8 for admission to Learning Support Systems. This is determined by the ACT/SAT score and the high school GPA. The higher the GPA, the lower the ACT/SAT can be, and vice versa. Course requirements include 4 years of English, 4 years of science, 4 years of math, 3 years of social science, and 2 years of a foreign language. (Substitutions are allowed for foreign language if the student has documentation that supports the substitution.) Students may appeal an admission decision if they are denied and could be offered a probationary admission.

Additional Information

Student Support Services provides individual and group counseling, tutoring, advocacy, taped texts, advising, readers, learning lab, computer training, and referral for diagnosis of LD. The University Counseling Center provides study skills training; test-taking strategies; notetaking skills; textbook-reading skills; test anxiety and stress management, time management, and organizational techniques; thesis and dissertation writing; and personal counseling. Passport is a special section of the Personal and Academic Development Seminar Class offered through the Learning Support Program and is specifically designed for students with LD.

ADMISSIONS INFO FOR STUDENTS WITH LEARNING DIFFERENCES

Phone: 404-413-1560 • Fax: 404-413-1563 • Email: access@gsu.edu

SAT/ACT required: Yes (Test optional for 2021)
Interview required: No
Essay required: No
Additional application required: No
Documentation submitted to: Access and Accommodations Center

Special Ed. HS course work accepted: Yes
Separate application required for Programs/Services: No
Documentation required for:
LD: Psychoeducational evaluation
ADHD: Psychoeducational evaluation
ASD: Psychoeducational evaluation

Georgia State University

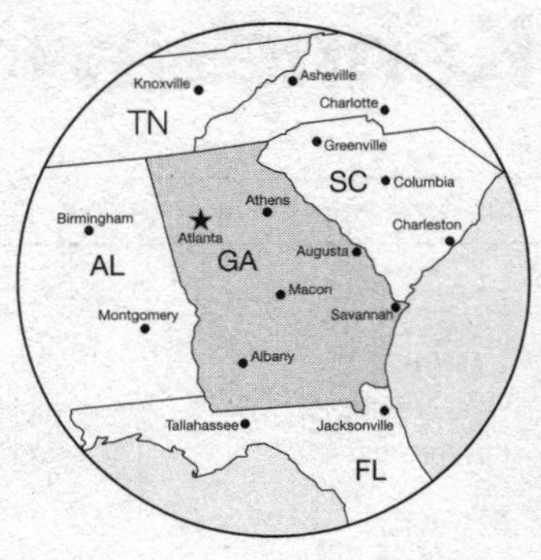

General Admissions

Very important factors include: rigor of secondary school record, academic GPA, standardized test scores. *Other factors include:* application essay, recommendation(s), talent/ability. High school diploma is required and GED is not accepted. *Academic units required:* 4 English, 4 math, 4 science, 2 science labs, 2 foreign language, 3 social studies. *Academic units recommended:* 4 English, 4 math, 4 science, 2 science labs, 2 foreign language, 3 social studies.

Accommodations or Services

Accommodations are decided upon an individual basis after a thorough review of appropriate, current documentation. The accommodations requests must be supported through the documentation provided and must be logically linked to the current impact of the condition on academic functioning.

Financial Aid

Students should submit: FAFSA. Applicants will be notified of awards on a rolling basis beginning 3/16. *Need-based scholarships/grants offered:* College/university scholarship or grant aid from institutional funds; Federal Pell; Private scholarships; SEOG; State scholarships/grants; United Negro College Fund. *Loan aid offered:* Direct PLUS loans; Direct Subsidized Stafford Loans; Direct Unsubsidized Stafford Loans. Federal Work-Study Program available. Institutional employment available.

Campus Life

Activities: Campus Ministries; Choral groups; Concert band; Dance; Drama/theater; International Student Organization; Jazz band; Literary magazine; Marching band; Model UN; Music ensembles; Musical theater; Opera; Pep band; Radio station; Student government; Student newspaper; Student-run film society; Symphony orchestra; Television station. **Organizations:** 520 registered organizations, 43 honor societies, 37 religious organizations, 17 fraternities, 17 sororities. **Athletics (Intercollegiate):** *Men:* baseball, basketball, cross-country, golf, soccer, tennis, track/field (outdoor), volleyball. *Women:* basketball, cross-country, golf, soccer, softball, tennis, track/field (outdoor), volleyball.

ACCOMMODATIONS

Allowed in exams:	
Calculators	Yes
Dictionary	Yes
Computer	Yes
Spell-checker	Yes
Extended test time	Yes
Scribe	Yes
Proctors	Yes
Oral exams	Yes
Note-takers	Yes
Support services for students with:	
LD	Yes
ADHD	Yes
ASD	Yes
Distraction-reduced environment	Yes
Recording of lecture allowed	Yes
Reading technology	Yes
Audio books	No
Other assistive technology	Yes
Priority registration	Yes
Added costs of services:	
For LD	No
For ADHD	No
For ASD	No
LD specialists	Yes
ADHD & ASD coaching	Yes
ASD specialists	No
Professional tutors	Yes
Peer tutors	Yes
Max. hours/week for services	Varies
How professors are notified of student approved accommodations	Student

COLLEGE GRADUATION REQUIREMENTS

Course waivers allowed	No
Course substitutions allowed	Yes

In what courses: Foreign Language on a case-by-case basis

Kennesaw State University

3391 Town Point Drive, Suite 1000, Kennesaw, GA 30144-5591 • Admissions: 770-423-6300 • Fax: 470-578-9169 **Support: CS**

CAMPUS

Type of school	Public
Environment	Town

STUDENTS

Undergrad enrollment	34,499
% male/female	53/48
% from out of state	13
% frosh live on campus	43

FINANCIAL FACTS

Annual in-state tuition	$4,450
Annual out-of-state tuition	$15,704
Room and board	$12,947
Required fees	$1,986

GENERAL ADMISSIONS INFO

Application fee	$40
Regular application deadline	6/1
Nonfall registration	Yes
Range SAT EBRW	530–620
Range SAT Math	530–620
Range ACT Composite	20–26

ACADEMICS

Student/faculty ratio	21:1
% students returning for sophomore year	80

Most classes have 20–29 students.

Programs/Services for Students with Learning Differences

Student Disability Services (SDS) is the contact point for students with disabilities to identify themselves, provide appropriate documentation, determine approved accommodations, and coordinate necessary academic accommodations and services. Academic Coaching is a service that is available to any students registered with SDS. Academic Coaching is a partnership between the student and a member of the SDS team that explores academic challenges and strategies to combat those challenges. Coaching focuses on time management, test preparation, procrastination, note-taking skills, motivation, and reading skills.

Admissions

Admissions for students with learning disabilities is the same as for all applicants, including standardized test scores, academic GPA, and required academic core courses. The average GPA is 3.38 and SAT Writing 579 and Math 563 and ACT English 23, Reading 25, Math 22. The minimum GPA is 2.5. Required courses include: 4 units of English, 4 units of math, 4 units of science, 3 units of social science, and 2 units of same foreign language.

Additional Information

SDS emails individual Course Accessibility Letters directly to faculty and the student. The letter will outline the accommodations approved for that student by SDS. The additional comments regarding the deficits of the specific disabilities, along with instructional tips provided in the letter, allow instructors to have a better picture of what barriers to instruction students with disabilities may face in a classroom. The instructional tips suggested are generally at the discretion of the instructor and are meant to give you greater insight into what is helpful. Additional information is also provided in the letter to provide faculty with helpful information in regards to reasonable implementation of accommodations.

ADMISSIONS INFO FOR STUDENTS WITH LEARNING DIFFERENCES

Phone: 470-578-2666 • Fax: 470-578-9111 • Email: sds@kennesaw.edu

SAT/ACT required: Yes (Test optional for 2021)
Interview required: No
Essay required: No
Additional application required: No
Documentation submitted to: Student Disability Services

Special Ed. HS course work accepted: Yes
Separate application required for Programs/Services: No
Documentation required for:
LD: Psychoeducational evaluation
ADHD: Psychoeducational evaluation
ASD: Psychoeducational evaluation

Kennesaw State University

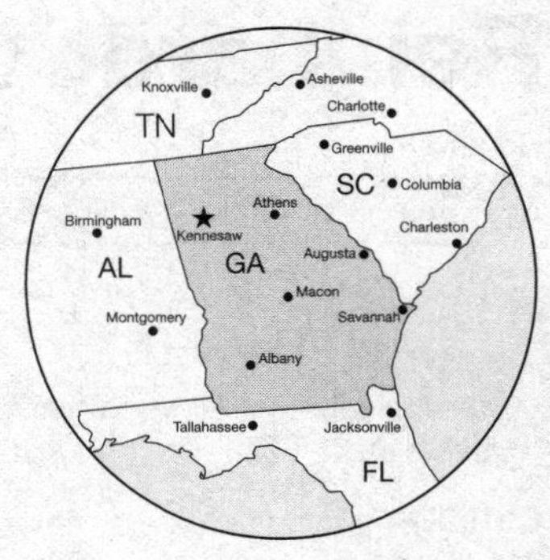

General Admissions

Very important factors include: academic GPA, standardized test scores. High school diploma is required and GED is not accepted. *Academic units required:* 4 English, 4 math, 4 science, 2 science labs, 2 foreign language, 1 social studies, 2 history. *Academic units recommended:* 4 English, 4 math, 4 science, 2 science labs, 2 foreign language, 1 social studies, 2 history.

Accommodations or Services

Accommodations are decided upon an individual basis after a thorough review of appropriate, current documentation. The accommodations requests must be supported through the documentation provided and must be logically linked to the current impact of the condition on academic functioning.

Financial Aid

Students should submit: CSS/Financial Aid PROFILE; FAFSA; Noncustodial PROFILE. Applicants will be notified of awards on a rolling basis beginning 2/15. *Need-based scholarships/grants offered:* College/university scholarship or grant aid from institutional funds; Federal Pell; Private scholarships; SEOG; State scholarships/grants; United Negro College Fund. *Loan aid offered:* Direct PLUS loans; Direct Subsidized Stafford Loans; Direct Unsubsidized Stafford Loans. Federal Work-Study Program available. Institutional employment available.

Campus Life

Activities: Campus Ministries; Choral groups; Concert band; Dance; Drama/theater; International Student Organization; Jazz band; Literary magazine; Marching band; Music ensembles; Musical theater; Opera; Pep band; Radio station; Student government; Student newspaper; Symphony orchestra. **Organizations:** 275 registered organizations, 18 honor societies, 35 religious organizations, 19 fraternities, 11 sororities. **Athletics (Intercollegiate):** *Men:* baseball, basketball, cross-country, golf, tennis, track/field (outdoor), track/field (indoor). *Women:* basketball, cheerleading, cross-country, golf, soccer, softball, tennis, track/field (outdoor), track/field (indoor), volleyball.

ACCOMMODATIONS

Allowed in exams:	
Calculators	Yes
Dictionary	Yes
Computer	Yes
Spell-checker	Yes
Extended test time	Yes
Scribe	Yes
Proctors	Yes
Oral exams	Yes
Note-takers	Yes
Support services for students with:	
LD	Yes
ADHD	Yes
ASD	Yes
Distraction-reduced environment	Yes
Recording of lecture allowed	Yes
Reading technology	Yes
Audio books	Yes
Other assistive technology	Yes
Priority registration	Yes
Added costs of services:	
For LD	No
For ADHD	No
For ASD	No
LD specialists	Yes
ADHD & ASD coaching	Yes
ASD specialists	No
Professional tutors	No
Peer tutors	Yes
Max. hours/week for services	Varies
How professors are notified of student approved accommodations	Both

COLLEGE GRADUATION REQUIREMENTS

Course waivers allowed	No
Course substitutions allowed	Yes
In what courses: Case-by-case situation	

Reinhardt University

7300 Reinhardt Circle, Waleska, GA 30183 • Admissions: 770-720-5526 • Fax: 770-720-5899 **Support: SP**

CAMPUS

Type of school	Private (nonprofit)
Environment	Rural

STUDENTS

Undergrad enrollment	1,432
% male/female	51/49
% from out of state	8
% frosh live on campus	74

FINANCIAL FACTS

Annual tuition	$24,228
Room and board	$10,920
Required fees	$900

GENERAL ADMISSIONS INFO

Application fee	$25
Regular application deadline	8/17
Nonfall registration	Yes

Admission may be deferred.

Range SAT EBRW	490–600
Range SAT Math	480–580
Range ACT Composite	18–24

ACADEMICS

Student/faculty ratio	12:1
% students returning for sophomore year	66

Most classes have 10–19 students.

Programs/Services for Students with Learning Differences

The Academic Support Office (ASO) provides assistance to students with specific learning abilities or attention deficit disorders. Students are enrolled in regular college courses. The program focuses on compensatory skills and provides special services in academic advising, group tutoring, assistance in writing assignments, note-taking, testing accommodations, and coordination of assistive learning technologies. Reinhardt's ASO was established in 1982 to provide assistance to students with learning disabilities who meet regular college entrance requirements, have a diagnosed LD, and may or may not have received any LD services in the past due to ineligibility for high school services, or a recent diagnosis.

Admissions

Applicants with learning disabilities should request an ASO admission packet from Admissions; if they choose to self disclose upon application, they should complete the regular application; note an interest in Academic Support; fill out the supplemental form from ASO; provide IEPs from as many years of high school, psychological evaluations documenting the disability, and three references addressing aptitude, motivation, ability to set realistic goals, interpersonal skills, and readiness for college; and submit SAT/ACT scores. Students applying to the ASO program may be asked to interview with the ASO faculty. Admission decisions are made by the Admission Office. Students choosing not to self-disclose upon application should request information from the ASO Director.

Additional Information

ASO Tutorial is a fee-based tutorial program where a student works one-on-one with a tutor in a specific subject in which the student needs more support. Tutors are seasoned faculty members who are proficient in working with students with learning disabilities and/or differing learning styles. Academic Coaching provides students with the tools needed for academic achievement such as study skills development, time management, organization, and test review. The B.O.L.D. Program is specifically geared for students who have specific needs due to LD and ADHD. Built around the concept of Universal Design, B.O.L.D. offers services that are individualized and go above and beyond the standard accommodations. The Strategic Education for Students with Autism Spectrum Disorders program (SEAD) provides students with individualized strategy instruction and support, group sessions focusing on social skills, and monthly social activities with peers.

ADMISSIONS INFO FOR STUDENTS WITH LEARNING DIFFERENCES

Phone: 770-720-5567 • Fax: 770-720-5602 • Email: AAA@reinhardt.edu

SAT/ACT required: No
Interview required: Yes
Essay required: No
Additional application required: No
Documentation submitted to: Academic Support Office

Special Ed. HS course work accepted: Yes
Separate application required for Programs/Services: No
Documentation required for:
LD: Psychoeducational evaluation
ADHD: Psychoeducational evaluation
ASD: Psychoeducational evaluation

Reinhardt University

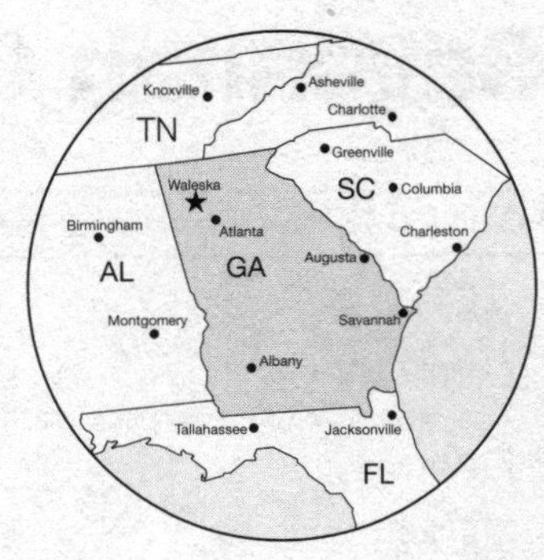

Georgia

General Admissions

Very important factors include: academic GPA, standardized test scores. *Important factors include:* rigor of secondary school record, class rank. High school diploma is required and GED is accepted. *Academic units required:* 4 English, 4 math, 3 science, 3 social studies. *Academic units recommended:* 2 foreign language.

Accommodations or Services

Accommodations are decided upon an individual basis after a thorough review of appropriate, current documentation. The accommodations requests must be supported through the documentation provided and must be logically linked to the current impact of the condition on academic functioning.

Financial Aid

Students should submit: FAFSA; State aid form. Applicants will be notified of awards on a rolling basis beginning 3/1. *Need-based scholarships/grants offered:* College/university scholarship or grant aid from institutional funds; Federal Pell; Private scholarships; SEOG; State scholarships/grants. *Loan aid offered:* Direct PLUS loans; Direct Subsidized Stafford Loans; Direct Unsubsidized Stafford Loans. Federal Work-Study Program available.

Campus Life

Activities: Campus Ministries; Choral groups; Concert band; Drama/theater; International Student Organization; Jazz band; Literary magazine; Music ensembles; Musical theater; Student government; Student newspaper; Student-run film society; Symphony orchestra; Television station; Yearbook. **Organizations:** 40 registered organizations, 12 honor societies, 5 religious organizations. **Athletics (Intercollegiate):** *Men:* baseball, basketball, cheerleading, cross-country, golf, soccer, tennis. *Women:* basketball, cheerleading, cross-country, golf, soccer, softball, tennis, volleyball.

ACCOMMODATIONS

Allowed in exams:	
Calculators	Yes
Dictionary	No
Computer	Yes
Spell-checker	Yes
Extended test time	Yes
Scribe	Yes
Proctors	Yes
Oral exams	Yes
Note-takers	Yes
Support services for students with:	
LD	Yes
ADHD	Yes
ASD	Yes
Distraction-reduced environment	Yes
Recording of lecture allowed	Yes
Reading technology	Yes
Audio books	Yes
Other assistive technology	Yes
Priority registration	Yes
Added costs of services:	
For LD	Yes
For ADHD	Yes
For ASD	Yes
LD specialists	Yes
ADHD & ASD coaching	Yes
ASD specialists	No
Professional tutors	Yes
Peer tutors	No
Max. hours/week for services	Unlimited
How professors are notified of student approved accommodations	Student and Director

COLLEGE GRADUATION REQUIREMENTS

Course waivers allowed	No
Course substitutions allowed	No

Savannah College of Art and Design

PO Box 3146, Savannah, GA 31402-3146 • Admissions: 912-525-5100 • Fax: 912-525-5986 **Support: S**

CAMPUS	
Type of school	Private (nonprofit)
Environment	City
STUDENTS	
Undergrad enrollment	12,167
% male/female	32/68
% from out of state	69
% frosh live on campus	87
FINANCIAL FACTS	
Annual tuition	$37,575
Room and board	$13,905
Required fees	$500
GENERAL ADMISSIONS INFO	
Application fee	$60
Regular application deadline	Rolling
Nonfall registration	Yes
Admission may be deferred.	
Range SAT EBRW	540–640
Range SAT Math	510–600
Range ACT Composite	21–27
ACADEMICS	
Student/faculty ratio	20:1
% students returning for sophomore year	84
Most classes have 10–19 students.	

Programs/Services for Students with Learning Differences

All reasonable accommodations are determined for students on an individual basis. In order to receive academic adjustments and/or reasonable accommodations, students must make an appointment with their accommodation specialist each term to make their specific accommodation requests known.

Admissions

Applicants who do not meet the standard criteria for admission are encouraged to submit supplementary materials. Exceptions to the general rules of admission may be made for applicants with exceptional drive and passion for the arts. Supplementary materials may include one or all of the following: One to three recommendations may be submitted by a teacher, counselor or community leader with whom the applicant has had immediate contact. Recommendations should address the applicant's level of commitment, as well as attributes such as creativity, initiative, motivation, character and academic achievement, to aid in assessing the applicant's reasonable potential for success as a student at SCAD. A Statement of Purpose should be no more than 500 words in length and should give an overview of the applicant's academic and personal experience, describing preparation for and commitment to further study at SCAD, as well as educational and professional goals and aspirations; students who submit portfolio, audition, riding or writing submission will have it scored according to a rubric relevant to the type of submission; résumé/list of achievements and awards; and a personal or telephone interview which may be scheduled by contacting the admission department.

Additional Information

The Office of Counseling and Student Support Services invites all students with a diagnosed disability and their parent or guardian to attend Jump Start, a special expanded orientation in Savannah, Georgia, held before the general SCAD orientation begins. Jump Start is designed to increase awareness of the services and resources available to students with disabilities, ease the transition to college and provide strategies for success at SCAD. In addition to excellent professor instruction, state-of-the-art specialized equipment and cutting-edge technology, SCAD students have access to a wealth of learning resources outside the classroom.

ADMISSIONS INFO FOR STUDENTS WITH LEARNING DIFFERENCES

Phone: 912-525-6971 • Email: accommodations@scad.edu

SAT/ACT required: Yes (Test optional for 2021)
Interview required: No
Essay required: No
Additional application required: No
Documentation submitted to: Office of Accommodation Services

Special Ed. HS course work accepted: Yes
Separate application required for Programs/Services: No
Documentation required for:
LD: Psychoeducational evaluation
ADHD: Psychoeducational evaluation
ASD: Psychoeducational evaluation

Savannah College of Art and Design

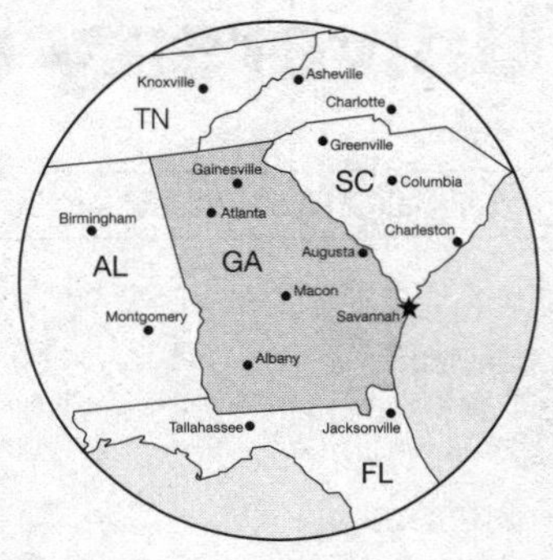

Georgia

General Admissions

Very important factors include: academic GPA. *Important factors include:* rigor of secondary school record, standardized test scores, level of applicant's interest. *Other factors include:* class rank, application essay, recommendation(s), interview, extracurricular activities, talent/ability, character/personal qualities. High school diploma is required and GED is accepted.

Accommodations or Services

Accommodations are decided upon an individual basis after a thorough review of appropriate, current documentation. The accommodations requests must be supported through the documentation provided and must be logically linked to the current impact of the condition on academic functioning.

Financial Aid

Students should submit: FAFSA. Applicants will be notified of awards on a rolling basis beginning 4/15. *Need-based scholarships/grants offered:* College/university scholarship or grant aid from institutional funds; Federal Pell; Private scholarships; SEOG; State scholarships/grants; United Negro College Fund. *Loan aid offered:* Direct PLUS loans; Direct Subsidized Stafford Loans; Direct Unsubsidized Stafford Loans. Federal Work-Study Program available. Institutional employment available.

Campus Life

Activities: Campus Ministries; Choral groups; Dance; Drama/theater; International Student Organization; Literary magazine; Music ensembles; Musical theater; Radio station; Student newspaper; Television station. **Organizations:** 105 registered organizations, 2 honor societies, 5 religious organizations. **Athletics (Intercollegiate):** *Men:* baseball, basketball, cross-country, equestrian sports, golf, lacrosse, soccer, swimming, tennis. *Women:* basketball, cross-country, equestrian sports, golf, lacrosse, soccer, softball, swimming, tennis, volleyball.

ACCOMMODATIONS

Allowed in exams:	
Calculators	Yes
Dictionary	Yes
Computer	Yes
Spell-checker	Yes
Extended test time	Yes
Scribe	Yes
Proctors	Yes
Oral exams	Yes
Note-takers	Yes
Support services for students with:	
LD	Yes
ADHD	Yes
ASD	Yes
Distraction-reduced environment	Yes
Recording of lecture allowed	Yes
Reading technology	Yes
Audio books	Yes
Other assistive technology	Yes
Priority registration	Yes
Added costs of services:	
For LD	No
For ADHD	No
For ASD	No
LD specialists	No
ADHD & ASD coaching	Yes
ASD specialists	No
Professional tutors	No
Peer tutors	Yes
Max. hours/week for services	Varies
How professors are notified of student approved accommodations	Student

COLLEGE GRADUATION REQUIREMENTS

Course waivers allowed	Yes
In what courses: Math, Foreign Languages	
Course substitutions allowed	Yes
In what courses: Math, Foreign Languages	

University of Georgia

Terrell Hall, 210 South Jackson Street, Athens, GA 30602-1633 • Admissions: 706-542-8776 **Support: CS**

CAMPUS

Type of school	Public
Environment	City

STUDENTS

Undergrad enrollment	29,848
% male/female	43/57
% from out of state	12
% frosh live on campus	98

FINANCIAL FACTS

Annual in-state tuition	$9,790
Annual out-of-state tuition	$28,830
Room and board	$10,328
Required fees	$2,290

GENERAL ADMISSIONS INFO

Application fee	$70
Regular application deadline	1/1
Nonfall registration	Yes

Admission may be deferred.

Range SAT EBRW	630–700
Range SAT Math	610–720
Range ACT Composite	27–32

ACADEMICS

Student/faculty ratio	17:1
% students returning for sophomore year	96

Most classes have 10–19 students.

Programs/Services for Students with Learning Differences

The Disability Resource Center (DRC) assists the University in fulfilling its commitment to educate and serve students with disabilities who qualify for admissions. The DRC coordinates and provides a variety of academic and support services to students, including students with Learning Disabilities (LDs), Attention Deficit Hyperactivity Disorder (ADHD), and Asperger Syndrome (AS). Its mission is to promote equal educational opportunities and a welcoming environment for students with disabilities at the University of Georgia. DRC staff members are dedicated professionals with a wide range of expertise in disability-related issues. These encompass disability specific accommodations, universal design, program access, assistive technology, alternative text, architectural access, and disability law. Staff can hold regular meetings with students to discuss and monitor academic progress, assist students in understanding their disability, make referrals to other campus and community resources, and consult with faculty as needed.

Admissions

There are no special admission criteria for students with disabilities. All students must meet the admission criteria set by the University. However, a student with a disability may disclose his/her diagnosis in a personal statement/essay to further explain test scores and/or grades received. The primary factors in admission are GPA, courses, the rigor of the courses, and the best score or combination of scores on the SAT or ACT. All applications are reviewed for conduct issues, recommendations, and satisfactory completion of all the required College Preparatory courses.

Additional Information

DRC staff refer students to campus resources as requested/necessary. The Academic Resource Center located in Milledge Hall provides a variety of academic assistance for all students on campus. The ARC has a peer-based tutor program that includes drop-in labs for chemistry, math, and physics, as well as appointment-based tutoring for more than 60 courses. ARC provides Academic Coaching, which is appointment-based programming for students who want to meet with a certified and trained academic coach to create a strategic learning plan for success. The ARC also has a Writing Center that is staffed with specialists who are experts in their field. Every fall, academic success workshops are offered on issues such as time management, stress management, and preparing for final exams.

ADMISSIONS INFO FOR STUDENTS WITH LEARNING DIFFERENCES

Phone: 706-542-8719 • Fax: 706-542-7719 • Email: drc@uga.edu

SAT/ACT required: Yes (Test optional for 2021)
Interview required: No
Essay required: Yes
Additional application required: No
Documentation submitted to: Disability Resource Center

Special Ed. HS course work accepted: Yes
Separate application required for Programs/Services: Yes
Documentation required for:
LD: Psychoeducational evaluation
ADHD: Psychoeducational evaluation
ASD: Psychoeducational evaluation

University of Georgia

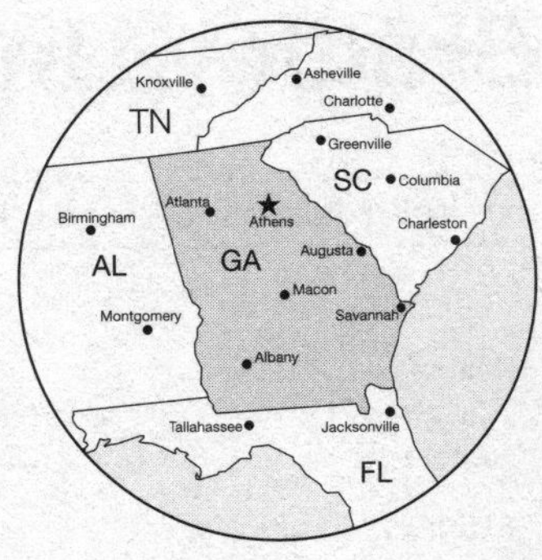

Georgia

General Admissions

Very important factors include: rigor of secondary school record, academic GPA. *Important factors include:* standardized test scores. *Other factors include:* application essay, recommendation(s), extracurricular activities, talent/ability, character/personal qualities, first generation, volunteer work, work experience. High school diploma is required and GED is accepted. *Academic units required:* 4 English, 4 math, 4 science, 2 science labs, 2 foreign language, 3 social studies. *Academic units recommended:* 4 English, 4 math, 4 science, 2 science labs, 3 foreign language, 3 social studies, 1 academic elective.

Accommodations or Services

Accommodations are decided upon an individual basis after a thorough review of appropriate, current documentation. The accommodations requests must be supported through the documentation provided and must be logically linked to the current impact of the condition on academic functioning.

Financial Aid

Students should submit: CSS/Financial Aid PROFILE; FAFSA; Noncustodial PROFILE. Applicants will be notified of awards on or about 4/1. *Need-based scholarships/grants offered:* College/university scholarship or grant aid from institutional funds; Federal Pell; Private scholarships; SEOG; State scholarships/grants. *Loan aid offered:* Direct PLUS loans; Direct Subsidized Stafford Loans; Direct Unsubsidized Stafford Loans. Federal Work-Study Program available. Institutional employment available.

Campus Life

Activities: Campus Ministries; Choral groups; Concert band; Dance; Drama/theater; International Student Organization; Jazz band; Literary magazine; Marching band; Model UN; Music ensembles; Musical theater; Opera; Pep band; Radio station; Student government; Student newspaper; Student-run film society; Symphony orchestra; Yearbook. **Organizations:** 746 registered organizations, 28 honor societies, 64 religious organizations, 37 fraternities, 29 sororities. **Athletics (Intercollegiate):** *Men:* baseball, basketball, cross-country, diving, football, golf, swimming, tennis, track/field (outdoor), track/field (indoor). *Women:* basketball, cross-country, diving, equestrian sports, golf, gymnastics, soccer, softball, swimming, tennis, track/field (outdoor), track/field (indoor), volleyball.

ACCOMMODATIONS

Allowed in exams:	
Calculators	Yes
Dictionary	No
Computer	Yes
Spell-checker	Yes
Extended test time	Yes
Scribe	Yes
Proctors	Yes
Oral exams	Yes
Note-takers	Yes
Support services for students with:	
LD	Yes
ADHD	Yes
ASD	Yes
Distraction-reduced environment	Yes
Recording of lecture allowed	Yes
Reading technology	Yes
Audio books	Yes
Other assistive technology	Yes
Priority registration	Yes
Added costs of services:	
For LD	No
For ADHD	No
For ASD	No
LD specialists	Yes
ADHD & ASD coaching	No
ASD specialists	No
Professional tutors	Yes
Peer tutors	Yes
Max. hours/week for services	Varies
How professors are notified of student approved accommodations	Student

COLLEGE GRADUATION REQUIREMENTS

Course waivers allowed	No
Course substitutions allowed	Yes
In what courses: Case-by-case basis	

Bradley University

1501 W. Bradley Avenue, Peoria, IL 61625 • Admissions: 309-677-1000 • Fax: 309-677-2797 **Support: CS**

CAMPUS	
Type of school	Private (nonprofit)
Environment	City
STUDENTS	
Undergrad enrollment	4,636
% male/female	49/51
% from out of state	18
% frosh live on campus	90
FINANCIAL FACTS	
Annual tuition	$35,060
Room and board	$11,280
Required fees	$420
GENERAL ADMISSIONS INFO	
Application fee	$0
Regular application deadline	7/27
Nonfall registration	Yes
Admission may be deferred.	
Range SAT EBRW	540–630
Range SAT Math	530–640
Range ACT Composite	22–28
ACADEMICS	
Student/faculty ratio	12:1
% students returning for sophomore year	85
Most classes have 10–19 students.	

Programs/Services for Students with Learning Differences

The Office of Student Access Services (SAS) is committed to the fulfillment of equal educational opportunity, academic freedom and human dignity for students with disabilities. The SAS exists to provide reasonable and appropriate accommodations for qualified students with documented disabilities, to assist students in self-advocacy, to educate the Bradley community about disabilities, and ensure compliance with federal and state law. Students are required to provide documentation of their disability prior to the provision of services.

Admissions

Students with learning disabilities must meet the same admission requirements as all applicants. ACT or SAT score is required. Mid 50% SAT 1040–1310 or ACT 22–28 and an average GPA of 3.6.

Additional Information

Professional Academic Coaching is provided through the Academic Success Center. Through one-on-one meetings, students work with professional staff to identify and address barriers to success and develop strategies and resources for more effective learning. Student Success Workshops are offered on a variety of topics such as time management, organization, note-taking, goal setting and motivation, memory and concentration, and test-taking strategies. Free peer tutoring is available to all students as well as fee-based private tutoring with certified tutors.

ADMISSIONS INFO FOR STUDENTS WITH LEARNING DIFFERENCES

Phone: 309-677-3654 • Fax: 309-677-3685 • Email: eagorman@bradley.edu

SAT/ACT required: No
Interview required: No
Essay required: Yes
Additional application required: No
Documentation submitted to: Student Access Services

Special Ed. HS course work accepted: Yes
Separate application required for Programs/Services: Yes
Documentation required for:
- **LD:** Psychoeducational evaluation
- **ADHD:** Psychoeducational evaluation
- **ASD:** Psychoeducational evaluation

Bradley University

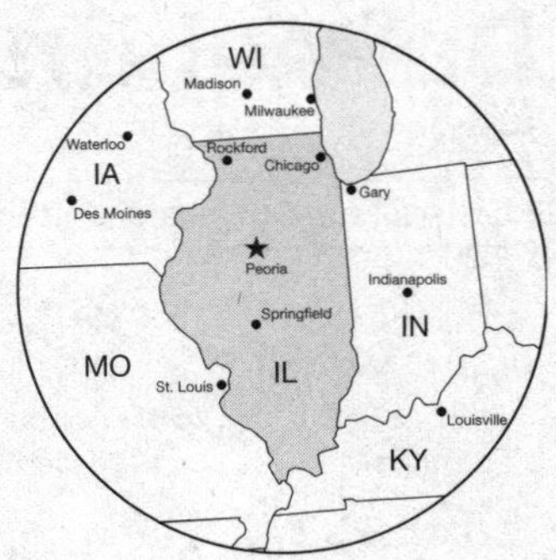

General Admissions

Very important factors include: rigor of secondary school record, academic GPA. *Important factors include:* class rank, standardized test scores. *Other factors include:* application essay, recommendation(s), interview, extracurricular activities, talent/ability, character/personal qualities, first generation, alumni/ae relation, geographical residence, racial/ethnic status, volunteer work, work experience, level of applicant's interest. High school diploma is required and GED is accepted. *Academic units required:* 4 English, 3 math, 2 science, 2 science labs, 2 social studies. *Academic units recommended:* 5 English, 4 math, 3 science, 3 science labs, 2 foreign language, 3 social studies, 2 history.

Accommodations or Services

Accommodations are decided upon an individual basis after a thorough review of appropriate, current documentation. The accommodations requests must be supported through the documentation provided and must be logically linked to the current impact of the condition on academic functioning.

Financial Aid

Students should submit: FAFSA. *Need-based scholarships/grants offered:* College/university scholarship or grant aid from institutional funds; Federal Pell; Private scholarships; SEOG; State scholarships/grants; United Negro College Fund. *Loan aid offered:* Direct PLUS loans; Direct Subsidized Stafford Loans; Direct Unsubsidized Stafford Loans. Federal Work-Study Program available. Institutional employment available.

Campus Life

Activities: Campus Ministries; Choral groups; Concert band; Dance; Drama/theater; International Student Organization; Jazz band; Literary magazine; Music ensembles; Musical theater; Pep band; Radio station; Student government; Student newspaper; Student-run film society; Symphony orchestra; Television station. **Organizations:** 245 registered organizations, 33 honor societies, 12 religious organizations, 15 fraternities, 12 sororities. **Athletics (Intercollegiate):** *Men:* baseball, basketball, cross-country, golf, soccer, tennis. *Women:* basketball, cross-country, golf, softball, tennis, track/field (outdoor), track/field (indoor), volleyball.

ACCOMMODATIONS

Allowed in exams:	
Calculators	Yes
Dictionary	Yes
Computer	Yes
Spell-checker	Yes
Extended test time	Yes
Scribe	Yes
Proctors	Yes
Oral exams	Yes
Note-takers	Yes
Support services for students with:	
LD	No
ADHD	No
ASD	No
Distraction-reduced environment	Yes
Recording of lecture allowed	Yes
Reading technology	Yes
Audio books	Yes
Other assistive technology	Yes
Priority registration	Yes
Added costs of services:	
For LD	No
For ADHD	No
For ASD	No
LD specialists	Yes
ADHD & ASD coaching	Yes
ASD specialists	No
Professional tutors	Yes
Peer tutors	Yes
Max. hours/week for services	Varies
How professors are notified of student approved accommodations	Both

COLLEGE GRADUATION REQUIREMENTS

Course waivers allowed	Yes
In what courses: Case-by-case basis	
Course substitutions allowed	Yes
In what courses: Case-by-case basis	

Illinois

DePaul University

1 East Jackson Boulevard, Chicago, IL 60604-2287 • Admissions: 312-362-8300 • Fax: 312-362-5749 **Support: SP**

CAMPUS

Type of school	Private (nonprofit)
Environment	Metropolis

STUDENTS

Undergrad enrollment	14,009
% male/female	47/53
% from out of state	25
% frosh live on campus	66

FINANCIAL FACTS

Annual tuition	$40,551
Room and board	$14,736
Required fees	$651

GENERAL ADMISSIONS INFO

Application fee	$0
Regular application deadline	2/1
Nonfall registration	Yes

Admission may be deferred.

Range SAT EBRW	540–650
Range SAT Math	530–640

ACADEMICS

Student/faculty ratio	16:1
% students returning for sophomore year	85

Most classes have 20–29 students.

Programs/Services for Students with Learning Differences

The Center for Students with Disabilities (CSD) is designed to service and support students with learning disabilities, attention deficit hyperactivity disorder, and all other disabilities. The immediate goals are to provide learning strategies based on students' strengths and weaknesses to assist students in the completion of course work. The ultimate goal is to impart academic and study skills that will enable the students to function independently in the academic environment and competitive job market. CSD provides intensive help on a one-on-one basis through Learning Specialist Clinician Services which is a fee-for-service available to students with learning disabilities. Learning Specialists meet with regularly to develop executive functioning skills and self-advocacy strategies that support expectations for academic success Learning Specialists do not facilitate accommodations for students; students are responsible for initiating and utilizing approved accommodations.

Admissions

There is no separate process for students with learning disabilities who wish to be considered for admission to the university. Students with learning disabilities must be first accepted to DePaul University before they can be accepted to the Center for Students with Disabilities (CSD). DePaul is Test Optional.

Additional Information

Student Success Coaching is a peer coaching program for first-year students to support the transition to college. Students meet on-on-one with to develop an action plan to establish goals, identify campus resources, improve time-management skills, and explore student organizations and opportunities for activities. There is an option to pay for additional support.

ADMISSIONS INFO FOR STUDENTS WITH LEARNING DIFFERENCES

Phone: 773-325-1677 • Fax: 773-325-3720 • Email: csd@depaul.edu

SAT/ACT required: No
Interview required: Yes
Essay required: No
Additional application required: Yes
Documentation submitted to: Center or Students with Disabilities

Special Ed. HS course work accepted: Yes
Separate application required for Programs/Services: Yes
Documentation required for:

- **LD:** Psychoeducational evaluation
- **ADHD:** Psychoeducational evaluation
- **ASD:** Psychoeducational evaluation

DePaul University

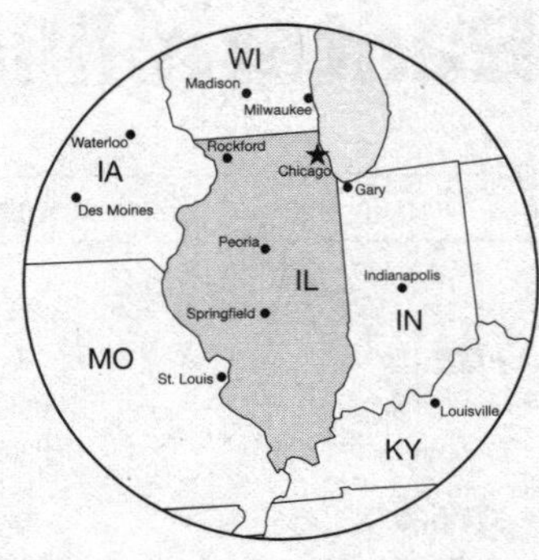

General Admissions

Very important factors include: rigor of secondary school record, academic GPA, standardized test scores. *Important factors include:* class rank, recommendation(s), extracurricular activities, talent/ability, character/personal qualities. *Other factors include:* application essay, interview, first generation, alumni/ae relation, geographical residence, state residency, religious affiliation/commitment, racial/ethnic status. High school diploma is required and GED is accepted. *Academic units required:* 4 English, 3 math, 3 science, 2 science labs, 2 unit from above areas or other academic areas. *Academic units recommended:* 4 English, 3 math, 3 science, 2 science labs, 2 foreign language.

Accommodations or Services

Accommodations are decided upon an individual basis after a thorough review of appropriate, current documentation. The accommodations requests must be supported through the documentation provided and must be logically linked to the current impact of the condition on academic functioning.

Financial Aid

Students should submit: FAFSA. *Need-based scholarships/grants offered:* College/university scholarship or grant aid from institutional funds; Federal Pell; Private scholarships; SEOG; State scholarships/grants. *Loan aid offered:* Direct PLUS loans; Direct Subsidized Stafford Loans; Direct Unsubsidized Stafford Loans. Federal Work-Study Program available. Institutional employment available.

Campus Life

Activities: Campus Ministries; Choral groups; Concert band; Dance; Drama/theater; International Student Organization; Jazz band; Literary magazine; Model UN; Music ensembles; Musical theater; Opera; Pep band; Radio station; Student government; Student newspaper; Student-run film society; Symphony orchestra. **Organizations:** 282 registered organizations, 24 honor societies, 18 religious organizations, 12 fraternities, 16 sororities. **Athletics (Intercollegiate):** *Men:* basketball, cross-country, golf, soccer, tennis, track/field (outdoor), track/field (indoor). *Women:* basketball, cross-country, soccer, softball, tennis, track/field (outdoor), track/field (indoor), volleyball.

ACCOMMODATIONS

Allowed in exams:	
Calculators	Yes
Dictionary	Yes
Computer	Yes
Spell-checker	Yes
Extended test time	Yes
Scribe	Yes
Proctors	Yes
Oral exams	Yes
Note-takers	Yes
Support services for students with:	
LD	Yes
ADHD	Yes
ASD	Yes
Distraction-reduced environment	Yes
Recording of lecture allowed	Yes
Reading technology	Yes
Audio books	Yes
Other assistive technology	Yes
Priority registration	Yes
Added costs of services:	
For LD	Yes
For ADHD	Yes
For ASD	Yes
LD specialists	Yes
ADHD & ASD coaching	Yes
ASD specialists	No
Professional tutors	No
Peer tutors	Yes
Max. hours/week for services	Varies
How professors are notified of student approved accommodations	Both

COLLEGE GRADUATION REQUIREMENTS

Course waivers allowed	No
Course substitutions allowed	No

Illinois

Eastern Illinois University

600 Lincoln Avenue, Charleston, IL 61920 • Admissions: 217-581-2223 • Fax: 217-581-7060 **Support: SP**

CAMPUS

Type of school	Public
Environment	Village

STUDENTS

Undergrad enrollment	6,229
% male/female	43/57
% from out of state	7
% frosh live on campus	89

FINANCIAL FACTS

Annual in-state tuition	$9,241
Annual out-of-state tuition	$11,551
Room and board	$9,864
Required fees	$2,822

GENERAL ADMISSIONS INFO

Application fee	$30
Regular application deadline	8/15
Nonfall registration	Yes

Admission may be deferred.

Range SAT EBRW	470–570
Range SAT Math	470–560
Range ACT Composite	18–23

ACADEMICS

Student/faculty ratio	14:1
% students returning for sophomore year	73

Most classes have 10–19 students.

Programs/Services for Students with Learning Differences

The Student Disability Services provides support to students with LD/ADHD as appropriate with documentation. The FOCUS Program is a free, one-to-one mentoring program for students with disabilities. FOCUS student mentors work with students to develop: strategies for studying; modes of communication with professors; time management skills; organization skills; note-taking skills. Eastern Illinois University's Students with Autism Transitional Education Program (STEP) focuses on providing enhanced support in three main skill set areas: academic, social and daily living STEP is a fee-based program limited to 20 students. Students must be admitted to the university in order to apply for STEP. Students who have enrolled in STEP for at least one semester can transition to STEP-Maintenance (M) at the discretion of the STEP administrators. STEP-M participants continue to receive support services at a less intense level.

Admissions

Applicants must have a high school grade-point average (GPA) of 2.5 on a 4.0 (unweighted scale) and SAT: 960 or ACT: 18. The Writing Section is not required. Any student who falls slightly below the criteria listed above, or had a noticeable decrease in semester GPA, is strongly encouraged to include a personal statement and letter of recommendation. The student should use the statement to provide more information as EIU reviews the application. Additional materials may be requested and used in the decision process.

Additional Information

The STEP Transition Program provides opportunities for growth through: Individualized peer mentorships that work to develop ASD skill sets; personalized campus tours focused on the individual's schedule/routine each semester; social skills groups that focus on utilizing interpersonal skills in the classroom and throughout the campus community; a positive educational work environment through regularly scheduled academic study tables; social events tailored to interests of the participants of the program to enhance the opportunity for friendships, active involvement on campus, and vocational skill development; physical fitness programs personalized to individual needs and abilities; residential support through trained residence assistants; single-room option for an additional fee that supports the opportunity to decompress and regulate (based on availability); early move-in date that allows for a calmer transition from the home to residence hall life; and regular daily-living skill trainings to ensure that students adequately

ADMISSIONS INFO FOR STUDENTS WITH LEARNING DIFFERENCES

Phone: 217-581-6583 • Fax: 217-581-7208 • Email: studentdisability@eiu.edu

SAT/ACT required: No
Interview required: No
Essay required: No
Additional application required: No
Documentation submitted to: Student Disability Services

Special Ed. HS course work accepted: Yes
Separate application required for Programs/Services: Yes
Documentation required for:
LD: Psychoeducational evaluation
ADHD Psychoeducational evaluation
ASD: Psychoeducational evaluation

Eastern Illinois University

adjust to adulthood. Regular contact with parents to allow for optimum teamwork between the individual, campus supports, and the family. There is a fee of $3,000 per semester.

General Admissions

Very important factors include: rigor of secondary school record, academic GPA, standardized test scores. *Other factors include:* class rank, application essay, recommendation(s), talent/ability, character/personal qualities. High school diploma is required and GED is accepted. *Academic units required:* 4 English, 3 math, 3 science, 3 science labs, 3 social studies, 2 academic electives. *Academic units recommended:* 2 foreign language.

Accommodations or Services

Accommodations are decided upon an individual basis after a thorough review of appropriate, current documentation. The accommodations requests must be supported through the documentation provided and must be logically linked to the current impact of the condition on academic functioning.

Financial Aid

Students should submit: Business/Farm Supplement; CSS/Financial Aid PROFILE; FAFSA; Noncustodial PROFILE. Applicants will be notified of awards on a rolling basis beginning 1/20. *Need-based scholarships/grants offered:* College/university scholarship or grant aid from institutional funds; Federal Pell; Private scholarships; SEOG; State scholarships/grants. *Loan aid offered:* Direct PLUS loans; Direct Subsidized Stafford Loans; Direct Unsubsidized Stafford Loans. Federal Work-Study Program available. Institutional employment available.

Campus Life

Activities: Campus Ministries; Choral groups; Concert band; Dance; Drama/theater; International Student Organization; Jazz band; Literary magazine; Marching band; Music ensembles; Musical theater; Pep band; Radio station; Student government; Student newspaper; Symphony orchestra; Television station; Yearbook. **Organizations:** 214 registered organizations, 20 honor societies, 16 religious organizations, 11 fraternities, 12 sororities. **Athletics (Intercollegiate):** *Men:* baseball, basketball, cross-country, football, golf, soccer, swimming, tennis, track/field (outdoor), track/field (indoor). *Women:* basketball, cross-country, golf, rugby, soccer, softball, swimming, tennis, track/field (outdoor), track/field (indoor), volleyball.

ACCOMMODATIONS

Allowed in exams:	
Calculators	Yes
Dictionary	Yes
Computer	Yes
Spell-checker	Yes
Extended test time	Yes
Scribe	No
Proctors	Yes
Oral exams	Yes
Note-takers	Yes
Support services for students with:	
LD	Yes
ADHD	Yes
ASD	Yes
Distraction-reduced environment	Yes
Recording of lecture allowed	Yes
Reading technology	Yes
Audio books	Yes
Other assistive technology	Yes
Priority registration	Yes
Added costs of services:	
For LD	No
For ADHD	No
For ASD	Yes
LD specialists	Yes
ADHD & ASD coaching	Yes
ASD specialists	Yes
Professional tutors	No
Peer tutors	Yes
Max. hours/week for services	Varies
How professors are notified of student approved accommodations	Student

COLLEGE GRADUATION REQUIREMENTS

Course waivers allowed	No
Course substitutions allowed	No

Illinois

Illinois State University

Office of Admissions, Normal, IL 61790-2200 • Admissions: 309-438-2181 • Fax: 309-438-3932 **Support: CS**

CAMPUS

Type of school	Public
Environment	City

STUDENTS

Undergrad enrollment	18,199
% male/female	45/55
% from out of state	2

FINANCIAL FACTS

Annual in-state tuition	$11,524
Annual out-of-state tuition	$23,048
Room and board	$9,850
Required fees	$3,308

GENERAL ADMISSIONS INFO

Application fee	$50
Regular application deadline	4/1
Nonfall registration	Yes

Admission may be deferred.

Range SAT EBRW	510–610
Range SAT Math	510–610
Range ACT Composite	20–26

ACADEMICS

Student/faculty ratio	19:1
% students returning for sophomore year	79

Most classes have 20–29 students.

Programs/Services for Students with Learning Differences

Illinois State University is dedicated to the principles of equal opportunity in education and accepts diversity as an affirmation of individual identity within a welcoming community. Student Access and Accommodation Services (SAAS) embraces the richness and value that disability brings to our campus community as it strengthens our learning, attitudes, and respect for each other. SAAS accomplished this through: 1) individual accommodation(s) to facilitate and support an accessible educational environment through inclusion of students with disabilities by removing or reducing barriers in the university setting; 2) collaborative partnerships with students, faculty, staff, members of the campus community, and university stakeholders to make Illinois State University accessible to everyone.

Admissions

Middle 50% ranges for 2018. The middle 50% ranges for admitted students are GPA: 3.07–3.83 on a 4.0 scale and SAT: 1020–1200 or ACT: 21–26. For students whose applications require further review, an optional academic personal statement may help Admissions come to the right decision. If a student chooses to submit a statement, it will be considered along with the transcript and test score information to determine eligibility for admission. If a student chooses to submit a statement, it should address the following: State why you feel Illinois State University is a good fit for your educational goals; Identify and explain your academic strengths and weaknesses; Explain any circumstances which affected your high school academic performance, if applicable. It may be in the student's best interest to complete the optional statement if the student falls below or in the lower end of one or all of the middle 50 percent ranges for admitted students.

Additional Information

Individualized LD/ADHD academic coaching is available to help students develop college level skills in the areas of note-taking, time management, reading strategies, study skills, and test taking. Meetings can be scheduled weekly, biweekly, or monthly. Academic coaching and peer-tutoring services are offered through the Julia N. Visor Academic Center.

ADMISSIONS INFO FOR STUDENTS WITH LEARNING DIFFERENCES

Phone: 309-438-5853 • Fax: 309-438-7713 • Email: ableisu@ilstu.edu

SAT/ACT required: No
Interview required: No
Essay required: Optional
Additional application required: No
Documentation submitted to: Student Access and Accommodations Services

Special Ed. HS course work accepted: Yes
Separate application required for Programs/Services: No
Documentation required for:
LD: Psychoeducational evaluation
ADHD: Psychoeducational evaluation
ASD: Psychoeducational evaluation

Illinois State University

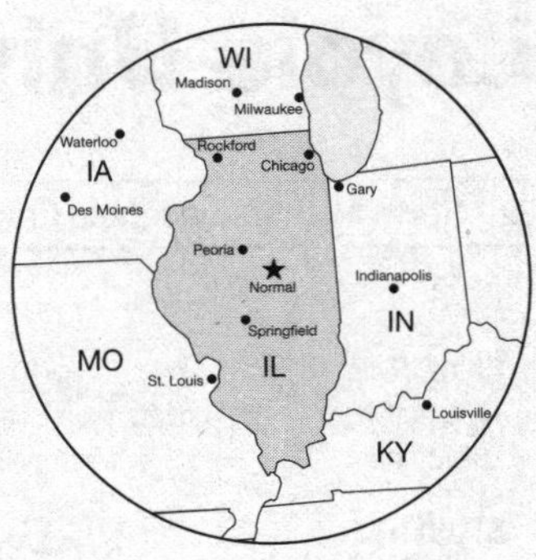

General Admissions

Very important factors include: academic GPA, standardized test scores. *Other factors include:* application essay, talent/ability, first generation, geographical residence, state residency, racial/ethnic status. High school diploma is required and GED is accepted. *Academic units required:* 8 English, 6 math, 4 science, 4 science labs, 4 foreign language, 4 social studies, 4 history, 4 visual/performing arts.

Accommodations or Services

Accommodations are decided upon an individual basis after a thorough review of appropriate, current documentation. The accommodations requests must be supported through the documentation provided and must be logically linked to the current impact of the condition on academic functioning.

Financial Aid

Students should submit: FAFSA. *Need-based scholarships/grants offered:* College/university scholarship or grant aid from institutional funds; Federal Nursing Scholarships; Federal Pell; Private scholarships; SEOG; State scholarships/grants. *Loan aid offered:* Direct PLUS loans; Direct Subsidized Stafford Loans; Direct Unsubsidized Stafford Loans. Federal Work-Study Program available. Institutional employment available.

Campus Life

Activities: Campus Ministries; Choral groups; Concert band; Dance; Drama/theater; International Student Organization; Jazz band; Literary magazine; Marching band; Model UN; Music ensembles; Musical theater; Opera; Pep band; Radio station; Student government; Student newspaper; Student-run film society; Symphony orchestra; Television station. **Organizations:** 370 registered organizations, 24 honor societies, 20 fraternities, 19 sororities. **Athletics (Intercollegiate):** *Men:* baseball, basketball, cheerleading, cross-country, football, golf, tennis, track/field (outdoor), track/field (indoor). *Women:* basketball, cheerleading, cross-country, diving, golf, gymnastics, soccer, softball, swimming, tennis, track/field (outdoor), track/field (indoor), volleyball.

ACCOMMODATIONS

Allowed in exams:	
Calculators	Yes
Dictionary	No
Computer	Yes
Spell-checker	Yes
Extended test time	Yes
Scribe	Yes
Proctors	Yes
Oral exams	Yes
Note-takers	Yes
Support services for students with:	
LD	Yes
ADHD	Yes
ASD	Yes
Distraction-reduced environment	Yes
Recording of lecture allowed	Yes
Reading technology	Yes
Audio books	Yes
Other assistive technology	Yes
Priority registration	Yes
Added costs of services:	
For LD	No
For ADHD	No
For ASD	No
LD specialists	Yes
ADHD & ASD coaching	Yes
ASD specialists	No
Professional tutors	No
Peer tutors	Yes
Max. hours/week for services	Varies
How professors are notified of student approved accommodations	Student

COLLEGE GRADUATION REQUIREMENTS

Course waivers allowed	No
Course substitutions allowed	Yes
In what courses: Case-by-case basis	

Illinois

Loyola University of Chicago

820 North Michigan Avenue, Chicago, IL 60611 • Admissions: 312-915-6500 • Fax: 312-915-7216 **Support: S**

CAMPUS	
Type of school	Private (nonprofit)
Environment	Metropolis
STUDENTS	
Undergrad enrollment	12,104
% male/female	33/67
% from out of state	39
% frosh live on campus	86
FINANCIAL FACTS	
Annual tuition	$45,500
Room and board	$15,020
Required fees	$1,398
GENERAL ADMISSIONS INFO	
Application fee	$0
Regular application deadline	Rolling
Nonfall registration	Yes
Range SAT EBRW	570–660
Range SAT Math	560–660
Range ACT Composite	25–30
ACADEMICS	
Student/faculty ratio	14:1
% students returning for sophomore year	86
Most classes have 10–19 students.	

Programs/Services for Students with Learning Differences

Any student with a documented disability is encouraged to register with the services for the Student Accessibility Center (SAC). Students are required to provide documentation from a medical provider, therapist, psychiatrist, etc. that clearly states their diagnosis. Additional information about symptoms and how their diagnosis impacts their college career is encouraged; supplemental documentation (IEP, 504 plans, documents from previous universities, etc.) are all accepted forms of supplemental documentation after an intake appointment to determine accommodations, students are registered with our office and work 1:1 as needed with an accessibility specialist.

Admissions

There is no separate application process for students with learning disabilities. All applicants must meet the same admission criteria. The average GPA is 3.6 and the mid 50% SAT is 1110–1320 or ACT 24–29.

Additional Information

UNIV 112: Strategies for Learning is a one-credit, semester long course designed to help students become strong learners in college. Students identify challenge areas, previous academic experiences, and motivations to create a plan for college success that includes developing learning strategies for test-prep, note-taking, study skills, and exam prep. One-on-one personalized Success Coaching is offered free to students who want to work on organization, time management, note-taking, test prep, and goal setting. UNIV 112 and Success Coaching are offered through Student Academic Services.

ADMISSIONS INFO FOR STUDENTS WITH LEARNING DIFFERENCES

Phone: 773-508-3700 • Fax: 773-508-7777 • Email: sac@luc.edu

SAT/ACT required: No
Interview required: No
Essay required: Yes
Additional application required: Yes
Documentation submitted to: Student Accessibility Center

Special Ed. HS course work accepted: Yes
Separate application required for Programs/Services: Yes
Documentation required for:
LD: Psychoeducational evaluation
ADHD: Psychoeducational evaluation
ASD: Psychoeducational evaluation

Loyola University of Chicago

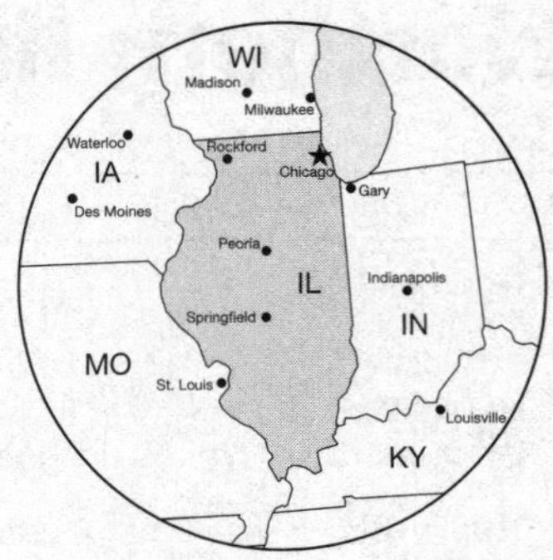

General Admissions

Very important factors include: rigor of secondary school record, academic GPA, standardized test scores. *Important factors include:* application essay, recommendation(s), extracurricular activities, character/personal qualities. *Other factors include:* class rank, interview, talent/ability, first generation, alumni/ae relation, geographical residence, state residency. High school diploma is required and GED is accepted. *Academic units required:* 4 English, 3 math, 3 science, 2 foreign language, 2 social studies, 1 history. *Academic units recommended:* 4 English, 4 math, 3 science, 2 foreign language, 2 social studies, 2 history, 3 academic electives.

Accommodations or Services

Accommodations are decided upon an individual basis after a thorough review of appropriate, current documentation. The accommodations requests must be supported through the documentation provided and must be logically linked to the current impact of the condition on academic functioning.

Financial Aid

Students should submit: FAFSA. Applicants will be notified of awards on a rolling basis beginning 3/1. *Need-based scholarships/grants offered:* College/university scholarship or grant aid from institutional funds; Federal Pell; Private scholarships; SEOG; State scholarships/grants. *Loan aid offered:* Direct PLUS loans; Direct Subsidized Stafford Loans; Direct Unsubsidized Stafford Loans. Institutional employment available.

Campus Life

Activities: Campus Ministries; Choral groups; Concert band; Dance; Drama/theater; International Student Organization; Jazz band; Literary magazine; Model UN; Music ensembles; Musical theater; Opera; Pep band; Radio station; Student government; Student newspaper; Student-run film society; Symphony orchestra; Television station. **Organizations:** 230 registered organizations, 9 honor societies, 7 religious organizations, 9 fraternities, 10 sororities. **Athletics (Intercollegiate):** *Men:* basketball, cheerleading, cross-country, golf, soccer, track/field (outdoor), track/field (indoor), volleyball. *Women:* basketball, cheerleading, cross-country, golf, soccer, softball, track/field (outdoor), track/field (indoor), volleyball.

ACCOMMODATIONS

Allowed in exams:	
Calculators	Yes
Dictionary	Yes
Computer	Yes
Spell-checker	Yes
Extended test time	Yes
Scribe	Yes
Proctors	Yes
Oral exams	Yes
Note-takers	Yes
Support services for students with:	
LD	Yes
ADHD	Yes
ASD	Yes
Distraction-reduced environment	Yes
Recording of lecture allowed	Yes
Reading technology	Yes
Audio books	Yes
Other assistive technology	Yes
Priority registration	Yes
Added costs of services:	
For LD	No
For ADHD	No
For ASD	No
LD specialists	No
ADHD & ASD coaching	Yes
ASD specialists	No
Professional tutors	No
Peer tutors	Yes
Max. hours/week for services	Varies
How professors are notified of student approved accommodations	Student

COLLEGE GRADUATION REQUIREMENTS

Course waivers allowed	No
Course substitutions allowed	Yes
In what courses: Foreign language	

Illinois

Northern Illinois University

1425 Lincoln Hwy, DeKalb, IL 60115 • Admissions: 815-753-0446 **Support: CS**

CAMPUS

Type of school	Public
Environment	Village

STUDENTS

Undergrad enrollment	12,131
% male/female	49/51
% from out of state	5
% frosh live on campus	89

FINANCIAL FACTS

Annual in-state tuition	$9,464
Annual out-of-state tuition	$9,464
Room and board	$10,880
Required fees	$2,888

GENERAL ADMISSIONS INFO

Application fee	$40
Regular application deadline	8/1
Nonfall registration	Yes
Range SAT EBRW	470–590
Range SAT Math	470–580
Range ACT Composite	19–25

ACADEMICS

Student/faculty ratio	13:1
% students returning for sophomore year	72

Most classes have 20–29 students.

Programs/Services for Students with Learning Differences

The Disability Resource Center (DRC) offers guidance, services and resources to help you succeed at NIU. The DRC will work with the student to determine needs and develop a plan to meet them. The Center works to provide reasonable and appropriate accommodations for students and the campus community. Exam accommodations, classroom accommodations, reformatting of course materials, and adaptive technology are a few of the accommodations offered. Promoting self-advocacy and communication skills, the focus is on helping students create collaborative relationships with faculty and staff. Faculty are integral to supporting students who are eligible for accommodations in the classroom. The Center works with faculty and department staff so accommodations are understood and implemented for student access and success.

Admissions

NIU's DRC does not have a program; therefore, there is not a separate admissions process. All new students seeking access/accommodations participate in an initial interview then develop an Accommodation Plan. General admission requires 4 years English, 2 years math, 2 years science, and 3 years social studies. The Chance Program is only available to Illinois residents from targeted schools or who participate in certain academic preparatory programs. The ACT or SAT is not required for admission.

Additional Information

The guiding mission of the CHANCE Program is to identify, recruit, admit, and assist otherwise capable students whose pre-college education has not fully enabled them to take maximum advantage of their potential and the opportunities of higher education at NIU. CHANCE services include: individual and group academic, personal and career counseling, academic monitoring and follow-up throughout the student's undergraduate career, tutorial assistance for courses, academic skills-enhancement courses, introductory university transition skills-building course taught by a counselor, and peer mentoring for freshmen and transfer students. The A+ Program offers peer-led small group workshops that focus on effective reading, time management, testing strategies, test anxiety, note-taking skills, learning styles. Peer Assisted Learning (PAL) is offered one-on-one or in small group settings.

ADMISSIONS INFO FOR STUDENTS WITH LEARNING DIFFERENCES

Phone: 815- 753-1303 • Fax: 815-753-9570 • Email: drc@niu.edu

SAT/ACT required: Yes (Test blind for 2021)
Interview required: No
Essay required: No
Additional application required: No
Documentation submitted to: Disability Resource Center

Special Ed. HS course work accepted: Yes
Separate application required for Programs/Services: No
Documentation required for:
LD: Psychoeducational evaluation
ADHD: Psychoeducational evaluation
ASD: Psychoeducational evaluation

Northern Illinois University

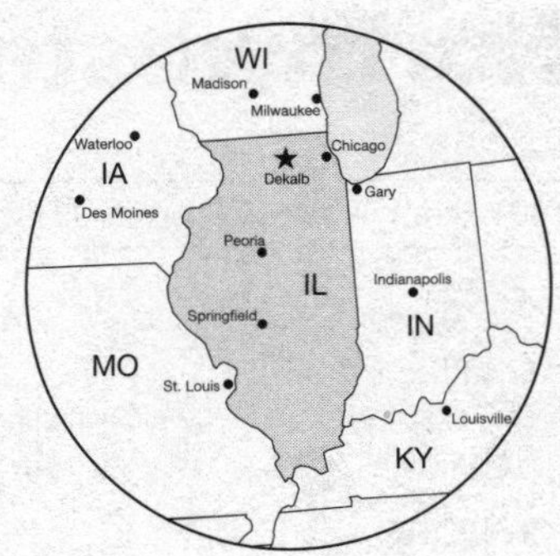

General Admissions

Very important factors include: rigor of secondary school record, class rank, standardized test scores. *Other factors include:* application essay, recommendation(s), interview, extracurricular activities, talent/ability, racial/ethnic status. High school diploma is required and GED is accepted. *Academic units required:* 4 English, 2 math, 2 science, 1 science lab, 1 foreign language, 2 social studies, 1 history. *Academic units recommended:* 4 math, 4 science, 2 science labs, 2 foreign language, 3 social studies.

Accommodations or Services

Accommodations are decided upon an individual basis after a thorough review of appropriate, current documentation. The accommodations requests must be supported through the documentation provided and must be logically linked to the current impact of the condition on academic functioning.

Financial Aid

Students should submit: FAFSA; Institution's own financial aid form. Applicants will be notified of awards on a rolling basis beginning 10/15. *Need-based scholarships/grants offered:* College/university scholarship or grant aid from institutional funds; Federal Nursing Scholarships; Federal Pell; Private scholarships; SEOG; State scholarships/grants. *Loan aid offered:* Direct PLUS loans; Direct Subsidized Stafford Loans; Direct Unsubsidized Stafford Loans. Federal Work-Study Program available. Institutional employment available.

Campus Life

Activities: Campus Ministries; Choral groups; Concert band; Dance; Drama/theater; International Student Organization; Jazz band; Marching band; Model UN; Music ensembles; Musical theater; Opera; Pep band; Radio station; Student government; Student newspaper; Student-run film society; Symphony orchestra; Television station. **Organizations:** 355 registered organizations, 23 religious organizations, 27 fraternities, 19 sororities. **Athletics (Intercollegiate):** *Men:* baseball, basketball, diving, football, golf, soccer, swimming, tennis, wrestling. *Women:* basketball, cross-country, golf, gymnastics, soccer, softball, swimming, tennis, volleyball.

ACCOMMODATIONS

Allowed in exams:	
Calculators	Yes
Dictionary	Yes
Computer	Yes
Spell-checker	Yes
Extended test time	Yes
Scribe	Yes
Proctors	Yes
Oral exams	Yes
Note-takers	Yes
Support services for students with:	
LD	Yes
ADHD	Yes
ASD	Yes
Distraction-reduced environment	Yes
Recording of lecture allowed	Yes
Reading technology	Yes
Audio books	Yes
Other assistive technology	Yes
Priority registration	Yes
Added costs of services:	
For LD	No
For ADHD	No
For ASD	No
LD specialists	No
ADHD & ASD coaching	Yes
ASD specialists	No
Professional tutors	No
Peer tutors	Yes
Max. hours/week for services	Varies
How professors are notified of student approved accommodations	Student

COLLEGE GRADUATION REQUIREMENTS

Course waivers allowed	Yes
In what courses: Case-by-case basis	
Course substitutions allowed	Yes
In what courses: Case-by-case basis	

Illinois

Northwestern University

1801 Hinman Ave., Evanston, IL 60204 • Admissions: 847-491-7271 **Support: CS**

CAMPUS	
Type of school	Private (nonprofit)
Environment	City
STUDENTS	
Undergrad enrollment	8,319
% male/female	49/51
% from out of state	69
% frosh live on campus	100
FINANCIAL FACTS	
Annual tuition	$56,286
Room and board	$17,616
Required fees	$474
GENERAL ADMISSIONS INFO	
Application fee	$75
Regular application deadline	1/1
Nonfall registration	Yes
Admission may be deferred.	
Range SAT EBRW	700–760
Range SAT Math	740–790
Range ACT Composite	33–35
ACADEMICS	
Student/faculty ratio	6:1
% students returning for sophomore year	98
Most classes have 10–19 students.	

Programs/Services for Students with Learning Differences

AccessibleNU is the campus resource that provides students with LD, ADHD, and all other disabilities the tools, reasonable accommodations, and support services needed to participate fully in the university environment. A wide range of services are provided to students with disabilities allowing them full access to programs and activities at Northwestern University. It is the responsibility of the student to provide documentation of disability, to inform the AccessibleNU office and to request accommodations and services if needed. A student who has a disability but has not registered with AccessibleNU is not entitled to services or accommodations.

Admissions

There is no special admissions procedure for students with learning disabilities or ADHD. All applicants must meet the general admission criteria. Most students have taken AP and honors courses in high school and been very successful in these competitive college-prep courses. ACT/SAT tests are required, and SAT Subject Tests are recommended. Foreign-language substitutions may be allowed and are decided on a case-by-case basis.

Additional Information

Undergraduate Program for Advancing Learning (UPAL) and Peer Academic Coaching is available through the office of Academic Support and Learning Advancement. UPAL provides sustained support during each quarter through a small group experience with peer mentoring. The focus is on enhancing a student's academic experiences at Northwestern. Individual Academic Coaching pairs trained undergraduate coaches with students to help with refining a student's approach to studying and learning including time management, organization skills, and accessing campus resources for success. Peer and TA tutoring in a variety of academic subjects is available free of charge.

ADMISSIONS INFO FOR STUDENTS WITH LEARNING DIFFERENCES

Phone: 847-467-5530 • Fax: 847-467-5531 • Email: accessiblenu@northwestern.edu

SAT/ACT required: Yes (Test optional for 2021)
Interview required: No
Essay required: Yes
Additional application required: No
Documentation submitted to: AccessibleNU

Special Ed. HS course work accepted: Yes
Separate application required for Programs/Services: No
Documentation required for:
LD: Psychoeducational evaluation
ADHD: Psychoeducational evaluation
ASD: Psychoeducational evaluation

Northwestern University

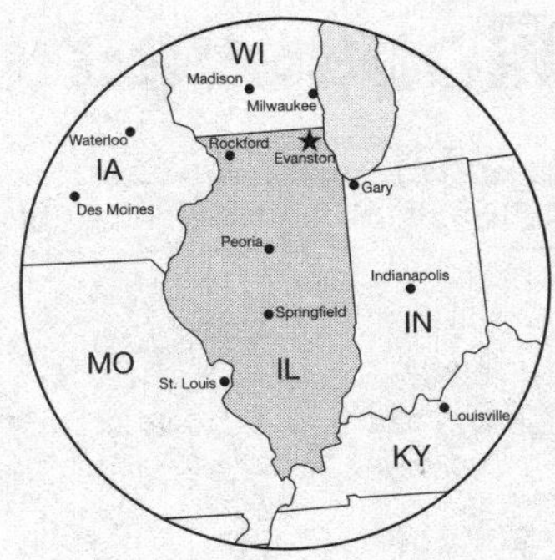

General Admissions

Very important factors include: rigor of secondary school record, class rank, academic GPA, standardized test scores. *Important factors include:* application essay, recommendation(s), extracurricular activities, talent/ability, character/personal qualities. *Other factors include:* interview, first generation, alumni/ae relation, racial/ethnic status, volunteer work, work experience, level of applicant's interest. High school diploma is required and GED is accepted. *Academic units recommended:* 4 English, 3 math, 2 science, 2 science labs, 2 foreign language, 2 social studies, 2 history, 1 academic elective.

Accommodations or Services

Accommodations are decided upon an individual basis after a thorough review of appropriate, current documentation. The accommodations requests must be supported through the documentation provided and must be logically linked to the current impact of the condition on academic functioning.

Financial Aid

Students should submit: FAFSA. Applicants will be notified of awards on a rolling basis beginning 11/1. *Need-based scholarships/grants offered:* College/university scholarship or grant aid from institutional funds; Federal Pell; SEOG; State scholarships/grants. *Loan aid offered:* Direct PLUS loans; Direct Subsidized Stafford Loans; Direct Unsubsidized Stafford Loans. Federal Work-Study Program available. Institutional employment available.

Campus Life

Activities: Campus Ministries; Choral groups; Concert band; Dance; Drama/theater; International Student Organization; Jazz band; Literary magazine; Marching band; Model UN; Music ensembles; Musical theater; Opera; Pep band; Radio station; Student government; Student newspaper; Student-run film society; Symphony orchestra; Television station; Yearbook. **Organizations:** 415 registered organizations, 23 honor societies, 29 religious organizations, 17 fraternities, 12 sororities. **Athletics (Intercollegiate):** *Men:* baseball, basketball, cheerleading, diving, football, golf, soccer, swimming, tennis, wrestling. *Women:* basketball, cheerleading, cross-country, diving, fencing, field hockey, golf, lacrosse, soccer, softball, swimming, tennis, volleyball.

ACCOMMODATIONS

Allowed in exams:	
Calculators	Yes
Dictionary	Yes
Computer	Yes
Spell-checker	Yes
Extended test time	Yes
Scribe	Yes
Proctors	Yes
Oral exams	Yes
Note-takers	Yes
Support services for students with:	
LD	Yes
ADHD	Yes
ASD	Yes
Distraction-reduced environment	Yes
Recording of lecture allowed	Yes
Reading technology	Yes
Audio books	Yes
Other assistive technology	Yes
Priority registration	Yes
Added costs of services:	
For LD	No
For ADHD	No
For ASD	No
LD specialists	Yes
ADHD & ASD coaching	No
ASD specialists	No
Professional tutors	No
Peer tutors	No
Max. hours/week for services	Usually one hour
How professors are notified of student approved accommodations	Student

COLLEGE GRADUATION REQUIREMENTS

Course waivers allowed	No
Course substitutions allowed	Yes
In what courses: Case-by-case basis	

Roosevelt University

430 South Michigan Avenue, Chicago, IL 60605 • Admissions: 877-277-5978 • Fax: 847-619-4216 **Support: SP**

CAMPUS

Type of school	Private (nonprofit)
Environment	Metropolis

STUDENTS

Undergrad enrollment	2,381
% male/female	34/66
% from out of state	34
% frosh live on campus	71

FINANCIAL FACTS

Annual tuition	$31,493
Room and board	$8,700
Required fees	$354

GENERAL ADMISSIONS INFO

Application fee	$25
Regular application deadline	Rolling
Nonfall registration	Yes

Admission may be deferred.

Range SAT EBRW	510–630
Range SAT Math	500–600
Range ACT Composite	21–27

ACADEMICS

Student/faculty ratio	11:1
% students returning for sophomore year	73

Most classes have 10–19 students.

Programs/Services for Students with Learning Differences

The Learning and Support Services Program (LSSP) is designed to assist students with learning differences in their pursuit of a college education. Students meet once or twice a week with a staff member of the Academic Success Center for individualized support on the development of compensatory strategies and self-advocacy skills. LSSP is a fee-based program. Students with learning disabilities need to register with Disability Services for accommodations.

Admissions

Applicants can self-report GPA and ACT or SAT. The Writing section is not required. There is no separate admissions process for students with learning disabilities. Though not initially required, a personal statement, essay, letters of recommendation, and/or official transcripts may be requested after initial review of your application.

Additional Information

The Learning and Support Services Program is available to students with learning disabilities, attention disorders, traumatic brain injury, and any other condition that presents learning disorders. Assistance is available in course selection, required course readings, assignments, and more. Depending on individual needs, tutoring assistance may include course related training, time management, organizational skills, to name a few. Students are highly encouraged to utilize other appropriate resources, such as counseling, career development, campus life, and tutoring center. Services and accommodations are available to undergraduate and graduate students. One-to-one peer mentoring is available through the Office of Academic Success and focuses on services fitted to the student's needs such as study support, organizational strategies, social support, test prep, and writing and proofreading assistance.

ADMISSIONS INFO FOR STUDENTS WITH LEARNING DIFFERENCES

Phone: 312-341-3811 • Fax: 312-341-2471 • Email: academicsuccess@roosevelt.edu

SAT/ACT required: No
Interview required: Yes
Essay required: Yes
Additional application required: No
Documentation submitted to: Academic Success Center

Special Ed. HS course work accepted: Yes
Separate application required for Programs/Services: Yes
Documentation required for:
LD: Psychoeducational evaluation
ADHD: Psychoeducational evaluation
ASD: Psychoeducational evaluation

Roosevelt University

General Admissions

Very important factors include: academic GPA, standardized test scores. *Other factors include:* rigor of secondary school record, class rank, application essay, recommendation(s), interview, extracurricular activities, talent/ability, character/personal qualities, first generation, alumni/ae relation, level of applicant's interest. High school diploma is required and GED is accepted. *Academic units required:* 4 English, 3 math, 2 science, 2 science labs, 2 social studies. *Academic units recommended:* 4 English, 4 math, 3 science, 3 science labs, 2 foreign language, 3 social studies, 2 history, 2 academic electives.

Accommodations or Services

Accommodations are decided upon an individual basis after a thorough review of appropriate, current documentation. The accommodations requests must be supported through the documentation provided and must be logically linked to the current impact of the condition on academic functioning.

Financial Aid

Students should submit: FAFSA; Institution's own financial aid form. *Need-based scholarships/grants offered:* College/university scholarship or grant aid from institutional funds; Federal Pell; Private scholarships; SEOG; State scholarships/grants. *Loan aid offered:* Direct PLUS loans; Direct Subsidized Stafford Loans; Direct Unsubsidized Stafford Loans. Federal Work-Study Program available. Institutional employment available.

Campus Life

Activities: Choral groups; Concert band; Dance; Drama/theater; International Student Organization; Jazz band; Literary magazine; Music ensembles; Musical theater; Opera; Pep band; Radio station; Student government; Student newspaper; Symphony orchestra. **Organizations:** 60 registered organizations, 6 honor societies, 3 religious organizations, 2 fraternities, 5 sororities.

ACCOMMODATIONS

Allowed in exams:	
Calculators	Yes
Dictionary	No
Computer	Yes
Spell-checker	Yes
Extended test time	Yes
Scribe	Yes
Proctors	Yes
Oral exams	No
Note-takers	Yes
Support services for students with:	
LD	Yes
ADHD	Yes
ASD	Yes
Distraction-reduced environment	Yes
Recording of lecture allowed	Yes
Reading technology	Yes
Audio books	Yes
Other assistive technology	Yes
Priority registration	No
Added costs of services:	
For LD	Yes
For ADHD	Yes
For ASD	Yes
LD specialists	Yes
ADHD & ASD coaching	Yes
ASD specialists	No
Professional tutors	No
Peer tutors	Yes
Max. hours/week for services	Varies
How professors are notified of student approved accommodations	Student

COLLEGE GRADUATION REQUIREMENTS

Course waivers allowed	Yes
In what courses: Case-by-case basis	
Course substitutions allowed	Yes
In what courses: Case-by-case basis	

Illinois

Southern Illinois University Carbondale

Undergraduate Admissions, Mailcode 4710, Carbondale, IL 62901 • Admissions: 618-536-4405 • Fax: 618-453-4609 **Support: SP**

CAMPUS

Type of school	Public
Environment	Town

STUDENTS

Undergrad enrollment	8,311
% male/female	53/47
% from out of state	18
% frosh live on campus	91

FINANCIAL FACTS

Annual in-state tuition	$9,638
Annual out-of-state tuition	$9,638
Room and board	$10,622

Required fees $5,466

GENERAL ADMISSIONS INFO

Application fee	$40
Regular application deadline	Rolling
Nonfall registration	Yes

Admission may be deferred.

Range SAT EBRW	540–710
Range SAT Math	530–710
Range ACT Composite	21–28

ACADEMICS

Student/faculty ratio	12:1
% students returning for sophomore year	75

Most classes have 10–19 students.

Programs/Services for Students with Learning Differences

Southern Illinois University provides students with disabilities equal opportunity and access to seek their educational goals through the Disability Support Services office. In addition, SIU offers the Achieve Program, a comprehensive program of support for students with LD, ADHD, ASD, and other learning differences.

Admissions

Applicants are eligible for automatic admissions if they are on track to complete the course requirements and who meet one of the following requirements: a cumulative GPA of 2.75, ranking in the top 10% of their graduating class, or test score equivalent of 23 ACT or 1140 SAT. The Achieve Program works with Admissions for students who are applying to Achieve and who do not meet these requirements through a holistic review process. The holistic review process also considers ACT or SAT subscores, high school rank, improvements in high school GPA from year to year, letters of recommendation, participation in service or extracurricular activities, and extenuating circumstances.

Additional Information

Achieve Program admissions process: Meet criteria for Achieve admission 1) Primary diagnosis of a learning disability, attention deficit disorder, or other learning difference, 2) IQ commensurate with college achievement, 3) Age-appropriate social and emotional maturity. In addition, students must complete an Achieve Program application and submit all required documentation and paperwork. The Achieve Program reviews and makes an initial decision about a candidate. If the candidate is a good fit, the candidate is invited to complete a staff interview. At the conclusion of the interview, staff will make a decision about acceptance into the Achieve Program.

ADMISSIONS INFO FOR STUDENTS WITH LEARNING DIFFERENCES

Phone: 618-453-5738 • Fax: 618-453-5700 • Email: DSS@siu.edu or achieve@siu.edu

SAT/ACT required: No (if GPA is above 2.75)
Interview required: Yes
Essay required: Yes
Additional application required: No
Documentation submitted to: Disability Support Services

Special Ed. HS course work accepted: Yes
Separate application required for Programs/Services: Yes
Documentation required for:
LD: Psychoeducational evaluation
ADHD: Psychoeducational evaluation
ASD: Psychoeducational evaluation

Southern Illinois University Carbondale

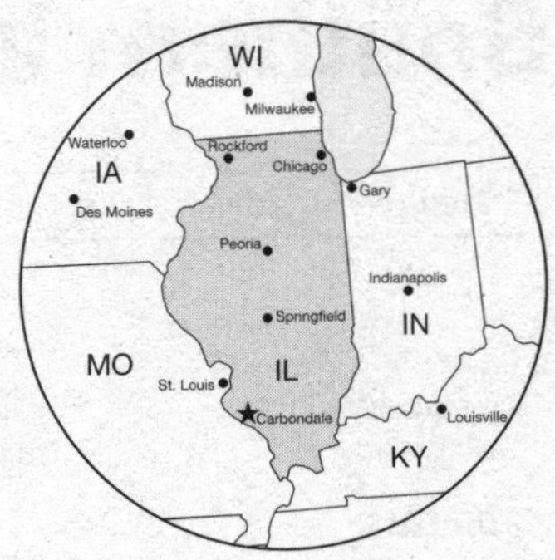

General Admissions

Very important factors include: academic GPA, standardized test scores. *Important factors include:* rigor of secondary school record. *Other factors include:* class rank, application essay, recommendation(s), extracurricular activities, talent/ability, character/personal qualities, volunteer work. High school diploma is required and GED is accepted. *Academic units required:* 4 English, 3 math, 3 science, 3 science labs, 3 social studies, 2 academic electives. *Academic units recommended:* 4 English, 4 math, 3 science, 3 science labs, 3 social studies, 2 academic electives.

Accommodations or Services

Accommodations are decided upon an individual basis after a thorough review of appropriate, current documentation. The accommodations requests must be supported through the documentation provided and must be logically linked to the current impact of the condition on academic functioning.

Financial Aid

Students should submit: FAFSA. *Need-based scholarships/grants offered:* College/university scholarship or grant aid from institutional funds; Federal Pell; Private scholarships; SEOG; State scholarships/grants. *Loan aid offered:* Direct PLUS loans; Direct Subsidized Stafford Loans; Direct Unsubsidized Stafford Loans. Federal Work-Study Program available. Institutional employment available.

Campus Life

Activities: Campus Ministries; Choral groups; Concert band; Dance; Drama/theater; International Student Organization; Jazz band; Literary magazine; Marching band; Model UN; Music ensembles; Musical theater; Opera; Pep band; Radio station; Student government; Student newspaper; Student-run film society; Symphony orchestra; Television station. **Organizations:** 299 registered organizations, 22 honor societies, 10 religious organizations, 20 fraternities, 10 sororities. **Athletics (Intercollegiate):** *Men:* baseball, basketball, cheerleading, cross-country, diving, football, golf, swimming, tennis, track/field (outdoor), track/field (indoor). *Women:* basketball, cheerleading, cross-country, diving, golf, softball, swimming, tennis, track/field (outdoor), track/field (indoor), volleyball.

ACCOMMODATIONS

Allowed in exams:	
Calculators	Yes
Dictionary	Yes
Computer	Yes
Spell-checker	Yes
Extended test time	Yes
Scribe	Yes
Proctors	Yes
Oral exams	Yes
Note-takers	Yes
Support services for students with:	
LD	Yes
ADHD	Yes
ASD	Yes
Distraction-reduced environment	Yes
Recording of lecture allowed	Yes
Reading technology	Yes
Audio books	Yes
Other assistive technology	Yes
Priority registration	Yes
Added costs of services:	
For LD	Yes
For ADHD	Yes
For ASD	Yes
LD specialists	Yes
ADHD & ASD coaching	Yes
ASD specialists	Yes
Professional tutors	No
Peer tutors	Yes
Max. hours/week for services	20
How professors are notified of student approved accommodations	Both

COLLEGE GRADUATION REQUIREMENTS

Course waivers allowed	Yes
In what courses: Case-by case basis	
Course substitutions allowed	Yes
In what courses: Case-by case basis	

Illinois

Southern Illinois University—Edwardsville

Il State Rte 157, Edwardsville, IL 62026-1047 • Admissions: 618-650-3705 • Fax: 618-650-5013 **Support: S**

CAMPUS

Type of school	Public
Environment	Town

STUDENTS

Undergrad enrollment	10,400
% male/female	46/54
% from out of state	16
% frosh live on campus	62

FINANCIAL FACTS

Annual in-state tuition	$9,123
Annual out-of-state tuition	$9,123
Room and board	$9,881
Required fees	$3,096

GENERAL ADMISSIONS INFO

Application fee	$40
Regular application deadline	7/1
Nonfall registration	Yes

Admission may be deferred.

Range SAT EBRW	510–610
Range SAT Math	510–610
Range ACT Composite	20–26

ACADEMICS

Student/faculty ratio	15:1
% students returning for sophomore year	79

Most classes have 10–19 students.

Programs/Services for Students with Learning Differences

Accessible Campus Community & Equitable Student Support (ACCESS) provides reasonable accommodations to ensure that diverse learners have access to the University and its programs through intentional interventions, programs, and services in order to meet federal guidelines, encourage personal growth, and increase effective communication.

Admissions

Students with learning disabilities are required to submit the same general application form as all other students. Students should submit documentation of their learning disability in order to receive services once enrolled. This documentation should be sent to DSS. Regular admissions criteria recommended: 4 years of English, 3 years of math, 3 years of science, 3 years of social science, 2 years of a foreign language or electives (students with deficiencies need to check with the Office of Admissions); grade point average of 2.5/4.0 and an ACT minimum of 18 (the average is 22.4) or SAT of 860-890. Students not meeting this criteria are encouraged to apply and may be subject to additional review.

Additional Information

The Learning Support Service is available to help students with disabilities improve their time management skills and develop effective study strategies. Current resources include advocacy, priority registration, books in alternate format, extended time testing assistance in writing/ready exams, and volunteer note takers. In addition, the ACCESS staff members act as liaisons with faculty and staff regarding learning disabilities and accommodations needed by students. Services and accommodations are available for undergraduate and graduate students.

ADMISSIONS INFO FOR STUDENTS WITH LEARNING DIFFERENCES

Phone: 618-650-3726 • Fax: 618-650-5691 • Email: myaccess@siue.edu

SAT/ACT required: Yes (Test optional for 2021)
Interview required: No
Essay required: No
Additional application required: Yes
Documentation submitted to: ACCESS

Special Ed. HS course work accepted: Yes
Separate application required for Programs/Services: No
Documentation required for:
LD: Psychoeducational evaluation
ADHD: Psychoeducational evaluation
ASD: Psychoeducational evaluation

Southern Illinois University—Edwardsville

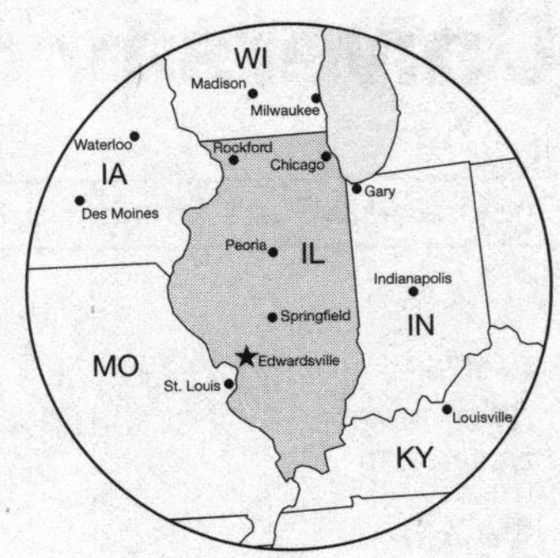

General Admissions

Very important factors include: academic GPA, standardized test scores. *Important factors include:* rigor of secondary school record, class rank. High school diploma is required and GED is accepted. *Academic units required:* 4 English, 3 math, 3 science, 3 science labs, 3 social studies, 2 academic electives. *Academic units recommended:* 2 foreign language.

Accommodations or Services

Accommodations are decided upon an individual basis after a thorough review of appropriate, current documentation. The accommodations requests must be supported through the documentation provided and must be logically linked to the current impact of the condition on academic functioning.

Financial Aid

Students should submit: FAFSA. *Need-based scholarships/grants offered:* College/university scholarship or grant aid from institutional funds; Federal Nursing Scholarships; Federal Pell; Private scholarships; SEOG; State scholarships/grants. *Loan aid offered:* Direct PLUS loans; Direct Subsidized Stafford Loans; Direct Unsubsidized Stafford Loans. Federal Work-Study Program available. Institutional employment available.

Campus Life

Activities: Campus Ministries; Choral groups; Concert band; Dance; Drama/theater; International Student Organization; Jazz band; Literary magazine; Music ensembles; Musical theater; Opera; Pep band; Radio station; Student government; Student newspaper; Symphony orchestra. **Organizations:** 302 registered organizations, 18 honor societies, 10 religious organizations, 13 fraternities, 9 sororities. **Athletics (Intercollegiate):** *Men:* baseball, basketball, cross-country, golf, soccer, tennis, track/field (outdoor), track/field (indoor), wrestling. *Women:* basketball, cross-country, golf, soccer, softball, tennis, track/field (outdoor), track/field (indoor), volleyball.

ACCOMMODATIONS

Allowed in exams:	
Calculators	Yes
Dictionary	Yes
Computer	Yes
Spell-checker	No
Extended test time	Yes
Scribe	Yes
Proctors	Yes
Oral exams	Yes
Note-takers	Yes
Support services for students with:	
LD	Yes
ADHD	Yes
ASD	Yes
Distraction-reduced environment	Yes
Recording of lecture allowed	Yes
Reading technology	Yes
Audio books	Yes
Other assistive technology	Yes
Priority registration	Yes
Added costs of services:	
For LD	No
For ADHD	No
For ASD	No
LD specialists	No
ADHD & ASD coaching	No
ASD specialists	No
Professional tutors	No
Peer tutors	Yes
Max. hours/week for services	Varies
How professors are notified of student approved accommodations	Student

COLLEGE GRADUATION REQUIREMENTS

Course waivers allowed	No
Course substitutions allowed	Yes
In what courses: Case-by-case basis	

Illinois

University of Illinois at Springfield

One University Plaza, Springfield, IL 62703-5407 • Admissions: 217-206-4847 • Fax: 217-206-6620 **Support: S**

CAMPUS	
Type of school	Public
Environment	City
STUDENTS	
Undergrad enrollment	2,613
% male/female	49/51
% from out of state	12
% frosh live on campus	83
FINANCIAL FACTS	
Annual in-state tuition	$9,503
Annual out-of-state tuition	$19,117
Room and board	$9,760
Required fees	$2,418
GENERAL ADMISSIONS INFO	
Application fee	$50
Regular application deadline	Start of Term
Nonfall registration	Yes
Admission may be deferred.	
Range SAT EBRW	500–610
Range SAT Math	495–610
Range ACT Composite	19–26
ACADEMICS	
Student/faculty ratio	13:1
% students returning for sophomore year	79
Most classes have 10–19 students.	

Programs/Services for Students with Learning Differences

The Office of Disability Services (ODS) provides students with accommodations. The Center for Academic Success is designed to offer students one-stop academic support. The Learning Hub under the Center offers free academic support services. Through a peer-tutoring program, it offers one-to-one appointments in writing, math, accounting, economics, science, and academic skills.

Admissions

Admissions is the same for all students. In addition to the transcript and ACT or SAT, applicants submit the personal and academic statement, which are viewed as an applicant's opportunity to speak on his or her own behalf. The statement should address any circumstances (positive or negative) that may have affected the applicant's high school experience and that are not readily apparent from academic records or standardized test scores.

Additional Information

The Learning Hub is part of the Center for Academic Success. The writing resources provide academic assistance for the writing of effective essays and research papers and serve students at every level through one-to-one tutoring, workshops, and requested presentations where students learn together outside of formal classes. They will not simply proofread a paper for grammatical or citation mistakes. Rather, tutors will walk students through primary concerns such as argument, logic, organization, clarity, and flow, before then working on secondary concerns including grammar and mechanics. Services are free, but students are limited in the number of hours per week they can ask for tutoring in specific courses. There are 30 state of the art testing stations available to proctor make-up exams, exam re-takes, online student exams, and certification exams.

ADMISSIONS INFO FOR STUDENTS WITH LEARNING DIFFERENCES

Phone: 217-206-6666 or 217-206-6668 • Fax: 217-206-7154 • Email: ods@uis.edu

SAT/ACT required: Yes (Test optional for 2021)
Interview required: No
Essay required: Yes
Additional application required: No
Documentation submitted to: Office of Disability Services

Special Ed. HS course work accepted: Yes
Separate application required for Programs/Services: No
Documentation required for:
LD: Psychoeducational evaluation
ADHD: Psychoeducational evaluation
ASD: Psychoeducational evaluation

University of Illinois at Springfield

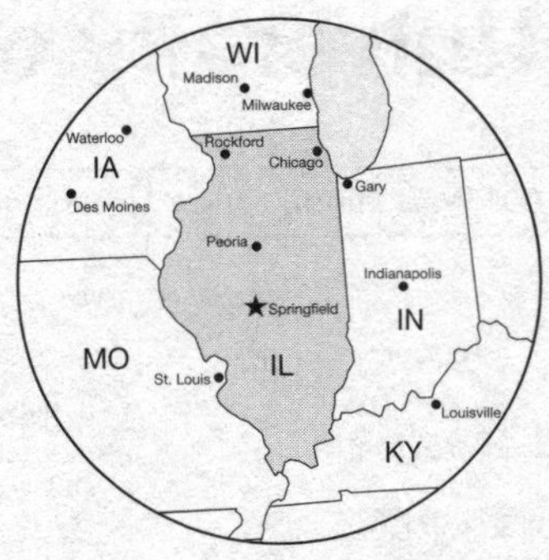

General Admissions

Very important factors include: rigor of secondary school record, academic GPA, standardized test scores. *Important factors include:* class rank. *Other factors include:* application essay, recommendation(s), extracurricular activities, character/personal qualities, volunteer work, work experience, level of applicant's interest. High school diploma is required and GED is accepted. *Academic units required:* 4 English, 3 math, 3 science, 1 science lab, 2 foreign language, 3 social studies. *Academic units recommended:* 4 English, 4 math, 3 science, 1 science lab, 2 foreign language, 3 social studies, 3 history.

Accommodations or Services

Accommodations are decided upon an individual basis after a thorough review of appropriate, current documentation. The accommodations requests must be supported through the documentation provided and must be logically linked to the current impact of the condition on academic functioning.

Financial Aid

Students should submit: FAFSA. Applicants will be notified of awards on a rolling basis beginning 2/1. *Need-based scholarships/grants offered:* College/university scholarship or grant aid from institutional funds; Federal Pell; Private scholarships; SEOG; State scholarships/grants. *Loan aid offered:* Direct PLUS loans; Direct Subsidized Stafford Loans; Direct Unsubsidized Stafford Loans. Federal Work-Study Program available. Institutional employment available.

Campus Life

Activities: Campus Ministries; Choral groups; Concert band; Dance; Drama/theater; International Student Organization; Jazz band; Model UN; Music ensembles; Pep band; Radio station; Student government; Student newspaper; Student-run film society. **Organizations:** 85 registered organizations, 8 honor societies, 8 religious organizations, 6 fraternities, 5 sororities. **Athletics (Intercollegiate):** *Men:* basketball, golf, soccer, tennis. *Women:* basketball, cheerleading, golf, soccer, softball, tennis, volleyball.

ACCOMMODATIONS

Allowed in exams:	
Calculators	Yes
Dictionary	Yes
Computer	No
Spell-checker	Yes
Extended test time	Yes
Scribe	Yes
Proctors	Yes
Oral exams	Yes
Note-takers	Yes
Support services for students with:	
LD	Yes
ADHD	Yes
ASD	Yes
Distraction-reduced environment	Yes
Recording of lecture allowed	Yes
Reading technology	Yes
Audio books	Yes
Other assistive technology	Yes
Priority registration	Yes
Added costs of services:	
For LD	No
For ADHD	No
For ASD	No
LD specialists	No
ADHD & ASD coaching	No
ASD specialists	No
Professional tutors	Yes
Peer tutors	Yes
Max. hours/week for services	Varies
How professors are notified of student approved accommodations	Student

COLLEGE GRADUATION REQUIREMENTS

Course waivers allowed	Yes
In what courses: Math and foreign language	
Course substitutions allowed	Yes
In what courses: Math and foreign language	

Illinois

University of Illinois at Urbana-Champaign

901 West Illinois Street, Urbana, IL 61801-3028 • Admissions: 217-333-0302 • Fax: 217-244-4614 **Support: CS**

CAMPUS

Type of school	Public
Environment	City

STUDENTS

Undergrad enrollment	34,120
% male/female	54/46
% from out of state	10
% frosh live on campus	99

FINANCIAL FACTS

Annual in-state tuition	$12,036
Annual out-of-state tuition	$29,178
Room and board	$11,480
Required fees	$4,174

GENERAL ADMISSIONS INFO

Application fee	$50
Regular application deadline	1/5
Nonfall registration	No

Admission may be deferred.

Range SAT EBRW	600–700
Range SAT Math	620–780
Range ACT Composite	27–33

ACADEMICS

Student/faculty ratio	20:1
% students returning for sophomore year	91

Most classes have 10–19 students.

Programs/Services for Students with Learning Differences

The Office of Disability Resources & Educational Services (DRES) has a learning disability specialist on staff who works with students on compensatory strategies in test preparation, test taking, reading comprehension, and written expression. Four licensed clinical psychologists (three as access specialists and one as a clinical counselor) and other mental health professionals who are on staff to provide supports and services given the large growth in the number of students with ADHD, acquired brain injury, Autism Spectrum Disorders, and psychiatric disabilities. DRES provides students with academic accommodations and access. Also provided are support services including academic skills/strategies training, case management, and coaching for organization, time management, structure, prioritizing, and motivation. In addition, students can learn to use various types of assistive technology to help in their academics. Academic consultation and screening is also offered for any University of Illinois student who is experiencing difficulty with their academic course work and suspects that he or she may have an undiagnosed disability such as ADHD or a learning disability.

Admissions

Students self-report their GPA and ACT/SAT. Students select which college they are applying to in the university and the admission criteria will vary by college. Applicants with LD/ADHD are expected to meet the same criteria as all other applicants. However, applicants can self-disclose challenges or obstacles faced that may have had an impact on their academic record.

Additional Information

Most DRES students contact professors and set up their own accommodations; however, with many of our students with autism, we may email their professors for them, role-play to practice talking to instructors, or meet with the student and their professors to discuss accommodations. DRES will check in with their professors on a regular basis to be proactive about solving problems and serve as consultants with faculty, departments, and housing to provide recommendations for accommodations for unique classroom requirements or problem behaviors. Graduation rate for students on the autism spectrum is 85%, which is consistent with the University of Illinois graduation rate. Most of these students are employed or go on to graduate school.

ADMISSIONS INFO FOR STUDENTS WITH LEARNING DIFFERENCES

Phone: 217-333-4603 • Fax: 217-244-0014 • Email: disability@illinois.edu

SAT/ACT required: Yes (Test optional for 2021)
Interview required: No
Essay required: Yes
Additional application required: No
Documentation submitted to: Disability Resources and Educational Services

Special Ed. HS course work accepted: Yes
Separate application required for Programs/Services: Yes
Documentation required for:
LD: Psychoeducational evaluation
ADHD: Psychoeducational evaluation
ASD: Psychoeducational evaluation

University of Illinois at Urbana-Champaign

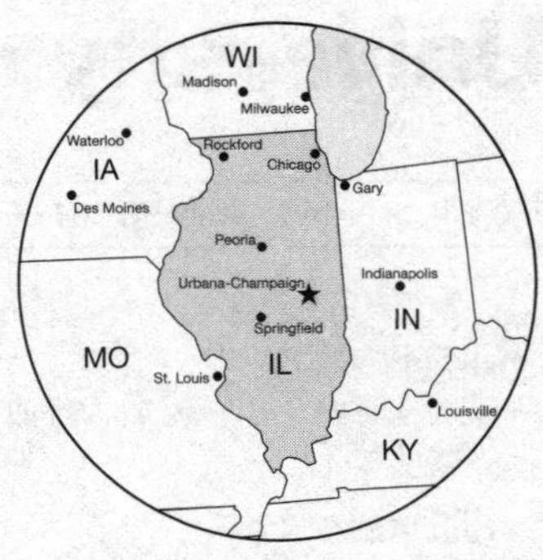

General Admissions

Very important factors include: rigor of secondary school record, academic GPA. *Important factors include:* application essay, standardized test scores, extracurricular activities, talent/ability. *Other factors include:* class rank, character/personal qualities, first generation, geographical residence, state residency, racial/ethnic status, volunteer work, work experience. High school diploma is required and GED is accepted. *Academic units required:* 4 English, 3 math, 2 science, 2 science labs, 2 foreign language, 2 social studies, 2 academic electives. *Academic units recommended:* 4 English, 4 math, 4 science, 4 science labs, 4 foreign language, 4 social studies, 4 academic electives.

Accommodations or Services

Accommodations are decided upon an individual basis after a thorough review of appropriate, current documentation. The accommodations requests must be supported through the documentation provided and must be logically linked to the current impact of the condition on academic functioning.

Financial Aid

Students should submit: FAFSA. Applicants will be notified of awards on a rolling basis beginning 3/31. *Need-based scholarships/grants offered:* College/university scholarship or grant aid from institutional funds; Federal Pell; Private scholarships; SEOG; State scholarships/grants; United Negro College Fund. *Loan aid offered:* Direct PLUS loans; Direct Subsidized Stafford Loans; Direct Unsubsidized Stafford Loans. Federal Work-Study Program available. Institutional employment available.

Campus Life

Activities: Choral groups; Concert band; Dance; Drama/theater; International Student Organization; Jazz band; Literary magazine; Marching band; Music ensembles; Musical theater; Opera; Pep band; Radio station; Student government; Student newspaper; Student-run film society; Symphony orchestra; Television station; Yearbook. **Organizations:** 1400 registered organizations. **Athletics (Intercollegiate):** *Men:* baseball, basketball, cheerleading, cross-country, football, golf, gymnastics, tennis, track/field (outdoor), wrestling. *Women:* basketball, cheerleading, cross-country, diving, golf, gymnastics, soccer, softball, swimming, tennis, track/field (outdoor), volleyball.

ACCOMMODATIONS

Allowed in exams:	
Calculators	Yes
Dictionary	Yes
Computer	Yes
Spell-checker	Yes
Extended test time	Yes
Scribe	Yes
Proctors	Yes
Oral exams	Yes
Note-takers	Yes
Support services for students with:	
LD	Yes
ADHD	Yes
ASD	Yes
Distraction-reduced environment	Yes
Recording of lecture allowed	Yes
Reading technology	Yes
Audio books	Yes
Other assistive technology	Yes
Priority registration	Yes
Added costs of services:	
For LD	No
For ADHD	No
For ASD	No
LD specialists	Yes
ADHD & ASD coaching	Yes
ASD specialists	Yes
Professional tutors	Yes
Peer tutors	Yes
Max. hours/week for services	Varies
How professors are notified of student approved accommodations	Student

COLLEGE GRADUATION REQUIREMENTS

Course waivers allowed	No
Course substitutions allowed	Yes

In what courses: Case-by-case basis

Illinois

University of St. Francis

500 Wilcox Street, Joliet, IL 60435 • Admissions: 815-740-5037 • Fax: 815-740-5078 **Support: S**

CAMPUS	
Type of school	Private (nonprofit)
Environment	City
STUDENTS	
Undergrad enrollment	1,648
% male/female	34/66
% from out of state	9
% frosh live on campus	46
FINANCIAL FACTS	
Annual tuition	$35,000
Room and board	$10,210
GENERAL ADMISSIONS INFO	
Application fee	$0
Regular application deadline	8/1
Nonfall registration	Yes
Admission may be deferred.	
Range SAT EBRW	520–600
Range SAT Math	510–620
Range ACT Composite	20–27
ACADEMICS	
Student/faculty ratio	13:1
% students returning for sophomore year	81
Most classes have 10–19 students.	

Programs/Services for Students with Learning Differences

The Office of Disability Services as part of the Academic Resource Center (ACR) works with students who required accommodations for learning differences. The ACR offers opportunities and support services to enhance learning, improve skills, and promote academic success. ACR provides tutoring that focuses both on course content and study habits. Services are offered free of charge.

Admissions

Applicants with learning disabilities must meet the same criteria for admissions as all other applicants. Students are automatically admissible with a 2.5 GPA or above and the following courses: 4 years English, 3 years math, 2 years social studies, 2 years science. They must also have 3 years from two of these courses: foreign language, computer science, or music.

Additional Information

Supplemental Instruction (SI) offers regularly scheduled reviews, discussions, study strategies, and exam preparation for many courses. Each session is guided by an SI leader, who has successfully taken the course and knows what the professor. SI is offered in informal small groups. All peer tutors have been recommended by faculty in their specific subject area and are trained by the College Reading and Learning Association (CRLA). Tutoring is offered free of charge.

ADMISSIONS INFO FOR STUDENTS WITH LEARNING DIFFERENCES

Phone: 815-740-3204 • Fax: 815-740-3726 • Email: salag@stfrancis.edu

SAT/ACT required: Yes (Test optional for 2021)
Interview required: No
Essay required: No
Additional application required: No
Documentation submitted to: Office of Disability Service

Special Ed. HS course work accepted: Yes
Separate application required for Programs/Services: No
Documentation required for:
LD: Psychoeducational evaluation
ADHD: Psychoeducational evaluation
ASD: Psychoeducational evaluation

University of St. Francis

General Admissions

Very important factors include: rigor of secondary school record, academic GPA, standardized test scores. *Other factors include:* class rank, application essay, recommendation(s), interview. High school diploma is required and GED is accepted. *Academic units required:* 4 English, 3 math, 2 science, 1 science lab, 2 social studies, 3 academic electives, 3 unit from above areas or other academic areas.

Accommodations or Services

Accommodations are decided upon an individual basis after a thorough review of appropriate, current documentation. The accommodations requests must be supported through the documentation provided and must be logically linked to the current impact of the condition on academic functioning.

Financial Aid

Students should submit: FAFSA; Institution's own financial aid form. *Need-based scholarships/grants offered:* College/university scholarship or grant aid from institutional funds; Federal Pell; Private scholarships; SEOG; State scholarships/grants; United Negro College Fund. *Loan aid offered:* Direct PLUS loans; Direct Subsidized Stafford Loans; Direct Unsubsidized Stafford Loans. Federal Work-Study Program available. Institutional employment available.

Campus Life

Activities: Campus Ministries; Choral groups; Dance; Drama/theater; International Student Organization; Music ensembles; Musical theater; Opera; Radio station; Student government; Student newspaper; Symphony orchestra; Television station. **Organizations:** 65 registered organizations, 19 honor societies, 2 religious organizations, 1 fraternity, 1 sorority. **Athletics (Intercollegiate):** *Men:* baseball, basketball, cross-country, football, golf, soccer, tennis, track/field (outdoor), track/field (indoor). *Women:* basketball, cheerleading, cross-country, golf, soccer, softball, tennis, track/field (outdoor), track/field (indoor), volleyball.

ACCOMMODATIONS

Allowed in exams:	
Calculators	Yes
Dictionary	Yes
Computer	Yes
Spell-checker	Yes
Extended test time	Yes
Scribe	Yes
Proctors	Yes
Oral exams	Yes
Note-takers	Yes
Support services for students with:	
LD	Yes
ADHD	Yes
ASD	Yes
Distraction-reduced environment	Yes
Recording of lecture allowed	Yes
Reading technology	Yes
Audio books	Yes
Other assistive technology	Yes
Priority registration	Yes
Added costs of services:	
For LD	No
For ADHD	No
For ASD	No
LD specialists	No
ADHD & ASD coaching	No
ASD specialists	No
Professional tutors	Yes
Peer tutors	Yes
Max. hours/week for services	Varies
How professors are notified of student approved accommodations	Director

COLLEGE GRADUATION REQUIREMENTS

Course waivers allowed	Yes
In what courses: Case-by-case basis	
Course substitutions allowed	Yes
In what courses: Case-by-case basis	

Illinois

Western Illinois University

1 University Circle, Macomb, IL 61455-1390 • Admissions: 309-298-3157 • Fax: 309-298-3111 **Support: CS**

CAMPUS	
Type of school	Public
Environment	Village
STUDENTS	
Undergrad enrollment	5,958
% male/female	47/53
% from out of state	12
% frosh live on campus	89
FINANCIAL FACTS	
Annual in-state tuition	$8,883
Annual out-of-state tuition	$8,883
Room and board	$10,100
Required fees	$2,841
GENERAL ADMISSIONS INFO	
Application fee	$30
Regular application deadline	Rolling
Nonfall registration	Yes
Admission may be deferred.	
Range SAT EBRW	480–580
Range SAT Math	470–570
Range ACT Composite	18–25
ACADEMICS	
Student/faculty ratio	13:1
% students returning for sophomore year	68
Most classes have 10–19 students.	

Programs/Services for Students with Learning Differences

Disability Resources facilitates equal access to University classes, program, and activities for students with disabilities. DR works with students to determine disability and hear requests for reasonable accommodations. All requests for accommodations must be reasonable both at the institutional level and at the individual level. Students self-identify and follow the necessary procedures to connect with DR to apply for accommodations.

Admissions

Applicants who do not meet the academic profile for admissions are encouraged to submit a personal statement which addresses their academic goals and how they plan to realize those goals at WIU. The statement may also explain any extenuating circumstances that may have affected their academic performance in high school. Letters of support will also be considered. Students may also be admitted through the Office for Academic Services. Students must have a minimum ACT of 16 or a minimum SAT score of 880 (with a GPA equal to or greater than 2.0/4.0 scale) to be eligible. Admission requirements for the Office of Academic Services are on a sliding scale: lower ACT or SAT scores require a greater GPA, higher ACT or SAT scores allow for a somewhat lower GPA, with a 2.0 minimum.

Additional Information

The University Advising and Academic Support Center offers support and academic skill development. Academic Success Coaching (ASC) is for students who seek additional support in reaching their academic potential through an interactive process that focuses on the areas of organization, goal setting, motivation, time management, success strategies, school/life balance and connecting with resources. The Turning Point Peer Mentor Program focuses on the transition from high school to college to address issues such as self-advocacy, study skills, time management, and organization skills.

ADMISSIONS INFO FOR STUDENTS WITH LEARNING DIFFERENCES

Phone: 309-298-1884 • Fax: 309-298-2361 • Email: SDSC@wiu.edu

SAT/ACT required: No (depending on GPA))
Interview required: No
Essay required: No
Additional application required: No
Documentation submitted to: Student Development and Success Center

Special Ed. HS course work accepted: Yes
Separate application required for Programs/Services: No
Documentation required for:
LD: Psychoeducational evaluation
ADHD: Psychoeducational evaluation
ASD: Psychoeducational evaluation

Western Illinois University

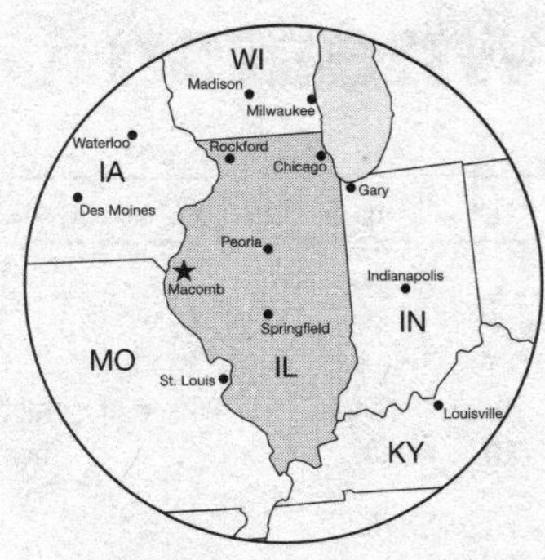

General Admissions

Very important factors include: academic GPA, standardized test scores. *Other factors include:* rigor of secondary school record. High school diploma is required and GED is accepted. *Academic units required:* 4 English, 3 math, 3 science, 3 social studies, 2 academic electives.

Accommodations or Services

Accommodations are decided upon an individual basis after a thorough review of appropriate, current documentation. The accommodations requests must be supported through the documentation provided and must be logically linked to the current impact of the condition on academic functioning.

Financial Aid

Students should submit: FAFSA. *Need-based scholarships/grants offered:* College/university scholarship or grant aid from institutional funds; Federal Pell; Private scholarships; SEOG; State scholarships/grants. *Loan aid offered:* Direct PLUS loans; Direct Subsidized Stafford Loans; Direct Unsubsidized Stafford Loans. Federal Work-Study Program available. Institutional employment available.

Campus Life

Activities: Campus Ministries; Choral groups; Concert band; Dance; Drama/theater; International Student Organization; Jazz band; Literary magazine; Marching band; Model UN; Music ensembles; Musical theater; Opera; Pep band; Radio station; Student government; Student newspaper; Student-run film society; Symphony orchestra; Television station. **Organizations:** 273 registered organizations, 15 honor societies, 11 religious organizations, 16 fraternities, 10 sororities. **Athletics (Intercollegiate):** *Men:* baseball, basketball, cross-country, diving, football, golf, soccer, swimming, tennis, track/field (outdoor), track/field (indoor). *Women:* basketball, cheerleading, cross-country, diving, golf, soccer, softball, swimming, tennis, track/field (outdoor), track/field (indoor), volleyball.

ACCOMMODATIONS

Allowed in exams:	
Calculators	Yes
Dictionary	Yes
Computer	Yes
Spell-checker	Yes
Extended test time	Yes
Scribe	Yes
Proctors	Yes
Oral exams	Yes
Note-takers	Yes
Support services for students with:	
LD	Yes
ADHD	Yes
ASD	Yes
Distraction-reduced environment	Yes
Recording of lecture allowed	Yes
Reading technology	Yes
Audio books	Yes
Other assistive technology	Yes
Priority registration	Yes
Added costs of services:	
For LD	No
For ADHD	No
For ASD	No
LD specialists	Yes
ADHD & ASD coaching	No
ASD specialists	No
Professional tutors	No
Peer tutors	Yes
Max. hours/week for services	Varies
How professors are notified of student approved accommodations	Both

COLLEGE GRADUATION REQUIREMENTS

Course waivers allowed	Yes
In what courses: Case-by-case basis	
Course substitutions allowed	Yes
In what courses: Case-by-case basis	

Illinois

Wheaton College (IL)

501 College Avenue, Wheaton, IL 60187 • Admissions: 630-752-5011 • Fax: 630-752-5285 **Support: S**

CAMPUS

Type of school	Private (nonprofit)
Environment	Town

STUDENTS

Undergrad enrollment	2,358
% male/female	46/54
% from out of state	73
% frosh live on campus	99

FINANCIAL FACTS

Annual tuition	$39,100
Room and board	$10,990

GENERAL ADMISSIONS INFO

Application fee	$50
Regular application deadline	1/1
Nonfall registration	Yes

Admission may be deferred.

Range SAT EBRW	620–720
Range SAT Math	600–720
Range ACT Composite	26–32

ACADEMICS

Student/faculty ratio	10:1
% students returning for sophomore year	93

Most classes have 10–19 students.

Programs/Services for Students with Learning Differences

Learning and Accessibility Services enhances and enriches the way students learn and approach classes and also has resources for students with learning differences that impact academics or campus life. Through one-on-one strategic meetings and academic workshops/seminars students have the opportunity to develop new strategies, build existing skills, and figure out how they are uniquely wired in order to maximize their learning experience. A series of workshops are offered each year that cover topics such as management, strategies for reading and note-taking, paper-writing and research, how to get the most out of test preparation, and overcoming procrastination and perfectionism and more.

Admissions

Wheaton College seeks applicants with a committed Christian experience, high academic ability, moral character, personal integrity, and concern for others. The average GPA is 3.7. The mid 50% SAT is 1240–1550 or ACT 27–32. Applicants with learning disabilities must meet the same admission requirements as all applicants.

Additional Information

Individual meetings are available by appointment to offer accountability, coaching and accommodation advocacy. Academic counseling is available for all students. Accommodation approval and services for students with documented learning including assessment screening for potential learning challenges are available and can include: learning style assessment, academic coaching and accountability, and strategic learning improvement information.

ADMISSIONS INFO FOR STUDENTS WITH LEARNING DIFFERENCES

Phone: 630-752-5615 • Fax: 630-752-7226 • Email: jennifer.nicodem@wheaton.edu

SAT/ACT required: No
Interview required: No
Essay required: Yes
Additional application required: No
Documentation submitted to: Learning and Accessibility Services
Special Ed. HS course work accepted: Yes
Separate application required for Programs/Services: No
Documentation required for:
LD: Psychoeducational evaluation
ADHD: Psychoeducational evaluation
ASD: Psychoeducational evaluation

Wheaton College (IL)

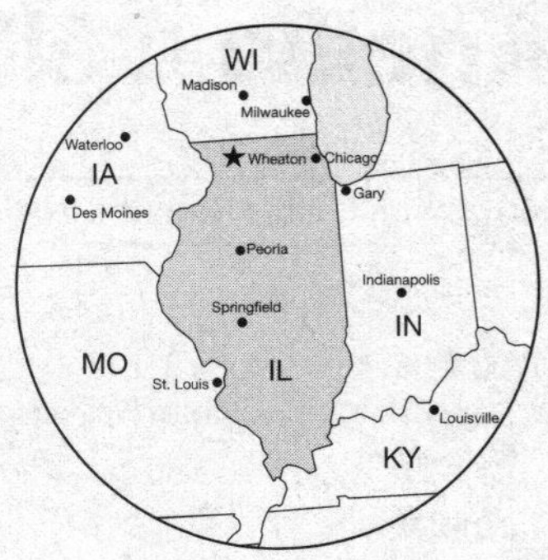

General Admissions

Very important factors include: rigor of secondary school record, academic GPA, application essay, standardized test scores, recommendation(s), character/personal qualities, religious affiliation/commitment. *Important factors include:* interview, extracurricular activities, talent/ability. *Other factors include:* class rank, first generation, alumni/ae relation, geographical residence, state residency, racial/ethnic status, work experience, level of applicant's interest. High school diploma is required and GED is accepted. *Academic units required:* 4 English, 3 math, 3 science, 2 foreign language, 3 social studies. *Academic units recommended:* 4 English, 4 math, 4 science, 3 foreign language, 4 social studies.

Accommodations or Services

Accommodations are decided upon an individual basis after a thorough review of appropriate, current documentation. The accommodations requests must be supported through the documentation provided and must be logically linked to the current impact of the condition on academic functioning.

Financial Aid

Students should submit: FAFSA. *Need-based scholarships/grants offered:* College/university scholarship or grant aid from institutional funds; Federal Pell; Private scholarships; SEOG; State scholarships/grants. *Loan aid offered:* Direct PLUS loans; Direct Subsidized Stafford Loans; Direct Unsubsidized Stafford Loans. Federal Work-Study Program available. Institutional employment available.

Campus Life

Activities: Campus Ministries; Choral groups; Concert band; Dance; Drama/theater; International Student Organization; Jazz band; Literary magazine; Model UN; Music ensembles; Musical theater; Opera; Pep band; Student government; Student newspaper; Student-run film society; Symphony orchestra. **Organizations:** 95 registered organizations, 13 honor societies, 16 religious organizations. **Athletics (Intercollegiate):** *Men:* baseball, basketball, cross-country, football, golf, soccer, swimming, tennis, track/field (outdoor), track/field (indoor), wrestling. *Women:* basketball, cross-country, golf, soccer, softball, swimming, tennis, track/field (outdoor), track/field (indoor), volleyball, water polo.

ACCOMMODATIONS

Allowed in exams:	
Calculators	Yes
Dictionary	Yes
Computer	Yes
Spell-checker	No
Extended test time	Yes
Scribe	Yes
Proctors	Yes
Oral exams	Yes
Note-takers	Yes
Support services for students with:	
LD	Yes
ADHD	Yes
ASD	Yes
Distraction-reduced environment	Yes
Recording of lecture allowed	Yes
Reading technology	Yes
Audio books	Yes
Other assistive technology	Yes
Priority registration	No
Added costs of services:	
For LD	No
For ADHD	No
For ASD	No
LD specialists	No
ADHD & ASD coaching	Yes
ASD specialists	No
Professional tutors	No
Peer tutors	Yes
Max. hours/week for services	Varies
How professors are notified of student approved accommodations	Both

COLLEGE GRADUATION REQUIREMENTS

Course waivers allowed	No
Course substitutions allowed	Yes

In what courses: Foreign language substitution

Ancilla College

9601 Union Road, Plymouth, IN 46513 • Admissions: 579-936-8898 ext. 330 **Support: SP**

CAMPUS	
Type of school	Private (Non-profit)
Environment	Town
STUDENTS	
Undergrad enrollment	386
% male/female	38/62
% from out of state	10
% frosh live on campus	65
FINANCIAL FACTS	
Annual tuition	$18,700
Room and board	$16,550
GENERAL ADMISSIONS INFO	
Regular application deadline	3/1
Nonfall registration	Yes
Range SAT EBRW	440–520
Range SAT Math	420–520
Range ACT Composite	14–21
ACADEMICS	
Student/faculty ratio	11:1
% students returning for sophomore year	45

Programs/Services for Students with Learning Differences

The Autism Program at Ancilla College (APAC) is a fee-based college level program designed to help students diagnosed with Autism Spectrum Disorder build academic, independent, social, and workplace skills and knowledge. APAC is intended for students who may struggle with communication and social interactions in an educational environment, but are also academically capable of pursing a college-level education. Students must be admitted to Ancilla College to be considered for APAC.

Admissions

Students applying for the Autism Program at Ancilla College must also meet the requirements for admission and be accepted to Ancilla College. This includes a cumulative GPA of at least 2.0 on a 4.0 scale, a preferred high school curriculum of 4 years of English, 3 years of math, 2 years of science, and 2 years of social studies. APAC applicants must submit the application to APAC along with psychological evaluation dated within the past three years, a copy of the IEP or #504 if applicable, and a teacher recommendation form. They must also meet with APAC staff.

Additional Information

The Center for Student Achievement works in partnership with the college community to assist all students in becoming active, responsible, and successful learners. Tutoring services are offered for all students in every subject. All students have access to the Writing and Math Lab. The Autism Program (APAC) focuses on students' needs outside of the classroom. The program has optional campus housing for APAC students.

ADMISSIONS INFO FOR STUDENTS WITH LEARNING DIFFERENCES

Phone: 574-936-8898 (ext. 364) • Fax: 574-935-1773 • Email: kristen.robson@ancilla.edu

SAT/ACT required: No
Interview required: No
Essay required: No
Additional application required: No
Documentation submitted to: ADA Coordinator or APAC

Special Ed. HS course work accepted: Yes
Separate application required for Programs/Services: Yes
Documentation required for:
LD: Psychoeducational evaluation
ADHD: Psychoeducational evaluation
ASD: Psychoeducational evaluation

Ancilla College

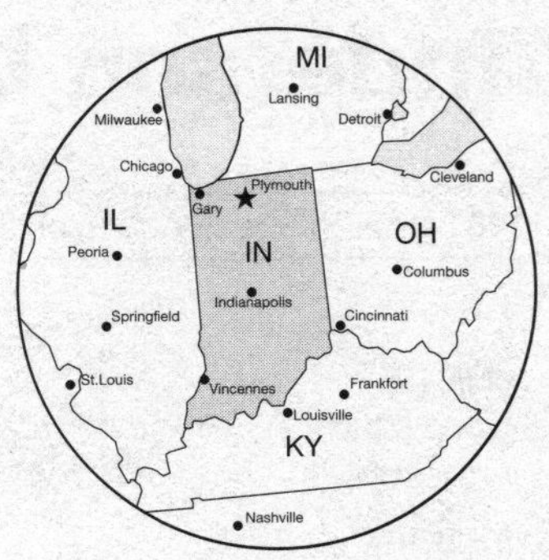

General Admissions

Freshman admission requirements: High school diploma is required, and GED is accepted. *Academic units recommended:* 4 English, 3 math, 2 science, 2 social studies. Ancilla College will use your ACT or SAT scores to qualify you for an academic scholarship, but they are not required for admission.

Accommodations or Services

Accommodations are decided upon an individual basis after a thorough review of appropriate, current documentation. The accommodations requests must be supported through the documentation provided and must be logically linked to the current impact of the condition on academic functioning.

Financial Aid

Students should submit: FAFSA. Applicants will be notified of awards on a rolling basis beginning 3/1. *Need-based scholarships/grants offered:* College/university scholarship or grant aid from institutional funds; Federal Pell; Private scholarships; SEOG; State scholarships/grants. *Loan aid offered:* Direct PLUS loans; Direct Subsidized Stafford Loans; Direct Unsubsidized Stafford Loans. Federal Work-Study Program available. Institutional employment available

Campus Life

Activities: Campus Ministries; Choral groups. **Athletics (Intercollegiate):** *Men:* baseball, basketball, bowling, cross-country, diving, golf, lacrosse, soccer, swimming, wrestling. *Women:* basketball, bowling cross-country, diving, lacrosse, soccer, softball, swimming.

ACCOMMODATIONS

Allowed in exams:	
Calculators	Yes
Dictionary	Yes
Computer	Yes
Spell-checker	Yes
Extended test time	Yes
Scribe	Yes
Proctors	Yes
Oral exams	No
Note-takers	Yes
Support services for students with:	
LD	Yes
ADHD	Yes
ASD	Yes
Distraction-reduced environment	Yes
Recording of lecture allowed	Yes
Reading technology	Yes
Audio books	No
Other assistive technology	Yes
Priority registration	Yes
Added costs of services:	
For LD	No
For ADHD	No
For ASD	Yes
LD specialists	No
ADHD & ASD coaching	Yes
ASD specialists	Yes
Professional tutors	Yes
Peer tutors	Yes
Max. hours/week for services	Varies
How professors are notified of student approved accommodations	Both

COLLEGE GRADUATION REQUIREMENTS

Course waivers allowed	No
Course substitutions allowed	No

Anderson University (IN)

1100 East Fifth Street, Anderson, IN 46012-3495 • Admissions: 765-641-4080 • Fax: 765-641-4091 **Support: CS**

CAMPUS

Type of school	Private (nonprofit)
Environment	Town

STUDENTS

Undergrad enrollment	1,311
% male/female	42/58
% from out of state	22
% frosh live on campus	87

FINANCIAL FACTS

Annual tuition	$26,820
Room and board	$10,640
Required fees	$3,160

GENERAL ADMISSIONS INFO

Application fee	$0
Regular application deadline	Rolling
Nonfall registration	Yes

Admission may be deferred.

Range SAT EBRW	500–580
Range SAT Math	500–580
Range ACT Composite	20–25

ACADEMICS

Student/faculty ratio	10:1
% students returning for sophomore year	69

Most classes have 10–19 students.

Programs/Services for Students with Learning Differences

The Bridges program aims to provide students with learning disabilities and/or ADHD an extra layer of support during the transition from high school to college. First-years enrolled in the program are typically limited to a lighter course load during their first semester. A two-credit-hour college survival skills/study skills class, taught by a DSS staff member, provides an extra layer of support during the transitions of the first semester. Students are fully integrated into the university and are expected to meet the same academic standards as all other students. Students requesting consideration for the Bridges program must notify Disability Services for Students and/or provide admissions documentation of a specific learning disability and/or ADHD. Students applying for the program are required to have a personal interview with the program director.

Admissions

Students with specific learning disabilities who apply to Anderson do so through the regular admission channels. Also considered in the evaluation of each application is the student's seriousness of purpose; personality and character; expressed willingness to live within the standards of the Anderson University community; and service to school, church, and community. Documentation of a specific learning disability must be included with the application. Students are encouraged to self-disclose because they may qualify for special consideration and be admitted through the LD program. Failure to disclose could result in nonacceptance based on standardized class scores, GPA, etc. Upon request for consideration for the program, prospective students are expected to make an on-campus visit, at which time a personal interview is arranged with the program director. All applicants are considered on an individual basis.

Additional Information

Anderson University offers the Bridges program to help students with specific learning disabilities and/or ADHD achieve their educational goals. The Kissinger Academic Center for Excellence is a place where students are supported in achieving their academic goals and empowered to help one another.

ADMISSIONS INFO FOR STUDENTS WITH LEARNING DIFFERENCES

Phone: 765-641-3851 • Fax: 765-641-3851 • Email: tjcoplin@anderson.edu

SAT/ACT required: No
Interview required: No
Essay required: Recommended
Additional application required: No
Documentation submitted to: Disability Services for Students

Special Ed. HS course work accepted: Yes
Separate application required for Programs/Services: Yes
Documentation required for:
LD: Psychoeducational evaluation
ADHD: Psychoeducational evaluation
ASD: Psychoeducational evaluation

Anderson University (IN)

General Admissions

Very important factors include: rigor of secondary school record, recommendation(s), religious affiliation/commitment. *Important factors include:* class rank, academic GPA, standardized test scores, interview, extracurricular activities, character/personal qualities, volunteer work. *Other factors include:* application essay, talent/ability, first generation, alumni/ae relation, racial/ethnic status, level of applicant's interest. High school diploma is required and GED is accepted. *Academic units required:* 4 English, 3 math, 3 science, 3 science labs, 2 foreign language, 1 social studies, 1 history. *Academic units recommended:* 4 English, 4 math, 4 science, 4 science labs, 3 foreign language, 2 social studies, 2 history, 5 academic electives, 1 computer science, 1 visual/performing arts.

Accommodations or Services

Accommodations are decided upon an individual basis after a thorough review of appropriate, current documentation. The accommodations requests must be supported through the documentation provided and must be logically linked to the current impact of the condition on academic functioning.

Financial Aid

Students should submit: FAFSA. *Need-based scholarships/grants offered:* College/university scholarship or grant aid from institutional funds; Federal Pell; Private scholarships; SEOG; State scholarships/grants. *Loan aid offered:* Direct PLUS loans; Direct Subsidized Stafford Loans; Direct Unsubsidized Stafford Loans. Federal Work-Study Program available.

Campus Life

Activities: Campus Ministries; Choral groups; Concert band; Dance; Drama/theater; International Student Organization; Jazz band; Literary magazine; Model UN; Music ensembles; Musical theater; Opera; Pep band; Radio station; Student government; Student newspaper; Symphony orchestra; Yearbook. **Organizations:** 42 registered organizations, 16 honor societies, 15 religious organizations. **Athletics (Intercollegiate):** *Men:* baseball, basketball, cheerleading, cross-country, football, golf, soccer, tennis, track/field (outdoor). *Women:* basketball, cheerleading, cross-country, golf, soccer, softball, tennis, track/field (outdoor), volleyball.

ACCOMMODATIONS

Allowed in exams:	
Calculators	Yes
Dictionary	No
Computer	Yes
Spell-checker	Yes
Extended test time	Yes
Scribe	Yes
Proctors	No
Oral exams	No
Note-takers	Yes
Support services for students with:	
LD	Yes
ADHD	Yes
ASD	Yes
Distraction-reduced environment	Yes
Recording of lecture allowed	Yes
Reading technology	Yes
Audio books	Yes
Other assistive technology	Yes
Priority registration	No
Added costs of services:	
For LD	No
For ADHD	No
For ASD	No
LD specialists	Yes
ADHD & ASD coaching	No
ASD specialists	No
Professional tutors	Yes
Peer tutors	Yes
Max. hours/week for services	Varies
How professors are notified of student approved accommodations	Student

COLLEGE GRADUATION REQUIREMENTS

Course waivers allowed	No
Course substitutions allowed	Yes

In what courses: Case-by-case basis

Indiana

Earlham College

801 National Road, West Richmond, IN 47374-4095 • Admissions: 765-983-1600 • Fax: 765-983-1560 **Support: S**

CAMPUS

Type of school	Private (nonprofit)
Environment	Town

STUDENTS

Undergrad enrollment	927
% male/female	43/57
% from out of state	90
% frosh live on campus	87

FINANCIAL FACTS

Annual tuition	$47,106
Room and board	$11,347
Required fees	$985

GENERAL ADMISSIONS INFO

Application fee	$0
Regular application deadline	2/1
Nonfall registration	Yes

Admission may be deferred.

Range SAT EBRW	550–680
Range SAT Math	550–690
Range ACT Composite	23–30

ACADEMICS

Student/faculty ratio	10:1
% students returning for sophomore year	80

Most classes have 10–19 students.

Programs/Services for Students with Learning Differences

Earlham College is committed to providing equal access to its programs, activities and services. Students with disabilities are provided accommodations through an individualized and interactive process. The director of the Academic Enrichment Center (AEC) is the 504 Coordinator for students and is responsible for assisting students with obtaining disability status and reasonable accommodations. The college expects students with disabilities to take an active role in communicating their needs since students can best describe their strengths and challenges. The college also recognizes that it is most effective when the disclosure of disabilities are made prior to students' arriving on campus.

Admissions

The admissions application process for students with disabilities is the same as that of other students. Disclosure of student's disability is voluntary and optional. Registering with Disability Services is a separate process from the admission application. The Academic Enrichment Center (AEC) is the College's disability services office, with the Director serving as the 504 Coordinator for students. Students can start the registration process with AEC once they have accepted the admission offer. Earlham evaluates in a holistic way, and there are no cutoffs for GPA. Each applicant must submit an original piece of writing that demonstrates writing skills and style and highlights the student's thinking process. The college is test optional, so neither ACT nor SAT is required for admission.

Additional Information

AEC provides group tutoring and one-to-one tutors for courses not supported by group tutoring sessions. The Writing Center provides drop-in service or individual in-depth consultations. Students may also request a meeting with the director of the AEC to develop time-management and study skills. All services are offered free of charge.

ADMISSIONS INFO FOR STUDENTS WITH LEARNING DIFFERENCES

Phone: 765-983-1390 • Email: yanpe@earlham.edu

SAT/ACT required: No
Interview required: No
Essay required: Yes
Additional application required: No
Documentation submitted to: Academic Enrichment Center

Special Ed. HS course work accepted: Yes
Separate application required for Programs/Services: No
Documentation required for:
LD: Psychoeducational evaluation
ADHD: Psychoeducational evaluation
ASD: Psychoeducational evaluation

Earlham College

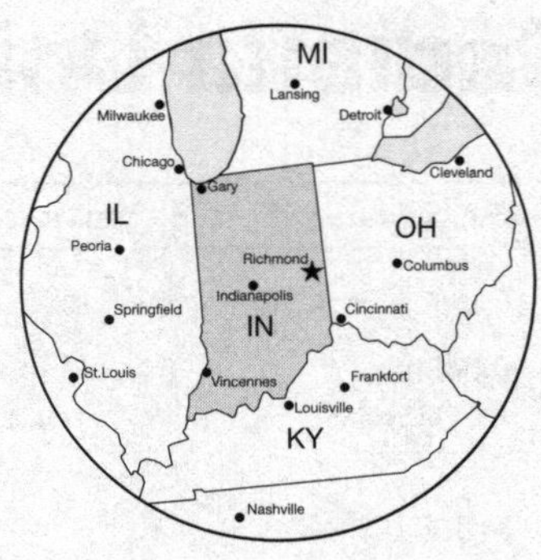

General Admissions

Very important factors include: rigor of secondary school record, academic GPA. *Important factors include:* application essay, extracurricular activities, character/personal qualities. *Other factors include:* class rank, standardized test scores, recommendation(s), interview, talent/ability, racial/ethnic status, volunteer work, work experience. High school diploma is required and GED is accepted. *Academic units required:* 4 English, 3 math, 3 science, 2 science labs, 2 foreign language, 2 social studies, 2 history. *Academic units recommended:* 4 English, 4 math, 4 science, 2 science labs, 2 foreign language, 2 social studies, 2 history.

Accommodations or Services

Accommodations are decided upon an individual basis after a thorough review of appropriate, current documentation. The accommodations requests must be supported through the documentation provided and must be logically linked to the current impact of the condition on academic functioning.

Financial Aid

Students should submit: FAFSA. *Need-based scholarships/grants offered:* College/university scholarship or grant aid from institutional funds; Federal Pell; Private scholarships; SEOG; State scholarships/grants. *Loan aid offered:* Direct PLUS loans; Direct Subsidized Stafford Loans; Direct Unsubsidized Stafford Loans. Federal Work-Study Program available. Institutional employment available.

Campus Life

Activities: Campus Ministries; Choral groups; Dance; Drama/theater; International Student Organization; Literary magazine; Music ensembles; Radio station; Student government; Student newspaper; Symphony orchestra. **Organizations:** 60 registered organizations, 1 honor society, 8 religious organizations. **Athletics (Intercollegiate):** *Men:* baseball, basketball, cross-country, football, soccer, tennis, track/field (outdoor), track/field (indoor). *Women:* basketball, cross-country, field hockey, soccer, tennis, track/field (outdoor), track/field (indoor), volleyball.

ACCOMMODATIONS

Allowed in exams:	
Calculators	Yes
Dictionary	No
Computer	Yes
Spell-checker	No
Extended test time	Yes
Scribe	Yes
Proctors	Yes
Oral exams	No
Note-takers	Yes
Support services for students with:	
LD	Yes
ADHD	Yes
ASD	No
Distraction-reduced environment	Yes
Recording of lecture allowed	Yes
Reading technology	Yes
Audio books	Yes
Other assistive technology	Yes
Priority registration	Yes
Added costs of services:	
For LD	No
For ADHD	No
For ASD	No
LD specialists	No
ADHD & ASD coaching	No
ASD specialists	No
Professional tutors	No
Peer tutors	Yes
Max. hours/week for services	Varies
How professors are notified of student approved accommodations	Student

COLLEGE GRADUATION REQUIREMENTS

Course waivers allowed	No
Course substitutions allowed	Yes
In what courses: Case-by-case basis	

Indiana University Bloomington

940 E. Seventh Street, Bloomington, IN 47405 • Admissions: 812-855-0661 • Fax: 812-855-5102 **Support: S**

CAMPUS

Type of school	Public
Environment	City

STUDENTS

Undergrad enrollment	32,794
% male/female	51/49
% from out of state	36
% frosh live on campus	98

FINANCIAL FACTS

Annual in-state tuition	$9,575
Annual out-of-state tuition	$35,140
Room and board	$10,830
Required fees	$1,372

GENERAL ADMISSIONS INFO

Application fee	$65
Regular application deadline	2/1
Nonfall registration	Yes

Admission may be deferred.

Range SAT EBRW	580–670
Range SAT Math	570–690
Range ACT Composite	24–31

ACADEMICS

Student/faculty ratio	16:1
% students returning for sophomore year	90

Most classes have 20–29 students.

Programs/Services for Students with Learning Differences

The Office of Disability Services for Students (DSS) ensures that students with disabilities have the tools, support services, and resources that allow equal access and reasonable accommodations to be successful at Indiana University Bloomington. Prospective students are encouraged to contact DSS early in the admissions process with any questions or concerns and for assistance tracking paperwork through the admissions office. Eligibility is based on an individual evaluation and will include review of the documentation sent with the DSS registration. A list of reasonable accommodation(s) will be reviewed by both the Coordinator and the student in order to decide how these modifications will avoid reducing academic expectations.

Admissions

The middle 50% range for GPA for admitted freshmen is 3.57–4.0. The cumulative GPA, as well as the grades earned in the 34 courses required for admission, will be an important part of the application review process. If a high school computes a weighted GPA and includes this GPA on a transcript, IU will consider it for both the admission and scholarship processes. The middle 50% range of SAT scores is 1180–1370. The middle 50% range for the ACT composite is 25–31.

Additional Information

Accommodations can be made to provide: test modifications, referrals to tutors, peer note-takers, books on tape, adaptive technology, and priority registration for students needing books on tape. Students must provide appropriate documentation and submit request for services. Students need to request a letter from the Office of Disability Services for Students (DSS) to give to their professors. No course requirements are waived automatically. Students who have difficulty with math or foreign language should discuss with DSS. The Student Academic Center offers workshops, courses for credit, and individualized academic assessments. No fees.

ADMISSIONS INFO FOR STUDENTS WITH LEARNING DIFFERENCES

Phone: 812-855-7578 • Fax: 812-855-7650 • Email: iubdss@indiana.edu

SAT/ACT required: No
Interview required: No
Essay required: Yes
Additional application required: No
Documentation submitted to: Disability Services for Students

Special Ed. HS course work accepted: Yes
Separate application required for Programs/Services: No
Documentation required for:
LD: Psychoeducational evaluation
ADHD: Psychoeducational evaluation
ASD: Psychoeducational evaluation

Indiana University Bloomington

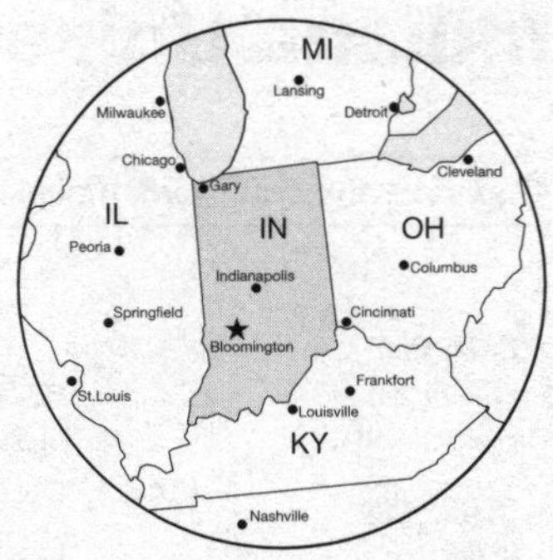

General Admissions

Very important factors include: rigor of secondary school record, class rank, academic GPA, standardized test scores. *Important factors include:* application essay, *Other factors include:* recommendation(s), interview, extracurricular activities, talent/ability, character/personal qualities, first generation, alumni/ae relation, geographical residence, state residency, racial/ethnic status, volunteer work, work experience. High school diploma is required and GED is accepted. *Academic units required:* 4 English, 3.5 math, 3 science, 2 science labs, 2 foreign language, 3 social studies, 1.5 academic electives.

Accommodations or Services

Accommodations are decided upon an individual basis after a thorough review of appropriate, current documentation. The accommodations requests must be supported through the documentation provided and must be logically linked to the current impact of the condition on academic functioning.

Financial Aid

Students should submit: FAFSA. Applicants will be notified of awards on or about 3/1. *Need-based scholarships/grants offered:* College/university scholarship or grant aid from institutional funds; Federal Pell; Private scholarships; SEOG; State scholarships/grants. *Loan aid offered:* Direct PLUS loans; Direct Subsidized Stafford Loans; Direct Unsubsidized Stafford Loans. Federal Work-Study Program available. Institutional employment available.

Campus Life

Activities: Campus Ministries; Choral groups; Concert band; Dance; Drama/theater; International Student Organization; Jazz band; Literary magazine; Marching band; Model UN; Music ensembles; Musical theater; Opera; Pep band; Radio station; Student government; Student newspaper; Symphony orchestra; Television station; Yearbook. **Organizations:** 830 registered organizations, 43 honor societies, 51 religious organizations, 35 fraternities, 33 sororities. **Athletics (Intercollegiate):** *Men:* baseball, basketball, cheerleading, cross-country, diving, football, golf, soccer, swimming, tennis, track/field (outdoor), wrestling. *Women:* basketball, cheerleading, cross-country, diving, field hockey, golf, soccer, softball, swimming, tennis, track/field (outdoor), volleyball, water polo.

ACCOMMODATIONS

Allowed in exams:	
Calculators	Yes
Dictionary	Yes
Computer	Yes
Spell-checker	Yes
Extended test time	Yes
Scribe	Yes
Proctors	Yes
Oral exams	Yes
Note-takers	Yes
Support services for students with:	
LD	Yes
ADHD	Yes
ASD	Yes
Distraction-reduced environment	Yes
Recording of lecture allowed	Yes
Reading technology	Yes
Audio books	Yes
Other assistive technology	Yes
Priority registration	Yes
Added costs of services:	
For LD	No
For ADHD	No
For ASD	No
LD specialists	No
ADHD & ASD coaching	No
ASD specialists	No
Professional tutors	Yes
Peer tutors	Yes
Max. hours/week for services	Varies
How professors are notified of student approved accommodations	Student

COLLEGE GRADUATION REQUIREMENTS

Course waivers allowed	Yes
In what courses: Case-by-case basis	
Course substitutions allowed	No

Indiana

Indiana University—Purdue University Indianapolis

425 University Boulevard, Indianapolis, IN 46202 • Admissions: 317-274-4591 • Fax: 317-278-1862 **Support: S**

CAMPUS

Type of school	Public
Environment	Metropolis

STUDENTS

Undergrad enrollment	20,500
% male/female	42/58
% from out of state	6
% frosh live on campus	37

FINANCIAL FACTS

Annual in-state tuition	$9,944
Annual out-of-state tuition	$31,626
Room and board	$10,152

GENERAL ADMISSIONS INFO

Application fee	$65
Regular application deadline	5/1
Nonfall registration	Yes

Admission may be deferred.

Range SAT EBRW	500–600
Range SAT Math	500–600
Range ACT Composite	19–25

ACADEMICS

Student/faculty ratio	15:1
% students returning for sophomore year	73

Most classes have 10–19 students.

Programs/Services for Students with Learning Differences

Adaptive Educational Services (AES) is the IUPUI office dedicated to working with students with documented disabilities to ensure that these students receive the appropriate accommodations so they have an equal opportunity to be successful at higher education. AES receives and evaluates students' documentation of disabilities in order to determine the correct accommodations and services students are entitled to receive. AES provides some accommodations for students and directs them to alternative campus or off-campus groups that can provide other assistance. AES serves as an advocate for students with disabilities, working as a mediator with faculty over classroom issues and with administrators regarding campus policies, and it also encourages the university to expand its vision and policies regarding persons with disabilities.

Admissions

Admissions requirements are the same for all applicants. IUPUI is test optional and ACT or SAT scores are not required. Applicants typically have at least a 2.8 GPA and 19 ACT or 1000 SAT. Applicants must submit a 200–400 word essay. Applicants who do not submit test scores are expected to have a 3.0 GPA. Applicants who do not meet the GPA or test score can be reviewed holistically. Emphasis will be placed on high school curriculum, grades, and essay. The average GPA is 3.49, and the average test scores are 22 ACT or 1120 SAT.

Additional Information

The Bepko Learning Center provides resources to help students improve their study skills including academic success coaches, academic mentoring, and tutoring. Academic success workshops are facilitated by academic success coaches which address a variety of topics: time management, goal setting, note-taking strategies, reading strategies, test-taking strategies, and general study strategies.

ADMISSIONS INFO FOR STUDENTS WITH LEARNING DIFFERENCES

Phone: 317-274-3241 • Fax: 317-278-2051 • Email: kjmccrac@iupui.edu

SAT/ACT required: Yes (Test optional for 2021)
Interview required: No
Essay required: No
Additional application required: No
Documentation submitted to: AES

Special Ed. HS course work accepted: Yes
Separate application required for Programs/Services: No
Documentation required for:
LD: Psychoeducational evaluation
ADHD: Psychoeducational evaluation
ASD: Psychoeducational evaluation

Indiana University—Purdue University Indianapolis

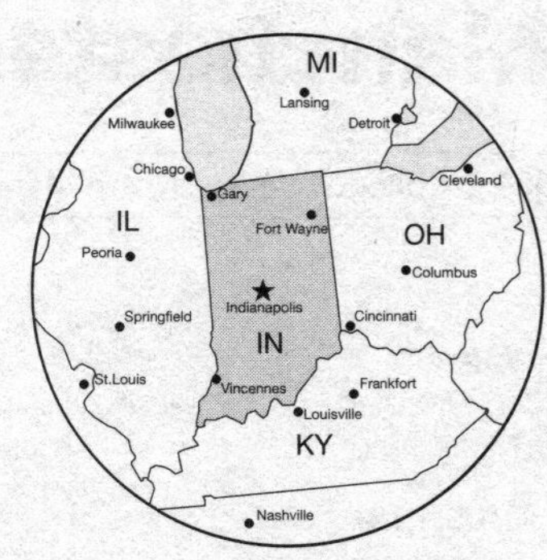

General Admissions

Very important factors include: rigor of secondary school record, academic GPA, standardized test scores. *Other factors include:* class rank, application essay, character/personal qualities, first generation, volunteer work, work experience. High school diploma is required and GED is accepted. *Academic units required:* 4 English, 3 math, 3 science, 3 science labs, 3 social studies, 7 academic electives.

Accommodations or Services

Accommodations are decided upon an individual basis after a thorough review of appropriate, current documentation. The accommodations requests must be supported through the documentation provided and must be logically linked to the current impact of the condition on academic functioning.

Financial Aid

Students should submit: FAFSA. Applicants will be notified of awards on a rolling basis beginning 2/1. *Need-based scholarships/grants offered:* College/university scholarship or grant aid from institutional funds; Federal Pell; Private scholarships; SEOG; State scholarships/grants. *Loan aid offered:* Direct PLUS loans; Direct Subsidized Stafford Loans; Direct Unsubsidized Stafford Loans. Federal Work-Study Program available. Institutional employment available.

Campus Life

Activities: Campus Ministries; Choral groups; Dance; Drama/theater; International Student Organization; Jazz band; Literary magazine; Model UN; Music ensembles; Pep band; Student government; Student newspaper; Student-run film society; Symphony orchestra. **Organizations:** 566 registered organizations, 28 honor societies, 34 religious organizations, 14 fraternities, 16 sororities. **Athletics (Intercollegiate):** *Men:* basketball, cross-country, diving, golf, soccer, swimming, tennis. *Women:* basketball, cross-country, diving, golf, soccer, softball, swimming, tennis, volleyball.

ACCOMMODATIONS

Allowed in exams:	
Calculators	Yes
Dictionary	Yes
Computer	Yes
Spell-checker	Yes
Extended test time	Yes
Scribe	Yes
Proctors	Yes
Oral exams	Yes
Note-takers	Yes
Support services for students with:	
LD	Yes
ADHD	Yes
ASD	Yes
Distraction-reduced environment	Yes
Recording of lecture allowed	Yes
Reading technology	Yes
Audio books	No
Other assistive technology	Yes
Priority registration	Yes
Added costs of services:	
For LD	No
For ADHD	No
For ASD	No
LD specialists	No
ADHD & ASD coaching	No
ASD specialists	No
Professional tutors	Yes
Peer tutors	Yes
Max. hours/week for services	Varies
How professors are notified of student approved accommodations	Student

COLLEGE GRADUATION REQUIREMENTS

Course waivers allowed	Yes
In what courses: Case-by-case basis	
Course substitutions allowed	Yes
In what courses: Case-by-case basis	

Indiana

Manchester University

604 E. College Avenue, North Manchester, IN 46962 • Admissions: 260-982-5055 • Fax: 260-982-5239 **Support: CS**

CAMPUS

Type of school	Private (nonprofit)
Environment	Rural

STUDENTS

Undergrad enrollment	1,071
% male/female	46/54
% from out of state	18
% frosh live on campus	95

FINANCIAL FACTS

Annual tuition	$33,178
Room and board	$10,122
Required fees	$1,258

GENERAL ADMISSIONS INFO

Application fee	$0
Regular application deadline	7/27
Nonfall registration	Yes

Admission may be deferred.

ACADEMICS

Student/faculty ratio	12:1
% students returning for sophomore year	67

Most classes have 10–19 students.

Programs/Services for Students with Learning Differences

Manchester University does not have a specific program for students with learning disabilities. The college is, however, very sensitive to all students. The key word at Manchester University is "success," which means graduating in 4 years. The college wants all students to be able to complete their degree in 4 years. The college does provide support services to students identified as disabled to allow them to be successful. The goal is to assist students in their individual needs.

Admissions

Students with learning disabilities submit the regular application form and are required to meet the same admission criteria as all other applicants. Students are admitted to the college and use the support services as they choose. If special consideration for admission is requested, it is done individually, based on potential for graduation from the college. Manchester considers a wide range of information in making individual admission decisions. Students are encouraged to provide information beyond what is required on the application form if they believe it will strengthen their application or help the college to understand the students' performance or potential. Students who self-disclose the existence of a learning disability and are denied can ask to appeal the decision and have their application reviewed in a "different" way. The key question that will be asked is if the student can graduate in 4 years or, at the most, 5 years.

Additional Information

The Success Center provides tutoring for all students at the college. A course is offered presenting college level study skills with opportunities for students to apply these skills in their current course texts. Specific topics include time management, note-taking, vocabulary, text study techniques, test-taking, and memory strategies. Academic coaches are available to talk with students to identify areas of weaknesses and ways of improving. Course-specific peer tutoring is offered throughout the semester.

ADMISSIONS INFO FOR STUDENTS WITH LEARNING DIFFERENCES

Phone: 260-982-5076 • Fax: 260-982-5888 • Email: mlmiller02@manchester.edu

SAT/ACT required: No
Interview required: Yes
Essay required: No
Additional application required: No
Documentation submitted to: Academic Support Services

Special Ed. HS course work accepted: Yes
Separate application required for Programs/Services: No
Documentation required for:
LD: Psychoeducational evaluation
ADHD: Psychoeducational evaluation
ASD: Psychoeducational evaluation

Manchester University

General Admissions

Very important factors include: rigor of secondary school record, class rank, academic GPA, recommendation(s). *Important factors include:* extracurricular activities, talent/ability, character/personal qualities. *Other factors include:* standardized test scores, interview, alumni/ae relation, volunteer work, work experience, level of applicant's interest. High school diploma is required and GED is accepted. *Academic units required:* 4 English, 2 math, 2 science, 2 science labs, 1 social studies, 1 history, 2 academic electives. *Academic units recommended:* 4 English, 3 math, 3 science, 2 science labs, 2 foreign language, 2 social studies, 2 history, 2 academic electives, 1 computer science, 1 visual/ performing arts.

Accommodations or Services

Accommodations are decided upon an individual basis after a thorough review of appropriate, current documentation. The accommodations requests must be supported through the documentation provided and must be logically linked to the current impact of the condition on academic functioning.

Financial Aid

Students should submit: FAFSA. *Need-based scholarships/grants offered:* College/university scholarship or grant aid from institutional funds; Federal Pell; Private scholarships; SEOG; State scholarships/grants. *Loan aid offered:* Direct PLUS loans; Direct Subsidized Stafford Loans; Direct Unsubsidized Stafford Loans. Federal Work-Study Program available. Institutional employment available.

Campus Life

Activities: Campus Ministries; Choral groups; Concert band; Dance; Drama/theater; International Student Organization; Jazz band; Literary magazine; Model UN; Music ensembles; Opera; Pep band; Radio station; Student government; Student newspaper; Symphony orchestra; Yearbook. **Organizations:** 61 registered organizations, 5 honor societies, 4 religious organizations. **Athletics (Intercollegiate):** *Men:* baseball, basketball, cheerleading, cross-country, football, golf, soccer, tennis, track/field (outdoor), wrestling. *Women:* basketball, cheerleading, cross-country, golf, soccer, softball, tennis, track/field (outdoor), volleyball.

ACCOMMODATIONS

Allowed in exams:	
Calculators	Yes
Dictionary	No
Computer	Yes
Spell-checker	Yes
Extended test time	Yes
Scribe	Yes
Proctors	Yes
Oral exams	Yes
Note-takers	Yes
Support services for students with:	
LD	Yes
ADHD	Yes
ASD	Yes
Distraction-reduced environment	Yes
Recording of lecture allowed	Yes
Reading technology	Yes
Audio books	No
Other assistive technology	Yes
Priority registration	No
Added costs of services:	
For LD	No
For ADHD	No
For ASD	No
LD specialists	Yes
ADHD & ASD coaching	No
ASD specialists	No
Professional tutors	Yes
Peer tutors	Yes
Max. hours/week for services	Unlimited
How professors are notified of student approved accommodations	Student and Disability Office

COLLEGE GRADUATION REQUIREMENTS

Course waivers allowed	No
Course substitutions allowed	No

Indiana

University of Indianapolis

1400 East Hanna Avenue, Indianapolis, IN 46227-3697 • Admissions: 317-788-3216 • Fax: 317-788-3300 **Support: SP**

CAMPUS

Type of school	Private (nonprofit)
Environment	Metropolis

STUDENTS

Undergrad enrollment	4,402
% male/female	37/63
% from out of state	14
% frosh live on campus	77

FINANCIAL FACTS

Annual tuition	$30,888
Room and board	$10,972
Required fees	$1,380

GENERAL ADMISSIONS INFO

Application fee	$25
Regular application deadline	8/2
Nonfall registration	Yes

Admission may be deferred.

Range SAT EBRW	490–600
Range SAT Math	490–590
Range ACT Composite	19–25

ACADEMICS

% students returning for sophomore year	73

Most classes have 10–19 students.

Programs/Services for Students with Learning Differences

The University of Indianapolis offers a full support program called BUILD (Baccalaureate for University of Indianapolis Learning Disabled). The goal of this program is to help students with learning disabilities reach their academic potential. This program is designed for students who are diagnosed with a specific learning disability, attention-deficit/hyperactivity disorder, mental health issues, or Autism Spectrum Disorder. The BUILD program offers in-depth accommodations. Services are comprehensive, and staff is knowledgeable about learning disabilities.

Admissions

Admission to the BUILD program occurs after a student has been accepted to the university. Students with LD must meet the university admissions requirements. However, consideration is given for individual strengths and weaknesses. The student must submit the following to the Office of Admissions: university application for admission, high school transcript, and SAT or ACT scores. The student must submit the following to the BUILD Program: current documentation regarding I.Q. scores, reading and math proficiency level, primary learning style, and major learning difficulty. After BUILD reviews the information, interviews will be arranged for those applicants being considered for final selection into the BUILD Program. Acceptance into BUILD is determined by the program director.

Additional Information

The BUILD program supports self-advocacy. Students are expected to function independently, attend class, and interact with professors. BUILD tutorial sessions are to support student academic endeavors. Tutors will assist students, review class information, discern main concepts, set goals, and recommend skills to reach goals. Students are expected to attend each tutorial session having already attempted homework and reading assignments.

ADMISSIONS INFO FOR STUDENTS WITH LEARNING DIFFERENCES

Phone: 317-788-3536 • Fax: 317-788-3585 • Email: build@uindy.edu

SAT/ACT required: Yes (Test optional through 2022)
Interview required: Yes, for BUILD
Essay required: Yes
Additional application required: Yes
Documentation submitted to: BUILD

Special Ed. HS course work accepted: Yes
Separate application required for Programs/Services: Yes
Documentation required for:
- **LD:** Psychoeducational evaluation
- **ADHD:** Psychoeducational evaluation
- **ASD:** Psychoeducational evaluation

University of Indianapolis

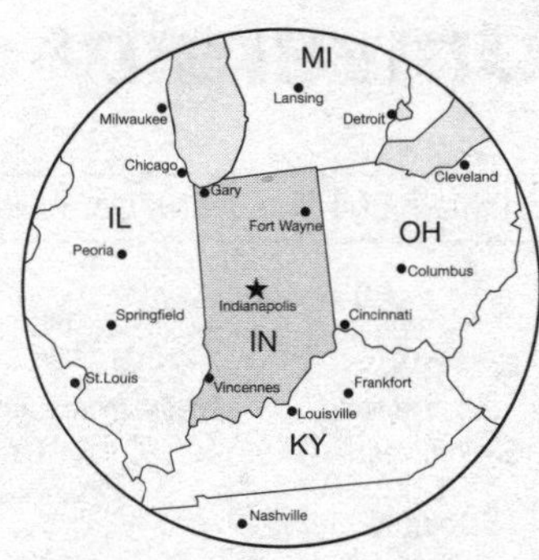

General Admissions

Very important factors include: rigor of secondary school record, academic GPA. *Important factors include:* standardized test scores. *Other factors include:* class rank, recommendation(s), interview, talent/ability. High school diploma is required and GED is accepted. *Academic units required:* 4 English, 3 math, 2 science, 1 science lab, 2 foreign language, 2 social studies, 1 history, 3 academic electives, 1 computer science, 2 visual/performing arts. *Academic units recommended:* 4 English, 3 math, 3 science, 2 science labs, 3 foreign language, 2 social studies, 1 history, 3 academic electives, 1 computer science, 2 visual/performing arts.

Accommodations or Services

Accommodations are decided upon an individual basis after a thorough review of appropriate, current documentation. The accommodations requests must be supported through the documentation provided and must be logically linked to the current impact of the condition on academic functioning.

Financial Aid

Students should submit: FAFSA. *Need-based scholarships/grants offered:* College/university scholarship or grant aid from institutional funds; Federal Pell; Private scholarships; SEOG; State scholarships/grants. *Loan aid offered:* Direct PLUS loans; Direct Subsidized Stafford Loans; Direct Unsubsidized Stafford Loans. Federal Work-Study Program available. Institutional employment available.

Campus Life

Activities: Campus Ministries; Choral groups; Concert band; Dance; Drama/theater; International Student Organization; Jazz band; Literary magazine; Music ensembles; Musical theater; Opera; Pep band; Radio station; Student government; Student newspaper; Television station; Yearbook. **Organizations:** 53 registered organizations, 14 honor societies, 4 religious organizations. **Athletics (Intercollegiate):** *Men:* baseball, basketball, cross-country, diving, football, golf, soccer, swimming, tennis, track/field (outdoor), wrestling. *Women:* basketball, cross-country, diving, golf, soccer, softball, swimming, tennis, track/field (outdoor), volleyball.

ACCOMMODATIONS

Allowed in exams:	
Calculators	Yes
Dictionary	Yes
Computer	Yes
Spell-checker	Yes
Extended test time	Yes
Scribe	Yes
Proctors	Yes
Oral exams	Yes
Note-takers	Yes
Support services for students with:	
LD	Yes
ADHD	Yes
ASD	Yes
Distraction-reduced environment	Yes
Recording of lecture allowed	Yes
Reading technology	Yes
Audio books	Yes
Other assistive technology	Yes
Priority registration	Yes
Added costs of services:	
For LD	Yes
For ADHD	Yes
For ASD	Yes
LD specialists	Yes
ADHD & ASD coaching	No
ASD specialists	No
Professional tutors	No
Peer tutors	Yes
Max. hours/week for services	Varies
How professors are notified of student approved accommodations	Student

COLLEGE GRADUATION REQUIREMENTS

Course waivers allowed	No
Course substitutions allowed	No

University of Notre Dame

220 Main Building, Notre Dame, IN 46556 • Admissions: 574-631-7505 • Fax: 574-631-8865 **Support: S**

CAMPUS

Type of school	Private (nonprofit)
Environment	City

STUDENTS

Undergrad enrollment	8,731
% male/female	52/48
% from out of state	93
% frosh live on campus	100

FINANCIAL FACTS

Annual tuition	$57,192
Room and board	$15,984
Required fees	$507

GENERAL ADMISSIONS INFO

Application fee	$80
Regular application deadline	1/1
Nonfall registration	Yes

Admission may be deferred.

Range SAT EBRW	680–760
Range SAT Math	720–790
Range ACT Composite	32–35

ACADEMICS

Student/faculty ratio	9:1
% students returning for sophomore year	98

Most classes have 10–19 students.

Programs/Services for Students with Learning Differences

It is the mission of Disability Services to ensure that Notre Dame students with disabilities have access to the programs and facilities of the university. Disability Services is committed to forming partnerships with students to share the responsibility of meeting individual needs. At the University of Notre Dame, students with disabilities may use a variety of services intended to reduce the effects that a disability may have on their educational experience. Services do not lower course standards or alter essential degree requirements, but instead give students an equal opportunity to demonstrate their academic abilities. Students can initiate a request for services by registering with Disability Services and providing information that documents the disability. Individual assistance is provided in selecting the services that will provide access to the academic programs and facilities of the university.

Admissions

All applicants must meet the same admission criteria. Essays are the most enjoyable part of the application reading process that helps UND learn about important decisions you've made, adventures you've survived, lessons you've learned, family traditions you've experienced, challenges you've faced, and embarrassing moments you've overcome. Interviews are not offered.

Additional Information

Services for students with learning disabilities or Attention Deficit Disorder include taped textbooks, note-takers, exam modifications, assistance with developing time management skills and learning strategies, and screening and referral for diagnostic testing. Students may substitute American Sign Language for Foreign Language requirement. Tutors are available for all students from other resources. There is also a Writing Center for all students.

ADMISSIONS INFO FOR STUDENTS WITH LEARNING DIFFERENCES

Phone: 574-631-7141 • Fax: 574-631-2133 • Email: showland@nd.edu

SAT/ACT required: Yes (Test optional for 2021)
Interview required: No
Essay required: Yes
Additional application required: No
Documentation submitted to: Disability Services

Special Ed. HS course work accepted: Yes
Separate application required for Programs/Services: No
Documentation required for:
LD: Psychoeducational evaluation
ADHD: Psychoeducational evaluation
ASD: Psychoeducational evaluation

University of Notre Dame

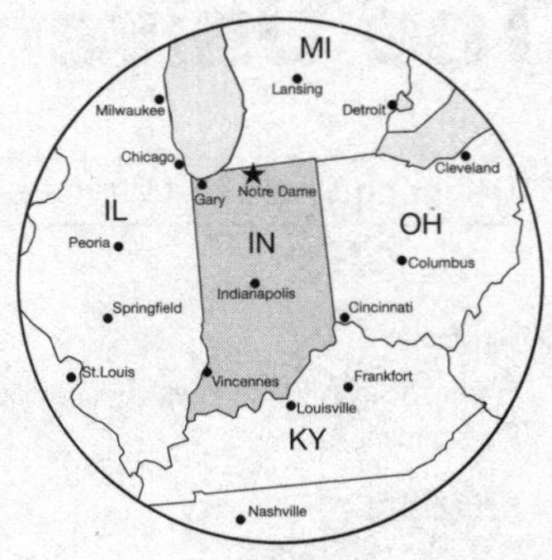

General Admissions

Very important factors include: rigor of secondary school record. *Important factors include:* class rank, academic GPA, application essay, standardized test scores, recommendation(s), extracurricular activities, talent/ability, character/personal qualities, alumni/ae relation, volunteer work. *Other factors include:* first generation, religious affiliation/commitment, racial/ethnic status, work experience, level of applicant's interest. High school diploma is required and GED is accepted. *Academic units required:* 4 English, 3 math, 2 science, 2 science labs, 2 foreign language, 2 history, 3 academic electives. *Academic units recommended:* 4 English, 4 math, 4 science, 2 science labs, 4 foreign language, 4 history.

Accommodations or Services

Accommodations are decided upon an individual basis after a thorough review of appropriate, current documentation. The accommodations requests must be supported through the documentation provided and must be logically linked to the current impact of the condition on academic functioning.

Financial Aid

Students should submit: CSS/Financial Aid PROFILE; FAFSA; Noncustodial PROFILE. *Need-based scholarships/grants offered:* College/university scholarship or grant aid from institutional funds; Federal Pell; Private scholarships; SEOG; State scholarships/grants. *Loan aid offered:* Direct PLUS loans; Direct Subsidized Stafford Loans; Direct Unsubsidized Stafford Loans. Federal Work-Study Program available. Institutional employment available.

Campus Life

Activities: Campus Ministries; Choral groups; Concert band; Dance; Drama/theater; International Student Organization; Jazz band; Literary magazine; Marching band; Model UN; Music ensembles; Musical theater; Opera; Pep band; Radio station; Student government; Student newspaper; Student-run film society; Symphony orchestra; Television station; Yearbook. **Organizations:** 440 registered organizations, 10 honor societies, 9 religious organizations. **Athletics (Intercollegiate):** *Men:* baseball, basketball, cross-country, diving, fencing, football, golf, ice hockey, lacrosse, soccer, swimming, tennis, track/field (outdoor). *Women:* basketball, crew/rowing, cross-country, diving, fencing, golf, lacrosse, soccer, softball, swimming, tennis, track/field (outdoor), volleyball.

ACCOMMODATIONS

Allowed in exams:	
Calculators	Yes
Dictionary	Yes
Computer	No
Spell-checker	Yes
Extended test time	Yes
Scribe	Yes
Proctors	Yes
Oral exams	Yes
Note-takers	Yes
Support services for students with:	
LD	Yes
ADHD	Yes
ASD	Yes
Distraction-reduced environment	Yes
Recording of lecture allowed	Yes
Reading technology	Yes
Audio books	Yes
Other assistive technology	Yes
Priority registration	Yes
Added costs of services:	
For LD	No
For ADHD	No
For ASD	No
LD specialists	No
ADHD & ASD coaching	No
ASD specialists	No
Professional tutors	No
Peer tutors	Yes
Max. hours/week for services	Varies
How professors are notified of student approved accommodations	Student

COLLEGE GRADUATION REQUIREMENTS

Course waivers allowed	No
Course substitutions allowed	No

The University of Saint Francis

2701 Spring Street, Fort Wayne, IN 46808 • Admissions: 260-399-8000 **Support: S**

CAMPUS

Type of school	Private (nonprofit)
Environment	City

STUDENTS

Undergrad enrollment	1,741
% male/female	30/70
% from out of state	11
% frosh live on campus	46

FINANCIAL FACTS

Annual tuition	$31,290
Room and board	$10,490
Required fees	$1,130

GENERAL ADMISSIONS INFO

Application fee	$0
Regular application deadline	Rolling
Nonfall registration	Yes

Admission may be deferred.

Range SAT EBRW	478–590
Range SAT Math	470–580
Range ACT Composite	18–25

ACADEMICS

Student/faculty ratio	11:1
% students returning for sophomore year	69

Most classes have 10–19 students.

Programs/Services for Students with Learning Differences

Students with documented disabilities enjoy access to all university educational programs and activities through accommodations, adjustments, and coordinated services. The Student Accessibility Services office works collaboratively with students with documented disabilities to ensure equal access.

Admissions

For admission to the University of Saint Francis, incoming students should meet the following requirements: graduate from an accredited high school; rank in the upper half of the high school graduation class; have a 2.3 grade point average on a 4.0 scale; and earn an SAT score of 1000 or above or an ACT composite score of 21 or above. Candidates who do not meet the criteria for automatic admission to the University of Saint Francis may still apply for admission. Applications for admission will be reviewed by the Academic Review Committee.

Additional Information

The Academic and Career Development Center provides support to students with disabilities through tutoring and study skills resources, Mentoring for Academic Progress (MAP), and Student Accessibility Services.

ADMISSIONS INFO FOR STUDENTS WITH LEARNING DIFFERENCES

Phone: 260-399-8065 • Fax: 260-399-8161 • Email: gburgess@sf.edu

SAT/ACT required: Yes (Test optional for 2021)
Interview required: No
Essay required: No
Additional application required: Yes
Documentation submitted to: Student Accessibility Services

Special Ed. HS course work accepted: Yes
Separate application required for Programs/Services: Yes
Documentation required for:
LD: Psychoeducational evaluation
ADHD: Psychoeducational evaluation
ASD: Psychoeducational evaluation

The University of Saint Francis

General Admissions

Very important factors include: rigor of secondary school record, academic GPA, standardized test scores. *Important factors include:* class rank. *Other factors include:* application essay, recommendation(s), interview, extracurricular activities, volunteer work, work experience, level of applicant's interest. High school diploma is required and GED is accepted. *Academic units required:* 4 English, 3 math, 2 science, 2 social studies, 1 history, 1 academic elective. *Academic units recommended:* 4 English, 4 math, 3 science, 3 social studies, 1 history, 4 academic electives.

Accommodations or Services

Accommodations are decided upon an individual basis after a thorough review of appropriate, current documentation. The accommodations requests must be supported through the documentation provided and must be logically linked to the current impact of the condition on academic functioning.

Financial Aid

Students should submit: FAFSA. *Need-based scholarships/grants offered:* College/university scholarship or grant aid from institutional funds; Federal Pell; Private scholarships; SEOG; State scholarships/grants. *Loan aid offered:* Direct PLUS loans; Direct Subsidized Stafford Loans; Direct Unsubsidized Stafford Loans. Federal Work-Study Program available. Institutional employment available.

Campus Life

Activities: Campus Ministries; Choral groups; Concert band; Dance; Drama/theater; Jazz band; Literary magazine; Marching band; Music ensembles; Musical theater; Pep band; Student government; Student-run film society. **Organizations:** 36 registered organizations, 6 honor societies, 1 religious organization.

ACCOMMODATIONS

Allowed in exams:	
Calculators	Yes
Dictionary	Yes
Computer	Yes
Spell-checker	Yes
Extended test time	Yes
Scribe	Yes
Proctors	Yes
Oral exams	Yes
Note-takers	Yes
Support services for students with:	
LD	Yes
ADHD	Yes
ASD	Yes
Distraction-reduced environment	Yes
Recording of lecture allowed	Yes
Reading technology	Yes
Audio books	Yes
Other assistive technology	Yes
Priority registration	Yes
Added costs of services:	
For LD	No
For ADHD	No
For ASD	No
LD specialists	No
ADHD & ASD coaching	No
ASD specialists	No
Professional tutors	Yes
Peer tutors	Yes
Max. hours/week for services	Varies
How professors are notified of student approved accommodations	Student

COLLEGE GRADUATION REQUIREMENTS

Course waivers allowed	No
Course substitutions allowed	No

University of Southern Indiana

8600 University Boulevard, Evansville, IN 47712 • Admissions: 812-464-1765 • Fax: 812-465-7154 **Support: S**

CAMPUS

Type of school	Public
Environment	City

STUDENTS

Undergrad enrollment	7,094
% male/female	37/63
% from out of state	16
% frosh live on campus	70

FINANCIAL FACTS

Annual in-state tuition	$8,706
Annual out-of-state tuition	$20,242
Room and board	$9,514

GENERAL ADMISSIONS INFO

Application fee	$40
Regular application deadline	8/15
Nonfall registration	Yes

Admission may be deferred.

Range SAT EBRW	490–590
Range SAT Math	490–580
Range ACT Composite	19–25

ACADEMICS

Student/faculty ratio	17:1
% students returning for sophomore year	67

Most classes have 20–29 students.

Programs/Services for Students with Learning Differences

USI Disability Resources (DR) coordinates services and academic accommodations for USI students with disabilities to ensure equal access. DR reviews documentation for eligibility, collaborates with students to determine appropriate accommodations, and assists with implementing accommodations.

Admissions

Admissions criteria are the same for all students; however, the admissions office will always work with students on an individual basis if needed. In general, students with a 3.6 GPA or higher are admitted with honors. Students with a 2.0–3.5 GPA are admitted in good standing, and students with a GPA below a 2.0 are accepted conditionally. The conditional admissions procedure is for new freshmen who earned below a 2.0 in English, math, science, and social studies. The following are required for those admitted conditionally: freshman seminar; 2.0 GPA; registration through the University Division rather than a specific major; enrollment in no more than 12 credit hours. ACT/SAT scores are used for placement purposes.

Additional Information

Skills classes are offered in basic grammar, algebra review, reading, and study skills. Credit is given for the hours, but the grades are Pass/No Pass. There are no paid note-takers, but special supplies and copy services are provided at no charge to allow the students to get copies of other students' notes. Other services include assistance obtaining alternative-format textbooks; test accommodations; and advocacy and counseling. Students can be paired with an academic coach for assistance and support. Academic coaches offer individualized weekly sessions that focus on a variety of topics: time management, note-taking, textbook reading, memory, and concentration. Subject-based peer tutoring is provided to all students.

ADMISSIONS INFO FOR STUDENTS WITH LEARNING DIFFERENCES

Phone: 812-464-1961 • Fax: 812-464-1935 • Email: rfstone@usi.edu

SAT/ACT required: Yes (Test optional for 2021)
Interview required: No
Essay required: No
Additional application required: No
Documentation submitted to: Disability Resources

Special Ed. HS course work accepted: Yes
Separate application required for Programs/Services: No
Documentation required for:
LD: Psychoeducational evaluation
ADHD: Psychoeducational evaluation
ASD: Psychoeducational evaluation

University of Southern Indiana

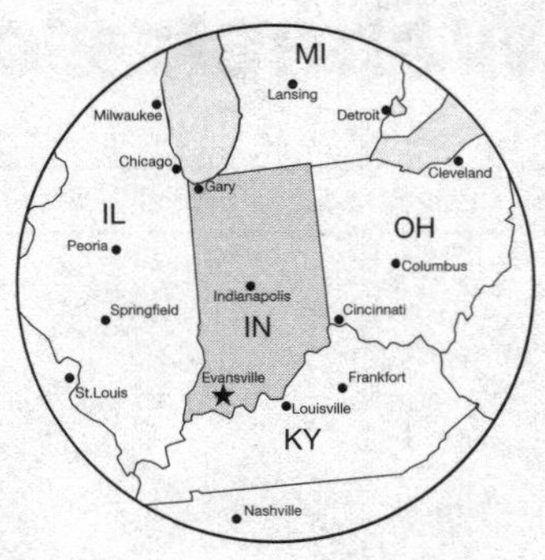

General Admissions

Very important factors include: academic GPA, standardized test scores. *Important factors include:* class rank. *Other factors include:* rigor of secondary school record, application essay, recommendation(s), interview, extracurricular activities, talent/ability, character/personal qualities, volunteer work. High school diploma is required and GED is accepted. *Academic units recommended:* 4 English, 4 math, 2 science, 2 foreign language, 2 social studies, 2 history, 2 academic electives.

Accommodations or Services

Accommodations are decided upon an individual basis after a thorough review of appropriate, current documentation. The accommodations requests must be supported through the documentation provided and must be logically linked to the current impact of the condition on academic functioning.

Financial Aid

Students should submit: FAFSA. *Need-based scholarships/grants offered:* College/university scholarship or grant aid from institutional funds; Federal Nursing Scholarships; Federal Pell; Private scholarships; SEOG; State scholarships/grants; United Negro College Fund. *Loan aid offered:* Direct PLUS loans; Direct Subsidized Stafford Loans; Direct Unsubsidized Stafford Loans. Federal Work-Study Program available. Institutional employment available.

Campus Life

Activities: Campus Ministries; Choral groups; Dance; Drama/theater; International Student Organization; Jazz band; Literary magazine; Pep band; Radio station; Student government; Student newspaper; Television station. **Organizations:** 151 registered organizations, 9 honor societies, 11 religious organizations, 6 fraternities, 7 sororities. **Athletics (Intercollegiate):** *Men:* baseball, basketball, cross-country, golf, soccer, tennis, track/field (outdoor), track/field (indoor). *Women:* basketball, cross-country, golf, soccer, softball, tennis, track/field (outdoor), track/field (indoor), volleyball.

ACCOMMODATIONS

Allowed in exams:	
Calculators	Yes
Dictionary	Yes
Computer	Yes
Spell-checker	Yes
Extended test time	Yes
Scribe	Yes
Proctors	Yes
Oral exams	Yes
Note-takers	Yes
Support services for students with:	
LD	Yes
ADHD	Yes
ASD	Yes
Distraction-reduced environment	Yes
Recording of lecture allowed	Yes
Reading technology	Yes
Audio books	Yes
Other assistive technology	Yes
Priority registration	Yes
Added costs of services:	
For LD	No
For ADHD	No
For ASD	No
LD specialists	No
ADHD & ASD coaching	No
ASD specialists	No
Professional tutors	No
Peer tutors	Yes
Max. hours/week for services	Varies
How professors are notified of student approved accommodations	Student

COLLEGE GRADUATION REQUIREMENTS

Course waivers allowed	No
Course substitutions allowed	Yes
In what courses: Case-by-case basis	

Indiana

Wabash College

P.O. Box 352, Crawfordsville, IN 47933 • Admissions: 765-361-6225 • Fax: 765-361-6437 **Support: S**

CAMPUS

Type of school	Private (nonprofit)
Environment	Village

STUDENTS

Undergrad enrollment	866
% male/female	100/0
% from out of state	20
% frosh live on campus	99

FINANCIAL FACTS

Annual tuition	$45,000
Room and board	$10,900
Required fees	$850

GENERAL ADMISSIONS INFO

Application fee	$50
Regular application deadline	7/1
Nonfall registration	Yes

Admission may be deferred.

Range SAT EBRW	560–650
Range SAT Math	560–670
Range ACT Composite	23–29

ACADEMICS

Student/faculty ratio	10:1
% students returning for sophomore year	91

Most classes have fewer than 10 students.

Programs/Services for Students with Learning Differences

Disability Services is the most helpful to students with special needs when students identify their needs before they begin classes. Once the student is on campus, the coordinator is available to work with him at any point in the academic year. Students vary in their need for consultation and guidance by the coordinator. It is the decision of the student whether or not to request accommodation, and it is his responsibility to provide acceptable documentation and notify the relevant staff members of his condition and of his desire for accommodation(s).

Admissions

Admissions requires students to submit an ACT or SAT score. Mid 50% SAT 1100–1300 or ACT 23–28. Most admitted students have a B+ GPA and those below a 3.25 GPA are less likely to be admitted.

Additional Information

Most students who self-disclose provide documentation of ADHD. The director of academic support services provides study skills guidance to any Wabash student in time management, test-taking, note-taking, reading, and other academic skills usually grouped under this heading.

ADMISSIONS INFO FOR STUDENTS WITH LEARNING DIFFERENCES

Phone: 765-361-6347 • Fax: 765-361-6432 • Email: thrushh@wabash.edu

SAT/ACT required: Yes (Test optional for 2021)
Interview required: No
Essay required: No
Additional application required: No
Documentation submitted to: Disability Services

Special Ed. HS course work accepted: Yes
Separate application required for Programs/Services: No
Documentation required for:
LD: Psychoeducational evaluation
ADHD: Psychoeducational evaluation
ASD: Psychoeducational evaluation

Wabash College

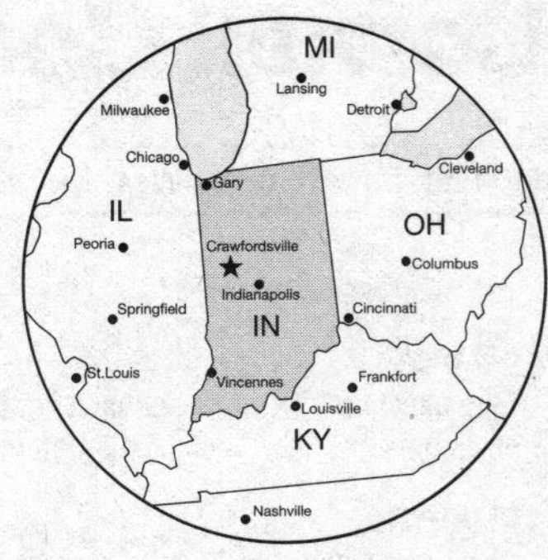

General Admissions

Very important factors include: rigor of secondary school record, class rank, academic GPA, level of applicant's interest. *Important factors include:* standardized test scores, interview, extracurricular activities, talent/ability. *Other factors include:* application essay, recommendation(s), character/personal qualities, first generation, alumni/ae relation, geographical residence, racial/ethnic status, volunteer work, work experience. High school diploma is required and GED is accepted. *Academic units recommended:* 4 English, 4 math, 2 science, 2 science labs, 2 foreign language, 2 social studies, 2 history, 2 academic electives.

Accommodations or Services

Accommodations are decided upon an individual basis after a thorough review of appropriate, current documentation. The accommodations requests must be supported through the documentation provided and must be logically linked to the current impact of the condition on academic functioning.

Financial Aid

Students should submit: FAFSA. Applicants will be notified of awards on a rolling basis beginning 1/1. *Need-based scholarships/grants offered:* College/university scholarship or grant aid from institutional funds; Federal Pell; Private scholarships; SEOG; State scholarships/grants; United Negro College Fund. *Loan aid offered:* Direct PLUS loans; Direct Subsidized Stafford Loans; Direct Unsubsidized Stafford Loans. Federal Work-Study Program available. Institutional employment available.

Campus Life

Activities: Campus Ministries; Choral groups; Dance; Drama/theater; International Student Organization; Jazz band; Literary magazine; Music ensembles; Pep band; Radio station; Student government; Student newspaper; Student-run film society; Yearbook. **Organizations:** 66 registered organizations, 9 honor societies, 3 religious organizations, 10 fraternities. **Athletics (Intercollegiate):** *Men:* baseball, basketball, cross-country, diving, football, golf, soccer, swimming, tennis, track/field (outdoor), track/field (indoor), wrestling.

ACCOMMODATIONS

Allowed in exams:	
Calculators	Yes
Dictionary	Yes
Computer	Yes
Spell-checker	Yes
Extended test time	Yes
Scribe	Yes
Proctors	Yes
Oral exams	Yes
Note-takers	Yes
Support services for students with:	
LD	Yes
ADHD	Yes
ASD	Yes
Distraction-reduced environment	Yes
Recording of lecture allowed	Yes
Reading technology	Yes
Audio books	Yes
Other assistive technology	Yes
Priority registration	No
Added costs of services:	
For LD	No
For ADHD	No
For ASD	No
LD specialists	No
ADHD & ASD coaching	No
ASD specialists	No
Professional tutors	No
Peer tutors	Yes
Max. hours/week for services	Varies
How professors are notified of student approved accommodations	Both

COLLEGE GRADUATION REQUIREMENTS

Course waivers allowed	Yes
In what courses: Case-by-case situation	
Course substitutions allowed	Yes
In what courses: Case-by-case situation	

Indiana

Cornell College

600 First Street South, West Mount Vernon, IA 52314-1098 • Admissions: 319-895-4215 • Fax: 319-895-4451 **Support: S**

CAMPUS

Type of school	Private (nonprofit)
Environment	Rural

STUDENTS

Undergrad enrollment	1,017
% male/female	53/47
% from out of state	67
% frosh live on campus	97

FINANCIAL FACTS

Annual tuition	$45,288
Room and board	$10,150
Required fees	$626

GENERAL ADMISSIONS INFO

Application fee	$0
Regular application deadline	5/1
Nonfall registration	No

Admission may be deferred.

Range SAT EBRW	540–675
Range SAT Math	560–670
Range ACT Composite	23–29

ACADEMICS

Student/faculty ratio	12:1
% students returning for sophomore year	81

Most classes have 10–19 students.

Programs/Services for Students with Learning Differences

Cornell College makes reasonable accommodations for persons with disabilities. Students should notify the Coordinator of Academic Support and Advising and their course instructor of any disability-related accommodations within the first three days of the term for which the accommodations are required, due to the fast pace of the block format. Students must provide documentation that accurately describes their current situation, which includes the diagnosis and information about who diagnosed the student and when this was done; the functional limitations of their diagnosis; and the recommended accommodations. This information should be submitted to the Coordinator of Academic Support and Advising by August 1 of the year they are enrolling. Students must also meet in person with the Coordinator of Academic Support and Advising for an intake meeting to finalized accommodations.

Admissions

Students with a disability can contact Academic Support and Advising early in the admission process to have questions answered. Students can apply with no ACT/SAT test and should choose the "No Test" option and be prepared to answer additional questions. Students also have the option to submit a portfolio instead of or in addition to test scores to showcase skills, talents, and why they will flourish at Cornell. Students can use the portfolio to show what they do to excel—maybe it's a photo journal of a community project they led, a portfolio of paintings or drawings, a recording of performing on stage, or something so creative the college does not even know it exists.

Additional Information

Due to the pace of the block plan, students need to talk to their professors as early in the block as possible about the implementation of their accommodations. Students are encouraged to seek out help proactively through the Center for Teaching and Learning, as the 18 days in class pass quickly. Support is available to students through the Center for Teaching and Learning—they simply need to come to the library and ask for help. Students also have access to counseling services through the Health Center.

ADMISSIONS INFO FOR STUDENTS WITH LEARNING DIFFERENCES

Phone: 319-895-4382 • Fax: 319-895-5187 • Email: Bpaulsen@cornellcollege.edu

SAT/ACT required: No
Interview required: No
Essay required: Yes
Additional application required: No
Documentation submitted to: Accessibility and Disability Services

Special Ed. HS course work accepted: No
Separate application required for Programs/Services: No
Documentation required for:
LD: Psychoeducational evaluation
ADHD: Psychoeducational evaluation
ASD: Psychoeducational evaluation

Cornell College

General Admissions

Very important factors include: academic GPA. *Important factors include:* application essay, standardized test scores. *Other factors include:* rigor of secondary school record, class rank, recommendation(s), interview, extracurricular activities, character/personal qualities, first generation, alumni/ae relation, geographical residence, state residency, racial/ethnic status, volunteer work, work experience, level of applicant's interest. High school diploma is required and GED is accepted. *Academic units recommended:* 4 English, 3 math, 3 science, 1 science lab, 2 foreign language, 3 social studies. Institution is test optional.

Accommodations or Services

Accommodations are decided upon an individual basis after a thorough review of appropriate, current documentation. The accommodations requests must be supported through the documentation provided and must be logically linked to the current impact of the condition on academic functioning.

Financial Aid

Students should submit: FAFSA. *Need-based scholarships/grants offered:* College/university scholarship or grant aid from institutional funds; Federal Pell; SEOG; State scholarships/grants. *Loan aid offered:* Direct PLUS loans; Direct Subsidized Stafford Loans; Direct Unsubsidized Stafford Loans. Federal Work-Study Program available. Institutional employment available.

Campus Life

Activities: Campus Ministries; Choral groups; Concert band; Dance; Drama/theater; International Student Organization; Jazz band; Literary magazine; Music ensembles; Musical theater; Radio station; Student government; Student newspaper; Symphony orchestra; Yearbook. **Organizations:** 63 registered organizations, 16 honor societies, 6 religious organizations, 8 fraternities, 7 sororities. **Athletics (Intercollegiate):** *Men:* baseball, basketball, cross-country, football, golf, soccer, tennis, track/field (outdoor), track/field (indoor), wrestling. *Women:* basketball, cross-country, golf, soccer, softball, tennis, track/field (outdoor), track/field (indoor), volleyball.

ACCOMMODATIONS

Allowed in exams:	
Calculators	Yes
Dictionary	Yes
Computer	Yes
Spell-checker	Yes
Extended test time	Yes
Scribe	Yes
Proctors	Yes
Oral exams	Yes
Note-takers	Yes
Support services for students with:	
LD	Yes
ADHD	Yes
ASD	Yes
Distraction-reduced environment	Yes
Recording of lecture allowed	Yes
Reading technology	Yes
Audio books	Yes
Other assistive technology	No
Priority registration	No
Added costs of services:	
For LD	No
For ADHD	No
For ASD	No
LD specialists	No
ADHD & ASD coaching	No
ASD specialists	No
Professional tutors	No
Peer tutors	Yes
Max. hours/week for services	Varies
How professors are notified of student approved accommodations	Director

COLLEGE GRADUATION REQUIREMENTS

Course waivers allowed	No
Course substitutions allowed	Yes

In what courses: Student works with institution to determine course substitutions

Iowa

Drake University

2507 University Avenue, Des Moines, IA 50311-4505 • Admissions: 515-271-2011 • Fax: 515-271-2831 **Support: S**

CAMPUS

Type of school	Private (nonprofit)
Environment	Metropolis

STUDENTS

Undergrad enrollment	2,954
% male/female	41/59
% from out of state	69
% frosh live on campus	97

FINANCIAL FACTS

Annual tuition	$44,188
Room and board	$11,152
Required fees	$178

GENERAL ADMISSIONS INFO

Application fee	$0
Regular application deadline	3/1
Nonfall registration	Yes

Admission may be deferred.

Range SAT EBRW	560–680
Range SAT Math	560–680
Range ACT Composite	24–30

ACADEMICS

Student/faculty ratio	10:1
% students returning for sophomore year	89

Most classes have 10–19 students.

Programs/Services for Students with Learning Differences

The Student Disability Services facilitates and enhances the opportunity for students with any type of disability to successfully complete their postsecondary education. The SDS is committed to enriching the academic experience of Drake students with disabilities through individualized assessment of accommodations and resource needs. It is the students' responsibility to self-identify a learning disability; to provide documentation of their disability; and to request the accommodations that they need.

Admissions

There is no special admission process for students with learning disabilities. All applicants are expected to meet the same admission criteria. Students must be admitted and enrolled in the university prior to seeking accommodations or services for a learning disability. Admissions reviews each application for admission individually, there is no single, inflexible set of standards—such as GPA or test score. Instead, first-year students can choose the Standard Application or Test-Flexible Application. The Standard Application path provides a holistic admission review of the traditional admission measurements: transcript, ACT or SAT score, essay, and the other parts of your application. The Test-Flexible Application path requires an interview in lieu of an ACT or SAT; first-year students can only choose this path if they have a cumulative GPA of 3.0 or higher (on a weighted or unweighted scale) and are not pursuing pre-pharmacy, pre-athletic training, pre-occupational therapy, or the National Alumni Scholarship.

Additional Information

The SDS can offer students appointments at the pre-admission and pre-enrollment stages; review of Drake's policies and procedures regarding students with disabilities; identification and coordination of classroom accommodations; assessment of service needs; note-takers, scribes, and readers; referral to appropriate campus resources; advocacy and liaison with the university community; and training on the use of assistive technology. Services provided by the SDS do not lower any course standards or change any requirements of a particular degree.

ADMISSIONS INFO FOR STUDENTS WITH LEARNING DIFFERENCES

Phone: 515-271-1835 • Fax: 515-271-2376 • Email: michelle.laughlin@drake.edu

SAT/ACT required: No
Interview required: No
Essay required: Yes
Additional application required: No
Documentation submitted to: Student Disability Services

Special Ed. HS course work accepted: Yes
Separate application required for Programs/Services: No
Documentation required for:
- **LD:** Psychoeducational evaluation
- **ADHD:** Psychoeducational evaluation
- **ASD:** Psychoeducational evaluation

Drake University

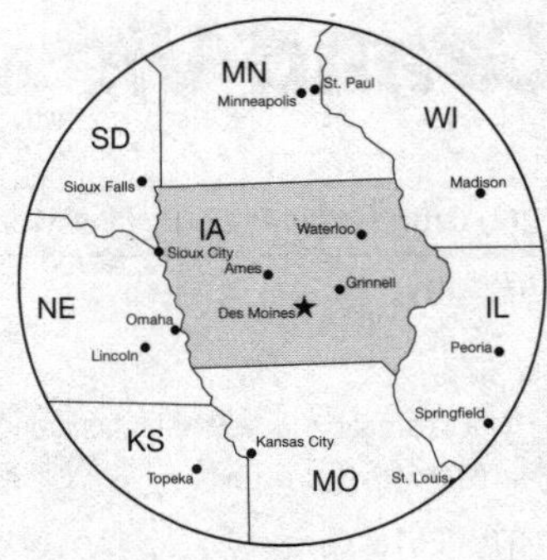

General Admissions

Very important factors include: rigor of secondary school record, academic GPA. *Important factors include:* standardized test scores, interview. *Other factors include:* class rank, application essay, recommendation(s), extracurricular activities, talent/ability, character/personal qualities, alumni/ae relation, racial/ethnic status, volunteer work, work experience, level of applicant's interest. High school diploma is required and a GED is accepted. *Academic units recommended:* 4 English, 3 math, 2 science, 1 science lab, 2 foreign language, 4 social studies. Applicants may choose to complete an essay or an admission interview, in lieu of submitting a test score.

Accommodations or Services

Accommodations are decided upon an individual basis after a thorough review of appropriate, current documentation. The accommodations requests must be supported through the documentation provided and must be logically linked to the current impact of the condition on academic functioning.

Financial Aid

Students should submit: FAFSA. *Need-based scholarships/grants offered:* College/university scholarship or grant aid from institutional funds; Federal Pell; Private scholarships; SEOG; State scholarships/grants. *Loan aid offered:* Direct PLUS loans; Direct Subsidized Stafford Loans; Direct Unsubsidized Stafford Loans. Federal Work-Study Program available. Institutional employment available.

Campus Life

Activities: Choral groups; Concert band; Dance; Drama/theater; International Student Organization; Jazz band; Literary magazine; Marching band; Model UN; Music ensembles; Musical theater; Pep band; Radio station; Student government; Student newspaper; Symphony orchestra. **Organizations:** 160 registered organizations, 24 honor societies, 10 religious organizations, 9 fraternities, 5 sororities. **Athletics (Intercollegiate):** *Men:* basketball, cheerleading, cross-country, football, golf, soccer, tennis, track/field (outdoor), track/field (indoor). *Women:* basketball, cheerleading, crew/rowing, cross-country, golf, soccer, softball, tennis, track/field (outdoor), track/field (indoor), volleyball.

ACCOMMODATIONS

Allowed in exams:	
Calculators	Yes
Dictionary	Yes
Computer	Yes
Spell-checker	Yes
Extended test time	Yes
Scribe	Yes
Proctors	Yes
Oral exams	Yes
Note-takers	Yes
Support services for students with:	
LD	Yes
ADHD	Yes
ASD	Yes
Distraction-reduced environment	Yes
Recording of lecture allowed	Yes
Reading technology	Yes
Audio books	Yes
Other assistive technology	Yes
Priority registration	No
Added costs of services:	
For LD	No
For ADHD	No
For ASD	No
LD specialists	No
ADHD & ASD coaching	No
ASD specialists	No
Professional tutors	No
Peer tutors	Yes
Max. hours/week for services	Unlimited
How professors are notified of student approved accommodations	Student

COLLEGE GRADUATION REQUIREMENTS

Course waivers allowed	No
Course substitutions allowed	No

Grand View University

1200 Grandview Avenue, Des Moines, IA 50316-1599 • Admissions: 515-263-2810 • Fax: 515-263-2974 **Support: CS**

CAMPUS	
Type of school	Private (nonprofit)
Environment	Village
STUDENTS	
Undergrad enrollment	1800
% male/female	42/58
% from out of state	13
% frosh live on campus	85
FINANCIAL FACTS	
Annual tuition	$28,588
Room and board	$9,334
Required fees	$736
GENERAL ADMISSIONS INFO	
Application fee	$0
Regular application deadline	8/15
Nonfall registration	Yes
Admission may be deferred.	
Range SAT EBRW	440-590
Range SAT Math	450-590
Range ACT Composite	18–23
ACADEMICS	
Student/faculty ratio	12:1
% students returning for sophomore year	68
Most classes have 10–19 students.	

Programs/Services for Students with Learning Differences

Grand View provides services to students with learning differences through the Disability Services office. Accommodations are decided upon an individual basis after a thorough review of appropriate, current documentation. The accommodations requests must be supported through the documentation provided and must be logically linked to the current impact of the condition on academic functioning.

Admissions

There is no special admissions process for students with LD and ADHD. There is a freshman academy for students who do not have sufficient preparation to undertake college work but show potential for success in college. Grand View has a personalized admission and enrollment policy. Consideration may be given to: class rank and test scores; quality of high school curriculum completed; co-curricular achievement; and maturity and seriousness of purpose as displayed through church, community, school, work, and family activities. Students planning to attend Grand View University are encouraged to pursue a college-preparatory course of study in high school. It is recommended that students complete: four years of English, three years of math, three years of science, three years of social science, and two years of foreign language. Admission to a particular program or major may be governed by different standards.

Additional Information

Academic Enrichment Center provides resources which complement classroom instruction enabling students to optimize their academic experience. Students can receive help with reading comprehension, study skills, organizational skills, developing a personal management plan, test-taking strategies, writing skills, personalized instruction in math, and peer tutoring. The Career Center provides services, resources, and educational opportunities by assisting students in developing, evaluating, initiating, and implementing personal career and life plans. Faculty members serve as academic advisors. Core courses can have substitutions options. Other services or accommodations offered for students with appropriate documentation include the use of calculators, computers, or spellcheckers; extended testing time; scribes; proctors; oral exams; notetakers; a distraction-free environment for taking tests; tape-recording of lectures; and services for students with ADHD.

ADMISSIONS INFO FOR STUDENTS WITH LEARNING DIFFERENCES

Phone: 515-263-2971 • Fax: 515-263-2824 • Email: mrjohnson@grandview.edu

SAT/ACT required: No (depending on GPA)
Interview required: No
Essay required: Yes
Additional application required: No
Documentation submitted to: Academic Success

Special Ed. HS course work accepted: Yes
Separate application required for Programs/Services: No
Documentation required for:
LD: Psychoeducational evaluation
ADHD: Psychoeducational evaluation
ASD: Psychoeducational evaluation

Grand View University

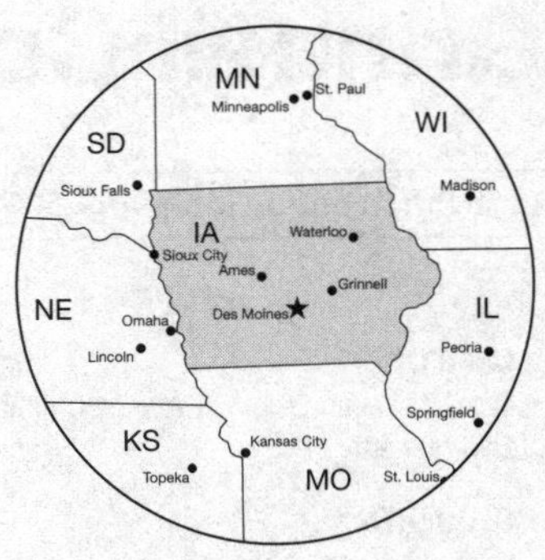

General Admissions

Very important factors include: rigor of secondary school record, class rank, academic GPA, character/personal qualities. *Important factors include:* standardized test scores. *Other factors include:* extracurricular activities, talent/ability, alumni/ae relation, volunteer work, work experience. High school diploma is required, and GED is accepted. *Academic units recommended:* 4 English, 3 math, 3 science, 2 foreign language, 3 social studies.

Accommodations or Services

Accommodations are decided upon an individual basis after a thorough review of appropriate, current documentation. The accommodations requests must be supported through the documentation provided and must be logically linked to the current impact of the condition on academic functioning.

Financial Aid

Students should submit: FAFSA *Need-based scholarships/grants offered:* College/university scholarship or grant aid from institutional funds; Federal Pell; Private scholarships; SEOG; State scholarships/grants. Federal Work-Study Program available. Institutional employment available.

Campus Life

Activities: Campus Ministries; Choral groups; Concert band; Dance; Drama/theater; International Student Organization; Jazz band; Literary magazine; Music ensembles; Pep band; Radio station; Student government; Student newspaper; Television station. **Organizations:** 28 registered organizations, 1 religious organization. **Athletics (Intercollegiate):** *Men:* baseball, basketball, cross-country, golf, soccer. *Women:* basketball, cross-country, golf, soccer, softball, volleyball.

ACCOMMODATIONS

Allowed in exams:	
Calculators	Yes
Dictionary	Yes
Computer	Yes
Spell-checker	Yes
Extended test time	Yes
Scribe	Yes
Proctors	Yes
Oral exams	Yes
Note-takers	Yes
Support services for students with:	
LD	Yes
ADHD	Yes
ASD	Yes
Distraction-reduced environment	Yes
Recording of lecture allowed	Yes
Reading technology	Yes
Audio books	Yes
Other assistive technology	Yes
Priority registration	No
Added costs of services:	
For LD	No
For ADHD	No
For ASD	No
LD specialists	Yes
ADHD & ASD coaching	No
ASD specialists	No
Professional tutors	No
Peer tutors	Yes
Max. hours/week for services	Unlimited
How professors are notified of student approved accommodations	Student in collaboration with the director

COLLEGE GRADUATION REQUIREMENTS

Course waivers allowed	No
Course substitutions allowed	Yes

In what courses: Student works with institution to determine course substitutions

Iowa

Grinnell College

1115 8th Avenue, Grinnell, IA 50112-1690 • Admissions: 641-269-3600 • Fax: 641-269-4800 **Support: S**

CAMPUS

Type of school	Private (nonprofit)
Environment	Village

STUDENTS

Undergrad enrollment	1,716
% male/female	46/54
% from out of state	91
% frosh live on campus	100

FINANCIAL FACTS

Annual tuition	$56,188
Room and board	$13,864
Required fees	$492

GENERAL ADMISSIONS INFO

Application fee	$0
Regular application deadline	1/15
Nonfall registration	No

Admission may be deferred.

Range SAT EBRW	670–740
Range SAT Math	700–790
Range ACT Composite	31–34

ACADEMICS

Student/faculty ratio	9:1
% students returning for sophomore year	96

Most classes have 10–19 students.

Programs/Services for Students with Learning Differences

Grinnell College's commitment to creating a diverse, multicultural campus community includes many students, faculty, and staff with disabilities. Using universal design principles, Grinnell tries to remove as many barriers as possible and make accommodations for disabilities when needed. They provide accommodations and support for Grinnellians with disabilities such as learning, psychiatric, physical, or sensory disabilities. They offer many services to all students that can be of help to those with disabilities, including mentoring, technology, academic skills training, and career services.

Admissions

Admission Criteria is the same for all students. Admission to Grinnell is highly selective, and while there is no single factor that guarantees admission, it helps to have taken a challenging, balanced high school curriculum. The recommended secondary school program is: 4 years of English, 4 years of mathematics (at least through pre-calculus), 3 years of social studies, 3 years of lab science, and 3 years of a foreign language. First-year applicants may interview beginning in February of their junior years and until mid-December of their senior years. Interviews are not required for admission, and applicants may only interview once. ACT/ SAT required.

Additional Information

The Academic Advising office staff will work with students on nearly any academic concern. Students can go to the office for instruction on study skills and time management, to receive peer tutoring, to get support for managing their academic obligations while dealing with a personal or medical concern, or to apply for a leave of absence. A wide range of resources includes speech to text, text to speech, Braille, tactile graphics, etc. All students receive Read & Write Gold 11 software.

ADMISSIONS INFO FOR STUDENTS WITH LEARNING DIFFERENCES

Phone: 641-269-3089 • Email: wilkeaut@grinnell.edu

SAT/ACT required: Yes (Test optional for 2021)
Interview required: Recommended
Essay required: Yes
Additional application required: No
Documentation submitted to: Accessibility and Disability Services

Special Ed. HS course work accepted: No
Separate application required for Programs/Services: No
Documentation required for:
LD: Psychoeducational evaluation
ADHD: Psychoeducational evaluation
ASD: Psychoeducational evaluation

Grinnell College

General Admissions

Very important factors include: rigor of secondary school record, class rank, academic GPA, recommendation(s). *Important factors include:* application essay, standardized test scores, extracurricular activities, talent/ability. *Other factors include:* interview, character/personal qualities, first generation, alumni/ae relation, geographical residence, state residency, racial/ethnic status, volunteer work, work experience, level of applicant's interest. High school diploma is required and GED is accepted. *Academic units recommended:* 4 English, 4 math, 3 science, 3 science labs, 3 foreign language, 3 social studies, 3 history. For the 2020–21 admission cycle Grinnell College will adopt a test optional admission policy. Check with institution for current policy.

Accommodations or Services

Accommodations are decided upon an individual basis after a thorough review of appropriate, current documentation. The accommodations requests must be supported through the documentation provided and must be logically linked to the current impact of the condition on academic functioning.

Financial Aid

Students should submit: FAFSA; CSS/Financial Aid PROFILE. *Need-based scholarships/grants offered:* College/university scholarship or grant aid from institutional funds; Federal Pell; Private scholarships; SEOG; State scholarships/grants. *Loan aid offered:* Direct PLUS loans; Direct Subsidized Stafford Loans; Direct Unsubsidized Stafford Loans. Federal Work-Study Program available. Institutional employment available.

Campus Life

Activities: Campus Ministries; Choral groups; Concert band; Dance; Drama/theater; International Student Organization; Jazz band; Literary magazine; Model UN; Music ensembles; Musical theater; Pep band; Radio station; Student government; Student newspaper; Student-run film society; Symphony orchestra; Yearbook. **Organizations:** 110 registered organizations, 2 honor societies, 5 religious organizations. **Athletics (Intercollegiate):** *Men:* baseball, basketball, cross-country, diving, football, golf, soccer, swimming, tennis, track/field (outdoor), track/field (indoor). *Women:* basketball, cross-country, diving, golf, soccer, softball, swimming, tennis, track/field (outdoor), track/field (indoor), volleyball.

ACCOMMODATIONS

Allowed in exams:	
Calculators	Yes
Dictionary	Yes
Computer	Yes
Spell-checker	Yes
Extended test time	Yes
Scribe	Yes
Proctors	Yes
Oral exams	Yes
Note-takers	Yes
Support services for students with:	
LD	Yes
ADHD	Yes
ASD	Yes
Distraction-reduced environment	Yes
Recording of lecture allowed	Yes
Reading technology	Yes
Audio books	Yes
Other assistive technology	Yes
Priority registration	Yes
Added costs of services:	
For LD	No
For ADHD	No
For ASD	No
LD specialists	Yes
ADHD & ASD coaching	Yes
ASD specialists	No
Professional tutors	No
Peer tutors	Yes
Max. hours/week for services	Varies
How professors are notified of student approved accommodations	Student and Disability Office

COLLEGE GRADUATION REQUIREMENTS

Course waivers allowed	No
Course substitutions allowed	Yes

In what courses: Student works with institution to determine course substitutions

Iowa

Iowa State University

100 Enrollment Services Center, Ames, IA 50011-2011 • Admissions: 515-294-5836 • Fax: 515-294-2592 **Support: CS**

CAMPUS	
Type of school	Public
Environment	Town
STUDENTS	
Undergrad enrollment	28,294
% male/female	57/43
% from out of state	40
% frosh live on campus	93
FINANCIAL FACTS	
Annual in-state tuition	$9,320
Annual out-of-state tuition	$24,508
Room and board	$9,149
Required fees	$1,278
GENERAL ADMISSIONS INFO	
Application fee	$40
Regular application deadline	3/1
Nonfall registration	Yes
Admission may be deferred.	
Range SAT EBRW	540–650
Range SAT Math	560–690
Range ACT Composite	22–28
ACADEMICS	
Student/faculty ratio	19:1
% students returning for sophomore year	87
Most classes have 20–29 students.	

Programs/Services for Students with Learning Differences

ISU is committed to providing equal opportunities and facilitating the personal growth and development of all students. Staff from the Student Accessibility Services Office assists students with issues relating to the documented disability. A thorough review of most current LD evaluation and documentation is completed to determine the possible accommodations needed. SAS staff also offers assistance in articulating needs to faculty and staff and may serve as a liaison in student/staff negotiations. Documentation should include current diagnosis, functional limitations, and relevant information about the student and examiner's qualifications; behavioral observation of the way students present themselves, verbal and nonverbal communication, interpersonal skills and behavior during testing; a narrative describing developmental and educational history; and a description of the effect of the disability on learning is required. Recommendations concerning possible accommodations are welcomed.

Admissions

Students are admitted directly if they meet the Regent Admission Index (RAI) score. There are two mathematical formulas for computing student's RAI scores, the primary RAI formula (for students whose high school provides class rank) and the Alternative RAI formula (for students whose high school does not provide class rank. Students with LD who feel their academic record does not reflect their ability to succeed may request to be considered on an individual basis. These students should submit a letter requesting special consideration and provide a description of how the disability impacts academic performance, services used in high school, and documentation of the disability.

Additional Information

Counselors work one-on-one to evaluate and identify problem study habits and devise strategies to improve them. The Student Support Services is located in the Academic Success Center (ASC). ASC coordinates services including counseling, teaching reading, and study skills, and provides a list of tutors. The Writing Center is available to all students. The LD specialist provides information about readers, note-takers, and scribes. Peer Supplemental Instruction (SI) is an academic assistance program attached to very difficult courses. SI leaders attend classes and conduct biweekly sessions to help students learn and study the course material. Student Support Services is a federally funded program for students with LD and others qualified to receive academic support in the form of free tutoring and skill-building workshops.

ADMISSIONS INFO FOR STUDENTS WITH LEARNING DIFFERENCES

Phone: 515-294-7220 • Email: smoats@iastate.edu

SAT/ACT required: Yes (Test optional for 2021)
Interview required: No
Essay required: No
Additional application required: Yes
Documentation submitted to: Student Accessibility Services

Special Ed. HS course work accepted: No
Separate application required for Programs/Services: Yes
Documentation required for:
LD: Psychoeducational evaluation
ADHD: Psychoeducational evaluation
ASD: Psychoeducational evaluation

Iowa State University

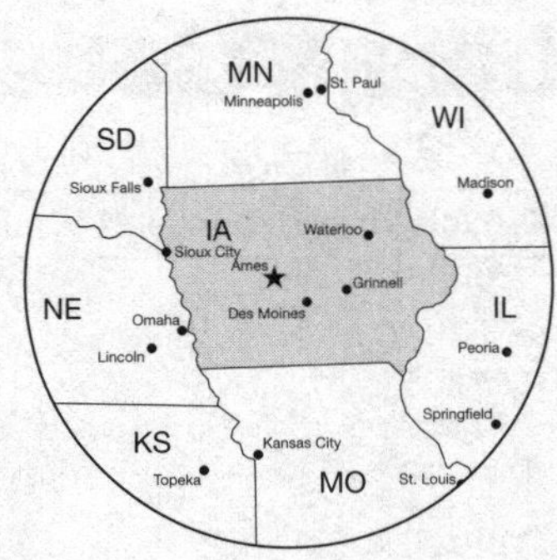

General Admissions

Very important factors include: rigor of secondary school record, class rank, academic GPA, standardized test scores. *Other factors include:* recommendation(s), interview, extracurricular activities, talent/ability, character/personal qualities, geographical residence, state residency, volunteer work, work experience. High school diploma is required, and GED is accepted. *Academic units required:* 4 English, 3 math, 3 science, 2 science labs, 2 foreign language, 2 social studies. *Academic units recommended:* 4 English, 4 math, 4 science, 3 science labs, 3 foreign language, 4 social studies. Iowa State University will be test-optional for Fall 2021 freshman applicants. This temporary waiver of Iowa State's normal admission requirements has been granted by the Board of Regents, State of Iowa.

Accommodations or Services

Accommodations are decided upon an individual basis after a thorough review of appropriate, current documentation. The accommodations requests must be supported through the documentation provided and must be logically linked to the current impact of the condition on academic functioning.

Financial Aid

Students should submit: FAFSA. Applicants will be notified of awards on a rolling basis beginning 3/15. *Need-based scholarships/grants offered:* College/university scholarship or grant aid from institutional funds; Federal Pell; SEOG; State scholarships/grants. *Loan aid offered:* Direct PLUS loans; Direct Subsidized Stafford Loans; Direct Unsubsidized Stafford Loans. Federal Work-Study Program available. Institutional employment available.

Campus Life

Activities: Campus Ministries; Choral groups; Concert band; Dance; Drama/theater; International Student Organization; Jazz band; Literary magazine; Marching band; Model UN; Music ensembles; Musical theater; Pep band; Radio station; Student government; Student newspaper; Student-run film society; Symphony orchestra; Television station. **Organizations:** 898 registered organizations, 28 honor societies, 39 religious organizations, 44 fraternities, 36 sororities. **Athletics (Intercollegiate):** *Men:* basketball, cross-country, football, golf, track/field (outdoor), track/field (indoor), wrestling. *Women:* basketball, cross-country, diving, golf, gymnastics, soccer, softball, swimming, tennis, track/field (outdoor), track/field (indoor), volleyball.

ACCOMMODATIONS

Allowed in exams:	
Calculators	Yes
Dictionary	Yes
Computer	Yes
Spell-checker	Yes
Extended test time	Yes
Scribe	Yes
Proctors	Yes
Oral exams	Yes
Note-takers	Yes
Support services for students with:	
LD	Yes
ADHD	Yes
ASD	Yes
Distraction-reduced environment	Yes
Recording of lecture allowed	Yes
Reading technology	Yes
Audio books	Yes
Other assistive technology	No
Priority registration	No
Added costs of services:	
For LD	No
For ADHD	No
For ASD	No
LD specialists	No
ADHD & ASD coaching	Yes
ASD specialists	No
Professional tutors	No
Peer tutors	Yes
Max. hours/week for services	Varies
How professors are notified of student approved accommodations	Student

COLLEGE GRADUATION REQUIREMENTS

Course waivers allowed	No
Course substitutions allowed	No

Loras College

1450 Alta Vista, Dubuque, IA 52001 • Admissions: 563-588-7236 • Fax: 563-588-7119 **Support: SP**

CAMPUS	
Type of school	Private (nonprofit)
Environment	Town
STUDENTS	
Undergrad enrollment	1,412
% male/female	55/45
% from out of state	59
% frosh live on campus	94
FINANCIAL FACTS	
Annual tuition	$33,500
Room and board	$8,600
Required fees	$1,738
GENERAL ADMISSIONS INFO	
Application fee	$0
Regular application deadline	Rolling
Nonfall registration	Yes
Admission may be deferred.	
Range SAT EBRW	480–575
Range SAT Math	485–570
Range ACT Composite	20–25
ACADEMICS	
Student/faculty ratio	12:1
% students returning for sophomore year	78
Most classes have 20–29 students.	

Programs/Services for Students with Learning Differences

Loras College provides the supportive, comprehensive Lynch Program for the motivated individual with a learning disability or AD/HD. Students can be successful in Loras' competitive environment if they have had adequate preparation, are willing to work with program staff, and take responsibility for their own learning. The Enhanced Program staff has a specialist to serve as guides and advocates, encouraging and supporting students to become independent learners. The specialist also serves as the student's advisor for a two-credit class called Learning Strategies both semesters of the first year. Students with LD or ADHD who are enrolled in college-preparatory courses in high school are the most appropriate candidates for the Loras program.

Admissions

Students interested in the Enhanced Program should apply simultaneously to the College and the Enhanced Program. The Enhanced Program Application and current documentation should be submitted to the Lynch Learning Center. After the materials are reviewed, appropriate candidates will be invited for an official interview with a Lynch Learning Center staff member. All application materials for the Enhanced Program must be received by December 15, the priority application date. Students are encouraged to apply early in their senior year.

Additional Information

The Autism Specific Program ARCH is designed to help students with ASD thrive emotionally, academically and socially. Through the four-year program, students work directly with Certified Autism Specialists. Students meet weekly with their coach and attend weekly study table sessions and bi-monthly mentoring meetings. Students have access to smart pens and speech to text software.

ADMISSIONS INFO FOR STUDENTS WITH LEARNING DIFFERENCES

Phone: 563-588-7134 • Email: lynn.gallagher@loras.edu

SAT/ACT required: No
Interview required: Yes
Essay required: Yes
Additional application required: Yes
Documentation submitted to: Lynch Learning Center

Special Ed. HS course work accepted: Yes
Separate application required for Programs/Services: Yes
Documentation required for:
- **LD:** Psychoeducational evaluation
- **ADHD:** Psychoeducational evaluation
- **ASD:** Psychoeducational evaluation

Loras College

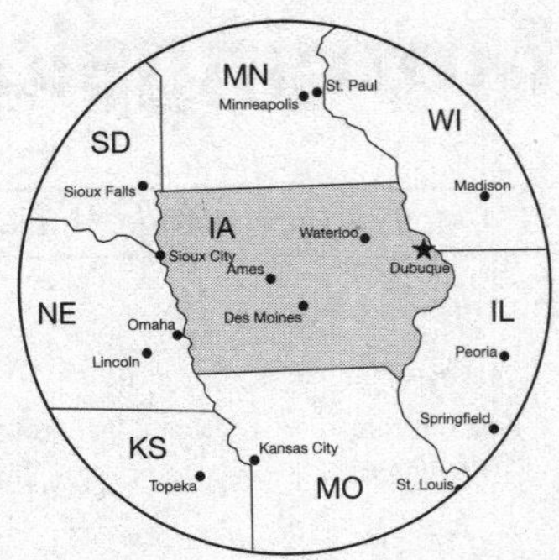

General Admissions

Very important factors include: rigor of secondary school record, academic GPA, standardized test scores. *Other factors include:* class rank, application essay, recommendation(s), interview, extracurricular activities, character/personal qualities, racial/ethnic status, volunteer work, work experience, level of applicant's interest. High school diploma is required and a GED is accepted. *Academic units recommended:* 4 English, 4 math, 3 science, 2 science labs, 3 social studies, 2 academic electives. Test optional policy is dependent on weighted high school GPA.

Accommodations or Services

Accommodations are decided upon an individual basis after a thorough review of appropriate, current documentation. The accommodations requests must be supported through the documentation provided and must be logically linked to the current impact of the condition on academic functioning.

Financial Aid

Students should submit: CSS/Financial Aid PROFILE; FAFSA. Applicants will be notified of awards on a rolling basis beginning 2/1. *Need-based scholarships/grants offered:* College/university scholarship or grant aid from institutional funds; Federal Pell; Private scholarships; SEOG; State scholarships/grants. *Loan aid offered:* Direct PLUS loans; Direct Subsidized Stafford Loans; Direct Unsubsidized Stafford Loans. Federal Work-Study Program available. Institutional employment available.

Campus Life

Activities: Campus Ministries; Choral groups; Concert band; Dance; Drama/theater; International Student Organization; Jazz band; Literary magazine; Music ensembles; Pep band; Radio station; Student government; Student newspaper; Television station; Yearbook. **Organizations:** 58 registered organizations, 3 honor societies, 7 religious organizations, 1 fraternity, 1 sorority. **Athletics (Intercollegiate):** *Men:* baseball, basketball, cross-country, diving, football, golf, soccer, swimming, tennis, track/field (outdoor), track/field (indoor), wrestling. *Women:* basketball, cross-country, diving, golf, soccer, softball, swimming, tennis, track/field (outdoor), track/field (indoor), volleyball.

ACCOMMODATIONS

Allowed in exams:	
Calculators	Yes
Dictionary	Yes
Computer	Yes
Spell-checker	Yes
Extended test time	Yes
Scribe	Yes
Proctors	Yes
Oral exams	Yes
Note-takers	Yes
Support services for students with:	
LD	Yes
ADHD	Yes
ASD	Yes
Distraction-reduced environment	Yes
Recording of lecture allowed	Yes
Reading technology	Yes
Audio books	Yes
Other assistive technology	Yes
Priority registration	Yes
Added costs of services:	
For LD	Yes
For ADHD	Yes
For ASD	Yes
LD specialists	Yes
ADHD & ASD coaching	Yes
ASD specialists	No
Professional tutors	No
Peer tutors	Yes
Max. hours/week for services	Varies
How professors are notified of student approved accommodations	Student

COLLEGE GRADUATION REQUIREMENTS

Course waivers allowed	Yes
In what courses: Student works with institution to determine course waivers	
Course substitutions allowed	No

Iowa

Morningside College

1501 Morningside Avenue, Sioux City, IA 51106-1751 • Admissions: 712-274-5511 • Fax: 712-274-5101 **Support: CS**

CAMPUS	
Type of school	Private (nonprofit)
Environment	City
STUDENTS	
Undergrad enrollment	1,212
% male/female	46/54
% from out of state	32
% frosh live on campus	94
FINANCIAL FACTS	
Annual tuition	$32,460
Room and board	$10,110
Required fees	$1,510
GENERAL ADMISSIONS INFO	
Application fee	$25
Nonfall registration	Yes
Admission may be deferred.	
Range ACT Composite	19–25
ACADEMICS	
Student/faculty ratio	13:1
% students returning for sophomore year	71
Most classes have 10–19 students.	

Programs/Services for Students with Learning Differences

Morningside recognizes that students with different learning styles may need assistance in order to be truly successful. Students requesting accommodations should submit documentation to the Associate Dean of Academic Affairs. This documentation may include but is not necessarily limited to the following: high school records; specific plans recommended by qualified professionals and/or consultants; and satisfactory medical determination as required.

Admissions

Morningside's selective admissions program is based on: class rank, college preparatory coursework, GPA, ACT or SAT, essay participation recommended but not required, character, and personal abilities. Students with ACT of 20 or SAT of 1410, and either ranked in the top half of their class or have achieved a high school GPA of 2.5 meet the academic standards for admissions. First-year students who have been out of high school more than 5 years are not required to submit ACT or SAT test scores but are required to take math and/or English placement assessments. Students who have not completed high school may be admitted on the basis of a GED score.

Additional Information

Reasonable accommodations for students might include the following: note-taking, copies of instructor's notes, tape-recording of class, reasonable equipment modification, preferential seating, books on tape, test-taking accommodations, word processor adaptations, and reader service. The Academic Support Center is open to all students. Academic Support Center staff helps students improve or strengthen their academics by providing free assistance in writing techniques. Writing specialists are available to help students with the basics as well as help proficient writers who want assistance for particular writing assignments or projects. Staff and student tutors are available in the Academic Support Center for students who want help in areas such as accounting, biology, chemistry, economics, history, math, science, religion, and sociology. The Krone Advising Center houses a team of full-time, professional, first-year advisers.

ADMISSIONS INFO FOR STUDENTS WITH LEARNING DIFFERENCES

Phone: 712-274-5030, ext: 5388 • Fax: 712-274-5358 • Email: lopez@morningside.edu

SAT/ACT required: Yes
Interview required: Yes
Essay required: Yes
Additional application required: No
Documentation submitted to: Associate Dean for Academic Affairs

Special Ed. HS course work accepted: Yes
Separate application required for Programs/Services: No
Documentation required for:
LD: Psychoeducational evaluation
ADHD: Psychoeducational evaluation
ASD: Psychoeducational evaluation

Morningside College

General Admissions

Very important factors include: rigor of secondary school record, class rank, academic GPA, standardized test scores, recommendation(s). *Important factors include:* interview, extracurricular activities, talent/ability. *Other factors include:* application essay. High school diploma is required and a GED is accepted. *Academic units recommended:* 3 English, 2 math, 2 science, 3 social studies.

Accommodations or Services

Accommodations are decided upon an individual basis after a thorough review of appropriate, current documentation. The accommodations requests must be supported through the documentation provided and must be logically linked to the current impact of the condition on academic functioning.

Financial Aid

Students should submit: FAFSA. *Need-based scholarships/grants offered:* College/university scholarship or grant aid from institutional funds; Federal Pell; Private scholarships; SEOG; State scholarships/grants. *Loan aid offered:* Federal Work-Study Program available. Institutional employment available.

Campus Life

Activities: Campus Ministries; Choral groups; Concert band; Dance; Drama/theater; International Student Organization; Jazz band; Literary magazine; Marching band; Music ensembles; Musical theater; Pep band; Radio station; Student government; Student newspaper; Television station; Yearbook. **Organizations:** 40 registered organizations, 15 honor societies, 10 religious organizations, 2 fraternities, 1 sorority. **Athletics (Intercollegiate):** *Men:* baseball, basketball, cheerleading, cross-country, football, golf, soccer, swimming, tennis, track/field (outdoor), track/field (indoor), wrestling. *Women:* basketball, cheerleading, cross-country, golf, soccer, softball, swimming, tennis, track/field (outdoor), track/field (indoor), volleyball.

ACCOMMODATIONS

Allowed in exams:	
Calculators	Yes
Dictionary	Yes
Computer	Yes
Spell-checker	Yes
Extended test time	Yes
Scribe	Yes
Proctors	Yes
Oral exams	Yes
Note-takers	Yes
Support services for students with:	
LD	Yes
ADHD	Yes
ASD	Yes
Distraction-reduced environment	Yes
Recording of lecture allowed	Yes
Reading technology	Yes
Audio books	Yes
Other assistive technology	No
Priority registration	No
Added costs of services:	
For LD	No
For ADHD	No
For ASD	No
LD specialists	No
ADHD & ASD coaching	No
ASD specialists	No
Professional tutors	Yes
Peer tutors	Yes
Max. hours/week for services	Unlimited
How professors are notified of student approved accommodations	Associate Dean

COLLEGE GRADUATION REQUIREMENTS

Course waivers allowed	No
Course substitutions allowed	No

Iowa

St. Ambrose University

Admissions and Welcome Center 310 West Locust Street, Davenport, IA 52803-2898 • Admissions: 563-333-6300 • Fax: 563-333-6038 **Support: CS**

CAMPUS

Type of school	Private (nonprofit)
Environment	City

STUDENTS

Undergrad enrollment	2,260
% male/female	45/55
% from out of state	66
% frosh live on campus	95

FINANCIAL FACTS

Annual tuition	$32,478
Room and board	$11,354
Required fees	$280

GENERAL ADMISSIONS INFO

Application fee	$0
Nonfall registration	Yes

Admission may be deferred.

Range SAT EBRW	490–590
Range SAT Math	510–600
Range ACT Composite	20–25

ACADEMICS

Student/faculty ratio	11:1
% students returning for sophomore year	76

Most classes have 20 students.

Programs/Services for Students with Learning Differences

At St. Ambrose University, students are encouraged to register with the Accessibility Resource Center (ARC) to devise a plan for success! ARC staff assist students in selecting courses and provide advice regarding the academic and non-academic course requirements. Students receive support in practicing self-advocacy with faculty and others when identifying and requesting appropriate accommodations. These accommodations include alternative exam arrangements, assistive technology, books in alternative format, assistive listening devices, a disability service provider, course substitution, note-takers, and sign language interpreters. Students are encouraged to meet with ARC staff to discuss additional resources and other reasonable accommodations.

Admissions

Applicants can be admitted with a GPA of 2.5 or above and an ACT of 20 or above or a 1000 or above on the SAT. If applicants can't satisfy both requirements, students may qualify for Conditional Admission. Minimum requirements for Conditional/Provisional status are a 2.0 cumulative GPA and 18 on the ACT or 940 on the SAT. These students will have their academic progress monitored each semester by the SAU Board of Studies, which is composed of SAU faculty. The LD specialist or SDS director acts as academic advisor for students with disabilities during their first year.

Additional Information

A four-week Summer Transition Program is available for college-bound students with learning disabilities, Asperger's, and/or ADHD who have completed their junior year in high school. Students do not have to be admitted to St. Ambrose to participate in this program, and completion of the program does not guarantee admission to St. Ambrose University. Students take either Intro to Psychology or Intro to Sociology, and engage in sessions where they receive instruction on study skills, note-taking, textbook reading, and memorization strategies.

ADMISSIONS INFO FOR STUDENTS WITH LEARNING DIFFERENCES

Phone: 563-333-6275 • Email: SaddlerRyanC@sau.edu

SAT/ACT required: No
Interview required: No
Essay required: Yes
Additional application required: Yes
Documentation submitted to: Accessibility Resource Center

Special Ed. HS course work accepted: Yes
Separate application required for Programs/Services: Yes
Documentation required for:
LD: Psychoeducational evaluation
ADHD: Psychoeducational evaluation
ASD: Psychoeducational evaluation

St. Ambrose University

General Admissions

Very important factors include: rigor of secondary school record, class rank, academic GPA, standardized test scores. *Other factors include:* application essay, recommendation(s), interview, extracurricular activities, talent/ability, character/personal qualities, first generation, alumni/ae relation, racial/ethnic status, volunteer work. High school diploma is required and a GED is accepted. *Academic units recommended:* 4 English, 3 math, 2 science, 2 science labs, 1 foreign language, 1 social studies, 1 history, 4 academic electives. Test scores are required for admission to specific programs and eligibility for top academic scholarships.

Accommodations or Services

Accommodations are decided upon an individual basis after a thorough review of appropriate, current documentation. The accommodations requests must be supported through the documentation provided and must be logically linked to the current impact of the condition on academic functioning.

Financial Aid

Students should submit: FAFSA. *Need-based scholarships/grants offered:* College/university scholarship or grant aid from institutional funds; Federal Pell; Private scholarships; SEOG; State scholarships/grants. *Loan aid offered:* Direct PLUS loans; Direct Subsidized Stafford Loans; Direct Unsubsidized Stafford Loans. Federal Work-Study Program available. Institutional employment available.

Campus Life

Activities: Campus Ministries; Choral groups; Concert band; Dance; Drama/theater; International Student Organization; Jazz band; Literary magazine; Marching band; Model UN; Music ensembles; Musical theater; Pep band; Radio station; Student government; Student newspaper; Television station. **Organizations:** 84 registered organizations, 15 honor societies, 3 religious organizations. **Athletics (Intercollegiate):** *Men:* baseball, basketball, bowling, cheerleading, cross-country, football, golf, soccer, tennis, track/field (outdoor), track/field (indoor), volleyball. *Women:* basketball, bowling, cheerleading, cross-country, golf, soccer, softball, tennis, track/field (outdoor), track/field (indoor), volleyball.

ACCOMMODATIONS

Allowed in exams:	
Calculators	Yes
Dictionary	Yes
Computer	Yes
Spell-checker	Yes
Extended test time	Yes
Scribe	Yes
Proctors	Yes
Oral exams	Yes
Note-takers	Yes
Support services for students with:	
LD	Yes
ADHD	Yes
ASD	Yes
Distraction-reduced environment	Yes
Recording of lecture allowed	Yes
Reading technology	Yes
Audio books	Yes
Other assistive technology	Yes
Priority registration	No
Added costs of services:	
For LD	No
For ADHD	No
For ASD	No
LD specialists	Yes
ADHD & ASD coaching	Yes
ASD specialists	Yes
Professional tutors	No
Peer tutors	Yes
Max. hours/week for services	Varies
How professors are notified of student approved accommodations	Student

COLLEGE GRADUATION REQUIREMENTS

Course waivers allowed	No
Course substitutions allowed	Yes

In what courses: Student will work with institution to determine course substitutions

Iowa

University of Iowa

108 Calvin Hall, Iowa City, IA 52242 • Admissions: 319-335-3847 • Fax: 319-333-1535 **Support: CS**

CAMPUS	
Type of school	Public
Environment	City
STUDENTS	
Undergrad enrollment	23,482
% male/female	46/54
% from out of state	32
% frosh live on campus	94
FINANCIAL FACTS	
Annual in-state tuition	$9,830
Annual out-of-state tuition	$31,793
Room and board	$11590
Required fees	$1,533
GENERAL ADMISSIONS INFO	
Application fee	$40
Regular application deadline	5/1
Nonfall registration	Yes
Admission may be deferred.	
Range SAT EBRW	560–660
Range SAT Math	570–680
Range ACT Composite	22–29
ACADEMICS	
Student/faculty ratio	15:1
% students returning for sophomore year	86
Most classes have 10–19 students.	

Programs/Services for Students with Learning Differences

University of Iowa's Student Disability Services (SDS) facilitates individualized academic accommodations for eligible students. Each student has an assigned staff adviser who assists the student in identifying appropriate course accommodations, communicating classroom needs to faculty, accessing other related services and resources. Students with LD/ADHD who need disability services are encouraged to register with SDS as soon as possible. Students are encouraged to schedule an on-campus interview with the LD/ADHD coordinator to learn more about disability services for students with LD-ADHD and about the university.

Admissions

Students are admitted directly if they meet the Regent Admission Index (RAI) score. There are two mathematical formulas for computing student's RAI scores, the primary RAI formula (for students whose high school class rank) and the Alternative RAI formula (for students whose high school does not provide class rank. Students with LD who feel their academic record does not reflect their ability to succeed may request to be considered on an individual basis. These students should submit a letter requesting special consideration and provide a description of how the disability impacts academic performance, services used in high school, and documentation of the disability.

Additional Information

The University of Iowa also offers the REACH Program. This is a transition certificate program for college students with disabilities, such as autism, intellectual disabilities, and learning disabilities. UI REACH provides a Big Ten college experience and empowers young adults to become independent members of the community. Coursework, campus life, and career experiences prepare students to reach their full potential. Students requesting disability-related services from Student Disability Services are required to provide satisfactory evidence of their eligibility for services. Services are determined on a case-by-case basis. They include priority registration for courses, assistance in communicating with faculty and administrators, facilitation of classroom accommodations. Students have access to assistive services including Jaws and FM systems.

ADMISSIONS INFO FOR STUDENTS WITH LEARNING DIFFERENCES

Phone: 319-335-1462 • Fax: 319-335-3973 • Email: sds-info@uiowa.edu

SAT/ACT required: Yes (Test optional for 2021)
Interview required: No
Essay required: No
Additional application required: No
Documentation submitted to: Student Disabilities Services

Special Ed. HS course work accepted: No
Separate application required for Programs/Services: No
Documentation required for:
LD: Psychoeducational evaluation
ADHD: Psychoeducational evaluation
ASD: Psychoeducational evaluation

University of Iowa

General Admissions

Very important factors include: rigor of secondary school record, class rank, academic GPA, standardized test scores. *Other factors include:* recommendation(s), talent/ability, character/personal qualities, state residency. High school diploma is required and a GED is accepted. *Academic units required:* 4 English, 3 math, 3 science, 2 foreign language, 3 social studies. *Academic units recommended:* 4 math. Students entering in Fall 2021 may be admitted without a test score.

Accommodations or Services

Accommodations are decided upon an individual basis after a thorough review of appropriate, current documentation. The accommodations requests must be supported through the documentation provided and must be logically linked to the current impact of the condition on academic functioning.

Financial Aid

Students should submit: FAFSA. *Need-based scholarships/grants offered:* College/university scholarship or grant aid from institutional funds; Federal Pell; Private scholarships; SEOG; State scholarships/grants. *Loan aid offered:* Direct PLUS loans; Direct Subsidized Stafford Loans; Direct Unsubsidized Stafford Loans. Federal Work-Study Program available. Institutional employment available.

Campus Life

Activities: Campus Ministries; Choral groups; Concert band; Dance; Drama/theater; International Student Organization; Jazz band; Literary magazine; Marching band; Model UN; Music ensembles; Musical theater; Opera; Pep band; Radio station; Student government; Student newspaper; Student-run film society; Symphony orchestra; Television station. **Organizations:** 500 registered organizations, 18 honor societies, 21 religious organizations, 27 fraternities, 23 sororities. **Athletics (Intercollegiate):** *Men:* baseball, basketball, cheerleading, cross-country, diving, football, golf, gymnastics, swimming, tennis, track/field (outdoor), track/field (indoor), wrestling. *Women:* basketball, cheerleading, crew/rowing, cross-country, diving, field hockey, golf, gymnastics, soccer, softball, swimming, tennis, track/field (outdoor), track/field (indoor), volleyball.

ACCOMMODATIONS

Allowed in exams:	
Calculators	Yes
Dictionary	No
Computer	Yes
Spell-checker	Yes
Extended test time	Yes
Scribe	Yes
Proctors	Yes
Oral exams	No
Note-takers	Yes
Support services for students with:	
LD	Yes
ADHD	Yes
ASD	Yes
Distraction-reduced environment	Yes
Recording of lecture allowed	Yes
Reading technology	Yes
Audio books	Yes
Other assistive technology	Yes
Priority registration	Yes
Added costs of services:	
For LD	No
For ADHD	No
For ASD	No
LD specialists	No
ADHD & ASD coaching	No
ASD specialists	No
Professional tutors	No
Peer tutors	Yes
Max. hours/week for services	Varies
How professors are notified of student approved accommodations	Student

COLLEGE GRADUATION REQUIREMENTS

Course waivers allowed	No
Course substitutions allowed	Yes

In what courses: Student will work with institutions to determine course substitutions

Iowa

University of Northern Iowa

1227 West 27th Street, Cedar Falls, IA 50614-0018 • Admissions: 319-273-2281• Fax: 319-273-2885 **Support: S**

CAMPUS

Type of school	Public
Environment	Town

STUDENTS

Undergrad enrollment	8,973
% male/female	41/59
% from out of state	6
% frosh live on campus	92

FINANCIAL FACTS

Annual in-state tuition	$8,938
Annual out-of-state tuition	$19,480
Room and board	$9,160
Required fees	$1,273

GENERAL ADMISSIONS INFO

Application fee	$40
Regular application deadline	8/15
Nonfall registration	Yes

Admission may be deferred.

Range ACT Composite	20–25

ACADEMICS

Student/faculty ratio	17:1
% students returning for sophomore year	83

Most classes have 20–29 students.

Programs/Services for Students with Learning Differences

Student Accessibility Services (SAS) views disabilities as an integral part of the rich diversity at the University of Northern Iowa. The SAS office works collaboratively with students, faculty, and staff to create an accessible educational environment for students. A majority of the students connected with SAS have invisible disabilities, like anxiety, depression, learning disabilities, etc. Whether a student has previously utilized accommodations or received a new diagnosis and needs to request accommodations for the first time, SAS is available to support students at any point in their college careers.

Admissions

Admission is based on the Regent Admission Index (RAI). Applicants who achieve at least a 245 RAI score and who meet the minimum high school course requirements are guaranteed admission. Applicants who achieve less than a 245 RAI score but meet the minimum high school course requirements will be considered for admission on an individual basis. Applicants must also meet the minimum course requirements including 4 years English, 3 years math (including equivalents of algebra, geometry, and algebra II), 3 years science, 3 years social studies, and 2 years of electives. Students with disabilities follow the same admissions process as students without disabilities.

Additional Information

Accommodations for students are determined by Student Accessibility Services (SAS) staff on a case-by-case basis after reviewing both the student self-report and supporting documentation. Once SDS has received both pieces of information, the student will be invited to have a one-on-one meeting with one of the professional staff in order to finalize eligibility for services. In addition to the academic accommodations, SAS also offers an academic coaching program to students registered for academic accommodations. This program helps students with time management, prioritization, goal setting, and other academic success strategies.

ADMISSIONS INFO FOR STUDENTS WITH LEARNING DIFFERENCES

Phone: 319-273-2677 • Fax: 319-273-7576 • Email: accessibilityservices@uni.edu

SAT/ACT required: Yes (Test optional for 2021)
Interview required: No
Essay required: No
Additional application required: Yes
Documentation submitted to: Student Accessibility Services

Special Ed. HS course work accepted: No
Separate application required for Programs/Services: Yes
Documentation required for:
LD: Psychoeducational evaluation
ADHD: Psychoeducational evaluation
ASD: Psychoeducational evaluation

University of Northern Iowa

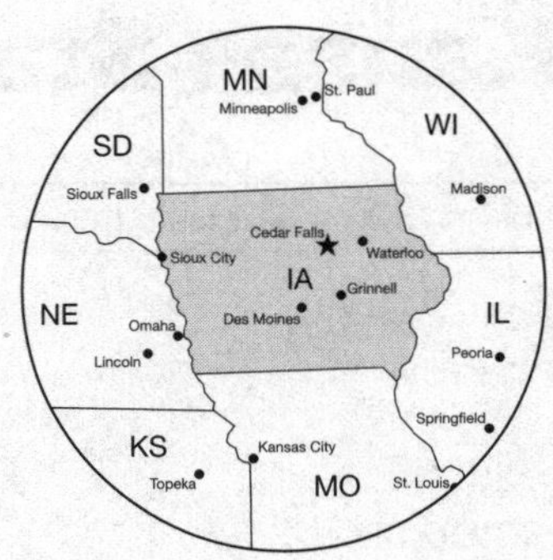

General Admissions

Very important factors include: rigor of secondary school record, class rank, academic GPA, standardized test scores. *Other factors include:* recommendation(s), interview, talent/ability, first generation. High school diploma is required and a GED is accepted. *Academic units required:* 4 English, 3 math, 3 science, 3 social studies, 2 academic electives. *Academic units recommended:* 1 science lab, 2 foreign language. The Iowa Board of Regents has issued a temporary, one-year waiver to the ACT/SAT testing requirement due to the ongoing pandemic concerns for Fall 2021.

Accommodations or Services

Accommodations are decided upon an individual basis after a thorough review of appropriate, current documentation. The accommodations requests must be supported through the documentation provided and must be logically linked to the current impact of the condition on academic functioning.

Financial Aid

Students should submit: FAFSA. Applicants will be notified of awards on a rolling basis beginning 2/15. *Need-based scholarships/grants offered:* College/university scholarship or grant aid from institutional funds; Federal Pell; Private scholarships; SEOG; State scholarships/grants. *Loan aid offered:* Direct PLUS loans; Direct Subsidized Stafford Loans; Direct Unsubsidized Stafford Loans. Federal Work-Study Program available. Institutional employment available.

Campus Life

Activities: Campus Ministries; Choral groups; Concert band; Dance; Drama/theater; International Student Organization; Jazz band; Literary magazine; Marching band; Model UN; Music ensembles; Musical theater; Opera; Pep band; Radio station; Student government; Student newspaper; Symphony orchestra; Yearbook. **Organizations:** 260 registered organizations, 17 honor societies, 17 religious organizations, 4 fraternities, 5 sororities. **Athletics (Intercollegiate):** *Men:* basketball, cross-country, football, golf, track/field (outdoor), track/field (indoor), wrestling. *Women:* basketball, cross-country, diving, golf, soccer, softball, swimming, tennis, track/field (outdoor), track/field (indoor), volleyball.

ACCOMMODATIONS

Allowed in exams:	
Calculators	Yes
Dictionary	No
Computer	Yes
Spell-checker	Yes
Extended test time	Yes
Scribe	Yes
Proctors	Yes
Oral exams	Yes
Note-takers	Yes
Support services for students with:	
LD	Yes
ADHD	Yes
ASD	Yes
Distraction-reduced environment	Yes
Recording of lecture allowed	Yes
Reading technology	Yes
Audio books	Yes
Other assistive technology	Yes
Priority registration	Yes
Added costs of services:	
For LD	No
For ADHD	No
For ASD	No
LD specialists	No
ADHD & ASD coaching	Yes
ASD specialists	No
Professional tutors	No
Peer tutors	Yes
Max. hours/week for services	Varies
How professors are notified of student approved accommodations	Student

COLLEGE GRADUATION REQUIREMENTS

Course waivers allowed	No
Course substitutions allowed	Yes

In what courses: Student will work with institution to determine course substitutions

Iowa

Kansas State University

119 Anderson Hall, Manhattan, KS 66506 • Admissions: 785-532-6250 • Fax: 785-532-6393 **Support: CS**

CAMPUS

Type of school	Public
Environment	Town

STUDENTS

Undergrad enrollment	17,210
% male/female	52/48
% from out of state	21
% frosh live on campus	75

FINANCIAL FACTS

Annual In-State Tuition	$9,375
Annual Out-of-State Tuition	$25,251
Room and board	$13,540
Required fees	$1,065

GENERAL ADMISSIONS INFO

Application fee	$40
Nonfall registration	Yes
Range ACT Composite	22–28

ACADEMICS

Student/faculty ratio	18:1
% students returning for sophomore year	86

Most classes have 10–19 students.

Programs/Services for Students with Learning Differences

KSU is committed to providing equal access and opportunity to all campus programs and services for students with disabilities. Students who are requesting services and accommodations are asked to submit documentation in order to establish the presence of a disability and support the reasonableness of requested accommodations. Documentation must clearly demonstrate the current, functional limitations in the learning or living environment. Scholarships are available to students who meet the requirements.

Admissions

To be considered for qualified admissions you must complete a pre-college curriculum with at least a 2.0 GPA (2.5 for non-residents) AND achieve one of the following: 21 or higher composite score on the ACT assessment OR 980 or higher on the SAT I, CR + M, OR rank in the top third of your graduating class AND, if applicable, achieve a 2.0 GPA or higher on all college credit taken in high school. Students who don't meet these requirements should apply early for full consideration. Additional information may be requested.

Additional Information

The Academic Assistance Center provides a variety of academic support services, including learning skills instruction, computer-assisted mathematics practice, academic counseling, credit by examination, entrance and professional examinations, and tutoring in a variety of K-State courses. Students experiencing academic difficulties are aided directly by a member of the Academic Assistance Center staff. Students have access to assistive services including, Writing Pens, ZoomText, Read and Write Software, and Dictation Software. There is also the opportunity to join the Delta Alpha Pi Honorary Society for Students with Disabilities, as well as to participate in a Workforce Recruitment campaign.

ADMISSIONS INFO FOR STUDENTS WITH LEARNING DIFFERENCES

Phone: 785-532-6441• Fax: 785-532-6457 • Email: accesscenter@ksu.edu

SAT/ACT required: No (Not required with a 3.3 GPA)
Interview required: No
Essay required: Yes
Additional application required: Yes
Documentation submitted to: Academic Assistance Center

Special Ed. HS course work accepted: Yes
Separate application required for Programs/Services: Yes
Documentation required for:
LD: Psychoeducational evaluation
ADHD: Psychoeducational evaluation
ASD: Psychoeducational evaluation

Kansas State University

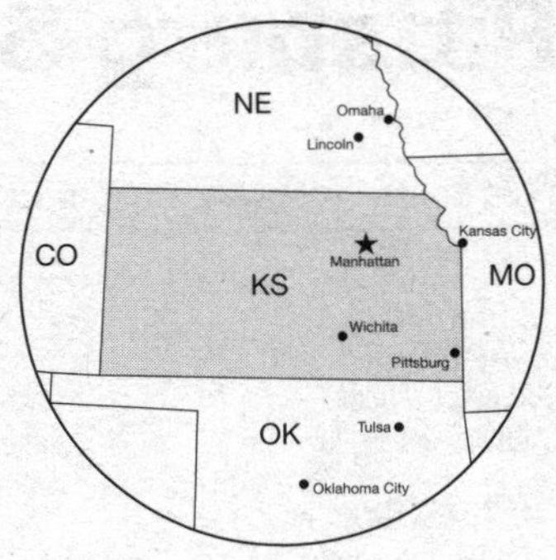

General Admissions

Very important factors include: rigor of secondary school record, class rank, academic GPA, standardized test scores. *Important factors include:* level of applicant's interest. *Other factors include:* recommendation(s). High school diploma is required and a GED is accepted. *Academic units required:* 4 English, 3 math, 3 science, 3 social studies, 3 academic electives. Institution is test optional depending on GPA.

Accommodations or Services

Accommodations are decided upon an individual basis after a thorough review of appropriate, current documentation. The accommodations requests must be supported through the documentation provided and must be logically linked to the current impact of the condition on academic functioning.

Financial Aid

Students should submit: FAFSA. Applicants will be notified of awards on a rolling basis beginning 1/1. *Need-based scholarships/grants offered:* College/university scholarship or grant aid from institutional funds; Federal Pell; Private scholarships; SEOG; State scholarships/grants. *Loan aid offered:* Direct PLUS loans; Direct Subsidized Stafford Loans; Direct Unsubsidized Stafford Loans. Federal Work-Study Program available. Institutional employment available.

Campus Life

Activities: Campus Ministries; Choral groups; Concert band; Dance; Drama/theater; International Student Organization; Jazz band; Marching band; Music ensembles; Musical theater; Pep band; Radio station; Student government; Student newspaper; Symphony orchestra; Television station; Yearbook. **Organizations:** 594 registered organizations, 36 honor societies, 37 religious organizations, 28 fraternities, 16 sororities. **Athletics (Intercollegiate):** *Men:* baseball, basketball, cheerleading, cross-country, football, golf, track/field (outdoor), track/field (indoor). *Women:* basketball, cheerleading, crew/rowing, cross-country, equestrian sports, golf, tennis, track/field (outdoor), track/field (indoor), volleyball.

ACCOMMODATIONS

Allowed in exams:	
Calculators	Yes
Dictionary	Yes
Computer	Yes
Spell-checker	Yes
Extended test time	Yes
Scribe	Yes
Proctors	Yes
Oral exams	Yes
Note-takers	Yes
Support services for students with:	
LD	Yes
ADHD	Yes
ASD	Yes
Distraction-reduced environment	Yes
Recording of lecture allowed	Yes
Reading technology	Yes
Audio books	Yes
Other assistive technology	Yes
Priority registration	Yes
Added costs of services:	
For LD	No
For ADHD	No
For ASD	No
LD specialists	No
ADHD & ASD coaching	Yes
ASD specialists	No
Professional tutors	No
Peer tutors	No
Max. hours/week for services	Varies
How professors are notified of student approved accommodations	Student and Disability Office

COLLEGE GRADUATION REQUIREMENTS

Course waivers allowed	Yes
In what courses: math, foreign language	
Course substitutions allowed	Yes
In what courses: math, foreign language	

Pittsburg State University

1701 South Broadway, Pittsburg, KS 66762 • Admissions: 620-235-4251 • Fax: 620-235-6003 **Support: CS**

CAMPUS

Type of school	Public
Environment	Village

STUDENTS

Undergrad enrollment	5,181
% male/female	50/50
% from out of state	34

FINANCIAL FACTS

Annual in-state tuition	$7,338
Annual out-of-state tuition	$18,682
Room and board	$7,996
Required fees	$1,644

GENERAL ADMISSIONS INFO

Application fee	$30
Regular application deadline	Rolling
Nonfall registration	Yes

Admission may be deferred.

Range SAT EBRW	480–600
Range SAT Math	440–590
Range ACT Composite	19–24

ACADEMICS

Student/faculty ratio	17:1
% students returning for sophomore year	75

Most classes have 10–19 students.

Programs/Services for Students with Learning Differences

The Center for Student Accommodations provides reasonable accommodations to currently enrolled Pittsburg State University students with a diagnosed disability. Once students are admitted and enrolled, they must contact the Center for Student Accommodations to schedule an appointment, complete the application, and submit documentation from a licensed healthcare professional, psychologist, or psychiatrist of their diagnosis. Students are required to contact the Student Accommodations office at the beginning of each semester to make arrangements for accommodations.

Admissions

Pittsburg State University uses a "Qualified Admissions" formula for admissions. Kansas and out-of-state freshmen under the age of 21 may be granted automatic admissions with a 2.0 (2.5 for non-residents) or higher grade point average (GPA) on a 4.0 Scale. They must also have an ACT composite score of 21 or higher (SAT of 1060 or higher), OR rank in the top one-third of graduating class. Course requirements include: 4 years English, 4 years math, 3 years science, 3 years social studies, and 3 years electives. Students admitted to PSU generally have an ACT composite score of 21 or higher (SAT of 1060 or higher) If applicable, students should achieve at least a 2.0 GPA on a 4.0 scale on all transferable college credits.

Additional Information

The Center for Student Accommodation provides services determined on an individual basis. They match the student with the appropriate service. The Center for Student Accommodations can also provide study skill strategies and direct students to other appropriate university support services. Students have access to assistive technology including, Communication Access Real-time Translation (CART) and Read and Write.

ADMISSIONS INFO FOR STUDENTS WITH LEARNING DIFFERENCES

Phone: 620-235-6578 • Fax: 620-235-4190 • Email: csa@pittstate.edu

SAT/ACT required: No (depending on GPA)
Interview required: No
Essay required: Yes
Additional application required: Yes
Documentation submitted to: Center for Student Accommodation

Special Ed. HS course work accepted: Yes
Separate application required for Programs/Services: Yes
Documentation required for:
LD: Psychoeducational evaluation
ADHD: Psychoeducational evaluation
ASD: Psychoeducational evaluation

Pittsburg State University

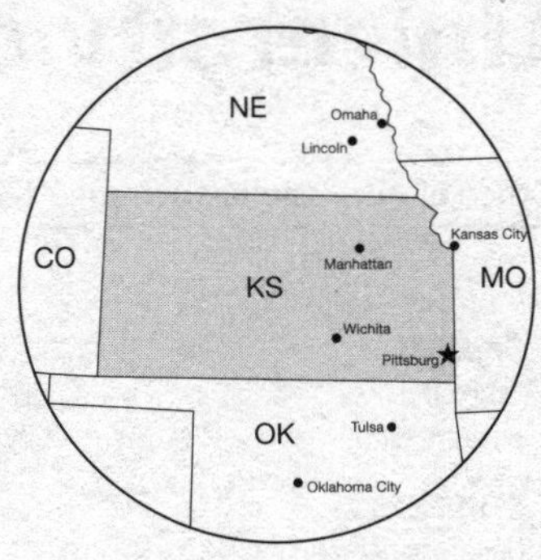

General Admissions

Very important factors include: rigor of secondary school record, class rank, academic GPA, standardized test scores. High school diploma is required and a GED is accepted. *Academic units required:* 4 English, 4 math, 3 science, 3 social studies, 3 academic electives. Qualified Admissions criteria for those pursuing postsecondary admission at a Kansas public university summer 2021 or later: ACT score of 21+ or a cumulative 2.25+ GPA.

Accommodations or Services

Accommodations are decided upon an individual basis after a thorough review of appropriate, current documentation. The accommodations requests must be supported through the documentation provided and must be logically linked to the current impact of the condition on academic functioning.

Financial Aid

Students should submit: FAFSA. *Need-based scholarships/grants offered:* College/university scholarship or grant aid from institutional funds; Federal Nursing Scholarships; Federal Pell; Private scholarships; SEOG; State scholarships/grants. *Loan aid offered:* Direct PLUS loans; Direct Subsidized Stafford Loans; Direct Unsubsidized Stafford Loans. Federal Work-Study Program available. Institutional employment available.

Campus Life

Activities: Campus Ministries; Choral groups; Dance; Drama/theater; International Student Organization; Literary magazine; Marching band; Music ensembles; Musical theater; Opera; Radio station; Student government; Student newspaper; Symphony orchestra; Television station; Yearbook. **Organizations:** 150 registered organizations, 19 honor societies, 5 religious organizations, 7 fraternities, 3 sororities. **Athletics (Intercollegiate):** *Men:* baseball, basketball, cheerleading, cross-country, football, golf, track/field (outdoor), track/field (indoor). *Women:* basketball, cheerleading, cross-country, softball, track/field (outdoor), track/field (indoor), volleyball.

ACCOMMODATIONS

Allowed in exams:	
Calculators	Yes
Dictionary	Yes
Computer	Yes
Spell-checker	Yes
Extended test time	Yes
Scribe	Yes
Proctors	Yes
Oral exams	Yes
Note-takers	Yes
Support services for students with:	
LD	Yes
ADHD	Yes
ASD	Yes
Distraction-reduced environment	Yes
Recording of lecture allowed	Yes
Reading technology	Yes
Audio books	Yes
Other assistive technology	Yes
Priority registration	No
Added costs of services:	
For LD	No
For ADHD	No
For ASD	No
LD specialists	No
ADHD & ASD coaching	Yes
ASD specialists	No
Professional tutors	No
Peer tutors	Yes
Max. hours/week for services	Varies
How professors are notified of student approved accommodations	Director

COLLEGE GRADUATION REQUIREMENTS

Course waivers allowed	No
Course substitutions allowed	No

University of Kansas

Office of Admissions, Lawrence, KS 66045-7576 • Admissions: 785-864-3911 • Fax: 785-864-5017 **Support: S**

CAMPUS

Type of school	Public
Environment	City

STUDENTS

Undergrad enrollment	19,667
% male/female	48/52
% from out of state	29
% frosh live on campus	68

FINANCIAL FACTS

Annual in-state tuition	$10,092
Annual out-of-state tuition	$26,960
Room and board	$10,350
Required fees	$1,074

GENERAL ADMISSIONS INFO

Application fee	$40
Regular application deadline	8/19
Nonfall registration	Yes

Admission may be deferred.

Range SAT EBRW	560–660
Range SAT Math	540–670
Range ACT Composite	22–29

ACADEMICS

Student/faculty ratio	17:1
% students returning for sophomore year	86

Most classes have 10–19 students.

Programs/Services for Students with Learning Differences

The Academic Achievement and Access Center (AAAC) facilitates appropriate academic accommodations and auxiliary aids and services that are necessary to afford an individual with a disability an equal opportunity to participate in the University's programs and activities. Specifically, students must provide written documentation from a qualified professional on the nature and impact of the disability. The student and the AAAC will then engage in an interactive process to determine what, if any, accommodations are appropriate based on the student's disability and individual needs. The AAAC assists students with disabilities by facilitating accommodations that remove barriers to their academic success. They authorize reasonable and appropriate accommodations for qualified students with documented disabilities, assist students in self-advocacy, educate the University of Kansas about disabilities, and ensure compliance with federal and state law.

Admissions

All applications are welcomed; all students interested in the University of Kansas complete an application, which will be reviewed individually by KU's admissions staff. The review covers these factors: cumulative high school GPA, ACT or SAT scores, GPA in the core curriculum, and strength of courses. Freshmen are assured admission into KU's College of Liberal Arts & Sciences, School of Journalism, or School of Social Welfare if they meet one of these combinations: an ACT score of at least 21 or an SAT score of at least 1060 plus a GPA of at least 3.25; an ACT score of at least 24 or an SAT score of at least 1160 plus a GPA of at least 3.0; or 3.4 GPA on a 4.0 scale, no test scores required. Applicants not able to take the ACT or SAT due to test cancellations are encouraged to apply to KU for a holistic review. Applicants can update their KU application after they have taken the ACT or SAT. Test scores are required for some majors, the University Honors Program, and scholarships.

Additional Information

Skill workshops are available in study skills, time management, stress management, and preparing for exams. Disability Resources also serves as an advocate or liaison for students. Tutoring services for students who meet qualifications are available through Supportive Educational Services at no cost. Tutoring Services offered through the Academic Achievement and Access Center are also available in most challenging entry level courses for a fee. Services and accommodations are available for undergraduate and graduate students. KU is a Read and Write Campus. All students have access to Read and Write software.

ADMISSIONS INFO FOR STUDENTS WITH LEARNING DIFFERENCES

Phone: 785-864-4064 • Fax: 785-864-2817 • Email: achieve@ku.edu/ access@ku.edu

SAT/ACT required: Yes
Interview required: Yes
Essay required: Yes
Additional application required: No
Documentation submitted to: Academic Achievement and Access Center
Special Ed. HS course work accepted: Yes
Separate application required for Programs/Services: No
Documentation required for:
LD: Psychoeducational evaluation
ADHD: Psychoeducational evaluation
ASD: Psychoeducational evaluation

University of Kansas

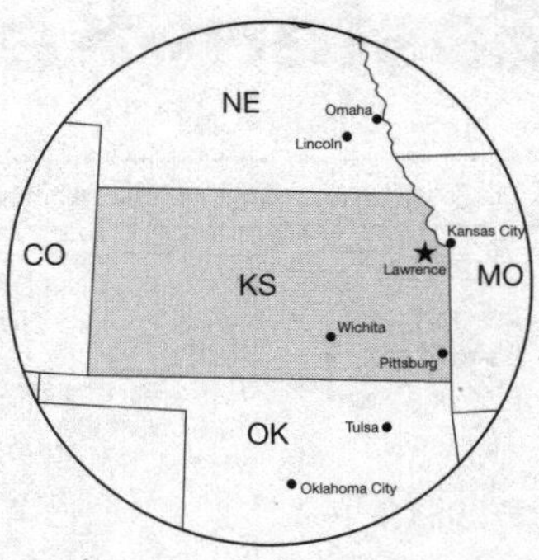

General Admissions

Very important factors include: academic GPA, standardized test scores. *Other factors include:* rigor of secondary school record, class rank, application essay, extracurricular activities, talent/ability, character/personal qualities, first generation, alumni/ae relation, geographical residence, state residency, racial/ethnic status, volunteer work, work experience, level of applicant's interest. High school diploma is required and a GED is accepted. *Academic units required:* 4 English, 3 math, 3 science, 1 science lab, 3 social studies, 3 academic electives. *Academic units recommended:* 4 English, 4 math, 3 science, 3 social studies, 3 academic electives. Test scores are required for admission to some majors, the University Honors Program, and scholarship consideration.

Accommodations or Services

Accommodations are decided upon an individual basis after a thorough review of appropriate, current documentation. The accommodations requests must be supported through the documentation provided and must be logically linked to the current impact of the condition on academic functioning.

Financial Aid

Students should submit: FAFSA. *Need-based scholarships/grants offered:* College/university scholarship or grant aid from institutional funds; Federal Pell; Private scholarships; SEOG; State scholarships/grants. *Loan aid offered:* Direct PLUS loans; Direct Subsidized Stafford Loans; Direct Unsubsidized Stafford Loans. Federal Work-Study Program available. Institutional employment available.

Campus Life

Activities: Choral groups; Concert band; Dance; Drama/theater; International Student Organization; Jazz band; Literary magazine; Marching band; Model UN; Music ensembles; Musical theater; Opera; Pep band; Radio station; Student government; Student newspaper; Symphony orchestra; Television station. **Organizations:** 582 registered organizations, 28 honor societies, 39 religious organizations, 26 fraternities, 17 sororities. **Athletics (Intercollegiate):** *Men:* baseball, basketball, cross-country, football, golf, track/field (outdoor), track/field (indoor). *Women:* basketball, crew/rowing, cross-country, diving, golf, soccer, softball, swimming, tennis, track/field (outdoor), track/field (indoor), volleyball.

ACCOMMODATIONS

Allowed in exams:	
Calculators	Yes
Dictionary	Yes
Computer	Yes
Spell-checker	Yes
Extended test time	Yes
Scribe	Yes
Proctors	Yes
Oral exams	Yes
Note-takers	Yes
Support services for students with:	
LD	Yes
ADHD	Yes
ASD	Yes
Distraction-reduced environment	Yes
Recording of lecture allowed	Yes
Reading technology	Yes
Audio books	Yes
Other assistive technology	Yes
Priority registration	Yes
Added costs of services:	
For LD	No
For ADHD	No
For ASD	No
LD specialists	Yes
ADHD & ASD coaching	No
ASD specialists	No
Professional tutors	Yes
Peer tutors	Yes
Max. hours/week for services	Varies
How professors are notified of student approved accommodations	Student

COLLEGE GRADUATION REQUIREMENTS

Course waivers allowed	No
Course substitutions allowed	Yes

In what courses: Student will work with institution to determine course substitutions

Eastern Kentucky University

521 Lancaster Ave. Charles Douglas Whitlock Bldg SSB CPO 54, Richmond, KY 40475 • Admissions: 859-622-2106 • Fax: 859-622-8024 **Support: CS**

CAMPUS

Type of school	Public
Environment	Town

STUDENTS

Undergrad enrollment	12,662
% male/female	43/57
% from out of state	15
% frosh live on campus	76

FINANCIAL FACTS

Annual in-state tuition	$9,266
Annual out-of-state tuition	$19,338
Room and board	$10,173
Required fees	$540

GENERAL ADMISSIONS INFO

Application fee	$35
Regular application deadline	8/1
Nonfall registration	Yes

Admission may be deferred.

Range SAT EBRW	490–590
Range SAT Math	500–580
Range ACT Composite	20–26

ACADEMICS

Student/faculty ratio	15:1
% students returning for sophomore year	75

Most classes have 10–19 students.

Programs/Services for Students with Learning Differences

The Center for Student Accessibility is home to Project Success. Project SUCCESS responds effectively and efficiently to the individual educational needs of eligible university students with learning disabilities through a cost-effective, flexible program of peer tutors, academic coaching, focus groups, and assistive technology. Upon admittance, Project SUCCESS develops an individualized program of services that serves to enhance the academic success of each student. The services a student utilizes will be determined in a conference between the student and the program director. At the core of the program is Academic Coaching and individualized tutoring services.

Admissions

Students who meet the following criteria will be granted full admission to the University: have graduated from an accredited high school earning a minimum cumulative high school grade point average of 2.5 on a 4.0 scale; OR have submitted a minimum ACT composite score of 20 or SAT combined verbal/critical reading score of 950 or higher AND meet the Kentucky Pre-College Curriculum and have submitted an official six-semester high school transcript, or a General Equivalency Diploma (GED), or documentation indicating completion of an EKU approved home-school or distance learning high school program.

Additional Information

Project SUCCESS services provided include academic coaching, one-on one tutoring, note-taking services, e-texts, test accommodations, advocacy, weekly seminars. Skills classes are offered in study skills, reading skills, weekly workshops in transition, time management, learning and study strategies, test-taking skills, developmental math, developmental reading, and developmental writing. "Planning to Win" is a summer transition program specifically designed for high school junior and graduating seniors with learning disabilities, attention deficit disorder and other cognitive disorders. The program is geared towards high school students who are planning to attend college in the fall as well as those who are only exploring post-secondary educational options at any college. Students attend three days of educational and inspiring workshops, fellowship with current college students, and spend two nights in an EKU residence hall. The Planning to Win Program is focused on students; however, parents and interested educators are also welcome.

ADMISSIONS INFO FOR STUDENTS WITH LEARNING DIFFERENCES

Phone: 859-622-2933 • Fax: 859-622-6794 • Email: accessibility@eku.edu

SAT/ACT required: No
Interview required: Yes
Essay required: Yes
Additional application required: No
Documentation submitted to: Center for Student Accessibility

Special Ed. HS course work accepted: Yes
Separate application required for Programs/Services: No
Documentation required for:
LD: Psychoeducational evaluation
ADHD: Psychoeducational evaluation
ASD: Psychoeducational evaluation

Eastern Kentucky University

Kentucky

General Admissions

Very important factors include: rigor of secondary school record, academic GPA, standardized test scores. High school diploma is required and a GED is accepted. *Academic units required:* 4 English, 3 math, 3 science, 1 science lab, 2 foreign language, 3 social studies, 7 academic electives, 2 units from above areas or other academic areas.

Accommodations or Services

Accommodations are decided upon an individual basis after a thorough review of appropriate, current documentation. The accommodations requests must be supported through the documentation provided and must be logically linked to the current impact of the condition on academic functioning.

Financial Aid

Students should submit: FAFSA. *Need-based scholarships/grants offered:* College/university scholarship or grant aid from institutional funds; Federal Pell; Private scholarships; SEOG; State scholarships/grants. *Loan aid offered:* Direct PLUS loans; Direct Subsidized Stafford Loans; Direct Unsubsidized Stafford Loans. Federal Work-Study Program available. Institutional employment available.

Campus Life

Activities: Campus Ministries; Choral groups; Concert band; Dance; Drama/theater; International Student Organization; Jazz band; Literary magazine; Marching band; Music ensembles; Musical theater; Pep band; Radio station; Student government; Student newspaper; Student-run film society; Symphony orchestra; Yearbook. **Organizations:** 178 registered organizations, 30 honor societies, 11 religious organizations, 16 fraternities, 13 sororities. **Athletics (Intercollegiate):** *Men:* baseball, basketball, cheerleading, cross-country, football, golf, tennis, track/field (outdoor), track/field (indoor). *Women:* basketball, cheerleading, cross-country, golf, soccer, softball, tennis, track/field (outdoor), track/field (indoor), volleyball.

ACCOMMODATIONS

Allowed in exams:	
Calculators	Yes
Dictionary	Yes
Computer	Yes
Spell-checker	Yes
Extended test time	Yes
Scribe	Yes
Proctors	Yes
Oral exams	Yes
Note-takers	Yes
Support services for students with:	
LD	Yes
ADHD	Yes
ASD	Yes
Distraction-reduced environment	Yes
Recording of lecture allowed	Yes
Reading technology	Yes
Audio books	Yes
Other assistive technology	Yes
Priority registration	Yes
Added costs of services:	
For LD	No
For ADHD	No
For ASD	No
LD specialists	Yes
ADHD & ASD coaching	No
ASD specialists	No
Professional tutors	No
Peer tutors	Yes
Max. hours/week for services	6
How professors are notified of student approved accommodations	Student

COLLEGE GRADUATION REQUIREMENTS

Course waivers allowed	Yes
In what courses: Case-by-case basis	
Course substitutions allowed	Yes
In what courses: Case-by-case basis	

Murray State University

102 Curris Center, Murray, KY 42071-0009 • Admissions: 270-809-3741 • Fax: 270-809-3780 **Support: SP**

CAMPUS

Type of school	Public
Environment	Village

STUDENTS

Undergrad enrollment	8,215
% male/female	39/61
% from out of state	29
% frosh live on campus	77

FINANCIAL FACTS

Annual in-state tuition	$9,168
Annual out-of-state tuition	$13,920
Room and board	$9,284

GENERAL ADMISSIONS INFO

Application fee	$40
Regular application deadline	8/18
Nonfall registration	Yes

Admission may be deferred.

Range SAT EBRW	550–650
Range SAT Math	530–650
Range ACT Composite	21–28

ACADEMICS

Student/faculty ratio	15:1
% students returning for sophomore year	76

Most classes have 10–19 students.

Programs/Services for Students with Learning Differences

The Office of Student Disability Services provides accommodations and services to students with documented disabilities. These disabilities can include, but are not limited to: cognitive disabilities (i.e., learning disabilities, attention deficit disorders, and traumatic brain injury), psychological impairments, seizure disorders, autism, sensory disorders, mobility impairments, and other physical or health impairments. Through an interactive process between the student and SDS staff, student's eligibility for accommodations will be determined following a review of their reasonable documentation. SDS staff will work to ensure appropriate accommodations are in place in order for the student to have equal access to the University's resources and academic programs. Additionally, OSD serves to educate the University community about the kinds of practices and processes that will allow students, parents, and community members to feel welcomed and included with the campus of Murray State University.

Admissions

Students with learning disabilities must meet the same admissions requirements as all other students at the institution. However, an admissions appeal process is available for students not meeting minimum admissions requirements. Applicants are admitted with a GPA of 3.0 or higher and no ACT/SAT test score is required for admission decision. Applicants can also be admitted with a GPA of 2.0–2.99 with an ACT composite score of 18 or higher (SAT 960 or higher). There may be additional options for students who do not meet the general admission standards.

Additional Information

The Office of Student Disability Services offers a more comprehensive level of academic support for up to 50 incoming freshmen each fall semester. This program, called Project PASS (Program for Achieving Student Success), includes the following areas of support: scheduling assistance during summer orientation, an early move-in program, specialized support classes, and Project Mentor (individualized assistance with learning effective strategies for organizing and studying course material). There are no fees for Project PASS, except for the early move-in program and Project Mentor.

ADMISSIONS INFO FOR STUDENTS WITH LEARNING DIFFERENCES

Phone: 270-809-2018 • Fax: 270-809-4339 • Email: vwilson@murraystate.edu / msu.studentdisabilities@murraystate.edu

SAT/ACT required: No (depending on GPA)
Interview required: No
Essay required: Yes
Additional application required: Yes
Documentation submitted to: Office of Student Disability Services

Special Ed. HS course work accepted: Yes
Separate application required for Programs/Services: Yes
Documentation required for:
LD: Psychoeducational evaluation
ADHD: Psychoeducational evaluation
ASD: Psychoeducational evaluation

Murray State University

Kentucky

General Admissions

Very important factors include: rigor of secondary school record, class rank, academic GPA, standardized test scores. High school diploma is required and a GED is accepted. *Academic units required:* 4 English, 3 math, 3 science, 1 science lab, 2 foreign language, 3 social studies, 3 history, 5 academic electives, 1 unit from above areas or other academic areas. *Academic units recommended:* 4 math, 4 science, 1 computer science. Test optional depending on GPA.

Accommodations or Services

Accommodations are decided upon an individual basis after a thorough review of appropriate, current documentation. The accommodations requests must be supported through the documentation provided and must be logically linked to the current impact of the condition on academic functioning.

Financial Aid

Students should submit: FAFSA. *Need-based scholarships/grants offered:* College/university scholarship or grant aid from institutional funds; Federal Pell; Private scholarships; SEOG; State scholarships/grants. *Loan aid offered:* Direct PLUS loans; Direct Subsidized Stafford Loans; Direct Unsubsidized Stafford Loans. Federal Work-Study Program available. Institutional employment available.

Campus Life

Activities: Campus Ministries; Choral groups; Concert band; Dance; Drama/theater; International Student Organization; Jazz band; Literary magazine; Marching band; Model UN; Music ensembles; Musical theater; Opera; Pep band; Radio station; Student government; Student newspaper; Student-run film society; Symphony orchestra; Television station. **Organizations:** 162 registered organizations, 16 honor societies, 12 religious organizations, 12 fraternities, 11 sororities. **Athletics (Intercollegiate):** *Men:* baseball, basketball, bowling, cheerleading, cross-country, equestrian sports, football, golf, horseback riding, riflery, rodeo, tennis. *Women:* basketball, cheerleading, cross-country, equestrian sports, golf, horseback riding, riflery, rodeo, soccer, softball, tennis, track/field (outdoor), volleyball.

ACCOMMODATIONS

Allowed in exams:	
Calculators	Yes
Dictionary	Yes
Computer	Yes
Spell-checker	Yes
Extended test time	Yes
Scribe	Yes
Proctors	Yes
Oral exams	Yes
Note-takers	Yes
Support services for students with:	
LD	Yes
ADHD	Yes
ASD	Yes
Distraction-reduced environment	Yes
Recording of lecture allowed	Yes
Reading technology	Yes
Audio books	Yes
Other assistive technology	Yes
Priority registration	Yes
Added costs of services:	
For LD	No
For ADHD	No
For ASD	No
LD specialists	No
ADHD & ASD coaching	Yes
ASD specialists	No
Professional tutors	No
Peer tutors	Yes
Max. hours/week for services	Varies
How professors are notified of student approved accommodations	Student and Disability Office

COLLEGE GRADUATION REQUIREMENTS

Course waivers allowed	No
Course substitutions allowed	Yes

In what courses: Student will work with institution to determine course substitutions

Thomas More University

333 Thomas More Pkwy., Crestview Hills, KY 41017-3495 • Admissions: 859-344-3332 • Fax: 859-344-3444 **Support: S**

CAMPUS

Type of school	Private (nonprofit)
Environment	Village

STUDENTS

Undergrad enrollment	2,030
% male/female	47/53
% from out of state	41

FINANCIAL FACTS

Annual tuition	$30,550
Room and board	$9,000
Required fees	$1,540

GENERAL ADMISSIONS INFO

Application fee	$0
Nonfall registration	Yes
Range SAT EBRW	500–580
Range SAT Math	510–560
Range ACT Composite	19–25

ACADEMICS

Student/faculty ratio	16:1
% students returning for sophomore year	59

Most classes have 10–19 students.

Programs/Services for Students with Learning Differences

Thomas More University's Student Support Services program is committed to the individual academic, personal, cultural/social, and financial needs of the student. It is committed to promoting sensitivity and cultural awareness of the population served and to promoting varied on/off campus services and events that enhance the student's educational opportunities. A variety of support services are offered, including developmental courses, peer tutoring, and individual counseling. Students with deficits in speech/language, study skills, written expression, ongoing additional skills, perceptual skills, reading, speaking, math, fine motor, and ADHD with or without LD are admissible.

Admissions

The ACT/SAT are only used for placement. Course requirements are English: 4 credits, foreign language: 2 credits, social science: 3 credits, mathematics: 3 credits, science: 3 credits, arts appreciation: 1 credit, and computer literacy: 1 credit. Applicants lacking some of these units may be admitted at the discretion of the Admissions Committee. The Institute for Learning Differences (ILD) helps students develop an IEP plan, and the strategic learning specialists can then provide students with the tools needed to meet the academic demands of college. While the program is designed for students who have a primary diagnosis of ADHD, language-based learning disability, or ASD yet have otherwise normal intellectual ability, it may serve other qualified students.

Additional Information

The Institute for Learning Differences, a division of the Thomas More Success Center, offers a comprehensive fee-based program designed to support students with documented learning differences on their journey to achieve a college education. The Institute for Learning Differences (ILD) is designed for students with a diagnosed learning difference who have at least average intellectual learning abilities. This fee-based program provides best practices and researched-based approaches to best support those students striving for college success. To ensure our team is fully prepared to best serve the students in the program, the applications are carefully evaluated to identify whose needs best match the services offered by the ILD. All applicants must submit supporting documents as well as an application for admissions to Thomas More University.

ADMISSIONS INFO FOR STUDENTS WITH LEARNING DIFFERENCES

Phone: 859-344-3582 • Fax: 859-344-3690 • Email:/ild@thomasmore.edu

SAT/ACT required: No
Interview required: Yes
Essay required: Yes
Additional application required: Yes
Documentation submitted to: Disability Services for traditional accommodations; Institute for Learning Differences for fee-based services

Special Ed. HS course work accepted: Yes
Separate application required for Programs/Services: Yes
Documentation required for:
LD: Psychoeducational evaluation
ADHD: Psychoeducational evaluation
ASD: Psychoeducational evaluation

Thomas More University

Kentucky

General Admissions

Very important factors include: academic GPA, standardized test scores. *Important factors include:* rigor of secondary school record. *Other factors include:* class rank, application essay, recommendation(s), interview, extracurricular activities, talent/ability, character/personal qualities, volunteer work. High school diploma is required and a GED is accepted. *Academic units required:* 4 English, 3 math, 3 science, 1 science lab, 2 foreign language, 3 social studies. *Academic units recommended:* 2 visual/performing arts. For Fall 2021, Thomas More University has implemented a test-optional admissions policy for first-year applicants.

Accommodations or Services

Accommodations are decided upon an individual basis after a thorough review of appropriate, current documentation. The accommodations requests must be supported through the documentation provided and must be logically linked to the current impact of the condition on academic functioning.

Financial Aid

Students should submit: FAFSA. *Need-based scholarships/grants offered:* College/university scholarship or grant aid from institutional funds; Federal Pell; Private scholarships; SEOG; United Negro College Fund.

Campus Life

Activities: Campus Ministries; Choral groups; Dance; Drama/theater; International Student Organization; Literary magazine; Marching band; Music ensembles; Student government. **Organizations:** 40 registered organizations, 10 honor societies, 1 religious organization, 1 fraternity.

ACCOMMODATIONS

Allowed in exams:	
Calculators	Yes
Dictionary	Yes
Computer	Yes
Spell-checker	No
Extended test time	Yes
Scribe	Yes
Proctors	Yes
Oral exams	Yes
Note-takers	Yes
Support services for students with:	
LD	Yes
ADHD	Yes
ASD	Yes
Distraction-reduced environment	Yes
Recording of lecture allowed	Yes
Reading technology	Yes
Audio books	Yes
Other assistive technology	Yes
Priority registration	No
Added costs of services:	
For LD	Yes
For ADHD	Yes
For ASD	Yes
LD specialists	Yes
ADHD & ASD coaching	Yes
ASD specialists	Yes
Professional tutors	Yes
Peer tutors	Yes
Max. hours/week for services	Unlimited
How professors are notified of student approved accommodations	Yes

COLLEGE GRADUATION REQUIREMENTS

Course waivers allowed	No
Course substitutions allowed	No

University of Kentucky

100 W.D. Funkhouser Building, Lexington, KY 40506 • Admissions: 859-257-2000 • Fax: 859-257-3823 **Support: CS**

CAMPUS

Type of school	Public
Environment	City

STUDENTS

Undergrad enrollment	22,236
% male/female	44/56
% from out of state	36
% frosh live on campus	89

FINANCIAL FACTS

Annual in-state tuition	$12,360
Annual out-of-state tuition	$30,680
Room and board	$13,210
Required fees	$1,349

GENERAL ADMISSIONS INFO

Application fee	$50
Regular application deadline	2/15
Nonfall registration	Yes

Admission may be deferred.

Range SAT EBRW	540–650
Range SAT Math	530–670
Range ACT Composite	22–29

ACADEMICS

Student/faculty ratio	16:1
% students returning for sophomore year	85

Most classes have 20–29 students.

Programs/Services for Students with Learning Differences

The University of Kentucky Disability Resource Center partners with qualified students with disabilities to assist them in gaining equal access to institutional programs and services consistent with their unique needs. The center seeks to responsibly advocate the needs of students with disabilities to the campus community through consultation and outreach efforts with administration, faculty, students, and university partners. The DRC provides services to the university community so students with disabilities have an equal opportunity to fully participate in all aspects of university life. The DRC serves students with a wide array of disabilities, and their website provides valuable information for students, parents, faculty, and staff related to various responsibilities, services, and programs of the office. The university nurtures a diverse community characterized by fairness and equal opportunity.

Admissions

Admission for freshman applicants is based on a holistic review including high school grades, national college admission test results, successful completion of pre-college curriculum, essays, and academic letters of recommendation. Applicants may submit official scores from either the ACT or the SAT. Most undergraduate majors at UK permit applicants to be directly admitted to their program as part of the general undergraduate admission process. However, some colleges and programs at UK require an admission process separate from general undergraduate admission to the University. These selective admission majors and programs may require test scores or higher GPA than general admission, the minimum requirements for in-state applicants, a separate application, a portfolio, or an interview. Applicants admitted with a cumulative unweighted high school GPA between 2.00-2.49 on a 4.0 scale will be required to enter into a Wildcat Success Plan (learning contract) with the University of Kentucky prior to enrollment.

Additional Information

Students have access to assistive technology including software programs that read aloud, dictate and write, and enlarge text. All accommodations are determined based on individual documentation and need.

ADMISSIONS INFO FOR STUDENTS WITH LEARNING DIFFERENCES

Phone: 859-257-2754 • Fax: 859-257-1980 • Email: dtbeac1@uky.edu/drc@uky.edu

SAT/ACT required: Yes (Test optional through 2022)
Interview required: No
Essay required: Yes
Additional application required: Yes
Documentation submitted to: Disability Resource Center

Special Ed. HS course work accepted: No
Separate application required for Programs/Services: Yes
Documentation required for:
LD: Psychoeducational evaluation
ADHD: Psychoeducational evaluation
ASD: Psychoeducational evaluation

University of Kentucky

General Admissions

Very important factors include: rigor of secondary school record, academic GPA, standardized test scores. *Important factors include:* application essay, recommendation(s). *Other factors include:* class rank, interview, extracurricular activities, talent/ability, character/personal qualities, alumni/ae relation, geographical residence, state residency, volunteer work. High school diploma is required and a GED is accepted. *Academic units required:* 4 English, 3 math, 3 science, 1 science lab, 3 foreign language, 3 social studies, 7 academic electives, 1 visual/performing arts, 1 unit from above areas or other academic areas. The University of Kentucky is implementing a test optional policy for the 2021–22 academic year.

Accommodations or Services

Accommodations are decided upon an individual basis after a thorough review of appropriate, current documentation. The accommodations requests must be supported through the documentation provided and must be logically linked to the current impact of the condition on academic functioning.

Financial Aid

Students should submit: FAFSA. Applicants will be notified of awards on a rolling basis beginning 2/15. *Need-based scholarships/grants offered:* College/university scholarship or grant aid from institutional funds; Federal Pell; Private scholarships; SEOG; State scholarships/grants. *Loan aid offered:* Direct PLUS loans; Direct Subsidized Stafford Loans; Direct Unsubsidized Stafford Loans. Federal Work-Study Program available.

Campus Life

Activities: Campus Ministries; Choral groups; Concert band; Dance; Drama/theater; International Student Organization; Jazz band; Literary magazine; Marching band; Model UN; Music ensembles; Musical theater; Opera; Pep band; Radio station; Student government; Student newspaper; Symphony orchestra; Television station; Yearbook. **Organizations:** 348 registered organizations, 28 honor societies, 20 religious organizations, 19 fraternities, 16 sororities. **Athletics (Intercollegiate):** *Men:* baseball, basketball, cheerleading, cross-country, diving, football, golf, riflery, soccer, swimming, tennis, track/field (outdoor), track/field (indoor). *Women:* basketball, cheerleading, cross-country, diving, golf, gymnastics, riflery, soccer, softball, swimming, tennis, track/field (outdoor), track/field (indoor), volleyball.

ACCOMMODATIONS

Allowed in exams:	
Calculators	No
Dictionary	No
Computer	Yes
Spell-checker	No
Extended test time	Yes
Scribe	Yes
Proctors	Yes
Oral exams	Yes
Note-takers	No
Support services for students with:	
LD	Yes
ADHD	Yes
ASD	Yes
Distraction-reduced environment	Yes
Recording of lecture allowed	Yes
Reading technology	Yes
Audio books	Yes
Other assistive technology	Yes
Priority registration	Yes
Added costs of services:	
For LD	No
For ADHD	No
For ASD	No
LD specialists	No
ADHD & ASD coaching	No
ASD specialists	No
Professional tutors	No
Peer tutors	No
Max. hours/week for services	Varies
How professors are notified of student approved accommodations	Student

COLLEGE GRADUATION REQUIREMENTS

Course waivers allowed	No
Course substitutions allowed	Yes

In what courses: Student will work with institution to determine course substitutions

Western Kentucky University

Potter Hall 117, Bowling Green, KY 42101-1020 • Admissions: 270-745-2551 • Fax: 270-745-6133 **Support: CS**

CAMPUS

Type of school	Public
Environment	Town

STUDENTS

Undergrad enrollment	15,895
% male/female	40/60
% from out of state	28
% frosh live on campus	83

FINANCIAL FACTS

Annual in-state tuition	$10,802
Annual out-of-state tuition	$26,496
Room and board	$8,432
Required fees	$200

GENERAL ADMISSIONS INFO

Application fee	$45
Regular application deadline	8/1
Nonfall registration	Yes

Admission may be deferred.

Range SAT EBRW	500–620
Range SAT Math	490–600
Range ACT Composite	19–27

ACADEMICS

Student/faculty ratio	18:1
% students returning for sophomore year	73

Most classes have 10–19 students.

Programs/Services for Students with Learning Differences

The purpose of SARC is to coordinate services and accommodations for students with documented disabilities. This office supports equity among students, ensuring they have access to the complete Western Kentucky University experience. SARC also works to increase awareness among all members of the University so that students with disabilities are able to achieve academic success based on their abilities. Students use an online system for managing accommodations and services. This system is used to share Faculty Notification Letters and coordinate note-taking services.

Admissions

Students admitted to WKU may be placed in an appropriate academic support program based on academic needs at the time of admission. Students will be notified regarding any academic placement by the appropriate office. ACT or SAT is required only when the minimum GPA or class rank is not met. To be admitted, a student must have at least a 2.0 unweighted high school GPA. Those with a GPA below 2.5 must achieve a Composite Admission Index (CAI) score of at least 60. Those with a 2.5 unweighted high school GPA or greater are not required to submit ACT or SAT scores for admission purposes. Students admitted to WKU may be placed in an appropriate academic support program based on academic needs at the time of admission. Students who have between a 2.0–2.49 unweighted high school GPA and achieve the required CAI score, will be admitted to WKU via the Summer Scholars Program.

Additional Information

Testing accommodations, such as extended time, quiet room, and use of computer assistive technology are provided. There are strict guidelines that need to be followed in order to schedule exam accommodations. For students registered for note-taking accommodations they can use the recording devices, note-taker applications for each class, or request a notetaker for each class. The student is responsible for working in partnership with potential classmates, course instructors, and the SARC to secure a classroom Notetaker. Students have access to assistive technology including, Video Relay, Video Phone, Captioned Phone, JAWS, Read Write Gold, Dragon Naturally Speaking, Talking Calculator, Intellikeys Adaptive Keyboard, Orbit Trackball Mouse, and Zoomtext Screen Magnifier.

ADMISSIONS INFO FOR STUDENTS WITH LEARNING DIFFERENCES

Phone: 270-745-5004 • Email: robert.unseld@wku.edu

SAT/ACT required: No (depending on GPA)
Interview required: Yes
Essay required: Yes
Additional application required: No
Documentation submitted to: Student Accessibility Resource Center
Special Ed. HS course work accepted: Yes
Separate application required for Programs/Services: No
Documentation required for:
LD: Psychoeducational evaluation
ADHD: Psychoeducational evaluation
ASD: Psychoeducational evaluation

Western Kentucky University

Kentucky

General Admissions

Very important factors include: academic GPA, standardized test scores. High school diploma is required and a GED is accepted. *Academic units required:* 4 English, 3 math, 3 science, 3 social studies, 7 academic electives, 1 visual/performing arts. *Academic units recommended:* 2 foreign language. Beginning with the spring 2021 semester, WKU will no longer require standardized test scores, such as the ACT or SAT, for most applicants for admission.

Accommodations or Services

Accommodations are decided upon an individual basis after a thorough review of appropriate, current documentation. The accommodations requests must be supported through the documentation provided and must be logically linked to the current impact of the condition on academic functioning.

Financial Aid

Students should submit: CSS/Financial Aid PROFILE; FAFSA; Noncustodial PROFILE. Applicants will be notified of awards on a rolling basis beginning 12/21. *Need-based scholarships/grants offered:* College/university scholarship or grant aid from institutional funds; Federal Pell; Private scholarships; SEOG; State scholarships/grants; United Negro College Fund. *Loan aid offered:* Direct PLUS loans; Direct Subsidized Stafford Loans; Direct Unsubsidized Stafford Loans. Federal Work-Study Program available. Institutional employment available.

Campus Life

Activities: Campus Ministries; Choral groups; Concert band; Dance; Drama/theater; International Student Organization; Jazz band; Literary magazine; Marching band; Model UN; Music ensembles; Musical theater; Opera; Pep band; Radio station; Student government; Student newspaper; Student-run film society; Symphony orchestra; Television station; Yearbook. **Organizations:** 366 registered organizations, 25 honor societies, 35 religious organizations, 19 fraternities, 16 sororities. **Athletics (Intercollegiate):** *Men:* baseball, basketball, cross-country, diving, football, golf, riflery, swimming, tennis, track/field (outdoor), track/field (indoor). *Women:* basketball, cross-country, diving, golf, riflery, soccer, swimming, tennis, track/field (outdoor), track/field (indoor), volleyball.

ACCOMMODATIONS

Allowed in exams:	
Calculators	Yes
Dictionary	Yes
Computer	Yes
Spell-checker	Yes
Extended test time	Yes
Scribe	Yes
Proctors	Yes
Oral exams	Yes
Note-takers	Yes
Support services for students with:	
LD	Yes
ADHD	Yes
ASD	Yes
Distraction-reduced environment	Yes
Recording of lecture allowed	Yes
Reading technology	Yes
Audio books	Yes
Other assistive technology	Yes
Priority registration	Yes
Added costs of services:	
For LD	Yes
For ADHD	Yes
For ASD	Yes
LD specialists	Yes
ADHD & ASD coaching	Yes
ASD specialists	Yes
Professional tutors	Yes
Peer tutors	Yes
Max. hours/week for services	20
How professors are notified of student approved accommodations	Student and Disability Office

COLLEGE GRADUATION REQUIREMENTS

Course waivers allowed	Yes
In what courses: Case-by-case basis	
Course substitutions allowed	Yes
In what courses: Case-by-case basis	

Louisiana College

1140 College Drive, Pineville, LA 71359-0566 • Admissions: 318-487-7259 **Support: SP**

CAMPUS

Type of school	Private (nonprofit)
Environment	Town

STUDENTS

Undergrad enrollment	1,004
% male/female	53/47
% from out of state	12
% frosh live on campus	78

FINANCIAL FACTS

Annual tuition	$17,500
Room and board	$5,646
Required fees	

GENERAL ADMISSIONS INFO

Application fee	$25
Regular application deadline	8/15
Nonfall registration	Yes

Admission may be deferred.

Range SAT EBRW	460–540
Range SAT Math	450–520
Range ACT Composite	18–23

ACADEMICS

Student/faculty ratio	10:1
% students returning for sophomore year	65

Most classes have 10–19 students.

Programs/Services for Students with Learning Differences

Students may choose to enroll in the Student Success Center Special Services. Through this program, extensive individualized tutoring is arranged. Assistance can be provided with note taking, study skills, time management, research, paper writing, etc. Audio books are available. Test accommodations can be arranged, e.g., in a distraction-free environment or with extended time.

Admissions

Prospective students with learning differences would benefit greatly from contacting the Student Success Center and speaking personally with the Director. To be admitted unconditionally, applicants must fulfill one of the following criteria: (1) At least a 20 on the ACT or a 1030 on the SAT and a GPA of 2.0 on a 4.0 scale in the academic core subjects. (2) A minimum of 17 on the ACT or 900 on the SAT and a GPA of 2.5 out of 4.0 in academic core subjects. (3) A minimum of 18 on the ACT or 940 on the SAT and a GPA of 2.3 on a 4.0 in academic core subjects. (4) A minimum of 19 on the ACT or 980 on the SAT and a GPA of 2.2 on a 4.0 in academic core subjects. Students will also need a high school diploma with 4 years English, 4 years math, 3 years science (with at least 2 units of lab), 3 years social studies (with at least 1 unit focusing on the United States and 1 unit on the world). The remaining 10 units may be earned from the following academic areas: English, math, science, social studies, foreign language, humanities, fine/performing arts, physical education, health, and computer science (provided a substantial programming or mathematical component is established).

Additional Information

Tutoring sessions are conducted in most subjects taken by Level I students. Additional tutorial help is available at the higher levels as needed. The PASS staff will carefully work with individual professors and the student's academic advisor to coordinate and accommodate the student's learning needs. Students admitted to PASS will remain in the program as long as they are at Louisiana College. Noncompliance with any component of the program may result in a student's dismissal from the program. Skills classes are offered in study techniques, test-taking strategies, and time management through orientation, and private tutoring from a PASS staff member. Incoming freshmen are encouraged to attend one summer session (5 weeks) to become familiar with the campus and college life. There is an additional fee for the PASS program that ranges from $450–$850 per semester, depending on the level of support provided.

ADMISSIONS INFO FOR STUDENTS WITH LEARNING DIFFERENCES

Phone: 318-487-7629 • Email: jolynn.mcconley@lacollege.edu

SAT/ACT required: Yes
Interview required: No
Essay required: Yes
Additional application required: No
Documentation submitted to: Student Success Center Special Services

Special Ed. HS course work accepted: Yes
Separate application required for Programs/Services: No
Documentation required for:
LD: Psychoeducational evaluation
ADHD: Psychoeducational evaluation
ASD: Psychoeducational evaluation

Louisiana College

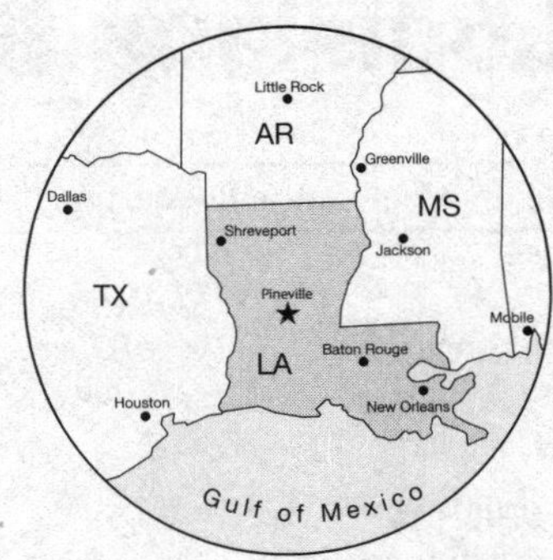

General Admissions

Very important factors include: academic GPA, standardized test scores. *Other factors include:* rigor of secondary school record. High school diploma is required and GED is accepted. *Academic units required:* 4 English, 4 math, 3 science, 2 science labs, 3 social studies, 8 unit from above areas or other academic areas.

Accommodations or Services

Accommodations are decided upon an individual basis after a thorough review of appropriate, current documentation. The accommodations requests must be supported through the documentation provided and must be logically linked to the current impact of the condition on academic functioning.

Financial Aid

Students should submit: FAFSA. *Need-based scholarships/grants offered:* College/university scholarship or grant aid from institutional funds; Federal Pell; Private scholarships; SEOG; State scholarships/grants. *Loan aid offered:* Direct PLUS loans; Direct Subsidized Stafford Loans; Direct Unsubsidized Stafford Loans. Federal Work-Study Program available. Institutional employment available.

Campus Life

Activities: Campus Ministries; Choral groups; Concert band; Drama/theater; Jazz band; Marching band; Music ensembles; Musical theater; Opera; Pep band; Radio station; Student government; Symphony orchestra. **Organizations:** 12 registered organizations, 13 honor societies, 6 religious organizations.

ACCOMMODATIONS

Allowed in exams:	
Calculators	Yes
Dictionary	Yes
Computer	Yes
Spell-checker	Yes
Extended test time	Yes
Scribe	Yes
Proctors	Yes
Oral exams	Yes
Note-takers	Yes
Support services for students with:	
LD	Yes
ADHD	Yes
ASD	Yes
Distraction-reduced environment	Yes
Recording of lecture allowed	Yes
Reading technology	Yes
Audio books	Yes
Other assistive technology	Yes
Priority registration	No
Added costs of services:	
For LD	No
For ADHD	No
For ASD	No
LD specialists	Yes
ADHD & ASD coaching	Yes
ASD specialists	No
Professional tutors	No
Peer tutors	Yes
Max. hours/week for services	Varies
How professors are notified of student approved accommodations	Student and Disability Office

COLLEGE GRADUATION REQUIREMENTS

Course waivers allowed	No
Course substitutions allowed	No

Louisiana

Louisiana State University—Baton Rouge

Pleasant Hall, Baton Rouge, LA 70803 • Admissions: 225-578-1175 • Fax: 225-578-4433 **Support: S**

CAMPUS

Type of school	Public
Environment	City

STUDENTS

Undergrad enrollment	25,826
% male/female	47/53
% from out of state	17
% frosh live on campus	70

FINANCIAL FACTS

Annual in-state tuition	$11,962
Annual out-of-state tuition	$28,639
Room and board	$12,174

GENERAL ADMISSIONS INFO

Application fee	$50
Regular application deadline	4/15
Nonfall registration	Yes

Admission may be deferred.

Range SAT EBRW	530–640
Range SAT Math	530–640
Range ACT Composite	23–28

ACADEMICS

Student/faculty ratio	20:1
% students returning for sophomore year	83

Most classes have 10–19 students.

Programs/Services for Students with Learning Differences

The purpose of Disability Services (DS) is to assist any student who finds his or her disability to be a barrier to achieving educational and/ or personal goals. The office provides support services to students with learning disabilities. These services are provided to encourage students with LD/ADHD to achieve success in college. The consequences of a disability may include specialized requirements; therefore, the particular needs of each student are considered on an individual basis. DS dedicates its efforts to meeting both the needs of students with disabilities and the interests of faculty, staff, and the university as a whole. It is the practice of DS that issues concerning accommodations of students with disabilities in academic and other programs and activities be resolved between the student requesting the accommodation and the university employee representing the department within which the academic program or service is located. After intervention, if the student does not find the provision of an accommodation satisfactory, the student may file a formal grievance.

Admissions

Students interested in Ogden Honors College consideration and top scholarships should complete the writing section. Students who are borderline to meeting admission requirements are still encouraged to apply. Other factors considered for admission may include choice of degree program, rank in class, credit in advanced placement or honors courses, rigor of the high school curriculum, and grade trends.

Additional Information

Specialized support services are based on individual disability-based needs. Services available include disability management counseling; adaptive equipment loan; note-takers; referral for tutoring; assistance with enrollment and registration; liaison assistance and referral to on-campus and off-campus resources; supplemental orientation to the campus; and advocacy on behalf of students with campus faculty, staff, and students. The Learning Assistance Center is open to all students on campus.

ADMISSIONS INFO FOR STUDENTS WITH LEARNING DIFFERENCES

Phone: 225-578-5919 • Fax: 225-578-4560 • Email: bjcornw@lsu.edu/ disability@lsu.edu

SAT/ACT required: Yes
Interview required: No
Essay required: Yes
Additional application required: No
Documentation submitted to: Disability Services

Special Ed. HS course work accepted: Yes
Separate application required for Programs/Services: No
Documentation required for:
LD: Psychoeducational evaluation
ADHD: Psychoeducational evaluation
ASD: Psychoeducational evaluation

Louisiana State University— Baton Rouge

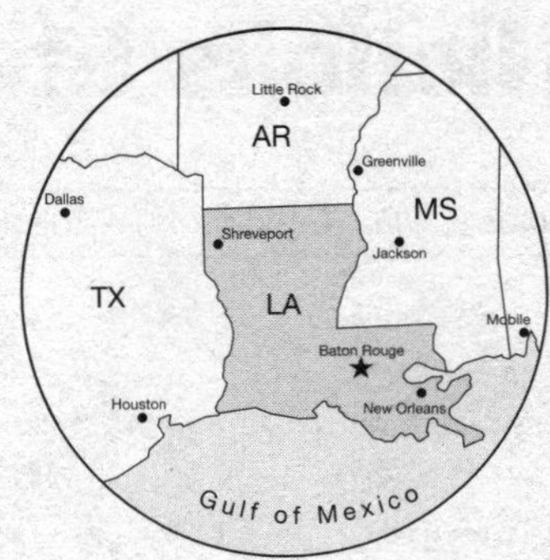

General Admissions

Very important factors include: rigor of secondary school record, academic GPA, standardized test scores. *Important factors include:* talent/ability. *Other factors include:* class rank, application essay, recommendation(s), interview, extracurricular activities, first generation, alumni/ae relation, level of applicant's interest. High school diploma is required and a GED is accepted. *Academic units required:* 4 English, 4 math, 4 science, 2 foreign language, 3 social studies, 1 history, 1 visual/performing arts.

Accommodations or Services

Accommodations are decided upon an individual basis after a thorough review of appropriate, current documentation. The accommodations requests must be supported through the documentation provided and must be logically linked to the current impact of the condition on academic functioning.

Financial Aid

Students should submit: FAFSA; Institution's own financial aid form. *Need-based scholarships/grants offered:* College/university scholarship or grant aid from institutional funds; Federal Pell; Private scholarships; SEOG; State scholarships/grants. *Loan aid offered:* Direct PLUS loans; Direct Subsidized Stafford Loans; Direct Unsubsidized Stafford Loans. Federal Work-Study Program available. Institutional employment available.

Campus Life

Activities: Campus Ministries; Choral groups; Concert band; Dance; Drama/theater; International Student Organization; Jazz band; Literary magazine; Marching band; Music ensembles; Musical theater; Opera; Pep band; Radio station; Student government; Student newspaper; Student-run film society; Symphony orchestra; Television station; Yearbook. **Organizations:** 572 registered organizations, 27 honor societies, 44 religious organizations, 22 fraternities, 14 sororities. **Athletics (Intercollegiate):** *Men:* baseball, basketball, cheerleading, cross-country, diving, football, golf, swimming, tennis, track/field (outdoor), track/field (indoor). *Women:* basketball, cheerleading, cross-country, diving, golf, gymnastics, soccer, softball, swimming, tennis, track/field (outdoor), track/field (indoor), volleyball.

ACCOMMODATIONS

Allowed in exams:	
Calculators	Yes
Dictionary	No
Computer	Yes
Spell-checker	Yes
Extended test time	Yes
Scribe	Yes
Proctors	Yes
Oral exams	Yes
Note-takers	Yes
Support services for students with:	
LD	Yes
ADHD	Yes
ASD	Yes
Distraction-reduced environment	Yes
Recording of lecture allowed	Yes
Reading technology	Yes
Audio books	Yes
Other assistive technology	Yes
Priority registration	No
Added costs of services:	
For LD	No
For ADHD	No
For ASD	No
LD specialists	No
ADHD & ASD coaching	No
ASD specialists	No
Professional tutors	No
Peer tutors	No
Max. hours/week for services	Varies
How professors are notified of student approved accommodations	Student

COLLEGE GRADUATION REQUIREMENTS

Course waivers allowed	Yes
In what courses: Foreign Languages	
Course substitutions allowed	Yes
In what courses: Foreign Languages	

Louisiana

Nicholls State University

P.O. Box 2004, Thibodaux, LA 70310 • Admissions: 985-448-4507 • Fax: 985-448-4929 **Support: S**

CAMPUS	
Type of school	Public
Environment	Village
STUDENTS	
Undergrad enrollment	5,573
% male/female	36/64
% from out of state	5
% frosh live on campus	43
FINANCIAL FACTS	
Annual in-state tuition	$4,922
Annual out-of-state tuition	$6,015
Room and board	$9,938
Required fees	$3,030
GENERAL ADMISSIONS INFO	
Application fee	$20
Regular application deadline	8/1
Nonfall registration	Yes
Admission may be deferred.	
Range SAT EBRW	430–540
Range SAT Math	440–550
Range ACT Composite	20–24
ACADEMICS	
Student/faculty ratio	19:1
% students returning for sophomore year	73
Most classes have 20–29 students.	

Programs/Services for Students with Learning Differences

Nicholls State offers the Bridge to Independence program, a two-year certificate program designed to provide add-on services to help students with ASD successfully transition to college life and further develop their social skills and campus friendships. To qualify for the program, students will first need to apply and be accepted to Nicholls based on admission requirements (such as GPA, ACT scores, and high school curriculum). Degree program students who participate in the Bridge program will: attend weekly social skill seminars, receive systematic monitoring of their academic, behavioral and social performance, be provided with academic coaches and peer mentors to help them successfully progress toward earning their college degree, receive liaison services between the Bridge program and their faculty members, participate in campus activities and organizations, and receive assistance coordinating any necessary student or academic services such as counseling or tutoring.

Admissions

Applications will be reviewed on an individual basis and an admissions decision will be made considering each applicant's potential for success and will include factors such as ACT score, special talents, and the University's commitment to a demographically diverse student population. Students who receive their GED or graduate from non-accredited homeschool programs and are under the age of 25 must submit ACT scores with a minimum 23 composite score and demonstrate no need for remedial coursework in order to be admitted.

Additional Information

The Dyslexia Center provides a support system; equipment; remediation; academic planning; resources; and assistance. Accommodation forms with appropriate classroom and testing accommodations are given to professors. Typical accommodations may include extended time; use of an electronic dictionary; oral reader; or use of a computer. Other campus services include the Student Access Center (SAC); Office for Students with Disabilities; the Testing Center for special testing accommodations such as extended time or a quiet room; the Tutorial and Academic Enhancement Center for tutoring assistance; and the university counseling center.

ADMISSIONS INFO FOR STUDENTS WITH LEARNING DIFFERENCES

Phone: 985-448-4430 • Email: studentaccess@nicholls.edu

SAT/ACT required: Yes
Interview required: Yes
Essay required: Yes
Additional application required: No
Documentation submitted to: Student Access Center (SAC)
Special Ed. HS course work accepted: Yes
Separate application required for Programs/Services: No
Documentation required for:
- **LD:** Psychoeducational evaluation
- **ADHD:** Psychoeducational evaluation
- **ASD:** Psychoeducational evaluation

Nicholls State University

General Admissions

Very important factors include: rigor of secondary school record. *Important factors include:* standardized test scores. *Other factors include:* class rank, academic GPA, talent/ability. High school diploma is required and a GED is accepted. *Academic units required:* 4 English, 3 math, 3 science, 2 foreign language, 1 social studies, 2 history, 2 academic electives.

Accommodations or Services

Accommodations are decided upon an individual basis after a thorough review of appropriate, current documentation. The accommodations requests must be supported through the documentation provided and must be logically linked to the current impact of the condition on academic functioning.

Financial Aid

Students should submit: FAFSA. *Need-based scholarships/grants offered:* College/university scholarship or grant aid from institutional funds; Federal Pell; Private scholarships; SEOG; State scholarships/grants. *Loan aid offered:* Direct PLUS loans; Direct Subsidized Stafford Loans; Direct Unsubsidized Stafford Loans. Federal Work-Study Program available. Institutional employment available.

Campus Life

Activities: Choral groups; Concert band; Dance; Drama/theater; Jazz band; Literary magazine; Marching band; Music ensembles; Musical theater; Radio station; Student government; Student newspaper; Student-run film society; Television station; Yearbook. **Organizations:** 121 registered organizations, 24 honor societies, 6 religious organizations, 10 fraternities, 5 sororities. **Athletics (Intercollegiate):** *Men:* baseball, basketball, cross-country, football, golf, tennis. *Women:* basketball, cross-country, golf, soccer, softball, tennis, track/field (outdoor), track/field (indoor), volleyball.

ACCOMMODATIONS	
Allowed in exams:	
Calculators	Yes
Dictionary	Yes
Computer	Yes
Spell-checker	Yes
Extended test time	Yes
Scribe	Yes
Proctors	Yes
Oral exams	Yes
Note-takers	Yes
Support services for students with:	
LD	Yes
ADHD	Yes
ASD	Yes
Distraction-reduced environment	Yes
Recording of lecture allowed	Yes
Reading technology	Yes
Audio books	Yes
Other assistive technology	Yes
Priority registration	Yes
Added costs of services:	
For LD	No
For ADHD	No
For ASD	No
LD specialists	No
ADHD & ASD coaching	No
ASD specialists	No
Professional tutors	No
Peer tutors	No
Max. hours/week for services	Varies
How professors are notified of student approved accommodations	Student

COLLEGE GRADUATION REQUIREMENTS	
Course waivers allowed	No
Course substitutions allowed	No

Tulane University

6823 St. Charles Avenue, New Orleans, LA 70118 • Admissions: 504-865-5731 • Fax: 504-862-8715 **Support: CS**

CAMPUS

Type of school	Private (nonprofit)
Environment	Metropolis

STUDENTS

Undergrad enrollment	6,968
% male/female	41/59
% from out of state	80
% frosh live on campus	98

FINANCIAL FACTS

Annual tuition	$58,850
Room and board	$16,248

GENERAL ADMISSIONS INFO

Application fee	$0
Regular application deadline	11/15
Nonfall registration	Yes

Admission may be deferred.

Range SAT EBRW	660–750
Range SAT Math	700–770
Range ACT Composite	31–33

ACADEMICS

Student/faculty ratio	8:1
% students returning for sophomore year	93

Programs/Services for Students with Learning Differences

The Goldman Office of Disability Services (ODS) is committed to providing equal access and a friendly environment for all who study and work at Tulane University. ODS offers accommodations and modifications of the academic or work environment to students and employees with psychological, medical/physical, and learning/developmental disabilities. Staff members work collaboratively to develop an individualized plan that gives each student the same opportunity for success as their peers.

Admissions

For admission to the Goldman ODS services, applicants must complete the Request for Accommodation form, submit supporting documentation, meet with ODS staff to discuss approved accommodations and implementation of those accommodations, and meet with ODs staff as needed for ongoing support. No audition or portfolio is required for admission to the university, but the inclusion of a portfolio is helpful.

Additional Information

Tulane offers assistive technology to students, including closed captioning services for students with hearing impairments. The process begins by connecting with the Goldman Center and completing an application. After the Center receives a request and documentation, the student will be contacted by a Goldman Center staff person to set up a Welcome Meeting. Meetings can be held remotely (by Zoom video chat or by phone) or in person based on the student's preference.

ADMISSIONS INFO FOR STUDENTS WITH LEARNING DIFFERENCES

Phone: 504-862-8433 • Fax: 504-862-8435 • Email: goldman@tulane.edu

SAT/ACT required: Yes (Test optional for 2021)
Interview required: No
Essay required: Yes
Additional application required: No
Documentation submitted to: Goldman Office of Disability Services

Special Ed. HS course work accepted: Yes
Separate application required for Programs/Services: No
Documentation required for:
- **LD:** Psychoeducational evaluation
- **ADHD:** Psychoeducational evaluation
- **ASD:** Psychoeducational evaluation

Tulane University

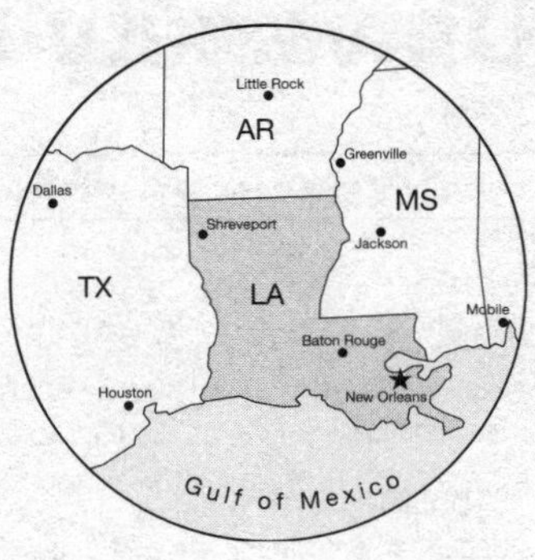

General Admissions

Very important factors include: rigor of secondary school record, class rank, academic GPA, standardized test scores. *Important factors include:* application essay, recommendation(s), character/personal qualities. *Other factors include:* interview, extracurricular activities, talent/ability, first generation, alumni/ae relation, volunteer work, work experience, level of applicant's interest. High school diploma is required and a GED is accepted. *Academic units recommended:* 4 English, 3 math, 3 science, 3 science labs, 3 foreign language, 3 social studies.

Accommodations or Services

Accommodations are decided upon an individual basis after a thorough review of appropriate, current documentation. The accommodations requests must be supported through the documentation provided and must be logically linked to the current impact of the condition on academic functioning. Submitting test scores for the SAT or ACT will be an optional, not required, part of the admission process for students applying this fall for a spot in Tulane University's 2021 entering class.

Financial Aid

Students should submit: FAFSA. Applicants will be notified of awards on a rolling basis beginning 12/15. *Need-based scholarships/grants offered:* College/university scholarship or grant aid from institutional funds; Federal Pell; Private scholarships; SEOG; State scholarships/grants. *Loan aid offered:* Direct PLUS loans; Direct Subsidized Stafford Loans; Direct Unsubsidized Stafford Loans. Federal Work-Study Program available. Institutional employment available.

Campus Life

Activities: Campus Ministries; Choral groups; Concert band; Dance; Drama/theater; International Student Organization; Jazz band; Literary magazine; Marching band; Model UN; Music ensembles; Musical theater; Pep band; Radio station; Student government; Student newspaper; Student-run film society; Symphony orchestra; Television station; Yearbook. **Organizations:** 250 registered organizations, 43 honor societies, 11 religious organizations, 12 fraternities, 12 sororities. **Athletics (Intercollegiate):** *Men:* baseball, basketball, cross-country, football, tennis, track/field (outdoor). *Women:* basketball, cross-country, diving, golf, swimming, tennis, track/field (outdoor), track/field (indoor), volleyball.

ACCOMMODATIONS

Allowed in exams:	
Calculators	Yes
Dictionary	Yes
Computer	Yes
Spell-checker	Yes
Extended test time	Yes
Scribe	Yes
Proctors	Yes
Oral exams	Yes
Note-takers	Yes
Support services for students with:	
LD	Yes
ADHD	Yes
ASD	Yes
Distraction-reduced environment	Yes
Recording of lecture allowed	Yes
Reading technology	Yes
Audio books	Yes
Other assistive technology	Yes
Priority registration	Yes
Added costs of services:	
For LD	No
For ADHD	No
For ASD	No
LD specialists	No
ADHD & ASD coaching	Yes
ASD specialists	No
Professional tutors	Yes
Peer tutors	Yes
Max. hours/week for services	Varies
How professors are notified of student approved accommodations	Student

COLLEGE GRADUATION REQUIREMENTS

Course waivers allowed	Yes
In what courses: Foreign language	
Course substitutions allowed	Yes
In what courses: Foreign language	

Louisiana

University of New Orleans

University of New Orleans Privateer Enrollment Center, New Orleans, LA 70148 • Admissions: 504-280-6595 • Fax: 504-280-3973 **Support: S**

CAMPUS	
Type of school	Public
Environment	Metropolis
STUDENTS	
Undergrad enrollment	6,713
% male/female	49/51
% from out of state	7
% frosh live on campus	27
FINANCIAL FACTS	
Annual in-state tuition	$6,960
Annual out-of-state tuition	$11,796
Room and board	$9,245
Required fees	$2,394
GENERAL ADMISSIONS INFO	
Application fee	$25
Regular application deadline	8/15
Nonfall registration	Yes
Range SAT EBRW	520–630
Range SAT Math	500–610
Range ACT Composite	20–25
ACADEMICS	
Student/faculty ratio	20:1
% students returning for sophomore year	68
Most classes have 10–19 students.	

Programs/Services for Students with Learning Differences

The Office of Disability Services (ODS) at UNO coordinates all services and programs. In addition to serving its primary function as a liaison between the student and the university, the office provides a limited number of direct services to students with all kinds of permanent and temporary disabilities. Services begin when a student registered with the university contacts the ODS office, provides documentation of the disability, and requests assistance. ODS encourages student independence, program accessibility, and a psychologically supportive environment, so students may achieve their educational objectives. ODS also seeks to educate the campus community about disability issues.

Admissions

Students with LD should submit the general application form and are expected to meet the same admission standards as all other applicants. In-state applicants must have all of the following: (1) a minimum 18 ACT English (500 SAT Evidence-Based Reading and Writing), (2) a minimum 19 ACT Math (510 SAT Math), (3) a completed Louisiana Board of Regents' high school Core 4 curriculum (19 units), and (4) a minimum 2.0 grade point average on a 4.0 scale. In-state first-years must either have the Louisiana Core 4 with a GPA of at least 2.5 OR a composite ACT of 23 (1140 SAT). Out-of-state applicants have the same requirements—with an equivalent to the Louisiana Core 4 curriculum. Out-of-state first-years must do one of the following: fulfill the in-state first-year requirements OR complete 17 or 18 credits from the Core 4 curriculum with a core average of 2.5 and a composite of 23 ACT (1140 SAT) OR have a minimum 26 ACT composite. The University may choose to admit students not meeting all requirements.

Additional Information

Privateer Pathways is designed for students who, because of their ACT or SAT scores, need additional support in mathematics and/or English. Skills will be developed through the strategic delivery of academic support to students. The programs cover aspects such as time management, academic honesty, and financial aid. Bi-weekly Success Coaching is also available to first-year students. Each student will be individually evaluated for program eligibility based on high school transcripts and test scores. Participants will receive academic advising on courses required as part of the Pathways program.

ADMISSIONS INFO FOR STUDENTS WITH LEARNING DIFFERENCES

Phone: 504-280-7327 • Fax: 504-280-3972 • Email: aaking@uno.edu

SAT/ACT required: Yes (Test optional for 2021))
Interview required: No
Essay required: Yes
Additional application required: No
Documentation submitted to: Office of Student Accountability, Advocacy and Disability Services

Special Ed. HS course work accepted: Yes
Separate application required for Programs/Services: No
Documentation required for:
LD: Psychoeducational evaluation
ADHD: Psychoeducational evaluation
ASD: Psychoeducational evaluation

University of New Orleans

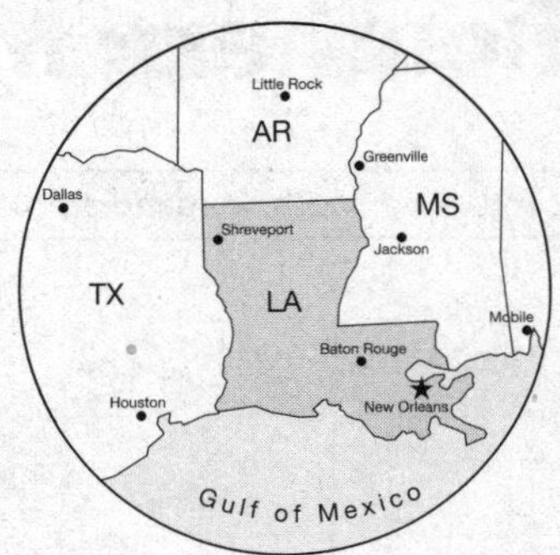

General Admissions

Very important factors include: academic GPA, standardized test scores. High school diploma is required and a GED is accepted. *Academic units required:* 4 English, 4 math, 4 science, 2 foreign language, 4 social studies, 1 visual/performing arts.

Accommodations or Services

Accommodations are decided upon an individual basis after a thorough review of appropriate, current documentation. The accommodations requests must be supported through the documentation provided and must be logically linked to the current impact of the condition on academic functioning.

Financial Aid

Students should submit: FAFSA. Applicants will be notified of awards on a rolling basis beginning 3/1. *Need-based scholarships/grants offered:* College/university scholarship or grant aid from institutional funds; Federal Pell; Private scholarships; SEOG; State scholarships/grants; United Negro College Fund. *Loan aid offered:* Direct PLUS loans; Direct Subsidized Stafford Loans; Direct Unsubsidized Stafford Loans. Federal Work-Study Program available. Institutional employment available.

Campus Life

Activities: Campus Ministries; Choral groups; Concert band; Dance; Drama/theater; International Student Organization; Jazz band; Literary magazine; Model UN; Music ensembles; Musical theater; Pep band; Radio station; Student government; Student newspaper; Student-run film society. **Organizations:** 101 registered organizations, 9 honor societies, 5 religious organizations, 8 fraternities, 7 sororities. **Athletics (Intercollegiate):** *Men:* baseball, basketball, diving, golf, swimming, tennis. *Women:* basketball, diving, swimming, tennis, volleyball.

Louisiana

ACCOMMODATIONS

Allowed in exams:	
Calculators	Yes
Dictionary	Yes
Computer	Yes
Spell-checker	Yes
Extended test time	Yes
Scribe	Yes
Proctors	Yes
Oral exams	Yes
Note-takers	Yes
Support services for students with:	
LD	Yes
ADHD	Yes
ASD	Yes
Distraction-reduced environment	Yes
Recording of lecture allowed	Yes
Reading technology	Yes
Audio books	No
Other assistive technology	Yes
Priority registration	No
Added costs of services:	
For LD	No
For ADHD	No
For ASD	No
LD specialists	No
ADHD & ASD coaching	No
ASD specialists	No
Professional tutors	No
Peer tutors	Yes
Max. hours/week for services	Varies
How professors are notified of student approved accommodations	Student

COLLEGE GRADUATION REQUIREMENTS

Course waivers allowed	No
Course substitutions allowed	No

Southern Maine Community College

2 Fort Road South, Portland, ME 04106 • Admissions: 207-741-5800 • Fax: 207-741-5760 **Support: S**

CAMPUS

Type of school	Public
Environment	Town

STUDENTS

Undergrad enrollment	6,384
% male/female	44/56
% from out of state	9

FINANCIAL FACTS

Annual in-state tuition	$3,784
Annual out-of-state tuition	$6,604
Room and board	$9,488

GENERAL ADMISSIONS INFO

Application fee	$20
Regular application deadline	Open

ACADEMICS

Student/faculty ratio	17:1
% students returning for sophomore year	57

Programs/Services for Students with Learning Differences

The Disability Services program at Southern Maine is designed to offer academic support to students through various individualized services. Students can get professional faculty tutoring in their most difficult courses; learn about their specific learning style; improve concentration and memory; study more efficiently for tests; learn how to better manage their time; learn the basic skills that are the foundation of their specific technology; and use a computer toward processing, Internet research, and other computer applications

Admissions

All students must meet the same admission criteria. There is no special admissions process for students with learning disabilities. All students have access to disability services, including those with a diagnosed learning disability. Some students are required to take the Accuplacer tests for placement into many courses. Students are exempt from the English portion with an SAT Critical Reading score of 450+ or ACT of 21. Students are exempt from the Math portion of Accuplacer with SAT 490 Math or ACT 21.

Additional Information

TRIO Student Support Services are available to eligible students. As a TRIO SSS participant, students receive one-on-one support from their own dedicated Success Coach. Each semester, students regularly meet with their TRIO Coach to: develop your college success plan; set academic and other goals; address any challenges; and provide students with the skills and resources needed to succeed. TRIO Coaches collaborate with SMCC staff and faculty advisors to ensure student success. Students must complete a separate application for TRIO SSS.

ADMISSIONS INFO FOR STUDENTS WITH LEARNING DIFFERENCES

Phone: 207-741-5923 • Email: disabilityservices@smccme.edu

SAT/ACT required: No
Interview required: No
Essay required: No
Additional application required: No
Documentation submitted to: Counseling and Disability Services

Special Ed. HS course work accepted: Yes
Separate application required for Programs/Services: No
Documentation required for:
LD: Psychoeducational evaluation
ADHD: Psychoeducational evaluation
ASD: Psychoeducational evaluation

Southern Maine Community College

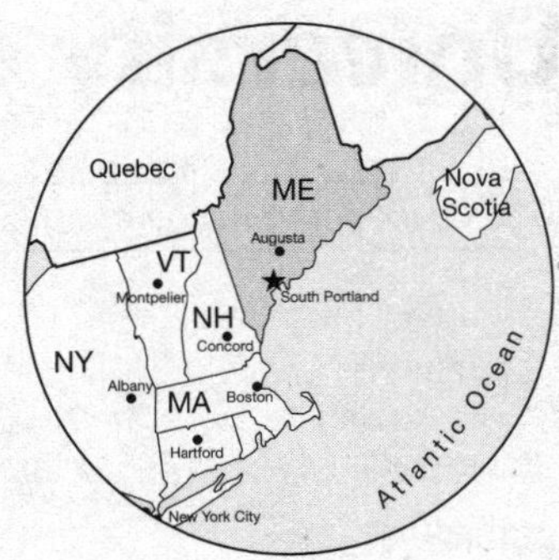

General Admissions

Other factors include: state residency. High school diploma is required and a GED is accepted.

Accommodations or Services

Accommodations are decided upon an individual basis after a thorough review of appropriate, current documentation. The accommodations requests must be supported through the documentation provided and must be logically linked to the current impact of the condition on academic functioning.

Financial Aid

Students should submit: FAFSA. *Need-based scholarships/grants offered:* College/university scholarship or grant aid from institutional funds; Federal Pell; Private scholarships; State scholarships/grants. *Loan aid offered:* Direct PLUS loans; Direct Subsidized Stafford Loans; Direct Unsubsidized Stafford Loans.

Campus Life

Activities: Choral groups; Drama/theater; Literary magazine; Student government; Student newspaper. **Organizations:** 1 honor society.

ACCOMMODATIONS

Allowed in exams:	
Calculators	Yes
Dictionary	Yes
Computer	Yes
Spell-checker	Yes
Extended test time	Yes
Scribe	Yes
Proctors	Yes
Oral exams	Yes
Note-takers	Yes
Support services for students with:	
LD	Yes
ADHD	Yes
ASD	Yes
Distraction-reduced environment	Yes
Recording of lecture allowed	Yes
Reading technology	Yes
Audio books	No
Other assistive technology	Yes
Priority registration	No
Added costs of services:	
For LD	No
For ADHD	No
For ASD	No
LD specialists	No
ADHD & ASD coaching	No
ASD specialists	No
Professional tutors	No
Peer tutors	Yes
Max. hours/week for services	Varies
How professors are notified of student approved accommodations	Student and Disability Office

COLLEGE GRADUATION REQUIREMENTS

Course waivers allowed	Yes
In what courses: Student will work with institution to determine course waivers	
Course substitutions allowed	Yes
In what courses: Student will work with institution to determine course substitutions	

Maine

University of Maine

5713 Chadbourne Hall, Orono, ME 04469-5713 • Admissions: 207-581-1561 • Fax: 207-581-1213 **Support: S**

CAMPUS

Type of school	Public
Environment	Village

STUDENTS

Undergrad enrollment	8,832
% male/female	54/46
% from out of state	33
% frosh live on campus	89

FINANCIAL FACTS

Annual in-state tuition	$9,000
Annual out-of-state tuition	$29,310
Room and board	$10,966
Required fees	$2,438

GENERAL ADMISSIONS INFO

Application fee	$0
Regular application deadline	2/1
Nonfall registration	Yes

Admission may be deferred.

Range SAT EBRW	530–630
Range SAT Math	520–620
Range ACT Composite	21–27

ACADEMICS

Student/faculty ratio	15:1
% students returning for sophomore year	74

Most classes have 10–19 students.

Programs/Services for Students with Learning Differences

The primary goal of the University of Maine Student Accessibility Services (SAS) is to create educational access for students with disabilities at UMaine by providing or coordinating disability accommodations, giving information about the University and available resources to students and families, and educating the campus community. Some of the services provided or coordinated for students with disabilities include testing accommodations, note takers, ordering alternate format texts, classroom relocation, advice on disability issues, and housing-related accommodations. The staff of SAS promotes self-determination and personal responsibility for students with disabilities by educating them about their rights and responsibilities so that they can make informed choices in order to meet or exceed the standards expected of all students at the University of Maine.

Admissions

All students applying to the University of Maine have the same admissions process for accessing disability services. Student must submit documents to the office of SAS. Courses required include: 4 years English, 3–4 years math (at least algebra I and II, and geometry; some programs require advanced mathematics), 2–3 years lab science (some programs require specific science courses), 2 years foreign language, and 2–3 years social studies. Computer science and fine arts courses are strongly recommended.

Additional Information

DSS does not provide tutoring as an accommodation. Students are referred to the UMaine Tutoring Center. This program provides small group tutoring for 100 and 200 level courses. These tutorials are study skills based and do not reteach the classroom material. Currently, students are only assigned a tutor for one class each semester. Students who want one on one tutoring have the option to recruit and hire tutors on their own. Additionally, UMaine has both a Math Lab and a Writing Center that are open to all students. They are staffed by upper-class students in math and English. The Math Lab is open on a drop-in basis whereas the Writing Center is available both for drop-ins and by appointment.

ADMISSIONS INFO FOR STUDENTS WITH LEARNING DIFFERENCES

Phone: 207-581-2319 • Fax: 207-581-9420 • Email: shenry@maine.edu

SAT/ACT required: Yes (Test optional through 2022)
Interview required: No
Essay required: Yes
Additional application required: No
Documentation submitted to: Student Accessibility Services

Special Ed. HS course work accepted: No
Separate application required for Programs/Services: No
Documentation required for:
LD: Psychoeducational evaluation
ADHD: Psychoeducational evaluation
ASD: Psychoeducational evaluation

University of Maine

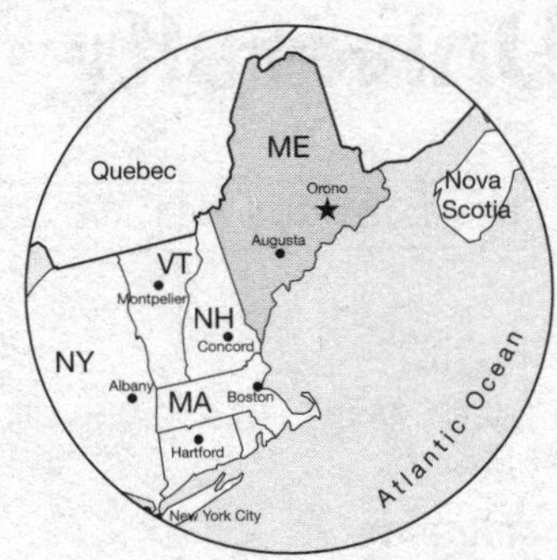

General Admissions

Very important factors include: rigor of secondary school record, class rank, academic GPA, standardized test scores. *Important factors include:* application essay, recommendation(s). *Other factors include:* interview, extracurricular activities, talent/ability, character/personal qualities, volunteer work, work experience. High school diploma is required and a GED is accepted. *Academic units required:* 4 English, 3 math, 2 science, 2 science labs, 2 social studies, 4 academic electives. *Academic units recommended:* 4 English, 4 math, 4 science, 3 science labs, 2 foreign language, 2 social studies, 1 history, 4 academic electives.

Accommodations or Services

Accommodations are decided upon an individual basis after a thorough review of appropriate, current documentation. The accommodations requests must be supported through the documentation provided and must be logically linked to the current impact of the condition on academic functioning.

Financial Aid

Students should submit: FAFSA. *Need-based scholarships/grants offered:* College/university scholarship or grant aid from institutional funds; Federal Pell; Private scholarships; SEOG; State scholarships/grants. *Loan aid offered:* Direct PLUS loans; Direct Subsidized Stafford Loans; Direct Unsubsidized Stafford Loans. Federal Work-Study Program available. Institutional employment available.

Campus Life

Activities: Campus Ministries; Choral groups; Concert band; Dance; Drama/theater; International Student Organization; Jazz band; Literary magazine; Marching band; Model UN; Music ensembles; Musical theater; Opera; Pep band; Radio station; Student government; Student newspaper; Student-run film society; Symphony orchestra. **Organizations:** 168 registered organizations, 11 honor societies, 8 religious organizations, 17 fraternities, 9 sororities. **Athletics (Intercollegiate):** *Men:* baseball, basketball, cross-country, diving, football, ice hockey, soccer, swimming, track/field (outdoor), track/field (indoor). *Women:* basketball, cross-country, diving, field hockey, ice hockey, soccer, softball, swimming, track/field (outdoor), track/field (indoor), volleyball.

ACCOMMODATIONS

Allowed in exams:	
Calculators	Yes
Dictionary	No
Computer	Yes
Spell-checker	Yes
Extended test time	Yes
Scribe	Yes
Proctors	Yes
Oral exams	Yes
Note-takers	Yes
Support services for students with:	
LD	Yes
ADHD	Yes
ASD	Yes
Distraction-reduced environment	Yes
Recording of lecture allowed	Yes
Reading technology	Yes
Audio books	Yes
Other assistive technology	Yes
Priority registration	No
Added costs of services:	
For LD	No
For ADHD	No
For ASD	No
LD specialists	No
ADHD & ASD coaching	No
ASD specialists	No
Professional tutors	No
Peer tutors	Yes
Max. hours/week for services	Varies
How professors are notified of student approved accommodations	Student

COLLEGE GRADUATION REQUIREMENTS

Course waivers allowed	No
Course substitutions allowed	Yes
In what courses: Case-by-case basis	

University of New England

11 Hills Beach Road, Biddeford, ME 04005-9599 • Admissions: 207-602-2847 • Fax: 207-602-5900 **Support: S**

CAMPUS

Type of school	Private (nonprofit)
Environment	Town

STUDENTS

Undergrad enrollment	4,275
% male/female	31/69
% from out of state	73
% frosh live on campus	95

FINANCIAL FACTS

Annual in-state tuition	$37,390
Room and board	$14,410
Required fees	$1,360

GENERAL ADMISSIONS INFO

Application fee	$40
Regular application deadline	2/15
Nonfall registration	Yes

Admission may be deferred.

Range SAT EBRW	520–620
Range SAT Math	520–610
Range ACT Composite	21–27

ACADEMICS

Student/faculty ratio	13:1
% students returning for sophomore year	82

Most classes have 10–19 students.

Programs/Services for Students with Learning Differences

The Student Access Center works to ensure that the University promotes respect for individual differences and that no person who meets the academic and technical standards needed for admission and continued enrollment at UNE is denied benefits or subjected to discrimination due to a disability. Toward this end, and in conjunction with federal and state laws, the University provides reasonable accommodations for qualified students.

Admissions

The University of New England is test optional. UNE has an Early Assurance Program designed to offer talented undergraduate students with well-defined career aspirations the opportunity to receive automatic acceptance into certain UNE graduate programs when admitted as a first-year. Qualified applicants declare their intent to pursue a graduate or professional degree by selecting their intended Early Assurance designation on the Common Application or on UNE's online application. If a student is accepted to UNE and also accepted into the Early Assurance program, they may then move directly into their chosen UNE graduate program, as long as the progression requirements are met during their undergraduate studies.

Additional Information

The Student Academic Success Center (SASC) provides a comprehensive array of academic support services including placement testing, courses, workshops, and tutoring. The mission of the Student Academic Success Center is to assist students to become independent learners so that they are able to meet the University's academic standards and attain their personal educational goals. In the Student Academic Success Center, professional staff members help students develop and maintain the skills they need to meet the challenges of undergraduate and graduate study. This is accomplished through individual consultations, workshops, and classroom presentations. The SASC Learning Specialist's time is spent working with students to assess progress and effectiveness in implementing practices designed to enable success. SASC provides a staff of peer, graduate, and professional tutors to support a wide selection of undergraduate courses. Students have access to assistive technology, including smart pens for note taking assistance.

ADMISSIONS INFO FOR STUDENTS WITH LEARNING DIFFERENCES

Phone: 207-602-2815 • Fax: 207-602-5971 • Email: hpatterson@une.edu

SAT/ACT required: No
Interview required: No
Essay required: Yes
Additional application required: No
Documentation submitted to: Student Access Center
Special Ed. HS course work accepted: Yes
Separate application required for Programs/Services: No
Documentation required for:
LD: Psychoeducational evaluation
ADHD: Psychoeducational evaluation
ASD: Psychoeducational evaluation

University of New England

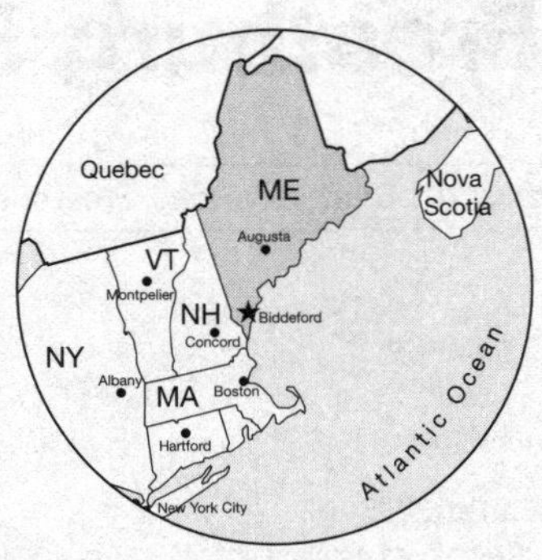

General Admissions

Very important factors include: rigor of secondary school record, academic GPA. *Important factors include:* class rank. *Other factors include:* application essay, standardized test scores, recommendation(s), extracurricular activities, talent/ability, character/personal qualities, alumni/ae relation, geographical residence, volunteer work, work experience. High school diploma is required and a GED is accepted. *Academic units required:* 4 English, 3 math, 3 science, 2 science labs, 2 social studies, 2 history. *Academic units recommended:* 4 math, 4 science, 3 science labs, 2 foreign language, 4 social studies, 4 history, 4 academic electives.

Accommodations or Services

Accommodations are decided upon an individual basis after a thorough review of appropriate, current documentation. The accommodations requests must be supported through the documentation provided and must be logically linked to the current impact of the condition on academic functioning.

Financial Aid

Students should submit: FAFSA. *Need-based scholarships/grants offered:* College/university scholarship or grant aid from institutional funds; Federal Pell; Private scholarships; SEOG; State scholarships/grants. *Loan aid offered:* Direct PLUS loans; Direct Subsidized Stafford Loans; Direct Unsubsidized Stafford Loans. Federal Work-Study Program available. Institutional employment available.

Campus Life

Activities: Campus Ministries; Dance; Drama/theater; International Student Organization; Jazz band; Literary magazine; Music ensembles; Musical theater; Pep band; Student government; Student newspaper; Yearbook. **Organizations:** 70 registered organizations, 3 honor societies, 6 religious organizations. **Athletics (Intercollegiate):** *Men:* basketball, cross-country, golf, lacrosse, soccer. *Women:* basketball, cross-country, field hockey, golf, lacrosse, soccer, softball, swimming, volleyball.

ACCOMMODATIONS

Allowed in exams:	
Calculators	Yes
Dictionary	Yes
Computer	Yes
Spell-checker	Yes
Extended test time	Yes
Scribe	Yes
Proctors	Yes
Oral exams	No
Note-takers	Yes
Support services for students with:	
LD	Yes
ADHD	Yes
ASD	Yes
Distraction-reduced environment	Yes
Recording of lecture allowed	Yes
Reading technology	Yes
Audio books	Yes
Other assistive technology	Yes
Priority registration	Yes
Added costs of services:	
For LD	No
For ADHD	No
For ASD	No
LD specialists	No
ADHD & ASD coaching	No
ASD specialists	No
Professional tutors	No
Peer tutors	No
Max. hours/week for services	Varies
How professors are notified of student approved accommodations	Student

COLLEGE GRADUATION REQUIREMENTS

Course waivers allowed	No
Course substitutions allowed	No

Frostburg State University

FSU, 101 Braddock Road, Frostburg, MD 21532 • Admissions: 301-687-4201 • Fax: 301-687-7074 **Support: S**

CAMPUS

Type of school	Public
Environment	Village

STUDENTS

Undergrad enrollment	4,638
% male/female	48/52
% from out of state	9
% frosh live on campus	97

FINANCIAL FACTS

Annual in-state tuition	$6,834
Annual out-of-state tuition	$21,320
Room and board	$10,574
Required fees	$2,766

GENERAL ADMISSIONS INFO

Application fee	$45
Nonfall registration	Yes
Range SAT EBRW	470–570
Range SAT Math	460–550
Range ACT Composite	17–23

ACADEMICS

Student/faculty ratio	16:1
% students returning for sophomore year	77

Most classes have 10–19 students.

Programs/Services for Students with Learning Differences

Frostburg State University provides comprehensive support services for students with disabilities to assist them in achieving their potential. To be eligible for the services, admitted students must provide recent and appropriate documentation relating to their disability. Some of the services provided are extended time for testing, note takers, advocacy, electronic texts, priority registration, readers and scribes, and assistive technology. The goal of the program is to provide appropriate support services to enhance learning and to strive for student self-advocacy and understanding of and independence in their learning styles.

Admissions

There is no special admission procedure for students with learning disabilities. All students must complete the mainstream program in high school and meet all of the requirements for the university and the state. There is a Student Support Services/Disabled Student Services information form that must be completed by students to enroll in these programs. Admission to FSU is determined by the Admissions Office, which assesses an applicant's likelihood of success in a regular college program with support service assistance.

Additional Information

Student Support Services (SSS), TRIO program, is an educational opportunity project which helps students with disabilities achieve their academic and personal goals. SSS acts as an advocate for qualified students, plans, and coordinates services and provides programs which help students develop the academic, interpersonal and social skills they need for success at Frostburg.

ADMISSIONS INFO FOR STUDENTS WITH LEARNING DIFFERENCES

Phone: 301-687-4483 • Email: hhveith@frostburg.edu

SAT/ACT required: Yes (Test optional for 2021)
Interview required: No
Essay required: No
Additional application required: No
Documentation submitted to: Student Support Services

Special Ed. HS course work accepted: No
Separate application required for Programs/Services: No
Documentation required for:
LD: Psychoeducational evaluation
ADHD: Psychoeducational evaluation
ASD: Psychoeducational evaluation

Frostburg State University

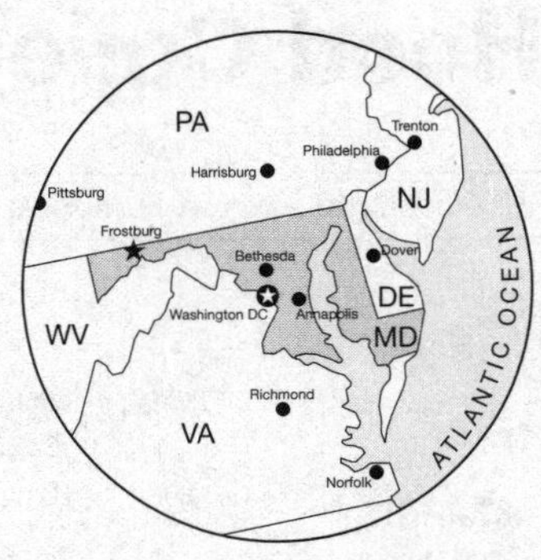

General Admissions

Very important factors include: rigor of secondary school record, academic GPA, standardized test scores. *Important factors include:* recommendation(s), interview. *Other factors include:* extracurricular activities, talent/ability, character/personal qualities, alumni/ae relation. High school diploma is required and a GED is accepted. *Academic units required:* 4 English, 3 math, 3 science, 2 science labs, 2 foreign language, 3 history.

Accommodations or Services

Accommodations are decided upon an individual basis after a thorough review of appropriate, current documentation. The accommodations requests must be supported through the documentation provided and must be logically linked to the current impact of the condition on academic functioning.

Financial Aid

Students should submit: FAFSA. Applicants will be notified of awards on a rolling basis beginning 2/1. *Need-based scholarships/grants offered:* College/university scholarship or grant aid from institutional funds; Federal Pell; Private scholarships; SEOG; State scholarships/grants. *Loan aid offered:* Direct PLUS loans; Direct Subsidized Stafford Loans; Direct Unsubsidized Stafford Loans. Federal Work-Study Program available. Institutional employment available.

Campus Life

Activities: Campus Ministries; Choral groups; Dance; Drama/theater; International Student Organization; Jazz band; Literary magazine; Marching band; Model UN; Music ensembles; Pep band; Radio station; Student government; Student newspaper; Television station; Yearbook. **Organizations:** 95 registered organizations, 18 honor societies, 6 religious organizations, 9 fraternities, 6 sororities. **Athletics (Intercollegiate):** *Men:* baseball, basketball, cross-country, diving, football, golf, soccer, swimming, tennis, track/field (outdoor), track/field (indoor). *Women:* basketball, cross-country, diving, field hockey, lacrosse, soccer, softball, swimming, tennis, track/field (outdoor), track/field (indoor), volleyball.

ACCOMMODATIONS

Allowed in exams:	
Calculators	Yes
Dictionary	Yes
Computer	Yes
Spell-checker	Yes
Extended test time	Yes
Scribe	Yes
Proctors	Yes
Oral exams	Yes
Note-takers	Yes
Support services for students with:	
LD	Yes
ADHD	Yes
ASD	Yes
Distraction-reduced environment	Yes
Recording of lecture allowed	Yes
Reading technology	Yes
Audio books	Yes
Other assistive technology	Yes
Priority registration	Yes
Added costs of services:	
For LD	No
For ADHD	No
For ASD	No
LD specialists	No
ADHD & ASD coaching	Yes
ASD specialists	No
Professional tutors	Yes
Peer tutors	Yes
Max. hours/week for services	Varies
How professors are notified of student approved accommodations	Student

COLLEGE GRADUATION REQUIREMENTS

Course waivers allowed	No
Course substitutions allowed	Yes

In what courses: Student will work with institution to determine course substitutions

Maryland

Hood College

401 Rosemont Avenue, Frederick, MD 21701 • Admissions: 301-696-3400 • Fax: 301-696-3819 **Support: S**

CAMPUS

Type of school	Private (nonprofit)
Environment	Town

STUDENTS

Undergrad enrollment	1,126
% male/female	37/63
% from out of state	26
% frosh live on campus	82

FINANCIAL FACTS

Annual tuition	$41,680
Room and board	$13,010
Required fees	$620

GENERAL ADMISSIONS INFO

Application fee	$0
Regular application deadline	3/1
Nonfall registration	Yes
Range SAT EBRW	510–610
Range SAT Math	490–600
Range ACT Composite	19–24

ACADEMICS

Student/faculty ratio	10:1
% students returning for sophomore year	75

Most classes have 10–19 students.

Programs/Services for Students with Learning Differences

Hood College is a community that welcomes all those who seek to succeed. Hood presents a diverse face, one that embraces students with disabilities and celebrates the fact that differences come in many varieties. An assessment for learning disabilities should be current (i.e., within the last five years for learning disabilities, the last six months for psychiatric disabilities, and the last three years for all other disabilities, including AD/HD. This does not apply to physical or sensory disabilities of a permanent or unchanging nature), and it should suggest the specific accommodations deemed necessary to participate in the academic programs at Hood College.

Admissions

General admission criteria include a minimum 2.75 GPA in core academic courses including 4 years English, 3 years math, 3 years science, 3 years social studies, and 2 years of a foreign language (substitutions are allowed in foreign language if appropriate). The average GPA of admitted students is a 3.5. Hood College's admission process is highly individualized. In addition to the application, essay, transcript, and letter of recommendation, students are strongly encouraged to submit their resume, additional writing sample, online portfolio, or schedule an interview.

Additional Information

The Office of Accessibility Services (OAS) provides accommodations, education, consultation, and advocacy support for qualified students with disabilities at Hood College. Hood College provides academic accommodations for students to ensure equal access. These accommodations are provided with guidance from Sections 504 and 508 of the Rehabilitation Act of 1973, the Americans with Disabilities Act of 1990 (ADA), as amended by the ADA Amendments Act of 2008, the Fair Housing Act, and other applicable federal and state regulations that prohibit discrimination on the basis of disability.

ADMISSIONS INFO FOR STUDENTS WITH LEARNING DIFFERENCES

Phone: 301-696-3421 • Email: gmuer@hood.edu

SAT/ACT required: No
Interview required: No
Essay required: Yes
Additional application required: No
Documentation submitted to: Office of Accessibility Services

Special Ed. HS course work accepted: Yes
Separate application required for Programs/Services: Yes
Documentation required for:
LD: Psychoeducational evaluation
ADHD: Psychoeducational evaluation
ASD: Psychoeducational evaluation

Hood College

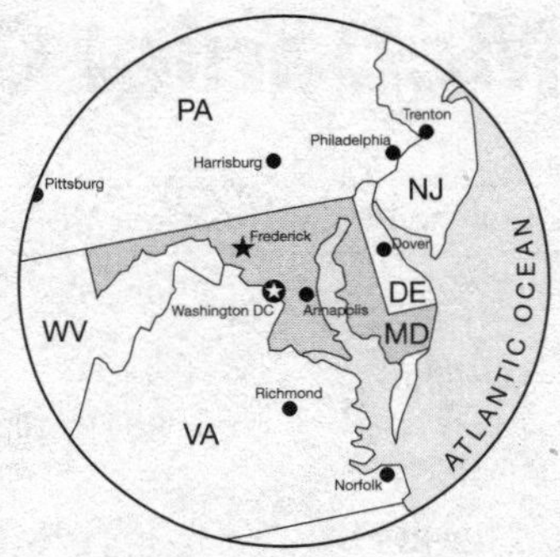

General Admissions

Very important factors include: rigor of secondary school record, academic GPA. *Important factors include:* application essay, interview, extracurricular activities, character/personal qualities, alumni/ae relation. *Other factors include:* class rank, standardized test scores, recommendation(s), talent/ability, volunteer work, work experience, level of applicant's interest. High school diploma is required and a GED is accepted. *Academic units required:* 4 English, 3 math, 3 science, 2 science labs, 2 foreign language, 3 social studies, 1 academic elective. *Academic units recommended:* 4 English, 4 math, 3 science, 2 science labs, 3 foreign language, 3 social studies, 2 academic electives.

Accommodations or Services

Accommodations are decided upon an individual basis after a thorough review of appropriate, current documentation. The accommodations requests must be supported through the documentation provided and must be logically linked to the current impact of the condition on academic functioning.

Financial Aid

Students should submit: FAFSA. Applicants will be notified of awards on a rolling basis beginning 12/1. *Need-based scholarships/grants offered:* College/university scholarship or grant aid from institutional funds; Federal Pell; Private scholarships; SEOG; State scholarships/grants. *Loan aid offered:* Direct PLUS loans; Direct Subsidized Stafford Loans; Direct Unsubsidized Stafford Loans. Federal Work-Study Program available. Institutional employment available.

Campus Life

Activities: Campus Ministries; Choral groups; Dance; Drama/theater; International Student Organization; Jazz band; Literary magazine; Model UN; Music ensembles; Musical theater; Radio station; Student government; Student newspaper; Television station. **Organizations:** 50 registered organizations, 16 honor societies, 8 religious organizations. **Athletics (Intercollegiate):** *Men:* basketball, cross-country, golf, lacrosse, soccer, swimming, tennis, track/field (outdoor). *Women:* basketball, cross-country, field hockey, golf, lacrosse, soccer, softball, swimming, tennis, track/field (outdoor), volleyball.

ACCOMMODATIONS

Allowed in exams:	
Calculators	Yes
Dictionary	Yes
Computer	Yes
Spell-checker	Yes
Extended test time	Yes
Scribe	Yes
Proctors	Yes
Oral exams	Yes
Note-takers	Yes
Support services for students with:	
LD	Yes
ADHD	Yes
ASD	Yes
Distraction-reduced environment	Yes
Recording of lecture allowed	Yes
Reading technology	Yes
Audio books	No
Other assistive technology	No
Priority registration	No
Added costs of services:	
For LD	No
For ADHD	No
For ASD	No
LD specialists	No
ADHD & ASD coaching	No
ASD specialists	No
Professional tutors	No
Peer tutors	Yes
Max. hours/week for services	Varies
How professors are notified of student approved accommodations	Student and Disability Office

COLLEGE GRADUATION REQUIREMENTS

Course waivers allowed	No
Course substitutions allowed	Yes

In what courses: Student will work directly with institution to determine course substitutions

Maryland

McDaniel College

2 College Hill, Westminster, MD 21157 • Admissions: 410-857-2230 **Support: CS**

CAMPUS

Type of school	Private (nonprofit)
Environment	Town

STUDENTS

Undergrad enrollment	1,680
% male/female	49/51
% from out of state	32
% frosh live on campus	95

FINANCIAL FACTS

Annual tuition	$45,876
Room and board	$12,246
Required fees	$975

GENERAL ADMISSIONS INFO

Application fee	$0
Regular application deadline	7/15
Nonfall registration	Yes

Admission may be deferred.

Range SAT EBRW	500–600
Range SAT Math	488–590
Range ACT Composite	19–25

ACADEMICS

Student/faculty ratio	12:1
% students returning for sophomore year	77

Most classes have 10–19 students.

Programs/Services for Students with Learning Differences

Student Academic Support Services (SASS) ensures that all students with documented disabilities receive appropriate academic accommodations. The Mentorship Advantage Program (MAP) offers interactive workshops on topics such as socialization, organization, assistive technology, time management, resume writing, and interviewing. The Providing Academic Support for Success (PASS) program offers students the opportunity to learn alongside their peers and is supported by Graduate Assistants three evenings a week. The Academic Skills Program (ASP), a fee based opportunity ($3,150 annual fee), provides students with weekly consultation with an Academic Counselor, academic skills tutoring with a SASS graduate assistant, use of supervised study/computer lab, learning style, and priority registration.

Admissions

The admission process is the same for all applicants. General admission criteria include a minimum 2.8 GPA in core academic courses including 4 years English, 3 years math, 3 years science, 3 years social studies, and 3 years of a foreign language (substitutions are allowed in foreign language if appropriate). Students with a 3.5 GPA do not have to submit an ACT or SAT. The average ACT is 21 and the average SAT is 1000. Any documentation for LD or ADHD should be sent to ASC to be used after a student is admitted and enrolled.

Additional Information

McDaniel "Step Ahead" is an optional 5-day summer bridge opportunity offered for first-year students with disabilities. Intensive workshops, team building activities and field trips are available for students to familiarize themselves with the resources, staff and peers who comprise and utilize McDaniel's SASS. Each participant is matched with a peer mentor. Some typical accommodations offered by the SASS include: note takers, alternative testing arrangements such as extra time, books on tape, computer with speech input, separate testing room, tape recorder, foreign language substitution, and math substitution.

ADMISSIONS INFO FOR STUDENTS WITH LEARNING DIFFERENCES

Phone: 410-857-2504 • Fax: 410-386-4617 • Email: sass@mcdaniel.edu

SAT/ACT required: No
Interview required: No
Essay required: Yes
Additional application required: No
Documentation submitted to: Academic Skills Center

Special Ed. HS course work accepted: No
Separate application required for Programs/Services: No
Documentation required for:
LD: Psychoeducational evaluation
ADHD: Psychoeducational evaluation
ASD: Psychoeducational evaluation

McDaniel College

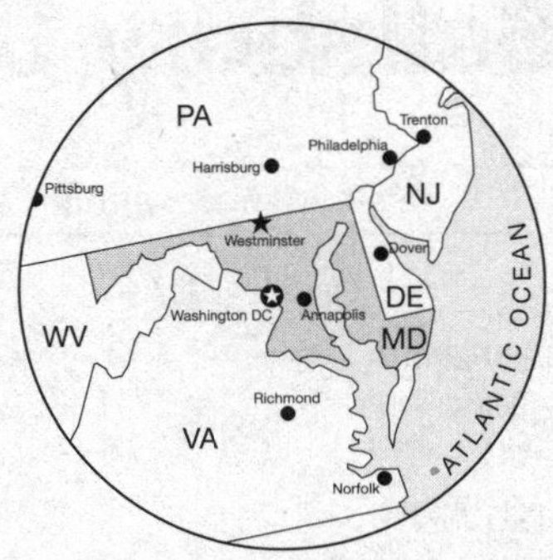

General Admissions

Very important factors include: rigor of secondary school record, academic GPA. *Important factors include:* application essay, recommendation(s). *Other factors include:* class rank, interview, extracurricular activities, talent/ability, character/personal qualities, first generation, alumni/ae relation, volunteer work, work experience. High school diploma is required and a GED is accepted. *Academic units required:* 4 English, 3 math, 3 science, 3 science labs, 3 foreign language, 3 social studies. *Academic units recommended:* 4 English, 4 math, 4 science, 4 foreign language, 3 social studies.

Accommodations or Services

Accommodations are decided upon an individual basis after a thorough review of appropriate, current documentation. The accommodations requests must be supported through the documentation provided and must be logically linked to the current impact of the condition on academic functioning.

Financial Aid

Students should submit: CSS/Financial Aid PROFILE; FAFSA; Noncustodial PROFILE; State aid form. Applicants will be notified of awards on or about 4/1. *Need-based scholarships/grants offered:* College/university scholarship or grant aid from institutional funds; Federal Pell; Private scholarships; SEOG; State scholarships/grants. *Loan aid offered:* Direct PLUS loans; Direct Subsidized Stafford Loans; Direct Unsubsidized Stafford Loans. Federal Work-Study Program available. Institutional employment available.

Campus Life

Activities: Campus Ministries; Choral groups; Concert band; Dance; Drama/theater; International Student Organization; Jazz band; Literary magazine; Model UN; Music ensembles; Musical theater; Pep band; Radio station; Student government; Student newspaper; Student-run film society; Television station; Yearbook. **Organizations:** 90 registered organizations, 28 honor societies, 3 religious organizations, 5 fraternities, 6 sororities. **Athletics (Intercollegiate):** *Men:* baseball, basketball, cross-country, football, golf, lacrosse, soccer, swimming, tennis, track/field (outdoor), track/field (indoor), volleyball, wrestling. *Women:* basketball, cross-country, field hockey, golf, lacrosse, soccer, softball, swimming, tennis, track/field (outdoor), track/field (indoor), volleyball.

ACCOMMODATIONS

Allowed in exams:	
Calculators	Yes
Dictionary	Yes
Computer	Yes
Spell-checker	Yes
Extended test time	Yes
Scribe	Yes
Proctors	Yes
Oral exams	Yes
Note-takers	Yes
Support services for students with:	
LD	Yes
ADHD	Yes
ASD	Yes
Distraction-reduced environment	Yes
Recording of lecture allowed	Yes
Reading technology	Yes
Audio books	Yes
Other assistive technology	Yes
Priority registration	Yes
Added costs of services:	
For LD	Yes
For ADHD	Yes
For ASD	Yes
LD specialists	Yes
ADHD & ASD coaching	No
ASD specialists	No
Professional tutors	Yes
Peer tutors	Yes
Max. hours/week for services	Unlimited
How professors are notified of student approved accommodations	Student

COLLEGE GRADUATION REQUIREMENTS

Course waivers allowed	Yes
In what courses: Foreign Language	
Course substitutions allowed	Yes
In what courses: Foreign Language	

Maryland

Salisbury University

1101 Camden Avenue, Salisbury, MD 21801 • Admissions: 410-543-6161 • Fax: 410-546-6016 **Support: S**

CAMPUS

Type of school	Public
Environment	Town

STUDENTS

Undergrad enrollment	7,686
% male/female	44/56
% from out of state	13
% frosh live on campus	88

FINANCIAL FACTS

Annual in-state tuition	$7,488
Annual out-of-state tuition	$18,190
Room and board	$12,476
Required fees	$2,780

GENERAL ADMISSIONS INFO

Application fee	$50
Regular application deadline	1/15
Nonfall registration	Yes

Admission may be deferred.

Range SAT EBRW	570–640
Range SAT Math	550–640
Range ACT Composite	19–23

ACADEMICS

Student/faculty ratio	15:1
% students returning for sophomore year	81

Most classes have 20–29 students.

Programs/Services for Students with Learning Differences

The Disability Resource Center (DRC) aims to inform, educate and support students with disabilities in ways which allow them to achieve their educational, career, and life goals on the basis of their personal skills, abilities, interests, and values. Equity in access, rights of privacy, and the integrity of academic programs, policies, and practices are emphasized by the DRC.

Admissions

Applicants must submit the completed application for admission, official high school transcripts, essay, and letter(s) of recommendation. Standardized SAT or ACT test scores are required for applicants with a weighted grade point average of 3.5 or less on a 4.0 scale. Applicants choosing to exclude standardized test scores should provide evidence of individual achievements and/or experiences which would not be evident from a review of the official high school transcripts. Leadership qualities, community service, artistic talent, athletic talent, and diversity of background, including cultural, experiential, and geographic, are additional factors used in the holistic review of each applicant.

Additional Information

Once the DRC evaluates the submitted disability documentation, confirm that documentation meets the necessary criteria for receiving reasonable accommodations, and receives the student's completed intake form, the student should contact the DRC in order to schedule an Intake Conference. At this meeting, the student and DRC staff member will discuss the student's accommodation plans, strategies for a successful academic career, and campus resources and services, among other topics. All documentation submitted should contain a comprehensive written evaluation, prepared by a qualified professional, and should include a statement of diagnosis of a disability, a description of that disability, and a description of the nature and severity of the student's disability.

ADMISSIONS INFO FOR STUDENTS WITH LEARNING DIFFERENCES

Phone: 410-548-6083 • Fax: 410-543-6088 • Email: disabilitysupport@salisbury.edu

SAT/ACT required: No
Interview required: No
Essay required: Yes
Additional application required: Yes
Documentation submitted to: Disability Resource Center

Special Ed. HS course work accepted: No
Separate application required for Programs/Services: Yes
Documentation required for:
LD: Psychoeducational evaluation
ADHD: Psychoeducational evaluation
ASD: Psychoeducational evaluation

Salisbury University

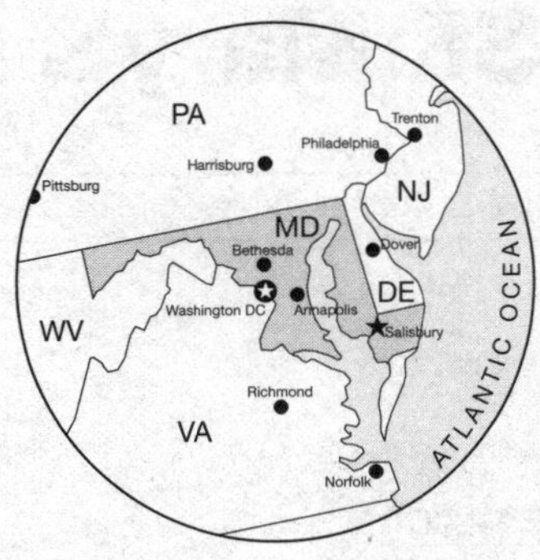

General Admissions

Very important factors include: rigor of secondary school record, academic GPA. *Important factors include:* class rank, standardized test scores. *Other factors include:* application essay, recommendation(s), extracurricular activities, talent/ability, character/personal qualities, first generation, alumni/ae relation, geographical residence, state residency, racial/ethnic status, volunteer work, work experience, level of applicant's interest. High school diploma is required and a GED is accepted. *Academic units required:* 4 English, 4 math, 3 science, 2 science labs, 2 foreign language, 3 social studies. *Academic units recommended:* 4 English, 4 math, 4 science, 3 science labs, 3 foreign language, 3 social studies, 3 academic electives.

Accommodations or Services

Accommodations are decided upon an individual basis after a thorough review of appropriate, current documentation. The accommodations requests must be supported through the documentation provided and must be logically linked to the current impact of the condition on academic functioning.

Financial Aid

Students should submit: FAFSA. *Need-based scholarships/grants offered:* College/university scholarship or grant aid from institutional funds; Federal Pell; Private scholarships; SEOG; State scholarships/grants. *Loan aid offered:* Direct PLUS loans; Direct Subsidized Stafford Loans; Direct Unsubsidized Stafford Loans. Federal Work-Study Program available. Institutional employment available.

Campus Life

Activities: Campus Ministries; Choral groups; Concert band; Dance; Drama/theater; International Student Organization; Jazz band; Literary magazine; Model UN; Music ensembles; Musical theater; Opera; Pep band; Radio station; Student government; Student newspaper; Student-run film society; Symphony orchestra; Television station. **Organizations:** 121 registered organizations, 30 honor societies, 9 religious organizations, 11 fraternities, 7 sororities. **Athletics (Intercollegiate):** *Men:* baseball, basketball, cross-country, football, lacrosse, soccer, swimming, tennis, track/field (outdoor). *Women:* basketball, cross-country, field hockey, lacrosse, soccer, softball, swimming, tennis, track/field (outdoor), volleyball.

ACCOMMODATIONS

Allowed in exams:	
Calculators	Yes
Dictionary	Yes
Computer	Yes
Spell-checker	Yes
Extended test time	Yes
Scribe	Yes
Proctors	Yes
Oral exams	Yes
Note-takers	Yes
Support services for students with:	
LD	Yes
ADHD	Yes
ASD	Yes
Distraction-reduced environment	Yes
Recording of lecture allowed	Yes
Reading technology	Yes
Audio books	Yes
Other assistive technology	Yes
Priority registration	Yes
Added costs of services:	
For LD	No
For ADHD	No
For ASD	No
LD specialists	No
ADHD & ASD coaching	Yes
ASD specialists	No
Professional tutors	No
Peer tutors	Yes
Max. hours/week for services	Varies
How professors are notified of student approved accommodations	Student

COLLEGE GRADUATION REQUIREMENTS

Course waivers allowed	Yes
In what courses: Case-by-case basis.	
Course substitutions allowed	Yes
In what courses: Case-by-case basis.	

Maryland

St. Mary's College of Maryland

47645 College Drive, St. Mary's City, MD 20686-3001 • Admissions: 240-895-5000 • Fax: 240-895-5001 **Support: S**

CAMPUS	
Type of school	Public
Environment	Rural
STUDENTS	
Undergrad enrollment	1,491
% male/female	41/59
% from out of state	5
% frosh live on campus	91
FINANCIAL FACTS	
Annual in-state tuition	$12,116
Annual out-of-state tuition	$28,192
Room and board	$13,595
Required fees	$3,008
GENERAL ADMISSIONS INFO	
Application fee	$50
Regular application deadline	1/5
Nonfall registration	Yes
Admission may be deferred.	
Range SAT EBRW	540–650
Range SAT Math	520–640
Range ACT Composite	21–29
ACADEMICS	
Student/faculty ratio	9:1
% students returning for sophomore year	85
Most classes have 10–19 students.	

Programs/Services for Students with Learning Differences

The Office of Accessibility Services uses an interactive process including a student self-disclosure survey, an intake interview designed to learn more about their experiences and barriers. Supporting documentation is used to give additional context; because documentation presents a barrier, in some situations, SMCM will support accommodations through self-disclosure and intake only. OAS will provide services to students with various differences, including specific learning, neurodevelopmental, medical, mental health, low incidence, and temporary disabilities

Admissions

The admissions criteria is the same for all students. Students who prefer to disclose a learning disability can contact their Admissions Counselor. Each Admissions Counselor has the opportunity to bring students to an Admissions Committee that has flexibility in interpreting scores.

Additional Information

Students have access to assistive technology including, speech-to-text software, FM systems, special chairs, special tech tables, video taping, Skype, JAWS, and Irlen Method. Most reasonable requests made by licensed clinical specialists or students during accommodation discussion have been reported as successful in high school.

ADMISSIONS INFO FOR STUDENTS WITH LEARNING DIFFERENCES

Phone: 240-895-4917 • Email: adasupport@smcm.edu

SAT/ACT required: No
Interview required: No
Essay required: Yes
Additional application required: No
Documentation submitted to: Office of Accessibility Services

Special Ed. HS course work accepted: Yes
Separate application required for Programs/Services: No
Documentation required for:
LD: Psychoeducational evaluation
ADHD: Psychoeducational evaluation
ASD: Psychoeducational evaluation

St. Mary's College of Maryland

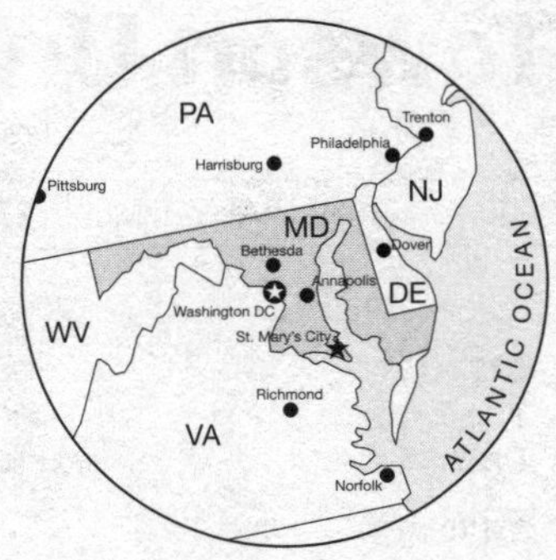

General Admissions

Very important factors include: rigor of secondary school record, academic GPA, application essay, standardized test scores, recommendation(s). *Important factors include:* class rank, extracurricular activities, talent/ability, character/personal qualities. *Other factors include:* interview, first generation, alumni/ae relation, geographical residence, state residency, racial/ethnic status, work experience, level of applicant's interest. High school diploma is required and a GED is accepted. *Academic units required:* 4 English, 3 math, 3 science, 2 science labs, 2 social studies, 1 history. *Academic units recommended:* 4 math, 4 foreign language, 3 social studies.

Accommodations or Services

Accommodations are decided upon an individual basis after a thorough review of appropriate, current documentation. The accommodations requests must be supported through the documentation provided and must be logically linked to the current impact of the condition on academic functioning.

Financial Aid

Students should submit: FAFSA. Applicants will be notified of awards on a rolling basis beginning 12/1. *Need-based scholarships/grants offered:* College/university scholarship or grant aid from institutional funds; Federal Pell; Private scholarships; SEOG; State scholarships/grants. *Loan aid offered:* Direct PLUS loans; Direct Subsidized Stafford Loans; Direct Unsubsidized Stafford Loans. Federal Work-Study Program available. Institutional employment available.

Campus Life

Activities: Campus Ministries; Choral groups; Dance; Drama/theater; Jazz band; Literary magazine; Music ensembles; Radio station; Student government; Student newspaper; Symphony orchestra. **Organizations:** 99 registered organizations, 12 honor societies, 4 religious organizations. **Athletics (Intercollegiate):** *Men:* baseball, basketball, cross-country, lacrosse, sailing, soccer, swimming, tennis. *Women:* basketball, cross-country, field hockey, lacrosse, sailing, soccer, swimming, tennis, volleyball.

ACCOMMODATIONS

Allowed in exams:	
Calculators	Yes
Dictionary	Yes
Computer	Yes
Spell-checker	Yes
Extended test time	Yes
Scribe	Yes
Proctors	Yes
Oral exams	Yes
Note-takers	Yes
Support services for students with:	
LD	Yes
ADHD	Yes
ASD	Yes
Distraction-reduced environment	Yes
Recording of lecture allowed	Yes
Reading technology	Yes
Audio books	Yes
Other assistive technology	Yes
Priority registration	Yes
Added costs of services:	
For LD	No
For ADHD	No
For ASD	No
LD specialists	No
ADHD & ASD coaching	Yes
ASD specialists	No
Professional tutors	No
Peer tutors	Yes
Max. hours/week for services	Varies
How professors are notified of student approved accommodations	Student and Disability Office

COLLEGE GRADUATION REQUIREMENTS

Course waivers allowed	No
Course substitutions allowed	Yes

In what courses: Student will work with institution to determine substitutions

Maryland

Towson University

8000 York Road, Towson, MD 21252-0001 • Admissions: 410-704-2113 • Fax: 410-704-3030 **Support: CS**

CAMPUS

Type of school	Public
Environment	Metropolis

STUDENTS

Undergrad enrollment	19,619
% male/female	41/59
% from out of state	11
% frosh live on campus	84

FINANCIAL FACTS

Annual in-state tuition	$9,440
Annual out-of-state tuition	$23,208
Room and board	$23,464
Required fees	$3,236

GENERAL ADMISSIONS INFO

Application fee	$45
Regular application deadline	1/15
Nonfall registration	Yes

Admission may be deferred.

Range SAT EBRW	540–620
Range SAT Math	520–600
Range ACT Composite	20–25

ACADEMICS

Student/faculty ratio	16:1
% students returning for sophomore year	86

Most classes have 20–29 students.

Programs/Services for Students with Learning Differences

Accessibility & Disability Services (ADS) at Towson University provides leadership in promoting equal access to educational opportunities to students with disabilities. ADS collaborates with students, faculty, and staff to identify and remove barriers to foster an all-inclusive campus. The office provides individual services and facilitates accommodations to students with disabilities, and offers institution-wide guidance, consultation, and training on disability-related topics. ADS provides accommodations and services to students with various disabilities and some temporary impairments that substantially limit one or more major life activities. Eligibility for accommodations is established through a variety of information sources, including the student's self-report, observation and interaction with the student, previous accommodations received and the particular accommodations requested, the unique characteristics of a course or program, as well as documentation from external sources, such as psychologists, educational professionals, and health care providers.

Admissions

The admissions criteria is the same for all students. Students who prefer to disclose a learning disability begin by working through their Admissions Counselor. Each Admissions Counselor has the opportunity to bring students to an Admissions Committee that has flexibility in interpreting scores. Upon admission to Towson, students must submit an application along with documentation of disability to ADS. An ADS Specialist will contact the student to schedule a meeting for a personal interview to discuss disability, reasonable accommodations, and support services.

Additional Information

The College Orientation & Life Activities Program (COLA) is a fee-based program designed for TU students with autism who would like support in adjusting to college life. The COLA program focuses on supporting students in addressing challenges, developing strengths, exploring opportunities, and planning for success as a TU student. Support is tailored to each COLA student's self-determined goals in independent living, social experiences, academic success, and work exploration. Two levels of services are offered: COLA Regular, $4,000/semester and COLA Lite, $2,200/semester.

ADMISSIONS INFO FOR STUDENTS WITH LEARNING DIFFERENCES

Phone: 410-704-2638 • Fax: 410-704-4247 • Email: swillemin@towson.edu

SAT/ACT required: No
Interview required: No
Essay required: Yes
Additional application required: Yes
Documentation submitted to: Disability Support Services

Special Ed. HS course work accepted: Yes
Separate application required for Programs/Services: Yes
Documentation required for:
LD: Psychoeducational evaluation
ADHD: Psychoeducational evaluation
ASD: Psychoeducational evaluation

Towson University

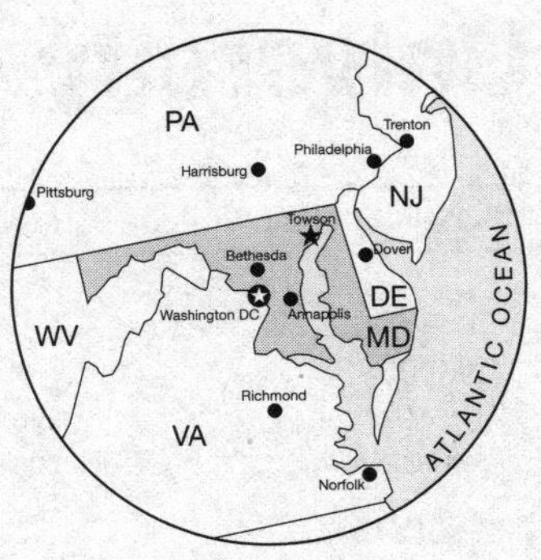

General Admissions

Very important factors include: academic GPA, standardized test scores. *Important factors include:* rigor of secondary school record. *Other factors include:* class rank, application essay, recommendation(s), talent/ability, first generation. High school diploma is required and a GED is accepted. *Academic units required:* 4 English, 4 math, 3 science, 2 science labs, 2 foreign language, 3 social studies, 6 academic electives.

Accommodations or Services

Accommodations are decided upon an individual basis after a thorough review of appropriate, current documentation. The accommodations requests must be supported through the documentation provided and must be logically linked to the current impact of the condition on academic functioning.

Financial Aid

Students should submit: FAFSA; State aid form. *Need-based scholarships/grants offered:* College/university scholarship or grant aid from institutional funds; Federal Pell; Private scholarships; SEOG; State scholarships/grants. *Loan aid offered:* Direct PLUS loans; Direct Subsidized Stafford Loans; Direct Unsubsidized Stafford Loans. Federal Work-Study Program available. Institutional employment available.

Campus Life

Activities: Campus Ministries; Choral groups; Concert band; Dance; Drama/theater; International Student Organization; Jazz band; Literary magazine; Marching band; Model UN; Music ensembles; Musical theater; Opera; Pep band; Radio station; Student government; Student newspaper; Student-run film society; Symphony orchestra; Television station. **Organizations:** 323 registered organizations, 22 honor societies, 27 religious organizations, 25 fraternities, 17 sororities. **Athletics (Intercollegiate):** *Men:* baseball, basketball, cheerleading, cross-country, diving, football, golf, lacrosse, soccer, swimming, tennis. *Women:* basketball, cheerleading, cross-country, diving, field hockey, gymnastics, lacrosse, soccer, softball, swimming, tennis, track/field (outdoor), volleyball.

ACCOMMODATIONS

Allowed in exams:	
Calculators	Yes
Dictionary	No
Computer	Yes
Spell-checker	Yes
Extended test time	Yes
Scribe	Yes
Proctors	Yes
Oral exams	Yes
Note-takers	Yes
Support services for students with:	
LD	Yes
ADHD	Yes
ASD	Yes
Distraction-reduced environment	Yes
Recording of lecture allowed	Yes
Reading technology	Yes
Audio books	Yes
Other assistive technology	Yes
Priority registration	Yes
Added costs of services:	
For LD	No
For ADHD	No
For ASD	Not
LD specialists	Yes
ADHD & ASD coaching	Yes
ASD specialists	Yes
Professional tutors	Yes
Peer tutors	Yes
Max. hours/week for services	Unlimited
How professors are notified of student approved accommodations	Student

COLLEGE GRADUATION REQUIREMENTS

Course waivers allowed	No
Course substitutions allowed	Yes

In what courses: Student will work with institution to determine course substitutions

Maryland

University of Maryland, College Park

Mitchell Building, College Park, MD 20742-5235 • Admissions: 301-314-8385 • Fax: 301-314-9693 **Support: CS**

CAMPUS

Type of school	Public
Environment	Metropolis

STUDENTS

Undergrad enrollment	30,511
% male/female	52/48
% from out of state	23
% frosh live on campus	92

FINANCIAL FACTS

Annual in-state tuition	$8,824
Annual out-of-state tuition	$34,936
Room and board	$12,935
Required fees	$1,955

GENERAL ADMISSIONS INFO

Application fee	$75
Regular application deadline	1/2
Nonfall registration	Yes

Admission may be deferred.

Range SAT EBRW	630–720
Range SAT Math	650–760
Range ACT Composite	29–33

ACADEMICS

Student/faculty ratio	18:1
% students returning for sophomore year	95

Most classes have 10–19 students.

Programs/Services for Students with Learning Differences

The goal of the Disability Support Services is to coordinate services that ensure individuals with disabilities equal access to University programs. This goal is accomplished by: providing and coordinating individually tailored direct services to students, faculty and staff, and campus visitors who have disabilities; providing consultation to university staff regarding the Adaptive Technology needs of students and staff who have disabilities; and providing support and information to students and staff, which promotes the development of advocacy and negotiation skills.

Admissions

Applicants must use the Coalition Application for Access and Affordability and Success to apply. Academic merit is assessed on the basis of each applicant's achievements and potential in a broad range of academic categories, as influenced by the opportunities and challenges faced by the applicant. These categories include: Educational Performance, Potential for College Success, Potential to Promote Beneficial Educational Outcomes and to Contribute to Campus and Community Life, and Students' Persistence and Commitment to Educational Success. The review process considers more than 26 factors.

Additional Information

Learning Assistance Service (LAS) is the academic support unit of the University Counseling Center. LAS exists to help students achieve their academic goals by providing a range of services. LAS also provides Academic Success Workshop series to help students become successful, active learners. Workshops focus on helping students manage their time and improve their approach to studying and learning at UM. LAS offers learning strategy courses to help develop college-level learning strategies.

ADMISSIONS INFO FOR STUDENTS WITH LEARNING DIFFERENCES

Phone: 301-314-7682 • Fax: 301-405-0813 • Email: jahutch@umd.edu

SAT/ACT required: Yes (Test optional for 2021)
Interview required: No
Essay required: Yes
Additional application required: No
Documentation submitted to: Disability Support Services

Special Ed. HS course work accepted: Yes
Separate application required for Programs/Services: No
Documentation required for:
LD: Psychoeducational evaluation
ADHD: Psychoeducational evaluation
ASD: Psychoeducational evaluation

University of Maryland, College Park

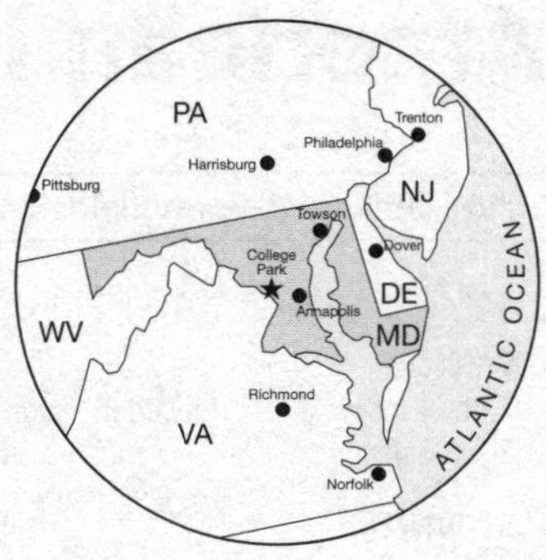

General Admissions

Very important factors include: rigor of secondary school record, academic GPA, standardized test scores. *Important factors include:* class rank, application essay, recommendation(s), talent/ability, first generation, state residency. *Other factors include:* extracurricular activities, character/personal qualities, alumni/ae relation, geographical residence, racial/ethnic status, volunteer work, work experience. High school diploma is required and a GED is accepted. *Academic units required:* 4 English, 4 math, 3 science, 2 science labs, 2 foreign language, 3 social studies. *Academic units recommended:* 4 English, 4 math, 3 science, 2 science labs, 2 foreign language, 3 social studies.

Accommodations or Services

Accommodations are decided upon an individual basis after a thorough review of appropriate, current documentation. The accommodations requests must be supported through the documentation provided and must be logically linked to the current impact of the condition on academic functioning.

Financial Aid

Students should submit: FAFSA. *Need-based scholarships/grants offered:* College/university scholarship or grant aid from institutional funds; Federal Pell; Private scholarships; SEOG; State scholarships/grants. *Loan aid offered:* Direct PLUS loans; Direct Subsidized Stafford Loans; Direct Unsubsidized Stafford Loans. Federal Work-Study Program available. Institutional employment available.

Campus Life

Activities: Campus Ministries; Choral groups; Concert band; Dance; Drama/theater; International Student Organization; Jazz band; Literary magazine; Marching band; Model UN; Music ensembles; Musical theater; Opera; Pep band; Radio station; Student government; Student newspaper; Student-run film society; Symphony orchestra; Television station; Yearbook. **Organizations:** 724 registered organizations, 49 honor societies, 52 religious organizations, 32 fraternities, 24 sororities. **Athletics (Intercollegiate):** *Men:* baseball, basketball, cross-country, football, golf, lacrosse, soccer, swimming, tennis, track/field (outdoor), track/field (indoor), wrestling. *Women:* basketball, cheerleading, cross-country, field hockey, golf, gymnastics, lacrosse, soccer, softball, swimming, tennis, track/field (outdoor), track/field (indoor), volleyball, water polo.

ACCOMMODATIONS

Allowed in exams:	
Calculators	Yes
Dictionary	Yes
Computer	Yes
Spell-checker	Yes
Extended test time	Yes
Scribe	Yes
Proctors	Yes
Oral exams	Yes
Note-takers	Yes
Support services for students with:	
LD	Yes
ADHD	Yes
ASD	Yes
Distraction-reduced environment	Yes
Recording of lecture allowed	Yes
Reading technology	Yes
Audio books	Yes
Other assistive technology	Yes
Priority registration	Yes
Added costs of services:	
For LD	No
For ADHD	No
For ASD	No
LD specialists	Yes
ADHD & ASD coaching	Yes
ASD specialists	No
Professional tutors	No
Peer tutors	Yes
Max. hours/week for services	Varies
How professors are notified of student approved accommodations	Student

COLLEGE GRADUATION REQUIREMENTS

Course waivers allowed	No
Course substitutions allowed	Yes
In what courses: Student works with institution to determine course substitutions	

American International College

1000 State Street, Springfield, MA 01109-3184 • Admissions: 413-205-3201 • Fax: 413-205-3051 **Support: SP**

CAMPUS

Type of school	Private (nonprofit)
Environment	City

STUDENTS

Undergrad enrollment	1,341
% male/female	38/62
% from out of state	35

FINANCIAL FACTS

Annual tuition	$38,220
Room and board	$14,840
Required fees	$60

GENERAL ADMISSIONS INFO

Application fee	$0
Regular application deadline	Rolling
Nonfall registration	Yes

Admission may be deferred.

ACADEMICS

Student/faculty ratio	18:1
% students returning for sophomore year	69

Most classes have 20–29 students.

Programs/Services for Students with Learning Differences

Supportive Learning Services (SLS) has been an integral part of the American International College campus since 1977. AIC values their students' individual strengths above all things and truly believes they can achieve their dreams if given the right tools. This fee-based program provides the required tools, along with ongoing support and encouragement in the form of regular, individualized professional tutoring and academic coaching, group study sessions facilitated by professional educators, and skill-based workshops. SLS tutors work closely with college faculty and staff using a proactive advising model to support students. Assistance is available to each student in the program for the duration of his or her college career.

Admissions

In addition to the standard AIC application, applicants to SLSP need to provide a recently administered Wechsler Adult Intelligence Scale, relevant diagnostic material, any supportive assistance they've received in the past and ACT or SAT scores. AIC evaluates high school coursework, grades, and standardized test scores. However, they are equally interested in student activities, personal statements, and letters of recommendations.

Additional Information

Their expert staff reviews each student's documentation and gets to know them through a personal interview. Tutors then work creatively to find the best way to help them improve vital academic skills like: goal setting, organization and planning, note-taking, time management, and study skills, like volume reading and writing and Test taking. In addition to helping build academic skills, SLS staff can help students develop and practice self-advocacy skills and explore technologies that support academic success. Collegiate Disability Services (CDS), housed with SLS, ensures that all qualified students with disabilities receive accommodations and services that support an accessible, equitable, and inclusive learning and living environment at American International College. CDS staff works closely with Academics and Student Life to reduce or eliminate any disadvantages that may occur as a result of an individual's disability.

ADMISSIONS INFO FOR STUDENTS WITH LEARNING DIFFERENCES

Phone: 413-205-3426 • Fax: 413-205-3908 • Email: accessibility.Services@aic.edu

SAT/ACT required: No
Interview required: Yes
Essay required: Yes
Additional application required: No
Documentation submitted to: Supportive Learning Services Program

Special Ed. HS course work accepted: No
Separate application required for Programs/Services: No
Documentation required for:
LD: Psychoeducational evaluation
ADHD: Psychoeducational evaluation
ASD: Psychoeducational evaluation

American International College

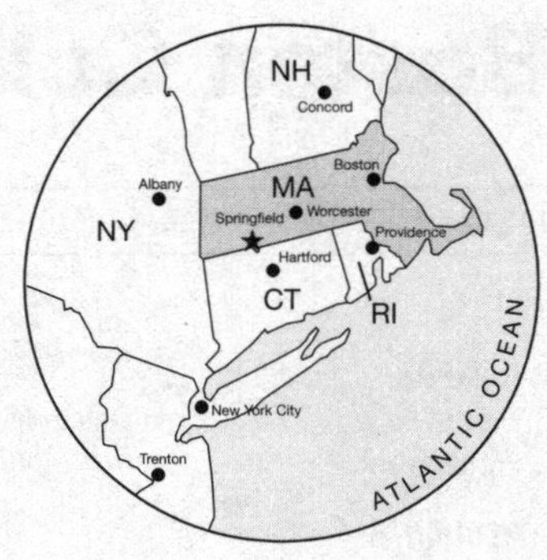

General Admissions

Very important factors include: academic GPA, standardized test scores. *Important factors include:* rigor of secondary school record. *Other factors include:* application essay, recommendation(s), extracurricular activities, talent/ability, character/personal qualities, first generation, alumni/ae relation, volunteer work, work experience, level of applicant's interest. High school diploma is required and a GED is accepted. *Academic units recommended:* 4 English, 3 math, 2 science, 2 science labs, 1 foreign language, 2 social studies, 4 academic electives.

Accommodations or Services

Accommodations are decided upon an individual basis after a thorough review of appropriate, current documentation. The accommodations requests must be supported through the documentation provided and must be logically linked to the current impact of the condition on academic functioning.

Financial Aid

Students should submit: FAFSA. Applicants will be notified of awards on a rolling basis beginning 3/15. *Need-based scholarships/grants offered:* College/university scholarship or grant aid from institutional funds; Federal Nursing Scholarships; Federal Pell; Private scholarships; SEOG; State scholarships/grants. *Loan aid offered:* Direct PLUS loans; Direct Subsidized Stafford Loans; Direct Unsubsidized Stafford Loans. Federal Work-Study Program available. Institutional employment available.

Campus Life

Activities: Campus Ministries; Dance; Drama/theater; International Student Organization; Literary magazine; Model UN; Pep band; Student government; Student newspaper; Yearbook. **Organizations:** 45 registered organizations, 5 honor societies, 1 religious organization, 3 fraternities, 3 sororities. **Athletics (Intercollegiate):** *Men:* baseball, basketball, cheerleading, cross-country, football, golf, ice hockey, lacrosse, soccer, tennis, track/field (outdoor), track/field (indoor), wrestling. *Women:* basketball, cheerleading, cross-country, field hockey, lacrosse, soccer, softball, tennis, track/field (outdoor), track/field (indoor), volleyball.

ACCOMMODATIONS

Allowed in exams:	
Calculators	Yes
Dictionary	No
Computer	Yes
Spell-checker	Yes
Extended test time	Yes
Scribe	Yes
Proctors	Yes
Oral exams	Yes
Note-takers	No
Support services for students with:	
LD	Yes
ADHD	Yes
ASD	Yes
Distraction-reduced environment	Yes
Recording of lecture allowed	Yes
Reading technology	Yes
Audio books	Yes
Other assistive technology	Yes
Priority registration	Yes
Added costs of services:	
For LD	Yes
For ADHD	Yes
For ASD	Yes
LD specialists	Yes
ADHD & ASD coaching	Yes
ASD specialists	No
Professional tutors	Yes
Peer tutors	No
Max. hours/week for services	5
How professors are notified of student approved accommodations	Student and Disability Office

COLLEGE GRADUATION REQUIREMENTS

Course waivers allowed	No
Course substitutions allowed	No

Boston College

140 Commonwealth Avenue, Chestnut Hill, MA 02467-3809 • Admissions: 617-552-3100 • Fax: 617-552-0798 **Support: CS**

CAMPUS

Type of school	Private (nonprofit)
Environment	City

STUDENTS

Undergrad enrollment	9,370
% male/female	47/53
% from out of state	73
% frosh live on campus	99

FINANCIAL FACTS

Annual tuition	$59,050
Room and board	$14,826
Required fees	$1,130

GENERAL ADMISSIONS INFO

Application fee	$80
Regular application deadline	1/1
Nonfall registration	Yes

Admission may be deferred.

Range SAT EBRW	660–730
Range SAT Math	680–770
Range ACT Composite	31–34

ACADEMICS

Student/faculty ratio	11:1
% students returning for sophomore year	95

Most classes have 10–19 students.

Programs/Services for Students with Learning Differences

The Connors Family Learning Center offers special services to students with learning disabilities and tutoring and skills workshops to all Boston College students. Students may request professional and peer tutoring through the center and receive access to additional support for documenting learning differences.

Admissions

All students are evaluated for admissions through general requirements. Admission is very competitive and the mid 50% SAT score is 1415–1520 and ACT 33–35. There is a required supplemental essay for all applicants and those students applying to the Human-Centered Engineering major have a specific essay prompt. Students who are requesting services must submit a registration form to the Disability Services Office and request an intake appointment by June 1st of the admissions year. For entry to the program through the CFLC, students must engage with this office directly.

Additional Information

Students are advised to inform their academic advisor about their disability. When possible, choose small, structured classes with professors who use multi-modal methods of instruction, provide a detailed syllabus, present information in an organized manner, and use various ways to evaluate student performance. Students should be knowledgeable about their disability and comfortable describing it to advocate effectively. Students are responsible for informing professors of needs early in the semester to obtain appropriate accommodations.

ADMISSIONS INFO FOR STUDENTS WITH LEARNING DIFFERENCES

Phone: 617-552-8055 • Fax: 617-552-6075 • Email: dugganka@bc.edu

SAT/ACT required: Yes (Test optional for 2021)
Interview required: No
Essay required: Yes
Additional application required: No
Documentation submitted to: The Connors Family Learning Center

Special Ed. HS course work accepted: Yes
Separate application required for Programs/Services: No
Documentation required for:
- **LD:** Psychoeducational evaluation
- **ADHD:** Psychoeducational evaluation
- **ASD:** Psychoeducational evaluation

Boston College

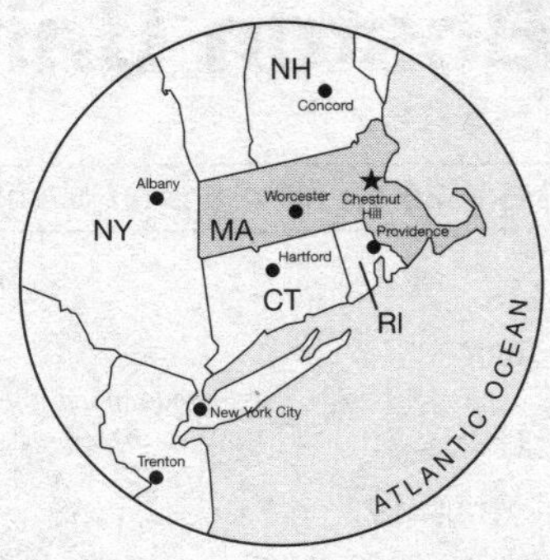

General Admissions

Very important factors include: rigor of secondary school record, academic GPA, standardized test scores. *Important factors include:* class rank, application essay, recommendation(s), extracurricular activities, talent/ability, character/personal qualities, alumni/ae relation, religious affiliation/commitment, volunteer work. *Other factors include:* first generation, racial/ethnic status, work experience. High school diploma is required and GED is accepted. *Academic units recommended:* 4 English, 4 math, 4 science, 4 science labs, 4 foreign language, 4 social studies, 4 history.

Accommodations or Services

Accommodations are decided upon an individual basis after a thorough review of appropriate, current documentation. The accommodations requests must be supported through the documentation provided and must be logically linked to the current impact of the condition on academic functioning.

Financial Aid

Students should submit: FAFSA; CSS/Financial Aid PROFILE; Noncustodial CSS. *Need-based scholarships/grants offered:* College/university scholarship or grant aid from institutional funds; Federal Pell; Private scholarships; SEOG; State scholarships/grants. *Loan aid offered:* Direct PLUS loans; Direct Subsidized Stafford Loans; Direct Unsubsidized Stafford Loans. Federal Work-Study Program available. Institutional employment available.

Campus Life

Activities: Campus Ministries; Choral groups; Concert band; Dance; Drama/theater; International Student Organization; Jazz band; Literary magazine; Marching band; Music ensembles; Musical theater; Pep band; Radio station; Student government; Student newspaper; Student-run film society; Symphony orchestra; Television station; Yearbook. **Organizations:** 300 registered organizations, 12 honor societies, 14 religious organizations. **Athletics (Intercollegiate):** *Men:* baseball, basketball, cross-country, diving, fencing, football, golf, ice hockey, lacrosse, sailing, skiing (downhill/alpine), soccer, swimming, tennis, track/field (outdoor), track/field (indoor). *Women:* basketball, crew/rowing, cross-country, diving, fencing, field hockey, golf, ice hockey, lacrosse, sailing, skiing (downhill/alpine), soccer, softball, swimming, tennis, track/field (outdoor), track/field (indoor), volleyball.

ACCOMMODATIONS

Allowed in exams:	
Calculators	Yes
Dictionary	No
Computer	Yes
Spell-checker	Yes
Extended test time	Yes
Scribe	Yes
Proctors	Yes
Oral exams	Yes
Note-takers	Yes
Support services for students with:	
LD	No
ADHD	Yes
ASD	No
Distraction-reduced environment	Yes
Recording of lecture allowed	No
Reading technology	No
Audio books	Yes
Other assistive technology	No
Priority registration	Yes
Added costs of services:	
For LD	No
For ADHD	No
For ASD	No
LD specialists	Yes
ADHD & ASD coaching	No
ASD specialists	No
Professional tutors	No
Peer tutors	Yes
Max. hours/week for services	Varies
How professors are notified of student approved accommodations	Student and Disability Office

COLLEGE GRADUATION REQUIREMENTS

Course waivers allowed	No
Course substitutions allowed	Yes

In what courses: Student will work with institution to determine course substitutions

Massachusetts

Boston University

233 Bay State Road, Boston, MA 02215 • Admissions: 617-353-2300 **Support: CS**

CAMPUS

Type of school	Private (nonprofit)
Environment	Metropolis

STUDENTS

Undergrad enrollment	17,983
% male/female	41/59
% from out of state	72
% frosh live on campus	99

FINANCIAL FACTS

Annual tuition	$56,584
Room and board	$16,640
Required fees	$1,218

GENERAL ADMISSIONS INFO

Application fee	$80
Regular application deadline	1/4
Nonfall registration	Yes

Admission may be deferred.

Range SAT EBRW	650–720
Range SAT Math	690–790
Range ACT Composite	30–34

ACADEMICS

Student/faculty ratio	10:1
% students returning for sophomore year	94

Most classes have 10–19 students.

Programs/Services for Students with Learning Differences

The Office of Disability Services (ODS) is committed to assisting individuals with disabilities in achieving fulfillment and success in all aspects of university life. The primary objective of ODS is to foster academic excellence, personal responsibility, and leadership growth in students with disabilities through vigorous programming and the provision of reasonable accommodations. The university does not waive program requirements or permit substitutions for required courses. Several degree programs have foreign language or mathematics requirements.

Admissions

The Office of Admissions makes all admissions decisions on an individual basis. BU expects that students with disabilities, including those with LD, will meet the same competitive admissions criteria as their peers without disabilities. There are no special admissions procedures for applicants with LD. ODS does not participate in any way in the application process or in admissions decisions. Admission is based on the strength of a student's secondary school record.

Additional Information

The Office of Disability Services provides academic accommodations and services to students with learning and attentional disabilities. Disability Services arranges for academic accommodations for students with learning differences. Such accommodations may include the use of a note taker, course materials in alternative formats, reduced course load, or possibly examination-related accommodations such as extended time or a distraction-reduced environment. Students seeking accommodations must provide appropriate medical documentation of their disability so that Disability Services can determine the student's eligibility for accommodations; and if the student is eligible, determine appropriate academic accommodations.

ADMISSIONS INFO FOR STUDENTS WITH LEARNING DIFFERENCES

Phone: 617-353-3658 • Fax: 617-353-9646 • Email: access@bu.edu

SAT/ACT required: Yes (Test optional for 2021)
Interview required: No
Essay required: Yes
Additional application required: No
Documentation submitted to: Office of Disability Services

Special Ed. HS course work accepted: No
Separate application required for Programs/Services: No
Documentation required for:
LD: Psychoeducational evaluation
ADHD: Psychoeducational evaluation
ASD: Psychoeducational evaluation

Boston University

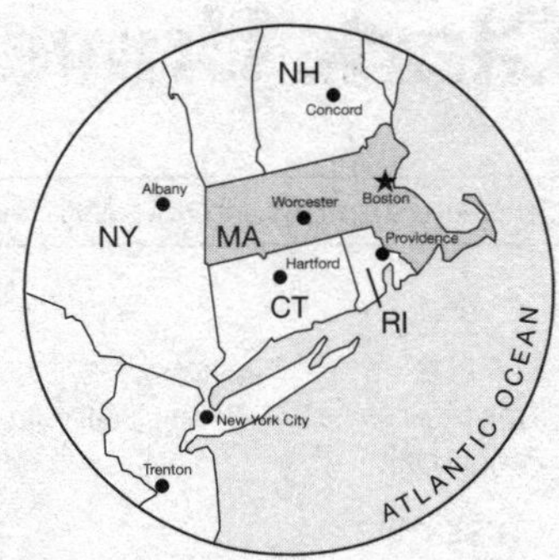

General Admissions

Very important factors include: rigor of secondary school record. *Important factors include:* class rank, academic GPA, application essay, standardized test scores, recommendation(s), extracurricular activities, character/ personal qualities, alumni/ae relation. *Other factors include:* first generation, geographical residence, state residency, racial/ethnic status, volunteer work, work experience. High school diploma is required and a GED is accepted. *Academic units required:* 4 English, 3 math, 3 science, 3 science labs, 2 foreign language, 3 social studies. *Academic units recommended:* 4 English, 4 math, 4 science, 4 science labs, 4 foreign language, 4 social studies.

Accommodations or Services

Accommodations are decided upon an individual basis after a thorough review of appropriate, current documentation. The accommodations requests must be supported through the documentation provided and must be logically linked to the current impact of the condition on academic functioning.

Financial Aid

Students should submit: FAFSA; CSS Financial Aid/PROFILE; Non-custodial (Divorced/Separated) Parent's Statement. *Need-based scholarships/grants offered:* College/university scholarship or grant aid from institutional funds; Federal Pell; Private scholarships; SEOG; State scholarships/grants. *Loan aid offered:* Direct PLUS loans; Direct Subsidized Stafford Loans; Direct Unsubsidized Stafford Loans. Federal Work-Study Program available. Institutional employment available.

Campus Life

Activities: Campus Ministries; Choral groups; Concert band; Dance; Drama/theater; International Student Organization; Jazz band; Literary magazine; Marching band; Model UN; Music ensembles; Musical theater; Opera; Pep band; Radio station; Student government; Student newspaper; Student-run film society; Symphony orchestra; Television station; Yearbook. **Organizations:** 450 registered organizations, 10 honor societies, 19 religious organizations, 8 fraternities, 13 sororities. **Athletics (Intercollegiate):** *Men:* basketball, crew/rowing, cross-country, diving, golf, ice hockey, soccer, swimming, tennis, track/field (outdoor), track/field (indoor), wrestling. *Women:* basketball, crew/rowing, cross-country, diving, field hockey, golf, ice hockey, lacrosse, soccer, softball, swimming, tennis, track/field (outdoor), track/field (indoor).

ACCOMMODATIONS

Allowed in exams:	
Calculators	No
Dictionary	No
Computer	Yes
Spell-checker	Yes
Extended test time	Yes
Scribe	Yes
Proctors	Yes
Oral exams	Yes
Note-takers	Yes
Support services for students with:	
LD	Yes
ADHD	Yes
ASD	Yes
Distraction-reduced environment	Yes
Recording of lecture allowed	Yes
Reading technology	No
Audio books	Yes
Other assistive technology	Yes
Priority registration	No
Added costs of services:	
For LD	Yes
For ADHD	Yes
For ASD	Yes
LD specialists	Yes
ADHD & ASD coaching	No
ASD specialists	No
Professional tutors	No
Peer tutors	No
Max. hours/week for services	Varies
How professors are notified of student approved accommodations	Student

COLLEGE GRADUATION REQUIREMENTS

Course waivers allowed	No
Course substitutions allowed	No

Clark University

950 Main Street, Worcester, MA 01610-1477 • Admissions: 508-793-7431 • Fax: 508-793-8821 **Support: CS**

CAMPUS

Type of school	Private (nonprofit)
Environment	City

STUDENTS

Undergrad enrollment	2,349
% male/female	39/61
% from out of state	61
% frosh live on campus	98

FINANCIAL FACTS

Annual tuition	$48,250
Room and board	$9,800
Required fees	$352

GENERAL ADMISSIONS INFO

Application fee	$60
Regular application deadline	1/15
Nonfall registration	Yes

Admission may be deferred.

Range SAT EBRW	600–60
Range SAT Math	580–690
Range ACT Composite	27–31

ACADEMICS

Student/faculty ratio	11:1
% students returning for sophomore year	86

Most classes have 10–19 students.

Programs/Services for Students with Learning Differences

Clark University is committed to providing equal access to otherwise qualified students with disabilities who are able to effectively function in a rigorous, campus-based, liberal-arts environment. University provides a support service for qualified students who register with Student Accessibility Services. The director of Student Accessibility Services works with students to coordinate academic accommodations and services on campus. Student Accessibility Services is located in the Goddard Library.

Admissions

Students with disabilities should self-advocate for their needs and self-identify during the admissions process. By doing so admissions can help applicants get connected with appropriate resources on campus.

Additional Information

An early orientation program 2 days prior to general orientation is designed to meet the needs of entering students with LD. This program is highly recommended as it provides intensive exposure to academic services on campus. Students take a reading comprehension and writing exam, and results are used to match students to the most appropriate academic program. Graduate students work with students on time management and organizational skills. Although note-takers are available, Special Services supplements this accommodation with the taping of lectures and highly recommends that students use a cassette recorder with a count.

ADMISSIONS INFO FOR STUDENTS WITH LEARNING DIFFERENCES

Phone: 508-798-4368 • Fax: 508-421-3700 • Email: tsawicki@clarku.edu

SAT/ACT required: No
Interview required: No
Essay required: Yes
Additional application required: No
Documentation submitted to: Student Accessibility Services

Special Ed. HS course work accepted: No
Separate application required for Programs/Services: No
Documentation required for:
- **LD:** Psychoeducational evaluation
- **ADHD:** Psychoeducational evaluation
- **ASD:** Psychoeducational evaluation

Clark University

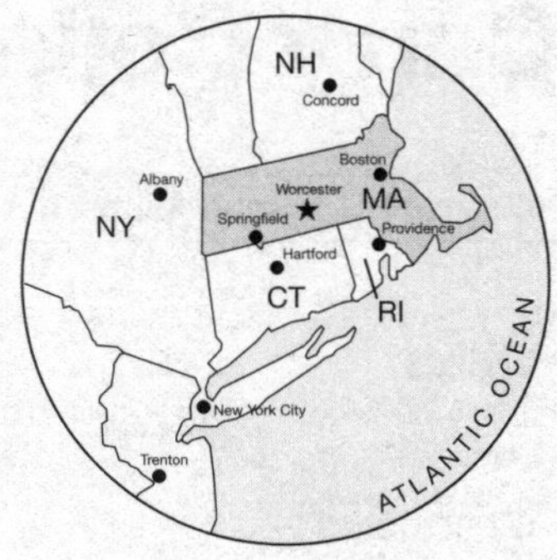

General Admissions

Very important factors include: rigor of secondary school record, academic GPA, recommendation(s). *Important factors include:* application essay, extracurricular activities, talent/ability, character/personal qualities, volunteer work. *Other factors include:* class rank, standardized test scores, interview, first generation, alumni/ae relation, geographical residence, racial/ethnic status, work experience, level of applicant's interest. High school diploma is required and a GED is accepted. *Academic units recommended:* 4 English, 3 math, 3 science, 2 science labs, 2 foreign language, 2 social studies, 2 history.

Accommodations or Services

Accommodations are decided upon an individual basis after a thorough review of appropriate, current documentation. The accommodations requests must be supported through the documentation provided and must be logically linked to the current impact of the condition on academic functioning.

Financial Aid

Students should submit: FAFSA; State aid form. Applicants will be notified of awards on a rolling basis beginning 12/1. *Need-based scholarships/grants offered:* College/university scholarship or grant aid from institutional funds; Federal Pell; SEOG; State scholarships/grants. *Loan aid offered:* Direct PLUS loans; Direct Subsidized Stafford Loans; Direct Unsubsidized Stafford Loans. Federal Work-Study Program available. Institutional employment available.

Campus Life

Activities: Campus Ministries; Choral groups; Concert band; Dance; Drama/theater; International Student Organization; Jazz band; Literary magazine; Marching band; Model UN; Music ensembles; Musical theater; Pep band; Radio station; Student government; Student newspaper; Student-run film society; Symphony orchestra; Television station; Yearbook. **Organizations:** 130 registered organizations, 10 honor societies, 7 religious organizations. **Athletics (Intercollegiate):** *Men:* baseball, basketball, crew/rowing, cross-country, diving, lacrosse, soccer, swimming, tennis. *Women:* basketball, crew/rowing, cross-country, diving, field hockey, soccer, softball, swimming, tennis, volleyball.

ACCOMMODATIONS

Allowed in exams:	
Calculators	Yes
Dictionary	Yes
Computer	Yes
Spell-checker	Yes
Extended test time	Yes
Scribe	Yes
Proctors	Yes
Oral exams	Yes
Note-takers	Yes
Support services for students with:	
LD	Yes
ADHD	Yes
ASD	Yes
Distraction-reduced environment	Yes
Recording of lecture allowed	Yes
Reading technology	Yes
Audio books	Yes
Other assistive technology	Yes
Priority registration	Yes
Added costs of services:	
For LD	No
For ADHD	No
For ASD	No
LD specialists	Yes
ADHD & ASD coaching	Yes
ASD specialists	Yes
Professional tutors	Yes
Peer tutors	No
Max. hours/week for services	Varies
How professors are notified of student approved accommodations	Student and Disability Office

COLLEGE GRADUATION REQUIREMENTS

Course waivers allowed — Yes

In what courses: All students must complete graduation requirements. These requirements are waived/replaced in only exceptional circumstances and all cases are considered on an individual basis based on documentation of disability.

Course substitutions allowed — Yes

In what courses: All students must complete graduation requirements. These requirements are waived/replaced in only exceptional circumstances and all cases are considered on an individual basis based on documentation of disability.

Curry College

1071 Blue Hill Avenue, Milton, MA 02186 • Admissions: 617-333-2210 • Fax: 617-333-2114 **Support: SP**

CAMPUS

Type of school	Private (nonprofit)
Environment	Village

STUDENTS

Undergrad enrollment	2,312
% male/female	41/59
% from out of state	32

FINANCIAL FACTS

Annual tuition	$40,080
Room and board	$16,085
Required fees	$1,975

GENERAL ADMISSIONS INFO

Application fee	$50
Nonfall registration	Yes

Admission may be deferred.

Range SAT EBRW	470–560
Range SAT Math	470–550
Range ACT Composite	19–23

ACADEMICS

Student/faculty ratio	11:1
% students returning for sophomore year	65

Most classes have 10–19 students.

Programs/Services for Students with Learning Differences

The Program for Advancement of Learning (PAL) at Curry College is a comprehensive individualized program for students with specific learning disabilities and ADHD. Students in PAL participate fully in Curry College course work and extracurricular activities. The goal of PAL is to facilitate students' understanding of their individual learning styles and help them achieve independence as learners. Students' empowerment is developed via intensive study of their own strengths, needs, and learning styles. The PAL 3-week summer program is strongly recommended for new students.

Admissions

Courses required include 4 English, 3 math, 2 science, 2 science lab, 1 social studies, 1 history, and 5 electives. For admission into PAL, applicants must submit a recent diagnostic evaluation describing a Specific Learning Disability and/or ADHD. In addition, an IEP or its equivalent is requested, if available. On-campus interviews are strongly recommended and may be required of some applicants. Space is limited for the program. Students applying to PAL are not required to submit SAT or ACT. Students may also respond to an "Optional" Supplement. Admission decisions are made jointly by PAL and the Office of Admissions.

Additional Information

PAL students must commit to the program for at least 1 year and have the option to continue with full or partial support beyond the first year. A 3-week 3-credit summer PAL summer session is strongly recommended. Students meet regularly with their own PAL instructor who is a learning specialist. The focus is on using the student's strengths to improve skills in areas such as listening, speaking, reading, writing, organization and time management, note-taking, and test-taking. Students also receive help with readings, papers, and assignments for classes as the basis for learning about their unique learning style. The specialist reviews diagnostic testing to help the student understand the profile of strengths and needs. Students earn three credits toward graduation for the first year. Skills classes, for credit, are offered through the Academic Enrichment Center in developmental reading, writing, and math. Another special offering is diagnostic testing, which is available through the Educational Diagnostic Center at PAL.

ADMISSIONS INFO FOR STUDENTS WITH LEARNING DIFFERENCES

Phone: 617-333-2250 • Fax: 617-333-2018 • Email: pal@curry.edu

SAT/ACT required: No
Interview required: No, but strongly recommended
Essay required: Yes
Additional application required: No
Documentation submitted to: Program for the Advancement of Learning (PAL)

Special Ed. HS course work accepted: Yes
Separate application required for Programs/Services: No
Documentation required for:
LD: Psychoeducational evaluation
ADHD: Psychoeducational evaluation
ASD: Psychoeducational evaluation

Curry College

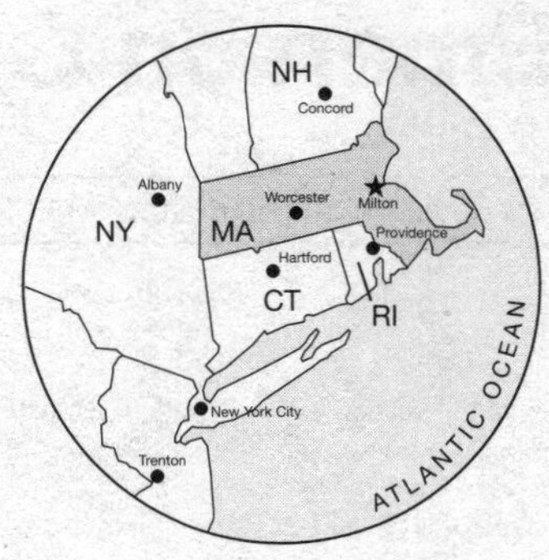

General Admissions

Very important factors include: rigor of secondary school record. *Important factors include:* academic GPA, application essay, standardized test scores, recommendation(s), interview, extracurricular activities, character/personal qualities. *Other factors include:* class rank, talent/ability, alumni/ae relation, volunteer work, work experience, level of applicant's interest. High school diploma is required and a GED is accepted. *Academic units required:* 4 English, 3 math. *Academic units recommended:* 2 science, 1 science lab, 2 foreign language, 2 social studies, 2 history.

Accommodations or Services

Accommodations are decided upon an individual basis after a thorough review of appropriate, current documentation. The accommodations requests must be supported through the documentation provided and must be logically linked to the current impact of the condition on academic functioning.

Financial Aid

Students should submit: FAFSA. *Need-based scholarships/grants offered:* College/university scholarship or grant aid from institutional funds; Federal Pell; Private scholarships; SEOG; State scholarships/grants. *Loan aid offered:* Direct PLUS loans; Direct Subsidized Stafford Loans; Direct Unsubsidized Stafford Loans.

Campus Life

Activities: Campus Ministries; Choral groups; Dance; Drama/theater; International Student Organization; Literary magazine; Music ensembles; Radio station; Student government; Student newspaper; Student-run film society; Television station; Yearbook. **Organizations:** 1 honor society, 2 religious organizations. **Athletics (Intercollegiate):** *Men:* baseball, basketball, cheerleading, football, ice hockey, lacrosse, soccer, tennis. *Women:* basketball, cheerleading, cross-country, lacrosse, soccer, softball, tennis.

ACCOMMODATIONS

Allowed in exams:	
Calculators	Yes
Dictionary	Yes
Computer	Yes
Spell-checker	Yes
Extended test time	Yes
Scribe	Yes
Proctors	Yes
Oral exams	Yes
Note-takers	Yes
Support services for students with:	
LD	Yes
ADHD	Yes
ASD	Yes
Distraction-reduced environment	Yes
Recording of lecture allowed	Yes
Reading technology	Yes
Audio books	Yes
Other assistive technology	Yes
Priority registration	No
Added costs of services:	
For LD	Yes
For ADHD	Yes
For ASD	Yes
LD specialists	Yes
ADHD & ASD coaching	No
ASD specialists	No
Professional tutors	Yes
Peer tutors	Yes
Max. hours/week for services	2.5
How professors are notified of student approved accommodations	Student

COLLEGE GRADUATION REQUIREMENTS

Course waivers allowed	No
Course substitutions allowed	Yes

In what courses: Student will work with institution to determine course substitutions

Emerson College

120 Boylston Street, Boston, MA 02116-4624 • Admissions: 617-824-8600 • Fax: 617-824-8609 **Support: CS**

CAMPUS	
Type of school	Private (nonprofit)
Environment	Metropolis
STUDENTS	
Undergrad enrollment	3,871
% male/female	39/61
% from out of state	70
% frosh live on campus	99
FINANCIAL FACTS	
Annual tuition	$48,560
Room and board	$18,400
Required fees	$872
GENERAL ADMISSIONS INFO	
Application fee	$65
Regular application deadline	1/15
Nonfall registration	Yes
Admission may be deferred.	
Range SAT EBRW	610–700
Range SAT Math	590–710
Range ACT Composite	27–31
ACADEMICS	
Student/faculty ratio	13:1
% students returning for sophomore year	89
Most classes have 10–19 students.	

Programs/Services for Students with Learning Differences

Emerson College is committed to providing equal access to its academic programs and social activities for all qualified students with disabilities. One of the primary goals of the Student Accessibility Services (SAS) is to foster a welcoming and accessible environment for students across the campus. Emerson's SAS offers academic accommodations and related services to qualified students with documented physical, medical, visual, hearing, learning, and psychological disabilities. Students with disabilities are not required to register with the SAS, but in order to receive accommodations they must self-identify to the SAS and request accommodations.

Admissions

Emerson College accepts the Common Application with a required Supplement. Admission is competitive. In choosing candidates for the entering class, we look for students who present academic promise in their secondary school record, recommendations, and writing competency, as well as personal qualities as seen in extracurricular activities, community involvement, and demonstrated leadership. There is no separate application for students with learning disabilities.

Additional Information

Emerson College offers academic support services, free of charge, to all undergraduate and graduate Emerson students. The College's Writing & Academic Resource Center (WARC) consists of three full-time professionals, graduate assistant writing tutors, and peer tutors. The professional staff provides academic counseling and support with study strategies and time management to individuals seeking academic support.

ADMISSIONS INFO FOR STUDENTS WITH LEARNING DIFFERENCES

Phone: 617-824-8500 • Fax: 617-824-8941 • Email: sas@emerson.edu

SAT/ACT required: No
Interview required: No
Essay required: Yes
Additional application required: No
Documentation submitted to: Student Accessibility Services

Special Ed. HS course work accepted: No
Separate application required for Programs/Services: No
Documentation required for:
LD: Psychoeducational evaluation
ADHD: Psychoeducational evaluation
ASD: Psychoeducational evaluation

Emerson College

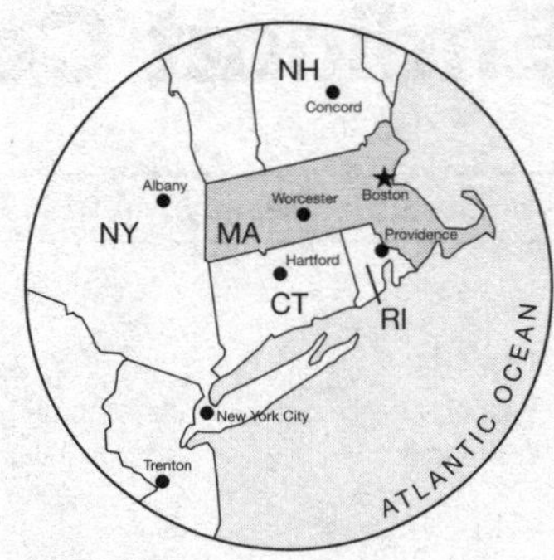

General Admissions

Very important factors include: academic GPA, application essay. *Important factors include:* rigor of secondary school record, class rank, recommendation(s), extracurricular activities, talent/ability, character/personal qualities. *Other factors include:* standardized test scores, first generation, alumni/ae relation, geographical residence, racial/ethnic status, volunteer work, work experience. High school diploma is required and a GED is accepted. *Academic units required:* 4 English, 3 math, 3 science, 3 foreign language, 3 social studies. *Academic units recommended:* 4 English, 3 math, 3 science, 3 foreign language, 3 social studies, 4 academic electives.

Accommodations or Services

Accommodations are decided upon an individual basis after a thorough review of appropriate, current documentation. The accommodations requests must be supported through the documentation provided and must be logically linked to the current impact of the condition on academic functioning.

Financial Aid

Students should submit: FAFSA. Applicants will be notified of awards on a rolling basis beginning 3/15. *Need-based scholarships/grants offered:* College/university scholarship or grant aid from institutional funds; Federal Pell; Private scholarships; SEOG; State scholarships/grants. *Loan aid offered:* Direct PLUS loans; Direct Subsidized Stafford Loans; Direct Unsubsidized Stafford Loans. Federal Work-Study Program available. Institutional employment available.

Campus Life

Activities: Campus Ministries; Choral groups; Dance; Drama/theater; International Student Organization; Literary magazine; Model UN; Music ensembles; Musical theater; Radio station; Student government; Student newspaper; Student-run film society; Television station; Yearbook. **Organizations:** 80 registered organizations. **Athletics (Intercollegiate):** *Men:* baseball, basketball, cross-country, golf, lacrosse, soccer, tennis, track/field (indoor), volleyball. *Women:* basketball, cross-country, golf, lacrosse, soccer, softball, tennis, track/field (indoor), volleyball.

ACCOMMODATIONS

Allowed in exams:	
Calculators	Yes
Dictionary	Yes
Computer	Yes
Spell-checker	Yes
Extended test time	Yes
Scribe	Yes
Proctors	Yes
Oral exams	No
Note-takers	Yes
Support services for students with:	
LD	Yes
ADHD	Yes
ASD	Yes
Distraction-reduced environment	Yes
Recording of lecture allowed	Yes
Reading technology	Yes
Audio books	No
Other assistive technology	Yes
Priority registration	No
Added costs of services:	
For LD	No
For ADHD	No
For ASD	No
LD specialists	Yes
ADHD & ASD coaching	No
ASD specialists	No
Professional tutors	No
Peer tutors	Yes
Max. hours/week for services	4
How professors are notified of student approved accommodations	Student

COLLEGE GRADUATION REQUIREMENTS

Course waivers allowed	Yes
In what courses: Quantitative reasoning (math), world languages	
Course substitutions allowed	Yes
In what courses: Quantitative reasoning (math), world languages	

Endicott College

376 Hale Street, Beverly, MA 01915 • Admissions: 978-921-1000 • Fax: 978-232-2520 **Support: S**

CAMPUS

Type of school	Private (nonprofit)
Environment	Town

STUDENTS

Undergrad enrollment	3,322
% male/female	37/63
% from out of state	48
% frosh live on campus	98

FINANCIAL FACTS

Annual tuition	$34,470
Room and board	$16,130
Required fees	$850

GENERAL ADMISSIONS INFO

Application fee	$50
Regular application deadline	2/15
Nonfall registration	Yes

Admission may be deferred.

Range SAT EBRW	550–630
Range SAT Math	540–610
Range ACT Composite	22–27

ACADEMICS

Student/faculty ratio	13:1
% students returning for sophomore year	86

Most classes have 10–19 students.

Programs/Services for Students with Learning Differences

Endicott College, through the Division of Academic Success and the Center for Accessibility Services, provides reasonable accommodations to qualified students. Accommodations provide qualified individuals with an equal opportunity to obtain the same benefit or privileges as those available to a similarly situated individual without a disability. Students requesting accommodations must self-identify and provide appropriate documentation of their disability. Eligibility for reasonable and appropriate accommodations will be determined on an individual basis.

Admissions

Endicott College looks for students who present academic promise in their secondary school record, recommendations, and writing competency, as well as personal qualities as seen in extracurricular activities, community involvement, and demonstrated leadership. The average GPA is a 3.4. Endicott College, which is test-optional, believes that the grades earned in high school are the most important factor in the admission decision. The minimum GPA for the nursing program is a 3.0. The college recommends that students have 4 years English, 3 years math, 3 years science, 3 years social studies, and 2 years foreign language. Engineering applicants must have 5 years of math and can take math the summer prior to entering college.

Additional Information

To request an accommodation, students must complete the online request form. Endicott will consider any information (including, but not limited to, a description of needs; records of past accommodations and services from high school or another college; formal psychological or medical evaluations, letters from past health, education, or service providers) when evaluating requests for accommodation. This information is needed to develop an understanding of how conditions are likely to affect the student.

ADMISSIONS INFO FOR STUDENTS WITH LEARNING DIFFERENCES

Phone: 978-998-7746 • Fax: 978-232-2150 • Email: cgalatis@endicott.edu

SAT/ACT required: No
Interview required: No
Essay required: Yes
Additional application required: Yes
Documentation submitted to: Center for Accessibility Services

Special Ed. HS course work accepted: Yes
Separate application required for Programs/Services: No
Documentation required for:
LD: Psychoeducational evaluation
ADHD: Psychoeducational evaluation
ASD: Psychoeducational evaluation

Endicott College

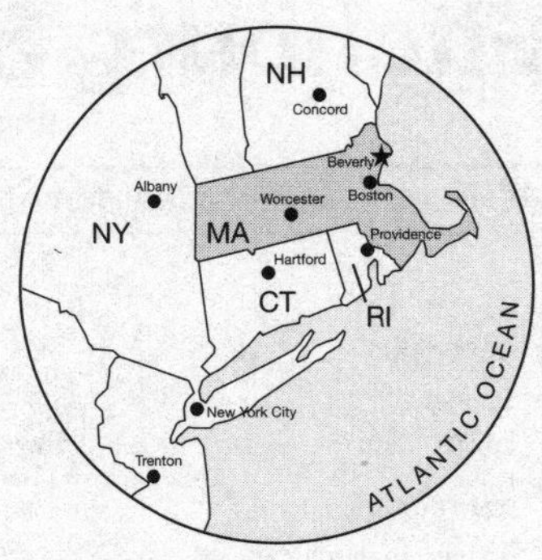

General Admissions

Very important factors include: rigor of secondary school record, academic GPA, character/personal qualities. *Important factors include:* class rank, application essay, standardized test scores, extracurricular activities, talent/ability, alumni/ae relation, geographical residence. *Other factors include:* recommendation(s), interview, first generation, state residency, racial/ethnic status, level of applicant's interest. High school diploma is required and a GED is accepted. *Academic units recommended:* 4 English, 3 math, 2 science, 2 social studies, 1 history, 4 academic electives.

Accommodations or Services

Accommodations are decided upon an individual basis after a thorough review of appropriate, current documentation. The accommodations requests must be supported through the documentation provided and must be logically linked to the current impact of the condition on academic functioning.

Financial Aid

Students should submit: FAFSA*Need-based scholarships/grants offered:* College/university scholarship or grant aid from institutional funds; Federal Pell; Private scholarships; SEOG; State scholarships/grants. *Loan aid offered:* Direct PLUS loans; Direct Subsidized Stafford Loans; Direct Unsubsidized Stafford Loans. Federal Work-Study Program available. Institutional employment available.

Campus Life

Activities: Campus Ministries; Choral groups; Dance; Drama/theater; International Student Organization; Jazz band; Literary magazine; Model UN; Music ensembles; Musical theater; Pep band; Radio station; Student government; Student newspaper; Television station; Yearbook. **Organizations:** 62 registered organizations, 16 honor societies, 2 religious organizations. **Athletics (Intercollegiate):** *Men:* baseball, basketball, cross-country, equestrian sports, football, golf, lacrosse, soccer, tennis, volleyball. *Women:* basketball, cross-country, equestrian sports, field hockey, lacrosse, soccer, softball, tennis, volleyball.

ACCOMMODATIONS

Allowed in exams:	
Calculators	Yes
Dictionary	Yes
Computer	Yes
Spell-checker	Yes
Extended test time	Yes
Scribe	Yes
Proctors	Yes
Oral exams	Yes
Note-takers	Yes
Support services for students with:	
LD	Yes
ADHD	Yes
ASD	Yes
Distraction-reduced environment	Yes
Recording of lecture allowed	Yes
Reading technology	Yes
Audio books	Yes
Other assistive technology	Yes
Priority registration	No
Added costs of services:	
For LD	No
For ADHD	No
For ASD	No
LD specialists	Yes
ADHD & ASD coaching	No
ASD specialists	No
Professional tutors	Yes
Peer tutors	Yes
Max. hours/week for services	Varies
How professors are notified of student approved accommodations	Director

COLLEGE GRADUATION REQUIREMENTS

Course waivers allowed	No
Course substitutions allowed	No

Fitchburg State College

160 Pearl Street, Fitchburg, MA 01420-2697 • Admissions: 978-665-3144 • Fax: 978-665-4540 **Support: S**

CAMPUS

Type of school	Public
Environment	Town

STUDENTS

Undergrad enrollment	4,044
% male/female	47/53
% from out of state	8
% frosh live on campus	68

FINANCIAL FACTS

Annual in-state tuition	$970
Annual out-of-state tuition	$7,050
Room and board	$8,256
Required fees	$7,624

GENERAL ADMISSIONS INFO

Application fee	$50
Regular application deadline	8/21
Nonfall registration	Yes

Admission may be deferred.

Range SAT EBRW	490–580
Range SAT Math	500–570
Range ACT Composite	10–24

ACADEMICS

Student/faculty ratio	13:1
% students returning for sophomore year	74

Most classes have 20–29 students.

Programs/Services for Students with Learning Differences

The Disability Services Office provides support services and programs for students with disabilities. Disability Services will verify student eligibility for accommodations and for coordinating accommodations across campus. Students must request services themselves and must provide appropriate documentation to support the need for such services. Once students have obtained copies of their disability documentation from their high school or medical provider, to support the need for such services, they should meet with staff in the Disability Services office to register for services. Documentation must clearly state the diagnosis, describe the symptoms that impact the student's ability to function in the educational environment and provide specific recommendations for accommodations.

Admissions

Students requesting a waiver of ACT/SAT or foreign language requirement must submit the Psychoeducational testing (within 3 years) with 504 Plan or IEP. Office of Admissions forwards testing to the Office of Disability Services for review who informs Admissions if a student meets the criteria for the waiver(s). If so, the applicant does not need to submit ACT/SAT or proof of completion of foreign language. (However, he or she must complete two additional college prep electives to substitute for the foreign language.) The university wants a weighted GPA of 3.0, however, it considers GPAs between 2.0–2.9 if students submit SAT/ACT scores meeting the sliding scale requirements. Applicants not meeting the sliding scale requirements will be considered on an individual basis for a limited number of admission exceptions. Applicants who meet the 3.0 GPA requirements do not have to use the sliding scale for admission, but still must submit competitive SAT/ACT scores if they are applying within 3 years of high school graduation.

Additional Information

The Office of Disability Services provides support services, programs, and academic accommodations for students with documented disabilities. Some examples of academic accommodations include: testing accommodations, materials in an alternate format, adaptive software and computer equipment, assistive listening devices, sign language interpreters, reduced course load waiver (below 12 credits), academic skill building workshops, support with the development of leadership, self-advocacy, and self-determination skills. To be eligible for academic accommodations, students must request services themselves and must provide appropriate documentation to support the need for such services. Requests for accommodations must be made in a timely manner and must be reasonable given the nature of the disability.

ADMISSIONS INFO FOR STUDENTS WITH LEARNING DIFFERENCES

Phone: 978-665-4029 • Fax: 978-665-4786 • Email: disabilityserviceslist@fitchburgstate.edu

SAT/ACT required: No
Interview required: No
Essay required: Yes
Additional application required: No
Documentation submitted to: Disability Services
Special Ed. HS course work accepted: Yes
Separate application required for Programs/Services: No
Documentation required for:
- **LD:** Psychoeducational evaluation
- **ADHD:** Psychoeducational evaluation
- **ASD:** Psychoeducational evaluation

Fitchburg State College

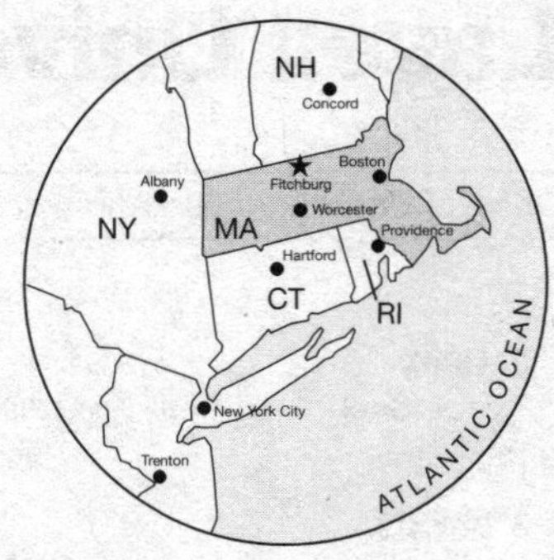

General Admissions

Very important factors include: rigor of secondary school record. *Important factors include:* academic GPA, application essay, standardized test scores. *Other factors include:* recommendation(s), extracurricular activities, talent/ability, character/personal qualities, alumni/ae relation, volunteer work, work experience, level of applicant's interest. High school diploma is required and a GED is accepted. *Academic units required:* 4 English, 3 math, 3 science, 2 science labs, 2 foreign language, 1 social studies, 1 history, 2 academic electives.

Accommodations or Services

Accommodations are decided upon an individual basis after a thorough review of appropriate, current documentation. The accommodations requests must be supported through the documentation provided and must be logically linked to the current impact of the condition on academic functioning.

Financial Aid

Students should submit: FAFSA. *Need-based scholarships/grants offered:* College/university scholarship or grant aid from institutional funds; Federal Pell; Private scholarships; SEOG; State scholarships/grants. *Loan aid offered:* Direct PLUS loans; Direct Subsidized Stafford Loans; Direct Unsubsidized Stafford Loans. Federal Work-Study Program available. Institutional employment available.

Campus Life

Activities: Choral groups; Concert band; Dance; Drama/theater; Jazz band; Literary magazine; Model UN; Radio station; Student government; Student newspaper; Student-run film society. **Organizations:** 60 registered organizations, 12 honor societies, 1 religious organization, 2 fraternities, 3 sororities. **Athletics (Intercollegiate):** *Men:* baseball, basketball, cross-country, football, ice hockey, soccer, track/field (outdoor), track/field (indoor). *Women:* basketball, cross-country, field hockey, lacrosse, soccer, softball, track/field (outdoor), track/field (indoor).

ACCOMMODATIONS

Allowed in exams:	
Calculators	Yes
Dictionary	Yes
Computer	Yes
Spell-checker	Yes
Extended test time	Yes
Scribe	Yes
Proctors	Yes
Oral exams	Yes
Note-takers	Yes
Support services for students with:	
LD	Yes
ADHD	Yes
ASD	Yes
Distraction-reduced environment	Yes
Recording of lecture allowed	Yes
Reading technology	Yes
Audio books	No
Other assistive technology	Yes
Priority registration	No
Added costs of services:	
For LD	No
For ADHD	No
For ASD	No
LD specialists	No
ADHD & ASD coaching	No
ASD specialists	No
Professional tutors	Yes
Peer tutors	Yes
Max. hours/week for services	Varies
How professors are notified of student approved accommodations	Student

COLLEGE GRADUATION REQUIREMENTS

Course waivers allowed	No
Course substitutions allowed	Yes

In what courses: Student will work with instituion to determine course substitution

Massachusetts

Lasell University

Office of Undergraduate Admissions, Newton, MA 02466 • Admissions: 617-243-2225 • Fax: 617-243-2380 **Support: S**

CAMPUS

Type of school	Private (nonprofit)
Environment	City

STUDENTS

Undergrad enrollment	1,639
% male/female	36/64
% from out of state	43
% frosh live on campus	89

FINANCIAL FACTS

Annual tuition	$37,500
Room and board	$16,000
Required fees	$1,500

GENERAL ADMISSIONS INFO

Application fee	$40
Regular application deadline	Rolling
Nonfall registration	No

Admission may be deferred.

Range SAT EBRW	490–580
Range SAT Math	490–590
Range ACT Composite	20–25

ACADEMICS

Student/faculty ratio	13:1
% students returning for sophomore year	68

Most classes have 10–19 students.

Programs/Services for Students with Learning Differences

Lasell University provides appropriate and reasonable accommodations to ensure that no student is discriminated against on the basis of his/her disability. Students with learning disabilities are very capable individuals who experience some kind of challenge that may call for reasonable accommodations to foster success in the classroom. Academic accommodations are determined on an individual basis, facilitated by the AAC Director, making use of submitted comprehensive disability documentation as well as confidential consultation with the student. The determined accommodations may differ from those previously provided to a student, as the accommodations must appropriately address the current impact of the disability on the student's performance in a collegiate setting.

Admissions

All applicants must indicate whether they are electing to apply using ACT/SAT scores or as a test-optional applicant. Once an applicant indicates the decision to submit or not submit test scores, this decision cannot be reversed. Students who apply as test optional must submit an essay or have an interview. This essay or interview is graded and used to help the committee make an admission decision.

Additional Information

Students must complete the Lasell University Learning Disability Registration & Accommodation Request form and gather comprehensive learning disability documentation. Students are advised to review the General Information for Students with Disabilities for more detailed information about the kind of paperwork you need to submit. Students will communicate academic accommodation needs with faculty at the beginning of the semester. Students have access to assistive technology including, Kurzweil and Dragon Naturally Speaking Software

ADMISSIONS INFO FOR STUDENTS WITH LEARNING DIFFERENCES

Phone: 617-243-2115 • Email: slamphere@lasell.edu

SAT/ACT required: No
Interview required: No
Essay required: Yes
Additional application required: No
Documentation submitted to: Disabilities Services

Special Ed. HS course work accepted: Yes
Separate application required for Programs/Services: No
Documentation required for:
LD: Psychoeducational evaluation
ADHD: Psychoeducational evaluation
ASD: Psychoeducational evaluation

Lasell University

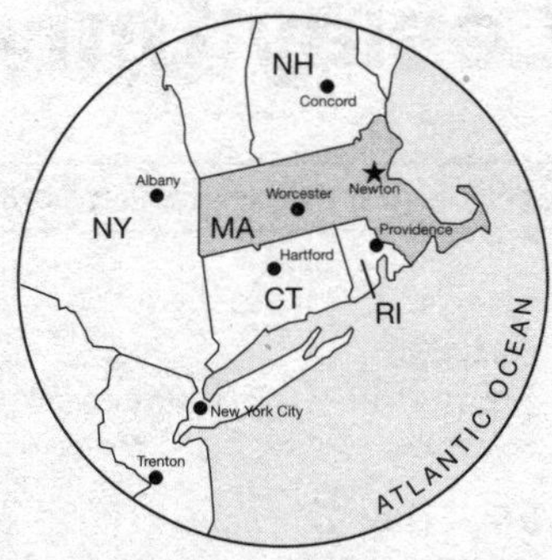

General Admissions

Very important factors include: rigor of secondary school record, academic GPA, interview. *Important factors include:* application essay, recommendation(s), extracurricular activities, volunteer work. *Other factors include:* standardized test scores, talent/ability, character/personal qualities, alumni/ae relation, level of applicant's interest. High school diploma is required and a GED is accepted. *Academic units required:* 4 English, 3 math, 2 science, 2 science labs, 1 social studies, 1 history. *Academic units recommended:* 4 English, 4 math, 3 science, 3 science labs, 2 foreign language, 2 social studies, 2 history. Lasell does not require applicants to submit test results for admission to undergraduate programs.

Accommodations or Services

Accommodations are decided upon an individual basis after a thorough review of appropriate, current documentation. The accommodations requests must be supported through the documentation provided and must be logically linked to the current impact of the condition on academic functioning.

Financial Aid

Students should submit: FAFSA. *Need-based scholarships/grants offered:* College/university scholarship or grant aid from institutional funds; Federal Pell; Private scholarships; SEOG; State scholarships/grants. *Loan aid offered:* Direct PLUS loans; Direct Subsidized Stafford Loans; Direct Unsubsidized Stafford Loans. Federal Work-Study Program available. Institutional employment available.

Campus Life

Activities: Choral groups; Dance; Drama/theater; International Student Organization; Jazz band; Literary magazine; Music ensembles; Musical theater; Radio station; Student government; Student newspaper; Yearbook. **Organizations:** 71 registered organizations, 4 honor societies, 1 religious organization. **Athletics (Intercollegiate):** *Men:* basketball, cross-country, lacrosse, soccer, volleyball. *Women:* basketball, cross-country, field hockey, lacrosse, soccer, softball, volleyball.

ACCOMMODATIONS

Allowed in exams:	
Calculators	Yes
Dictionary	Yes
Computer	Yes
Spell-checker	Yes
Extended test time	Yes
Scribe	Yes
Proctors	No
Oral exams	No
Note-takers	Yes
Support services for students with:	
LD	Yes
ADHD	Yes
ASD	Yes
Distraction-reduced environment	Yes
Recording of lecture allowed	Yes
Reading technology	Yes
Audio books	Yes
Other assistive technology	Yes
Priority registration	No
Added costs of services:	
For LD	No
For ADHD	No
For ASD	No
LD specialists	No
ADHD & ASD coaching	No
ASD specialists	No
Professional tutors	No
Peer tutors	No
Max. hours/week for services	Varies
How professors are notified of student approved accommodations	Student and Disability Office

COLLEGE GRADUATION REQUIREMENTS

Course waivers allowed	No
Course substitutions allowed	Yes
In what courses:	

Massachusetts

Lesley University

Lesley University Undergraduate Admission, Cambridge, MA 02140 • Admissions: 617-349-8800 • Fax: 617-349-8810 **Support: S**

CAMPUS

Type of school	Private (nonprofit)
Environment	Metropolis

STUDENTS

Undergrad enrollment	2,128
% male/female	23/77
% from out of state	38

FINANCIAL FACTS

Annual tuition	$29,200
Room and board	$16,630
Required fees	$750

GENERAL ADMISSIONS INFO

Application fee	$0
Regular application deadline	Rolling
Nonfall registration	Yes

Admission may be deferred.

Range SAT EBRW	510–620
Range SAT Math	490–590
Range ACT Composite	20–26

ACADEMICS

Student/faculty ratio	10:1
% students returning for sophomore year	81

Most classes have 10–19 students.

Programs/Services for Students with Learning Differences

Lesley University is committed to providing equal or equally effective alternative access to academic, social, cultural, and recreational programs for all qualified individuals with disabilities. The Disability Services team works with faculty, staff, and students to make appropriate adjustments to provide this access. Educational access includes the provision of classroom accommodations, auxiliary aids, and services. Accommodations allow all students equal opportunities inside the classroom, around campus, and at university-sponsored events off campus.

Admissions

Students should have a strong academic background. Most students admitted to Lesley have a 3.1 average GPA and have taken the following required high school coursework: 4 years of English, 3 years of math, including Algebra II, 3 years of science, including 2 or more lab courses, 3 years of history/social sciences, including U.S. History, a fourth year of math, science, and social science, and at least 2 years of a foreign language is strongly recommended.

Additional Information

Students should request disability-related accommodations by contacting the appropriate Disability Services director in advance of each semester, submitting the relevant documentation, working with Disability Services to determine reasonable accommodations, and providing the disability accommodation letter to their instructors to sign. The Threshold Program at Lesley University is a non-degree postsecondary program for young adults with diverse learning, developmental, and intellectual disabilities. There is a 2-year certificate program with a guided transition. Students may have learning, intellectual, or developmental disabilities. Students live in the residence hall and attend classes or work and have one-on-one assistance. These students would have difficulty in a traditional college program but are motivated to experience life on a college campus with the help of a paraprofessional.

ADMISSIONS INFO FOR STUDENTS WITH LEARNING DIFFERENCES

Phone: 617-349-8572 via Relay 711 • Fax: 617-349-8558 • Email: dnewman@lesley.edu

SAT/ACT required: No
Interview required: No
Essay required: Yes
Additional application required: No
Documentation submitted to: Disability Support Services

Special Ed. HS course work accepted: Yes
Separate application required for Programs/Services: No
Documentation required for:
LD: Psychoeducational evaluation
ADHD: Psychoeducational evaluation
ASD: Psychoeducational evaluation

Lesley University

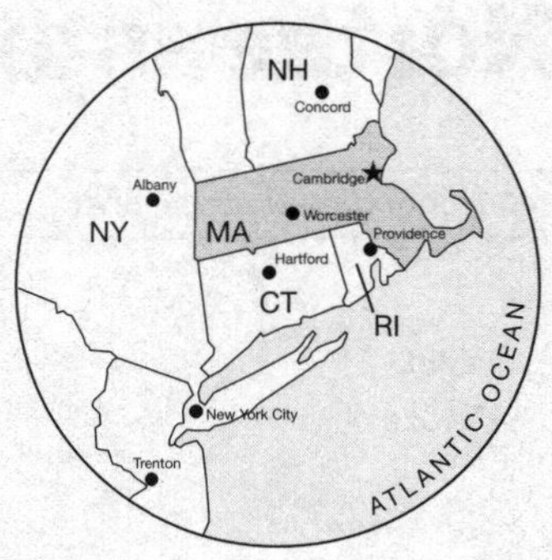

General Admissions

Very important factors include: rigor of secondary school record, academic GPA, interview. *Important factors include:* class rank, application essay, standardized test scores, recommendation(s), extracurricular activities, talent/ability, character/personal qualities, volunteer work. *Other factors include:* first generation, alumni/ae relation, racial/ethnic status, work experience. High school diploma is required and a GED is accepted. *Academic units required:* 4 English, 3 math, 3 science, 2 science labs, 1 social studies, 1 history, 4 academic electives. *Academic units recommended:* 4 English, 4 math, 4 science, 2 science labs, 2 foreign language, 2 social studies, 2 history.

Accommodations or Services

Accommodations are decided upon an individual basis after a thorough review of appropriate, current documentation. The accommodations requests must be supported through the documentation provided and must be logically linked to the current impact of the condition on academic functioning.

Financial Aid

Students should submit: Business/Farm Supplement; CSS/Financial Aid PROFILE; FAFSA. *Need-based scholarships/grants offered:* College/university scholarship or grant aid from institutional funds; Federal Pell; Private scholarships; SEOG; State scholarships/grants. *Loan aid offered:* Direct PLUS loans; Direct Subsidized Stafford Loans; Direct Unsubsidized Stafford Loans. Federal Work-Study Program available. Institutional employment available.

Campus Life

Activities: Campus Ministries; Choral groups; Dance; Drama/theater; International Student Organization; Literary magazine; Musical theater; Student government; Student newspaper. **Organizations:** 25 registered organizations, 2 honor societies, 2 religious organizations. **Athletics (Intercollegiate):** *Men:* basketball, cross-country, soccer, tennis, volleyball. *Women:* basketball, crew/rowing, cross-country, soccer, softball, tennis, volleyball.

ACCOMMODATIONS

Allowed in exams:	
Calculators	Yes
Dictionary	Yes
Computer	Yes
Spell-checker	Yes
Extended test time	Yes
Scribe	Yes
Proctors	No
Oral exams	No
Note-takers	
Support services for students with:	
LD	Yes
ADHD	Yes
ASD	Yes
Distraction-reduced environment	Yes
Recording of lecture allowed	Yes
Reading technology	Yes
Audio books	Yes
Other assistive technology	Yes
Priority registration	Yes
Added costs of services:	
For LD	No
For ADHD	No
For ASD	No
LD specialists	No
ADHD & ASD coaching	Yes
ASD specialists	No
Professional tutors	No
Peer tutors	Yes
Max. hours/week for services	Varies
How professors are notified of student approved accommodations	

COLLEGE GRADUATION REQUIREMENTS

Course waivers allowed	No
Course substitutions allowed	No

Northeastern University

360 Huntington Avenue, Boston, MA 02115 • Admissions: 617-373-2200 • Fax: 617-373-8780 **Support: SP**

CAMPUS

Type of school	Private (nonprofit)
Environment	Metropolis

STUDENTS

Undergrad enrollment	18,359
% male/female	49/51
% from out of state	73
% frosh live on campus	99

FINANCIAL FACTS

Annual tuition	$ 54,360
Room and board	$17,092
Required fees	$1,092

GENERAL ADMISSIONS INFO

Application fee	$75
Regular application deadline	1/1
Nonfall registration	Yes

Admission may be deferred.

Range SAT EBRW	680–750
Range SAT Math	710–790
Range ACT Composite	32–35

ACADEMICS

Student/faculty ratio	14:1
% students returning for sophomore year	96

Most classes have 10–19 students.

Programs/Services for Students with Learning Differences

For students with documented learning disabilities and/or ADHD, Northeastern offers both a comprehensive program and basic support services. The Learning Disabilities Program (LDP) is a comprehensive academic support program for students with LD and/or ADHD. Students meet with an LDP specialist for two regularly scheduled, one-hour appointments each week. Content for meetings includes time management, organization, reading and writing strategies, exam preparation, and metacognitive skills. The LDP is a fee-based service and requires an additional application and interview. The Disability Resource Center (DRC) offers accommodations to students with disabilities, including exam accommodations, note-taking services, and alternate format text. Students registered with the DRC may also meet with a disability specialist for support in using accommodations and other disability-related needs. There is no charge for basic support services.

Admissions

There is no separate or different admissions process for students with disabilities. However, students who are interested in the Learning Disabilities Program (LDP) must apply to the LDP as well as the University. Students are encouraged to submit an application to the LDP immediately upon their decision to attend the University. The LDP also requires an interview for acceptance to the program.

Additional Information

Students who are interested in basic services, including accommodations, are encouraged to provide documentation to the Disability Resource Center (DRC) while their applications are being reviewed by the Admissions Office. In this way, the DRC can provide feedback on the documentation as soon as the student is accepted to NU. Students have access to assistive technology including, Read and Write Gold and ZoomText.

ADMISSIONS INFO FOR STUDENTS WITH LEARNING DIFFERENCES

Phone: 617-373-2675 • Fax: 617-373-7500 • Email: DRC@northeastern.edu

SAT/ACT required: Yes (Test optional for 2021)
Interview required: Yes
Essay required: Yes
Additional application required: Yes
Documentation submitted to: Disability Resource Center and Learning Disabilities Program for fee-based services

Special Ed. HS course work accepted: Yes
Separate application required for Programs/Services: Yes
Documentation required for:
LD: Psychoeducational evaluation
ADHD: Psychoeducational evaluation
ASD: Psychoeducational evaluation

Northeastern University

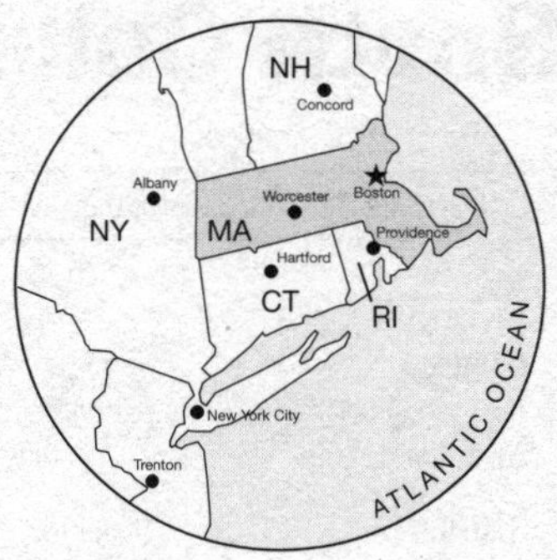

General Admissions

Very important factors include: rigor of secondary school record, academic GPA, application essay, standardized test scores, recommendation(s). *Important factors include:* extracurricular activities, talent/ability, character/personal qualities, volunteer work. *Other factors include:* class rank, first generation, geographical residence, racial/ethnic status, level of applicant's interest. High school diploma is required and a GED is accepted. *Academic units required:* 4 English, 3 math, 3 science, 2 science labs, 2 foreign language, 3 social studies, 2 history. *Academic units recommended:* 4 math, 4 science.

Accommodations or Services

Accommodations are decided upon an individual basis after a thorough review of appropriate, current documentation. The accommodations requests must be supported through the documentation provided and must be logically linked to the current impact of the condition on academic functioning.

Financial Aid

Students should submit: FAFSA; CSS/Financial Aid PROFILE; Noncustodial CSS form. *Need-based scholarships/grants offered:* College/university scholarship or grant aid from institutional funds; Federal Pell; Private scholarships; SEOG; State scholarships/grants. *Loan aid offered:* Direct PLUS loans; Direct Subsidized Stafford Loans; Direct Unsubsidized Stafford Loans. Federal Work-Study Program available. Institutional employment available.

Campus Life

Activities: Choral groups; Concert band; Dance; Drama/theater; International Student Organization; Jazz band; Literary magazine; Model UN; Music ensembles; Musical theater; Pep band; Radio station; Student government; Student newspaper; Student-run film society; Symphony orchestra; Television station; Yearbook. **Organizations:** 400 registered organizations, 22 religious organizations. **Athletics (Intercollegiate):** *Men:* baseball, basketball, crew/rowing, cross-country, ice hockey, soccer, track/field (outdoor), track/field (indoor). *Women:* basketball, crew/rowing, cross-country, diving, field hockey, ice hockey, soccer, swimming, track/field (outdoor), track/field (indoor), volleyball.

ACCOMMODATIONS

Allowed in exams:	
Calculators	Yes
Dictionary	Yes
Computer	Yes
Spell-checker	Yes
Extended test time	Yes
Scribe	Yes
Proctors	Yes
Oral exams	Yes
Note-takers	Yes
Support services for students with:	
LD	Yes
ADHD	Yes
ASD	Yes
Distraction-reduced environment	Yes
Recording of lecture allowed	Yes
Reading technology	Yes
Audio books	Yes
Other assistive technology	Yes
Priority registration	No
Added costs of services:	
For LD	Yes
For ADHD	Yes
For ASD	Yes
LD specialists	Yes
ADHD & ASD coaching	No
ASD specialists	No
Professional tutors	Yes
Peer tutors	Yes
Max. hours/week for services	Varies
How professors are notified of student approved accommodations	Student

COLLEGE GRADUATION REQUIREMENTS

Course waivers allowed	No
Course substitutions allowed	Yes

In what courses: Student will work with institution to determine course substitutions

Massachusetts

Smith College

7 College Lane, Northampton, MA 01063 • Admissions: 413-585-2500 • Fax: 413-585-2527 **Support: S**

CAMPUS

Type of school	Private (nonprofit)
Environment	Town

STUDENTS

Undergrad enrollment	2,531
% male/female	0/100
% from out of state	81
% frosh live on campus	100

FINANCIAL FACTS

Annual tuition	$55,830
Room and board	$18,760
Required fees	$284

GENERAL ADMISSIONS INFO

Application fee	$0
Regular application deadline	1/15
Nonfall registration	No

Admission may be deferred.

Range SAT EBRW	670–740
Range SAT Math	660–780
Range ACT Composite	30–33

ACADEMICS

Student/faculty ratio	9:1
% students returning for sophomore year	94

Most classes have 10–19 students.

Programs/Services for Students with Learning Differences

Smith College is both philosophically committed and legally required to enable students with documented disabilities to participate in college programs by providing reasonable accommodations for them. The Office of Disabilities Services (ODS) facilitates the provision of services and offers services aimed to eliminate barriers through modification of the program when necessary. A student may voluntarily register with ODS by completing a disability identification form and providing documentation of the disability, after which proper accommodations will be determined. Students with disabilities who need academic services are asked to make their needs known and file timely request forms for accommodations in course work each semester with ODS. Students are encouraged to tell professors about the accommodations needed. The college is responsible for providing that, within certain limits, students are not denied the opportunity to participate in college programs on the basis of a disability. The college will provide support services to students with appropriate evaluations and documentation. Students should contact the ODS for consultation and advice. Through the ODS office there are Peer Mentors.

Admissions

There is no special admissions procedure for students with learning disabilities. ACT/SAT are optional. Students may release scores at their discretion. Leniency may be granted in regard to a high school's waiving of foreign language requirements due to a learning disability. High school courses recommended are 4 years of English composition and literature, 3 years of a foreign language (or 2 years in each of 2 languages), 3 years of math, 3 years of science, and 2 years of history. Essays are required and help them understand how the student thinks, writes and what they are about.

Additional Information

The support services assist students to meet their requirements through modifications to programs when necessary. Courses are available in quantitative skills, study skills, and time management skills. The Special Needs Action Group for Support is a cross-disability, student-led group that meets regularly to provide support and peer mentoring and plan activities. Support services include readers, note-takers, scribes, assistive listening devices, typists, computing software and hardware, books on tape, writing counseling, peer tutoring, and time management/study skills training. If peer tutors are not available, other tutorial services may be sought.

ADMISSIONS INFO FOR STUDENTS WITH LEARNING DIFFERENCES

Phone: 413-585-2071 • Fax: 413-585-4498 • Email: lrausche@smith.edu

SAT/ACT required: No
Interview required: Yes
Essay required: Yes
Additional application required: No
Documentation submitted to: Office of Disability Services

Special Ed. HS course work accepted: No
Separate application required for Programs/Services: No
Documentation required for:
LD: Psychoeducational evaluation
ADHD: Psychoeducational evaluation
ASD: Psychoeducational evaluation

Smith College

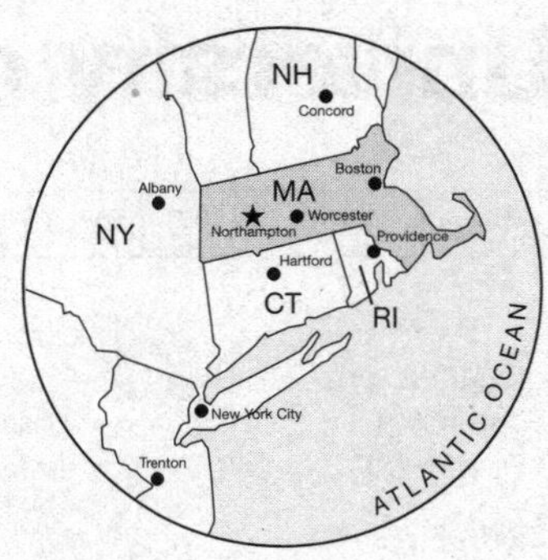

General Admissions

Very important factors include: rigor of secondary school record, academic GPA, application essay, recommendation(s), character/personal qualities. *Important factors include:* class rank, interview, extracurricular activities, talent/ability. *Other factors include:* standardized test scores, first generation, alumni/ae relation, racial/ethnic status, volunteer work, work experience. High school diploma or equivalent is not required. *Academic units recommended:* 4 English, 3 math, 3 science, 3 science labs, 3 foreign language, 2 history, 1 academic elective.

Accommodations or Services

Accommodations are decided upon an individual basis after a thorough review of appropriate, current documentation. The accommodations requests must be supported through the documentation provided and must be logically linked to the current impact of the condition on academic functioning.

Financial Aid

Students should submit: FAFSA; Institution's own financial aid form; CSS/Financial Aid PROFILE. *Need-based scholarships/grants offered:* College/university scholarship or grant aid from institutional funds; Federal Pell; Private scholarships; SEOG; State scholarships/grants. *Loan aid offered:* Direct PLUS loans; Direct Subsidized Stafford Loans; Direct Unsubsidized Stafford Loans. Federal Work-Study Program available. Institutional employment available.

Campus Life

Activities: Campus Ministries; Choral groups; Concert band; Dance; Drama/theater; International Student Organization; Jazz band; Literary magazine; Model UN; Music ensembles; Musical theater; Radio station; Student government; Student newspaper; Symphony orchestra; Television station; Yearbook. **Organizations:** 100 registered organizations, 3 honor societies, 9 religious organizations. **Athletics (Intercollegiate):** *Women:* basketball, crew/rowing, cross-country, diving, equestrian sports, field hockey, lacrosse, skiing (downhill/alpine), soccer, softball, squash, swimming, tennis, track/field (outdoor), track/field (indoor), volleyball.

ACCOMMODATIONS

Allowed in exams:	
Calculators	Yes
Dictionary	No
Computer	Yes
Spell-checker	Yes
Extended test time	Yes
Scribe	Yes
Proctors	No
Oral exams	Yes
Note-takers	Yes
Support services for students with:	
LD	Yes
ADHD	Yes
ASD	Yes
Distraction-reduced environment	Yes
Recording of lecture allowed	Yes
Reading technology	Yes
Audio books	Yes
Other assistive technology	Yes
Priority registration	Yes
Added costs of services:	
For LD	No
For ADHD	No
For ASD	No
LD specialists	No
ADHD & ASD coaching	No
ASD specialists	No
Professional tutors	Yes
Peer tutors	Yes
Max. hours/week for services	Unlimited
How professors are notified of student approved accommodations	Student and Disability Office

COLLEGE GRADUATION REQUIREMENTS

Course waivers allowed	No
Course substitutions allowed	Yes
In what courses: Student will work with institution to determine course substitutions	

University of Massachusetts-Amherst

University Admissions Center, Amherst, MA 01003 • Admissions: 413-545-0222 • Fax: 413-545-4312 **Support: CS**

CAMPUS

Type of school	Public
Environment	Town

STUDENTS

Undergrad enrollment	23,907
% male/female	50/50
% from out of state	17
% frosh live on campus	99

FINANCIAL FACTS

Annual in-state tuition	$15,791
Annual out-of-state tuition	$35,779
Room and board	$13,432
Required fees	$648

GENERAL ADMISSIONS INFO

Application fee	$80
Regular application deadline	1/15
Nonfall registration	Yes

Admission may be deferred.

Range SAT EBRW	590–680
Range SAT Math	600–710
Range ACT Composite	26–32

ACADEMICS

Student/faculty ratio	17:1
% students returning for sophomore year	91

Most classes have 10–19 students.

Programs/Services for Students with Learning Differences

Disability Services' understands that disability as an identity is experienced differently by each person and henceforth value the information that students share with us regarding their disability and accommodation needs in addition to the diagnostic documentation they provide. Students struggling academically who think they may need testing for a learning disability can apply for a scholarship through our department to cover some or all of their testing costs. Disability Services works closely with all departments on campus to ensure accessibility compliance.

Admissions

It is at the student's discretion whether or not they disclose as a person with a disability when they apply for admission. The university is test optional. Courses required for admission include: 4 years English, 4 years math (including a math during senior year), 3 years science, 2 years social science (including 1 history), and 2 years of foreign language (in the same language). Grade trend is very important as are the courses taken that relate to the intended college major. Applicants to the College of Engineering, Isenberg School of Management, or the Computer Science major must have four years of math including an advanced math course, such as pre-calculus, calculus, or trigonometry. Applicants to the College of Engineering must also have chemistry and physics.

Additional Information

Students with a disability are encouraged to register with Disability Services upon their decision to attend the university. Disability Services provides a Spring Orientation for parents and accepted students who have identified themselves as people with disabilities, prior to the deposit deadline. The Massachusetts Inclusive Concurrent Enrollment Initiative (MAICEI) provides high school students aged 18–21 with significant (typically autism or intellectual) disabilities the opportunity to have a college experience alongside their non-disabled peers. MAICEI students are supported by the MAICEI Program Coordinator, Educational Coaches, and Peer Mentors. The goal of the University of Massachusetts Amherst MAICEI Program is to enhance the academic success, career development, and independence skills of its participants.

ADMISSIONS INFO FOR STUDENTS WITH LEARNING DIFFERENCES

Phone: 413-545-0892 • Fax: 413-577-0122 • Email: notify@admin.umass.edu

SAT/ACT required: Yes (Test optional through 2023)
Interview required: No
Essay required: Yes
Additional application required: Yes
Documentation submitted to: Disability Services

Special Ed. HS course work accepted: Yes
Separate application required for Programs/Services: Yes
Documentation required for:
LD: Psychoeducational evaluation
ADHD: Psychoeducational evaluation
ASD: Psychoeducational evaluation

University of Massachusetts-Amherst

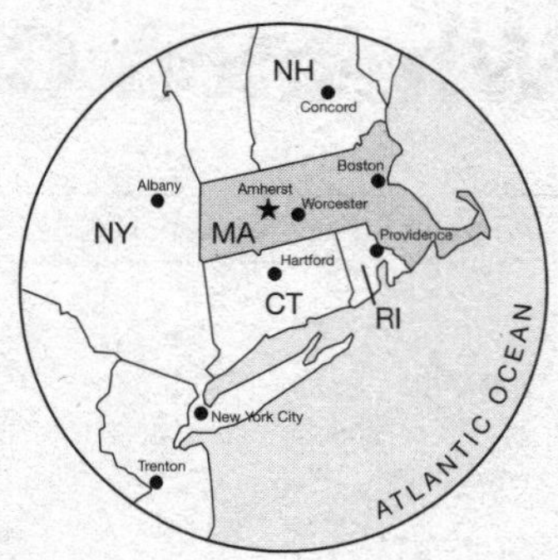

General Admissions

Very important factors include: rigor of secondary school record, academic GPA, standardized test scores. *Important factors include:* class rank, application essay, recommendation(s), extracurricular activities, talent/ability, character/personal qualities, first generation. *Other factors include:* alumni/ae relation, geographical residence, state residency, racial/ethnic status, volunteer work. High school diploma is required and a GED is accepted. *Academic units required:* 4 English, 4 math, 3 science, 2 science labs, 2 foreign language, 2 social studies, 2 academic electives.

Accommodations or Services

Accommodations are decided upon an individual basis after a thorough review of appropriate, current documentation. The accommodations requests must be supported through the documentation provided and must be logically linked to the current impact of the condition on academic functioning.

Financial Aid

Students should submit: FAFSA. *Need-based scholarships/grants offered:* College/university scholarship or grant aid from institutional funds; Federal Pell; Private scholarships; SEOG; State scholarships/grants. *Loan aid offered:* Direct PLUS loans; Direct Subsidized Stafford Loans; Direct Unsubsidized Stafford Loans. Federal Work-Study Program available. Institutional employment available.

Campus Life

Activities: Campus Ministries; Choral groups; Concert band; Dance; Drama/theater; International Student Organization; Jazz band; Literary magazine; Marching band; Model UN; Music ensembles; Musical theater; Opera; Pep band; Radio station; Student government; Student newspaper; Student-run film society; Symphony orchestra; Television station. **Organizations:** 500 registered organizations, 38 honor societies, 22 religious organizations, 22 fraternities, 14 sororities. **Athletics (Intercollegiate):** *Men:* baseball, basketball, cross-country, diving, football, ice hockey, lacrosse, soccer, swimming, track/field (outdoor), track/field (indoor). *Women:* basketball, crew/rowing, cross-country, diving, field hockey, lacrosse, soccer, softball, swimming, tennis, track/field (outdoor), track/field (indoor).

ACCOMMODATIONS

Allowed in exams:	
Calculators	Yes
Dictionary	Yes
Computer	Yes
Spell-checker	Yes
Extended test time	Yes
Scribe	Yes
Proctors	Yes
Oral exams	Yes
Note-takers	Yes
Support services for students with:	
LD	Yes
ADHD	Yes
ASD	Yes
Distraction-reduced environment	Yes
Recording of lecture allowed	Yes
Reading technology	Yes
Audio books	Yes
Other assistive technology	Yes
Priority registration	Yes
Added costs of services:	
For LD	No
For ADHD	No
For ASD	No
LD specialists	Yes
ADHD & ASD coaching	No
ASD specialists	No
Professional tutors	No
Peer tutors	No
Max. hours/week for services	Varies
How professors are notified of student approved accommodations	Director

COLLEGE GRADUATION REQUIREMENTS

Course waivers allowed	No
Course substitutions allowed	Yes

In what courses: Student will work with institution to determine course substitutions

Massachusetts

Wheaton College (MA)

26 E Main Street, Norton, MA 02766 • Admissions: 508-286-8251 • Fax: 508-286-8271 **Support: S**

CAMPUS	
Type of school	Private (nonprofit)
Environment	Village
STUDENTS	
Undergrad enrollment	1,774
% male/female	40/60
% from out of state	63
% frosh live on campus	98
FINANCIAL FACTS	
Annual tuition	$55,904
Room and board	$14,378
Required fees	$462
GENERAL ADMISSIONS INFO	
Application fee	$60
Regular application deadline	1/15
Nonfall registration	Yes
Admission may be deferred.	
Range SAT EBRW	600–680
Range SAT Math	550–660
Range ACT Composite	27–32
ACADEMICS	
Student/faculty ratio	11:1
% students returning for sophomore year	83
Most classes have 10–19 students.	

Programs/Services for Students with Learning Differences

Wheaton College encourages life-long learning by assisting students to become self-advocates and independent learners. The college does not have a special program for students with LD. The Assistant Dean for College Skills serves as the 504/ADA coordinator. Students with LD can access services through the dean. The Academic Advising Center houses the Dean of Academic Advising who holds drop-in office hours and assists students with petitions to the Committee on Admissions and Academic Standing, Orientation, and Probation; general advising; and incomplete grade resolution. The advising staff can assist with pressing advising questions. Students also have access to tutors, peer advisors, and preceptors who offer assistance with study strategies. All students have access to these services.

Admissions

All applicants must meet the same admission standards. Students with LD may choose to meet with the Assistant Dean for College Skills. It is strongly suggested that students take 4 years of English, 3–4 years of math, 3–4 years of a foreign language, 2 years of social studies, and 3–4 years of science. Students are encouraged to take AP and honors courses and courses in visual/performing arts. Wheaton will accept courses taken in the special education department. Students with LD are encouraged to self-disclose and provide current documentation. All LD testing information should be sent to both admissions and support services.

Additional Information

Contact: Accessibility Services Autumn Grant. Abilities 1st! is pre orientation gives students the opportunity to move into their dorm two days before the rest of the class, learn about the Writing Center, Library Information Services and Assistive Technology, and First Year Seminar (FYS). Students have access to assistive technology including screen reader (i.e., JAWS or Voiceover) for quizzes, exams, in-class assignments. Additionally there are assistive listening devices, communication access real-time translation, text to speech software, specialized magnifiers, and tactile boards.

ADMISSIONS INFO FOR STUDENTS WITH LEARNING DIFFERENCES

Phone: 508-286-8215 • Fax: 508-286-5621 • Email: grant_autumn@wheatoncollege.edu

SAT/ACT required: No
Interview required: No
Essay required: Yes
Additional application required: No
Documentation submitted to: Learning and Accessibility Services

Special Ed. HS course work accepted: No
Separate application required for Programs/Services: No
Documentation required for:
LD: Psychoeducational evaluation
ADHD: Psychoeducational evaluation
ASD: Psychoeducational evaluation

Wheaton College (MA)

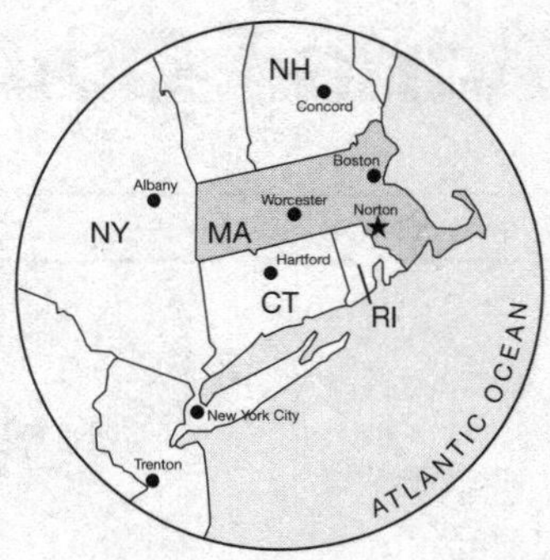

General Admissions

Very important factors include: rigor of secondary school record, academic GPA, application essay, recommendation(s), character/personal qualities. *Important factors include:* extracurricular activities, talent/ability, alumni/ae relation. *Other factors include:* class rank, standardized test scores, interview, first generation, geographical residence, state residency, racial/ethnic status, volunteer work, work experience. High school diploma is required and a GED is accepted. *Academic units required:* 4 English. *Academic units recommended:* 4 math, 4 science, 4 foreign language, 4 social studies, 4 history.

Accommodations or Services

Accommodations are decided upon an individual basis after a thorough review of appropriate, current documentation. The accommodations requests must be supported through the documentation provided and must be logically linked to the current impact of the condition on academic functioning.

Financial Aid

Students should submit: FAFSA; CSS/Financial Aid PROFILE; Noncustodial CSS form. *Need-based scholarships/grants offered:* College/university scholarship or grant aid from institutional funds; Federal Pell; Private scholarships; SEOG; State scholarships/grants. *Loan aid offered:* Direct PLUS loans; Direct Subsidized Stafford Loans; Direct Unsubsidized Stafford Loans. Federal Work-Study Program available. Institutional employment available.

Campus Life

Activities: Campus Ministries; Choral groups; Dance; Drama/theater; International Student Organization; Jazz band; Literary magazine; Model UN; Music ensembles; Musical theater; Radio station; Student government; Student newspaper; Student-run film society; Symphony orchestra; Yearbook. **Organizations:** 110 registered organizations, 10 honor societies, 5 religious organizations. **Athletics (Intercollegiate):** *Men:* baseball, basketball, cross-country, diving, lacrosse, soccer, swimming, tennis, track/field (outdoor), track/field (indoor). *Women:* basketball, cross-country, diving, field hockey, lacrosse, soccer, softball, swimming, synchronized swimming, tennis, track/field (outdoor), track/field (indoor), volleyball.

ACCOMMODATIONS

Allowed in exams:	
Calculators	Yes
Dictionary	No
Computer	Yes
Spell-checker	No
Extended test time	Yes
Scribe	Yes
Proctors	Yes
Oral exams	Yes
Note-takers	Yes
Support services for students with:	
LD	Yes
ADHD	Yes
ASD	Yes
Distraction-reduced environment	Yes
Recording of lecture allowed	Yes
Reading technology	Yes
Audio books	Yes
Other assistive technology	Yes
Priority registration	Yes
Added costs of services:	
For LD	No
For ADHD	No
For ASD	No
LD specialists	No
ADHD & ASD coaching	No
ASD specialists	No
Professional tutors	No
Peer tutors	Yes
Max. hours/week for services	Varies
How professors are notified of student approved accommodations	Student

COLLEGE GRADUATION REQUIREMENTS

Course waivers allowed	No
Course substitutions allowed	Yes

In what courses: Students will work with institution to determine course substitution

Massachusetts

Adrian College

110 South Madison Street, Adrian, MI 49221 • Admissions: 517-265-5161 • Fax: 517-264-3331 **Support: CS**

CAMPUS

Type of school	Private (nonprofit)
Environment	Town

STUDENTS

Undergrad enrollment	1,828
% male/female	50/50
% from out of state	25
% frosh live on campus	92

FINANCIAL FACTS

Annual tuition	$37,809
Room and board	$11,720
Required fees	$1,025

GENERAL ADMISSIONS INFO

Application fee	$0
Regular application deadline	Rolling
Nonfall registration	No

Admission may be deferred.

Range SAT EBRW	480–580
Range SAT Math	480–520
Range ACT Composite	19–24

ACADEMICS

Student/faculty ratio	13:1
% students returning for sophomore year	64

Most classes have 10–19 students.

Programs/Services for Students with Learning Differences

Adrian College has extensive academic support services for all students with disabilities. The more the students are mainstreamed in high school, the greater their chances of success at Adrian. There is no special or separate curriculum for students with learning disabilities.

Admissions

Students with learning disabilities must meet regular admission criteria. Students should demonstrate the ability to do college-level work through an acceptable GPA in college-preparatory classes (average 3.22) including four years English, three years math, social studies, science, and language, and ACT (average 20–25) or SAT. Furthermore, by their senior year in high school, students should, for the most part, be mainstreamed. Courses taken in special education will be considered for admission. The applications of students who self-disclose are reviewed by Academic Services staff, not to determine admissions, but to start a documentation file.

Additional Information

Adrian does not have a specific program for students with learning differences. Academic Services Department offers a wide variety of services for students such as: assistance developing time management plans, effective reading strategies, note-taking, and test-taking skills. Course adaptations help to make courses more understandable. Skills classes are available in reading, math, study skills and research paper writing, and students are granted credit toward their GPA. Tutorial assistance is available for all students. P.R.I.D.E. (Promoting the Rights of Individuals Everywhere) communicates information about the difficulties and accomplishments of people with disabilities.

ADMISSIONS INFO FOR STUDENTS WITH LEARNING DIFFERENCES

Phone: 517-265-5161, ext. 4093 • Fax: 517-264-3331

SAT/ACT required: Yes
Interview required: No
Essay required: No
Additional application required: No
Documentation submitted to: ACCESS, Academic Services

Special Ed. HS course work accepted: Yes
Separate application required for Programs/Services: No
Documentation required for:
LD: Psychoeducational evaluation
ADHD: Psychoeducational evaluation
ASD: Psychoeducational evaluation

Adrian College

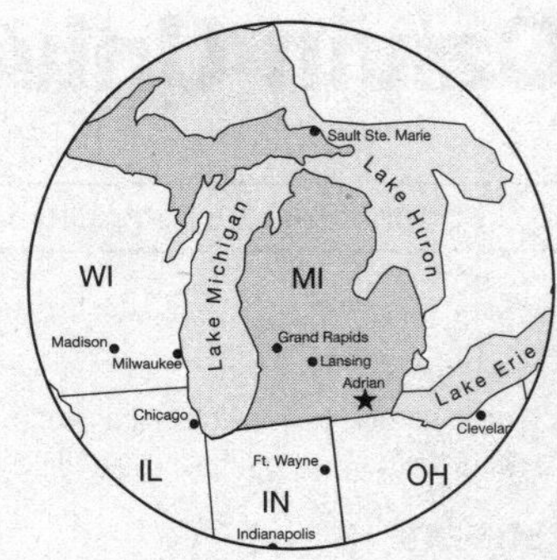

Michigan

General Admissions

Very important factors include: rigor of secondary school record, class rank. *Important factors include:* academic GPA, standardized test scores, talent/ability. *Other factors include:* interview, extracurricular activities, character/personal qualities, alumni/ae relation, volunteer work, work experience, level of applicant's interest. High school diploma is required and GED is accepted. *Academic units recommended:* 4 English, 3 math, 2 science, 1 science lab, 2 foreign language, 1 social studies, 1 history, 2 academic electives.

Accommodations or Services

Accommodations are decided upon an individual basis after a thorough review of appropriate, current documentation. The accommodations requests must be supported through the documentation provided and must be logically linked to the current impact of the condition on academic functioning.

Financial Aid

Students should submit: FAFSA. *Need-based scholarships/grants offered:* College/university scholarship or grant aid from institutional funds; Federal Pell; Private scholarships; SEOG; State scholarships/grants. *Loan aid offered:* Federal Work-Study Program available. Institutional employment available.

Campus Life

Activities: Campus Ministries; Choral groups; Concert band; Dance; Drama/theater; International Student Organization; Jazz band; Literary magazine; Marching band; Music ensembles; Musical theater; Pep band; Radio station; Student government; Student newspaper; Symphony orchestra; Yearbook. **Organizations:** 68 registered organizations, 13 honor societies, 8 religious organizations, 4 fraternities, 3 sororities. **Athletics (Intercollegiate):** *Men:* baseball, basketball, cross-country, football, golf, ice hockey, lacrosse, soccer, tennis, track/field (outdoor). *Women:* basketball, bowling, cross-country, golf, ice hockey, lacrosse, soccer, softball, tennis, track/field (outdoor), volleyball.

ACCOMMODATIONS

Allowed in exams:	
Calculators	No
Dictionary	Yes
Computer	Yes
Spell-checker	Yes
Extended test time	Yes
Scribe	Yes
Proctors	Yes
Oral exams	Yes
Note-takers	Yes
Support services for students with:	
LD	Yes
ADHD	Yes
ASD	Yes
Distraction-reduced environment	Yes
Recording of lecture alowed	Yes
Reading technology	Yes
Audio books	Yes
Other assistive technology	Yes
Priority registration	No
Added costs of services:	
For LD	No
For ADHD	No
For ASD	No
LD specialists	Yes
ADHD & ASD coaching	No
ASD specialists	No
Professional tutors	No
Peer tutors	Yes
Max. hours/week for services	Varies
How professors are notified of student approved accommodations	Student and Disability Office

COLLEGE GRADUATION REQUIREMENTS

Course waivers allowed	No
Course substitutions allowed	No

Calvin University

3201 Burton Street S.E., Grand Rapids, MI 49546 • Admissions: 616-526-6106 • Fax: 616-526-6777 **Support: CS**

CAMPUS

Type of school	Private (nonprofit)
Environment	Metropolis

STUDENTS

Undergrad enrollment	3,732
% male/female	46/54
% from out of state	33
% frosh live on campus	94

FINANCIAL FACTS

Annual tuition	$37,600
Room and board	$10,800
Required fees	$206

GENERAL ADMISSIONS INFO

Application fee	$35
Regular application deadline	8/15
Nonfall registration	Yes

Admission may be deferred.

Range SAT EBRW	570–670
Range SAT Math	570–690
Range ACT Composite	24–30

ACADEMICS

Student/faculty ratio	13:1
% students returning for sophomore year	85

Most classes have 20–29 students.

Programs/Services for Students with Learning Differences

Calvin is committed to supporting all students with disabilities. Calvin provides assistance for students with visual, auditory, and mobility impairments, as well as learning disabilities, chronic health conditions, and psychological and temporary disabilities. Students interested in receiving accommodations are asked to meet with a disability coordinator who will discuss the documentation required for each specific student's unique situation.

Admissions

There are no special admissions criteria for students with LD. Applicants are expected to have an ACT of 20 (19 English and 20 Math) or SAT of 940 (470 Critical Reading and 470 Math). The mid 50 percent for ACT is 23–25, and for SAT, it is 1090–1320. Courses required include: 3 English, 1 algebra, 1 geometry, and a minimum of 2 in any two of the following fields: social science, language, or natural science; one foreign language, math, social science, and natural science fields must include at least 3 years of study. The mid 50 percent GPA is 3.3–3.9. The Access Program provides an alternate entry track for first-time students who show promise of being successful at Calvin, but who cannot meet all of the admissions standards. The students are provided with placement testing in math and/or English, special advising, and enrollment in a college thinking and learning course during their first semester at Calvin. Depending on the outcome of the placement testing, additional developmental courses may be required as a condition of admission.

Additional Information

The Knights Scholars Program provides tools for students to make a successful transition to college and achieve academic success. The program includes academic advising, personalized coursework, and peer coaches. Students are admitted to the program by a committee upon admissions or through direct communication with the program director.

ADMISSIONS INFO FOR STUDENTS WITH LEARNING DIFFERENCES

Phone: 616-526-6155 • Fax: 616-526-7066 • Email: successcenter@calvin.edu

SAT/ACT required: No
Interview required: No
Essay required: Yes
Additional application required: No
Documentation submitted to: Disability Services

Special Ed. HS course work accepted: No
Separate application required for Programs/Services: No
Documentation required for:
LD: Psychoeducational evaluation
ADHD: Psychoeducational evaluation
ASD: Psychoeducational evaluation

Calvin University

Michigan

General Admissions

Very important factors include: rigor of secondary school record, academic GPA, standardized test scores, religious affiliation/commitment. *Important factors include:* application essay, recommendation(s), extracurricular activities, character/personal qualities. *Other factors include:* class rank, volunteer work, work experience, level of applicant's interest. High school diploma is required and GED is accepted. *Academic units required:* 3 English, 3 math, 2 science, 2 social studies, 3 academic electives. *Academic units recommended:* 4 English, 3 math, 2 science, 1 science lab, 2 foreign language, 3 social studies, 3 academic electives.

Accommodations or Services

Accommodations are decided upon an individual basis after a thorough review of appropriate, current documentation. The accommodations requests must be supported through the documentation provided and must be logically linked to the current impact of the condition on academic functioning.

Financial Aid

Students should submit: FAFSA. Applicants will be notified of awards on a rolling basis beginning 3/10. *Need-based scholarships/grants offered:* College/university scholarship or grant aid from institutional funds; Federal Pell; Private scholarships; SEOG; State scholarships/grants. *Loan aid offered:* Direct PLUS loans; Direct Subsidized Stafford Loans; Direct Unsubsidized Stafford Loans. Federal Work-Study Program available. Institutional employment available.

Campus Life

Activities: Campus Ministries; Choral groups; Concert band; Dance; Drama/theater; International Student Organization; Jazz band; Literary magazine; Music ensembles; Pep band; Student government; Student newspaper; Student-run film society; Symphony orchestra; Yearbook. **Organizations:** 80 registered organizations, 6 honor societies, 5 religious organizations. **Athletics (Intercollegiate):** *Men:* baseball, basketball, cross-country, diving, golf, soccer, swimming, tennis, track/field (outdoor). *Women:* basketball, cross-country, diving, golf, soccer, softball, swimming, tennis, track/field (outdoor), volleyball.

ACCOMMODATIONS

Allowed in exams:	
Calculators	Yes
Dictionary	Yes
Computer	Yes
Spell-checker	Yes
Extended test time	Yes
Scribe	Yes
Proctors	Yes
Oral exams	Yes
Note-takers	Yes
Support services for students with:	
LD	Yes
ADHD	Yes
ASD	Yes
Distraction-reduced environment	Yes
Recording of lecture alowed	Yes
Reading technology	Yes
Audio books	Yes
Other assistive technology	Yes
Priority registration	Yes
Added costs of services:	
For LD	No
For ADHD	No
For ASD	No
LD specialists	No
ADHD & ASD coaching	Yes
ASD specialists	No
Professional tutors	No
Peer tutors	Yes
Max. hours/week for services	Varies
How professors are notified of student approved accommodations	Student

COLLEGE GRADUATION REQUIREMENTS

Course waivers allowed	No
Course substitutions allowed	Yes
In what courses: Case-by-case basis	

Eastern Michigan University

401 Pierce Hall, Ypsilanti, Michigan 48197 • Admissions: 734-487-3060 **Support: S**

CAMPUS

Type of school	Public
Environment	Town

STUDENTS

Undergrad enrollment	14,872
% male/female	40/60
% from out of state	10
% frosh live on campus	68

FINANCIAL FACTS

Annual in-state tuition	$11,778
Annual out-of-state tuition	$11,778
Room and board	$10,696

GENERAL ADMISSIONS INFO

Application fee	$35
Regular application deadline	Rolling
Nonfall registration	Yes
Range SAT EBRW	490–600
Range SAT Math	480–590
Range ACT Composite	19–25

ACADEMICS

Student/faculty ratio	14:1
% students returning for sophomore year	70

Programs/Services for Students with Learning Differences

Students with learning differences are encouraged to contact the Disability Resource Center (DRC) and complete the "DRC Initial Questionnaire." Following completion of the questionnaire, students should schedule an appointment with a DRC Case Manager. Supporting documentation should be submitted to the DRC, after which a case manager will provide a Letter of Accommodation.

Admissions

All applicants must meet the same admission criteria. The ACT or SAT is required for admission. The average GPA is 3.28 and an ACT score of 22 and SAT score of 1100. If applicants have a high GPA, they may be admitted even if their test score is below the average. Applicants with a high ACT or SAT test score may be admitted with a lower-than-average GPA. Students are encouraged to provide additional information to support their application.

Additional Information

The College Supports Program (CSP) at Eastern Michigan University is aimed at increasing admissions, retention, and matriculation for students with Autism Spectrum Disorder (ASD) through a fee-for-service supportive program. The program includes assistance in academic and social-emotional growth, helps students develop the daily living skills needed for independence, and supports executive functioning skills; it has a separate application process.

ADMISSIONS INFO FOR STUDENTS WITH LEARNING DIFFERENCES

Phone: 734-487-2470 • Email: drc@emich.edu

SAT/ACT required: No (depending on GPA)
Interview required: No
Essay required: No
Additional application required: No
Documentation submitted to: Disability Resource Center (DRC)

Special Ed. HS course work accepted: Yes
Separate application required for Programs/Services: No
Documentation required for:
LD: Psychoeducational evaluation
ADHD: Psychoeducational evaluation
ASD: Psychoeducational evaluation

Eastern Michigan University

General Admissions

Very important factors include: academic GPA, standardized test scores. *Important factors include:* rigor of secondary school record. *Other factors include:* application essay, recommendation(s). High school diploma is required and a GED is accepted. *Academic units recommended:* 4 English, 4 math, 4 science, 2 foreign language, 2 social studies, 1 history, 4 electives.

Accommodations or Services

Accommodations are decided upon an individual basis after a thorough review of appropriate, current documentation. The accommodations requests must be supported through the documentation provided and must be logically linked to the current impact of the condition on academic functioning.

Financial Aid

Students should submit: FAFSA. *Need-based scholarships/grants offered:* College/university scholarship or grant aid from institutional funds; Federal Pell; Private scholarships; SEOG; State scholarships/grants. *Loan aid offered:* Direct PLUS loans; Direct Subsidized Stafford Loans; Direct Unsubsidized Stafford Loans. Federal Work-Study Program available. Institutional employment available.

Campus Life

Activities: Campus Ministries; Choral groups; Concert band; Dance; Drama/theater; International Student Organization; Jazz band; Literary magazine; Marching band; Model UN; Music ensembles; Musical theater; Opera; Pep band; Radio station; Student government; Student newspaper; Student-run film society; Symphony orchestra. **Organizations:** 247 registered organizations, 9 honor societies, 17 religious organizations. **Athletics (Intercollegiate):** *Men:* baseball, basketball, football, ice hockey, soccer, tennis. *Women:* basketball, cross-country, golf, gymnastics, soccer, softball, tennis, track/field (outdoor), track/field (indoor), volleyball.

ACCOMMODATIONS

Allowed in exams:	
Calculators	Yes
Dictionary	Yes
Computer	Yes
Spell-checker	Yes
Extended test time	Yes
Scribe	Yes
Proctors	Yes
Oral exams	Yes
Note-takers	Yes
Support services for students with:	
LD	Yes
ADHD	Yes
ASD	Yes
Distraction-reduced environment	Yes
Recording of lecture allowed	Yes
Reading technology	Yes
Audio books	Yes
Other assistive technology	Yes
Priority registration	Yes
Added costs of services:	
For LD	No
For ADHD	No
For ASD	Yes
LD specialists	Yes
ADHD & ASD coaching	Yes
ASD specialists	Yes
Professional tutors	No
Peer tutors	Yes
Max. hours/week for services	Varies
How professors are notified of student approved accommodations	Both

COLLEGE GRADUATION REQUIREMENTS

Course waivers allowed	No
Course substitutions allowed	No

Ferris State University

1201 South State Street, Big Rapids, MI 49307 • Admissions: 231-591-2100 • Fax: 231-591-3944 **Support: CS**

CAMPUS

Type of school	Public
Environment	Village

STUDENTS

Undergrad enrollment	10,398
% male/female	48/52
% from out of state	5
% frosh live on campus	82

FINANCIAL FACTS

Annual in-state tuition	$12,930
Annual out-of-state tuition	$12,930
Room and board	$10,340

GENERAL ADMISSIONS INFO

Application fee	$0
Regular application deadline	8/1
Nonfall registration	Yes

Admission may be deferred.

Range SAT EBRW	470–590
Range SAT Math	460–580
Range ACT Composite	18–25

ACADEMICS

Student/faculty ratio	16:1
% students returning for sophomore year	76

Most classes have 10–19 students.

Programs/Services for Students with Learning Differences

Ferris State University is committed to a policy of equal opportunity for qualified students. The mission of Disabilities Services is to serve and advocate for students with disabilities, empowering them for selfreliance and independence. Ferris State does not have a program for students with learning disabilities, but does provide a variety of support services and accommodations for students with documented learning disabilities. To obtain support services, students will complete a request for services application and a copy of the documentation of the disability. Documentation for LD/ADHD must be dated within five years and be submitted by a qualified professional. Professional development is offered to faculty and staff.

Admissions

Students with learning disabilities must submit the general application form and should meet the same entrance criteria as all students. ACT scores are used for placement only and may not have an adverse effect on applicants with disabilities. Students with LD/ADHD are encouraged to self-disclose and provide information as to the extent of the disability. Sometimes a pre-admission interview is required if the GPA is questionable. In general, students should have a 2.0 GPA, but some programs require a higher GPA and specific courses. Diverse curricula offerings and a flexible admissions policy allow for the admission of most high school graduates and transfer students. Some programs are selective in nature and require the completion of specific courses and/or a minimum GPA.

Additional Information

Disability Services provides services and accommodations to students with LD or ADHD with appropriate documentation. These could include calculators for exams; Dragon Naturally Speaking extended testing times; electronic text; spellchecker for essay tests or exams; note-takers; word processing for essay tests; use of student supplied recording device in class; quiet areas for testing; educational counseling; and JAWS. The Academic Support Center offers tutoring for most courses.

ADMISSIONS INFO FOR STUDENTS WITH LEARNING DIFFERENCES

Phone: 231-591-3057 • Fax: 231-591-3939 • Email: ecds@ferris.edu

SAT/ACT required: No
Interview required: Yes
Essay required: Yes
Additional application required: No
Documentation submitted to: Disability Services

Special Ed. HS course work accepted: No
Separate application required for Programs/Services: No
Documentation required for:
LD: Psychoeducational evaluation
ADHD: Psychoeducational evaluation
ASD: Psychoeducational evaluation

Ferris State University

Michigan

General Admissions

Very important factors include: rigor of secondary school record. *Important factors include:* academic GPA, standardized test scores, character/personal qualities. *Other factors include:* class rank, first generation, alumni/ae relation, geographical residence, volunteer work, work experience. High school diploma is required and GED is accepted. *Academic units recommended:* 4 English, 4 math, 3 science, 2 foreign language, 3 social studies, 1 academic elective, 1 visual/performing arts.

Accommodations or Services

Accommodations are decided upon an individual basis after a thorough review of appropriate, current documentation. The accommodations requests must be supported through the documentation provided and must be logically linked to the current impact of the condition on academic functioning.

Financial Aid

Students should submit: FAFSA*Need-based scholarships/grants offered:* College/university scholarship or grant aid from institutional funds; Federal Pell; Private scholarships; SEOG; State scholarships/grants. *Loan aid offered:* Direct PLUS loans; Direct Subsidized Stafford Loans; Direct Unsubsidized Stafford Loans. Federal Work-Study Program available. Institutional employment available.

Campus Life

Activities: Campus Ministries; Choral groups; Concert band; Dance; Drama/theater; International Student Organization; Jazz band; Music ensembles; Musical theater; Opera; Pep band; Radio station; Student government; Student newspaper; Student-run film society; Symphony orchestra; Television station. **Organizations:** 240 registered organizations, 19 honor societies, 10 religious organizations, 5 fraternities, 3 sororities. **Athletics (Intercollegiate):** *Men:* basketball, cheerleading, cross-country, football, golf, ice hockey, tennis, track/field (outdoor). *Women:* basketball, cheerleading, cross-country, golf, soccer, softball, tennis, track/field (outdoor), volleyball.

ACCOMMODATIONS

Allowed in exams:	
Calculators	Yes
Dictionary	Yes
Computer	Yes
Spell-checker	Yes
Extended test time	Yes
Scribe	Yes
Proctors	No
Oral exams	Yes
Note-takers	Yes
Support services for students with:	
LD	Yes
ADHD	Yes
ASD	Yes
Distraction-reduced environment	Yes
Recording of lecture allowed	Yes
Reading technology	Yes
Audio books	Yes
Other assistive technology	Yes
Priority registration	Yes
Added costs of services:	
For LD	No
For ADHD	No
For ASD	No
LD specialists	No
ADHD & ASD coaching	Yes
ASD specialists	No
Professional tutors	No
Peer tutors	Yes
Max. hours/week for services	Varies
How professors are notified of student approved accommodations	Student and Disability Office

COLLEGE GRADUATION REQUIREMENTS

Course waivers allowed	No
Course substitutions allowed	No

Grand Valley State University

1 Campus Drive, Allendale, MI 49401 • Admissions: 616-331-2025 • Fax: 616-331-2000 **Support: S**

CAMPUS

Type of school	Public
Environment	City

STUDENTS

Undergrad enrollment	21,112
% male/female	40/60
% from out of state	8
% frosh live on campus	86

FINANCIAL FACTS

Annual in-state tuition	$13,576
Annual out-of-state tuition	$19,168
Room and board	$9,732
Required fees	

GENERAL ADMISSIONS INFO

Application fee	$30
Regular application deadline	5/1
Nonfall registration	Yes
Range SAT EBRW	520–630
Range SAT Math	520–620
Range ACT Composite	21–26

ACADEMICS

Student/faculty ratio	16:1
% students returning for sophomore year	85

Most classes have 20–29 students.

Programs/Services for Students with Learning Differences

Skills assistance provides students with strategies for collegiate success through individual preparation and guidance with a learning skills curriculum specialist. This program is designed for students in DSR who have a desire to improve academic performance or be more successful. This service is provided to identify and explore the unique learning characteristics of students who feel that their own study efforts are not reflected in the academic performance. The goal of Learning Skills assistance is to help students get the most out of their learning experiences as motivated and organized learners at Grand Valley State University. Students may meet with the learning skills curriculum specialist throughout the academic year.

Admissions

All applicants must meet the general admission criteria for admission. Students with learning disabilities are encouraged to self-disclose in the application process. ACT or SAT scores are not currently required for admission. Applicants should indicate whether they are submitting test scores. Students can submit test scores at a later date to be considered for scholarships. Grand Valley takes a holistic approach to reviewing applications, using several factors in evaluating academic fit. These factors include grade point average (GPA), academic rigor, short answer response on the admissions application, and standardized test scores when presented.

Additional Information

Applicants are reviewed under the same requirements. The university factors in high school courses including 4 years English, 3 years science, 3 years math, 3 years social science, and 2 years foreign language. The middle 50% admitted have a GPA between 3.4–3.9, ACT between 21–26 or SAT between 1050–1240. The university is test optional for 2021 and will review this policy for future years. Grade trend is important plus other factors such as leadership, talent, and activities.

ADMISSIONS INFO FOR STUDENTS WITH LEARNING DIFFERENCES

Phone: 616-331-2490 • Fax: 616-331-3880 • Email: dsr@gvsu.edu

SAT/ACT required: Yes (Test blind for 2021)
Interview required: No
Essay required: No
Additional application required: Yes
Documentation submitted to: DSR

Special Ed. HS course work accepted: No
Separate application required for Programs/Services: Yes
Documentation required for:
LD: Psychoeducational evaluation
ADHD: Psychoeducational evaluation
ASD: Psychoeducational evaluation

Grand Valley State University

General Admissions

Very important factors include: rigor of secondary school record, academic GPA. *Important factors include:* standardized test scores. *Other factors include:* class rank, application essay, recommendation(s), extracurricular activities, talent/ability, first generation, alumni/ae relation, volunteer work, work experience. High school diploma is required and GED is accepted. *Academic units required:* 4 English, 3 math, 3 science, 2 science labs, 2 foreign language, 3 social studies.

Accommodations or Services

Accommodations are decided upon an individual basis after a thorough review of appropriate, current documentation. The accommodations requests must be supported through the documentation provided and must be logically linked to the current impact of the condition on academic functioning.

Financial Aid

Students should submit: FAFSA; Institution's own financial aid form; State aid form. Applicants will be notified of awards on a rolling basis beginning 3/1. *Need-based scholarships/grants offered:* College/university scholarship or grant aid from institutional funds; Federal Pell; Private scholarships; SEOG; State scholarships/grants. *Loan aid offered:* Direct PLUS loans; Direct Subsidized Stafford Loans; Direct Unsubsidized Stafford Loans. Federal Work-Study Program available. Institutional employment available.

Campus Life

Activities: Campus Ministries; Choral groups; Concert band; Dance; Drama/theater; International Student Organization; Jazz band; Literary magazine; Marching band; Music ensembles; Musical theater; Pep band; Radio station; Student government; Student newspaper; Symphony orchestra; Television station. **Organizations:** 407 registered organizations, 20 honor societies, 16 religious organizations, 14 fraternities, 14 sororities. **Athletics (Intercollegiate):** *Men:* baseball, basketball, cross-country, diving, football, golf, swimming, tennis, track/field (outdoor), track/field (indoor). *Women:* basketball, cross-country, diving, golf, soccer, softball, swimming, tennis, track/field (outdoor), track/field (indoor), volleyball.

ACCOMMODATIONS

Allowed in exams:	
Calculators	Yes
Dictionary	Yes
Computer	Yes
Spell-checker	Yes
Extended test time	Yes
Scribe	Yes
Proctors	Yes
Oral exams	Yes
Note-takers	Yes
Support services for students with:	
LD	Yes
ADHD	Yes
ASD	Yes
Distraction-reduced environment	Yes
Recording of lecture allowed	Yes
Reading technology	Yes
Audio books	Yes
Other assistive technology	Yes
Priority registration	Yes
Added costs of services:	
For LD	No
For ADHD	No
For ASD	No
LD specialists	Yes
ADHD & ASD coaching	Yes
ASD specialists	No
Professional tutors	Yes
Peer tutors	Yes
Max. hours/week for services	Varies
How professors are notified of student approved accommodations	Student

COLLEGE GRADUATION REQUIREMENTS

Course waivers allowed	No
Course substitutions allowed	No

Lake Superior State University

650 W. Easterday Avenue, Sault Ste. Marie, MI 49783-1699 • Admissions: 906-635-2231 • Fax: 906-635-6669 **Support: S**

CAMPUS

Type of school	Public
Environment	City

STUDENTS

Undergrad enrollment	1,984
% male/female	46/54
% from out of state	7
% frosh live on campus	72

FINANCIAL FACTS

Annual in-state tuition	$12,456
Annual out-of-state tuition	$12,456
Room and board	$10,472
Required fees	$205

GENERAL ADMISSIONS INFO

Application fee	$0
Regular application deadline	Rolling
Nonfall registration	Yes

Admission may be deferred.

Range SAT EBRW	490-590
Range SAT Math	480-570
Range ACT Composite	18–23

ACADEMICS

Student/faculty ratio	17:1
% students returning for sophomore year	68

Most classes have 10–19 students.

Programs/Services for Students with Learning Differences

The Accessibility Services (AS) office is available to help students with disabilities participate fully in the university's programs, services, and activities. It is the policy of the university that persons with disabilities have access to any program, service, or activity offered by the university that is comparable to the access received by persons without disabilities, unless such access would place an undue burden upon the university. If technologies or other products are needed to provide access to university programs, services, or activities, AS will make every reasonable effort to purchase such products; if these products cannot be purchased, AS will make provisions for effective alternatives that meet the accessibility requirements.

Admissions

Lake Superior State University is an open-admission-policy institution. It has few admission thresholds and admits all applicants so long as certain minimum requirements are met. ACT or SAT is not required for admission.

Additional Information

The Academic Success Center (ASC) provides free academic support to all students. Services provided include small group tutoring, a Writing Center available for students to have drop in sessions or appointments for longer assignments, a Math Center for tutoring, the LSSU Mentoring that connects students with mentors, Supplemental Instruction courses for historically challenging courses, and the Aleks Math Program that provides two options for satisfying beginning math and prerequisites.

ADMISSIONS INFO FOR STUDENTS WITH LEARNING DIFFERENCES

Phone: 906-635-2355 • Email: accessibility@lssu.edu

SAT/ACT required: No
Interview required: No
Essay required: No
Additional application required: No
Documentation submitted to: Accessibility Services

Special Ed. HS course work accepted: No
Separate application required for Programs/Services: No
Documentation required for:
LD: Psychoeducational evaluation
ADHD: Psychoeducational evaluation
ASD: Psychoeducational evaluation

Lake Superior State University

Michigan

General Admissions

Very important factors include: rigor of secondary school record, academic GPA, standardized test scores. *Other factors include:* class rank, recommendation(s), interview, geographical residence. High school diploma is required and GED is accepted. *Academic units recommended:* 4 English, 3 math, 3 science, 3 science labs, 2 foreign language, 2 social studies, 1 history.

Accommodations or Services

Accommodations are decided upon an individual basis after a thorough review of appropriate, current documentation. The accommodations requests must be supported through the documentation provided and must be logically linked to the current impact of the condition on academic functioning.

Financial Aid

Students should submit: FAFSA*Need-based scholarships/grants offered:* College/university scholarship or grant aid from institutional funds; Federal Nursing Scholarships; Federal Pell; Private scholarships; SEOG; State scholarships/grants. *Loan aid offered:* Direct PLUS loans; Direct Subsidized Stafford Loans; Direct Unsubsidized Stafford Loans.

Campus Life

Activities: Campus Ministries; Choral groups; Dance; Drama/theater; International Student Organization; Literary magazine; Model UN; Pep band; Radio station; Student government; Student newspaper. **Organizations:** 60 registered organizations, 4 fraternities, 4 sororities. **Athletics (Intercollegiate):** *Men:* basketball, cross-country, ice hockey, tennis, track/field (outdoor), track/field (indoor). *Women:* basketball, cross-country, softball, tennis, track/field (outdoor), track/field (indoor), volleyball.

ACCOMMODATIONS

Allowed in exams:	
Calculators	Yes
Dictionary	Yes
Computer	Yes
Spell-checker	Yes
Extended test time	Yes
Scribe	Yes
Proctors	Yes
Oral exams	Yes
Note-takers	Yes
Support services for students with:	
LD	Yes
ADHD	Yes
ASD	Yes
Distraction-reduced environment	Yes
Recording of lecture alowed	Yes
Reading technology	Yes
Audio books	Yes
Other assistive technology	Yes
Priority registration	Yes
Added costs of services:	
For LD	No
For ADHD	No
For ASD	No
LD specialists	No
ADHD & ASD coaching	No
ASD specialists	No
Professional tutors	Yes
Peer tutors	Yes
Max. hours/week for services	Varies
How professors are notified of student approved accommodations	Student

COLLEGE GRADUATION REQUIREMENTS

Course waivers allowed	No
Course substitutions allowed	No

Michigan State University

250 Administration Building, East Lansing, MI 48824 • Admissions: 517-355-8332 • Fax: 517-353-1647 **Support: CS**

CAMPUS

Type of school	Public
Environment	City

STUDENTS

Undergrad enrollment	38,950
% male/female	49/51
% from out of state	14
% frosh live on campus	95

FINANCIAL FACTS

Annual in-state tuition	$16,650
Annual out-of-state tuition	$41,002
Room and board	$10,522

GENERAL ADMISSIONS INFO

Application fee	$65
Regular application deadline	Rolling
Nonfall registration	Yes

Admission may be deferred.

Range SAT EBRW	550–650
Range SAT Math	550–670
Range ACT Composite	23–29

ACADEMICS

Student/faculty ratio	16:1
% students returning for sophomore year	92

Most classes have 20–29 students.

Programs/Services for Students with Learning Differences

The Resource Center for Persons with Disabilities (RCPD) specialists work closely with students to coordinate accommodations. Documentation establishing the presence of a disability and explaining the nature and degree to which the disability affects major life activities including learning is essential for RCPD staff to accurately assess a condition and determine what accommodations would most effectively facilitate full participation at MSU. Students with disabilities must therefore provide medical/psychological documentation indicating the presence of a disability that substantially limits a major life activity.

Admissions

Freshman admission is based on: academic performance in high school, strength and quality of curriculum, recent trends in academic performance, class rank, Standardized test results, English language proficiency for non-U.S. citizens or permanent residents whose first language is not English, leadership, talents, conduct and diversity of experience. The mid 50% of admitted students have a 3.5–4.0 GPA, 23–29 ACT or 1130–1310 SAT. MSU is test optional for 2021 and will review this policy for future years.

Additional Information

BOND offers structured opportunities for social and communication development for students with autism. Students can connect with others facing similar challenges. The BOND program offers peer mentoring, skill-building events, and social outings. Additionally, the Stern Tutoring and Alternative Techniques for Education (STATE) program provides tutoring to students with learning disabilities who are academically at risk. STATE provides tutoring and peer mentoring as well as strategies for academic success. Finally, the Runge Family Endowment for Students with Learning Differences recognizes the role RCPD plays in welcoming students, reassuring families, and advancing successes for students growing through challenges. This endowment assists students with learning differences by helping to fund programming aimed at providing structure, learning strategies, and academic tutoring.

ADMISSIONS INFO FOR STUDENTS WITH LEARNING DIFFERENCES

Phone: 517-884-7273 • Fax: 517-432-3191 • Email: mjh@msu.edu

SAT/ACT required: Yes (Test optional for 2021)
Interview required: No
Essay required: Not Applicable
Additional application required: Yes
Documentation submitted to: RCPD

Special Ed. HS course work accepted: No
Separate application required for Programs/Services: Yes
Documentation required for:
LD: Psychoeducational evaluation
ADHD: Psychoeducational evaluation
ASD: Psychoeducational evaluation

Michigan State University

Michigan

General Admissions

Very important factors include: academic GPA, application essay, standardized test scores. *Important factors include:* rigor of secondary school record. *Other factors include:* class rank, recommendation(s), interview, extracurricular activities, talent/ability, character/personal qualities, first generation, alumni/ae relation, geographical residence, state residency, volunteer work, work experience, level of applicant's interest. High school diploma is required and GED is accepted. *Academic units required:* 4 English, 3 math, 3 science, 1 science lab, 2 foreign language, 3 social studies. *Academic units recommended:* 4 English, 3 math, 3 science, 2 foreign language, 3 social studies.

Accommodations or Services

Accommodations are decided upon an individual basis after a thorough review of appropriate, current documentation. The accommodations requests must be supported through the documentation provided and must be logically linked to the current impact of the condition on academic functioning.

Financial Aid

Students should submit: FAFSA; State aid form. Applicants will be notified of awards on or about 4/1. *Need-based scholarships/grants offered:* College/university scholarship or grant aid from institutional funds; Federal Pell; Private scholarships; SEOG; State scholarships/grants; United Negro College Fund. *Loan aid offered:* Direct PLUS loans; Direct Subsidized Stafford Loans; Direct Unsubsidized Stafford Loans. Federal Work-Study Program available. Institutional employment available.

Campus Life

Activities: Campus Ministries; Choral groups; Concert band; Dance; Drama/theater; International Student Organization; Jazz band; Literary magazine; Marching band; Model UN; Music ensembles; Musical theater; Opera; Pep band; Radio station; Student government; Student newspaper; Student-run film society; Symphony orchestra; Television station; Yearbook. **Organizations:** 700 registered organizations, 47 honor societies, 50 religious organizations, 38 fraternities, 23 sororities. **Athletics (Intercollegiate):** *Men:* baseball, basketball, cheerleading, cross-country, diving, football, golf, ice hockey, soccer, swimming, tennis, track/field (outdoor), track/field (indoor), wrestling. *Women:* basketball, cheerleading, crew/rowing, cross-country, diving, field hockey, golf, gymnastics, soccer, softball, swimming, tennis, track/field (outdoor), track/field (indoor), volleyball.

ACCOMMODATIONS

Allowed in exams:	
Calculators	Yes
Dictionary	No
Computer	Yes
Spell-checker	Yes
Extended test time	Yes
Scribe	Yes
Proctors	Yes
Oral exams	Yes
Note-takers	Yes
Support services for students with:	
LD	Yes
ADHD	Yes
ASD	Yes
Distraction-reduced environment	Yes
Recording of lecture alowed	Yes
Reading technology	Yes
Audio books	Yes
Other assistive technology	Yes
Priority registration	Yes
Added costs of services:	
For LD	No
For ADHD	No
For ASD	No
LD specialists	Yes
ADHD & ASD coaching	Yes
ASD specialists	Yes
Professional tutors	Yes
Peer tutors	Yes
Max. hours/week for services	2
How professors are notified of student approved accommodations	Student

COLLEGE GRADUATION REQUIREMENTS

Course waivers allowed	No
Course substitutions allowed	Yes
In what courses: Case-by-case basis	

Michigan Technological University

1400 Townsend Drive, Houghton, MI 49931 • Admissions: 906-487-2335 • Fax: 906-487-2125 **Support: CS**

CAMPUS	
Type of school	Public
Environment	Village
STUDENTS	
Undergrad enrollment	5,688
% male/female	72/28
% from out of state	22
% frosh live on campus	94
FINANCIAL FACTS	
Annual in-state tuition	$16,130
Annual out-of-state tuition	$36,432
Room and board	$11,314
Required fees	$306
GENERAL ADMISSIONS INFO	
Application fee	$0
Regular application deadline	Rolling
Nonfall registration	Yes
Range SAT EBRW	580–680
Range SAT Math	590–690
Range ACT Composite	25–30
ACADEMICS	
Student/faculty ratio	12:1
% students returning for sophomore year	84

Most classes have 10–19 students.

Programs/Services for Students with Learning Differences

To be eligible for services, students with disabilities must identify themselves and present professional documentation/evaluation to the Coordinator for Student Disability Services. Documentation should be recent, on letterhead and describe the current impact of the disability.

Admissions

All applicants must meet the same admission criteria. There is no separate admission process for students with disabilities. The average GPA is 3.8, 26.7 ACT or 1200 SAT. Michigan Tech does not recompute the GPA but will use either weighted or unweighted GPA, whichever is higher. Students applying for 2021 who have a 3.0 or higher cumulative GPA will be considered equally for admission whether or not scores are submitted. Students with a cumulative GPA below 3.0 must submit official test scores. Michigan Tech does not super score. Official scores are required for students who wish to be considered for merit-based scholarships.

Additional Information

Counseling Services offers support groups dependent on student interests and participation. Students run their own Autism Support group, The Spectrum Connection. Career Services works with Spectrum students on transitioning to careers. Student Disability Services provides support and resources for students with or without a documented disability. Students do not need to have documentation of a disability to discuss strategies for college success with the coordinator of student disability services; incoming students should make an appointment as early as possible in their first semester.

ADMISSIONS INFO FOR STUDENTS WITH LEARNING DIFFERENCES

Phone: 906-487-2212 • Fax: 906-487-3060 • Email: sds@mtu.edu

SAT/ACT required: Yes (Test optional for 2021)
Interview required: No
Essay required: No
Additional application required: No
Documentation submitted to: Student Disability Services

Special Ed. HS course work accepted: Yes
Separate application required for Programs/Services: No
Documentation required for:
LD: Psychoeducational evaluation
ADHD: Psychoeducational evaluation
ASD: Psychoeducational evaluation

Michigan Technological University

Michigan

General Admissions

Very important factors include: academic GPA, standardized test scores. *Important factors include:* rigor of secondary school record. *Other factors include:* application essay, recommendation(s), extracurricular activities, talent/ability, character/personal qualities. High school diploma is required and GED is accepted. *Academic units required:* 3 English, 3 math, 2 science. *Academic units recommended:* 4 English, 4 math, 3 science, 2 foreign language, 3 social studies, 2 academic electives, 1 computer science.

Accommodations or Services

Accommodations are decided upon an individual basis after a thorough review of appropriate, current documentation. The accommodations requests must be supported through the documentation provided and must be logically linked to the current impact of the condition on academic functioning.

Financial Aid

Students should submit: FAFSA. *Need-based scholarships/grants offered:* College/university scholarship or grant aid from institutional funds; Federal Pell; Private scholarships; SEOG; State scholarships/grants. *Loan aid offered:* Direct PLUS loans; Direct Subsidized Stafford Loans; Direct Unsubsidized Stafford Loans. Federal Work-Study Program available. Institutional employment available.

Campus Life

Activities: Campus Ministries; Choral groups; Concert band; Dance; Drama/theater; International Student Organization; Jazz band; Literary magazine; Music ensembles; Musical theater; Pep band; Radio station; Student government; Student newspaper; Student-run film society; Symphony orchestra. **Organizations:** 244 registered organizations, 15 honor societies, 7 religious organizations, 12 fraternities, 7 sororities. **Athletics (Intercollegiate):** *Men:* basketball, cross-country, football, ice hockey, skiing (Nordic/cross-country), tennis, track/field (outdoor). *Women:* basketball, cross-country, skiing (Nordic/cross-country), tennis, track/field (outdoor), volleyball.

ACCOMMODATIONS

Allowed in exams:	
Calculators	Yes
Dictionary	Yes
Computer	Yes
Spell-checker	Yes
Extended test time	Yes
Scribe	Yes
Proctors	Yes
Oral exams	Yes
Note-takers	Yes
Support services for students with:	
LD	Yes
ADHD	Yes
ASD	Yes
Distraction-reduced environment	Yes
Recording of lecture allowed	Yes
Reading technology	Yes
Audio books	Yes
Other assistive technology	Yes
Priority registration	Yes
Added costs of services:	
For LD	No
For ADHD	No
For ASD	No
LD specialists	Yes
ADHD & ASD coaching	Yes
ASD specialists	No
Professional tutors	No
Peer tutors	Yes
Max. hours/week for services	Varies
How professors are notified of student approved accommodations	Student and Disability Office

COLLEGE GRADUATION REQUIREMENTS

Course waivers allowed	No
Course substitutions allowed	No

Northern Michigan University

1401 Presque Isle Avenue, Marquette, MI 49855 • Admissions: 906-227-2650 • Fax: 906-227-1747 **Support: S**

CAMPUS

Type of school	Public
Environment	Village

STUDENTS

Undergrad enrollment	7,136
% male/female	44/56
% from out of state	23
% frosh live on campus	83

FINANCIAL FACTS

Annual in-state tuition	$12,232
Annual out-of-state tuition	$17,980
Room and board	$11,072

GENERAL ADMISSIONS INFO

Application fee	$35
Regular application deadline	Rolling
Nonfall registration	Yes

Admission may be deferred.

Range SAT EBRW	Test Blind
Range SAT Math	Test Blind
Range ACT Composite	Test Blind

ACADEMICS

Student/faculty ratio	20:1
% students returning for sophomore year	76

Most classes have 20–29 students.

Programs/Services for Students with Learning Differences

Disability Services (DS) provides services and accommodations to all students with disabilities. Disability Services provides assistance and accommodations to students who have documented disabilities. Accommodation requests are reviewed on an individual basis. Students are required to meet with the Coordinator of Disability Services and provide appropriate documentation, which includes a diagnosis, symptoms of the disability, test scores and data that support the diagnosis, and recommendations regarding classroom accommodations. Students with ADHD must provide appropriate documentation through a written report submitted by a medical doctor, psychiatrist, psychologist, counselor, or school psychologist to receive appropriate accommodations.

Admissions

There are no special admissions for students with learning disabilities. All students submit the same general application and are expected to have a high school GPA of at least 2.25. There are no specific high school courses required for admissions, though the university recommends 4 years English, 4 years math, 3 years history/social studies, 3 years science, 3 years foreign language, 2 years fine or performing arts, and 1 year computer instruction. Applicants not meeting all of the criteria will be fully considered by the Admission Review Committee. Applicants may be asked to take a preadmission test or supply further information.

Additional Information

The coordinator of DS works one-on-one with students as needed and will also meet with students who do not have specific documentation if they request assistance. Skill classes are offered in reading, writing, math, study skills, sociocultural development, and interpersonal growth. No course waivers are granted for graduation requirements from NMU. Substitutions, however, are granted when appropriate. Student Support Services provides each student with an individual program of educational support services, including academic advising; basic skill building in reading, math, and writing; counseling; career advisement; developmental skill building; mentoring; support groups and study groups; tutoring from paraprofessionals; specialized tutors; group tutoring or supplemental instruction; and workshops on personal development and study skills improvement.

ADMISSIONS INFO FOR STUDENTS WITH LEARNING DIFFERENCES

Phone: 906-227-1700 • Fax: 906-227-1714

SAT/ACT required: Yes (Test blind for 2021)
Interview required: No
Essay required: No
Additional application required: No
Documentation submitted to: Disability Services

Special Ed. HS course work accepted: Yes
Separate application required for Programs/Services: No
Documentation required for:
LD: Psychoeducational evaluation
ADHD: Psychoeducational evaluation
ASD: Psychoeducational evaluation

Northern Michigan University

General Admissions

Very important factors include: academic GPA, standardized test scores. High school diploma is required and GED is accepted. *Academic units recommended:* 4 English, 4 math, 4 science, 2 foreign language, 4 social studies.

Accommodations or Services

Accommodations are decided upon an individual basis after a thorough review of appropriate, current documentation. The accommodations requests must be supported through the documentation provided and must be logically linked to the current impact of the condition on academic functioning.

Financial Aid

Students should submit: FAFSA. *Need-based scholarships/grants offered:* College/university scholarship or grant aid from institutional funds; Federal Pell; Private scholarships; SEOG; State scholarships/grants. *Loan aid offered:* Direct PLUS loans; Direct Subsidized Stafford Loans; Direct Unsubsidized Stafford Loans. Federal Work-Study Program available. Institutional employment available.

Campus Life

Activities: Campus Ministries; Choral groups; Concert band; Dance; Drama/theater; International Student Organization; Jazz band; Literary magazine; Marching band; Model UN; Music ensembles; Musical theater; Opera; Pep band; Radio station; Student government; Student newspaper; Student-run film society; Symphony orchestra; Television station. **Organizations:** 300 registered organizations, 8 honor societies, 20 religious organizations, 2 fraternities, 4 sororities. **Athletics (Intercollegiate):** *Men:* basketball, football, golf, ice hockey, skiing (Nordic/cross-country). *Women:* basketball, cross-country, diving, skiing (Nordic/cross-country), soccer, swimming, track/field (outdoor), track/field (indoor), volleyball.

ACCOMMODATIONS

Allowed in exams:	
Calculators	Yes
Dictionary	Yes
Computer	Yes
Spell-checker	Yes
Extended test time	Yes
Scribe	Yes
Proctors	Yes
Oral exams	Yes
Note-takers	Yes
Support services for students with:	
LD	Yes
ADHD	Yes
ASD	Yes
Distraction-reduced environment	Yes
Recording of lecture alowed	Yes
Reading technology	No
Audio books	Yes
Other assistive technology	Yes
Priority registration	No
Added costs of services:	
For LD	No
For ADHD	No
For ASD	No
LD specialists	No
ADHD & ASD coaching	No
ASD specialists	No
Professional tutors	No
Peer tutors	Yes
Max. hours/week for services	2–4
How professors are notified of student approved accommodations	Student

COLLEGE GRADUATION REQUIREMENTS

Course waivers allowed	No
Course substitutions allowed	Yes
In what courses: Case-by-case basis	

University of Michigan—Ann Arbor

515 E. Jefferson St., Ann Arbor, MI 48109-1316 • Admissions: 734-764-7433 • Fax: 734-936-0740 **Support: CS**

CAMPUS	
Type of school	Public
Environment	City
STUDENTS	
Undergrad enrollment	31,046
% male/female	50/50
% from out of state	41
% frosh live on campus	97
FINANCIAL FACTS	
Annual in-state tuition	$17,948
Annual out-of-state tuition	$55,928
Room and board	$12,034
GENERAL ADMISSIONS INFO	
Application fee	$75
Regular application deadline	2/1
Nonfall registration	Yes
Admission may be deferred.	
Range SAT EBRW	660–740
Range SAT Math	680–790
Range ACT Composite	31–34
ACADEMICS	
Student/faculty ratio	15:1
% students returning for sophomore year	97
Most classes have 10–19 students.	

Programs/Services for Students with Learning Differences

SSD offers selected student services that are not provided by other University of Michigan offices or outside organizations. SSD assists students in negotiating disability-related barriers to the pursuit of their education; strives to improve access to university programs, activities, and facilities; and promotes increased awareness of disability issues on campus. SSD encourages inquiries for information and will confidentially discuss concerns.

Admissions

Students with learning disabilities are expected to meet the same admission requirements as their peers. There is no set minimum GPA as it is contingent on several other factors. For students with learning disabilities, the admissions office will accept letters of recommendation from LD specialists. When applying for admission to the University of Michigan, students with learning disabilities are encouraged to self-identify on the application form or by writing a cover letter. The university is highly selective in the admission process and applicants are encouraged to take the most rigorous curriculum offered in their high school. For the 2020–21 application cycle, students who are unable to provide standardized test scores are encouraged to apply and will not be disadvantaged in the application process. Applications will be reviewed with the information a student is able to provide.

Additional Information

Academic Coaching is available to students with learning disabilities through SSD. Academic Coaching is a working partnership that focuses on the "process of learning." Together with a professional coach, students examine their learning styles, habits of working, and current difficulties or barriers to success. Then together this team (coach and student) works to create and put in place more effective strategies than are the norm. The aim is to heighten awareness of what it takes to achieve academic success and anchor this with new strategies, a supportive relationship, and personal accountability.

ADMISSIONS INFO FOR STUDENTS WITH LEARNING DIFFERENCES

Phone: 734-763-3000 • Fax: 734-936-3947 • Email: ssdoffice@umich.edu

SAT/ACT required: Yes (Test optional for 2021)
Interview required: No
Essay required: Yes
Additional application required: No
Documentation submitted to: SSD

Special Ed. HS course work accepted: No
Separate application required for Programs/Services: No
Documentation required for:
LD: Psychoeducational evaluation
ADHD: Psychoeducational evaluation
ASD: Psychoeducational evaluation

University of Michigan—Ann Arbor

Michigan

General Admissions

Very important factors include: rigor of secondary school record, academic GPA. *Important factors include:* application essay, standardized test scores, recommendation(s), character/personal qualities, first generation. *Other factors include:* extracurricular activities, talent/ability, alumni/ae relation, geographical residence, state residency, volunteer work, work experience, level of applicant's interest. High school diploma is required and GED is accepted. *Academic units required:* 4 English, 3 math, 3 science, 1 science lab, 2 foreign language, 1 social study, 3 history. *Academic units recommended:* 4 English, 4 math, 4 science, 1 science lab, 4 foreign language, 1 social study, 3 history, 1 computer science, 2 visual/performing arts.

Accommodations or Services

Accommodations are decided upon an individual basis after a thorough review of appropriate, current documentation. The accommodations requests must be supported through the documentation provided and must be logically linked to the current impact of the condition on academic functioning.

Financial Aid

Students should submit: FAFSA. *Need-based scholarships/grants offered:* College/university scholarship or grant aid from institutional funds; Federal Pell; Private scholarships; SEOG; State scholarships/grants. *Loan aid offered:* Direct PLUS loans; Direct Subsidized Stafford Loans; Direct Unsubsidized Stafford Loans. Federal Work-Study Program available. Institutional employment available.

Campus Life

Activities: Campus Ministries; Choral groups; Concert band; Dance; Drama/theater; International Student Organization; Jazz band; Literary magazine; Marching band; Model UN; Music ensembles; Musical theater; Opera; Pep band; Radio station; Student government; Student newspaper; Student-run film society; Symphony orchestra; Television station; Yearbook. **Organizations:** 1500 registered organizations, 38 honor societies, 89 religious organizations, 29 fraternities, 28 sororities. **Athletics (Intercollegiate):** *Men:* baseball, basketball, cheerleading, cross-country, diving, football, golf, gymnastics, ice hockey, swimming, tennis, track/field (outdoor), track/field (indoor), wrestling. *Women:* basketball, cheerleading, crew/rowing, cross-country, diving, field hockey, golf, gymnastics, soccer, softball, swimming, tennis, track/field (outdoor), track/field (indoor), volleyball, water polo.

ACCOMMODATIONS

Allowed in exams:	
Calculators	Yes
Dictionary	Yes
Computer	Yes
Spell-checker	Yes
Extended test time	Yes
Scribe	Yes
Proctors	Yes
Oral exams	No
Note-takers	Yes
Support services for students with:	
LD	Yes
ADHD	Yes
ASD	Yes
Distraction-reduced environment	Yes
Recording of lecture allowed	Yes
Reading technology	Yes
Audio books	No
Other assistive technology	Yes
Priority registration	No
Added costs of services:	
For LD	No
For ADHD	No
For ASD	No
LD specialists	Yes
ADHD & ASD coaching	No
ASD specialists	No
Professional tutors	Yes
Peer tutors	Yes
Max. hours/week for services	Varies
How professors are notified of student approved accommodations	Student

COLLEGE GRADUATION REQUIREMENTS

Course waivers allowed	No
Course substitutions allowed	No

Western Michigan University

1903 W Michigan Ave., Kalamazoo, MI 49008-5211 • Admissions: 269-387-2000 • Fax: 269-387-2096 **Support: CS**

CAMPUS

Type of school	Public
Environment	City

STUDENTS

Undergrad enrollment	16,801
% male/female	51/49
% from out of state	14.9
% frosh live on campus	87

FINANCIAL FACTS

Annual in-state tuition	$13,380
Annual out-of-state tuition	$16,494
Room and board	$10,826

GENERAL ADMISSIONS INFO

Application fee	$40
Regular application deadline	Rolling
Nonfall registration	Yes
Range SAT EBRW	500–610
Range SAT Math	500–600
Range ACT Composite	19–26

ACADEMICS

Student/faculty ratio	16:1
% students returning for sophomore year	78

Most classes have 20–29 students.

Programs/Services for Students with Learning Differences

Disability Services for Students (DSS) makes education accessible to all students, regardless of issues or challenges faced. DSS advocates for students to have the appropriate tools and/or accommodations to be successful.

Admissions

The average WMU freshman has a 3.4 high school GPA and a 23 ACT or 1090 SAT. WMU does not require letters of recommendation, resumes, or personal statements. There is no separate application process for students with learning disabilities but students are encouraged to self-disclose if they wish to do so.

Additional Information

Western Michigan University's Autism Spectrum Services Center (ASC) provides transition support for students with ASD and other disabilities. The fee for this program includes weekly one-on-one meetings with an ASC coordinator or graduate student, workshops, and organized social events, and it promotes increased communication between students and faculty.

ADMISSIONS INFO FOR STUDENTS WITH LEARNING DIFFERENCES

Phone: 269-387-2116 • Email: vpsa-dsrs@wmich.edu

SAT/ACT required: Yes (Test optional for 2021)
Interview required: No
Essay required: No
Additional application required: No
Documentation submitted to: Disability Services for Students

Special Ed. HS course work accepted: No
Separate application required for Programs/Services: Yes
Documentation required for:
LD: Psychoeducational evaluation
ADHD: Psychoeducational evaluation
ASD: Psychoeducational evaluation

Western Michigan University

Michigan

General Admissions

Very important factors include: academic GPA, standardized test scores. *Important factors include:* rigor of secondary school record. *Other factors include:* application essay, recommendation(s), extracurricular activities. High school diploma is required and GED is accepted. *Academic units recommended:* 4 English, 3 math, 3 science, 2 foreign language, 3 social studies.

Accommodations or Services

Accommodations are decided upon an individual basis after a thorough review of appropriate, current documentation. The accommodations requests must be supported through the documentation provided and must be logically linked to the current impact of the condition on academic functioning.

Financial Aid

Students should submit: FAFSA. *Need-based scholarships/grants offered:* College/university scholarship or grant aid from institutional funds; Federal Pell; Private scholarships; SEOG; State scholarships/grants. *Loan aid offered:* Direct PLUS loans; Direct Subsidized Stafford Loans; Direct Unsubsidized Stafford Loans. Federal Work-Study Program available. Institutional employment available.

Campus Life

Activities: Campus Ministries; Choral groups; Concert band; Dance; Drama/theater; International Student Organization; Jazz band; Literary magazine; Marching band; Model UN; Music ensembles; Musical theater; Opera; Pep band; Radio station; Student government; Student newspaper; Student-run film society; Symphony orchestra. **Organizations:** 418 registered organizations, 17 honor societies, 47 religious organizations, 19 fraternities, 14 sororities. **Athletics (Intercollegiate):** *Men:* baseball, basketball, football, ice hockey, soccer, tennis. *Women:* basketball, cross-country, golf, gymnastics, soccer, softball, tennis, track/field (outdoor), track/field (indoor), volleyball.

ACCOMMODATIONS

Allowed in exams:	
Calculators	Yes
Dictionary	Yes
Computer	Yes
Spell-checker	Yes
Extended test time	Yes
Scribe	Yes
Proctors	Yes
Oral exams	Yes
Note-takers	Yes
Support services for students with:	
LD	Yes
ADHD	Yes
ASD	Yes
Distraction-reduced environment	Yes
Recording of lecture alowed	Yes
Reading technology	Yes
Audio books	Yes
Other assistive technology	Yes
Priority registration	Yes
Added costs of services:	
For LD	No
For ADHD	No
For ASD	Yes
LD specialists	Yes
ADHD & ASD coaching	Yes
ASD specialists	Yes
Professional tutors	No
Peer tutors	Yes
Max. hours/week for services	Varies
How professors are notified of student approved accommodations	Student

COLLEGE GRADUATION REQUIREMENTS

Course waivers allowed	No
Course substitutions allowed	No

Augsburg University

2211 Riverside Avenue, Minneapolis, MN 55454 • Admissions: 612-330-1001 • Fax: 612-330-1590 **Support: SP**

CAMPUS

Type of school	Private (nonprofit)
Environment	Metropolis

STUDENTS

Undergrad enrollment	2,512
% male/female	44/56
% from out of state	11
% frosh live on campus	65

FINANCIAL FACTS

Annual tuition	$39,395
Room and board	$10,885
Required fees	$710

GENERAL ADMISSIONS INFO

Regular application deadline	Rolling
Nonfall registration	Yes

Admission may be deferred.

Range SAT EBRW	540–650
Range SAT Math	520–660
Range ACT Composite	18–23

ACADEMICS

Student/faculty ratio	12:1
% students returning for sophomore year	72

Most classes have 10–19 students.

Programs/Services for Students with Learning Differences

Disability Resources (CLASS) provides those academic services needed to accommodate individuals with learning, attentional, psychiatric or other cognitive-based disabilities, as well as students with physical disabilities and other health concerns including temporary disabilities. The foundation of CLASS, however, is deeply rooted in the promotion of student independence and the personal realization of one's full potential. Augsburg students who are eligible to receive CLASS services, once admitted, will work one-on-one with a CLASS Disability Specialist. The Specialist will work to provide academic guidance and service-related assistance whenever appropriate. No additional or supplemental fee is required for CLASS services.

Admissions

Students with disabilities are evaluated for admission to Augsburg College according to the same criteria and standards as other applicants. Once admitted to the college, students with disabilities complete the same General Education Core Curriculum and must meet the same essential course requirements (with or without reasonable academic accommodations) as students without disabilities. Students do not need to disclose their learning difference to Admissions, and it is not taken into consideration in admission decisions. Any documentation of a learning disability should be sent directly to CLASS and not included with the application to the college.

Additional Information

To establish eligibility for services students must submit appropriate documentation for a cognitive-related disability that usually includes a current psychological, psychoeducational, or neuro-psychological evaluation. In some cases, they may ask for a treating clinician to complete and return the Verification of Disability form as a supplement to other documentation. If a student has an Autism Spectrum Disorder, they should fill out and return the PDD questionnaire in an effort to identify how the Pervasive Developmental Disorder diagnosis is currently and uniquely impacting the student. Students do not need to wait until they have been accepted to the college before determining their eligibility for CLASS services. They will review documentation for any prospective student who has applied for admission to Augsburg and will contact students about their eligibility once they have reviewed the documentation.

ADMISSIONS INFO FOR STUDENTS WITH LEARNING DIFFERENCES

Phone: 612-330-1053 • Fax: 612-330-1137 • Email: class@augsburg.edu

SAT/ACT required: No
Interview required: Yes
Essay required: Yes
Additional application required: No
Documentation submitted to: CLASS

Special Ed. HS course work accepted: No
Separate application required for Programs/Services: No
Documentation required for:
LD: Psychoeducational evaluation
ADHD: Psychoeducational evaluation
ASD: Psychoeducational evaluation

Augsburg University

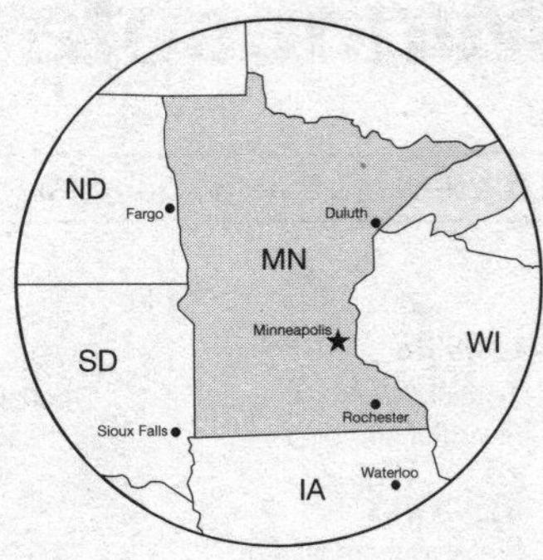

General Admissions

Very important factors include: rigor of secondary school record, class rank, academic GPA, application essay, recommendation(s). *Important factors include:* standardized test scores, extracurricular activities, alumni/ae relation. *Other factors include:* interview, talent/ability, first generation, volunteer work, work experience. High school diploma is required and GED is accepted. *Academic units required:* 4 English, 3 math, 3 science, 2 foreign language, 2 social studies. *Academic units recommended:* 4 social studies, 2 history.

Accommodations or Services

Accommodations are decided upon an individual basis after a thorough review of appropriate, current documentation. The accommodations requests must be supported through the documentation provided and must be logically linked to the current impact of the condition on academic functioning.

Financial Aid

Students should submit: FAFSA; State aid form. Applicants will be notified of awards on a rolling basis beginning 4/1. *Need-based scholarships/grants offered:* College/university scholarship or grant aid from institutional funds; Federal Pell; Private scholarships; SEOG; State scholarships/grants. *Loan aid offered:* Direct PLUS loans; Direct Subsidized Stafford Loans; Direct Unsubsidized Stafford Loans. Institutional employment available.

Campus Life

Activities: Campus Ministries; Choral groups; Concert band; Dance; Drama/theater; International Student Organization; Jazz band; Literary magazine; Music ensembles; Opera; Radio station; Student government; Student newspaper; Yearbook. **Organizations:** 35 registered organizations, 1 honor society, 1 religious organization. **Athletics (Intercollegiate):** *Men:* baseball, basketball, cross-country, football, golf, ice hockey, soccer, tennis, track/field (outdoor), track/field (indoor), wrestling. *Women:* basketball, cheerleading, cross-country, golf, ice hockey, soccer, softball, swimming, tennis, track/field (outdoor), track/field (indoor), volleyball.

ACCOMMODATIONS

Allowed in exams:	
Calculators	Yes
Dictionary	Yes
Computer	Yes
Spell-checker	Yes
Extended test time	Yes
Scribe	Yes
Proctors	Yes
Oral exams	Yes
Note-takers	Yes
Support services for students with:	
LD	Yes
ADHD	Yes
ASD	Yes
Distraction-reduced environment	Yes
Recording of lecture alowed	Yes
Reading technology	Yes
Audio books	Yes
Other assistive technology	Yes
Priority registration	No
Added costs of services:	
For LD	No
For ADHD	No
For ASD	No
LD specialists	Yes
ADHD & ASD coaching	No
ASD specialists	No
Professional tutors	No
Peer tutors	Yes
Max. hours/week for services	Varies
How professors are notified of student approved accommodations	Student

COLLEGE GRADUATION REQUIREMENTS

Course waivers allowed	No
Course substitutions allowed	Yes
In what courses: Case-by-case basis	

Minnesota

Minnesota State University, Moorhead

1104 Seventh Avenue, South Moorhead, MN 56563 • Admissions: 218-477-2161 • Fax: 218-477-4374 **Support: S**

CAMPUS

Type of school	Public
Environment	City

STUDENTS

Undergrad enrollment	4,675
% male/female	39/61
% from out of state	31
% frosh live on campus	88

FINANCIAL FACTS

Annual in-state tuition	$7,632
Annual out-of-state tuition	$15,262
Room and board	$9,864
Required fees	$1,000

GENERAL ADMISSIONS INFO

Application fee	$20
Regular application deadline	Rolling
Nonfall registration	Yes

Admission may be deferred.

Range ACT Composite	19–24

ACADEMICS

Student/faculty ratio	19:1
% students returning for sophomore year	76

Most classes have 20–29 students.

Programs/Services for Students with Learning Differences

The Disability Resource Center (DRC) addresses the needs of students who have disabilities. The purpose of the DRC is to provide services and accommodations to students with documented disabilities, work closely with faculty and staff in an advisory capacity, assist in the development of reasonable accommodations for students, and provide equal access for otherwise qualified individuals with disabilities. A student with a documented learning disability may be eligible for services. DRC will assist in the development of reasonable accommodations for students with disabilities. To be eligible to receive services, students must provide appropriate documentation. This documentation should identify the nature and extent of the disability and provide information on the functional limitations as related to the academic environment. The documentation should provide recommended reasonable accommodations. Requests that would alter the academic standards are not granted. Students are responsible for monitoring their progress with faculty, requesting assistance, and meeting university standards.

Admissions

All applicants must meet the same admission criteria, which is to have at least a 21 or higher composite on the ACT (or 1060 on the SAT), OR a cumulative 3.0 GPA (out of a 4.0 scale), OR to have a rank in the top 50% of their high school class. Course requirements include 4 years English, 3 years math, 3 years science, 3 years social studies, 2 years world language, and 2 years of world culture or the arts. Students can be admitted if deficient in course requirements. If denied admission, there is an appeal process.

Additional Information

Examples of general accommodations or services include the following: extended test times, reduced distraction testing environments, taped texts, note-taking, assistive technology, scribes, readers, tape-recording lectures, faculty liaisons, strategy development, priority registration, and individual support. Study skills courses are offered and students may earn credits for these courses. Services and accommodations are available for undergraduate and graduate students.

ADMISSIONS INFO FOR STUDENTS WITH LEARNING DIFFERENCES

Phone: 218-477-4318 • Fax: 218-477-2420 • Email: accessibility@mnstate.edu

SAT/ACT required: No
Interview required: No
Essay required: No
Additional application required: No
Documentation submitted to: Disability Resource Center

Special Ed. HS course work accepted: Yes
Separate application required for Programs/Services: No
Documentation required for:
LD: Psychoeducational evaluation
ADHD: Psychoeducational evaluation
ASD: Psychoeducational evaluation

Minnesota State University, Moorhead

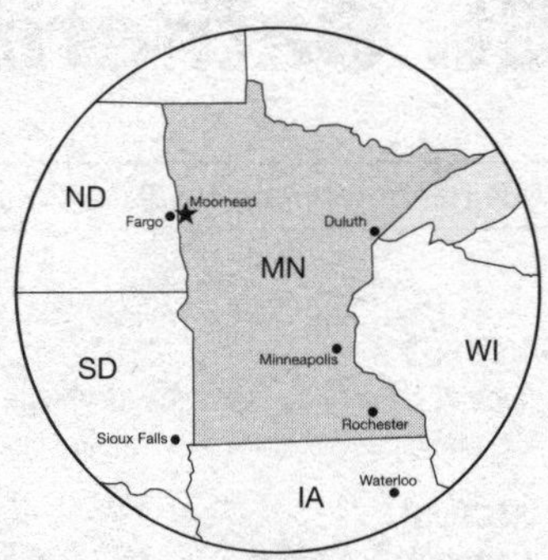

General Admissions

Very important factors include: class rank, academic GPA, standardized test scores. *Other factors include:* rigor of secondary school record, application essay, recommendation(s). High school diploma is required and GED is accepted. *Academic units required:* 4 English, 3 math, 3 science, 3 science lab, 2 foreign language, 2 social studies, 1 history, 2 visual/performing arts.

Accommodations or Services

Accommodations are decided upon an individual basis after a thorough review of appropriate, current documentation. The accommodations requests must be supported through the documentation provided and must be logically linked to the current impact of the condition on academic functioning.

Financial Aid

Students should submit: FAFSA. Applicants will be notified of awards on a rolling basis beginning 12/1. *Need-based scholarships/grants offered:* College/university scholarship or grant aid from institutional funds; Private scholarships; State scholarships/grants. *Loan aid offered:* Direct PLUS loans; Direct Subsidized Stafford Loans; Direct Unsubsidized Stafford Loans. Federal Work-Study Program available. Institutional employment available.

Campus Life

Activities: Campus Ministries; Choral groups; Concert band; Dance; Drama/theater; International Student Organization; Jazz band; Literary magazine; Model UN; Music ensembles; Musical theater; Pep band; Radio station; Student government; Student newspaper; Student-run film society; Television station. **Organizations:** 130 registered organizations, 7 honor societies, 11 religious organizations, 2 sororities. **Athletics (Intercollegiate):** *Men:* basketball, cross-country, football, track/field (outdoor), track/field (indoor), wrestling. *Women:* basketball, cross-country, golf, soccer, softball, swimming, tennis, track/field (outdoor), track/field (indoor), volleyball.

ACCOMMODATIONS

Allowed in exams:	
Calculators	Yes
Dictionary	Yes
Computer	Yes
Spell-checker	Yes
Extended test time	Yes
Scribe	Yes
Proctors	Yes
Oral exams	Rarely
Note-takers	Yes
Support services for students with:	
LD	Yes
ADHD	Yes
ASD	Yes
Distraction-reduced environment	Yes
Recording of lecture alowed	Yes
Reading technology	Yes
Audio books	Yes
Other assistive technology	Yes
Priority registration	Yes
Added costs of services:	
For LD	No
For ADHD	No
For ASD	No
LD specialists	Yes
ADHD & ASD coaching	No
ASD specialists	No
Professional tutors	No
Peer tutors	Yes
Max. hours/week for services	1
How professors are notified of student approved accommodations	Student and Disability Office

COLLEGE GRADUATION REQUIREMENTS

Course waivers allowed	Yes
In what courses: Depends on the disability and requirements of the student's major	
Course substitutions allowed	Yes
In what courses: Depends on the disability and requirements of the student's major	

Minnesota

St. Catherine University

2004 Randolph Avenue, Saint Paul, MN 55105 • Admissions: 651-690-6000 • Fax: 651-690-8868 **Support: CS**

CAMPUS

Type of school	Private (nonprofit)
Environment	Metropolis

STUDENTS

Undergrad enrollment	3,153
% male/female	5/95
% from out of state	17
% frosh live on campus	67

FINANCIAL FACTS

Annual tuition	$44,480
Room and board	$9,300
Required fees	$894

GENERAL ADMISSIONS INFO

Application fee	$0
Regular application deadline	Rolling
Nonfall registration	Yes

Admission may be deferred.

Range SAT EBRW	570–640
Range SAT Math	510–630
Range ACT Composite	23–25

ACADEMICS

Student/faculty ratio	11:1
% students returning for sophomore year	80

Most classes have 10–19 students.

Programs/Services for Students with Learning Differences

St. Catherine University has two campuses where learning support is available. The Academic Success Center (Minneapolis Campus) provides a wide range of academic support. It offers individual and group tutoring, both online and in person with peer tutors and professional staff. The O'Neill Center for Academic Development (St. Paul campus) provides individual academic support through the Writing/Reading Center, the Math/Science Center, the Disability Resources Center, and Student Mentors.

Admissions

There is no special admission procedure for students with learning disabilities, though the college tends to give special consideration if students self-disclose this information. Disclosure can help explain test scores, difficulties with certain course work, and so on. Saint Catherine University does not discriminate on the basis of disability in admission. A student may be accepted on a conditional basis to a program that provides special advising, limited course load, and a course in strategies for success.

Additional Information

To access services, the student and Access Consultant discuss the anticipated demands of the courses for which the student is registered and develop accommodation letters. The letters identify the learning strategies and accommodations that will be used. For example, texts in alternative formats, testing accommodations, and note-takers are some of the more frequently offered accommodations. The specific nature of the disability is not addressed the student delivers the accommodation letters to her professors. Some students meet with Access Consultants on a weekly basis for time management and study strategies. Within the O'Neill Center, a student may access assistance in writing, math and science courses.

ADMISSIONS INFO FOR STUDENTS WITH LEARNING DIFFERENCES

Phone: 651-590-6563 • Fax: 651-690-6718 • Email: oneill_center@stkate.edu

SAT/ACT required: No
Interview required: No
Essay required: Yes
Additional application required: No
Documentation submitted to: O'Neill Learning Center

Special Ed. HS course work accepted: Yes
Separate application required for Programs/Services: No
Documentation required for:
LD: Psychoeducational evaluation
ADHD: Psychoeducational evaluation
ASD: Psychoeducational evaluation

St. Catherine University

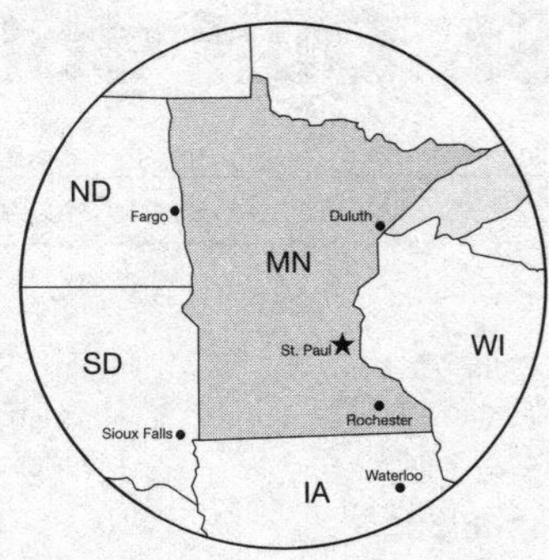

General Admissions

Very important factors include: rigor of secondary school record. *Important factors include:* class rank, academic GPA, application essay, standardized test scores, recommendation(s). *Other factors include:* interview, first generation, level of applicant's interest. High school diploma is required and GED is accepted. *Academic units recommended:* 4 English, 3 math, 2 science, 4 foreign language, 2 social studies.

Accommodations or Services

Accommodations are decided upon an individual basis after a thorough review of appropriate, current documentation. The accommodations requests must be supported through the documentation provided and must be logically linked to the current impact of the condition on academic functioning.

Financial Aid

Students should submit: FAFSA; Institution's own financial aid form. Applicants will be notified of awards on a rolling basis beginning 3/1. *Need-based scholarships/grants offered:* College/university scholarship or grant aid from institutional funds; Federal Nursing Scholarships; Federal Pell; Private scholarships; SEOG; State scholarships/grants. *Loan aid offered:* Direct PLUS loans; Direct Subsidized Stafford Loans; Direct Unsubsidized Stafford Loans. Federal Work-Study Program available. Institutional employment available.

Campus Life

Activities: Campus Ministries; Choral groups; Dance; Drama/theater; International Student Organization; Literary magazine; Music ensembles; Musical theater; Radio station; Student government; Student newspaper. **Organizations:** 40 registered organizations, 24 honor societies, 4 religious organizations, 1 sorority. **Athletics (Intercollegiate):** *Women:* basketball, cross-country, diving, ice hockey, soccer, softball, swimming, tennis, track/field (outdoor), track/field (indoor), volleyball.

ACCOMMODATIONS

Allowed in exams:	
Calculators	Yes
Dictionary	Yes
Computer	Yes
Spell-checker	Yes
Extended test time	Yes
Scribe	Yes
Proctors	Yes
Oral exams	Yes
Note-takers	Yes
Support services for students with:	
LD	Yes
ADHD	Yes
ASD	Yes
Distraction-reduced environment	Yes
Recording of lecture allowed	Yes
Reading technology	Yes
Audio books	Yes
Other assistive technology	Yes
Priority registration	Yes
Added costs of services:	
For LD	No
For ADHD	No
For ASD	No
LD specialists	Yes
ADHD & ASD coaching	No
ASD specialists	No
Professional tutors	No
Peer tutors	Yes
Max. hours/week for services	Unlimited
How professors are notified of student approved accommodations	Student and Disability Office

COLLEGE GRADUATION REQUIREMENTS

Course waivers allowed	No
Course substitutions allowed	Yes
In what courses: Case-by-case basis	

Minnesota

St. Olaf College

1520 St. Olaf Avenue, Northfield, MN 55057 • Admissions: 507-786-3025 • Fax: 507-786-3832 **Support: S**

CAMPUS

Type of school	Private (nonprofit)
Environment	Village

STUDENTS

Undergrad enrollment	3,072
% male/female	42/58
% from out of state	52
% frosh live on campus	100

FINANCIAL FACTS

Annual tuition	$51,450
Room and board	$11,660

GENERAL ADMISSIONS INFO

Application fee	$35
Regular application deadline	1/15
Nonfall registration	No

Admission may be deferred.

Range SAT EBRW	590–710
Range SAT Math	600–720
Range ACT Composite	26–32

ACADEMICS

Student/faculty ratio	12:1
% students returning for sophomore year	91

Most classes have 10–19 students.

Programs/Services for Students with Learning Differences

The goal of the services at St. Olaf is to provide equal access to a St. Olaf education for all students with disabilities. The purpose is to create and maintain an environment in which students may achieve their fullest potential, limited to the least extent possible by individual disabilities. All faculty, staff, and students of the college are expected to adhere to this philosophy of equal access to educational opportunity and assume broad responsibility for its implementation. In order to receive services through Student Disability Services, students must provide a clear statement of diagnosed disability.

Admissions

All applicants must meet the same competitive admission criteria. There is no separate application process for students with learning disabilities or attention deficit disorder. It's recommended that students have a strong academic curriculum. Once admitted, students with documented disabilities should have their current documentation sent to the Student Disability Services Office.

Additional Information

Academic Coaching is available and offered free of charge for students who wish to learn more about managing time, learning styles and strategies, study skills or strategies, accountability, test-taking strategies, test-taking anxiety, note taking strategies, and more. St. Olaf also offers Supplemental Instruction (SI) for courses that are historically difficult. SI is provided by peer leaders who have taken the specific course and are trained in helping students learn and retain new information.

ADMISSIONS INFO FOR STUDENTS WITH LEARNING DIFFERENCES

Phone: 507-756-3288 • Fax: 507-786-3923 • Email: glampe@stolaf.edu

SAT/ACT required: No
Interview required: No
Essay required: No
Additional application required: No
Documentation submitted to: Disability and Access

Special Ed. HS course work accepted: Yes
Separate application required for Programs/Services: No
Documentation required for:
LD: Psychoeducational evaluation
ADHD: Psychoeducational evaluation
ASD: Psychoeducational evaluation

St. Olaf College

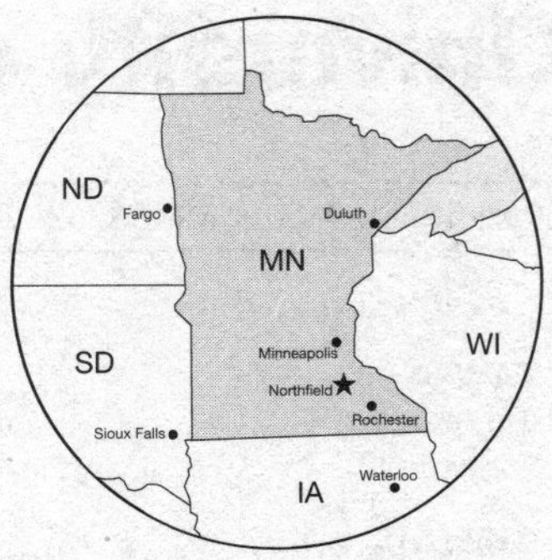

General Admissions

Very important factors include: rigor of secondary school record, academic GPA, application essay. *Important factors include:* class rank, standardized test scores, recommendation(s), interview, extracurricular activities, talent/ability, character/personal qualities. *Other factors include:* first generation, alumni/ae relation, geographical residence, state residency, religious affiliation/commitment, racial/ethnic status, volunteer work, work experience, level of applicant's interest. High school diploma is required and GED is accepted. *Academic units recommended:* 4 English, 4 math, 4 science, 2 science labs, 4 foreign language, 4 social studies.

Accommodations or Services

Accommodations are decided upon an individual basis after a thorough review of appropriate, current documentation. The accommodations requests must be supported through the documentation provided and must be logically linked to the current impact of the condition on academic functioning.

Financial Aid

Students should submit: FAFSA. *Need-based scholarships/grants offered:* College/university scholarship or grant aid from institutional funds; Federal Pell; Private scholarships; SEOG; State scholarships/grants. *Loan aid offered:* Direct Subsidized Stafford Loans; Direct Unsubsidized Stafford Loans. Federal Work-Study Program available. Institutional employment available.

Campus Life

Activities: Campus Ministries; Choral groups; Concert band; Dance; Drama/theater; International Student Organization; Jazz band; Literary magazine; Model UN; Music ensembles; Musical theater; Opera; Pep band; Radio station; Student government; Student newspaper; Student-run film society; Symphony orchestra. **Organizations:** 221 registered organizations, 20 honor societies, 15 religious organizations. **Athletics (Intercollegiate):** *Men:* baseball, basketball, cross-country, diving, football, golf, ice hockey, skiing (downhill/alpine), skiing (Nordic/cross-country), soccer, swimming, tennis, track/field (outdoor), track/field (indoor), wrestling. *Women:* basketball, cross-country, diving, golf, ice hockey, skiing (downhill/alpine), skiing (Nordic/cross-country), soccer, softball, swimming, tennis, track/field (outdoor), track/field (indoor), volleyball.

ACCOMMODATIONS

Allowed in exams:	
Calculators	Yes
Dictionary	Yes
Computer	Yes
Spell-checker	Yes
Extended test time	Yes
Scribe	Yes
Proctors	Yes
Oral exams	Yes
Note-takers	Yes
Support services for students with:	
LD	Yes
ADHD	Yes
ASD	Yes
Distraction-reduced environment	Yes
Recording of lecture alowed	Yes
Reading technology	Yes
Audio books	Yes
Other assistive technology	Yes
Priority registration	No
Added costs of services:	
For LD	No
For ADHD	No
For ASD	No
LD specialists	Yes
ADHD & ASD coaching	Yes
ASD specialists	Yes
Professional tutors	No
Peer tutors	Yes
Max. hours/week for services	Unlimited
How professors are notified of student approved accommodations	Student

COLLEGE GRADUATION REQUIREMENTS

Course waivers allowed	No
Course substitutions allowed	Yes
In what courses: Case-by-case basis	

University of Minnesota, Morris

600 E 4th St., Morris, MN 56267 • Admissions: 320-589-6035 • Fax: 320-589-6051 **Support: S**

CAMPUS

Type of school	Public
Environment	Rural

STUDENTS

Undergrad enrollment	1,499
% male/female	42/58
% from out of state	20
% frosh live on campus	95

FINANCIAL FACTS

Annual in-state tuition	$12,324
Annual out-of-state tuition	$14,378
Room and board	$8,632
Required fees	$1,254

GENERAL ADMISSIONS INFO

Application fee	$35
Regular application deadline	3/15
Nonfall registration	Yes

Admission may be deferred.

Range SAT EBRW	540–660
Range SAT Math	550–600
Range ACT Composite	21–28

ACADEMICS

Student/faculty ratio	11:1
% students returning for sophomore year	79

Most classes have 10–19 students.

Programs/Services for Students with Learning Differences

The Disability Resource Center (DRC) promotes access and equity for all students, faculty, staff, and guests of the University of Minnesota Morris. The DRC Coordinator uses documentation to better understand a student's experience of their condition, identify impacts in an academic setting, and make informed decisions to determine reasonable and appropriate accommodations. When additional information is needed to determine accommodations, the DRC Coordinator can help the student obtain what is necessary, which may require the student to sign a release of information for current providers. If the student is not working with a provider, the Coordinator can provide referral information to the student. Students are responsible for the cost of assessments and appointments with providers.

Admissions

All applicants are expected to meet the same admission criteria. There is no separate application for students with learning disabilities. Course requirements include 4 years English, 4 years math, 3 years science, 3 years social studies, and 2 years foreign language. Applicants missing the foreign language requirement will not be denied admission if they are otherwise admissible. The average ACT is 22–27 or SAT 1080–1350.

Additional Information

The Peer Assisted Learning (PAL) program is designed to aid students with courses historically considered difficult. PAL facilitators meet with students on a regularly scheduled basis, out of class, to conduct group review sessions. Participation is voluntary. Students are encouraged to contact the DRC as early as possible to discuss reasonable accommodations or services. The DRC Coordinator and students will discuss how the disability impacts academics and student life. The primary responsibility of the Coordinator is to determine students' eligibility for services and to facilitate the process of identifying appropriate and reasonable accommodations.

ADMISSIONS INFO FOR STUDENTS WITH LEARNING DIFFERENCES

Phone: 320-589-6178 • Fax: 320-589-6473 • Email: hoekstra@morris.umn.edu

SAT/ACT required: Yes (Test optional for 2021)
Interview required: No
Essay required: No
Additional application required: Yes
Documentation submitted to: DRC

Special Ed. HS course work accepted: Yes
Separate application required for Programs/Services: Yes
Documentation required for:
LD: Psychoeducational evaluation
ADHD: Psychoeducational evaluation
ASD: Psychoeducational evaluation

University of Minnesota, Morris

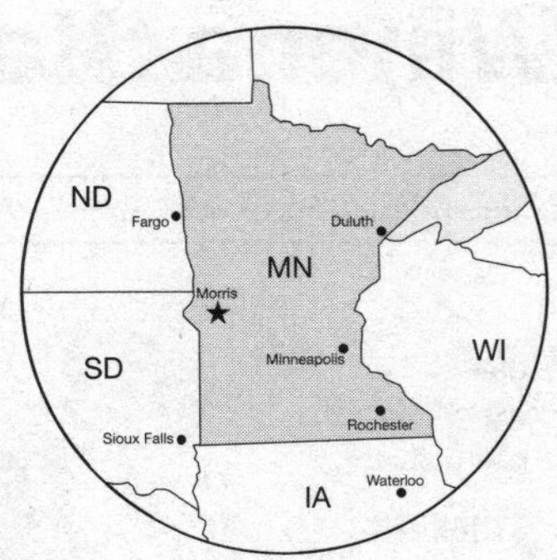

General Admissions

Very important factors include: rigor of secondary school record, class rank, academic GPA, standardized test scores. *Important factors include:* extracurricular activities, talent/ability, character/personal qualities, volunteer work, work experience. *Other factors include:* application essay, recommendation(s), interview, first generation. High school diploma is required and GED is accepted. *Academic units required:* 4 English, 4 math, 3 science, 2 foreign language, 3 social studies.

Accommodations or Services

Accommodations are decided upon an individual basis after a thorough review of appropriate, current documentation. The accommodations requests must be supported through the documentation provided and must be logically linked to the current impact of the condition on academic functioning.

Financial Aid

Students should submit: FAFSA; Institution's own financial aid form. *Need-based scholarships/grants offered:* College/university scholarship or grant aid from institutional funds; Federal Pell; Private scholarships; SEOG; State scholarships/grants. *Loan aid offered:* Direct PLUS loans; Direct Subsidized Stafford Loans; Direct Unsubsidized Stafford Loans. Federal Work-Study Program available. Institutional employment available.

Campus Life

Activities: Campus Ministries; Choral groups; Concert band; Dance; Drama/theater; International Student Organization; Jazz band; Literary magazine; Music ensembles; Musical theater; Radio station; Student government; Student newspaper; Symphony orchestra. **Organizations:** 100 registered organizations, 5 honor societies, 12 religious organizations. **Athletics (Intercollegiate):** *Men:* baseball, basketball, football, golf, tennis, track/field (outdoor), track/field (indoor). *Women:* basketball, cross-country, diving, golf, soccer, softball, swimming, tennis, track/field (outdoor), track/field (indoor), volleyball.

ACCOMMODATIONS

Allowed in exams:	
Calculators	Yes
Dictionary	Yes
Computer	Yes
Spell-checker	Yes
Extended test time	Yes
Scribe	Yes
Proctors	Yes
Oral exams	Yes
Note-takers	Yes
Support services for students with:	
LD	Yes
ADHD	Yes
ASD	Yes
Distraction-reduced environment	Yes
Recording of lecture alowed	Yes
Reading technology	Yes
Audio books	Yes
Other assistive technology	Yes
Priority registration	Yes
Added costs of services:	
For LD	No
For ADHD	No
For ASD	No
LD specialists	No
ADHD & ASD coaching	Yes
ASD specialists	No
Professional tutors	No
Peer tutors	Yes
Max. hours/week for services	Varies
How professors are notified of student approved accommodations	Student and Disability Office

COLLEGE GRADUATION REQUIREMENTS

Course waivers allowed	Yes
In what courses: Students may submit a petition for a waiver to be determined by a committee	
Course substitutions allowed	Yes
In what courses: Students may submit a petition for a waiver to be determined by a committee	

Minnesota

Winona State University

600 E 4th St., Morris, MN 56267 • Admissions: 320-589-6035 • Fax: 320-589-6051 **Support: S**

CAMPUS

Type of school	Public
Environment	Rural

STUDENTS

Undergrad enrollment	6,972
% male/female	34/66
% from out of state	29

FINANCIAL FACTS

Annual in-state tuition	$7,720
Annual out-of-state tuition	$13,900
Room and board	$9,190
Required fees	$1,114

GENERAL ADMISSIONS INFO

Application fee	$20
Regular application deadline	7/13
Nonfall registration	Yes

Admission may be deferred.

Range SAT EBRW	490–580
Range SAT Math	510–630
Range ACT Composite	19–24

ACADEMICS

Student/faculty ratio	19:1
% students returning for sophomore year	75

Most classes have 10–19 students.

Programs/Services for Students with Learning Differences

"Helping Students Succeed" is the motto of WSU's Access Services. Many academic resources are offered free of charge to qualified students. Examples of academic accommodations include but are not limited to extended time on exams, low distraction test environment and alternate format textbooks.

Admissions

ACT score of 21 or better with class rank in top 2/3 of high school class or Top 50 percent of graduating class with an ACT score of 18–20. Course requirements include: 4 years English, 4 years math, 3 years science, 3 years social studies, 2 years foreign language (American Sign Language is accepted), and 1 additional year of an elective. The student's academic transcript will be reviewed to see that they have completed the Minnesota State University Preparation Requirements. Admissions decisions are processed in 15 to 20 days.

Additional Information

Students are encouraged to contact the DRC as early as possible to discuss reasonable accommodations or services. The DRC Coordinator and students will discuss how the disability impacts academics and student life. The primary responsibility of the Coordinator is to determine students' eligibility for services and to facilitate the process of identifying appropriate and reasonable accommodations.

ADMISSIONS INFO FOR STUDENTS WITH LEARNING DIFFERENCES

Phone: 320-589-6178 • Fax: 320-589-6473 • Email: hoekstra@morris.umn.edu

SAT/ACT required: No (depending on GPA)
Interview required: No
Essay required: No
Additional application required: Yes
Documentation submitted to: DRC

Special Ed. HS course work accepted: Yes
Separate application required for Programs/Services: Yes
Documentation required for:
LD: Psychoeducational evaluation
ADHD: Psychoeducational evaluation
ASD: Psychoeducational evaluation

Winona State University

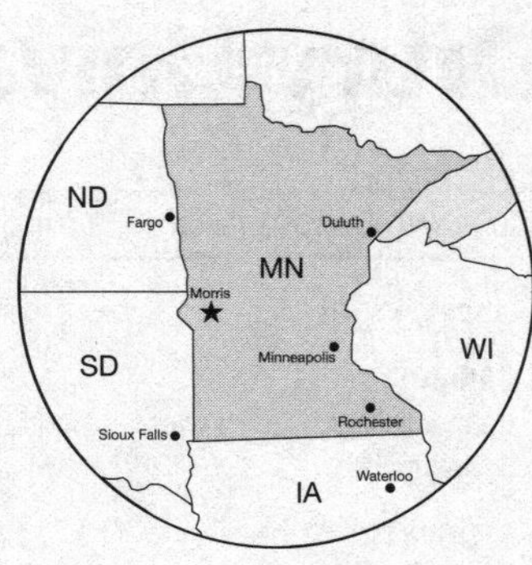

General Admissions

Very important factors include: rigor of secondary school record, class rank, academic GPA, standardized test scores. *Important factors include:* extracurricular activities, talent/ability, character/personal qualities, volunteer work, work experience. *Other factors include:* application essay, recommendation(s), interview, first generation. High school diploma is required and GED is accepted. *Academic units required:* 4 English, 4 math, 3 science, 2 foreign language, 3 social studies.

Accommodations or Services

Accommodations are decided upon an individual basis after a thorough review of appropriate, current documentation. The accommodations requests must be supported through the documentation provided and must be logically linked to the current impact of the condition on academic functioning.

Financial Aid

Students should submit: FAFSA; Institution's own financial aid form. *Need-based scholarships/grants offered:* College/university scholarship or grant aid from institutional funds; Federal Pell; Private scholarships; SEOG; State scholarships/grants. *Loan aid offered:* Direct PLUS loans; Direct Subsidized Stafford Loans; Direct Unsubsidized Stafford Loans. Federal Work-Study Program available. Institutional employment available.

Campus Life

Activities: Campus Ministries; Choral groups; Concert band; Dance; Drama/theater; International Student Organization; Jazz band; Literary magazine; Music ensembles; Musical theater; Radio station; Student government; Student newspaper; Symphony orchestra. **Organizations:** 100 registered organizations, 5 honor societies, 12 religious organizations. **Athletics (Intercollegiate):** *Men:* baseball, basketball, football, golf, tennis, track/field (outdoor), track/field (indoor). *Women:* basketball, cross-country, diving, golf, soccer, softball, swimming, tennis, track/field (outdoor), track/field (indoor), volleyball.

ACCOMMODATIONS

Allowed in exams:	
Calculators	Yes
Dictionary	Yes
Computer	Yes
Spell-checker	Yes
Extended test time	Yes
Scribe	Yes
Proctors	Yes
Oral exams	Yes
Note-takers	Yes
Support services for students with:	
LD	Yes
ADHD	Yes
ASD	Yes
Distraction-reduced environment	Yes
Recording of lecture alowed	Yes
Reading technology	Yes
Audio books	Yes
Other assistive technology	Yes
Priority registration	Yes
Added costs of services:	
For LD	No
For ADHD	No
For ASD	No
LD specialists	No
ADHD & ASD coaching	Yes
ASD specialists	No
Professional tutors	No
Peer tutors	Yes
Max. hours/week for services	Varies
How professors are notified of student approved accommodations	Student and Disability Office

COLLEGE GRADUATION REQUIREMENTS

Course waivers allowed: Yes

In what courses: Students may submit a petition for a waiver to be determined by a committee

Course substitutions allowed: Yes

In what courses: Students may submit a petition for a waiver to be determined by a committee

Minnesota

Drury University

900 North Benton Avenue, Springfield, MO 65802-3712 • Admissions: 417-873-7205 • Fax: 417-866-3873 **Support: S**

CAMPUS

Type of school	Private (nonprofit)
Environment	Metropolis

STUDENTS

Undergrad enrollment	1,477
% male/female	42/58
% from out of state	20
% frosh live on campus	81

FINANCIAL FACTS

Annual tuition	$29,900
Room and board	$9,236
Required fees	$1,315

GENERAL ADMISSIONS INFO

Application fee	$0
Regular application deadline	8/3
Nonfall registration	Yes

Admission may be deferred.

Range SAT EBRW	520–620
Range SAT Math	525–605
Range ACT Composite	22–28

ACADEMICS

Student/faculty ratio	13:1
% students returning for sophomore year	79

Most classes have 10–19 students.

Programs/Services for Students with Learning Differences

Disability Support Services helps ensure an equitable college experience for Drury Students with disabilities. Academic accommodations are available at no cost to students who can provide documentation of a disability and can demonstrate that the requested accommodations are necessary for participation in university programs within established guidelines. Academic accommodations coordinated by Disability Support Services include, but are not limited to: extended time during exams, testing in a low-distraction environment, out-of-class testing, audio textbooks and materials, student note-takers, preferential seating, tape recorded lectures, sign language interpreters, adjustable tables, and seating. Disability Support Services also offers information and referral services concerning the many programs of the University and Springfield community.

Admissions

The university is test optional and standardized tests are not required for admission. However, if an applicant does not submit either the ACT or SAT the applicant will need to write a 250 word essay for admission answering one of these four topics: 1) Describe a community with which you identify. 2) Explain a time that you have gone beyond and left an impact on a group or person and the world around you. 3) Define success. 4) Describe a challenge you have faced and overcome. Drury is very flexible in admission and students can take classes without enrolling in the college. Drury partners with many colleges to allow students to transfer with limited difficulty. Fusion is a Drury College program that can be customized to meet individual priorities but has some foundational courses required by all students.

Additional Information

Disability Support Services Office provides services for students who qualify based upon appropriate documentation. Accommodations include: extended time during exams, testing in a distraction-free environment, audio textbooks, student note-takers, preferential seating, tape recorded lectures, priority registration, peer mentors to help provide peer guidance as you make the transition to Drury University, and help developing self-advocacy skills.

ADMISSIONS INFO FOR STUDENTS WITH LEARNING DIFFERENCES

Phone: 417-873-7457 • Fax: 417-873-6833 • Email: ederr@drury.edu

SAT/ACT required: No
Interview required: No
Essay required: No
Additional application required: Yes
Documentation submitted to: DSS

Special Ed. HS course work accepted: Yes
Separate application required for Programs/Services: Yes
Documentation required for:
- **LD:** Psychoeducational evaluation
- **ADHD:** Psychoeducational evaluation
- **ASD:** Psychoeducational evaluation

Drury University

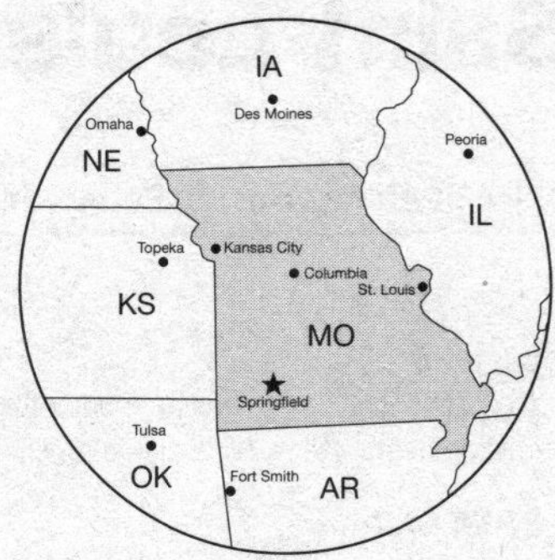

General Admissions

Very important factors include: academic GPA, standardized test scores. *Important factors include:* rigor of secondary school record, talent/ability. *Other factors include:* application essay, recommendation(s), interview, extracurricular activities, character/personal qualities, first generation, alumni/ae relation, religious affiliation/commitment, racial/ethnic status, volunteer work, work experience, level of applicant's interest. High school diploma is required and GED is accepted. *Academic units required:* 3 math. *Academic units recommended:* 4 English, 3 math, 3 science, 2 foreign language, 3 social studies.

Accommodations or Services

Accommodations are decided upon an individual basis after a thorough review of appropriate, current documentation. The accommodations requests must be supported through the documentation provided and must be logically linked to the current impact of the condition on academic functioning.

Financial Aid

Students should submit: FAFSA. *Need-based scholarships/grants offered:* College/university scholarship or grant aid from institutional funds; Federal Pell; Private scholarships; SEOG; State scholarships/grants. *Loan aid offered:* Direct PLUS loans; Direct Subsidized Stafford Loans; Direct Unsubsidized Stafford Loans. Federal Work-Study Program available. Institutional employment available.

Campus Life

Activities: Campus Ministries; Choral groups; Concert band; Dance; Drama/theater; International Student Organization; Jazz band; Model UN; Music ensembles; Musical theater; Pep band; Radio station; Student government; Student newspaper; Symphony orchestra; Television station. **Organizations:** 74 registered organizations, 9 honor societies, 5 religious organizations, 4 fraternities, 4 sororities. **Athletics (Intercollegiate):** *Men:* baseball, basketball, cheerleading, cross-country, diving, golf, soccer, softball, swimming, tennis. *Women:* basketball, cheerleading, cross-country, diving, golf, soccer, softball, swimming, tennis, volleyball.

ACCOMMODATIONS

Allowed in exams:	
Calculators	Yes
Dictionary	Yes
Computer	Yes
Spell-checker	Yes
Extended test time	Yes
Scribe	Yes
Proctors	Yes
Oral exams	Yes
Note-takers	Yes
Support services for students with:	
LD	Yes
ADHD	Yes
ASD	Yes
Distraction-reduced environment	Yes
Recording of lecture allowed	Yes
Reading technology	No
Audio books	Yes
Other assistive technology	No
Priority registration	Yes
Added costs of services:	
For LD	No
For ADHD	No
For ASD	No
LD specialists	Yes
ADHD & ASD coaching	Yes
ASD specialists	Yes
Professional tutors	No
Peer tutors	Yes
Max. hours/week for services	varies
How professors are notified of student approved accommodations	Student

COLLEGE GRADUATION REQUIREMENTS

Course waivers allowed	No
Course substitutions allowed	No

Missouri

Saint Louis University

Office of Admissions, DuBourg Hall, Saint Louis, MO 63103 • Admissions: 314-977-2500 • Fax: 314-977-7136 **Support: S**

CAMPUS

Type of school	Private (nonprofit)
Environment	Metropolis

STUDENTS

Undergrad enrollment	7,127
% male/female	40/60
% from out of state	61
% frosh live on campus	92

FINANCIAL FACTS

Annual tuition	$46,400
Room and board	$12,920
Required fees	$724

GENERAL ADMISSIONS INFO

Application fee	$0
Regular application deadline	Rolling
Nonfall registration	Yes

Admission may be deferred.

Range SAT EBRW	590–680
Range SAT Math	580–700
Range ACT Composite	25–30

ACADEMICS

Student/faculty ratio	9:1
% students returning for sophomore year	91

Most classes have 20–29 students.

Programs/Services for Students with Learning Differences

Students at St Louis University are expected to self-identify and apply for accommodations through Disability Services. Accommodations must be renewed annually. The university partners with students, faculty, academic departments, and service providers to facilitate equal access to and opportunity to participate in all university programs, services, and experiences. Aids and services are coordinated to meet the needs of students with disabilities to create a safe and supportive campus community for everyone.

Admissions

Saint Louis University is test optional and does not require the ACT or SAT for admission. Saint Louis admissions is selective with an acceptance rate of 58%. Students that get into Saint Louis who submit scores have an average SAT score between 1180–1370 or an average ACT score of 25–31. The average GPA is 3.9.

Additional Information

Students with LD are responsible for contacting Disability Services in order to learn about the accommodation process on campus and to receive academic accommodations within the classroom. Student Support Services (SSS) works with students throughout their time at SLU, from assisting with their transition to college to planning for what comes after their bachelor's degree is in hand. They do this in a variety of ways and strive to provide the students with quality programming and support during their journey. SSS goals for students include: successful transition, academic success, and developing sense of self. Applicants will have both a primary advisor in their college and a SSS advisor. Students are expected to meet with advisers at least once each semester. Standing tutoring appointments allow students to meet with the same tutor at the same day and time each week for the entire semester. SSS also has its own writing consultant to help students with papers and to grow skills in the writing process.

ADMISSIONS INFO FOR STUDENTS WITH LEARNING DIFFERENCES

Phone: 314-977-3484 • Fax: 314-977-3486 • Email: disability_services@slu.edu

SAT/ACT required: Yes (Test optional for 2021)
Interview required: No
Essay required: Yes
Additional application required: No
Documentation submitted to: Disability Services in the Student Success Center

Special Ed. HS course work accepted: No
Separate application required for Programs/Services: No
Documentation required for:
LD: Psychoeducational evaluation
ADHD: Psychoeducational evaluation
ASD: Psychoeducational evaluation

Saint Louis University

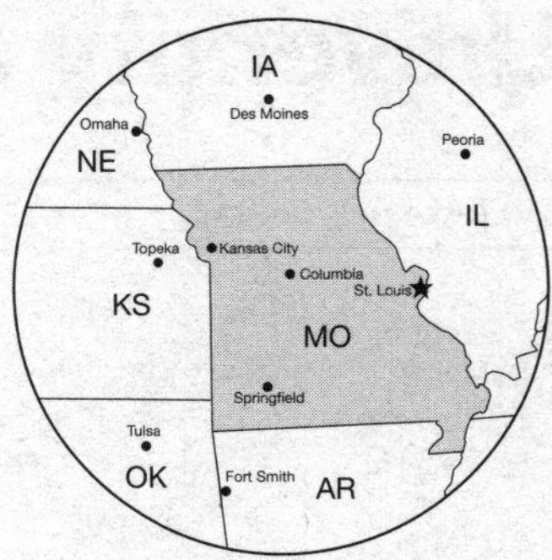

General Admissions

Very important factors include: academic GPA, standardized test scores. *Important factors include:* rigor of secondary school record, application essay, extracurricular activities, talent/ability, character/personal qualities, volunteer work. *Other factors include:* recommendation(s), interview, work experience. High school diploma is required and GED is accepted. *Academic units required:* 4 English, 4 math, 3 science, 3 foreign language, 3 social studies, 3 academic electives. *Academic units recommended:* 4 English, 4 math, 3 science, 3 foreign language, 3 social studies, 3 academic electives.

Accommodations or Services

Accommodations are decided upon an individual basis after a thorough review of appropriate, current documentation. The accommodations requests must be supported through the documentation provided and must be logically linked to the current impact of the condition on academic functioning.

Financial Aid

Students should submit: FAFSA. Applicants will be notified of awards on a rolling basis beginning 4/1. *Need-based scholarships/grants offered:* College/university scholarship or grant aid from institutional funds; Federal Nursing Scholarships; Federal Pell; Private scholarships; SEOG; State scholarships/grants. *Loan aid offered:* Direct PLUS loans; Direct Subsidized Stafford Loans; Direct Unsubsidized Stafford Loans. Federal Work-Study Program available. Institutional employment available.

Campus Life

Activities: Campus Ministries; Choral groups; Dance; Drama/theater; International Student Organization; Jazz band; Literary magazine; Model UN; Music ensembles; Musical theater; Pep band; Radio station; Student government; Student newspaper; Symphony orchestra; Television station. **Athletics (Intercollegiate):** *Men:* baseball, basketball, cross-country, diving, soccer, swimming, tennis, track/field (outdoor), track/field (indoor). *Women:* basketball, cross-country, diving, field hockey, soccer, softball, swimming, tennis, track/field (outdoor), track/field (indoor), volleyball.

ACCOMMODATIONS

Allowed in exams:	
Calculators	Yes
Dictionary	Yes
Computer	Yes
Spell-checker	Yes
Extended test time	Yes
Scribe	Yes
Proctors	Yes
Oral exams	Yes
Note-takers	Yes
Support services for students with:	
LD	No
ADHD	Yes
ASD	No
Distraction-reduced environment	Yes
Recording of lecture allowed	Yes
Reading technology	Yes
Audio books	No
Other assistive technology	Yes
Priority registration	Yes
Added costs of services:	
For LD	No
For ADHD	No
For ASD	No
LD specialists	No
ADHD & ASD coaching	No
ASD specialists	No
Professional tutors	No
Peer tutors	Yes
Max. hours/week for services	Varies
How professors are notified of student approved accommodations	Student and Disability Office

COLLEGE GRADUATION REQUIREMENTS

Course waivers allowed — Yes
In what courses: Varies

Course substitutions allowed — Yes
In what courses: Varies

Missouri

University of Missouri

230 Jesse Hall, Columbia, MO 65211 • Admissions: 573-882-7786 • Fax: 573-882-7887 **Support: CS**

CAMPUS

Type of school	Public
Environment	City

STUDENTS

Undergrad enrollment	21,933
% male/female	47/53
% from out of state	20
% frosh live on campus	93

FINANCIAL FACTS

Annual in-state tuition	$13,264
Annual out-of-state tuition	$30,468
Room and board	$10,668

GENERAL ADMISSIONS INFO

Application fee	$55
Regular application deadline	Rolling
Nonfall registration	Yes

Admission may be deferred.

Range SAT EBRW	560–660
Range SAT Math	560–680
Range ACT Composite	23–29

ACADEMICS

Student/faculty ratio	17:1
% students returning for sophomore year	88

Most classes have 20–29 students.

Programs/Services for Students with Learning Differences

Reasonable accommodations, auxiliary aids, and support services are provided by the Office of Disability Services (ODS) to ensure that any student with a disability will have equal access to the educational programs and activities at the university. MU does not have a standalone program oriented to students with specific learning disabilities; all students with disabilities are supported through ODS. Students with disabilities (including specific learning disabilities or ADD/ADHD) are required to adhere to the same academic standards as other students at the university. Students with disabilities have the responsibility to self-identify and are encouraged to request accommodations through ODS as early as possible.

Admissions

There are no special admissions for students with learning disabilities. University of Missouri has a pilot program starting for applicants in the fall of 2021. Applicants will need to complete specific courses with good grades and provide a minimum test score or apply without test scores but submit a personal statement and resume. Some opportunities may be limited for applicants electing a review without test scores. The university shares that providing a test score does allow for accurate course placement and maximizes chances for scholarships and may improve chances of admission. Applicants can submit test scores at a later date. For applicants who submit test scores of 24+ ACT or 1160+ SAT the required GPA is 2.0; those with scores as low as an ACT of 17 or SAT 920–960 will need a 3.65 GPA.

Additional Information

Auxiliary aids and classroom accommodations include note-takers, lab assistants, readers, and assistive technology. Testing accommodations include time extensions, distraction-reduced environments, readers, scribes, or adaptive equipment. Coordinators can offer support and counseling in the areas of time management, study skills, learning styles, and other academic and social issues. Group support is also available. The Learning Center works cooperatively with ODS to provide individual tutoring free of charge. Other services include writing assistance, math assistance, test reviews, help with reading comprehension, and study skills training.

ADMISSIONS INFO FOR STUDENTS WITH LEARNING DIFFERENCES

Phone: 573-882-4696 • Fax: 573-884-5002 • Email: disabilitycenter@missouri.edu

SAT/ACT required: Yes (Test optional for 2021)
Interview required: No
Essay required: No
Additional application required: No
Documentation submitted to: Office of Disability Services

Special Ed. HS course work accepted: Yes
Separate application required for Programs/Services: No
Documentation required for:
LD: Psychoeducational evaluation
ADHD: Psychoeducational evaluation
ASD: Psychoeducational evaluation

University of Missouri

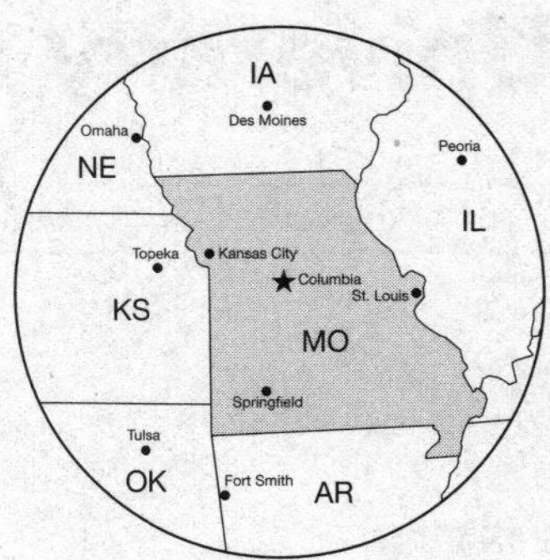

General Admissions

Very important factors include: class rank, academic GPA, standardized test scores. *Other factors include:* rigor of secondary school record, application essay, recommendation(s), talent/ability. High school diploma is required and GED is accepted. *Academic units required:* 4 English, 4 math, 3 science, 1 science lab, 2 foreign language, 3 social studies, 1 fine arts.

Accommodations or Services

Accommodations are decided upon an individual basis after a thorough review of appropriate, current documentation. The accommodations requests must be supported through the documentation provided and must be logically linked to the current impact of the condition on academic functioning.

Financial Aid

Students should submit: FAFSA. *Need-based scholarships/grants offered:* College/university scholarship or grant aid from institutional funds; Federal Nursing Scholarships; Federal Pell; Private scholarships; SEOG; State scholarships/grants. *Loan aid offered:* Direct PLUS loans; Direct Subsidized Stafford Loans; Direct Unsubsidized Stafford Loans. Federal Work-Study Program available. Institutional employment available.

Campus Life

Activities: Campus Ministries; Choral groups; Concert band; Dance; Drama/theater; International Student Organization; Jazz band; Literary magazine; Marching band; Model UN; Music ensembles; Musical theater; Opera; Pep band; Radio station; Student government; Student newspaper; Student-run film society; Symphony orchestra; Television station; Yearbook. **Organizations:** 600 registered organizations, 31 honor societies, 40 religious organizations, 31 fraternities, 23 sororities. **Athletics (Intercollegiate):** *Men:* baseball, basketball, cross-country, diving, football, golf, swimming, track/field (outdoor), track/field (indoor), wrestling. *Women:* basketball, cheerleading, cross-country, diving, golf, gymnastics, soccer, softball, swimming, tennis, track/field (outdoor), track/field (indoor), volleyball.

ACCOMMODATIONS

Allowed in exams:	
Calculators	Yes
Dictionary	Yes
Computer	Yes
Spell-checker	Yes
Extended test time	Yes
Scribe	Yes
Proctors	Yes
Oral exams	Yes
Note-takers	Yes
Support services for students with:	
LD	Yes
ADHD	Yes
ASD	Yes
Distraction-reduced environment	Yes
Recording of lecture allowed	Yes
Reading technology	Yes
Audio books	Yes
Other assistive technology	Yes
Priority registration	Yes
Added costs of services:	
For LD	No
For ADHD	No
For ASD	No
LD specialists	Yes
ADHD & ASD coaching	Yes
ASD specialists	No
Professional tutors	Yes
Peer tutors	Yes
Max. hours/week for services	Unlimited
How professors are notified of student approved accommodations	Student

COLLEGE GRADUATION REQUIREMENTS

Course waivers allowed	No
Course substitutions allowed	Yes
In what courses: Case-by-case basis	

University of Missouri—Kansas City

5100 Rockhill Road, Kansas City, MO 64114 • Admissions: 816-235-1111 • Fax: 816-235-5544 **Support: S**

CAMPUS

Type of school	Public
Environment	Metropolis

STUDENTS

Undergrad enrollment	7,426
% male/female	43/57
% from out of state	21
% frosh live on campus	49

FINANCIAL FACTS

Annual in-state tuition	$10,146
Annual out-of-state tuition	$25,186
Room and board	$11,748

GENERAL ADMISSIONS INFO

Application fee	$45
Regular application deadline	6/1
Nonfall registration	Yes

Admission may be deferred.

Range SAT EBRW	500–650
Range SAT Math	480–680
Range ACT Composite	21–28

ACADEMICS

Student/faculty ratio	16:1
% students returning for sophomore year	76

Most classes have 10–19 students.

Programs/Services for Students with Learning Differences

The Office of Services for Students with Disabilities' mission is to educate and support the UMKC community to understand the unique challenges, myths, and stereotypes faced by people with disabilities; recognize the unique contributions that people with disabilities make to society; and accept and engage people with disabilities in the daily flow of life. They also provide reasonable accommodations to help students demonstrate their abilities, knowledge, and skills.

Admissions

There is no special admission for students with disabilities. Students may be automatically admitted with a 2.5 GPA and 19 ACT. The School of Engineering requires a 3.0 GPA and 24 ACT with 25 math subscore. Under the test optional process, students with a 2.75 GPA may be fully admitted with no test score to UMKC. However, note that the following programs require a test score: Architectural Studies, Conservatory, School of Computing and Engineering, School of Dentistry, School of Medicine, School of Nursing and Health Studies, School of Pharmacy, and the Honors College.

Additional Information

Student Disability Services provides reasonable accommodations to students with appropriate documentation. Students must self-disclose and contact the Office of Student Disability Services.

ADMISSIONS INFO FOR STUDENTS WITH LEARNING DIFFERENCES

Phone: 816-235-5696 • Fax: 816-235-6363 • Email: laurentr@umkc.edu

SAT/ACT required: No
Interview required: No
Essay required: No
Additional application required: No
Documentation submitted to: SDS

Special Ed. HS course work accepted: Yes
Separate application required for Programs/Services: No
Documentation required for:
LD: Psychoeducational evaluation
ADHD: Psychoeducational evaluation
ASD: Psychoeducational evaluation

University of Missouri—Kansas City

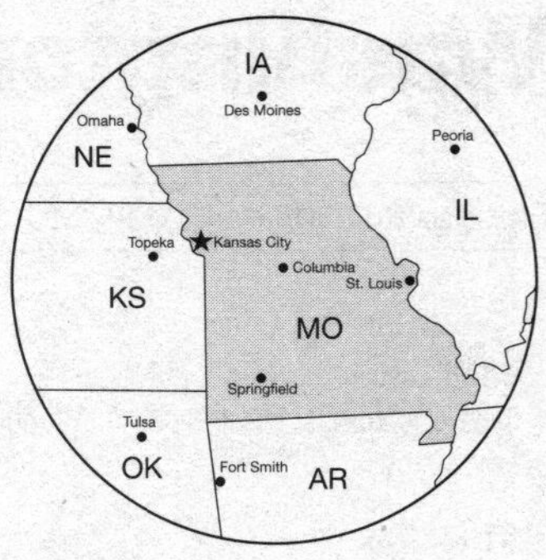

General Admissions

Very important factors include: rigor of secondary school record, class rank, academic GPA. *Other factors include:* application essay, standardized test scores, recommendation(s), interview, extracurricular activities, talent/ability, character/personal qualities, first generation, volunteer work, work experience. High school diploma is required and GED is accepted. *Academic units required:* 4 English, 4 math, 3 science, 1 science lab, 2 foreign language, 3 social studies, 1 visual/performing art.

Accommodations or Services

Accommodations are decided upon an individual basis after a thorough review of appropriate, current documentation. The accommodations requests must be supported through the documentation provided and must be logically linked to the current impact of the condition on academic functioning.

Financial Aid

Students should submit: FAFSA. *Need-based scholarships/grants offered:* College/university scholarship or grant aid from institutional funds; Federal Nursing Scholarships; Federal Pell; Private scholarships; SEOG; State scholarships/grants; United Negro College Fund. *Loan aid offered:* Direct PLUS loans; Direct Subsidized Stafford Loans; Direct Unsubsidized Stafford Loans. Federal Work-Study Program available. Institutional employment available.

Campus Life

Activities: Campus Ministries; Choral groups; Concert band; Dance; Drama/theater; International Student Organization; Jazz band; Literary magazine; Model UN; Music ensembles; Musical theater; Opera; Pep band; Radio station; Student government; Student newspaper; Student-run film society; Symphony orchestra. **Organizations:** 338 registered organizations, 32 honor societies, 13 religious organizations, 5 fraternities, 7 sororities. **Athletics (Intercollegiate):** *Men:* basketball, cheerleading, cross-country, golf, riflery, soccer, tennis, track/field (outdoor). *Women:* basketball, cheerleading, cross-country, golf, riflery, softball, tennis, track/field (outdoor), volleyball.

ACCOMMODATIONS

Allowed in exams:	
Calculators	Yes
Dictionary	Yes
Computer	Yes
Spell-checker	Yes
Extended test time	Yes
Scribe	Yes
Proctors	Yes
Oral exams	Yes
Note-takers	Yes
Support services for students with:	
LD	Yes
ADHD	Yes
ASD	Yes
Distraction-reduced environment	Yes
Recording of lecture alowed	Yes
Reading technology	Yes
Audio books	Yes
Other assistive technology	Yes
Priority registration	Yes
Added costs of services:	
For LD	No
For ADHD	No
For ASD	No
LD specialists	No
ADHD & ASD coaching	Yes
ASD specialists	No
Professional tutors	No
Peer tutors	Yes
Max. hours/week for services	Varies
How professors are notified of student approved accommodations	Student

COLLEGE GRADUATION REQUIREMENTS

Course waivers allowed	No
Course substitutions allowed	Yes
In what courses: Case-by case-basis	

Missouri

Washington University in St. Louis

Campus Box 1089, St. Louis, MO 63130-4899 • Admissions: 314-935-6000 • Fax: 314-935-4290 **Support: CS**

CAMPUS

Type of school	Private (nonprofit)
Environment	City

STUDENTS

Undergrad enrollment	7,404
% male/female	47/53
% from out of state	89
% frosh live on campus	100

FINANCIAL FACTS

Annual tuition	$56,300
Room and board	$17,402
Required fees	$1,086

GENERAL ADMISSIONS INFO

Application fee	$75
Regular application deadline	1/2
Nonfall registration	No

Admission may be deferred.

Range SAT EBRW	720–760
Range SAT Math	760–800
Range ACT Composite	33–35

ACADEMICS

Student/faculty ratio	7:1
% students returning for sophomore year	97

Most classes have 10–19 students.

Programs/Services for Students with Learning Differences

Disability Resources assists students with disabilities by providing guidance and accommodations to ensure equal access to our campus, both physically and academically. In accordance with the ADA Amendments Act (ADAAA) and University policy, students must provide appropriate documentation to the Disability Resources (DR) office in a timely manner before they can be considered for accommodations. Students must submit a request for accommodation, including documentation of the disability, to Disability Resources. Disability Resources will then determine eligibility and work with each individual student to implement accommodations.

Admissions

There is no special admissions process for students with learning disabilities. Students may choose to voluntarily identify themselves in the admissions process. Courses required for all applicants include: 4 years English, 4 years math, 3–4 years science, 3–4 years history or social science, 2 years foreign language since 9th grade; the College of Arts & Sciences recommends both chemistry and physics for students considering pre-medicine or natural sciences. A portfolio is required for applicants to the College of Art. Portfolios are strongly encouraged for the College of Architecture.

Additional Information

The Center for Advanced Learning provides support services to help the students to succeed academically. These include: essential study and test-taking skills, access to peer mentors, executive functioning, and time management and study techniques, etc.

ADMISSIONS INFO FOR STUDENTS WITH LEARNING DIFFERENCES

Phone: 314-935-5970 • Fax: 314-935-7559 • Email: disabilityresources@wustl.edu

SAT/ACT required: Yes (Test optional for 2021)
Interview required: No
Essay required: Recommended
Additional application required: No
Documentation submitted to: Disability Resources

Special Ed. HS course work accepted: No
Separate application required for Programs/Services: No
Documentation required for:
LD: Psychoeducational evaluation
ADHD: Psychoeducational evaluation
ASD: Psychoeducational evaluation

Washington University in St. Louis

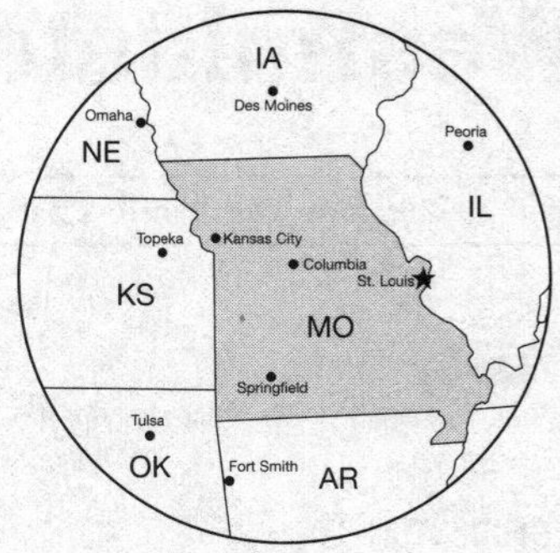

General Admissions

Very important factors include: rigor of secondary school record, class rank, academic GPA, application essay, standardized test scores, recommendation(s), extracurricular activities, talent/ability, character/personal qualities, volunteer work, work experience, level of applicant's interest. *Important factors include:* first generation. *Other factors include:* interview, alumni/ae relation, geographical residence, state residency, racial/ethnic status. High school diploma is required and GED is accepted. *Academic units required:* 4 English, 3 math, 3 science, 2 science labs, 2 foreign language, 2 social studies, 2 history. *Academic units recommended:* 4 English, 4 math, 4 science, 4 science labs, 4 foreign language, 4 social studies, 4 history.

Accommodations or Services

Accommodations are decided upon an individual basis after a thorough review of appropriate, current documentation. The accommodations requests must be supported through the documentation provided and must be logically linked to the current impact of the condition on academic functioning.

Financial Aid

Students should submit: CSS/Financial Aid PROFILE; FAFSA; Noncustodial PROFILE. *Need-based scholarships/grants offered:* College/university scholarship or grant aid from institutional funds; Federal Pell; Private scholarships; SEOG; State scholarships/grants; United Negro College Fund. *Loan aid offered:* Direct PLUS loans; Direct Subsidized Stafford Loans; Direct Unsubsidized Stafford Loans. Federal Work-Study Program available. Institutional employment available.

Campus Life

Activities: Campus Ministries; Choral groups; Concert band; Dance; Drama/theater; International Student Organization; Jazz band; Literary magazine; Model UN; Music ensembles; Musical theater; Opera; Pep band; Radio station; Student government; Student newspaper; Student-run film society; Symphony orchestra; Television station. **Organizations:** 380 registered organizations, 22 honor societies, 20 religious organizations, 15 fraternities, 10 sororities. **Athletics (Intercollegiate):** *Men:* baseball, basketball, cross-country, diving, football, soccer, swimming, tennis, track/field (outdoor), track/field (indoor). *Women:* basketball, cross-country, diving, golf, soccer, softball, swimming, tennis, track/field (outdoor), track/field (indoor), volleyball.

ACCOMMODATIONS

Allowed in exams:	
Calculators	Yes
Dictionary	Yes
Computer	Yes
Spell-checker	Yes
Extended test time	Yes
Scribe	Yes
Proctors	Yes
Oral exams	Yes
Note-takers	Yes
Support services for students with:	
LD	Yes
ADHD	Yes
ASD	Yes
Distraction-reduced environment	Yes
Recording of lecture allowed	Yes
Reading technology	Yes
Audio books	Yes
Other assistive technology	Yes
Priority registration	Yes
Added costs of services:	
For LD	No
For ADHD	No
For ASD	No
LD specialists	Yes
ADHD & ASD coaching	Yes
ASD specialists	Yes
Professional tutors	Yes
Peer tutors	Yes
Max. hours/week for services	Varies
How professors are notified of student approved accommodations	Student

COLLEGE GRADUATION REQUIREMENTS

Course waivers allowed	No
Course substitutions allowed	No

Westminster College (MO)

Champ Auditorium, Westminster College, Fulton, MO 65251 • Admissions: 573-592-5251 • Fax: 573-592-5255 **Support: SP**

CAMPUS

Type of school	Private (nonprofit)
Environment	Village

STUDENTS

Undergrad enrollment	655
% male/female	56/44
% from out of state	16
% frosh live on campus	88

FINANCIAL FACTS

Annual tuition	$28,330
Room and board	$10,842
Required fees	$2,550

GENERAL ADMISSIONS INFO

Application fee	$0
Regular application deadline	Rolling
Nonfall registration	Yes

Admission may be deferred.

Range SAT EBRW	530–590
Range SAT Math	500–600
Range ACT Composite	20–25

ACADEMICS

Student/faculty ratio	11:1
% students returning for sophomore year	77

Most classes have 10–19 students.

Programs/Services for Students with Learning Differences

One of the many supports offered through the Tomnitz Family Learning Opportunities Center is the Learning Differences Program (LDP). This program provides support that students with a diagnosed learning disorder need to be successful learners in the academic environment they share with regularly admitted students. The LDP's services are tailored to meet the specific needs of students that includes but is not limited to one-on-one academic advising; enrollment in supplemental courses designed to encourage and support academic success in the Humanities, Natural and Mathematical Sciences, and Social Sciences; extended-time testing; class notes; dictation; and access to a quiet and/or supportive study environment. There is an additional fee for each semester the student is in the program.

Admissions

There is a special application and admissions procedure for students with learning disabilities. Students submit a completed Westminster College application form and a separate application form for the LPD program. Appropriate documentation must be submitted, along with four teacher recommendations. Once all the information has been sent to the LPD, students will be able to have an in-person interview.

Additional Information

The College Transition Program (CTP) is designed specifically to support students with a diagnosis of Autism Spectrum Disorder who are high functioning. Besides academic support, social skills development, and advising, services includes communication with parents and instructors who have the students in their classroom. Students who are admitted to and enroll in the CTP pay an additional fee for each semester they are in the program.

ADMISSIONS INFO FOR STUDENTS WITH LEARNING DIFFERENCES

Phone: 573-592-5304 • Fax: 573-592-5191

SAT/ACT required: Yes (Test optional for 2021)
Interview required: Yes
Essay required: Recommended
Additional application required: No
Documentation submitted to: Learning Opportunity Center

Special Ed. HS course work accepted: Yes
Separate application required for Programs/Services: No
Documentation required for:
LD: Psychoeducational evaluation
ADHD: Psychoeducational evaluation
ASD: Psychoeducational evaluation

Westminster College (MO)

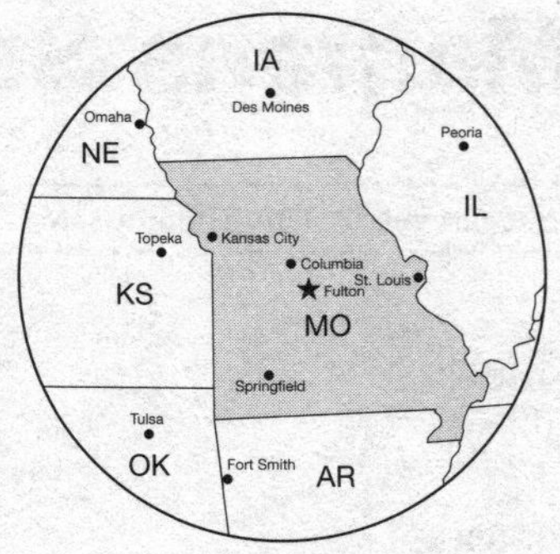

General Admissions

Very important factors include: rigor of secondary school record, standardized test scores, character/personal qualities. *Important factors include:* class rank, academic GPA, recommendation(s), extracurricular activities, volunteer work. *Other factors include:* application essay, interview, talent/ability, alumni/ae relation, work experience. High school diploma is required and GED is accepted. *Academic units required:* 4 English, 3 math, 2 science, 2 science labs. *Academic units recommended:* 2 foreign language, 2 social studies, 2 academic electives.

Accommodations or Services

Accommodations are decided upon an individual basis after a thorough review of appropriate, current documentation. The accommodations requests must be supported through the documentation provided and must be logically linked to the current impact of the condition on academic functioning.

Financial Aid

Students should submit: FAFSA. Applicants will be notified of awards on or about 2/1. *Need-based scholarships/grants offered:* College/university scholarship or grant aid from institutional funds; Federal Pell; Private scholarships; SEOG; State scholarships/grants. *Loan aid offered:* Direct PLUS loans; Direct Subsidized Stafford Loans; Direct Unsubsidized Stafford Loans. Federal Work-Study Program available. Institutional employment available.

Campus Life

Activities: Campus Ministries; Choral groups; Dance; Drama/theater; International Student Organization; Jazz band; Literary magazine; Model UN; Music ensembles; Pep band; Student government; Student newspaper. **Organizations:** 49 registered organizations, 15 honor societies, 2 religious organizations, 6 fraternities, 3 sororities. **Athletics (Intercollegiate):** *Men:* baseball, basketball, cheerleading, cross-country, football, golf, soccer, tennis, track/field (outdoor). *Women:* basketball, cheerleading, cross-country, golf, soccer, softball, tennis, track/field (outdoor), volleyball.

ACCOMMODATIONS

Allowed in exams:	
Calculators	Yes
Dictionary	Yes
Computer	Yes
Spell-checker	Yes
Extended test time	Yes
Scribe	Yes
Proctors	Yes
Oral exams	Yes
Note-takers	Yes
Support services for students with:	
LD	Yes
ADHD	Yes
ASD	Yes
Distraction-reduced environment	Yes
Recording of lecture allowed	Yes
Reading technology	Yes
Audio books	Yes
Other assistive technology	Yes
Priority registration	No
Added costs of services:	
For LD	Yes
For ADHD	Yes
For ASD	Yes
LD specialists	Yes
ADHD & ASD coaching	No
ASD specialists	No
Professional tutors	No
Peer tutors	Yes
Max. hours/week for services	Varies
How professors are notified of student approved accommodations	Student and Disability Office

COLLEGE GRADUATION REQUIREMENTS

Course waivers allowed	No
Course substitutions allowed	Yes
In what courses: Case-by-case basis	

Missouri

Montana State University Billings

1500 University Drive, Billings, MT 59101 • Admissions: 406-657-2158 • Fax: 406-657-2302 **Support: S**

CAMPUS	
Type of school	Public
Environment	City
STUDENTS	
Undergrad enrollment	4,031
% male/female	35/65
% from out of state	9
% frosh live on campus	31
FINANCIAL FACTS	
Annual in-state tuition	$6,040
Annual out-of-state tuition	$19,370
Room and board	$7,070
GENERAL ADMISSIONS INFO	
Application fee	$30
Regular application deadline	Rolling
Nonfall registration	Yes
Range ACT Composite	17–23
ACADEMICS	
Student/faculty ratio	14:1
% students returning for sophomore year	62
Most classes have 10–19 students.	

Programs/Services for Students with Learning Differences

The Disability Support Services (DSS) helps students with documented learning differences coordinate the provision of reasonable accommodations offered by the university.

Admissions

There is no special admission process for students with learning disabilities. All students must meet the same admission criteria. First-year applicants must meet one of the following conditions: ACT of 22 or SAT of 920, a 2.5 GPA, or a rank in the top half of the class.

Additional Information

Students must request services, provide documentation specifying a learning disability or ADHD, make an appointment for an intake with DSS, meet with professors at the beginning of each semester, and work closely with DSS. DSS must keep documentation and intake on file, make a determination of accommodations, issue identification cards to qualified students, and serve as a resource and a support system. Services include course and testing accommodations, alternative testing, priority scheduling, technical assistance, liaison and referral services, taped textbooks, and career, academic, and counseling referrals. The use of a computer, calculator, dictionary, or spellchecker is at the discretion of the individual professor and based on the documented needs of the student. Services and accommodations are available for undergraduate and graduate students.

ADMISSIONS INFO FOR STUDENTS WITH LEARNING DIFFERENCES

Phone: 406-657-2283 • Fax: 406-657-1658 • Email: tcarey@msubillings.edu

SAT/ACT required: Yes
Interview required: No
Essay required: Recommended
Additional application required: Yes
Documentation submitted to: Disability Support Services

Special Ed. HS course work accepted: No
Separate application required for Programs/Services: Yes
Documentation required for:
- **LD:** Psychoeducational evaluation
- **ADHD:** Psychoeducational evaluation
- **ASD:** Psychoeducational evaluation

Montana State University Billings

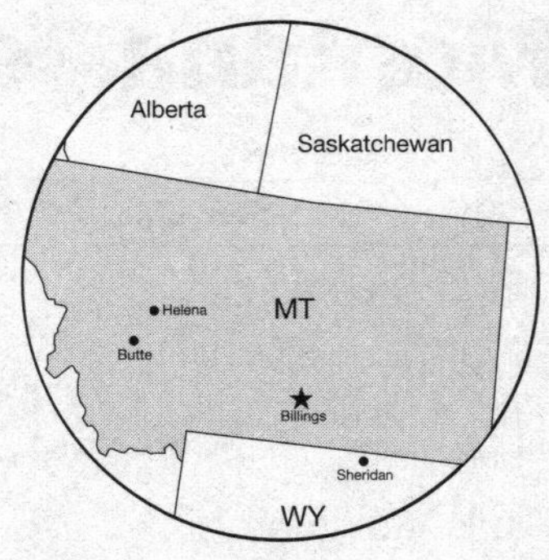

General Admissions

Very important factors include: rigor of secondary school record, class rank, academic GPA, standardized test scores. *Other factors include:* character/personal qualities, work experience. High school diploma is required and GED is accepted. *Academic units required:* 4 English, 3 math, 2 science, 2 science labs, 3 social studies, 2 computer science, foreign language, visual/performing arts, or vocational education required.

Accommodations or Services

Accommodations are decided upon an individual basis after a thorough review of appropriate, current documentation. The accommodations requests must be supported through the documentation provided and must be logically linked to the current impact of the condition on academic functioning.

Financial Aid

Students should submit: FAFSA; Institution's own financial aid form. *Need-based scholarships/grants offered:* College/university scholarship or grant aid from institutional funds; Federal Pell; Private scholarships; SEOG; State scholarships/grants. *Loan aid offered:* Direct PLUS loans; Direct Subsidized Stafford Loans; Direct Unsubsidized Stafford Loans. Federal Work-Study Program available. Institutional employment available.

Campus Life

Activities: Campus Ministries; Choral groups; Concert band; Drama/theater; International Student Organization; Jazz band; Literary magazine; Music ensembles; Musical theater; Pep band; Radio station; Student government; Student newspaper; Symphony orchestra. **Organizations:** 53 registered organizations, 10 honor societies, 38 religious organizations. **Athletics (Intercollegiate):** *Men:* baseball, basketball, cross-country, golf, soccer, tennis, track/field (outdoor), track/field (indoor). *Women:* basketball, cross-country, golf, soccer, softball, tennis, track/field (outdoor), track/field (indoor), volleyball.

ACCOMMODATIONS

Allowed in exams:	
Calculators	Yes
Dictionary	Yes
Computer	Yes
Spell-checker	Yes
Extended test time	Yes
Scribe	Yes
Proctors	Yes
Oral exams	Yes
Note-takers	Yes
Support services for students with:	
LD	Yes
ADHD	Yes
ASD	Yes
Distraction-reduced environment	Yes
Recording of lecture alowed	Yes
Reading technology	Yes
Audio books	Yes
Other assistive technology	Yes
Priority registration	Yes
Added costs of services:	
For LD	No
For ADHD	No
For ASD	No
LD specialists	No
ADHD & ASD coaching	No
ASD specialists	No
Professional tutors	Yes
Peer tutors	Yes
Max. hours/week for services	Varies
How professors are notified of student approved accommodations	Student and Disability Office

COLLEGE GRADUATION REQUIREMENTS

Course waivers allowed	No
Course substitutions allowed	No

Montana

Montana Technological University

1300 West Park Street, Butte, MT 59701 • Admissions: 406-496-4256 • Fax: 406-496-4710 **Support: CS**

CAMPUS

Type of school	Public
Environment	Town

STUDENTS

Undergrad enrollment	1,493
% male/female	63/37
% from out of state	18
% frosh live on campus	60

FINANCIAL FACTS

Annual in-state tuition	$7,390
Annual out-of-state tuition	$22,540
Room and board	$10,198

GENERAL ADMISSIONS INFO

Application fee	$30
Regular application deadline	Rolling
Nonfall registration	Yes

Admission may be deferred.

Range SAT EBRW	530–620
Range SAT Math	550–640
Range ACT Composite	21–26

ACADEMICS

Student/faculty ratio	13:1
% students returning for sophomore year	79

Most classes have 10–19 students.

Programs/Services for Students with Learning Differences

All persons with disabilities have the right to participate fully and equally in the programs and services of Montana Technological University. The Disability Coordinators at the University are committed to making the appropriate accommodations. Montana Tech's student life counselors are resources for students with disabilities. The counselors are a general resource for all students who may need assistance. Availability of services from Disability Services is subject to a student's eligibility for these and any other services. Students must provide appropriate and current documentation prior to requesting and receiving services or accommodations. All faculty and staff at the college are responsible for assuring access by providing reasonable accommodations. The Montana Tech Learning Center offers a variety of services to help students achieve their full academic potential. Tutors are available to help all students with course work in an assortment of subject areas. The Learning Center addresses the importance of developing basic college success skills.

Admissions

There is no special admission process for students with LD or ADHD. The GED is accepted. Students must have 14 academic high school credits, including 4 years of English, 2 years of science, 3 years of math, 3 years of social studies, and 2 years from other academic areas, including foreign language, computer science, visual/performing arts, and vocational education. Interviews are not required, and special education courses in high school are not accepted. Students who do not meet any of the general admission criteria may ask to be evaluated considering other factors. Students with LD/ADHD are encouraged to self-disclose in the admissions process.

Additional Information

The following types of services are offered to students with disabilities: assistance in working with faculty members, text accommodation in concert with instructors, and access to assistive technology, note-taking, and career services. Documentation to receive services should be sent directly to Disability Services. Montana Tech offers compensatory classes for students with LD in both math and English. Services and accommodations are available for undergraduate and graduate students.

ADMISSIONS INFO FOR STUDENTS WITH LEARNING DIFFERENCES

Phone: 406-496-4129 • Fax: 406-496-4757 • Email: cvath@mtech.edu

SAT/ACT required: No
Interview required: No
Essay required: No
Additional application required: No
Documentation submitted to: Disability Services

Special Ed. HS course work accepted: No
Separate application required for Programs/Services: No
Documentation required for:
LD: Psychoeducational evaluation
ADHD: Psychoeducational evaluation
ASD: Psychoeducational evaluation

Montana Technological University

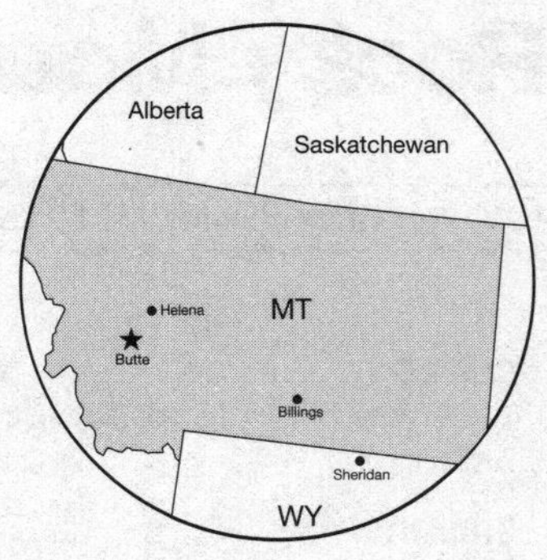

General Admissions

Very important factors include: class rank, academic GPA, standardized test scores. High school diploma is required and GED is accepted. *Academic units required:* 4 English, 3 math, 2 science, 2 science labs, 3 social studies, 2 unit from above areas or other academic areas. *Academic units recommended:* 4 math.

Accommodations or Services

Accommodations are decided upon an individual basis after a thorough review of appropriate, current documentation. The accommodations requests must be supported through the documentation provided and must be logically linked to the current impact of the condition on academic functioning.

Financial Aid

Students should submit: FAFSA. *Need-based scholarships/grants offered:* College/university scholarship or grant aid from institutional funds; Federal Pell; Private scholarships; SEOG; State scholarships/grants. *Loan aid offered:* Direct PLUS loans; Direct Subsidized Stafford Loans; Direct Unsubsidized Stafford Loans. Federal Work-Study Program available. Institutional employment available.

Campus Life

Activities: Campus Ministries; Choral groups; International Student Organization; Pep band; Radio station; Student government; Student newspaper. **Organizations:** 50 registered organizations, 3 honor societies. **Athletics (Intercollegiate):** *Men:* basketball, football, golf. *Women:* basketball, golf, volleyball.

ACCOMMODATIONS

Allowed in exams:	
Calculators	Yes
Dictionary	Yes
Computer	Yes
Spell-checker	Yes
Extended test time	Yes
Scribe	Yes
Proctors	Yes
Oral exams	Yes
Note-takers	Yes
Support services for students with:	
LD	Yes
ADHD	Yes
ASD	Yes
Distraction-reduced environment	Yes
Recording of lecture alowed	Yes
Reading technology	Yes
Audio books	Yes
Other assistive technology	Yes
Priority registration	Yes
Added costs of services:	
For LD	No
For ADHD	No
For ASD	No
LD specialists	Yes
ADHD & ASD coaching	No
ASD specialists	No
Professional tutors	No
Peer tutors	Yes
Max. hours/week for services	Unlimited
How professors are notified of student approved accommodations	Student and Disability Office

COLLEGE GRADUATION REQUIREMENTS

Course waivers allowed	No
Course substitutions allowed	No

Rocky Mountain College

1511 Poly Drive, Billings, MT 59102-1796 • Admissions: 406-657-1026 • Fax: 406-657-1189 **Support: CS**

CAMPUS	
Type of school	Private (nonprofit)
Environment	City
STUDENTS	
Undergrad enrollment	850
% male/female	51/49
% from out of state	42
% frosh live on campus	79
FINANCIAL FACTS	
Annual tuition	$29,976
Room and board	$8,596
Required fees	$610
GENERAL ADMISSIONS INFO	
Application fee	$35
Regular application deadline	Rolling
Nonfall registration	Yes
Admission may be deferred.	
Range SAT EBRW	480–590
Range SAT Math	450–580
Range ACT Composite	19–23
ACADEMICS	
Student/faculty ratio	10:1
% students returning for sophomore year	70
Most classes have 10–19 students.	

Programs/Services for Students with Learning Differences

Services for Academic Success (SAS) provides a comprehensive support program for students with LD. Students are responsible for identifying themselves, providing appropriate documentation, and requesting reasonable accommodations as soon as possible after enrolling. The program tailors services to meet the needs of the individuals. SAS welcomes applications from students who are committed to learning and who are excited about meeting the challenges of college with the support provided by the SAS staff. The SAS program is supported by a grant from the U.S. Department of Education and funds from Rocky Mountain College. The small size of the college, the caring attitude of the faculty, and the excellent support program all make Rocky a learning disability-friendly college.

Admissions

There is no special admissions application for students with learning disabilities. All applicants must meet the same criteria, which include an ACT of 21 or SAT of 1000, a GPA of 2.5, and the following recommended courses: 4 years of English, 3 years of math, 3 years of social science, 3 years of science, and 2 years of a foreign language. There is the opportunity to be considered for a conditional admission if scores or grades are below the cutoffs. To identify and provide necessary support services as soon as possible, students with disabilities are encouraged to complete a Services for Academic Success application when they are accepted. All documentation is confidential.

Additional Information

SAS provides a variety of services tailored to meet a student's individual needs. Services are free to participants and include developmental course work in reading, writing, and mathematics, study skills classes, tutoring in all subjects, academic, career, and personal counseling, graduate school counseling, accommodations for students with learning disabilities, alternative testing arrangements, taping of lectures or textbooks, cultural and academic enrichment opportunities, and advocacy. SAS staff meets with each student to talk about the supportive services the student needs and then develop a semester plan. Skills classes for college credit are offered in math, English, and studying techniques.

ADMISSIONS INFO FOR STUDENTS WITH LEARNING DIFFERENCES

Phone: 406-657-1128 • Fax: 406-259-9751

SAT/ACT required: Yes (Test optional for 2021)
Interview required: No
Essay required: No
Additional application required: No
Documentation submitted to: Services for Academic Success

Special Ed. HS course work accepted: No
Separate application required for Programs/Services: No
Documentation required for:
LD: Psychoeducational evaluation
ADHD: Psychoeducational evaluation
ASD: Psychoeducational evaluation

Rocky Mountain College

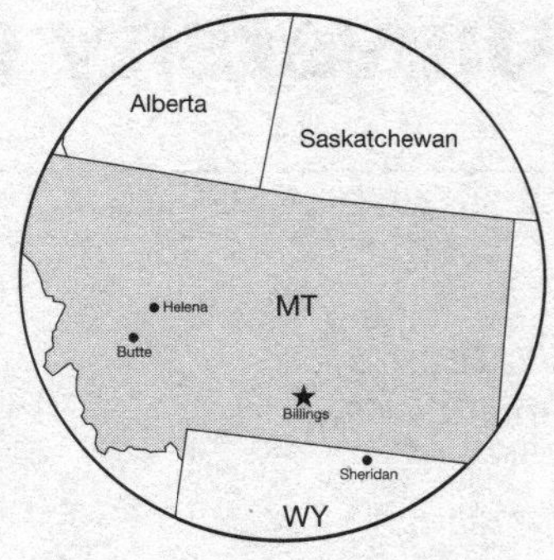

General Admissions

Very important factors include: academic GPA, standardized test scores, level of applicant's interest. *Important factors include:* rigor of secondary school record, application essay, recommendation(s). *Other factors include:* class rank, interview, extracurricular activities, talent/ability, character/personal qualities, first generation, alumni/ae relation, work experience. High school diploma is required and GED is accepted. *Academic units required:* 4 English, 4 math, 3 science, 3 social studies, 2 history, 3 academic electives.

Accommodations or Services

Accommodations are decided upon an individual basis after a thorough review of appropriate, current documentation. The accommodations requests must be supported through the documentation provided and must be logically linked to the current impact of the condition on academic functioning.

Financial Aid

Students should submit: FAFSA. Applicants will be notified of awards on a rolling basis beginning 1/15. *Need-based scholarships/grants offered:* College/university scholarship or grant aid from institutional funds; Federal Pell; Private scholarships; SEOG; State scholarships/grants. *Loan aid offered:* Direct PLUS loans; Direct Subsidized Stafford Loans; Direct Unsubsidized Stafford Loans. Federal Work-Study Program available. Institutional employment available.

Campus Life

Activities: Campus Ministries; Choral groups; Concert band; Drama/theater; International Student Organization; Jazz band; Music ensembles; Musical theater; Pep band; Student government; Student newspaper; Yearbook. **Organizations:** 13 registered organizations, 1 honor society, 4 religious organizations. **Athletics (Intercollegiate):** *Men:* basketball, cheerleading, football, golf, skiing (downhill/alpine). *Women:* basketball, cheerleading, golf, skiing (downhill/alpine), soccer, volleyball.

ACCOMMODATIONS

Allowed in exams:	
Calculators	Yes
Dictionary	Yes
Computer	Yes
Spell-checker	Yes
Extended test time	Yes
Scribe	Yes
Proctors	Yes
Oral exams	Yes
Note-takers	Yes
Support services for students with:	
LD	Yes
ADHD	Yes
ASD	Yes
Distraction-reduced environment	Yes
Recording of lecture alowed	Yes
Reading technology	Yes
Audio books	Yes
Other assistive technology	Yes
Priority registration	No
Added costs of services:	
For LD	No
For ADHD	No
For ASD	No
LD specialists	Yes
ADHD & ASD coaching	No
ASD specialists	No
Professional tutors	Yes
Peer tutors	Yes
Max. hours/week for services	Unlimited
How professors are notified of student approved accommodations	Student and Disability Office

COLLEGE GRADUATION REQUIREMENTS

Course waivers allowed	No
Course substitutions allowed	Yes
In what courses: Case-by-case basis	

Montana

University of Montana

32 Campus Drive, Missoula, MT 59812 • Admissions: 243-6266 • Fax: 406-243-5711 **Support: S**

CAMPUS

Type of school	Public
Environment	City

STUDENTS

Undergrad enrollment	7,515
% male/female	44/56
% from out of state	30
% frosh live on campus	76

FINANCIAL FACTS

Annual in-state tuition	$5,352
Annual out-of-state tuition	$24,144
Room and board	$9,966
Required fees	$2,002

GENERAL ADMISSIONS INFO

Application fee	$30
Regular application deadline	Rolling
Nonfall registration	Yes

Admission may be deferred.

Range SAT EBRW	535–635
Range SAT Math	520–610
Range ACT Composite	20–26

ACADEMICS

Student/faculty ratio	16:1
% students returning for sophomore year	71

Most classes have 10–19 students.

Programs/Services for Students with Learning Differences

Students interested in attending the University of Montana have to reach out and provide documentation to Disability Services. Once the information is received, Disability Services assigns a coordinator to the student. The Coordinator and the student collaborate to address barriers in the university program that may deny or limit full and equal program access. Students are encouraged to secure their rights through the student-coordinator relationship.

Admissions

There is no separate admission process for students with learning disabilities. Admitted students should have a 2.5 GPA and rank in the upper 50% of class (if the school ranks). Courses required include: 4 years English, 3 years math, 3 years social studies, 2 years science, and 2 years of foreign language. Students who do not meet the admission standards or those who meet the standards but have low test scores or a low-grade point average are encouraged to apply for admission. Applicants will be referred to the Admissions Committee to determine if they can be admitted on a "Conditional Status" or offered the opportunity to start at Missoula College.

Additional Information

The Academic Advising Center is an academic support arm within the Office for Student Success (OSS). The Center provides assistance to all students regarding registration support, academic petitions, and other campus resources. Examples include math lab, writing center, library assistance, health services including medical, counseling, dental, and pharmacy, tutoring services, study groups, academic and career advising, study skill courses, financial aid, housing, and leadership development programs.

ADMISSIONS INFO FOR STUDENTS WITH LEARNING DIFFERENCES

Phone: 406-243-2243 • Fax: 406-243-5330 • Email: dss@umontana.edu

SAT/ACT required: Yes (Test optional through Spring 2022)
Interview required: No
Essay required: Not Applicable
Additional application required: Yes
Documentation submitted to: OSS

Special Ed. HS course work accepted: Yes
Separate application required for Programs/Services: Yes
Documentation required for:
LD: Psychoeducational evaluation
ADHD: Psychoeducational evaluation
ASD: Psychoeducational evaluation

University of Montana

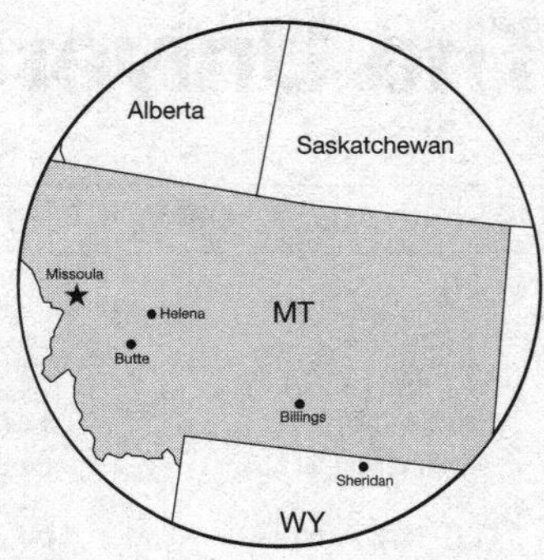

General Admissions

Very important factors include: rigor of secondary school record, class rank, academic GPA, standardized test scores. *Important factors include:* extracurricular activities, talent/ability. High school diploma is required and GED is accepted. *Academic units required:* 4 English, 3 math, 2 science, 2 science labs, 3 social studies, 2 history. *Academic units recommended:* 2 foreign language, 2 computer science, 2 visual/performing arts.

Accommodations or Services

Accommodations are decided upon an individual basis after a thorough review of appropriate, current documentation. The accommodations requests must be supported through the documentation provided and must be logically linked to the current impact of the condition on academic functioning.

Financial Aid

Students should submit: FAFSA. *Need-based scholarships/grants offered:* College/university scholarship or grant aid from institutional funds; Federal Pell; Private scholarships; SEOG; State scholarships/grants. *Loan aid offered:* Direct PLUS loans; Direct Subsidized Stafford Loans; Direct Unsubsidized Stafford Loans. Federal Work-Study Program available. Institutional employment available.

Campus Life

Activities: Campus Ministries; Choral groups; Concert band; Dance; Drama/theater; International Student Organization; Jazz band; Literary magazine; Marching band; Model UN; Music ensembles; Musical theater; Opera; Pep band; Radio station; Student government; Student newspaper; Symphony orchestra; Television station. **Organizations:** 150 registered organizations, 6 fraternities, 4 sororities. **Athletics (Intercollegiate):** *Men:* basketball, cheerleading, cross-country, football, tennis, track/field (outdoor), track/field (indoor). *Women:* basketball, cheerleading, cross-country, golf, soccer, tennis, track/field (outdoor), track/field (indoor), volleyball.

ACCOMMODATIONS

Allowed in exams:	
Calculators	Yes
Dictionary	No
Computer	Yes
Spell-checker	Yes
Extended test time	Yes
Scribe	Yes
Proctors	Yes
Oral exams	No
Note-takers	Yes
Support services for students with:	
LD	Yes
ADHD	Yes
ASD	Yes
Distraction-reduced environment	Yes
Recording of lecture alowed	Yes
Reading technology	Yes
Audio books	Yes
Other assistive technology	Yes
Priority registration	Yes
Added costs of services:	
For LD	No
For ADHD	No
For ASD	No
LD specialists	No
ADHD & ASD coaching	No
ASD specialists	No
Professional tutors	No
Peer tutors	Yes
Max. hours/week for services	Varies
How professors are notified of student approved accommodations	Student

COLLEGE GRADUATION REQUIREMENTS

Course waivers allowed — Yes

In what courses: Students can receive assistance with course substitution petition from Disability Services.

Course substitutions allowed — Yes

In what courses: Students can receive assistance with course substitution petition from Disability Services.

Montana

The University of Montana—Western

710 South Atlantic, Dillon, MT 59725 • Admissions: 406-683-7331 • Fax: 406-683-7493 **Support: S**

CAMPUS

Type of school	Public
Environment	Rural

STUDENTS

Undergrad enrollment	1,358
% male/female	37/63
% from out of state	26
% frosh live on campus	79

FINANCIAL FACTS

Annual in-state tuition	$4,523
Annual out-of-state tuition	$15,913
Room and board	$7,260
Required fees	$1,224

GENERAL ADMISSIONS INFO

Application fee	$30
Regular application deadline	Rolling
Nonfall registration	Yes

Admission may be deferred.

Range SAT EBRW	430–570
Range SAT Math	460–550
Range ACT Composite	17–22

ACADEMICS

Student/faculty ratio	17:1
% students returning for sophomore year	76

Most classes have 10–19 students.

Programs/Services for Students with Learning Differences

Once the student is enrolled at the U of Montana, Western, they need to request academic exceptions by going through the Student Affairs Office and the Dean of Students. These needs may be physical, social, and/or academic. Almost all services are free to the student. If an applicant has a documented learning disability and requests special accommodations for a class, he or she must contact the Dean of Students so that arrangements can be made. The professor of the class, the Dean, and the student will meet to set up an IEP for that class, and documentation will be kept on file in the Student Life Office.

Admissions

The college has no special requirements other than those outlined by the state Board of Regents: a valid high school diploma or GED. Criteria for general admission includes 4 years of English, 3 years of math, 3 years of science, 3 years of social studies, and 2 years from foreign language, computer science, visual/performing arts, or vocational education; a 2.5 GPA (minimum 2.0 for students with learning disabilities); a 20 ACT or 960 SAT; and ranking within the top 50 percent of the applicant's class. Students with documented learning disabilities may request waivers or substitutions in courses affected by the disability. Because Western Montana is a small university, each individual can set up an admissions plan. If a student does not meet admissions requirements they can be admitted provisionally if they provide satisfactory evidence that they are prepared to successfully pursue the special courses required.

Additional Information

Students who present appropriate documentation may be eligible for some of the following services or accommodations: the use of calculators, dictionaries, computers, or spellcheckers during tests; extended time on tests; distraction free environments for tests; proctors; scribes; oral exams; note-takers; tape recorders in class; books on tape; and priority registration. The Learning Center offers skill-building classes in reading, writing, and math. These classes do not count toward a student's GPA, but they do for athletic eligibility. The MOSSAIC program (Mentoring, Organization, and Social Support for Autism/All Inclusion on Campus) is a support program for university students diagnosed with ASD. There is an additional cost for weekly peer mentoring.

ADMISSIONS INFO FOR STUDENTS WITH LEARNING DIFFERENCES

Phone: 406-683-7565 • Fax: 406-683-7570

SAT/ACT required: Yes (Test optional for Fall 2021)
Interview required: No
Essay required: No
Additional application required: No
Documentation submitted to: Student Affairs Office

Special Ed. HS course work accepted: Yes
Separate application required for Programs/Services: No
Documentation required for:
LD: Psychoeducational evaluation
ADHD: Psychoeducational evaluation
ASD: Psychoeducational evaluation

The University of Montana—Western

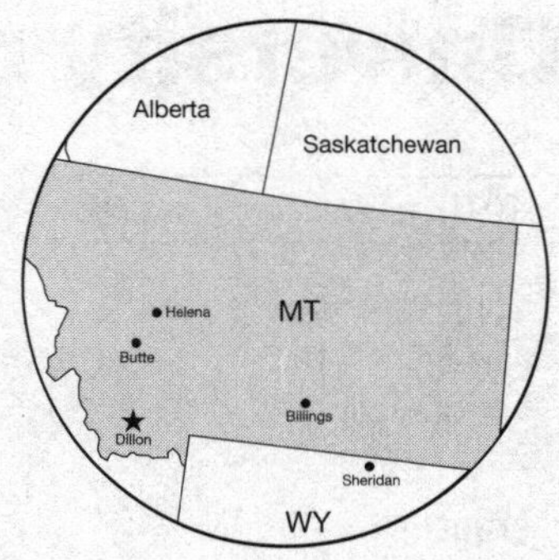

General Admissions

Very important factors include: rigor of secondary school record, class rank, academic GPA, standardized test scores. High school diploma is required and GED is accepted. *Academic units required:* 4 English, 3 math, 2 science, 2 science labs, 2 social studies, 1 history, 2 academic electives. *Academic units recommended:* 4 English, 4 math, 3 science, 2 science labs, 2 social studies, 1 history, 3 academic electives.

Accommodations or Services

Accommodations are decided upon an individual basis after a thorough review of appropriate, current documentation. The accommodations requests must be supported through the documentation provided and must be logically linked to the current impact of the condition on academic functioning.

Financial Aid

Students should submit: FAFSA. *Need-based scholarships/grants offered:* College/university scholarship or grant aid from institutional funds; Federal Pell; Private scholarships; SEOG; State scholarships/grants. *Loan aid offered:* Direct PLUS loans; Direct Subsidized Stafford Loans; Direct Unsubsidized Stafford Loans. Federal Work-Study Program available. Institutional employment available.

Campus Life

Activities: Campus Ministries; Choral groups; Drama/theater; Music ensembles; Musical theater; Radio station; Student government. **Organizations:** 25 registered organizations, 2 honor societies, 2 religious organizations. **Athletics (Intercollegiate):** *Men:* basketball, cheerleading, football, golf, rodeo. *Women:* basketball, cheerleading, golf, rodeo, volleyball.

ACCOMMODATIONS

Allowed in exams:	
Calculators	Yes
Dictionary	Yes
Computer	Yes
Spell-checker	Yes
Extended test time	Yes
Scribe	Yes
Proctors	Yes
Oral exams	Yes
Note-takers	Yes
Support services for students with:	
LD	Yes
ADHD	Yes
ASD	Yes
Distraction-reduced environment	Yes
Recording of lecture alowed	Yes
Reading technology	Yes
Audio books	Yes
Other assistive technology	Yes
Priority registration	Yes
Added costs of services:	
For LD	No
For ADHD	No
For ASD	No
LD specialists	No
ADHD & ASD coaching	No
ASD specialists	No
Professional tutors	No
Peer tutors	Yes
Max. hours/week for services	Unlimited
How professors are notified of student approved accommodations	Student and Disability Office

COLLEGE GRADUATION REQUIREMENTS

Course waivers allowed	Yes
In what courses: General education	
Course substitutions allowed	Yes
In what courses: General education	

Montana

University of Nebraska—Lincoln

1410 Q Street, Lincoln, NE 68588-0417 • Admissions: 402-472-2023 • Fax: 402-472-0670 **Support: S**

CAMPUS

Type of school	Public
Environment	City

STUDENTS

Undergrad enrollment	20,253
% male/female	52/48
% from out of state	25
% frosh live on campus	86

FINANCIAL FACTS

Annual in-state tuition	$7,770
Annual out-of-state tuition	$24,900
Room and board	$11,283
Required fees	$1,792

GENERAL ADMISSIONS INFO

Application fee	$45
Regular application deadline	5/1
Nonfall registration	Yes
Range SAT EBRW	560–670
Range SAT Math	560–690
Range ACT Composite	22–28

ACADEMICS

Student/faculty ratio	17:1
% students returning for sophomore year	81

Most classes have 20–29 students.

Programs/Services for Students with Learning Differences

Services for Students with Disabilities (SSD) facilitates equal and integrated access to the academic, social, cultural and recreational programs offered at the University of Nebraska—Lincoln. Services are designed to meet the unique educational needs of enrolled students with documented disabilities. The student needs to complete the SSD application in order to receive services. Students are encouraged to assess their needs realistically, to take advantage of appropriate support, and to be clear and proactive about gaining assistance. Any student who needs a reasonable accommodation based on a qualified disability is required to register with the SSD office for assistance. The Office of Services for Students with Disabilities also serves as a resource to UNL's administrative units and academic departments that have responsibility to accommodate faculty, staff, and campus visitors with disabilities.

Admissions

Students with disabilities are considered for admission on the same basis as all other applicants and must meet the same academic standards. First-year applicants should have a minimum of a 20 ACT or 1040 SAT or rank in the top 50% of their high school class or have a 3.0 GPA. Course requirements include: 4 years English, 4 years math, 3 years science, 3 years social studies, and 2 years foreign language.

Additional Information

UNL Disability Club is a registered student organization, open to all students and community members with or without disabilities. The objective of the UNL Disability Club is to: share information and resources pertinent to the educational advancement of students with disabilities; provide advocacy for students with disabilities; and promote a setting for students with disabilities to get to know each other and establish camaraderie. The university offers free tutoring, mentoring, and consulting services to all students.

ADMISSIONS INFO FOR STUDENTS WITH LEARNING DIFFERENCES

Phone: 402-472-3787 • Fax: 402-472-0080 • Email: gsimanek3@unl.edu

SAT/ACT required: No
Interview required: No
Essay required: Not Applicable
Additional application required: Yes
Documentation submitted to: SSD

Special Ed. HS course work accepted: No
Separate application required for Programs/Services: Yes
Documentation required for:
LD: Psychoeducational evaluation
ADHD: Psychoeducational evaluation
ASD: Psychoeducational evaluation

University of Nebraska—Lincoln

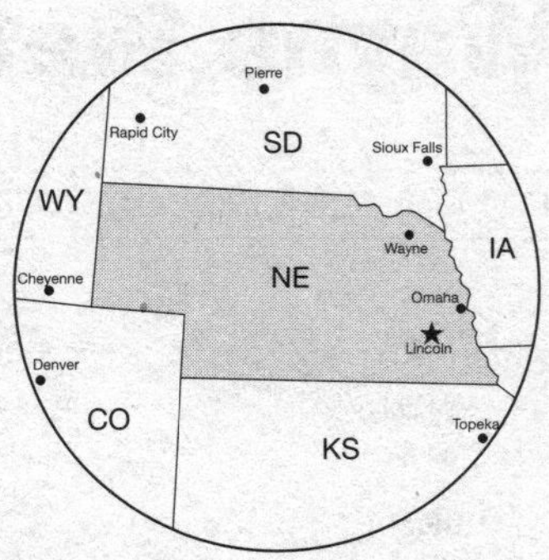

General Admissions

Very important factors include: class rank, academic GPA, standardized test scores. *Important factors include:* rigor of secondary school record. High school diploma is required and GED is accepted. *Academic units required:* 4 English, 4 math, 3 science, 1 science lab, 2 foreign language, 1 social studies, 2 history.

Accommodations or Services

Accommodations are decided upon an individual basis after a thorough review of appropriate, current documentation. The accommodations requests must be supported through the documentation provided and must be logically linked to the current impact of the condition on academic functioning.

Financial Aid

Students should submit: FAFSA. Applicants will be notified of awards on a rolling basis beginning 12/1. *Need-based scholarships/grants offered:* College/university scholarship or grant aid from institutional funds; Federal Pell; Private scholarships; SEOG; State scholarships/grants. *Loan aid offered:* Direct PLUS loans; Direct Subsidized Stafford Loans; Direct Unsubsidized Stafford Loans. Federal Work-Study Program available. Institutional employment available.

Campus Life

Activities: Campus Ministries; Choral groups; Concert band; Dance; Drama/theater; International Student Organization; Jazz band; Literary magazine; Marching band; Model UN; Music ensembles; Musical theater; Opera; Pep band; Radio station; Student government; Student newspaper; Student-run film society; Symphony orchestra; Television station. **Organizations:** 535 registered organizations, 29 honor societies, 31 religious organizations, 33 fraternities, 23 sororities. **Athletics (Intercollegiate):** *Men:* baseball, basketball, cross-country, football, golf, gymnastics, rodeo, tennis, track/field (outdoor), track/field (indoor), wrestling. *Women:* basketball, bowling, cross-country, diving, golf, gymnastics, riflery, rodeo, soccer, softball, swimming, tennis, track/field (outdoor), track/field (indoor), volleyball.

ACCOMMODATIONS

Allowed in exams:	
Calculators	Yes
Dictionary	Yes
Computer	Yes
Spell-checker	Yes
Extended test time	Yes
Scribe	Yes
Proctors	No
Oral exams	Yes
Note-takers	Yes
Support services for students with:	
LD	Yes
ADHD	Yes
ASD	Yes
Distraction-reduced environment	Yes
Recording of lecture allowed	Yes
Reading technology	Yes
Audio books	Yes
Other assistive technology	Yes
Priority registration	Yes
Added costs of services:	
For LD	No
For ADHD	No
For ASD	No
LD specialists	No
ADHD & ASD coaching	No
ASD specialists	No
Professional tutors	No
Peer tutors	No
Max. hours/week for services	Varies
How professors are notified of student approved accommodations	Student and Disability Office

COLLEGE GRADUATION REQUIREMENTS

Course waivers allowed	No
Course substitutions allowed	Yes
In what courses: Case-by-case basis	

Wayne State College

1111 Main Street, Wayne, NE 68787 • Admissions: 402-375-7234 • Fax: 402-375-7204 **Support: S**

CAMPUS

Type of school	Public
Environment	Rural

STUDENTS

Undergrad enrollment	2,829
% male/female	42/58
% from out of state	16
% frosh live on campus	94

FINANCIAL FACTS

Annual in-state tuition	$5,580
Annual out-of-state tuition	$11,160
Room and board	$8,210
Required fees	$1,848

GENERAL ADMISSIONS INFO

Application fee	$0
Regular application deadline	8/24
Nonfall registration	Yes

Admission may be deferred.

Range ACT Composite	18–25

ACADEMICS

Student/faculty ratio	21:1
% students returning for sophomore year	69

Most classes have 20–29 students.

Programs/Services for Students with Learning Differences

The Disability Services Program provides services for students with appropriate documentation. Disability services are offered through the Holland Academic Success Center and include determination of eligibility for services, referral to appropriate resources and responses to requests for accommodations. Accommodations can include exam accommodations, recorded books and campus reader service, learning strategies, support/ discussion groups, and screening and referral for evaluation.

Admissions

Admission to Wayne State College is open to all high school graduates or students with a GED or equivalent. High school special education courses are accepted. Required courses include 4 years English, 3 years math, 3 years social studies, and 3 years science. ACT or SAT score is used for course placement only.

Additional Information

Holland Academic Success Center coaches work one-on-one to help create academic goals. Specific plans for these goals are structured in weekly individual meetings throughout the semester. Academic Coaching: motivates students to take ownership of their academic success; focuses students on their academic goals and helps them identify the steps to reach them; develops time management skills; encourages use of all available campus resources; does not take the place of program advisors. Peer tutors, available through the Peer Tutor Program, are available to all the students at the University. Writing Tutors are also available to review papers before they are handed in to instructors.

ADMISSIONS INFO FOR STUDENTS WITH LEARNING DIFFERENCES

Phone: 402-375-7505 • Email: disabilityservices@wsc.edu

SAT/ACT required: No
Interview required: No
Essay required: No
Additional application required: No
Documentation submitted to: Disability Services

Special Ed. HS course work accepted: Yes
Separate application required for Programs/Services: No
Documentation required for:
LD: Psychoeducational evaluation
ADHD: Psychoeducational evaluation
ASD: Psychoeducational evaluation

Wayne State College

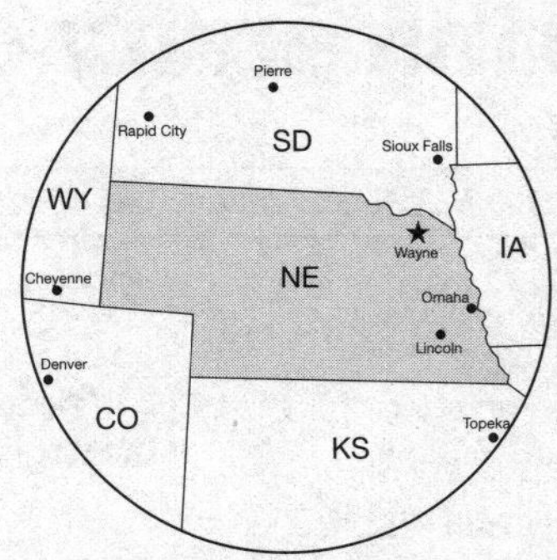

General Admissions

High school diploma is required and GED is accepted. *Academic units recommended:* 4 English, 3 math, 2 science, 2 foreign language, 3 social studies, 2 computer science, 2 visual/performing arts.

Accommodations or Services

Accommodations are decided upon an individual basis after a thorough review of appropriate, current documentation. The accommodations requests must be supported through the documentation provided and must be logically linked to the current impact of the condition on academic functioning.

Financial Aid

Students should submit: FAFSA. Applicants will be notified of awards on a rolling basis beginning 11/15. *Need-based scholarships/grants offered:* College/university scholarship or grant aid from institutional funds; Federal Pell; Private scholarships; SEOG; State scholarships/grants. *Loan aid offered:* Direct PLUS loans; Direct Subsidized Stafford Loans; Direct Unsubsidized Stafford Loans. Federal Work-Study Program available. Institutional employment available.

Campus Life

Activities: Campus Ministries; Choral groups; Concert band; Dance; Drama/theater; International Student Organization; Jazz band; Literary magazine; Marching band; Music ensembles; Musical theater; Pep band; Radio station; Student government; Student newspaper; Television station. **Organizations:** 100 registered organizations. **Athletics (Intercollegiate):** *Men:* baseball, basketball, cross-country, football, golf, track/field (outdoor), track/field (indoor). *Women:* basketball, cross-country, golf, soccer, softball, track/field (outdoor), track/field (indoor), volleyball.

ACCOMMODATIONS

Allowed in exams:	
Calculators	Yes
Dictionary	Yes
Computer	Yes
Spell-checker	Yes
Extended test time	Yes
Scribe	Yes
Proctors	Yes
Oral exams	Yes
Note-takers	Yes
Support services for students with:	
LD	Yes
ADHD	Yes
ASD	Yes
Distraction-reduced environment	Yes
Recording of lecture allowed	Yes
Reading technology	Yes
Audio books	Yes
Other assistive technology	Yes
Priority registration	Yes
Added costs of services:	
For LD	No
For ADHD	No
For ASD	No
LD specialists	No
ADHD & ASD coaching	No
ASD specialists	No
Professional tutors	No
Peer tutors	Yes
Max. hours/week for services	Unlimited
How professors are notified of student approved accommodations	Student

COLLEGE GRADUATION REQUIREMENTS

Course waivers allowed	No
Course substitutions allowed	No

University of Nevada, Las Vegas

4505 Maryland Parkway, Las Vegas, NV 89154-1021 • Admissions: 702-774-8658 • Fax: 702-774-8008 **Support: CS**

CAMPUS

Type of school	Public
Environment	Metropolis

STUDENTS

Undergrad enrollment	25,827
% male/female	43/57
% from out of state	17

FINANCIAL FACTS

Annual in-state tuition	$8,604
Annual out-of-state tuition	$24,258
Room and board	$10,924

GENERAL ADMISSIONS INFO

Application fee	$60
Regular application deadline	8/1
Nonfall registration	Yes

Admission may be deferred.

Range SAT EBRW	520–620
Range SAT Math	510–630
Range ACT Composite	19–25

ACADEMICS

Student/faculty ratio	20:1
% students returning for sophomore year	79

Most classes have 20–29 students.

Programs/Services for Students with Learning Differences

The Disability Resource Center (DRC) provides academic accommodations for students with documented disabilities who are otherwise qualified for university programs. Compliance with Section 504 requires that reasonable academic accommodations be made for students with disabilities. These accommodations might include note-taking, testing accommodations, books on tape, readers, assistive technology, housing adjustments, and dietary adjustments. To establish services, students will need to provide DRC with appropriate documentation of their disability. Appropriate accommodations will be determined after both a review of the reporting student's documentation of a disability as well as a discussion with that student to clarify his or her disability related needs.

Admissions

All applicants are expected to meet the same admission criteria. Freshmen applicants should have a weighted 3.0 grade point average (GPA) in the following high school academic courses: 4 years English, 3 years math, 3 years social science, and 3 years natural science with a total of 13 units. If a student has completed the 13 core high school courses but does not have a 3.0 GPA, the student may fulfill any of the following admission requirements to be admissible to UNLV: have a combined score from the SAT Critical Reading and Math sections of at least 1040, or an ACT composite score of at least 22, or a Nevada Advanced High School Diploma. If the applicant does not satisfy the minimum admission requirements, the student may still be eligible for admission.

Additional Information

The Disability Resource Center offers help to all students on campus who have a diagnosed disability. Following their evaluation, students meet with DRC specialists to develop a plan for services. Psychological services are available through the Counseling and Psychological Services Office. Assistance is provided year-round to active students. Students remain active by requesting service each semester. Services are available to undergraduate, graduate, and continuing education students.

ADMISSIONS INFO FOR STUDENTS WITH LEARNING DIFFERENCES

Phone: 702-895-0866 • Fax: 702-895-0651 • Email: drc@unlv.edu

SAT/ACT required: No
Interview required: No
Essay required: No
Additional application required: No
Documentation submitted to: DRC

Special Ed. HS course work accepted: No
Separate application required for Programs/Services: No
Documentation required for:
LD: Psychoeducational evaluation
ADHD: Psychoeducational evaluation
ASD: Psychoeducational evaluation

University of Nevada, Las Vegas

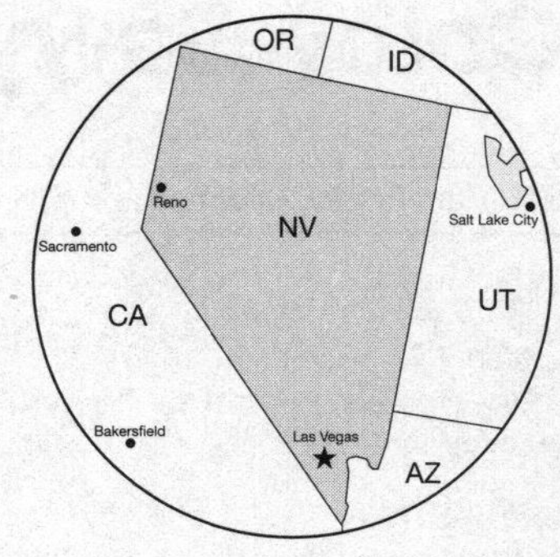

Nevada

General Admissions

Very important factors include: rigor of secondary school record, academic GPA. *Important factors include:* standardized test scores. High school diploma is required and GED is not accepted. *Academic units required:* 4 English, 3 math, 3 science, 2 science labs, 3 social studies.

Accommodations or Services

Accommodations are decided upon an individual basis after a thorough review of appropriate, current documentation. The accommodations requests must be supported through the documentation provided and must be logically linked to the current impact of the condition on academic functioning.

Financial Aid

Students should submit: FAFSA. *Need-based scholarships/grants offered:* College/university scholarship or grant aid from institutional funds; Federal Pell; Private scholarships; SEOG; State scholarships/grants. *Loan aid offered:* Direct PLUS loans; Direct Subsidized Stafford Loans; Direct Unsubsidized Stafford Loans. Federal Work-Study Program available. Institutional employment available.

Campus Life

Activities: Campus Ministries; Choral groups; Concert band; Dance; Drama/theater; International Student Organization; Jazz band; Literary magazine; Marching band; Model UN; Music ensembles; Musical theater; Opera; Pep band; Radio station; Student government; Student newspaper; Student-run film society; Symphony orchestra; Television station; Yearbook. **Organizations:** 24 honor societies, 14 religious organizations, 8 fraternities, 6 sororities. **Athletics (Intercollegiate):** *Men:* baseball, basketball, football, golf, soccer, swimming, tennis. *Women:* basketball, cross-country, equestrian sports, golf, soccer, softball, swimming, tennis, track/field (outdoor), volleyball.

ACCOMMODATIONS

Allowed in exams:	
Calculators	Yes
Dictionary	Yes
Computer	Yes
Spell-checker	Yes
Extended test time	Yes
Scribe	Yes
Proctors	Yes
Oral exams	Yes
Note-takers	Yes
Support services for students with:	
LD	Yes
ADHD	Yes
ASD	Yes
Distraction-reduced environment	Yes
Recording of lecture alowed	Yes
Reading technology	Yes
Audio books	Yes
Other assistive technology	Yes
Priority registration	Yes
Added costs of services:	
For LD	No
For ADHD	No
For ASD	No
LD specialists	Yes
ADHD & ASD coaching	No
ASD specialists	No
Professional tutors	No
Peer tutors	No
Max. hours/week for services	No
How professors are notified of student approved accommodations	Student

COLLEGE GRADUATION REQUIREMENTS

Course waivers allowed	No
Course substitutions allowed	Yes
In what courses: Case-by-case basis	

Colby-Sawyer College

541 Main Street, New London, NH 03257-7835 • Admissions: 603-526-3700 • Fax: 603-526-3452 **Support: CS**

CAMPUS

Type of school	Private (nonprofit)
Environment	Rural

STUDENTS

Undergrad enrollment	851
% male/female	29/71
% from out of state	63
% frosh live on campus	96

FINANCIAL FACTS

Annual tuition	$44,130
Room and board	$15,428

GENERAL ADMISSIONS INFO

Application fee	$0
Regular application deadline	Rolling
Nonfall registration	Yes

Admission may be deferred.

ACADEMICS

Student/faculty ratio	13:1
% students returning for sophomore year	71

Most classes have 10–19 students.

Programs/Services for Students with Learning Differences

Students at Colby-Sawyer College are at the center of everything the college does, and the college excels at providing an individualized learning experience. Opportunities for faculty contact and academic support services are plentiful and initiated by the student. The curriculum at Colby-Sawyer College is writing intensive and requires critical reading and thinking skills and quantitative literacy abilities. Through Access Resources (AR), Colby-Sawyer has Learning Specialists who provide services to students with documented disabilities. These specialists ensure that students have equal access to the curriculum. Additionally, expert coaches, Learning Consultants, available to all students requesting additional academic support or skill building.

Admissions

There is no special admissions process for students with learning disabilities. Access Resources (AR) does not accept disability documentation prior to the student receiving an acceptance to the college and submitting an enrollment deposit. During the application process, students do not disclose disability information, however, parents and students may schedule to meet with AR and bring documentation for review prior to acceptance. The ACT or SAT is optional and not required for admission. Courses required include 4 years English, 3 years math, 3 years science, and 3 years social studies; a foreign language is optional. Applicants are encouraged to be involved in leadership positions, organized clubs, volunteer services, or employment. An essay is required.

Additional Information

Each student has a faculty advisor and Class Dean in addition to support through the Dean of Studies Office. ADA Accommodations for students with documented disabilities are offered on an individualized basis. These include half-hour weekly meetings with a learning specialist for academic coaching, Live Scribe Echo Pens on loan, access to Kurzweil and Dragon Naturally Speaking at the Academic Development Center, and accommodations for testing.

ADMISSIONS INFO FOR STUDENTS WITH LEARNING DIFFERENCES

Phone: 603-526-3711 • Fax: 603-526-3115 • Email: accessresources@colby-sawyer.edu

SAT/ACT required: No
Interview required: No
Essay required: Yes
Additional application required: No
Documentation submitted to: Access Resource

Special Ed. HS course work accepted: Yes
Separate application required for Programs/Services: No
Documentation required for:
LD: Psychoeducational evaluation
ADHD: Psychoeducational evaluation
ASD: Psychoeducational evaluation

Colby-Sawyer College

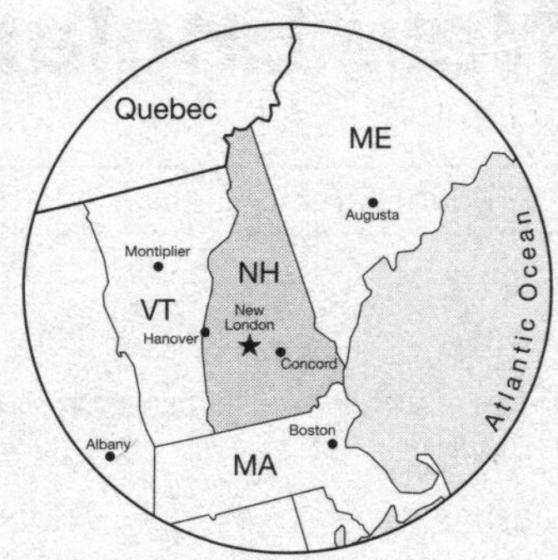

General Admissions

Very important factors include: rigor of secondary school record, academic GPA, interview. *Important factors include:* class rank, application essay, standardized test scores, recommendation(s), extracurricular activities, talent/ability, alumni/ae relation. *Other factors include:* first generation, geographical residence, state residency. High school diploma is required and GED is accepted. *Academic units recommended:* 4 English, 3 math, 3 science, 3 science labs, 2 foreign language, 3 social studies.

Accommodations or Services

Accommodations are decided upon an individual basis after a thorough review of appropriate, current documentation. The accommodations requests must be supported through the documentation provided and must be logically linked to the current impact of the condition on academic functioning.

Financial Aid

Students should submit: FAFSA. *Need-based scholarships/grants offered:* College/university scholarship or grant aid from institutional funds; Federal Pell; Private scholarships; SEOG; State scholarships/grants. *Loan aid offered:* Federal Work-Study Program available. Institutional employment available.

Campus Life

Activities: Choral groups; Dance; Drama/theater; Literary magazine; Musical theater; Radio station; Student government; Student newspaper; Yearbook. **Organizations:** 40 registered organizations, 5 honor societies, 1 religious organization. **Athletics (Intercollegiate):** *Men:* baseball, basketball, diving, equestrian sports, skiing (downhill/alpine), soccer, swimming, tennis, track/field (outdoor). *Women:* basketball, diving, equestrian sports, lacrosse, skiing (downhill/alpine), soccer, swimming, tennis, track/field (outdoor), volleyball.

ACCOMMODATIONS

Allowed in exams:	
Calculators	Yes
Dictionary	Yes
Computer	Yes
Spell-checker	Yes
Extended test time	Yes
Scribe	Yes
Proctors	Yes
Oral exams	No
Note-takers	Yes
Support services for students with:	
LD	Yes
ADHD	Yes
ASD	Yes
Distraction-reduced environment	Yes
Recording of lecture alowed	Yes
Reading technology	Yes
Audio books	Yes
Other assistive technology	Yes
Priority registration	No
Added costs of services:	
For LD	No
For ADHD	No
For ASD	No
LD specialists	Yes
ADHD & ASD coaching	Yes
ASD specialists	Yes
Professional tutors	Yes
Peer tutors	Yes
Max. hours/week for services	1 hour per class per week plus 3 writing consultations per paper
How professors are notified of student approved accommodations	Student

COLLEGE GRADUATION REQUIREMENTS

Course waivers allowed	No
Course substitutions allowed	No

New Hampshire

New England College

102 Bridge Street, Henniker, NH 03242 • Admissions: 603-428-2223 • Fax: 603-428-3155 **Support: CS**

CAMPUS

Type of school	Private (nonprofit)
Environment	Rural

STUDENTS

Undergrad enrollment	1,858
% male/female	41/59
% from out of state	78
% frosh live on campus	70

FINANCIAL FACTS

Annual tuition	$38,428
Room and board	$16,070

GENERAL ADMISSIONS INFO

Application fee	$0
Regular application deadline	Rolling
Nonfall registration	Yes

Admission may be deferred.

ACADEMICS

Student/faculty ratio	15:1
% students returning for sophomore year	58

Most classes have 10–19 students.

Programs/Services for Students with Learning Differences

Pathways Academic Success Services provides comprehensive academic support. All students are assigned a faculty advisor at the time of registration. The Office of Student Access and Accommodations (OSAA) supports students with disabilities, some of whom may have learning disabilities. The center provides individual or small group tutoring, academic counseling, and referral services. Tutoring is available in most subject areas. The center focuses primarily on helping students make a successful transition to New England College while supporting all students in their effort to become independent and successful learners. The support services meet the needs of students who do not require a formal, structured program, but who can find success when offered support and advocacy by a trained and experienced staff in conjunction with small classes and personal attention by faculty. Typically, these students have done well in mainstream programs in high school when given assistance.

Admissions

Students with learning disabilities submit the general New England College application. Students should have a 2.0 GPA. SAT/ACT results are optional. Course requirements include 4 years of English, 2 years of math, 2 years of science, and 2 years of social studies. Documentation of the learning disability should be submitted. An interview is recommended. Successful applicants have typically done well in mainstream programs in high school when given tutorial and study skills assistance.

Additional Information

Students may elect to use the Pathways Services with regular appointments or only occasionally in response to particular or difficult assignments. The center provides tutoring in content areas; computer facilities; study skills instruction; time management strategies; writing support in planning, editing, and proofreading; referrals to other college services; and one-on-one writing support for first-year students. Professional tutors work with students individually and in small groups.

ADMISSIONS INFO FOR STUDENTS WITH LEARNING DIFFERENCES

Phone: 603-428-2302 • Fax: 603-428-2433 • Email: access@nec.edu

SAT/ACT required: No
Interview required: As requested
Essay required: Required
Additional application required: No
Documentation submitted to: OSAA

Special Ed. HS course work accepted: No
Separate application required for Programs/Services: No
Documentation required for:
LD: Psychoeducational evaluation
ADHD: Psychoeducational evaluation
ASD: Psychoeducational evaluation

New England College

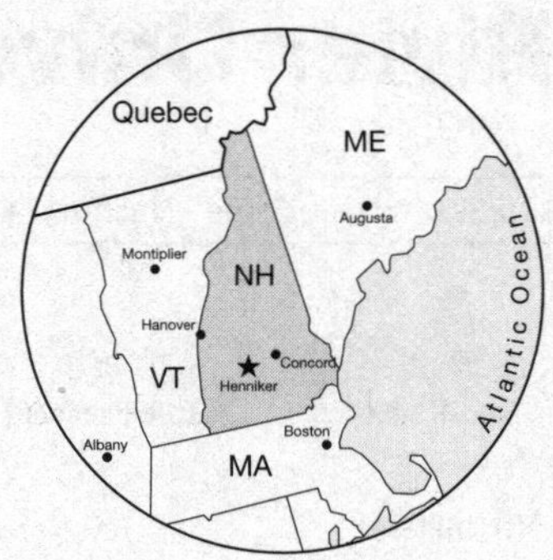

General Admissions

Very important factors include: academic GPA. *Important factors include:* volunteer work. *Other factors include:* rigor of secondary school record, class rank, application essay, recommendation(s), extracurricular activities, talent/ability, character/personal qualities, alumni/ae relation. High school diploma is required and GED is accepted. *Academic units recommended:* 4 English, 3 math, 3 science, 1 science lab, 3 social studies.

Accommodations or Services

Accommodations are decided upon an individual basis after a thorough review of appropriate, current documentation. The accommodations requests must be supported through the documentation provided and must be logically linked to the current impact of the condition on academic functioning.

Financial Aid

Students should submit: CSS/Financial Aid PROFILE; FAFSA. *Need-based scholarships/grants offered:* College/university scholarship or grant aid from institutional funds; Federal Pell; Private scholarships; SEOG; State scholarships/grants. *Loan aid offered:* Direct PLUS loans; Direct Subsidized Stafford Loans; Direct Unsubsidized Stafford Loans. Federal Work-Study Program available. Institutional employment available.

Campus Life

Activities: Drama/theater; International Student Organization; Literary magazine; Radio station; Student government; Student newspaper. **Organizations:** 26 registered organizations, 3 honor societies, 1 religious organization, 1 sorority. **Athletics (Intercollegiate):** *Men:* baseball, basketball, cross-country, ice hockey, lacrosse, soccer. *Women:* basketball, cheerleading, cross-country, field hockey, ice hockey, lacrosse, soccer, softball.

ACCOMMODATIONS

Allowed in exams:	
Calculators	Yes
Dictionary	Yes
Computer	Yes
Spell-checker	Yes
Extended test time	Yes
Scribe	No
Proctors	Yes
Oral exams	Yes
Note-takers	Yes
Support services for students with:	
LD	Yes
ADHD	Yes
ASD	Yes
Distraction-reduced environment	Yes
Recording of lecture allowed	Yes
Reading technology	Yes
Audio books	Yes
Other assistive technology	Yes
Priority registration	Yes
Added costs of services:	
For LD	No
For ADHD	No
For ASD	No
LD specialists	Yes
ADHD & ASD coaching	Yes
ASD specialists	No
Professional tutors	Yes
Peer tutors	Yes
Max. hours/week for services	Varies
How professors are notified of student approved accommodations	Director

COLLEGE GRADUATION REQUIREMENTS

Course waivers allowed	Yes
In what courses: Basic college Math requirement	
Course substitutions allowed	Yes
In what courses: Basic college Math requirement	

New Hampshire

Rivier University

420 South Main Street, Nashua, NH 03060 • Admissions: 603-897-8219 • Fax: 603-891-1799 **Support: S**

CAMPUS

Type of school	Private (nonprofit)
Environment	City

STUDENTS

Undergrad enrollment	1,438
% male/female	21/79
% from out of state	43
% frosh live on campus	48

FINANCIAL FACTS

Annual tuition	$33,410
Room and board	$12,112
Required fees	$600

GENERAL ADMISSIONS INFO

Application fee	$25
Regular application deadline	3/1
Nonfall registration	No

Admission may be deferred.

ACADEMICS

Student/faculty ratio	7:1
% students returning for sophomore year	62

Most classes have 10–19 students.

Programs/Services for Students with Learning Differences

Disability Services provides the opportunity for all individuals who meet academic requirements to be provided auxiliary services, facilitating their earning of a college education. To be eligible for support services, students are required to provide appropriate documentation of their disabilities to the coordinator of Disability Services. The documentation is reviewed in order to arrange for accommodations. To access services, students must contact the coordinator of Disability Services before the start of each semester to schedule an appointment and provide documentation; together the coordinator and the student will discuss and arrange for support services specifically related to the disability.

Admissions

There is no special admissions process for students with LD. All applicants must meet the same criteria. Students should have a combined SAT of 820, a GPA in the top 80 percent of their graduating class and take college-prep courses in high school. Courses required include 4 years of English, 2 years of a foreign language (though this may be substituted), 1 year of science, 3 years of math, 2 years of social science, and 4 years of academic electives. Applicants not meeting the general admission requirements may inquire about alternative admissions. The college offers a probational admit option that requires students to maintain a minimum 2.0 GPA their first semester.

Additional Information

Through the Office of Disability Services there is a range of supports. Students can request personal counseling; preferential registration; classroom accommodations including tape recording of lectures, extended times for test completion, testing free from distractions, and note-takers; student advocacy; a writing center for individualized instruction in writing; and individualized accommodations as developed by the coordinator of Disability Services with the student. Services and accommodations are available for undergraduate and graduate students.

ADMISSIONS INFO FOR STUDENTS WITH LEARNING DIFFERENCES

Phone: 603-897-8497 • Fax: 603-897-8887 • Email: disabilityservices@rivier.edu

SAT/ACT required: No
Interview required: No
Essay required: Yes
Additional application required: No
Documentation submitted to: Disability Services

Special Ed. HS course work accepted: No
Separate application required for Programs/Services: No
Documentation required for:
LD: Psychoeducational evaluation
ADHD: Psychoeducational evaluation
ASD: Psychoeducational evaluation

Rivier University

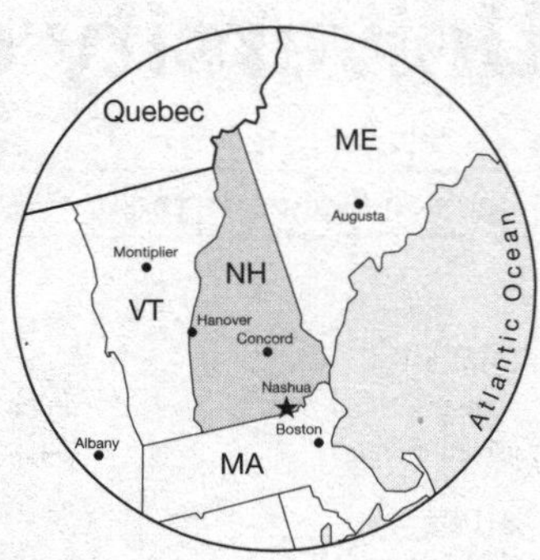

General Admissions

Very important factors include: rigor of secondary school record, academic GPA. *Important factors include:* class rank, application essay, standardized test scores, extracurricular activities, talent/ability, volunteer work, work experience. *Other factors include:* recommendation(s), interview, character/personal qualities. High school diploma is required and GED is accepted. *Academic units recommended:* 4 English, 3 math, 1 science, 1 science lab, 2 foreign language, 2 social studies, 1 history, 3 academic electives.

Accommodations or Services

Accommodations are decided upon an individual basis after a thorough review of appropriate, current documentation. The accommodations requests must be supported through the documentation provided and must be logically linked to the current impact of the condition on academic functioning.

Financial Aid

Students should submit: FAFSA. *Need-based scholarships/grants offered:* College/university scholarship or grant aid from institutional funds; Federal Pell; Private scholarships; SEOG; State scholarships/grants. *Loan aid offered:* Direct PLUS loans; Direct Subsidized Stafford Loans; Direct Unsubsidized Stafford Loans. Federal Work-Study Program available. Institutional employment available.

Campus Life

Activities: Campus Ministries; Choral groups; Dance; Drama/theater; International Student Organization; Model UN; Music ensembles; Student government; Television station; Yearbook. **Organizations:** 30 registered organizations, 2 honor societies, 2 religious organizations. **Athletics (Intercollegiate):** *Men:* baseball, basketball, cross-country, soccer, volleyball. *Women:* basketball, cross-country, soccer, softball, volleyball.

ACCOMMODATIONS

Allowed in exams:	
Calculators	Yes
Dictionary	No
Computer	Yes
Spell-checker	Yes
Extended test time	Yes
Scribe	Yes
Proctors	Yes
Oral exams	Yes
Note-takers	Yes
Support services for students with:	
LD	Yes
ADHD	Yes
ASD	Yes
Distraction-reduced environment	Yes
Recording of lecture allowed	Yes
Reading technology	Yes
Audio books	Yes
Other assistive technology	Yes
Priority registration	Yes
Added costs of services:	
For LD	No
For ADHD	No
For ASD	No
LD specialists	No
ADHD & ASD coaching	No
ASD specialists	No
Professional tutors	No
Peer tutors	Yes
Max. hours/week for services	Varies
How professors are notified of student approved accommodations	Student and Disability Office

COLLEGE GRADUATION REQUIREMENTS

Course waivers allowed	No
Course substitutions allowed	Yes
In what courses: Case-by-case basis	

University of New Hampshire

3 Garrison Avenue, Durham, NH 03824 • Admissions: 603-862-1360 • Fax: 603-862-0077 **Support: S**

CAMPUS

Type of school	Public
Environment	Village

STUDENTS

Undergrad enrollment	12,103
% male/female	44/56
% from out of state	52
% frosh live on campus	96

FINANCIAL FACTS

Annual in-state tuition	$15,520
Annual out-of-state tuition	$32,860
Room and board	$12,242
Required fees	$3,418

GENERAL ADMISSIONS INFO

Application fee	$50
Regular application deadline	2/1
Nonfall registration	Yes

Admission may be deferred.

Range SAT EBRW	540–640
Range SAT Math	530–630
Range ACT Composite	22–28

ACADEMICS

Student/faculty ratio	17:1
% students returning for sophomore year	86

Most classes have 20–29 students.

Programs/Services for Students with Learning Differences

Academic Assistance at the University can be supported by a number of programs. The Student Accessibility Services (SAS) provides assistance and accommodations based on the impact of the disability, and through a discussion with the student. The office serves students with documented disabilities on a case-by-case basis. Additionally, The Center for Academic Resources (CFAR) counselors are also available for drop-in consultation to help students address academic challenges and to find the right support resources on campus. They also offer Academic Mentors. All students with LD/ADHD must provide current and appropriate documentation to qualify for services. Through one to one meetings with SAS staff or a variety of workshops provided across campus, students can learn and further develop their self-advocacy skills, notetaking skills, exam preparation skills, organization and time management, and Assistive Technology (AT) Lab.

Admissions

Applicants have the option to submit SAT or ACT scores. Applicants who do not submit scores will be reviewed equally with those who do submit scores. Once an applicant indicates that no test score will be submitted, the applicant cannot change this decision during the admission process. Students planning to study music education, music history, music performance, or music theory are required to audition as part of the application process. Students planning to study theatre acting, dance, or musical theatre are also required to audition as part of the application process. The average GPA is between a B and B+. Courses required include: 4 years English, 3 years math, 3 years science, 3 years social science, and 2 years foreign language. Some majors have additional requirements.

Additional Information

Once students self-identify, they need to reach out to their instructors, with the support of the SAS to request accommodations. Often, as well, there are students on campus offering tutoring on a private fee basis. Each Department has a list of tutors available to support a student who is looking for help.

ADMISSIONS INFO FOR STUDENTS WITH LEARNING DIFFERENCES

Phone: 603-862-2607 • Fax: 603-862-4043 • Email: michael.shuttic@unh.edu

SAT/ACT required: No
Interview required: No
Essay required: Yes
Additional application required: Yes
Documentation submitted to: SAS

Special Ed. HS course work accepted: No
Separate application required for Programs/Services: Yes
Documentation required for:
LD: Psychoeducational evaluation
ADHD: Psychoeducational evaluation
ASD: Psychoeducational evaluation

University of New Hampshire

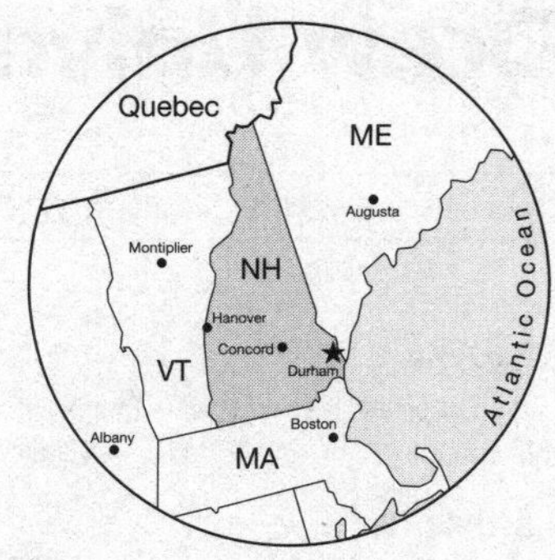

General Admissions

Very important factors include: rigor of secondary school record, academic GPA. *Important factors include:* recommendation(s). *Other factors include:* class rank, application essay, standardized test scores, extracurricular activities, talent/ability, character/personal qualities, first generation, alumni/ae relation, geographical residence, state residency, racial/ethnic status, volunteer work, work experience. High school diploma is required and GED is accepted. *Academic units required:* 4 English, 3 math, 3 science, 2 science labs, 2 foreign language, 3 social studies. *Academic units recommended:* 4 English, 4 math, 4 science, 3 science labs, 3 foreign language, 3 social studies, 1 visual/performing arts.

Accommodations or Services

Accommodations are decided upon an individual basis after a thorough review of appropriate, current documentation. The accommodations requests must be supported through the documentation provided and must be logically linked to the current impact of the condition on academic functioning.

Financial Aid

Students should submit: FAFSA. *Need-based scholarships/grants offered:* College/university scholarship or grant aid from institutional funds; Federal Pell; Private scholarships; SEOG; State scholarships/grants. *Loan aid offered:* Direct PLUS loans; Direct Subsidized Stafford Loans; Direct Unsubsidized Stafford Loans. Federal Work-Study Program available. Institutional employment available.

Campus Life

Activities: Campus Ministries; Choral groups; Concert band; Dance; Drama/theater; International Student Organization; Jazz band; Literary magazine; Marching band; Model UN; Music ensembles; Musical theater; Opera; Pep band; Radio station; Student government; Student newspaper; Student-run film society; Symphony orchestra; Yearbook. **Organizations:** 271 registered organizations, 25 honor societies, 9 religious organizations, 12 fraternities, 8 sororities. **Athletics (Intercollegiate):** *Men:* basketball, cross-country, football, ice hockey, skiing (downhill/alpine), skiing (Nordic/cross-country), soccer, track/field (outdoor), track/field (indoor). *Women:* basketball, cross-country, diving, field hockey, gymnastics, ice hockey, lacrosse, skiing (downhill/alpine), skiing (Nordic/cross-country), soccer, swimming, track/field (outdoor), track/field (indoor), volleyball.

ACCOMMODATIONS

Allowed in exams:	
Calculators	Yes
Dictionary	Yes
Computer	Yes
Spell-checker	Yes
Extended test time	Yes
Scribe	Yes
Proctors	Yes
Oral exams	Yes
Note-takers	Yes
Support services for students with:	
LD	Yes
ADHD	Yes
ASD	Yes
Distraction-reduced environment	Yes
Recording of lecture alowed	Yes
Reading technology	Yes
Audio books	Yes
Other assistive technology	Yes
Priority registration	Yes
Added costs of services:	
For LD	No
For ADHD	No
For ASD	No
LD specialists	No
ADHD & ASD coaching	Mentor
ASD specialists	No
Professional tutors	No
Peer tutors	Yes
Max. hours/week for services	Varies
How professors are notified of student approved accommodations	Student

COLLEGE GRADUATION REQUIREMENTS

Course waivers allowed	No
Course substitutions allowed	Yes
In what courses: Case-by-case basis	

New Hampshire

Drew University

36 Madison Avenue, Madison, NJ 07940-1493 • Admissions: 973-408-3739 • Fax: 973-408-3068 **Support: CS**

CAMPUS

Type of school	Private (nonprofit)
Environment	Village

STUDENTS

Undergrad enrollment	1,577
% male/female	40/60
% from out of state	33
% frosh live on campus	88

FINANCIAL FACTS

Annual tuition	$41,820
Room and board	$15,258
Required fees	$1,157

GENERAL ADMISSIONS INFO

Application fee	$40
Regular application deadline	2/1
Nonfall registration	Yes

Admission may be deferred.

Range SAT EBRW	570–650
Range SAT Math	535–650
Range ACT Composite	23–29

ACADEMICS

Student/faculty ratio	12:1
% students returning for sophomore year	85

Most classes have 10–19 students.

Programs/Services for Students with Learning Differences

The Office of Accessibility Resources (OAR) is available to students as soon as they are admitted. Academic accommodations are available based on a student's disability and individual needs. Services and accommodations are dependent upon students submitting a form that explains the nature of their needs as well as supporting documentation from a licensed professional (qualified in that disability). The student will then review these forms in a personal and confidential meeting with the Director of Accessibility Resources. Once the student has submitted the documentation, there is a review process and then a meeting with the Director of OAR. Academic Services connects students to coaching, peer-tutoring, and specialized advisement as well as career and personal counseling.

Admissions

All applicants are expected to meet the same admission criteria, and there is no separate process for students with disabilities. The university is test-optional, so neither the ACT nor SAT is required for admission. The minimum GPA is 2.5. Applicants should take a college-prep curriculum in high school.

Additional Information

There are a number of on-campus supports for all students including a Writing Center. Counseling services includes a Transition Workshop that helps students who are living on their own for the first time to manage issues that arise in their personal life. There is also, among other workshops, a hands-on procrastination seminar that teaches time-management skills, such as how to set and meet deadlines.

ADMISSIONS INFO FOR STUDENTS WITH LEARNING DIFFERENCES

Phone: 973-408-3962 • Fax: 973 408-3768 • Email: dgiroux@drew.edu

SAT/ACT required: No
Interview required: No
Essay required: No
Additional application required: No
Documentation submitted to: OAR

Special Ed. HS course work accepted: No
Separate application required for Programs/Services: No
Documentation required for:
LD: Psychoeducational evaluation
ADHD: Psychoeducational evaluation
ASD: Psychoeducational evaluation

Drew University

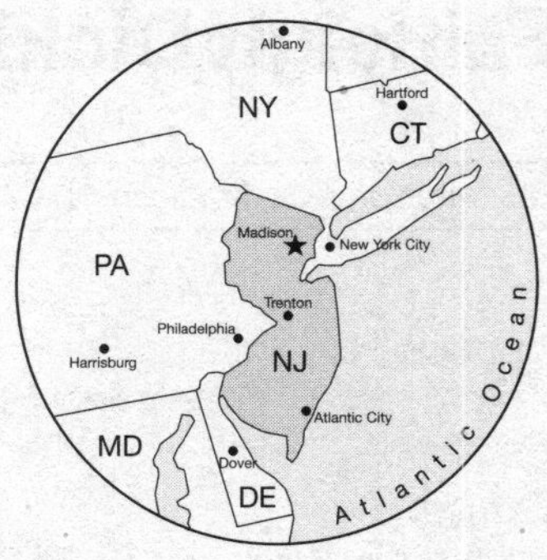

General Admissions

Very important factors include: rigor of secondary school record, academic GPA, interview. *Important factors include:* application essay, recommendation(s), extracurricular activities, talent/ability, character/personal qualities. *Other factors include:* class rank, standardized test scores, first generation, alumni/ae relation, racial/ethnic status, volunteer work, work experience, level of applicant's interest. High school diploma is required and GED is accepted. *Academic units recommended:* 4 English, 3 math, 2 science, 2 foreign language, 2 social studies, 2 history, 3 academic electives.

Accommodations or Services

Accommodations are decided upon an individual basis after a thorough review of appropriate, current documentation. The accommodations requests must be supported through the documentation provided and must be logically linked to the current impact of the condition on academic functioning.

Financial Aid

Students should submit: FAFSA. Applicants will be notified of awards on a rolling basis beginning 1/1. *Need-based scholarships/grants offered:* College/university scholarship or grant aid from institutional funds; Federal Pell; Private scholarships; SEOG; State scholarships/grants. *Loan aid offered:* Direct PLUS loans; Direct Subsidized Stafford Loans; Direct Unsubsidized Stafford Loans. Federal Work-Study Program available. Institutional employment available.

Campus Life

Activities: Campus Ministries; Choral groups; Dance; Drama/theater; International Student Organization; Jazz band; Literary magazine; Model UN; Music ensembles; Musical theater; Pep band; Radio station; Student government; Student newspaper; Student-run film society; Symphony orchestra; Yearbook. **Organizations:** 133 registered organizations, 17 honor societies, 8 religious organizations. **Athletics (Intercollegiate):** *Men:* baseball, basketball, cross-country, fencing, lacrosse, soccer, swimming, tennis. *Women:* basketball, cross-country, fencing, field hockey, lacrosse, soccer, softball, swimming, tennis.

ACCOMMODATIONS

Allowed in exams:	
Calculators	Yes
Dictionary	Yes
Computer	Yes
Spell-checker	Yes
Extended test time	Yes
Scribe	Yes
Proctors	Yes
Oral exams	Yes
Note-takers	Yes
Support services for students with:	
LD	Yes
ADHD	Yes
ASD	No
Distraction-reduced environment	Yes
Recording of lecture allowed	Yes
Reading technology	Yes
Audio books	Yes
Other assistive technology	Yes
Priority registration	Yes
Added costs of services:	
For LD	No
For ADHD	No
For ASD	No
LD specialists	Yes
ADHD & ASD coaching	Yes
ASD specialists	No
Professional tutors	No
Peer tutors	Yes
Max. hours/week for services	Varies
How professors are notified of student approved accommodations	Student

COLLEGE GRADUATION REQUIREMENTS

Course waivers allowed	Yes
In what courses: Depends on major	
Course substitutions allowed	Yes
In what courses: Depends on major	

Fairleigh Dickinson University, College at Florham

285 Madison Ave., Madison, NJ 07940 • Admissions: 800-338-8803 • Fax: 973-443-8088 **Support: SP**

CAMPUS	
Type of school	Private (nonprofit)
Environment	Village
STUDENTS	
Undergrad enrollment	2,620
% male/female	43/57
% from out of state	20
% frosh live on campus	79
FINANCIAL FACTS	
Annual tuition	$43,654
Room and board	$13,021
Required fees	$1,082
GENERAL ADMISSIONS INFO	
Application fee	$50
Regular application deadline	Rolling
Nonfall registration	Yes
ACADEMICS	
Student/faculty ratio	12:1
% students returning for sophomore year	80

Programs/Services for Students with Learning Differences

The Regional Center for College Students with Learning Disabilities offers a structured plan of support. Services are offered at no additional charge. Planning, learning strategies, professional tutors, counseling, and accommodations are the cornerstones of the Regional Center. The Program is staffed by professionals with services at both the Metropolitan Campus and the Campus of Florham. Assistance to students is intensive and the program is fully integrated into the coursework. Students are in touch with faculty on a regular basis. The program encourages involvement in the community, particularly service-type activities relevant to the students with LD. Performance data are routinely reviewed to identify students in need of more intensive help. Upon admission students are invited to attend a summer orientation session. During this time, students meet with center staff to develop an Individual Academic Plan.

Admissions

All applicants are expected to meet the same admission criteria. There is no separate application process for students with learning disabilities. The university is test optional and does not require the ACT or SAT in the application process.

Additional Information

First-years who are able to receive the support of the Regional Center will be able to have up to four academic support sessions per week. Additionally, students with an ASD diagnosis can apply for the two-year COMPASS Program for a fee per academic year. This is an individually tailored, comprehensive, academic, and social support program for a very limited number of college students with high functioning Autism Spectrum Disorder or Asperger's Syndrome. COMPASS is offered separately on each of FDU's two New Jersey campuses. The goals of this program are to help each student recognize and make use of existing academic and social strengths, to aid in the development of new abilities, and to promote progress toward a higher level of independent functioning. Students interested in COMPASS must first apply and be accepted to Fairleigh Dickinson University through the general application process at one of FDU's New Jersey campuses. Fee for COMPASS, $6,520 per semester.

ADMISSIONS INFO FOR STUDENTS WITH LEARNING DIFFERENCES

Phone: 973-443-8079 • Fax: 692-2813 • Email: hebert@fdu.edu

SAT/ACT required: No
Interview required: No
Essay required: Yes
Additional application required: Yes
Documentation submitted to: Regional Center

Special Ed. HS course work accepted: Yes
Separate application required for Programs/Services: No
Documentation required for:
LD: Psychoeducational evaluation
ADHD: Psychoeducational evaluation
ASD: Psychoeducational evaluation

Fairleigh Dickinson University, College at Florham

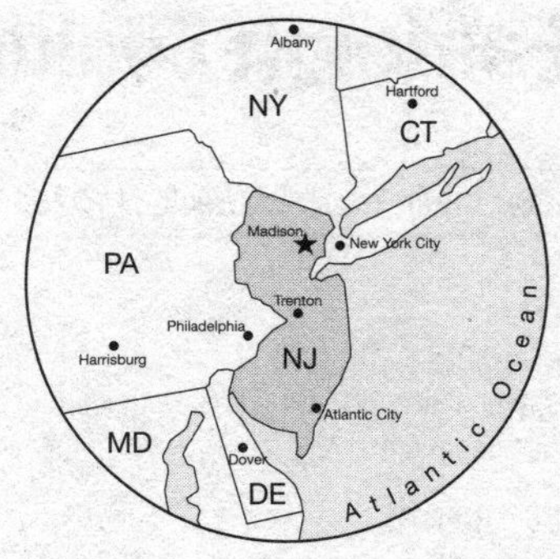

General Admissions

Very important factors include: academic GPA, standardized test scores. *Important factors include:* rigor of secondary school record, recommendation(s). *Other factors include:* class rank, application essay, interview, extracurricular activities, talent/ability, character/personal qualities, alumni/ae relation, volunteer work, level of applicant's interest. High school diploma is required and GED is accepted. *Academic units required:* 4 English, 3 math, 2 science, 2 science labs, 2 history, 3 academic electives. *Academic units recommended:* 4 English, 3 math, 3 science, 2 science labs, 2 foreign language, 2 history, 4 academic electives.

Accommodations or Services

Accommodations are decided upon an individual basis after a thorough review of appropriate, current documentation. The accommodations requests must be supported through the documentation provided and must be logically linked to the current impact of the condition on academic functioning.

Financial Aid

Students should submit: FAFSA. *Need-based scholarships/grants offered:* College/university scholarship or grant aid from institutional funds; Federal Pell; Private scholarships; SEOG; State scholarships/grants. *Loan aid offered:* Direct PLUS loans; Direct Subsidized Stafford Loans; Direct Unsubsidized Stafford Loans. Federal Work-Study Program available. Institutional employment available.

Campus Life

Activities: Campus Ministries; Choral groups; Dance; Drama/theater; International Student Organization; Literary magazine; Musical theater; Radio station; Student government; Student newspaper; Student-run film society. **Organizations:** 43 registered organizations, 9 honor societies, 3 religious organizations, 7 fraternities, 5 sororities. **Athletics (Intercollegiate):** *Men:* baseball, basketball, cross-country, football, golf, lacrosse, soccer, swimming, tennis. *Women:* basketball, cross-country, field hockey, lacrosse, soccer, softball, swimming, tennis, volleyball.

ACCOMMODATIONS

Allowed in exams:	
Calculators	Yes
Dictionary	Yes
Computer	Yes
Spell-checker	Yes
Extended test time	Yes
Scribe	Yes
Proctors	Yes
Oral exams	Yes
Note-takers	Yes
Support services for students with:	
LD	Yes
ADHD	Yes
ASD	Yes
Distraction-reduced environment	Yes
Recording of lecture allowed	Yes
Reading technology	Yes
Audio books	Yes
Other assistive technology	Yes
Priority registration	Yes
Added costs of services:	
For LD	No
For ADHD	No
For ASD	Yes
LD specialists	Yes
ADHD & ASD coaching	No
ASD specialists	Yes
Professional tutors	Yes
Peer tutors	No
Max. hours/week for services	4
How professors are notified of student approved accommodations	Student and Disability Office

COLLEGE GRADUATION REQUIREMENTS

Course waivers allowed	No
Course substitutions allowed	Yes
In what courses: Case-by-case basis	

New Jersey

Fairleigh Dickinson University, Metropolitan Campus

1000 River Road, Teaneck, NJ 07666-1966 • Admissions: 201-692-2553 • Fax: 201-692-7319 **Support: SP**

CAMPUS	
Type of school	Private (nonprofit)
Environment	Town
STUDENTS	
Undergrad enrollment	6,353 4,101
% male/female	42/58
% from out of state	13
% frosh live on campus	55
FINANCIAL FACTS	
Annual tuition	$41,154
Room and board	$14,556
Required fees	$1,082
GENERAL ADMISSIONS INFO	
Application fee	$50
Regular application deadline	Rolling
Nonfall registration	Yes
ACADEMICS	
Student/faculty ratio	14:1
% students returning for sophomore year	73

Programs/Services for Students with Learning Differences

Similar to the program offered on the Florham campus, The Regional Center for College Students with LD offers a structured plan of intensive advisement, academic support, and counseling services tailored to the unique needs of students with language-based disabilities. The Center offers students learning strategies, professional tutors, counseling, and classroom accommodations. Staffed by professionals at the Metropolitan Campus and the Campus of Florham, the LD program and special services are free. Assistance is intensive and the program fully integrated into the course work. Performance data is routinely reviewed to identify students in need of more intensive help. Upon admission students are invited to attend a summer orientation session.

Admissions

Admissions decisions are made independently by FDU Admissions and the LD Program Admissions Directors. Students must be admitted to the university before applications can be reviewed by the Regional Center. Criteria include documentation of a primary diagnosis of a language-based learning disability made by licensed professionals dated within 24 months of the application; evidence of adequate performance in mainstream college-prep high school courses; and evidence of motivation as reflected in recommendations. Students enrolled solely in special education high school classes are usually not admissible.

Additional Information

Students with a language-based learning disability enrolled at both the Metropolitan and Florham campuses during their undergraduate career are provided comprehensive professional support free of charge. Students are provided with structured plans of intensive academic support and counseling services specific to the unique learning needs of each student. Freshman can receive up to four support sessions a week per semester, sophomores three supports a semester, juniors and seniors one or two supports per semester.

ADMISSIONS INFO FOR STUDENTS WITH LEARNING DIFFERENCES

Phone: 201-692-2460 • Email: bbyrnes@fdu.edu

SAT/ACT required: No
Interview required: No
Essay required: Yes
Additional application required: No
Documentation submitted to: Regional Center

Special Ed. HS course work accepted: Yes
Separate application required for Programs/Services: No
Documentation required for:
LD: Psychoeducational evaluation
ADHD: Psychoeducational evaluation
ASD: Psychoeducational evaluation

Fairleigh Dickinson University, Metropolitan Campus

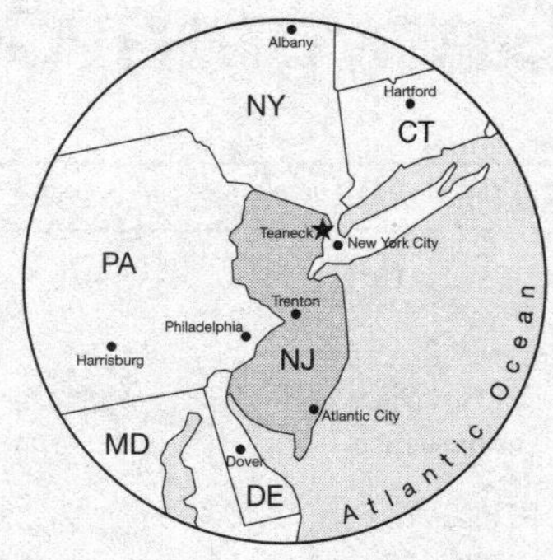

General Admissions

Very important factors include: academic GPA, standardized test scores. *Important factors include:* rigor of secondary school record, recommendation(s). *Other factors include:* class rank, application essay, interview, extracurricular activities, talent/ability, character/personal qualities, alumni/ae relation, volunteer work, level of applicant's interest. High school diploma is required and GED is accepted. *Academic units required:* 4 English, 3 math, 2 science, 2 science labs, 2 history, 3 academic electives. *Academic units recommended:* 4 English, 3 math, 3 science, 2 science labs, 2 foreign language, 2 history, 4 academic electives.

Accommodations or Services

Accommodations are decided upon an individual basis after a thorough review of appropriate, current documentation. The accommodations requests must be supported through the documentation provided and must be logically linked to the current impact of the condition on academic functioning.

Financial Aid

Students should submit: FAFSA. *Need-based scholarships/grants offered:* College/university scholarship or grant aid from institutional funds; Federal Pell; Private scholarships; SEOG; State scholarships/grants. *Loan aid offered:* Direct PLUS loans; Direct Subsidized Stafford Loans; Direct Unsubsidized Stafford Loans. Federal Work-Study Program available. Institutional employment available.

Campus Life

Activities: Campus Ministries; Choral groups; Dance; Drama/theater; International Student Organization; Literary magazine; Music ensembles; Musical theater; Radio station; Student government; Student newspaper; Student-run film society. **Organizations:** 79 registered organizations, 10 honor societies, 4 religious organizations, 5 fraternities, 7 sororities. **Athletics (Intercollegiate):** *Men:* baseball, basketball, cross-country, golf, soccer, tennis, track/field (indoor). *Women:* basketball, bowling, cross-country, fencing, golf, soccer, softball, tennis, track/field (indoor), volleyball.

ACCOMMODATIONS

Allowed in exams:	
Calculators	Yes
Dictionary	Yes
Computer	Yes
Spell-checker	Yes
Extended test time	Yes
Scribe	Yes
Proctors	Yes
Oral exams	Yes
Note-takers	No
Support services for students with:	
LD	Yes
ADHD	No
ASD	Yes
Distraction-reduced environment	Yes
Recording of lecture allowed	Yes
Reading technology	Yes
Audio books	Yes
Other assistive technology	Yes
Priority registration	Yes
Added costs of services:	
For LD	No
For ADHD	No
For ASD	No
LD specialists	Yes
ADHD & ASD coaching	No
ASD specialists	No
Professional tutors	Yes
Peer tutors	No
Max. hours/week for services	8
How professors are notified of student approved accommodations	Letter from Regional Center and student

COLLEGE GRADUATION REQUIREMENTS

Course waivers allowed	No
Course substitutions allowed	Yes
In what courses: Case-by-case basis	

New Jersey

Georgian Court University

900 Lakewood Avenue, Lakewood, NJ 08701-2697 • Admissions: 732-987-2700 • Fax: 732-987-2000 **Support: SP**

CAMPUS

Type of school	Private (nonprofit)
Environment	Town

STUDENTS

Undergrad enrollment	1,550
% male/female	25/75
% from out of state	7
% frosh live on campus	47

FINANCIAL FACTS

Annual tuition	$32,050
Room and board	$11,200
Required fees	$1,560

GENERAL ADMISSIONS INFO

Application fee	$40
Regular application deadline	8/1
Nonfall registration	Yes

Admission may be deferred.

Range SAT EBRW	480–580
Range SAT Math	478–580
Range ACT Composite	19–25

ACADEMICS

Student/faculty ratio	12:1
% students returning for sophomore year	79

Most classes have 10–19 students.

Programs/Services for Students with Learning Differences

The Academic Development and Support Center supports students' needs depending on the documentation the student shares with the Center. There is no fee for their services that can include free tutoring. However, The Learning Connection (TLC), located in the same center, is an assistance program designed to provide support for students with mild to moderate learning disabilities. The program is not one of remediation, but it is an individualized support program to assist candidates in becoming successful college students. Emphasis is placed on developing self-help strategies and study techniques. This is a fee based program of tutoring and coaching.

Admissions

The class rank and transcript should give evidence of the ability to succeed in college. Students must submit SAT scores. Conditional admission may be offered to some applicants. Students with learning disabilities should indicate on their application their wish to apply to the Learning Center. The Associate Director of Admissions is the liaison between the admissions staff and the TLC. Applicants are expected to have completed a rigorous high school curriculum in core courses including English, math, science, social studies and foreign language. The university is test optional and does not require the ACT or SAT for admission. However, applicants applying to the nursing program must submit test scores and have an ACT of 21 or higher or 1000 or higher on the SAT. No personal interview is required but informational interviews are offered at a student's request.

Additional Information

The Learning Connection offers individuals one-on-one support with a professional staff member known as an Academic Development Specialist. Students are guaranteed 2 hours of scheduled tutoring and coaching each week. The specialist will work with the student on time management, organizational skills, study strategies, and test-taking skills. The specialist will track the student's progress and assignments. Additionally, the student will receive support in the development of socialization and life skills. The student will develop a strong bond with the Academic Development Specialist.

ADMISSIONS INFO FOR STUDENTS WITH LEARNING DIFFERENCES

Phone: 732-987-2646 • Fax: 732-987-2026 • Email: lfahr@georgian.edu

SAT/ACT required: No
Interview required: Yes
Essay required: No
Additional application required: No
Documentation submitted to: The Learning Connection

Special Ed. HS course work accepted: No
Separate application required for Programs/Services: No
Documentation required for:
- **LD:** Psychoeducational evaluation
- **ADHD:** Psychoeducational evaluation
- **ASD:** Psychoeducational evaluation

Georgian Court University

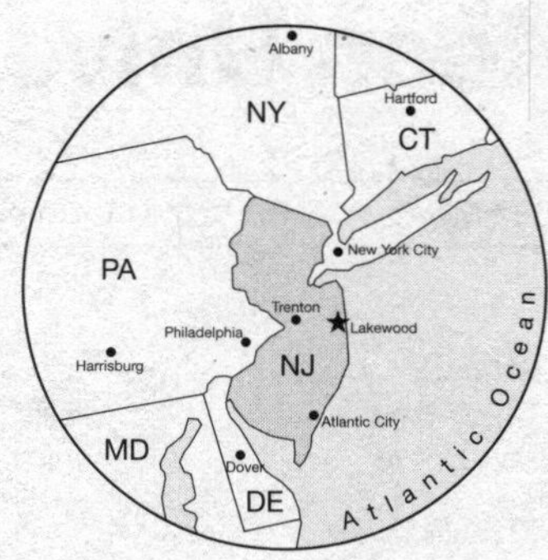

General Admissions

Very important factors include: rigor of secondary school record, academic GPA. *Important factors include:* standardized test scores. *Other factors include:* class rank, application essay, recommendation(s), interview, extracurricular activities, talent/ability, character/personal qualities, first generation, religious affiliation/commitment, volunteer work, work experience, level of applicant's interest. High school diploma is required and GED is accepted. *Academic units required:* 4 English, 2 math, 1 science, 1 science lab, 2 foreign language, 1 history, 6 academic electives.

Accommodations or Services

Accommodations are decided upon an individual basis after a thorough review of appropriate, current documentation. The accommodations requests must be supported through the documentation provided and must be logically linked to the current impact of the condition on academic functioning.

Financial Aid

Students should submit: FAFSA; State aid form. *Need-based scholarships/grants offered:* College/university scholarship or grant aid from institutional funds; Federal Pell; Private scholarships; SEOG; State scholarships/grants. *Loan aid offered:* Direct PLUS loans; Direct Subsidized Stafford Loans; Direct Unsubsidized Stafford Loans. Federal Work-Study Program available. Institutional employment available.

Campus Life

Activities: Campus Ministries; Choral groups; Concert band; Dance; Drama/theater; International Student Organization; Jazz band; Literary magazine; Model UN; Music ensembles; Student government; Student newspaper. **Organizations:** 40 registered organizations, 19 honor societies, 2 religious organizations. **Athletics (Intercollegiate):** *Men:* basketball, cross-country, lacrosse, soccer, track/field (outdoor).*Women:* basketball, cross-country, lacrosse, soccer, softball, tennis, track/field (outdoor), volleyball.

ACCOMMODATIONS

Allowed in exams:	
Calculators	Yes
Dictionary	Yes
Computer	Yes
Spell-checker	Yes
Extended test time	Yes
Scribe	Yes
Proctors	Yes
Oral exams	Yes
Note-takers	Yes
Support services for students with:	
LD	Yes
ADHD	Yes
ASD	Yes
Distraction-reduced environment	Yes
Recording of lecture alowed	Yes
Reading technology	Yes
Audio books	Yes
Other assistive technology	Yes
Priority registration	Yes
Added costs of services:	
For LD	Yes
For ADHD	Yes
For ASD	Yes
LD specialists	Yes
ADHD & ASD coaching	Yes
ASD specialists	Yes
Professional tutors	Yes
Peer tutors	Yes
Max. hours/week for services	Varies
How professors are notified of student approved accommodations	Student

COLLEGE GRADUATION REQUIREMENTS

Course waivers allowed	No
Course substitutions allowed	Yes
In what courses: Case-by-case basis	

Kean University

1000 Morris Ave, PO Box 411, Union, NJ 07083-0411 • Admissions: 908-737-7100 • Fax: 908-737-7105 **Support: CS**

CAMPUS

Type of school	Public
Environment	City

STUDENTS

Undergrad enrollment	11,947
% male/female	40/60
% from out of state	2
% frosh live on campus	38

FINANCIAL FACTS

Annual in-state tuition	$12,445
Annual out-of-state tuition	$19,621
Room and board	$14,472

GENERAL ADMISSIONS INFO

Application fee	$75
Regular application deadline	8/15
Nonfall registration	Yes

Admission may be deferred.

Range SAT EBRW	460–550
Range SAT Math	460–550
Range ACT Composite	17–23

ACADEMICS

Student/faculty ratio	17:1
% students returning for sophomore year	74

Most classes have 20–29 students.

Programs/Services for Students with Learning Differences

Disability Services provides support, accommodations, educational programs and activities to ensure that all students have the maximum possible opportunity to equal access to all areas of University life. Students with disabilities must provide current documentation that shows the functional limitations of their disability. Accommodations for classrooms, testing and residence life are provided to create equal access on campus. Services include accommodations, assistive technology training, alternate testing room, and a mentoring program.

Admissions

There is no special admissions process for students with LD. All applicants must meet the same admission criteria. Courses taken in special education may be considered. SAT/ACT is optional. The minimum GPA is 2.8 and the average GPA is 3.0. Kean requires two recommendations and a personal essay. Although students are asked to write about their educational and career objectives, they can also share noteworthy accomplishments in their lives or discuss something or someone who helped them become the person they are today. The student must be highly motivated, able to do college work, be of at least average intelligence, have a documented learning disability, have areas of academic strength, and make a commitment to work responsibly and attend classes, tutoring, workshops, and counseling sessions. Students are encouraged to apply by early March.

Additional Information

College Steps provides college support to students with learning disabilities, autism and executive functioning deficits. College Steps supports students in achieving success in college and work and life. Peer mentors are part of the program and help students transition into college and encourage students to get involved in clubs, activities, and social groups.

ADMISSIONS INFO FOR STUDENTS WITH LEARNING DIFFERENCES

Phone: 908-737-4910 • Fax: 908-737-4865 • Email: disabilityservices@kean.edu

SAT/ACT required: No
Interview required: Yes
Essay required: No
Additional application required: Yes
Documentation submitted to: Support Program/Services

Special Ed. HS course work accepted: No
Separate application required for Programs/Services: Yes
Documentation required for:
LD: Educational and Psychological evaluations
ADHD: Educational and Psychological evaluations as well as Medical Verification
ASD: Educational and Psychological evaluations

Kean University

General Admissions

Very important factors include: rigor of secondary school record, academic GPA. *Important factors include:* standardized test scores. *Other factors include:* application essay, recommendation(s), interview, extracurricular activities, talent/ability, character/personal qualities, alumni/ae relation, volunteer work, work experience. High school diploma is required and GED is accepted. *Academic units required:* 4 English, 3 math, 2 science, 2 science labs, 2 history, 5 academic electives. *Academic units recommended:* 4 English, 3 math, 2 science, 2 science labs, 2 foreign language, 2 social studies, 2 history, 5 academic electives.

Accommodations or Services

Accommodations are decided upon an individual basis after a thorough review of appropriate, current documentation. The accommodations requests must be supported through the documentation provided and must be logically linked to the current impact of the condition on academic functioning.

Financial Aid

Students should submit: FAFSA. Applicants will be notified of awards on a rolling basis beginning 1/31. *Need-based scholarships/grants offered:* College/university scholarship or grant aid from institutional funds; Federal Pell; Private scholarships; SEOG; State scholarships/grants. *Loan aid offered:* Direct PLUS loans; Direct Subsidized Stafford Loans; Direct Unsubsidized Stafford Loans. Federal Work-Study Program available. Institutional employment available.

Campus Life

Activities: Campus Ministries; Choral groups; Concert band; Dance; Drama/theater; International Student Organization; Jazz band; Literary magazine; Model UN; Music ensembles; Musical theater; Pep band; Radio station; Student government; Student newspaper; Student-run film society; Symphony orchestra; Television station; Yearbook. **Organizations:** 124 registered organizations, 30 honor societies, 8 religious organizations, 15 fraternities, 15 sororities. **Athletics (Intercollegiate):** *Men:* baseball, basketball, football, lacrosse, soccer, track/field (outdoor). *Women:* basketball, field hockey, lacrosse, soccer, softball, tennis, track/field (outdoor), volleyball.

ACCOMMODATIONS

Allowed in exams:	
Calculators	Yes
Dictionary	Yes
Computer	Yes
Spell-checker	Yes
Extended test time	Yes
Scribe	Yes
Proctors	Yes
Oral exams	Yes
Note-takers	Yes
Support services for students with:	
LD	Yes
ADHD	Yes
ASD	Yes
Distraction-reduced environment	Yes
Recording of lecture alowed	Yes
Reading technology	Yes
Audio books	Yes
Other assistive technology	Yes
Priority registration	Yes
Added costs of services:	
For LD	No
For ADHD	No
For ASD	No
LD specialists	Yes
ADHD & ASD coaching	Yes
ASD specialists	Yes
Professional tutors	No
Peer tutors	Yes
Max. hours/week for services	Varies
How professors are notified of student approved accommodations	Student

COLLEGE GRADUATION REQUIREMENTS

Course waivers allowed	No
Course substitutions allowed	Yes
In what courses: Case-by-case basis	

Monmouth University (NJ)

400 Cedar Ave, West Long Branch, NJ 07764-1898 Admissions: 732-571-3456 Fax: 732-263-5166 **Support: CS**

CAMPUS

Type of school	Private (nonprofit)
Environment	Village

STUDENTS

Undergrad enrollment	4,450
% male/female	41/59
% from out of state	26
% frosh live on campus	79

FINANCIAL FACTS

Annual tuition	$39,968
Room and board	$14,942
Required fees	$712

GENERAL ADMISSIONS INFO

Application fee	$50
Regular application deadline	Rolling
Nonfall registration	Yes

Admission may be deferred.

Range SAT EBRW	530–620
Range SAT Math	520–620
Range ACT Composite	21–27

ACADEMICS

Student/faculty ratio	12:1
% students returning for sophomore year	81

Most classes have 20–29 students.

Programs/Services for Students with Learning Differences

Monmouth University recognizes the special needs of students with disabilities who are capable, with appropriate assistance, of excelling in a demanding university environment. Reasonable support services and a nurturing environment contribute to their success. Monmouth's commitment is to provide a learning process and atmosphere that allows students to pursue their educational goals, realize their full potential, contribute actively to their community and society, and determine the direction of their lives. Students are enrolled in regular courses and are not isolated from the rest of the student body in any manner. Students with documented disabilities may request reasonable accommodations and/or auxiliary aids. It is important that students disclose their disability and provide the required documentation to Department of Disability Services for Students. Much of their success has to do with individual recognition of their specific learning needs, and a willingness to self-advocate in a student-driven program.

Admissions

All applicants are expected to meet the same admission requirements. There is no separate application process for students with learning disabilities. The university is currently test optional and will review this policy in future. Students should pursue a rigorous academic curriculum in high school and be involved in leadership, activities, and volunteering.

Additional Information

Monmouth University offers one course that is designed for students with disabilities. Transition to College is a one credit elective course geared toward incoming freshmen with disabilities. The course attempts to assist students in their transition by presenting material that will help them become independent learners. Topics include: learning styles, self-advocacy, organizational methods, and time management study skills.

ADMISSIONS INFO FOR STUDENTS WITH LEARNING DIFFERENCES

Phone: 732-571-3460 • Fax: 732-263-5126 • Email: jcarey@monmouth.edu

SAT/ACT required: Yes (Test optional for 2021)
Interview required: No
Essay required: No
Additional application required: No
Documentation submitted to: Department of Disability Services for Students

Special Ed. HS course work accepted: Yes
Separate application required for Programs/Services: No
Documentation required for:
LD: Psychoeducational evaluation
ADHD: Psychoeducational evaluation
ASD: Psychoeducational evaluation

Monmouth University (NJ)

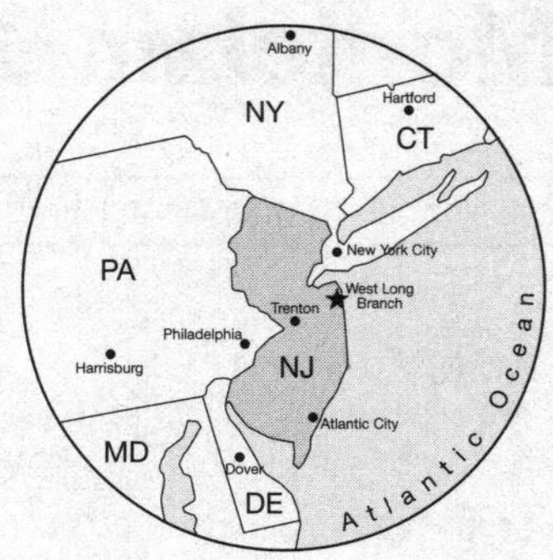

General Admissions

Very important factors include: rigor of secondary school record, academic GPA, standardized test scores. *Important factors include:* application essay, recommendation(s), extracurricular activities, volunteer work. *Other factors include:* character/personal qualities, alumni/ae relation. High school diploma is required and GED is accepted. *Academic units required:* 4 English, 3 math, 2 science, 1 science lab, 2 history, 5 academic electives. *Academic units recommended:* 4 English, 3 math, 2 science, 1 science lab, 2 foreign language, 2 social studies, 2 history, 5 academic electives.

Accommodations or Services

Accommodations are decided upon an individual basis after a thorough review of appropriate, current documentation. The accommodations requests must be supported through the documentation provided and must be logically linked to the current impact of the condition on academic functioning.

Financial Aid

Students should submit: FAFSA. *Need-based scholarships/grants offered:* College/university scholarship or grant aid from institutional funds; Federal Pell; Private scholarships; SEOG; State scholarships/grants. *Loan aid offered:* Direct PLUS loans; Direct Subsidized Stafford Loans; Direct Unsubsidized Stafford Loans. Federal Work-Study Program available. Institutional employment available.

Campus Life

Activities: Campus Ministries; Choral groups; Concert band; Dance; Drama/theater; International Student Organization; Jazz band; Literary magazine; Model UN; Music ensembles; Musical theater; Pep band; Radio station; Student government; Student newspaper; Television station; Yearbook. **Organizations:** 117 registered organizations, 26 honor societies, 6 religious organizations, 7 fraternities, 9 sororities. **Athletics (Intercollegiate):** *Men:* baseball, basketball, cross-country, football, golf, soccer, tennis, track/field (outdoor), track/field (indoor). *Women:* basketball, cross-country, field hockey, golf, lacrosse, soccer, softball, tennis, track/field (outdoor), track/field (indoor).

ACCOMMODATIONS

Allowed in exams:	
Calculators	Yes
Dictionary	Yes
Computer	Yes
Spell-checker	Yes
Extended test time	Yes
Scribe	Yes
Proctors	Yes
Oral exams	No
Note-takers	Yes
Support services for students with:	
LD	Yes
ADHD	Yes
ASD	Yes
Distraction-reduced environment	Yes
Recording of lecture allowed	Yes
Reading technology	Yes
Audio books	Yes
Other assistive technology	Yes
Priority registration	Yes
Added costs of services:	
For LD	No
For ADHD	No
For ASD	No
LD specialists	Yes
ADHD & ASD coaching	No
ASD specialists	No
Professional tutors	No
Peer tutors	Yes
Max. hours/week for services	Varies
How professors are notified of student approved accommodations	Student

COLLEGE GRADUATION REQUIREMENTS

Course waivers allowed	No
Course substitutions allowed	No

New Jersey

Montclair State University

One Normal Avenue, Montclair, NJ 07043-1624 • Admissions: 973-655-4444 • Fax: 973-655-7700 **Support: S**

CAMPUS

Type of school	Public
Environment	Town

STUDENTS

Undergrad enrollment	16,687
% male/female	39/61
% from out of state	4
% frosh live on campus	48

FINANCIAL FACTS

Annual in-state tuition	$12,082
Annual out-of-state tuition	$20,042
Room and board	$16,193
Required fees	$989

GENERAL ADMISSIONS INFO

Application fee	$65
Regular application deadline	3/1
Nonfall registration	Yes

Admission may be deferred.

Range SAT EBRW	500–600
Range SAT Math	490–580

ACADEMICS

Student/faculty ratio	17:1
% students returning for sophomore year	80

Most classes have 20–29 students.

Programs/Services for Students with Learning Differences

The Disability Resource Center (DRC) at the university helps students receive the accommodations and services necessary for success. The DRC provides assistance to students with physical, sensory, learning, psychological, neurological, and chronic medical disabilities. At the beginning of every semester, once the student has submitted the DRC registration form and has met with a staff person from the DRC, the student meets with the instructors of the classes they are taking and shares the accommodation form provided by DRC.

Admissions

The university considers a number of factors in evaluating applicants for admission. The most important factors include grades in rigorous courses, involvement in community service, student organizations, talent, and extracurricular activities. Courses recommended are 4 years of English, 3 years of math, 2 years of foreign language, 2 years of social science, and three additional courses in core subject areas. The strongest applicants have a 3.2 GPA or higher. The university is test optional and does not require an ACT or SAT for admissions.

Additional Information

The DRC provides accommodations and services. (Appropriate academic accommodations are determined on a case-by-case basis and must be supported by documentation.) Academic accommodations are note takers, readers, scribes, extended testing, textbooks on CD, equipment loans, and adaptive technology.

ADMISSIONS INFO FOR STUDENTS WITH LEARNING DIFFERENCES

Phone: 973-655-5431 • Fax: 973-655-5308 • Email: drc@mail.montclair.edu

SAT/ACT required: Yes
Interview required: No
Essay required: Not Applicable
Additional application required: No
Documentation submitted to: DRC

Special Ed. HS course work accepted: Yes
Separate application required for Programs/Services: Yes
Documentation required for:
- **LD:** Psychoeducational evaluation
- **ADHD:** Psychoeducational evaluation
- **ASD:** Psychoeducational evaluation

Montclair State University

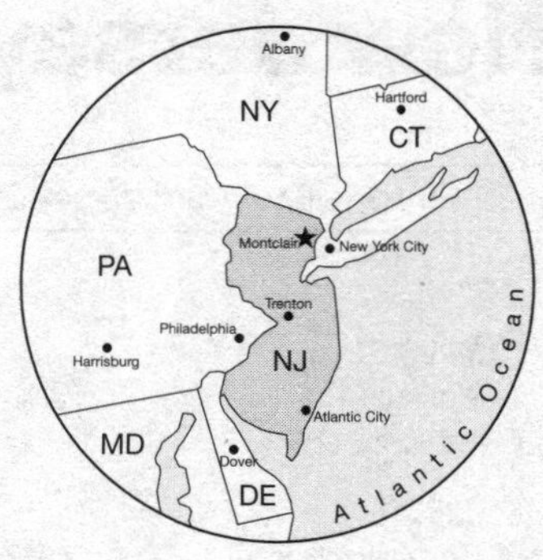

General Admissions

Very important factors include: rigor of secondary school record, academic GPA, recommendation(s). *Important factors include:* application essay, *Other factors include:* class rank, standardized test scores, extracurricular activities, talent/ability, character/personal qualities, religious affiliation/commitment, work experience. High school diploma is required and GED is accepted. *Academic units required:* 4 English, 3 math, 2 science, 2 science labs, 2 foreign language, 2 social studies, 3 academic electives.

Accommodations or Services

Accommodations are decided upon an individual basis after a thorough review of appropriate, current documentation. The accommodations requests must be supported through the documentation provided and must be logically linked to the current impact of the condition on academic functioning.

Financial Aid

Students should submit: FAFSA; State aid form. *Need-based scholarships/grants offered:* College/university scholarship or grant aid from institutional funds; Federal Pell; Private scholarships; SEOG; State scholarships/grants. *Loan aid offered:* Direct PLUS loans; Direct Subsidized Stafford Loans; Direct Unsubsidized Stafford Loans. Federal Work-Study Program available. Institutional employment available.

Campus Life

Activities: Campus Ministries; Choral groups; Concert band; Dance; Drama/theater; International Student Organization; Jazz band; Literary magazine; Marching band; Music ensembles; Musical theater; Opera; Pep band; Radio station; Student government; Student newspaper; Student-run film society; Symphony orchestra; Television station; Yearbook. **Organizations:** 160 registered organizations, 4 honor societies, 8 religious organizations, 19 fraternities, 17 sororities. **Athletics (Intercollegiate):** *Men:* baseball, basketball, diving, football, lacrosse, soccer, swimming, track/field (outdoor). *Women:* basketball, diving, field hockey, lacrosse, soccer, softball, swimming, track/field (outdoor), volleyball.

ACCOMMODATIONS

Allowed in exams:	
Calculators	Yes
Dictionary	Yes
Computer	Yes
Spell-checker	Yes
Extended test time	Yes
Scribe	Yes
Proctors	Yes
Oral exams	Yes
Note-takers	Yes
Support services for students with:	
LD	Yes
ADHD	Yes
ASD	Yes
Distraction-reduced environment	Yes
Recording of lecture allowed	Yes
Reading technology	Yes
Audio books	Yes
Other assistive technology	Yes
Priority registration	Yes
Added costs of services:	
For LD	No
For ADHD	No
For ASD	No
LD specialists	No
ADHD & ASD coaching	No
ASD specialists	No
Professional tutors	No
Peer tutors	Yes
Max. hours/week for services	Varies
How professors are notified of student approved accommodations	Student

COLLEGE GRADUATION REQUIREMENTS

Course waivers allowed	No
Course substitutions allowed	Yes
In what courses: Case-by-case basis	

New Jersey

New Jersey City University

2039 Kennedy Boulevard, Jersey City, NJ 07305 • Admissions: 201-800-6855 **Support: CS**

CAMPUS

Type of school	Public
Environment	City

STUDENTS

Undergrad enrollment	5,962
% male/female	42/58
% from out of state	1
% frosh live on campus	21

FINANCIAL FACTS

Annual in-state tuition	$12,413
Annual out-of-state tuition	$22,221
Room and board	$14,574
Required fees	$165

GENERAL ADMISSIONS INFO

Application fee	$55
Regular application deadline	Rolling
Nonfall registration	Yes

Admission may be deferred.

Range SAT EBRW	430–540
Range SAT Math	430–540

ACADEMICS

Student/faculty ratio	14:1
% students returning for sophomore year	73

Most classes have 20–29 students.

Programs/Services for Students with Learning Differences

Students with Disabilities are served by the Office of Specialized Services for Student with Disabilities at New Jersey City University. The Office of Specialized Services (OSS) provides NJCU students with disabilities equal access to college programs The OSS assists students, on an individual basis, in securing reasonable accommodations, including, but not limited to alternate testing arrangements, adaptive technology, and assistance in arranging other support services (e.g., books on tape, and note-taking support) supported by documentation. It is the student's responsibility to self-identify and request services.

Admissions

There is no separate application for students with disabilities. All applicants are expected to meet the same admission standards. Applicants must submit 2 letters of recommendations. Students may also write an essay to describe aspirations and motivations. ACT or SAT required. The average GPA is 2.9. Applicants should pursue a college-prep curriculum in high school.

Additional Information

Students requesting academic adjustments are required to submit appropriate and recent documentation of their disability. Students wishing to obtain accommodations may do so by contacting the OSS Director. Additionally, the Center for Student Success (CSS) provides: individual and small group peer tutoring in basic English and math; study halls in basic English and math; workshops on study skills, learning styles, information literacy, financial literacy, and success strategies; Access to computer-based learning skills materials and resources; referrals to on-campus academic and personal assistance programs; co-curricular transcript application; learning and study skills strategies; and exposure to leadership opportunities.

ADMISSIONS INFO FOR STUDENTS WITH LEARNING DIFFERENCES

Phone: 201-200-2091

SAT/ACT required: Yes
Interview required: No
Essay required: No
Additional application required: No
Documentation submitted to: OSS

Special Ed. HS course work accepted: Yes
Separate application required for Programs/Services: No
Documentation required for:
- **LD:** Psychoeducational evaluation
- **ADHD:** Psychoeducational evaluation
- **ASD:** Psychoeducational evaluation

New Jersey City University

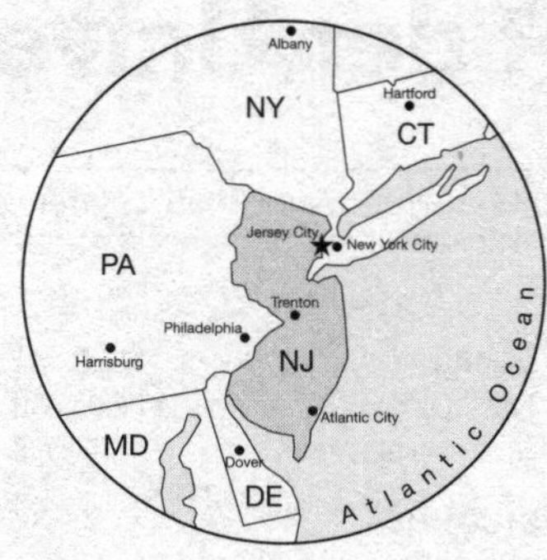

General Admissions

Very important factors include: rigor of secondary school record, class rank, academic GPA. *Important factors include:* extracurricular activities. High school diploma is required and GED is accepted. *Academic units required:* 4 English, 4 math, 4 science, 2 science labs, 4 social studies. *Academic units recommended:* 4 English, 4 math, 4 science, 3 science labs, 2 foreign language, 4 social studies.

Accommodations or Services

Accommodations are decided upon an individual basis after a thorough review of appropriate, current documentation. The accommodations requests must be supported through the documentation provided and must be logically linked to the current impact of the condition on academic functioning.

Financial Aid

Students should submit: FAFSA. Applicants will be notified of awards on a rolling basis beginning 2/15. *Need-based scholarships/grants offered:* College/university scholarship or grant aid from institutional funds; Federal Pell. *Loan aid offered:* Direct PLUS loans; Direct Subsidized Stafford Loans; Direct Unsubsidized Stafford Loans. Federal Work-Study Program available. Institutional employment available.

Campus Life

Activities: Concert band; Drama/theater; Jazz band; Student government; Symphony orchestra; Yearbook. **Organizations:** 23 registered organizations. **Athletics (Intercollegiate):** *Men:* baseball, basketball, cross-country, soccer, track/field (outdoor), track/field (indoor), volleyball. *Women:* basketball, bowling, cross-country, soccer, softball, track/field (outdoor), track/field (indoor), volleyball.

ACCOMMODATIONS

Allowed in exams:	
Calculators	Yes
Dictionary	Yes
Computer	Yes
Spell-checker	Yes
Extended test time	Yes
Scribe	Yes
Proctors	Yes
Oral exams	Yes
Note-takers	Yes
Support services for students with:	
LD	Yes
ADHD	Yes
ASD	Yes
Distraction-reduced environment	Yes
Recording of lecture allowed	Yes
Reading technology	Yes
Audio books	Yes
Other assistive technology	Yes
Priority registration	Yes
Added costs of services:	
For LD	No
For ADHD	No
For ASD	No
LD specialists	Yes
ADHD & ASD coaching	Yes
ASD specialists	No
Professional tutors	No
Peer tutors	Yes
Max. hours/week for services	Unlimited
How professors are notified of student approved accommodations	Student and Disability Office

COLLEGE GRADUATION REQUIREMENTS

Course waivers allowed	No
Course substitutions allowed	Yes

In what courses: Case-by-case basis

New Jersey

Rider University

2083 Lawrenceville Road, Lawrenceville, NJ 08648-3099 • Admissions: 609-896-5042 • Fax: 609-895-6645 **Support: CS**

CAMPUS

Type of school	Private (nonprofit)
Environment	Village

STUDENTS

Undergrad enrollment	3,763
% male/female	44/56
% from out of state	23
% frosh live on campus	83

FINANCIAL FACTS

Annual tuition	$45,120
Room and board	$15,500
Required fees	$740

GENERAL ADMISSIONS INFO

Application fee	$50
Regular application deadline	Rolling
Nonfall registration	Yes

Admission may be deferred.

Range SAT EBRW	510–600
Range SAT Math	510–600
Range ACT Composite	19–26

ACADEMICS

Student/faculty ratio	10:1
% students returning for sophomore year	77

Most classes have 10–19 students.

Programs/Services for Students with Learning Differences

Student Accessibility and Support Services (SASS) helps students to access academic support. Students have to initiate contact and provide appropriate documentation. The Academic Success Center (ASC) offers all qualifying students free programs and services. The staff is made up of trained professionals, peers tutors, and peer assistants. There is a Student Writing Tutors support program through ACS that helps students improve their writing process.

Admissions

Admissions performs a holistic review of an application. ACT or SAT scores are not required for admission. There is a required audition for some performing arts programs. Course requirements include 4 English, 3 years math and 9 year-long credits in humanities, foreign language, math, social science, or science.

Additional Information

There is supplemental instruction to assist students in specific courses. Peer tutors collaborate with course professors and help guide the student in study techniques. Rider University also offers an 8-week summer program on campus for young adults with a range of developmental disabilities. Students work on effective communication and problem solving.

ADMISSIONS INFO FOR STUDENTS WITH LEARNING DIFFERENCES

Phone: 609-895-5492 • Fax: 609-895-5507 • Email: Blandfor@Rider.edu

SAT/ACT required: No
Interview required: No
Essay required: No
Additional application required: No
Documentation submitted to: SASS

Special Ed. HS course work accepted: No
Separate application required for Programs/Services: No
Documentation required for:
LD: Psychoeducational evaluation
ADHD: Psychoeducational evaluation
ASD: Psychoeducational evaluation

Rider University

General Admissions

Very important factors include: rigor of secondary school record, academic GPA, application essay, recommendation(s). *Other factors include:* class rank, standardized test scores, interview, extracurricular activities, talent/ability, character/personal qualities, alumni/ae relation, geographical residence, state residency, volunteer work, work experience, level of applicant's interest. High school diploma is required and GED is accepted. *Academic units required:* 4 English, 3 math. *Academic units recommended:* 4 science, 4 science labs, 2 foreign language, 2 social studies, 2 history.

Accommodations or Services

Accommodations are decided upon an individual basis after a thorough review of appropriate, current documentation. The accommodations requests must be supported through the documentation provided and must be logically linked to the current impact of the condition on academic functioning.

Financial Aid

Students should submit: FAFSA. *Need-based scholarships/grants offered:* College/university scholarship or grant aid from institutional funds; Federal Pell; Private scholarships; SEOG; State scholarships/grants. *Loan aid offered:* Direct PLUS loans; Direct Subsidized Stafford Loans; Direct Unsubsidized Stafford Loans. Federal Work-Study Program available. Institutional employment available.

Campus Life

Activities: Campus Ministries; Choral groups; Concert band; Dance; Drama/theater; International Student Organization; Literary magazine; Model UN; Music ensembles; Musical theater; Opera; Pep band; Radio station; Student government; Student newspaper; Student-run film society; Symphony orchestra; Television station; Yearbook. **Organizations:** 251 registered organizations, 15 honor societies, 5 religious organizations, 6 fraternities, 9 sororities. **Athletics (Intercollegiate):** *Men:* baseball, basketball, cheerleading, cross-country, diving, golf, soccer, swimming, tennis, track/field (outdoor), wrestling. *Women:* basketball, cheerleading, cross-country, diving, field hockey, soccer, softball, swimming, tennis, track/field (outdoor), volleyball.

ACCOMMODATIONS

Allowed in exams:	
Calculators	Yes
Dictionary	Yes
Computer	Yes
Spell-checker	Yes
Extended test time	Yes
Scribe	Yes
Proctors	Yes
Oral exams	Yes
Note-takers	Yes
Support services for students with:	
LD	Yes
ADHD	Yes
ASD	Yes
Distraction-reduced environment	Yes
Recording of lecture alowed	Yes
Reading technology	Yes
Audio books	Yes
Other assistive technology	Yes
Priority registration	Yes
Added costs of services:	
For LD	No
For ADHD	No
For ASD	No
LD specialists	No
ADHD & ASD coaching	Yes
ASD specialists	No
Professional tutors	Yes
Peer tutors	Yes
Max. hours/week for services	Varies
How professors are notified of student approved accommodations	Student

COLLEGE GRADUATION REQUIREMENTS

Course waivers allowed	No
Course substitutions allowed	Yes
In what courses: Case-by-case basis	

New Jersey

Seton Hall University

400 S Orange Ave, South Orange, NJ 07079 • Admissions: 973-761900 • Fax: 973-275-2339 **Support: CS**

CAMPUS	
Type of school	Private (nonprofit)
Environment	Village
STUDENTS	
Undergrad enrollment	6,102
% male/female	48/52
% from out of state	34
% frosh live on campus	74
FINANCIAL FACTS	
Annual tuition	$42,920
Room and board	$15,368
Required fees	$1,820
GENERAL ADMISSIONS INFO	
Application fee	$55
Regular application deadline	3/1
Nonfall registration	Yes
Admission may be deferred.	
Range SAT EBRW	580–660
Range SAT Math	570–670
Range ACT Composite	24–29
ACADEMICS	
% students returning for sophomore year	83

Programs/Services for Students with Learning Differences

The Disability Support Services (DSS) provides students with disabilities equal access to all university programs and activities. It works collaboratively with academic departments and student affairs offices to engage and support the intellectual and social development of students with disabilities. Accommodations are provided based on submission of appropriate documentation, which is reviewed by DSS staff in compliance with university policy.

Admissions

There is no special admission process for students with learning disabilities, and all applicants must meet the same admission criteria. The average GPA is 3.6. The average ACT is 26 and SAT is 1235. Grades and test scores are most important for admission. The admission office also values demonstrated interest in the university. This includes visiting the campus, attending admission programs, opening emails sent from the college, and the time an applicant takes to get to know Seton Hall.

Additional Information

In coordinating its activities with other departments of the university (such as Residence Life and Academic Services), Student Support Services works to assure that the university remains in compliance with all federal laws and regulations. The DSS office provides the following services to individuals with LD (with appropriate documentation): reduced course load, extended time to complete assignments, tape recorders, note-taking, taped texts, readers, extended time for in class assignments, assistive technology (calculator, word processor, etc.), extended time for testing, and a distraction-reduced environment. The recommendation from DSS is that students meet with their instructor at least one week before each scheduled exam to determine how exam accommodations will be implemented.

ADMISSIONS INFO FOR STUDENTS WITH LEARNING DIFFERENCES

Phone: 973-313-6003 • Fax: 973-761-9185 • Email: dss@shu.edu

SAT/ACT required: Yes (Test optional for 2021)
Interview required: No
Essay required: No
Additional application required: No
Documentation submitted to: Disability Support Services

Special Ed. HS course work accepted: No
Separate application required for Programs/Services: No
Documentation required for:
- **LD:** Psychoeducational evaluation
- **ADHD:** Psychoeducational evaluation
- **ASD:** Psychoeducational evaluation

Seton Hall University

General Admissions

High school diploma is required and GED is accepted. *Academic units required:* 4 English, 3 math, 1 science, 1 science lab, 2 foreign language, 2 social studies, 4 academic electives.

Accommodations or Services

Accommodations are decided upon an individual basis after a thorough review of appropriate, current documentation. The accommodations requests must be supported through the documentation provided and must be logically linked to the current impact of the condition on academic functioning.

Financial Aid

Students should submit: FAFSA. *Need-based scholarships/grants offered:* College/university scholarship or grant aid from institutional funds; Federal Pell; Private scholarships; SEOG; State scholarships/grants. *Loan aid offered:* Direct PLUS loans; Direct Subsidized Stafford Loans; Direct Unsubsidized Stafford Loans. Federal Work-Study Program available. Institutional employment available.

Campus Life

Organizations: 100 registered organizations, 13 honor societies, 3 religious organizations, 11 fraternities, 11 sororities. **Athletics (Intercollegiate):** *Men:* baseball, basketball, cross-country, diving, golf, soccer, swimming, track/field (outdoor). *Women:* basketball, cross-country, diving, soccer, softball, swimming, tennis, track/field (outdoor).

ACCOMMODATIONS

Allowed in exams:	
Calculators	Yes
Dictionary	Yes
Computer	Yes
Spell-checker	Yes
Extended test time	Yes
Scribe	Yes
Proctors	Yes
Oral exams	Yes
Note-takers	Yes
Support services for students with:	
LD	Yes
ADHD	Yes
ASD	Yes
Distraction-reduced environment	Yes
Recording of lecture allowed	Yes
Reading technology	Yes
Audio books	Yes
Other assistive technology	Yes
Priority registration	No
Added costs of services:	
For LD	No
For ADHD	No
For ASD	No
LD specialists	Yes
ADHD & ASD coaching	No
ASD specialists	No
Professional tutors	Yes
Peer tutors	Yes
Max. hours/week for services	Varies
How professors are notified of student approved accommodations	Student

COLLEGE GRADUATION REQUIREMENTS

Course waivers allowed	Yes
In what courses: Mathematics and world languages.	
Course substitutions allowed	Yes
In what courses. Mathematics and world languages	

New Mexico Institute of Mining & Technology

801 Leroy Place, Socorro, NM 87801 • Admissions: 575-835-5424 • Fax: 575-835-5989 **Support: S**

CAMPUS

Type of school	Public
Environment	Village

STUDENTS

Undergrad enrollment	1,321
% male/female	67/33
% from out of state	10
% frosh live on campus	89

FINANCIAL FACTS

Annual in-state tuition	$7,031
Annual out-of-state tuition	$22,860
Room and board	$8,624
Required fees	$1,330

GENERAL ADMISSIONS INFO

Application fee	$15
Regular application deadline	8/1
Nonfall registration	Yes

Admission may be deferred.

Range SAT EBRW	580–690
Range SAT Math	590–690
Range ACT Composite	23–29

ACADEMICS

Student/faculty ratio	11:1
% students returning for sophomore year	77

Most classes have 10–19 students.

Programs/Services for Students with Learning Differences

New Mexico Tech does not have a specific program for students with LD. The first step to receive accommodations is sending appropriate documentation to Disability Resource Center (DRC). Students need to complete the First-Time Request, which will be reviewed, and then the DRC Academic Coach will ask the student to come to their office where there will be a review of the specific needs of the student. Additional services for students with disabilities are available in the Counseling and Student Health Center. Students must present recent documentation completed within the previous 3 years. The documentation should be sent to the DRC. New Mexico Tech sends a letter to all admitted students asking those with disabilities to contact the Disability Resource Center. There is a special application required after admission and enrollment to receive services or accommodations. The counseling staff works with students with disabilities on an individual basis to accommodate their special needs. Students may also use the counseling service to reduce their stress, think through problems or difficulties, clarify options, and express and explore feelings.

Admissions

There is no special admission process for students with LD. The minimum GPA is a 2.5. The college requires an ACT composite score of 21 or higher or an SAT score of 970 or higher. The GED is accepted with a score of 50 or higher. High school course requirements include 4 years of English, 2 years of science (including biology, physics, chemistry, and earth science), 3 years of math, and 3 years of social science, of which one must be history. Students are encouraged to self-disclose their disability during the admission process.

Additional Information

Students will work with staff to determine appropriate accommodations or services. These services may include note-takers, coordinating of academic accommodations, extended time for tests, calculators in exams, skills classes in study strategies and time management, and tutorial services available for all students on campus.

ADMISSIONS INFO FOR STUDENTS WITH LEARNING DIFFERENCES

Phone: 575-835-6619 • Fax: 575-835-5959 • Email: counseling@nmt.edu

SAT/ACT required: Yes
Interview required: No
Essay required: No
Additional application required: No
Documentation submitted to: Office for Counseling and Disability Services

Special Ed. HS course work accepted: Yes
Separate application required for Programs/Services: No
Documentation required for:
LD: Psychoeducational evaluation
ADHD: Psychoeducational evaluation
ASD: Psychoeducational evaluation

New Mexico Institute of Mining & Technology

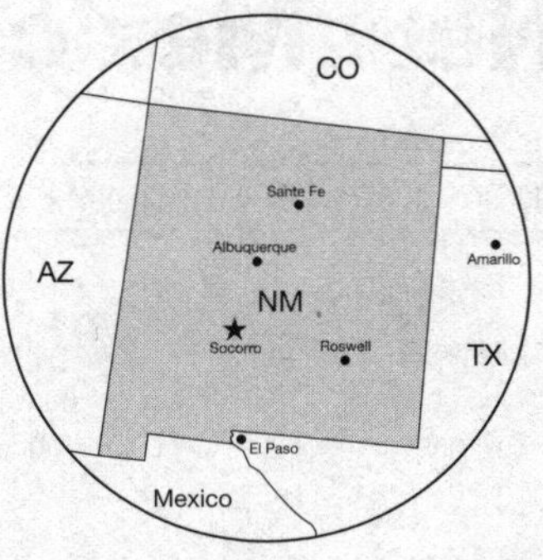

General Admissions

Very important factors include: rigor of secondary school record, academic GPA, standardized test scores. *Other factors include:* class rank, extracurricular activities, talent/ability. High school diploma is required and GED is accepted. *Academic units required:* 4 English, 3 math, 2 science, 2 science labs, 2 social studies, 1 history, 3 academic electives. *Academic units recommended:* 4 English, 4 math, 4 science, 3 science labs, 2 foreign language, 3 social studies, 1 history.

Accommodations or Services

Accommodations are decided upon an individual basis after a thorough review of appropriate, current documentation. The accommodations requests must be supported through the documentation provided and must be logically linked to the current impact of the condition on academic functioning.

Financial Aid

Students should submit: CSS/Financial Aid PROFILE; FAFSA; Noncustodial PROFILE;. Applicants will be notified of awards on or about 4/1. *Need-based scholarships/grants offered:* College/university scholarship or grant aid from institutional funds; Federal Pell; Private scholarships; SEOG; State scholarships/grants. *Loan aid offered:* Direct PLUS loans; Direct Subsidized Stafford Loans; Direct Unsubsidized Stafford Loans. Federal Work-Study Program available. Institutional employment available.

Campus Life

Activities: Choral groups; Concert band; Dance; Drama/theater; International Student Organization; Jazz band; Music ensembles; Musical theater; Radio station; Student government; Student newspaper. **Organizations:** 60 registered organizations, 7 honor societies, 3 religious organizations.

ACCOMMODATIONS

Allowed in exams:	
Calculators	Yes
Dictionary	No
Computer	Yes
Spell-checker	Yes
Extended test time	Yes
Scribe	Yes
Proctors	Yes
Oral exams	Yes
Note-takers	Yes
Support services for students with:	
LD	Yes
ADHD	Yes
ASD	Yes
Distraction-reduced environment	Yes
Recording of lecture alowed	Yes
Reading technology	Yes
Audio books	Yes
Other assistive technology	Yes
Priority registration	Yes
Added costs of services:	
For LD	No
For ADHD	No
For ASD	No
LD specialists	No
ADHD & ASD coaching	No
ASD specialists	No
Professional tutors	No
Peer tutors	Yes
Max. hours/week for services	Unlimited
How professors are notified of student approved accommodations	Student and Disability Office

COLLEGE GRADUATION REQUIREMENTS

Course waivers allowed	No
Course substitutions allowed	No

New Mexico State University

PO Box 30001, Las Cruces, NM 88003-8001 • Admissions: 575-646-3121 • Fax: 575-646-6330 **Support: S**

CAMPUS	
Type of school	Public
Environment	City
STUDENTS	
Undergrad enrollment	11,153
% male/female	44/56
% from out of state	26
% frosh live on campus	62
FINANCIAL FACTS	
Annual in-state tuition	$8,044
Annual out-of-state tuition	$25,666
Room and board	$10,228
GENERAL ADMISSIONS INFO	
Application fee	$20
Regular application deadline	Rolling
Nonfall registration	Yes
Range SAT EBRW	480–580
Range SAT Math	470–570
Range ACT Composite	18–23
ACADEMICS	
Student/faculty ratio	16:1
% students returning for sophomore year	75
Most classes have 10–19 students.	

Programs/Services for Students with Learning Differences

The Coordinator at the Accessibility Services Department is the first contact for a student seeking accommodations. Students need to provide documentation of a diagnosis of a disability to the Student Success Services office. They provide direct assistance to students and work with the student and the faculty to identify accommodations. The functional limitations identified need to support the request for accommodations. Campus Tutoring Services offers academic support services by highly trained accredited tutors. These services are free and offer individual and small group tutoring.

Admissions

There is no special admissions criteria for students with disabilities. Admissions looks for a minimum 2.75 GPA, ACT of 21 or SAT of 1060 or rank in the top 20% of the class. Applicants who do not meet NMSU Las Cruces's admission requirements may apply to participate in the Aggie Pathway to an undergraduate degree offered at any of the NMSU community colleges. Aggie Pathway students may transition to the NMSU Las Cruces campus after successful completion of any required developmental education courses and 24 degree credits with a 2.5 cumulative college GPA.

Additional Information

Academic advisors are available to assist students in developing their educational plan that will lead to academic, career, and personal aspirations. Financial aid advisors guide students through the financial aid process and help students find the best options for their needs.

ADMISSIONS INFO FOR STUDENTS WITH LEARNING DIFFERENCES

Phone: 505-277-3506 • Fax: 505-277-3750 • Email: arcsrvs@unm.edu

SAT/ACT required: Yes (Test optional for 2021)
Interview required: No
Essay required: No
Additional application required: Yes
Documentation submitted to: Accessibility Services Department
Special Ed. HS course work accepted: Yes
Separate application required for Programs/Services: Yes
Documentation required for:
LD: Psychoeducational evaluation
ADHD: Psychoeducational evaluation
ASD: Psychoeducational evaluation

New Mexico State University

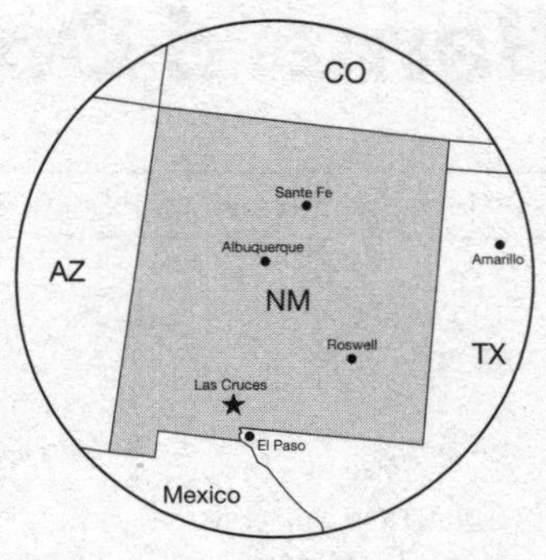

General Admissions

Very important factors include: academic GPA, standardized test scores. *Other factors include:* rigor of secondary school record, class rank. High school diploma is required and GED is accepted. *Academic units required:* 4 English, 4 math, 2 science, 2 science labs, 1 foreign language.

Accommodations or Services

Accommodations are decided upon an individual basis after a thorough review of appropriate, current documentation. The accommodations requests must be supported through the documentation provided and must be logically linked to the current impact of the condition on academic functioning.

Financial Aid

Students should submit: FAFSA. *Need-based scholarships/grants offered:* College/university scholarship or grant aid from institutional funds; Federal Pell; Private scholarships; SEOG; State scholarships/grants. *Loan aid offered:* Direct PLUS loans; Direct Subsidized Stafford Loans; Direct Unsubsidized Stafford Loans. Federal Work-Study Program available. Institutional employment available.

Campus Life

Activities: Campus Ministries; Choral groups; Concert band; Dance; Drama/theater; International Student Organization; Jazz band; Literary magazine; Marching band; Model UN; Music ensembles; Musical theater; Opera; Pep band; Radio station; Student government; Student newspaper; Symphony orchestra; Television station. **Organizations:** 327 registered organizations, 23 honor societies, 17 religious organizations, 10 fraternities, 5 sororities. **Athletics (Intercollegiate):** *Men:* baseball, basketball, cross-country, football, golf, tennis. *Women:* basketball, cross-country, golf, softball, swimming, tennis, track/field (outdoor), volleyball.

ACCOMMODATIONS

Allowed in exams:	
Calculators	Yes
Dictionary	No
Computer	Yes
Spell-checker	No
Extended test time	Yes
Scribe	Yes
Proctors	Yes
Oral exams	Yes
Note-takers	Yes
Support services for students with:	
LD	Yes
ADHD	Yes
ASD	Yes
Distraction-reduced environment	Yes
Recording of lecture alowed	Yes
Reading technology	Yes
Audio books	Yes
Other assistive technology	Yes
Priority registration	Yes
Added costs of services:	
For LD	No
For ADHD	No
For ASD	No
LD specialists	No
ADHD & ASD coaching	No
ASD specialists	No
Professional tutors	Yes
Peer tutors	Yes
Max. hours/week for services	Unlimited
How professors are notified of student approved accommodations	Student

COLLEGE GRADUATION REQUIREMENTS

Course waivers allowed	No
Course substitutions allowed	Yes
In what courses: Case-by-case basis	

Barnard College

3009 Broadway, New York, NY 10027 • Admissions: 212-854-2014 • Fax: 212-280-8797 **Support: S**

CAMPUS

Type of school	Private (nonprofit)
Environment	Metropolis

STUDENTS

Undergrad enrollment	2,631
% male/female	0/100
% from out of state	73
% frosh live on campus	91

FINANCIAL FACTS

Annual tuition	$55,781
Room and board	$15,691
Required fees	$1,698

GENERAL ADMISSIONS INFO

Application fee	$75
Regular application deadline	1/1
Nonfall registration	No

Admission may be deferred.

Range SAT EBRW	670–750
Range SAT Math	670–770
Range ACT Composite	31–34

ACADEMICS

Student/faculty ratio	9:1
% students returning for sophomore year	95

Most classes have 10–19 students.

Programs/Services for Students with Learning Differences

The Center for Accessibility Resources & Disability Services' (CARDS) mission is to provide support services to students, faculty, and staff that encourage Barnard students with disabilities to become self-sufficient in managing their own accommodations. In 1978, Barnard established a program to provide services for students with disabilities that enhance their educational, pre-professional, and personal development. CARDS serves students with visual, mobility, and hearing disabilities, and students with invisible disabilities such as chronic medical conditions, learning disabilities/ADD, psychiatric disabilities and substance use/recovery. CARDS works with and empowers students with disabilities in order to coordinate support services that enable equal access to education and college life. Responding to the mandate of Section 504 of the Rehabilitation Act of 1973, and with contributions from public, private and College resources, the campus has become increasingly accessible. CARDS works to ensure that reasonable accommodations are made to provide programmatic and physical access.

Admissions

Students are held to the same admissions criteria as students without any needs for accommodations.

Additional Information

To register with CARDS, you will need to have an intake session with its director or accommodations coordinator. Call the office at 212-854-4634 to set up an appointment time. Accommodations are not retroactive, so accommodations for classes or exams can only be set up after your intake meeting, which is why it's important to register with CARDS early in the semester to use your accommodations for all your coursework. Students may register throughout the semester, however, no intake meetings are conducted during midterm exams, final exams, or the last two weeks of the semester unless a student has a brand new diagnosis that was just found out in the last two weeks of the semester. It's imperative that CARDS has at least two weeks prior to final exams to get accommodations set up for students, so in this case, meet with them for accommodations for the following semester after final exams end. At your appointment, CARDS staff will likely spend some time chatting with you in order to get to know you and your needs. CARDS staff will explain policies and procedures for accessing accommodations, complete an intake packet with you, and create an accommodation plan for you!

ADMISSIONS INFO FOR STUDENTS WITH LEARNING DIFFERENCES

Phone: 212-854-4634 • Fax: 212-280-8768 • Email: cards@barnard.edu

SAT/ACT required: Yes (Test-optional for 2021 admission)
Interview required: No
Essay required: Yes
Additional application required: No
Documentation submitted to: Center for Accessibility & Resources Center

Special Ed. HS course work accepted: Yes
Separate application required for Programs/Services: No
Documentation required for:
LD: Psychoeducational evaluation
ADHD: Psychoeducational evaluation
ASD: Psychoeducational evaluation

Barnard College

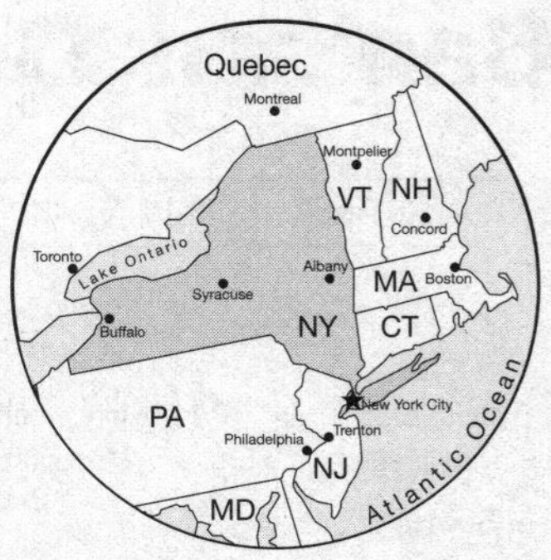

General Admissions

Very Important factors include: rigor of secondary school record, academic GPA, application essay, recommendation(s), character/personal qualities. *Important factors include:* class rank, standardized test scores, extracurricular activities, talent/ability, volunteer work. *Other factors include:* interview, first generation, alumni/ae relation, geographical residence, racial/ethnic status, level of applicant's interest. High school diploma is required and a GED is accepted. *Academic units recommended:* 4 English, 3 math, 3 science, 3 foreign language, 3 history.

Accommodations or Services

Accommodations are decided upon an individual basis after a thorough review of appropriate, current documentation. The accommodations requests must be supported through the documentation provided and must be logically linked to the current impact of the condition on academic functioning.

Financial Aid

Students should submit: CSS/Financial Aid PROFILE; FAFSA; Noncustodial PROFILE; State aid form. *Need-based scholarships/grants offered:* College/ university scholarship or grant aid from institutional funds; Federal Pell; Private scholarships; SEOG; State scholarships/grants. *Loan aid offered:* Direct PLUS loans; Direct Subsidized Stafford Loans; Direct Unsubsidized Stafford Loans. Federal Work-Study Program available. Institutional employment available.

Campus Life

Activities: Campus Ministries; Choral groups; Concert band; Dance; Drama/ theater; International Student Organization; Jazz band; Literary magazine; Marching band; Model UN; Music ensembles; Musical theater; Opera; Pep band; Radio station; Student government; Student newspaper; Student-run film society; Symphony orchestra; Yearbook. **Organizations:** 100 registered organizations, 1 honor society, 75 religious organizations, 10 sororities. **Athletics (Intercollegiate):** *Women:* archery, basketball, crew/rowing, cross-country, diving, fencing, field hockey, golf, lacrosse, soccer, softball, swimming, tennis, track/field (outdoor), volleyball.

ACCOMMODATIONS

Allowed in exams:	
Calculators	Yes
Dictionary	Yes
Computer	Yes
Spell-checker	Yes
Extended test time	Yes
Scribe	Yes
Proctors	Yes
Oral exams	No
Note-takers	Yes
Support services for students with:	
LD	Yes
ADHD	Yes
ASD	Yes
Distraction-reduced environment	Yes
Recording of lecture allowed	Yes
Reading technology	No
Audio books	Yes
Other assistive technology	No
Priority registration	No
Added costs of services:	
For LD	No
For ADHD	No
For ASD	No
LD specialists	No
ADHD & ASD coaching	Yes
ASD specialists	No
Professional tutors	No
Peer tutors	Yes
Max. hours/week for services	Varies
How professors are notified of student approved accommodations	Center for Assessibility & Disability Resources

COLLEGE GRADUATION REQUIREMENTS

Course waivers allowed	Yes
In what courses: Foreign Language on a case-by-case basis	
Course substitutions allowed	No

Canisius College

2001 Main Street, Buffalo, NY 14208 • Admissions: 716-888-2200 • Fax: 716-888-3230 **Support: S**

CAMPUS

Type of school	Private (nonprofit)
Environment	Metropolis

STUDENTS

Undergrad enrollment	2,213
% male/female	52/48
% from out of state	12
% frosh live on campus	63

FINANCIAL FACTS

Annual tuition	$27,940
Room and board	$11,526
Required fees	$1,488

GENERAL ADMISSIONS INFO

Application fee	$0
Regular application deadline	Rolling
Nonfall registration	Yes

Admission may be deferred.

Range SAT EBRW	510–630
Range SAT Math	520–640
Range ACT Composite	20–27

ACADEMICS

Student/faculty ratio	11:1
% students returning for sophomore year	84

Most classes have 10–19 students.

Programs/Services for Students with Learning Differences

Academic Mentor Program offers assistance to students with a variety of issues that may arise through their academic career. Academic Mentors meet regularly with students and assist with better time management, handling of courses, study skills, etc., to help achieve academic success. Accessibility Support is committed to creating equal access for all Canisius students with disabilities. It is our goal to help meet the needs of individuals registered and documented through the office, whether the disability is permanent or temporary.

Admissions

There is no special admissions criteria for students with learning disabilities. When reviewing the application for admission, the Admissions Committee looks for students with at least a solid B average in a college preparatory program of study. Rigor of curriculum, including the types of courses being taken in the senior year, is considered the most important factor in the admissions decision.

Additional Information

Students must self-identify with the GRIFF Center for Academic Engagement, complete the Accessibility Support intake form, and provide current documentation. The student then meets with a professional in AS to discuss the accommodations, and to become familiar with the procedures. Students can receive alternative texts, note takers, readers, talking calculators, and assistive listening devices. The Griff Center Proctor Site is a designated area for students that need testing accommodations due to a disability or to make up a missed exam. Test accommodations are determined on a case-by-case basis.

ADMISSIONS INFO FOR STUDENTS WITH LEARNING DIFFERENCES

Phone: 716-888-2476 • Fax: 716-888-3212 • Email: rapones@canisius.edu

SAT/ACT required: Yes (Test-optional for 2021 admission)
Interview required: No
Essay required: Yes
Additional application required: No
Documentation submitted to: Griff Center for Student Success, Accessibility Support

Special Ed. HS course work accepted: Yes
Separate application required for Programs/Services: No
Documentation required for:
LD: Psychoeducational evaluation
ADHD: Psychoeducational evaluation
ASD: Psychoeducational evaluation

Canisius College

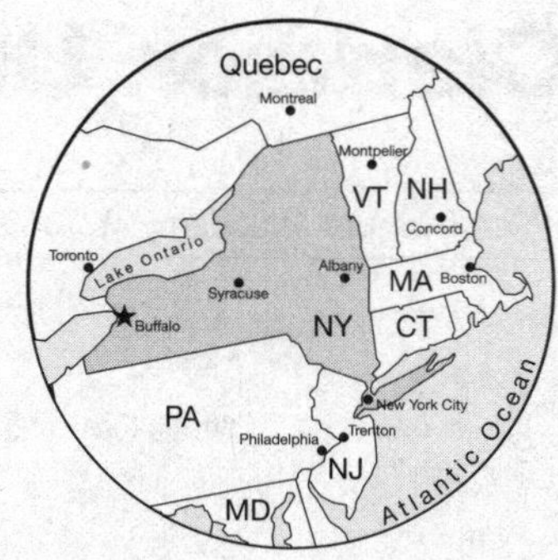

General Admissions

Very Important factors include: rigor of secondary school record, academic GPA, standardized test scores. *Important factors include:* application essay, recommendation(s), extracurricular activities, volunteer work. *Other factors include:* class rank, interview, talent/ability, character/personal qualities, first generation, alumni/ae relation, work experience, level of applicant's interest. High school diploma is required and a GED is accepted. *Academic units required:* 4 English, 3 math, 3 science, 2 science labs, 2 foreign language, 4 social studies. *Academic units recommended:* 4 English, 4 math, 4 science, 2 science labs, 4 foreign language, 4 social studies, 4 academic electives.

Accommodations or Services

Accommodations are decided upon an individual basis after a thorough review of appropriate, current documentation. The accommodations requests must be supported through the documentation provided and must be logically linked to the current impact of the condition on academic functioning.

Financial Aid

Students should submit: FAFSA; Institution's own financial aid form. Applicants will be notified of awards on a rolling basis beginning 12/1. *Need-based scholarships/grants offered:* College/university scholarship or grant aid from institutional funds; Federal Pell; Private scholarships; SEOG; State scholarships/grants; United Negro College Fund. *Loan aid offered:* Direct PLUS loans; Direct Subsidized Stafford Loans; Direct Unsubsidized Stafford Loans. Federal Work-Study Program available. Institutional employment available.

Campus Life

Activities: Campus Ministries; Choral groups; Concert band; Dance; Drama/theater; International Student Organization; Jazz band; Literary magazine; Marching band; Model UN; Music ensembles; Musical theater; Pep band; Radio station; Student government; Student newspaper; Student-run film society; Symphony orchestra; Television station; Yearbook. **Organizations:** 140 registered organizations, 17 honor societies, 2 religious organizations, 1 fraternity, 1 sorority. **Athletics (Intercollegiate):** *Men:* baseball, basketball, cross-country, diving, golf, ice hockey, lacrosse, soccer, swimming. *Women:* basketball, cross-country, diving, lacrosse, soccer, softball, swimming, synchronized swimming, volleyball.

ACCOMMODATIONS

Allowed in exams:	
Calculators	Yes
Dictionary	Yes
Computer	Yes
Spell-checker	Yes
Extended test time	Yes
Scribe	Yes
Proctors	Yes
Oral exams	Yes
Note-takers	Yes
Support services for students with:	
LD	Yes
ADHD	Yes
ASD	Yes
Distraction-reduced environment	Yes
Recording of lecture allowed	Yes
Reading technology	Yes
Audio books	Yes
Other assistive technology	Yes
Priority registration	No
Added costs of services:	
For LD	No
For ADHD	No
For ASD	No
LD specialists	No
ADHD & ASD coaching	Yes
ASD specialists	No
Professional tutors	Yes
Peer tutors	No
Max. hours/week for services	Varies
How professors are notified of student approved accommodations	Director

COLLEGE GRADUATION REQUIREMENTS

Course waivers allowed	Yes
In what courses: Based on applicable documentation mainly math and foreign languages.	
Course substitutions allowed	Yes
In what courses: Based on applicable documentation mainly math and foreign languages.	

Clarkson University

Holcroft House, Potsdam, NY 13699 • Admissions: 315-268-6480 • Fax: 315-268-7647 **Support: S**

CAMPUS

Type of school	Private (nonprofit)
Environment	Village

STUDENTS

Undergrad enrollment	2,982
% male/female	69/31
% from out of state	31
% frosh live on campus	94

FINANCIAL FACTS

Annual tuition	$51,454
Room and board	$17,118
Required fees	$1,270

GENERAL ADMISSIONS INFO

Application fee	$50
Regular application deadline	1/15
Nonfall registration	Yes

Admission may be deferred.

Range SAT EBRW	560–660
Range SAT Math	600–690
Range ACT Composite	23–30

ACADEMICS

Student/faculty ratio	14:1
% students returning for sophomore year	91

Most classes have 10–19 students.

Programs/Services for Students with Learning Differences

For AccessABILITY Services to determine if a student's condition meets the standard defined by the law, an evaluative intake interview will be conducted with the student and any additional documentation supplied will be reviewed. All decisions are made on a case-by-case basis and any additional information requested following the intake interview will be used to determine the current functional limitations caused by the disability and reasonable modifications in an academic or residential setting. Decisions made by the Office of AccessABILITY.

Admissions

The admission process and criteria are the same for all students applying to Clarkson. Disability status will not be a consideration in admission decisions.

Additional Information

The services following services are offered free of charge to all Clarkson University students but are not specifically designed for students with disabilities. Student Support Services (SSS) offers academic support for qualifying students. Some of the available services include weekly small group tutoring, practice exams, and workshops. Individual academic counseling is available for students seeking assistance in such areas as development and strengthening of study techniques, improving motivation, and dealing with test taking stress and time-management skills. The Writing Center offers one-on-one help with academic and personal projects, like essays, reports, and labs.

ADMISSIONS INFO FOR STUDENTS WITH LEARNING DIFFERENCES

Phone: 315-268-7643 • Fax: 315-268-6643 • Email: kmpearson@clarkson.edu

SAT/ACT required: No
Interview required: No
Essay required: Yes
Additional application required: No
Documentation submitted to: Office of Accommodative Services

Special Ed. HS course work accepted: Yes
Separate application required for Programs/Services: No
Documentation required for:
LD: Psychoeducational evaluation
ADHD: Psychoeducational evaluation
ASD: Psychoeducational evaluation

Clarkson University

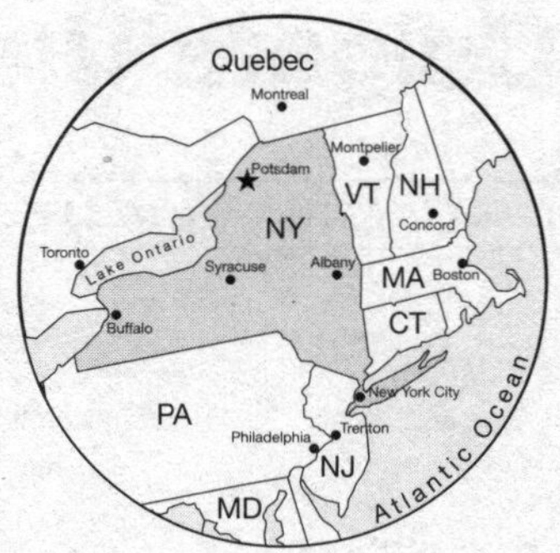

General Admissions

Very Important factors include: rigor of secondary school record, academic GPA. *Important factors include:* class rank, standardized test scores, recommendation(s), extracurricular activities, volunteer work. *Other factors include:* application essay, talent/ability, character/personal qualities, first generation, alumni/ae relation, work experience, level of applicant's interest. High school diploma is required and a GED is accepted. *Academic units required:* 4 English, 3 math, 1 science, 4 unit from above areas or other academic areas. *Academic units recommended:* 4 math, 4 science.

Accommodations or Services

Accommodations are decided upon an individual basis after a thorough review of appropriate, current documentation. The accommodations requests must be supported through the documentation provided and must be logically linked to the current impact of the condition on academic functioning.

Financial Aid

Students should submit: FAFSA; State aid form. *Need-based scholarships/grants offered:* College/university scholarship or grant aid from institutional funds; Federal Pell; Private scholarships; SEOG; State scholarships/grants. *Loan aid offered:* Direct PLUS loans; Direct Subsidized Stafford Loans; Direct Unsubsidized Stafford Loans. Federal Work-Study Program available. Institutional employment available.

Campus Life

Activities: Choral groups; Concert band; Dance; Drama/theater; International Student Organization; Jazz band; Model UN; Music ensembles; Musical theater; Pep band; Radio station; Student government; Student newspaper; Student-run film society; Symphony orchestra; Television station; Yearbook. **Organizations:** 231 registered organizations, 24 honor societies, 5 religious organizations, 9 fraternities, 4 sororities. **Athletics (Intercollegiate):** *Men:* baseball, basketball, cross-country, diving, golf, ice hockey, lacrosse, skiing (downhill/alpine), skiing (Nordic/cross-country), soccer, swimming. *Women:* basketball, cross-country, diving, ice hockey, lacrosse, skiing (downhill/alpine), skiing (Nordic/cross-country), soccer, swimming, volleyball.

ACCOMMODATIONS

Allowed in exams:	
Calculators	Yes
Dictionary	Yes
Computer	Yes
Spell-checker	Yes
Extended test time	Yes
Scribe	Yes
Proctors	Yes
Oral exams	Yes
Note-takers	Yes
Support services for students with:	
LD	Yes
ADHD	Yes
ASD	Yes
Distraction-reduced environment	Yes
Recording of lecture allowed	Yes
Reading technology	Yes
Audio books	Yes
Other assistive technology	Yes
Priority registration	Yes
Added costs of services:	
For LD	NO
For ADHD	No
For ASD	No
LD specialists	No
ADHD & ASD coaching	No
ASD specialists	No
Professional tutors	No
Peer tutors	Yes
Max. hours/week for services	Varies
How professors are notified of student approved accommodations	Student and Disability Office

COLLEGE GRADUATION REQUIREMENTS

Course waivers allowed	Yes
In what courses: on a case-by-case basis	
Course substitutions allowed	Yes
In what courses: on a case-by-case basis	

Colgate University

13 Oak Drive, Hamilton, NY 13346 • Admissions: 315-228-7401 • Fax: 315-228-7524 **Support: S**

CAMPUS

Type of school	Private (nonprofit)
Environment	Rural

STUDENTS

Undergrad enrollment	2,980
% male/female	45/55
% from out of state	74
% frosh live on campus	100

FINANCIAL FACTS

Annual tuition	$59,655
Room and board	$15,035
Required fees	$360

GENERAL ADMISSIONS INFO

Application fee	$60
Regular application deadline	1/15
Nonfall registration	No

Admission may be deferred.

Range SAT EBRW	660–730
Range SAT Math	670–770
Range ACT Composite	31–34

ACADEMICS

Student/faculty ratio	9:1
% students returning for sophomore year	95

Most classes have 10–19 students.

Programs/Services for Students with Learning Differences

Colgate provides for a small student body a liberal arts education that will expand individual potential and ability to participate effectively in society's affairs. There are many resources available for all students. Colgate's goal is to offer resources and services within the campus-wide support system that are responsive to the various talents, needs, and preferences of students with disabilities. For the university to understand and prepare for the accommodations that may be requested, students are asked to complete a confidential self-assessment questionnaire and provide appropriate documentation about their disability. The Director of Academic Support and Disability Services works with students and faculty to assure that the needs of students with disabilities are met, serves as clearinghouse for information about disabilities, provides training and individual consultation for all members of the Colgate community, and provides academic counseling and individualized instruction. Seeking help early and learning to be a self-advocate are essential to college success.

Admissions

There is no special admission process for students with learning disabilities. The Office of Admissions reviews the applications of all candidates for admission. The admissions staff looks for evidence of substantial achievement in a rigorous secondary school curriculum, one counselor recommendation, standardized testing, a personalized essay, and extracurricular involvement.

Additional Information

Students are encouraged to seek help early; meet with professors at the beginning of each semester to discuss approaches and accommodations that will meet their needs; and seek assistance from the Director of Academic Support and Disability Services, administrative advisor, and faculty advisor. Modifications in the curriculum are made on an individual basis. Colgate provides services in support of academic work on an as-needed basis, such as assistance with note-takers, tape-recorded lectures, tutors, readers, and assistive technology. There is a Writing and Speaking Center and tutoring, and skills help is available in writing, reading, and study strategies. Services and accommodations are available for undergraduate and graduate students. Students must complete a Special Needs Identification Form.

ADMISSIONS INFO FOR STUDENTS WITH LEARNING DIFFERENCES

Phone: 315-228-7375 • Fax: 315 410-5635 • Email: lwaldman@colgate.edu

SAT/ACT required: Yes (Test optional through 2023)
Interview required: No
Essay required: No
Additional application required: No
Documentation submitted to: Academic Support & Disability Services

Special Ed. HS course work accepted: Yes
Separate application required for Programs/Services: No
Documentation required for:
LD: Psychoeducational evaluation
ADHD: Psychoeducational evaluation
ASD: Psychoeducational evaluation

Colgate University

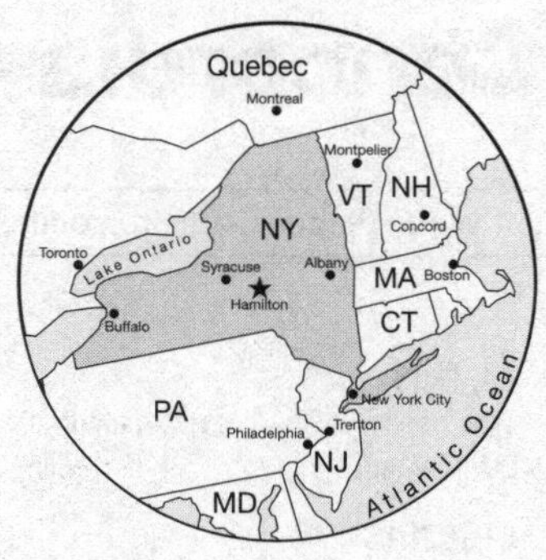

General Admissions

Very Important factors include: rigor of secondary school record, class rank, academic GPA. *Important factors include:* application essay, standardized test scores, recommendation(s), extracurricular activities, talent/ability, character/personal qualities. *Other factors include:* first generation, alumni/ae relation, geographical residence, racial/ethnic status, volunteer work, work experience. High school diploma is required and a GED is accepted. *Academic units required:* 4 English, 3 math, 3 science, 2 science labs, 3 foreign language, 3 social studies. *Academic units recommended:* 4 English, 4 math, 4 science, 4 science labs, 4 foreign language, 4 social studies.

Accommodations or Services

Accommodations are decided upon an individual basis after a thorough review of appropriate, current documentation. The accommodations requests must be supported through the documentation provided and must be logically linked to the current impact of the condition on academic functioning.

Financial Aid

Students should submit: CSS/Financial Aid PROFILE; FAFSA; Noncustodial PROFILE. *Need-based scholarships/grants offered:* College/university scholarship or grant aid from institutional funds; Federal Pell; SEOG. *Loan aid offered:* Direct PLUS loans; Direct Subsidized Stafford Loans; Direct Unsubsidized Stafford Loans. Federal Work-Study Program available. Institutional employment available.

Campus Life

Activities: Campus Ministries; Choral groups; Concert band; Dance; Drama/theater; International Student Organization; Jazz band; Literary magazine; Model UN; Music ensembles; Musical theater; Opera; Pep band; Radio station; Student government; Student newspaper; Symphony orchestra; Yearbook. **Organizations:** 167 registered organizations, 12 honor societies, 10 religious organizations, 5 fraternities, 3 sororities. **Athletics (Intercollegiate):** *Men:* basketball, crew/rowing, cross-country, diving, football, golf, ice hockey, lacrosse, soccer, swimming, tennis, track/field (outdoor). *Women:* basketball, crew/rowing, cross-country, diving, field hockey, ice hockey, lacrosse, soccer, softball, swimming, tennis, track/field (outdoor), volleyball.

ACCOMMODATIONS

Allowed in exams:	
Calculators	Yes
Dictionary	Yes
Computer	Yes
Spell-checker	Yes
Extended test time	Yes
Scribe	Yes
Proctors	Yes
Oral exams	Yes
Note-takers	Yes
Support services for students with:	
LD	No
ADHD	No
ASD	No
Distraction-reduced environment	Yes
Recording of lecture allowed	Yes
Reading technology	Yes
Audio books	Yes
Other assistive technology	Yes
Priority registration	No
Added costs of services:	
For LD	No
For ADHD	No
For ASD	No
LD specialists	No
ADHD & ASD coaching	Yes
ASD specialists	No
Professional tutors	Yes
Peer tutors	Yes
Max. hours/week for services	Varies
How professors are notified of student approved accommodations	Student

COLLEGE GRADUATION REQUIREMENTS

Course waivers allowed	No
Course substitutions allowed	Yes
In what courses: Case-by-case basis	

Concordia College (NY)

171 White Plains Road, Bronxville, NY 10708 • Admissions: 914-337-9300 • Fax: 914-395-4636 **Support: SP**

CAMPUS

Type of school	Private (nonprofit)
Environment	Village

STUDENTS

Undergrad enrollment	1,281
% male/female	21/79
% from out of state	24

FINANCIAL FACTS

Annual tuition	$34,500
Room and board	$13,983
Required fees	$1,500

GENERAL ADMISSIONS INFO

Application fee	$60
Regular application deadline	3/15
Nonfall registration	Yes

Admission may be deferred.

Range SAT EBRW	450–570
Range SAT Math	400–550
Range ACT Composite	17–22

ACADEMICS

Student/faculty ratio	12:1
% students returning for sophomore year	64

Programs/Services for Students with Learning Differences

Concordia Connection is a program for students with LD who have demonstrated the potential to earn a college degree. Their commitment is to provide an intimate, supportive, and caring environment where students with special learning needs can experience college as a successful and rewarding endeavor. This is a mainstream program. Students are fully integrated into the college. During the fall and spring semesters, students are registered for four or five classes. Additionally, students are registered for a one-credit independent study, which incorporates a weekly, 1-hour group session with the director and staff that focuses on the development of individualized learning strategies. Progress is monitored, and an assessment of learning potential and academic levels is provided. The program's director coordinates support services and works with the assigned freshman advisor to assure an optimal course plan each semester. A summer orientation and academic seminar is required for all new Concordia Connection students.

Admissions

Students wishing to apply should submit the following documents to the Admissions Office: a Concordia application and the student's current transcript; SAT/ACT scores; documentation of LD; recommendations from an LD specialist and a guidance counselor; and an essay describing the nature of the LD, the effect on learning patterns, and the student's reason for pursuing college. Visits are encouraged. Applicants must be high school graduates, have a diagnosed LD, have college-prep courses, and be committed to being successful. General admissions criteria include a B average, ACT/SAT scores (used to assess strengths and weaknesses rather than for acceptance or denial), and college-preparatory courses in high school (foreign language is recommended but not required). Students with LD who self-disclose and provide documentation will be reviewed by the Admissions Office and the director of Concordia Connection.

Additional Information

The Concordia Connection provides services to all students. These include test-taking modifications, taped text books, computer access, and tutoring. Although there are no charges for students requesting peer tutoring, there is a $6,000 charge for program services. Skills courses for credit are offered in time management, organizational skills, and study skills. The 1-day summer orientation helps students get acquainted with support services, get exposure to academic expectations, review components and requirements of the freshman year, develop group cohesion, and explore individualized needs and strategies for seeking assistance.

ADMISSIONS INFO FOR STUDENTS WITH LEARNING DIFFERENCES

Phone: 914-337-9300, ext: 2361 • Fax: 914-395-4500 • Email: nastacia.brown@concordia-ny.edu

SAT/ACT required: No
Interview required: No
Essay required: Yes
Additional application required: No
Documentation submitted to: Admissions

Special Ed. HS course work accepted: Yes
Separate application required for Programs/Services: Yes
Documentation required for:
LD: Psychoeducational evaluation
ADHD: Psychoeducational evaluation
ASD: Psychoeducational evaluation

Concordia College (NY)

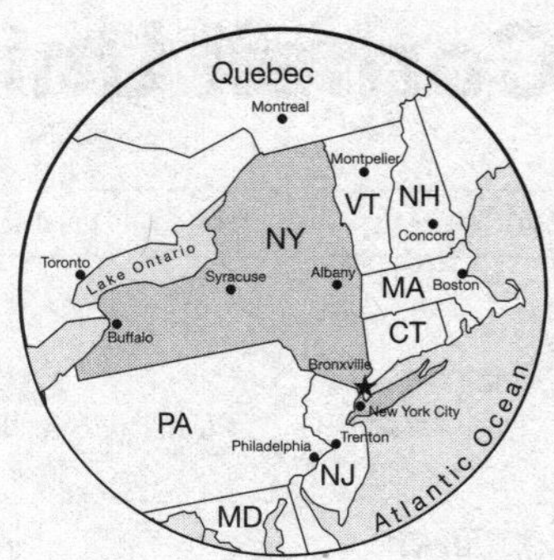

General Admissions

Very Important factors include: rigor of secondary school record. *Important factors include:* class rank, standardized test scores, interview, character/personal qualities. *Other factors include:* application essay, recommendation(s), extracurricular activities, talent/ability, alumni/ae relation, religious affiliation/commitment, volunteer work, work experience. High school diploma is required and a GED is accepted.

Accommodations or Services

Accommodations are decided upon an individual basis after a thorough review of appropriate, current documentation. The accommodations requests must be supported through the documentation provided and must be logically linked to the current impact of the condition on academic functioning.

Financial Aid

Students should submit: FAFSA. *Need-based scholarships/grants offered:* College/university scholarship or grant aid from institutional funds; Federal Pell; Private scholarships; SEOG; State scholarships/grants. *Loan aid offered:* Direct PLUS loans; Direct Subsidized Stafford Loans; Direct Unsubsidized Stafford Loans. Federal Work-Study Program available. Institutional employment available.

Campus Life

Activities: Choral groups; Concert band; Dance; Drama/theater; International Student Organization; Jazz band; Literary magazine; Music ensembles; Musical theater; Student government; Student newspaper; Yearbook. **Organizations:** 35 registered organizations, 1 honor society, 3 religious organizations. **Athletics (Intercollegiate):** *Men:* baseball, basketball, soccer, tennis, volleyball. *Women:* basketball, soccer, softball, tennis, volleyball.

ACCOMMODATIONS

Allowed in exams:	
Calculators	Yes
Dictionary	Yes
Computer	Yes
Spell-checker	Yes
Extended test time	Yes
Scribe	Yes
Proctors	Yes
Oral exams	Yes
Note-takers	Yes
Support services for students with:	
LD	Yes
ADHD	Yes
ASD	Yes
Distraction-reduced environment	Yes
Recording of lecture allowed	Yes
Reading technology	Yes
Audio books	No
Other assistive technology	Yes
Priority registration	Yes
Added costs of services:	
For LD	Yes
For ADHD	Yes
For ASD	Yes
LD specialists	Yes
ADHD & ASD coaching	No
ASD specialists	Yes
Professional tutors	Yes
Peer tutors	Yes
Max. hours/week for services	10
How professors are notified of student approved accommodations	Student and Disability Office

COLLEGE GRADUATION REQUIREMENTS

Course waivers allowed	No
Course substitutions allowed	Yes
In what courses: Case-by-case basis	

Cornell University

410 Thurston Ave., Ithaca, NY 14850 • Admissions: 607-255-5241 • Fax: 607-255-0659 **Support: S**

CAMPUS

Type of school	Private (nonprofit)
Environment	Town

STUDENTS

Undergrad enrollment	14,976
% male/female	46/54
% from out of state	64
% frosh live on campus	99

FINANCIAL FACTS

Annual tuition	$58,586
Room and board	$14,671
Required fees	$656

GENERAL ADMISSIONS INFO

Application fee	$80
Regular application deadline	1/2
Nonfall registration	Yes

Admission may be deferred.

Range SAT EBRW	680–760
Range SAT Math	720–800
Range ACT Composite	32–35

ACADEMICS

Student/faculty ratio	9:1
% students returning for sophomore year	97

Most classes have 10–19 students.

Programs/Services for Students with Learning Differences

Cornell University strives to be an accessible community where students with disabilities have an equitable opportunity to fully participate in all aspects of university life. Students with disabilities must submit requests for disability services to the Student Disability Services (SDS) office. The SDS staff is responsible for determining appropriate and effective federally mandated support services for eligible students. The university provides support services for a broad range of disabilities. There is not a specific program designed for students with learning disabilities. Once a student has been approved for disability services, many units across campus are responsible for fulfilling access needs. Students are directly involved in the process of arranging accommodations with instructors and for following established procedures for using disability services.

Admissions

Cornell does not have a special admissions process for students with learning disabilities. All students applying to Cornell are expected to meet admissions criteria.

Additional Information

Admitted students with disabilities are encouraged to register for disability services online at sds.cornell.edu The Learning Strategies Center is the main support center for all undergraduates at the University. LSC strives to engage students in the learning process and support their efforts to become more successful and independent learners through tutoring services, study groups, tips for time management, and supplemental course instruction.

ADMISSIONS INFO FOR STUDENTS WITH LEARNING DIFFERENCES

Phone: 607-254-4545 • Fax: 607-255-1562 • Email: sds_cu@cornell.edu

SAT/ACT required: Yes (Test-optional for 2021)
Interview required: No
Essay required: Yes
Additional application required: No
Documentation submitted to: Student Disability Services

Special Ed. HS course work accepted: Yes
Separate application required for Programs/Services: No
Documentation required for:
LD: Psychoeducational evaluation
ADHD: Psychoeducational evaluation
ASD: Psychoeducational evaluation

Cornell University

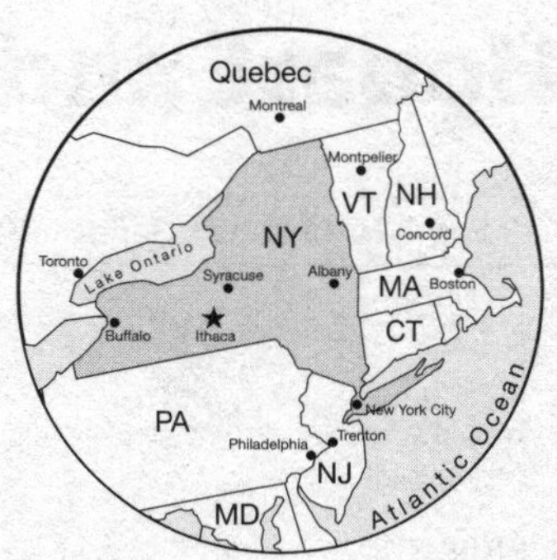

General Admissions

Very Important factors include: rigor of secondary school record, academic GPA, application essay, standardized test scores, recommendation(s), extracurricular activities, talent/ability, character/personal qualities. *Important factors include:* class rank. *Other factors include:* interview, first generation, alumni/ae relation, geographical residence, state residency, racial/ethnic status, volunteer work, work experience. High school diploma or equivalent is not required.

Accommodations or Services

Accommodations are decided upon an individual basis after a thorough review of appropriate, current documentation. The accommodations requests must be supported through the documentation provided and must be logically linked to the current impact of the condition on academic functioning.

Financial Aid

Students should submit: CSS/Financial Aid PROFILE; FAFSA; Noncustodial PROFILE. *Need-based scholarships/grants offered:* College/university scholarship or grant aid from institutional funds; Federal Pell; Private scholarships; SEOG; State scholarships/grants. *Loan aid offered:* Direct PLUS loans; Direct Subsidized Stafford Loans; Direct Unsubsidized Stafford Loans. Federal Work-Study Program available. Institutional employment available.

Campus Life

Activities: Campus Ministries; Choral groups; Concert band; Dance; Drama/theater; International Student Organization; Jazz band; Literary magazine; Marching band; Model UN; Music ensembles; Musical theater; Pep band; Radio station; Student government; Student newspaper; Student-run film society; Symphony orchestra; Television station; Yearbook. **Organizations:** 1275 registered organizations, 15 honor societies, 26 religious organizations, 37 fraternities, 19 sororities. **Athletics (Intercollegiate):** *Men:* baseball, basketball, crew/rowing, cross-country, diving, football, golf, ice hockey, lacrosse, polo, soccer, squash, swimming, tennis, track/field (outdoor), track/field (indoor), wrestling. *Women:* basketball, crew/rowing, cross-country, diving, equestrian sports, fencing, field hockey, gymnastics, ice hockey, lacrosse, polo, soccer, softball, squash, swimming, tennis, track/field (outdoor), track/field (indoor), volleyball.

ACCOMMODATIONS

Allowed in exams:	
Calculators	Yes
Dictionary	Yes
Computer	Yes
Spell-checker	Yes
Extended test time	Yes
Scribe	Yes
Proctors	Yes
Oral exams	Yes
Note-takers	Yes
Support services for students with:	
LD	Yes
ADHD	Yes
ASD	Yes
Distraction-reduced environment	Yes
Recording of lecture allowed	Yes
Reading technology	Yes
Audio books	Yes
Other assistive technology	Yes
Priority registration	Not Applicable
Added costs of services:	
For LD	No
For ADHD	No
For ASD	No
LD specialists	No
ADHD & ASD coaching	No
ASD specialists	No
Professional tutors	No
Peer tutors	Not Applicable
Max. hours/week for services	Varies
How professors are notified of student approved accommodations	Student

COLLEGE GRADUATION REQUIREMENTS

Course waivers allowed	No
Course substitutions allowed	No

Hobart and William Smith Colleges

629 South Main Street, Geneva, NY 14456 • Admissions: 315-781-3622 • Fax: 315-781-3914 **Support: CS**

CAMPUS

Type of school	Private (nonprofit)
Environment	Village

STUDENTS

Undergrad enrollment	2,036
% male/female	48/52
% from out of state	61
% frosh live on campus	100

FINANCIAL FACTS

Annual tuition	$57,400
Room and board	$16,650
Required fees	$1,250

GENERAL ADMISSIONS INFO

Application fee	$0
Regular application deadline	2/1
Nonfall registration	Yes

Admission may be deferred.

Range SAT EBRW	590–670
Range SAT Math	590–690
Range ACT Composite	26–30

ACADEMICS

Student/faculty ratio	10:1
% students returning for sophomore year	88

Most classes have 10–19 students.

Programs/Services for Students with Learning Differences

Hobart and William Smith Colleges cultivate an inclusive and supporting learning community that values the diverse learning styles of our students. The Office of Disability Services in the Center for Teaching and Learning (CTL) is committed to providing students with disabilities access to HWS programs and activities. We strive to provide the appropriate individualized accommodations necessary for students with disabilities to succeed. The Office of Disability Services seeks to promote academic achievement, extracurricular involvement, and help students with disabilities take full advantage of the academic and extracurricular opportunities available at HWS. The Coordinator of Disability Services works independently and in cooperation with other administrative offices and academic departments to: identify and implement individualized accommodations while fostering the academic and personal development of students; ensure the appropriateness of disability-related accommodations in specific courses; and assist HWS and establishing policies, procedures, and facilities that are in compliance with state and federal disability laws.

Admissions

The admissions process for students with learning differences is the same. Students are welcome to disclose their LD/ADHD/ASD status, but it is not required.

Additional Information

Hobart and William Smith Colleges welcome students with learning differences and disabilities. Our admissions process is centered upon getting to know students as individuals. We welcome the opportunity to learn from students about their accomplishments, challenges they have faced, and how they have succeeded. An admissions interview is the perfect format to share that information.

ADMISSIONS INFO FOR STUDENTS WITH LEARNING DIFFERENCES

Phone: 315-781-3351 • Fax: 315-781-3862 • Email: ctl@hws.edu

SAT/ACT required: No
Interview required: No
Essay required: Yes
Additional application required: No
Documentation submitted to: Office of Disability Services

Special Ed. HS course work accepted: Yes
Separate application required for Programs/Services: No
Documentation required for:
- **LD:** Psychoeducational evaluation
- **ADHD:** Psychoeducational evaluation
- **ASD:** Psychoeducational evaluation

Hobart and William Smith Colleges

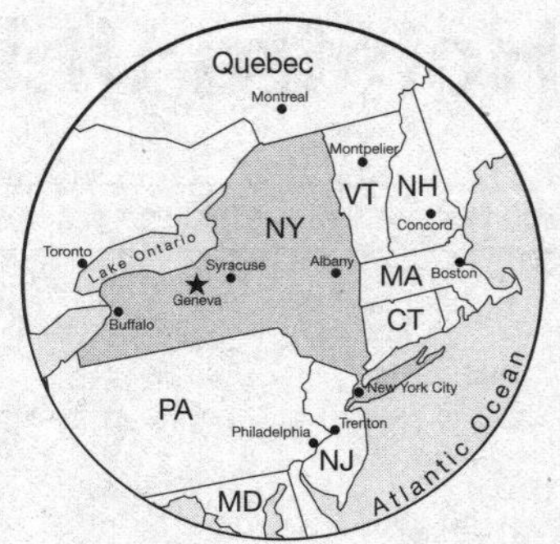

General Admissions

Very Important factors include: rigor of secondary school record, academic GPA. *Important factors include:* application essay, recommendation(s), interview, extracurricular activities. *Other factors include:* class rank, character/personal qualities, alumni/ae relation, geographical residence, state residency, religious affiliation/commitment, racial/ethnic status, level of applicant's interest. High school diploma is required and a GED is accepted. *Academic units required:* 4 English, 3 math, 3 science, 2 science labs, 2 foreign language, 2 social studies, 2 academic electives. *Academic units recommended:* 3 foreign language, 3 social studies, 4 academic electives.

Accommodations or Services

Accommodations are decided upon an individual basis after a thorough review of appropriate, current documentation. The accommodations requests must be supported through the documentation provided and must be logically linked to the current impact of the condition on academic functioning.

Financial Aid

Students should submit: FAFSA. Applicants will be notified of awards on a rolling basis beginning 3/15. *Need-based scholarships/grants offered:* College/university scholarship or grant aid from institutional funds; Federal Pell; Private scholarships; SEOG; State scholarships/grants. *Loan aid offered:* Direct PLUS loans; Direct Subsidized Stafford Loans; Direct Unsubsidized Stafford Loans. Federal Work-Study Program available. Institutional employment available.

Campus Life

Activities: Campus Ministries; Choral groups; Concert band; Dance; Drama/theater; International Student Organization; Jazz band; Literary magazine; Music ensembles; Radio station; Student government; Student newspaper; Student-run film society. **Organizations:** 112 registered organizations, 12 honor societies, 1 religious organization, 6 fraternities, 1 sorority. **Athletics (Intercollegiate):** *Men:* basketball, crew/rowing, cross-country, football, golf, ice hockey, lacrosse, sailing, soccer, squash, tennis. *Women:* basketball, crew/rowing, cross-country, diving, field hockey, golf, lacrosse, sailing, soccer, squash, swimming, tennis.

ACCOMMODATIONS

Allowed in exams:	
Calculators	Yes
Dictionary	Yes
Computer	Yes
Spell-checker	Yes
Extended test time	Yes
Scribe	Yes
Proctors	Yes
Oral exams	Yes
Note-takers	Yes
Support services for students with:	
LD	Yes
ADHD	Yes
ASD	Yes
Distraction-reduced environment	Yes
Recording of lecture allowed	Yes
Reading technology	Yes
Audio books	Yes
Other assistive technology	Yes
Priority registration	No
Added costs of services:	
For LD	No
For ADHD	No
For ASD	No
LD specialists	Yes
ADHD & ASD coaching	No
ASD specialists	No
Professional tutors	No
Peer tutors	Yes
Max. hours/week for services	Varies
How professors are notified of student approved accommodations	Student

COLLEGE GRADUATION REQUIREMENTS

Course waivers allowed	Yes
In what courses: foreign language	
Course substitutions allowed	Yes
In what courses: foreign language	

Hofstra University

100 Hofstra University, Hempstead, NY 11549 • Admissions: 516-463-6700 • Fax: 516-463-5100 **Support: SP**

CAMPUS

Type of school	Private (nonprofit)
Environment	City

STUDENTS

Undergrad enrollment	6,400
% male/female	45/55
% from out of state	37
% frosh live on campus	67

FINANCIAL FACTS

Annual tuition	$46,450
Room and board	$16,428
Required fees	$1,060

GENERAL ADMISSIONS INFO

Application fee	$70
Regular application deadline	Rolling
Nonfall registration	Yes

Admission may be deferred.

Range SAT EBRW	580–660
Range SAT Math	580–680
Range ACT Composite	25–30

ACADEMICS

Student/faculty ratio	13:1
% students returning for sophomore year	83

Most classes have 10–19 students.

Programs/Services for Students with Learning Differences

The mission of Student Access Services is to provide disability related education, services, and resources to the Hofstra Community. SAS ensures equal access to education for all Hofstra students, regardless of disability, in compliance with federal law and in keeping with Hofstra's long-standing commitment to equality and access in its programs and services. We respectfully serve our students by facilitating barrier-free educational opportunities and assisting them in becoming independent, self-advocating learners. Students who are applying to the fee-based PALS program may be asked to provide documentation and come to campus for a personal interview to determine if the PALS program is the right fit.

Admissions

Students are held to the same admission criteria as any other student who is looking for admission to the University. Students may be required to interview with the admission staff and /or the disabilities staff to asses a fit for the University. After a full review is conducted an admission decision will be reached.

Additional Information

Enrollment in PALS is a two-semester (one-year) commitment. Students enrolled in PALS are billed a one-time, $13,000 charge during their first year at Hofstra. However, this one-time fee entitles the student to continue meeting with a learning specialist for the duration of his or her academic program at Hofstra. PALS students are also eligible for reasonable accommodations through SAS. Reasonable accommodations are adjustments to Hofstra University programs, policies and practices that "level the playing field" for students with disabilities. Reasonable accommodations may include extended time on examinations; testing in a smaller, proctored environment; and supplemental note-taking services. As with learning strategies, accommodations are based on each student's disability-related needs and careful review of comprehensive disability documentation.

ADMISSIONS INFO FOR STUDENTS WITH LEARNING DIFFERENCES

Phone: 516-463-7075 • Fax: 516-463-7070 • Email: SAS@hostra.edu

SAT/ACT required: No
Interview required: No
Essay required: Recommended
Additional application required: No
Documentation submitted to: Student Access Services

Special Ed. HS course work accepted: Yes
Separate application required for Programs/Services: Yes
Documentation required for:
LD: Psychoeducational evaluation
ADHD: Psychoeducational evaluation
ASD: Psychoeducational evaluation

Hofstra University

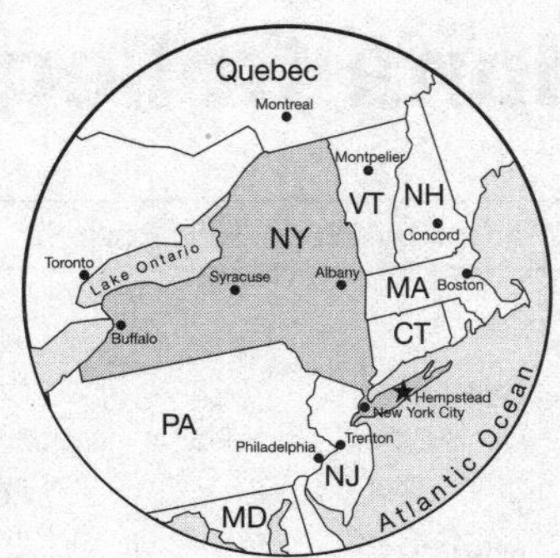

General Admissions

Very Important factors include: rigor of secondary school record, class rank, academic GPA, application essay, recommendation(s). *Important factors include:* interview, extracurricular activities, talent/ability, character/personal qualities. *Other factors include:* standardized test scores, first generation, alumni/ae relation, geographical residence, racial/ethnic status, volunteer work, work experience, level of applicant's interest. High school diploma is required and a GED is accepted. *Academic units required:* 4 English, 3 math, 3 science, 1 science lab, 2 foreign language, 3 social studies. *Academic units recommended:* 4 math, 4 science, 2 science labs, 3 foreign language, 4 social studies.

Accommodations or Services

Accommodations are decided upon an individual basis after a thorough review of appropriate, current documentation. The accommodations requests must be supported through the documentation provided and must be logically linked to the current impact of the condition on academic functioning.

Financial Aid

Students should submit: FAFSA. *Need-based scholarships/grants offered:* College/university scholarship or grant aid from institutional funds; Federal Pell; Private scholarships; SEOG; State scholarships/grants; United Negro College Fund. *Loan aid offered:* Direct PLUS loans; Direct Subsidized Stafford Loans; Direct Unsubsidized Stafford Loans. Federal Work-Study Program available. Institutional employment available.

Campus Life

Activities: Campus Ministries; Choral groups; Concert band; Dance; Drama/theater; Jazz band; Literary magazine; Model UN; Music ensembles; Musical theater; Opera; Pep band; Radio station; Student government; Student newspaper; Student-run film society; Symphony orchestra; Television station. **Organizations:** 223 registered organizations, 39 honor societies, 6 religious organizations, 10 fraternities, 10 sororities. **Athletics (Intercollegiate):** *Men:* baseball, basketball, cross-country, golf, lacrosse, soccer, tennis, wrestling. *Women:* basketball, cross-country, field hockey, golf, lacrosse, soccer, softball, tennis, volleyball.

ACCOMMODATIONS

Allowed in exams:	
Calculators	Yes
Dictionary	Yes
Computer	Yes
Spell-checker	Yes
Extended test time	Yes
Scribe	Yes
Proctors	Yes
Oral exams	Yes
Note-takers	Yes
Support services for students with:	
LD	Yes
ADHD	Yes
ASD	Yes
Distraction-reduced environment	Yes
Recording of lecture allowed	Yes
Reading technology	Yes
Audio books	Yes
Other assistive technology	Yes
Priority registration	No
Added costs of services:	
For LD	Yes
For ADHD	Yes
For ASD	Yes
LD specialists	Yes
ADHD & ASD coaching	Yes
ASD specialists	Yes
Professional tutors	No
Peer tutors	Yes
Max. hours/week for services	Varies
How professors are notified of student approved accommodations	Student

COLLEGE GRADUATION REQUIREMENTS

Course waivers allowed	No
Course substitutions allowed	Yes

In what courses: Case-by-case basis

Iona College

715 North Avenue, New Rochelle, NY 10801 • Admissions: 914-633-2502 • Fax: 914-633-2182 **Support: SP**

CAMPUS

Type of school	Private (nonprofit)
Environment	City

STUDENTS

Undergrad enrollment	2,743
% male/female	52/48
% from out of state	23
% frosh live on campus	62

FINANCIAL FACTS

Annual tuition	$37,972
Room and board	$15,736
Required fees	$2,200

GENERAL ADMISSIONS INFO

Application fee	$50
Regular application deadline	2/15
Nonfall registration	Yes

Admission may be deferred.

Range SAT EBRW	500–590
Range SAT Math	490–580
Range ACT Composite	20–26

ACADEMICS

Student/faculty ratio	14:1
% students returning for sophomore year	72

Most classes have 20–29 students.

Programs/Services for Students with Learning Differences

The College Assistance Program (CAP) of Iona College is an optional, fee-based program that offers comprehensive support and services for students with learning disabilities, AD/HD, traumatic brain injuries, or are on the autism spectrum. In addition to encouraging success by providing instruction tailored to individual strengths and needs, the program emphasizes broadly applicable strategies that cross academic disciplines. The team of professional learning specialists who work with CAP students is devoted to the support and guidance of each student. They train students to incorporate appropriate skills-based strategies which cross the disciplines. The goal is for students to gradually practice these skills until they are able to master them independently. With success comes self-confidence and a greater ability to plan and achieve academic, personal, and career goals. Additionally, the CAP counselor assists students with academic coaching, stress management, and career and internship planning. Students take the standard full-time course requirements for baccalaureate degree programs.

Admissions

To be a realistic candidate for admission, an applicant should have taken: 4 years English, 2 years foreign language, 4 years math, 3 years natural science (including two laboratory sciences) and 3 years social studies. Iona College prefers to see students who have maintained at least a solid B/B+ (85–89) average in high school.

Additional Information

In addition to tuition, CAP students are required to pay separate program fees. The current fee per semester is $1,770. During the early part of the summer, all entering CAP freshmen participate in this transition program where a number of skills are addressed. The aim is to provide students with a solid foundation from which the college experience can begin with confidence. The fee is $1,375. An experienced staff instructs and guides students in intensive writing instruction, study skills, organizational and time-management skills. Individual learning styles are explored and opportunities are provided to practice self-advocacy. In addition, several workshops are offered in areas that meet the students' specific needs. CAP works with each student to create an individual schedule that blends both interests and abilities with Iona's Core Curriculum. Consideration is given to matching the student's learning strengths with a professor's teaching style.

ADMISSIONS INFO FOR STUDENTS WITH LEARNING DIFFERENCES

Phone: 914-633-2366 • Fax: 914-633-2230 • Email: access@iona.edu

SAT/ACT required: No
Interview required: Yes
Essay required: Yes
Additional application required: No
Documentation submitted to: Accessibility Services Office

Special Ed. HS course work accepted: Yes
Separate application required for Programs/Services: Yes
Documentation required for:
- **LD:** Psychoeducational evaluation
- **ADHD:** Psychoeducational evaluation
- **ASD:** Psychoeducational evaluation

Iona College

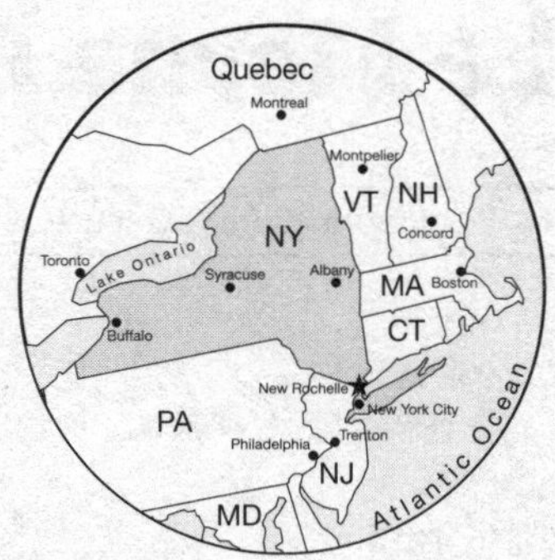

Both students and staff agree that the summer transition program facilitates a successful transition from high school to college. Students engage in an average two hours per week of skills-based tutoring with a learning specialist. Students are also encouraged to participate in weekly group tutoring. Students who are enrolled in CAP register early and receive help with course selection and registration. The CAP counselor offers academic coaching, time management, and stress management strategies, based on the individual needs of each student. Students are encouraged to meet with the counselor on a regular basis until they are able to manage these strategies on their own. CAP arranges for students to study in groups for many of the core classes.

General Admissions

Very Important factors include: rigor of secondary school record, academic GPA. *Important factors include:* character/personal qualities. *Other factors include:* class rank, application essay, standardized test scores, recommendation(s), interview, extracurricular activities, talent/ability, first generation, alumni/ae relation, geographical residence, volunteer work, work experience. High school diploma is required and a GED is accepted. *Academic units required:* 4 English, 3 math, 3 science, 2 science labs, 2 foreign language, 2 social studies, 1 history, 1 academic elective. *Academic units recommended:* 4 math, 2 history, 3 academic electives.

Accommodations or Services

Accommodations are decided upon an individual basis after a thorough review of appropriate, current documentation. The accommodations requests must be supported through the documentation provided and must be logically linked to the current impact of the condition on academic functioning.

Financial Aid

Students should submit: FAFSA; State aid form. *Need-based scholarships/grants offered:* College/university scholarship or grant aid from institutional funds; Federal Pell; Private scholarships; SEOG; State scholarships/grants. *Loan aid offered:* Direct PLUS loans; Direct Subsidized Stafford Loans; Direct Unsubsidized Stafford Loans. Federal Work-Study Program available. Institutional employment available.

Campus Life

Activities: Campus Ministries; Choral groups; Concert band; Dance; Drama/theater; International Student Organization; Literary magazine; Model UN; Music ensembles; Musical theater; Pep band; Radio station; Student government; Student newspaper; Student-run film society; Television station; Yearbook. **Organizations:** 80 registered organizations, 26 honor societies, 3 religious organizations, 3 fraternities, 5 sororities. **Athletics (Intercollegiate):** *Men:* baseball, basketball, crew/rowing, cross-country, diving, golf, soccer, swimming, track/field (outdoor), track/field (indoor), water polo. *Women:* basketball, crew/rowing, cross-country, diving, lacrosse, soccer, softball, swimming, track/field (outdoor), track/field (indoor), volleyball, water polo.

ACCOMMODATIONS

Allowed in exams:	
Calculators	Yes
Dictionary	Yes
Computer	Yes
Spell-checker	Yes
Extended test time	Yes
Scribe	Yes
Proctors	Yes
Oral exams	Yes
Note-takers	Yes
Support services for students with:	
LD	Yes
ADHD	Yes
ASD	Yes
Distraction-reduced environment	Yes
Recording of lecture allowed	Yes
Reading technology	Yes
Audio books	Yes
Other assistive technology	Yes
Priority registration	Yes
Added costs of services:	
For LD	Yes
For ADHD	Yes
For ASD	Yes
LD specialists	Yes
ADHD & ASD coaching	Yes
ASD specialists	Yes
Professional tutors	Yes
Peer tutors	Yes
Max. hours/week for services	Varies
How professors are notified of student approved accommodations	Student

COLLEGE GRADUATION REQUIREMENTS

Course waivers allowed	Yes
In what courses: Foreign language if documented in student's evaluation.	
Course substitutions allowed	Yes
In what courses: Foreign language if documented in student's evaluation.	

Le Moyne College

1419 Salt Springs Rd., Syracuse, NY 13214-1301 • Admissions: 315-445-4300 • Fax: 315-445-4711 **Support: S**

CAMPUS

Type of school	Private (nonprofit)
Environment	City

STUDENTS

Undergrad enrollment	2,642
% male/female	40/60
% from out of state	7
% frosh live on campus	79

FINANCIAL FACTS

Annual tuition	$34,910
Room and board	$14,470
Required fees	$1,000

GENERAL ADMISSIONS INFO

Application fee	$0
Regular application deadline	Rolling
Nonfall registration	Yes

Admission may be deferred.

Range SAT EBRW	533–640
Range SAT Math	540–640
Range ACT Composite	22–28

ACADEMICS

Student/faculty ratio	12:1
% students returning for sophomore year	87

Most classes have 10–19 students.

Programs/Services for Students with Learning Differences

Academic support services for students with disabilities are coordinated by the Director of Disability Support Services in the Academic Support Center. Students with Special Needs have access to the same support services provided to all students—individual sessions with professionals in the Academic Support Center (ASC) regarding study skills and learning strategies, ASC Workshops provided each fall semester, and individual and small- group tutoring in writing, mathematics, foreign languages, economics, and the natural sciences. In addition, students with disabilities receive individualized services through the ASC. Our goal is to create collaborative partnerships that put students in the driver's seat of their education to enhance their chances for academic success.

Admissions

Le Moyne College is a test-optional school. Strength of the academic program (both the level and the courses taken) is the single most important factor in the admission decision.

Additional Information

Upon receiving a student's documentation, a file is set up in DSS and students meet with the Director to do a formal intake and find out which accommodations fit the student's needs. Each semester, the Director meets with all students with disabilities in order to set up their academic diagnostic tests, make referrals to appropriate diagnosticians, provide supplemental academic advising, assist students in developing self-advocacy skills, and provide liaison and advocacy measures between students and faculty or staff.

ADMISSIONS INFO FOR STUDENTS WITH LEARNING DIFFERENCES

Phone: 315-445-4118 • Fax: 315-445-6014 • Email: dss@lemoyne.edu

SAT/ACT required: No
Interview required: No
Essay required: Required
Additional application required: No
Documentation submitted to: Disability Support Services

Special Ed. HS course work accepted: Yes
Separate application required for Programs/Services: No
Documentation required for:
- **LD:** Psychoeducational evaluation
- **ADHD:** Psychoeducational evaluation
- **ASD:** Psychoeducational evaluation

Le Moyne College

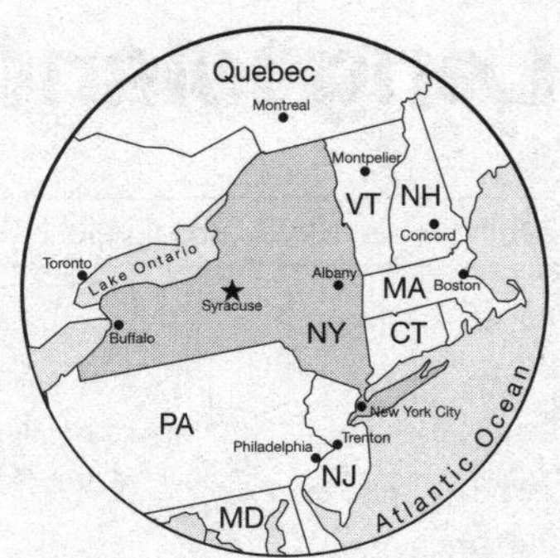

General Admissions

Very Important factors include: rigor of secondary school record, academic GPA. *Important factors include:* class rank, application essay, recommendation(s), interview, extracurricular activities, talent/ability. *Other factors include:* standardized test scores, character/personal qualities, alumni/ae relation, geographical residence, state residency, volunteer work, level of applicant's interest. High school diploma is required and a GED is accepted. *Academic units required:* 4 English, 3 math, 3 science, 3 foreign language, 4 social studies. *Academic units recommended:* 4 math, 4 science, 3 science labs.

Accommodations or Services

Accommodations are decided upon an individual basis after a thorough review of appropriate, current documentation. The accommodations requests must be supported through the documentation provided and must be logically linked to the current impact of the condition on academic functioning.

Financial Aid

Students should submit: FAFSA; State aid form. *Need-based scholarships/grants offered:* College/university scholarship or grant aid from institutional funds; Federal Pell; Private scholarships; SEOG; State scholarships/grants. *Loan aid offered:* Direct PLUS loans; Direct Subsidized Stafford Loans; Direct Unsubsidized Stafford Loans. Federal Work-Study Program available. Institutional employment available.

Campus Life

Activities: Campus Ministries; Choral groups; Concert band; Dance; Drama/theater; International Student Organization; Jazz band; Literary magazine; Model UN; Music ensembles; Musical theater; Radio station; Student government; Student newspaper; Student-run film society; Symphony orchestra; Television station; Yearbook. **Organizations:** 108 registered organizations, 21 honor societies, 9 religious organizations. **Athletics (Intercollegiate):** *Men:* baseball, basketball, cross-country, diving, golf, lacrosse, soccer, swimming, tennis. *Women:* basketball, cross-country, diving, golf, lacrosse, soccer, softball, swimming, tennis, volleyball.

ACCOMMODATIONS

Allowed in exams:	
Calculators	Yes
Dictionary	Yes
Computer	Yes
Spell-checker	Yes
Extended test time	Yes
Scribe	Not Applicable
Proctors	Yes
Oral exams	No
Note-takers	Yes
Support services for students with:	
LD	No
ADHD	No
ASD	No
Distraction-reduced environment	Yes
Recording of lecture allowed	Yes
Reading technology	Yes
Audio books	Yes
Other assistive technology	Yes
Priority registration	Yes
Added costs of services:	
For LD	Yes
For ADHD	Yes
For ASD	Yes
LD specialists	No
ADHD & ASD coaching	No
ASD specialists	No
Professional tutors	No
Peer tutors	Yes
Max. hours/week for services	Varies
How professors are notified of student approved accommodations	Student

COLLEGE GRADUATION REQUIREMENTS

Course waivers allowed	No
Course substitutions allowed	Yes
In what courses: Case-by-case basis	

Long Island University Post

720 Northern Blvd., Brookville, NY 11548 • Admissions: 516-299-2900 • Fax: 516-299-2137 **Support: SP**

CAMPUS

Type of school	Private (nonprofit)
Environment	Metropolis

STUDENTS

Undergrad enrollment	6,164
% male/female	33/67
% from out of state	11.6
% frosh live on campus	42

FINANCIAL FACTS

Annual tuition	$37,182
Room and board	$14,664
Required fees	$1,954

GENERAL ADMISSIONS INFO

Application fee	$50
Regular application deadline	Rolling
Nonfall registration	Yes

Admission may be deferred.

Range SAT EBRW	540–640
Range SAT Math	540–650
Range ACT Composite	22–28

ACADEMICS

Student/faculty ratio	12:1
% students returning for sophomore year	75

Most classes have 10–19 students.

Programs/Services for Students with Learning Differences

It is the mission of LIU Post to ensure that students with disabilities have equal access to all aspects of university life. All students who identify as having a disability are encouraged to contact our Learning Support Center, which houses the Academic Resource Program and Disability Support Services, where they will be given information and assistance in deciding whether the services will best meet the individual needs of the student. The Academic Resource Program is a comprehensive, structured, fee-based support program for students who have a learning disability and/or ADHD.

Admissions

For standard admission, students must have a minimum GPA of 2.5. In the past, the school also looked for an SAT score of 1000 or ACT score of 19.

Additional Information

The fee for the Academic Resource Program is $2,000 per semester, which is in addition to the cost for tuition, room and board, and books. Learning assistants help freshmen make the transition from high school to college. They assist all Academic Resource Program students in time management, organizational skills, note-taking techniques, study skills, and other necessary learning strategies. Each student is responsible for his or her attendance and participation in these sessions. Freshmen and sophomores meet with a learning assistant for two hours per week. Students are welcome to schedule more hours if necessary. Juniors and seniors are given the opportunity to schedule and contract more flexible hours with the ARP staff. Auxiliary aids and ancillary services are provided at no charge.

ADMISSIONS INFO FOR STUDENTS WITH LEARNING DIFFERENCES

Phone: 516-299-3057 • Fax: 516-299-2126 • Email: postlearningsupport@liu.edu

SAT/ACT required: No
Interview required: Yes
Essay required: Required
Additional application required: Yes
Documentation submitted to: Disability Support Services

Special Ed. HS course work accepted: Yes
Separate application required for Programs/Services: Yes
Documentation required for:
LD: Psychoeducational evaluation
ADHD: Psychoeducational evaluation
ASD: Psychoeducational evaluation

Long Island University Post

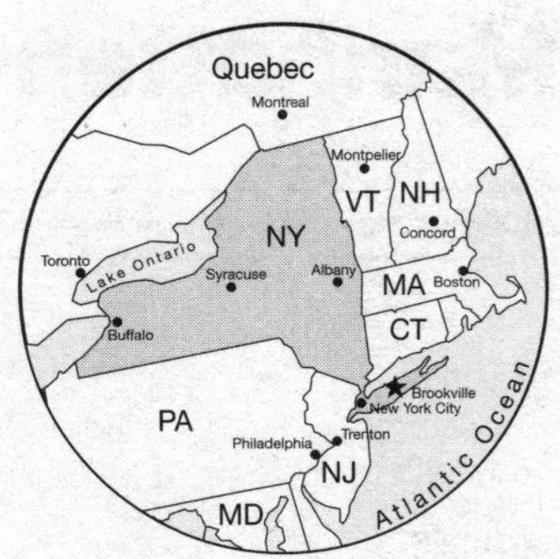

General Admissions

Very Important factors include: rigor of secondary school record, class rank, academic GPA, standardized test scores, talent/ability, character/personal qualities. *Important factors include:* application essay, interview, extracurricular activities, volunteer work. *Other factors include:* recommendation(s), first generation, alumni/ae relation, work experience. High school diploma is required and a GED is accepted. *Academic units recommended:* 4 English, 3 math, 3 science, 3 science labs, 2 foreign language, 4 social studies.

Accommodations or Services

Accommodations are decided upon an individual basis after a thorough review of appropriate, current documentation. The accommodations requests must be supported through the documentation provided and must be logically linked to the current impact of the condition on academic functioning.

Financial Aid

Students should submit: FAFSA; State aid form. *Need-based scholarships/grants offered:* College/university scholarship or grant aid from institutional funds; Federal Pell; Private scholarships; SEOG; State scholarships/grants; United Negro College Fund. *Loan aid offered:* Direct PLUS loans; Direct Subsidized Stafford Loans; Direct Unsubsidized Stafford Loans. Federal Work-Study Program available. Institutional employment available.

Campus Life

Activities: Campus Ministries; Choral groups; Concert band; Dance; Drama/theater; International Student Organization; Jazz band; Literary magazine; Marching band; Model UN; Music ensembles; Musical theater; Pep band; Radio station; Student government; Student newspaper; Student-run film society; Symphony orchestra; Television station; Yearbook. **Organizations:** 68 registered organizations, 20 honor societies, 3 religious organizations, 5 fraternities, 4 sororities. **Athletics (Intercollegiate):** *Men:* baseball, basketball, cross-country, football, soccer, tennis, track/field (outdoor), track/field (indoor), volleyball. *Women:* basketball, cross-country, field hockey, soccer, softball, swimming, tennis, track/field (outdoor), track/field (indoor), volleyball.

ACCOMMODATIONS

Allowed in exams:	
Calculators	Yes
Dictionary	No
Computer	Yes
Spell-checker	Yes
Extended test time	Yes
Scribe	Yes
Proctors	Yes
Oral exams	Yes
Note-takers	Yes
Support services for students with:	
LD	Yes
ADHD	Yes
ASD	Yes
Distraction-reduced environment	Yes
Recording of lecture allowed	Yes
Reading technology	Yes
Audio books	No
Other assistive technology	No
Priority registration	No
Added costs of services:	
For LD	Yes
For ADHD	Yes
For ASD	Yes
LD specialists	Yes
ADHD & ASD coaching	Yes
ASD specialists	No
Professional tutors	No
Peer tutors	Yes
Max. hours/week for services	Varies
How professors are notified of student approved accommodations	Student

COLLEGE GRADUATION REQUIREMENTS

Course waivers allowed	No
Course substitutions allowed	Yes
In what courses: Case-by-case basis	

Manhattanville College

2900 Purchase Street, Purchase, NY 10577 • Admissions: 914-323-5464 • Fax: 914-694-1732 **Support: SP**

CAMPUS	
Type of school	Private (nonprofit)
Environment	Town
STUDENTS	
Undergrad enrollment	1,504
% male/female	42/58
% from out of state	25
% frosh live on campus	63
FINANCIAL FACTS	
Annual tuition	$38,880
Room and board	$14,810
Required fees	$1,450
GENERAL ADMISSIONS INFO	
Application fee	$50
Regular application deadline	Rolling
Nonfall registration	Yes
Admission may be deferred.	
Range SAT EBRW	490–580
Range SAT Math	490–590
Range ACT Composite	19–27
ACADEMICS	
Student/faculty ratio	11:1
% students returning for sophomore year	70
Most classes have 10–19 students.	

Programs/Services for Students with Learning Differences

The Valiant Learning Support Program (VLSP) is a fee-based program designed to assist college-ready students to navigate the academic challenges of the college curriculum. This program offers students customized learning strategy sessions with highly trained, professional. Learning Specialists provide each student enrolled in VSLP with 3 hours of 1:1 academic support on a weekly basis, which may include working with the students on writing skills, reading comprehension skills, executive functioning skills such as time management and prioritization, and study skills. Learning Specialists use the student's own coursework to support students in their efforts to take ownership of their own learning and partner with students to promote self-advocacy and self-determination. The fee for VLSP is $3,600 per semester. PAC Program The Pathways and Connections Program (PAC) is an innovative and comprehensive fee-based program designed to assist college-ready students on the Autism Spectrum. The program focuses on executive functioning skills in the social realm and supports students with transitional skills and integration into the campus community. The PAC Program components include individual, customized meetings with PAC Coordinator, weekly group sessions, peer mentoring, social events—on and off-campus. Students may apply to VLSP and/or PAC after they have been accepted by the College and have made a deposit.

Admissions

The Admissions process is the same for all students. Submitting test scores is optional. A personal essay and two letters of recommendations are required; a personal interview is strongly encouraged and may be required in some cases. Students may apply to VLSP and PAC after they have been admitted to the college and have made a deposit.

Additional Information

The Director of the Center for Student Accommodations will meet individually with each student to talk about what accommodations are most appropriate along with a review of the documentation of disability. Developing the most appropriate accommodations is an ongoing process and accommodations can be changed or adjusted if the need arises. Students at the college level are responsible to self-disclose and initiate the accommodations process.

ADMISSIONS INFO FOR STUDENTS WITH LEARNING DIFFERENCES

Phone: 914-323-7129 • Fax: 914-694-1732 • Email: Alyssa.CampoCarman@mville.edu

SAT/ACT required: No
Interview required: In some cases
Essay required: Yes
Additional application required: No
Documentation submitted to: Center for Student Accommodations

Special Ed. HS course work accepted: Yes
Separate application required for Programs/Services: Yes
Documentation required for:
- **LD:** Psychoeducational evaluation
- **ADHD:** Psychoeducational evaluation
- **ASD:** Psychoeducational evaluation

Manhattanville College

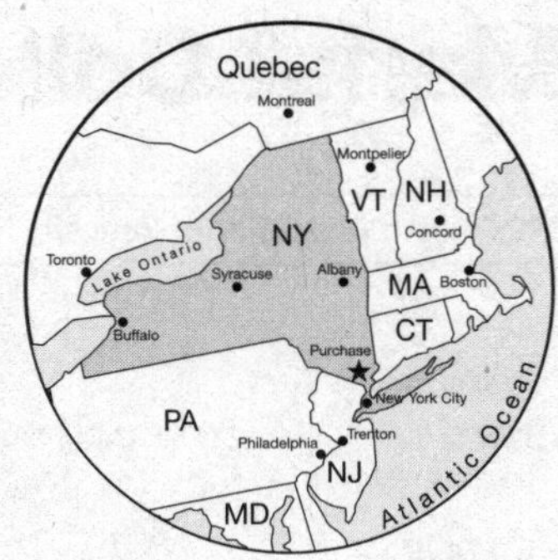

General Admissions

Very Important factors include: rigor of secondary school record, academic GPA, application essay, recommendation(s), extracurricular activities, talent/ability, character/personal qualities, alumni/ae relation, level of applicant's interest. *Important factors include:* geographical residence. *Other factors include:* class rank, standardized test scores, interview, first generation, state residency, work experience. High school diploma is required and a GED is accepted. *Academic units required:* 4 English, 3 math, 2 science, 2 social studies, 5 academic electives.

Accommodations or Services

Accommodations are decided upon an individual basis after a thorough review of appropriate, current documentation. The accommodations requests must be supported through the documentation provided and must be logically linked to the current impact of the condition on academic functioning.

Financial Aid

Students should submit: FAFSA; Institution's own financial aid form;. Applicants will be notified of awards on a rolling basis beginning 5/1. *Need-based scholarships/grants offered:* College/university scholarship or grant aid from institutional funds; Federal Pell; Private scholarships; SEOG; State scholarships/grants; United Negro College Fund. *Loan aid offered:* Direct PLUS loans; Direct Subsidized Stafford Loans; Direct Unsubsidized Stafford Loans. Federal Work-Study Program available. Institutional employment available.

Campus Life

Activities: Campus Ministries; Choral groups; Concert band; Dance; Drama/theater; International Student Organization; Jazz band; Literary magazine; Model UN; Music ensembles; Musical theater; Opera; Radio station; Student government; Student newspaper; Student-run film society. **Organizations:** 50 registered organizations, 3 honor societies, 4 religious organizations. **Athletics (Intercollegiate):** *Men:* baseball, basketball, golf, ice hockey, lacrosse, soccer, tennis. *Women:* basketball, cheerleading, field hockey, ice hockey, lacrosse, soccer, softball, tennis, volleyball.

ACCOMMODATIONS

Allowed in exams:	
Calculators	Yes
Dictionary	No
Computer	Yes
Spell-checker	Yes
Extended test time	Yes
Scribe	Yes
Proctors	Yes
Oral exams	Yes
Note-takers	Yes
Support services for students with:	
LD	Yes
ADHD	Yes
ASD	Yes
Distraction-reduced environment	Yes
Recording of lecture allowed	Yes
Reading technology	Yes
Audio books	Yes
Other assistive technology	Yes
Priority registration	No
Added costs of services:	
For LD	Yes
For ADHD	Yes
For ASD	Yes
LD specialists	Yes
ADHD & ASD coaching	Yes
ASD specialists	No
Professional tutors	Yes
Peer tutors	Yes
Max. hours/week for services	Varies
How professors are notified of student approved accommodations	Student

COLLEGE GRADUATION REQUIREMENTS

Course waivers allowed	No
Course substitutions allowed	Yes
In what courses: Case-by-case basis	

Marist College

3399 North Road, Poughkeepsie, NY 12601-1387 • Admissions: 845-575-3226 • Fax: 845-575-3215 **Support: SP**

CAMPUS

Type of school	Private (nonprofit)
Environment	Town

STUDENTS

Undergrad enrollment	5,460
% male/female	42/58
% from out of state	48
% frosh live on campus	98

FINANCIAL FACTS

Annual tuition	$42,430
Room and board	$16,380

GENERAL ADMISSIONS INFO

Application fee	$50
Regular application deadline	2/1
Nonfall registration	Yes

Admission may be deferred.

Range SAT EBRW	580–660
Range SAT Math	580–670
Range ACT Composite	25–30

ACADEMICS

Student/faculty ratio	16:1
% students returning for sophomore year	88

Most classes have 20–29 students.

Programs/Services for Students with Learning Differences

The Learning Support Program provides a complement of academic services that are designed to meet the individual needs of students. The Program focuses on the development and use of strategies that will promote independence and personal success. Students are expected to serve as their own advocates in a continually increasing fashion. Students are enrolled in credit-bearing courses and complete degree requirements required by all students. Learning Disability Specialists work closely with faculty and administration to assist the students. Each individual is encouraged to openly discuss his or her learning needs with appropriate faculty at the start of the semester. Specialists frequently assist students in preparation for this meeting. Participation in the Program is available to students on a continual basis for as long as the Specialist and student mutually agree is necessary. Students are expected to assume increasingly higher levels of responsibility for their academic success and to function independently as soon as possible beyond the freshman year. The Learning Support Program is a fee-based program.

Admissions

Students wishing to participate in the Learning Disabilities Support Program must apply to Marist College by submitting a regular application to the Undergraduate Admissions Office. In addition, a separate Application for the Learning Disabilities Support Program must be completed.

Additional Information

The Program emphasizes the development of compensatory strategies. Each student is assigned to work one-on-one with a Learning Specialist. Freshmen meet with the Specialist twice a week. The goals of each session are individualized and typical sessions concentrate on Improving skills in writing, note taking, organization, time management, and test-taking strategies. The Specialist establishes a plan for necessary and appropriate academic accommodations. Students who are a good fit for the Program typically possess a knowledge and acceptance of their learning disability, ADD, or ADHD, a willingness to accept assistance and access support, an ability to independently implement strategies taught in sessions, self-motivation a desire to participate in the Program, and sound study skills and work habits. There is a fee for the program. There is no charge for students with documentation who are not in the program and are just requesting reasonable accommodations.

ADMISSIONS INFO FOR STUDENTS WITH LEARNING DIFFERENCES

Phone: 845-575-3000 • Fax: 845.575.3011 • Email: accommodations@marist.edu

SAT/ACT required: No
Interview required: Yes
Essay required: Yes
Additional application required: No
Documentation submitted to: Office of Accommodations and Accessibility

Special Ed. HS course work accepted: Yes
Separate application required for Programs/Services: Yes
Documentation required for:
LD: Psychoeducational evaluation
ADHD: Psychoeducational evaluation
ASD: Psychoeducational evaluation

Marist College

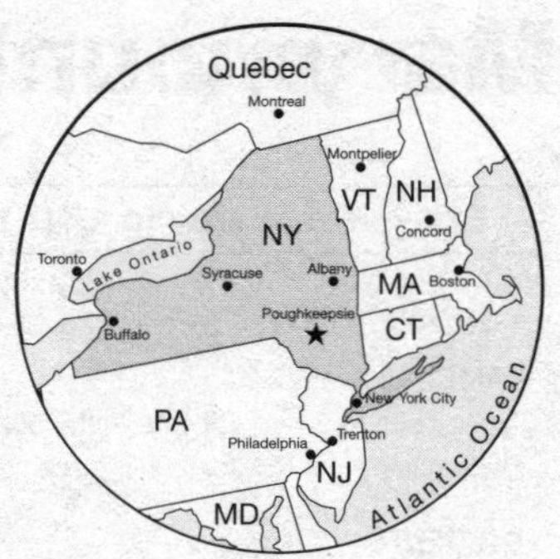

General Admissions

Very Important factors include: rigor of secondary school record, academic GPA. *Important factors include:* class rank, application essay, recommendation(s), extracurricular activities, talent/ability, character/personal qualities, geographical residence, state residency, volunteer work. *Other factors include:* standardized test scores, first generation, alumni/ae relation, racial/ethnic status, level of applicant's interest. High school diploma is required and a GED is accepted. *Academic units required:* 4 English, 3 math, 3 science, 2 science labs, 2 foreign language, 2 social studies, 1 history, 2 academic electives. *Academic units recommended:* 4 math, 4 science, 3 science labs, 3 foreign language.

Accommodations or Services

Accommodations are decided upon an individual basis after a thorough review of appropriate, current documentation. The accommodations requests must be supported through the documentation provided and must be logically linked to the current impact of the condition on academic functioning.

Financial Aid

Students should submit: FAFSA. *Need-based scholarships/grants offered:* College/university scholarship or grant aid from institutional funds; Federal Pell; Private scholarships; SEOG; State scholarships/grants. *Loan aid offered:* Direct PLUS loans; Direct Subsidized Stafford Loans; Direct Unsubsidized Stafford Loans. Federal Work-Study Program available. Institutional employment available.

Campus Life

Activities: Campus Ministries; Choral groups; Concert band; Dance; Drama/theater; International Student Organization; Jazz band; Literary magazine; Marching band; Model UN; Music ensembles; Musical theater; Pep band; Radio station; Student government; Student newspaper; Symphony orchestra; Television station. **Organizations:** 81 registered organizations, 20 honor societies, 5 religious organizations, 3 fraternities, 4 sororities. **Athletics (Intercollegiate):** *Men:* baseball, basketball, crew/rowing, cross-country, diving, football, lacrosse, soccer, swimming, tennis, track/field (outdoor). *Women:* basketball, crew/rowing, cross-country, diving, lacrosse, soccer, softball, swimming, tennis, track/field (outdoor), volleyball, water polo.

ACCOMMODATIONS	
Allowed in exams:	
Calculators	Yes
Dictionary	No
Computer	Yes
Spell-checker	No
Extended test time	Yes
Scribe	Yes
Proctors	Yes
Oral exams	No
Note-takers	Yes
Support services for students with:	
LD	Yes
ADHD	Yes
ASD	Yes
Distraction-reduced environment	Yes
Recording of lecture allowed	Yes
Reading technology	Yes
Audio books	Yes
Other assistive technology	Yes
Priority registration	No
Added costs of services:	
For LD	Yes
For ADHD	Yes
For ASD	Yes
LD specialists	Yes
ADHD & ASD coaching	No
ASD specialists	No
Professional tutors	No
Peer tutors	Yes
Max. hours/week for services	Varies
How professors are notified of student approved accommodations	Student

COLLEGE GRADUATION REQUIREMENTS	
Course waivers allowed	No
Course substitutions allowed	No

Marymount Manhattan College

221 East 71 Street, New York, NY 10021 • Admissions: 212-517-0430 • Fax: 212-517-0448 **Support: SP**

CAMPUS

Type of school	Private (nonprofit)
Environment	Metropolis

STUDENTS

Undergrad enrollment	1,892
% male/female	21/79
% from out of state	72
% frosh live on campus	79

FINANCIAL FACTS

Annual tuition	$ 35,680
Room and board	$ 18,894
Required fees	$1,730

GENERAL ADMISSIONS INFO

Application fee	$60
Regular application deadline	Rolling
Nonfall registration	Yes

Admission may be deferred.

Range SAT EBRW	510–620
Range SAT Math	470–580
Range ACT Composite	20–27

ACADEMICS

Student/faculty ratio	11:1
% students returning for sophomore year	69

Most classes have 10–19 students.

Programs/Services for Students with Learning Differences

The Academic Access Program includes a full range of support services that center on academic and personal growth for students with learning disabilities. Students who have been admitted to the full-time program are required to demonstrate commitment to overcoming learning difficulties through regular attendance and tutoring. Academic advisement and counseling is provided to assist in developing a program plan suited to individual needs. The college is looking for highly motivated students with a commitment to compensate for their learning disabilities and to fully participate in the tutoring program. Once admitted into the program, students receive a program plan suited to their needs, based on a careful examination of the psychoeducational evaluations. Full time students sign a contract to regularly attend tutoring provided by professionals experienced within the field of LD. In addition to assisting students in the development of skills and strategies for their coursework, LD specialists coach participants in the attitudes and behavior necessary for college success. Professors assist learning specialists in carefully monitoring students' progress throughout the academic year and arranging for accommodations. This is a fee-based program.

Admissions

Admission to Marymount Manhattan College's Program for Academic Access is based on a diagnosis of dyslexia, ADHD, or other primary learning disability; intellectual potential within the average to superior range; and a serious commitment in attitude and work habits to meeting the program and college academic requirements. Prospective students are required to submit the following: high school transcript or GED. Students are expected to have college prep courses in high school but foreign language is not required for admission; ACT or SAT are required; results of a recent complete Psychoeducational evaluation; letters of recommendation from teachers, tutors, or counselors; and have a personal interview. Students may be admitted to the college through the Program for Academic Access. Students interested in being considered for admission through the program must self-disclose their LD/ADHD in a personal statement with the application. There is no fixed deadline for the application, however, there are a limited number of slots available. Completed files received by mid-January are at an advantage to be eligible for selection.

ADMISSIONS INFO FOR STUDENTS WITH LEARNING DIFFERENCES

Phone: 212-774-0724 • Fax: 212-774-4875 • Email: dnash@mmm.edu

SAT/ACT required: Yes (Test optional for Fall 2021)
Interview required: Yes
Essay required: Yes
Additional application required: No
Documentation submitted to: Academic Access and Disability Services

Special Ed. HS course work accepted: Yes
Separate application required for Programs/Services: No
Documentation required for:
LD: Psychoeducational evaluation
ADHD: Psychoeducational evaluation
ASD: Psychoeducational evaluation

Marymount Manhattan College

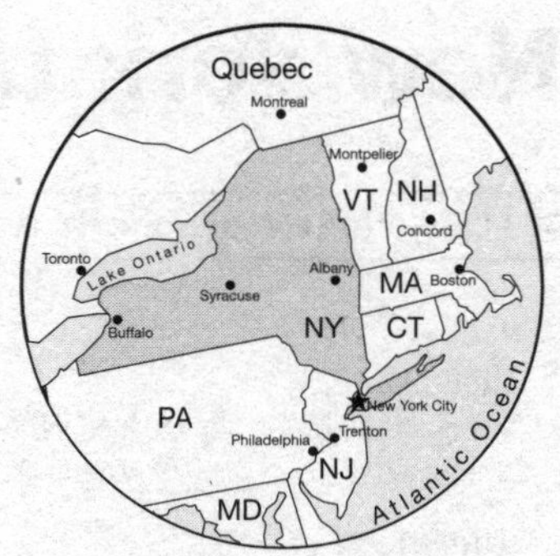

Additional Information

LD professionals associated with the program. Students have access to two hours of tutoring per week with a learning specialist, drop-in tutoring, and monthly parent meetings. Classes are offered in study skills, reading, and vocabulary development. Workshops are provided to help with overcoming procrastination, and to help with effectiveness. The Academic Access Program is fee based—$3,000 per semester.

General Admissions

Very Important factors include: rigor of secondary school record, academic GPA, standardized test scores. *Important factors include:* application essay, recommendation(s), talent/ability, character/personal qualities. *Other factors include:* interview, extracurricular activities, first generation, alumni/ae relation, geographical residence, state residency, volunteer work, work experience. High school diploma is required and a GED is accepted. *Academic units required:* 4 English, 3 math, 3 science, 3 social studies, 4 academic electives. *Academic units recommended:* 2 science labs, 2 foreign language.

Accommodations or Services

Accommodations are decided upon an individual basis after a thorough review of appropriate, current documentation. The accommodations requests must be supported through the documentation provided and must be logically linked to the current impact of the condition on academic functioning.

Financial Aid

Students should submit: FAFSA. *Need-based scholarships/grants offered:* College/university scholarship or grant aid from institutional funds; Federal Pell; Private scholarships; SEOG; State scholarships/grants. *Loan aid offered:* Direct PLUS loans; Direct Subsidized Stafford Loans; Direct Unsubsidized Stafford Loans. Federal Work-Study Program available. Institutional employment available.

Campus Life

Activities: Campus Ministries; Choral groups; Dance; Drama/theater; International Student Organization; Musical theater; Radio station; Student government; Student newspaper; Yearbook. **Organizations:** 3 religious organizations.

ACCOMMODATIONS	
Allowed in exams:	
Calculators	Yes
Dictionary	Yes
Computer	Yes
Spell-checker	Yes
Extended test time	Yes
Scribe	Yes
Proctors	Yes
Oral exams	Yes
Note-takers	Yes
Support services for students with:	
LD	Yes
ADHD	Yes
ASD	Yes
Distraction-reduced environment	Yes
Recording of lecture allowed	Yes
Reading technology	Yes
Audio books	Yes
Other assistive technology	Yes
Priority registration	Yes
Added costs of services:	
For LD	Yes
For ADHD	Yes
For ASD	Yes
LD specialists	Yes
ADHD & ASD coaching	Yes
ASD specialists	No
Professional tutors	Yes
Peer tutors	Yes
Max. hours/week for services	2
How professors are notified of student approved accommodations	Student

COLLEGE GRADUATION REQUIREMENTS	
Course waivers allowed	No
Course substitutions allowed	No

New York University

383 Lafayette St., New York, NY 10012 • Admissions: 212-998-4500 • Fax: 212-995-4902 **Support: CS**

CAMPUS

Type of school	Private (nonprofit)
Environment	Metropolis

STUDENTS

Undergrad enrollment	26,612
% male/female	42/58
% from out of state	67
% frosh live on campus	89

FINANCIAL FACTS

Annual tuition	$52,206
Room and board	$19,244
Required fees	$2,676

GENERAL ADMISSIONS INFO

Application fee	$80
Regular application deadline	1/1
Nonfall registration	Yes

Admission may be deferred.

Range SAT EBRW	660–740
Range SAT Math	690–790
Range ACT Composite	30–34

ACADEMICS

Student/faculty ratio	9:1
% students returning for sophomore year	94

Most classes have 10–19 students.

Programs/Services for Students with Learning Differences

The Henry and Lucy Moses Center for Students with Disabilities (CSD) works with students with a documented disability or disabilities who register with the office to obtain appropriate accommodations and services. This process is designed to encourage independence, backed by a strong system of support. Each student who is approved through CSD works with a staff specialist to develop an individualized and reasonable accommodation plan. Reasonable accommodations are adjustments to policy, practice, and programs that "level the playing field" for students with disabilities and provide equal access to NYU's programs and activities. Accommodation plans and other related services are based on each student's disability documentation and NYU program requirements and are therefore determined on a case-by-case basis.

Admissions

There is no special application process for students with disabilities applying to NYU, although a student may voluntarily disclose their disability during the admissions process. Disclosing a disability has no impact on the admissions decision. Applicants to programs in Steinhardt School of Culture, Education, and Human Development and our Tisch School of the Arts, which requires an audition or portfolio, are not required to submit ACT/SAT for consideration and doing so is entirely optional. For other programs, NYU has a flexible testing policy, and applicants can submit one of the following: SAT or ACT (no essay test required), 3 SAT Subject Tests, 3 AP Exams, International Baccalaureate (IB) Diploma, 3 IB higher-level exam scores if not an IB Diploma candidate, or certain international qualifications showing completion of a secondary education.

Additional Information

Once students submit an application for accommodations, they will be contacted by a Disability Specialist within 2–3 business days to set up a meeting to discuss appropriate and reasonable accommodations. The University Learning Centers provide free individual and group review sessions for specific courses as well as academic coaching and skills workshops. The Moses Center annually provides a limited number of tuition awards made possible by grant funding to registered students with disabilities based on applicant's financial need, severity of disability, and academic qualifications.

ADMISSIONS INFO FOR STUDENTS WITH LEARNING DIFFERENCES

Phone: 212-998-4980 • Fax: 212-995-4114 • Email: mosescsa@nyu.edu

SAT/ACT required: Yes (Test optional for 2021)
Interview required: No
Essay required: Yes
Additional application required: No
Documentation submitted to: Moses Center for Students with Disabilities

Special Ed. HS course work accepted: Yes
Separate application required for Programs/Services: No
Documentation required for:
LD: Psychoeducational evaluation
ADHD: Psychoeducational evaluation
ASD: Psychoeducational evaluation

New York University

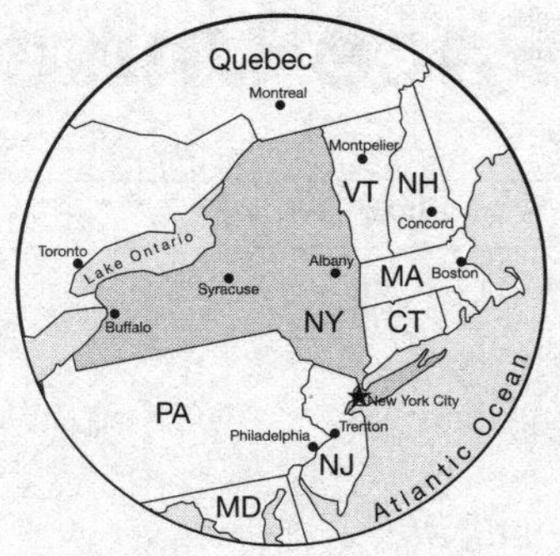

General Admissions

Very Important factors include: rigor of secondary school record, class rank, academic GPA, standardized test scores, talent/ability. *Important factors include:* application essay, recommendation(s), extracurricular activities, character/personal qualities. *Other factors include:* interview, first generation, alumni/ae relation, geographical residence, racial/ethnic status, volunteer work, work experience, level of applicant's interest. High school diploma is required and a GED is accepted. *Academic units required:* 4 English, 3 math, 3 science, 3 science labs, 3 foreign language, 3 social studies, 3 history. *Academic units recommended:* 4 English, 4 math, 4 science, 4 science labs, 4 foreign language, 4 social studies, 4 history.

Accommodations or Services

Accommodations are decided upon an individual basis after a thorough review of appropriate, current documentation. The accommodations requests must be supported through the documentation provided and must be logically linked to the current impact of the condition on academic functioning.

Financial Aid

Students should submit: CSS/Financial Aid PROFILE; FAFSA; Noncustodial PROFILE. *Need-based scholarships/grants offered:* College/university scholarship or grant aid from institutional funds; Federal Nursing Scholarships; Federal Pell; Private scholarships; SEOG; State scholarships/grants. *Loan aid offered:* Direct PLUS loans; Direct Subsidized Stafford Loans; Direct Unsubsidized Stafford Loans. Federal Work-Study Program available. Institutional employment available.

Campus Life

Activities: Campus Ministries; Choral groups; Concert band; Dance; Drama/theater; International Student Organization; Jazz band; Literary magazine; Model UN; Music ensembles; Musical theater; Opera; Pep band; Radio station; Student government; Student newspaper; Student-run film society; Symphony orchestra; Television station; Yearbook. **Organizations:** 609 registered organizations, 14 honor societies, 41 religious organizations, 23 fraternities, 14 sororities. **Athletics (Intercollegiate):** *Men:* basketball, cross-country, diving, fencing, golf, soccer, swimming, tennis, track/field (outdoor), track/field (indoor), volleyball, wrestling. *Women:* basketball, cross-country, diving, fencing, golf, soccer, swimming, tennis, track/field (outdoor), track/field (indoor), volleyball.

ACCOMMODATIONS

Allowed in exams:	
Calculators	Yes
Dictionary	Yes
Computer	Yes
Spell-checker	Yes
Extended test time	Yes
Scribe	Yes
Proctors	Yes
Oral exams	No
Note-takers	Yes
Support services for students with:	
LD	Yes
ADHD	Yes
ASD	Yes
Distraction-reduced environment	Yes
Recording of lecture allowed	Yes
Reading technology	Yes
Audio books	No
Other assistive technology	Yes
Priority registration	Yes
Added costs of services:	
For LD	No
For ADHD	No
For ASD	No
LD specialists	Yes
ADHD & ASD coaching	No
ASD specialists	No
Professional tutors	Yes
Peer tutors	Yes
Max. hours/week for services	Varies
How professors are notified of student approved accommodations	Student

COLLEGE GRADUATION REQUIREMENTS

Course waivers allowed	No
Course substitutions allowed	Yes
In what courses: Case-by-case basis	

Pace University

1 Pace Plaza, New York, NY 10038 • Admissions: 212-346-1323 • Fax: 212-346-1040 **Support: SP**

CAMPUS	
Type of school	Private (nonprofit)
Environment	Metropolis
STUDENTS	
Undergrad enrollment	8,238
% male/female	38/62
% from out of state	46
% frosh live on campus	73
FINANCIAL FACTS	
Annual tuition	$45,832
Room and board	$20,146
Required fees	$1,852
GENERAL ADMISSIONS INFO	
Application fee	$50
Regular application deadline	2/1
Nonfall registration	Yes
Admission may be deferred.	
Range SAT EBRW	530–620
Range SAT Math	520–610
Range ACT Composite	21–27
ACADEMICS	
Student/faculty ratio	14:1
% students returning for sophomore year	78
Most classes have 10–19 students.	

Programs/Services for Students with Learning Differences

The OASIS Program, a comprehensive fee-for-service support program for students with autism, Asperger Syndrome, learning disabilities, nonverbal learning differences, and related challenges. Accommodations in courses are provided. However, the work is not modified, and Oasis students learn alongside their peers in an academically rigorous setting. Students participating in OASIS receive the following support services: daily meetings with an academic coach to assist with organization and management of their studies; an education coordinator to assist with course selection/ registration; housing coordinator to help students navigate residential life; a social coach to assist with the "social literacy" course; a social coordinator to assist students as they integrate into the social activities within the wider college community.

Admissions

The same rigorous admission and academic standards apply to students with and without a disability. For students applying to OASIS, submitting test scores is optional.

Additional Information

To request an accommodation for a disability, a student must self-identify and register with the Student Accessibility Services Office for his or her campus. The student will be responsible for providing documentation and meeting with a member of the Student Accessibility Services Office staff to discuss their accommodation requests and be oriented to office policies and procedures for accessing accommodations. The OASIS program has a separate application process. Applicants for OASIS go through a special admissions process in which they are evaluated by the admissions team during a personal interview.

ADMISSIONS INFO FOR STUDENTS WITH LEARNING DIFFERENCES

Phone: 212-346-1526 • Fax: 914-773-3639 • Email: jsaccoccio@pace.edu

SAT/ACT required: No (for most programs)
Interview required: No
Essay required: Yes
Additional application required: No
Documentation submitted to: Student Accessibility Services

Special Ed. HS course work accepted: Yes
Separate application required for Programs/Services: Yes
Documentation required for:
LD: Psychoeducational evaluation
ADHD: Psychoeducational evaluation
ASD: Psychoeducational evaluation

Pace University

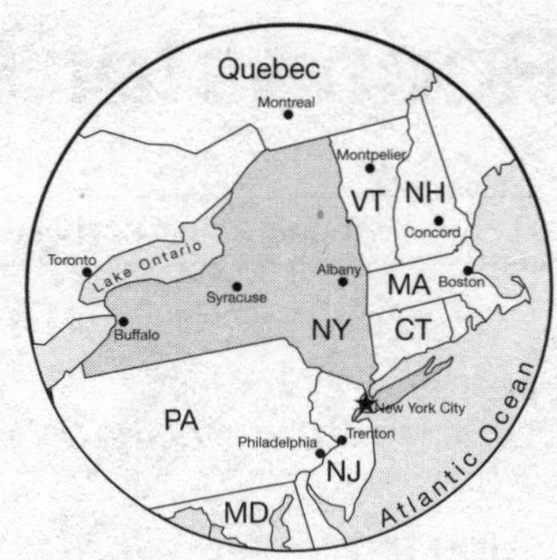

General Admissions

Very Important factors include: rigor of secondary school record, application essay, standardized test scores. *Important factors include:* class rank, academic GPA, recommendation(s). *Other factors include:* interview, extracurricular activities, talent/ability, character/personal qualities, alumni/ae relation, volunteer work, work experience. High school diploma is required and a GED is accepted. *Academic units required:* 4 English, 3 math, 2 science labs, 2 foreign language, 3 history, 2 academic electives.

Accommodations or Services

Accommodations are decided upon an individual basis after a thorough review of appropriate, current documentation. The accommodations requests must be supported through the documentation provided and must be logically linked to the current impact of the condition on academic functioning.

Financial Aid

Students should submit: FAFSA. Applicants will be notified of awards on a rolling basis beginning 1/20. *Need-based scholarships/grants offered:* College/university scholarship or grant aid from institutional funds; Federal Nursing Scholarships; Federal Pell; Private scholarships; SEOG; State scholarships/grants. *Loan aid offered:* Direct PLUS loans; Direct Subsidized Stafford Loans; Direct Unsubsidized Stafford Loans. Federal Work-Study Program available. Institutional employment available.

Campus Life

Activities: Choral groups; Dance; Drama/theater; International Student Organization; Literary magazine; Model UN; Musical theater; Radio station; Student government; Student newspaper; Student-run film society; Television station; Yearbook. **Organizations:** 196 registered organizations, 34 honor societies, 3 religious organizations, 10 fraternities, 11 sororities. **Athletics (Intercollegiate):** *Men:* baseball, basketball, cross-country, football, golf, lacrosse, swimming, tennis, track/field (outdoor), track/field (indoor). *Women:* basketball, cheerleading, cross-country, equestrian sports, soccer, softball, swimming, tennis, track/field (outdoor), track/field (indoor), volleyball.

ACCOMMODATIONS

Allowed in exams:	
Calculators	Yes
Dictionary	Yes
Computer	Yes
Spell-checker	Yes
Extended test time	Yes
Scribe	Yes
Proctors	Yes
Oral exams	Yes
Note-takers	Yes
Support services for students with:	
LD	Yes
ADHD	Yes
ASD	Yes
Distraction-reduced environment	Yes
Recording of lecture allowed	Yes
Reading technology	Yes
Audio books	Yes
Other assistive technology	Yes
Priority registration	Yes
Added costs of services:	
For LD	Yes
For ADHD	Yes
For ASD	Yes
LD specialists	Yes
ADHD & ASD coaching	Yes
ASD specialists	Yes
Professional tutors	No
Peer tutors	Yes
Max. hours/week for services	Varies
How professors are notified of student approved accommodations	Student

COLLEGE GRADUATION REQUIREMENTS

Course waivers allowed	Yes
In what courses: Determined on a case-by-case basis	
Course substitutions allowed	Yes
In what courses: Determined on a case-by-case basis	

Rochester Institute of Technology

60 Lomb Memorial Drive, Rochester, NY 14623-5604 • Admissions: 585-475-6631 • Fax: 585-475-7424 **Support: SP**

CAMPUS

Type of school	Private (nonprofit)
Environment	City

STUDENTS

Undergrad enrollment	12,623
% male/female	67/33
% from out of state	48
% frosh live on campus	96

FINANCIAL FACTS

Annual tuition	$ 50,564
Room and board	$13,976
Required fees	$676

GENERAL ADMISSIONS INFO

Application fee	$65
Regular application deadline	1/15
Nonfall registration	Yes

Admission may be deferred.

Range SAT EBRW	600–690
Range SAT Math	620–720
Range ACT Composite	27–32

ACADEMICS

Student/faculty ratio	13:1
% students returning for sophomore year	89

Most classes have 10–19 students.

Programs/Services for Students with Learning Differences

The Spectrum Support Program provides innovative supports that positively impact the college experience for RIT students, particularly those with Autism Spectrum Disorders. RIT is committed to helping students build connections that will assist them in achieving academic, social, and career success. The program seeks to create a campus culture of acceptance and support through collaboration, consultation, and training. Enrollment in the Spectrum Support Program has increased since its inception and averages 30 new incoming students each fall. The Program provides services to incoming freshmen and continues to provide support even as students transition out of RIT. In addition the RIT Disability Services Office provides reasonable accommodations to students with LD, ADHD, and other health-related disabilities.

Admissions

Most students applying to RIT choose a specific major as part of the admission process. In addition, all colleges offer undeclared options and the University Studies program is available to applicants with interests in two or more colleges. Admission requirements and entrance exam score ranges vary from one major to another. Applicants for the Spectrum Support Program (SSP) must meet all the academic requirements of admission to RIT and be matriculated into an undergraduate program. A Pre-baccalaureate Studies Option is also available for students who may need additional preparation before entering a bachelor's degree program.

Additional Information

SSP does not require specific documentation of an Autism Spectrum Disorder as a condition of enrollment in SSP, however, students should identify as a member of the community of students on the autism spectrum at RIT. The Spectrum Support Program provides support in academic skills, social competence, self-care, self-advocacy, and executive functioning. Support is provided through one on one coaching, small group seminars, social events, and collaboration with cross-campus partners. There is a different fee structure for students who are entering freshmen and students continuing after freshmen year and depends on sessions once or twice a week or twice monthly. A pre-orientation program is offered three-days prior to fall New Student Orientation and assists program enrolled students in transitioning to RIT. Separate registration and fees apply.

ADMISSIONS INFO FOR STUDENTS WITH LEARNING DIFFERENCES

Phone: 585-475-6988 • Fax: 585-475-2915 • Email: dso@rit.edu

SAT/ACT required: No
Interview required: No
Essay required: Yes
Additional application required: No
Documentation submitted to: Disability Services Office

Special Ed. HS course work accepted: Yes
Separate application required for Programs/Services: No
Documentation required for:
LD: Psychoeducational evaluation
ADHD: Psychoeducational evaluation
ASD: Psychoeducational evaluation

Rochester Institute of Technology

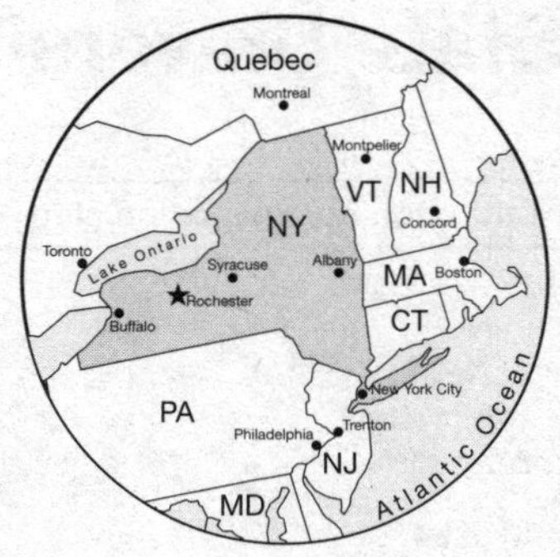

General Admissions

Very Important factors include: rigor of secondary school record, academic GPA. *Important factors include:* class rank, standardized test scores. *Other factors include:* application essay, recommendation(s), interview, extracurricular activities, talent/ability, character/personal qualities, first generation, alumni/ae relation, geographical residence, racial/ethnic status, volunteer work, work experience, level of applicant's interest. High school diploma is required and a GED is accepted. *Academic units required:* 4 English, 2 math, 2 science, 1 science lab, 4 social studies, 10 academic electives. *Academic units recommended:* 4 English, 3 math, 3 science, 2 science labs, 3 foreign language, 4 social studies, 5 academic electives.

Accommodations or Services

Accommodations are decided upon an individual basis after a thorough review of appropriate, current documentation. The accommodations requests must be supported through the documentation provided and must be logically linked to the current impact of the condition on academic functioning.

Financial Aid

Students should submit: FAFSA. Applicants will be notified of awards on a rolling basis beginning 2/1. *Need-based scholarships/grants offered:* College/university scholarship or grant aid from institutional funds; Federal Pell; Private scholarships; SEOG; State scholarships/grants. *Loan aid offered:* Direct PLUS loans; Direct Subsidized Stafford Loans; Direct Unsubsidized Stafford Loans. Federal Work-Study Program available. Institutional employment available.

Campus Life

Activities: Campus Ministries; Choral groups; Concert band; Dance; Drama/theater; International Student Organization; Jazz band; Literary magazine; Music ensembles; Musical theater; Pep band; Radio station; Student government; Student newspaper; Student-run film society; Symphony orchestra; Yearbook. **Organizations:** 300 registered organizations, 9 honor societies, 10 religious organizations, 19 fraternities, 10 sororities. **Athletics (Intercollegiate):** *Men:* baseball, basketball, crew/rowing, cross-country, diving, ice hockey, lacrosse, soccer, swimming, tennis, track/field (outdoor), track/field (indoor), wrestling. *Women:* basketball, cheerleading, crew/rowing, cross-country, diving, ice hockey, lacrosse, soccer, softball, swimming, tennis, track/field (outdoor), track/field (indoor), volleyball.

ACCOMMODATIONS

Allowed in exams:	
Calculators	Yes
Dictionary	Yes
Computer	Yes
Spell-checker	Yes
Extended test time	Yes
Scribe	Yes
Proctors	Yes
Oral exams	Yes
Note-takers	Yes
Support services for students with:	
LD	Yes
ADHD	Yes
ASD	Yes
Distraction-reduced environment	Yes
Recording of lecture allowed	Yes
Reading technology	Yes
Audio books	Yes
Other assistive technology	Yes
Priority registration	Yes
Added costs of services:	
For LD	No
For ADHD	No
For ASD	No
LD specialists	Yes
ADHD & ASD coaching	Yes
ASD specialists	Yes
Professional tutors	No
Peer tutors	Yes
Max. hours/week for services	Varies
How professors are notified of student approved accommodations	Director

COLLEGE GRADUATION REQUIREMENTS

Course waivers allowed	No
Course substitutions allowed	No

State University of New York—Alfred State College

Huntington Administration Bldg., Alfred, NY 14802 • Admissions: 607-587-4215 • Fax: 607-587-4299 **Support: CS**

CAMPUS

Type of school	Public
Environment	Rural

STUDENTS

Undergrad enrollment	3,760
% male/female	63/37
% from out of state	4
% frosh live on campus	79

FINANCIAL FACTS

Annual in-state tuition	$7,070
Annual out-of-state tuition	$11,040
Room and board	$13,060
Required fees	$1,782

GENERAL ADMISSIONS INFO

Application fee	$50
Regular application deadline	Rolling
Nonfall registration	Yes

Admission may be deferred.

Range SAT EBRW	470–580
Range SAT Math	470–590
Range ACT Composite	18–25

ACADEMICS

Student/faculty ratio	18:1
% students returning for sophomore year	78

Most classes have 10–19 students.

Programs/Services for Students with Learning Differences

Alfred State welcomes all students who meet admissions criteria, regardless of disability status. Students with documented disabilities are highly encouraged to self-disclose and submit appropriate documentation to the Office of Accessibility Services (OAS). Appropriate documentation includes Psychological Evaluations and/or medical documentation. IEP's are not accepted as a stand-alone document to determine eligibility for services. Appropriate accommodations are determined on an individual basis and are based upon the submitted documentation and subsequent discussion with the student. The coordinator/counselor of Accessibility Services meets with the student to determine which support services can further the student's academic success. The Student Success Center offers tutoring by peer and professional tutors.

Admissions

Admissions criteria do not vary regardless of a documented learning difference. Assistance is available for those students who need it, upon request.

Additional Information

The Educational Opportunity Program (EOP) and Alfred State Opportunity Program (ASOP) offer opportunities to high school graduates or the equivalent who do not meet normally applied admission criteria, but who have the potential for college success. The ASOP is considered an extended program, which means students might take an additional year to complete degree requirements. This Associates Degree program allows those students to enter directly in the baccalaureate degree program. A student can take a lighter course load and be given other support services. The EOP is also an extended program with courses that are paced to accommodate student success. Students study full-time, participating in regular tutoring and academic advising.

ADMISSIONS INFO FOR STUDENTS WITH LEARNING DIFFERENCES

Phone: 607-587-4506 • Fax: 607-587-4298 • Email: ryanma@alfredstate.edu

SAT/ACT required: Yes (Test optional for 2021)
Interview required: No
Essay required: Recommended
Additional application required: No
Documentation submitted to: OAS

Special Ed. HS course work accepted: Yes
Separate application required for Programs/Services: No
Documentation required for:
LD: Psychoeducational evaluation
ADHD: Psychoeducational evaluation and/or medical documentation outlining functional limitations of student
ASD: Psychoeducational evaluation and/or medical documentation outlining functional limitations of student

State University of New York— Alfred State College

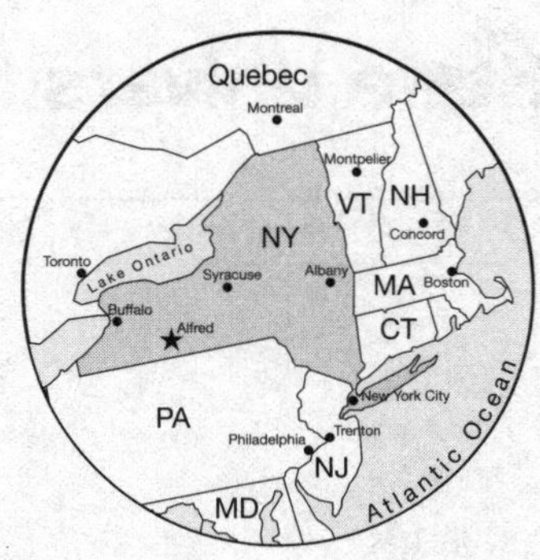

General Admissions

Very Important factors include: rigor of secondary school record, academic GPA, standardized test scores. *Other factors include:* application essay, recommendation(s), interview, extracurricular activities, talent/ability, character/personal qualities, volunteer work, work experience, level of applicant's interest. High school diploma is required and a GED is accepted.

Accommodations or Services

Accommodations are decided upon an individual basis after a thorough review of appropriate, current documentation. The accommodations requests must be supported through the documentation provided and must be logically linked to the current impact of the condition on academic functioning.

Financial Aid

Students should submit: FAFSA; Institution's own financial aid form. Applicants will be notified of awards on a rolling basis beginning 3/15. *Need-based scholarships/grants offered:* College/university scholarship or grant aid from institutional funds; Federal Pell; Private scholarships; SEOG; State scholarships/grants. *Loan aid offered:* Direct PLUS loans; Direct Subsidized Stafford Loans; Direct Unsubsidized Stafford Loans. Federal Work-Study Program available. Institutional employment available.

Campus Life

Activities: Campus Ministries; Choral groups; Concert band; Dance; Drama/theater; International Student Organization; Jazz band; Literary magazine; Music ensembles; Musical theater; Pep band; Radio station; Student government; Student newspaper; Symphony orchestra; Yearbook. **Organizations:** 125 registered organizations, 5 honor societies, 4 religious organizations, 6 fraternities, 6 sororities. **Athletics (Intercollegiate):** *Men:* baseball, basketball, cheerleading, cross-country, football, lacrosse, soccer, swimming, track/field (outdoor), wrestling. *Women:* basketball, cheerleading, cross-country, soccer, softball, swimming, track/field (outdoor), volleyball.

ACCOMMODATIONS

Allowed in exams:	
Calculators	Yes
Dictionary	Yes
Computer	Yes
Spell-checker	Yes
Extended test time	Yes
Scribe	Yes
Proctors	Yes
Oral exams	Yes
Note-takers	Yes
Support services for students with:	
LD	Yes
ADHD	Yes
ASD	Yes
Distraction-reduced environment	Yes
Recording of lecture allowed	Yes
Reading technology	Yes
Audio books	Yes
Other assistive technology	Yes
Priority registration	Yes
Added costs of services:	
For LD	No
For ADHD	No
For ASD	No
LD specialists	Yes
ADHD & ASD coaching	Yes
ASD specialists	No
Professional tutors	Yes
Peer tutors	Yes
Max. hours/week for services	Varies
How professors are notified of student approved accommodations	Director

COLLEGE GRADUATION REQUIREMENTS

Course waivers allowed	No
Course substitutions allowed	No

State University of New York—Binghamton University

PO Box 6001, Binghamton, NY 13902-6001 • Admissions: 607-777-2171 • Fax: 607-777-4445 **Support CS**

CAMPUS

Type of school	Public
Environment	City

STUDENTS

Undergrad enrollment	13,693
% male/female	51/49
% from out of state	7
% frosh live on campus	98

FINANCIAL FACTS

Annual in-state tuition	$6,870
Annual out-of-state tuition	$23,710
Room and board	$15,058
Required fees	$2,934

GENERAL ADMISSIONS INFO

Application fee	$50
Regular application deadline	1/15
Nonfall registration	Yes

Admission may be deferred.

Range SAT EBRW	640–711
Range SAT Math	650–720
Range ACT Composite	28–31

ACADEMICS

Student/faculty ratio	19:1
% students returning for sophomore year	91

Most classes have 10–19 students.

Programs/Services for Students with Learning Differences

Services for Students with Disabilities (SSD) provides a wide range of assistance to enrolled students with learning or other disabilities. The office is part of the Division of Student Affairs and interfaces with offices and departments throughout the University. Students who register with the office are connected with staff who partner with them to determine reasonable accommodations and support services. Student Support Services promotes academic success and personal growth for students with disabilities. Students should understand that part of their responsibility as a student at Binghamton is to reach out for services before the classes begin. Early registration will make them eligible for the one-day Transition Program, where the rights of that student is discussed. Spring admissions is also allowed.

Admissions

Binghamton University welcomes applications from all qualified individuals. While there are no special admissions procedures or academic programs expressly for students with disabilities, the Services for Students with Disabilities Office provides a wide range of support services to enrolled students. Diagnostic tests are not required for admissions, but students are encouraged to meet with the director of Services for Students with Disabilities and provide documentation to determine appropriate accommodations. Through nonmatriculated enrollment, students can take courses but are not enrolled in a degree program. If they do well, they may then apply for matriculation, using credits earned toward their degree. General admission criteria includes 4 years of English, 3 years of math, 2 years of social science, 2 years of science, and 2 years of 2 foreign languages or 3 years of 1 foreign language. The mid 50 percent score range on the SAT is 1100–1330.

Additional Information

The first step in connecting with SSD is to submit documentation related to the disability. The documentation should provide information related to the present functional impact of the disability. During the intake appointments policies and procedures regarding access to accommodations at Binghamton University is outlined. Examples of what is available for no fee for the student are: JAWS, Kurzweil Reader, Smart Pens, and more. There is also free tutoring services, personal mentoring and counseling, and study skills and time management development.

ADMISSIONS INFO FOR STUDENTS WITH LEARNING DIFFERENCES

Phone: 607-777-2686 • Fax: 607-777-6893 • Email: ssd@binghamton.edu

SAT/ACT required: Yes (Test optional for 2021)
Interview required: No
Essay required: No
Additional application required: Yes
Documentation submitted to: SSD

Special Ed. HS course work accepted: No
Separate application required for Programs/Services: Yes
Documentation required for:
LD: Psychoeducational evaluation
ADHD: Psychoeducational evaluation
ASD: Psychoeducational evaluation

State University of New York—Binghamton University

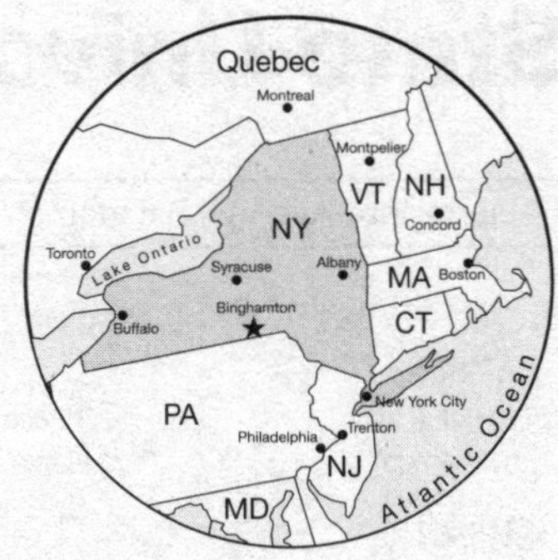

General Admissions

Very Important factors include: rigor of secondary school record, academic GPA, standardized test scores. *Important factors include:* class rank, application essay, recommendation(s), extracurricular activities. *Other factors include:* talent/ability, character/personal qualities, first generation, alumni/ae relation, geographical residence, state residency, racial/ethnic status, volunteer work, work experience, level of applicant's interest. *Freshman admission requirements:* High school diploma is required and GED is accepted. *Academic units required:* 4 English, 3 math, 2 science, 3 foreign language, 2 social studies. *Academic units recommended:* 4 math, 4 science, 4 social studies, 4 history.

Accommodations or Services

Accommodations are decided upon an individual basis after a thorough review of appropriate, current documentation. The accommodations requests must be supported through the documentation provided and must be logically linked to the current impact of the condition on academic functioning.

Financial Aid

Students should submit: FAFSA. Applicants will be notified of awards on a rolling basis beginning 2/15. *Need-based scholarships/grants offered:* College/university scholarship or grant aid from institutional funds; Federal Pell; Private scholarships; SEOG; State scholarships/grants. *Loan aid offered:* Direct PLUS loans; Direct Subsidized Stafford Loans; Direct Unsubsidized Stafford Loans. Federal Work-Study Program available. Institutional employment available.

Campus Life

Activities: Campus Ministries; Choral groups; Concert band; Dance; Drama/theater; International Student Organization; Jazz band; Literary magazine; Model UN; Music ensembles; Musical theater; Opera; Radio station; Student government; Student newspaper; Student-run film society; Symphony orchestra; Television station; Yearbook. **Organizations:** 373 registered organizations, 28 honor societies, 14 religious organizations, 36 fraternities, 17 sororities. **Athletics (Intercollegiate):** *Men:* baseball, basketball, cross-country, diving, golf, lacrosse, soccer, swimming, tennis, track/field (outdoor), track/field (indoor), wrestling. *Women:* basketball, cross-country, diving, lacrosse, soccer, softball, swimming, tennis, track/field (outdoor), track/field (indoor), volleyball.

ACCOMMODATIONS

Allowed in exams:	
Calculators	Yes
Dictionary	No
Computer	Yes
Spell-checker	Yes
Extended test time	Yes
Scribe	Yes
Proctors	Yes
Oral exams	Yes
Note-takers	Yes
Support services for students with:	
LD	Yes
ADHD	Yes
ASD	Yes
Distraction-reduced environment	Yes
Recording of lecture allowed	Yes
Reading technology	Yes
Audio books	Yes
Other assistive technology	Yes
Priority registration	Yes
Added costs of services:	
For LD	No
For ADHD	No
For ASD	No
LD specialists	Yes
ADHD & ASD coaching	No
ASD specialists	No
Professional tutors	No
Peer tutors	Yes
Max. hours/week for services	Varies
How professors are notified of student approved accommodations	Student

COLLEGE GRADUATION REQUIREMENTS

Course waivers allowed	No
Course substitutions allowed	Yes
In what courses: Case-by-case situation	

State University of New York—Potsdam

44 Pierrepont Avenue, Potsdam, NY 13676 • Admissions: 315-267-2180 • Fax: 315-267-2163 **Support: S**

CAMPUS

Type of school	Public
Environment	Village

STUDENTS

Undergrad enrollment	3,055
% male/female	38/62
% from out of state	4
% frosh live on campus	92

FINANCIAL FACTS

Annual in-state-tuition	$7,070
Annual out-of-state tuition	$16,980
Room and board	$13,900

GENERAL ADMISSIONS INFO

Application fee	$50
Regular application deadline	7/16
Nonfall registration	Yes

Admission may be deferred.

Range SAT EBRW	520–625
Range SAT Math	510–620
Range ACT Composite	20–27

ACADEMICS

Student/faculty ratio	11:1
% students returning for sophomore year	73

Most classes have 10–19 students.

Programs/Services for Students with Learning Differences

The State University of New York College—Potsdam is committed to the full inclusion of all individuals who can benefit from educational opportunities. Accommodative Services provides academic accommodations for all qualified students who have documented learning, emotional, and/or physical disabilities and a need for accommodations. The ultimate goal is to promote individuals' independence within the academic atmosphere of the university. Students are assisted in this process by the support services and programs available to all Potsdam students. Students must submit (written) documentation of the disability and the need for accommodations. After forwarding documentation, students are encouraged to make an appointment to meet with the coordinator to discuss accommodations. All accommodations are determined on an individual basis. Accommodative Services makes every effort to ensure access to academic accommodations.

Admissions

In most cases the minimum GPA requirement is an 80 on a 0–100 scale or a 2.5 on a 4.0 scale. The average GPA is 88.2. However, students falling below these figures should speak with an Admissions Counselor before ruling out Potsdam. Courses recommended include 4 years English, 3 years mathematics, 3 years science, 4 years social science, 3 years foreign language, and 1 year of fine or performing arts. The ACT/ SAT is not required.

Additional Information

Accommodations available through Accommodative Services include note-takers; test readers/books on tape; alternative testing such as extended time and/or distraction-reduced environment, exam readers/ scribes, and use of word processor with spellchecker; and lending of some equipment. Additional services can include special registration and academic advising. Accommodative Services will assist students requesting non-academic auxiliary aids or services in locating the appropriate campus resources to address the request. The College Counseling Center provides psychological services. The early warning system asks each instructor to indicate at midpoint in each semester if a student is making unsatisfactory academic progress. Results of this inquiry are sent to the student and advisor. Student Support Services provides academic support, peer mentoring, and counseling. Tutoring is available for all students one-on-one or in small groups.

ADMISSIONS INFO FOR STUDENTS WITH LEARNING DIFFERENCES

Phone: 315-267-3267 • Fax: 315-267-3268 • Email: oas@potsdam.edu

SAT/ACT required: No
Interview required: No
Essay required: No
Additional application required: No
Documentation submitted to: Accommodations Services Office

Special Ed. HS course work accepted: No
Separate application required for Programs/Services: No
Documentation required for:
LD: Psychoeducational evaluation
ADHD: Psychoeducational evaluation
ASD: Psychoeducational evaluation

State University of New York—Potsdam

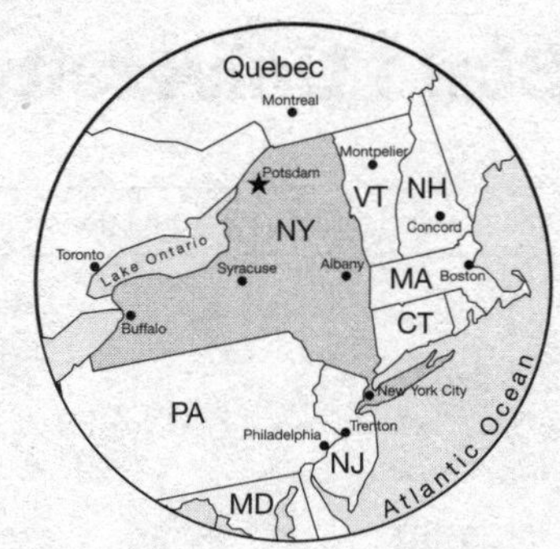

General Admissions

Important factors include: rigor of secondary school record, academic GPA, application essay, recommendation(s). *Other factors include:* standardized test scores, interview, extracurricular activities, talent/ability, character/personal qualities, volunteer work, work experience, level of applicant's interest. High school diploma is required and a GED is accepted. *Academic units recommended:* 4 English, 3 math, 3 science, 3 foreign language, 4 social studies, 1 visual/performing arts.

Accommodations or Services

Accommodations are decided upon an individual basis after a thorough review of appropriate, current documentation. The accommodations requests must be supported through the documentation provided and must be logically linked to the current impact of the condition on academic functioning.

Financial Aid

Students should submit: FAFSA; State aid form. *Need-based scholarships/grants offered:* College/university scholarship or grant aid from institutional funds; Federal Pell; Private scholarships; SEOG; State scholarships/grants. *Loan aid offered:* Direct PLUS loans; Direct Subsidized Stafford Loans; Direct Unsubsidized Stafford Loans. Federal Work-Study Program available. Institutional employment available.

Campus Life

Activities: Campus Ministries; Choral groups; Concert band; Dance; Drama/theater; International Student Organization; Jazz band; Literary magazine; Music ensembles; Musical theater; Opera; Pep band; Radio station; Student government; Student newspaper; Symphony orchestra. **Organizations:** 90 registered organizations, 21 honor societies, 6 religious organizations, 2 fraternities, 7 sororities. **Athletics (Intercollegiate):** *Men:* basketball, cross-country, diving, equestrian sports, golf, ice hockey, lacrosse, soccer, swimming. *Women:* basketball, cross-country, diving, equestrian sports, ice hockey, lacrosse, soccer, softball, swimming, tennis, volleyball.

ACCOMMODATIONS

Allowed in exams:	
Calculators	Yes
Dictionary	Yes
Computer	Yes
Spell-checker	Yes
Extended test time	Yes
Scribe	Yes
Proctors	Yes
Oral exams	Yes
Note-takers	Yes
Support services for students with:	
LD	Yes
ADHD	Yes
ASD	Yes
Distraction-reduced environment	Yes
Recording of lecture allowed	Yes
Reading technology	Yes
Audio books	Yes
Other assistive technology	Yes
Priority registration	Yes
Added costs of services:	
For LD	No
For ADHD	No
For ASD	No
LD specialists	No
ADHD & ASD coaching	No
ASD specialists	No
Professional tutors	No
Peer tutors	Yes
Max. hours/week for services	Varies
How professors are notified of student approved accommodations	Student and Disability Office

COLLEGE GRADUATION REQUIREMENTS

Course waivers allowed	Yes
In what courses: Case-by-case basis	
Course substitutions allowed	Yes
In what courses: Case-by-case basis	

State University of New York—Stony Brook University

Office of Undergraduate Admissions, Stony Brook, NY 11794-1901 • Admissions: 631-632-6868 • Fax: 631-632-9898 **Support: S**

CAMPUS

Type of school	Public
Environment	Town

STUDENTS

Undergrad enrollment	17,767
% male/female	51/49
% from out of state	6
% frosh live on campus	82

FINANCIAL FACTS

Annual in-state tuition	$7,070
Annual out-of-state tuition	$24,740
Room and board	$14,278
Required fees	$3,105

GENERAL ADMISSIONS INFO

Application fee	$50
Regular application deadline	1/15
Nonfall registration	Yes

Admission may be deferred.

Range SAT EBRW	590–690
Range SAT Math	640–750
Range ACT Composite	26–32

ACADEMICS

Student/faculty ratio	19:1
% students returning for sophomore year	89

Most classes have 10–19 students.

Programs/Services for Students with Learning Differences

Disability Support Services (DSS) coordinates advocacy and support services for students with disabilities. These services assist integrating students' needs with the resources available at the university to eliminate physical or programmatic barriers and ensure an accessible academic environment. All information and documentation of student disabilities is confidential. Students are responsible for identifying and documenting their disabilities through the DSS office. Students receive assistance, recruitment of readers, interpreters, note-takers, test accommodations, and counseling. A learning disabilities specialist is available to refer students for diagnostic testing and educational programming, meet accommodation needs, and provide in-service training to the university community. A Supported Education Program offering individual counseling and group sessions is available for students with psychological disabilities. Students who anticipate requiring assistance should contact Disability Support Services as early as possible to allow time for implementing recommended services.

Admissions

Admissions looks for a strong high school academic. The ACT/ SAT is required. Students who show evidence of leadership, special talents or interests, and other personal qualities through extracurricular activities, volunteer work, and other non-academic pursuits will receive special consideration. Freshman applicants admitted to the University but not initially accepted into their major of choice may apply for admission into the major after satisfying the requirements.

Additional Information

Every semester the student should go to the DSS to meet with a counselor and fill out an accommodation request form to generate a letter to each professor that explains the accommodations. Types of services and accommodations available are pre-registration advisement, liaising with faculty and staff, taped texts, learning strategies and time management training, assistance in locating tutors, assistance in arranging for note-takers and readers, tutorial computer programs, proctoring and/or modified administration of exams, support groups, referrals to appropriate campus resources, peer advising, and aid in vocational decision making. Services and accommodations are available to undergraduate and graduate students. No skills classes are offered.

ADMISSIONS INFO FOR STUDENTS WITH LEARNING DIFFERENCES

Phone: 631-632-6748 • Fax: 631-632-6747 • Email: sasc@stonybrook.edu

SAT/ACT required: Yes (Test optional through 2022)
Interview required: No
Essay required: No
Additional application required: No
Documentation submitted to: Disability Support Services

Special Ed. HS course work accepted: Yes
Separate application required for Programs/Services: No
Documentation required for:
LD: Psychoeducational evaluation
ADHD: Psychoeducational evaluation
ASD: Psychoeducational evaluation

State University of New York— Stony Brook University

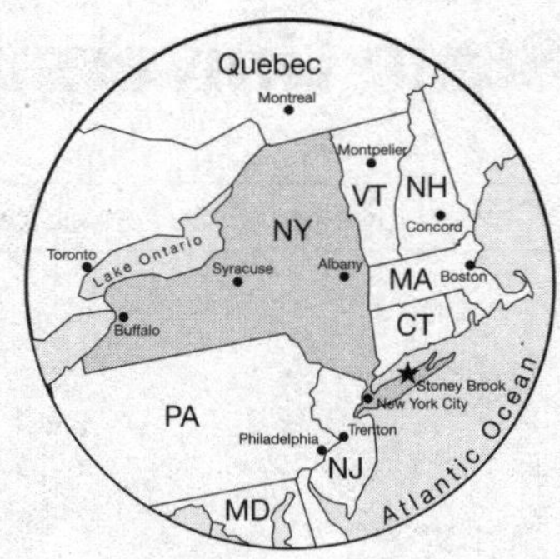

General Admissions

Very Important factors include: rigor of secondary school record, academic GPA, standardized test scores. *Important factors include:* application essay, recommendation(s). *Other factors include:* class rank, interview, extracurricular activities, talent/ability, character/personal qualities, first generation, alumni/ae relation, geographical residence, state residency, volunteer work, work experience, level of applicant's interest. High school diploma is required and a GED is accepted. *Academic units required:* 4 English, 4 math, 4 science, 4 social studies. *Academic units recommended:* 4 English, 4 math, 4 science, 3 foreign language, 4 social studies.

Accommodations or Services

Accommodations are decided upon an individual basis after a thorough review of appropriate, current documentation. The accommodations requests must be supported through the documentation provided and must be logically linked to the current impact of the condition on academic functioning.

Financial Aid

Students should submit: FAFSA; State aid form. *Need-based scholarships/grants offered:* College/university scholarship or grant aid from institutional funds; Federal Pell; Private scholarships; SEOG; State scholarships/grants. *Loan aid offered:* Direct PLUS loans; Direct Subsidized Stafford Loans; Direct Unsubsidized Stafford Loans. Federal Work-Study Program available. Institutional employment available.

Campus Life

Activities: Campus Ministries; Choral groups; Concert band; Dance; Drama/theater; International Student Organization; Jazz band; Literary magazine; Marching band; Model UN; Music ensembles; Musical theater; Opera; Pep band; Radio station; Student government; Student newspaper; Student-run film society; Symphony orchestra; Television station. **Organizations:** 351 registered organizations, 8 honor societies, 19 religious organizations, 15 fraternities, 13 sororities. **Athletics (Intercollegiate):** *Men:* baseball, basketball, cross-country, diving, football, lacrosse, soccer, swimming, tennis, track/field (outdoor), track/field (indoor). *Women:* basketball, cross-country, diving, lacrosse, soccer, softball, swimming, tennis, track/field (outdoor), track/field (indoor), volleyball.

ACCOMMODATIONS

Allowed in exams:	
Calculators	Yes
Dictionary	No
Computer	Yes
Spell-checker	Yes
Extended test time	Yes
Scribe	Yes
Proctors	Yes
Oral exams	No
Note-takers	Yes
Support services for students with:	
LD	No
ADHD	No
ASD	No
Distraction-reduced environment	Yes
Recording of lecture allowed	Yes
Reading technology	Yes
Audio books	Yes
Other assistive technology	Yes
Priority registration	Yes
Added costs of services:	
For LD	No
For ADHD	No
For ASD	No
LD specialists	No
ADHD & ASD coaching	No
ASD specialists	No
Professional tutors	No
Peer tutors	Yes
Max. hours/week for services	Varies
How professors are notified of student approved accommodations	Student and Disability Office

COLLEGE GRADUATION REQUIREMENTS

Course waivers allowed	Yes
In what courses: Case-by-case basis	
Course substitutions allowed	Yes
In what courses: Case-by-case basis	

New York

State University of New York—University at Albany

Office of Undergraduate Admissions, Albany, NY 12222 • Admissions: 518-442-5435 • Fax: 518-442-5383 **Support: CS**

CAMPUS

Type of school	Public
Environment	City

STUDENTS

Undergrad enrollment	13,153
% male/female	48/52
% from out of state	4
% frosh live on campus	91

FINANCIAL FACTS

Annual in-state tuition	$7,070
Annual out-of-state tuition	$24,660
Room and board	$14,640
Required fees	$2,956

GENERAL ADMISSIONS INFO

Application fee	$50
Regular application deadline	3/1
Nonfall registration	Yes

Admission may be deferred.

Range SAT EBRW	550–620
Range SAT Math	540–630
Range ACT Composite	22–28

ACADEMICS

Student/faculty ratio	18:1
% students returning for sophomore year	82

Most classes have 10–19 students.

Programs/Services for Students with Learning Differences

Reasonable accommodations will be provided for students with documented disabilities through the Disability Resource Center. Students are responsible for providing the University with documentation of the disability. Documentation must be submitted to the DRC. The mission of the DRC is to empower individual students, using appropriate supportive services, as well as acting as an expert resource for the university community.

Admissions

The average GPA is 92.2 (3.6/4.0). The middle 50% were between 88% and 96% (3.2–3.8). Freshman applicants must take the SAT or ACT and the middle 50% scored between 1150 and 1310 SAT and 23 to 27 on ACT. Academic performance is important but not the only factor used. Academic performance in high school is considered to be the best predictor of academic success, but it is not the only factor that will play a role in a student's experience as an undergraduate. The admissions committee looks at the whole person, recognizing special talents and interests outside the classroom as well as in it.

Additional Information

Academic coaching is available through the Academic Support Center. Academic coaches work with students to help them pinpoint areas of stress and then develop personalized strategies and plans for success. Tutoring services—both drop in and on-line—are offered free to all students. The Center for Autism and Related Disabilities((CARD Albany) is a university-affiliated resource center that provides evidence-based training and support to families and professionals and contributes knowledge to the field of Autism Spectrum Disorders.

ADMISSIONS INFO FOR STUDENTS WITH LEARNING DIFFERENCES

Phone: 518-442-5490 • Fax: 518-442-5400 • Email: cmalloch@albany.edu

SAT/ACT required: Yes (Test optional through 2022)
Interview required: No
Essay required: No
Additional application required: No
Documentation submitted to: Disability Resource Center

Special Ed. HS course work accepted: Yes
Separate application required for Programs/Services: No
Documentation required for:
LD: Psychoeducational evaluation
ADHD: Psychoeducational evaluation
ASD: Psychoeducational evaluation

State University of New York— University at Albany

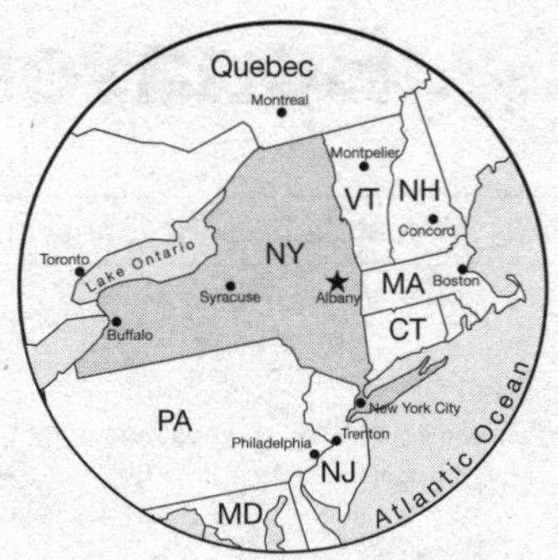

General Admissions

Very Important factors include: rigor of secondary school record, class rank, academic GPA, standardized test scores, recommendation(s), character/personal qualities. *Important factors include:* application essay. *Other factors include:* extracurricular activities, talent/ability, first generation, alumni/ae relation, geographical residence, volunteer work, work experience, level of applicant's interest. High school diploma is required and a GED is accepted. *Academic units required:* 4 English, 2 math, 2 science, 2 science labs, 1 foreign language, 3 social studies, 2 history, 4 academic electives. *Academic units recommended:* 4 math, 3 science, 3 science labs, 3 foreign language.

Accommodations or Services

Accommodations are decided upon an individual basis after a thorough review of appropriate, current documentation. The accommodations requests must be supported through the documentation provided and must be logically linked to the current impact of the condition on academic functioning.

Financial Aid

Students should submit: FAFSA. *Need-based scholarships/grants offered:* College/university scholarship or grant aid from institutional funds; Federal Pell; Private scholarships; SEOG; State scholarships/grants. *Loan aid offered:* Direct PLUS loans; Direct Subsidized Stafford Loans; Direct Unsubsidized Stafford Loans. Federal Work-Study Program available. Institutional employment available.

Campus Life

Activities: Campus Ministries; Choral groups; Concert band; Dance; Drama/theater; International Student Organization; Jazz band; Literary magazine; Marching band; Model UN; Music ensembles; Musical theater; Pep band; Radio station; Student government; Student newspaper; Student-run film society; Symphony orchestra; Television station; Yearbook. **Organizations:** 210 registered organizations, 22 honor societies, 15 religious organizations, 17 fraternities, 17 sororities. **Athletics (Intercollegiate):** *Men:* baseball, basketball, cross-country, football, lacrosse, soccer, track/field (outdoor), track/field (indoor). *Women:* basketball, cross-country, field hockey, golf, lacrosse, soccer, softball, tennis, track/field (outdoor), track/field (indoor), volleyball.

ACCOMMODATIONS

Allowed in exams:	
Calculators	Yes
Dictionary	Yes
Computer	Yes
Spell-checker	Yes
Extended test time	Yes
Scribe	Yes
Proctors	Yes
Oral exams	Yes
Note-takers	Yes
Support services for students with:	
LD	Yes
ADHD	Yes
ASD	Yes
Distraction-reduced environment	Yes
Recording of lecture allowed	Yes
Reading technology	Yes
Audio books	Yes
Other assistive technology	Yes
Priority registration	Yes
Added costs of services:	
For LD	No
For ADHD	No
For ASD	No
LD specialists	Yes
ADHD & ASD coaching	No
ASD specialists	No
Professional tutors	No
Peer tutors	Yes
Max. hours/week for services	Varies
How professors are notified of student approved accommodations	Student

COLLEGE GRADUATION REQUIREMENTS

Course waivers allowed	No
Course substitutions allowed	Yes
In what courses: Case-by-case basis	

St. Bonaventure University

3261 West State Road St., Bonaventure, NY 14778 • Admissions: 716-375-2434 • Fax: 716-375-4005 **Support: S**

CAMPUS

Type of school	Private (nonprofit)
Environment	Village

STUDENTS

Undergrad enrollment	1,787
% male/female	53/47
% from out of state	25
% frosh live on campus	98

FINANCIAL FACTS

Annual tuition	$35,450
Room and board	$13,770
Required fees	$1,065

GENERAL ADMISSIONS INFO

Application fee	$0
Regular application deadline	7/1
Nonfall registration	Yes

Admission may be deferred.

Range SAT EBRW	510–620
Range SAT Math	520–620
Range ACT Composite	19–26

ACADEMICS

Student/faculty ratio	12:1
% students returning for sophomore year	84

Most classes have 20–29 students.

Programs/Services for Students with Learning Differences

Under Section 504 of the Federal Rehabilitation Act of 1973 and the Americans with Disabilities Act (ADA) of 1990, St. Bonaventure University is mandated to make reasonable accommodations for otherwise qualified students with disabilities. Specific accommodations will be arranged individually with each student depending upon the type and extent of the disability. St. Bonaventure provides services to students with identified disabilities. It is expected that a student with a disability, with appropriate accommodations, will be able to meet the basic requirements of a liberal arts education. Students with identified disabilities are required to complete the same admissions process as other applicants to St. Bonaventure. The Coordinator of Disability Support Services (DSS) does not diagnose disabilities. Students with disabilities are required to provide documentation of the disability. A student with a disability is required to meet with the Coordinator of DSS if he or she wishes to have academic accommodations arranged for the semester. It is the student's responsibility to deliver accommodation letters to his or her professors after accommodations have been arranged. Accommodations are set up on a semester-by-semester basis; it is the student's responsibility to contact the Coordinator of DSS at the beginning of each semester to ensure appropriate accommodations can be made. The student is encouraged to discuss his or her disability with his or her professors and to arrange for specific accommodations for test-taking and other course requirements. It is the responsibility of the professor to provide alternative testing accommodations to eligible students with disabilities who request them; however, if an Exam Proctoring Form is filled out five business days prior to the exam, the exam may be proctored in the Teaching and Learning Center during regular business hours. A student applying for a course substitution should contact the Coordinator of DSS for assistance. All disability information is confidential.

Admissions

St. Bonaventure University, has a rolling admissions policy and review applications throughout the year. SBU evaluates the highest sub scores for each test and uses highest test score for the admission. Other considerations include a personal essay and additional recommendations. There is not a formula to determine admissibility to St. Bonaventure University. The admission committee reviews each applicant's qualifications individually, considering a variety of characteristics that indicate academic preparation and potential for success. and look carefully at applicants who have achieved

ADMISSIONS INFO FOR STUDENTS WITH LEARNING DIFFERENCES

Phone: 716-375-2065 • Fax: 716-375-2071 • Email: aspencer@sbu.edu

SAT/ACT required: No
Interview required: Not Applicable
Essay required: Not Applicable
Additional application required: Not Applicable
Documentation submitted to: Disability Support Services

Special Ed. HS course work accepted: Yes
Separate application required for Programs/Services: Not Applicable
Documentation required for:
LD: Psychoeducational evaluation
ADHD: Psychoeducational evaluation
ASD: Psychoeducational evaluation

St. Bonaventure University

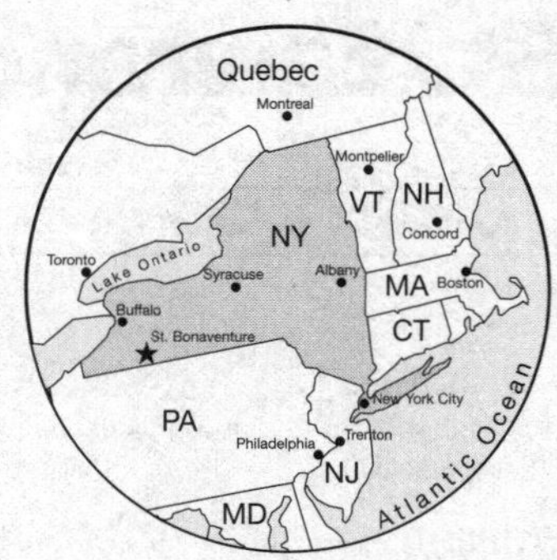

academic success in high school and those who have demonstrated significant promise but have yet to show the world their full potential. An average GPA is 90% and average ACT 25 or SAT 1135.

Additional Information
Students with LD may obtain assistance with assessing learning strengths and weaknesses and consult one-on-one or in groups to acquire a greater command of a subject, get help with a specific assignment, or discuss academic challenges. Services might include, but are not limited to: alternative testing arrangements, taped texts and classes, access to word processors/spellchecker, note-takers, tutors, peer mentors, time management and study skills training, and weekly individual appointments. Assistance can be offered in requesting books on tape. Tutoring services are available to all students and are not intended to be a substitute for independent study or preparation.

General Admissions
Very important factors include: rigor of secondary school record, academic GPA, recommendation(s), character/personal qualities. *Important factors include:* application essay, standardized test scores, extracurricular activities, talent/ability. *Other factors include:* class rank, interview, first generation, alumni/ae relation, geographical residence, state residency, work experience, level of applicant's interest. High school diploma is required and GED is accepted. *Academic units recommended:* 4 English, 3 math, 3 science, 3 science labs, 2 foreign language, 4 social studies.

Accommodations or Services
Accommodations are decided upon an individual basis after a thorough review of appropriate, current documentation. The accommodations requests must be supported through the documentation provided and must be logically linked to the current impact of the condition on academic functioning.

Financial Aid
Students should submit: FAFSA. Applicants will be notified of awards on or about 4/15. *Need-based scholarships/grants offered:* College/university scholarship or grant aid from institutional funds; Federal Pell; Private scholarships; SEOG; State scholarships/grants. *Loan aid offered:* Direct PLUS loans; Direct Subsidized Stafford Loans; Direct Unsubsidized Stafford Loans. Federal Work-Study Program available. Institutional employment available.

Campus Life
Activities: Campus Ministries; Choral groups; Concert band; Dance; Drama/theater; International Student Organization; Jazz band; Literary magazine; Model UN; Music ensembles; Pep band; Radio station ; Student government; Student newspaper; Television station. **Organizations:** 60 registered organizations, 15 honor societies, 4 religious organizations, on campus. **Athletics (Intercollegiate):** *Men:* baseball, basketball, cross-country, diving, golf, soccer, swimming, tennis. *Women:* basketball, cross-country, diving, lacrosse, soccer, softball, swimming, tennis.

ACCOMMODATIONS

Allowed in exams:	
Calculators	Yes
Dictionary	Yes
Computer	Yes
Spell-checker	Yes
Extended test time	Yes
Scribe	Yes
Proctors	Yes
Oral exams	Yes
Note-takers	Yes
Support services for students with:	
LD	Yes
ADHD	Yes
ASD	Yes
Distraction-reduced environment	Yes
Recording of lecture allowed	Yes
Reading technology	Yes
Audio books	Yes
Other assistive technology	No
Priority registration	Yes
Added costs of services:	
For LD	No
For ADHD	No
For ASD	No
LD specialists	No
ADHD & ASD coaching	No
ASD specialists	No
Professional tutors	Yes
Peer tutors	Yes
Max. hours/week for services	Varies
How professors are notified of student approved accommodations	Student

COLLEGE GRADUATION REQUIREMENTS

Course waivers allowed	No
Course substitutions allowed	Yes
In what courses: Case by case basis	

St. Lawrence University

23 Romoda Drive, Canton, NY 13617 • Admissions: 315-229-5261 • Fax: 315-229-5818 **Support: S**

CAMPUS

Type of school	Private (nonprofit)
Environment	Village

STUDENTS

Undergrad enrollment	2,392
% male/female	45/55
% from out of state	61
% frosh live on campus	100

FINANCIAL FACTS

Annual tuition	$58,330
Room and board	$15,150
Required fees	$420

GENERAL ADMISSIONS INFO

Application fee	$60
Regular application deadline	2/1
Nonfall registration	Yes

Admission may be deferred.

Range SAT EBRW	580–670
Range SAT Math	580–680
Range ACT Composite	24–30

ACADEMICS

Student/faculty ratio	11:1
% students returning for sophomore year	90

Most classes have 10–19 students.

Programs/Services for Students with Learning Differences

The student Accessibility Services (SAS) office provides advisors to help develop each student's individual education plan. It's the responsibility of the student to inform professors at the beginning of each semester. Every effort is made to individually and appropriately serve students to enable them to attain success and reach their goals. The staff is made up of three professionals who provide a wide range of support services and accommodations for students with disabilities. Students must identify themselves as having a disability. Each student must provide appropriate documentation that clearly supports the disability and specifically recommends accommodations that relate specifically to the manifestations of the individual's condition. The accommodations assigned to each student are made on case-by-case basis.

Admissions

Students with disabilities operate through the same admissions process and criteria as the general applicant body. An interview is recommended and can be done off campus with an alumni representative. Students are also required to submit one counselor and two teacher recommendations. St. Lawrence is test optional and ACT or SAT scores are not required for admission.

Additional Information

The Office of Academic and Advising Programs supports developing organizational skills, study skills, test-taking strategies, and other support depending on the student's needs. Peer tutors are free. Students need to be self-starters (to seek out the service early and follow through). As soon as possible, students should provide the official documents that describe the learning disability, the office helps develop the IEP—and notify the professors about the learning disability. Academic requirements required for graduation are waived. Services and accommodations are available for undergraduate and graduate students.

ADMISSIONS INFO FOR STUDENTS WITH LEARNING DIFFERENCES

Phone: 315-229-5537 • Fax: 315-229-7453 • Email: mmccluskey@stlawu.edu

SAT/ACT required: No
Interview required: No
Essay required: Yes
Additional application required: No
Documentation submitted to: SAS

Special Ed. HS course work accepted: No
Separate application required for Programs/Services: No
Documentation required for:
LD: Psychoeducational evaluation
ADHD: Psychoeducational evaluation
ASD: Psychoeducational evaluation

St. Lawrence University

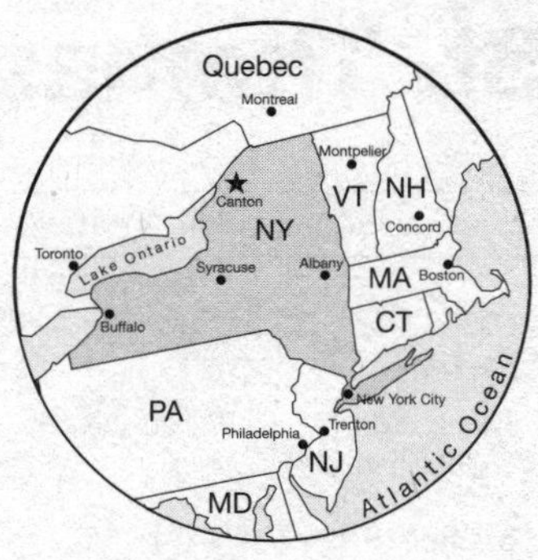

General Admissions

Very important factors include: rigor of secondary school record, academic GPA, application essay, recommendation(s), character/personal qualities. *Important factors include:* class rank, interview, extracurricular activities. *Other factors include:* standardized test scores, talent/ability, first generation, alumni/ae relation, geographical residence, volunteer work, work experience, level of applicant's interest. High school diploma is required and GED is accepted. *Academic units recommended:* 4 English, 4 math, 4 science, 4 foreign language, 2 social studies, 2 history.

Accommodations or Services

Accommodations are decided upon an individual basis after a thorough review of appropriate, current documentation. The accommodations requests must be supported through the documentation provided and must be logically linked to the current impact of the condition on academic functioning.

Financial Aid

Students should submit: FAFSA. *Need-based scholarships/grants offered:* College/university scholarship or grant aid from institutional funds; Federal Pell; Private scholarships; SEOG; State scholarships/grants. *Loan aid offered:* Direct PLUS loans; Direct Subsidized Stafford Loans; Direct Unsubsidized Stafford Loans. Federal Work-Study Program available. Institutional employment available.

Campus Life

Activities: Campus Ministries; Choral groups; Concert band; Dance; Drama/theater; International Student Organization; Jazz band; Literary magazine; Model UN; Music ensembles; Musical theater; Radio station; Student government; Student newspaper; Student-run film society; Yearbook. **Organizations:** 117 registered organizations, 22 honor societies, 4 religious organizations, 2 fraternities, 4 sororities. **Athletics (Intercollegiate):** *Men:* baseball, basketball, crew/rowing, cross-country, equestrian sports, football, golf, ice hockey, lacrosse, skiing (downhill/alpine), skiing (Nordic/cross-country), soccer, squash, swimming, tennis, track/field (outdoor), track/field (indoor). *Women:* basketball, crew/rowing, cross-country, equestrian sports, field hockey, golf, ice hockey, lacrosse, skiing (downhill/alpine), skiing (Nordic/cross-country), soccer, softball, squash, swimming, tennis, track/field (outdoor), track/field (indoor), volleyball.

ACCOMMODATIONS

Allowed in exams:	
Calculators	Yes
Dictionary	No
Computer	Yes
Spell-checker	Yes
Extended test time	Yes
Scribe	Yes
Proctors	Yes
Oral exams	Yes
Note-takers	Yes
Support services for students with:	
LD	Yes
ADHD	Yes
ASD	Yes
Distraction-reduced environment	Yes
Recording of lecture allowed	Yes
Reading technology	Yes
Audio books	Yes
Other assistive technology	Yes
Priority registration	No
Added costs of services:	
For LD	No
For ADHD	No
For ASD	No
LD specialists	No
ADHD & ASD coaching	No
ASD specialists	No
Professional tutors	No
Peer tutors	Yes
Max. hours/week for services	Varies
How professors are notified of student approved accommodations	Student

COLLEGE GRADUATION REQUIREMENTS

Course waivers allowed	No
Course substitutions allowed	No

St. Thomas Aquinas College

125 Route 340, Sparkill, NY 10976 • Admissions: 845-398-4100 • Fax: 845-398-4372 **Support: CS**

CAMPUS

Type of school	Private (nonprofit)
Environment	Village

STUDENTS

Undergrad enrollment	1,797
% male/female	50/50
% from out of state	21
% frosh live on campus	65

FINANCIAL FACTS

Annual tuition	$34,400
Room and board	$14,780
Required fees	$800

GENERAL ADMISSIONS INFO

Application fee	$30
Regular application deadline	Rolling
Nonfall registration	Yes

Admission may be deferred.

Range SAT EBRW	450–580
Range SAT Math	440–580
Range ACT Composite	17–23

ACADEMICS

Student/faculty ratio	16:1
% students returning for sophomore year	71

Most classes have 20–29 students.

Programs/Services for Students with Learning Differences

The Pathways Program offers individualized and interpersonal services that are comprehensive and specialized. The goal of the program is to help students better develop learning strategies in alignment with their learning difference and/or ADHD. There is a director and trained staff who support one-on-one mentoring, seminars, and workshops. A mentor is assigned to each student and is available to help with time management, editing papers, and reviewing concepts from courses the student is attending.

Admissions

Pathways has an application and admissions process that is additional to the colleges. Admissions to Pathways is competitive. Students must be accepted by the college before their Pathways application is evaluated; however, students should apply to the college and to Pathways at the same time. The following must be submitted to Pathways: a completed Pathways application; for applicants who were classified, the most recent IEP: and a comprehensive diagnostic assessment including an adult intelligence test, measures of achievement/educational skills, and specific effects of the LD/ ADHD on the student's current academic performance. Reports are required; scores on an IEP are insufficient documentation. Students must also have a personal interview with Pathways staff. Transfer applications are accepted.

Additional Information

The Pathways Program requires incoming freshman students to attend a four-day residential program on campus in the summer prior to starting college. One of the goals of the summer program is to help students feel comfortable transitioning to college. During the four days they will meet other students, take a course for credit, and, through that class, learn the expectations of the professors they will be meeting throughout the rest of their college experience. The summer introduces students to study skills, organization, note-taking, and test-taking strategies to help them transition from high school to college.

ADMISSIONS INFO FOR STUDENTS WITH LEARNING DIFFERENCES

Phone: 845-398-4087 • Fax: 845-398-4151 • Email: aschlinc@stac.edu

SAT/ACT required: Yes (Test optional for 2021)
Interview required: Yes
Essay required: No
Additional application required: No
Documentation submitted to: Pathways Program

Special Ed. HS course work accepted: No
Separate application required for Programs/Services: Yes
Documentation required for:
LD: Psychoeducational evaluation
ADHD: Psychoeducational evaluation
ASD: Psychoeducational evaluation

St. Thomas Aquinas College

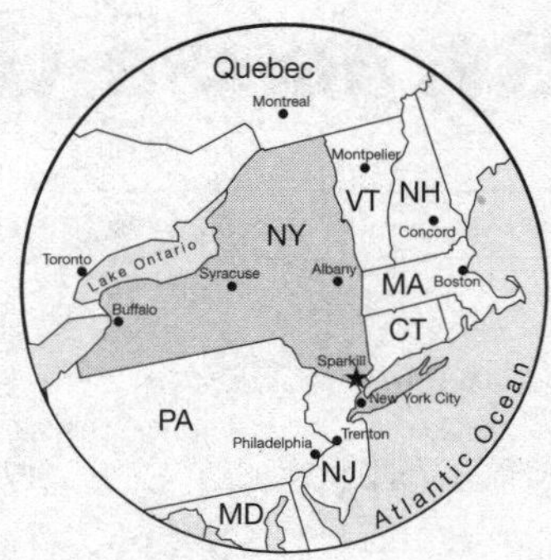

General Admissions

Very important factors include: rigor of secondary school record. *Important factors include:* recommendation(s), interview, extracurricular activities, talent/ability. *Other factors include:* academic GPA, application essay, standardized test scores, alumni/ae relation, volunteer work, work experience, level of applicant's interest. High school diploma is required and GED is accepted. *Academic units required:* 4 English, 3 math, 3 science, 2 science labs, 3 foreign language, 4 social studies, 2 history, 1 academic elective. *Academic units recommended:* 4 English, 3 math, 3 science, 2 science labs, 3 foreign language, 4 social studies, 2 history, 1 academic elective.

Accommodations or Services

Accommodations are decided upon an individual basis after a thorough review of appropriate, current documentation. The accommodations requests must be supported through the documentation provided and must be logically linked to the current impact of the condition on academic functioning.

Financial Aid

Students should submit: FAFSA; State aid form. *Need-based scholarships/grants offered:* College/university scholarship or grant aid from institutional funds; Federal Pell; Private scholarships; SEOG; State scholarships/grants. *Loan aid offered:* Direct PLUS loans; Direct Subsidized Stafford Loans; Direct Unsubsidized Stafford Loans. Federal Work-Study Program available. Institutional employment available.

Campus Life

Activities: Campus Ministries; Choral groups; Concert band; Dance; Drama/theater; Literary magazine; Music ensembles; Musical theater; Radio station; Student government; Student newspaper; Yearbook. **Organizations:** 35 registered organizations, 8 honor societies. **Athletics (Intercollegiate):** *Men:* baseball, basketball, cross-country, golf, soccer, tennis, track/field (outdoor), track/field (indoor). *Women:* basketball, cross-country, lacrosse, soccer, softball, tennis, track/field (outdoor).

ACCOMMODATIONS

Allowed in exams:	
Calculators	Yes
Dictionary	No
Computer	Yes
Spell-checker	Yes
Extended test time	Yes
Scribe	Yes
Proctors	Yes
Oral exams	No
Note-takers	Yes
Support services for students with:	
LD	Yes
ADHD	Yes
ASD	Yes
Distraction-reduced environment	Yes
Recording of lecture allowed	Yes
Reading technology	Yes
Audio books	Yes
Other assistive technology	Yes
Priority registration	Yes
Added costs of services:	
For LD	No
For ADHD	No
For ASD	No
LD specialists	Yes
ADHD & ASD coaching	Yes
ASD specialists	No
Professional tutors	Yes
Peer tutors	No
Max. hours/week for services	Varies
How professors are notified of student approved accommodations	Student

COLLEGE GRADUATION REQUIREMENTS

Course waivers allowed	No
Course substitutions allowed	Yes
In what courses: Case by case basis	

Syracuse University

100 Crouse-Hinds Hall, Syracuse, NY 13244-2130 • Admissions: 315-443-3611 • Fax: 315-443-4226 **Support: SP**

CAMPUS

Type of school	Private (nonprofit)
Environment	City

STUDENTS

Undergrad enrollment	14,854
% male/female	47/53
% from out of state	63
% frosh live on campus	99

FINANCIAL FACTS

Annual tuition	$54,270
Room and board	$16,356
Required fees	$1,656

GENERAL ADMISSIONS INFO

Application fee	$85
Regular application deadline	1/1
Nonfall registration	Yes

Admission may be deferred.

Range SAT EBRW	580–670
Range SAT Math	600–710
Range ACT Composite	26–30

ACADEMICS

Student/faculty ratio	15:1
% students returning for sophomore year	92

Most classes have 10–19 students.

Programs/Services for Students with Learning Differences

The Center for Disability Resources (CDR) assigns students counselors throughout their college experience. The counselors help students develop and implement a plan that will support their disability related issues. There is also an academic support and tutoring program arranged through the Center for Academic Achievement (CLASS). The coordinator of this program helps students who need exam and other academic accommodations, including technology support, professional tutoring, guidance and mentoring, note-taking assistance, and skill development.

Admissions

All students must meet regular admission standards and submit the general application form. General admission criteria include 4 years English, 3–4 years math, 3–4 years science, 3–4 years social studies, and 2 years foreign language. Syracuse is test optional and ACT or SAT is not currently required for admission. Many colleges within the university have their own college-specific admission requirements and typically the ACT or SAT is not required for theater or music applicants. Applicants apply to one of nine undergraduate colleges, depending upon the program of study of interest. Applicants are encouraged to identify a second major option.

Additional Information

On Track is a fee-based program providing enhanced academic support for students with Attention Deficit Hyperactivity Disorder (ADHD) and Learning Disabilities (LD). The goal of this program will be to address both academic and social-emotional readiness. Students in On Track meet regularly with a specially trained coach for academic monitoring or support, guidance in connecting with other university and community services, and counseling focused on building independence and executive function. The program aims to assist students as they transition to the standard university support systems by their second year, where they receive follow up support with "step down" services through the Center for Disability Services. There is also the Taishoff Center, where students with intellectual disabilities can attend University College through InclusiveU.

ADMISSIONS INFO FOR STUDENTS WITH LEARNING DIFFERENCES

Phone: 315-443-4498 • Fax: 315-443-1312 • Email: disabilityservices@syr.edu

SAT/ACT required: Yes (Test optional for 2021)
Interview required: No
Essay required: Yes
Additional application required: Yes
Documentation submitted to: CDR

Special Ed. HS course work accepted: No
Separate application required for Programs/Services: Yes
Documentation required for:
- **LD:** Psychoeducational evaluation
- **ADHD:** Psychoeducational evaluation
- **ASD:** Psychoeducational evaluation

Syracuse University

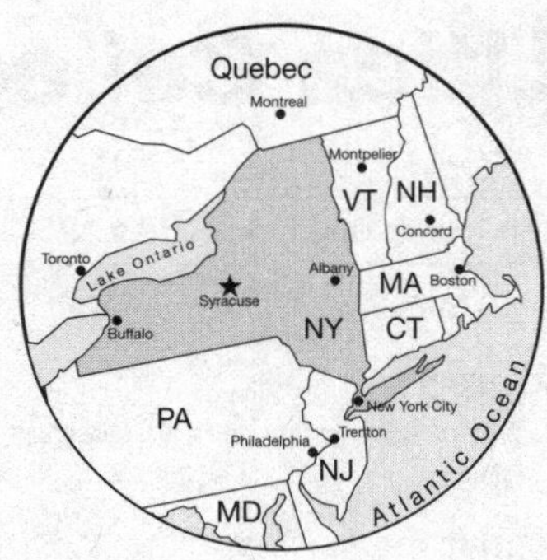

General Admissions

Very important factors include: rigor of secondary school record, class rank, academic GPA, application essay, standardized test scores, recommendation(s), interview, extracurricular activities, talent/ability, character/personal qualities, volunteer work, level of applicant's interest. *Other factors include:* first generation, alumni/ae relation, geographical residence, state residency, racial/ethnic status, work experience. High school diploma is required and GED is accepted. *Academic units recommended:* 4 English, 4 math, 4 science, 4 science labs, 3 foreign language, 4 social studies, 4 history.

Accommodations or Services

Accommodations are decided upon an individual basis after a thorough review of appropriate, current documentation. The accommodations requests must be supported through the documentation provided and must be logically linked to the current impact of the condition on academic functioning.

Financial Aid

Students should submit: FAFSA; Institution's own financial aid form. Applicants will be notified of awards on a rolling basis beginning 4/1. *Need-based scholarships/grants offered:* College/university scholarship or grant aid from institutional funds; Federal Pell; Private scholarships; SEOG; State scholarships/grants. *Loan aid offered:* Direct PLUS loans; Direct Subsidized Stafford Loans; Direct Unsubsidized Stafford Loans. Federal Work-Study Program available. Institutional employment available.

Campus Life

Activities: Campus Ministries; Choral groups; Concert band; Dance; Drama/theater; International Student Organization; Jazz band; Literary magazine; Marching band; Model UN; Music ensembles; Musical theater; Opera; Pep band; Radio station; Student government; Student newspaper; Student-run film society; Symphony orchestra; Television station; Yearbook. **Organizations:** 311 registered organizations, 34 honor societies, 28 religious organizations, 26 fraternities, 22 sororities. **Athletics (Intercollegiate):** *Men:* basketball, cheerleading, crew/rowing, cross-country, diving, football, lacrosse, soccer, swimming, track/field (outdoor). *Women:* basketball, cheerleading, crew/rowing, cross-country, diving, field hockey, ice hockey, lacrosse, soccer, softball, swimming, tennis, track/field (outdoor), volleyball.

ACCOMMODATIONS

Allowed in exams:	
Calculators	Yes
Dictionary	No
Computer	Yes
Spell-checker	Yes
Extended test time	Yes
Scribe	Yes
Proctors	Yes
Oral exams	Yes
Note-takers	Yes
Support services for students with:	
LD	Yes
ADHD	Yes
ASD	Yes
Distraction-reduced environment	Yes
Recording of lecture allowed	Yes
Reading technology	Yes
Audio books	Yes
Other assistive technology	Yes
Priority registration	Yes
Added costs of services:	
For LD	Yes
For ADHD	Yes
For ASD	Yes
LD specialists	Yes
ADHD & ASD coaching	Yes
ASD specialists	Yes
Professional tutors	Yes
Peer tutors	Yes
Max. hours/week for services	7
How professors are notified of student approved accommodations	Student and Disability Office

COLLEGE GRADUATION REQUIREMENTS

Course waivers allowed	Yes
In what courses: Math and foreign language, reviewed on a case by case basis.	
Course substitutions allowed	Yes
In what courses: Math and foreign language, reviewed on a case by case basis.	

Utica College

1600 Burrstone Road, Utica, NY 13502-4892 • Admissions: 315-792-3006 • Fax: 315-792-3003 **Support: CS**

CAMPUS

Type of school	Private (nonprofit)
Environment	City

STUDENTS

Undergrad enrollment	3,488
% male/female	41/59
% from out of state	14
% frosh live on campus	73

FINANCIAL FACTS

Annual tuition	$21,560
Room and board	$12,108
Required fees	$700

GENERAL ADMISSIONS INFO

Application fee	$40
Regular application deadline	Rolling
Nonfall registration	Yes

Admission may be deferred.

Range SAT EBRW	500–600
Range SAT Math	510–610
Range ACT Composite	20–26

ACADEMICS

Student/faculty ratio	13:1
% students returning for sophomore year	71

Most classes have 10–19 students.

Programs/Services for Students with Learning Differences

The Office of Learning Services provides academic support and advisement to students who identify themselves as disabled and who provide appropriate supporting documentation. Accommodations are determined on a case-by-case basis based on supportive documentation provided by the student. Students are responsible for initiating a request for accommodations; for providing documentation of a disability; and for contacting the Office of Learning Services as early as possible upon admission. The Office of Learning Services professional staff members determine eligibility for services based on documentation; consult with students about appropriate accommodations; assist students in self-monitoring the effectiveness of the accommodations; coordinate auxiliary services; provide information regarding rights and responsibilities of students; provide individualized educational advising; and serve as advocates for the student.

Admissions

Utica College does not require the ACT or SAT except for specific programs. Students are evaluated on an individualized basis. Students should have four years of English, three years of social studies, three years of math, three years of science, and two years of foreign language. Documentation of a disability should be sent to the Office of Learning Services. Students are not required to self-disclose the disability during the admission process.

Additional Information

The Office of Learning Services provides accommodations to students with disabilities based on appropriate and current documentation. Services may include priority registration, specific skill remediation, learning and study strategy development, referrals for diagnostic evaluation, time-management strategies, and professional tutoring. Accommodations may include such items as: use of a tape recorder; time extensions for tests and/or alternative testing methods; note-takers; and separate location for tests. An accommodation letter is generated for each student stating what accommodations are appropriate in each individual case. It is the responsibility of the students to meet with their instructors to discuss their disability and their accommodations.

ADMISSIONS INFO FOR STUDENTS WITH LEARNING DIFFERENCES

Phone: 315-792-3032 • Fax: 315-792-3003 • Email: jcborner@utica.edu

SAT/ACT required: No
Interview required: No
Essay required: Yes
Additional application required: No
Documentation submitted to: Office of Learning Services

Special Ed. HS course work accepted: No
Separate application required for Programs/Services: No
Documentation required for:
LD: Psychoeducational evaluation
ADHD: Psychoeducational evaluation
ASD: Psychoeducational evaluation

Utica College

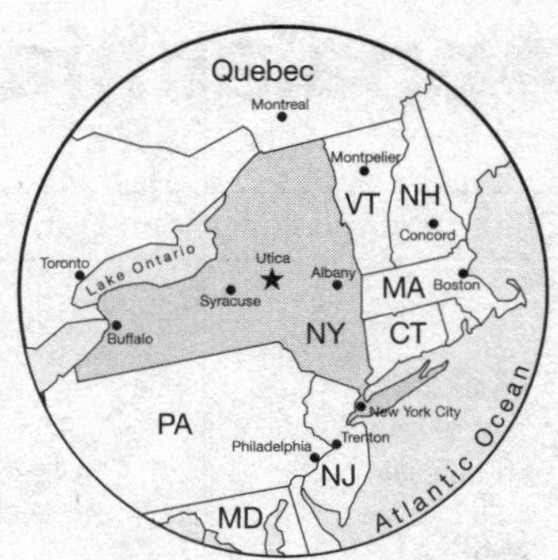

General Admissions

Very important factors include: rigor of secondary school record, academic GPA. *Important factors include:* application essay, standardized test scores. *Other factors include:* class rank, recommendation(s), interview, extracurricular activities, talent/ability, character/personal qualities, first generation, alumni/ae relation, volunteer work, work experience. High school diploma is required and GED is accepted. *Academic units required:* 4 English, 3 math, 3 science, 1 foreign language, 4 social studies, 3.5 academic electives, 1 visual/performing arts, 2.5 unit from above areas or other academic areas.

Accommodations or Services

Accommodations are decided upon an individual basis after a thorough review of appropriate, current documentation. The accommodations requests must be supported through the documentation provided and must be logically linked to the current impact of the condition on academic functioning.

Financial Aid

Students should submit: FAFSA; State aid form. *Need-based scholarships/grants offered:* College/university scholarship or grant aid from institutional funds; Federal Pell; Private scholarships; SEOG; State scholarships/grants. *Loan aid offered:* Direct PLUS loans; Direct Subsidized Stafford Loans; Direct Unsubsidized Stafford Loans. Federal Work-Study Program available. Institutional employment available.

Campus Life

Activities: Campus Ministries; Choral groups; Concert band; Dance; Drama/theater; International Student Organization; Jazz band; Literary magazine; Music ensembles; Radio station; Student government; Student newspaper; Television station; Yearbook. **Organizations:** 80 registered organizations, 8 honor societies, 3 religious organizations, 3 fraternities, 4 sororities. **Athletics (Intercollegiate):** *Men:* baseball, basketball, cross-country, diving, football, golf, ice hockey, lacrosse, soccer, swimming, tennis, track/field (outdoor). *Women:* basketball, cross-country, diving, field hockey, ice hockey, lacrosse, soccer, softball, swimming, tennis, track/field (outdoor), volleyball, water polo.

ACCOMMODATIONS

Allowed in exams:	
Calculators	Yes
Dictionary	Yes
Computer	Yes
Spell-checker	Yes
Extended test time	Yes
Scribe	Yes
Proctors	Yes
Oral exams	Yes
Note-takers	Yes
Support services for students with:	
LD	Yes
ADHD	Yes
ASD	Yes
Distraction-reduced environment	Yes
Recording of lecture allowed	Yes
Reading technology	Yes
Audio books	Yes
Other assistive technology	Yes
Priority registration	Yes
Added costs of services:	
For LD	No
For ADHD	No
For ASD	No
LD specialists	Yes
ADHD & ASD coaching	No
ASD specialists	No
Professional tutors	No
Peer tutors	Yes
Max. hours/week for services	Varies
How professors are notified of student approved accommodations	Student and Disability Office

COLLEGE GRADUATION REQUIREMENTS

Course waivers allowed	No
Course substitutions allowed	Yes
In what courses: Case by case basis	

Appalachian State University

Office of Admissions, Boone, NC 28608-2004 • Admissions: 828-262-2120 • Fax: 828-262-3296 **Support: CS**

CAMPUS

Type of school	Public
Environment	Village

STUDENTS

Undergrad enrollment	17,518
% male/female	44/56
% from out of state	9
% frosh live on campus	99

FINANCIAL FACTS

Annual in-state tuition	$7,710
Annual out-of-state tuition	$22,517
Room and board	$7,414

GENERAL ADMISSIONS INFO

Application fee	$65
Regular application deadline	3/1
Nonfall registration	Yes

Admission may be deferred.

Range SAT EBRW	560–640
Range SAT Math	540–630
Range ACT Composite	22–28

ACADEMICS

Student/faculty ratio	16:1
% students returning for sophomore year	88

Most classes have 20–29 students.

Programs/Services for Students with Learning Differences

The Office of Disability Services (ODS) is the central service that determines the needs of students based on appropriate documentation and helps coordinate suitable academic accommodations. ODS works with students to ensure that they are provided equal access at ASU by providing reasonable accommodations. Additionally, the Scholars with Diverse Abilities (SDAP) program is a two-year program that helps students determine their academic and career goals. The program is inclusive on the University campus.

Admissions

Individuals with disabilities must be accepted to the University through the established admissions process required of all applicants. Admission is based solely on the University's requirements; neither the nature nor severity of a disability is considered in the admission process. The mid 50% of applicants have a weighted GPA of 3.9–4.5, ACT of 21–28, and SAT of 1120–1290. The minimum requirements for the North Carolina University system of which Appalachian State belongs are a 2.5 GPA and a 17 ACT or a 880 SAT. The university is test optional and does not required the submission of ACT or SAT for admission.

Additional Information

The Support the Student Learning Center is home to As-U-R, an intensive support program focusing on supporting students with executive functioning challenges. As-U-R provides a variety of supports and resources for students, including strategic tutoring and peer mentoring, learning strategy instruction tailored to the needs of college students, drop-in assistance, quiet study rooms, specific training to address executive function challenges, access to assistive technology, transition assistance for incoming, as well as graduating students, and coordination of individualized services. Academic Strategy Instruction includes one-on-one appointments on study skills topics and are free to all students.

ADMISSIONS INFO FOR STUDENTS WITH LEARNING DIFFERENCES

Phone: 828-262-3056 • Fax: 828-262-7904 • Email: ods@appstate.edu

SAT/ACT required: Yes (Test optional for 2021)
Interview required: No
Essay required: No
Additional application required: No
Documentation submitted to: ODS

Special Ed. HS course work accepted: No
Separate application required for Programs/Services: No
Documentation required for:
- **LD:** Psychoeducational evaluation
- **ADHD:** Psychoeducational evaluation
- **ASD:** Psychoeducational evaluation

Appalachian State University

General Admissions

Very important factors include: rigor of secondary school record, class rank, academic GPA, standardized test scores. *Important factors include:* application essay, extracurricular activities, talent/ability, character/personal qualities, volunteer work. *Other factors include:* first generation, alumni/ae relation. High school diploma is required and GED is accepted. *Academic units required:* 4 English, 4 math, 3 science, 1 science lab, 2 foreign language, 1 social studies, 1 history.

Accommodations or Services

Accommodations are decided upon an individual basis after a thorough review of appropriate, current documentation. The accommodations requests must be supported through the documentation provided and must be logically linked to the current impact of the condition on academic functioning.

Financial Aid

Students should submit: FAFSA. *Need-based scholarships/grants offered:* College/university scholarship or grant aid from institutional funds; Federal Pell; Private scholarships; SEOG; State scholarships/grants. *Loan aid offered:* Direct PLUS loans; Direct Subsidized Stafford Loans; Direct Unsubsidized Stafford Loans. Federal Work-Study Program available. Institutional employment available.

Campus Life

Activities: Campus Ministries; Choral groups; Concert band; Dance; Drama/theater; International Student Organization; Jazz band; Literary magazine; Marching band; Model UN; Music ensembles; Musical theater; Opera; Pep band; Radio station; Student government; Student newspaper; Student-run film society; Symphony orchestra; Television station. **Organizations:** 383 registered organizations, 18 honor societies, 26 religious organizations, 18 fraternities, 14 sororities. **Athletics (Intercollegiate):** *Men:* baseball, basketball, cross-country, football, golf, soccer, tennis, track/field (outdoor), track/field (indoor), wrestling. *Women:* basketball, cross-country, field hockey, golf, soccer, softball, tennis, track/field (outdoor), track/field (indoor), volleyball.

ACCOMMODATIONS

Allowed in exams:	
Calculators	Yes
Dictionary	No
Computer	Yes
Spell-checker	Yes
Extended test time	Yes
Scribe	Yes
Proctors	Yes
Oral exams	Yes
Note-takers	Yes
Support services for students with:	
LD	Yes
ADHD	Yes
ASD	Yes
Distraction-reduced environment	Yes
Recording of lecture allowed	Yes
Reading technology	Yes
Audio books	Yes
Other assistive technology	Yes
Priority registration	Yes
Added costs of services:	
For LD	No
For ADHD	No
For ASD	No
LD specialists	Yes
ADHD & ASD coaching	Yes
ASD specialists	Yes
Professional tutors	No
Peer tutors	Yes
Max. hours/week for services	Varies
How professors are notified of student approved accommodations	Student

COLLEGE GRADUATION REQUIREMENTS

Course waivers allowed	Yes
In what courses: Case-by-case basis	
Course substitutions allowed	Yes
In what courses: Case-by-case basis	

Brevard College

One Brevard College Drive, Brevard, NC 28712 • Admissions: 828-884-8300 • Fax: 828-884-3790 **Support: CS**

CAMPUS

Type of school	Private (nonprofit)
Environment	Village

STUDENTS

Undergrad enrollment	751
% male/female	55/45
% from out of state	43
% frosh live on campus	94

FINANCIAL FACTS

Annual tuition	$28,400
Room and board	$10,400
Required fees	$1,850

GENERAL ADMISSIONS INFO

Application fee	$0
Regular application deadline	Rolling
Nonfall registration	Yes

Admission may be deferred.

ACADEMICS

Student/faculty ratio	11:1
% students returning for sophomore year	65

Most classes have fewer than 10 students.

Programs/Services for Students with Learning Differences

The Director of Student Accessibility and Disability Services (SADS) oversees educational accommodations for students with appropriate documentation. There is a Request for Academic Accommodation Form to be completed by the student and returned to the office (SADS). The student will be invited to a "Welcome Meeting," where all students needing accommodations attend. It is the student's responsibility to schedule an appointment prior to the beginning of each semester. Students can be granted extended time on tests, alternative testing environment, note-takers, and alternative book formats.

Admissions

There is no special admission process for students with LD. Brevard asks for quite a bit of information from applicants and from those who know the applicants and their learning style. Applicants must provide official transcripts, letters of recommendation from college counselor or dean, a teacher of English, and one other teacher or adult who has worked with the student and knows the student well. Brevard is test optional and does not require students to submit the ACT or SAT. The average GPA is 3.0. Brevard looks for strong verbal ability as represented in an applicant's writing sample(s). This gives the college a chance to know what the student struggles with, what the student feels confident about, what the student wants to achieve by earning a degree. Conditional admission status is available for students who display some, but not all, of the indicators of success as a post-secondary liberal arts student.

Additional Information

With the help of the John Gardner Institute for Excellence in Undergraduate Education, the college has developed the BC CARES partnership. The campus life department and academic affairs is focused on helping students navigate success inside the classroom and on campus. The staff has taken on the roles of mentors, giving first year students supplemental instruction. They are the check-in coaches for new students. Additionally, there is a Writing and Math Lab that is staffed by instructors and peer tutors who work one-on-one with students.

ADMISSIONS INFO FOR STUDENTS WITH LEARNING DIFFERENCES

Phone: 828-884-8131 • Fax: 828-884-8293 • Email: Kathleen.Koontz@brevard.edu

SAT/ACT required: No
Interview required: No
Essay required: No
Additional application required: No
Documentation submitted to: SADS

Special Ed. HS course work accepted: No
Separate application required for Programs/Services: No
Documentation required for:
LD: Psychoeducational evaluation
ADHD: Psychoeducational evaluation
ASD: Psychoeducational evaluation

Brevard College

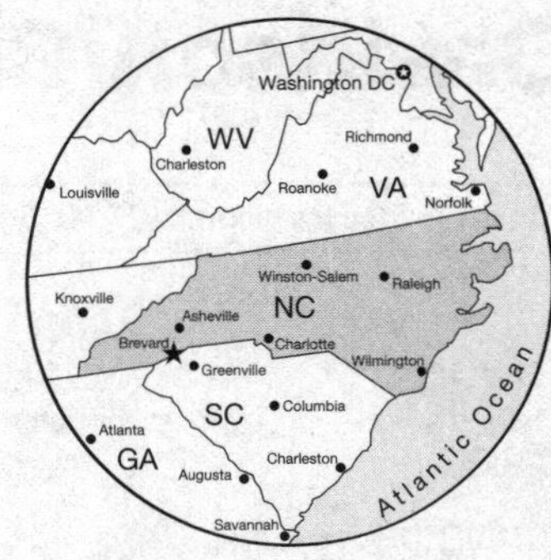

North Carolina

General Admissions

Very important factors include: rigor of secondary school record, academic GPA, level of applicant's interest. *Important factors include:* class rank, application essay, interview, extracurricular activities, talent/ability, character/personal qualities, volunteer work. *Other factors include:* standardized test scores, recommendation(s), alumni/ae relation, work experience. High school diploma is required and GED is accepted. *Academic units recommended:* 4 English, 3 math, 3 science, 1 science lab, 2 foreign language, 4 social studies, 1 history, 4 academic electives.

Accommodations or Services

Accommodations are decided upon an individual basis after a thorough review of appropriate, current documentation. The accommodations requests must be supported through the documentation provided and must be logically linked to the current impact of the condition on academic functioning.

Financial Aid

Students should submit: CSS/Financial Aid PROFILE; FAFSA; Institution's own financial aid form; Noncustodial PROFILE. Applicants will be notified of awards on or about 3/27. *Need-based scholarships/grants offered:* College/university scholarship or grant aid from institutional funds; Federal Pell; Private scholarships; SEOG; State scholarships/grants. *Loan aid offered:* Direct PLUS loans; Direct Subsidized Stafford Loans; Direct Unsubsidized Stafford Loans. Federal Work-Study Program available. Institutional employment available.

Campus Life

Activities: Campus Ministries; Choral groups; Concert band; Dance; Drama/theater; Jazz band; Literary magazine; Music ensembles; Musical theater; Opera; Pep band; Student government; Student newspaper; Yearbook. **Organizations:** 32 registered organizations, 3 honor societies, 1 religious organization. **Athletics (Intercollegiate):** *Men:* baseball, basketball, cheerleading, cross-country, cycling, football, golf, soccer, tennis, track/field (outdoor). *Women:* basketball, cheerleading, cross-country, cycling, golf, soccer, softball, tennis, track/field (outdoor), volleyball.

ACCOMMODATIONS

Allowed in exams:	
Calculators	Yes
Dictionary	Yes
Computer	Yes
Spell-checker	Yes
Extended test time	Yes
Scribe	Yes
Proctors	Yes
Oral exams	Yes
Note-takers	Yes
Support services for students with:	
LD	Yes
ADHD	Yes
ASD	Yes
Distraction-reduced environment	Yes
Recording of lecture allowed	Yes
Reading technology	Yes
Audio books	Yes
Other assistive technology	Yes
Priority registration	Yes
Added costs of services:	
For LD	No
For ADHD	No
For ASD	No
LD specialists	Yes
ADHD & ASD coaching	Yes
ASD specialists	No
Professional tutors	No
Peer tutors	Yes
Max. hours/week for services	Varies
How professors are notified of student approved accommodations	Student

COLLEGE GRADUATION REQUIREMENTS

Course waivers allowed	No
Course substitutions allowed	Yes
In what courses: Case by case basis	

Davidson College

PO Box 7156, Davidson, NC 28035-7156 • Admissions: 704-894-2230 • Fax: 704-894-2016 **Support: CS**

CAMPUS

Type of school	Private (nonprofit)
Environment	Village

STUDENTS

Undergrad enrollment	1,837
% male/female	51/49
% from out of state	78
% frosh live on campus	100

FINANCIAL FACTS

Annual tuition	$54,520
Room and board	$15,225
Required fees	$540

GENERAL ADMISSIONS INFO

Application fee	$50
Regular application deadline	1/7
Nonfall registration	Yes

Admission may be deferred.

Range SAT EBRW	650–730
Range SAT Math	660–755
Range ACT Composite	30–33

ACADEMICS

Student/faculty ratio	9:1
% students returning for sophomore year	95

Most classes have 10–19 students.

Programs/Services for Students with Learning Differences

The Academic Access and Disability Resources Office (AADR) collaborates with the Dean of Students Office to help students who have appropriate documentation receive accommodations. The student has to write to the AADR requesting support for their learning difference. Their accommodations will be based on current documentation but is not guaranteed unless the AADR approves. If the learning plan recommends adjustment to academic requirements, the recommendation is considered by the Curriculum Requirements Committee and may result in the approval of the recommendation or the substitution of the academic requirement. All students seeking accommodations on the basis of a LD must provide recent documentation. The Dean of Students, with the student's permission, will notify professors of an individual student's need for adaptations. Accommodations are not universal in nature, but are designed to meet the specific need of the individual to offset a specific disability.

Admissions

There is no special admission process for students with LD, though the Admissions Office may seek comments from support staff knowledgeable about LD. Students are encouraged to self-disclose their ADHD. The admission process is very competitive, and the disclosure can help the Admissions Office more fairly evaluate the transcript. This disclosure could address any specific academic issues related to the LD, such as no foreign language in high school because of the specific LD or lower grades in math as a result of a math disability. Students have completed at least 4 years of English, 3 years of math, 2 years of the same foreign language, 2 years of science, and 2 years of history/social studies. Interviews are not required or recommended. Davidson is test optional and does not required the ACT or SAT to be admitted.

Additional Information

Support services and accommodations available include, but are not limited to: extended time on tests, referrals for appropriate diagnostic evaluation; individual coaching and instruction in compensatory strategies and study skills; consultation with faculty and staff; student support groups as requested; classroom accommodations such as taped texts, note-takers, use of tape recorders, use of computers with spellcheckers, and individual space for study or test-taking; reduced course loads; and course substitutions or waivers (rarely).

ADMISSIONS INFO FOR STUDENTS WITH LEARNING DIFFERENCES

Phone: 704-894-2225 • Fax: 704-894-2849 • Email: admission@davidson.edu

SAT/ACT required: No
Interview required: No
Essay required: No
Additional application required: No
Documentation submitted to: AADR

Special Ed. HS course work accepted: No
Separate application required for Programs/Services: No
Documentation required for:
LD: Psychoeducational evaluation
ADHD: Psychoeducational evaluation
ASD: Psychoeducational evaluation

Davidson College

North Carolina

General Admissions

Very important factors include: rigor of secondary school record, recommendation(s), character/personal qualities, volunteer work. *Important factors include:* application essay, standardized test scores, extracurricular activities, talent/ability. *Other factors include:* class rank, academic GPA, alumni/ae relation. High school diploma is required and GED is not accepted. *Academic units required:* 4 English, 3 math, 2 science, 2 foreign language, 2 unit from above areas or other academic areas. *Academic units recommended:* 4 math, 4 science, 4 foreign language.

Accommodations or Services

Accommodations are decided upon an individual basis after a thorough review of appropriate, current documentation. The accommodations requests must be supported through the documentation provided and must be logically linked to the current impact of the condition on academic functioning.

Financial Aid

Students should submit: Business/Farm Supplement; CSS/Financial Aid PROFILE; FAFSA; Noncustodial PROFILE. *Need-based scholarships/grants offered:* College/university scholarship or grant aid from institutional funds; Federal Pell; Private scholarships; SEOG; State scholarships/grants. *Loan aid offered:* Direct PLUS loans; Direct Subsidized Stafford Loans; Direct Unsubsidized Stafford Loans. Federal Work-Study Program available. Institutional employment available.

Campus Life

Activities: Campus Ministries; Choral groups; Dance; Drama/theater; International Student Organization; Jazz band; Literary magazine; Music ensembles; Musical theater; Pep band; Radio station; Student government; Student newspaper; Symphony orchestra; Yearbook. **Organizations:** 168 registered organizations, 15 honor societies, 16 religious organizations, 8 fraternities, 6 sororities. **Athletics (Intercollegiate):** *Men:* baseball, basketball, cross-country, diving, football, golf, soccer, swimming, tennis, track/field (outdoor), wrestling. *Women:* basketball, cross-country, diving, field hockey, lacrosse, soccer, swimming, tennis, track/field (outdoor), volleyball.

ACCOMMODATIONS

Allowed in exams:	
Calculators	Yes
Dictionary	Yes
Computer	Yes
Spell-checker	Yes
Extended test time	Yes
Scribe	Yes
Proctors	Yes
Oral exams	No
Note-takers	Yes
Support services for students with:	
LD	Yes
ADHD	Yes
ASD	Yes
Distraction-reduced environment	Yes
Recording of lecture allowed	Yes
Reading technology	Yes
Audio books	Yes
Other assistive technology	Yes
Priority registration	Yes
Added costs of services:	
For LD	No
For ADHD	No
For ASD	No
LD specialists	Yes
ADHD & ASD coaching	Yes
ASD specialists	No
Professional tutors	No
Peer tutors	Yes
Max. hours/week for services	Varies
How professors are notified of student approved accommodations	Student and Disability Office

COLLEGE GRADUATION REQUIREMENTS

Course waivers allowed	No
Course substitutions allowed	Yes
In what courses: Case by case basis	

Duke University

2138 Campus Drive, Durham, NC 27708 • Admissions: 919-684-3214 • Fax: 919-668-1661 **Support: CS**

CAMPUS

Type of school	Private (nonprofit)
Environment	Metropolis

STUDENTS

Undergrad enrollment	6,596
% male/female	50/50
% from out of state	85
% frosh live on campus	100

FINANCIAL FACTS

Annual tuition	$57,934
Room and board	$17,584

GENERAL ADMISSIONS INFO

Application fee	$85
Regular application deadline	1/3
Nonfall registration	No

Admission may be deferred.

Range SAT EBRW	710–770
Range SAT Math	740–800
Range ACT Composite	33–35

ACADEMICS

Student/faculty ratio	6:1
% students returning for sophomore year	98

Most classes have 10–19 students.

Programs/Services for Students with Learning Differences

Duke University provides significant academic support services for students through the Academic Resource Center (ARC). Students who submit appropriate documentation of their learning disability to the ARC clinical director are eligible for assistance in obtaining reasonable academic adjustments and auxiliary aids. In addition, the ARC clinical director and instructors can provide individualized instruction in academic skills and learning strategies, academic support counseling, and referrals for other services. Students with learning disabilities voluntarily access and use the services of the ARC, just as they might access and use other campus resources. Student interactions with the ARC staff are confidential.

Admissions

There is no special admission process for students with LD. All applicants must meet the general Duke admission criteria. Most applicants are in the top 10% of their class and have completed a demanding curriculum including many AP and honors courses. Students must submit two teacher and one counselor recommendation. Applicants may also submit one optional personal recommendation from a coach, a director, or a teacher from an elective. Some students choose to disclose a disability in their application because it is an important element of their experiences or to share how they dealt with an obstacle. Duke considers this information in understanding a student's achievements and evaluates accomplishments within the context of opportunities or challenges presented to that student. Duke does not use information to deny admission to a student. Duke University is currently test optional.

Additional Information

At the ARC there are learning consultants who help with time management, test preparation, class and course strategies, problem solving, and learning alternatives. There are some learning consultants that have an area of expertise and work with a student to identify strategies for problem solving for a particular course. Peer tutors are available as well. Sessions are generally one hour in length, and students can request more than one hour.

ADMISSIONS INFO FOR STUDENTS WITH LEARNING DIFFERENCES

Phone: 919-684-5917 • Fax: 919-684-5917 • Email: admissions@duke.edu

SAT/ACT required: No
Interview required: Yes
Essay required: Yes
Additional application required: Yes
Documentation submitted to: ARC

Special Ed. HS course work accepted: Yes
Separate application required for Programs/Services: Yes
Documentation required for:
LD: Psychoeducational evaluation
ADHD: Psychoeducational evaluation
ASD: Psychoeducational evaluation

Duke University

North Carolina

General Admissions

Very important factors include: rigor of secondary school record, academic GPA, application essay, standardized test scores, recommendation(s), extracurricular activities, talent/ability, character/personal qualities. *Other factors include:* interview, first generation, alumni/ae relation, geographical residence, state residency, religious affiliation/commitment, racial/ethnic status, volunteer work, work experience, level of applicant's interest. High school diploma is required and GED is not accepted. *Academic units recommended:* 4 English, 3 math, 3 science, 3 foreign language, 3 social studies.

Accommodations or Services

Accommodations are decided upon an individual basis after a thorough review of appropriate, current documentation. The accommodations requests must be supported through the documentation provided and must be logically linked to the current impact of the condition on academic functioning.

Financial Aid

Students should submit: FAFSA. Applicants will be notified of awards on a rolling basis beginning 3/1. *Need-based scholarships/grants offered:* College/university scholarship or grant aid from institutional funds; Federal Pell; Private scholarships; SEOG; State scholarships/grants. *Loan aid offered:* Direct PLUS loans; Direct Subsidized Stafford Loans; Direct Unsubsidized Stafford Loans. Federal Work-Study Program available. Institutional employment available.

Campus Life

Activities: Campus Ministries; Choral groups; Concert band; Dance; Drama/theater; International Student Organization; Jazz band; Literary magazine; Marching band; Model UN; Music ensembles; Musical theater; Opera; Pep band; Radio station; Student government; Student newspaper; Student-run film society; Symphony orchestra; Television station. **Organizations:** 200 registered organizations, 10 honor societies, 25 religious organizations, 21 fraternities, 14 sororities. **Athletics (Intercollegiate):** *Men:* baseball, basketball, cross-country, diving, fencing, football, golf, lacrosse, soccer, swimming, tennis, track/field (outdoor), track/field (indoor), volleyball, wrestling. *Women:* basketball, crew/rowing, cross-country, diving, fencing, field hockey, golf, lacrosse, soccer, swimming, tennis, track/field (outdoor), track/field (indoor), volleyball.

ACCOMMODATIONS

Allowed in exams:	
Calculators	Yes
Dictionary	Yes
Computer	Yes
Spell-checker	Yes
Extended test time	Yes
Scribe	Yes
Proctors	Yes
Oral exams	Yes
Note-takers	Yes
Support services for students with:	
LD	Yes
ADHD	Yes
ASD	Yes
Distraction-reduced environment	Yes
Recording of lecture allowed	Yes
Reading technology	Yes
Audio books	Yes
Other assistive technology	Yes
Priority registration	No
Added costs of services:	
For LD	No
For ADHD	No
For ASD	No
LD specialists	Yes
ADHD & ASD coaching	Yes
ASD specialists	No
Professional tutors	No
Peer tutors	Yes
Max. hours/week for services	Unlimited
How professors are notified of student approved accommodations	Student and Disability Office

COLLEGE GRADUATION REQUIREMENTS

Course waivers allowed	No
Course substitutions allowed	No

East Carolina University

Office of Undergraduate Admissions, Greenville, NC 27858-4353 • Admissions: 252-328-6640 • Fax: 252-328-6945 **Support: CS**

CAMPUS

Type of school	Public
Environment	City

STUDENTS

Undergrad enrollment	23,081
% male/female	43/57
% from out of state	9
% frosh live on campus	94

FINANCIAL FACTS

Annual in-state tuition	$7,239
Annual out-of-state tuition	$23,516
Room and board	$10,136

GENERAL ADMISSIONS INFO

Application fee	$75
Regular application deadline	3/1
Nonfall registration	Yes

Admission may be deferred.

Range SAT EBRW	520–600
Range SAT Math	510–590
Range ACT Composite	19–24

ACADEMICS

Student/faculty ratio	18:1
% students returning for sophomore year	82

Most classes have 20–29 students.

Programs/Services for Students with Learning Differences

Disability Support Services (DSS) provides accommodation information to students who complete the Request for Accommodation form. The accommodations can vary depending on the needs of the student who has presented them with the appropriate evaluation from a professional. DSS requires an in-take meeting prior to receiving services. Once the student has had the meeting, they are given a letter to take to their instructors to notify them of accommodations. Tests for classes can be taken at the DSS office once the student completes the Alternative Testing Request. It is also the responsibility of the student to request electronic books prior to attending classes.

Admissions

Although the STEPP Program (Supporting Transition and Education Through Planning and Partnership) has some flexibility in alternate admissions criteria, students who fall short of requirements in multiple areas or who are significantly below standards in a requirement are generally less competitive candidates. In particular, it's important to ensure that applicants complete 2 years of the same foreign language and 4 years of math (Algebra 1, Geometry, Algebra 2, and an "advanced math" course that requires Algebra 2 as a prerequisite) before you graduate from high school. Students should begin their application to STEPP 18 months before enrolling. STEPP's application process considers traditional admissions criteria and seeks to admit students who show a readiness for college and are willing to actively use the support being offered.

Additional Information

The STEPP Program is designed for students with specific learning disabilities. The program offers academic, social, and life-skills support. The program is limited to 10 each year, and there is no additional fee to participate. First year students are required to attend a "boot camp" with their parents to introduce them to the college experience at the university. The student will be required to take five courses provided by STEPP in addition to their academic requirements. There are required study halls, a graduate student mentor, tutors available in certain subjects, and on-going advising. The STEPP Program will also help with supporting a designated residence hall to promote the student meeting other students outside of the program.

ADMISSIONS INFO FOR STUDENTS WITH LEARNING DIFFERENCES

Phone: 252-737-1016 • Fax: 252-737-1192 • Email: dssdept@ecu.edu

SAT/ACT required: Yes (Test optional for 2021)
Interview required: No
Essay required: No
Additional application required: Yes
Documentation submitted to: Disability Support Services

Special Ed. HS course work accepted: No
Separate application required for Programs/Services: Yes
Documentation required for:
LD: Psychoeducational evaluation
ADHD: Psychoeducational evaluation
ASD: Psychoeducational evaluation

East Carolina University

General Admissions

Very important factors include: rigor of secondary school record, academic GPA, standardized test scores, state residency. *Important factors include:* class rank. *Other factors include:* application essay, extracurricular activities, talent/ability, character/personal qualities, first generation, alumni/ae relation, volunteer work, work experience, level of applicant's interest. High school diploma is required and GED is accepted. *Academic units required:* 4 English, 4 math, 3 science, 1 science lab, 2 foreign language, 1 social studies, 1 history. *Academic units recommended:* 4 English, 4 math, 3 science, 1 science lab, 2 foreign language, 2 social studies, 1 history, 1 visual/performing arts.

Accommodations or Services

Accommodations are decided upon an individual basis after a thorough review of appropriate, current documentation. The accommodations requests must be supported through the documentation provided and must be logically linked to the current impact of the condition on academic functioning.

Financial Aid

Students should submit: FAFSA. *Need-based scholarships/grants offered:* College/university scholarship or grant aid from institutional funds; Federal Nursing Scholarships; Federal Pell; Private scholarships; SEOG; State scholarships/grants. *Loan aid offered:* Direct PLUS loans; Direct Subsidized Stafford Loans; Direct Unsubsidized Stafford Loans. Federal Work-Study Program available. Institutional employment available.

Campus Life

Activities: Campus Ministries; Choral groups; Concert band; Dance; Drama/theater; International Student Organization; Jazz band; Literary magazine; Marching band; Model UN; Music ensembles; Musical theater; Opera; Pep band; Radio station; Student government; Student newspaper; Student-run film society; Symphony orchestra; Television station; Yearbook. **Organizations:** 425 registered organizations, 21 honor societies, 28 religious organizations, 23 fraternities, 14 sororities. **Athletics (Intercollegiate):** *Men:* baseball, basketball, cheerleading, cross-country, diving, football, golf, swimming, tennis, track/field (outdoor). *Women:* basketball, cheerleading, cross-country, diving, golf, soccer, softball, swimming, tennis, track/field (outdoor), volleyball.

ACCOMMODATIONS

Allowed in exams:	
Calculators	Yes
Dictionary	Yes
Computer	Yes
Spell-checker	Yes
Extended test time	Yes
Scribe	Yes
Proctors	Yes
Oral exams	Yes
Note-takers	Yes
Support services for students with:	
LD	Yes
ADHD	Yes
ASD	Yes
Distraction-reduced environment	Yes
Recording of lecture allowed	Yes
Reading technology	Yes
Audio books	Yes
Other assistive technology	Yes
Priority registration	Yes
Added costs of services:	
For LD	No
For ADHD	No
For ASD	No
LD specialists	Yes
ADHD & ASD coaching	Yes
ASD specialists	No
Professional tutors	No
Peer tutors	Yes
Max. hours/week for services	Varies
How professors are notified of student approved accommodations	Student

COLLEGE GRADUATION REQUIREMENTS

Course waivers allowed	No
Course substitutions allowed	No

Elon University

50 Campus Drive, Elon, NC 27244-2010 • Admissions: 336-278-3566 • Fax: 336-278-7699 **Support: S**

CAMPUS	
Type of school	Private (nonprofit)
Environment	Town
STUDENTS	
Undergrad enrollment	6,277
% male/female	40/60
% from out of state	81
% frosh live on campus	99
FINANCIAL FACTS	
Annual tuition	$37,921
Room and board	$$13,141
GENERAL ADMISSIONS INFO	
Application fee	$60
Regular application deadline	1/1
Nonfall registration	Yes
Admission may be deferred.	
Range SAT EBRW	590–660
Range SAT Math	570–660
Range ACT Composite	25–30
ACADEMICS	
Student/faculty ratio	12:1
% students returning for sophomore year	91
Most classes have 10–19 students.	

Programs/Services for Students with Learning Differences

Elon University's Disabilities Resource (DR) program supports students with different needs and accommodations. Faculty, staff, administrators, and students work together to find approaches and accommodations that enable students to benefit from the wide variety of programs and activities on campus. DR helps students to connect with instructors and also engages the instructors in understanding the needs of each individual student.

Admissions

Students with disabilities must meet the same admissions criteria as other applicants. There is no special admission process. Most important factors in admissions are academic rigor, grades, Elon is test optional and does not require the ACT or SAT for admission. GPA is converted to 4.0 scale, and then Elon gives weight to honors, AP, or IB courses. Courses required include 4 years English, 3 years math, 2 years foreign language, 3 years social studies, and 3 years science. Students may be admitted with one deficiency. Disclosing a disability is totally up to the applicant.

Additional Information

Students must provide current documentation to request accommodations. They are encouraged to be proactive and develop an ongoing conversation with their professors and service providers. Every student is assigned an advisor, a professor or an administrator who helps students get information regarding programs, tutors, and special needs. All students have access to The Tutoring Center and Writing Center. Waivers for foreign language or math courses are never approved. However, students may request a foreign language substitution. Documentation is required that demonstrates the presence of deficits that make learning a foreign language extremely difficult, as well as, a history of poor grades in the subject. Students who have never taken such classes will be asked to enroll; performance will be evaluated before the end of the drop/add period and a decision will be made regarding the substitution.

ADMISSIONS INFO FOR STUDENTS WITH LEARNING DIFFERENCES

Phone: 336 278-6500 • Fax: 336-278-6672 • Email: swise2@elon.edu

SAT/ACT required: No
Interview required: No
Essay required: Yes
Additional application required: No
Documentation submitted to: The Office of Disabilities Resources

Special Ed. HS course work accepted: No
Separate application required for Programs/Services: No
Documentation required for:
LD: Psychoeducational evaluation
ADHD: Psychoeducational evaluation
ASD: Psychoeducational evaluation

Elon University

North Carolina

General Admissions

Very important factors include: rigor of secondary school record, academic GPA, application essay, standardized test scores, recommendation(s). *Important factors include:* extracurricular activities, talent/ability, alumni/ae relation. *Other factors include:* class rank, character/personal qualities, first generation, geographical residence, state residency, racial/ethnic status, level of applicant's interest. High school diploma is required and GED is accepted. *Academic units required:* 4 English, 3 math, 3 science, 1 science lab, 2 foreign language, 2 social studies, 1 history. *Academic units recommended:* 4 English, 4 math, 3 science, 1 science lab, 3 foreign language, 2 social studies, 1 history.

Accommodations or Services

Accommodations are decided upon an individual basis after a thorough review of appropriate, current documentation. The accommodations requests must be supported through the documentation provided and must be logically linked to the current impact of the condition on academic functioning.

Financial Aid

Students should submit: CSS/Financial Aid PROFILE; FAFSA. *Need-based scholarships/grants offered:* College/university scholarship or grant aid from institutional funds; Federal Pell; Private scholarships; SEOG; State scholarships/grants; United Negro College Fund. *Loan aid offered:* Direct PLUS loans; Direct Subsidized Stafford Loans; Direct Unsubsidized Stafford Loans. Federal Work-Study Program available. Institutional employment available.

Campus Life

Activities: Campus Ministries; Choral groups; Concert band; Dance; Drama/theater; International Student Organization; Jazz band; Literary magazine; Marching band; Model UN; Music ensembles; Musical theater; Pep band; Radio station; Student government; Student newspaper; Student-run film society; Symphony orchestra; Television station; Yearbook. **Organizations:** 284 registered organizations, 27 honor societies, 27 religious organizations, 13 fraternities, 13 sororities. **Athletics (Intercollegiate):** *Men:* baseball, basketball, cheerleading, cross-country, football, golf, soccer, tennis. *Women:* basketball, cheerleading, cross-country, golf, soccer, softball, tennis, track/field (outdoor), track/field (indoor), volleyball.

ACCOMMODATIONS

Allowed in exams:	
Calculators	Yes
Dictionary	Yes
Computer	Yes
Spell-checker	Yes
Extended test time	Yes
Scribe	Yes
Proctors	Yes
Oral exams	No
Note-takers	Yes
Support services for students with:	
LD	Yes
ADHD	Yes
ASD	Yes
Distraction-reduced environment	Yes
Recording of lecture allowed	Yes
Reading technology	Yes
Audio books	Yes
Other assistive technology	Yes
Priority registration	Yes
Added costs of services:	
For LD	No
For ADHD	No
For ASD	No
LD specialists	No
ADHD & ASD coaching	No
ASD specialists	No
Professional tutors	No
Peer tutors	Yes
Max. hours/week for services	Unlimited
How professors are notified of student approved accommodations	Student and Disability Office

COLLEGE GRADUATION REQUIREMENTS

Course waivers allowed	No
Course substitutions allowed	Yes
In what courses: Case by case basis	

Guilford College

5800 West Friendly Avenue, Greensboro, NC 27410 • Admissions: 336-316-2100 • Fax: 336-316-2954 **Support: CS**

CAMPUS

Type of school	Private (nonprofit)
Environment	City

STUDENTS

Undergrad enrollment	1,525
% male/female	47/53
% from out of state	28
% frosh live on campus	89

FINANCIAL FACTS

Annual tuition	$39,400
Room and board	$12,200
Required fees	$720

GENERAL ADMISSIONS INFO

Application fee	$0
Regular application deadline	Rolling
Nonfall registration	Yes

Admission may be deferred.

Range SAT EBRW	510–590
Range SAT Math	460–580
Range ACT Composite	17–24

ACADEMICS

Student/faculty ratio	12:1
% students returning for sophomore year	66

Most classes have 10–19 students.

Programs/Services for Students with Learning Differences

The Accessibility Resource Center (ARC) oversees programs and services for students with documented learning differences with the goal to help them become self-advocates. Once a student completes an ARC Registration Agreement form, they will need to make an appointment with the ARC director. During the meeting, they will discuss what academic services and accommodations the student will need. In turn, the student is responsible for communicating and negotiating with each of their professors.

Admissions

Students with learning differences meet the same criteria for admissions. There are three ways to apply to Guilford College: the Guilford College Application, the Common Application, and the CFNC Application. A personal essay is required of each applicant. Guilford College is test optional. Disclosure of learning differences is not required, but if an admitted student self-discloses, the schools works to connect them with the Accessibility Resource Center prior to entry, so they can set up necessary accommodations and services needed to succeed.

Additional Information

The Learning Commons is the study space for the Learning and Writing Center, open to all students. The Commons offers academic coaching service that includes helping students develop learning strategies, assignment help, and writing assistance. There is drop-in tutoring for specific subjects and weekly meetings with course-specific tutors. There are professional tutors for support in general writing, studying and reading skills, and time management development, as well as peer tutors for course-specific tutoring.

ADMISSIONS INFO FOR STUDENTS WITH LEARNING DIFFERENCES

Phone: 336-316-2837 • Fax: 336-316-2946 • Email: mongiovika@guilford.edu

SAT/ACT required: No
Interview required: No
Essay required: Yes
Additional application required: No
Documentation submitted to: Accessibility Resource Center

Special Ed. HS course work accepted: Yes
Separate application required for Programs/Services: No
Documentation required for:
LD: Psychoeducational evaluation
ADHD: Psychoeducational evaluation
ASD: Psychoeducational evaluation

Guilford College

North Carolina

General Admissions

Important factors include: rigor of secondary school record, class rank, academic GPA, application essay, standardized test scores, character/personal qualities. *Other factors include:* recommendation(s), interview, extracurricular activities, talent/ability, first generation, alumni/ae relation, geographical residence, state residency, religious affiliation/commitment, racial/ethnic status, work experience. High school diploma is required and GED is accepted. *Academic units recommended:* 4 English, 3 math, 3 science, 2 foreign language, 3 social studies.

Accommodations or Services

Accommodations are decided upon an individual basis after a thorough review of appropriate, current documentation. The accommodations requests must be supported through the documentation provided and must be logically linked to the current impact of the condition on academic functioning.

Financial Aid

Students should submit: FAFSA; Institution's own financial aid form. *Need-based scholarships/grants offered:* College/university scholarship or grant aid from institutional funds; Federal Pell; Private scholarships; SEOG; State scholarships/grants. *Loan aid offered:* Direct PLUS loans; Direct Subsidized Stafford Loans; Direct Unsubsidized Stafford Loans. Federal Work-Study Program available. Institutional employment available.

Campus Life

Activities: Campus Ministries; Choral groups; Drama/theater; International Student Organization; Jazz band; Music ensembles; Pep band; Radio station; Student government; Student newspaper; Student-run film society; Yearbook. **Organizations:** 54 registered organizations, 1 honor society, 5 religious organizations. **Athletics (Intercollegiate):** *Men:* baseball, basketball, cross-country, football, golf, lacrosse, rugby, soccer, tennis. *Women:* basketball, cross-country, lacrosse, rugby, soccer, softball, swimming, tennis, volleyball.

ACCOMMODATIONS

Allowed in exams:	
Calculators	Yes
Dictionary	Yes
Computer	Yes
Spell-checker	Yes
Extended test time	Yes
Scribe	Yes
Proctors	Yes
Oral exams	Yes
Note-takers	Yes
Support services for students with:	
LD	Yes
ADHD	Yes
ASD	Yes
Distraction-reduced environment	Yes
Recording of lecture allowed	Yes
Reading technology	Yes
Audio books	Yes
Other assistive technology	Yes
Priority registration	No
Added costs of services:	
For LD:	No
For ADHD:	No
For ASD:	No
LD specialists	No
ADHD & ASD coaching	Yes
ASD specialists	No
Professional tutors	Yes
Peer tutors	Yes
Max. hours/week for services	Varies
How professors are notified of student approved accommodations	Student and Disability Office

COLLEGE GRADUATION REQUIREMENTS

Course waivers allowed	Yes
In what courses: Math/Quantitative Literacy	
Course substitutions allowed	Yes
In what courses: Math/Quantitative Literacy	

High Point University

One University Parkway, High Point, NC 27268 • Admissions: 336-841-9216 • Fax: 336-888-6382 **Support: SP**

CAMPUS

Type of school	Private (nonprofit)
Environment	City

STUDENTS

Undergrad enrollment	4,561
% male/female	44/56
% from out of state	74
% frosh live on campus	98

FINANCIAL FACTS

Annual tuition	$38,080
Room and board	$15,438

GENERAL ADMISSIONS INFO

Application fee	$50
Regular application deadline	3/1
Nonfall registration	Yes

Admission may be deferred.

Range SAT EBRW	550–630
Range SAT Math	540–630
Range ACT Composite	22–28

ACADEMICS

Student/faculty ratio	15:1
% students returning for sophomore year	83

Most classes have 10–19 students.

Programs/Services for Students with Learning Differences

Learning Excellence is a fee-based academic support program. This program offers individualized support for students who feel they need help with transitioning to college, time management and organization, study skill development, and strategy development for learning differences. This program is one semester long, and a student must be sure to reapply each semester for this program. There is a limited number of students that are accepted into the Learning Excellence Program. Accommodations are based on the documentation required by the program, which includes, but is not limited to a written report by a qualified professional indicating the diagnosis, symptom or condition, the history of the student's disability, and recommendations directly linked to impact the diagnosis has on the students learning.

Admissions

High Point University is test optional and does not require the ACT or SAT for admission. High Point asks applicants to submit one letter of recommendation. Course requirements include 4 years English, 3 years math, 3 years social studies, 3 years science, and 2 years foreign language.

Additional Information

Academic Services are available on campus for all students. Besides academic advising, there is tutorial support provided by undergraduate peer tutors and supplemental instruction tutoring, as well as student success workshops. These workshops include study planning, writing tips, leadership, mastering math, and time management. Through this office there is small group tutoring for specific subjects.

ADMISSIONS INFO FOR STUDENTS WITH LEARNING DIFFERENCES

Phone: 336-841-9026 • Fax: 336-888-6324 • Email: rberger@highpoint.edu

SAT/ACT required: No
Interview required: No
Essay required: Yes
Additional application required: No
Documentation submitted to: Learning Excellence

Special Ed. HS course work accepted: No
Separate application required for Programs/Services: Yes
Documentation required for:
LD: Psychoeducational evaluation
ADHD: Psychoeducational evaluation
ASD: Psychoeducational evaluation

High Point University

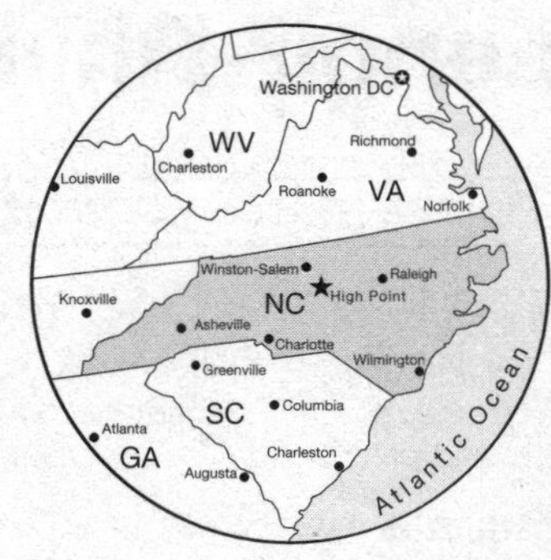

North Carolina

General Admissions

Very important factors include: academic GPA. *Important factors include:* rigor of secondary school record, application essay, standardized test scores, recommendation(s), interview, extracurricular activities, talent/ability, character/personal qualities, volunteer work. *Other factors include:* class rank, first generation, alumni/ae relation. High school diploma is required and GED is accepted. *Academic units required:* 4 English, 3 math, 3 science, 1 science lab, 2 foreign language, 3 social studies. *Academic units recommended:* 4 English, 4 math, 3 science, 1 science lab, 3 foreign language, 3 social studies.

Accommodations or Services

Accommodations are decided upon an individual basis after a thorough review of appropriate, current documentation. The accommodations requests must be supported through the documentation provided and must be logically linked to the current impact of the condition on academic functioning.

Financial Aid

Students should submit: FAFSA; State aid form. *Need-based scholarships/grants offered:* College/university scholarship or grant aid from institutional funds; Federal Pell; Private scholarships; SEOG; State scholarships/grants. *Loan aid offered:* Direct PLUS loans; Direct Subsidized Stafford Loans; Direct Unsubsidized Stafford Loans. Federal Work-Study Program available. Institutional employment available.

Campus Life

Activities: Campus Ministries; Choral groups; Concert band; Dance; Drama/theater; International Student Organization; Jazz band; Literary magazine; Model UN; Music ensembles; Musical theater; Opera; Pep band; Radio station; Student government; Student newspaper; Student-run film society; Symphony orchestra; Television station; Yearbook. **Organizations:** 139 registered organizations, 23 honor societies, 6 religious organizations, 6 fraternities, 10 sororities. **Athletics (Intercollegiate):** *Men:* baseball, basketball, cheerleading, cross-country, golf, soccer, tennis, track/field (outdoor), track/field (indoor). *Women:* basketball, cheerleading, cross-country, golf, soccer, tennis, track/field (outdoor), track/field (indoor), volleyball.

ACCOMMODATIONS

Allowed in exams:	
Calculators	Yes
Dictionary	No
Computer	Yes
Spell-checker	No
Extended test time	Yes
Scribe	Yes
Proctors	Yes
Oral exams	Yes
Note-takers	Yes
Support services for students with:	
LD	Yes
ADHD	Yes
ASD	Yes
Distraction-reduced environment	Yes
Recording of lecture allowed	Yes
Reading technology	Yes
Audio books	Yes
Other assistive technology	Yes
Priority registration	Yes
Added costs of services:	
For LD	Yes
For ADHD	Yes
For ASD	Yes
LD specialists	Yes
ADHD & ASD coaching	Yes
ASD specialists	No
Professional tutors	Yes
Peer tutors	Yes
Max. hours/week for services	Varies
How professors are notified of student approved accommodations	Student and Disability Office

COLLEGE GRADUATION REQUIREMENTS

Course waivers allowed	No
Course substitutions allowed	Yes
In what courses: Foreign Language	

Lenoir-Rhyne University

524 7th Ave NE, Hickory, NC 28603 • Admissions: 828-328-7300 **Support: S**

CAMPUS

Type of school	Private (nonprofit)
Environment	Town

STUDENTS

Undergrad enrollment	1846
% male/female	41/59
% from out of state	17
% frosh live on campus	65

FINANCIAL FACTS

Annual tuition	$39,900
Room and board	$12,700

GENERAL ADMISSIONS INFO

Application fee	$35
Regular application deadline	Rolling
Nonfall registration	Yes

Admission may be deferred.

Range SAT EBRW	480–590
Range SAT Math	490–580
Range ACT Composite	18–24

ACADEMICS

Student/faculty ratio	12:1
% students returning for sophomore year	72

Most classes have 20–29 students.

Programs/Services for Students with Learning Differences

The Lohr Learning Commons and Academic Support Programs is the central department where students with appropriate documentation can request academic services. The Academic Support Services and Resources offers individual and group tutoring provide by trained peer tutors. There are academic coaching sessions with professional staff on a variety of topics. There is no additional fee for these services. The Writing Center provides assistance in developing and organizing ideas and help in choosing a topic or generating ideas. With appropriate documentation, students with LD/ADHD may be eligible for some of the following services or accommodations: the use of calculators, dictionary, computer or spellcheck in exams; extended time on tests; distraction-free environment; scribe; proctor; oral exams; note taker; tape recorder in class; books on tape; and substitution of the foreign language requirement. Extensive documentation is required for foreign language substitution.

Admissions

All students are required to meet the same admissions criteria whether they are a student with a learning difference or not. They should apply as all other students. Applicants must submit a score for either the ACT or SAT. Course requirements include at least 4 years of English and math, 1 year of science (plus chemistry for nursing students), and 1 year of social studies.

Additional Information

The Office of Student Success supports all students on campus. Their services include time management, skill development, study skill techniques, and academic and major exploration. Academic coaching provides students with targeted academic support. Appointments usually last 30 minutes to one hour and focus on topics, including learning and study strategies, time management, organization, and goal setting.

ADMISSIONS INFO FOR STUDENTS WITH LEARNING DIFFERENCES

Phone: 828-328-7296 • Fax: 828-267-3441 • Email: sherry.proctor@lr.edu

SAT/ACT required: Yes
Interview required: No
Essay required: Yes
Additional application required: No
Documentation submitted to: Lohr Learning Commons

Special Ed. HS course work accepted: No
Separate application required for Programs/Services: No
Documentation required for:
LD: Psychoeducational evaluation
ADHD: Psychoeducational evaluation
ASD: Psychoeducational evaluation

Lenoir-Rhyne University

General Admissions

Very important factors include: academic GPA, standardized test scores. *Important factors include:* rigor of secondary school record, class rank, application essay, recommendation(s), extracurricular activities, character/personal qualities, volunteer work, work experience. High school diploma is required and GED is accepted. *Academic units required:* 4 English, 3 math, 1 science, 1 science lab, 2 foreign language, 1 history. *Academic units recommended:* 4 English, 4 math, 2 science, 1 science lab, 3 foreign language, 2 history.

Accommodations or Services

Accommodations are decided upon an individual basis after a thorough review of appropriate, current documentation. The accommodations requests must be supported through the documentation provided and must be logically linked to the current impact of the condition on academic functioning.

Financial Aid

Students should submit: FAFSA. *Need-based scholarships/grants offered:* College/university scholarship or grant aid from institutional funds; Federal Pell; Private scholarships; SEOG; State scholarships/grants. *Loan aid offered:* Direct PLUS loans; Direct Subsidized Stafford Loans; Direct Unsubsidized Stafford Loans. Federal Work-Study Program available. Institutional employment available.

Campus Life

Activities: Campus Ministries; Choral groups; Concert band; Dance; Drama/theater; International Student Organization; Jazz band; Literary magazine; Marching band; Model UN; Music ensembles; Musical theater; Pep band; Radio station; Student government; Student newspaper; Student-run film society; Symphony orchestra; Yearbook. **Organizations:** 57 registered organizations, 12 honor societies, 7 religious organizations, 4 fraternities, 5 sororities. **Athletics (Intercollegiate):** *Men:* baseball, basketball, cheerleading, cross-country, football, golf, soccer. *Women:* basketball, cheerleading, cross-country, golf, soccer, softball, volleyball.

ACCOMMODATIONS

Allowed in exams:	
Calculators	Yes
Dictionary	Yes
Computer	Yes
Spell-checker	Yes
Extended test time	Yes
Scribe	Yes
Proctors	Yes
Oral exams	Yes
Note-takers	Yes
Support services for students with:	
LD	Yes
ADHD	Yes
ASD	Yes
Distraction-reduced environment	Yes
Recording of lecture allowed	Yes
Reading technology	Yes
Audio books	Yes
Other assistive technology	Yes
Priority registration	No
Added costs of services:	
For LD	No
For ADHD	No
For ASD	No
LD specialists	No
ADHD & ASD coaching	No
ASD specialists	No
Professional tutors	Yes
Peer tutors	Yes
Max. hours/week for services	Varies
How professors are notified of student approved accommodations	Student and Disability Office

COLLEGE GRADUATION REQUIREMENTS

Course waivers allowed	No
Course substitutions allowed	Yes
In what courses: Case by case basis	

North Carolina State University

Box 7103, Raleigh, NC 27695 • Admissions: 919-515-2434 • Fax: 919-515-5039 **Support: S**

CAMPUS

Type of school	Public
Environment	Metropolis

STUDENTS

Undergrad enrollment	24,238
% male/female	53/47
% from out of state	9
% frosh live on campus	97

FINANCIAL FACTS

Annual in-state tuition	$9,100
Annual out-of-state tuition	$29,220
Room and board	$11,601

GENERAL ADMISSIONS INFO

Application fee	$85
Regular application deadline	1/15
Nonfall registration	Yes

Admission may be deferred.

Range SAT EBRW	620–690
Range SAT Math	630–730
Range ACT Composite	27–32

ACADEMICS

Student/faculty ratio	14:1
% students returning for sophomore year	94

Most classes have 20–29 students.

Programs/Services for Students with Learning Differences

The Disability Resource Office (DRO) determines appropriate academic adjustments and accommodations for students with disabilities. Once approved for accommodations, at the beginning of each semester the student must follow the DRO process, including providing an Accommodation Letter to each instructor. The Disability Resource Office helps students and their parents make a smooth transition from high school to the university.

Admissions

All students (with and without disabilities) are admitted under the same standards set by the university. Students applying to NC State for fall 2021 do not have to submit either the ACT or SAT. The average GPA is 3.8 and an average 29.3 ACT or 1337 SAT. Course requirements include 4 years English, 4 years math, 2 years foreign language, 3 science, and 2 social studies.

Additional Information

All enrolled students may receive services and accommodations through the coordinator of learning disabilities of the DSO if they present appropriate documentation. The documentation should include a written report with a statement specifying areas of learning disabilities. Services and accommodations available with appropriate documentation include extended testing times for exams; reduced distraction testing environments; use of calculators, dictionaries, computers, or spellcheckers during exams; proctors; note-takers; audio format; assistive technology; and priority registration. Scribes are provided either by the department of the course or through the DRO.

ADMISSIONS INFO FOR STUDENTS WITH LEARNING DIFFERENCES

Phone: 919-515-7653 • Fax: 919-513-2840 • Email: disability@ncsu.edu

SAT/ACT required: No
Interview required: No
Essay required: Yes
Additional application required: No
Documentation submitted to: Disability Resources Office

Special Ed. HS course work accepted: No
Separate application required for Programs/Services: No
Documentation required for:
- **LD:** Psychoeducational evaluation
- **ADHD:** Psychoeducational evaluation
- **ASD:** Psychoeducational evaluation

North Carolina State University

North Carolina

General Admissions

Very important factors include: rigor of secondary school record, class rank, academic GPA, standardized test scores. *Other factors include:* application essay, recommendation(s), extracurricular activities, talent/ability, character/personal qualities, first generation, alumni/ae relation, geographical residence, state residency, racial/ethnic status, volunteer work, work experience, level of applicant's interest. High school diploma is required and GED is accepted. *Academic units required:* 4 English, 4 math, 3 science, 1 science lab, 2 foreign language, 1 social studies, 1 history. *Academic units recommended:* 4 English, 4 math, 3 science, 1 science lab, 2 foreign language, 1 social studies, 1 history.

Accommodations or Services

Accommodations are decided upon an individual basis after a thorough review of appropriate, current documentation. The accommodations requests must be supported through the documentation provided and must be logically linked to the current impact of the condition on academic functioning.

Financial Aid

Students should submit: FAFSA. Applicants will be notified of awards on a rolling basis beginning 4/1. *Need-based scholarships/grants offered:* College/university scholarship or grant aid from institutional funds; Federal Pell; Private scholarships; SEOG; State scholarships/grants; United Negro College Fund. *Loan aid offered:* Direct PLUS loans; Direct Subsidized Stafford Loans; Direct Unsubsidized Stafford Loans. Federal Work-Study Program available. Institutional employment available.

Campus Life

Activities: Campus Ministries; Choral groups; Concert band; Dance; Drama/theater; International Student Organization; Jazz band; Literary magazine; Marching band; Model UN; Music ensembles; Musical theater; Pep band; Radio station; Student government; Student newspaper; Student-run film society; Symphony orchestra; Yearbook. **Organizations:** 646 registered organizations, 20 honor societies, 63 religious organizations, 29 fraternities, 20 sororities. **Athletics (Intercollegiate):** *Men:* baseball, basketball, cheerleading, cross-country, diving, football, golf, riflery, soccer, swimming, tennis, track/field (outdoor), track/field (indoor), wrestling. *Women:* basketball, cheerleading, cross-country, diving, golf, gymnastics, riflery, soccer, softball, swimming, tennis, track/field (outdoor), track/field (indoor), volleyball.

ACCOMMODATIONS

Allowed in exams:	
Calculators	Yes
Dictionary	Yes
Computer	Yes
Spell-checker	Yes
Extended test time	Yes
Scribe	Yes
Proctors	Yes
Oral exams	Yes
Note-takers	Yes
Support services for students with:	
LD	Yes
ADHD	Yes
ASD	Yes
Distraction-reduced environment	Yes
Recording of lecture allowed	Yes
Reading technology	Yes
Audio books	Yes
Other assistive technology	Yes
Priority registration	Yes
Added costs of services:	
For LD	No
For ADHD	No
For ASD	No
LD specialists	No
ADHD & ASD coaching	No
ASD specialists	No
Professional tutors	No
Peer tutors	Yes
Max. hours/week for services	Varies
How professors are notified of student approved accommodations	Director

COLLEGE GRADUATION REQUIREMENTS

Course waivers allowed	No
Course substitutions allowed	No

St. Andrews University

1700 Dogwood Mile, Laurinburg, NC 28352 • Admissions: 910-277-5555 • Fax: 910-277-5020 **Support: S**

CAMPUS

Type of school	Private (nonprofit)
Environment	Rural

STUDENTS

Undergrad enrollment	758
% male/female	44/56
% from out of state	39

FINANCIAL FACTS

Annual tuition	$28,680
Room and board	$10,300
Required fees	$1,000

GENERAL ADMISSIONS INFO

Application fee	$35
Regular application deadline	Rolling
Nonfall registration	Yes
Range SAT EBRW	370–580
Range SAT Math	400-580
Range ACT Composite	15–24

ACADEMICS

% students returning for sophomore year	49

Most classes have 10–19 students.

Programs/Services for Students with Learning Differences

The Office of Disability Services and The Center for Academic Success offer a range of support services for students with disabilities. These services are meant to help students devise strategies for meeting college demands and to foster independence, responsibility, and self advocacy. The Office of Disability Services responds to each request for services and helps students develop a viable plan for personal success. The Center for Academic Success (CAS) offers weekly tutoring sessions, walk-in assistance, and by-appointment mentoring and tutoring sessions. The Writing Center is a free resource to all students to assist with writing assignments. There are tutors available at the center to help with writing assignments and editing of written work. Additionally, there are quiet study rooms for students who need to study away from their dorms.

Admissions

Each application is reviewed on an individual basis. Prospective students are strongly encouraged to visit the campus. Students with learning disabilities complete the regular admissions application. There are no minimum test scores or GPA. The admissions office considers extracurricular activities with an emphasis on leadership, volunteerism, and service. Some applicants may be required to submit additional information including an essay, recommendations, resume, sample of scholarly work, or an interview.

Additional Information

Student Success Center is a resource for all students. This Center provides additional guidance, support, and developmental instruction. This is a place where students can receive referrals for academic support, where a list of peer-to-peer tutors and freshman academic advising is available.

ADMISSIONS INFO FOR STUDENTS WITH LEARNING DIFFERENCES

Phone: 910-277-5667 • Fax: 910-277-5746 • Email: admissions@sapc.edu

SAT/ACT required: Yes (Test optional for 2021)
Interview required: No
Essay required: No
Additional application required: No
Documentation submitted to: Student Success Center

Special Ed. HS course work accepted: No
Separate application required for Programs/Services: No
Documentation required for:
LD: Psychoeducational evaluation
ADHD: Psychoeducational evaluation
ASD: Psychoeducational evaluation

St. Andrews University

North Carolina

General Admissions

Important factors include: academic GPA, standardized test scores, extracurricular activities, character/personal qualities. *Other factors include:* rigor of secondary school record, class rank, application essay, recommendation(s), interview, talent/ability, first generation, volunteer work, work experience. High school diploma is required and GED is accepted. *Academic units required:* 3 English, 3 math, 3 science, 1 foreign language, 3 social studies.

Accommodations or Services

Accommodations are decided upon an individual basis after a thorough review of appropriate, current documentation. The accommodations requests must be supported through the documentation provided and must be logically linked to the current impact of the condition on academic functioning.

Financial Aid

Students should submit: FAFSA. *Need-based scholarships/grants offered:* College/university scholarship or grant aid from institutional funds; Federal Pell; Private scholarships; SEOG; State scholarships/grants. *Loan aid offered:* Direct PLUS loans; Direct Subsidized Stafford Loans; Direct Unsubsidized Stafford Loans. Federal Work-Study Program available. Institutional employment available.

Campus Life

Organizations: 30 registered organizations, 3 honor societies, 1 religious organization. **Athletics (Intercollegiate):** *Men:* baseball, basketball, cross-country, equestrian sports, golf, horseback riding, lacrosse, soccer, track/field (outdoor), wrestling. *Women:* basketball, cross-country, equestrian sports, horseback riding, lacrosse, soccer, softball, track/field (outdoor), volleyball, wrestling.

ACCOMMODATIONS

Allowed in exams:	
Calculators	Yes
Dictionary	Yes
Computer	Yes
Spell-checker	Yes
Extended test time	Yes
Scribe	Yes
Proctors	Yes
Oral exams	Yes
Note-takers	Yes
Support services for students with:	
LD	Yes
ADHD	Yes
ASD	Yes
Distraction-reduced environment	Yes
Recording of lecture allowed	Yes
Reading technology	Yes
Audio books	Yes
Other assistive technology	Yes
Priority registration	No
Added costs of services:	
For LD	No
For ADHD	No
For ASD	No
LD specialists	No
ADHD & ASD coaching	No
ASD specialists	No
Professional tutors	No
Peer tutors	Yes
Max. hours/week for services	Varies
How professors are notified of student approved accommodations	Student

COLLEGE GRADUATION REQUIREMENTS

Course waivers allowed	No
Course substitutions allowed	Yes
In what courses: Case by case basis	

University of North Carolina at Asheville

One University Heights, Asheville, NC 28804-8502 • Admissions: 828-251-6481 • Fax: 828-251-6482 **Support: S**

CAMPUS

Type of school	Public
Environment	Town

STUDENTS

Undergrad enrollment	3,286
% male/female	43/57
% from out of state	11
% frosh live on campus	96

FINANCIAL FACTS

Annual in-state tuition	$4,246
Annual out-of-state tuition	$21,594
Room and board	$9,950
Required fees	$3,220

GENERAL ADMISSIONS INFO

Application fee	$75
Regular application deadline	8/1
Nonfall registration	Yes

Admission may be deferred.

Range SAT EBRW	560–650
Range SAT Math	530–620
Range ACT Composite	22–27

ACADEMICS

Student/faculty ratio	13:1
% students returning for sophomore year	73

Most classes have 10–19 students.

Programs/Services for Students with Learning Differences

The goal of the Office of Academic Accessibility (OAA) is to provide students with disabilities equal access to university courses, programs, services, and activities in a self-reliant manner when possible. The Office is in charge of helping students with any questions about how to find tutors, communicate with professors, and general educational advice. There is an online Student Application and a review of the documentation. Documentation should include a brief diagnostic statement identifying the disability, description of the current functional impact to student's experiences, and assessment method(s) used and assessment score reports used.

Admissions

Admissions criteria and procedures for the university are the same for students with and without disabilities. NCS is test optional and does not require the submission of the ACT or SAT for admission. The committee reviews each application and looks specifically at the quality of the student's high school curriculum, performance, grade trend and class rank (if provided), and scores on ACT or SAT. Qualitative factors such as the essay, activities, honors achieved, leadership roles, special talents and abilities, are also important in the review process. Applicants not admitted during the formal admission process to UNC Asheville may appeal the university's decision. These students are encouraged to contact the assigned Admissions Counselor to get help with the appeal. This counselor will advocate for the student's appeal and help the student submit the appropriate materials to provide the best chance for the appeal to be granted.

Additional Information

The Academic Success Center gives students the ability to take care of essential student business and receive services in one convenient location. Academic accessibility meets individual needs by coordinating and implementing internal policies regarding programs, services, and activities for individuals with disabilities. The office functions as a source of information, educational outreach, and advice, as well as a communication link for individuals with disabilities.

ADMISSIONS INFO FOR STUDENTS WITH LEARNING DIFFERENCES

Phone: 828-250-3979 • Fax: 828-251-6492 • Email: caogburn@unca.edu

SAT/ACT required: Yes (Test optional for 2021)
Interview required: No
Essay required: Yes
Additional application required: Yes
Documentation submitted to: OAA

Special Ed. HS course work accepted: Yes
Separate application required for Programs/Services: Yes
Documentation required for:
LD: Psychoeducational evaluation
ADHD: Psychoeducational evaluation
ASD: Psychoeducational evaluation

University of North Carolina at Asheville

North Carolina

General Admissions

Very important factors include: rigor of secondary school record, class rank, academic GPA, application essay, standardized test scores, recommendation(s). *Important factors include:* extracurricular activities, talent/ability, character/personal qualities. *Other factors include:* first generation, alumni/ae relation, geographical residence, state residency, racial/ethnic status, volunteer work, work experience, level of applicant's interest. High school diploma is required and GED is not accepted. *Academic units required:* 4 English, 4 math, 3 science, 1 science lab, 2 foreign language, 2 social studies.

Accommodations or Services

Accommodations are decided upon an individual basis after a thorough review of appropriate, current documentation. The accommodations requests must be supported through the documentation provided and must be logically linked to the current impact of the condition on academic functioning.

Financial Aid

Students should submit: FAFSA. Applicants will be notified of awards on a rolling basis beginning 12/15. *Need-based scholarships/grants offered:* College/university scholarship or grant aid from institutional funds; Federal Pell; Private scholarships; SEOG; State scholarships/grants. *Loan aid offered:* Direct PLUS loans; Direct Subsidized Stafford Loans; Direct Unsubsidized Stafford Loans. Federal Work-Study Program available. Institutional employment available.

Campus Life

Activities: Campus Ministries; Choral groups; Concert band; Dance; Drama/theater; International Student Organization; Jazz band; Literary magazine; Model UN; Music ensembles; Musical theater; Pep band; Radio station; Student government; Student newspaper; Student-run film society. **Organizations:** 79 registered organizations, 2 honor societies, 9 religious organizations, 2 fraternities, 2 sororities. **Athletics (Intercollegiate):** *Men:* baseball, basketball, cheerleading, cross-country, soccer, tennis, track/field (outdoor). *Women:* basketball, cheerleading, cross-country, soccer, tennis, track/field (outdoor), volleyball.

ACCOMMODATIONS

Allowed in exams:	
Calculators	Yes
Dictionary	Yes
Computer	Yes
Spell-checker	Yes
Extended test time	Yes
Scribe	Yes
Proctors	Yes
Oral exams	Yes
Note-takers	Yes
Support services for students with:	
LD	Yes
ADHD	Yes
ASD	Yes
Distraction-reduced environment	Yes
Recording of lecture allowed	Yes
Reading technology	Yes
Audio books	Yes
Other assistive technology	Yes
Priority registration	Yes
Added costs of services:	
For LD	No
For ADHD	No
For ASD	No
LD specialists	No
ADHD & ASD coaching	No
ASD specialists	No
Professional tutors	No
Peer tutors	Yes
Max. hours/week for services	Varies
How professors are notified of student approved accommodations	Student

COLLEGE GRADUATION REQUIREMENTS

Course waivers allowed — Yes

In what courses: Math, foreign language, and others on an individual basis.

Course substitutions allowed — Yes

In what courses: Math, foreign language, and others on an individual basis.

University of North Carolina at Chapel Hill

Jackson Hall, Chapel Hill, NC 27599-2200 • Admissions: 919-962-2211 • Fax: 919-962-3045 **Support: CS**

CAMPUS

Type of school	Public
Environment	Town

STUDENTS

Undergrad enrollment	19,034
% male/female	40/60
% from out of state	14
% frosh live on campus	99

FINANCIAL FACTS

Annual in-state tuition	$7,019
Annual out-of-state tuition	$34,198
Room and board	$11,526
Required fees	$2,027

GENERAL ADMISSIONS INFO

Application fee	$85
Regular application deadline	1/15
Nonfall registration	No

Admission may be deferred.

Range SAT EBRW	650–730
Range SAT Math	650–760
Range ACT Composite	27–33

ACADEMICS

Student/faculty ratio	13:1
% students returning for sophomore year	96

Most classes have 10–19 students.

Programs/Services for Students with Learning Differences

The Learning Center and Accessibility Resources & Service (ARS) provides reasonable accommodations, resources and services to undergraduate and graduate/professional students with disabilities. They are not involved with the admissions process to the university. Documentation should be submitted to the Accessibility Resources & Services. A committee led by the Director of Disabilities Services reviews all the documentation. Each accommodation is evaluated on a case-by-case basis. ARS staff will work with the student to determine specific accommodations. They will help to reach out to professors to evaluate if the course is able to provide reasonable accommodations in the way the class is taught.

Admissions

Students with disabilities are expected to meet the same standards of academic admission criteria and academic performance as other students. The University of North Carolina at Chapel Hill is part of the UNC system, and there are general minimum requirements for all of the colleges in the system. However, UNC Chapel Hill is very selective in the admission process. The typical applicant has taken many honors and AP and IB courses and has demonstrated a high-level of involvement in leadership, volunteerism, and extracurricular activities. UNC is test optional and may review this decision in the future.

Additional Information

The Learning Disability Services (LDS) is available to students with Learning Disabilities and Attention Deficit Disorder. It is important that students understand the impact of their learning difference on their academic success. They should be able to self-advocate with the direction of the LDS and understand what tools and strategies are necessary to enhance learning in the classroom. The peer tutors are undergraduate students who have done well in a particular course.

ADMISSIONS INFO FOR STUDENTS WITH LEARNING DIFFERENCES

Phone: 919-962-3954 • Fax: 919-843-5609 • Email: ars@unc.edu

SAT/ACT required: Yes (Test optional for 2021)
Interview required: No
Essay required: Yes
Additional application required: Yes
Documentation submitted to: ARS

Special Ed. HS course work accepted: No
Separate application required for Programs/Services: Yes
Documentation required for:
- **LD:** Psychoeducational evaluation
- **ADHD:** Psychoeducational evaluation
- **ASD:** Psychoeducational evaluation

University of North Carolina at Chapel Hill

North Carolina

General Admissions

Very important factors include: rigor of secondary school record, application essay, standardized test scores, recommendation(s), extracurricular activities, talent/ability, character/personal qualities, state residency. *Important factors include:* class rank, academic GPA, volunteer work, work experience. *Other factors include:* first generation, alumni/ae relation, racial/ethnic status. High school diploma is required and GED is not accepted. *Academic units required:* 4 English, 4 math, 3 science, 1 science lab, 2 foreign language, 1 social studies, 1 history, 1 academic elective.

Accommodations or Services

Accommodations are decided upon an individual basis after a thorough review of appropriate, current documentation. The accommodations requests must be supported through the documentation provided and must be logically linked to the current impact of the condition on academic functioning.

Financial Aid

Students should submit: FAFSA;. Applicants will be notified of awards on a rolling basis beginning 3/1. *Need-based scholarships/grants offered:* College/university scholarship or grant aid from institutional funds; Federal Pell; Private scholarships; SEOG; State scholarships/grants. *Loan aid offered:* Direct PLUS loans; Direct Subsidized Stafford Loans; Direct Unsubsidized Stafford Loans. Federal Work-Study Program available. Institutional employment available.

Campus Life

Activities: Campus Ministries; Choral groups; Concert band; Dance; Drama/theater; International Student Organization; Jazz band; Literary magazine; Marching band; Model UN; Music ensembles; Musical theater; Opera; Pep band; Radio station; Student government; Student newspaper; Student-run film society; Symphony orchestra; Television station; Yearbook. **Organizations:** 836 registered organizations, 30 honor societies, 47 religious organizations, 30 fraternities, 24 sororities. **Athletics (Intercollegiate):** *Men:* baseball, basketball, cross-country, diving, fencing, football, golf, lacrosse, soccer, swimming, tennis, track/field (outdoor), track/field (indoor), wrestling. *Women:* basketball, crew/rowing, cross-country, diving, fencing, field hockey, golf, gymnastics, lacrosse, soccer, softball, swimming, tennis, track/field (outdoor), track/field (indoor), volleyball.

ACCOMMODATIONS

Allowed in exams:	
Calculators	Yes
Dictionary	Yes
Computer	Yes
Spell-checker	Yes
Extended test time	Yes
Scribe	Yes
Proctors	Yes
Oral exams	Yes
Note-takers	Yes
Support services for students with:	
LD	Yes
ADHD	Yes
ASD	Yes
Distraction-reduced environment	Yes
Recording of lecture allowed	Yes
Reading technology	Yes
Audio books	Yes
Other assistive technology	Yes
Priority registration	Yes
Added costs of services:	
For LD	No
For ADHD	No
For ASD	No
LD specialists	Yes
ADHD & ASD coaching	Yes
ASD specialists	No
Professional tutors	No
Peer tutors	Yes
Max. hours/week for services	10
How professors are notified of student approved accommodations	Student and Disability Office

COLLEGE GRADUATION REQUIREMENTS

Course waivers allowed	No
Course substitutions allowed	Yes
In what courses: Case by case basis	

University of North Carolina at Greensboro

PO Box 26170, Greensboro, NC 27402-6170 • Admissions: 336-334-5243 • Fax: 336-334-4180 **Support: CS**

CAMPUS

Type of school	Public
Environment	City

STUDENTS

Undergrad enrollment	16,106
% male/female	33/67
% from out of state	3
% frosh live on campus	79

FINANCIAL FACTS

Annual in-state tuition	$7,403
Annual out-of-state tuition	$22,562
Room and board	$9,264

GENERAL ADMISSIONS INFO

Application fee	$65
Regular application deadline	3/1
Nonfall registration	Yes
Range SAT EBRW	500–590
Range SAT Math	500–570
Range ACT Composite	19–24

ACADEMICS

Student/faculty ratio	16:1
% students returning for sophomore year	75

Most classes have 20–29 students.

Programs/Services for Students with Learning Differences

The Office of Accessibility Resources and Services (OARS) help students understand their learning needs and styles. Specific accommodations are unique to every student. Modifications can include extended time, a reader, and scribe. The staff teaches the students organization and management skills. Additionally, the staff serves as advocates at times where the student may need to explain to the professors the type of accommodations necessary in the classroom.

Admissions

Individuals with disabilities enter the University through the established admissions procedures that are required of all applicants. Neither the nature nor the severity of one's disability is used as a criterion for admission. An applicant's admission is based solely on academic qualifications. The University of North Carolina system has minimum admission requirements for all colleges in the system. Each college also has its own admission criteria. The average GPA at UNC Greensboro is 3.8. The average ACT is 23 and the middle 50% SAT is 1030–1220. The university is currently test optional and may review this policy for future admission cycles. Course requirements include 4 years English, 4 years math, 3 years science, 2 years social science, and 2 years foreign language. Students not accepted could be matched with a NC university that has admission slots available for qualified students.

Additional Information

The Academic Achievement Center provides tutoring, supplemental instruction, and academic skill development. Services such as tutoring, academic skills, coaching, supplemental instruction, and workshops. Students registered with the Office of Accessibility Resources and Services have access to support to help them better understand their specific learning styles. The Student Success Center offers free tutoring for all students in 100-200 level courses.

ADMISSIONS INFO FOR STUDENTS WITH LEARNING DIFFERENCES

Phone: 336-334-5440 • Fax: 336-334-4415 • Email: oars@uncg.edu

SAT/ACT required: Yes (Test optional for 2021)
Interview required: No
Essay required: Yes
Additional application required: Yes
Documentation submitted to: OARS

Special Ed. HS course work accepted: No
Separate application required for Programs/Services: Yes
Documentation required for:
LD: Psychoeducational evaluation
ADHD: Psychoeducational evaluation
ASD: Psychoeducational evaluation

University of North Carolina at Greensboro

North Carolina

General Admissions

Very important factors include: rigor of secondary school record, academic GPA. *Important factors include:* standardized test scores. *Other factors include:* class rank, application essay, recommendation(s), extracurricular activities, volunteer work. High school diploma is required and GED is accepted. *Academic units required:* 4 English, 4 math, 3 science, 1 science lab, 2 foreign language, 2 social studies.

Accommodations or Services

Accommodations are decided upon an individual basis after a thorough review of appropriate, current documentation. The accommodations requests must be supported through the documentation provided and must be logically linked to the current impact of the condition on academic functioning.

Financial Aid

Students should submit: FAFSA; Institution's own financial aid form. Applicants will be notified of awards on a rolling basis beginning 4/1. *Need-based scholarships/grants offered:* College/university scholarship or grant aid from institutional funds; Federal Pell; Private scholarships; SEOG; State scholarships/grants. *Loan aid offered:* Direct PLUS loans; Direct Subsidized Stafford Loans; Direct Unsubsidized Stafford Loans. Federal Work-Study Program available. Institutional employment available.

Campus Life

Activities: Campus Ministries; Choral groups; Concert band; Dance; Drama/theater; International Student Organization; Jazz band; Literary magazine; Music ensembles; Musical theater; Opera; Pep band; Radio station; Student government; Student newspaper; Student-run film society; Symphony orchestra. **Organizations:** 195 registered organizations, 39 honor societies, 36 religious organizations, 39 fraternities, 36 sororities. **Athletics (Intercollegiate):** *Men:* baseball, basketball, cross-country, golf, soccer, tennis, wrestling. *Women:* basketball, cross-country, golf, soccer, softball, tennis, volleyball.

ACCOMMODATIONS

Allowed in exams:	
Calculators	Yes
Dictionary	Yes
Computer	Yes
Spell-checker	Yes
Extended test time	Yes
Scribe	Yes
Proctors	Yes
Oral exams	Yes
Note-takers	Yes
Support services for students with:	
LD	Yes
ADHD	Yes
ASD	Yes
Distraction-reduced environment	Yes
Recording of lecture allowed	Yes
Reading technology	Yes
Audio books	Yes
Other assistive technology	Yes
Priority registration	No
Added costs of services:	
For LD	No
For ADHD	No
For ASD	No
LD specialists	Yes
ADHD & ASD coaching	Yes
ASD specialists	No
Professional tutors	No
Peer tutors	Yes
Max. hours/week for services	Varies
How professors are notified of student approved accommodations	Student

COLLEGE GRADUATION REQUIREMENTS

Course waivers allowed	No
Course substitutions allowed	Yes
In what courses: Case by case basis	

University of North Carolina—Charlotte

9201 University City Boulevard, Charlotte, NC 28223-0001 • Admissions: 704-687-5507 • Fax: 704-687-6483 **Support: CS**

CAMPUS

Type of school	Public
Environment	Metropolis

STUDENTS

Undergrad enrollment	24,070
% male/female	53/47
% from out of state	5
% frosh live on campus	77

FINANCIAL FACTS

Annual in-state tuition	$3,812
Annual out-of-state tuition	$17,246
Room and board	$11,100
Required fees	$3,232

GENERAL ADMISSIONS INFO

Application fee	$75
Regular application deadline	6/1
Nonfall registration	Yes

Range SAT EBRW	560–640
Range SAT Math	560–650
Range ACT Composite	22–26

ACADEMICS

Student/faculty ratio	19:1
% students returning for sophomore year	83

Most classes have 20–29 students.

Programs/Services for Students with Learning Differences

The Office of Disability Services is the main campus office that helps to determine accommodations. Testing accommodations are specific to the student. Examples of common accommodations include extended time, distraction-free environment, scribes, and more. Through collaboration with the institution's diverse community, Disability Services facilitates accommodations, discourse, and engagement to promote a universally accessible learning environment for all.

Admissions

All applicants must meet the same admission criteria. The middle 50% GPA for admitted students is 3.2–3.7 unweighted or 3.8–4.5 weighted. The mid 50% ACT is 22–27 or SAT 1130–1280. Admission decisions are based on GPA, courses (including senior year courses) and may depend on the identified major. Business, nursing, computing & informatics, and engineering are more competitive. The university is currently test optional and may review this policy in future years. Required high school courses include 4 years English, 4 years math, 3 years science, 2 years social studies, and 2 years foreign language.

Additional Information

The Peer Assisted Learning program offers students additional academic group study support lead by Peer Leaders, who are current students who have completed the course successfully. Tutorial Services are provided in course-specific academic subjects. Services are free and available to any enrolled undergraduate student. **Students Obtaining Success (SOS)** is a peer-based mentoring program for students experiencing academic difficulties or on academic probation. SOS is a semester-long program and is individually tailored to help students identify unique challenges and improve academic performance. SOS empowers students to identify strengths and challenges, develop academic and personal success strategies, and connect with appropriate campus resources. 49er Rebound is a program to assist students who are experiencing academic difficulty at UNC Charlotte and helps them return to school.

ADMISSIONS INFO FOR STUDENTS WITH LEARNING DIFFERENCES

Phone: 704-687-0040 • Fax: 704-687-1395 • Email: disability@uncc.edu

SAT/ACT required: Yes (Test optional for 2021)
Interview required: No
Essay required: Yes
Additional application required: No
Documentation submitted to: No

Special Ed. HS course work accepted: No
Separate application required for Programs/Services: Yes
Documentation required for:
LD: Psychoeducational evaluation
ADHD: Psychoeducational evaluation
ASD: Psychoeducational evaluation

University of North Carolina—Charlotte

North Carolina

General Admissions

Very important factors include: rigor of secondary school record, academic GPA, standardized test scores. *Other factors include:* extracurricular activities, talent/ability, character/personal qualities, geographical residence, state residency, work experience, level of applicant's interest. High school diploma is required and GED is accepted. *Academic units required:* 4 English, 4 math, 3 science, 1 science lab, 2 foreign language, 1 social studies, 1 history. *Academic units recommended:* 3 foreign language.

Accommodations or Services

Accommodations are decided upon an individual basis after a thorough review of appropriate, current documentation. The accommodations requests must be supported through the documentation provided and must be logically linked to the current impact of the condition on academic functioning.

Financial Aid

Students should submit: FAFSA. Applicants will be notified of awards on a rolling basis beginning 3/15. *Need-based scholarships/grants offered:* College/university scholarship or grant aid from institutional funds; Federal Pell; Private scholarships; SEOG; State scholarships/grants; United Negro College Fund. *Loan aid offered:* Direct PLUS loans; Direct Subsidized Stafford Loans; Direct Unsubsidized Stafford Loans. Federal Work-Study Program available. Institutional employment available.

Campus Life

Activities: Campus Ministries; Choral groups; Concert band; Dance; Drama/theater; International Student Organization; Jazz band; Literary magazine; Marching band; Model UN; Music ensembles; Musical theater; Opera; Pep band; Radio station; Student government; Student newspaper; Student-run film society; Symphony orchestra; Television station. **Organizations:** 363 registered organizations, 14 honor societies, 47 religious organizations, 22 fraternities, 16 sororities. **Athletics (Intercollegiate):** *Men:* baseball, basketball, cross-country, golf, soccer, tennis, track/field (outdoor). *Women:* basketball, cross-country, soccer, softball, tennis, track/field (outdoor), volleyball.

ACCOMMODATIONS

Allowed in exams:	
Calculators	Yes
Dictionary	Yes
Computer	Yes
Spell-checker	Yes
Extended test time	Yes
Scribe	Yes
Proctors	Yes
Oral exams	Yes
Note-takers	Yes
Support services for students with:	
LD	Yes
ADHD	Yes
ASD	Yes
Distraction-reduced environment	Yes
Recording of lecture allowed	Yes
Reading technology	Yes
Audio books	Yes
Other assistive technology	Yes
Priority registration	Yes
Added costs of services:	
For LD	No
For ADHD	No
For ASD	No
LD specialists	Yes
ADHD & ASD coaching	Yes
ASD specialists	No
Professional tutors	No
Peer tutors	Yes
Max. hours/week for services	Varies
How professors are notified of student approved accommodations	Student

COLLEGE GRADUATION REQUIREMENTS

Course waivers allowed	No
Course substitutions allowed	No

University of North Carolina—Wilmington

601 South College Rd., Wilmington, NC 28403-5904 • Admissions: 910-962-3243 • Fax: 910-962-3038 **Support: CS**

CAMPUS	
Type of school	Public
Environment	City
STUDENTS	
Undergrad enrollment	14,785
% male/female	37/63
% from out of state	12
% frosh live on campus	93
FINANCIAL FACTS	
Annual in-state tuition	$4,440
Annual out-of-state tuition	$18,508
Room and board	$11,346
Required fees	$2,738
GENERAL ADMISSIONS INFO	
Application fee	$80
Regular application deadline	2/1
Nonfall registration	Yes
Admission may be deferred.	
Range SAT EBRW	590–660
Range SAT Math	580–660
Range ACT Composite	22–27
ACADEMICS	
Student/faculty ratio	18:1
% students returning for sophomore year	86
Most classes have 20–29 students.	

Programs/Services for Students with Learning Differences

It is up to the students to register with the Disability Resource Center (DRC) by making an appointment with a staff member to discuss the student's academic needs. Each semester the student must work with the DRC in order to request similar or different accommodations since different classes may require different accommodations. Students with disabilities are expected to maintain the same responsibility for their education as other students. This includes maintaining the same academic levels, attending class, maintaining appropriate behavior, and providing notification of any special needs. It is the student's responsibility to utilize the services and keep in close contact with the Disability Resource Center. DRC does not do any formal assessments but does have a referral list available.

Admissions

Courses required include: 4 English, 4 math, 2 foreign language, 3 science, and 2 social studies. UNC Wilmington is test optional and applicants can decide whether or not to submit a score. This policy may change in the future and applicants should check with the admission policy every year for standardized testing. The middle 50% ACT composite is 24–27. Middle 50% SAT is 200–1310. UNCW superscores either test. The middle 50% weighted GPA is 3.8–4.4 (A/B average). The minimum GPA for the UNC System is a 2.5, but these applicants are unlikely to be admitted. A GPA will not be recalculated, however, it is reviewed in the context of the student's high school's individual grading scale (regional college reps are familiar with high schools). Class rank will be considered, if provided (not in classes less than 50 students).

Additional Information

The University Learning Center provides academic support through reasonable accommodations such as tutoring and deciding what to study and how to study. The tutoring is free, and most tutoring is one-on-one. There are also small groups sessions. Writing consultations are available for all academic writing. There is also Supplemental Instruction (SI), which is peer-facilitated group review sessions hosted by students who have already taken the specific course.

ADMISSIONS INFO FOR STUDENTS WITH LEARNING DIFFERENCES

Phone: 910-962-7555 • Fax: 910-962-7556 • Email: stonec@uncw.edu

SAT/ACT required: Yes (Test optional for 2021)
Interview required: No
Essay required: Yes
Additional application required: No
Documentation submitted to: DRC

Special Ed. HS course work accepted: No
Separate application required for Programs/Services: No
Documentation required for:
LD: Psychoeducational evaluation
ADHD: Psychoeducational evaluation
ASD: Psychoeducational evaluation

University of North Carolina—Wilmington

General Admissions

Very important factors include: rigor of secondary school record, academic GPA, application essay, standardized test scores, recommendation(s). *Important factors include:* class rank. *Other factors include:* extracurricular activities, talent/ability, character/personal qualities, first generation, alumni/ae relation, geographical residence, state residency, racial/ethnic status, volunteer work, work experience, level of applicant's interest. High school diploma is required and GED is accepted. *Academic units required:* 4 English, 4 math, 3 science, 1 science lab, 2 foreign language, 1 social studies, 1 history.

Accommodations or Services

Accommodations are decided upon an individual basis after a thorough review of appropriate, current documentation. The accommodations requests must be supported through the documentation provided and must be logically linked to the current impact of the condition on academic functioning.

Financial Aid

Students should submit: FAFSA. *Need-based scholarships/grants offered:* College/university scholarship or grant aid from institutional funds; Federal Nursing Scholarships; Federal Pell; Private scholarships; SEOG; State scholarships/grants; United Negro College Fund. *Loan aid offered:* Direct PLUS loans; Direct Subsidized Stafford Loans; Direct Unsubsidized Stafford Loans. Federal Work-Study Program available. Institutional employment available.

Campus Life

Activities: Campus Ministries; Choral groups; Concert band; Dance; Drama/theater; International Student Organization; Literary magazine; Model UN; Music ensembles; Pep band; Radio station; Student government; Student newspaper; Student-run film society; Television station. **Organizations:** 272 registered organizations, 15 honor societies, 19 religious organizations, 15 fraternities, 14 sororities. **Athletics (Intercollegiate):** *Men:* baseball, basketball, cheerleading, cross-country, diving, golf, soccer, swimming, tennis, track/field (outdoor). *Women:* basketball, cheerleading, cross-country, diving, golf, soccer, softball, swimming, tennis, track/field (outdoor), volleyball.

ACCOMMODATIONS

Allowed in exams:	
Calculators	Yes
Dictionary	No
Computer	Yes
Spell-checker	Yes
Extended test time	Yes
Scribe	Yes
Proctors	Yes
Oral exams	Yes
Note-takers	Yes
Support services for students with:	
LD	Yes
ADHD	Yes
ASD	Yes
Distraction-reduced environment	Yes
Recording of lecture allowed	Yes
Reading technology	Yes
Audio books	Yes
Other assistive technology	Yes
Priority registration	No
Added costs of services:	
For LD	No
For ADHD	No
For ASD	No
LD specialists	Yes
ADHD & ASD coaching	No
ASD specialists	Yes
Professional tutors	Yes
Peer tutors	Yes
Max. hours/week for services	Varies
How professors are notified of student approved accommodations	Student and Disability Office

COLLEGE GRADUATION REQUIREMENTS

Course waivers allowed	No
Course substitutions allowed	No

Wake Forest University

P.O. Box 7305 Reynolda Station, Winston-Salem, NC 27109 • Admissions: 336-758-5201• Fax: 336-758-4324 **Support: CS**

CAMPUS

Type of school	Private (nonprofit)
Environment	City

STUDENTS

Undergrad enrollment	5,287
% male/female	47/53
% from out of state	78
% frosh live on campus	99

FINANCIAL FACTS

Annual tuition	$56,722
Room and board	$17,334
Required fees	$1,038

GENERAL ADMISSIONS INFO

Application fee	$65
Regular application deadline	1/1
Nonfall registration	No
Range SAT EBRW	650–720
Range SAT Math	670–770
Range ACT Composite	30–33

ACADEMICS

Student/faculty ratio	10:1
% students returning for sophomore year	94

Most classes have 10–19 students.

Programs/Services for Students with Learning Differences

The Learning Assistance Center (LAC) and Disability Services (LC-DS) offers support for academic success to all students. Once students are enrolled at Wake Forest, all students are required to meet the same standards for graduation. The University endeavors to provide facilities that follow all laws and regulations regarding access for individuals with disabilities. For students with documented disabilities, the program director will work with the student and professors to help implement any approved course accommodations. The students with learning disabilities have a series of conferences with staff members who specialize in academic skills and who help design an overall study plan to improve scholastic performance in those areas needing assistance.

Admissions

Wake Forest is test optional and does not require the submission of ACT or SAT during the admission process, nor are students disadvantaged by not submitting scores. If students want their scores to be evaluated, they can submit these during the admission process. Wake Forest states that there has been no difference in academic achievement at Wake Forest between those who submitted scores and those who declined to do so. Wake Forest College considers the application of any qualified student, regardless of disability, on the basis of the selection criteria established which include personal and academic merit. Personal interviews are encouraged.

Additional Information

The Learning Assistance Program staff will assist students with learning disabilities to learn new approaches to studying and methods for improving reading comprehension, note-taking, time management, study organization, memory, motivation, and self-modification. In addition to one-on-one tutoring in many academic subjects, the LAC provides collaborative learning groups comprised of two to five students. Accommodations are determined based on appropriate documentation. The tutors are advanced undergraduates or graduate students who have demonstrated mastery of specific subject areas and are supervised by the LAC staff for their tutoring activities. The LAC also offers all students individual academic counseling to help develop study, organization, and time management strategies that are important for successful college-level learning. There are also other campus resources and help centers including a Chemistry Center, a Math Center, and a Writing Center.

ADMISSIONS INFO FOR STUDENTS WITH LEARNING DIFFERENCES

Phone: 336-758-5929 • Fax: 336-758-1991 • Email: admissions@wfu.edu

SAT/ACT required: No
Interview required: No
Essay required: Yes
Additional application required: No
Documentation submitted to: LC-DS

Special Ed. HS course work accepted: No
Separate application required for Programs/Services: No
Documentation required for:
LD: Psychoeducational evaluation
ADHD: Psychoeducational evaluation
ASD: Psychoeducational evaluation

Wake Forest University

North Carolina

General Admissions

Very important factors include: rigor of secondary school record, class rank, academic GPA, application essay, character/personal qualities. *Important factors include:* recommendation(s), interview, extracurricular activities, talent/ability. *Other factors include:* standardized test scores, first generation, alumni/ae relation, geographical residence, state residency, religious affiliation/commitment, racial/ethnic status, volunteer work, level of applicant's interest. High school diploma is required and GED is accepted. *Academic units required:* 4 English, 3 math, 1 science, 2 foreign language, 2 social studies. *Academic units recommended:* 4 English, 4 math, 4 science, 4 foreign language, 4 social studies.

Accommodations or Services

Accommodations are decided upon an individual basis after a thorough review of appropriate, current documentation. The accommodations requests must be supported through the documentation provided and must be logically linked to the current impact of the condition on academic functioning.

Financial Aid

Students should submit: CSS/Financial Aid PROFILE; FAFSA; Noncustodial PROFILE; State aid form. *Need-based scholarships/grants offered:* College/university scholarship or grant aid from institutional funds; Federal Pell; Private scholarships; SEOG; State scholarships/grants; United Negro College Fund. *Loan aid offered:* Direct PLUS loans; Direct Subsidized Stafford Loans; Direct Unsubsidized Stafford Loans. Federal Work-Study Program available. Institutional employment available.

Campus Life

Activities: Campus Ministries; Choral groups; Concert band; Dance; Drama/theater; International Student Organization; Jazz band; Literary magazine; Marching band; Model UN; Music ensembles; Musical theater; Pep band; Radio station; Student government; Student newspaper; Student-run film society; Symphony orchestra; Television station; Yearbook. **Organizations:** 168 registered organizations, 16 honor societies, 16 religious organizations, 14 fraternities, 9 sororities. **Athletics (Intercollegiate):** *Men:* baseball, basketball, cheerleading, cross-country, football, golf, soccer, tennis, track/field (outdoor), track/field (indoor). *Women:* basketball, cheerleading, cross-country, field hockey, golf, soccer, tennis, track/field (outdoor), track/field (indoor), volleyball.

ACCOMMODATIONS

Allowed in exams:	
Calculators	No
Dictionary	Yes
Computer	Yes
Spell-checker	Yes
Extended test time	Yes
Scribe	No
Proctors	No
Oral exams	No
Note-takers	No
Support services for students with:	
LD	Yes
ADHD	Yes
ASD	Yes
Distraction-reduced environment	Yes
Recording of lecture allowed	Yes
Reading technology	Yes
Audio books	Yes
Other assistive technology	Yes
Priority registration	No
Added costs of services:	
For LD	No
For ADHD	No
For ASD	No
LD specialists	Yes
ADHD & ASD coaching	No
ASD specialists	No
Professional tutors	No
Peer tutors	Yes
Max. hours/week for services	Varies
How professors are notified of student approved accommodations	Student and Director

COLLEGE GRADUATION REQUIREMENTS

Course waivers allowed	No
Course substitutions allowed	Yes
In what courses: Case by case basis	

Western Carolina University

102 Camp Building, Cullowhee, NC 28723 • Admissions: 828-227-7317 • Fax: 828-227-7319 **Support: CS**

CAMPUS

Type of school	Public
Environment	Rural

STUDENTS

Undergrad enrollment	10,469
% male/female	45/55
% from out of state	10

FINANCIAL FACTS

Annual in-state tuition	$1,000
Annual out-of-state tuition	$5,000
Room and board	$10,845
Required fees	$3,353

GENERAL ADMISSIONS INFO

Application fee	$65
Regular application deadline	3/1
Nonfall registration	Yes
Range SAT EBRW	510–610
Range SAT Math	510–590
Range ACT Composite	20–25

ACADEMICS

Student/faculty ratio	17:1
% students returning for sophomore year	78

Most classes have 20–29 students.

Programs/Services for Students with Learning Differences

The Office of Accessibility Resources (OAS) attempts to respond to the needs of students with learning disabilities by making services and assistive technologies available as needed. Students must submit current documentation. The Disability Coordinator conducts the initial intake meeting with the student to review services and documentation required. This is the person that approves accommodations.

Admissions

Students with learning disabilities are admitted under the same standards as students who do not have learning disabilities. Most applicants are admitted through the standard admission process. Courses required include 4 years English, 4 years math, 3 years science, 2 years social science, and 2 years foreign language. The average GPA is 3.7. Some students who do not meet the standard admission guidelines may be offered an opportunity to enroll through the Academic Success Program (ASP). This program provides a full year of support to motivate and help students develop skills to excel in college.

Additional Information

Examples of services or accommodations are the use of calculators, dictionaries, computers, or spellcheckers during exams; extended time on tests; quiet environments; scribes; proctors; oral exams; note-takers; tape recorders in class; text in alternate format; and priority registration. All students have access to tutoring, writing and math centers, and a technology assistance center. ASP is a conditional admission program that usually requires attendance at a summer program prior to entering as a freshman.

ADMISSIONS INFO FOR STUDENTS WITH LEARNING DIFFERENCES

Phone: 828-227-3886 • Fax: 828-227-7602 • Email: pperrott@wcu.edu

SAT/ACT required: Yes
Interview required: No
Essay required: No
Additional application required: Yes
Documentation submitted to: OAS

Special Ed. HS course work accepted: No
Separate application required for Programs/Services: Yes
Documentation required for:
LD: Psychoeducational evaluation
ADHD: Psychoeducational evaluation
ASD: Psychoeducational evaluation

Western Carolina University

General Admissions

Very important factors include: rigor of secondary school record, class rank, academic GPA, standardized test scores, level of applicant's interest. *Important factors include:* application essay, recommendation(s), extracurricular activities, talent/ability, character/personal qualities. *Other factors include:* interview, first generation, geographical residence, state residency. High school diploma is required and GED is accepted. *Academic units required:* 4 English, 4 math, 3 science, 3 science labs, 2 foreign language, 2 social studies, 1 history, 4 academic electives. *Academic units recommended:* 4 English, 4 math, 3 science, 3 science labs, 2 foreign language, 2 social studies, 1 history, 8 academic electives.

Accommodations or Services

Accommodations are decided upon an individual basis after a thorough review of appropriate, current documentation. The accommodations requests must be supported through the documentation provided and must be logically linked to the current impact of the condition on academic functioning.

Financial Aid

Students should submit: CSS/Financial Aid PROFILE; FAFSA; Noncustodial PROFILE. Applicants will be notified of awards on a rolling basis beginning 12/15. *Need-based scholarships/grants offered:* College/university scholarship or grant aid from institutional funds; Federal Pell; Private scholarships; SEOG; State scholarships/grants. *Loan aid offered:* Direct PLUS loans; Direct Subsidized Stafford Loans; Direct Unsubsidized Stafford Loans. Federal Work-Study Program available. Institutional employment available.

Campus Life

Activities: Campus Ministries; Choral groups; Concert band; Dance; Drama/theater; International Student Organization; Jazz band; Literary magazine; Marching band; Model UN; Music ensembles; Musical theater; Pep band; Radio station; Student government; Student newspaper; Student-run film society; Television station. **Organizations:** 150 registered organizations, 7 honor societies, 17 religious organizations, 13 fraternities, 9 sororities. **Athletics (Intercollegiate):** *Men:* baseball, basketball, cheerleading, cross-country, football, golf, track/field (outdoor), track/field (indoor). *Women:* basketball, cheerleading, cross-country, golf, soccer, softball, tennis, track/field (outdoor), track/field (indoor), volleyball.

ACCOMMODATIONS

Allowed in exams:	
Calculators	Yes
Dictionary	Yes
Computer	Yes
Spell-checker	Yes
Extended test time	Yes
Scribe	Yes
Proctors	Yes
Oral exams	Yes
Note-takers	Yes
Support services for students with:	
LD	Yes
ADHD	Yes
ASD	Yes
Distraction-reduced environment	Yes
Recording of lecture allowed	Yes
Reading technology	Yes
Audio books	No
Other assistive technology	Yes
Priority registration	Yes
Added costs of services:	
For LD	No
For ADHD	No
For ASD	No
LD specialists	Yes
ADHD & ASD coaching	No
ASD specialists	No
Professional tutors	Yes
Peer tutors	Yes
Max. hours/week for services	Varies
How professors are notified of student approved accommodations	Student

COLLEGE GRADUATION REQUIREMENTS

Course waivers allowed	Yes
In what courses: Individually considered	
Course substitutions allowed	Yes
In what courses: Individually considered	

North Dakota State University

PO Box 6050 Dept 2832, Fargo, ND 58108 • Admissions: 701-231-8643 • Fax: 701-231-8802 **Support: S**

CAMPUS

Type of school	Public
Environment	City

STUDENTS

Undergrad enrollment	10,831
% male/female	53/47
% from out of state	58
% frosh live on campus	94

FINANCIAL FACTS

Annual in-state tuition	$8,606
Annual out-of-state tuition	$12,909
Room and board	$8,878
Required fees	$1,427

GENERAL ADMISSIONS INFO

Application fee	$0
Regular application deadline	8/1
Nonfall registration	Yes

Admission may be deferred.

Range SAT EBRW	530–630
Range SAT Math	510–640
Range ACT Composite	21–26

ACADEMICS

Student/faculty ratio	16:1
% students returning for sophomore year	79

Most classes have 20–29 students.

Programs/Services for Students with Learning Differences

NDSU Disability Services DS) offers support and accommodations to students with diagnosed disabilities. Once students have been approved for accommodations, they utilize the Bison Accessibility Portal to make arrangements for the accommodations they have been approved for through DS. Students will need to make requests for accommodations every semester.

Admissions

Students with learning disabilities submit the general application and are expected to meet the same admission standards as all other applicants. Most admitted students have a 2.5 GPA or higher. North Dakota State University is test optional and no ACT or SAT is required to be admitted. This policy may change in future years. Courses required include 4 years English, 3 years math, 3 years lab science, 3 years social science, and 1 year in a core subject area or world language (including foreign languages, Native American languages, or American Sign Language). Students who do not meet these minimum guidelines will still be considered if there is evidence in the student's academic record that demonstrates a high probability of success.

Additional Information

Skills courses are offered. A technology lab/resource room is available for student use. Individual, career, and academic counseling along with support groups are available through the NDSU Counseling Center. Student Support Services Program provides tutoring and small group instruction in study strategies, reading, computers, math, and science. Additionally there is mentoring/coaching available.

ADMISSIONS INFO FOR STUDENTS WITH LEARNING DIFFERENCES

Phone: 701-231-8463 • Fax: 701-231-8520 • Email: ndsu.disability.services@ndsu.edu

SAT/ACT required: Yes (Test optional through 2022)
Interview required: No
Essay required: Recommended
Additional application required: No
Documentation submitted to: Disability Services

Special Ed. HS course work accepted: No
Separate application required for Programs/Services: No
Documentation required for:
- **LD:** Psychoeducational evaluation
- **ADHD:** Psychoeducational evaluation
- **ASD:** Psychoeducational evaluation

North Dakota State University

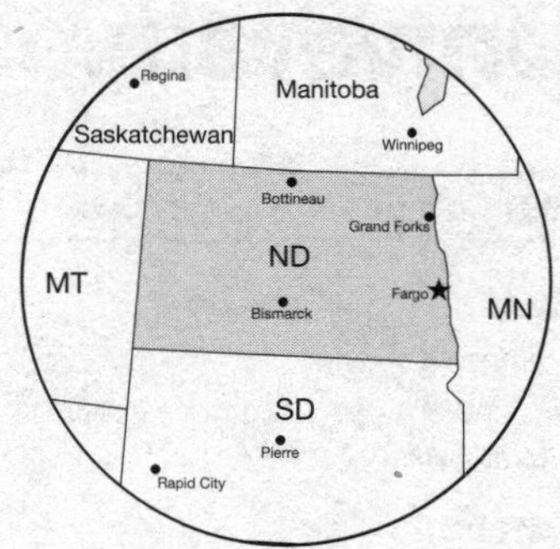

General Admissions

Very important factors include: academic GPA, standardized test scores. High school diploma is required and GED is accepted. *Academic units required:* 4 English, 3 math, 3 science, 3 science labs, 3 social studies.

Accommodations or Services

Accommodations are decided upon an individual basis after a thorough review of appropriate, current documentation. The accommodations requests must be supported through the documentation provided and must be logically linked to the current impact of the condition on academic functioning.

Financial Aid

Students should submit: FAFSA. *Need-based scholarships/grants offered:* College/university scholarship or grant aid from institutional funds; Federal Pell; Private scholarships; SEOG; State scholarships/grants. *Loan aid offered:* Direct PLUS loans; Direct Subsidized Stafford Loans; Direct Unsubsidized Stafford Loans. Federal Work-Study Program available. Institutional employment available.

Campus Life

Activities: Campus Ministries; Choral groups; Concert band; Dance; Drama/theater; International Student Organization; Jazz band; Marching band; Model UN; Music ensembles; Musical theater; Opera; Pep band; Radio station; Student government; Student newspaper; Symphony orchestra; Television station. **Organizations:** 300 registered organizations, 23 honor societies, 22 religious organizations, 12 fraternities, 3 sororities. **Athletics (Intercollegiate):** *Men:* baseball, basketball, cross-country, football, golf, track/field (outdoor), track/field (indoor), wrestling. *Women:* basketball, cross-country, golf, soccer, softball, track/field (outdoor), track/field (indoor), volleyball.

ACCOMMODATIONS

Allowed in exams:	
Calculators	Yes
Dictionary	Yes
Computer	Yes
Spell-checker	Yes
Extended test time	Yes
Scribe	Yes
Proctors	Yes
Oral exams	Yes
Note-takers	Yes
Support services for students with:	
LD	Yes
ADHD	Yes
ASD	Yes
Distraction-reduced environment	Yes
Recording of lecture allowed	Yes
Reading technology	Yes
Audio books	No
Other assistive technology	Yes
Priority registration	Yes
Added costs of services:	
For LD:	No
For ADHD:	No
For ASD:	No
LD specialists	No
ADHD & ASD coaching	No
ASD specialists	No
Professional tutors	No
Peer tutors	Yes
Max. hours/week for services	Unlimited
How professors are notified of student approved accommodations	Student

COLLEGE GRADUATION REQUIREMENTS

Course waivers allowed	Yes
In what courses: Case by case basis	
Course substitutions allowed	Yes
In what courses: Case by case basis	

North Dakota

University of Jamestown

6081 College Lane, Jamestown, ND 58405-0001 • Admissions: 701-252-3467 • Fax: 701-253-4318 **Support: S**

CAMPUS

Type of school	Private (nonprofit)
Environment	Village

STUDENTS

Undergrad enrollment	905
% male/female	55/45
% from out of state	60
% frosh live on campus	95

FINANCIAL FACTS

Annual tuition	$22,718
Room and board	$8,316
Required fees	$780

GENERAL ADMISSIONS INFO

Application fee	$0
Regular application deadline	Rolling
Nonfall registration	Yes

Admission may be deferred.

Range SAT EBRW	480–560
Range SAT Math	470–560
Range ACT Composite	19–25

ACADEMICS

Student/faculty ratio	10:1
% students returning for sophomore year	70

Most classes have 10–19 students.

Programs/Services for Students with Learning Differences

Students must register with the University of Jamestown Office of Disability Services (ODS) after completing the application. The Student Success Center (SSC) includes advising, tutor services, and disability services. The SSC helps to coordinate reasonable accommodations for qualified students with disabilities to ensure their access to the university curriculum, and to support and educate faculty and staff regarding the legal and moral issues of accommodating students with disabilities and the implementation of reasonable accommodations for students with disabilities.

Admissions

Students with learning disabilities must meet the same admission requirements as all other applicants. The minimum GPA is 2.5 and 19 ACT or 990 SAT. Students who do not meet these automatic admission criteria are still encouraged to apply. These students will be reviewed based on their transcripts, planned major, and a short essay describing plans for success in college.

Additional Information

In addition to one-on-one tutoring, the Student Success Center offers several study sessions each semester. If more on-on-one attention is needed beyond a study group, students complete a tutor request form and the Center does their best to line up with a one-on-one tutor. The UJ Writing Center is available to review course writing requirements, including evaluating the writing for self-reflection, research, drafting, and revising. Writing consultants are experienced in navigating this process and provide support.

ADMISSIONS INFO FOR STUDENTS WITH LEARNING DIFFERENCES

Phone: 701-252-3467 • Fax: 701-253-4318 • Email: jolynch@uj.edu

SAT/ACT required: Yes
Interview required: No
Essay required: No
Additional application required: Yes
Documentation submitted to: ODS

Special Ed. HS course work accepted: Yes
Separate application required for Programs/Services: Yes
Documentation required for:
- **LD:** Psychoeducational evaluation
- **ADHD:** Psychoeducational evaluation
- **ASD:** Psychoeducational evaluation

University of Jamestown

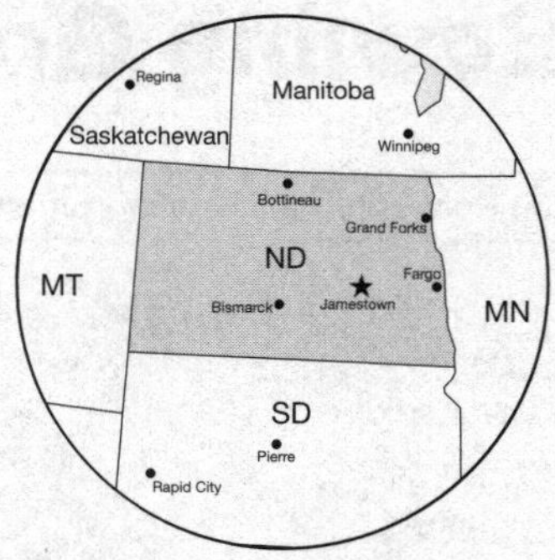

General Admissions

Very important factors include: academic GPA, standardized test scores. *Important factors include:* rigor of secondary school record. *Other factors include:* class rank, application essay, recommendation(s), alumni/ae relation, level of applicant's interest. High school diploma is required and GED is accepted. *Academic units recommended:* 4 English, 3 math, 4 science, 2 foreign language, 3 social studies.

Accommodations or Services

Accommodations are decided upon an individual basis after a thorough review of appropriate, current documentation. The accommodations requests must be supported through the documentation provided and must be logically linked to the current impact of the condition on academic functioning.

Financial Aid

Students should submit: FAFSA. *Need-based scholarships/grants offered:* Federal Pell; Private scholarships; SEOG; State scholarships/grants. *Loan aid offered:* Direct PLUS loans; Direct Subsidized Stafford Loans; Direct Unsubsidized Stafford Loans. Federal Work-Study Program available. Institutional employment available.

Campus Life

Activities: Campus Ministries; Choral groups; Concert band; Drama/theater; International Student Organization; Jazz band; Literary magazine; Music ensembles; Musical theater; Pep band; Student government; Student newspaper. **Organizations:** 26 registered organizations, 5 honor societies, 2 religious organizations. **Athletics (Intercollegiate):** *Men:* baseball, basketball, cross-country, football, golf, track/field (outdoor), track/field (indoor), wrestling. *Women:* basketball, cross-country, golf, soccer, softball, track/field (outdoor), track/field (indoor), volleyball, wrestling.

ACCOMMODATIONS

Allowed in exams:	
Calculators	Yes
Dictionary	Yes
Computer	Yes
Spell-checker	Yes
Extended test time	Yes
Scribe	Yes
Proctors	Yes
Oral exams	Yes
Note-takers	Yes
Support services for students with:	
LD	Yes
ADHD	Yes
ASD	Yes
Distraction-reduced environment	Yes
Recording of lecture allowed	Yes
Reading technology	Yes
Audio books	Yes
Other assistive technology	Yes
Priority registration	No
Added costs of services:	
For LD	No
For ADHD	No
For ASD	No
LD specialists	No
ADHD & ASD coaching	No
ASD specialists	No
Professional tutors	No
Peer tutors	Yes
Max. hours/week for services	Varies
How professors are notified of student approved accommodations	Student and Disability Office

COLLEGE GRADUATION REQUIREMENTS

Course waivers allowed	Yes
In what courses: Case by case basis by petition	
Course substitutions allowed	Yes
In what courses: Case by case basis by petition	

North Dakota

Bowling Green State University

200 University Hall, Bowling Green, OH 43403-0085 • Admissions: 419-372-2478 • Fax: 419-372-6955 **Support: S**

CAMPUS

Type of school	Public
Environment	Town

STUDENTS

Undergrad enrollment	13,772
% male/female	44/56
% from out of state	11
% frosh live on campus	90

FINANCIAL FACTS

Annual in-state tuition	$9,973
Annual out-of-state tuition	$17,962
Room and board	$10,396
Required fees	$2,154

GENERAL ADMISSIONS INFO

Application fee	$45
Regular application deadline	7/15
Nonfall registration	Yes
Range SAT EBRW	500–610
Range SAT Math	510–600
Range ACT Composite	20–25

ACADEMICS

Student/faculty ratio	17:1
% students returning for sophomore year	77

Most classes have 20–29 students.

Programs/Services for Students with Learning Differences

The FLY (Falcon Learning Your Way) Program is a fee-based academic support program that provides a comprehensive range of enhanced services to Bowling Green State University students transitioning from high school to college who have learning and/or attention challenges. The range of services in the FLY Program facilitates student learning, self-advocacy, and independence. Students take ownership of their education through working with a Learning Specialist to create an individualized Falcon Learning Plan; engaging in strategies for time management, organization, reading and writing; utilizing tutoring by peer tutors who are internationally certified by the College Reading and Learning Association; and accessing assistive technology in the BGSU Learning Commons. Learning Commons is open to all BGSU students, and the extent of participation is determined by the student. The lab provides a tutorial service and additional support in the development of efficient techniques for studying, reading textbooks, taking notes, time management, and strategies for effective test-taking and text-preparation.

Admissions

Students must submit a general application to the university prior to submitting an application to the FLY Program. After students have been admitted, they may complete the application to the FLY Program. Students should submit documentation of their disability to Accessibility Services and to the FLY Program. BGSU is test optional and may require standardized tests in future years.

Additional Information

The FLY Program provides learning specialists who help students create an individualized Falcon Learning Plan and meet with students weekly. FLY Program services include regularly scheduled meetings with a learning specialist, tutoring plans, mid-term monitoring and progress reporting, workshops in study skills, time management and coping strategies, and information about other campus resources. Students also have access to accommodations granted by Accessibility Services. There is a special orientation for FLY Program participants before their freshman year. The fee for the FLY Program is $2,500 per semester. General services include priority registration and advising.

ADMISSIONS INFO FOR STUDENTS WITH LEARNING DIFFERENCES

Phone: 419-372-8495 • Fax: 419-372-8496 • Email: access@bgsu.edu

SAT/ACT required: Yes (Test optional for 2021)
Interview required: No
Essay required: No
Additional application required: Yes
Documentation submitted to: Accessibility Services and FLY

Special Ed. HS course work accepted: Yes
Separate application required for Programs/Services: Yes
Documentation required for:
- **LD:** Psychoeducational evaluation
- **ADHD:** Psychoeducational evaluation
- **ASD:** Psychoeducational evaluation

Bowling Green State University

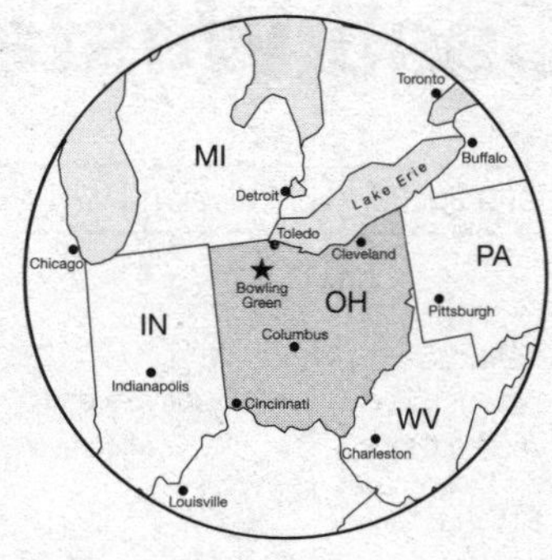

General Admissions

Very important factors include: rigor of secondary school record, academic GPA, standardized test scores. *Important factors include:* class rank. *Other factors include:* application essay, recommendation(s), interview, extracurricular activities, talent/ability, character/personal qualities, first generation, alumni/ae relation, racial/ethnic status, volunteer work, work experience, level of applicant's interest. High school diploma is required and GED is accepted. *Academic units recommended:* 4 English, 3 math, 3 science, 2 science labs, 2 foreign language, 3 social studies, 1 visual/performing arts.

Accommodations or Services

Accommodations are decided upon an individual basis after a thorough review of appropriate, current documentation. The accommodations requests must be supported through the documentation provided and must be logically linked to the current impact of the condition on academic functioning.

Financial Aid

Students should submit: FAFSA. Applicants will be notified of awards on a rolling basis beginning 4/12. *Need-based scholarships/grants offered:* College/university scholarship or grant aid from institutional funds; Federal Pell; Private scholarships; SEOG; State scholarships/grants. *Loan aid offered:* Direct PLUS loans; Direct Subsidized Stafford Loans; Direct Unsubsidized Stafford Loans. Federal Work-Study Program available. Institutional employment available.

Campus Life

Activities: Campus Ministries; Choral groups; Concert band; Dance; Drama/theater; International Student Organization; Jazz band; Literary magazine; Marching band; Model UN; Music ensembles; Musical theater; Opera; Pep band; Radio station; Student government; Student newspaper; Student-run film society; Symphony orchestra; Television station; Yearbook. **Organizations:** 335 registered organizations, 12 honor societies, 14 religious organizations, 20 fraternities, 17 sororities. **Athletics (Intercollegiate):** *Men:* baseball, basketball, cross-country, football, golf, ice hockey, soccer. *Women:* basketball, cross-country, golf, gymnastics, soccer, softball, swimming, tennis, track/field (outdoor), track/field (indoor), volleyball.

ACCOMMODATIONS

Allowed in exams:	
Calculators	Yes
Dictionary	No
Computer	Yes
Spell-checker	Yes
Extended test time	Yes
Scribe	Yes
Proctors	Yes
Oral exams	Yes
Note-takers	Yes
Support services for students with:	
LD	Yes
ADHD	Yes
ASD	Yes
Distraction-reduced environment	Yes
Recording of lecture alowed	Yes
Reading technology	Yes
Audio books	Yes
Other assistive technology	Yes
Priority registration	Yes
Added costs of services:	
For LD	No
For ADHD	No
For ASD	No
LD specialists	No
ADHD & ASD coaching	No
ASD specialists	No
Professional tutors	Yes
Peer tutors	No
Max. hours/week for services	Varies
How professors are notified of student approved accommodations	Student

COLLEGE GRADUATION REQUIREMENTS

Course waivers allowed	No
Course substitutions allowed	Yes
In what courses: Case by case basis	

Case Western Reserve University

10900 Euclid Ave, Cleveland, OH 44106-7055 • Admissions: 216-368-4450 • Fax: 216-368-5111 **Support: S**

CAMPUS

Type of school	Private (nonprofit)
Environment	Metropolis

STUDENTS

Undergrad enrollment	5,269
% male/female	54/46
% from out of state	72
% frosh live on campus	97

FINANCIAL FACTS

Annual tuition	$52,448
Room and board	$16,874
Required fees	$500

GENERAL ADMISSIONS INFO

Application fee	$70
Regular application deadline	1/15
Nonfall registration	Yes

Admission may be deferred.

Range SAT EBRW	640–720
Range SAT Math	700–790
Range ACT Composite	30–34

ACADEMICS

Student/faculty ratio	11:1
% students returning for sophomore year	93

Most classes have 10–19 students.

Programs/Services for Students with Learning Differences

Students at CWRU are not required to disclose disability information to anyone. However, in order to use services and appropriate accommodations, students should notify Disability Resources so that staff members that are aware of a disability. Students decide who needs to know about their disability. Disability Resources is the only department that will determine eligibility. Disability Resources will work closely with students and design an individual plan for accommodations. Included in that plan are strategies for disclosure to professors as well as identifying specific accommodations that will be needed for each course.

Admissions

Admission counselors review academics, life experiences and interests. Applicants should complete a minimum of: 4 years English, 3 years math, 3 years science, 3 years social studies, and 2 years foreign language. Applicants considering engineering or the sciences should have an additional year of math and laboratory science. Liberal arts majors should consider an additional year of social studies and foreign language. Students can submit self-reported scores by completing the form on their applicant portal. Enrolling students will confirm their testing with official score reports. CWRU "superscore" students' test results on SAT or ACT. Middle 50%) SAT is 1310–1470 or ACT 30–34.

Additional Information

Disability Resources and the Office of Accommodated Testing and Services (OATS) are committed to providing required course material in alternate formats for students with approved accommodations. Students who are denied eligibility or who are dissatisfied with an accommodation method may request that the Associate Director of Disability Resources reconsider the decision. Services available can include note-takers, alternate format for print materials, scheduling assistance, assistive technology, testing accommodations, and testing information.

ADMISSIONS INFO FOR STUDENTS WITH LEARNING DIFFERENCES

Phone: 216-368-5230 • Fax: 216-368-8826 • Email: disability@case.edu

SAT/ACT required: Yes (Test optional for 2021)
Interview required: No
Essay required: No
Additional application required: No
Documentation submitted to: Disability Resources

Special Ed. HS course work accepted: Yes
Separate application required for Programs/Services: No
Documentation required for:
LD: Psychoeducational evaluation
ADHD: Psychoeducational evaluation
ASD: Psychoeducational evaluation

Case Western Reserve University

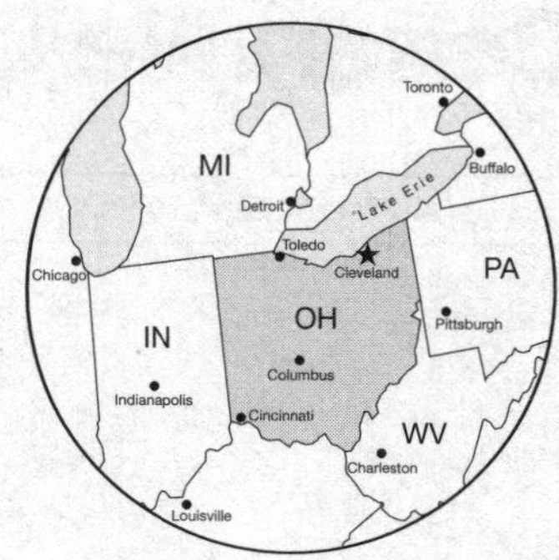

General Admissions

Very important factors include: rigor of secondary school record, class rank, academic GPA, standardized test scores, extracurricular activities. *Important factors include:* application essay, recommendation(s), interview, talent/ability, character/personal qualities, racial/ethnic status, volunteer work. *Other factors include:* first generation, alumni/ae relation, work experience, level of applicant's interest. *Freshman admission requirements:* High school diploma is required and GED is accepted. *Academic units required:* 4 English, 3 math, 3 science, 2 science labs, 2 foreign language, 3 social studies. *Academic units recommended:* 4 math, 3 science labs, 3 foreign language, 4 social studies.

Accommodations or Services

Accommodations are decided upon an individual basis after a thorough review of appropriate, current documentation. The accommodations requests must be supported through the documentation provided and must be logically linked to the current impact of the condition on academic functioning.

Financial Aid

Students should submit: CSS/Financial Aid PROFILE; FAFSA; Institution's own financial aid form; Noncustodial PROFILE. *Need-based scholarships/grants offered:* College/university scholarship or grant aid from institutional funds; Federal Pell; Private scholarships; SEOG; State scholarships/grants. *Loan aid offered:* Direct PLUS loans; Direct Subsidized Stafford Loans; Direct Unsubsidized Stafford Loans. Federal Work-Study Program available. Institutional employment available.

Campus Life

Activities: Campus Ministries; Choral groups; Concert band; Dance; Drama/theater; International Student Organization; Jazz band; Literary magazine; Marching band; Model UN; Music ensembles; Musical theater; Pep band; Radio station; Student government; Student newspaper; Student-run film society; Symphony orchestra; Yearbook. **Organizations:** 249 registered organizations, 8 honor societies, 7 religious organizations, 18 fraternities, 9 sororities. **Athletics (Intercollegiate):** *Men:* baseball, basketball, cross-country, football, soccer, swimming, tennis, track/field (outdoor), track/field (indoor), wrestling. *Women:* basketball, cross-country, soccer, softball, swimming, tennis, track/field (outdoor), track/field (indoor), volleyball.

ACCOMMODATIONS

Allowed in exams:	
Calculators	Yes
Dictionary	No
Computer	Yes
Spell-checker	No
Extended test time	Yes
Scribe	Yes
Proctors	Yes
Oral exams	Yes
Note-takers	Yes
Support services for students with:	
LD	Yes
ADHD	Yes
ASD	Yes
Distraction-reduced environment	Yes
Recording of lecture allowed	Yes
Reading technology	Yes
Audio books	Yes
Other assistive technology	Yes
Priority registration	Yes
Added costs of services:	
For LD	No
For ADHD	No
For ASD	No
LD specialists	No
ADHD & ASD coaching	Yes
ASD specialists	No
Professional tutors	No
Peer tutors	Yes
Max. hours/week for services	Varies
How professors are notified of student approved accommodations	Student and Director

COLLEGE GRADUATION REQUIREMENTS

Course waivers allowed	No
Course substitutions allowed	Yes
In what courses: Case by case basis	

Cedarville University

251 N. Main Street, Cedarville, OH 45314 • Admissions: 937-766-7700 • Fax: 937-766-7575 **Support: CS**

CAMPUS

Type of school	Private (nonprofit)
Environment	Rural

STUDENTS

Undergrad enrollment	3,869
% male/female	46/54
% from out of state	59
% frosh live on campus	96

FINANCIAL FACTS

Annual tuition	$32,364
Room and board	$7,922
Required fees	$200

GENERAL ADMISSIONS INFO

Application fee	$30
Regular application deadline	8/1
Nonfall registration	Yes

Admission may be deferred.

Range SAT EBRW	580–680
Range SAT Math	540–670
Range ACT Composite	23–29

ACADEMICS

Student/faculty ratio	16:1
% students returning for sophomore year	85

Most classes have 10–19 students.

Programs/Services for Students with Learning Differences

Disability Services is part of the Academic Enrichment Center, also known as the Cove. The Cove provides academic resources and support to all students, while Disability Services exists to ensure that students who are impacted by a disability are provided the access that they need. Disability Services is the office designated by Cedarville University to evaluate accommodation requests related to the impact of a diagnosed disability and determine reasonable accommodations for qualified students with disabilities.

Admissions

3.0 GPA, 22 ACT, + file review; if below but close to criteria, students are placed into foundation courses. Cedarville University seeks motivated student who know Christ personally and want to grow academically. Some academic departments require specific credentials, an interview, or audition for admission to their majors. Liberal arts majors are admitted provisionally with 27 ACT or 1280 SAT and a 3.5 high school GPA. However, they must maintain at least a 3.3 GPA and supply two faculty recommendations at the end of the freshman year in order to stay in the program. Nursing Majors need a 24 ACT or 1170 SAT and show a strong commitment to leading a godly lifestyle and a desire to use nursing as ministry for Christ. Engineering applicants need ACT Math sub-score of 25 or higher or an SAT Math sub-score of 620 or higher to declare one of the engineering majors. Students not meeting this requirement but wishing to declare an engineering major will be identified simply as Engineering students until they have competed Calculus I and Digital Logic Design with a "C". Music and Worship majors must audition.

Additional Information

The Cove offers several options for students who need academic support. Students can customize learning experiences to fit needs. Academic Peer Coaches (APCs) are available for 20 weekly sessions provided by Academic Peer Coaches (APCs). APCs are students who lead weekly review and drop-in sessions for a course, working closely with the professor. Students can attend one of the more than 10 tutoring hours in The Cove's tutoring lab each week for math and chemistry courses. There are also study groups and Individual tutoring. Students can apply for a tutor in a study group or individual setting for any course that does not have an APC or tutoring lab.

ADMISSIONS INFO FOR STUDENTS WITH LEARNING DIFFERENCES

Phone: 937-766-7700 • Fax: 937-766-7419 • Email: disabilityservices@cedarville.edu

SAT/ACT required: Yes (Test optional through 2023)
Interview required: No
Essay required: No
Additional application required: No
Documentation submitted to: Disability Services

Special Ed. HS course work accepted: No
Separate application required for Programs/Services: No
Documentation required for:
LD: Psychoeducational evaluation
ADHD: Psychoeducational evaluation
ASD: Psychoeducational evaluation

Cedarville University

General Admissions

Very important factors include: rigor of secondary school record, academic GPA, standardized test scores, recommendation(s), character/personal qualities. *Important factors include:* church leader recommendation, class rank, application essay, alumni/ae relation. *Other factors include:* extracurricular activities, talent/ability, first generation, geographical residence, state residency, volunteer work, work experience. *Freshman admission requirements:* High school diploma is required and GED is accepted. *Academic units recommended:* 4 English, 3 math, 3 science, 2 science labs, 3 foreign language, 2 social studies, 2 history.

Accommodations or Services

Accommodations are decided upon an individual basis after a thorough review of appropriate, current documentation. The accommodations requests must be supported through the documentation provided and must be logically linked to the current impact of the condition on academic functioning.

Financial Aid

Students should submit: FAFSA. Applicants will be notified of awards on a rolling basis beginning 2/1. *Need-based scholarships/grants offered:* College/university scholarship or grant aid from institutional funds; Federal Nursing Scholarships; Federal Pell; Private scholarships; SEOG; State scholarships/grants. *Loan aid offered:* Direct PLUS loans; Direct Subsidized Stafford Loans; Direct Unsubsidized Stafford Loans. Federal Work-Study Program available. Institutional employment available.

Campus Life

Activities: Campus Ministries; Choral groups; Concert band; Dance; Drama/theater; International Student Organization; Jazz band; Model UN; Music ensembles; Musical theater; Pep band; Radio station; Student government; Student newspaper; Student-run film society; Symphony orchestra; Yearbook. **Organizations:** 144 registered organizations, 5 honor societies, 12 religious organizations. **Athletics (Intercollegiate):** *Men:* baseball, basketball, cheerleading, cross-country, golf, soccer, tennis, track/field (outdoor), track/field (indoor). *Women:* basketball, cheerleading, cross-country, soccer, softball, tennis, track/field (outdoor), track/field (indoor), volleyball.

ACCOMMODATIONS

Allowed in exams:	
Calculators	Yes
Dictionary	Yes
Computer	Yes
Spell-checker	Yes
Extended test time	Yes
Scribe	Yes
Proctors	Yes
Oral exams	Yes
Note-takers	Yes
Support services for students with:	
LD	Yes
ADHD	Yes
ASD	Yes
Distraction-reduced environment	Yes
Recording of lecture alowed	Yes
Reading technology	Yes
Audio books	Yes
Other assistive technology	Yes
Priority registration	Yes
Added costs of services:	
For LD	Yes
For ADHD	No
For ASD	No
LD specialists	No
ADHD & ASD coaching	Yes
ASD specialists	No
Professional tutors	No
Peer tutors	Yes
Max. hours/week for services	Varies
How professors are notified of student approved accommodations	Student and Director

COLLEGE GRADUATION REQUIREMENTS

Course waivers allowed	Yes
In what courses: Case-by-case basis for math and foreign language	
Course substitutions allowed	Yes
In what courses: Case-by-case basis for math and foreign language	

Ohio

Central Ohio Technical College

1179 University Drive, Newark, OH 43055 • Admissions: 740-366-9494 • Fax: 740-366-9290 **Support: CS**

CAMPUS	
Type of school	Public
Environment	Town
STUDENTS	
Undergrad enrollment	3,513
% male/female	29/71
% from out of state	1
% frosh live on campus	1
FINANCIAL FACTS	
Annual in-state tuition	$4,776
Annual out-of-state tuition	$7,536
GENERAL ADMISSIONS INFO	
Application fee	$0
Regular application deadline	Rolling
Nonfall registration	Yes
ACADEMICS	
Student/faculty ratio	16:1
% students returning for sophomore year	48

Programs/Services for Students with Learning Differences

Student Life-Disability Services (SL-DS) is a support unit for students of Central Ohio Technical College and The Ohio State University at Newark. SL-DS provides free programs and services designed to help students have full access to college life. All students are encouraged to contact the SL-DS in the early stages of their college planning. Preadmission services include information about academic support services, specialized equipment, transition issues, admission requirements, and meetings with staff counselors.

Admissions

Admission is open to all applicants with a high school diploma or the GED, except in health programs. There are no specific course requirements. ACT/SAT tests are not required. The application process is the same for all students. There is no requirement to provide disability-related information to the Admissions Office. Documentation of your disability should be sent directly to SL-DS. Eligibility for services/accommodations is a separate process from admissions. All prospective students are encouraged to contact SL-DS in the early stages of their college planning. Preadmission services include information about academic support services, transition issues, admission requirements, and appropriate documentation (copy of last IEP or results of last psychoeducational battery) and meetings with staff disability professionals.

Additional Information

The learning specialist has a face-to-face meeting with the student in order to provide that student an opportunity to discuss personal academic challenges and receive individual advice tailored to their particular needs. The areas of support include planning, time management, prioritizing, study skills and techniques, goal setting, effective use of resources including peer-assisted learning, faculty support and communication, technology, and e-learning. There is a Math Learning Center dedicated to providing services to students to help improve their math skills, and a Testing Center where students receive accommodation and a distraction free environment to take their exams.

ADMISSIONS INFO FOR STUDENTS WITH LEARNING DIFFERENCES

Phone: 740-366-9441 • Fax: 740-364-9646 • Email: ada-osu@osu.edu

SAT/ACT required: No
Interview required: No
Essay required: No
Additional application required: No
Documentation submitted to: Student Life-Disability Services

Special Ed. HS course work accepted: No
Separate application required for Programs/Services: No
Documentation required for:
LD: Psychoeducational evaluation
ADHD: Psychoeducational evaluation
ASD: Psychoeducational evaluation

Central Ohio Technical College

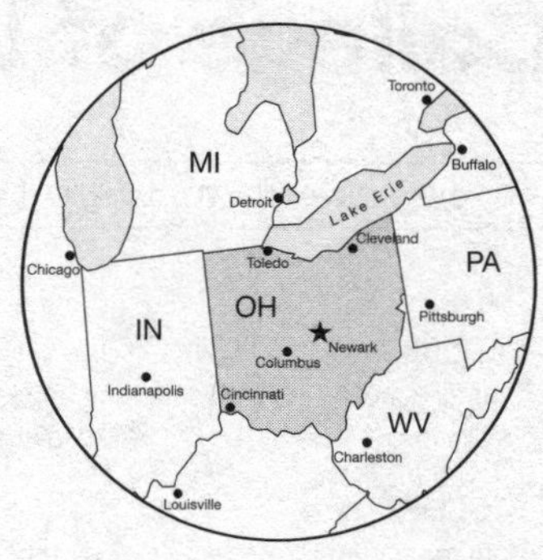

General Admissions

Freshman admission requirements: High school diploma is required and GED is accepted.

Accommodations or Services

Accommodations are decided upon an individual basis after a thorough review of appropriate, current documentation. The accommodations requests must be supported through the documentation provided and must be logically linked to the current impact of the condition on academic functioning.

Financial Aid

Students should submit: FAFSA. Applicants will be notified of awards on a rolling basis beginning 2/15. *Need-based scholarships/grants offered:* College/university scholarship or grant aid from institutional funds; Federal Pell; Private scholarships; SEOG; State scholarships/grants. *Loan aid offered:* Direct PLUS loans; Direct Subsidized Stafford Loans; Direct Unsubsidized Stafford Loans. Federal Work-Study Program available. Institutional employment available.

Campus Life

Activities: Choral groups; Drama/theater; Music ensembles; Student government; Student newspaper.

ACCOMMODATIONS

Allowed in exams:	
Calculators	Yes
Dictionary	No
Computer	Yes
Spell-checker	Yes
Extended test time	Yes
Scribe	Yes
Proctors	Yes
Oral exams	Yes
Note-takers	Yes
Support services for students with:	
LD	Yes
ADHD	Yes
ASD	Yes
Distraction-reduced environment	Yes
Recording of lecture alowed	Yes
Reading technology	Yes
Audio books	Yes
Other assistive technology	Yes
Priority registration	Yes
Added costs of services:	
For LD	No
For ADHD	No
For ASD	No
LD specialists	Yes
ADHD & ASD coaching	No
ASD specialists	No
Professional tutors	Yes
Peer tutors	Yes
Max. hours/week for services	Varies
How professors are notified of student approved accommodations	Student

COLLEGE GRADUATION REQUIREMENTS

Course waivers allowed	No
Course substitutions allowed	No

College of Wooster

847 College Avenue, Wooster, OH 44691 • Admissions: 330-263-2322 • Fax: 330-263-2621 **Support: CS**

CAMPUS

Type of school	Private (nonprofit)
Environment	Town

STUDENTS

Undergrad enrollment	1,942
% male/female	46/54
% from out of state	65
% frosh live on campus	100

FINANCIAL FACTS

Annual tuition	$54,000
Room and board	$12,750

GENERAL ADMISSIONS INFO

Application fee	$0
Regular application deadline	2/15
Non fall registration	Yes

Admission may be deferred.

Range SAT EBRW	580–680
Range SAT Math	570–700
Range ACT Composite	24–31

ACADEMICS

Student/faculty ratio	10:1
% students returning for sophomore year	86

Most classes have fewer than 10 students.

Programs/Services for Students with Learning Differences

The Learning Center offers many resources for students. Its goal is to help students thrive and learn skills that will take them beyond college. The staff helps students develop stronger time management skills, and test-prep strategies and help with note-taking methods. New students to the Learning Center should fill out the Clockwork online registration form.

Admissions

There is no special admissions procedure for students with learning differences. The average GPA is 3.7. Students are also evaluated by their extracurricular activities and performance on standardized tests.

Additional Information

There are programs and workshops offered throughout the year to support students with learning differences. For example, there is a series of workshops presented by APEX for incoming freshman that focus on transitioning to college and developing study skills. The Learning Center's contribution to the series has included sessions on time management, test-taking strategies, and reading skills. Study hall is offered at critical times during the semester. Peer tutors are available, and there is assistance in the Math and Writing Center.

ADMISSIONS INFO FOR STUDENTS WITH LEARNING DIFFERENCES

Phone: 330-263-2595 • Fax: 330-263-3829 • Email: alarson@wooster.edu

SAT/ACT required: Optional
Interview required: No
Essay required: Yes
Additional application required: Yes
Documentation submitted to: The Learning Center

Special Ed. HS course work accepted: No
Separate application required for Programs/Services: No
Documentation required for:
- **LD:** Psychoeducational evaluation
- **ADHD:** Psychoeducational evaluation
- **ASD:** Psychoeducational evaluation

College of Wooster

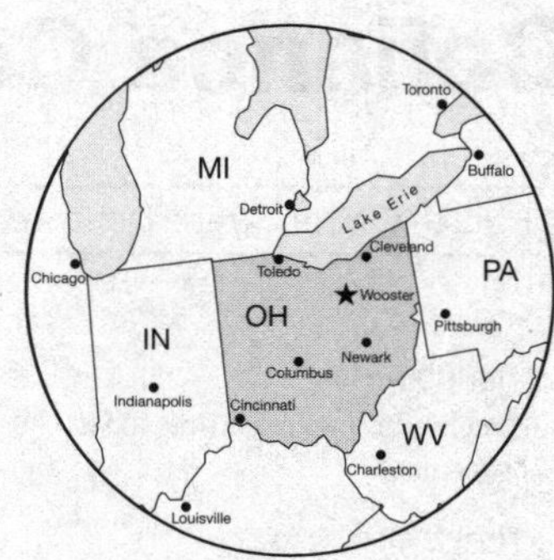

General Admissions

Very important factors include: rigor of secondary school record, academic GPA. *Important factors include:* class rank, application essay, standardized test scores, recommendation(s), interview, extracurricular activities, character/personal qualities. *Other factors include:* talent/ability, first generation, alumni/ae relation, geographical residence, state residency, racial/ethnic status, volunteer work, work experience. *Freshman admission requirements:* High school diploma is required and GED is accepted. *Academic units required:* 4 English, 3 math, 3 science, 2 science labs, 2 foreign language, 3 social studies, 1 academic elective.

Accommodations or Services

Accommodations are decided upon an individual basis after a thorough review of appropriate, current documentation. The accommodations requests must be supported through the documentation provided and must be logically linked to the current impact of the condition on academic functioning.

Financial Aid

Students should submit: FAFSA, CSS/Financial Aid PROFILE. *Need-based scholarships/grants offered:* College/university scholarship or grant aid from institutional funds; Federal Pell; Private scholarships; SEOG; State scholarships/grants. *Loan aid offered:* Direct PLUS loans; Direct Subsidized Stafford Loans; Direct Unsubsidized Stafford Loans. Federal Work-Study Program available. Institutional employment available.

Campus Life

Activities: Campus Ministries; Choral groups; Concert band; Dance; Drama/theater; International Student Organization; Jazz band; Literary magazine; Marching band; Model UN; Music ensembles; Musical theater; Radio station; Student government; Student newspaper; Student-run film society; Symphony orchestra; Yearbook. **Organizations:** 125 registered organizations, 5 honor societies, 8 religious organizations, 4 fraternities, 7 sororities. **Athletics (Intercollegiate):** *Men:* baseball, basketball, cross-country, diving, football, golf, lacrosse, soccer, swimming, tennis, track/field (outdoor), track/field (indoor). *Women:* basketball, cross-country, diving, field hockey, lacrosse, soccer, softball, swimming, tennis, track/field (outdoor), track/field (indoor), volleyball.

ACCOMMODATIONS

Allowed in exams:	
Calculators	Yes
Dictionary	Yes
Computer	Yes
Spell-checker	Yes
Extended test time	Yes
Scribe	Yes
Proctors	Yes
Oral exams	Yes
Note-takers	Yes
Support services for students with:	
LD	Yes
ADHD	Yes
ASD	Yes
Distraction-reduced environment	Yes
Recording of lecture allowed	Yes
Reading technology	Yes
Audio books	Yes
Other assistive technology	Yes
Priority registration	Yes
Added costs of services:	
For LD	No
For ADHD	No
For ASD	No
LD specialists	Yes
ADHD & ASD coaching	No
ASD specialists	No
Professional tutors	No
Peer tutors	Yes
Max. hours/week for services	Varies
How professors are notified of student approved accommodations	Student

COLLEGE GRADUATION REQUIREMENTS

Course waivers allowed	Yes
In what courses: Foreign language	
Course substitutions allowed	Yes
In what courses: Course-by-course basis	

Ohio

Defiance College

701 North Clinton Street, Defiance, OH 43512-1695 • Admissions: 419-783-2359 • Fax: 419-783-2468 **Support: CS**

CAMPUS

Type of school	Private (nonprofit)
Environment	Village

STUDENTS

Undergrad enrollment	513
% male/female	55/45
% from out of state	41
% frosh live on campus	84

FINANCIAL FACTS

Annual tuition	$33,260
Room and board	$10,540
Required fees	$740

GENERAL ADMISSIONS INFO

Application fee	$25
Regular application deadline	Rolling
Nonfall registration	Yes

Admission may be deferred.

Range SAT EBRW	440–520
Range SAT Math	450–530
Range ACT Composite	17–21

ACADEMICS

Student/faculty ratio	9:1
% students returning for sophomore year	46

Most classes have 10–19 students.

Programs/Services for Students with Learning Differences

Defiance College offers services and resources to students who have documented disabilities requiring accommodations to ensure equal access. The Accessibility Services (AS) office is located in the Carrer Development Office. The AS is the college's designated office that maintains disability-related documents, certifies for services, determines reasonable accommodations, and coordinates services for students with disabilities. A student can request a tutor, receive writing support, and get help with developing study skills.

Admissions

There is no special admissions for students with disabilities. Most applicants have a 3.0 GPA or better. Applicants must submit either an ACT or SAT score. In addition to academic achievement, Defiance considers other factors that influence performance such as the caliber of the high school, rigor of courses, and involvement in extracurricular activities. Successful applicants typically submit transcripts that include in-depth work in English, math, foreign language, science, and social studies.

Additional Information

Defiance College's ASD Affinity Program accepts academically qualified students who might need assistance navigating the residential campus and would like social and academic support. The program provides campus housing with help from trained residential advisors and peers. Documentation of ASD (DSM) is required, as well as testing that indicates average intellectual ability (80+).

ADMISSIONS INFO FOR STUDENTS WITH LEARNING DIFFERENCES

Phone: 419-783-2359 • Fax: 419-783-2468 • Email: admissions@defiance.edu

SAT/ACT required: No
Interview required: No
Essay required: Yes
Additional application required: No
Documentation submitted to: ASD
Special Ed. HS course work accepted: No
Separate application required for Programs/Services: After Admissions
Documentation required for:
LD: IEP, Psychoeducational testing
ADHD: Psychoeducational testing or letter from appropriate physician
ASD: Psychoeducational evaluation and additional IEP

Defiance College

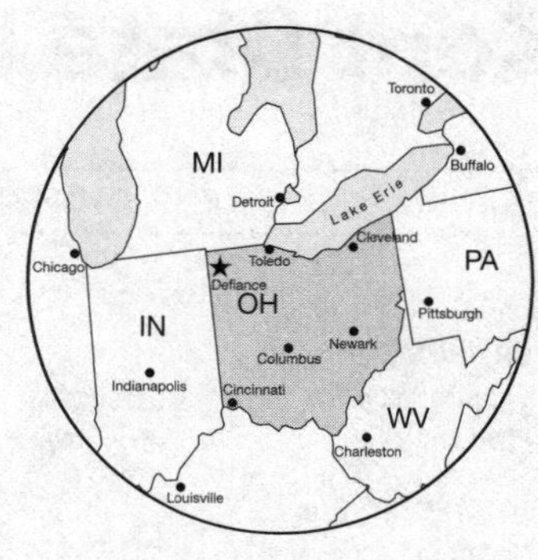

General Admissions

Very important factors include: rigor of secondary school record, academic GPA, standardized test scores. *Other factors include:* class rank, application essay, recommendation(s), interview, extracurricular activities, character/personal qualities, volunteer work, work experience. *Freshman admission requirements:* High school diploma is required and GED is accepted. *Academic units recommended:* 4 English, 3 math, 3 science, 2 science labs, 2 foreign language, 2 social studies, 2 visual/performing arts.

Accommodations or Services

Accommodations are decided upon an individual basis after a thorough review of appropriate, current documentation. The accommodations requests must be supported through the documentation provided and must be logically linked to the current impact of the condition on academic functioning. Documentation includes testing outcome from a WAIS, a Woodcock-Johnson from a third party, and an IEP.

Financial Aid

Students should submit: FAFSA. *Need-based scholarships/grants offered:* College/university scholarship or grant aid from institutional funds; Federal Pell; Private scholarships; SEOG; State scholarships/grants. *Loan aid offered:* Direct PLUS loans; Direct Subsidized Stafford Loans; Direct Unsubsidized Stafford Loans. Federal Work-Study Program available. Institutional employment available.

Campus Life

Activities: Campus Ministries; Choral groups; Concert band; Dance; Drama/theater; Jazz band; Literary magazine; Marching band; Music ensembles; Musical theater; Pep band; Student government; Student newspaper. **Organizations:** 36 registered organizations, 3 honor societies, 2 religious organizations, 1 fraternity, 1 sorority. **Athletics (Intercollegiate):** *Men:* baseball, basketball, cross-country, football, golf, soccer, tennis, track/field (outdoor), track/field (indoor). *Women:* basketball, cross-country, golf, soccer, softball, tennis, track/field (outdoor), track/field (indoor), volleyball.

ACCOMMODATIONS

Allowed in exams:	
Calculators	Yes
Dictionary	Yes
Computer	Yes
Spell-checker	Yes
Extended test time	Yes
Scribe	No
Proctors	Yes
Oral exams	No
Note-takers	Yes
Support services for students with:	
LD	Yes
ADHD	Yes
ASD	Yes
Distraction-reduced environment	Yes
Recording of lecture alowed	Yes
Reading technology	Yes
Audio books	Yes
Other assistive technology	Yes
Priority registration	Yes
Added costs of services:	
For LD	No
For ADHD	No
For ASD	No
LD specialists	Yes
ADHD & ASD coaching	Yes
ASD specialists	No
Professional tutors	Yes
Peer tutors	Yes
Max. hours/week for services	No
How professors are notified of student approved accommodations	Director

COLLEGE GRADUATION REQUIREMENTS

Course waivers allowed	Yes
In what courses Case by case basis	
Course substitutions allowed	Yes
In what courses Case by case basis	

Ohio

Kent State University—Kent Campus

161 Schwartz Center, Kent, OH 44242-0001 • Admissions: 330-672-2444 • Fax: 330-672-2499 **Support: CS**

CAMPUS

Type of school	Public
Environment	Town

STUDENTS

Undergrad enrollment	21,431
% male/female	38/62
% from out of state	16
% frosh live on campus	81

FINANCIAL FACTS

Annual in-state tuition	$11,432
Annual out-of-state tuition	$20,308
Room and board	$12,084
Required fees	$156

GENERAL ADMISSIONS INFO

Application fee	$50
Regular application deadline	5/1
Nonfall registration	Yes

Admission may be deferred.

Range SAT EBRW	530–620
Range SAT Math	510–610
Range ACT Composite	20–26

ACADEMICS

Student/faculty ratio	19:1
% students returning for sophomore year	81

Most classes have 10–19 students.

Programs/Services for Students with Learning Differences

The Office of Student Accessibility Services serves students with specific learning disabilities, such as ADD and ADHD, and other disabilities. Students will need to present appropriate documentation. Kent State also offers two programs (a 2-year and 4-year) for students with intellectual and developmental disabilities through the Career and Community Studies (CCS).

Admissions

Students with Learning Disabilities and ADHD must meet the same admission requirements as all applicants. The mean GPA is 3.4 and the mean ACT is 23 and SAT of 1130. Some academic programs have additional requirements. Core courses required are 4 English, 4 math, 3 science, 3 social studies, 2 foreign language, and 1 art (or additional unit of foreign language). Admissions may defer students who do not meet admissions criteria but who demonstrate areas of promise for successful college study. Deferred applicants may begin their college coursework at one of seven regional campuses of Kent State University.

Additional Information

Career and Community Studies (CCS) is a college-based, transition, non-degree program for students with intellectual and developmental disabilities. In this program, students will be guided through academic pursuits, peer socialization, and career discovery and preparation. CCS integrates inclusive classes, a typical college experience, and a transition curriculum to assist students in achieving a future life after the program. The CCS program is for students who have completed high school requirements and are at least 18 years of age. The first year of the program is foundational, offering courses on disability issues, personal development, health and wellness, and preparation for a rigorous college experience. In the second year, students participate in college-level courses and other campus opportunities. There is also an additional 2-year program that focuses on career-field specialization with courses on independent living, life-long learning competencies, and career development and employment, as well as internships in the community where students can apply their learning in jobs. The programs are non-degree and require 60 credits to graduate.

ADMISSIONS INFO FOR STUDENTS WITH LEARNING DIFFERENCES

Phone: 330-672-3391 • Fax: 330-672-3763 • Email: sas@kent.edu

SAT/ACT required: No for fall 2021. Yes for future cycles.
Interview required: No
Essay required: Yes
Additional application required: No
Documentation submitted to: CCS

Special Ed. HS course work accepted: Yes
Separate application required for Programs/Services: No
Documentation required for:
LD: Psychoeducational evaluation
ADHD: Psychoeducational evaluation
ASD: Psychoeducational evaluation

Kent State University—Kent Campus

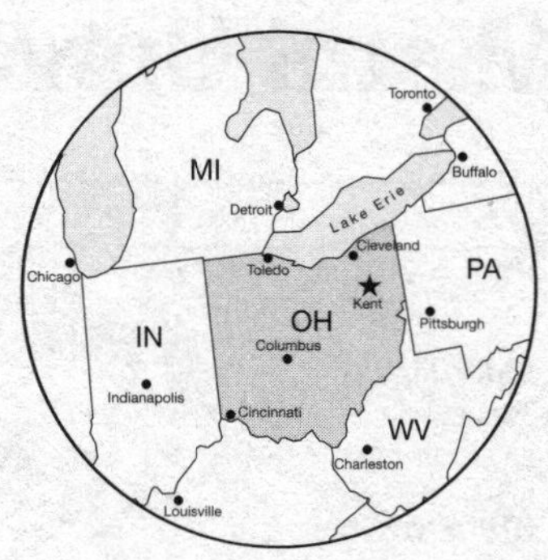

General Admissions

Very important factors include: academic GPA, standardized test scores. *Important factors include:* rigor of secondary school record. *Other factors include:* application essay, recommendation(s), interview, talent/ability, level of applicant's interest. *Freshman admission requirements:* High school diploma is required and GED is accepted. *Academic units recommended:* 4 English, 4 math, 3 science, 2 science labs, 2 foreign language, 3 social studies, 1 visual/performing arts.

Accommodations or Services

Accommodations are decided upon an individual basis after a thorough review of appropriate, current documentation. The accommodations requests must be supported through the documentation provided and must be logically linked to the current impact of the condition on academic functioning. Students must complete an SAS application and submit all available documentation and additional information for review by an access consultant.

Financial Aid

Students should submit: FAFSA. *Need-based scholarships/grants offered:* College/university scholarship or grant aid from institutional funds; Federal Pell; Private scholarships; SEOG; State scholarships/grants. *Loan aid offered:* Direct PLUS loans; Direct Subsidized Stafford Loans; Direct Unsubsidized Stafford Loans. Federal Work-Study Program available. Institutional employment available.

Campus Life

Activities: Campus Ministries; Choral groups; Concert band; Dance; Drama/theater; International Student Organization; Jazz band; Literary magazine; Marching band; Model UN; Music ensembles; Musical theater; Opera; Pep band; Radio station; Student government; Student newspaper; Symphony orchestra; Television station. **Organizations:** 423 registered organizations, 7 honor societies, 21 religious organizations, 19 fraternities, 8 sororities. **Athletics (Intercollegiate):** *Men:* baseball, basketball, cheerleading, cross-country, football, golf, track/field (outdoor), track/field (indoor), wrestling. *Women:* basketball, cheerleading, cross-country, field hockey, football, golf, gymnastics, soccer, softball, track/field (outdoor), track/field (indoor), volleyball.

ACCOMMODATIONS

Allowed in exams:	
Calculators	Yes
Dictionary	Yes
Computer	Yes
Spell-checker	Yes
Extended test time	Yes
Scribe	Yes
Proctors	Yes
Oral exams	Yes
Note-takers	Yes
Support services for students with:	
LD	Yes
ADHD	Yes
ASD	Yes
Distraction-reduced environment	Yes
Recording of lecture allowed	Yes
Reading technology	Yes
Audio books	Yes
Other assistive technology	Yes
Priority registration	Yes
Added costs of services:	
For LD	No
For ADHD	No
For ASD	No
LD specialists	Yes
ADHD & ASD coaching	No
ASD specialists	Yes
Professional tutors	Yes
Peer tutors	Yes
Max. hours/week for services	Varies
How professors are notified of student approved accommodations	Student

COLLEGE GRADUATION REQUIREMENTS

Course waivers allowed	No
Course substitutions allowed	Yes
In what courses: Varies	

Ohio

Miami University (OH)

301 S. Campus Avenue, Oxford, OH 45056 • Admissions: 513-529-2531 • Fax: 513-529-1550 **Support: CS**

CAMPUS

Type of school	Public
Environment	Village

STUDENTS

Undergrad enrollment	17,246
% male/female	50/50
% from out of state	34
% frosh live on campus	98

FINANCIAL FACTS

Annual in-state tuition	$13,136
Annual out-of-state tuition	$33,563
Room and board	$14,510
Required fees	$2,887

GENERAL ADMISSIONS INFO

Application fee	$50
Regular application deadline	2/1
Nonfall registration	Yes

Admission may be deferred.

Range SAT EBRW	600–680
Range SAT Math	610–730
Range ACT Composite	26–31

ACADEMICS

Student/faculty ratio	17:1
% students returning for sophomore year	90

Most classes have 20–29 students.

Programs/Services for Students with Learning Differences

The Student Disability Services (SDS) coordinates university and community resources to meet the academic and personal needs of students with LD, assists faculty in understanding the characteristics and needs of these students, and provides services on an individual basis to students with appropriate documentation. For example, students can schedule an exam on Students Accessing Miami (SAM). This is the same system where student documents for SDS registration and the alternative testing contract with faculty are processed. Appropriate services and accommodations are determined through a flexible, interactive process that involves the student and the coordinator. Arrangements are made through dialogue with faculty and staff responsible for implementing many of these services or accommodations. Decisions about services and accommodations for students with LD are made on the basis of the disability documentation and the functional limitations caused by the disability, as well as the current needs of the student. Students with ADHD must meet with the LD coordinator to initiate services after discussing disability-related needs and providing documentation of the disability and its impact on learning.

Admissions

Students with LD are admitted through the regular admission process; therefore, it is important to ensure that the information in the application accurately reflects a student's academic ability and potential. Students may self-disclose LD or ADHD on their application. The review process is comprehensive and individualized and considers many variables including class rank, commitment to social service, demonstrated leadership, employment, extenuating circumstances, extracurriculars, first generation, GPA, grade trends, high school profile, legacy status, and letter(s) of recommendation.

Additional Information

Services for students with LD include priority registration, classroom accommodations such as test modifications, extended exam times, liaison with faculty, campus advocacy, counseling, and career awareness. In addition, students with LD can utilize services through the Rinella Learning Center, which works with students encountering academic difficulties. Its tutorial assistance program provides peer tutors. The Bernard B. Rinella Jr. Learning Center has special services designed to help students experiencing academic problems. In meeting with a learning specialist, students' existing learning strategies will be assessed, and new effective strategies will be

ADMISSIONS INFO FOR STUDENTS WITH LEARNING DIFFERENCES

Phone: 513-529-1541 • Fax: 513-529-8595 • Email: zeisleja@miamioh.edu

SAT/ACT required: Yes (Test optional for 2021)
Interview required: No
Essay required: Yes
Additional application required: No
Documentation submitted to: The Rinella Learning Center

Special Ed. HS course work accepted: No
Separate application required for Programs/Services: No
Documentation required for:
LD: Psychoeducational evaluation
ADHD: Psychoeducational evaluation
ASD: Psychoeducational evaluation

Miami University (OH)

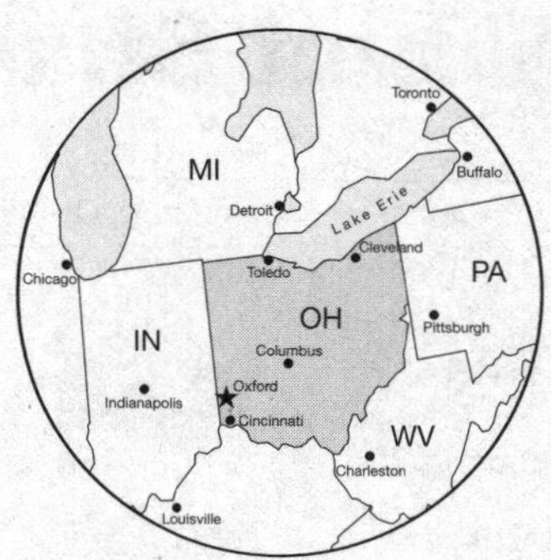

introduced. Topics including time management, notetaking, test taking, writing, and organization will be covered. New study strategies will be reinforced through individual conferences with a learning specialist, peer mentoring, and/or tutoring.

General Admissions

Very important factors include: rigor of secondary school record, class rank, academic GPA, application essay, standardized test scores, recommendation(s), talent/ability, character/personal qualities. *Other factors include:* extracurricular activities, first generation, alumni/ae relation, geographical residence, state residency, volunteer work, work experience. *Freshman admission requirements:* High school diploma is required and GED is accepted. *Academic units recommended:* 4 English, 4 math, 3 science, 2 foreign language, 2 social studies, 1 history, 1 visual/performing arts.

Accommodations or Services

Accommodations are decided upon an individual basis after a thorough review of appropriate, current documentation. The accommodations requests must be supported through the documentation provided and must be logically linked to the current impact of the condition on academic functioning.

Financial Aid

Students should submit: FAFSA. *Need-based scholarships/grants offered:* College/university scholarship or grant aid from institutional funds; Federal Pell; Private scholarships; SEOG; State scholarships/grants. *Loan aid offered:* Direct PLUS loans; Direct Subsidized Stafford Loans; Direct Unsubsidized Stafford Loans. Federal Work-Study Program available. Institutional employment available.

Campus Life

Activities: Campus Ministries; Choral groups; Concert band; Dance; Drama/theater; International Student Organization; Jazz band; Literary magazine; Marching band; Model UN; Music ensembles; Musical theater; Opera; Pep band; Radio station; Student government; Student newspaper; Student-run film society; Symphony orchestra; Television station; Yearbook. **Organizations:** 735 registered organizations, 27 honor societies, 25 religious organizations, 25 fraternities, 20 sororities. **Athletics (Intercollegiate):** *Men:* baseball, basketball, cross-country, diving, football, golf, ice hockey, swimming, track/field (outdoor). *Women:* basketball, cross-country, diving, field hockey, soccer, softball, swimming, tennis, track/field (outdoor), volleyball.

ACCOMMODATIONS

Allowed in exams:	
Calculators	Yes
Dictionary	Yes
Computer	Yes
Spell-checker	Yes
Extended test time	Yes
Scribe	Yes
Proctors	Yes
Oral exams	Yes
Note-takers	Yes
Support services for students with:	
LD	Yes
ADHD	Yes
ASD	Yes
Distraction-reduced environment	Yes
Recording of lecture alowed	Yes
Reading technology	Yes
Audio books	Yes
Other assistive technology	Yes
Priority registration	Yes
Added costs of services:	
For LD	No
For ADHD	No
For ASD	No
LD specialists	Yes
ADHD & ASD coaching	Yes
ASD specialists	Yes
Professional tutors	Yes
Peer tutors	Yes
Max. hours/week for services	Varies
How professors are notified of student approved accommodations	Student and Director

COLLEGE GRADUATION REQUIREMENTS

Course waivers allowed	No
Course substitutions allowed	Yes
In what courses: Varies	

Ohio

Mount St. Joseph University

5701 Delhi Road, Cincinnati, OH 45233 • Admissions: 513-244-4531 • Fax: 513-244-4629 **Support: SP**

CAMPUS

Type of school	Private (nonprofit)
Environment	Metropolis

STUDENTS

Undergrad enrollment	1,450
% male/female	40/60
% from out of state	34

FINANCIAL FACTS

Annual tuition	$31,100
Room and board	$9,920

GENERAL ADMISSIONS INFO

Application fee	$25
Regular application deadline	Rolling
Nonfall registration	Yes

Admission may be deferred.

Range SAT EBRW	510–580
Range SAT Math	490–570
Range ACT Composite	20–23

ACADEMICS

Student/faculty ratio	7:1
% students returning for sophomore year	72

Most classes have 10–19 students.

Programs/Services for Students with Learning Differences

Project EXCEL is a fee-based comprehensive academic support program for students with learning disabilities enrolled in the college. The program's goals are to assist students in the transition from a secondary program to a college curriculum and to promote the development of learning strategies and compensatory skills that will enable students to achieve success in a regular academic program. The structure of the program and supportive environment at the Mount give Project EXCEL its singular quality. Project EXCEL offers students individualized attention and a variety of support services to meet specific needs, including supervised tutoring by professional tutors; monitoring of student progress; instruction in learning strategies, time management, and coping skills; and academic advising with attention to the students' specific learning needs. Students admitted to the program must maintain a 2.3 overall GPA, and their progress is evaluated on an ongoing basis.

Admissions

Admission to Project EXCEL is multi-stepped, including: an interview with the program director; completed general admission application; completed Project EXCEL forms (general information, applicant goal and self-assessment, and educational data completed by high school); psychoeducational evaluation; transcript; ACT minimum of 15 or SAT of 700–740; and a recommendation. The application is reviewed by the Project EXCEL Director and Project EXCEL Admission Committee. The diagnostic evaluation must indicate the presence of specific LD and provide reasonable evidence that the student can successfully meet college academic requirements. Academic performance problems that exist concomitantly with a diagnosed ADD/ADHD will be considered in the review of the student's diagnostic profile. Students can be admitted to the college through Project EXCEL. Students not meeting all EXCEL admission requirements may be admitted part-time or on a probationary basis. Apply early. Other students not meeting admission requirements can take up to 6 hours per semester to a maximum of 13 hours. At that point, if they have a 2.0+ GPA they are admitted to the college.

Additional Information

Project EXCEL is a comprehensive academic support system for students with specific learning disabilities. Initiated in 1982, Project EXCEL has proven to be a highly successful intervention program. Students whose primary disability is a specific learning disability and/or ADHD may apply to Project

ADMISSIONS INFO FOR STUDENTS WITH LEARNING DIFFERENCES

Phone: 513-244-4623 • Fax: 513-244-4629 • Email: meghann.littrell@msj.edu

SAT/ACT required: Yes (Test optional for 2021)
Interview required: Yes
Essay required: No
Additional application required: Yes
Documentation submitted to: Project Excel

Special Ed. HS course work accepted: No
Separate application required for Programs/Services: Yes
Documentation required for:
LD: Psychoeducational evaluation
ADHD: Psychoeducational evaluation
ASD: Psychoeducational evaluation

Mount St. Joseph University

EXCEL. A fee-for-service program, Project EXCEL addresses the needs of this specific group of students through a comprehensive academic support system. Students must be admitted to Mount St. Joseph University before applying for Project EXCEL. As a Project EXCEL student, you'll discover your academic strengths, address learning challenges, and acquire new skills.

General Admissions

Very important factors include: rigor of secondary school record, academic GPA, standardized test scores. *Important factors include:* extracurricular activities, volunteer work, work experience, level of applicant's interest. *Other factors include:* class rank, application essay, recommendation(s), interview, talent/ability, character/personal qualities. High school diploma is required and GED is accepted. *Academic units required:* 4 English, 3 math, 2 science, 2 science labs, 2 foreign language, 1 visual/performing arts. *Academic units recommended:* 3 social studies, 3 history.

Accommodations or Services

Accommodations are decided upon an individual basis after a thorough review of appropriate, current documentation. The accommodations requests must be supported through the documentation provided and must be logically linked to the current impact of the condition on academic functioning.

Financial Aid

Students should submit: Institution's own financial aid form, FAFSA. *Need-based scholarships/grants offered:* College/university scholarship or grant aid from institutional funds; Federal Pell; Private scholarships; SEOG; State scholarships/grants. *Loan aid offered:* Direct PLUS loans; Direct Subsidized Stafford Loans; Direct Unsubsidized Stafford Loans. Federal Work-Study Program available. Institutional employment available.

Campus Life

Activities: Campus Ministries; Choral groups; Concert band; Dance; Drama/theater; Jazz band; Literary magazine; Marching band; Musical theater; Pep band; Student government; Student newspaper. **Organizations:** 44 registered organizations, 13 honor societies, 1 religious organization, 1 fraternity. **Athletics (Intercollegiate):** *Men:* baseball, basketball, cross-country, football, golf, lacrosse, soccer, tennis, track/field (outdoor), track/field (indoor), volleyball, wrestling. *Women:* basketball, cheerleading, cross-country, golf, lacrosse, soccer, softball, tennis, track/field (outdoor), track/field (indoor), volleyball.

ACCOMMODATIONS

Allowed in exams:	
Calculators	Yes
Dictionary	Yes
Computer	Yes
Spell-checker	No
Extended test time	Yes
Scribe	Yes
Proctors	Yes
Oral exams	Yes
Note-takers	Yes
Support services for students with:	
LD	Yes
ADHD	Yes
ASD	Yes
Distraction-reduced environment	Yes
Recording of lecture alowed	Yes
Reading technology	Yes
Audio books	Yes
Other assistive technology	Yes
Priority registration	Yes
Added costs of services:	
For LD	Yes
For ADHD	Yes
For ASD	No
LD specialists	Yes
ADHD & ASD coaching	No
ASD specialists	No
Professional tutors	Yes
Peer tutors	Yes
Max. hours/week for services	21
How professors are notified of student approved accommodations	Student

COLLEGE GRADUATION REQUIREMENTS

Course waivers allowed	Yes
In what courses: Foreign language	
Course substitutions allowed	Yes
In what courses: Foreign language	

Ohio

Muskingum University

163 Stormont Street, New Concord, OH 43762 • Admissions: 740-826-8137 • Fax: 614-826-8100 **Support: SP**

CAMPUS	
Type of school	Private (nonprofit)
Environment	Rural
STUDENTS	
Undergrad enrollment	1,603
% male/female	44/56
% from out of state	11
% frosh live on campus	75
FINANCIAL FACTS	
Annual tuition	$28,700
Room and board	$11,860
Required fees	$790
GENERAL ADMISSIONS INFO	
Application fee	$0
Regular application deadline	8/1
Nonfall registration	Yes
Admission may be deferred.	
Range SAT EBRW	450–560
Range SAT Math	440–560
Range ACT Composite	18–23
ACADEMICS	
Student/faculty ratio	13:1
% students returning for sophomore year	72
Most classes have 10–19 students.	

Programs/Services for Students with Learning Differences

The PLUS Program provides college students who have a learning disability support. The PLUS Program philosophy is designed to empower rather than rescue students. Based on their past educational experiences, students may view this as a considerable change. This can result in a shift in mindset for the student that encompasses looking at what is working, discovering possibilities, and using strengths and interests to enhance performance. The PLUS Program encourages students to take control of their learning process, which the university views as a crucial component of the college experience. The PLUS learning consultants empower students to develop academic and social skills, leading to self-direction, confidence, and independence. The PLUS Program reflects the university's commitment to the ultimate success of its students.

Admissions

Students should have a university preparatory curriculum. Generally, 4 years of English, 2 years of math, at least 2 years of science with lab, and social sciences are recommended for admissions. To apply to the PLUS Program, an applicant should complete all materials required for regular admission to the university. In addition, PLUS applicants should submit a recent comprehensive evaluation, which includes aptitude testing, achievement testing, and a diagnostic summary. Admission to the university and the PLUS Program are based upon application materials and a personal interview. Rolling admissions apply. Due to the great demand for the PLUS Program services, early application is strongly advised.

Additional Information

The PLUS program does not use peer tutors but has full-time professional tutors. Through learning strategy instruction, the learning consultants provide systematic and explicit instruction in learning strategies that are embedded in course content. Learning strategy instruction areas include time and materials management, organization, test taking, note-taking, reading, writing, memory, and study skills, among others. Learning consultants help students recognize the factors that influence success and understand their unique learning profile. Students participating in the Full PLUS Program receive an average of one contact hour per week for each eligible course for an average total of 3–4 hours per week. Maintenance PLUS Program students receive one half hour of PLUS tutorial services per week for each eligible course. Both levels of service are provided with additional services, including a primary learning consultant who acts as liaison to home, faculty, and others, guidance to promote favorable number

ADMISSIONS INFO FOR STUDENTS WITH LEARNING DIFFERENCES

Phone: 740-826-8284 • Fax: 740-826-8285 • Email: deo@muskingum.edu

SAT/ACT required: Yes (Test optional for 2021)
Interview required: Yes
Essay required: Yes
Additional application required: No
Documentation submitted to: PLUS Program

Special Ed. HS course work accepted: Yes
Separate application required for Programs/Services: No
Documentation required for:
LD: Psychoeducational evaluation
ADHD: Psychoeducational evaluation
ASD: Psychoeducational evaluation

Muskingum University

of courses, optimal course selection and balanced course load, and continuing services to provide a range of individual support for short-term needs. Muskingum University offers the First Step Transition Program, a two-week summer transition program to help bridge the gap between high school and university life.

General Admissions

Very important factors include: rigor of secondary school record, academic GPA. *Important factors include:* class rank, standardized test scores. *Other factors include:* application essay, recommendation(s), interview, extracurricular activities, talent/ability, character/personal qualities, alumni/ae relation, geographical residence, racial/ethnic status, work experience. *Freshman admission requirements:* High school diploma is required and GED is accepted. *Academic units required:* 4 English, 2 math, 2 science, 1 science lab, 2 foreign language, 2 social studies. *Academic units recommended:* 4 English, 3 math, 3 science, 2 science labs, 2 foreign language, 3 social studies.

Accommodations or Services

Accommodations are decided upon an individual basis after a thorough review of appropriate, current documentation. The accommodations requests must be supported through the documentation provided and must be logically linked to the current impact of the condition on academic functioning.

Financial Aid

Students should submit: FAFSA; State aid form. Applicants will be notified of awards on a rolling basis beginning 2/1. *Need-based scholarships/grants offered:* College/university scholarship or grant aid from institutional funds; Federal Pell; Private scholarships; SEOG; State scholarships/grants. *Loan aid offered:* Direct PLUS loans; Direct Subsidized Stafford Loans; Direct Unsubsidized Stafford Loans. Federal Work-Study Program available. Institutional employment available.

Campus Life

Activities: Campus Ministries; Choral groups; Concert band; Dance; Drama/theater; International Student Organization; Jazz band; Literary magazine; Marching band; Model UN; Music ensembles; Musical theater; Pep band; Radio station; Student government; Student newspaper; Symphony orchestra; Television station. **Organizations:** 96 registered organizations, 26 honor societies, 5 religious organizations, 6 fraternities, 6 sororities. **Athletics (Intercollegiate):** *Men:* baseball, basketball, cheerleading, cross-country, football, golf, soccer, tennis, track/field (outdoor), track/field (indoor), wrestling. *Women:* basketball, cheerleading, cross-country, golf, soccer, softball, tennis, track/field (outdoor), track/field (indoor), volleyball.

ACCOMMODATIONS

Allowed in exams:	
Calculators	Yes
Dictionary	Yes
Computer	Yes
Spell-checker	Yes
Extended test time	Yes
Scribe	Yes
Proctors	Yes
Oral exams	Yes
Note-takers	Yes
Support services for students with:	
LD	Yes
ADHD	Yes
ASD	Yes
Distraction-reduced environment	Yes
Recording of lecture alowed	Yes
Reading technology	Yes
Audio books	Yes
Other assistive technology	Yes
Priority registration	Yes
Added costs of services:	
For LD	Yes
For ADHD	Yes
For ASD	Yes
LD specialists	Yes
ADHD & ASD coaching	Yes
ASD specialists	No
Professional tutors	Yes
Peer tutors	No
Max. hours/week for services	3–4
How professors are notified of student approved accommodations	Student

COLLEGE GRADUATION REQUIREMENTS

Course waivers allowed	No
Course substitutions allowed	No

Oberlin College

101 North Professor Street, Oberlin, OH 44074 • Admissions: 440-775-8411 • Fax: 440-775-6905 **Support: CS**

CAMPUS

Type of school	Private (nonprofit)
Environment	Village

STUDENTS

Undergrad enrollment	2,846
% male/female	42/58
% from out of state	81
% frosh live on campus	99

FINANCIAL FACTS

Annual tuition	$57,654
Room and board	$17,334
Required fees	$900

GENERAL ADMISSIONS INFO

Application fee	$0
Regular application deadline	1/15
Nonfall registration	No

Admission may be deferred.

Range SAT EBRW	650–730
Range SAT Math	630–750
Range ACT Composite	29–33

ACADEMICS

Student/faculty ratio	11:1
% students returning for sophomore year	91

Most classes have 10–19 students.

Programs/Services for Students with Learning Differences

The Disability Resources at the Center for Student Success (DRCSS) provide services and coordinates accommodations to meet the needs of students who have disabilities. The program's philosophy is one that encourages self-advocacy. To verify a diagnosed LD, a student must provide a psychological assessment, educational test results, and a recent copy of an IEP. DRCSS determines eligibility. Students requesting services are interviewed by a learning disability counselor before a service plan is developed or initiated. Oberlin students on the Spectrum (OSOS) is a new advocacy and support group started by students and supported by the college.

Admissions

There is no special admissions procedure for students with LD. All applicants must meet the same admission requirements. Courses required include 4 years of English, 3 of math and at least 3 years of social science and science. The average GPA is typically a B average or better. It is generally true that candidates who show great promise as musicians have also performed at a high level in academic courses in secondary school. On occasion, however, the demands on a talented musician are so great as to effect performance in the classroom. This talent is more important than academic achievement in determining admission to the conservatory.

Additional Information

The Learning Resource Center and the Adaptive Technology Center are available for all students. Skills classes are offered for college credit in reading, study skills, and writing. DRCSS can arrange one or all of the following services for students with learning disabilities: quiet space for exams; extended examination times, up to twice the time typically allotted, based on diagnosis; oral exams; scribes; individual academic, personal, and vocational counseling; computer resources for additional academic skill development and assistance; alternate text; priority academic scheduling; peer tutoring; new student orientation assistance; and faculty/staff consultation. In addition, DRCSS can provide information about other support services sponsored by the college.

ADMISSIONS INFO FOR STUDENTS WITH LEARNING DIFFERENCES

Phone: 440-775-8464 • Fax: 440-775-5589

SAT/ACT required: Yes (Test optional through 2022)
Interview required: No
Essay required: No
Additional application required: No
Documentation submitted to: Disability Resources at the Center for Student Success

Special Ed. HS course work accepted: Yes
Separate application required for Programs/Services: No
Documentation required for:
- **LD:** Psychoeducational evaluation
- **ADHD:** Psychoeducational evaluation
- **ASD:** Psychoeducational evaluation

Oberlin College

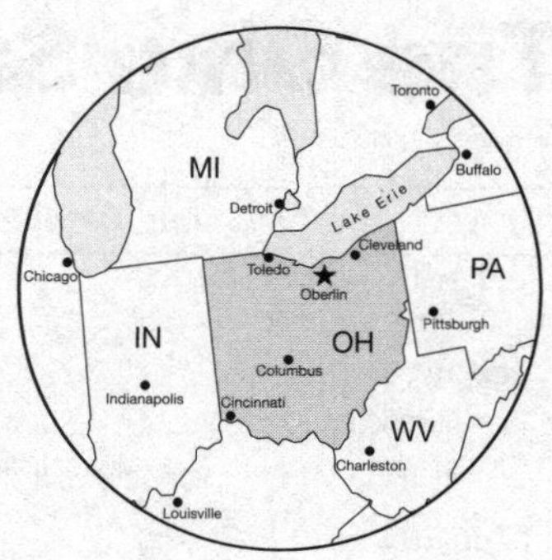

General Admissions

Very important factors include: rigor of secondary school record, class rank, academic GPA, standardized test scores. *Important factors include:* extracurricular activities, talent/ability, character/personal qualities, first generation. *Other factors include:* application essay, recommendation(s), interview, alumni/ae relation, racial/ethnic status, volunteer work, work experience, level of applicant's interest. *Freshman admission requirements:* High school diploma is required and GED is not accepted. *Academic units required:* 4 English, 3 math, 3 science, 3 foreign language, 3 social studies. *Academic units recommended:* 4 science.

Accommodations or Services

Accommodations are decided upon an individual basis after a thorough review of appropriate, current documentation. The accommodations requests must be supported through the documentation provided and must be logically linked to the current impact of the condition on academic functioning.

Financial Aid

Students should submit: Business/Farm Supplement; CSS/Financial Aid PROFILE; FAFSA; Institution's own financial aid form; Noncustodial PROFILE. *Need-based scholarships/grants offered:* College/university scholarship or grant aid from institutional funds; Federal Pell; Private scholarships; SEOG; State scholarships/grants. *Loan aid offered:* Direct PLUS loans; Direct Subsidized Stafford Loans; Direct Unsubsidized Stafford Loans. Federal Work-Study Program available. Institutional employment available.

Campus Life

Activities: Campus Ministries; Choral groups; Concert band; Dance; Drama/theater; International Student Organization; Jazz band; Literary magazine; Marching band; Music ensembles; Musical theater; Opera; Pep band; Radio station; Student government; Student newspaper; Student-run film society; Symphony orchestra; Yearbook. **Organizations:** 200 registered organizations, 3 honor societies, 12 religious organizations. **Athletics (Intercollegiate):** *Men:* baseball, basketball, cross-country, diving, football, golf, lacrosse, soccer, swimming, tennis, track/field (outdoor), track/field (indoor). *Women:* basketball, cross-country, diving, field hockey, golf, lacrosse, soccer, softball, swimming, tennis, track/field (outdoor), track/field (indoor), volleyball.

ACCOMMODATIONS

Allowed in exams:	
Calculators	Yes
Dictionary	Yes
Computer	Yes
Spell-checker	Yes
Extended test time	Yes
Scribe	Yes
Proctors	Yes
Oral exams	Yes
Note-takers	Yes
Support services for students with:	
LD	Yes
ADHD	Yes
ASD	Yes
Distraction-reduced environment	Yes
Recording of lecture alowed	Yes
Reading technology	Yes
Audio books	Yes
Other assistive technology	Yes
Priority registration	Yes
Added costs of services:	
For LD	No
For ADHD	No
For ASD	No
LD specialists	Yes
ADHD & ASD coaching	No
ASD specialists	Yes
Professional tutors	No
Peer tutors	Yes
Max. hours/week for services	Varies
How professors are notified of student approved accommodations	Student and Director

COLLEGE GRADUATION REQUIREMENTS

Course waivers allowed	No
Course substitutions allowed	Yes
In what courses: Case by case basis	

Ohio

The Ohio State University—Columbus

281 West Lane, Columbus, OH 43210 • Admissions: 614-292-3980 • Fax: 614-292-3980 **Support: CS**

CAMPUS

Type of school	Public
Environment	Metropolis

STUDENTS

Undergrad enrollment	45,657
% male/female	51/49
% from out of state	19
% frosh live on campus	93

FINANCIAL FACTS

Annual in-state tuition	$11,518
Annual out-of-state tuition	$33,502
Room and board	$13,066

GENERAL ADMISSIONS INFO

Application fee	$60
Regular application deadline	2/1
Nonfall registration	Yes

Admission may be deferred.

Range SAT EBRW	600–690
Range SAT Math	650–770
Range ACT Composite	28–32

ACADEMICS

Student/faculty ratio	19:1
% students returning for sophomore year	94

Most classes have 20–29 students.

Programs/Services for Students with Learning Differences

The Office for Disability Services (ODS) at Ohio State University offers a variety of services for students with documented disabilities, including learning disabilities, hearing or visual impairments, attention deficit disorders, and psychiatric or medical disabilities. The mission of ODS is to provide and coordinate support services and programs that enable students with disabilities to maximize their educational potential. ODS serves as a resource to all members of the university community so that students with disabilities can freely and actively participate in all facets of university life.

Admissions

There is no separate process for students with documentation, however, there can be an appeal process if denied admissions. Students can begin registration with Student Life Disability Services upon acceptance. However, consideration can be given to students with LD with support from ODS in instances where the student's rank, GPA or lack of courses, such as foreign language, have affected performance in high school. In addition to looking for students who have taken a rigorous high school curriculum, OSU also considers leadership, extracurricular activities, talent, first-generation status, challenges, and those who would benefit from support services on campus. Course requirements include 4 years English, 3 years math (4 recommended), 3 years science, 2 years social studies, 2 years foreign language, and 1 year of fine or performing arts.

Additional Information

Transition. Success. Independence. (TOPS) is a 2–4 year Workforce Development Certificate program. It offers students with developmental disabilities a unique opportunity to engage in OSU academic coursework and work experiences while developing independent living skills and participating in campus and community organizations, social activities, and events. Potential applicants are interested in lifelong learning and will benefit from experiences gained at OSU. Prerequisite criteria are: a high school graduate with traditional diploma or certificate of completion, ability to benefit from curricula to improve academic, employment, social and independent living outcomes, demonstration of functional communication skills, and a desire to continue learning. ACE (Autism College Experience) is a program to help students with autism or similar communication difficulties navigate the college experience.

ADMISSIONS INFO FOR STUDENTS WITH LEARNING DIFFERENCES

Phone: 614-292-3307 • Fax: 614-292-4190 • Email: slds@osu.edu

SAT/ACT required: Yes (Test optional for 2021)
Interview required: No
Essay required: Yes
Additional application required: No
Documentation submitted to: Office for Disability Services

Special Ed. HS course work accepted: No
Separate application required for Programs/Services: No
Documentation required for:
LD: Psychoeducational evaluation
ADHD: Psychoeducational evaluation
ASD: Psychoeducational evaluation

The Ohio State University—Columbus

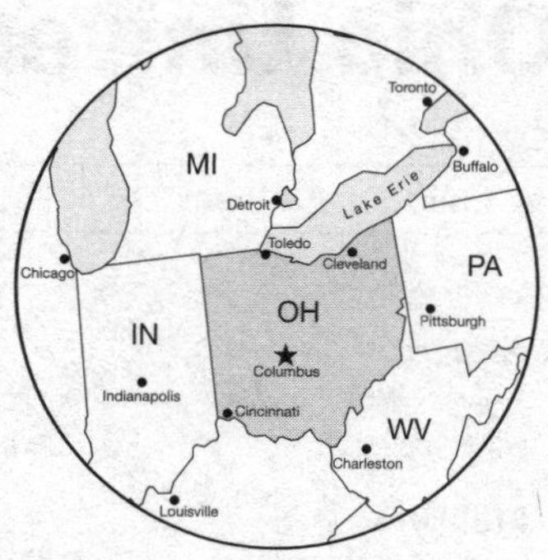

General Admissions

Very important factors include: rigor of secondary school record, class rank, academic GPA, standardized test scores. *Important factors include:* application essay, extracurricular activities, talent/ability, first generation. *Other factors include:* recommendation(s), character/personal qualities, geographical residence, state residency, racial/ethnic status. *Freshman admission requirements:* High school diploma is required and GED is accepted. *Academic units required:* 4 English, 3 math, 3 science, 3 science labs, 2 foreign language, 2 social studies, 1 academic elective, 1 visual/performing arts. *Academic units recommended:* 4 English, 4 math, 3 science, 3 science labs, 3 foreign language, 3 social studies, 1 academic elective, 1 visual/performing arts.

Accommodations or Services

Accommodations are decided upon an individual basis after a thorough review of appropriate, current documentation. The accommodations requests must be supported through the documentation provided and must be logically linked to the current impact of the condition on academic functioning.

Financial Aid

Students should submit: FAFSA. *Need-based scholarships/grants offered:* College/university scholarship or grant aid from institutional funds; Federal Pell; Private scholarships; SEOG; State scholarships/grants. *Loan aid offered:* Direct PLUS loans; Direct Subsidized Stafford Loans; Direct Unsubsidized Stafford Loans. Federal Work-Study Program available. Institutional employment available.

Campus Life

Activities: Campus Ministries; Choral groups; Concert band; Dance; Drama/theater; International Student Organization; Jazz band; Literary magazine; Marching band; Model UN; Music ensembles; Musical theater; Opera; Pep band; Radio station; Student government; Student newspaper; Student-run film society; Symphony orchestra; Television station. **Organizations:** 1449 registered organizations, 46 honor societies, 63 religious organizations, 38 fraternities, 26 sororities. **Athletics (Intercollegiate):** *Men:* baseball, basketball, cheerleading, cross-country, diving, fencing, football, golf, gymnastics, ice hockey, lacrosse, pistol, riflery, soccer, swimming, tennis, track/field (outdoor), track/field (indoor), volleyball, wrestling. *Women:* baseball, basketball, cheerleading, crew/rowing, cross-country, diving, fencing, field hockey, golf, gymnastics, ice hockey, lacrosse, pistol, riflery, soccer, softball, swimming, synchronized swimming, tennis, track/field (outdoor), track/field (indoor), volleyball.

ACCOMMODATIONS

Allowed in exams:	
Calculators	Yes
Dictionary	Yes
Computer	Yes
Spell-checker	Yes
Extended test time	Yes
Scribe	Yes
Proctors	Yes
Oral exams	Yes
Note-takers	Yes
Support services for students with:	
LD	Yes
ADHD	Yes
ASD	Yes
Distraction-reduced environment	Yes
Recording of lecture allowed	Yes
Reading technology	Yes
Audio books	Yes
Other assistive technology	Yes
Priority registration	Yes
Added costs of services:	
For LD	No
For ADHD	No
For ASD	No
LD specialists	Yes
ADHD & ASD coaching	No
ASD specialists	Yes
Professional tutors	No
Peer tutors	Yes
Max. hours/week for services	Varies
How professors are notified of student approved accommodations	Student and Director

COLLEGE GRADUATION REQUIREMENTS

Course waivers allowed	No
Course substitutions allowed	Yes
In what courses: Varies	

Ohio University—Athens

120 Chubb Hall, Athens, OH 45701 • Admissions: 740-593-4100 • Fax: 740-593-0560 **Support: S**

CAMPUS

Type of school	Public
Environment	Town

STUDENTS

Undergrad enrollment	20,406
% male/female	40/60
% from out of state	12
% frosh live on campus	95

FINANCIAL FACTS

Annual in-state tuition	$12,612
Annual out-of-state tuition	$22,406
Room and board	$12,172

GENERAL ADMISSIONS INFO

Application fee	$50
Regular application deadline	2/1
Nonfall registration	Yes

Admission may be deferred.

Range SAT EBRW	530–640
Range SAT Math	520–620
Range ACT Composite	21–26

ACADEMICS

Student/faculty ratio	16:1
% students returning for sophomore year	82

Most classes have 10–19 students.

Programs/Services for Students with Learning Differences

Student Accessibility Services assists students in transition to college through determination of reasonable accommodations, referral to pertinent resources to support student success, assist students in developing self-advocacy skills, and to serve as a central point of contact for navigating the college experience. Accessibility Coordinators are available and willing to meet upon a student's request; however, progress is not formally monitored by the SAS.

Admissions

Applicants with LD meet the same admission criteria as all other applicants. General admission Students not meeting the admission criteria are encouraged to self-disclose by writing a narrative explaining the impact of the disability. The average ACT is 22–26 and SAT of 1090–1240. The average GPA is 3.5. Admissions considers curriculum, class rank, GPA, and ACT/SAT. Some programs have more selective criteria. Courses required are 4 English, 4 math, 3 science, 3 social studies, 2 foreign language, 1 visual or performing arts, and 4 additional electives.

Additional Information

SAS has coaching support for students on the autism spectrum. The program provides an additional layer of individualized support. Coaches work individually with students on five key competency areas to develop the skills and strategies necessary to succeed in college. As students progress, the program's focus shifts from adjustment to the college environment to the pursuit of optimal independence and the transition to the workforce. Coaches are experienced, upper class student-employees trained to serve as an additional resource for students with ASD through ASPeCT (Autism Spectrum Peer Coaching Team).

ADMISSIONS INFO FOR STUDENTS WITH LEARNING DIFFERENCES

Phone: 740-593-2620 • Fax: 740-593-0790 • Email: disabilities@ohio.edu

SAT/ACT required: Yes (Test optional for 2021)
Interview required: No
Essay required: Yes
Additional application required: Yes
Documentation submitted to: Student Accessibility Services

Special Ed. HS course work accepted: Yes
Separate application required for Programs/Services: Yes
Documentation required for:
- **LD:** Psychoeducational evaluation
- **ADHD:** Psychoeducational evaluation
- **ASD:** Psychoeducational evaluation

Ohio University—Athens

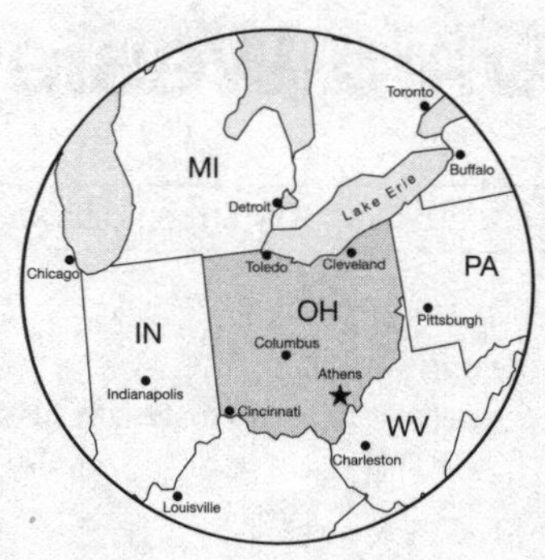

General Admissions

Very important factors include: rigor of secondary school record, academic GPA, standardized test scores. *Important factors include:* class rank, application essay, first generation. *Other factors include:* recommendation(s), interview, extracurricular activities, talent/ability, character/personal qualities, alumni/ae relation, geographical residence, state residency, volunteer work, work experience. *Freshman admission requirements:* High school diploma is required and GED is accepted. *Academic units required:* 4 English, 4 math, 3 science, 2 foreign language, 3 social studies, 4 academic electives, 1 unit from above areas or other academic areas. *Academic units recommended:* 1 visual/performing arts.

Accommodations or Services

Accommodations are decided upon an individual basis after a thorough review of appropriate, current documentation. The accommodations requests must be supported through the documentation provided and must be logically linked to the current impact of the condition on academic functioning.

Financial Aid

Students should submit: FAFSA; State aid form. Applicants will be notified of awards on a rolling basis beginning 3/15. *Need-based scholarships/grants offered:* College/university scholarship or grant aid from institutional funds; Federal Pell; Private scholarships; SEOG; State scholarships/grants. *Loan aid offered:* Direct PLUS loans; Direct Subsidized Stafford Loans; Direct Unsubsidized Stafford Loans. Federal Work-Study Program available. Institutional employment available.

Campus Life

Activities: Campus Ministries; Choral groups; Concert band; Dance; Drama/theater; International Student Organization; Jazz band; Literary magazine; Marching band; Music ensembles; Musical theater; Opera; Pep band; Radio station; Student government; Student newspaper; Student-run film society; Symphony orchestra; Television station; Yearbook. **Organizations:** 639 registered organizations, 24 honor societies, 28 religious organizations, 18 fraternities, 13 sororities. **Athletics (Intercollegiate):** *Men:* baseball, basketball, cheerleading, cross-country, football, golf, wrestling. *Women:* basketball, cheerleading, cross-country, diving, field hockey, golf, soccer, softball, swimming, track/field (outdoor), volleyball.

ACCOMMODATIONS

Allowed in exams:	
Calculators	Yes
Dictionary	Yes
Computer	Yes
Spell-checker	Yes
Extended test time	Yes
Scribe	Yes
Proctors	Yes
Oral exams	No
Note-takers	Yes
Support services for students with:	
LD	Yes
ADHD	Yes
ASD	Yes
Distraction-reduced environment	Yes
Recording of lecture allowed	Yes
Reading technology	Yes
Audio books	Yes
Other assistive technology	Yes
Priority registration	Yes
Added costs of services:	
For LD	No
For ADHD	No
For ASD	No
LD specialists	No
ADHD & ASD coaching	Yes
ASD specialists	Yes
Professional tutors	No
Peer tutors	No
Max. hours/week for services	Varies
How professors are notified of student approved accommodations	Student

COLLEGE GRADUATION REQUIREMENTS

Course waivers allowed	No
Course substitutions allowed	Yes
In what courses: Case by case basis	

Ohio

Ohio Wesleyan University

61 South Sandusky Street, Delaware, OH 43015 • Admissions: 740-368-3020 • Fax: 740-368-3314 **Support: CS**

CAMPUS

Type of school	Private (nonprofit)
Environment	Town

STUDENTS

Undergrad enrollment	1,494
% male/female	44/56
% from out of state	36
% frosh live on campus	91

FINANCIAL FACTS

Annual tuition	$46,870
Room and board	$12,800
Required fees	$260

GENERAL ADMISSIONS INFO

Application fee	$0
Regular application deadline	3/1
Nonfall registration	Yes

Admission may be deferred.

ACADEMICS

Student/faculty ratio	10:1
% students returning for sophomore year	78

Most classes have 10–19 students.

Programs/Services for Students with Learning Differences

The Disability Services Center (DSC) works to structure and deliver services that help a student to access accommodations. They review documentation, help students to receive reasonable accommodations for classroom learning and exams, provide educational counseling, consult with faculty on student need, assist in self-monitoring, and provide technical assistance.

Admissions

Admissions to Ohio Wesleyan University is the same for all students. Successful candidates for admission usually rank in the top quarter of their high school classes and have a minimum B average in their academic course work. Admissions to the university is offered on a selective basis. With few exceptions, the majors required for graduation require the completion of 8–15 courses. Double majors and minors are encouraged.

Additional Information

BISHOP ACCESS is a fee-based academic coaching program to help students who need additional level of academic and out-of-class support. There are weekly individual meetings, peer tutoring, and communication with parents. An academic coach works one-on-one and in small groups with students to help them navigate university life and complete school work that requires planning, goal-setting, and managing time. Students need to complete the application form and documentation of learning-related difficulty.

ADMISSIONS INFO FOR STUDENTS WITH LEARNING DIFFERENCES

Phone: 740-368-3990 • Fax: 740-368-3959

SAT/ACT required: Optional
Interview required: No
Essay required: Yes
Additional application required: No
Documentation submitted to: DSC

Special Ed. HS course work accepted: No
Separate application required for Programs/Services: No
Documentation required for:
- **LD:** Psychoeducational evaluation
- **ADHD:** Psychoeducational evaluation
- **ASD:** Psychoeducational evaluation

Ohio Wesleyan University

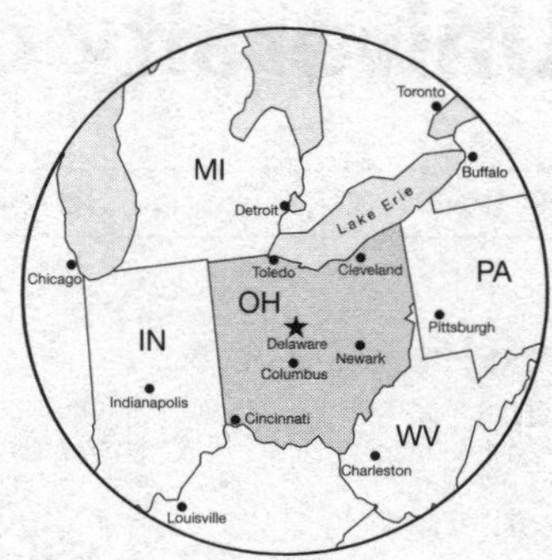

General Admissions

Very important factors include: rigor of secondary school record, academic GPA, application essay, recommendation(s), interview, character/personal qualities. *Important factors include:* class rank, standardized test scores, extracurricular activities, talent/ability. *Other factors include:* first generation, alumni/ae relation, geographical residence, volunteer work, work experience, level of applicant's interest. *Freshman admission requirements:* High school diploma is required and GED is accepted. *Academic units required:* 4 English, 3 math, 3 science, 2 foreign language, 3 social studies. *Academic units recommended:* 4 English, 4 math, 4 science, 3 foreign language, 4 social studies.

Accommodations or Services

Accommodations are decided upon an individual basis after a thorough review of appropriate, current documentation. The accommodations requests must be supported through the documentation provided and must be logically linked to the current impact of the condition on academic functioning.

Financial Aid

Students should submit: FAFSA. Applicants will be notified of awards on a rolling basis beginning 3/1. *Need-based scholarships/grants offered:* College/university scholarship or grant aid from institutional funds; Federal Pell; Private scholarships; SEOG; State scholarships/grants. *Loan aid offered:* Direct PLUS loans; Direct Subsidized Stafford Loans; Direct Unsubsidized Stafford Loans. Federal Work-Study Program available. Institutional employment available.

Campus Life

Activities: Campus Ministries; Choral groups; Dance; Drama/theater; International Student Organization; Jazz band; Literary magazine; Marching band; Model UN; Music ensembles; Musical theater; Opera; Pep band; Radio station; Student government; Student newspaper; Symphony orchestra; Yearbook. **Athletics (Intercollegiate):** *Men:* baseball, basketball, cross-country, diving, football, golf, lacrosse, sailing, soccer, swimming, tennis, track/field (outdoor), track/field (indoor). *Women:* basketball, cross-country, diving, field hockey, lacrosse, sailing, soccer, softball, swimming, tennis, track/field (outdoor), track/field (indoor), volleyball.

ACCOMMODATIONS

Allowed in exams:	
Calculators	Yes
Computer	Yes
Spell-checker	Yes
Extended test time	Yes
Scribe	No
Proctors	Yes
Oral exams	Yes
Note-takers	Yes
Support services for students with:	
LD	Yes
ADHD	Yes
ASD	Yes
Distraction-reduced environment	Yes
Recording of lecture alowed	Yes
Reading technology	Yes
Audio books	Yes
Other assistive technology	Yes
Priority registration	Yes
Added costs of services:	
For LD	No
For ADHD	No
For ASD	No
LD specialists	Yes
ADHD & ASD coaching	Yes
ASD specialists	No
Professional tutors	No
Peer tutors	Yes
Max. hours/week for services	Varies
How professors are notified of student approved accommodations	DSC

COLLEGE GRADUATION REQUIREMENTS

Course waivers allowed	Yes
In what courses: Case by case basis	
Course substitutions allowed	Yes
In what courses: Case by case basis	

Ohio

University of Cincinnati

P.O. Box 210091, Cincinnati, OH 45221-0091 • Admissions: 513-556-1100 • Fax: 513-556-1105 **Support: CS**

CAMPUS

Type of school	Public
Environment	Metropolis

STUDENTS

Undergrad enrollment	26,731
% male/female	50/50
% from out of state	17
% frosh live on campus	82

FINANCIAL FACTS

Annual in-state tuition	$12,138
Annual out-of-state tuition	$ 27,472
Room and board	$11,530
Required fees	$1,678

GENERAL ADMISSIONS INFO

Application fee	$50
Regular application deadline	3/1
Nonfall registration	Yes

Admission may be deferred.

Range SAT EBRW	560–660
Range SAT Math	560–690
Range ACT Composite	23–29

ACADEMICS

Student/faculty ratio	17:1
% students returning for sophomore year	86

Most classes have 20–29 students.

Programs/Services for Students with Learning Differences

Accessibility Resources (AR) supports students with disabilities through the delivery of reasonable accommodations and support services. Students with disabilities who need academic accommodations or other specialized services while attending UC will receive reasonable accommodations to meet their individual needs as well as advocacy assistance on disability-related issues. Students submit their documentation of disability to AR, complete a Student Self Report Form, and then interviews with the Director. There is a Writing Center for one-on-one appointments with a tutor, help in developing study skills with a tutor, and a Math Lab that offers small group tutoring.

Admissions

There is no special admission procedure for students with learning disabilities. The university is test optional and does not require the ACT or SAT for admission except for applicants to the university Honors Program, College of Nursing, and the Early Childhood Education Program. The University of Cincinnati has three campuses that offer different programs and opportunities. Applicants should be certain to select the correct campus on their application.

Additional Information

The Transition and Access Program (TAP) provides a four-year college experience for individuals with mild to moderate intellectual or developmental disabilities (ID/DD). Students live in the residence halls, attend classes, engage in vocational internships and participate in an active social life. TAP's mission is to enhance the quality of life of students through advocacy, access, and research. Applicants must have: a cognitive assessment with documented intellectual or developmental disability; a high school diploma and be age 18 or older; basic academic skills; the ability to learn and participate in inclusive classrooms and work settings; and the interest and ability to pursue educational, employment, and life experiences through post-secondary education. The cost of the program is approximately $26,000 per year.

ADMISSIONS INFO FOR STUDENTS WITH LEARNING DIFFERENCES

Phone: 513-556-6823 • Fax: 513-556-1383 • Email: disabisv@ucmail.uc.edu

SAT/ACT required: Yes (Test optional through 2022)
Interview required: No
Essay required: Yes
Additional application required: No
Documentation submitted to: Accessibility Resources

Special Ed. HS course work accepted: Yes
Separate application required for Programs/Services: No
Documentation required for:
LD: Psychoeducational evaluation
ADHD: Psychoeducational evaluation
ASD: Psychoeducational evaluation

University of Cincinnati

General Admissions

Very important factors include: rigor of secondary school record, academic GPA, standardized test scores. *Important factors include:* application essay, recommendation(s), talent/ability. *Other factors include:* class rank, extracurricular activities, character/personal qualities, first generation, geographical residence, state residency, racial/ethnic status, volunteer work, work experience. *Freshman admission requirements:* High school diploma is required and GED is not accepted. *Academic units required:* 4 English, 4 math, 3 science, 3 social studies, 5 unit from above areas or other academic areas. *Academic units recommended:* 2 foreign language.

Accommodations or Services

Accommodations are decided upon an individual basis after a thorough review of appropriate, current documentation. The accommodations requests must be supported through the documentation provided and must be logically linked to the current impact of the condition on academic functioning.

Financial Aid

Students should submit: FAFSA. *Need-based scholarships/grants offered:* College/university scholarship or grant aid from institutional funds; Federal Pell; Private scholarships; SEOG; State scholarships/grants; United Negro College Fund. *Loan aid offered:* Direct PLUS loans; Direct Subsidized Stafford Loans; Direct Unsubsidized Stafford Loans. Federal Work-Study Program available. Institutional employment available.

Campus Life

Activities: Campus Ministries; Choral groups; Concert band; Dance; Drama/theater; International Student Organization; Jazz band; Marching band; Model UN; Music ensembles; Musical theater; Opera; Pep band; Radio station; Student government; Student newspaper; Student-run film society; Symphony orchestra. **Organizations:** 981 registered organizations, 25 honor societies, 13 religious organizations, 28 fraternities, 17 sororities. **Athletics (Intercollegiate):** *Men:* baseball, basketball, cheerleading, cross-country, diving, football, golf, soccer, swimming, track/field (outdoor). *Women:* basketball, cheerleading, cross-country, diving, golf, lacrosse, soccer, swimming, tennis, track/field (outdoor), track/field (indoor), volleyball.

ACCOMMODATIONS

Allowed in exams:	
Calculators	Yes
Dictionary	Yes
Computer	Yes
Spell-checker	Yes
Extended test time	Yes
Scribe	Yes
Proctors	Yes
Oral exams	No
Note-takers	Yes
Support services for students with:	
LD	Yes
ADHD	Yes
ASD	Yes
Distraction-reduced environment	Yes
Recording of lecture alowed	Yes
Reading technology	Yes
Audio books	Yes
Other assistive technology	Yes
Priority registration	Yes
Added costs of services:	
For LD	No
For ADHD	No
For ASD	No
LD specialists	Yes
ADHD & ASD coaching	No
ASD specialists	No
Professional tutors	No
Peer tutors	Yes
Max. hours/week for services	Varies
How professors are notified of student approved accommodations	Student and Director

COLLEGE GRADUATION REQUIREMENTS

Course waivers allowed	No
Course substitutions allowed	Yes
In what courses: Case by case basis	

University of Dayton

300 College Park, Dayton, OH 45469-1669 • Admissions: 937-229-4411 • Fax: 937-229-4729 **Support: CS**

CAMPUS

Type of school	Private (nonprofit)
Environment	City

STUDENTS

Undergrad enrollment	8,483
% male/female	52/48
% from out of state	50
% frosh live on campus	93

FINANCIAL FACTS

Annual tuition	$44,890
Room and board	$14,580

GENERAL ADMISSIONS INFO

Application fee	$0
Regular application deadline	3/1
Nonfall registration	Yes

Admission may be deferred.

Range SAT EBRW	560–650
Range SAT Math	560–670
Range ACT Composite	23–29

ACADEMICS

Student/faculty ratio	14:1
% students returning for sophomore year	89

Most classes have 20–29 students.

Programs/Services for Students with Learning Differences

The Learning Teaching Center's Office of Learning Resources (OLR) focus is to provide all students with disabilities an equitable opportunity to participate freely and actively in all areas of university life. Accommodations decisions are made primarily based on interactive interview with the student and review of supporting documentation when needed. Many accommodations are provided using assistive software/technology and electronic services. There is no fee for any provided services.

Admissions

All applicants must meet the same admission criteria. The University of Dayton looks at the grades received in high school and may even request the 7th semester grades. Students are encouraged to take a rigorous curriculum in college prep courses. The university is test optional, so neither the ACT or SAT is required for admissions. Recommendation from a high school guidance counselor are very helpful. It is important to demonstrate interest in the university by attending an official campus visit or event in your area or joining virtual tours and events. Based on the overall academic quality of applicants and the requirements for a particular major or division, the admission committee may choose to admit a student to a different academic program.

Additional Information

The (FIRST) Fully Integrated Resource, Support and Transition program provides academic support integrated into a regular schedule of courses. This program is offered to a small number of students who have signed the FIRST program contract understanding that there are expectations that have to be accepted. The goal is to teach students metacognitive skills to help them succeed in college. The credit hours for these courses will apply toward the student's total credit hours for graduation. Additionally, because the university recognizes that students have individually unique academic and personal strengths and weaknesses, the Office of Learning Resources (OLR) provides support services to students such as drop-in tutoring (peer-facilitated), with additional support models (Supplemental Instruction) linked to specific classes, and writing support across the curriculum. All OLR support services are provided free of charge. OLR services are most effective if the student takes advantage of them before he or she falls too far behind or receives too many low grades.

ADMISSIONS INFO FOR STUDENTS WITH LEARNING DIFFERENCES

Phone: 937-229-2066 • Fax: 937-229-3270 • Email: eharrison1@udayton.edu

SAT/ACT required: Optional
Interview required: No
Essay required: No
Additional application required: Yes
Documentation submitted to: OLR

Special Ed. HS course work accepted: Yes
Separate application required for Programs/Services: Yes
Documentation required for:
LD: Psychoeducational evaluation
ADHD: Psychoeducational evaluation
ASD: Psychoeducational evaluation

University of Dayton

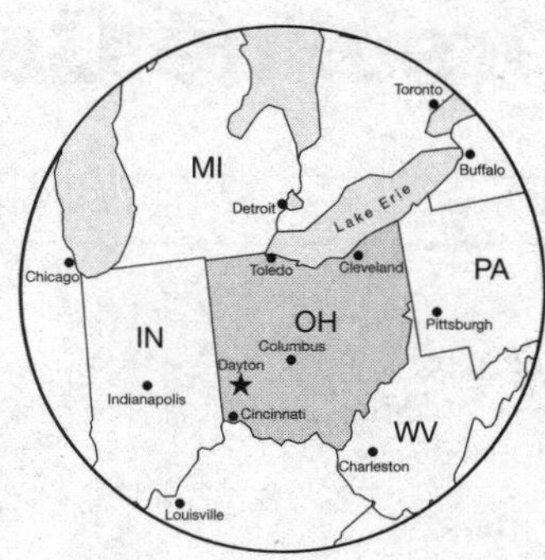

General Admissions

Very important factors include: rigor of secondary school record, class rank, academic GPA, application essay, standardized test scores. *Important factors include:* recommendation(s), extracurricular activities, character/personal qualities, alumni/ae relation. *Other factors include:* talent/ability, first generation, racial/ethnic status, volunteer work, work experience. *Freshman admission requirements:* High school diploma is required and GED is accepted. *Academic units recommended:* 4 English, 4 math, 4 science, 1 science lab, 2 foreign language, 4 social studies, 4 history, 4 computer science, 4 visual/performing arts.

Accommodations or Services

Accommodations are decided upon an individual basis after a thorough review of appropriate, current documentation. The accommodations requests must be supported through the documentation provided and must be logically linked to the current impact of the condition on academic functioning.

Financial Aid

Students should submit: FAFSA. *Need-based scholarships/grants offered:* College/university scholarship or grant aid from institutional funds; Federal Pell; Private scholarships; SEOG; State scholarships/grants. *Loan aid offered:* . Federal Work-Study Program available. Institutional employment available.

Campus Life

Activities: Campus Ministries; Choral groups; Concert band; Dance; Drama/theater; International Student Organization; Jazz band; Literary magazine; Marching band; Model UN; Music ensembles; Musical theater; Opera; Pep band; Radio station; Student government; Student newspaper; Symphony orchestra; Television station; Yearbook. **Organizations:** 267 registered organizations, 16 honor societies, 11 religious organizations, 10 fraternities, 11 sororities. **Athletics (Intercollegiate):** *Men:* baseball, basketball, cheerleading, cross-country, football, golf, soccer, tennis. *Women:* basketball, cheerleading, crew/rowing, cross-country, golf, soccer, softball, tennis, track/field (outdoor), track/field (indoor), volleyball.

ACCOMMODATIONS

Allowed in exams:	
Calculators	Yes
Dictionary	No
Computer	Yes
Spell-checker	Yes
Extended test time	Yes
Scribe	Yes
Proctors	Yes
Oral exams	No
Note-takers	Yes
Support services for students with:	
LD	Yes
ADHD	Yes
ASD	Yes
Distraction-reduced environment	Yes
Recording of lecture allowed	Yes
Reading technology	Yes
Audio books	Yes
Other assistive technology	Yes
Priority registration	Yes
Added costs of services:	
For LD	No
For ADHD	No
For ASD	No
LD specialists	Yes
ADHD & ASD coaching	Yes
ASD specialists	No
Professional tutors	No
Peer tutors	Yes
Max. hours/week for services	Varies
How professors are notified of student approved accommodations	Student

COLLEGE GRADUATION REQUIREMENTS

Course waivers allowed	No
Course substitutions allowed	Yes
In what courses Math, foreign language, and physical education	

Ohio

Ursuline College

2550 Lander Road, Pepper Pike, OH 44124-4398 • Admissions: 440-449-4203 • Fax: 440-684-6138 **Support: SP**

CAMPUS

Type of school	Private (nonprofit)
Environment	City

STUDENTS

Undergrad enrollment	651
% male/female	7/93
% from out of state	13
% frosh live on campus	56

FINANCIAL FACTS

Annual tuition	$34,290
Room and board	$11,232
Required fees	$400

GENERAL ADMISSIONS INFO

Application fee	$0
Regular application deadline	Rolling
Nonfall registration	Yes

Admission may be deferred.

Range SAT EBRW	480–560
Range SAT Math	470–550
Range ACT Composite	17–23

ACADEMICS

Student/faculty ratio	7:1
% students returning for sophomore year	75

Most classes have 10–19 students.

Programs/Services for Students with Learning Differences

Ursuline College is a small Catholic college committed to helping students with learning disabilities succeed in their courses and become independent learners. The Program for Students with Learning Disabilities (FOCUS) is a voluntary, comprehensive fee-paid program. The goals of the FOCUS program include providing a smooth transition to college life, helping students learn to apply the most appropriate learning strategies in college courses, and teaching self-advocacy skills. To be eligible for FOCUS admission, a student must present documentation of an LD conducted within the last 3 years. Students must have average to above-average intellectual ability and an appropriate academic foundation to succeed in a 4-year liberal arts college.

Admissions

To participate in the FOCUS program, students must first meet with the LD specialist to discuss whether the program is suitable for them. Students must then meet the requirements for clear or conditional admission to the college. Students with learning disabilities usually meet the same requirements for admission to the college as all other students. A student may receive a "conditional" admission if the GPA and ACT are lower. Students with conditional admission are limited to 12 credit hours per semester for the first year. The final admission decision is made by the Office of Admissions. Ursuline College admits candidates who demonstrate potential for success in rigorous academic work. Qualified applicants are admitted regardless of sex, race, religion, color, age, veteran status, national or ethnic origin, sexual orientation, gender identity or expression, or physical ability. All applications are reviewed on a need-blind basis, which means admission decisions are based solely on a student's academic and extracurricular merits, not on his or her family's financial circumstances. Ursuline's admission committee seeks to identify and admit students who will add character to the college community while succeeding academically and reserves the right to deny admission to any applicant.

Additional Information

The fee-based FOCUS program is offered in multiple phases to better meet individual students' needs. Staff have in-service training in order to understand how to accommodate students with special needs. The FOCUS program is broken down into the following four stages: FOCUS STAGE 1: One guaranteed weekly meeting with a disability specialist to cover all areas of academic progress, co-advising on academic courses majors, mid-term progress monitoring and monthly communication with faculty,

ADMISSIONS INFO FOR STUDENTS WITH LEARNING DIFFERENCES

Phone: 440-449-2046 • Email: ekohut@ursuline.edu

SAT/ACT required: Yes (Test optional for 2021)
Interview required: No
Essay required: Yes
Additional application required: Yes
Documentation submitted to: FOCUS

Special Ed. HS course work accepted: No
Separate application required for Programs/Services: Yes
Documentation required for:
LD: Psychoeducational evaluation
ADHD: Psychoeducational evaluation
ASD: Psychoeducational evaluation

Ursuline College

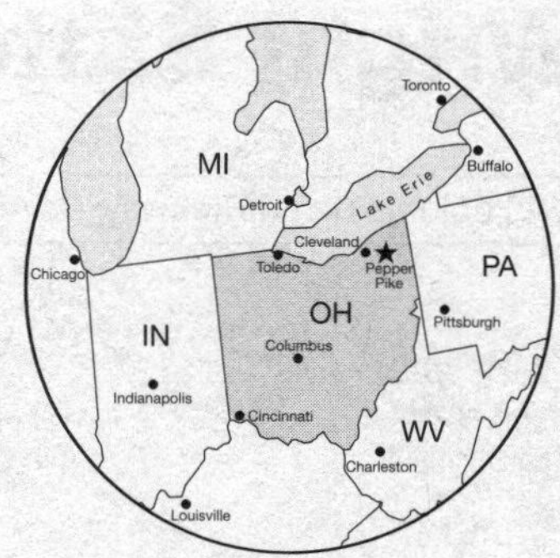

and priority registration. FOCUS STAGE 2: Incoming special orientation with the disability specialist, two guaranteed weekly meetings with a disability specialist to cover all areas of academic progress, co-advising on courses and majors, academic and social support, mid-term progress monitoring, biweekly communication with faculty, and priority registration. FOCUS STAGE 3: Students meet with the disability specialist a minimum of 3 times per week, bi-weekly monitoring and communication with faculty, co-advising on academic courses, majors, and priority registration. Academic and social support are provided. FOCUS STAGE 4: For students who are transitioning out of college.

General Admissions

Very important factors include: academic GPA, standardized test scores. *Other factors include:* rigor of secondary school record, class rank, application essay, recommendation(s), interview, alumni/ae relation. *Freshman admission requirements:* High school diploma is required and GED is accepted. *Academic units recommended:* 4 English, 3 math, 3 science, 2 science labs, 2 foreign language, 3 social studies, 1 visual/performing arts.

Accommodations or Services

Accommodations are decided upon an individual basis after a thorough review of appropriate, current documentation. The accommodations requests must be supported through the documentation provided and must be logically linked to the current impact of the condition on academic functioning.

Financial Aid

Students should submit: FAFSA; Institution's own financial aid form. Applicants will be notified of awards on a rolling basis beginning 2/1. *Need-based scholarships/grants offered:* College/university scholarship or grant aid from institutional funds; Federal Nursing Scholarships; Federal Pell; Private scholarships; SEOG; State scholarships/grants. *Loan aid offered:* Direct PLUS loans; Direct Subsidized Stafford Loans; Direct Unsubsidized Stafford Loans. Federal Work-Study Program available.

Campus Life

Activities: Campus Ministries; Drama/theater; Literary magazine; Student government. **Organizations:** 23 registered organizations, 4 honor societies. **Athletics (Intercollegiate):** *Women:* basketball, bowling, cross-country, golf, soccer, softball, swimming, tennis, track/field (outdoor), volleyball.

ACCOMMODATIONS

Allowed in exams:	
Calculators	Yes
Dictionary	Yes
Computer	Yes
Spell-checker	Yes
Extended test time	Yes
Scribe	Yes
Proctors	Yes
Oral exams	Yes
Note-takers	Yes
Support services for students with:	
LD	Yes
ADHD	Yes
ASD	Yes
Distraction-reduced environment	Yes
Recording of lecture alowed	Yes
Reading technology	Yes
Audio books	Yes
Other assistive technology	Yes
Priority registration	Yes
Added costs of services:	
For LD	Yes
For ADHD	Yes
For ASD	Yes
LD specialists	Yes
ADHD & ASD coaching	Yes
ASD specialists	No
Professional tutors	Yes
Peer tutors	Yes
Max. hours/week for services	Varies
How professors are notified of student approved accommodations	Student

COLLEGE GRADUATION REQUIREMENTS

Course waivers allowed	No
Course substitutions allowed	Yes
In what courses: Case by case basis	

Ohio

Wright State University

3640 Colonel Glenn Highway, Dayton, OH 45435 • Admissions: 937-775-5700 • Fax: 937-775-4410 **Support: CS**

CAMPUS

Type of school	Public
Environment	City

STUDENTS

Undergrad enrollment	9,585
% male/female	47/53
% from out of state	2
% frosh live on campus	51

FINANCIAL FACTS

Annual in-state tuition	$9,962
Annual out-of-state tuition	$19,380
Room and board	$9,622
Required fees	$926

GENERAL ADMISSIONS INFO

Application fee	$30
Regular application deadline	Rolling
Nonfall registration	Yes

Admission may be deferred.

Range SAT EBRW	490–620
Range SAT Math	480–610
Range ACT Composite	18–25

ACADEMICS

Student/faculty ratio	13:1
% students returning for sophomore year	63

Most classes have 10–19 students.

Programs/Services for Students with Learning Differences

The Office of Disability (ODS) staff members work with admitted Wright State students to ensure equal access to university programs and services. Whether they are making the transition from high school, community college, or another university, students should be aware of the process to request accommodations and/or auxiliary aids on the basis of a disability or temporary health condition. Services are supportive in nature, designed to provide the academic support necessary for students to have an equal opportunity for a college education. The application for accommodations from the Office of Disability Services is separate from the application for admission to the university. ODS does not participate in the university admission process.

Admissions

There is no special admissions process for students with learning disabilities. All students are required to have a college preparatory curriculum which includes: one (1) year of fine arts course, two (2) years of a foreign language, four (4) years of math, three (3) years of science, three (3) years of social studies, and four (4) years of English.

Additional Information

RASE Transition Coach Program is a fee-based program that provides support to students on the Autism Spectrum. Students are assigned a transition coach to work with them, one-on-one, for up to 5 hours per week. The transition coaches are experienced undergraduate or graduate students who are available as a resource for students on the Autism Spectrum. Coaches work with students on transition competency areas to develop the structure and framework necessary to be successful in college. The coach's focus can include assisting the student with learning self-advocacy skills, accessing campus resources and services, and problem solving. RASE program costs $750 per semester for year one and $300 per semester for additional years. PreFlight is a residential bridge program that will supply a variety of benefits including: early move-in, writing workshop, and engagement in college transition success programming.

ADMISSIONS INFO FOR STUDENTS WITH LEARNING DIFFERENCES

Phone: 937-775-5680 • Fax: 937-775-5699 • Email: disability_services@wright.edu

SAT/ACT required: Yes (Test optional for 2021)
Interview required: No
Essay required: No
Additional application required: No
Documentation submitted to: ODS

Special Ed. HS course work accepted: No
Separate application required for Programs/Services: Yes
Documentation required for:
- **LD:** Psychoeducational evaluation
- **ADHD:** Psychoeducational evaluation
- **ASD:** Psychoeducational evaluation

Wright State University

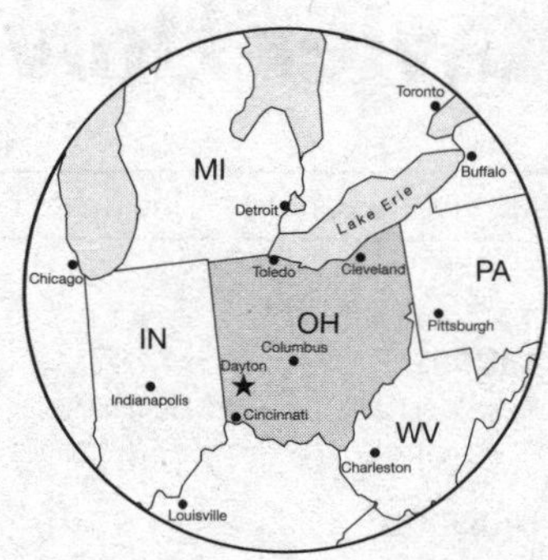

General Admissions

Very important factors include: rigor of secondary school record, academic GPA, standardized test scores. *Important factors include:* class rank. *Other factors include:* recommendation(s), state residency. *Freshman admission requirements:* High school diploma is required and GED is accepted. *Academic units required:* 4 English, 4 math, 3 science, 3 science labs, 3 social studies. *Academic units recommended:* 2 foreign language, 1 visual/performing arts.

Accommodations or Services

Accommodations are decided upon an individual basis after a thorough review of appropriate, current documentation. The accommodations requests must be supported through the documentation provided and must be logically linked to the current impact of the condition on academic functioning.

Financial Aid

Students should submit: FAFSA. *Need-based scholarships/grants offered:* College/university scholarship or grant aid from institutional funds; Federal Nursing Scholarships; Federal Pell; Private scholarships; SEOG; State scholarships/grants; United Negro College Fund. *Loan aid offered:* Direct PLUS loans; Direct Subsidized Stafford Loans; Direct Unsubsidized Stafford Loans. Federal Work-Study Program available. Institutional employment available.

Campus Life

Activities: Campus Ministries; Choral groups; Concert band; Dance; Drama/theater; International Student Organization; Jazz band; Literary magazine; Model UN; Music ensembles; Musical theater; Opera; Pep band; Radio station; Student government; Student newspaper; Symphony orchestra; Television station. **Organizations:** 205 registered organizations, 12 honor societies, 18 religious organizations, 9 fraternities, 11 sororities. **Athletics (Intercollegiate):** *Men:* baseball, basketball, cheerleading, cross-country, diving, golf, soccer, swimming, tennis. *Women:* basketball, cheerleading, cross-country, diving, soccer, softball, swimming, tennis, track/field (outdoor), volleyball.

ACCOMMODATIONS

Allowed in exams:	
Calculators	Yes
Dictionary	Yes
Computer	Yes
Spell-checker	Yes
Extended test time	Yes
Scribe	Yes
Proctors	Yes
Oral exams	Yes
Note-takers	Yes
Support services for students with:	
LD	Yes
ADHD	Yes
ASD	Yes
Distraction-reduced environment	Yes
Recording of lecture alowed	Yes
Reading technology	Yes
Audio books	Yes
Other assistive technology	Yes
Priority registration	No
Added costs of services:	
For LD	No
For ADHD	No
For ASD	Yes
LD specialists	Yes
ADHD & ASD coaching	Yes
ASD specialists	Yes
Professional tutors	Yes
Peer tutors	Yes
Max. hours/week for services	Varies
How professors are notified of student approved accommodations	Student

COLLEGE GRADUATION REQUIREMENTS

Course waivers allowed	Yes
In what courses: Considered on a case by case basis, however waivers are traditionally not offered.	
Course substitutions allowed	Yes
In what courses: Considered on a case by case basis, however waivers are traditionally not offered.	

Xavier University (OH)

3800 Victory Parkway, Cincinnati, OH 45207-5311 • Admissions: 513-745-3301 • Fax: 513-745-4319 **Support: CS**

CAMPUS

Type of school	Private (nonprofit)
Environment	Metropolis

STUDENTS

Undergrad enrollment	5,010
% male/female	46/54
% from out of state	57
% frosh live on campus	91

FINANCIAL FACTS

Annual tuition	$42,230
Room and board	$13,310
Required fees	$230

GENERAL ADMISSIONS INFO

Application fee	$35
Regular application deadline	Rolling
Nonfall registration	Yes

Admission may be deferred.

Range SAT EBRW	540–640
Range SAT Math	530–640
Range ACT Composite	22–28

ACADEMICS

Student/faculty ratio	11:1
% students returning for sophomore year	83

Most classes have 20–29 students.

Programs/Services for Students with Learning Differences

Xavier University is committed to providing equal access and reasonable accommodations to students with disabilities. The Office of Disability Services(ODS) provides academic accommodations and support services to provide equal access to educational opportunities. The office works closely with students and faculty, providing services and academic assistance to students with documented disabilities. The student has an obligation to self-identify that he or she has a disability and needs accommodations. Through a collaborative process, the Director of Disability Services will help determine reasonable and appropriate accommodations. For each accommodation the students requests, there will be an automatic note to the professor of the course the student is taking.

Admissions

All applicants must meet the same admission requirements. The average high school GPA of the admitted freshman class at Xavier University was 3.6. The university is test optional and applicants do not have to submit the ACT or SAT for admission. For those who do submit test scores, the average SAT score is between 1070–1250 or an average ACT score is 22–28.

Additional Information

The X-Path Program is established to provide individualized support for students on the autism spectrum or with related disorders. Support and coaching is tailored to the needs of each participating student to promote the development of academic competence, social integration, and self-advocacy. The mission of the X-Path Program is to increase opportunities for success for students who have autism and related disorders. Each student will work directly with the Accommodation and Support Coordinator and will also be assigned to a Peer Coach. The X-Path Program is for students on the Autism Spectrum. To be considered for this optional, fee-based program, applicants must meet the following criteria: be admitted to Xavier University through the Office of Undergraduate Admissions, be registered with the Office of Disability Services, and submit a completed online X-Path Program application. Applications will be reviewed to ensure that the program requirements are met and to assess whether the X-Path Program would be an appropriate option for the applicant's specific needs. Applicants may be contacted by program staff for an in-person or phone interview. All applicants accepted to the X-Path Program will receive a contract for program participation. The fee for participation in the X-Path Program is $1,500 per semester. Applicants may apply for financial assistance. All financial aid decisions will be determined by Xavier's Office of Student Financial Assistance.

ADMISSIONS INFO FOR STUDENTS WITH LEARNING DIFFERENCES

Phone: 513-745-3280 • Fax: 513-745-3387 • Email: disabilityservices@xavier.edu

SAT/ACT required: No
Interview required: No
Essay required: Yes
Additional application required: Yes
Documentation submitted to: ODS

Special Ed. HS course work accepted: Yes
Separate application required for Programs/Services: Yes
Documentation required for:
LD: Psychoeducational evaluation
ADHD: Psychoeducational evaluation
ASD: Psychoeducational evaluation

Xavier University (OH)

General Admissions

Very important factors include: rigor of secondary school record, academic GPA. *Important factors include:* application essay, standardized test scores, recommendation(s), extracurricular activities, character/personal qualities, volunteer work. *Other factors include:* class rank, talent/ability, first generation, alumni/ae relation, work experience, level of applicant's interest. *Freshman admission requirements:* High school diploma is required and GED is accepted. *Academic units recommended:* 4 English, 3 math, 3 science, 2 foreign language, 3 social studies, 5 academic electives, 1 unit from above areas or other academic areas.

Accommodations or Services

Accommodations are decided upon an individual basis after a thorough review of appropriate, current documentation. The accommodations requests must be supported through the documentation provided and must be logically linked to the current impact of the condition on academic functioning.

Financial Aid

Students should submit: FAFSA. Applicants will be notified of awards on a rolling basis beginning 1/1. *Need-based scholarships/grants offered:* College/university scholarship or grant aid from institutional funds; Federal Pell; Private scholarships; SEOG; State scholarships/grants; United Negro College Fund. *Loan aid offered:* Direct PLUS loans; Direct Subsidized Stafford Loans; Direct Unsubsidized Stafford Loans. Federal Work-Study Program available. Institutional employment available.

Campus Life

Activities: Campus Ministries; Choral groups; Concert band; Dance; Drama/theater; International Student Organization; Literary magazine; Model UN; Music ensembles; Musical theater; Pep band; Student government; Student newspaper; Television station. **Organizations:** 167 registered organizations, 9 honor societies, 4 religious organizations. **Athletics (Intercollegiate):** *Men:* baseball, basketball, cheerleading, cross-country, golf, soccer, swimming, tennis, track/field (outdoor), track/field (indoor). *Women:* basketball, cheerleading, cross-country, golf, soccer, swimming, tennis, track/field (outdoor), track/field (indoor), volleyball.

ACCOMMODATIONS

Allowed in exams:	
Calculators	Yes
Dictionary	Yes
Computer	Yes
Spell-checker	Yes
Extended test time	Yes
Scribe	Yes
Proctors	Yes
Oral exams	Yes
Note-takers	Yes
Support services for students with:	
LD	Yes
ADHD	Yes
ASD	Yes
Distraction-reduced environment	Yes
Recording of lecture alowed	Yes
Reading technology	Yes
Audio books	Yes
Other assistive technology	Yes
Priority registration	Yes
Added costs of services:	
For LD	No
For ADHD	No
For ASD	Yes
LD specialists	Yes
ADHD & ASD coaching	Yes
ASD specialists	No
Professional tutors	No
Peer tutors	Yes
Max. hours/week for services	Varies
How professors are notified of student approved accommodations	Student

COLLEGE GRADUATION REQUIREMENTS

Course waivers allowed: Yes
In what courses: Foreign language

Course substitutions allowed: Yes
In what courses: Varies

Oklahoma State University

219 Student Union, Stillwater, OK 74078 • Admissions: 405-744-5358 • Fax: 405-744-7092 **Support: S**

CAMPUS	
Type of school	Public
Environment	Town
STUDENTS	
Undergrad enrollment	19,766
% male/female	50/50
% from out of state	27
% frosh live on campus	82
FINANCIAL FACTS	
Annual in-state tuition	$13,280
Annual out-of-state tuition	$28,800
Room and board	$9,340
GENERAL ADMISSIONS INFO	
Application fee	$40
Regular application deadline	Rolling
Nonfall registration	Yes
Admission may be deferred.	
Range SAT EBRW	530–635
Range SAT Math	510–630
Range ACT Composite	21–28
ACADEMICS	
Student/faculty ratio	18:1
% students returning for sophomore year	83
Most classes have 10–19 students.	

Programs/Services for Students with Learning Differences

Student Accessibility Services (SAS) provides assistance that will allow equal opportunity and equal access to education. Academic support services can include classroom/testing accommodations, accessible textbooks, access to/assistance with assistive technology, and other services. Once the documentation has been received and reviewed, the student can set up an intake meeting to discuss accommodations and resources available. In order to set up academic accommodations, there will need to be a face-to-face meeting. For students beginning in the fall semester, this meeting typically occurs the summer before school starts (preferably before or after orientation), or schedule an intake meeting for the first or second week of the semester.

Admissions

There is no special admissions policy for students with LD. Students qualify for assured admission if they meet one of the following criteria: 1) have a 3.0 GPA or better unweighted and rank in the top 33% of their high school graduating class, 2) or have a 3.0 GPA or better in the 15-unit core and have a 21 ACT/1060 SAT or better, or 3) have a 24 ACT/1160 SAT or better. Students who apply without a test score need to submit essays and fill out the leadership resume as part of their completed application for admission. Consideration for most OSU scholarships will require a test score submission.

Additional Information

Tutoring at the Learning and Student Success Opportunity Center (LASSO) is open to all Oklahoma State University students at no additional charge. These are peer tutors available to students and are hired by the university in every course. Each tutor has an outstanding qualification and has gone through extensive tutor training. Supplemental Instruction sessions engage students in challenging courses with cutting-edge learning techniques.

ADMISSIONS INFO FOR STUDENTS WITH LEARNING DIFFERENCES

Phone: 405-744-7116 • Fax: 405-744-1143 • Email: accessibility@okstate.edu

SAT/ACT required: Yes (Test optional for 2021)
Interview required: No
Essay required: No
Additional application required: No
Documentation submitted to: Student Accessibility Services

Special Ed. HS course work accepted: No
Separate application required for Programs/Services: No
Documentation required for:
LD: Psychoeducational evaluation
ADHD: Psychoeducational evaluation
ASD: Psychoeducational evaluation

Oklahoma State University

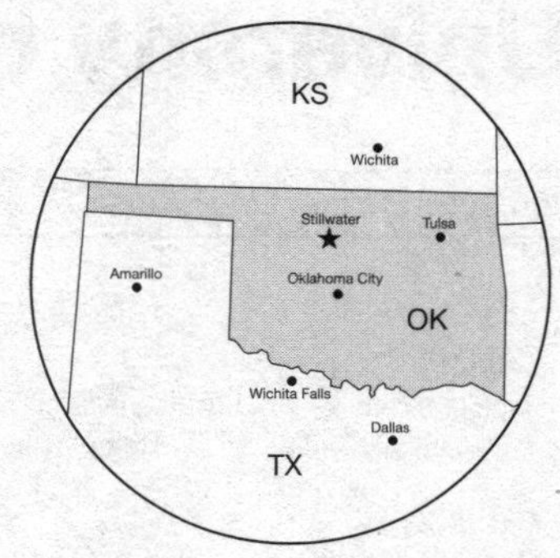

General Admissions

Very important factors include: class rank, academic GPA, standardized test scores. *Important factors include:* application essay, *Other factors include:* recommendation(s). *Freshman admission requirements:* High school diploma is required and GED is accepted. *Academic units required:* 4 English, 3 math, 3 science, 3 science labs, 2 social studies, 1 history.

Accommodations or Services

Accommodations are decided upon an individual basis after a thorough review of appropriate, current documentation. The accommodations requests must be supported through the documentation provided and must be logically linked to the current impact of the condition on academic functioning.

Financial Aid

Students should submit: FAFSA. Applicants will be notified of awards on a rolling basis beginning 3/15. *Need-based scholarships/grants offered:* College/university scholarship or grant aid from institutional funds; Federal Pell; Private scholarships; SEOG; State scholarships/grants. *Loan aid offered:* Direct PLUS loans; Direct Subsidized Stafford Loans; Direct Unsubsidized Stafford Loans. Federal Work-Study Program available. Institutional employment available.

Campus Life

Activities: Campus Ministries; Choral groups; Concert band; Dance; Drama/theater; International Student Organization; Jazz band; Literary magazine; Marching band; Model UN; Music ensembles; Musical theater; Opera; Pep band; Radio station; Student government; Student newspaper; Student-run film society; Symphony orchestra; Television station. **Organizations:** 518 registered organizations, 36 honor societies, 25 religious organizations, 27 fraternities, 18 sororities. **Athletics (Intercollegiate):** *Men:* baseball, basketball, cross-country, football, golf, tennis, track/field (outdoor), wrestling. *Women:* basketball, cross-country, equestrian sports, golf, soccer, softball, tennis, track/field (outdoor).

ACCOMMODATIONS

Allowed in exams:	
Calculators	Yes
Dictionary	Yes
Computer	Yes
Spell-checker	Yes
Extended test time	Yes
Scribe	Yes
Proctors	Yes
Oral exams	Yes
Note-takers	Yes
Support services for students with:	
LD	Yes
ADHD	Yes
ASD	Yes
Distraction-reduced environment	Yes
Recording of lecture alowed	Yes
Reading technology	Yes
Audio books	Yes
Other assistive technology	Yes
Priority registration	No
Added costs of services:	
For LD	No
For ADHD	No
For ASD	No
LD specialists	No
ADHD & ASD coaching	No
ASD specialists	No
Professional tutors	No
Peer tutors	Yes
Max. hours/week for services	Unlimited
How professors are notified of student approved accommodations	Director

COLLEGE GRADUATION REQUIREMENTS

Course waivers allowed	No
Course substitutions allowed	Yes
In what courses: Math and foreign language	

Oklahoma

University of Tulsa

800 South Tucker Drive, Tulsa, OK 74104 • Admissions: 918-631-2307 • Fax: 918-631-5003 **Support: CS**

CAMPUS

Type of school	Private (nonprofit)
Environment	Metropolis

STUDENTS

Undergrad enrollment	3,268
% male/female	54/46
% from out of state	43
% frosh live on campus	81

FINANCIAL FACTS

Annual tuition	$42,950
Room and board	$12,062
Required fees	$1,135

GENERAL ADMISSIONS INFO

Application fee	$50
Regular application deadline	Rolling
Nonfall registration	Yes

Admission may be deferred.

Range SAT EBRW	550–670
Range SAT Math	540–690
Range ACT Composite	24–31

ACADEMICS

Student/faculty ratio	10:1
% students returning for sophomore year	87

Most classes have 10–19 students.

Programs/Services for Students with Learning Differences

The Center for Student Academic Support (CSAS) aims to help students develop self-advocacy skills that will serve them throughout life. Additionally, students registered with CSAS who are diagnosed on the spectrum can request additional help. These services include, but are not limited to, academic success coaching, tutoring, and workshops. For students with an autism diagnosis, there is the Social Opportunities Program (SOP). This program individualizes the support and offers skill-building groups, social events, help with transitioning to college, time management, and more.

Admissions

All students must meet the general admissions requirements. Students with disabilities are not required to disclose information about the disability, but may voluntarily disclose or request information from CSAS. The university does not consider disabilities in the decision-making process, even if there is knowledge of the disability, without a request and disclosure by the applicant. All students must meet the general admissions requirements. General admission requirements include: 4 years of English, 3 years of math, 4 years of science, and 2 years of foreign language. No course substitutions are allowed. Conditional admission is available for freshmen and probational admission is an option for transfer students.

Additional Information

Coaches work one-on-one with students to provide accountability for coursework and partner with students to create individualized academic success plans as they pursue their academic goals. Academic coaching meetings typically occur once a week for around 30 minutes. Topics covered may include the following: time-management, study skills, test-taking skills, test preparation, prioritization, motivation, test anxiety, learning styles, memory and concentration, presentation strategies, stress management and anxiety, organization, and note taking strategies. The coaches also organizes monthly small group workshops and activities for students, as well as peer mentoring.

ADMISSIONS INFO FOR STUDENTS WITH LEARNING DIFFERENCES

Phone: 918-631-2315 • Fax: 918-631-3459 • Email: tawny-rigsby@utulsa.edu

SAT/ACT required: Yes (Test optional for 2021)
Interview required: No
Essay required: No
Additional application required: Yes
Documentation submitted to: Center for Student Academic Support

Special Ed. HS course work accepted: No
Separate application required for Programs/Services: Yes
Documentation required for:
LD: Psychoeducational evaluation
ADHD: Psychoeducational evaluation
ASD: Psychoeducational evaluation

University of Tulsa

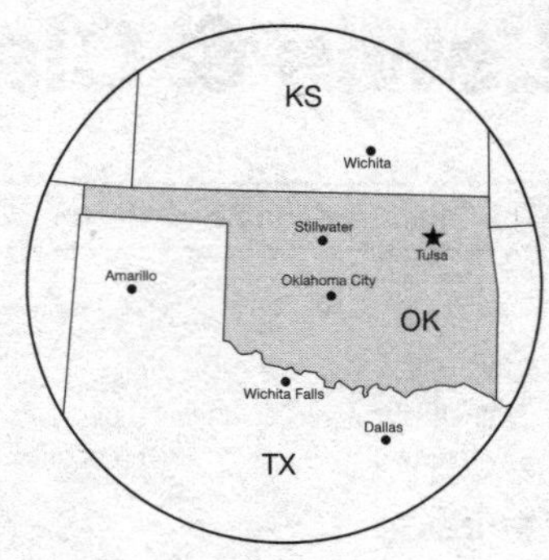

General Admissions

Very important factors include: rigor of secondary school record, academic GPA, standardized test scores. *Important factors include:* class rank, application essay, recommendation(s), interview. *Other factors include:* extracurricular activities, talent/ability, character/personal qualities, first generation, alumni/ae relation, racial/ethnic status, volunteer work, work experience. *Freshman admission requirements:* High school diploma is required and GED is accepted. *Academic units recommended:* 4 English, 4 math, 3 science, 3 science labs, 2 foreign language, 3 social studies, 1 computer science, 1 visual/performing arts.

Accommodations or Services

Accommodations are decided upon an individual basis after a thorough review of appropriate, current documentation. The accommodations requests must be supported through the documentation provided and must be logically linked to the current impact of the condition on academic functioning.

Financial Aid

Students should submit: FAFSA. *Need-based scholarships/grants offered:* College/university scholarship or grant aid from institutional funds; Federal Pell; Private scholarships; SEOG; State scholarships/grants. *Loan aid offered:* Direct PLUS loans; Direct Subsidized Stafford Loans; Direct Unsubsidized Stafford Loans. Federal Work-Study Program available. Institutional employment available.

Campus Life

Activities: Campus Ministries; Choral groups; Concert band; Dance; Drama/theater; International Student Organization; Jazz band; Literary magazine; Marching band; Music ensembles; Musical theater; Opera; Pep band; Radio station; Student government; Student newspaper; Student-run film society; Symphony orchestra; Television station. **Organizations:** 200 registered organizations, 35 honor societies, 19 religious organizations, 7 fraternities, 8 sororities. **Athletics (Intercollegiate):** *Men:* basketball, cheerleading, cross-country, football, golf, soccer, tennis, track/field (outdoor), track/field (indoor). *Women:* basketball, cheerleading, crew/rowing, cross-country, golf, soccer, softball, tennis, track/field (outdoor), track/field (indoor), volleyball.

ACCOMMODATIONS

Allowed in exams:	
Calculators	Yes
Dictionary	Yes
Computer	Yes
Spell-checker	Yes
Extended test time	Yes
Scribe	Yes
Proctors	Yes
Oral exams	Yes
Note-takers	Yes
Support services for students with:	
LD	Yes
ADHD	Yes
ASD	Yes
Distraction-reduced environment	Yes
Recording of lecture allowed	Yes
Reading technology	Yes
Audio books	Yes
Other assistive technology	Yes
Priority registration	Yes
Added costs of services:	
For LD	No
For ADHD	No
For ASD	No
LD specialists	Yes
ADHD & ASD coaching	Yes
ASD specialists	Yes
Professional tutors	Yes
Peer tutors	Yes
Max. hours/week for services	10
How professors are notified of student approved accommodations	Student

COLLEGE GRADUATION REQUIREMENTS

Course waivers allowed	Yes
In what courses: Varies	
Course substitutions allowed	Yes
In what courses: Varies	

Oklahoma

Lewis & Clark College

0615 S Palatine Hill Road, Portland, OR 97219-7899 • Admissions: 503-768-7040 • Fax: 503-768-7055 **Support: S**

CAMPUS	
Type of school	Private (nonprofit)
Environment	Metropolis
STUDENTS	
Undergrad enrollment	1,965
% male/female	39/61
% from out of state	88
% frosh live on campus	99
FINANCIAL FACTS	
Annual tuition	$54,832
Room and board	$13,145
Required fees	$360
GENERAL ADMISSIONS INFO	
Application fee	$0
Regular application deadline	1/15
Nonfall registration	Yes
Admission may be deferred.	
Range SAT EBRW	630–710
Range SAT Math	590–690
Range ACT Composite	27–31
ACADEMICS	
Student/faculty ratio	11:1
% students returning for sophomore year	82
Most classes have 20–29 students.	

Programs/Services for Students with Learning Differences

Lewis & Clark is committed to serving the needs of our students with disabilities and learning differences. Professional staff in the office of Student Support Services are available to ensure that students receive all of the benefits of a comprehensive selection of services. The office also provides advising and advocacy for students with disabilities and support for students who seek advice on academic strategies. Services, advising, and accommodations are always the result of an active partnership between students and Student Support Services staff. The student is responsible for providing professional testing and evaluation results, and recommendations for accommodations must be included in the report. The Director of Student Support Services must approve accommodations for a disability.

Admissions

The admissions process and criteria are the same for all applicants, regardless of learning differences. When admitting new students, admissions staff look for individuals from diverse backgrounds, with diverse talents and interests—students who will not only meet the rigorous academic challenges of a Lewis & Clark education, but will also take full advantage of the opportunities for individual achievement and growth offered here.The university is test optional and students do not need to submit ACT or SAT for admission. A personal interview or other forms of expressed interest are recommended but not required.

Additional Information

In order to access accommodations, students need to meet with a representative from the Student Support Services Office and provide their documentation. For students on the spectrum, the office will discuss ways to advocate to professors, support the student's learning style, and assist in reaching out to other students in the Lewis & Clark community. Additionally, Student Support Services works with students on effective study strategies, test-taking skills, and curriculum planning that fits their learning style. The Writing Center has peer consultants to help with writing skills. There is free peer-to-peer tutoring. The Keck Interactive Learning Center provides drop-in assistance for all languages taught on campus.

ADMISSIONS INFO FOR STUDENTS WITH LEARNING DIFFERENCES

Phone: 503-768-7192 • Fax: 503-768-7197 • Email: access@lclark.edu

SAT/ACT required: No
Interview required: Recommended
Essay required: Yes
Additional application required: No
Documentation submitted to: Student Support Services

Special Ed. HS course work accepted: No
Separate application required for Programs/Services: No
Documentation required for:
LD: Psychoeducational assessments
ADHD: Psychoeducational evaluation
ASD: Psychoeducational evaluation

Lewis & Clark College

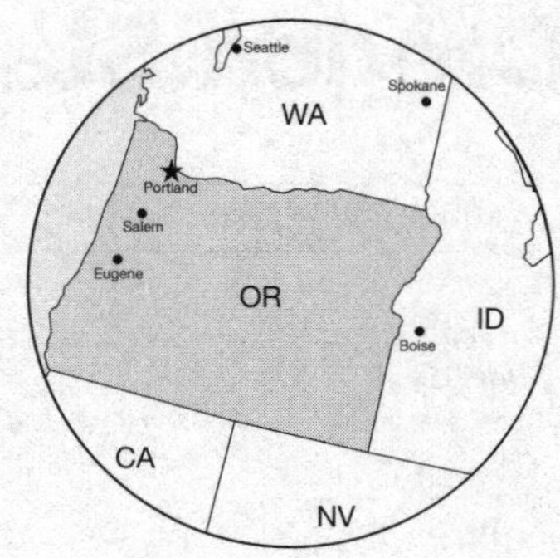

General Admissions

Very important factors include: rigor of secondary school record, academic GPA. *Important factors include:* application essay, standardized test scores, recommendation(s), extracurricular activities, talent/ability, character/personal qualities, volunteer work. *Other factors include:* class rank, interview, first generation, alumni/ae relation, geographical residence, racial/ethnic status, level of applicant's interest. *Freshman admission requirements:* High school diploma is required and GED is accepted. *Academic units recommended:* 4 English, 4 math, 3 science, 2 science labs, 2 foreign language, 3 social studies, 1 visual/performing arts.

Accommodations or Services

Accommodations are decided upon an individual basis after a thorough review of appropriate, current documentation. The accommodations requests must be supported through the documentation provided and must be logically linked to the current impact of the condition on academic functioning.

Financial Aid

Students should submit: CSS/Financial Aid PROFILE; FAFSA. *Need-based scholarships/grants offered:* College/university scholarship or grant aid from institutional funds; Federal Pell; Private scholarships; SEOG; State scholarships/grants. *Loan aid offered:* Direct PLUS loans; Direct Subsidized Stafford Loans; Direct Unsubsidized Stafford Loans. Federal Work-Study Program available. Institutional employment available.

Campus Life

Activities: Campus Ministries; Choral groups; Concert band; Dance; Drama/theater; International Student Organization; Jazz band; Literary magazine; Model UN; Music ensembles; Musical theater; Pep band; Radio station; Student government; Student newspaper; Symphony orchestra. **Organizations:** 167 registered organizations, 2 honor societies, 7 religious organizations. **Athletics (Intercollegiate):** *Men:* baseball, basketball, crew/rowing, cross-country, football, golf, swimming, tennis, track/field (outdoor). *Women:* basketball, crew/rowing, cross-country, golf, soccer, softball, swimming, tennis, track/field (outdoor), volleyball.

ACCOMMODATIONS

Allowed in exams:	
Calculators	Yes
Dictionary	Yes
Computer	Yes
Spell-checker	Yes
Extended test time	Yes
Scribe	Yes
Proctors	Yes
Oral exams	Yes
Note-takers	Yes
Support services for students with:	
LD	Yes
ADHD	Yes
ASD	Yes
Distraction-reduced environment	Yes
Recording of lecture alowed	Yes
Reading technology	Yes
Audio books	Yes
Other assistive technology	Yes
Priority registration	No
Added costs of services:	
For LD	No
For ADHD	No
For ASD	No
LD specialists	Yes
ADHD & ASD coaching	Yes
ASD specialists	No
Professional tutors	No
Peer tutors	Yes
Max. hours/week for services	Varies
How professors are notified of student approved accommodations	Director

COLLEGE GRADUATION REQUIREMENTS

Course waivers allowed	No
Course substitutions allowed	Yes
In what courses: Varies	

Oregon State University

104 Kerr Administration Building, Corvallis, OR 97331-2106 • Admissions: 541-737-4411 • Fax: 541-737-2482 **Support: CS**

CAMPUS

Type of school	Public
Environment	Town

STUDENTS

Undergrad enrollment	26,247
% male/female	53/47
% from out of state	33
% frosh live on campus	91

FINANCIAL FACTS

Annual in-state tuition	$12,165
Annual out-of-state tuition	$32,355
Room and board	$13,200

GENERAL ADMISSIONS INFO

Application fee	$65
Regular application deadline	9/1
Nonfall registration	Yes

Admission may be deferred.

Range SAT EBRW	550–660
Range SAT Math	530–660
Range ACT Composite	21–28

ACADEMICS

Student/faculty ratio	18:1
% students returning for sophomore year	85

Most classes have 20–29 students.

Programs/Services for Students with Learning Differences

Disability Access Services (DAS) facilitates access to university programs and services for students with disabilities through accommodations, education, consultation and advocacy. Accommodations are determined on a case-by-case basis depending on the student's documentation. DAS recommends that students meet with their academic advisor every term. DAS will send a specific notification to a student's professor each term letting that person know about the need for an accommodation. Additionally, there is an Academic Success Center where a student can receive tutoring, coaching, writing support, and help with developing study strategies.

Admissions

Oregon State's admission requirements are the same for all students. Admission assessment will consider all achievements, both academic and non-academic, to enroll students with a broad range of characteristics and perspectives. Considerations include but are not limited to academic achievement, creativity, initiative, motivation, leadership, persistence, service to others, intellectual curiosity, exceptional personal or academic recognition, unusual talent or ability, substantial experience with other cultures, and ability to overcome significant challenges. The university is test optional, so students do not need either the ACT or SAT for admission.

Additional Information

Coaching sessions are available in the Academic Success Center to all students registered with DAS. Coaching provides students with individualized strategies based on the students' impacts. Individual sessions focus on strategies, techniques, and resources. Some common topics may include time management, study skills, managing a course load, or navigating the college environment as a student with a disability. There is no set number of Coaching sessions, as they are based on the students need. Counseling and Psychological Services (CAPS) provides individual services that can help students develop effective habits to compensate for poor focus, distractibility, disorganization, and/or difficulty completing tasks, whether caused by ADHD/ADD or by other conditions. They can also help with issues of poor self-esteem, lack of self-confidence, anxiety and/or depression that can accompany ADHD.

ADMISSIONS INFO FOR STUDENTS WITH LEARNING DIFFERENCES

Phone: 541-737-4098 • Fax: 541-737-7354 • Email: disability.services@oregonstate.edu

SAT/ACT required: Yes (Test optional for 2021)
Interview required: No
Essay required: Yes
Additional application required: Yes
Documentation submitted to: DAS

Special Ed. HS course work accepted: No
Separate application required for Programs/Services: Yes
Documentation required for:
LD: Psychoeducational evaluation
ADHD: Psychoeducational evaluation
ASD: Psychoeducational evaluation

Oregon State University

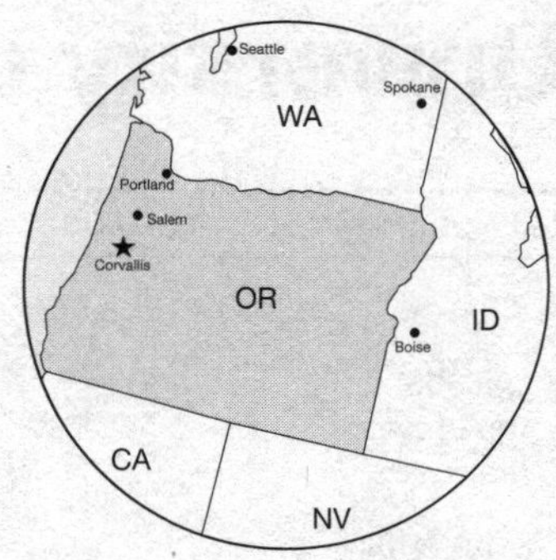

General Admissions

Very important factors include: academic GPA. *Important factors include:* rigor of secondary school record, application essay, talent/ability, character/personal qualities, volunteer work, work experience. *Other factors include:* class rank, standardized test scores, recommendation(s), extracurricular activities, level of applicant's interest. *Freshman admission requirements:* High school diploma is required and GED is accepted. *Academic units required:* 4 English, 3 math, 3 science, 2 science labs, 2 foreign language, 3 social studies. *Academic units recommended:* 3 science labs.

Accommodations or Services

Accommodations are decided upon an individual basis after a thorough review of appropriate, current documentation. The accommodations requests must be supported through the documentation provided and must be logically linked to the current impact of the condition on academic functioning.

Financial Aid

Students should submit: FAFSA. *Need-based scholarships/grants offered:* College/university scholarship or grant aid from institutional funds; Federal Pell; Private scholarships; SEOG; State scholarships/grants. *Loan aid offered:* Direct PLUS loans; Direct Subsidized Stafford Loans; Direct Unsubsidized Stafford Loans. Federal Work-Study Program available. Institutional employment available.

Campus Life

Activities: Campus Ministries; Choral groups; Concert band; Dance; Drama/theater; International Student Organization; Jazz band; Literary magazine; Marching band; Model UN; Music ensembles; Musical theater; Opera; Pep band; Radio station; Student government; Student newspaper; Student-run film society; Symphony orchestra; Television station; Yearbook. **Organizations:** 400 registered organizations, 12 honor societies, 28 religious organizations, 27 fraternities, 22 sororities. **Athletics (Intercollegiate):** *Men:* baseball, basketball, crew/rowing, football, golf, soccer, wrestling. *Women:* basketball, crew/rowing, cross-country, golf, gymnastics, soccer, softball, swimming, track/field (outdoor), volleyball.

ACCOMMODATIONS

Allowed in exams:	
Calculators	Yes
Dictionary	No
Computer	Yes
Spell-checker	Yes
Extended test time	Yes
Scribe	Yes
Proctors	Yes
Oral exams	Yes
Note-takers	Yes
Support services for students with:	
LD	Yes
ADHD	Yes
ASD	Yes
Distraction-reduced environment	Yes
Recording of lecture alowed	Yes
Reading technology	Yes
Audio books	Yes
Other assistive technology	Yes
Priority registration	Yes
Added costs of services:	
For LD	No
For ADHD	No
For ASD	No
LD specialists	Yes
ADHD & ASD coaching	Yes
ASD specialists	No
Professional tutors	No
Peer tutors	Yes
Max. hours/week for services	Varies
How professors are notified of student approved accommodations	Director

COLLEGE GRADUATION REQUIREMENTS

Course waivers allowed	No
Course substitutions allowed	Yes
In what courses: Varies	

University of Oregon

1217 University of Oregon Eugene, OR 97403-1217 • Admissions: 541-346-3201 • Fax: 541-346-5815 **Support: CS**

CAMPUS	
Type of school	Public
Environment	City
STUDENTS	
Undergrad enrollment	18,743
% male/female	46/54
% from out of state	43
% frosh live on campus	93
FINANCIAL FACTS	
Annual in-state tuition	$10,755
Annual out-of-state tuition	$35,367
Room and board	$12,783
Required fees	$2,361
GENERAL ADMISSIONS INFO	
Application fee	$65
Regular application deadline	1/15
Nonfall registration	Yes
Admission may be deferred.	
Range SAT EBRW	560–660
Range SAT Math	540–650
Range ACT Composite	22–28
ACADEMICS	
Student/faculty ratio	16:1
% students returning for sophomore year	86
Most classes have 10–19 students.	

Programs/Services for Students with Learning Differences

At the University of Oregon, the Accessible Education Center (AEC) supportsstudents with currently documented disabilities. During university orientation programs students discuss their needs, challenges, educational goals, and available services. Accommodations are determined on a case-by-case basis after admission and an individual appointment. A faculty notification letter outlining suggested accommodations is provided and is shared at the student's discretion.

Admissions

Students with disabilities must meet the same admission criteria as all other applicants. However, in exceptional cases, students who would otherwise not be admissible may be offered admissions by the Disability Review Committee based on a documented disability. Students not meeting the regular admission requirements who have extenuating circumstances due to any disability may request additional consideration of their application by a special committee. A completed application form, a graded writing sample, two letters of recommendation, and documentation of the disability with information about how it has influenced the student's ability to meet minimum admission requirements are required for special consideration based on disability. The university is test optional and students do not have to submit the ACT or SAT for admission.

Additional Information

Students are encouraged to take an active role in registering for and utilizing services. Once admitted, students should meet with AEC to review documentation and discuss educational goals. Typical support includes academic accommodations, including additional testing time, text to speech formats, and distraction reduced testing environments; permission to record lectures, and access to classmate notes. There is an opportunity for classroom relocation, adaptive technology, support with academic planning, time management, and organizational strategies. In addition to working individually with each student, groups are available for students with ADHD to talk with others about their challenges and develop a support group of peers. There is also a Social Connectedness Group that facilitates peer-directed social groups as a space for people on the autism spectrum as a way to socialize in a fashion that is most comfortable for them.

ADMISSIONS INFO FOR STUDENTS WITH LEARNING DIFFERENCES

Phone: 541-346-1155 • Fax: 541-346-6013 • Email: uoaec@uoregon.edu

SAT/ACT required: Yes (Test optional for 2021)
Interview required: No
Essay required: Yes
Additional application required: No
Documentation submitted to: AEC

Special Ed. HS course work accepted: No
Separate application required for Programs/Services: No
Documentation required for:
LD: Psychoeducational evaluation
ADHD: Psychoeducational evaluation
ASD: Psychoeducational evaluation

University of Oregon

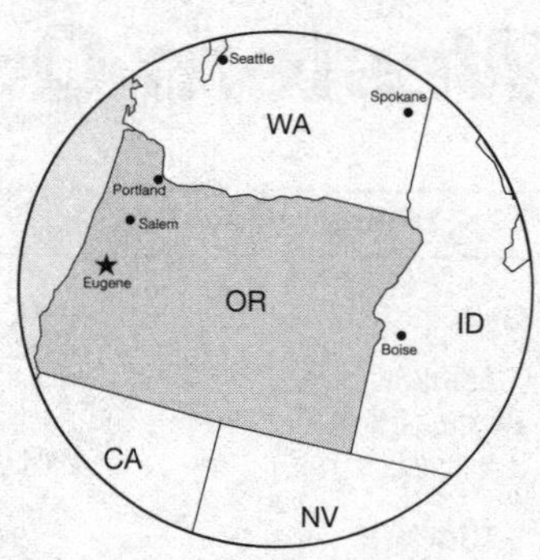

General Admissions

Very important factors include: rigor of secondary school record, academic GPA. *Important factors include:* application essay, standardized test scores. *Other factors include:* class rank, recommendation(s), extracurricular activities, talent/ability, character/personal qualities, first generation, geographical residence, state residency, racial/ethnic status, volunteer work, work experience. *Freshman admission requirements:* High school diploma is required and GED is accepted. *Academic units required:* 4 English, 3 math, 3 science, 2 foreign language, 3 social studies. *Academic units recommended:* 1 science lab, 1 visual/performing arts.

Accommodations or Services

Accommodations are decided upon an individual basis after a thorough review of appropriate, current documentation. The accommodations requests must be supported through the documentation provided and must be logically linked to the current impact of the condition on academic functioning.

Financial Aid

Students should submit: FAFSA;. Applicants will be notified of awards on a rolling basis beginning 12/15. *Need-based scholarships/grants offered:* College/university scholarship or grant aid from institutional funds; Federal Pell; Private scholarships; SEOG; State scholarships/grants. *Loan aid offered:* Direct PLUS loans; Direct Subsidized Stafford Loans; Direct Unsubsidized Stafford Loans. Federal Work-Study Program available. Institutional employment available.

Campus Life

Activities: Campus Ministries; Choral groups; Concert band; Dance; Drama/theater; International Student Organization; Jazz band; Literary magazine; Marching band; Music ensembles; Musical theater; Opera; Pep band; Radio station; Student government; Student newspaper; Student-run film society; Symphony orchestra; Television station. **Organizations:** 250 registered organizations, 21 honor societies, 19 fraternities, 18 sororities. **Athletics (Intercollegiate):** *Men:* baseball, basketball, cross-country, football, golf, tennis, track/field (outdoor). *Women:* basketball, cross-country, golf, gymnastics, lacrosse, soccer, softball, tennis, track/field (outdoor), volleyball.

ACCOMMODATIONS

Allowed in exams:	
Calculators	Yes
Dictionary	No
Computer	Yes
Spell-checker	Yes
Extended test time	Yes
Scribe	Yes
Proctors	Yes
Oral exams	Yes
Note-takers	Yes
Support services for students with:	
LD	Yes
ADHD	Yes
ASD	Yes
Distraction-reduced environment	Yes
Recording of lecture allowed	Yes
Reading technology	Yes
Audio books	Yes
Other assistive technology	Yes
Priority registration	Yes
Added costs of services:	
For LD	No
For ADHD	No
For ASD	No
LD specialists	Yes
ADHD & ASD coaching	Yes
ASD specialists	No
Professional tutors	No
Peer tutors	Yes
Max. hours/week for services	Varies
How professors are notified of student approved accommodations	Student and Director of AEC

COLLEGE GRADUATION REQUIREMENTS

Course waivers allowed	No
Course substitutions allowed	Yes
In what courses: Varies	

Western Oregon University

345 N. Monmouth Avenue, Monmouth, OR 97361 • Admissions: 503-838-8211 • Fax: 503-838-8067 **Support: CS**

CAMPUS

Type of school	Public
Environment	Village

STUDENTS

Undergrad enrollment	4,343
% male/female	36/64
% from out of state	22
% frosh live on campus	88

FINANCIAL FACTS

Annual in-state tuition	$8,280
Annual out-of-state tuition	$27,090
Room and board	$10,803
Required fees	$1,866

GENERAL ADMISSIONS INFO

Application fee	$60
Regular application deadline	Rolling
Nonfall registration	Yes
Range SAT EBRW	480–590
Range SAT Math	480–570
Range ACT Composite	17–23

ACADEMICS

Student/faculty ratio	12:1
% students returning for sophomore year	74

Most classes have 10–19 students.

Programs/Services for Students with Learning Differences

The Office of Disability Services (ODS) provides reasonable accommodations. These goals are realized by providing support services. ODS strives to meet the individual needs of students with disabilities. The Student Enrichment Program (SEP) is designed to help students find success in college. The program's goals are to help SEP students develop writing, math, learning, and critical thinking skills; maintain the necessary GPA to achieve individual goals; develop interpersonal communication skills; and achieve autonomy and maintain a sense of self-worth. Academic advising and assistance working with various departments on campus is available. There is also a Summer Bridge program to support new students' orientation to the college campus.

Admissions

The admission process is the same for all applicants. Students should have a 3.0 GPA. If the GPA is between 2.8–2.9 applicants should submit a letter from recommendation from a school counselor or teacher. Applicants should also have a "C" or higher, as well as 4 years English, 3 years math, 3 years social science, and 2 years in foreign language. Standardized tests are not required with a 3.0 GPA. For students with a GPA between 2.8–2.9, they must have an ACT of 23 or 1130 SAT. Test scores are also required for some scholarships, NCAA Division II, and the Honors Program.

Additional Information

Skills classes are offered in academic survival strategies (no credit) and critical thinking (college credit). Other services include advocacy, computer stations, note-takers, readers and taping services, alternative testing, advisement, and assistance with registration. CEP offers counseling; basic math courses; advising; individualized instruction in reading, study skills, writing, and critical thinking; monitor programs; and workshops on study skills, research writing, math anxiety, rapid reading, note-taking, and time management. Services and accommodations are available for undergraduate and graduate students.

ADMISSIONS INFO FOR STUDENTS WITH LEARNING DIFFERENCES

Phone: 503-838-8250 • Fax: 503-838-8721 • Email: ods@wou.edu

SAT/ACT required: No
Interview required: No
Essay required: No
Additional application required: Yes
Documentation submitted to: ODS

Special Ed. HS course work accepted: No
Separate application required for Programs/Services: Yes
Documentation required for:
LD: Psychoeducational evaluation
ADHD: Psychoeducational evaluation
ASD: Psychoeducational evaluation

Western Oregon University

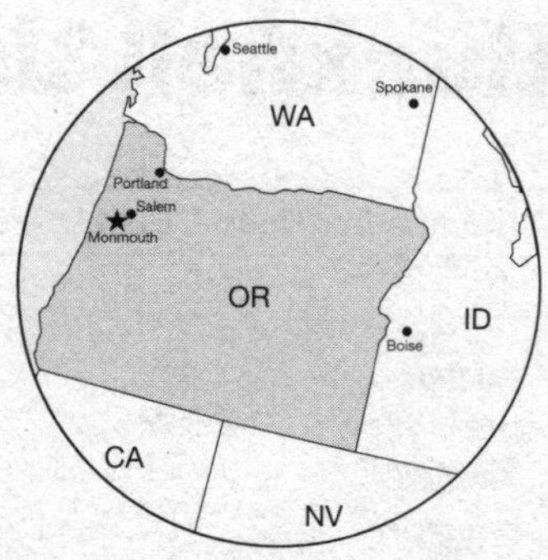

General Admissions

Very important factors include: rigor of secondary school record, class rank, academic GPA. *Important factors include:* recommendation(s), talent/ability. *Other factors include:* application essay, standardized test scores, character/personal qualities, first generation. *Freshman admission requirements:* High school diploma is required and GED is accepted. *Academic units required:* 4 English, 3 math, 2 foreign language, 3 social studies. *Academic units recommended:* 4 English, 3 math, 2 foreign language, 3 social studies.

Accommodations or Services

Accommodations are decided upon an individual basis after a thorough review of appropriate, current documentation. The accommodations requests must be supported through the documentation provided and must be logically linked to the current impact of the condition on academic functioning.

Financial Aid

Students should submit: FAFSA. Applicants will be notified of awards on a rolling basis beginning 5/1. *Need-based scholarships/grants offered:* College/university scholarship or grant aid from institutional funds; Federal Pell; Private scholarships; SEOG; State scholarships/grants; United Negro College Fund. *Loan aid offered:* Direct PLUS loans; Direct Subsidized Stafford Loans; Direct Unsubsidized Stafford Loans. Federal Work-Study Program available.

Campus Life

Activities: Campus Ministries; Choral groups; Concert band; Dance; Drama/theater; International Student Organization; Jazz band; Literary magazine; Marching band; Model UN; Music ensembles; Musical theater; Pep band; Radio station; Student government; Student newspaper. **Organizations:** 50 registered organizations, 4 honor societies, 6 religious organizations. **Athletics (Intercollegiate):** *Men:* baseball, basketball, cheerleading, cross-country, football, track/field (outdoor). *Women:* basketball, cheerleading, cross-country, soccer, softball, track/field (outdoor), volleyball.

ACCOMMODATIONS

Allowed in exams:	
Calculators	Yes
Dictionary	Yes
Computer	Yes
Spell-checker	Yes
Extended test time	Yes
Scribe	Yes
Proctors	Yes
Oral exams	Yes
Note-takers	Yes
Support services for students with:	
LD	Yes
ADHD	Yes
ASD	Yes
Distraction-reduced environment	Yes
Recording of lecture alowed	Yes
Reading technology	Yes
Audio books	Yes
Other assistive technology	Yes
Priority registration	Yes
Added costs of services:	
For LD	No
For ADHD	No
For ASD	No
LD specialists	Yes
ADHD & ASD coaching	No
ASD specialists	No
Professional tutors	No
Peer tutors	Yes
Max. hours/week for services	Varies
How professors are notified of student approved accommodations	Student and Director

COLLEGE GRADUATION REQUIREMENTS

Course waivers allowed	No
Course substitutions allowed	Yes
In what courses: Case by case basis	

Oregon

Bucknell University

Office of Admissions, 1 Dent Drive, Lewisburg, PA 17837 • Admissions: 570-577-3000 • Fax: 570-577-3538 **Support: CS**

CAMPUS

Type of school	Private (nonprofit)
Environment	Village

STUDENTS

Undergrad enrollment	3,608
% male/female	49/51
% from out of state	79
% frosh live on campus	100

FINANCIAL FACTS

Annual tuition	$57,882
Room and board	$14,174
Required fees	$320

GENERAL ADMISSIONS INFO

Application fee	$40
Regular application deadline	1/15
Nonfall registration	No

Admission may be deferred.

Range SAT EBRW	620–700
Range SAT Math	635–730
Range ACT Composite	28–32

ACADEMICS

Student/faculty ratio	9:1
% students returning for sophomore year	92

Most classes have 10–19 students.

Programs/Services for Students with Learning Differences

The Office of Accessibility Resources (OAR) provides support and help to students navigating communication with faculty and staff. The office is committed to providing a strong support system for individuals with disabilities, and ensuring that no otherwise qualified individual with a disability will be denied participation in or the benefits of any of the programs on the basis of a disability. Support is individualized on a case-by-case basis. Documentation required can be found on the website.

Admissions

Students should apply directly to their preferred college. ACT or SAT is required for admission. Subject Tests are not required but can be submitted. Students are encouraged to reach out to the Director of OAR and request a meeting. The director will meet with the student regarding academic concerns and work on developing appropriate accommodations. Applicants must apply to the College of Arts & Sciences, College of Engineering, or the Freeman College of Management. Bucknell is test optional, so students do not need to submit either the ACT or SAT.

Additional Information

The Office of Accessibility Resources (OAR) meet with students regarding academic concerns; consult regarding approved accommodations and make the appropriate referrals to on and off campus available resources when needed; discuss with registered students about how to talk to professors regarding accommodation needs; meet with registered students and professors to discuss the approved reasonable accommodations for specific academic needs; discuss assistive technology and other academic adjustments; and assist with arranging testing accommodations. The OAR Testing Center is a secondary option for registered students to take quizzes and tests.

ADMISSIONS INFO FOR STUDENTS WITH LEARNING DIFFERENCES

Phone: 570-577-1188 • Fax: 570-577-1826 • Email: hf007@bucknell.edu

SAT/ACT required: No
Interview required: No
Essay required: Yes
Additional application required: Yes
Documentation submitted to: OAR

Special Ed. HS course work accepted: Yes
Separate application required for Programs/Services: Yes
Documentation required for:
LD: Psychoeducational evaluation
ADHD: Psychoeducational evaluation
ASD: Psychoeducational evaluation

Bucknell University

Pennsylvania

General Admissions

Very important factors include: rigor of secondary school record, academic GPA, application essay, standardized test scores, talent/ability, character/personal qualities. *Important factors include:* recommendation(s), extracurricular activities, volunteer work. *Other factors include:* class rank, first generation, alumni/ae relation, geographical residence, religious affiliation/commitment, racial/ethnic status. *Freshman admission requirements:* High school diploma is required and GED is accepted. *Academic units required:* 4 English, 3 math, 2 science, 2 foreign language, 2 social studies, 2 history, 1 academic elective. *Academic units recommended:* 4 English, 4 math, 2 science, 2 science labs, 4 foreign language, 2 social studies, 2 history, 1 academic elective.

Accommodations or Services

Accommodations are decided upon an individual basis after a thorough review of appropriate, current documentation. The accommodations requests must be supported through the documentation provided and must be logically linked to the current impact of the condition on academic functioning.

Financial Aid

Students should submit: CSS/Financial Aid PROFILE; FAFSA. *Need-based scholarships/grants offered:* College/university scholarship or grant aid from institutional funds; Federal Pell; Private scholarships; SEOG; State scholarships/grants. *Loan aid offered:* Direct PLUS loans; Direct Subsidized Stafford Loans; Direct Unsubsidized Stafford Loans. Federal Work-Study Program available. Institutional employment available.

Campus Life

Activities: Campus Ministries; Choral groups; Concert band; Dance; Drama/theater; International Student Organization; Jazz band; Literary magazine; Model UN; Music ensembles; Musical theater; Opera; Pep band; Radio station; Student government; Student newspaper; Student-run film society; Symphony orchestra; Yearbook. **Organizations:** 190 registered organizations, 12 honor societies, 9 religious organizations, 9 fraternities, 9 sororities. **Athletics (Intercollegiate):** *Men:* baseball, basketball, cross-country, diving, football, golf, lacrosse, soccer, swimming, tennis, track/field (outdoor), track/field (indoor), water polo, wrestling. *Women:* basketball, crew/rowing, cross-country, diving, field hockey, golf, lacrosse, soccer, softball, swimming, tennis, track/field (outdoor), track/field (indoor), volleyball, water polo.

ACCOMMODATIONS

Allowed in exams:	
Calculators	Yes
Dictionary	No
Computer	Yes
Spell-checker	Yes
Extended test time	Yes
Scribe	Yes
Proctors	Yes
Oral exams	Yes
Note-takers	Yes
Support services for students with:	
LD	Yes
ADHD	Yes
ASD	Yes
Distraction-reduced environment	Yes
Recording of lecture allowed	Yes
Reading technology	Yes
Audio books	Yes
Other assistive technology	Yes
Priority registration	No
Added costs of services:	
For LD	No
For ADHD	No
For ASD	No
LD specialists	Yes
ADHD & ASD coaching	Yes
ASD specialists	No
Professional tutors	Yes
Peer tutors	Yes
Max. hours/week for services	Varies
How professors are notified of student approved accommodations	Student and Director

COLLEGE GRADUATION REQUIREMENTS

Course waivers allowed	No
Course substitutions allowed	Yes
In what courses: Varies	

Chatham University

1 Woodland Road, Pittsburgh, PA 15232 • Admissions: 412-365-1825 • Fax: 412-365-1609 **Support: CS**

CAMPUS

Type of school	Private (nonprofit)
Environment	Metropolis

STUDENTS

Undergrad enrollment	1,152
% male/female	29/71
% from out of state	23
% frosh live on campus	86

FINANCIAL FACTS

Annual tuition	$39,902
Room and board	$12,618

GENERAL ADMISSIONS INFO

Application fee	$35
Regular application deadline	8/1
Nonfall registration	Yes

Admission may be deferred.

Range SAT EBRW	530–650
Range SAT Math	520–620
Range ACT Composite	23–28

ACADEMICS

Student/faculty ratio	10:1
% students returning for sophomore year	80

Most classes have 10–19 students.

Programs/Services for Students with Learning Differences

The Office of Academic and Accessibility Resources (OAAR) supports all students depending on their needs. The university accommodates students with learning differences on a case-by-case basis. Chatham does not offer a specialized curriculum but works to provide reasonable accommodations in a way that does not substantially alter course content. The PACE Center for Disability Services uses a holistic approach to disability support services and a student-centered academic support model that provides peer-to-peer assistance across disciplines. The PACE Center Director is in charge of reviewing students' documentation and writes official accommodations letters. The center collaborates with faculty, staff, and students within the Chatham community.

Admissions

The Office of Admission reviews each application holistically to determine whether a student will be successful at Chatham. Each application is given careful consideration before an admission decision is reached. Chatham University has a test-optional policy. If the student chooses not to submit scores, they should send the following in addition to the application: a resume, graded writing sample, and participate in an interview.

Additional Information

Accommodations are determined on a case-by-case basis and are implemented only after the student's needs are documented. Documentation of a disability can take a variety of forms. Students are encouraged to make an appointment with the director to discuss any challenges they may face in regards to their educational program. Academic accommodations for students with disabilities may include, but are not limited to, alternate text formats, distraction-limited setting for testing, extended time for testing, note-taker services, and screen reading software. Other PACE services available for students with disabilities include academic skills coaching, learning style assessment, procrastination management, self-advocacy development, study strategies analysis, time management planning, tutoring, and supplemental instruction.

ADMISSIONS INFO FOR STUDENTS WITH LEARNING DIFFERENCES

Phone: 412-365-1611 • Fax: 412-365-1660 • Email: ckerr@chatham.edu

SAT/ACT required: No
Interview required: No
Essay required: Yes
Additional application required: No
Documentation submitted to: PACE Center

Special Ed. HS course work accepted: Yes
Separate application required for Programs/Services: No
Documentation required for:
LD: Pyschoeducational evaluation
ADHD: Pyschoeducational evaluation
ASD: Pyschoeducational evaluation

Chatham University

Pennsylvania

General Admissions

Very important factors include: rigor of secondary school record. *Important factors include:* academic GPA, application essay, *Other factors include:* class rank, standardized test scores, recommendation(s), interview, extracurricular activities, talent/ability, character/personal qualities, first generation, alumni/ae relation, geographical residence, volunteer work, work experience, level of applicant's interest. *Freshman admission requirements:* High school diploma is required and GED is accepted. *Academic units required:* 4 English, 2 math, 2 science, 3 unit from above areas or other academic areas. *Academic units recommended:* 4 English, 3 math, 3 science, 2 foreign language, 3 social studies.

Accommodations or Services

Accommodations are decided upon an individual basis after a thorough review of appropriate, current documentation. The accommodations requests must be supported through the documentation provided and must be logically linked to the current impact of the condition on academic functioning.

Financial Aid

Students should submit: FAFSA. *Need-based scholarships/grants offered:* College/university scholarship or grant aid from institutional funds; Federal Pell; Private scholarships; SEOG; State scholarships/grants. *Loan aid offered:* Direct PLUS loans; Direct Subsidized Stafford Loans; Direct Unsubsidized Stafford Loans. Federal Work-Study Program available. Institutional employment available.

Campus Life

Activities: Campus Ministries; Choral groups; Drama/theater; International Student Organization; Literary magazine; Student government; Student newspaper; Symphony orchestra. **Organizations:** 56 registered organizations, 10 honor societies, 4 religious organizations. **Athletics (Intercollegiate):** baseball, basketball, cross-country, diving, ice hockey, lacrosse, soccer, squash, swimming, track/field (outdoor), track/field (indoor). *Women:* basketball, cross-country, ice hockey, soccer, softball, swimming, tennis, volleyball, water polo.

ACCOMMODATIONS

Allowed in exams:	
Calculators	Yes
Dictionary	Yes
Computer	Yes
Spell-checker	Yes
Extended test time	Yes
Scribe	Yes
Proctors	Yes
Oral exams	Yes
Note-takers	Yes
Support services for students with:	
LD	Yes
ADHD	Yes
ASD	Yes
Distraction-reduced environment	Yes
Recording of lecture alowed	Yes
Reading technology	Yes
Audio books	Yes
Other assistive technology	Yes
Priority registration	No
Added costs of services:	
For LD	No
For ADHD	No
For ASD	No
LD specialists	No
ADHD & ASD coaching	Yes
ASD specialists	No
Professional tutors	Yes
Peer tutors	Yes
Max. hours/week for services	Varies
How professors are notified of student approved accommodations	Student and Director

COLLEGE GRADUATION REQUIREMENTS

Course waivers allowed	No
Course substitutions allowed	Yes
In what courses: Case by case basis	

Drexel University

3141 Chestnut Street, Main Building, Philadelphia, PA 19104 • Admissions: 215-895-2400 • Fax: 215-895-1285 **Support: CS**

CAMPUS

Type of school	Private (nonprofit)
Environment	Metropolis

STUDENTS

Undergrad enrollment	15,346
% male/female	52/48
% from out of state	51
% frosh live on campus	88

FINANCIAL FACTS

Annual tuition	$53,868
Room and board	$16,008
Required fees	$2,405

GENERAL ADMISSIONS INFO

Application fee	$50
Regular application deadline	1/15
Nonfall registration	Yes

Admission may be deferred.

Range SAT EBRW	590–680
Range SAT Math	600–710
Range ACT Composite	25–31

ACADEMICS

Student/faculty ratio	11:1
% students returning for sophomore year	89

Most classes have 10–19 students.

Programs/Services for Students with Learning Differences

Drexel University does not have a specific learning disability program, but services are provided through the Office of Disability Resources (ODR). The professional staff works closely with the students who have special needs to ensure that they have the opportunity to participate fully in Drexel University's programs and activities. Drexel's ODR offers an individualized transition program for students with disabilities upon request. Students need to contact the ODR before they arrive on campus. Students are eligible for electronic books, distraction-free environment for test-taking, extended time on tests, breaks during testing, note-taker, and access to power points and overheads before class begins.

Admissions

The regular admission requirements are the same for all students, and there is no special process for students with learning disabilities or any other type of disability. Students are encouraged to-self disclose and provide current documentation of their disabilities to the ODR. General admission criteria include recommended courses of 4 years of English, 3 years of math, 1 year of science, 1 year of social studies, 7 electives (chosen from English, math, science, social studies, foreign language, history, or mechanical drawing). The university is test flexible which means students can submit several different tests such as ACT, SAT, IB, or Subject Tests. The average GPA is 3.4 and an interview is recommended.

Additional Information

The Dragon Scholars Program (DSP) helps first year students transition to college by providing support and skill develop for approaching college level classes and facilitating peer networking through participation in a diverse learning community. This is a customized service that includes mentoring and coaching. The Drexel Autism Support Program (DASP) provides a peer-mediated community of practice for current Drexel students that promotes academic excellence, self-advocacy, and social integration. DASP does not require its participants to provide documentation of a diagnosis or disability. Disability Resources use the ClockWork system to process new student accommodations. Additionally, students will register to take exams with Disability Resources, request alternative format/accessible books and materials, and request note-taking services, using this system.

ADMISSIONS INFO FOR STUDENTS WITH LEARNING DIFFERENCES

Phone: 215-895-1401 • Fax: 215-895-1402 • Email: disability@drexel.edu

SAT/ACT required: Yes (Test optional for 2021)
Interview required: No
Essay required: Yes
Additional application required: No
Documentation submitted to: ODR

Special Ed. HS course work accepted: No
Separate application required for Programs/Services: No
Documentation required for:
LD: Psychoeducational evaluation
ADHD: Psychoeducational evaluation
ASD: Psychoeducational evaluation

Drexel University

Pennsylvania

General Admissions

Very important factors include: rigor of secondary school record, class rank, academic GPA, standardized test scores. *Important factors include:* application essay, recommendation(s), character/personal qualities. *Other factors include:* interview, extracurricular activities, talent/ability, first generation, alumni/ae relation, volunteer work, work experience, level of applicant's interest. *Freshman admission requirements:* High school diploma is required and GED is accepted. *Academic units required:* 3 math, 1 science, 1 science lab. *Academic units recommended:* 1 foreign language.

Accommodations or Services

Accommodations are decided upon an individual basis after a thorough review of appropriate, current documentation. The accommodations requests must be supported through the documentation provided and must be logically linked to the current impact of the condition on academic functioning.

Financial Aid

Students should submit: CSS/Financial Aid PROFILE; FAFSA. *Need-based scholarships/grants offered:* College/university scholarship or grant aid from institutional funds; Federal Pell; Private scholarships; SEOG; State scholarships/grants. *Loan aid offered:* Direct PLUS loans; Direct Subsidized Stafford Loans; Direct Unsubsidized Stafford Loans. Federal Work-Study Program available. Institutional employment available.

Campus Life

Activities: Campus Ministries; Choral groups; Concert band; Dance; Drama/theater; Jazz band; Literary magazine; Model UN; Music ensembles; Musical theater; Pep band; Radio station; Student government; Student newspaper; Student-run film society; Symphony orchestra; Television station; Yearbook. **Organizations:** 367 registered organizations, 9 honor societies, 19 religious organizations, 20 fraternities, 11 sororities. **Athletics (Intercollegiate):** *Men:* basketball, cheerleading, crew/rowing, diving, golf, lacrosse, soccer, swimming, tennis, wrestling. *Women:* basketball, cheerleading, crew/rowing, diving, field hockey, lacrosse, soccer, softball, swimming, tennis, volleyball.

ACCOMMODATIONS

Allowed in exams:	
Calculators	Yes
Dictionary	No
Computer	Yes
Spell-checker	Yes
Extended test time	Yes
Scribe	Yes
Proctors	Yes
Oral exams	Yes
Note-takers	Yes
Support services for students with:	
LD	Yes
ADHD	Yes
ASD	Yes
Distraction-reduced environment	Yes
Recording of lecture alowed	Yes
Reading technology	Yes
Audio books	Yes
Other assistive technology	Yes
Priority registration	Yes
Added costs of services:	
For LD	No
For ADHD	No
For ASD	No
LD specialists	Yes
ADHD & ASD coaching	Yes
ASD specialists	Yes
Professional tutors	Yes
Peer tutors	Yes
Max. hours/week for services	Varies
How professors are notified of student approved accommodations	Student

COLLEGE GRADUATION REQUIREMENTS

Course waivers allowed	No
Course substitutions allowed	No

East Stroudsburg University of Pennsylvania

200 Prospect Street East Stroudsburg, PA 18301-2999 • Admissions: 570-422-3542 • Fax: 570-422-3933 **Support: CS**

CAMPUS

Type of school	Public
Environment	Village

STUDENTS

Undergrad enrollment	5,417
% male/female	44/56
% from out of state	19
% frosh live on campus	79

FINANCIAL FACTS

Annual in-state tuition	$8,288
Annual out-of-state tuition	$17,616
Room and board	$6,658
Required fees	$1,646

GENERAL ADMISSIONS INFO

Application fee	$25
Regular application deadline	5/1
Nonfall registration	Yes
Range SAT EBRW	460–560
Range SAT Math	450–540
Range ACT Composite	17–21

ACADEMICS

Student/faculty ratio	19:1
% students returning for sophomore year	67

Most classes have 20–29 students.

Programs/Services for Students with Learning Differences

The Office of Accessible Services Individualized for Students (OASIS) supports students with documented disabilities. OASIS helps coordinate academics and housing accommodations. East Stroudsburg University of Pennsylvania is committed to providing equal educational access to otherwise qualified students with disabilities. Students with learning disabilities may work individually or in groups with the disabilities specialist. All students enrolled in the university have the opportunity to take skills classes in reading, composition, and math. Other services include workshops in time management and test taking strategies that are offered to all students. Note-taking support includes recording lectures, professors notes, peer notes, and use of smart pens.

Admissions

Students with LD file the general application and are encouraged to complete the section titled "Disabilities Information" and forward documentation of their disability to the Office of Disability Services. For general admission, academic achievement is the primary factor considered in the selection process. ESU looks for a good match between what each applicant can contribute to the university and how the university can meet each applicant's expectations through a whole- person assessment. ESU is interested in student contributions to their school and community, activities and achievements, aspirations, and anything else that would help evaluate potential success at ESU.

Additional Information

The Learning Center provides individual and group tutoring by peer tutors free of charge to ESU students. Tutors are assigned on a first-come, first-served basis, and students must complete and submit a request form in order to receive tutoring. East Stroudsburg University is the home of the Alpha Chapter of Delta Alpha Pi International Honor Society, an international honor society for students with disabilities who have achieved academic success. Services and accommodations are available for undergraduate and graduate students. The Career, Independent Living, and Learning Studies (CILLS) is a non-degree certificate program designed to help young adults with intellectual disabilities them lead productive lives. There are living accommodations in off-campus housing.

ADMISSIONS INFO FOR STUDENTS WITH LEARNING DIFFERENCES

Phone: 570-422-3954 • Fax: 717-422-3898 • Email: oasis@esu.edu

SAT/ACT required: No
Interview required: No
Essay required: Yes
Additional application required: No
Documentation submitted to: Office of Disability Services

Special Ed. HS course work accepted: Yes
Separate application required for Programs/Services: No
Documentation required for:
LD: Psychoeducational evaluation
ASD: Psychoeducational evaluation
ADHD: Psychoeducational evaluation

East Stroudsburg University of Pennsylvania

Pennsylvania

General Admissions

Very important factors include: rigor of secondary school record, class rank, academic GPA, standardized test scores. *Freshman admission requirements:* High school diploma is required and GED is accepted. *Academic units recommended:* 3 English, 3 math, 3 science, 1 science lab, 1 foreign language, 3 social studies.

Accommodations or Services

Accommodations are decided upon an individual basis after a thorough review of appropriate, current documentation. The accommodations requests must be supported through the documentation provided and must be logically linked to the current impact of the condition on academic functioning.

Financial Aid

Students should submit: FAFSA. Applicants will be notified of awards on or about 4/1. *Need-based scholarships/grants offered:* College/university scholarship or grant aid from institutional funds; Federal Pell; Private scholarships; SEOG; State scholarships/grants. *Loan aid offered:* Direct PLUS loans; Direct Subsidized Stafford Loans; Direct Unsubsidized Stafford Loans. Federal Work-Study Program available. Institutional employment available.

Campus Life

Activities: Campus Ministries; Choral groups; Concert band; Dance; Drama/theater; International Student Organization; Jazz band; Literary magazine; Marching band; Music ensembles; Musical theater; Pep band; Radio station; Student government; Student newspaper; Symphony orchestra. **Organizations:** 110 registered organizations, 28 honor societies, 3 religious organizations, 5 fraternities, 5 sororities. **Athletics (Intercollegiate):** *Men:* baseball, basketball, cross-country, football, soccer, tennis, track/field (outdoor), track/field (indoor), wrestling. *Women:* basketball, cross-country, field hockey, golf, lacrosse, soccer, softball, swimming, tennis, track/field (outdoor), track/field (indoor), volleyball.

ACCOMMODATIONS

Allowed in exams:	
Calculators	Yes
Dictionary	Yes
Computer	Yes
Spell-checker	Yes
Extended test time	Yes
Scribe	Yes
Proctors	Yes
Oral exams	No
Note-takers	Yes
Support services for students with:	
LD	Yes
ADHD	Yes
ASD	Yes
Distraction-reduced environment	Yes
Recording of lecture alowed	Yes
Reading technology	Yes
Audio books	Yes
Other assistive technology	Yes
Priority registration	Yes
Added costs of services:	
For LD	No
For ADHD	No
For ASD	No
LD specialists	Yes
ADHD & ASD coaching	Yes
ASD specialists	No
Professional tutors	Yes
Peer tutors	Yes
Max. hours/week for services	2
How professors are notified of student approved accommodations	Student

COLLEGE GRADUATION REQUIREMENTS

Course waivers allowed	No
Course substitutions allowed	No

Edinboro University of Pennsylvania

200 East Normal Street, Edinboro, PA 16444 • Admissions: 814-732-2761 • Fax: 814-732-2420 **Support: CS**

CAMPUS

Type of school	Public
Environment	Rural

STUDENTS

Undergrad enrollment	3,399
% male/female	42/58
% from out of state	10
% frosh live on campus	68

FINANCIAL FACTS

Annual in-state tuition	$9,985
Annual out-of-state tuition	$12,932
Room and board	$10,600

GENERAL ADMISSIONS INFO

Application fee	$30
Regular application deadline	Rolling
Nonfall registration	Yes

Admission may be deferred.

Range SAT EBRW	490–520
Range SAT Math	480–570
Range ACT Composite	18–23

ACADEMICS

Student/faculty ratio	15:1
% students returning for sophomore year	71

Most classes have 20–29 students.

Programs/Services for Students with Learning Differences

Edinboro is actively involved in providing services for students with learning disabilities. The Office for Accessibility Services (OAS) provides services that are individually directed by the program staff according to expressed needs. There are different levels of services offered depending on the student's needs. Level 1 offers supervised study sessions with trained peer advisors up to 10 hours per week; writing specialist by appointment one to two hours weekly; required appointment every two weeks with professional staff to review progress; and all services in Basic Service. Level 2 includes peer advising up to three hours weekly and all services in Basic Service. Basic Service provides assistance in arranging academic accommodations, including alternate test arrangements; priority scheduling; consultation with staff; and an alternate format of textbooks. Level 1 and 2 are fee-for-service levels.

Admissions

Students with LD submit the general application form. Upon receipt of the application by the Admissions Office, it is suggested that students identify any special services that may be required and contact the OAS so that a personal interview may be scheduled. Occasionally, OAS staff are asked for remarks on certain files, but it is not part of the admission decision. ACT or SAT score is required for admission. Admission to the Honors program is automatic with a 1200 SAT or 25 ACT and 3.5 GPA OR 1100 SAT or 22 ACT and 3.8 GPA.

Additional Information

The Office for Students with Disabilities has developed the Boro Autism Support Initiative for Success (BASIS) program in order to provide opportunities to otherwise qualified degree seeking college students with Autism Spectrum Disorders (ASD) to achieve excellence in all areas of their university experience. BASIS is an individualized support program available for enrolled Edinboro University students. The BASIS team will work with students to identify individual needs and provide support in 5 key areas: Academics, Communication, Daily Living Skills, Employment Readiness, Social Skills. BASIS is a fee-based program.

ADMISSIONS INFO FOR STUDENTS WITH LEARNING DIFFERENCES

Phone: 814-732-2462 • Fax: 814-732-2866 • Email: OAS@edinboro.edu

SAT/ACT required: Yes (Test optional for 2021)
Interview required: No
Essay required: No
Additional application required: No
Documentation submitted to: OAS

Special Ed. HS course work accepted: Yes
Separate application required for Programs/Services: No
Documentation required for:
LD: Psychoeducational evaluation
ADHD: Psychoeducational evaluation
ASD: Psychoeducational evaluation

Edinboro University of Pennsylvania

Pennsylvania

General Admissions

Very important factors include: rigor of secondary school record, class rank, academic GPA, standardized test scores. *Other factors include:* application essay, recommendation(s), interview, extracurricular activities, talent/ability, character/personal qualities, volunteer work, work experience. *Freshman admission requirements:* High school diploma is required and GED is accepted. *Academic units recommended:* 4 English, 3 math, 3 science, 2 foreign language, 4 social studies, 1 computer science.

Accommodations or Services

Accommodations are decided upon an individual basis after a thorough review of appropriate, current documentation. The accommodations requests must be supported through the documentation provided and must be logically linked to the current impact of the condition on academic functioning.

Financial Aid

Students should submit: FAFSA. *Need-based scholarships/grants offered:* College/university scholarship or grant aid from institutional funds; Federal Pell; Private scholarships; SEOG; State scholarships/grants. *Loan aid offered:* Direct Subsidized Stafford Loans; Direct Unsubsidized Stafford Loans. Federal Work-Study Program available. Institutional employment available.

Campus Life

Activities: Campus Ministries; Choral groups; Dance; Drama/theater; International Student Organization; Jazz band; Literary magazine; Marching band; Music ensembles; Opera; Radio station; Student government; Student newspaper; Student-run film society; Television station. **Organizations:** 175 registered organizations, 13 honor societies, 8 religious organizations, 7 fraternities, 7 sororities. **Athletics (Intercollegiate):** *Men:* basketball, cross-country, football, swimming, track/field (outdoor), track/field (indoor), wheel-chair basketball, wrestling. *Women:* basketball, cross-country, lacrosse, soccer, softball, swimming, track/field (outdoor), track/field (indoor), volleyball.

ACCOMMODATIONS

Allowed in exams:	
Calculators	Yes
Dictionary	Yes
Computer	Yes
Spell-checker	Yes
Extended test time	Yes
Scribe	Yes
Proctors	Yes
Oral exams	Yes
Note-takers	No
Support services for students with:	
LD	Yes
ADHD	Yes
ASD	Yes
Distraction-reduced environment	Yes
Recording of lecture alowed	Yes
Reading technology	Yes
Audio books	Yes
Other assistive technology	Yes
Priority registration	Yes
Added costs of services:	
For LD	No
For ADHD	No
For ASD	No
LD specialists	Yes
ADHD & ASD coaching	Yes
ASD specialists	Yes
Professional tutors	No
Peer tutors	Yes
Max. hours/week for services	8
How professors are notified of student approved accommodations	Student

COLLEGE GRADUATION REQUIREMENTS

Course waivers allowed	No
Course substitutions allowed	Yes
In what courses: Varies	

Gannon University

109 University Square, Erie, PA 16541 • Admissions: 814-871-7407 • Fax: 814-871-5826 **Support: CS**

CAMPUS

Type of school	Private (nonprofit)
Environment	City

STUDENTS

Undergrad enrollment	2,866
% male/female	39/61
% from out of state	28
% frosh live on campus	68

FINANCIAL FACTS

Annual tuition	$33,560
Room and board	$14,310
Required fees	$966

GENERAL ADMISSIONS INFO

Application fee	$25
Regular application deadline	Rolling
Nonfall registration	Yes

Admission may be deferred.

Range SAT EBRW	520–620
Range SAT Math	510–620
Range ACT Composite	19–26

ACADEMICS

Student/faculty ratio	13:1
% students returning for sophomore year	82

Most classes have 20–29 students.

Programs/Services for Students with Learning Differences

The Office of Disability Services (ODS) supports students with appropriate documentation and helps them receive academic accommodations. These documents have to come directly from the person/agency that did the testing. All material is reviewed on a case-by-case basis by the professional staff. Students seeking assistance have to contact the Disability Office once they have been accepted to the university. Students are responsible for self-disclosure, providing current documentation, and obtaining disability services. Students may also come to the Student Success Center, which is open to all students for additional support.

Admissions

Admissions is based on several factors including academic courses, grades, rank in class, and counselor recommendation. ACT/SAT test required. The minimum GPA and test scores required very based on the academic program and the university will notify the applicants if they do not meet the minimum requirements. Personal statement/essay is optional but recommended as it assists the university in evaluating eligibility beyond test scores and academic record. Courses required include 16 units of which 4 must be in English. Students diagnosed with a learning disability and who are interested in the Gannon's Program will also need: personal letters of recommendation from teachers, counselor or school administrators and scores from the testing agency. Records from any professional with whom the student has worked, such as psychologist, physician, reading specialist or math specialist. Students admitted conditionally must enter as undeclared majors until they can achieve a 2.0 GPA.

Additional Information

Features of the program may include biweekly or more as needed, tutoring sessions with the program instructors and tutors to review course material, and focus on specific needs. Additional services available are taping of classes, extended time on exams, and scribes as prescribed. Students are required to monitor their own progress and communicate their needs to instructors/specialists.

ADMISSIONS INFO FOR STUDENTS WITH LEARNING DIFFERENCES

Phone: 814-871-7000 • Fax: 814-871-7422 • Email: kanter002@gannon.edu

SAT/ACT required: Yes (Test optional for 2021)
Interview required: No
Essay required: Recommended
Additional application required: No
Documentation submitted to: Office of Disability Services

Special Ed. HS course work accepted: No
Separate application required for Programs/Services: No
Documentation required for:
LD: Psychoeducational evaluation
ADHD: Psychoeducational evaluation
ASD: Psychoeducational evaluation

Gannon University

General Admissions

Very important factors include: rigor of secondary school record, academic GPA, standardized test scores. *Other factors include:* class rank, application essay, recommendation(s), interview, extracurricular activities, character/personal qualities, alumni/ae relation, work experience. *Freshman admission requirements:* High school diploma is required and GED is accepted. *Academic units required:* 4 English, 2 math, 2 science, 2 science labs, 2 social studies, 1 history, 3 academic electives. *Academic units recommended:* 4 English, 4 math, 4 science, 3 science labs, 2 foreign language, 2 social studies, 1 history, 3 academic electives, 1 computer science, 1 visual/performing arts.

Accommodations or Services

Accommodations are decided upon an individual basis after a thorough review of appropriate, current documentation. The accommodations requests must be supported through the documentation provided and must be logically linked to the current impact of the condition on academic functioning.

Financial Aid

Students should submit: FAFSA. *Need-based scholarships/grants offered:* College/university scholarship or grant aid from institutional funds; Federal Nursing Scholarships; Federal Pell; Private scholarships; SEOG; State scholarships/grants. *Loan aid offered:* Direct PLUS loans; Direct Subsidized Stafford Loans; Direct Unsubsidized Stafford Loans. Federal Work-Study Program available. Institutional employment available.

Campus Life

Activities: Campus Ministries; Choral groups; Concert band; Dance; Drama/theater; International Student Organization; Literary magazine; Model UN; Pep band; Radio station; Student government; Student newspaper. **Organizations:** 91 registered organizations, 16 honor societies, 5 religious organizations, 7 fraternities, 5 sororities. **Athletics (Intercollegiate):** *Men:* baseball, basketball, cheerleading, cross-country, football, golf, soccer, swimming, water polo, wrestling. *Women:* basketball, cheerleading, cross-country, golf, lacrosse, soccer, softball, swimming, volleyball, water polo.

ACCOMMODATIONS

Allowed in exams:	
Calculators	No
Dictionary	No
Computer	Yes
Spell-checker	No
Extended test time	Yes
Scribe	Yes
Proctors	Yes
Oral exams	No
Note-takers	Yes
Support services for students with:	
LD	Yes
ADHD	Yes
ASD	Yes
Distraction-reduced environment	Yes
Recording of lecture allowed	Yes
Reading technology	Yes
Audio books	Yes
Other assistive technology	Yes
Priority registration	Yes
Added costs of services:	
For LD	No
For ADHD	No
For ASD	No
LD specialists	Yes
ADHD & ASD coaching	No
ASD specialists	No
Professional tutors	Yes
Peer tutors	Yes
Max. hours/week for services	Varies
How professors are notified of student approved accommodations	Student and Director

COLLEGE GRADUATION REQUIREMENTS

Course waivers allowed	No
Course substitutions allowed	Yes
In what courses: Varies	

Kutztown University of Pennsylvania

15200 Kutztown Rd., Kutztown, PA 19530-0730 • Admissions: 610-683-4060 • Fax: 610-683-1375 **Support: SP**

CAMPUS

Type of school	Public
Environment	Rural

STUDENTS

Undergrad enrollment	6,862
% male/female	45/55
% from out of state	12
% frosh live on campus	90

FINANCIAL FACTS

Annual in-state tuition	$7,716
Annual out-of-state tuition	$11,574
Room and board	$10,660
Required fees	$3,547

GENERAL ADMISSIONS INFO

Application fee	$35
Regular application deadline	Rolling
Nonfall registration	Yes

Admission may be deferred.

Range SAT EBRW	490–580
Range SAT Math	480–560
Range ACT Composite	18–24

ACADEMICS

Student/faculty ratio	17:1
% students returning for sophomore year	74

Most classes have 20–29 students.

Programs/Services for Students with Learning Differences

Kutztown University welcomes academically qualified students with disabilities to participate in its educational programs and is committed to providing access to its programs and services for all qualified individuals. Upon acceptance to Kutztown University, students should complete and submit the Accommodation Request Form from the Disability Service Office (DSO). The university offers the My Place program for students on the autism spectrum. This program focuses on supporting executive functioning skills, career development, social skill development, and independent college living.

Admissions

There is no special admissions process for students with learning disabilities. All applicants are expected to meet the same admission criteria. Course requirements include: 4 years English, 3 years math, 3 years science, and 3 years social studies. Conditional admission is available.

Additional Information

My Place offers three programs. The Residential Program provides a minimum of 6 contact hours a week. Students remain in the program for at least one year. This program concentrates on college adjustment, study strategies, classroom expectations, self-advocacy, and career planning. The Residential Program offers one-on-one coaching and group activities. Students are expected to participate in at least four social/group activities each semester. The Commuter/Continuing Program is for students who have participated in the Residential Program for one year. This program focuses on self-advocacy, study skills, classroom and workplace etiquette, and career plans and offers one hour of coaching weekly and two hours of structured study time and other activities. The Transition Program is the final program and focuses on students nearing graduation, internship/job search, graduate school planning, and transition to employment. There is one hour of coaching weekly.

ADMISSIONS INFO FOR STUDENTS WITH LEARNING DIFFERENCES

Phone: 610-683-4108 • Fax: 610-683-1520 • Email: DSO@kutztown.edu

SAT/ACT required: Yes (Test optional for 2021)
Interview required: No
Essay required: No
Additional application required: Yes
Documentation submitted to: DSO

Special Ed. HS course work accepted: No
Separate application required for Programs/Services: Yes
Documentation required for:
LD: Psychoeducational evaluation
ADHD: Psychoeducational evaluation
ASD: Psychoeducational evaluation

Kutztown University of Pennsylvania

Pennsylvania

General Admissions

Very important factors include: rigor of secondary school record, class rank, standardized test scores. *Other factors include:* academic GPA, recommendation(s), talent/ability. *Freshman admission requirements:* High school diploma is required and GED is accepted. *Academic units required:* 4 English, 3 math, 3 science, 2 science labs, 3 social studies.

Accommodations or Services

Accommodations are decided upon an individual basis after a thorough review of appropriate, current documentation. The accommodations requests must be supported through the documentation provided and must be logically linked to the current impact of the condition on academic functioning.

Financial Aid

Students should submit: FAFSA. *Need-based scholarships/grants offered:* College/university scholarship or grant aid from institutional funds; Federal Pell; Private scholarships; SEOG; State scholarships/grants. *Loan aid offered:* Direct PLUS loans; Direct Subsidized Stafford Loans; Direct Unsubsidized Stafford Loans. Federal Work-Study Program available. Institutional employment available.

Campus Life

Activities: Campus Ministries; Choral groups; Concert band; Dance; Drama/theater; International Student Organization; Jazz band; Literary magazine; Marching band; Model UN; Music ensembles; Musical theater; Radio station; Student government; Student newspaper; Student-run film society; Symphony orchestra; Television station; Yearbook. **Organizations:** 239 registered organizations, 13 honor societies, 7 religious organizations, 10 fraternities, 6 sororities. **Athletics (Intercollegiate):** *Men:* baseball, basketball, cross-country, football, tennis, track/field (outdoor), track/field (indoor), wrestling. *Women:* basketball, bowling, cross-country, field hockey, golf, lacrosse, soccer, softball, swimming, tennis, track/field (outdoor), track/field (indoor), volleyball.

ACCOMMODATIONS

Allowed in exams:	
Calculators	Yes
Dictionary	Yes
Computer	Yes
Spell-checker	Yes
Extended test time	Yes
Scribe	Yes
Proctors	Yes
Oral exams	No
Note-takers	Yes
Support services for students with:	
LD	Yes
ADHD	Yes
ASD	Yes
Distraction-reduced environment	Yes
Recording of lecture allowed	Yes
Reading technology	Yes
Audio books	Yes
Other assistive technology	Yes
Priority registration	Yes
Added costs of services:	
For LD	No
For ADHD	No
For ASD	Yes
LD specialists	Yes
ADHD & ASD coaching	Yes
ASD specialists	Yes
Professional tutor	Yes
Peer tutors	Yes
Max. hours/week for services	Varies
How professors are notified of student approved accommodations	Student

COLLEGE GRADUATION REQUIREMENTS

Course waivers allowed	No
Course substitutions allowed	Yes
In what courses: Case by case basis	

Lehigh University

27 Memorial Drive, West Bethlehem, PA 18015 • Admissions: 610-758-3100 • Fax: 610-758-4361 **Support: CS**

CAMPUS

Type of school	Private (nonprofit)
Environment	City

STUDENTS

Undergrad enrollment	5,164
% male/female	54/46
% from out of state	73
% frosh live on campus	99

FINANCIAL FACTS

Annual tuition	$54,490
Room and board	$15,720
Required fees	$720

GENERAL ADMISSIONS INFO

Application fee	$70
Regular application deadline	1/1
Nonfall registration	Yes

Admission may be deferred.

Range SAT EBRW	620–690
Range SAT Math	660–760
Range ACT Composite	29–33

ACADEMICS

Student/faculty ratio	9:1
% students returning for sophomore year	93

Most classes have 10–19 students.

Programs/Services for Students with Learning Differences

Disability Support Services (DSS) supports and enhances Lehigh University's educational mission and its commitment to maintaining an inclusive and equitable community by providing equal access and reasonable accommodations to qualified students with disabilities. If a student is not certain whether he or she has a learning disability, the Director of Academic Support Services can conduct a comprehensive intake interview and screening process. If a complete diagnostic evaluation seems appropriate, the student will be provided with referrals to community-based professionals who can perform a comprehensive evaluation at the student's expense. It is the responsibility of students to self-identify. Students who are eligible for accommodations must sign a professor notification and accommodation form at the beginning of each semester that students are requesting accommodations.

Admissions

There is no special admission process for students with learning disabilities. All applicants must meet the same admission criteria. An on-campus interview is recommended. Applicants' evaluations are based on many factors, including a challenging college prep curriculum that included AP and honors courses. Lehigh University adopted a test optional policy for the SAT or ACT during the 2020–21 year. With the exception of prospective student-athletes and applicants to the accelerated dental program with SUNY Optometry, first-year and transfer applicants for the fall 2021 semester can choose whether or not to submit SAT/ACT test scores for consideration. The mid 50% who submit test scores have SAT 1350–1480 and ACT 31–34.

Additional Information

Requests for reasonable accommodations are reviewed during an interactive process involving students, DSS and faculty when applicable. The Peer Mentor Program assists first-year students with the transition from high school to a competitive university. First-year students are matched with a peer mentor by college and/or major, and these tutors have taken the classes in which they are tutoring. Program participation is voluntary, and students may choose to withdraw from the program at any time. The Center for Writing and Math provides assistance with any writing assignments, including brainstorming, rough-draft preparations, and critiques of final draft and assistance in calculus and other math courses.

ADMISSIONS INFO FOR STUDENTS WITH LEARNING DIFFERENCES

Phone: 610-758-4152 • Fax: 610-758-5293 • Email: maz317@lehigh.edu

SAT/ACT required: No
Interview required: No
Essay required: Yes
Additional application required: No
Documentation submitted to: DDS

Special Ed. HS course work accepted: No
Separate application required for Programs/Services: No
Documentation required for:
LD: Psychoeducational evaluation
ADHD: Psychoeducational evaluation
ASD: Psychoeducational evaluation

Lehigh University

Pennsylvania

General Admissions

Very important factors include: rigor of secondary school record, class rank, academic GPA, standardized test scores, talent/ability, character/personal qualities. *Important factors include:* application essay, recommendation(s), extracurricular activities, first generation, geographical residence, racial/ethnic status, volunteer work. *Other factors include:* interview, alumni/ae relation, work experience. *Freshman admission requirements:* High school diploma is required and GED is accepted. *Academic units required:* 4 English, 3 math, 2 science, 2 science labs, 2 foreign language, 2 social studies, 2 history, 2 academic electives. *Academic units recommended:* 4 English, 4 math, 4 science, 3 science labs, 3 foreign language, 3 social studies, 2 history, 2 academic electives, 1 computer science, 1 visual/performing arts.

Accommodations or Services

Accommodations are decided upon an individual basis after a thorough review of appropriate, current documentation. The accommodations requests must be supported through the documentation provided and must be logically linked to the current impact of the condition on academic functioning.

Financial Aid

Students should submit: CSS/Financial Aid PROFILE; FAFSA; Noncustodial PROFILE. *Need-based scholarships/grants offered:* College/university scholarship or grant aid from institutional funds; Federal Pell; Private scholarships; State scholarships/grants. *Loan aid offered:* Direct PLUS loans; Direct Subsidized Stafford Loans; Direct Unsubsidized Stafford Loans. Federal Work-Study Program available. Institutional employment available.

Campus Life

Activities: Campus Ministries; Choral groups; Concert band; Dance; Drama/theater; International Student Organization; Jazz band; Literary magazine; Marching band; Model UN; Music ensembles; Musical theater; Pep band; Radio station; Student government; Student newspaper; Student-run film society; Symphony orchestra; Yearbook. **Organizations:** 150 registered organizations, 18 honor societies, 14 religious organizations, 14 fraternities, 10 sororities. **Athletics (Intercollegiate):** *Men:* baseball, basketball, cross-country, diving, football, golf, lacrosse, soccer, swimming, tennis, track/field (outdoor), track/field (indoor), wrestling. *Women:* basketball, crew/rowing, cross-country, diving, field hockey, golf, lacrosse, soccer, softball, swimming, tennis, track/field (outdoor), track/field (indoor), volleyball.

ACCOMMODATIONS

Allowed in exams:	
Calculators	Yes
Dictionary	Yes
Computer	Yes
Spell-checker	Yes
Extended test time	Yes
Scribe	Yes
Proctors	Yes
Oral exams	Yes
Note-takers	Yes
Support services for students with:	
LD	Yes
ADHD	Yes
ASD	Yes
Distraction-reduced environment	Yes
Recording of lecture alowed	Yes
Reading technology	Yes
Audio books	Yes
Other assistive technology	Yes
Priority registration	Yes
Added costs of services:	
For LD	No
For ADHD	No
For ASD	No
LD specialists	Yes
ADHD & ASD coaching	Yes
ASD specialists	No
Professional tutors	No
Peer tutors	Yes
Max. hours/week for services	Varies
How professors are notified of student approved accommodations	Student

COLLEGE GRADUATION REQUIREMENTS

Course waivers allowed	No
Course substitutions allowed	No

Mercyhurst University

501 East 38th Street, Erie, PA 16546 • Admissions: 814-824-2202 • Fax: 814-824-2071 **Support: SP**

CAMPUS	
Type of school	Private (nonprofit)
Environment	City
STUDENTS	
Undergrad enrollment	2,378
% male/female	41/59
% from out of state	51
% frosh live on campus	88
FINANCIAL FACTS	
Annual tuition	$38,580
Room and board	$12,500
Required fees	$2,770
GENERAL ADMISSIONS INFO	
Application fee	$0
Regular application deadline	Rolling
Nonfall registration	Yes
Admission may be deferred.	
Range SAT EBRW	510–610
Range SAT Math	520–610
Range ACT Composite	20–26
ACADEMICS	
Student/faculty ratio	14:1
% students returning for sophomore year	79
Most classes have 20–29 students.	

Programs/Services for Students with Learning Differences

The Learning Differences Program (LDP) supports students who have an identified learning difference. The Academic Advantage Program (AAP) is available for students who need a more structured program. There is also a Summer PASS Program for incoming freshman in the LDP. It is a three-week program that consists of living on campus, earning college credit, and developing a higher level of academic skills and abilities. The mission of the Autism Initiative at Mercyhurst (AIM) is to facilitate and support the adjustment and progression of college students on the autism spectrum. AIM seeks to broaden its participants' vocational opportunities and enhance social and community engagement. The program strives to emphasize students' abilities within the academic, social, emotional, and independent living domains and to build new skills in area of deficits.

Admissions

Mercyhurst University evaluates applicants in terms of their academic abilities, leadership and extracurricular involvement, and the potential contributions they might make as members of our campus community. Generally, we look for students who took a college preparatory curriculum in high school, completing 4 units of English, 5 units of social studies, 3 units of mathematics, 2 units of science (with corresponding labs), and 2 units of foreign language. These are strongly recommended minimums, though your admissions counselor will consider the totality of your high school curriculum when evaluating your application.

Additional Information

The Academic Advantage Program is available for an additional fee and includes intensive academic support. It is designed to help with the transition and adjustment to college life. There is one-to-one assistance to help students define their college goals and educational needs. This is an individualized plan that also looks to support study skills development. The AAP schedules weekly student meetings with trained academic counselors, who is available to consult with parents at mid-term and end of semesters at the student's request. The AIM Enhanced Services for students on the autism spectrum provides weekly meetings, peer mentoring, priority for specialized housing arrangements to live with a roommate and have space to self-regulate and build living skills, chaperoned social opportunities, individual social skills training, student-centered behavior plans, academic support through Autism Support Networking, guidance in career planning, and access to a variety of activities and adventures.

ADMISSIONS INFO FOR STUDENTS WITH LEARNING DIFFERENCES

Phone: 814-824-2000 • Fax: 814-824-2589 • Email: eruggiero@mercyhurst.edu

SAT/ACT required: No
Interview required: No
Essay required: Recommended
Additional application required: Yes
Documentation submitted to: LDP

Special Ed. HS course work accepted: Yes
Separate application required for Programs/Services: Yes
Documentation required for:
LD: Psychoeducational evaluation
ADHD: Psychological evaluation
ASD: Psychoeducational evaluation

Mercyhurst University

Pennsylvania

General Admissions

Very important factors include: rigor of secondary school record, class rank, academic GPA, standardized test scores. *Important factors include:* application essay, recommendation(s), interview, extracurricular activities, talent/ability, character/personal qualities. *Other factors include:* alumni/ae relation, geographical residence, state residency, religious affiliation/commitment, racial/ethnic status, volunteer work, work experience, level of applicant's interest. *Freshman admission requirements:* High school diploma is required and GED is accepted. *Academic units required:* 4 English, 3 math, 2 science, 1 science lab, 2 foreign language, 5 social studies. *Academic units recommended:* 4 English, 3 math, 3 science, 2 science labs, 2 foreign language, 5 social studies.

Accommodations or Services

Accommodations are decided upon an individual basis after a thorough review of appropriate, current documentation. The accommodations requests must be supported through the documentation provided and must be logically linked to the current impact of the condition on academic functioning.

Financial Aid

Students should submit: FAFSA; State aid form. Applicants will be notified of awards on a rolling basis beginning 2/15. *Need-based scholarships/grants offered:* College/university scholarship or grant aid from institutional funds; Federal Pell; Private scholarships; SEOG; State scholarships/grants. *Loan aid offered:* Direct PLUS loans; Direct Subsidized Stafford Loans; Direct Unsubsidized Stafford Loans. Federal Work-Study Program available. Institutional employment available.

Campus Life

Activities: Campus Ministries; Choral groups; Dance; Drama/theater; International Student Organization; Jazz band; Literary magazine; Model UN; Music ensembles; Musical theater; Pep band; Radio station; Student government; Student newspaper; Television station; Yearbook. **Organizations:** 80 registered organizations, 9 honor societies, 2 religious organizations. **Athletics (Intercollegiate):** *Men:* baseball, basketball, cheerleading, crew/rowing, cross-country, football, golf, ice hockey, lacrosse, soccer, tennis, volleyball, water polo, wrestling. *Women:* basketball, cheerleading, crew/rowing, cross-country, field hockey, golf, ice hockey, lacrosse, soccer, softball, tennis, volleyball, water polo.

ACCOMMODATIONS

Allowed in exams:	
Calculators	Yes
Dictionary	No
Computer	Yes
Spell-checker	Yes
Extended test time	Yes
Scribe	Yes
Proctors	Yes
Oral exams	Yes
Note-takers	Yes
Support services for students with:	
LD	Yes
ADHD	Yes
ASD	Yes
Distraction-reduced environment	Yes
Recording of lecture alowed	No
Reading technology	Yes
Audio books	No
Other assistive technology	Yes
Priority registration	Yes
Added costs of services:	
For LD	Yes
For ADHD	No
For ASD	Yes
LD specialists	Yes
ADHD & ASD coaching	Yes
ASD specialists	Yes
Professional tutors	Yes
Peer tutors	Yes
Max. hours/week for services	Varies
How professors are notified of student approved accommodations	Student and Director

COLLEGE GRADUATION REQUIREMENTS

Course waivers allowed	Yes
In what courses: Foreign language	
Course substitutions allowed	Yes
In what courses: Foreign language	

Messiah College

1 College Avenue, Mechanicsburg, PA 17055 • Admissions: 717-691-6000 • Fax: 717-691-2307 **Support: S**

CAMPUS

Type of school	Private (nonprofit)
Environment	Village

STUDENTS

Undergrad enrollment	2,579
% male/female	40/60
% from out of state	35
% frosh live on campus	93

FINANCIAL FACTS

Annual tuition	$36,340
Room and board	$10,900
Required fees	$840

GENERAL ADMISSIONS INFO

Application fee	$50
Regular application deadline	Rolling
Nonfall registration	Yes
Range SAT EBRW	560–660
Range SAT Math	530–650
Range ACT Composite	23–30

ACADEMICS

Student/faculty ratio	12:1
% students returning for sophomore year	89

Most classes have 10–19 students.

Programs/Services for Students with Learning Differences

Messiah College is a Christian college committed to providing reasonable accommodations to qualified students with disabilities. Students who feel they may qualify for services should meet with the Office of Academic Accessibility (OAA) staff. At that meeting, staff will discuss the documentation process, services available, and their educational goals. Services/accommodations are granted to create an equal opportunity for student success, but do not in any way waive class expectations. Students are required to submit documentation from a qualified educational evaluator stating the diagnosis, how such a diagnosis creates a "substantial impairment" and in which life activities, and a list of accommodations that will be needed by the student in order to benefit from the support.

Admissions

All applicants must meet the same admission criteria. All applicants are asked to write a 200–350-word essay in response to the question "Why are you interested in attending a faith-based college that affirms and integrates Christian beliefs?" Messiah is test optional and does not require the ACT or SAT in the admission process. Courses should include 4 years English, 2 years math, 2 years social studies, 2 years science, 2 years foreign language, and 3 years of electives. Students are encouraged to enroll in a rigorous 4-year curriculum. Students with disabilities are encouraged to self-disclose and request an interview with the OAA Director, but not to include documentation of the disability in the actual admission application.

Additional Information

Commonly provided accommodations by OAA include extended time for test-taking, proctored exams in an alternate location, note-taking assistance, disability coaching support, advocacy with instructors, alternate format textbooks, transition services, peer tutoring, and referral source for other required services. Other accommodations are considered on an individual basis. The Learning Center also offers assistance with time management, motivation, goal setting, reading skills, learning theory, and taking exams, in addition to providing a range of tutorial services through trained peer tutors. The Writing Center provides peer tutors for written projects.

ADMISSIONS INFO FOR STUDENTS WITH LEARNING DIFFERENCES

Phone: 717-796-5382 • Fax: 717-796-5217 • Email: aslody@messiah.edu

SAT/ACT required: No
Interview required: No
Essay required: Yes
Additional application required: No
Documentation submitted to: OAA

Special Ed. HS course work accepted: No
Separate application required for Programs/Services: No
Documentation required for:
- **LD:** Psychoeducational evaluation
- **ADHD:** Psychoeducational evaluation
- **ASD:** Psychoeducational evaluation

Messiah College

General Admissions

Very important factors include: rigor of secondary school record, class rank, academic GPA, standardized test scores, extracurricular activities, talent/ability, character/personal qualities, religious affiliation/commitment. *Important factors include:* application essay, volunteer work. *Other factors include:* recommendation(s), alumni/ae relation, racial/ethnic status, work experience, level of applicant's interest. *Freshman admission requirements:* High school diploma is required and GED is accepted. *Academic units required:* 4 English, 2 math, 2 science, 2 science labs, 2 foreign language, 2 social studies, 4 academic electives. *Academic units recommended:* 4 English, 3 math, 3 science, 3 science labs, 2 foreign language, 2 social studies, 2 history, 4 academic electives.

Accommodations or Services

Accommodations are decided upon an individual basis after a thorough review of appropriate, current documentation. The accommodations requests must be supported through the documentation provided and must be logically linked to the current impact of the condition on academic functioning.

Financial Aid

Students should submit: FAFSA. Applicants will be notified of awards on a rolling basis beginning 3/1. *Need-based scholarships/grants offered:* College/university scholarship or grant aid from institutional funds; Federal Nursing Scholarships; Federal Pell; Private scholarships; SEOG; State scholarships/grants. *Loan aid offered:* Direct PLUS loans; Direct Subsidized Stafford Loans; Direct Unsubsidized Stafford Loans. Federal Work-Study Program available. Institutional employment available.

Campus Life

Activities: Campus Ministries; Choral groups; Concert band; Dance; Drama/theater; International Student Organization; Jazz band; Literary magazine; Music ensembles; Musical theater; Pep band; Radio station; Student government; Student newspaper; Student-run film society; Symphony orchestra; Television station; Yearbook. **Organizations:** 75 registered organizations, 4 honor societies, 8 religious organizations. **Athletics (Intercollegiate):** *Men:* baseball, basketball, cross-country, golf, lacrosse, soccer, swimming, tennis, track/field (outdoor), track/field (indoor), ultimate frisbee, wrestling. *Women:* basketball, cross-country, field hockey, lacrosse, soccer, softball, swimming, tennis, track/field (outdoor), track/field (indoor), volleyball.

ACCOMMODATIONS

Allowed in exams:	
Calculators	Yes
Dictionary	No
Computer	Yes
Spell-checker	Yes
Extended test time	Yes
Scribe	Yes
Proctors	Yes
Oral exams	Yes
Note-takers	Yes
Support services for students with:	
LD	Yes
ADHD	Yes
ASD	Yes
Distraction-reduced environment	Yes
Recording of lecture allowed	Yes
Reading technology	Yes
Audio books	No
Other assistive technology	Yes
Priority registration	Yes
Added costs of services:	
For LD	No
For ADHD	No
For ASD	No
LD specialists	No
ADHD & ASD coaching	No
ASD specialists	No
Professional tutors	No
Peer tutors Yes	
Max. hours/week for services	Varies
How professors are notified of student approved accommodations	Student

COLLEGE GRADUATION REQUIREMENTS

Course waivers allowed	No
Course substitutions allowed	Yes
In what courses: Varies	

Millersville University of Pennsylvania

P.O. Box 1002, Millersville, PA 17551-0302 • Admissions: 717-871-4625 • Fax: 717-871-7973 **Support: CS**

CAMPUS

Type of school	Public
Environment	Village

STUDENTS

Undergrad enrollment	6,615
% male/female	42/58
% from out of state	8
% frosh live on campus	77

FINANCIAL FACTS

Annual in-state tuition	$9,570
Annual out-of-state tuition	$19,290
Room and board	$14,106
Required fees	$2,680

GENERAL ADMISSIONS INFO

Application fee	$50
Regular application deadline	Rolling
Nonfall registration	Yes

Admission may be deferred.

Range SAT EBRW	490–600
Range SAT Math	490–570
Range ACT Composite	19–25

ACADEMICS

Student/faculty ratio	19:1
% students returning for sophomore year	77

Most classes have 20–29 students.

Programs/Services for Students with Learning Differences

The Office of Learning Services supports students through advocacy, assistive technology, collaboration, and direct services with the university community. The Director of the Office of Learning Services reviews the documentation report submitted by the student and works with the student to complete a list of accommodations. This office coordinates tutoring services through the Tutoring Center, as well.

Admissions

Typical first year students have a solid B average in high school. ACT or SAT scores are not required for admission. Applicants are required to submit a personal statement. Recommendations are not required but could be helpful in the admission review of applicants with borderline academic qualifications.

Additional Information

The Office of Learning Services coordinates academic accommodations and related services for students with learning and physical disabilities. Students must complete a Special Assistance Request Form. Learning Services offer student learners with academic accommodations, individualized learning assistance, peer tutoring, tutor training, auxiliary aids, assistive technology, academic skills workshops, and individualized programming to promote independent and successful learners for the future.

ADMISSIONS INFO FOR STUDENTS WITH LEARNING DIFFERENCES

Phone: 717-871-5554 • Fax: 717-871-7943 • Email: Learning.Services@millersville.edu

SAT/ACT required: Yes (Test optional for 2021)
Interview required: No
Essay required: Yes
Additional application required: No
Documentation submitted to: Office of Learning Services

Special Ed. HS course work accepted: Yes
Separate application required for Programs/Services: No
Documentation required for:
LD: Psychoeducational evaluation
ADHD: Psychoeducational evaluation
ASD: Psychoeducational evaluation

Millersville University of Pennsylvania

Pennsylvania

General Admissions

Very important factors include: rigor of secondary school record, class rank, academic GPA. *Important factors include:* application essay, standardized test scores, talent/ability, character/personal qualities. *Other factors include:* recommendation(s), extracurricular activities, first generation, racial/ethnic status, volunteer work, work experience, level of applicant's interest. *Freshman admission requirements:* High school diploma is required and GED is accepted. *Academic units required:* 4 English, 3 math, 3 science, 2 science labs, 3 social studies, 2 history. *Academic units recommended:* 4 English, 3 math, 3 science, 2 science labs, 2 foreign language, 3 social studies, 2 history, 4 academic electives.

Accommodations or Services

Accommodations are decided upon an individual basis after a thorough review of appropriate, current documentation. The accommodations requests must be supported through the documentation provided and must be logically linked to the current impact of the condition on academic functioning.

Financial Aid

Students should submit: FAFSA. *Need-based scholarships/grants offered:* College/university scholarship or grant aid from institutional funds; Federal Pell; Private scholarships; SEOG; State scholarships/grants. *Loan aid offered:* Direct PLUS loans; Direct Subsidized Stafford Loans; Direct Unsubsidized Stafford Loans. Federal Work-Study Program available. Institutional employment available.

Campus Life

Activities: Campus Ministries; Choral groups; Concert band; Dance; Drama/theater; International Student Organization; Jazz band; Literary magazine; Marching band; Music ensembles; Musical theater; Radio station; Student government; Student newspaper; Student-run film society; Symphony orchestra; Television station. **Organizations:** 208 registered organizations, 15 honor societies, 10 religious organizations, 9 fraternities, 8 sororities. **Athletics (Intercollegiate):** *Men:* baseball, basketball, cross-country, football, golf, soccer, tennis, track/field (outdoor), track/field (indoor), wrestling. *Women:* basketball, cheerleading, cross-country, field hockey, lacrosse, soccer, softball, swimming, tennis, track/field (outdoor), track/field (indoor), volleyball.

ACCOMMODATIONS

Allowed in exams:	
Calculators	Yes
Dictionary	Yes
Computer	Yes
Spell-checker	Yes
Extended test time	Yes
Scribe	Yes
Proctors	Yes
Oral exams	Yes
Note-takers	Yes
Support services for students with:	
LD	Yes
ADHD	Yes
ASD	Yes
Distraction-reduced environment	Yes
Recording of lecture alowed	Yes
Reading technology	Yes
Audio books	Yes
Other assistive technology	Yes
Priority registration	Yes
Added costs of services:	
For LD	No
For ADHD	No
For ASD	No
LD specialists	No
ADHD & ASD coaching	Yes
ASD specialists	No
Professional tutors	No
Peer tutors	Yes
Max. hours/week for services	Varies
How professors are notified of student approved accommodations	Director

COLLEGE GRADUATION REQUIREMENTS

Course waivers allowed	Yes
In what courses: Foreign language and others determined by academic departments	
Course substitutions allowed	Yes
In what courses: Foreign language and others determined by academic departments	

Misericordia University

301 Lake Street, Dallas, PA 18612 • Admissions: 570-674-6264 • Fax: 570-675-2441 **Support: SP**

CAMPUS

Type of school	Private (nonprofit)
Environment	Town

STUDENTS

Undergrad enrollment	1,942
% male/female	32/68
% from out of state	28
% frosh live on campus	84

FINANCIAL FACTS

Annual tuition	$34,100
Room and board	$14,520
Required fees	$1,840

GENERAL ADMISSIONS INFO

Application fee	$35
Regular application deadline	Rolling
Nonfall registration	Yes

Admission may be deferred.

Range SAT EBRW	520–610
Range SAT Math	530–610
Range ACT Composite	22–27

ACADEMICS

Student/faculty ratio	10:1
% students returning for sophomore year	82

Most classes have 10–19 students.

Programs/Services for Students with Learning Differences

The Alternative Learners Project (ALP) provides support to students with learning disabilities. The Alternative Learning Manager and full-time coordinators serve a population of approximately 40 students with disabilities per year. All students who participate in ALP are enrolled in regular college courses. "Learning Strategies" are designed to make students more efficient learners, and accommodations are designed to work around students' disabilities whenever possible. Upon entry, each student develops a program of accommodation (POA) and participates in individual weekly meetings with a program coordinator. The ultimate goal of ALP is to help students with learning differences succeed independently in college.

Admissions

Misericordia University's experience with students with learning disabilities is that students who are highly motivated and socially mature have an excellent chance to be successful. Each applicant has to submit a standard application to the Admissions Office. In addition, students must send a written cover letter to the ALP Manager summarizing the disability, and indicate a desire to participate in the ALP. Additionally, a copy of the Psychoeducational report should be submitted along with the high school transcript and three letters of recommendation (one should be written by a special education professional, if appropriate). Class rank is usually above the top 60 percent. ACT/SAT scores are not required by the university and are not used in the ALP Admissions decision. Students and their parents are invited to campus for an interview. Following the interview, the ALP Manager reviews all information and notifies the student directly regarding admission to the program.

Additional Information

The ALP students can participate in the BRIDGE Program. The BRIDGE program brings ALP students to campus one week prior to the start of freshman year and features a series of assessments and workshops designed to assist students in identifying both strengths and needs in their learning styles. They receive training in the use of the Learning Strategies Curriculum, designed to help students become more effective and efficient learners. The ALP staff works with students to establish their Program of Accommodations.

ADMISSIONS INFO FOR STUDENTS WITH LEARNING DIFFERENCES

Phone: 570-674-3026 • Fax: 570-674-6205 • Email: kricardo@misericordia@edu

SAT/ACT required: Yes (Test optional for 2021)
Interview required: Yes
Essay required: Yes
Additional application required: No
Documentation submitted to: Alternative Learners Project (ALP)

Special Ed. HS course work accepted: Yes
Separate application required for Programs/Services: No
Documentation required for:
LD: Psychoeducational evaluation
ADHD: Psychoeducational evaluation
ASD: Psychoeducational evaluation

Misericordia University

Pennsylvania

General Admissions

Very important factors include: rigor of secondary school record, academic GPA, standardized test scores. *Important factors include:* class rank, extracurricular activities, character/personal qualities, volunteer work. *Other factors include:* application essay, recommendation(s), interview, first generation, alumni/ae relation, geographical residence, work experience, level of applicant's interest. *Freshman admission requirements:* High school diploma is required and GED is accepted. *Academic units required:* 4 English, 4 math, 4 science, 4 social studies.

Accommodations or Services

Accommodations are decided upon an individual basis after a thorough review of appropriate, current documentation. The accommodations requests must be supported through the documentation provided and must be logically linked to the current impact of the condition on academic functioning.

Financial Aid

Students should submit: FAFSA. *Need-based scholarships/grants offered:* College/university scholarship or grant aid from institutional funds; Federal Pell; Private scholarships; SEOG; State scholarships/grants. *Loan aid offered:* Direct PLUS loans; Direct Subsidized Stafford Loans; Direct Unsubsidized Stafford Loans. Federal Work-Study Program available. Institutional employment available.

Campus Life

Activities: Campus Ministries; Choral groups; Dance; Drama/theater; Jazz band; Literary magazine; Music ensembles; Radio station; Student government; Student newspaper; Television station; Yearbook. **Organizations:** 40 registered organizations, 15 honor societies, 1 religious organization. **Athletics (Intercollegiate):** *Men:* baseball, basketball, cross-country, golf, lacrosse, soccer, swimming, tennis, track/field (outdoor). *Women:* basketball, cheerleading, cross-country, field hockey, lacrosse, soccer, softball, swimming, tennis, track/field (outdoor), volleyball.

ACCOMMODATIONS

Allowed in exams:	
Calculators	Yes
Dictionary	Yes
Computer	Yes
Spell-checker	Yes
Extended test time	Yes
Scribe	Yes
Proctors	Yes
Oral exams	Yes
Note-takers	Yes
Support services for students with:	
LD	Yes
ADHD	Yes
ASD	Yes
Distraction-reduced environment	Yes
Recording of lecture alowed	Yes
Reading technology	Yes
Audio books	Yes
Other assistive technology	Yes
Priority registration	Yes
Added costs of services:	
For LD	No
For ADHD	No
For ASD	No
LD specialists	Yes
ADHD & ASD coaching	No
ASD specialists	No
Professional tutors	No
Peer tutors	Yes
Max. hours/week for services	10
How professors are notified of student approved accommodations	Program coordinators

COLLEGE GRADUATION REQUIREMENTS

Course waivers allowed	No
Course substitutions allowed	No

Muhlenberg College

2400 West Chew Street, Allentown, PA 18104-5596 • Admissions: 484-664-3200 • Fax: 484-664-3032 **Support: S**

CAMPUS

Type of school	Private (nonprofit)
Environment	City

STUDENTS

Undergrad enrollment	2,190
% male/female	39/61
% from out of state	73
% frosh live on campus	97

FINANCIAL FACTS

Annual tuition	$53,865
Room and board	$12,165
Required fees	$735

GENERAL ADMISSIONS INFO

Application fee	$50
Regular application deadline	2/1
Nonfall registration	Yes

Admission may be deferred.

Range SAT EBRW	580–680
Range SAT Math	570–660
Range ACT Composite	26–31

ACADEMICS

Student/faculty ratio	9:1
% students returning for sophomore year	88

Most classes have 10–19 students.

Programs/Services for Students with Learning Differences

The Office of Disability Services (ODS) supports students helping with access to programs and accommodations. Students with documented disorders may schedule a pre-advising appointment during the June Advising Event as long as the documentation was submitted to (ODS) in advance. Students must complete a multifaceted process and be approved prior to developing an Accommodations Plan. All requests are individually reviewed using a collaborative approach after the determination process is complete. Muhlenberg is committed to ensuring that all qualified students with disabilities are provided reasonable accommodations and services to ensure full access to programs and activities.

Admissions

There is no separate admission process for students with disabilities. All applicants must meet the same admission criteria. The average high school GPA of the admitted freshman class at Muhlenberg College is a 3.3. The college is test optional and does not require the ACT or SAT for admission.

Additional Information

The Academic Resource Center offers support to all students through a peer tutoring program, study skills workshops, and individual academic assistance. The ARC also provides support in organization and planning skills, development of effective learning strategies, and cultivation of critical thinking and problem solving skills.

ADMISSIONS INFO FOR STUDENTS WITH LEARNING DIFFERENCES

Phone: 484-664-3825 • Fax: 484-664-3697 • Email: pmoschini@muhlenberg.edu

SAT/ACT required: No
Interview required: No
Essay required: Yes
Additional application required: Yes
Documentation submitted to: ARC

Special Ed. HS course work accepted: No
Separate application required for Programs/Services: Yes
Documentation required for:
LD: Psychoeducational evaluation
ADHD: Psychoeducational evaluation
ASD: Psychoeducational evaluation

Muhlenberg College

Pennsylvania

General Admissions

Very important factors include: rigor of secondary school record, academic GPA, character/personal qualities. *Important factors include:* application essay, standardized test scores, recommendation(s), interview, extracurricular activities, talent/ability, volunteer work. *Other factors include:* class rank, first generation, alumni/ae relation, geographical residence, racial/ethnic status, level of applicant's interest. *Freshman admission requirements:* High school diploma is required and GED is accepted. *Academic units required:* 4 English, 3 math, 2 science, 2 science labs, 2 foreign language, 2 history, 1 academic elective. *Academic units recommended:* 4 English, 4 math, 3 science, 3 science labs, 4 foreign language, 2 social studies, 2 history, 1 academic elective.

Accommodations or Services

Accommodations are decided upon an individual basis after a thorough review of appropriate, current documentation. The accommodations requests must be supported through the documentation provided and must be logically linked to the current impact of the condition on academic functioning.

Financial Aid

Students should submit: CSS/Financial Aid PROFILE; FAFSA; Institution's own financial aid form; Noncustodial PROFILE. Applicants will be notified of awards on a rolling basis beginning 4/1. *Need-based scholarships/grants offered:* College/university scholarship or grant aid from institutional funds; Federal Pell; Private scholarships; SEOG; State scholarships/grants; United Negro College Fund. *Loan aid offered:* Direct PLUS loans; Direct Subsidized Stafford Loans; Direct Unsubsidized Stafford Loans. Federal Work-Study Program available. Institutional employment available.

Campus Life

Activities: Campus Ministries; Choral groups; Concert band; Dance; Drama/theater; International Student Organization; Jazz band; Literary magazine; Music ensembles; Musical theater; Opera; Pep band; Radio station; Student government; Student newspaper; Student-run film society; Symphony orchestra; Yearbook. **Organizations:** 123 registered organizations, 12 honor societies, 7 religious organizations, 3 fraternities, 5 sororities. **Athletics (Intercollegiate):** *Men:* baseball, basketball, cheerleading, cross-country, football, golf, lacrosse, soccer, tennis, track/field (outdoor), track/field (indoor), wrestling. *Women:* basketball, cheerleading, cross-country, field hockey, golf, lacrosse, soccer, softball, tennis, track/field (outdoor), track/field (indoor), volleyball.

ACCOMMODATIONS

Allowed in exams:	
Calculators	Yes
Dictionary	Yes
Computer	Yes
Spell-checker	Yes
Extended test time	Yes
Scribe	Yes
Proctors	Yes
Oral exams	Yes
Note-takers	Yes
Support services for students with:	
LD	Yes
ADHD	Yes
ASD	Yes
Distraction-reduced environment	Yes
Recording of lecture alowed	Yes
Reading technology	Yes
Audio books	Yes
Other assistive technology	Yes
Priority registration	Yes
Added costs of services:	
For LD	No
For ADHD	No
For ASD	No
LD specialists	No
ADHD & ASD coaching	No
ASD specialists	No
Professional tutors	No
Peer tutors	Yes
Max. hours/week for services	Varies
How professors are notified of student approved accommodations	Student

COLLEGE GRADUATION REQUIREMENTS

Course waivers allowed	No
Course substitutions allowed	Yes
In what courses: Case by case basis	

Neumann University

1 Neumann Drive, Aston, PA 19014-1298 • Admissions: 610-558-5616 • Fax: 610-361-2548 **Support: S**

CAMPUS

Type of school	Private (nonprofit)
Environment	Town

STUDENTS

Undergrad enrollment	1,793
% male/female	32/68
% from out of state	32
% frosh live on campus	81

FINANCIAL FACTS

Annual tuition	$31,500
Room and board	$13,680
Required fees	$1,460

GENERAL ADMISSIONS INFO

Application fee	$0
Regular application deadline	8/30
Nonfall registration	Yes

Admission may be deferred.

Range SAT EBRW	460–550
Range SAT Math	460–540
Range ACT Composite	16–20

ACADEMICS

Student/faculty ratio	14:1
% students returning for sophomore year	76

Most classes have 10–19 students.

Programs/Services for Students with Learning Differences

Neumann University is committed to providing equal education opportunities to all qualified students with disabilities, by providing appropriate and reasonable accommodations. Students are responsible for declaring their disabilities to the university in order to be eligible for accommodations or special services. The staff recognizes the individual strengths and talents of each student and motivates them to work to their fullest potential.

Admissions

There is no alternate application process for students with disabilities. All applicants are expected to meet the same admission criteria. Neumann University's undergraduate admissions have a rolling admissions policy. Interviews are not required, but strongly recommended. The ACT or SAT is only required if the GPA is low.

Additional Information

The Academic Resource Center offers tutoring services, There are professional writing tutors to help with the writing process and writing papers. There are academic coaches to help each student develop strategies for academic success. The Program for Success works individually with students to assist them in developing their academic goals. The counselors facilitate academic plans to help students become more successful.

ADMISSIONS INFO FOR STUDENTS WITH LEARNING DIFFERENCES

Phone: 610-361-5471 • Fax: 610-358-4564 • Email: disabilities@neumann.edu

SAT/ACT required: No
Interview required: No
Essay required: No
Additional application required: Yes
Documentation submitted to: DS

Special Ed. HS course work accepted: Yes
Separate application required for Programs/Services: Yes
Documentation required for:
LD: Psychoeducational evaluation
ADHD: Psychoeducational evaluation
ASD: Psychoeducational evaluation

Neumann University

Pennsylvania

General Admissions

Very important factors include: rigor of secondary school record, academic GPA, standardized test scores. *Important factors include:* application essay, recommendation(s), interview. *Other factors include:* extracurricular activities, talent/ability, character/personal qualities, first generation, alumni/ae relation, volunteer work, work experience, level of applicant's interest. *Freshman admission requirements:* High school diploma is required and GED is accepted. *Academic units required:* 4 English, 2 math, 2 science, 1 science lab, 2 foreign language, 2 social studies, 4 academic electives. *Academic units recommended:* 4 English, 2 math, 3 science, 2 science labs, 2 foreign language, 2 social studies, 4 academic electives.

Accommodations or Services

Accommodations are decided upon an individual basis after a thorough review of appropriate, current documentation. The accommodations requests must be supported through the documentation provided and must be logically linked to the current impact of the condition on academic functioning.

Financial Aid

Students should submit: FAFSA. *Need-based scholarships/grants offered:* College/university scholarship or grant aid from institutional funds; Federal Pell; Private scholarships; SEOG; State scholarships/grants. *Loan aid offered:* Direct PLUS loans; Direct Subsidized Stafford Loans; Direct Unsubsidized Stafford Loans. Federal Work-Study Program available.

Campus Life

Activities: Campus Ministries; Choral groups; Dance; Drama/theater; Jazz band; Literary magazine; Music ensembles; Musical theater; Pep band; Radio station; Student government; Student newspaper; Symphony orchestra; Television station. **Organizations:** 29 registered organizations, 15 honor societies. **Athletics (Intercollegiate):** *Men:* baseball, basketball, cross-country, golf, ice hockey, lacrosse, soccer, tennis. *Women:* basketball, cross-country, field hockey, ice hockey, lacrosse, soccer, softball, tennis, volleyball.

ACCOMMODATIONS

Allowed in exams:	
Calculators	Yes
Dictionary	No
Computer	Yes
Spell-checker	Yes
Extended test time	Yes
Scribe	Yes
Proctors	Yes
Oral exams	Yes
Note-takers	Yes
Support services for students with:	
LD	Yes
ADHD	Yes
ASD	Yes
Distraction-reduced environment	Yes
Recording of lecture allowed	Yes
Reading technology	Yes
Audio books	Yes
Other assistive technology	Yes
Priority registration	Yes
Added costs of services:	
For LD	No
For ADHD	No
For ASD	No
LD specialists	No
ADHD & ASD coaching	Yes
ASD specialists	No
Professional tutors	Yes
Peer tutors	Yes
Max. hours/week for services	20
How professors are notified of student approved accommodations	Student and Director

COLLEGE GRADUATION REQUIREMENTS

Course waivers allowed	Yes
In what courses: Varies	
Course substitutions allowed	Yes
In what courses: Varies	

Penn State University Park

201 Shields Building, University Park, PA 16802 • Admissions: 814-865-5471 • Fax: 814-863-7590 **Support: S**

CAMPUS

Type of school	Public
Environment	Town

STUDENTS

Undergrad enrollment	40,385
% male/female	53/47
% from out of state	34

FINANCIAL FACTS

Annual in-state tuition	$17,416
Annual out-of-state tuition	$34,480
Room and board	$11,884
Required fees	$1,034

GENERAL ADMISSIONS INFO

Application fee	$65
Regular application deadline	Rolling
Nonfall registration	Yes

Admission may be deferred.

Range SAT EBRW	580–670
Range SAT Math	580–700
Range ACT Composite	25–30

ACADEMICS

Student/faculty ratio	14:1
% students returning for sophomore year	94

Most classes have 20–29 students.

Programs/Services for Students with Learning Differences

Academic support services for students with learning disabilities is designed to ensure that students receive appropriate accommodations so that they can function independently and meet the academic demands of a competitive university. Students with learning disabilities should be able to complete college-level courses with the help of support services and classroom accommodations. To receive any of the support services, students must submit documentation of their learning disability to the learning disability specialist in the Student Disability Services (SDS) at Penn State.

Admissions

There is no special application process for students with learning disabilities or Attention Deficit Hyperactivity Disorder, and these students are considered for admission on the same basis as other applicants. The minimum 50 percent of admitted students have a GPA between 3.5 and 4.0. Penn State adopted a test optional policy for 2021. Submitted test scores have a mid 50% range for ACT between 26 and 30 or SAT between 1750 and 1990. Course requirements include 4 years English, 3 years math, 3 years science, 2 years foreign language, and 3 years social studies. If the applicant's high school grades and test scores are low, students may submit a letter explaining why their ability to succeed in college is higher than indicated by their academic records. The Admissions Office will consider this information as it is voluntarily provided. Once admitted, students with disabilities are encouraged to submit documentation of their learning disability to receive support services. Students may seek admission as a provisional or nondegree student if they do not meet criteria required for admission as a degree candidate. Any student may enroll as a nondegree student.

Additional Information

Students with LD are encouraged to participate in the Buddy Program; incoming students are matched with a senior buddy who is a current student with a disability and is available to share experiences with a junior buddy. Other services include providing audiotaped textbooks, arranging course substitutions with academic departments (when essential requirements are not involved), providing test accommodations, and providing individual counseling. Assistance with note-taking is offered through the ODS. Services are offered in a mainstream setting. The Learning Assistance Center operates a Math Center, Tutoring Center, Writing Center, and Computer Learning Center. Students may receive academic help either individually

ADMISSIONS INFO FOR STUDENTS WITH LEARNING DIFFERENCES

Phone: 814-863-1807 • Fax: 814-863-3217 • Email: edaccessibility@psu.edu

SAT/ACT required: Yes (Test optional for 2021)
Interview required: No
Essay required: Yes
Additional application required: No
Documentation submitted to: SDS

Special Ed. HS course work accepted: No
Separate application required for Programs/Services: Yes
Documentation required for:
LD: Psychoeducational evaluation
ADHD: Psychoeducational evaluation
ASD: Psychoeducational evaluation

Penn State University Park

or in small groups for a number of different courses. One-on-one academic assistance is available through the Office of Disability Services. Graduate students provide individual assistance with study skills, time management, and compensatory learning strategies.

General Admissions

Very important factors include: academic GPA, standardized test scores. *Important factors include:* rigor of secondary school record. *Other factors include:* class rank, application essay, extracurricular activities, talent/ability, character/personal qualities, alumni/ae relation, geographical residence, state residency, racial/ethnic status, volunteer work, work experience. *Freshman admission requirements:* High school diploma is required and GED is accepted. *Academic units required:* 4 English, 3 math, 3 science, 2 foreign language, 3 social studies. *Academic units recommended:* 3 foreign language.

Accommodations or Services

Accommodations are decided upon an individual basis after a thorough review of appropriate, current documentation. The accommodations requests must be supported through the documentation provided and must be logically linked to the current impact of the condition on academic functioning.

Financial Aid

Students should submit: FAFSA; Institution's own financial aid form. Applicants will be notified of awards on a rolling basis beginning 1/15. *Need-based scholarships/grants offered:* College/university scholarship or grant aid from institutional funds; Federal Pell; Private scholarships; SEOG; State scholarships/grants; United Negro College Fund. *Loan aid offered:* Direct PLUS loans; Direct Subsidized Stafford Loans; Direct Unsubsidized Stafford Loans. Federal Work-Study Program available. Institutional employment available.

Campus Life

Activities: Campus Ministries; Choral groups; Concert band; Dance; Drama/theater; International Student Organization; Jazz band; Literary magazine; Marching band; Model UN; Music ensembles; Musical theater; Opera; Pep band; Radio station; Student government; Student newspaper; Student-run film society; Symphony orchestra; Television station; Yearbook. **Organizations:** 1004 registered organizations, 36 honor societies, 57 religious organizations, 44 fraternities, 47 sororities. **Athletics (Intercollegiate):** *Men:* baseball, basketball, cheerleading, cross-country, diving, fencing, football, golf, gymnastics, lacrosse, soccer, swimming, tennis, track/field (outdoor), track/field (indoor), volleyball, wrestling. *Women:* basketball, cheerleading, cross-country, diving, fencing, field hockey, golf, gymnastics, lacrosse, soccer, softball, swimming, tennis, track/field (outdoor), track/field (indoor), volleyball.

ACCOMMODATIONS

Allowed in exams:	
Calculators	Yes
Dictionary	No
Computer	Yes
Spell-checker	Yes
Extended test time	Yes
Scribe	Yes
Proctors	Yes
Oral exams	Yes
Note-takers	Yes
Support services for students with:	
LD	Yes
ADHD	Yes
ASD	Yes
Distraction-reduced environment	Yes
Recording of lecture allowed	Yes
Reading technology	Yes
Audio books	No
Other assistive technology	Yes
Priority registration	Yes
Added costs of services:	
For LD	No
For ADHD	No
For ASD	No
LD specialists	No
ADHD & ASD coaching	No
ASD specialists	No
Professional tutors	No
Peer tutors	Yes
Max. hours/week for services	Varies
How professors are notified of student approved accommodations	Student

COLLEGE GRADUATION REQUIREMENTS

Course waivers allowed	No
Course substitutions allowed	Yes
In what courses: Varies	

Saint Joseph's University (PA)

5600 City Avenue, Philadelphia, PA 19131 • Admissions: 888-BE-A-HAWK • Fax: 610-660-1314 **Support: CS**

CAMPUS

Type of school	Private (nonprofit)
Environment	Metropolis

STUDENTS

Undergrad enrollment	4,678
% male/female	46/54
% from out of state	54
% frosh live on campus	96

FINANCIAL FACTS

Annual tuition	$47,740
Room and board	$14,840
Required fees	$200

GENERAL ADMISSIONS INFO

Application fee	$50
Regular application deadline	2/1
Nonfall registration	Yes

Admission may be deferred.

Range SAT EBRW	570–650
Range SAT Math	550–650
Range ACT Composite	23–29

ACADEMICS

Student/faculty ratio	10:1
% students returning for sophomore year	88

Most classes have 10–19 students.

Programs/Services for Students with Learning Differences

The Office of Student Disability Services (SDS) coordinates support services and determines reasonable academic adjustments based on demonstrated needs of students as supported by documentation from medical providers or current psychoeducational testing. The Success Center offers a variety of programs and services to meet the academic needs of the undergraduate and graduate student body. The Office of Learning Resources (OLR) runs the College Transition Coaching program to assist students in navigating the transition from high school to college.

Admissions

The admission process is designed to get to know the applicant as a whole person. The application is reviewed on the basis of academic and personal accomplishments, with primary consideration given to the high school record and strong academic performance in college preparatory courses. The university will also consider the personal essay, letter of academic recommendation, and extracurricular involvement. Submission of standardized test scores is optional. Students may still be reviewed as a test-optional applicant for admission to SJU only. Interviews are open to high school seniors to meet one-on-one with a representative from admissions. However, interviews are not required and those who cannot interview are not at a disadvantage.

Additional Information

Peer tutoring is offered in multiple subjects and there is supplemental instruction session in 6 subjects. They also help to organize study groups. There are appointments available for strategy development in approaching academic classes. There are note takers available, books in alternative formats, and exams in alternative formats. There is a learning specialist who sees students one-on-one to help improve time management, notetaking, and more.

ADMISSIONS INFO FOR STUDENTS WITH LEARNING DIFFERENCES

Phone: 610-660-1774 • Fax: 610-660-3053 • Email: cmecke@sju.edu

SAT/ACT required: No
Interview required: No
Essay required: No
Additional application required: No
Documentation submitted to: SDS

Special Ed. HS course work accepted: No
Separate application required for Programs/Services: No
Documentation required for:
LD: Psychoeducational evaluation
ADHD: Psychoeducational evaluation
ASD: Psychoeducational evaluation

Saint Joseph's University (PA)

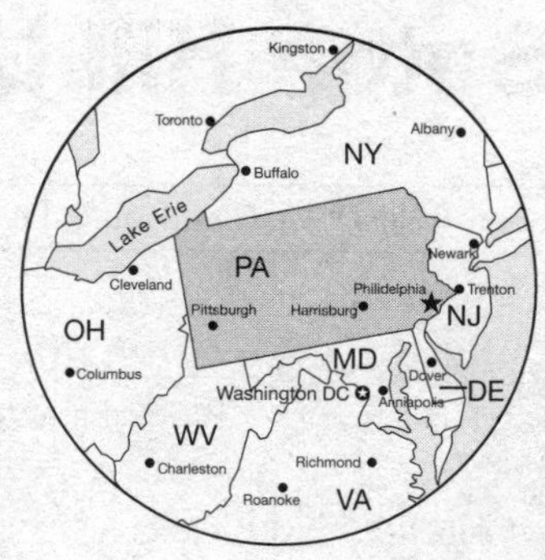

Pennsylvania

General Admissions

Very important factors include: rigor of secondary school record, class rank, academic GPA. *Important factors include:* application essay, standardized test scores, recommendation(s). *Other factors include:* interview, extracurricular activities, talent/ability, character/personal qualities, first generation, alumni/ae relation, geographical residence, racial/ethnic status, volunteer work, work experience, level of applicant's interest. *Freshman admission requirements:* High school diploma is required and GED is accepted. *Academic units required:* 4 English, 3 math, 3 science, 2 foreign language, 3 social studies, 5 academic electives.

Accommodations or Services

Accommodations are decided upon an individual basis after a thorough review of appropriate, current documentation. The accommodations requests must be supported through the documentation provided and must be logically linked to the current impact of the condition on academic functioning.

Financial Aid

Students should submit: FAFSA. *Need-based scholarships/grants offered:* College/university scholarship or grant aid from institutional funds; Federal Pell; Private scholarships; SEOG; State scholarships/grants. *Loan aid offered:* Direct PLUS loans; Direct Subsidized Stafford Loans; Direct Unsubsidized Stafford Loans. Federal Work-Study Program available. Institutional employment available.

Campus Life

Activities: Campus Ministries; Choral groups; Dance; Drama/theater; International Student Organization; Jazz band; Literary magazine; Music ensembles; Musical theater; Pep band; Radio station; Student government; Student newspaper; Student-run film society; Yearbook. **Organizations:** 90 registered organizations, 23 honor societies, 4 fraternities, 5 sororities. **Athletics (Intercollegiate):** *Men:* baseball, basketball, crew/rowing, cross-country, golf, lacrosse, soccer, tennis, track/field (outdoor), track/field (indoor). *Women:* basketball, crew/rowing, cross-country, field hockey, lacrosse, soccer, softball, tennis, track/field (outdoor), track/field (indoor).

ACCOMMODATIONS

Allowed in exams:	
Calculators	Yes
Dictionary	Yes
Computer	Yes
Spell-checker	Yes
Extended test time	Yes
Scribe	Yes
Proctors	Yes
Oral exams	Yes
Note-takers	Yes
Support services for students with:	
LD	Yes
ADHD	Yes
ASD	Yes
Distraction-reduced environment	Yes
Recording of lecture alowed	Yes
Reading technology	Yes
Audio books	Yes
Other assistive technology	Yes
Priority registration	Yes
Added costs of services:	
For LD	No
For ADHD	No
For ASD	No
LD specialists	Yes
ADHD & ASD coaching	Yes
ASD specialists	No
Professional tutors	No
Peer tutors	Yes
Max. hours/week for services	Varies
How professors are notified of student approved accommodations	Director

COLLEGE GRADUATION REQUIREMENTS

Course waivers allowed: Yes

In what courses: Foreign language, case-by-case basis

Course substitutions allowed: Yes

In what courses: Foreign language, case-by-case basis

Seton Hill University

1 Seton Hill Drive, Greensburg, PA 15601 • Admissions: 724-838-4255 • Fax: 724-830-1294 **Support: S**

CAMPUS

Type of school	Private (nonprofit)
Environment	Town

STUDENTS

Undergrad enrollment	1,728
% male/female	34/66
% from out of state	22
% frosh live on campus	80

FINANCIAL FACTS

Annual tuition	$37,396
Room and board	$12,300
Required fees	$550

GENERAL ADMISSIONS INFO

Application fee	$0
Regular application deadline	Rolling
Nonfall registration	Yes

Admission may be deferred.

ACADEMICS

Student/faculty ratio	14:1
% students returning for sophomore year	78

Most classes have 10–19 students.

Programs/Services for Students with Learning Differences

The Office of Disability Support Services (ODSS) offers academic support services to students with disabilities. The office works closely with students to assess individual needs and prepare a plan of accommodation, which may include note-takers, preferential seating, readers, extended time for testing, distraction-reduced testing environments, and access to special adaptive equipment and technology.

Admissions

Students with documented learning disabilities may request course substitutions for deficiencies in entrance courses based on the LD. Pre-admission interviews are not required but are recommended. The admissions office can also determine if an applicant might be appropriate to be admitted through the C.A.P.S Program. Within the C.A.P.S. Program there are two academic support programs, the pre-freshman year Opportunity Program, and Student Support Services. The Admissions Office primarily determines acceptance into these two programs. Students who feel they would benefit from the C.A.P.S. Program services may also apply by submitting an application that can be obtained through the C.A.P.S. Program Office. The university is test optional and does not require the ACT or SAT for admission.

Additional Information

The C.A.P.S. Program provides an academic coach who will meet with the student regularly through the first semester. After the first semester, the student remains a member of C.A.P.S. Program during their time at the university and can take advantage of the program's resources when they need it. The Opportunity Program is a week-long learning experience that prepares students for the university's demanding academic culture. It is designed to provide students with an academic experience that will ease their transition from high school to college. The program provides services that assist the students in maximizing and enhancing academic potential. Accommodations once in the college may include, but are not limited to, preferential seating, note-taking services, tape-recorded lectures, extended time for projects, extended time for quizzes and tests, testing in distraction-reduced environments, alternative testing formats, tutoring, counseling, course substitutions, use of assisted technologies (e.g., spellcheckers), computer based programs, and scribe services. Skills classes for college credit are offered in time management techniques, note-taking strategies, test-taking strategies, and text reading.

ADMISSIONS INFO FOR STUDENTS WITH LEARNING DIFFERENCES

Phone: 724-838-4295 • Fax: 724-830-4233 • Email: bassi@setonhill.edu

SAT/ACT required: No
Interview required: No
Essay required: No
Additional application required: No
Documentation submitted to: ODSS

Special Ed. HS course work accepted: No
Separate application required for Programs/Services: No
Documentation required for:
LD: Psychoeducational evaluation
ADHD: Psychoeducational evaluation
ASD: Psychoeducational evaluation

Seton Hill University

Pennsylvania

General Admissions

Very important factors include: rigor of secondary school record, academic GPA. *Important factors include:* class rank, standardized test scores, extracurricular activities, talent/ability, character/personal qualities. *Other factors include:* application essay, recommendation(s), interview, volunteer work, work experience. *Freshman admission requirements:* High school diploma is required and GED is accepted. *Academic units required:* 4 English, 2 math, 1 science, 1 science lab, 3 social studies, 4 academic electives. *Academic units recommended:* 2 foreign language.

Accommodations or Services

Accommodations are decided upon an individual basis after a thorough review of appropriate, current documentation. The accommodations requests must be supported through the documentation provided and must be logically linked to the current impact of the condition on academic functioning.

Financial Aid

Students should submit: FAFSA. *Need-based scholarships/grants offered:* College/university scholarship or grant aid from institutional funds; Federal Pell; Private scholarships; SEOG; State scholarships/grants. *Loan aid offered:* Direct PLUS loans; Direct Subsidized Stafford Loans; Direct Unsubsidized Stafford Loans. Federal Work-Study Program available. Institutional employment available.

Campus Life

Activities: Campus Ministries; Choral groups; Concert band; Dance; Drama/theater; International Student Organization; Jazz band; Literary magazine; Marching band; Model UN; Music ensembles; Musical theater; Pep band; Student government; Student newspaper; Symphony orchestra. **Organizations:** 40 registered organizations, 4 honor societies, 6 religious organizations. **Athletics (Intercollegiate):** *Men:* baseball, basketball, cross-country, football, lacrosse, soccer, track/field (outdoor), track/field (indoor), wrestling. *Women:* basketball, cross-country, equestrian sports, field hockey, golf, lacrosse, soccer, softball, tennis, track/field (outdoor), track/field (indoor), volleyball.

ACCOMMODATIONS

Allowed in exams:	
Calculators	Yes
Dictionary	Yes
Computer	Yes
Spell-checker	Yes
Extended test time	Yes
Scribe	Yes
Proctors	Yes
Oral exams	Yes
Note-takers	Yes
Support services for students with:	
LD	Yes
ADHD	Yes
ASD	Yes
Distraction-reduced environment	Yes
Recording of lecture alowed	Yes
Reading technology	Yes
Audio books	Yes
Other assistive technology	Yes
Priority registration	Yes
Added costs of services:	
For LD	No
For ADHD	No
For ASD	No
LD specialists	No
ADHD & ASD coaching	No
ASD specialists	No
Professional tutors	No
Peer tutors	Yes
Max. hours/week for services	Unlimited
How professors are notified of student approved accommodations	Student

COLLEGE GRADUATION REQUIREMENTS

Course waivers allowed: Yes
In what courses: All appropriate requests are reviewed and considered.

Course substitutions allowed: Yes
In what courses: All appropriate requests are reviewed and considered.

Temple University

1801 North Broad Street, Conwell Hall 103 (041-09), Philadelphia, PA 19122 • Admissions: 215-204-7200 • Fax: 215-204-5694 **Support: CS**

CAMPUS

Type of school	Public
Environment	Metropolis

STUDENTS

Undergrad enrollment	28,272
% male/female	46/54
% from out of state	21
% frosh live on campus	79

FINANCIAL FACTS

Annual in-state tuition	$18,859
Annual out-of-state tuition	$33,159
Room and board	$10,817
Required fees	$890

GENERAL ADMISSIONS INFO

Application fee	$55
Regular application deadline	2/1
Nonfall registration	Yes

Admission may be deferred.

Range SAT EBRW	570–660
Range SAT Math	550–660
Range ACT Composite	24–30

ACADEMICS

Student/faculty ratio	13:1
% students returning for sophomore year	89

Most classes have 10–19 students.

Programs/Services for Students with Learning Differences

Disability Resources and Services is a department within the Division of Student Affairs (DRS) that helps students arrange academic adjustments and accommodations. The Division of Student Affairs provides a variety of resources and services. In order to access these services, students should submit the most current and comprehensive documentation available. Staff will meet with students who do not have documentation. Students can access academic accommodations, housing access, orientation and placement assessment accommodations, communication access, assistive technology and alternate format materials, scholarships, career development, peer mentoring, and social skills development.

Admissions

When applying for admission to Temple, students with disabilities should follow the standard application process. The presence of a disability is not considered in admissions. Temple University is test optional. A policy called Temple Option provides a path for talented students whose potential for academic success is not accurately captured by standardized test scores. Students who choose the Temple Option will submit self-reflective, short-answers to a few specially designed, open-ended questions instead of their SAT or ACT scores.

Additional Information

Individualized learning support is available through the Learning Center in partnership with Disability Resources and Services for writing and STEM tutoring and academic coaching. Several student organizations and peer programs support student leadership development, including the Social Xchanges recreation group for students with ASD, SHOUT peer leadership, Eye to Eye (mentoring elementary school students with LD/ADHD), and Delta Alpha Pi honor society for students with disabilities.

ADMISSIONS INFO FOR STUDENTS WITH LEARNING DIFFERENCES

Phone: 215-204-1280 • Fax: 215-204-6794 • Email: drs@temple.edu

SAT/ACT required: No
Interview required: No
Essay required: Yes
Additional application required: No
Documentation submitted to: DRS
Special Ed. HS course work accepted: No
Separate application required for Programs/Services: No
Documentation required for:
LD: Psychoeducational evaluation
ADHD: Psychoeducational evaluation
ASD: Psychoeducational evaluation

Temple University

General Admissions

Very important factors include: rigor of secondary school record, academic GPA. *Other factors include:* class rank, application essay, standardized test scores, recommendation(s), extracurricular activities, talent/ability, character/personal qualities, first generation, alumni/ae relation, geographical residence, state residency, volunteer work, work experience. *Freshman admission requirements:* High school diploma is required and GED is accepted. *Academic units required:* 4 English, 3 math, 2 science, 1 science lab, 2 foreign language, 2 social studies, 1 history, 1 academic elective, 1 visual/performing arts. *Academic units recommended:* 4 English, 4 math, 3 science, 2 science labs, 2 foreign language, 2 social studies, 1 history, 3 academic electives, 1 visual/performing arts.

Accommodations or Services

Accommodations are decided upon an individual basis after a thorough review of appropriate, current documentation. The accommodations requests must be supported through the documentation provided and must be logically linked to the current impact of the condition on academic functioning.

Financial Aid

Students should submit: CSS/Financial Aid PROFILE; FAFSA. Applicants will be notified of awards on or about 4/1. *Need-based scholarships/grants offered:* College/university scholarship or grant aid from institutional funds; Federal Nursing Scholarships; Federal Pell; Private scholarships; SEOG; State scholarships/grants; United Negro College Fund. *Loan aid offered:* Direct PLUS loans; Direct Subsidized Stafford Loans; Direct Unsubsidized Stafford Loans. Federal Work-Study Program available. Institutional employment available.

Campus Life

Activities: Campus Ministries; Choral groups; Concert band; Dance; Drama/theater; International Student Organization; Jazz band; Literary magazine; Marching band; Model UN; Music ensembles; Musical theater; Opera; Pep band; Radio station; Student government; Student newspaper; Student-run film society; Symphony orchestra; Television station; Yearbook. **Organizations:** 361 registered organizations, 19 honor societies, 34 religious organizations, 16 fraternities, 15 sororities. **Athletics (Intercollegiate):** *Men:* baseball, basketball, cheerleading, crew/rowing, cross-country, football, golf, gymnastics, soccer, table tennis, tennis, track/field (outdoor), track/field (indoor). *Women:* basketball, cheerleading, crew/rowing, cross-country, fencing, field hockey, gymnastics, lacrosse, soccer, softball, table tennis, tennis, track/field (outdoor), track/field (indoor), volleyball.

ACCOMMODATIONS

Allowed in exams:	
Calculators	Yes
Dictionary	Yes
Computer	Yes
Spell-checker	Yes
Extended test time	Yes
Scribe	Yes
Proctors	Yes
Oral exams	Yes
Note-takers	Yes
Support services for students with:	
LD	Yes
ADHD	Yes
ASD	Yes
Distraction-reduced environment	Yes
Recording of lecture alowed	Yes
Reading technology	Yes
Audio books	Yes
Other assistive technology	Yes
Priority registration	Yes
Added costs of services:	
For LD	No
For ADHD	No
For ASD	No
LD specialists	Yes
ADHD & ASD coaching	Yes
ASD specialists	Yes
Professional tutors	No
Peer tutors	Yes
Max. hours/week for services	Varies
How professors are notified of student approved accommodations	Student

COLLEGE GRADUATION REQUIREMENTS

Course waivers allowed	Yes
In what courses: Math, foreign language, other courses as appropriate	
Course substitutions allowed	Yes
In what courses: Math, foreign language, other courses as appropriate	

University of Pittsburgh—Pittsburgh Campus

4227 Fifth Avenue, Pittsburgh, PA 15260 • Admissions: 412-624-7488 • Fax: 412-648-8815 **Support: CS**

CAMPUS

Type of school	Public
Environment	City

STUDENTS

Undergrad enrollment	19,017
% male/female	47/53
% from out of state	31
% frosh live on campus	96

FINANCIAL FACTS

Annual in-state tuition	$18,628
Annual out-of-state tuition	$32,656
Room and board	$11,050
Required fees	$1,090

GENERAL ADMISSIONS INFO

Application fee	$55
Regular application deadline	Rolling
Nonfall registration	Yes

Admission may be deferred.

Range SAT EBRW	630–700
Range SAT Math	630–740
Range ACT Composite	28–33

ACADEMICS

Student/faculty ratio	15:1
% students returning for sophomore year	93

Most classes have 10–19 students.

Programs/Services for Students with Learning Differences

At the University of Pittsburgh students are encouraged to self-disclose their disability with the Disability Resources and Services (DRS). Students with disabilities will be integrated as completely as possible into the University experience. Disability Resources and Services (DRS) partners with the student to develop a plan for obtaining accommodations. The student must complete a Student Application, attach appropriate documentation, and interview with a Disability Specialist who will review the application and documentation.

Admissions

Students with learning disabilities must meet the same admission criteria established for all applicants. U Pitt recommends that students submit any supplemental information that they feel will help the committee get to know them better. The committee is looking for students who are well-rounded both in and out of the classroom. The Personal Essay is optional. However, applicants should definitely submit a personal essay if they want special consideration in the review process due to extenuating circumstances affecting a term of lower grades. Recommendations are encouraged as these can help the admission office get to know the student better. Applicants will need to identify which of the four campuses they want to attend. The university adopted a test optional policy for 2021.

Additional Information

It is the student's responsibility to identify themselves to DRS and the request accommodations. Students are required to submit documentation of a disability as per the established documentation guidelines of the university. DRS services available may include exam accommodations, use of calculators, computer or spell checker in exams, scribes, proctors, controlled environments, alternative format, instructional strategy assistance, and assistive technology. There are three disability specialists on staff.

ADMISSIONS INFO FOR STUDENTS WITH LEARNING DIFFERENCES

Phone: 412-648-7890 • Fax: 412-624-3346 • Email: lculley@pitt.edu

SAT/ACT required: Yes (Test optional for 2021)
Interview required: No
Essay required: Yes
Additional application required: No
Documentation submitted to: Disability Resources and Services

Special Ed. HS course work accepted: No
Separate application required for Programs/Services: No
Documentation required for:
LD: Psychoeducational evaluation
ADHD: Psychoeducational evaluation
ASD: Psychoeducational evaluation

University of Pittsburgh—Pittsburgh Campus

Pennsylvania

General Admissions

Very important factors include: rigor of secondary school record, academic GPA, standardized test scores. *Important factors include:* application essay, *Other factors include:* class rank, recommendation(s), interview, extracurricular activities, talent/ability, character/personal qualities, first generation, alumni/ae relation, geographical residence, state residency, racial/ethnic status, volunteer work, work experience, level of applicant's interest. *Freshman admission requirements:* High school diploma is required and GED is not accepted. *Academic units required:* 4 English, 3 math, 3 science, 3 science labs, 2 foreign language, 2 social studies, 3 academic electives. *Academic units recommended:* 4 English, 4 math, 4 science, 4 science labs, 3 foreign language, 3 social studies, 5 academic electives.

Accommodations or Services

Accommodations are decided upon an individual basis after a thorough review of appropriate, current documentation. The accommodations requests must be supported through the documentation provided and must be logically linked to the current impact of the condition on academic functioning.

Financial Aid

Students should submit: FAFSA. *Need-based scholarships/grants offered:* College/university scholarship or grant aid from institutional funds; Federal Nursing Scholarships; Federal Pell; Private scholarships; SEOG; State scholarships/grants. *Loan aid offered:* Direct PLUS loans; Direct Subsidized Stafford Loans; Direct Unsubsidized Stafford Loans. Federal Work-Study Program available. Institutional employment available.

Campus Life

Activities: Campus Ministries; Choral groups; Concert band; Dance; Drama/theater; International Student Organization; Jazz band; Literary magazine; Marching band; Model UN; Music ensembles; Musical theater; Opera; Pep band; Radio station; Student government; Student newspaper; Student-run film society; Symphony orchestra; Television station. **Organizations:** 649 registered organizations, 30 honor societies, 24 fraternities, 12 sororities. **Athletics (Intercollegiate):** *Men:* baseball, basketball, cross-country, diving, football, soccer, swimming, track/field (outdoor), wrestling. *Women:* basketball, cross-country, diving, gymnastics, soccer, softball, swimming, tennis, track/field (outdoor), volleyball.

ACCOMMODATIONS

Allowed in exams:	
Calculators	Yes
Dictionary	Yes
Computer	Yes
Spell-checker	Yes
Extended test time	Yes
Scribe	Yes
Proctors	Yes
Oral exams	No
Note-takers	Yes
Support services for students with:	
LD	Yes
ADHD	Yes
ASD	Yes
Distraction-reduced environment	Yes
Recording of lecture allowed	Yes
Reading technology	Yes
Audio books	Yes
Other assistive technology	Yes
Priority registration	Yes
Added costs of services:	
For LD	No
For ADHD	No
For ASD	No
LD specialists	Yes
ADHD & ASD coaching	No
ASD specialists	No
Professional tutors	No
Peer tutors	Yes
Max. hours/week for services	Varies
How professors are notified of student approved accommodations	Student and Director

COLLEGE GRADUATION REQUIREMENTS

Course waivers allowed	No
Course substitutions allowed	Yes
In what courses: Case by case basis	

Widener University

1 University Place, Chester, PA 19013 • Admissions: 610-499-4126 • Fax: 610-499-4676 **Support: CS**

CAMPUS

Type of school	Private (nonprofit)
Environment	Town

STUDENTS

Undergrad enrollment	3,223
% male/female	43/57
% from out of state	41
% frosh live on campus	84

FINANCIAL FACTS

Annual tuition	$47,770
Room and board	$14,750
Required fees	$970

GENERAL ADMISSIONS INFO

Application fee	$0
Regular application deadline	Rolling
Nonfall registration	Yes

Admission may be deferred.

Range SAT EBRW	520–600
Range SAT Math	520–610
Range ACT Composite	20–25

ACADEMICS

Student/faculty ratio	13:1
% students returning for sophomore year	82

Most classes have 10–19 students.

Programs/Services for Students with Learning Differences

Student Accessibility Services (SAS) provides services to students with documented learning differences. The office serves as a campus advocate to ensure equal access to academic programs and campus life. Students wishing to use SAS must submit documentation that describes the nature of the learning disability including relevant evaluations and assessments. Each student has the option of meeting once or twice a week with a learning specialist in our academic coaching program. Typically, academic coaching sessions focus on time management, study skills, social and emotional adjustment, and academic planning. Disabilities Services serves as a campus advocate for the needs of students with LD by making sure that accommodations are provided when appropriate. Participation in our services is included in the basic tuition charge.

Admissions

Students with learning disabilities submit the same general application as all applicants. Admission decisions are made by the Office of Admissions. Students should submit their application, an essay, and recommendations. The university is test optional and ACT or SAT is not required for admission. There are no specific course requirements for admissions. High school GPA range is 2.0–4.0.

Additional Information

Academic Support & Advising pairs students with professors who serve as their advisor and mentor. The advisor offers guidance on which classes to take and help in finding an internship. Students can sign up for academic coaching to meet with counselors who can help them understand and accept their disabilities, individualize learning strategies, teach self-advocacy, and link the students with the other Academic Support Services available at Widener. This office assures that professors understand which accommodations are needed. The Writing Center provides assistance with writing assignments and is staffed by professors. The Math Center offers individualized and group tutoring and is staffed by professors and experienced tutors. In addition, the Tutoring Office provides individual and group tutoring for the majority of undergraduate Widener courses.

ADMISSIONS INFO FOR STUDENTS WITH LEARNING DIFFERENCES

Phone: 610-499-1266 • Fax: 610-499-1192 • Email: rross@widener.edu

SAT/ACT required: Yes (Test optional for 2021)
Interview required: No
Essay required: Yes
Additional application required: Yes
Documentation submitted to: Yes

Special Ed. HS course work accepted: Yes
Separate application required for Programs/Services: Yes
Documentation required for:
LD: Full psychoeducational evaluation
ADHD: Report from professional evaluation
ASD: Evaluation from professional evaluation

Widener University

Pennsylvania

General Admissions

Very important factors include: rigor of secondary school record, class rank, academic GPA, standardized test scores. *Other factors include:* application essay, recommendation(s), interview, extracurricular activities, talent/ability, character/personal qualities, alumni/ae relation, volunteer work, level of applicant's interest. *Freshman admission requirements:* High school diploma is required and GED is accepted. *Academic units required:* 4 English, 3 math, 3 science, 2 foreign language, 3 social studies, 3 academic electives. *Academic units recommended:* 4 English, 4 math, 4 science, 2 science labs, 2 foreign language, 4 social studies, 3 academic electives.

Accommodations or Services

Accommodations are decided upon an individual basis after a thorough review of appropriate, current documentation. The accommodations requests must be supported through the documentation provided and must be logically linked to the current impact of the condition on academic functioning.

Financial Aid

Students should submit: FAFSA. *Need-based scholarships/grants offered:* College/university scholarship or grant aid from institutional funds; Federal Pell; Private scholarships; SEOG; State scholarships/grants. *Loan aid offered:* Direct PLUS loans; Direct Subsidized Stafford Loans; Direct Unsubsidized Stafford Loans. Federal Work-Study Program available. Institutional employment available.

Campus Life

Activities: Campus Ministries; Choral groups; Concert band; Dance; Drama/theater; International Student Organization; Jazz band; Literary magazine; Marching band; Music ensembles; Pep band; Radio station; Student government; Student-run film society; Television station. **Organizations:** 80 registered organizations, 29 honor societies, 3 religious organizations, 5 fraternities, 6 sororities. **Athletics (Intercollegiate):** *Men:* baseball, basketball, cross-country, football, golf, lacrosse, soccer, swimming, tennis, track/field (outdoor), track/field (indoor). *Women:* basketball, cheerleading, cross-country, field hockey, lacrosse, soccer, softball, swimming, tennis, track/field (outdoor), track/field (indoor), volleyball.

ACCOMMODATIONS

Allowed in exams:	
Calculators	Yes
Dictionary	Yes
Computer	Yes
Spell-checker	Yes
Extended test time	Yes
Scribe	Yes
Proctors	Yes
Oral exams	Yes
Note-takers	Yes
Support services for students with:	
LD	Yes
ADHD	Yes
ASD	Yes
Distraction-reduced environment	Yes
Recording of lecture alowed	Yes
Reading technology	Yes
Audio books	No
Other assistive technology	Yes
Priority registration	Yes
Added costs of services:	
For LD	No
For ADHD	No
For ASD	No
LD specialists	Yes
ADHD & ASD coaching	No
ASD specialists	No
Professional tutors	Yes
Peer tutors	Yes
Max. hours/week for services	Unlimited
How professors are notified of student approved accommodations	Student

COLLEGE GRADUATION REQUIREMENTS

Course waivers allowed	No
Course substitutions allowed	No

Brown University

Brown University, Office of College Admission, Box 1876 Providence, RI 02912 • Admissions: 401-863-2378 • Fax: 401-863-9300 **Support: CS**

CAMPUS

Type of school	Private (nonprofit)
Environment	City

STUDENTS

Undergrad enrollment	6,834
% male/female	48/52
% from out of state	95
% frosh live on campus	100

FINANCIAL FACTS

Annual tuition	$59,254
Room and board	$15,908
Required fees	$1,442

GENERAL ADMISSIONS INFO

Application fee	$75
Regular application deadline	1/1
Nonfall registration	No

Admission may be deferred.

Range SAT EBRW	700–770
Range SAT Math	740–800
Range ACT Composite	33–35

ACADEMICS

Student/faculty ratio	6:1
% students returning for sophomore year	98

Most classes have 10–19 students.

Programs/Services for Students with Learning Differences

The Student and Employee Accessibility Services (SEAS) at Brown has a long history of providing accommodations and services to students with learning differences. The decision to self-identify and ask for accommodations is decided by the student. There is a registration process with SEAS that involves providing documentation and meeting with the office to discuss appropriate accommodations. Documentation guidelines are available on the SEAS website as well as information about services and accommodations: See SEAS website! https://www.brown.edu/campus-life/support/accessibility-services/

Admissions

Brown University is very selective in the admission process. Students with learning disabilities must meet the same admission criteria. Brown is test optional and applicants do not have to submit the ACT or SAT in the 2021 admission process. Applicants typically have pursued the most rigorous curriculum offered in their high school. Accomplished musicians or visual artist may include additional supplements with their application.

Additional Information

Brown's commitment to students with disabilities is based on awareness of what students require for success and seeks to foster an environment in which that success may be achieved. Group tutoring is offered for introductory courses in science, math, economics, and statistics. Students are assigned to small groups that meet weekly to review important or difficult topics covered in class that week. Tutors have either taken the course or proven competency, and have been trained by the Academic Support Staff. Students can receive assistance with quick questions in introductory and intermediate biology, chemistry, and physics. Students with disabilities who believe they may need accommodations should self-identify by registering with SEAS. SEAS staff will conduct a review and analysis prior to making a recommendation regarding the provision of reasonable accommodations. Requests for accommodations are evaluated individually, based on documentation, and completion of the registration process.

ADMISSIONS INFO FOR STUDENTS WITH LEARNING DIFFERENCES

Phone: 401-863-9588 • Fax: 401-863-1444 • Email: SEAS@brown.edu

SAT/ACT required: Yes (Test optional for 2021)
Interview required: Yes
Essay required: Yes
Additional application required: No
Documentation submitted to: SEAS

Special Ed. HS course work accepted: No
Separate application required for Programs/Services: No
Documentation required for:
LD: Psychoeducational evaluation
ADHD: Psychoeducational evaluation
ASD: Psychoeducational evaluation

Brown University

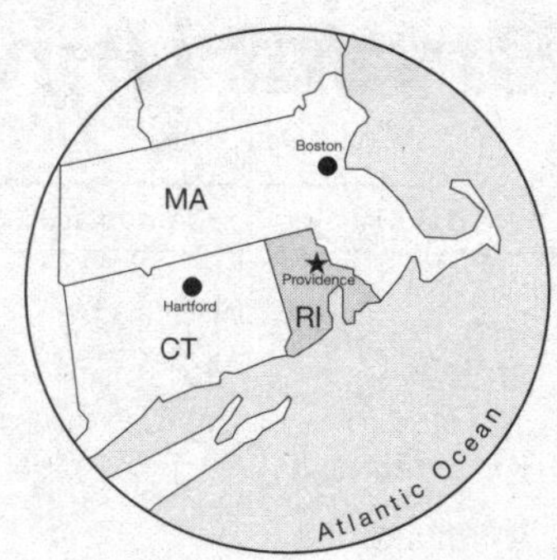

General Admissions

Very important factors include: rigor of secondary school record, class rank, academic GPA, application essay, standardized test scores, recommendation(s), talent/ability, character/personal qualities. *Important factors include:* extracurricular activities. *Other factors include:* interview, first generation, alumni/ae relation, geographical residence, state residency, racial/ethnic status, volunteer work, work experience. *Freshman admission requirements:* High school diploma is required and GED is accepted. *Academic units required:* 4 English, 3 math, 3 science, 2 science labs, 3 foreign language, 2 history, 1 academic elective. *Academic units recommended:* 4 English, 4 math, 4 science, 3 science labs, 4 foreign language, 1 social studies, 2 history, 1 academic elective, 1 visual/performing arts.

Accommodations or Services

Accommodations are decided upon an individual basis after a thorough review of appropriate, current documentation. The accommodations requests must be supported through the documentation provided and must be logically linked to the current impact of the condition on academic functioning.

Financial Aid

Students should submit: CSS/Financial Aid PROFILE; FAFSA; Noncustodial PROFILE. Applicants will be notified of awards on a rolling basis beginning 4/15. *Need-based scholarships/grants offered:* College/university scholarship or grant aid from institutional funds; Federal Pell; Private scholarships; SEOG; State scholarships/grants. *Loan aid offered:* Direct PLUS loans; Direct Subsidized Stafford Loans; Direct Unsubsidized Stafford Loans. Federal Work-Study Program available. Institutional employment available.

Campus Life

Activities: Campus Ministries; Choral groups; Concert band; Dance; Drama/theater; International Student Organization; Jazz band; Literary magazine; Marching band; Model UN; Music ensembles; Musical theater; Opera; Pep band; Radio station; Student government; Student newspaper; Student-run film society; Symphony orchestra; Television station; Yearbook. **Organizations:** 527 registered organizations, 3 honor societies, 25 religious organizations, 9 fraternities, 5 sororities. **Athletics (Intercollegiate):** *Men:* baseball, basketball, crew/rowing, cross-country, diving, fencing, football, golf, ice hockey, lacrosse, soccer, squash, swimming, tennis, track/field (outdoor), track/field (indoor), water polo, wrestling. *Women:* basketball, crew/rowing, cross-country, diving, equestrian sports, fencing, field hockey, golf, gymnastics, ice hockey, lacrosse, skiing (downhill/alpine), soccer, softball, squash, swimming, tennis, track/field (outdoor), track/field (indoor), volleyball, water polo.

ACCOMMODATIONS

Allowed in exams:	
Calculators	Yes
Dictionary	No
Computer	Yes
Spell-checker	Yes
Extended test time	Yes
Scribe	Yes
Proctors	Yes
Oral exams	Yes
Note-takers	Yes
Support services for students with:	
LD	Yes
ADHD	Yes
ASD	Yes
Distraction-reduced environment	Yes
Recording of lecture allowed	Yes
Reading technology	Yes
Audio books	Yes
Other assistive technology	Yes
Priority registration	No
Added costs of services:	
For ADHD	No
For ASD	No
For LD	No
LD specialists	No
ADHD & ASD coaching	Yes
ASD specialists	No
Professional tutors	No
Peer tutors	Yes
Max. hours/week for services	Varies
How professors are notified of student approved accommodations	Student

COLLEGE GRADUATION REQUIREMENTS

Course waivers allowed	Yes
In what courses: Varies	
Course substitutions allowed	Yes
In what courses: Varies	

Rhode Island

Bryant University

Office of Admission, 1150 Douglas Pike, Smithfield, RI 02917-1291 • Admissions: 401-232-6100 • Fax: 401-232-6731 **Support: CS**

CAMPUS

Type of school	Private (nonprofit)
Environment	Village

STUDENTS

Undergrad enrollment	3,259
% male/female	63/37
% from out of state	87
% frosh live on campus	94

FINANCIAL FACTS

Annual tuition	$45,966
Room and board	$16,204
Required fees	$897

GENERAL ADMISSIONS INFO

Application fee	$50
Regular application deadline	2/1
Nonfall registration	Yes

Admission may be deferred.

Range SAT EBRW	560–640
Range SAT Math	570–660
Range ACT Composite	25–29

ACADEMICS

Student/faculty ratio	13:1
% students returning for sophomore year	87

Most classes have 30–39 students.

Programs/Services for Students with Learning Differences

Bryant University offers services for students with learning disabilities. The Academic Center for Excellence (ACE) supports students with documentation of learning disability, and/or ADHD. The center provides study skills training to help students become self-reliant, independent, and confident learners. There is a peer tutoring program and study skills instruction by professional staff. Group sessions as a mode of instruction are encouraged and the staff engages in a partnership with students to help them achieve their goals. The learning specialist provides support for students who have submitted current (within 3 years) documentation and who also schedule an appointment with ACE at the start of each semester. Students are responsible for being proactive in reaching out to ACE for any academic needs that will facilitate success. In keeping with the philosophy of empowering Bryant students to achieve their goals of academic success, they also will receive assistance in learning how to access the comprehensive academic support services offered by the Academic Success Programs.

Admissions

Students are encouraged to self-disclose a learning challenge. All documentation should be sent to ACE. General admission criteria include an average GPA of 3.0. ACT/SAT are not required as Bryant is test optional. A minimum of 16 units with the following courses is recommended: 4 years of English; 4 years of college prep math, including a year beyond Algebra II; 2 years of history or social science; 2 years of lab sciences; 2 years of foreign language. Interviews are not required but are encouraged.

Additional Information

Students with documented learning differences need to submit documentation and request academic accommodations through Access Services in the Academic Center for Excellence. The Academic Success Programs are staffed by professionals in math and peer tutoring. The peer tutors are certified by the College Reading and Learning Association (CLRA) and are able to offer one-on-one appointments. The Learning Labs have specialists and peer tutors for math, economics, finance, and accounting assignment support. There is also a Student Support Network (SSN) for students if they experience difficulty in interpersonal peer relationships on campus. There is a training session available where students can have social skills support and meet new people through the groups focused on these needs. There is a separate online application for SSN.

ADMISSIONS INFO FOR STUDENTS WITH LEARNING DIFFERENCES

Phone: 401-232-6746 • Email: msaddlemire@bryant.edu

SAT/ACT required: No
Interview required: No
Essay required: Yes
Additional application required: Yes
Documentation submitted to: Academic Center for Excellence

Special Ed. HS course work accepted: No
Separate application required for Programs/Services: Yes
Documentation required for:
LD: Psychoeducational evaluation
ADHD: Psychoeducational evaluation
ASD: Psychoeducational evaluation

Bryant University

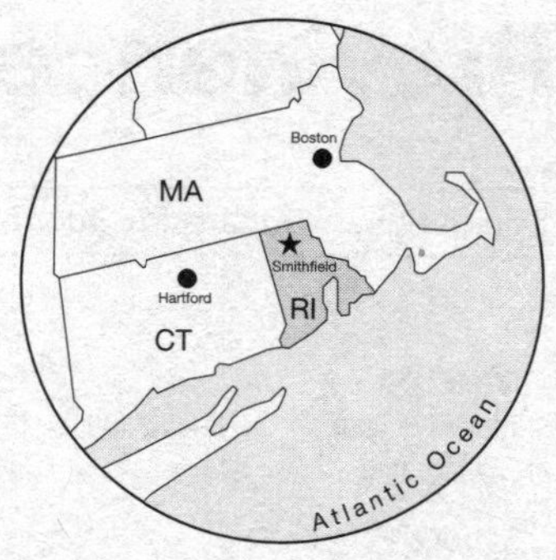

General Admissions

Very important factors include: rigor of secondary school record, academic GPA. *Important factors include:* class rank, application essay, standardized test scores, recommendation(s). *Other factors include:* interview, extracurricular activities, talent/ability, character/personal qualities, first generation, alumni/ae relation, geographical residence, state residency, racial/ethnic status, volunteer work, work experience, level of applicant's interest. *Freshman admission requirements:* High school diploma is required and GED is accepted. *Academic units required:* 4 English, 4 math, 2 science, 2 science labs, 2 foreign language, 2 history. *Academic units recommended:* 4 English, 4 math, 3 science, 2 science labs, 2 foreign language, 3 history.

Accommodations or Services

Accommodations are decided upon an individual basis after a thorough review of appropriate, current documentation. The accommodations requests must be supported through the documentation provided and must be logically linked to the current impact of the condition on academic functioning.

Financial Aid

Students should submit: FAFSA. *Need-based scholarships/grants offered:* College/university scholarship or grant aid from institutional funds; Federal Pell; Private scholarships; SEOG; State scholarships/grants. *Loan aid offered:* Direct PLUS loans; Direct Subsidized Stafford Loans; Direct Unsubsidized Stafford Loans. Federal Work-Study Program available. Institutional employment available.

Campus Life

Activities: Campus Ministries; Choral groups; Dance; Drama/theater; International Student Organization; Jazz band; Literary magazine; Music ensembles; Musical theater; Pep band; Radio station; Student government; Student newspaper; Television station; Yearbook. **Organizations:** 114 registered organizations, 14 honor societies, 6 religious organizations, 4 fraternities, 4 sororities. **Athletics (Intercollegiate):** *Men:* baseball, basketball, cross-country, football, golf, lacrosse, soccer, swimming, tennis, track/field (outdoor), track/field (indoor). *Women:* basketball, cross-country, field hockey, lacrosse, soccer, softball, swimming, tennis, track/field (outdoor), track/field (indoor), volleyball.

ACCOMMODATIONS

Allowed in exams:	
Calculators	Yes
Dictionary	No
Computer	Yes
Spell-checker	Yes
Extended test time	Yes
Scribe	Yes
Proctors	Yes
Oral exams	Yes
Note-takers	Yes
Support services for students with:	
LD	Yes
ADHD	Yes
ASD	Yes
Distraction-reduced environment	Yes
Recording of lecture allowed	Yes
Reading technology	Yes
Audio books	Yes
Other assistive technology	Yes
Priority registration	No
Added costs of services:	
For LD	No
For ADHD	No
For ASD	No
LD specialists	Yes
ADHD & ASD coaching	No
ASD specialists	No
Professional tutors	Yes
Peer tutors	Yes
Max. hours/week for services	Varies
How professors are notified of student approved accommodations	Student and Director

COLLEGE GRADUATION REQUIREMENTS

Course waivers allowed	No
Course substitutions allowed	No

Providence College

1 Cunningham Square, Providence, RI 02918 • Admissions: 401-865-2535 • Fax: 401-865-2826 **Support: CS**

CAMPUS

Type of school	Private (nonprofit)
Environment	City

STUDENTS

Undergrad enrollment	4,367
% male/female	46/56
% from out of state	91
% frosh live on campus	97

FINANCIAL FACTS

Annual tuition	$53,440
Room and board	$15,590
Required fees	$948

GENERAL ADMISSIONS INFO

Application fee	$65
Regular application deadline	1/15
Nonfall registration	Yes

Admission may be deferred.

Range SAT EBRW	610–670
Range SAT Math	600–680
Range ACT Composite	27–31

ACADEMICS

Student/faculty ratio	11:1
% students returning for sophomore year	91

Most classes have 20–29 students.

Programs/Services for Students with Learning Differences

The Director of the Office of Academic Services (OAS) and the faculty of the college are very supportive and diligent about providing comprehensive services. The (OAS) is the umbrella through which students can obtain a variety of services. After admission, the assistant director for Disability Services meets with the learning disabled students during the summer, prior to entry, to help them begin planning for freshman year. Students are monitored for four years. Through workshops and one-on-one meetings, the staff guides students through ways to engage professors with any questions or need for accommodations, The Tutoring Center offers group and individual tutoring, and peer tutors are available to support fellow students. The OAS also offers specialized support for student athletes who may need academic mentoring and life skills programming.

Admissions

There is no special admissions process for students with learning disabilities. However, an interview is highly recommended, during which individualized course work is examined. General course requirements include four years English, four years math, three years foreign language, two years lab science, two years social studies, and two years electives. The university is test optional and the ACT or SAT is not required for admission. Students should self-identify as learning disabled on their application.

Additional Information

The following services and accommodations are available for students presenting appropriate documentation: the use of calculators, dictionaries and computers during exams; extended time on tests; distraction-free testing environment; scribes; proctors; oral exams; note-takers; tape recorders in class; assistive technology; and priority registration. Skills seminars (for no credit) are offered in study techniques and test-taking strategies. All students have access to the Tutorial Center and Writing Center. Services and accommodations are available for undergraduate and graduate students.

ADMISSIONS INFO FOR STUDENTS WITH LEARNING DIFFERENCES

Phone: 401-865-2494 • Fax: 401-865-1219 • Email: OAS@providence.edu

SAT/ACT required: No
Interview required: Optional
Essay required: Yes
Additional application required: No
Documentation submitted to: Office of Academic Services

Special Ed. HS course work accepted: No
Separate application required for Programs/Services: No
Documentation required for:
LD: Psychoeducational evaluation
ADHD: Psychoeducational evaluation
ASD: Psychoeducational evaluation

Providence College

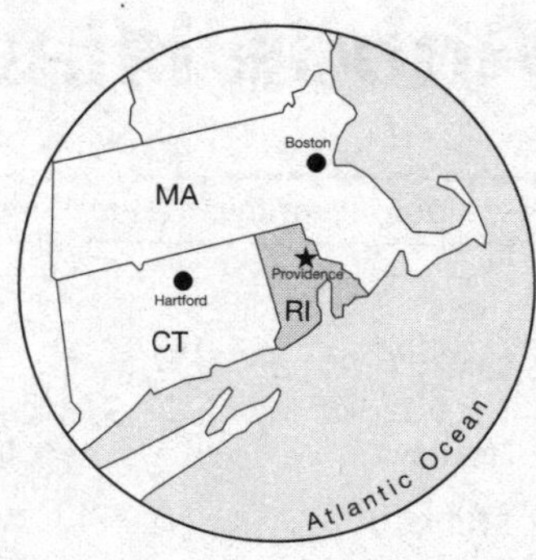

General Admissions

Very important factors include: rigor of secondary school record, academic GPA, application essay. *Important factors include:* recommendation(s), extracurricular activities, character/personal qualities. *Other factors include:* class rank, standardized test scores, talent/ability, first generation, alumni/ae relation, geographical residence, racial/ethnic status, volunteer work, work experience, level of applicant's interest. *Freshman admission requirements:* High school diploma is required and GED is not accepted. *Academic units required:* 4 English, 4 math, 3 science, 2 science labs, 3 foreign language, 2 social studies, 2 history. *Academic units recommended:* 4 English, 4 math, 4 science, 2 science labs, 4 foreign language, 2 social studies, 2 history.

Accommodations or Services

Accommodations are decided upon an individual basis after a thorough review of appropriate, current documentation. The accommodations requests must be supported through the documentation provided and must be logically linked to the current impact of the condition on academic functioning.

Financial Aid

Students should submit: FAFSA, CSS/Financial Aid PROFILE. *Need-based scholarships/grants offered:* College/university scholarship or grant aid from institutional funds; Federal Pell; Private scholarships; SEOG; State scholarships/grants; United Negro College Fund. *Loan aid offered:* Direct PLUS loans; Direct Subsidized Stafford Loans; Direct Unsubsidized Stafford Loans. Federal Work-Study Program available. Institutional employment available.

Campus Life

Activities: Campus Ministries; Choral groups; Concert band; Dance; Drama/theater; International Student Organization; Jazz band; Literary magazine; Music ensembles; Musical theater; Pep band; Radio station; Student government; Student newspaper; Student-run film society; Television station; Yearbook. **Organizations:** 125 registered organizations, 22 honor societies, 1 religious organization. **Athletics (Intercollegiate):** *Men:* basketball, cross-country, diving, ice hockey, lacrosse, soccer, swimming, track/field (outdoor), track/field (indoor). *Women:* basketball, cross-country, diving, field hockey, ice hockey, soccer, softball, swimming, tennis, track/field (outdoor), track/field (indoor), volleyball.

ACCOMMODATIONS

Allowed in exams:	
Calculators	Yes
Dictionary	Yes
Computer	Yes
Spell-checker	Yes
Extended test time	Yes
Scribe	Yes
Proctors	Yes
Oral exams	Yes
Note-takers	Yes
Support services for students with:	
LD	Yes
ADHD	Yes
ASD	Yes
Distraction-reduced environment	Yes
Recording of lecture allowed	Yes
Reading technology	Yes
Audio books	No
Other assistive technology	Yes
Priority registration	Yes
Added costs of services:	
For LD	No
For ADHD	No
For ASD	No
LD specialists	No
ADHD & ASD coaching	Yes
ASD specialists	Yes
Professional tutors	No
Peer tutors	Yes
Max. hours/week for services	Varies
How professors are notified of student approved accommodations	Student

COLLEGE GRADUATION REQUIREMENTS

Course waivers allowed	Yes
In what courses: Varies	
Course substitutions allowed	Yes
In what courses: Varies	

Rhode Island

Rhode Island College

600 Mount Pleasant Avenue, Providence, RI 02908 • Admissions: 401-456-8234 • Fax: 401-456-8817 **Support: CS**

CAMPUS

Type of school	Public
Environment	City

STUDENTS

Undergrad enrollment	6,432
% male/female	31/69
% from out of state	14
% frosh live on campus	38

FINANCIAL FACTS

Annual in-state tuition	$8,835
Annual out-of-state tuition	$23,310
Room and board	$11,597
Required fees	$1,25

GENERAL ADMISSIONS INFO

Application fee	$50
Regular application deadline	3/15
Nonfall registration	Yes
Range SAT EBRW	450–550
Range SAT Math	430–530
Range ACT Composite	16–19

ACADEMICS

Student/faculty ratio	13:1
% students returning for sophomore year	75

Most classes have 20–29 students.

Programs/Services for Students with Learning Differences

The Disability Center helps students with accommodations. Students with disabilities may self-identify at any point, but are encouraged to do so at admission. A registration card is sent to all new students. Filling out this card and returning it to the Office of Student Life starts the process. Faculty is responsible for stating at the beginning of each semester verbally or in writing that the instructor is available to meet individually with students who require accommodations. The college wants students to feel comfortable requesting assistance, and faculty and fellow students are encouraged to be friendly and supportive. The college feels that the presence of students with individual ways of learning and coping serves as a learning experience for the professor, student, and class.

Admissions

Admission requirements are the same for all applicants. Freshman requirements include 4 years of English, 2 years of a foreign language, 3 years of mathematics (Algebra I, Algebra II, and geometry), 2 years of social studies, 2 years of science (biology and chemistry or physics), 0.5 unit in the arts, and 4.5 additional college-preparatory units. Most accepted students rank in the upper 50% of their class. SAT or ACT scores required for admission. Students with LD/ADHD should submit the general application for admission. If a student does not meet admission requirements and is considered as a conditional admit, this would be done regardless of having an LD or ADHD.

Additional Information

The Disability Services Center (DSC) supports students with a variety of disability-related needs. For students with learning disabilities, support services may include testing accommodations, advocating and referring to campus staff if appropriate, and advocating for assistive technology. The Admissions Office does not forward documentation that a student submits with the college application to the Disability Services. The student must submit the documentation necessary for accommodations to the DSC separately.

There is also a Certificate of Undergraduate Study (CUS) in College and Career Attainment at Rhode Island College offers students with intellectual disability (ID) the opportunity to self-direct academic coursework and internships to enhance their skills and knowledge critical to a variety of career choices. The CUS includes internships extending student knowledge and skills across four vocational internship experiences.

ADMISSIONS INFO FOR STUDENTS WITH LEARNING DIFFERENCES

Phone: 401-456-8061 • Fax: 401-456-8702 • Email: dsc@ric.edu

SAT/ACT required: Yes (Test optional for 2021)
Interview required: No
Essay required: No
Additional application required: No
Documentation submitted to: DSC
Special Ed. HS course work accepted: No
Separate application required for Programs/Services: No
Documentation required for:
- **LD:** Psychoeducational evaluation
- **ADHD:** Psychoeducational evaluation
- **ASD:** Psychoeducational evaluation

Rhode Island College

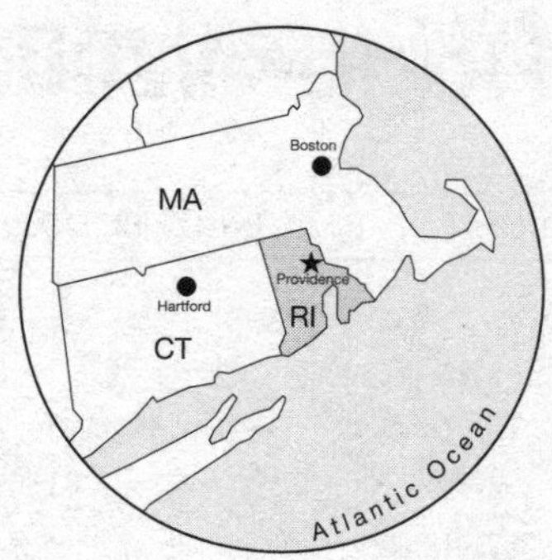

General Admissions

Very important factors include: rigor of secondary school record, class rank, academic GPA. *Important factors include:* application essay, standardized test scores, recommendation(s). *Other factors include:* interview, extracurricular activities, talent/ability, alumni/ae relation, volunteer work, work experience. *Freshman admission requirements:* High school diploma is required and GED is accepted. *Academic units required:* 4 English, 3 math, 2 science, 2 science labs, 2 foreign language, 2 social studies, 5 academic electives.

Accommodations or Services

Accommodations are decided upon an individual basis after a thorough review of appropriate, current documentation. The accommodations requests must be supported through the documentation provided and must be logically linked to the current impact of the condition on academic functioning.

Financial Aid

Students should submit: FAFSA, Institution's own financial aid form. *Need-based scholarships/grants offered:* College/university scholarship or grant aid from institutional funds; Federal Pell; Private scholarships; SEOG; State scholarships/grants. *Loan aid offered:* Direct PLUS loans; Direct Subsidized Stafford Loans; Direct Unsubsidized Stafford Loans. Federal Work-Study Program available. Institutional employment available.

Campus Life

Activities: Choral groups; Concert band; Dance; Drama/theater; International Student Organization; Jazz band; Literary magazine; Music ensembles; Musical theater; Radio station; Student government; Student newspaper; Student-run film society; Symphony orchestra; Television station. **Organizations:** 80 registered organizations, 14 honor societies, 2 fraternities, 3 sororities.

ACCOMMODATIONS

Allowed in exams:	
Calculators	Yes
Dictionary	Yes
Computer	Yes
Spell-checker	Yes
Extended test time	Yes
Scribe	Yes
Proctors	No
Oral exams	Yes
Note-takers	Yes
Support services for students with:	
LD	Yes
ADHD	Yes
ASD	Yes
Distraction-reduced environment	Yes
Recording of lecture allowed	Yes
Reading technology	Yes
Audio books	Yes
Other assistive technology	Yes
Priority registration	Yes
Added costs of services:	
For LD	No
For ADHD	No
For ASD	No
LD specialists	Yes
ADHD & ASD coaching	No
ASD specialists	No
Professional tutors	No
Peer tutors	Yes
Max. hours/week for services	Unlimited
How professors are notified of student approved accommodations	Student and Director

COLLEGE GRADUATION REQUIREMENTS

Course waivers allowed	Yes
In what courses: English and others if not required by student's major.	
Course substitutions allowed	Yes
In what courses: English and others if not required by student's major.	

Roger Williams University

1 Old Ferry Road, Bristol, RI 02809-2921 • Admissions: 401-254-3500 **Support: CS**

CAMPUS	
Type of school	Private (nonprofit)
Environment	Town
STUDENTS	
Undergrad enrollment	4,292
% male/female	49/51
% from out of state	78
% frosh live on campus	91
FINANCIAL FACTS	
Annual tuition	$37,944
Room and board	$15,698
Required fees	$330
GENERAL ADMISSIONS INFO	
Application fee	$55
Regular application deadline	2/1
Nonfall registration	Yes
Admission may be deferred.	
Range SAT EBRW	535–630
Range SAT Math	530–610
Range ACT Composite	22–27
ACADEMICS	
Student/faculty ratio	14:1
% students returning for sophomore year	85
Most classes have 20–29 students.	

Programs/Services for Students with Learning Differences

The Center for Student Academic Success (CSAS) offers academic advising and peer mentors who help to keep students on track with support, organizational, and study needs. The professional advisors meet regularly with students, and the Student Accessibility Services (SAS) works with students with documented disabilities. Peer mentors are assigned the first year to all students.

Admissions

Student with learning differences and/or disabilities of any type must meet the same admissions criteria as their non-disabled peers. Prospective students should be aware that RWU does not offer a program with a separate or additional application process. All students must complete the Common Application, one letter of recommendation, at minimum, is required, SAT and ACT are optional for all students applying except those who apply to the Department of Education. The average GPA is 3.2 on a 4.0 scale.

Additional Information

SAS is specifically dedicated to students with documentation. This support is available to eligible students once they request accommodations each semester. There is a test booking center to schedule exam accommodations, and alternative textbook support can be downloaded for a student into their portal. Class notes are sent to the student by a peer notetaker hired by the SAS, and other accommodations such as priority registration are available through the (SAS) as well. Students who disclose disabilities to SAS are most successful when they access the supports they need early on in their career at RWU and use services appropriately and independently.

ADMISSIONS INFO FOR STUDENTS WITH LEARNING DIFFERENCES

Phone: 401-254-3841• Email: lchoiniere@rwu.edu

SAT/ACT required: No
Interview required: No
Essay required: No
Additional application required: No
Documentation submitted to: SAS

Special Ed. HS course work accepted: No
Separate application required for Programs/Services: No
Documentation required for:
LD: Psychoeducational evaluation
ADHD: Psychoeducational evaluation
ASD: Psychoeducational evaluation

Roger Williams University

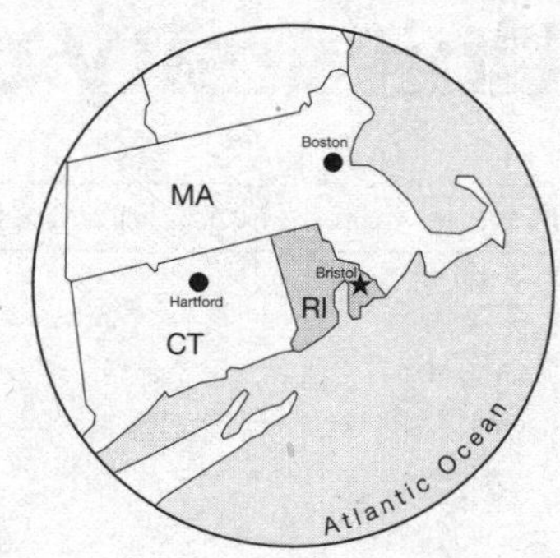

General Admissions

Very important factors include: rigor of secondary school record, academic GPA, application essay, recommendation(s), character/personal qualities. *Important factors include:* extracurricular activities, volunteer work. *Other factors include:* class rank, standardized test scores, interview, talent/ability, first generation, alumni/ae relation. *Freshman admission requirements:* High school diploma is required and GED is accepted. *Academic units required:* 4 English, 3 math, 3 science, 2 science labs, 3 social studies, 2 history, 2 academic electives. *Academic units recommended:* 4 math, 4 science, 2 foreign language, 3 social studies, 3 history, 3 academic electives.

Accommodations or Services

Accommodations are decided upon an individual basis after a thorough review of appropriate, current documentation. The accommodations requests must be supported through the documentation provided and must be logically linked to the current impact of the condition on academic functioning.

Financial Aid

Students should submit: FAFSA. Applicants will be notified of awards on or about 4/1. *Need-based scholarships/grants offered:* College/university scholarship or grant aid from institutional funds; Federal Pell; Private scholarships; SEOG; State scholarships/grants. *Loan aid offered:* Direct PLUS loans; Direct Subsidized Stafford Loans; Direct Unsubsidized Stafford Loans. Federal Work-Study Program available. Institutional employment available.

Campus Life

Activities: Choral groups; Dance; Drama/theater; International Student Organization; Literary magazine; Model UN; Music ensembles; Radio station; Student government; Student newspaper; Student-run film society; Yearbook. **Organizations:** 87 registered organizations, 17 honor societies, 2 religious organizations. **Athletics (Intercollegiate):** *Men:* baseball, basketball, cross-country, diving, equestrian sports, lacrosse, sailing, soccer, swimming, tennis, track/field (outdoor), track/field (indoor), wrestling. *Women:* basketball, cross-country, diving, equestrian sports, lacrosse, sailing, soccer, softball, swimming, tennis, track/field (outdoor), track/field (indoor), volleyball.

ACCOMMODATIONS

Allowed in exams:	
Calculators	Yes
Dictionary	No
Computer	Yes
Spell-checker	Yes
Extended test time	Yes
Scribe	Yes
Proctors	Yes
Oral exams	Yes
Note-takers	Yes
Support services for students with:	
LD	Yes
ADHD	Yes
ASD	Yes
Distraction-reduced environment	Yes
Recording of lecture alowed	Yes
Reading technology	No
Audio books	Yes
Other assistive technology	Yes
Priority registration	Yes
Added costs of services:	
For LD	No
For ADHD	No
For ASD	No
LD specialists	Yes
ADHD & ASD coaching	No
ASD specialists	No
Professional tutors	No
Peer tutors	Yes
Max. hours/week for services	Varies
How professors are notified of student approved accommodations	Student

COLLEGE GRADUATION REQUIREMENTS

Course waivers allowed	No
Course substitutions allowed	No

University of Rhode Island

14 Upper College Road, Kingston, RI 2881 • Admissions: 401-874-7100 • Fax: 401-874-5523 **Support: CS**

CAMPUS

Type of school	Public
Environment	Village

STUDENTS

Undergrad enrollment	13,671
% male/female	44/56
% from out of state	49
% frosh live on campus	92

FINANCIAL FACTS

Annual in-state tuition	$12,590
Annual out-of-state tuition	$29,710
Room and board	$12,510
Required fees	$1,976

GENERAL ADMISSIONS INFO

Application fee	$65
Regular application deadline	2/1
Nonfall registration	Yes

Admission may be deferred.

Range SAT EBRW	511–668
Range SAT Math	501–677
Range ACT Composite	20–29

ACADEMICS

Student/faculty ratio	16:1
% students returning for sophomore year	86

Most classes have 10–19 students.

Programs/Services for Students with Learning Differences

Disability Services for Students (DSS) will assist students in arranging accommodations, facilitate communication between students and professors, and help them to develop effective coping skills like time management, study skills, stress management, etc. Accommodations are provided case-by-case to meet the specific needs of individual students. Students are encouraged to have an on-going relationship with DSS and the professional staff is able to meet with students as often as desired. Students with LD/ADHD who want to access services or accommodations must provide DSS with current documentation and communicate what needs are requested. Students are also expected to keep up with their requested accommodations (pick up, deliver, and return letters in timely manner) and be involved in the decision-making process when it comes to their needs. Students are encouraged to make accommodation requests as early as possible and/or prior to the beginning of each semester.

Admissions

All applicants are expected to meet the general admission criteria. There is not a special process for students with LD/ADHD. General admission requirements expect students to rank in the upper 50% of their high school class and complete college preparatory courses including English, math, social studies, science and foreign language. If there is current documentation of a language-based LD, there is a waiver for the foreign language admissions requirement, but students must self-disclose during the admission process. Courses required for admission are 4 years English, 3 years math, 2 years science, 2 years social science or history, 2 years foreign language (American Sign Language is accepted), and 5 additional college prep courses.

Additional Information

Students need to provide the Disability Services for Students office with current documentation of their disability that includes: psychoeducational testing completed by a professional evaluator (see www.uri.edu/disabilityservices for more information). DSS will assist students in arranging for accommodations, help to facilitate communication between students and professors, and work with students to develop effective coping strategies. The S.T.A.R.T. URI Program is the bridge program for students with ASD entering the university. This summer program helps with the transition prior to entering the university in the fall. Its aim is to support academic and social skills. It is a 3-day program. The additional fees for the 3 days are for meals during attendance.

ADMISSIONS INFO FOR STUDENTS WITH LEARNING DIFFERENCES

Phone: 401-874-2098 • Fax: 401-874-5694 • Email: pramsdell@uri.edu

SAT/ACT required: Yes (Test optional for 2021)
Interview required: No
Essay required: Yes
Additional application required: No
Documentation submitted to: DSS

Special Ed. HS course work accepted: No
Separate application required for Programs/Services: No
Documentation required for:
LD: Psychoeducational evaluation
ADHD: Psychoeducational evaluation
ASD: Psychoeducational evaluation

University of Rhode Island

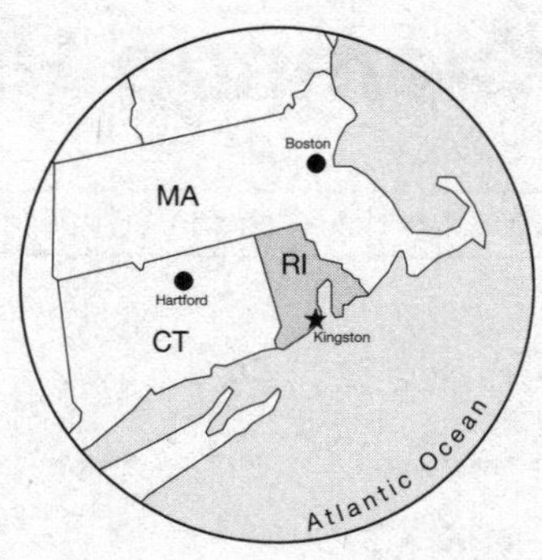

General Admissions

Very important factors include: rigor of secondary school record, academic GPA. *Important factors include:* standardized test scores. *Other factors include:* class rank, application essay, recommendation(s), extracurricular activities, talent/ability, character/personal qualities, first generation, alumni/ae relation, geographical residence, state residency, racial/ethnic status, volunteer work, work experience, level of applicant's interest. *Freshman admission requirements:* High school diploma is required and GED is accepted. *Academic units required:* 4 English, 3 math, 2 science, 1 science lab, 2 foreign language, 2 social studies, 5 academic electives.

Accommodations or Services

Accommodations are decided upon an individual basis after a thorough review of appropriate, current documentation. The accommodations requests must be supported through the documentation provided and must be logically linked to the current impact of the condition on academic functioning.

Financial Aid

Students should submit: FAFSA. *Need-based scholarships/grants offered:* College/university scholarship or grant aid from institutional funds; Federal Pell; Private scholarships; SEOG; State scholarships/grants; United Negro College Fund. *Loan aid offered:* Direct PLUS loans; Direct Subsidized Stafford Loans; Direct Unsubsidized Stafford Loans. Federal Work-Study Program available. Institutional employment available.

Campus Life

Activities: Campus Ministries; Choral groups; Concert band; Dance; Drama/theater; International Student Organization; Jazz band; Literary magazine; Marching band; Model UN; Music ensembles; Musical theater; Opera; Pep band; Radio station; Student government; Student newspaper; Student-run film society; Symphony orchestra; Television station; Yearbook. **Organizations:** 100 registered organizations, 40 honor societies, 12 religious organizations, 15 fraternities, 10 sororities. **Athletics (Intercollegiate):** *Men:* baseball, basketball, cheerleading, cross-country, football, golf, soccer, track/field (outdoor), track/field (indoor). *Women:* basketball, cheerleading, crew/rowing, cross-country, diving, soccer, softball, swimming, tennis, track/field (outdoor), track/field (indoor), volleyball.

ACCOMMODATIONS

Allowed in exams:	
Calculators	Yes
Dictionary	Yes
Computer	Yes
Spell-checker	Yes
Extended test time	Yes
Scribe	Yes
Proctors	Yes
Oral exams	Yes
Note-takers	Yes
Support services for students with:	
LD	Yes
ADHD	Yes
ASD	Yes
Distraction-reduced environment	Yes
Recording of lecture alowed	Yes
Reading technology	Yes
Audio books	Yes
Other assistive technology	Yes
Priority registration	Yes
Added costs of services:	
For LD	No
For ADHD	No
For ASD	No
LD specialists	Yes
ADHD & ASD coaching	Yes
ASD specialists	Yes
Professional tutors	No
Peer tutors	Yes
Max. hours/week for services	Varies
How professors are notified of student approved accommodations	Student

COLLEGE GRADUATION REQUIREMENTS

Course waivers allowed	No
Course substitutions allowed	Yes
In what courses: Varies	

Clemson University

105 Sikes Hall, Clemson, SC 29634-5124 • Admissions: 864-656-2287 • Fax: 864-656-2464 **Support: SP**

CAMPUS

Type of school	Public
Environment	Village

STUDENTS

Undergrad enrollment	20,185
% male/female	50/50
% from out of state	34
% frosh live on campus	98

FINANCIAL FACTS

Annual in-state tuition	$15,558
Annual out-of-state tuition	$38,550
Room and board	$11,414

GENERAL ADMISSIONS INFO

Application fee	$70
Regular application deadline	5/1
Nonfall registration	Yes

Admission may be deferred.

Range SAT EBRW	610–690
Range SAT Math	610–710
Range ACT Composite	27–32

ACADEMICS

Student/faculty ratio	16:1
% students returning for sophomore year	93

Most classes have 10–19 students.

Programs/Services for Students with Learning Differences

Student Accessibility Services coordinates the provision of reasonable accommodations for students with disabilities. Accommodations are individualized, flexible, and confidential based on the nature of the disability and the academic environment.

Admissions

All students must satisfy the same admission criteria for the university. There is no separate application process for students with disabilities. ACT/SAT are required. Students may request a waiver of the foreign language requirement by submitting a request to the exception committee. It is recommended that students self-disclose their learning disability if they need to explain the lack of a foreign language in their background or other information that will help admissions to understand their challenges. Music and theater require an audition. Interviews are not required, but students can meet with the admissions office.

Additional Information

Clemson offers the Spectrum Program for students with ASD focusing on building academics, social, and career development. An additional offering is the ClemsonLIFE Program, which offers a two-year basic program focusing on independent living skills. ClemsonLIFE also offers a two-year advanced program for students that have demonstrated the ability to safely live independently, sustain employment, and socially integrate during the basic program. The advanced program progresses with an emphasis on workplace experience, community integration, and independent living. Students who successfully complete the basic or advanced program receive a corresponding certificate of postsecondary education.

ADMISSIONS INFO FOR STUDENTS WITH LEARNING DIFFERENCES

Phone: 864-656-6848 • Email: studentaccess@lists.clemson.edu

SAT/ACT required: Yes (Test optional for 2021)
Interview required: No
Essay required: No
Additional application required: No
Documentation submitted to: Student Disability Services

Special Ed. HS course work accepted: Yes
Separate application required for Programs/Services: Yes
Documentation required for:
LD: Psychoeducational evaluation
ADHD: Psychoeducational evaluation
ASD: Psychoeducational evaluation

Clemson University

General Admissions

Very Important factors include: rigor of secondary school record, class rank, academic GPA, standardized test scores, state residency. *Other factors include:* application essay, recommendation(s), extracurricular activities, talent/ability, alumni/ae relation. *Freshman admission requirements:* High school diploma is required and GED is accepted. *Academic units required:* 4 English, 4 math, 3 science, 3 science labs, 2 foreign language, 1 social studies, 1 history, 2 academic electives, 1 computer science, 1 visual/performing arts, 1 unit from above areas or other academic areas. *Academic units recommended:* 4 science labs, 3 foreign language.

Accommodations or Services

Accommodations are decided upon an individual basis after a thorough review of appropriate, current documentation. The accommodations requests must be supported through the documentation provided.

Financial Aid

Students should submit: FAFSA. *Need-based scholarships/grants offered:* College/university scholarship or grant aid from institutional funds; Federal Pell; Private scholarships; SEOG; State scholarships/grants. *Loan aid offered:* Direct PLUS loans; Direct Subsidized Stafford Loans; Direct Unsubsidized Stafford Loans. Federal Work-Study Program available. Institutional employment available.

Campus Life

Activities: Campus Ministries; Choral groups; Concert band; Dance; Drama/theater; International Student Organization; Jazz band; Literary magazine; Marching band; Model UN; Music ensembles; Pep band; Radio station; Student government; Student newspaper; Television station; Yearbook. **Organizations:** 292 registered organizations, 23 honor societies, 24 religious organizations, 26 fraternities, 17 sororities. **Athletics (Intercollegiate):** *Men:* baseball, basketball, cheerleading, cross-country, diving, football, golf, soccer, swimming, tennis, track/field (outdoor), track/field (indoor). *Women:* basketball, cheerleading, crew/rowing, cross-country, diving, soccer, swimming, tennis, track/field (outdoor), track/field (indoor), volleyball.

ACCOMMODATIONS

Allowed in exams:	
Calculators	Yes
Dictionary	Yes
Computer	Yes
Spell-checker	Yes
Extended test time	Yes
Scribe	Yes
Proctors	Yes
Oral exams	Yes
Note-takers	Yes
Support services for students with:	
LD	Yes
ADHD	Yes
ASD	Yes
Distraction-reduced environment	Yes
Recording of lecture allowed	Yes
Reading technology	Yes
Audio books	Yes
Other assistive technology	Yes
Priority registration	Yes
Added costs of services:	
For LD	No
For ADHD	No
For ASD	No
LD specialists	No
ADHD & ASD coaching	Yes
ASD specialists	Yes
Professional tutors	No
Peer tutors	Yes
Max. hours/week for services	Unlimited
How professors are notified of student approved accommodations	Student

COLLEGE GRADUATION REQUIREMENTS

Course waivers allowed	No
Course substitutions allowed	No

College of Charleston

66 George Street, Charleston, SC 29424 • Admissions: 843-953-5670 • Fax: 843-953-6322 **Support: SP**

CAMPUS

Type of school	Public
Environment	City

STUDENTS

Undergrad enrollment	9,600
% male/female	36/64
% from out of state	35
% frosh live on campus	88

FINANCIAL FACTS

Annual in-state tuition	$12,518
Annual out-of-state tuition	$32,848
Room and board	$12,166
Required fees	$425

GENERAL ADMISSIONS INFO

Application fee	$50
Regular application deadline	2/15
Nonfall registration	Yes

Admission may be deferred.

Range SAT EBRW	550–640
Range SAT Math	530–620
Range ACT Composite	22–28

ACADEMICS

Student/faculty ratio	14:1
% students returning for sophomore year	81

Most classes have 20–29 students.

Programs/Services for Students with Learning Differences

The Center for Disability Services provides reasonable accommodations for students who self identify and present documentation supporting their accommodations.

Admissions

The College of Charleston admissions considers academic rigor, class rank, leadership, and extracurricular activities. ACT and SAT are not required but can be submitted if a student wishes to have test scores considered in the admission process. The middle 50% of applicants submitting scores have 1100–1250 (in-state applicants) and 1120–1280 (out-of-state applicants). For the ACT, the middle 50% had 21–27 (in-state applicants) or 24–29 (out-of-state applicants). Most applicants showed academic achievement in the A/B range. Courses required included 4 years English, 4 years math, 3 years lab science (4 recommended), 3 years of foreign language (2 in the same language), 3 years of social science, one year of fine arts, one year of PE or ROTC, and two years of additional electives (keyboarding not accepted). Some applicants can be considered who have not taken all of these required courses, but should submit a statement and relevant documentation from the high school explaining these deficits in course requirements. The College of Charleston also looks at leadership, special talents, activities, and honors. Senior year courses in progress are also reviewed to support overall academic preparedness and motivation.

Additional Information

Students Needing Access Parity (SNAP) is available to students with a documented disability. Approximately 850 students utilize the SNAP program. The additional application looks at academic and non-academic strengths, learning strategies, and past accommodations. The College of Charleston offers the Reach Program for students with mild intellectual and/or developmental disabilities that focuses on academics, socialization, independent living, and career development. The program accepts 12 students each year and includes traditional classes with support, on-campus housing, internships, campus clubs, and peer mentoring. Students applying to this program submit a student questionnaire, personal support questionnaire completed by the parent, transcript, current IEP, psycho-educational testing, and neuropsychological testing, along with three letters of recommendation.

ADMISSIONS INFO FOR STUDENTS WITH LEARNING DIFFERENCES

Phone: 843-953-1431 • Fax: 843-953-7731 • Email: mihaldf@cofc.edu

SAT/ACT required: No
Interview required: No
Essay required: Yes
Additional application required: Yes
Documentation submitted to: CSD

Special Ed. HS course work accepted: Yes
Separate application required for Programs/Services: Yes
Documentation required for:
LD: Psychoeducational evaluation
ADHD: Psychoeducational evaluation
ASD: Psychoeducational evaluation

College of Charleston

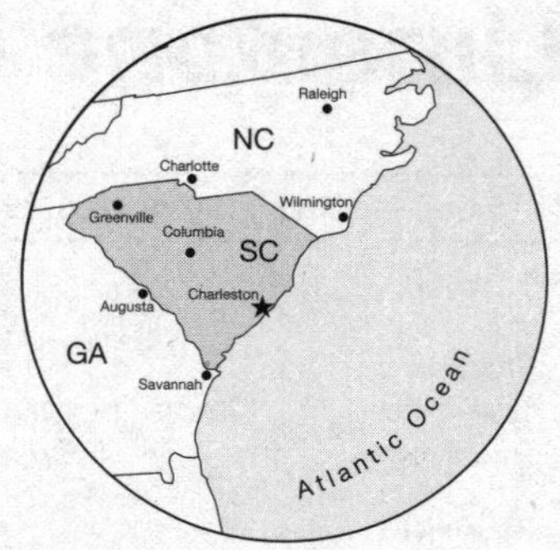

General Admissions

Very Important factors include: rigor of secondary school record, academic GPA, standardized test scores. *Important factors include:* class rank, talent/ ability, character/personal qualities, first generation, state residency. *Other factors include:* application essay, recommendation(s), extracurricular activities, alumni/ae relation, geographical residence, volunteer work, work experience, level of applicant's interest. *Freshman admission requirements:* High school diploma is required and GED is accepted. *Academic units required:* 4 English, 4 math, 3 science, 3 science labs, 3 foreign language, 2 social studies, 1 history, 3 academic electives, 1 visual/performing arts, 1 unit from above areas or other academic areas. *Academic units recommended:* 4 English, 4 math, 2 history, 1 computer science.

Accommodations or Services

Accommodations are decided upon an individual basis after a thorough review of appropriate, current documentation. The accommodations requests must be supported through the documentation provided and must be logically linked to the current impact of the condition on academic functioning.

Financial Aid

Students should submit: FAFSA. *Need-based scholarships/grants offered:* College/university scholarship or grant aid from institutional funds; Federal Pell; Private scholarships; SEOG; State scholarships/grants. *Loan aid offered:* Direct PLUS loans; Direct Subsidized Stafford Loans; Direct Unsubsidized Stafford Loans. Federal Work-Study Program available. Institutional employment available.

Campus Life

Activities: Campus Ministries; Choral groups; Dance; Drama/theater; International Student Organization; Jazz band; Literary magazine; Model UN; Music ensembles; Musical theater; Pep band; Radio station; Student government; Student newspaper; Symphony orchestra. **Organizations:** 225 registered organizations, 11 honor societies, 19 religious organizations, 12 fraternities, 14 sororities. **Athletics (Intercollegiate):** *Men:* baseball, basketball, cross-country, diving, golf, sailing, soccer, swimming, tennis. *Women:* basketball, cross-country, diving, equestrian sports, golf, sailing, soccer, softball, swimming, tennis, track/field (outdoor), track/field (indoor), volleyball.

ACCOMMODATIONS

Allowed in exams:	
Calculators	Yes
Dictionary	Yes
Computer	Yes
Spell-checker	Yes
Extended test time	Yes
Scribe	Yes
Proctors	Yes
Oral exams	Yes
Note-takers	Yes
Support services for students with:	
LD	Yes
ADHD	Yes
ASD	Yes
Distraction-reduced environment	Yes
Recording of lecture alowed	Yes
Reading technology	Yes
Audio books	Yes
Other assistive technology	Yes
Priority registration	Yes
Added costs of services:	
For LD	No
For ADHD	No
For ASD	No
LD specialists	Yes
ADHD & ASD coaching	Yes
ASD specialists	Yes
Professional tutors	Yes
Peer tutors	Yes
Max. hours/week for services	Varies
How professors are notified of student approved accommodations	Student

COLLEGE GRADUATION REQUIREMENTS

Course waivers allowed	No
Course substitutions allowed	Yes
In what courses: Case-by-case basis	

South Carolina

Limestone University

1115 College Drive, Gaffney, SC 29340-3799 • Admissions: 864-488-4549 • Fax: 864-487-8706 **Support: SP**

CAMPUS

Type of school	Private (nonprofit)
Environment	Town

STUDENTS

Undergrad enrollment	2,116
% male/female	55/45
% from out of state	36
% frosh live on campus	92

FINANCIAL FACTS

Annual tuition	$25,200
Room and board	$5,477
Required fees	$1,100

GENERAL ADMISSIONS INFO

Application fee	$25
Regular application deadline	8/25
Nonfall registration	Yes

Admission may be deferred.

Range SAT EBRW	490–580
Range SAT Math	480–580
Range ACT Composite	18–24

ACADEMICS

Student/faculty ratio	13:1
% students returning for sophomore year	67

Most classes have 10–19 students.

Programs/Services for Students with Learning Differences

The Office for Accessibility offers free services for self-identified students with documentation to determine eligibility. In addition, the Learning Enrichment and Achievement Program (LEAP) offers comprehensive student support services. This fee-based program offers weekly meeting with staff, organizational coaches, and learning specialists.

Admissions

Limestone University is test optional, so ACT or SAT scores are not required for admission. Students may submit scores if they feel these will help in an evaluation of their application. The minimum requirement for admission for the Limestone University Honors Program is an ACT 22 or SAT of 1100, 3.5 GPA, personal essay, 2 letters of recommendations (not required during the COVID-19 pandemic if counselors/teachers are not available to write). Students must be admitted to Limestone University as a fully admitted students or provisional admit prior to being considered by LEAP. Students must send a copy of their psychoeducational testing and participate in an interview with the director of the LEAP program.

Additional Information

Students utilizing the Learning Enrichment and Achievement Program (LEAP) also are enrolled in a study strategy course every semester and participate in scheduled consultations, meet with academic advisors, attend workshops, and take part in supervised study halls for a minimum of 10 hours a week. Students receive weekly and mid-term progress reports and have access to individual tutoring sessions. There is a fee associated with the LEAP program. In some cases, the Office for Vocational Rehabilitation will assist in funding the student's participation.

ADMISSIONS INFO FOR STUDENTS WITH LEARNING DIFFERENCES

Phone: 864-488-8377 • Fax: 864-487-8706

SAT/ACT required: Yes (Test optional for 2021)
Interview required: Yes
Essay required: No
Additional application required: Yes
Documentation submitted to: LEAP

Special Ed. HS course work accepted: Yes
Separate application required for Programs/Services: Yes
Documentation required for:
LD: Psychoeducational evaluation
ADHD: Psychoeducational evaluation
ASD: Psychoeducational evaluation

Limestone University

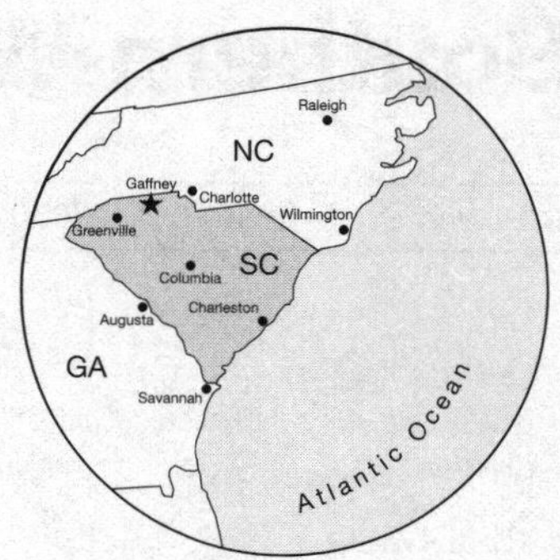

General Admissions

Very Important factors include: rigor of secondary school record, academic GPA, standardized test scores. *Important factors include:* class rank. *Other factors include:* recommendation(s), interview. *Freshman admission requirements:* High school diploma is required and GED is accepted. *Academic units required:* 4 English, 3 math, 2 science, 2 science labs, 3 social studies.

Accommodations or Services

Accommodations are decided upon an individual basis after a thorough review of appropriate, current documentation. The accommodations requests must be supported through the documentation provided and must be logically linked to the current impact of the condition on academic functioning.

Financial Aid

Students should submit: FAFSA. *Need-based scholarships/grants offered:* College/university scholarship or grant aid from institutional funds; Federal Pell; Private scholarships; SEOG; State scholarships/grants. *Loan aid offered:* Direct PLUS loans; Direct Subsidized Stafford Loans; Direct Unsubsidized Stafford Loans. Federal Work-Study Program available. Institutional employment available.

Campus Life

Activities: Campus Ministries; Choral groups; Concert band; Drama/theater; Jazz band; Literary magazine; Marching band; Music ensembles; Musical theater; Pep band; Student government; Yearbook. **Organizations:** 22 registered organizations, 5 honor societies, 3 religious organizations, 1 fraternity. **Athletics (Intercollegiate):** *Men:* baseball, basketball, cross-country, golf, lacrosse, soccer, swimming, tennis, track/field (outdoor), volleyball, wrestling. *Women:* basketball, cross-country, field hockey, golf, lacrosse, soccer, softball, swimming, tennis, track/field (outdoor), volleyball.

ACCOMMODATIONS

Allowed in exams:	
Calculators	Yes
Dictionary	Yes
Computer	Yes
Spell-checker	Yes
Extended test time	Yes
Scribe	Yes
Proctors	Yes
Oral exams	Yes
Note-takers	Yes
Support services for students with:	
LD	Yes
ADHD	Yes
ASD	Yes
Distraction-reduced environment	Yes
Recording of lecture allowed	Yes
Reading technology	Yes
Audio books	Yes
Other assistive technology	Yes
Priority registration	No
Added costs of services:	
For LD	Yes
For ADHD	Yes
For ASD	Yes
LD specialists	Yes
ADHD & ASD coaching	No
ASD specialists	Yes
Professional tutors	Yes
Peer tutors	Yes
Max. hours/week for services	Unlimited
How professors are notified of student approved accommodations	LEAP Staff

COLLEGE GRADUATION REQUIREMENTS

Course waivers allowed — No

In what courses: Foreign Language not required at Limestone.

Course substitutions allowed — No

In what courses: Foreign Language not required at Limestone.

South Carolina

Southern Wesleyan University

Wesleyan Drive, Central, SC 29630-1020 • Admissions: 864-644-5550 • Fax: 864-644-5972 **Support: CS**

CAMPUS

Type of school	Private (nonprofit)
Environment	Town

STUDENTS

Undergrad enrollment	1,150
% male/female	37/63
% from out of state	30
% frosh live on campus	81

FINANCIAL FACTS

Annual tuition	$24,926
Room and board	$9,072
Required fees	$750

GENERAL ADMISSIONS INFO

Application fee	$25
Regular application deadline	8/1
Nonfall registration	Yes

Admission may be deferred.

Range SAT EBRW	470–560
Range SAT Math	480–590
Range ACT Composite	17–23

ACADEMICS

Student/faculty ratio	14:1
% students returning for sophomore year	69

Most classes have 10–19 students.

Programs/Services for Students with Learning Differences

Southern Wesleyan University offers services to students with disabilities by coordinating the efforts of faculty and staff under the director of the Student Success Coordinator in the Student Success Center. The center offers free academic assistance, including peer tutors, writing coaches, online tutoring, and supplemental instruction. Peer tutoring is available in the Student Success Center by appointment, online reservation, or drop-in. Academic advising, career counseling, academic workshops, and mentoring are available as well. Academic support is also provided for any online students through Online Academic Support services.

Admissions

Southern Wesleyan University, is a Christ-centered, student-focused learning community devoted to transforming lives by challenging students to be dedicated scholars and servant-leaders who impact the world for Christ. All applicants must meet the same admission criteria. Courses taken in high school should include must have 4 years of English, 2 years of science, 2 years of social studies, and 2 years of math. Applicants should have a GPA of 2.3 (or rank in upper half of your graduating class at time of acceptance) and a composite SAT score of 860 (based on the critical reading/verbal and math sections) or an ACT score of 18.

Additional Information

Documentation of a disability is sent to the student Learning Services Coordinator. The student must request services each semester by discussing with the coordinator what accommodations are appropriate and needed in each course. The coordinator sends a letter to the professor of each course the student has identified for needed accommodation. The student also receives a copy and arranges the logistics and details with professors. Professors are available to students after class. Modifications can be made in test-taking, which could include extended time and a quiet place to take exams. Additionally, students may receive assistance with note-taking. All services are offered in response to students' requests.

ADMISSIONS INFO FOR STUDENTS WITH LEARNING DIFFERENCES

Phone: 864-644-5036 • Fax: 864-644-5979

SAT/ACT required: Yes (Test optional for 2021)
Interview required: No
Essay required: No
Additional application required: No
Documentation submitted to: Student Services Learning Coordinator

Special Ed. HS course work accepted: Yes
Separate application required for Programs/Services: No
Documentation required for:
LD: Psychoeducational evaluation
ADHD: Psychoeducational evaluation
ASD: Psychoeducational evaluation

Southern Wesleyan University

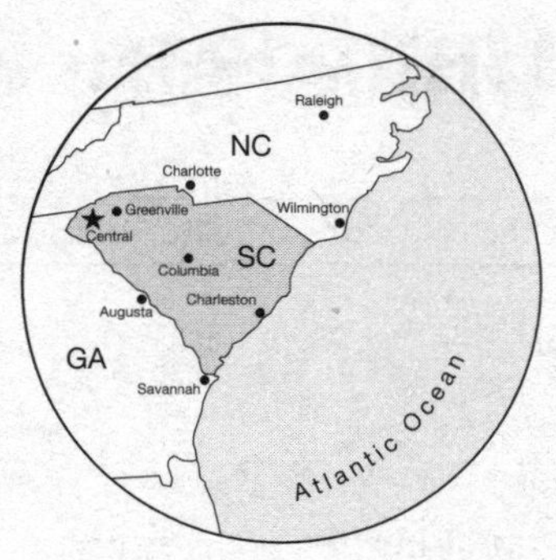

General Admissions

Very Important factors include: academic GPA, standardized test scores. *Important factors include:* rigor of secondary school record, class rank, talent/ability, character/personal qualities. *Other factors include:* recommendation(s). *Freshman admission requirements:* High school diploma is required and GED is accepted. *Academic units recommended:* 4 English, 2 math, 2 science, 2 social studies.

Accommodations or Services

Accommodations are decided upon an individual basis after a thorough review of appropriate, current documentation. The accommodations requests must be supported through the documentation provided and must be logically linked to the current impact of the condition on academic functioning.

Financial Aid

Students should submit: FAFSA. Applicants will be notified of awards on a rolling basis. *Need-based scholarships/grants offered:* College/university scholarship or grant aid from institutional funds; Federal Pell; Private scholarships; SEOG; State scholarships/grants. *Loan aid offered:* Direct PLUS loans; Direct Subsidized Stafford Loans; Direct Unsubsidized Stafford Loans. Federal Work-Study Program available. Institutional employment available.

Campus Life

Activities: Campus Ministries; Choral groups; Concert band; Drama/theater; Jazz band; Literary magazine; Music ensembles; Musical theater; Student government; Yearbook. **Organizations:** 12 registered organizations, 2 honor societies, 3 religious organizations. **Athletics (Intercollegiate):** *Men:* baseball, basketball, cross-country, golf, soccer. *Women:* basketball, cross-country, soccer, softball, volleyball.

ACCOMMODATIONS

Allowed in exams:	
Calculators	Yes
Dictionary	Yes
Computer	Yes
Spell-checker	Yes
Extended test time	Yes
Scribe	Yes
Proctors	Yes
Oral exams	Yes
Note-takers	Yes
Support services for students with:	
LD	Yes
ADHD	Yes
ASD	Yes
Distraction-reduced environment	Yes
Recording of lecture allowed	Yes
Reading technology	Yes
Audio books	Yes
Other assistive technology	Yes
Priority registration	No
Added costs of services:	
For LD	No
For ADHD	No
For ASD	No
LD specialists	Yes
ADHD & ASD coaching	Yes
ASD specialists	No
Professional tutors	Yes
Peer tutors	Yes
Max. hours/week for services	Varies
How professors are notified of student approved accommodations	Student and coordinator

COLLEGE GRADUATION REQUIREMENTS

Course waivers allowed	No
Course substitutions allowed	No

University of South Carolina—Columbia

Office of Undergraduate Admissions, Columbia, SC 29208 • Admissions: 803-777-7700 • Fax: 803-777-0101 **Support: CS**

CAMPUS

Type of school	Public
Environment	City

STUDENTS

Undergrad enrollment	27,066
% male/female	46/54
% from out of state	39
% frosh live on campus	94

FINANCIAL FACTS

Annual in-state tuition	$12,688
Annual out-of-state tuition	$33,928
Room and board	$12,435

GENERAL ADMISSIONS INFO

Application fee	$65
Regular application deadline	12/1
Nonfall registration	Yes

Admission may be deferred.

Range SAT EBRW	600–680
Range SAT Math	580–690
Range ACT Composite	25–31

ACADEMICS

Student/faculty ratio	17:1
% students returning for sophomore year	89

Most classes have 10–19 students.

Programs/Services for Students with Learning Differences

The university's Student Disability Resource Center (SDRC) provides educational support and assistance to students with LD who have potential for success in a competitive university setting. The SDRC is specifically designed to empower students with the confidence to become self-advocates and to take an active role in their education. The university works with each student on an individualized basis to match needs with appropriate tailored educational support and assistance. Student Disability Resource Center recommends and coordinates support services with faculty, administrators, advisors, and deans. All requests are based on documented diagnostic information regarding each student's specific learning disability. In order to use these accommodations, students will need to complete an application, which the SDRC staff will review alongside any other documentation. During the review, students will meet with the SDRC coordinator. After the application is approved, accommodations can be updated or modified.

Admissions

There is no special application or admission process for students with LD. The mid-range ACT scores are 25–30. SAT mid-range scores are 1200 to 1350. Admitted weighted GPAs are from 3.8 to 4.5. Applicants must have a cumulative C-plus average on defined college-preparatory courses, including 4 years of English, 4 years of math, 3 years of science, 2 years of the same foreign language, 4 years of electives, and 1 year of physical education. If denied admission, students may petition the Admissions Committee for an exception to the regular admissions requirements. Once admitted, students can contact the Educational Support Services Center to arrange an interview to determine which services are necessary to accommodate their needs.

Additional Information

Services are individually tailored to provide educational support and assistance. All requests are based on documented diagnostic information. The program is designed to provide educational support and assistance, including analysis of learning needs to determine appropriate interventions, consulting with the faculty about special academic needs, monitoring of progress by a staff member, study skills training, and tutorial referrals. Special program accommodations may include a reduced course load of 9–12 hours, waivers/substitutions for some courses, and expanded pass/fail options. Special classroom accommodations may include tape recorders, note-takers, and extended time on tests.

ADMISSIONS INFO FOR STUDENTS WITH LEARNING DIFFERENCES

Phone: 803-777-6142 Fax: 803-777-6741 Email: sadrc@mailbox.sc.edu

SAT/ACT required: Yes (Test optional for 2021)
Interview required: Yes
Essay required: Yes
Additional application required: No
Documentation submitted to: Office of Student Disability Services

Special Ed. HS course work accepted: Yes
Separate application required for Programs/Services: No
Documentation required for:
LD: Psychoeducational evaluation
ADHD: Psychoeducational evaluation
ASD: Psychoeducational evaluation

University of South Carolina—Columbia

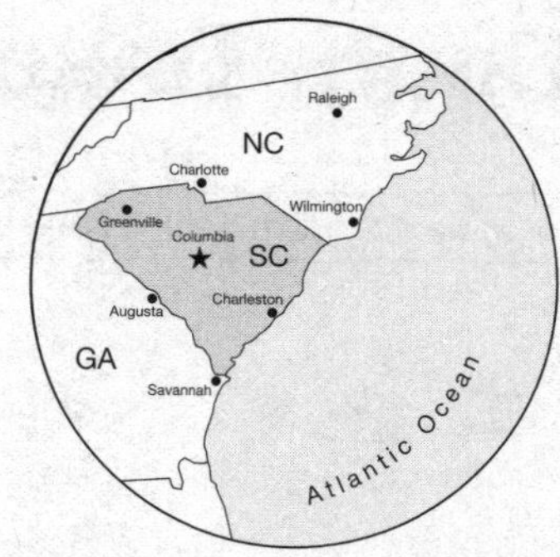

General Admissions

Very Important factors include: rigor of secondary school record, academic GPA, standardized test scores. *Other factors include:* class rank, application essay, recommendation(s), extracurricular activities, talent/ability, character/personal qualities, first generation, state residency, racial/ethnic status, volunteer work, work experience. *Freshman admission requirements:* High school diploma is required and GED is accepted. *Academic units required:* 4 English, 4 math, 3 science, 3 science labs, 2 foreign language, 2 social studies, 1 history, 2 academic electives, 1 visual/performing arts, 1 unit from above areas or other academic areas.

Accommodations or Services

Accommodations are decided upon an individual basis after a thorough review of appropriate, current documentation. The accommodations requests must be supported through the documentation provided and must be logically linked to the current impact of the condition on academic functioning.

Financial Aid

Students should submit: FAFSA *Need-based scholarships/grants offered:* College/university scholarship or grant aid from institutional funds; Federal Nursing Scholarships; Federal Pell; Private scholarships; SEOG; State scholarships/grants; United Negro College Fund. *Loan aid offered:* Direct PLUS loans; Direct Subsidized Stafford Loans; Direct Unsubsidized Stafford Loans. Federal Work-Study Program available. Institutional employment available.

Campus Life

Activities: Campus Ministries; Choral groups; Concert band; Dance; Drama/theater; International Student Organization; Jazz band; Literary magazine; Marching band; Music ensembles; Musical theater; Opera; Pep band; Radio station; Student government; Student newspaper; Student-run film society; Symphony orchestra; Television station. **Organizations:** 387 registered organizations, 28 honor societies, 31 religious organizations, 22 fraternities, 16 sororities. **Athletics (Intercollegiate):** *Men:* baseball, basketball, diving, football, golf, racquetball, soccer, softball, swimming, tennis, track/field (outdoor). *Women:* basketball, cross-country, diving, equestrian sports, golf, racquetball, soccer, softball, swimming, tennis, track/field (outdoor), volleyball.

ACCOMMODATIONS

Allowed in exams:	
Calculators	Yes
Dictionary	Yes
Computer	Yes
Spell-checker	Yes
Extended test time	Yes
Scribe	Yes
Proctors	Yes
Oral exams	No
Note-takers	Yes
Support services for students with:	
LD	Yes
ADHD	Yes
ASD	Yes
Distraction-reduced environment	Yes
Recording of lecture alowed	Yes
Reading technology	Yes
Audio books	Yes
Other assistive technology	Yes
Priority registration	Yes
Added costs of services:	
For LD	No
For ADHD	No
For ASD	No
LD specialists	Yes
ADHD & ASD coaching	No
ASD specialists	No
Professional tutors	No
Peer tutors	No
Max. hours/week for services	Varies
How professors are notified of student approved accommodations	Student

COLLEGE GRADUATION REQUIREMENTS

Course waivers allowed: Yes

In what courses: Students with learning disabilities may petition their college for substitution of the required foreign language if the requirement is not an integral part of the degree program.

Course substitutions allowed: Yes

In what courses: Students with learning disabilities may petition their college for substitution of the required foreign language if the requirement is not an integral part of the degree program.

South Carolina

South Dakota State University

Enrollment Services Center, Brookings, SD 57007 • Admissions: 605-688-4121 • Fax: 605-688-6891 **Support: S**

CAMPUS

Type of school	Public
Environment	Village

STUDENTS

Undergrad enrollment	10,067
% male/female	47/53
% from out of state	49

FINANCIAL FACTS

Annual in-state tuition	$9,200
Annual out-of-state tuition	$12,676
Room and board	$7,082

GENERAL ADMISSIONS INFO

Application fee	$20
Regular application deadline	last day to add classes
Nonfall registration	Yes
Range SAT EBRW	520–630
Range SAT Math	530–630
Range ACT Composite	19–26

ACADEMICS

Student/faculty ratio	17:1
% students returning for sophomore year	78

Most classes have 20–29 students.

Programs/Services for Students with Learning Differences

South Dakota State University is committed to providing equal opportunities for higher education to academically qualified students with LDs. All students, including those with disabilities, have access to skill development courses in the areas of general academic success skills, English composition, and mathematics. Free tutoring is available for all students in a wide variety of subject areas through the Wintrode Tutoring Program, an academic support program hosted by students who have successfully completed the same classes. Sessions consist of small group tutoring for up to four students and walk-in review sessions in select courses.

Admissions

Students with learning disabilities must meet the same admission criteria as all applicants. SDS looks for specific academic achievements when considering offering admissions to potential students. Students are recommended to have a high school cumulative GPA of 2.6 or higher or rank in the top 60% of the class. They should also complete the following core courses with a "C" average or above: 4 years of English, 3 years of advanced math (Algebra I and higher), 3 years of laboratory science, 3 years of social science, 1 year of fine arts (includes vocal, instrumental and studio arts), and basic computer skills (students should have basic keyboarding, word processing, spreadsheet, and Internet skills).

Additional Information

The Office of Disability Services provides assistance for students with a wide range of disabilities. Services include alternative text formats, note takers, assistive technology, alternative accommodations for exams (testing in a distraction-free environment or providing readers for exams), extended time for testing, and referrals to other resources. Tutoring and Supplemental Instruction (SI) is offered to all SDSU students through the Wintrode Tutoring & SI Program. SI offers a series of weekly review sessions for students. A Summer Bridge Program is also available before starting the first year. The program focuses on strengthening academic skills, developing a student network, learning about resources on campus, and promoting graduation in four years.

ADMISSIONS INFO FOR STUDENTS WITH LEARNING DIFFERENCES

Phone: 605-688-4504 • Fax: 605-688-4987 • Email: Nancy.Crooks@sdstate.edu

SAT/ACT required: No
Interview required: No
Essay required: No
Additional application required: No
Documentation submitted to: Disability Services

Special Ed. HS course work accepted: No
Separate application required for Programs/Services: No
Documentation required for:
LD: Psychoeducational evaluation
ADHD: Psychoeducational evaluation
ASD: Psychoeducational evaluation

South Dakota State University

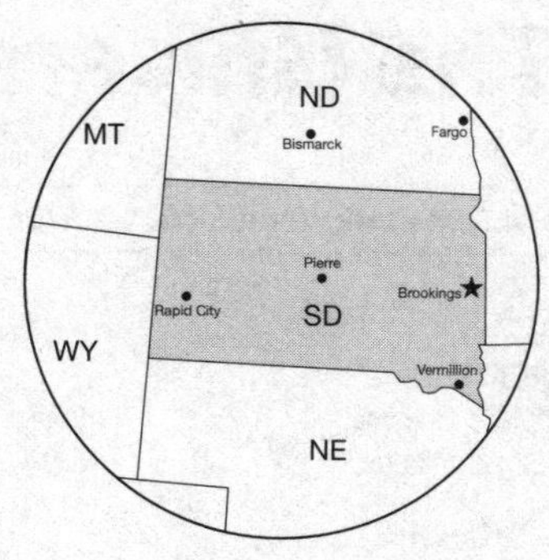

General Admissions

Very Important factors include: rigor of secondary school record, class rank, academic GPA, standardized test scores. *Other factors include:* application essay, recommendation(s). *Freshman admission requirements:* High school diploma is required and GED is accepted. *Academic units required:* 4 English, 3 math, 3 science, 3 science labs, 3 social studies, 1 visual/performing arts.

Accommodations or Services

Accommodations are decided upon an individual basis after a thorough review of appropriate, current documentation. The accommodations requests must be supported through the documentation provided and must be logically linked to the current impact of the condition on academic functioning.

Financial Aid

Students should submit: FAFSA. Applicants will be notified of awards on a rolling basis beginning 4/15. *Need-based scholarships/grants offered:* College/university scholarship or grant aid from institutional funds; Federal Pell; Private scholarships; SEOG; State scholarships/grants. *Loan aid offered:* Direct PLUS loans; Direct Subsidized Stafford Loans; Direct Unsubsidized Stafford Loans. Federal Work-Study Program available. Institutional employment available.

Campus Life

Activities: Campus Ministries; Choral groups; Concert band; Dance; Drama/theater; International Student Organization; Jazz band; Literary magazine; Marching band; Model UN; Music ensembles; Musical theater; Pep band; Radio station; Student government; Student newspaper; Symphony orchestra. **Organizations:** 200 registered organizations, 8 fraternities, 5 sororities. **Athletics (Intercollegiate):** *Men:* baseball, basketball, cross-country, diving, football, golf, swimming, tennis, track/field (outdoor), track/field (indoor), wrestling. *Women:* basketball, cross-country, diving, equestrian sports, golf, soccer, softball, swimming, tennis, track/field (outdoor), track/field (indoor), volleyball.

ACCOMMODATIONS

Allowed in exams:	
Calculators	Yes
Dictionary	Yes
Computer	Yes
Spell-checker	Yes
Extended test time	Yes
Scribe	Yes
Proctors	Yes
Oral exams	Yes
Note-takers	Yes
Support services for students with:	
LD	Yes
ADHD	Yes
ASD	Yes
Distraction-reduced environment	Yes
Recording of lecture allowed	Yes
Reading technology	Yes
Audio books	Yes
Other assistive technology	Yes
Priority registration	No
Added costs of services:	
For LD	No
For ADHD	No
For ASD	No
LD specialists	No
ADHD & ASD coaching	No
ASD specialists	No
Professional tutors	Yes
Peer tutors	Yes
Max. hours/week for services	Unlimited
How professors are notified of student approved accommodations	Student

COLLEGE GRADUATION REQUIREMENTS

Course waivers allowed	No
Course substitutions allowed	No

The University of South Dakota

414 East Clark, Vermillion, SD 57069 • Admissions: 605-677-5434 • Fax: 605-677-6323 **Support: S**

CAMPUS

Type of school	Public
Environment	Village

STUDENTS

Undergrad enrollment	7,475
% male/female	37/63
% from out of state	36
% frosh live on campus	85

FINANCIAL FACTS

Annual in-state tuition	$9,331
Annual out-of-state tuition	$12,807
Room and board	$8,032

GENERAL ADMISSIONS INFO

Application fee	$20
Regular application deadline	Rolling
Nonfall registration	Yes
Range SAT EBRW	500–600
Range SAT Math	500–600
Range ACT Composite	19–25

ACADEMICS

Student/faculty ratio	16:1
% students returning for sophomore year	77

Most classes have 10–19 students.

Programs/Services for Students with Learning Differences

The University of South Dakota Disability Services (USDDS) operates on the premise that students at the university are full participants in the process of obtaining appropriate accommodations for their disabilities. Students are encouraged to make their own decisions and become self-advocates for appropriate accommodations or services. USDDS's three main goals are to: (1) help students become self-advocates; (2) provide better transition services into and out of college; and (3) offer better instructional and support services. The university strives to ensure that all individuals with legally defined disabilities have access to the full range of the university's programs, services, and activities.

Admissions

For freshmen admission, students must have a minimum 2.6 GPA on a 4.0 scale in all high school courses, or be in the top 50% of their high school graduating class, and complete the following courses with a cumulative grade point average of a C or higher (2.0 on a 4.0 scale): 4 years of English, 3 years of advanced math (Algebra I or higher), 3 years of social science, 3 years of lab, and 1 year of fine arts. Other requirements apply for transfer admission and non-traditional admission. Non-traditional admission requirements apply for students who are age 24 or over and for those who did not graduate from high school.

Additional Information

Services are individualized for each student's learning needs. USDDS staff provides the following activities: planning, developing, delivering, and evaluating direct service programs, meeting individually with students and ensuring that students receive reasonable and appropriate accommodations that match their needs, consulting with faculty, and providing academic, career, and personal counseling referrals. Classroom accommodations include test modification, note-taking assistance, readers, books on tape, specialized computer facilities, and tutors.

ADMISSIONS INFO FOR STUDENTS WITH LEARNING DIFFERENCES

Phone: 605-688-4504 • Fax: 605-688-4987

SAT/ACT required: Yes (Test optional for 2021)
Interview required: No
Essay required: Yes
Additional application required: No
Documentation submitted to: Disability Services (DS)

Special Ed. HS course work accepted: Yes
Separate application required for Programs/Services: No
Documentation required for:
LD: Psychoeducational evaluation
ADHD: Psychoeducational evaluation
ASD: Psychoeducational evaluation

The University of South Dakota

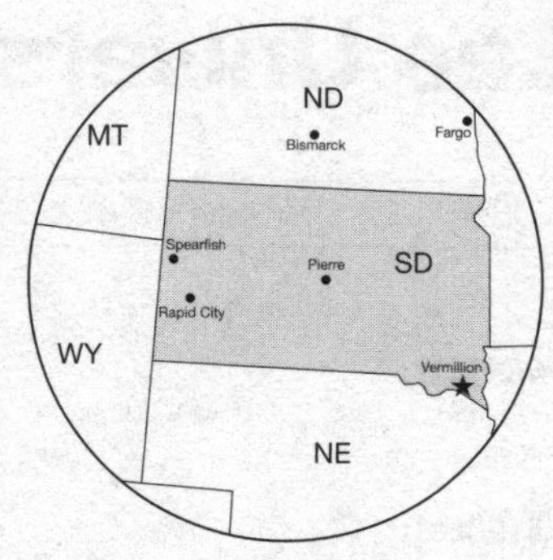

General Admissions

Very Important factors include: rigor of secondary school record, class rank, academic GPA, standardized test scores. *Other factors include:* application essay, recommendation(s). *Freshman admission requirements:* High school diploma is required and GED is accepted. *Academic units required:* 4 English, 3 math, 3 science labs, 3 social studies. *Academic units recommended:* 4 math, 4 science, 2 foreign language.

Accommodations or Services

Accommodations are decided upon an individual basis after a thorough review of appropriate, current documentation. The accommodations requests must be supported through the documentation provided and must be logically linked to the current impact of the condition on academic functioning.

Financial Aid

Students should submit: FAFSA; State aid form. Applicants will be notified of awards on a rolling basis beginning 11/1. *Need-based scholarships/grants offered:* College/university scholarship or grant aid from institutional funds; Federal Pell; Private scholarships; SEOG; State scholarships/grants; United Negro College Fund. *Loan aid offered:* Direct PLUS loans; Direct Subsidized Stafford Loans; Direct Unsubsidized Stafford Loans. Federal Work-Study Program available. Institutional employment available.

Campus Life

Activities: Campus Ministries; Choral groups; Concert band; Dance; Drama/theater; International Student Organization; Jazz band; Literary magazine; Marching band; Music ensembles; Musical theater; Opera; Pep band; Radio station; Student government; Student newspaper; Student-run film society; Symphony orchestra; Television station. **Organizations:** 144 registered organizations, 6 honor societies, 6 religious organizations, 7 fraternities, 3 sororities. **Athletics (Intercollegiate):** *Men:* basketball, cross-country, diving, football, golf, swimming, track/field (outdoor), track/field (indoor). *Women:* basketball, cross-country, diving, golf, soccer, softball, swimming, tennis, track/field (outdoor), track/field (indoor), volleyball.

ACCOMMODATIONS

Allowed in exams:	
Calculators	Yes
Dictionary	Yes
Computer	Yes
Spell-checker	Yes
Extended test time	Yes
Scribe	Yes
Proctors	Yes
Oral exams	Yes
Note-takers	Yes
Support services for students with:	
LD	Yes
ADHD	Yes
ASD	Yes
Distraction-reduced environment	Yes
Recording of lecture alowed	Yes
Reading technology	Yes
Audio books	Yes
Other assistive technology	Yes
Priority registration	No
Added costs of services:	
For LD	No
For ADHD	No
For ASD	No
LD specialists	Yes
ADHD & ASD coaching	No
ASD specialists	No
Professional tutors	No
Peer tutors	Yes
Max. hours/week for services	Unlimited
How professors are notified of student approved accommodations	Student

COLLEGE GRADUATION REQUIREMENTS

Course waivers allowed	No
Course substitutions allowed	No

Lee University

P.O. Box 3450, Cleveland, TN 37320-3450 • Admissions: 423-614-8500 • Fax: 423-614-8533 **Support: CS**

CAMPUS

Type of school	Private (nonprofit)
Environment	Town

STUDENTS

Undergrad enrollment	4,077
% male/female	39/61
% from out of state	52
% frosh live on campus	86

FINANCIAL FACTS

Annual tuition	$18,840
Room and board	$9,030
Required fees	$700

GENERAL ADMISSIONS INFO

Application fee	$25
Regular application deadline	Rolling
Nonfall registration	Yes

Admission may be deferred.

Range SAT EBRW	460–620
Range SAT Math	450–610
Range ACT Composite	21–28

ACADEMICS

Student/faculty ratio	15:1
% students returning for sophomore year	78

Most classes have 10–19 students.

Programs/Services for Students with Learning Differences

The Academic Support Office acts as a liaison between students with disabilities and the Lee University academic community. In compliance with Section 504 of the Rehabilitation Act of 1973, as amended, and the Americans with Disabilities Act (ADA) of 1990, and the amended ADA of 2011, the Academic Support Office works to ensure that students with physical, sensory, learning, and/or emotional disabilities have equal access to educational opportunities.

Admissions

Admission to Lee University is based on the completion of an official application and evidence that students possess the qualities needed for satisfactory achievement in terms of character, ability, academic foundation, purpose, and personality. The university admits students regardless of race, color, national origin, religious preference, or disability. To be eligible for admission, students must have received a diploma from an approved high school or a passing score on a GED test. Acceptance is based upon discernible qualities and potential without reference to any perceived notion of an ideal class. Lee is a Christian university offering liberal arts and professional education on both the baccalaureate and graduate levels through residential and distance programs. The curriculum integrates biblical truth as revealed in the Holy Scriptures with truth discovered through the study of arts and sciences and in the practice of various professions. Lee offers all students services through the Center for Student Success, focusing on coaching, learning, first year programs, academic support, calling and careers, and student success.

Additional Information

Accommodations can be made after meeting with the Director of Academic Support (DAC) as long as documentation is provided. Students are encouraged to initiate contact with the DAC coordinator early in the semester to determine the necessary accommodations. Students schedule regular meetings with the coordinator in order to monitor progress and/or determine the need for adjustments to the accommodations in courses. Services or resources provided include orientation to the DAC and orientation to the Adaptive Technology Center. Tutoring and mentoring is provided via one-on-one tutoring, small group tutoring, and lab tutoring. All tutors are trained, monitored, and evaluated. Student success coaching is available through a success coach. Support in time management, budgeting, career planning, test taking skills, study skills, stress management, campus involvement, and goal setting is available.

ADMISSIONS INFO FOR STUDENTS WITH LEARNING DIFFERENCES

Phone: 423-614-8181 • Email: lbradford@leeuniversity.edu

SAT/ACT required: No
Interview required: No
Essay required: No
Additional application required: Yes
Documentation submitted to: Academic Support Office

Special Ed. HS course work accepted: Yes
Separate application required for Programs/Services: Yes
Documentation required for:
LD: Psychoeducational evaluation
ADHD: Psychoeducational evaluation
ASD: Psychoeducational evaluation

Lee University

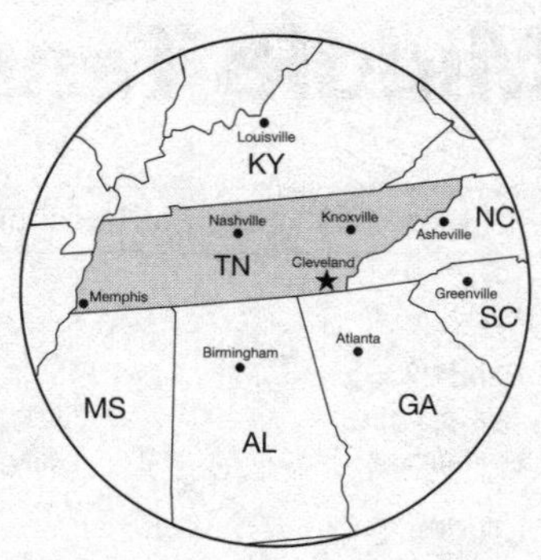

General Admissions

Very Important factors include: rigor of secondary school record, academic GPA, standardized test scores. *Important factors include:* class rank, character/personal qualities. *Other factors include:* application essay, recommendation(s), interview, extracurricular activities, talent/ability, first generation, alumni/ae relation. *Freshman admission requirements:* High school diploma is required and GED is accepted. *Academic units required:* 4 English, 3 math, 2 science, 1 foreign language, 2 social studies, 1 history. *Academic units recommended:* 4 English, 3 math, 2 science, 1 foreign language, 2 social studies, 1 history, 1 computer science.

Accommodations or Services

Accommodations are decided upon an individual basis after a thorough review of appropriate, current documentation. The accommodations requests must be supported through the documentation provided and must be logically linked to the current impact of the condition on academic functioning.

Financial Aid

Students should submit: FAFSA. *Need-based scholarships/grants offered:* College/university scholarship or grant aid from institutional funds; Federal Pell; Private scholarships; SEOG; State scholarships/grants. *Loan aid offered:* Direct PLUS loans; Direct Subsidized Stafford Loans; Direct Unsubsidized Stafford Loans. Federal Work-Study Program available. Institutional employment available.

Campus Life

Activities: Campus Ministries; Choral groups; Concert band; Drama/theater; International Student Organization; Jazz band; Literary magazine; Model UN; Music ensembles; Musical theater; Opera; Pep band; Student government; Student newspaper; Symphony orchestra; Yearbook. **Organizations:** 100 registered organizations, 17 honor societies, 15 religious organizations, 5 fraternities, 4 sororities. **Athletics (Intercollegiate):** *Men:* baseball, basketball, cheerleading, cross-country, golf, soccer, tennis. *Women:* basketball, cheerleading, cross-country, soccer, softball, tennis, volleyball.

ACCOMMODATIONS

Allowed in exams:	
Calculators	Yes
Dictionary	No
Computer	Yes
Spell-checker	Yes
Extended test time	Yes
Scribe	Yes
Proctors	Yes
Oral exams	Yes
Note-takers	Yes
Support services for students with:	
LD	Yes
ADHD	Yes
ASD	No
Distraction-reduced environment	Yes
Recording of lecture allowed	No
Reading technology	Yes
Audio books	Yes
Other assistive technology	Yes
Priority registration	Yes
Added costs of services:	
For LD	No
For ADHD	No
For ASD	No
LD specialists	Yes
ADHD & ASD coaching	Yes
ASD specialists	No
Professional tutors	No
Peer tutors	Yes
Max. hours/week for services	Varies
How professors are notified of student approved accommodations	Student

COLLEGE GRADUATION REQUIREMENTS

Course waivers allowed	No
Course substitutions allowed	No

Middle Tennessee State University

1301 East Main Street, Murfreesboro, TN 37132 • Admissions: 615-898-2111 • Fax: 615-898-5478 **Support: S**

CAMPUS

Type of school	Public
Environment	City

STUDENTS

Undergrad enrollment	18,093
% male/female	47/53
% from out of state	7
% frosh live on campus	46

FINANCIAL FACTS

Annual in-state tuition	$9,306
Annual out-of-state tuition	$28,606
Room and board	$9,286

GENERAL ADMISSIONS INFO

Application fee	$25
Regular application deadline	Rolling
Nonfall registration	Yes
Range SAT EBRW	510–640
Range SAT Math	500–620
Range ACT Composite	20–26

ACADEMICS

Student/faculty ratio	17:1
% students returning for sophomore year	75

Most classes have 10–19 students.

Programs/Services for Students with Learning Differences

The Disability & Access Center (DAC) offers support, advocacy, and services to students who learn differently. Students should complete a registration application to begin the process and provide medical documentation of their disability. Documentation is reviewed by DAC for completeness and appropriateness. Students meet with DAC staff to discuss accommodation needs. Appropriate accommodations are determined and displayed in a letter format. Students are responsible for notifying instructors and providing them copies of accommodation letters. Student and faculty discuss the best ways to implement the accommodations.

Admissions

Middle Tennessee State University is a comprehensive, innovative institution, attracting students to distinctive bachelor's, master's, specialist, and doctoral programs. Graduates are prepared to thrive in their chosen professions and a changing global society. Students and faculty generate, preserve, and disseminate knowledge and collaboratively promote excellence through teaching and learning, research, creative activity, and public engagement. Over 300 undergraduate and graduate degrees of study in diverse disciplines prepare students for high-demand careers. Highly trained and dedicated faculty members not only prepare students for their first job, but for careers that might not yet exist. The minimum GPA for admissions is 2.7. Students should have 4 years of English, 4 years of math, 3 years of science, 2 years of social studies, 2 years of foreign language, and 1 year of visual/performing arts. Course substitutions are not allowed. Students are encouraged to self-disclose a disability in a personal statement during the admission process, although this is not required.

Additional Information

The Disability & Access Center supports student success by promoting independence, cultural awareness, access, advocacy, and technological advances culminating in the understanding that disability is a natural part of the life experience.

ADMISSIONS INFO FOR STUDENTS WITH LEARNING DIFFERENCES

Phone: 615-898-2783 • Fax: 615-898-4893 • Email: dacemail@mtsu.edu

SAT/ACT required: No
Interview required: No
Essay required: No
Additional application required: Yes
Documentation submitted to: Support Program/Services

Special Ed. HS course work accepted: Yes
Separate application required for Programs/Services: Yes
Documentation required for:
- **LD:** Psychoeducational evaluation
- **ADHD:** Psychoeducational evaluation
- **ASD:** Psychoeducational evaluation

Middle Tennessee State University

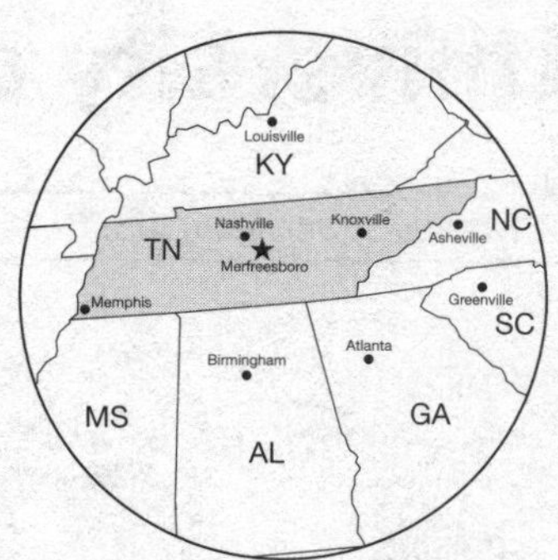

General Admissions

Very Important factors include: academic GPA, standardized test scores. *Other factors include:* rigor of secondary school record, application essay, recommendation(s), extracurricular activities, talent/ability, character/personal qualities, volunteer work, work experience, level of applicant's interest. High school diploma is required and GED is accepted. *Academic units required:* 4 English, 4 math, 3 science, 1 science lab, 2 foreign language, 1 social studies, 1 history, 1 visual/performing arts.

Accommodations or Services

Accommodations are decided upon an individual basis after a thorough review of appropriate, current documentation. The accommodations requests must be supported through the documentation provided and must be logically linked to the current impact of the condition on academic functioning.

Financial Aid

Students should submit: FAFSA. Applicants will be notified of awards on a rolling basis beginning 12/15. *Need-based scholarships/grants offered:* College/university scholarship or grant aid from institutional funds; Federal Pell; Private scholarships; SEOG; State scholarships/grants. *Loan aid offered:* Direct PLUS loans; Direct Subsidized Stafford Loans; Direct Unsubsidized Stafford Loans. Federal Work-Study Program available. Institutional employment available.

Campus Life

Activities: Campus Ministries; Choral groups; Concert band; Dance; Drama/theater; International Student Organization; Jazz band; Literary magazine; Marching band; Model UN; Music ensembles; Musical theater; Opera; Pep band; Radio station; Student government; Student newspaper; Student-run film society; Symphony orchestra;

ACCOMMODATIONS

Allowed in exams:	
Calculators	Yes
Dictionary	Yes
Computer	Yes
Spell-checker	Yes
Extended test time	Yes
Scribe	Yes
Proctors	Yes
Oral exams	Yes
Note-takers	Yes
Support services for students with:	
LD	Yes
ADHD	Yes
ASD	Yes
Distraction-reduced environment	Yes
Recording of lecture alowed	Yes
Reading technology	Yes
Audio books	Yes
Other assistive technology	Yes
Priority registration	Yes
Added costs of services:	
For LD	No
For ADHD	No
For ASD	No
LD specialists	No
ADHD & ASD coaching	No
ASD specialists	No
Professional tutors	No
Peer tutors	Yes
Max. hours/week for services	Varies
How professors are notified of student approved accommodations	Student and director

COLLEGE GRADUATION REQUIREMENTS

Course waivers allowed	Yes
In what courses: Math, foreign language, public speaking on a case-by-case basis	
Course substitutions allowed	Yes
In what courses: Math, foreign language, public speaking on a case-by-case basis	

University of Memphis

101 Wilder Tower, Memphis, TN 38152 • Admissions: 901-678-2111 • Fax: 901-678-3053 **Support: CS**

CAMPUS

Type of school	Public
Environment	Metropolis

STUDENTS

Undergrad enrollment	16,741
% male/female	39/61
% from out of state	10
% frosh live on campus	48

FINANCIAL FACTS

Annual in-state tuition	$8,208
Annual out-of-state tuition	$12,048
Room and board	$9,644
Required fees	$1,704

GENERAL ADMISSIONS INFO

Application fee	$25
Regular application deadline	7/1
Nonfall registration	Yes
Range SAT EBRW	440–570
Range SAT Math	440–590
Range ACT Composite	20–25

ACADEMICS

Student/faculty ratio	14:1
% students returning for sophomore year	76

Most classes have 20–29 students.

Programs/Services for Students with Learning Differences

The Disability Resources for Students (DRS) is designed to enhance academic strengths, provide support for areas of weakness, and build skills to help students with Learning, ADHD, and Autism Spectrum Disorders compete in the college environment. The program encourages development of life-long learning skills as well as personal responsibility for academic success. Training in college survival skills and regular meetings with the staff are emphasized during the first year to aid in the transition to college. Specific services are tailored to individual needs, considering one's strengths, weaknesses, course requirements, and learning styles. Students are integrated into regular classes and are held to the same academic standards as other students. However, academic accommodations are available to assist them in meeting requirements. DRS places responsibility on students to initiate services and follow through with services once they are arranged. Most students who use the appropriate services are successful in their academic pursuits.

Admissions

UofM uniquely provides two campus environments with over 250 areas of study that help students find their perfect match: UofM Lambuth or the Memphis Campus. Memphis has an acceptance rate of 84%. Students admitted typically have an average SAT score between 970–1210 or an average ACT score of 19–26. The following list of high school units represents the minimum high school academic requirements: English (4 units), visual and/or performing arts (1 unit), mathematics (3 units: Algebra I, Geometry, and Algebra II at least), natural and physical science (2 units: at least one unit of biology, chemistry, or physics), social studies (2 units: 1 unit must be U.S. history), and foreign language (2 units of the same language).

Additional Information

Some services are available to all students registered with DRS. However, academic services and accommodations are individually determined and based on the student's current functional limitations outlined in the medical or professional documentation, the student's compensatory skills, and the requirements of a particular course or program. The following general services are available to all students registered with DRS: early registration, orientation to using disability services, assistance with strategic class scheduling to enhance academic success, semester plan for accommodations and services, memos to faculty about disability needs, advocacy relating to disability access issues, information and guidance on academic, social,

ADMISSIONS INFO FOR STUDENTS WITH LEARNING DIFFERENCES

Phone: 901-678-2880 • Fax: 901-678-3070 • Email: vsails@memphis.edu

SAT/ACT required: Yes
Interview required: No
Essay required: No
Additional application required: No
Documentation submitted to: Disability Resources for Students

Special Ed. HS course work accepted: No
Separate application required for Programs/Services: No
Documentation required for:
LD: Psychoeducational evaluation
ADHD: Psychoeducational evaluation
ASD: Psychoeducational evaluation

University of Memphis

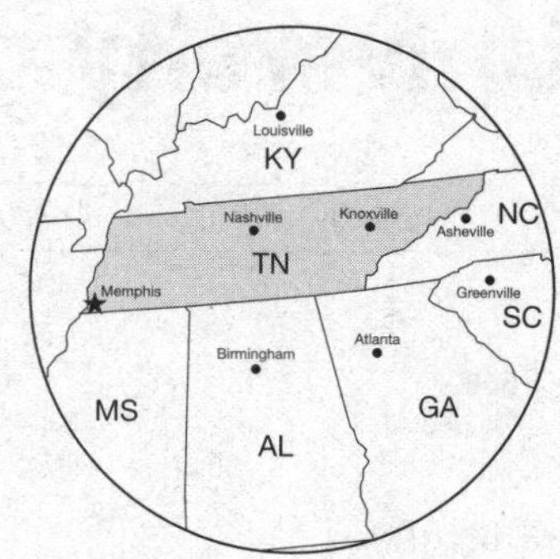

career, and personal issues, orientation to and use of the Assistive Technology Lab, referral to other university departments and community agencies, liaison with state and federal rehabilitation agencies, and information about specific opportunities for students with disabilities.

General Admissions

Very Important factors include: rigor of secondary school record, academic GPA, standardized test scores. *Other factors include:* application essay, recommendation(s), talent/ability, character/personal qualities, first generation, work experience. *Freshman admission requirements:* High school diploma is required and GED is accepted. *Academic units required:* 4 English, 3 math, 2 science, 1 science lab, 2 foreign language, 1 social studies, 1 history, 1 visual/performing arts.

Accommodations or Services

Accommodations are decided upon an individual basis after a thorough review of appropriate, current documentation. The accommodations requests must be supported through the documentation provided and must be logically linked to the current impact of the condition on academic functioning.

Financial Aid

Students should submit: FAFSA. Applicants will be notified of awards on a rolling basis beginning 6/1. *Need-based scholarships/grants offered:* College/university scholarship or grant aid from institutional funds; Federal Pell; Private scholarships; SEOG; State scholarships/grants. *Loan aid offered:* Direct PLUS loans; Direct Subsidized Stafford Loans; Direct Unsubsidized Stafford Loans. Federal Work-Study Program available. Institutional employment available.

Campus Life

Activities: Campus Ministries; Choral groups; Concert band; Dance; Drama/theater; International Student Organization; Jazz band; Literary magazine; Marching band; Music ensembles; Musical theater; Opera; Pep band; Radio station; Student government; Student newspaper; Symphony orchestra. **Organizations:** 186 registered organizations, 20 honor societies, 15 religious organizations, 15 fraternities, 10 sororities. **Athletics (Intercollegiate):** *Men:* baseball, basketball, cross-country, football, golf, riflery, soccer, tennis, track/field (outdoor). *Women:* basketball, cross-country, golf, riflery, soccer, softball, tennis, track/field (outdoor), volleyball.

ACCOMMODATIONS

Allowed in exams:	
Calculators	Yes
Dictionary	Yes
Computer	Yes
Spell-checker	Yes
Extended test time	Yes
Scribe	Yes
Proctors	Yes
Oral exams	Yes
Note-takers	Yes
Support services for students with:	
LD	Yes
ADHD	Yes
ASD	Yes
Distraction-reduced environment	Yes
Recording of lecture alowed	Yes
Reading technology	Yes
Audio books	Yes
Other assistive technology	Yes
Priority registration	Yes
Added costs of services:	
For LD	No
For ADHD	No
For ASD	No
LD specialists	Yes
ADHD & ASD coaching	Yes
ASD specialists	No
Professional tutors	Yes
Peer tutors	No
Max. hours/week for services	Varies
How professors are notified of student approved accommodations	Student

COLLEGE GRADUATION REQUIREMENTS

Course waivers allowed	No
Course substitutions allowed	Yes
In what courses: Case by case basis	

Tennessee

University of Tennessee at Martin

201 Hall-Moody, Martin, TN 38238 • Admissions: 731-881-7020 • Fax: 731-881-7029 **Support: CS**

CAMPUS

Type of school	Public
Environment	Village

STUDENTS

Undergrad enrollment	5,228
% male/female	40/60
% from out of state	9
% frosh live on campus	68

FINANCIAL FACTS

Annual in-state tuition	$8,214
Annual out-of-state tuition	$14,254
Room and board	$6,396
Required fees	$1,534

GENERAL ADMISSIONS INFO

Application fee	$30
Regular application deadline	Rolling
Nonfall registration	Yes

Admission may be deferred.

Range ACT Composite	21–26

ACADEMICS

Student/faculty ratio	15:1
% students returning for sophomore year	74

Most classes have 10–19 students.

Programs/Services for Students with Learning Differences

The university believes students with learning disabilities can achieve success in college without academic compromise and can become productive, self-sufficient members of society. Students must self-identify with the Office of Disability Services (ODS). Qualified students with learning disabilities should apply to ODS and submit their documentation once they have received an acceptance from the Office of Admissions. The students will need to make an appointment for an interview at ODS to review and formalize their accommodations. ODS has a list of accommodations and are willing to work with the student to access what is needed. ODS is designed to complement and supplement existing university support services available for all students.

Admissions

Applicants must meet regular admission criteria. Graduates from high schools with state accreditation may enter the university by meeting one of the following criteria: ACT 21+ or 980 SAT and GPA of 2.7, or ACT of 19+ or 900 SAT and GPA of 3.0 or above. Coursework should include: English (4 units), Algebra (2 units), advanced math (2 unit of geometry, trigonometry, calculus or advanced mathematics), natural/physical science (3 units; 1 must be a course in biology, chemistry or physics), U.S. history (1 unit), social studies (1 unit of world history, European history, or world geography, which may be fulfilled by completing 2 one-half unit courses), foreign language (2 units in the same language), and visual/performing arts (1 unit of theater arts, visual arts, music theory, music history, vocal music, instrumental music or art history).

Additional Information

The University is diligent in ensuring that students with disabilities are given equal access to all course materials and experiences. The Disability Service Office is available to students during the semester. In this partnership, the University provides the tools and resources, and the students provide the motivation and hard work. By working together, the students have the potential to reach their academic goals.

ADMISSIONS INFO FOR STUDENTS WITH LEARNING DIFFERENCES

Phone: 731-881-7719 • Fax: 731-881-7702 • Email: cboyd2@utm.edu

SAT/ACT required: Yes (Test optional for 2021)
Interview required: Yes
Essay required: No
Additional application required: Yes
Documentation submitted to: Disabiity Services Office

Special Ed. HS course work accepted: No
Separate application required for Programs/Services: Yes
Documentation required for:
LD: Psychoeducational evaluation
ADHD: Psychoeducational evaluation
ASD: Psychoeducational evaluation

University of Tennessee at Martin

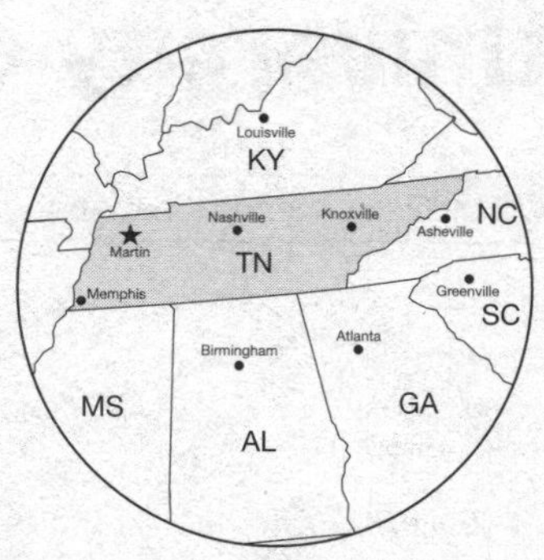

General Admissions

Very Important factors include: rigor of secondary school record, academic GPA, standardized test scores. *Freshman admission requirements:* High school diploma is required and GED is accepted. *Academic units required:* 4 English, 4 math, 3 science, 1 science lab, 2 foreign language, 1 social studies, 1 history, 1 visual/performing arts.

Accommodations or Services

Accommodations are decided upon an individual basis after a thorough review of appropriate, current documentation. The accommodations requests must be supported through the documentation provided and must be logically linked to the current impact of the condition on academic functioning.

Financial Aid

Students should submit: FAFSA; Institution's own financial aid form. Applicants will be notified of awards on a rolling basis beginning 12/15. *Need-based scholarships/grants offered:* College/university scholarship or grant aid from institutional funds; Federal Pell; Private scholarships; SEOG; State scholarships/grants. *Loan aid offered:* Direct PLUS loans; Direct Subsidized Stafford Loans; Direct Unsubsidized Stafford Loans. Federal Work-Study Program available. Institutional employment available.

Campus Life

Activities: Campus Ministries; Choral groups; Concert band; Dance; Drama/theater; International Student Organization; Jazz band; Literary magazine; Marching band; Model UN; Music ensembles; Musical theater; Pep band; Radio station; Student government; Student newspaper; Student-run film society; Television station; Yearbook. **Organizations:** 170 registered organizations, 18 honor societies, 12 religious organizations, 11 fraternities, 9 sororities. **Athletics (Intercollegiate):** *Men:* baseball, basketball, cross-country, football, golf, riflery, rodeo. *Women:* basketball, cheerleading, cross-country, equestrian sports, riflery, rodeo, soccer, softball, tennis, volleyball.

ACCOMMODATIONS

Allowed in exams:	
Calculators	Yes
Dictionary	Yes
Computer	Yes
Spell-checker	Yes
Extended test time	Yes
Scribe	Yes
Proctors	Yes
Oral exams	Yes
Note-takers	Yes
Support services for students with:	
LD	Yes
ADHD	Yes
ASD	Yes
Distraction-reduced environment	Yes
Recording of lecture alowed	Yes
Reading technology	Yes
Audio books	Yes
Other assistive technology	Yes
Priority registration	No
Added costs of services:	
For LD	No
For ADHD	No
For ASD	No
LD specialists	Yes
ADHD & ASD coaching	No
ASD specialists	No
Professional tutors	No
Peer tutors	Yes
Max. hours/week for services	Varies
How professors are notified of student approved accommodations	Student and director

COLLEGE GRADUATION REQUIREMENTS

Course waivers allowed	No
Course substitutions allowed	Yes
In what courses: Case by case basis	

University of Tennessee-Chattanooga

615 McCallie Avenue, Chattanooga, TN 37403 • Admissions: 423-425-4662 • Fax: 423-425-4157 **Support: SP**

CAMPUS

Type of school	Public
Environment	City

STUDENTS

Undergrad enrollment	10,297
% male/female	44/56
% from out of state	6
% frosh live on campus	79

FINANCIAL FACTS

Annual in-state tuition	$9,656
Annual out-of-state tuition	$25,774
Room and board	$9,500

GENERAL ADMISSIONS INFO

Application fee	$30
Regular application deadline	5/1
Nonfall registration	Yes

Admission may be deferred.

Range SAT EBRW	520–630
Range SAT Math	510–600
Range ACT Composite	21–26

ACADEMICS

Student/faculty ratio	19:1
% students returning for sophomore year	71

Most classes have 10–19 students.

Programs/Services for Students with Learning Differences

Disability Resource Center (DRC) at The University of Tennessee at Chattanooga is committed to ensuring that each individual has equal access to all educational opportunities and maximizes their potential regardless of the impact of their disability. DRC aims to support the ongoing development of an accessible university that embraces diversity and celebrates people's differences. This mission is accomplished by creating a physically, programmatically, and attitudinally accessible environment where people are accepted and expected to participate fully regardless of their disability.

Admissions

Students with disabilities submit a general application to the Admissions Office. If a course deficiency is due to impact of disability, an appeals committee will sometimes allow a probationary admittance if DRC works with prospective student to develop an accommodation plan. Students admitted on condition must earn at least a 2.0 GPA their first semester or suspension will result. The Dean of Admissions or admission committee may recommend conditions for acceptance. In order to receive accommodations in the classroom, students with disabilities need to submit application and documentation to the DRC. Application to the DRC is a separate process.

Additional Information

DRC does not, as a matter of policy, seek a waiver of any coursework on a student's behalf. Students admitted conditionally may be required to carry a reduced course load, take specific courses, have a specific advisor, and take specific programs of developmental study. The MOC program is a one week college experience prior to freshman year. There is also a five week Bridge program. Students apply to both programs and must be accepted to the University of Tennessee at Chattanooga. Additionally, the Mosaic Program is available to support students with autism. The curriculum includes four components of a graded courses, coaching, peer and professional mentorship, and supervised study hours. The first year focuses on independence, while year two addresses strengths and self-perceptions. Year three is focused on turning strengths into a career, and year four focuses on workplace skills. There is a fee and separate application process to this program.

ADMISSIONS INFO FOR STUDENTS WITH LEARNING DIFFERENCES

Phone: 423-425-4006 • Fax: 423-425-2288 • Email: michelle-rigler@utc.edu

SAT/ACT required: Yes (Test optional for 2021)
Interview required: No
Essay required: No
Additional application required: No
Documentation submitted to: Disability Resource Center

Special Ed. HS course work accepted: Yes
Separate application required for Programs/Services: No
Documentation required for:
LD: Psychoeducational evaluation
ADHD: Psychoeducational evaluation
ASD: Psychoeducational evaluation

University of Tennessee-Chattanooga

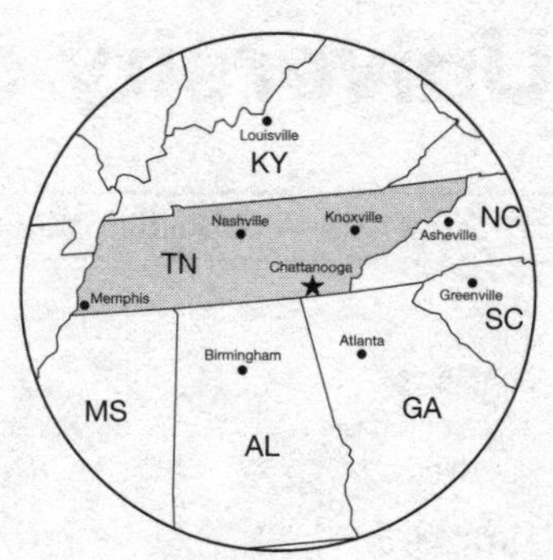

General Admissions

Very Important factors include: rigor of secondary school record, academic GPA, standardized test scores. *Important factors include:* character/personal qualities. *Other factors include:* application essay, recommendation(s), extracurricular activities, talent/ability, volunteer work, work experience. *Freshman admission requirements:* High school diploma is required and GED is accepted. *Academic units required:* 4 English, 4 math, 3 science, 3 science labs, 2 foreign language, 2 history, 1 visual/performing arts.

Accommodations or Services

Accommodations are decided upon an individual basis after a thorough review of appropriate, current documentation. The accommodations requests must be supported through the documentation provided and must be logically linked to the current impact of the condition on academic functioning.

Financial Aid

Students should submit: FAFSA; Institution's own financial aid form. Applicants will be notified of awards on a rolling basis beginning 1/1. *Need-based scholarships/grants offered:* College/university scholarship or grant aid from institutional funds; Federal Pell; Private scholarships; SEOG; State scholarships/grants. *Loan aid offered:* Direct PLUS loans; Direct Subsidized Stafford Loans; Direct Unsubsidized Stafford Loans. Federal Work-Study Program available. Institutional employment available.

Campus Life

Activities: Campus Ministries; Choral groups; Concert band; Dance; Drama/theater; International Student Organization; Jazz band; Literary magazine; Marching band; Model UN; Music ensembles; Musical theater; Opera; Pep band; Radio station; Student government; Student newspaper; Student-run film society; Symphony orchestra; Television station. **Organizations:** 125 registered organizations, 34 honor societies, 8 religious organizations, 14 fraternities, 11 sororities. **Athletics (Intercollegiate):** *Men:* basketball, cross-country, football, golf, tennis, track/field (outdoor), wrestling. *Women:* basketball, cross-country, golf, soccer, softball, tennis, track/field (outdoor), volleyball.

ACCOMMODATIONS

Allowed in exams:	
Calculators	Yes
Dictionary	Yes
Computer	Yes
Spell-checker	Yes
Extended test time	Yes
Scribe	Yes
Proctors	Yes
Oral exams	Yes
Note-takers	Yes
Support services for students with:	
LD	Yes
ADHD	Yes
ASD	Yes
Distraction-reduced environment	Yes
Recording of lecture alowed	Yes
Reading technology	Yes
Audio books	Yes
Other assistive technology	Yes
Priority registration	Yes
Added costs of services:	
For LD	No
For ADHD	No
For ASD	Yes
LD specialists	Yes
ADHD & ASD coaching	Yes
ASD specialists	Yes
Professional tutors	Yes
Peer tutors	No
Max. hours/week for services	Varies
How professors are notified of student approved accommodations	Student

COLLEGE GRADUATION REQUIREMENTS

Course waivers allowed	No
Course substitutions allowed	Yes
In what courses: Case by case basis	

University of Tennessee-Knoxville

320 Student Service Building, Knoxville, TN 37996-0230 • Admissions: 865-974-1111 **Support: SP**

CAMPUS

Type of school	Public
Environment	City

STUDENTS

Undergrad enrollment	23,152
% male/female	49/51
% from out of state	18
% frosh live on campus	91

FINANCIAL FACTS

Annual in-state tuition	$11,332
Annual out-of-state tuition	$29,522
Room and board	$11,482
Required fees	$1,932

GENERAL ADMISSIONS INFO

Application fee	$50
Regular application deadline	8/2
Nonfall registration	Yes

Admission may be deferred.

Range SAT EBRW	580–660
Range SAT Math	570–670
Range ACT Composite	24–30

ACADEMICS

Student/faculty ratio	17:1
% students returning for sophomore year	87

Most classes have 20–29 students.

Programs/Services for Students with Learning Differences

The mission of the Student Disability Services (SDS) is to provide each student with a disability an equal opportunity to participate in the university's programs and activities. Students who are requesting support services are required to submit documentation to verify eligibility under the ADA of 1990. The documentation must include medical or psychological information from a certified professional. It is each student's responsibility to meet the essential qualifications and institutional standards, disclose the disability in a timely manner, provide appropriate documentation, and inform SDS of accommodation needs. Students must also talk with professors about accommodations in the classroom, as needed, and inform SDS of barriers to a successful education. If accommodations are approved, the student is responsible for maintaining and returning borrowed equipment, keeping, cancelling or, rescheduling all appointments with SDS staff members, and monitoring their own progress towards graduation by staying actively involved in their academic planning and course selection.

Admissions

UT has a competitive but holistic admissions process that evaluates every part of a student's application, considering their experience and preparation in academic areas, as well as other factors, including rigor of high school curriculum, difficulty of senior-level coursework, extracurricular or leadership activities, awards, special talents or skills, optional supporting statement, and an optional letter(s) of recommendation. There is no special admission process for students with learning disabilities. The Office of Admissions makes every attempt to judge each application on its academic merits. If applicants believe that their academic record does not accurately reflect their situation, they should not include documentation with admission materials. Applicants who feel more information is needed to compete at an equal level with others seeking admission should consider voluntarily self-identifying the disability and the circumstances to the Admissions Office. Qualified candidates with a disability will not be denied admissions solely on the basis of their disability.

Additional Information

Disability Services works with each student on a case-by-case basis to determine and implement appropriate accommodations based on documentation. Services could include notetakers, alternative testing arrangements such as extra time, books on tape, computers with speech

ADMISSIONS INFO FOR STUDENTS WITH LEARNING DIFFERENCES

Phone: 865-974-6087 • Fax: 865-974-9552 • Email: sds@utk.edu

SAT/ACT required: Yes (Test optional for 2021)
Interview required: No
Essay required: No
Additional application required: Yes
Documentation submitted to: Support Program/Services

Special Ed. HS course work accepted: Yes
Separate application required for Programs/Services: Yes
Documentation required for:
LD: Psychoeducational evaluation
ADHD: Psychoeducational evaluation
ASD: Psychoeducational evaluation

University of Tennessee-Knoxville

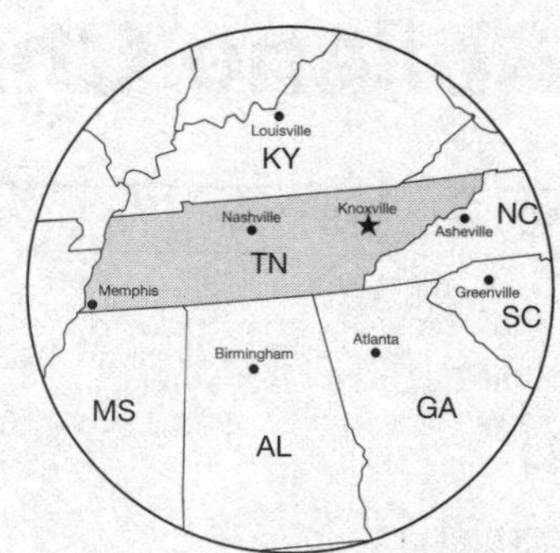

input, separate testing rooms, tape recorders, and foreign language substitutions. Content tutors are available on campus through different departments. The University of Tennessee offers the FUTURE Program, which is a two or three year vocational certificate program for students with intellectual and developmental disabilities, including autism. The program is designated as a Comprehensive Transition Program by the U.S. Department of Education. Courses focus on career exploration and workplace skills, digital literacy, and life skills. It also provides structured internships, modifications, and support to ensure student success in classes. Students participate in campus activities and events. Housing is offered for year two and three. FUTURE offers an inclusive experience, with fellow undergraduate students supporting students to be fully integrated into campus life.

General Admissions

Very Important factors include: academic GPA, standardized test scores. *Important factors include:* rigor of secondary school record, application essay, *Other factors include:* class rank, recommendation(s), extracurricular activities, talent/ability, character/personal qualities, first generation, alumni/ae relation, geographical residence, state residency, racial/ethnic status, volunteer work, work experience, level of applicant's interest. *Freshman admission requirements:* High school diploma is required and GED is accepted. *Academic units recommended:* 4 English, 4 math, 3 science, 3 science labs, 2 foreign language, 1 social studies, 1 history, 1 visual/performing arts.

Accommodations or Services

Accommodations are decided upon an individual basis after a thorough review of appropriate, current documentation. The accommodations requests must be supported through the documentation provided and must be logically linked to the current impact of the condition on academic functioning.

Financial Aid

Students should submit: FAFSA. *Need-based scholarships/grants offered:* College/university scholarship or grant aid from institutional funds; Federal Pell; Private scholarships; SEOG; State scholarships/grants. *Loan aid offered:* Direct PLUS loans; Direct Subsidized Stafford Loans; Direct Unsubsidized Stafford Loans. Federal Work-Study Program available.

Campus Life

Activities: Campus Ministries; Choral groups; Concert band; Dance; Drama/theater; International Student Organization; Jazz band; Literary magazine; Marching band; Model UN; Music ensembles; Musical theater; Opera; Pep band; Radio station; Student government; Student newspaper; Student-run film society; Symphony orchestra; Television station; Yearbook. **Organizations:** 481 registered organizations, 14 honor societies, 42 religious organizations, 25 fraternities, 20 sororities. **Athletics (Intercollegiate):** *Men:* baseball, basketball, cheerleading, cross-country, diving, football, golf, swimming, tennis, track/field (outdoor), track/field (indoor). *Women:* basketball, cheerleading, crew/rowing, cross-country, diving, golf, soccer, softball, swimming, tennis, track/field (outdoor), track/field (indoor), volleyball.

ACCOMMODATIONS

Allowed in exams:	
Calculators	Yes
Dictionary	Yes
Computer	Yes
Spell-checker	Yes
Extended test time	Yes
Scribe	Yes
Proctors	Yes
Oral exams	Yes
Note-takers	Yes
Support services for students with:	
LD	Yes
ADHD	Yes
ASD	Yes
Distraction-reduced environment	Yes
Recording of lecture allowed	Yes
Reading technology	Yes
Audio books	Yes
Other assistive technology	Yes
Priority registration	Yes
Added costs of services:	
For LD	No
For ADHD	No
For ASD	Yes
LD specialists	Yes
ADHD & ASD coaching	Yes
ASD specialists	Yes
Professional tutors	No
Peer tutors	Yes
Max. hours/week for services	Varies
How professors are notified of student approved accommodations	Student

COLLEGE GRADUATION REQUIREMENTS

Course waivers allowed	No
Course substitutions allowed	Yes
In what courses: Case by case basis	

Abilene Christian University

ACU Box 29000, Abilene, TX 79699 • Admissions: 325-674-2650 • Fax: 325-674-2130 **Support: CS**

CAMPUS

Type of school	Private (nonprofit)
Environment	City

STUDENTS

Undergrad enrollment	3,525
% male/female	40/60
% from out of state	15
% frosh live on campus	96

FINANCIAL FACTS

Annual tuition	$37,800
Room and board	$11,000

GENERAL ADMISSIONS INFO

Application fee	$50
Regular application deadline	2/15
Nonfall registration	Yes
Range SAT EBRW	520–630
Range SAT Math	500–600
Range ACT Composite	21–28

ACADEMICS

Student/faculty ratio	14:1
% students returning for sophomore year	79

Most classes have 10–19 students.

Programs/Services for Students with Learning Differences

ACU has a tradition and a vision for academic excellence for all of its students, including those with disabilities. Students with a documented disability are able to participate in the Alpha Scholars program, which provides academic accommodations, tutoring, academic coaching, and mentoring. When applying, a student's assessment report needs to be complete, including test scores and sub-scores, and should be no more than three years old. A student with ADD/ADHD can document their disability through a psychoeducational assessment or have the Documentation of Attention Deficit form completed by their prescribing health professional. To apply for Alpha Scholars, a student needs to fill out the online application at http://acu.edu/alpha.

Admissions

All students admitted to the university must meet the same criteria for admission. There is no special admission process for students with learning disabilities. Regular admissions criteria include college preparatory courses, such as 4 years of English, 3 years of math, 3 years of science, and 2 years of a foreign language. There is no specific GPA requirement. Some students not meeting the admission criteria may be admitted conditionally. Students admitted conditionally must take specified courses in a summer term and demonstrate motivation and ability. Students who complete their application before September 1 receive admissions notification by September 15.

Additional Information

Alpha Scholars Program provides opportunities for individual instruction in basic skills areas such as writing, math, or study skills. Students have access to assessment of learning preferences, strengths, and weaknesses, instruction and tutoring designed to fit the student's particular learning preferences and strengths and academic needs, classroom help if needed such as readers, notetakers, alternative testing arrangements, personal, career, and academic counseling, and workshops on topics such as time management skills, resume writing, career placement, and study skills. Excel peer tutoring is available to students for a fee.

ADMISSIONS INFO FOR STUDENTS WITH LEARNING DIFFERENCES

Phone: 325-674-2667 • Fax: 325-674-6847 • Email: eab16b@acu.edu

SAT/ACT required: No
Interview required: No
Essay required: No
Additional application required: Yes
Documentation submitted to: ACU

Special Ed. HS course work accepted: Yes
Separate application required for Programs/Services: Yes
Documentation required for:
- **LD:** Full psychoeducational assessment
- **ADHD:** Psychoeducational evaluation
- **ASD:** Psychoeducational evaluation

Abilene Christian University

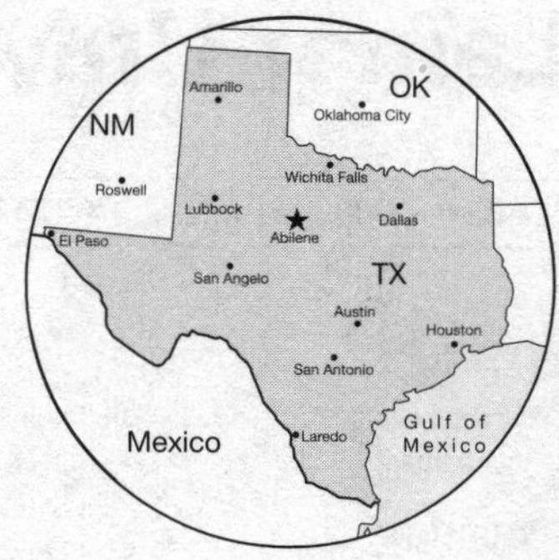

General Admissions

Very Important factors include: rigor of secondary school record, class rank, academic GPA, standardized test scores. *Important factors include:* talent/ability, character/personal qualities. *Other factors include:* application essay, recommendation(s), extracurricular activities, first generation, alumni/ae relation, volunteer work, work experience, level of applicant's interest. *Freshman admission requirements:* High school diploma is required and GED is accepted. *Academic units required:* 4 English, 3 math, 3 science, 2 science labs, 2 foreign language, 1 history. *Academic units recommended:* 4 English, 3 math, 3 science, 2 science labs, 2 foreign language, 1 history.

Accommodations or Services

Accommodations are decided upon an individual basis after a thorough review of appropriate, current documentation. The accommodations requests must be supported through the documentation provided and must be logically linked to the current impact of the condition on academic functioning.

Financial Aid

Students should submit: FAFSA. *Need-based scholarships/grants offered:* College/university scholarship or grant aid from institutional funds; Federal Pell; Private scholarships; SEOG; State scholarships/grants. *Loan aid offered:* Direct PLUS loans; Direct Subsidized Stafford Loans; Direct Unsubsidized Stafford Loans. Federal Work-Study Program available. Institutional employment available.

Campus Life

Activities: Campus Ministries; Choral groups; Concert band; Dance; Drama/theater; International Student Organization; Jazz band; Literary magazine; Marching band; Model UN; Music ensembles; Musical theater; Opera; Pep band; Radio station; Student government; Student newspaper; Symphony orchestra; Television station. **Organizations:** 114 registered organizations, 9 honor societies, 6 religious organizations, 7 fraternities, 7 sororities. **Athletics (Intercollegiate):** *Men:* baseball, basketball, cross-country, football, tennis, track/field (outdoor), track/field (indoor). *Women:* basketball, cross-country, soccer, softball, tennis, track/field (outdoor), track/field (indoor), volleyball.

ACCOMMODATIONS

Allowed in exams:	
Calculators	Yes
Dictionary	Yes
Computer	Yes
Spell-checker	Yes
Extended test time	Yes
Scribe	Yes
Proctors	Yes
Oral exams	No
Note-takers	Yes
Support services for students with:	
LD	Yes
ADHD	Yes
ASD	Yes
Distraction-reduced environment	Yes
Recording of lecture allowed	Yes
Reading technology	Yes
Audio books	Yes
Other assistive technology	Yes
Priority registration	No
Added costs of services:	
For LD	No
For ADHD	No
For ASD	No
LD specialists	Yes
ADHD & ASD coaching	Yes
ASD specialists	No
Professional tutors	No
Peer tutors	Yes
Max. hours/week for services	Varies
How professors are notified of student approved accommodations	Student

COLLEGE GRADUATION REQUIREMENTS

Course waivers allowed	No
Course substitutions allowed	No

Lamar University

P.O. Box 10009, Beaumont, TX 77710 • Admissions: 409-880-8888 • Fax: 409-880-8463 **Support: S**

CAMPUS

Type of school	Public
Environment	Village

STUDENTS

Undergrad enrollment	8,701
% male/female	42/58
% from out of state	2
% frosh live on campus	56

FINANCIAL FACTS

Annual in-state tuition	$10,464
Annual out-of-state tuition	$22,734
Room and board	$9,064

GENERAL ADMISSIONS INFO

Application fee	$25
Regular application deadline	Rolling
Nonfall registration	Yes
Range SAT EBRW	490–580
Range SAT Math	470–560
Range ACT Composite	17–23

ACADEMICS

Student/faculty ratio	18:1
% students returning for sophomore year	66

Most classes have 20–29 students.

Programs/Services for Students with Learning Differences

The Disability Resource Center (DRC) assures qualified students access to Lamar University's academic activities, programs, resources, and services. Students with disabilities may qualify for accommodations, academic adjustments, and/or assistive technology. Students are encouraged to contact the DRC to schedule an appointment with the Director or Communication Access Coordinator and complete an Accommodation Request Form and submit appropriate disability documentation that supports the accommodation requests. Individualized accommodation plans are developed for each student based on the needs identified.

Admissions

Applicants with learning disabilities and/or ADHD must meet the general admission requirements. Services will be offered to enrolled students who notify the Disability Resource Center. Students must be in top half of their class and complete fourteen credits to be admitted unconditionally, including 4years English, 3 years math (Algebra I–II and Geometry or higher), 2 years science (physical science, biology, chemistry, physics, or geology), 2.5 years social science, and 2.5 years electives (foreign language is recommended). A very limited number of applicants not meeting the prerequisites may be admitted on individual approval. Some students may be considered on an individual approval basis if they fail to meet unconditional admission. These students are subject to mandatory advisement. These students have a six-credit limit in summer and fourteen credit in fall term, and must successfully complete nine hours with a 2.0 GPA. Students must meet these provisions or leave for one year.

Additional Information

The Disability Resource Center offers a variety of services designed to assure qualified students access to the university's academic activities, programs, resources, and services. Services or accommodations could include priority registration, alternative testing accommodations, copying of class notes, classroom accommodations, notetakers, readers, and textbooks on tape. Professional staff assist students with questions, problem solving, adjustment, decision making, goal planning, and testing. Skills classes in study skills are offered, including developmental writing, reading, and math for credit. Students are referred to other offices and personnel in accord with the needs and intents of the individual. Services and accommodations are available for undergraduate and graduate students.

ADMISSIONS INFO FOR STUDENTS WITH LEARNING DIFFERENCES

Phone: 409-880-8347 • Fax: 409-880-2225

SAT/ACT required: Yes (Test optional for 2021)
Interview required: No
Essay required: No
Additional application required: No
Documentation submitted to: The Disability Resource Center

Special Ed. HS course work accepted: Yes
Separate application required for Programs/Services: Yes
Documentation required for:
LD: Psychoeducational evaluation
ADHD: Psychoeducational evaluation
ASD: Psychoeducational evaluation

Lamar University

General Admissions

Very important factors include: rigor of secondary school record, class rank. *Other factors include:* recommendations, extracurricular activities, talent/ability. *Freshman admission requirements:* High school diploma is required and GED is accepted. *Academic units required:* 4 English, 3 math, 2 science, 2.5 social studies, 2.5 academic electives. *Academic units recommended:* 2 foreign language.

Accommodations or Services

Accommodations are decided upon an individual basis after a thorough review of appropriate, current documentation. The accommodations requests must be supported through the documentation provided and must be logically linked to the current impact of the condition on academic functioning.

Financial Aid

Students should submit: FAFSA. Applicants will be notified of awards on a rolling basis beginning 11/1 *Need-based scholarships/grants offered:* College/university scholarship or grant aid from institutional funds; Federal Pell; Private scholarships; SEOG; State scholarships/grants. *Loan aid offered:* Direct PLUS loans; Direct Subsidized Stafford Loans; Direct Unsubsidized Stafford Loans. Federal Work-Study Program available. Institutional employment available.

Campus Life

Activities: Student government; Student newspaper. **Organizations:** 145 registered organizations, 11 fraternities, 8 sororities. **Athletics (Intercollegiate):** *Men:* baseball, basketball, cross-country, golf, tennis, track/field (outdoor). *Women:* basketball, cross-country, golf, tennis, track/field (outdoor), volleyball.

ACCOMMODATIONS

Allowed in exams:	
Calculators	Yes
Dictionary	Yes
Computer	Yes
Spell-checker	Yes
Extended test time	Yes
Scribe	Yes
Proctors	Yes
Oral exams	Yes
Note-takers	Yes
Support services for students with:	
LD	Yes
ADHD	Yes
ASD	Yes
Distraction-reduced environment	Yes
Recording of lecture alowed	Yes
Reading technology	Yes
Audio books	Yes
Other assistive technology	Yes
Priority registration	Yes
Added costs of services:	
For LD	No
For ADHD	No
For ASD	No
LD specialists	Yes
ADHD & ASD coaching	No
ASD specialists	No
Professional tutors	No
Peer tutors	Yes
Max. hours/week for services	15
How professors are notified of student approved accommodations	Student

COLLEGE GRADUATION REQUIREMENTS

Course waivers allowed	No
Course substitutions allowed	Yes
In what courses: Case by case basis	

Texas

Schreiner University

2100 Memorial Boulevard, Kerrville, TX 78028-5697 • Admissions: 830-792-7217 • Fax: (830) 792-7226 **Support: SP**

CAMPUS

Type of school	Private (nonprofit)
Environment	Town

STUDENTS

Undergrad enrollment	1,257
% male/female	44/56
% from out of state	3
% frosh live on campus	83

FINANCIAL FACTS

Annual tuition	$31,938
Room and board	$10,442

GENERAL ADMISSIONS INFO

Application fee	$25
Regular application deadline	8/1
Nonfall registration	Yes

Admission may be deferred.

Range SAT EBRW	470–560
Range SAT Math	450–550
Range ACT Composite	17–23

ACADEMICS

Student/faculty ratio	14:1
% students returning for sophomore year	64

Most classes have 10–19 students.

Programs/Services for Students with Learning Differences

Students admitted to the Learning Support Services (LSS) program must be highly motivated, have the intellectual potential for success in a rigorous academic program, and have the ability to meet the demands of college life. The program provides services to 60–70 students and is staffed by LD specialists and many tutors. Students with learning disabilities are enrolled in regular college courses and receive individual tutorial assistance in each subject. Students in the program are held to the same high standards and complete the same curriculum requirements as all other degree candidates. In addition to the LSS staff, the Schreiner University faculty is dedicated to helping students realize their full potential. Students with co-existing Autism Spectrum Disorders, traumatic brain injuries, intellectual disabilities, or severe psychological disorders are not eligible for the LSS program but may qualify for academic accommodations under Section 504.

Admissions

Students should have a GPA of 3.3 or higher. In addition, the student's involvement in high school and their community will be considered. Students who do not meet the minimum GPA requirement may be asked for additional documents to be reviewed by the admission committee for an admission decision. Applicants should be enrolled in regular, mainstream English courses in high school. Students need to take a college-preparatory curriculum. However, admission would not be denied to a qualified candidate if some coursework was not included. An interview is required and is an important part of the admissions decision. Applicants are considered individually and selected on the basis of their intellectual ability, motivation, academic preparation, and potential for success. The university has a test optional policy.

Additional Information

The Learning Support Services Program (LSS) is tailored to meet the needs of each participating student. Each LSS staff member is committed to helping students develop the independent study skills and strategies that are necessary for academic success. Individualized services may include study skills development, regularly scheduled tutoring for all classes, testing accommodations, such as readers, scribes, and extended time, use of recorded textbooks, arrangements made for note-takers in lecture classes, and a freshman seminar class that addresses issues of specific concern to college students with learning disabilities. The Student Academic Support

ADMISSIONS INFO FOR STUDENTS WITH LEARNING DIFFERENCES

Phone: 830-792-7258 • Email: jgallik@schreiner.edu

SAT/ACT required: No
Interview required: Yes
Essay required: Yes
Additional application required: No
Documentation submitted to: LSS

Special Ed. HS course work accepted: Yes
Separate application required for Programs/Services: Yes
Documentation required for:
LD: Psychoeducational evaluation
ADHD: Psychoeducational evaluation
ASD: Psychoeducational evaluation

Schreiner University

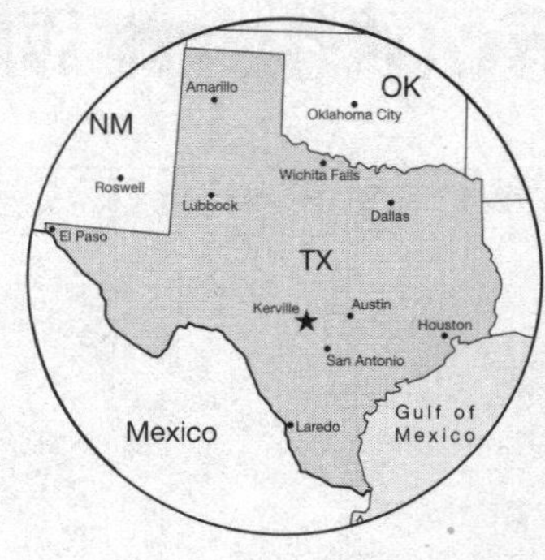

Texas

Center is also available to assist students through a variety of student-staffed programs and services including the Writing Center, Peer Tutoring Center, and supplemental instruction. All services provide academic support to students and promote lifelong learning practices.

General Admissions

Very Important factors include: class rank, academic GPA, standardized test scores. *Important factors include:* rigor of secondary school record, application essay, character/personal qualities, volunteer work, work experience, level of applicant's interest. *Other factors include:* recommendation(s), interview, extracurricular activities, talent/ability. *Freshman admission requirements:* High school diploma is required and GED is accepted. *Academic units recommended:* 4 English, 3 math, 3 science, 2 science labs, 2 foreign language, 2 social studies, 2 history, 3.5 academic electives, 1 computer science, 1 visual/performing arts.

Accommodations or Services

Accommodations are decided upon an individual basis after a thorough review of appropriate, current documentation. The accommodations requests must be supported through the documentation provided and must be logically linked to the current impact of the condition on academic functioning.

Financial Aid

Students should submit: FAFSA. *Need-based scholarships/grants offered:* College/university scholarship or grant aid from institutional funds; Federal Pell; Private scholarships; SEOG; State scholarships/grants. *Loan aid offered:* Direct PLUS loans; Direct Subsidized Stafford Loans; Direct Unsubsidized Stafford Loans. Federal Work-Study Program available. Institutional employment available.

Campus Life

Activities: Campus Ministries; Choral groups; Dance; Drama/theater; Literary magazine; Music ensembles; Musical theater; Pep band; Student government; Student newspaper; Symphony orchestra. **Organizations:** 38 registered organizations, 3 honor societies, 7 religious organizations, 2 fraternities, 2 sororities. **Athletics (Intercollegiate):** *Men:* baseball, basketball, golf, soccer, tennis. *Women:* basketball, cheerleading, golf, soccer, softball, tennis, volleyball.

ACCOMMODATIONS

Allowed in exams:	
Calculators	Yes
Dictionary	Yes
Computer	Yes
Spell-checker	Yes
Extended test time	Yes
Scribe	Yes
Proctors	Yes
Oral exams	Yes
Note-takers	Yes
Support services for students with:	
LD	Yes
ADHD	Yes
ASD	Yes
Distraction-reduced environment	Yes
Recording of lecture alowed	Yes
Reading technology	Yes
Audio books	Yes
Other assistive technology	Yes
Priority registration	No
Added costs of services:	
For LD	No
For ADHD	No
For ASD	No
LD specialists	Yes
ADHD & ASD coaching	Yes
ASD specialists	No
Professional tutors	Yes
Peer tutors	Yes
Max. hours/week for services	Varies
How professors are notified of student approved accommodations	Student and director

COLLEGE GRADUATION REQUIREMENTS

Course waivers allowed	No
Course substitutions allowed	No

Southern Methodist University

PO Box 750181, Dallas, TX 75275-0181 • Admissions: 214-768-2058 • Fax: 214-768-0103 **Support: CS**

CAMPUS

Type of school	Private (nonprofit)
Environment	Metropolis

STUDENTS

Undergrad enrollment	6,679
% male/female	51/49
% from out of state	55
% frosh live on campus	98

FINANCIAL FACTS

Annual tuition	$51,958
Room and board	$17,110
Required fees	$6,582

GENERAL ADMISSIONS INFO

Application fee	$60
Regular application deadline	7/31
Nonfall registration	Yes

Admission may be deferred.

Range SAT EBRW	640–720
Range SAT Math	660–760
Range ACT Composite	29–33

ACADEMICS

Student/faculty ratio	11:1
% students returning for sophomore year	91

Most classes have 10–19 students.

Programs/Services for Students with Learning Differences

The goal of Disability Accommodations & Success Strategies (DASS) is to provide students with documented disabilities services or reasonable accommodations in order to reduce the effects that a disability may have on their performance in a traditional academic setting. DASS provides individual attention and support for students needing assistance with various aspects of their campus experience such as notifying professors, arranging accommodations, referrals, and accessibility.

Admissions

The admissions committee weighs many factors during the course of the application process, including classroom performance, rigor of high school curriculum, quality of essays and recommendations, extracurricular activities, talents, character, and life experiences. Minimum high school course requirements include: 4 units of English, 3 units of math (algebra I, II, geometry), 3 units of social science, 3 units of science (of which 2 must be lab science), and 2 consecutive units of foreign language. There is no special admission process to the university for students with LD. If their standardized tests were administered under non-standard conditions, this will not weigh unfavorably into the admission decision. If a student plans to major or minor in music, dance, or theater, an audition is required.

Additional Information

DASS a offers academic coaching for students with diagnosed learning disabilities, a study and reading skills course called ORACLE, and a student-run organization called Students for New Learning. There are learning specialists available to work with students with learning differences free of charge. There are currently 380 students with learning disabilities and/or ADHD receiving services. Students need to request accommodations using the Accommodations Request Form. All communication with the student will then be through the student DASS link. In addition, all students have access to tutoring, writing centers, study skills workshops, and classes to improve reading rate, comprehension, and vocabulary. Skills classes are offered in time management, test strategies, notetaking strategies, organizational skills, concentration, memory, and test anxiety.

ADMISSIONS INFO FOR STUDENTS WITH LEARNING DIFFERENCES

Phone: 214-768-1470 • Fax: 214-768-1255 • Email: dass@smu.edu

SAT/ACT required: Yes (Test optional for 2021)
Interview required: No
Essay required: Yes
Additional application required: No
Documentation submitted to: Disability Accommodations & Success Strategies

Special Ed. HS course work accepted: Yes
Separate application required for Programs/Services: No
Documentation required for:
LD: Psychoeducational evaluation
ADHD: Psychoeducational evaluation
ASD: Psychoeducational evaluation

Southern Methodist University

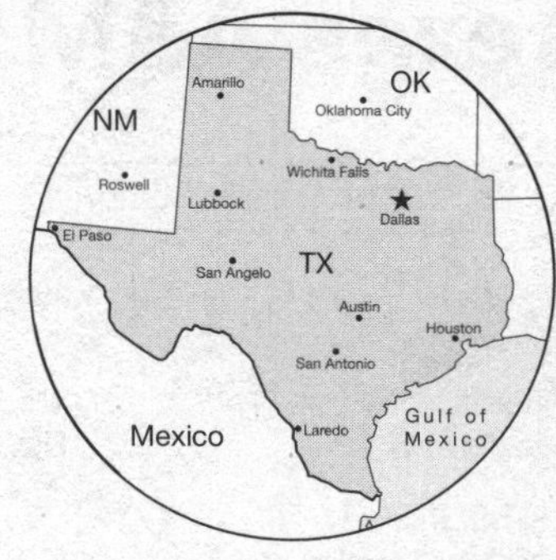

Texas

General Admissions

Very Important factors include: rigor of secondary school record, academic GPA, application essay, standardized test scores, recommendation(s). *Important factors include:* class rank, extracurricular activities, talent/ability, character/personal qualities. *Other factors include:* first generation, alumni/ae relation, racial/ethnic status, volunteer work, work experience, level of applicant's interest. *Freshman admission requirements:* High school diploma is required and GED is not accepted. *Academic units required:* 4 English, 3 math, 3 science, 2 science labs, 2 foreign language, 3 social studies. *Academic units recommended:* 4 English, 4 math, 3 science, 2 science labs, 3 foreign language, 3 history, 3 academic electives.

Accommodations or Services

Accommodations are decided upon an individual basis after a thorough review of appropriate, current documentation. The accommodations requests must be supported through the documentation provided and must be logically linked to the current impact of the condition on academic functioning.

Financial Aid

Students should submit: CSS/Financial Aid PROFILE; FAFSA; Noncustodial PROFILE. Applicants will be notified of awards on a rolling basis beginning 3/1. *Need-based scholarships/grants offered:* College/university scholarship or grant aid from institutional funds; Federal Pell; Private scholarships; SEOG; State scholarships/grants. *Loan aid offered:* Direct PLUS loans; Direct Subsidized Stafford Loans; Direct Unsubsidized Stafford Loans. Federal Work-Study Program available. Institutional employment available.

Campus Life

Activities: Campus Ministries; Choral groups; Concert band; Dance; Drama/theater; International Student Organization; Jazz band; Literary magazine; Marching band; Model UN; Music ensembles; Musical theater; Opera; Pep band; Radio station; Student government; Student newspaper; Student-run film society; Symphony orchestra; Television station; Yearbook. **Organizations:** 180 registered organizations, 16 honor societies, 27 religious organizations, 15 fraternities, 13 sororities. **Athletics (Intercollegiate):** *Men:* basketball, diving, football, golf, soccer, swimming, tennis, volleyball, water polo. *Women:* basketball, crew/rowing, cross-country, diving, equestrian sports, golf, soccer, swimming, tennis, track/field (outdoor), volleyball, water polo.

ACCOMMODATIONS

Allowed in exams:	
Calculators	Yes
Dictionary	Yes
Computer	Yes
Spell-checker	Yes
Extended test time	Yes
Scribe	Yes
Proctors	Yes
Oral exams	Yes
Note-takers	Yes
Support services for students with:	
LD	Yes
ADHD	Yes
ASD	Yes
Distraction-reduced environment	Yes
Recording of lecture allowed	Yes
Reading technology	Yes
Audio books	Yes
Other assistive technology	Yes
Priority registration	Yes
Added costs of services:	
For LD	No
For ADHD	No
For ASD	No
LD specialists	Yes
ADHD & ASD coaching	Yes
ASD specialists	No
Professional tutors	Yes
Peer tutors	Yes
Max. hours/week for services	Varies
How professors are notified of student approved accommodations	Student

COLLEGE GRADUATION REQUIREMENTS

Course waivers allowed	No
Course substitutions allowed	Yes
In what courses: Case by case basis	

Texas A&M University—College Station

P.O. Box 30014, College Station, TX 77843-3014 • Admissions: 979-845-1060 • Fax: 979-458-1808 **Support: SP**

CAMPUS

Type of school	Public
Environment	City

STUDENTS

Undergrad enrollment	53,123
% male/female	53/47
% from out of state	4
% frosh live on campus	72

FINANCIAL FACTS

Annual in-state tuition	$12,744
Annual out-of-state tuition	$40,476
Room and board	$11,400

GENERAL ADMISSIONS INFO

Application fee	$75
Regular application deadline	12/1
Nonfall registration	Yes
Range SAT EBRW	580–680
Range SAT Math	580–710
Range ACT Composite	26–31

ACADEMICS

Student/faculty ratio	19:1
% students returning for sophomore year	93

Most classes have 20–29 students.

Programs/Services for Students with Learning Differences

Disability Services offers accommodations coordination, evaluation referral, disability-related information, assistive technology services, sign language interpreting, and transcription services for academically related purposes. Although Disability Services does not offer disability evaluation and/or testing, tutoring, personal expenses, attendants or scholarships, Disability Services will provide other available resources. Students may request accommodations throughout the semester. It may take up to 2–3 weeks for the information to be reviewed and accommodations to be put in place. The Access Coordinator will contact students to set up an appointment to discuss possible accommodations.

Admissions

Applicants with learning disabilities submit the general application form and are considered under the same guidelines as all applicants. Students may have their application reviewed by requesting special consideration based on their disability and by providing letters of recommendation from their high school counselor stating what accommodations are needed in college to be successful. ACT or SAT are not required for admission. Students not meeting academic criteria for automatic admission may be offered admission to a summer provisional program. These students must take 9–12 credits and receive a grade of C in each of the courses.

Additional Information

Accommodations are provided on an individual basis as needs arise. Disability Resources offers accommodation coordination. The Academic Success Center offers on-campus, drop-in tutoring at TutorHubs located throughout campus. Tutoring is provided by undergraduate peer tutors. Aggie ACHIEVE (Academic Courses in Higher Inclusive Education and Vocational Experiences) is a four-year inclusive higher education program for young adults with intellectual and developmental disabilities to expand their interests and prepare for inclusive employment in the community. Students must have completed high school, be able to live independently, and fully participate in the program. Typically, 12 students are accepted. Aggie ACHIEVE students live on campus, participate in TAMU classes, join clubs and organizations, prepare for inclusive employment, and integrate fully into student life at Texas A&M University. There are fees associated with this program.

ADMISSIONS INFO FOR STUDENTS WITH LEARNING DIFFERENCES

Phone: 979-845-1637 • Fax: 979-458-1214 • Email: disability@tamu.edu

SAT/ACT required: Yes (Test optional for 2021)
Interview required: No
Essay required: Yes
Additional application required: No
Documentation submitted to: Academic Success Center

Special Ed. HS course work accepted: Yes
Separate application required for Programs/Services: Yes
Documentation required for:
LD: Psychoeducational evaluation
ADHD: Psychoeducational evaluation
ASD: Psychoeducational evaluation

Texas A&M University—College Station

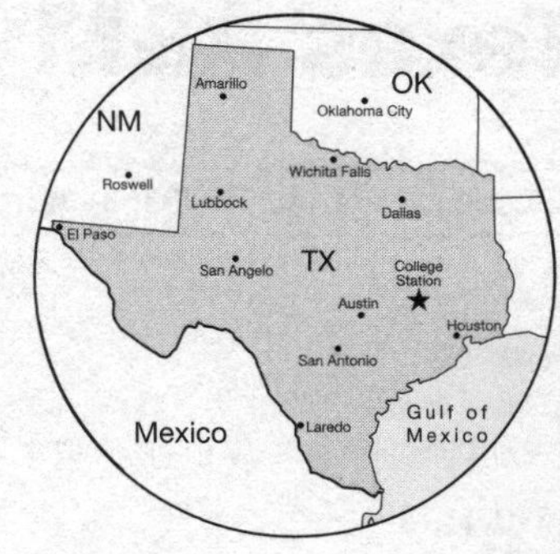

General Admissions

Very Important factors include: rigor of secondary school record, class rank, academic GPA, standardized test scores, extracurricular activities, talent/ability. *Important factors include:* application essay, first generation, geographical residence, state residency, volunteer work. *Other factors include:* recommendation(s), character/personal qualities, level of applicant's interest. *Freshman admission requirements:* High school diploma is required and GED is accepted. *Academic units required:* 4 English, 3 math, 3 science, 1 science lab, 2 foreign language, 3 social studies, 5 academic electives, 1 visual/performing arts, 1 unit from above areas or other academic areas. *Academic units recommended:* 4 English, 4 math, 4 science, 2 science labs, 2 foreign language, 4 social studies, 7 academic electives, 1 visual/performing arts.

Accommodations or Services

Accommodations are decided upon an individual basis after a thorough review of appropriate, current documentation. The accommodations requests must be supported through the documentation provided and must be logically linked to the current impact of the condition on academic functioning.

Financial Aid

Students should submit: FAFSA. *Need-based scholarships/grants offered:* College/university scholarship or grant aid from institutional funds; Federal Pell; Private scholarships; SEOG; State scholarships/grants. *Loan aid offered:* Direct PLUS loans; Direct Subsidized Stafford Loans; Direct Unsubsidized Stafford Loans. Federal Work-Study Program available. Institutional employment available.

Campus Life

Activities: Campus Ministries; Choral groups; Concert band; Dance; Drama/theater; International Student Organization; Jazz band; Literary magazine; Marching band; Music ensembles; Musical theater; Radio station; Student government; Student newspaper; Student-run film society; Symphony orchestra; Television station; Yearbook. **Organizations:** 1111 registered organizations, 33 honor societies, 86 religious organizations, 30 fraternities, 28 sororities. **Athletics (Intercollegiate):** *Men:* baseball, basketball, cross-country, diving, football, golf, riflery, swimming, tennis, track/field (outdoor), track/field (indoor). *Women:* basketball, cross-country, diving, equestrian sports, golf, riflery, soccer, softball, swimming, tennis, track/field (outdoor), track/field (indoor), volleyball.

ACCOMMODATIONS

Allowed in exams:	
Calculators	Yes
Dictionary	Yes
Computer	Yes
Spell-checker	Yes
Extended test time	Yes
Scribe	Yes
Proctors	Yes
Oral exams	Yes
Note-takers	Yes
Support services for students with:	
LD	Yes
ADHD	Yes
ASD	Yes
Distraction-reduced environment	Yes
Recording of lecture allowed	Yes
Reading technology	Yes
Audio books	Yes
Other assistive technology	Yes
Priority registration	Yes
Added costs of services:	
For LD	No
For ADHD	No
For ASD	No
LD specialists	Yes
ADHD & ASD coaching	Yes
ASD specialists	Yes
Professional tutors	No
Peer tutors	Yes
Max. hours/week for services	Varies
How professors are notified of student approved accommodations	Student

COLLEGE GRADUATION REQUIREMENTS

Course waivers allowed	No
Course substitutions allowed	Yes
In what courses: Case by case basis	

Texas A&M University—Kingsville

MSC 105, Kingsville, TX 78363 • Admissions: 361-593-2315 • Fax: 361-593-2195 **Support: S**

CAMPUS	
Type of school	Public
Environment	Town
STUDENTS	
Undergrad enrollment	6,178
% male/female	50/50
% from out of state	1
% frosh live on campus	64
FINANCIAL FACTS	
Annual in-state tuition	$9,694
Annual out-of-state tuition	$25,266
Room and board	$8,787
GENERAL ADMISSIONS INFO	
Application fee	$15
Regular application deadline	8/1
Nonfall registration	No
Admission may be deferred.	
Range SAT EBRW	470–560
Range SAT Math	470–560
Range ACT Composite	17–22
ACADEMICS	
Student/faculty ratio	17:1
% students returning for sophomore year	65
Most classes have 10–19 students.	

Programs/Services for Students with Learning Differences

The university is committed to providing an environment in which every student is encouraged to reach the highest level of personal and educational achievement. Students with documented disabilities must register with the Disability Resource Center (DRC) each semester in order to obtain accommodations and a letter of explanation to hand deliver to their instructors. Possible accommodations include counseling services, educational, vocational and personal consultations, tutoring, testing, and academic advising. Each freshman receives academic endorsement, developmental educational classes in writing, math, or reading, and access to tutoring or study groups. There are academic rescue programs for students in academic jeopardy. Additionally, students can enroll in no credit skills classes on topics including stress management and test anxiety.

Admissions

All applicants must meet the same general admission criteria. Students with LD are encouraged to self-disclose during the application process. There are two types of admission plans: conditional and unconditional. Students graduating in the top 10% of their high school class and completing a college preparatory high school program meet regular admission requirements. Top 10% students must also submit ACT or SAT scores to complete their admission file. The university is test optional for 2021 school year and this may be extended. Students who do not meet the assured admission criteria can be admitted through Texas A&M-Kingsville's individual review process. This process involves a holistic review of academic achievements, extracurricular activities, community service, talents, awards, and other factors that support a student's ability to succeed at Texas A&M-Kingsville. Applicants who are denied admission and wish to appeal need to submit a letter or email sent to admissions requesting the review and submit a personal statement of appeal and two recommendations from teachers in college prep courses.

Additional Information

Students with LD have access to notetakers, readers, writers, and other assistance that the university can provide. The Center for Student Success offers all students entering college as freshmen the University Success Course. The course is designed to assist freshman by enhancing their academic skills while introducing them to campus life at Texas A&M University-Kingsville. Also available is online tutoring, advising, and access to the University Writing Center. In addition, the PAL mentoring program is

ADMISSIONS INFO FOR STUDENTS WITH LEARNING DIFFERENCES

Phone: 361-593-3024 • Fax: 361-593-2006 • Email: angel.hoodye@tamuk.edu

SAT/ACT required: Yes (Test optional for 2021)
Interview required: Yes
Essay required: No
Additional application required: No
Documentation submitted to: Disability Resource Center (DRC)

Special Ed. HS course work accepted: Yes
Separate application required for Programs/Services: No
Documentation required for:
LD: Psychoeducational evaluation
ADHD: Psychoeducational evaluation
ASD: Psychoeducational evaluation

Texas A&M University—Kingsville

Texas

available to support students in making a successful transition to campus by creating educational and supportive relationships. The PAL Mentors support students by sharing skills and positive habits, guiding students to resources and opportunities on campus, and promoting positive decision making.

General Admissions

Very Important factors include: class rank, standardized test scores. *Freshman admission requirements:* High school diploma is required and GED is accepted *Academic units required:* 4 English, 4 math, 4 science, 2 foreign language, 4 social studies, 5.5 academic electives.

Accommodations or Services

Accommodations are decided upon an individual basis after a thorough review of appropriate, current documentation. The accommodations requests must be supported through the documentation provided and must be logically linked to the current impact of the condition on academic functioning.

Financial Aid

Students should submit: FAFSA; Institution's own financial aid form. Applicants will be notified of awards on a rolling basis beginning 5/1. *Need-based scholarships/grants offered:* College/university scholarship or grant aid from institutional funds; Federal Pell; Private scholarships; SEOG; State scholarships/grants. *Loan aid offered:* Direct PLUS loans; Direct Subsidized Stafford Loans; Direct Unsubsidized Stafford Loans; State loans.

Campus Life

Activities: Choral groups; Concert band; Dance; Drama/theater; Jazz band; Marching band; Music ensembles; Musical theater; Pep band; Radio station; Student government; Student newspaper; Television station.

ACCOMMODATIONS

Allowed in exams:	
Calculators	Yes
Dictionary	Yes
Computer	Yes
Spell-checker	Yes
Extended test time	Yes
Scribe	Yes
Proctors	Yes
Oral exams	Yes
Note-takers	Yes
Support services for students with:	
LD	Yes
ADHD	Yes
ASD	Yes
Distraction-reduced environment	Yes
Recording of lecture allowed	Yes
Reading technology	Yes
Audio books	Yes
Other assistive technology	Yes
Priority registration	Yes
Added costs of services:	
For LD	No
For ADHD	No
For ASD	No
LD specialists	No
ADHD & ASD coaching	No
ASD specialists	No
Professional tutors	No
Peer tutors	Yes
Max. hours/week for services	Varies
How professors are notified of student approved accommodations	Student

COLLEGE GRADUATION REQUIREMENTS

Course waivers allowed	Yes
In what courses: Case-by-case decision made by provost.	
Course substitutions allowed	Yes
In what courses: Case-by-case decision made by provost.	

Texas State University

429 North Guadalupe St., San Marcos, TX 78666 • Admissions: 512-245-2364 • Fax: 512-245-8044 **Support: CS**

CAMPUS	
Type of school	Public
Environment	Town
STUDENTS	
Undergrad enrollment	33,917
% male/female	42/58
% from out of state	2
% frosh live on campus	91
FINANCIAL FACTS	
Annual in-state tuition	$11,540
Annual out-of-state tuition	$23,820
Room and board	$10,880
GENERAL ADMISSIONS INFO	
Application fee	$75
Regular application deadline	5/1
Nonfall registration	Yes
Admission may be deferred.	
Range SAT EBRW	510–600
Range SAT Math	500–580
Range ACT Composite	19–25
ACADEMICS	
Student/faculty ratio	20:1
% students returning for sophomore year	76
Most classes have 20–29 students.	

Programs/Services for Students with Learning Differences

The Office of Disability Services (ODS) strives to be a model program serving students with disabilities in higher education. Specialized support services are based on the individual student disability based needs. Services available could include special groups registration, recorded textbooks, recording of textbooks not available on tape, arranging for special testing accommodations such as extended time and reader services, assistance in accessing adaptive computer equipment, assistance in locating volunteer readers and note-takers, liaison and advocacy between students, faculty and staff, referral for tutoring, disability management counseling, and information and referral to on- and off-campus resources.

Admissions

Students with LD must meet the same admission requirements as other applicants. Students applying should have completed 4 credits of English, 4 credits of math, 4 credits of science, 4 credits of social studies, 2 credits of foreign language, 1 credit of fine arts, and 1 credit of physical education. If the student does not meet the assured admission requirements and is ranked in the top 75% of the class, the application will be automatically reviewed through a holistic review process. Applications for Spring 2021, Summer 2021 and Fall 2021 from students who are unable to submit an ACT or SAT score due to reduced availability will also be reviewed, provided the student is ranked in the top 75% of their class. Texas State considers high school curriculum, admission essay(s), extracurricular involvement, leadership, community service, work experience, quality and competitive level of courses taken, and grades earned, in addition to other factors presented in the application.

Additional Information

Students will need to register for accommodations. The Student Learning Assistance Center is available to all students. Peer tutoring is offered for a fee. Supplemental Instruction (SI) is a nontraditional form of tutoring that focuses on collaboration, group study, and interaction for assisting students in undertaking "traditionally difficult" courses. SI targets courses with a minimum 30% rate of students that drop, withdraw, or fail, and then provides a trained peer who has successfully negotiated the course to assist its future students. Through 50-minute SI sessions, students are provided with course-specific learning and study strategies, note-taking and test-taking skills, as well as the opportunity for a structured study time with peers.

ADMISSIONS INFO FOR STUDENTS WITH LEARNING DIFFERENCES

Phone: 512-245-3451 • Fax: 512-245-3452 • Email: cr49669@txstate.edu

SAT/ACT required: Yes (Test optional for 2021)
Interview required: No
Essay required: No
Additional application required: No
Documentation submitted to: Office of Disability Services

Special Ed. HS course work accepted: Yes
Separate application required for Programs/Services: No
Documentation required for:
LD: Psychoeducational evaluation
ADHD: Psychoeducational evaluation
ASD: Psychoeducational evaluation

Texas State University

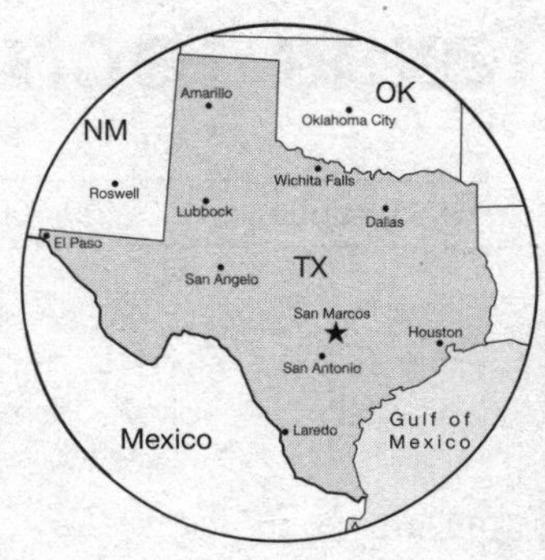

Texas

General Admissions

Very Important factors include: class rank, standardized test scores. *Other factors include:* rigor of secondary school record, application essay, extracurricular activities, talent/ability, first generation. *Freshman admission requirements:* High school diploma is required and GED is accepted. *Academic units required:* 4 English, 4 math, 4 science, 2 science labs, 2 foreign language, 2 social studies, 2 history, 6 academic electives, 1 visual/performing arts, 1 unit from above areas or other academic areas. *Academic units recommended:* 4 English, 4 math, 4 science, 2 science labs, 2 foreign language, 2 social studies, 2 history, 6 academic electives, 1 visual/performing arts.

Accommodations or Services

Accommodations are decided upon an individual basis after a thorough review of appropriate, current documentation. The accommodations requests must be supported through the documentation provided and must be logically linked to the current impact of the condition on academic functioning.

Financial Aid

Students should submit: FAFSA. Applicants will be notified of awards on a rolling basis beginning 3/1. *Need-based scholarships/grants offered:* College/university scholarship or grant aid from institutional funds; Federal Pell; Private scholarships; SEOG; State scholarships/grants. *Loan aid offered:* Direct PLUS loans; Direct Subsidized Stafford Loans; Direct Unsubsidized Stafford Loans. Federal Work-Study Program available. Institutional employment available.

Campus Life

Activities: Campus Ministries; Choral groups; Concert band; Dance; Drama/theater; International Student Organization; Jazz band; Literary magazine; Marching band; Model UN; Music ensembles; Musical theater; Opera; Pep band; Radio station; Student government; Student newspaper; Student-run film society; Symphony orchestra; Yearbook. **Organizations:** 455 registered organizations, 22 honor societies, 42 religious organizations, 19 fraternities, 13 sororities. **Athletics (Intercollegiate):** *Men:* baseball, basketball, cheerleading, cross-country, football, golf, track/field (outdoor). *Women:* basketball, cheerleading, cross-country, golf, soccer, softball, tennis, track/field (outdoor), volleyball.

ACCOMMODATIONS

Allowed in exams:	
Calculators	Yes
Dictionary	Yes
Computer	Yes
Spell-checker	Yes
Extended test time	Yes
Scribe	Yes
Proctors	Yes
Oral exams	Yes
Note-takers	Yes
Support services for students with:	
LD	Yes
ADHD	Yes
ASD	Yes
Distraction-reduced environment	Yes
Recording of lecture alowed	Yes
Reading technology	Yes
Audio books	Yes
Other assistive technology	Yes
Priority registration	Yes
Added costs of services:	
For LD	No
For ADHD	No
For ASD	No
LD specialists	Yes
ADHD & ASD coaching	Yes
ASD specialists	No
Professional tutors	No
Peer tutors	Yes
Max. hours/week for services	Varies
How professors are notified of student approved accommodations	Student and director

COLLEGE GRADUATION REQUIREMENTS

Course waivers allowed	No
Course substitutions allowed	Yes
In what courses: Case by case basis	

Texas Tech University

Box 45005, Lubbock, TX 79409-5005 • Admissions: 806-742-1480 • Fax: 806-742-0062 **Support: SP**

CAMPUS

Type of school	Public
Environment	Metropolis

STUDENTS

Undergrad enrollment	31,172
% male/female	52/48
% from out of state	6
% frosh live on campus	93

FINANCIAL FACTS

Annual in-state tuition	$11,600
Annual out-of-state tuition	$23,870
Room and board	$9,956

GENERAL ADMISSIONS INFO

Application fee	$75
Regular application deadline	8/1
Nonfall registration	Yes
Range SAT EBRW	540–630
Range SAT Math	530–630
Range ACT Composite	22–27

ACADEMICS

Student/faculty ratio	21:1
% students returning for sophomore year	87

Most classes have 20–29 students.

Programs/Services for Students with Learning Differences

Students with disabilities attending Texas Tech will find numerous programs designed to provide services and promote access to all phases of university activity. Programming is coordinated through the Dean of Students Office. Each student is encouraged to act as his or her own advocate and take the major responsibility for securing services and accommodations. The Disabled Student Services team, Dean of Students' Office, faculty, and staff are supportive in this effort. The TECHniques Center offers a fee-for-service program for students with learning disabilities, and the CASE program is support for students with autism or developmental disabilities.

Admissions

Students with disabilities must meet the exact same admissions standards as any other student. All students must have 4 years of English, 3 years of math, 2.5 years of social studies, 3 years of science, 2 years of foreign language, and 3.5 years of electives. Any applicant who scores a 1200 on the SAT or a 29 on the ACT is automatically admitted regardless of class rank. Some students are admissible who do not meet the stated requirements, but they must have a 2.0 GPA for a provisional admission. After a student is admitted, Disabled Student Services requires documentation that provides a diagnosis and an indication of the severity of the disability and offers recommendations for accommodations for students to receive services.

Additional Information

The TECHniques Center is a fee-for-service program offered by the Student Disability Services. The TECHniques Center provides supplemental academic support services to meet the needs of students with documented learning disabilities, ADD or ADHD, and/or Autism Spectrum Disorders. The goal is to help students become independent, learn to self-advocate, accomplish their educational goals, and make education accessible. The CASE program offers an innovative college support program for students diagnosed with autism and other developmental disabilities. With the support of the Burkhart Center for Autism Education and Research, the CASE program provides research-based, customized supports for students to facilitate their successful transition to college and the entrance into employment after graduation. Each student in CASE works with a learning specialist who assists and guides the students through their academic career. Learning specialists create personalized plans to identify each student's needs and build skills for independent living, social connections, and employment.

ADMISSIONS INFO FOR STUDENTS WITH LEARNING DIFFERENCES

Phone: 806-742-2405 • Fax: 806-742-4837 • Email: sds@ttu.edu

SAT/ACT required: Yes (Test optional for 2021)
Interview required: No
Essay required: No
Additional application required: Yes
Documentation submitted to: DSS or TECHniques or Case

Special Ed. HS course work accepted: Yes
Separate application required for Programs/Services: Yes
Documentation required for:
LD: Psychoeducational evaluation
ADHD: Psychoeducational evaluation
ASD: Psychoeducational evaluation

Texas Tech University

Texas

General Admissions

Very Important factors include: rigor of secondary school record, class rank, academic GPA, standardized test scores. *Important factors include:* application essay, recommendation(s), extracurricular activities, talent/ability, character/personal qualities, volunteer work. *Other factors include:* first generation, geographical residence, level of applicant's interest. *Freshman admission requirements:* High school diploma is required and GED is accepted. *Academic units required:* 4 English, 3 math, 3 science, 3 science labs, 2 foreign language, 5 academic electives, 1 visual/performing arts, 4 unit from above areas or other academic areas. *Academic units recommended:* 4 English, 4 math, 4 science, 4 science labs, 2 foreign language, 6 academic electives, 1 visual/performing arts.

Accommodations or Services

Accommodations are decided upon an individual basis after a thorough review of appropriate, current documentation. The accommodations requests must be supported through the documentation provided and must be logically linked to the current impact of the condition on academic functioning.

Financial Aid

Students should submit: FAFSA. *Need-based scholarships/grants offered:* College/university scholarship or grant aid from institutional funds; Federal Pell; Private scholarships; SEOG; State scholarships/grants; United Negro College Fund. *Loan aid offered:* Direct PLUS loans; Direct Subsidized Stafford Loans; Direct Unsubsidized Stafford Loans. Federal Work-Study Program available. Institutional employment available.

Campus Life

Activities: Campus Ministries; Choral groups; Concert band; Dance; Drama/theater; International Student Organization; Jazz band; Literary magazine; Marching band; Model UN; Music ensembles; Musical theater; Opera; Pep band; Radio station; Student government; Student newspaper; Student-run film society; Symphony orchestra; Television station; Yearbook. **Organizations:** 576 registered organizations, 33 honor societies, 47 religious organizations, 34 fraternities, 23 sororities. **Athletics (Intercollegiate):** *Men:* baseball, basketball, cross-country, football, golf, tennis, track/field (outdoor), track/field (indoor). *Women:* basketball, cross-country, golf, soccer, softball, tennis, track/field (outdoor), track/field (indoor), volleyball.

ACCOMMODATIONS

Allowed in exams:	
Calculators	Yes
Dictionary	No
Computer	Yes
Spell-checker	Yes
Extended test time	Yes
Scribe	Yes
Proctors	Yes
Oral exams	Yes
Note-takers	Yes
Support services for students with:	
LD	Yes
ADHD	Yes
ASD	Yes
Distraction-reduced environment	Yes
Recording of lecture alowed	Yes
Reading technology	Yes
Audio books	Yes
Other assistive technology	Yes
Priority registration	Yes
Added costs of services:	
For LD	Yes
For ADHD	Yes
For ASD	Yes
LD specialists	Yes
ADHD & ASD coaching	Yes
ASD specialists	Yes
Professional tutors	Yes
Peer tutors	Yes
Max. hours/week for services	Varies
How professors are notified of student approved accommodations	Student

COLLEGE GRADUATION REQUIREMENTS

Course waivers allowed	No
Course substitutions allowed	Yes
In what courses: Case by case basis	

University of Houston

Office of Admissions, Houston, TX 77204-2023 • Admissions: 713-743-1010 • Fax: 713-743-7542 **Support: SP**

CAMPUS

Type of school	Public
Environment	Metropolis

STUDENTS

Undergrad enrollment	37,689
% male/female	50/50
% from out of state	2
% frosh live on campus	45

FINANCIAL FACTS

Annual in-state tuition	$10,561
Annual out-of-state tuition	$25,831
Room and board	$9,750
Required fees	$1,008

GENERAL ADMISSIONS INFO

Application fee	$75
Regular application deadline	6/1
Nonfall registration	Yes
Range SAT EBRW	570–650
Range SAT Math	570–660
Range ACT Composite	22–27

ACADEMICS

Student/faculty ratio	23:1
% students returning for sophomore year	85

Most classes have 20–29 students.

Programs/Services for Students with Learning Differences

The Center for Students with DisABILITIES provides a wide variety of academic support services to students with all types of disabilities. The goal is to help ensure that these otherwise qualified students are able to successfully compete with non-disabled students by receiving equal educational opportunities in college as mandated by law. Through advocacy efforts and a deliberate, ongoing public education program, the staff strives to heighten the awareness of disability issues, educational rights, and abilities of persons who have disabilities.

Admissions

Admission is automatic for Texas residents in the top 15% of the class. Applicants who do not meet these admissions criteria will be reviewed in light of the applicant's academic rigor, community service, extracurricular activities, and surmounting obstacles to pursue higher education. Letters of reference from high school teachers, counselors, supervisors, and activity leaders along with personal statements are welcome additions to an applicant's file.

Additional Information

The Connecting to College (CtC) program provides additional support for UHCL students with Autism Spectrum Disorder (ASD) and related needs. The program is part of the Center for Autism and Developmental Disabilities and partners with the Student Success Center, Disability Services, Counseling Services, and Career Services to provide a team-based approach to supporting CtC students. Three levels of support are provided. This first level is open to all students and aims to connect students with student support services available. In Level 1, students meet with their CtC transition specialist a minimum of twice per semester. Students also participate in CtC group meetings every two weeks. Level 2 support focuses on social and behavioral expectations. Students meet once to twice a week with a transition specialist. Level 3 support is designed to provide immediate assistance to a student in crisis, personally or academically. The department of Communication Sciences also provides peer mentoring to students with ASD.

ADMISSIONS INFO FOR STUDENTS WITH LEARNING DIFFERENCES

Phone: 713-743-5400 • Fax: 713-743-5396 • Email: camoruso@uh.edu

SAT/ACT required: Yes (Test optional through 2022)
Interview required: No
Essay required: Yes
Additional application required: Yes
Documentation submitted to: UHCI

Special Ed. HS course work accepted: Yes
Separate application required for Programs/Services: Yes
Documentation required for:
- **LD:** Psychoeducational evaluation
- **ADHD:** Psychoeducational evaluation
- **ASD:** Psychoeducational evaluation

University of Houston

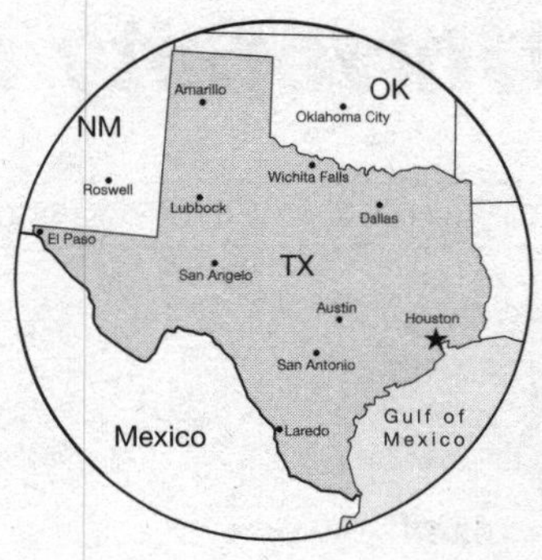

Texas

General Admissions

Very Important factors include: rigor of secondary school record, class rank, academic GPA, standardized test scores. *Other factors include:* application essay, recommendation(s), extracurricular activities, talent/ability, first generation, volunteer work, work experience. *Freshman admission requirements:* High school diploma is required and GED is accepted. *Academic units required:* 4 English, 3 math, 3 science, 2 science labs, 3 social studies. *Academic units recommended:* 4 math, 4 science, 2 foreign language, 1 history, 1 visual/performing arts.

Accommodations or Services

Accommodations are decided upon an individual basis after a thorough review of appropriate, current documentation. The accommodations requests must be supported through the documentation provided and must be logically linked to the current impact of the condition on academic functioning.

Financial Aid

Students should submit: FAFSA; Institution's own financial aid form. Applicants will be notified of awards on a rolling basis beginning 5/1. *Need-based scholarships/grants offered:* College/university scholarship or grant aid from institutional funds; Federal Pell; Private scholarships; SEOG; State scholarships/grants. *Loan aid offered:* Direct PLUS loans; Direct Subsidized Stafford Loans; Direct Unsubsidized Stafford Loans. Federal Work-Study Program available. Institutional employment available.

Campus Life

Activities: Campus Ministries; Choral groups; Concert band; Dance; Drama/theater; International Student Organization; Jazz band; Literary magazine; Marching band; Music ensembles; Musical theater; Opera; Pep band; Radio station; Student government; Student newspaper; Student-run film society; Symphony orchestra; Television station; Yearbook. **Organizations:** 491 registered organizations, 28 honor societies, 57 religious organizations, 22 fraternities, 18 sororities. **Athletics (Intercollegiate):** *Men:* baseball, basketball, cross-country, football, golf, track/field (outdoor), track/field (indoor). *Women:* basketball, cross-country, diving, soccer, softball, swimming, tennis, track/field (outdoor), track/field (indoor), volleyball.

ACCOMMODATIONS

Allowed in exams:	
Calculators	Yes
Dictionary	Yes
Computer	Yes
Spell-checker	Yes
Extended test time	Yes
Scribe	Yes
Proctors	Yes
Oral exams	Yes
Note-takers	Yes
Support services for students with:	
LD	Yes
ADHD	Yes
ASD	Yes
Distraction-reduced environment	Yes
Recording of lecture alowed	Yes
Reading technology	Yes
Audio books	Yes
Other assistive technology	Yes
Priority registration	Yes
Added costs of services:	
For LD	No
For ADHD	No
For ASD	No
LD specialists	Yes
ADHD & ASD coaching	Yes
ASD specialists	Yes
Professional tutors	Yes
Peer tutors	Yes
Max. hours/week for services	Varies
How professors are notified of student approved accommodations	Student

COLLEGE GRADUATION REQUIREMENTS

Course waivers allowed	No
Course substitutions allowed	Yes
In what courses: Case by case basis	

University of Texas at Austin

P.O. Box 8058, Austin, TX 78713-8058 • Admissions: 512-475-7399 • Fax: 512-475-7478 **Support: SP**

CAMPUS

Type of school	Public
Environment	Metropolis

STUDENTS

Undergrad enrollment	39,783
% male/female	45/55
% from out of state	5
% frosh live on campus	67

FINANCIAL FACTS

Annual in-state tuition	$10,824
Annual out-of-state tuition	$38,326
Room and board	$11,812

GENERAL ADMISSIONS INFO

Application fee	$75
Regular application deadline	12/1
Nonfall registration	Yes
Range SAT EBRW	620–720
Range SAT Math	610–760
Range ACT Composite	27–33

ACADEMICS

Student/faculty ratio	18:1
% students returning for sophomore year	96

Most classes have 10–19 students.

Programs/Services for Students with Learning Differences

Services for Students with Disabilities (SSD) provides a program of support and advocacy for students with LDs. Services offered include assistance with learning strategies, note-takers for lectures, scribes/readers, and extended time for in-class work. There is also a Tutoring and Learning Center whose free services include study skill assistance, subject area tutoring, life management skills, exam reviews, peer mentoring, and distance tutoring.

Admissions

Students with disabilities are expected to meet the same admissions criteria as all other students. It is up to the student whether he/she wants to self identify during the admissions process as having a disability. Please note that disability-related documentation sent to the Office of Admissions is not automatically forwarded to SSD. For students not otherwise eligible to enter due to grades or scores, a study skills class is required, plus other courses from a course list. The following criteria are considered for admission: class rank, strength of academic background, record of achievements, honors and awards, special accomplishments, work and service both in and out of school, essay(s), and required short answers. special circumstances that put the applicant's academic achievements into context, including socioeconomic status, experience in a single parent home, family responsibilities, experience overcoming adversity, cultural background, race and ethnicity, the language spoken in the applicant's home, and other information in the applicant's file are also considered. Recommendations (although not required) and the competitiveness of the major to which the student applies are additional factors.

Additional Information

There is a support group for UT students with ASD. Classroom accommodations include notetakers, assistive technology, scribes, readers, and extended testing times. The Longhorn TIES (Transition, Inclusion, Empower, Success) initiative supports the students on the autism spectrum through advocacy, connections, and training. Students who meet the eligibility requirements to receive support services will meet with the program administrator for bi-weekly coaching meetings. During coaching meetings, the program administrator supports development of skills and confidence in relation to self-advocacy in the following ways: introducing students to UT-Austin resources, assisting students with navigating new and challenging situations, helping them prioritize academic tasks, and providing other skill development training.

ADMISSIONS INFO FOR STUDENTS WITH LEARNING DIFFERENCES

Phone: 512-471-6259 • Fax: 512-475-7730 • Email: kelli.bradley@austin.utexas.edu

SAT/ACT required: Yes (Test optional for 2021)
Interview required: No
Essay required: Yes
Additional application required: No
Documentation submitted to: Services for Students with Disabilities

Special Ed. HS course work accepted: Yes
Separate application required for Programs/Services: No
Documentation required for:
LD: Psychoeducational evaluation
ADHD: Psychoeducational evaluation
ASD: Psychoeducational evaluation

University of Texas at Austin

General Admissions

Very Important factors include: rigor of secondary school record, class rank, academic GPA, application essay, standardized test scores, recommendation(s), extracurricular activities, talent/ability, character/personal qualities, first generation, geographical residence, state residency, religious affiliation/commitment, racial/ethnic status, volunteer work, and work experience. *Freshman admission requirements:* High school diploma is required and GED is accepted. *Academic units required:* 4 English, 4 math, 4 science, 2 foreign language, 4 social studies, 6 academic electives.

Accommodations or Services

Accommodations are decided upon an individual basis after a thorough review of appropriate, current documentation. The accommodations requests must be supported through the documentation provided and must be logically linked to the current impact of the condition on academic functioning.

Financial Aid

Students should submit: FAFSA; Institution's own financial aid form. Applicants will be notified of awards on a rolling basis beginning 4/1. *Need-based scholarships/grants offered:* College/university scholarship or grant aid from institutional funds; Federal Pell; Private scholarships; SEOG; State scholarships/grants. *Loan aid offered:* Direct PLUS loans; Direct Subsidized Stafford Loans; Direct Unsubsidized Stafford Loans. Federal Work-Study Program available. Institutional employment available.

Campus Life

Activities: Campus Ministries; Choral groups; Concert band; Dance; Drama/theater; International Student Organization; Jazz band; Literary magazine; Marching band; Model UN; Music ensembles; Musical theater; Opera; Pep band; Radio station; Student government; Student newspaper; Student-run film society; Symphony orchestra; Television station; Yearbook. **Organizations:** 1055 registered organizations, 5 honor societies, 96 religious organizations. **Athletics (Intercollegiate):** *Men:* baseball, basketball, cross-country, diving, football, golf, swimming, tennis, track/field (outdoor). *Women:* basketball, crew/rowing, cross-country, diving, golf, soccer, softball, swimming, tennis, track/field (outdoor), volleyball.

ACCOMMODATIONS

Allowed in exams:	
Calculators	Yes
Dictionary	Yes
Computer	Yes
Spell-checker	Yes
Extended test time	Yes
Scribe	Yes
Proctors	Yes
Oral exams	Yes
Note-takers	Yes
Support services for students with:	
LD	Yes
ADHD	Yes
ASD	Yes
Distraction-reduced environment	Yes
Recording of lecture alowed	Yes
Reading technology	Yes
Audio books	Yes
Other assistive technology	Yes
Priority registration	Yes
Added costs of services:	
For LD	No
For ADHD	No
For ASD	No
LD specialists	Yes
ADHD & ASD coaching	No
ASD specialists	Yes
Professional tutors	Yes
Peer tutors	Yes
Max. hours/week for services	Varies
How professors are notified of student approved accommodations	Student

COLLEGE GRADUATION REQUIREMENTS

Course waivers allowed	No
Course substitutions allowed	Yes
In what courses: Case by case basis	

Brigham Young University (UT)

A-153 ASB, Provo, UT 84602-1110 • Admissions: 801-422-2507 • Fax: 801-422-0005 **Support: S**

CAMPUS

Type of school	Private (nonprofit)
Environment	City

STUDENTS

Undergrad enrollment	31,292
% male/female	50/50
% from out of state	68
% frosh live on campus	63

FINANCIAL FACTS

Latter-day Saint Tuition	$5,970
Non-Latter-day Saint Tuition	$11,940
Room and board	$7,915

GENERAL ADMISSIONS INFO

Application fee	$35
Regular application deadline	12/15
Nonfall registration	Yes

Admission may be deferred.

Range SAT EBRW	610–710
Range SAT Math	600–710
Range ACT Composite	26–31

ACADEMICS

Student/faculty ratio	20:1
% students returning for sophomore year	90

Most classes have 20–29 students.

Programs/Services for Students with Learning Differences

The University Accessibility Center works to provide individualized programs to meet the specific needs of each student with a disability, assist in developing strengths to address academic challenges, and make arrangements for accommodations and special services as required.

Admissions

There is no special admission process for students with learning disabilities. Suggested courses include 4 years English, 3–4 years math, 2–3 years science, 2 years history or government, 2 years foreign language, and 2 years of literature or writing. Evaluations are made on an individualized basis with a system weighted for college-prep courses and core classes.

Additional Information

The University Accessibility Center offers services to students with learning differences. The Reaching Educational And Career Hopes (REACH) Program assists students with disabilities in making the transition from BYU to the workforce. Also, the Accessibility Lab offers various services to students with disabilities such as providing access to different assistive technology and proctoring exams. Services and accommodations are available for undergraduate and graduate students.

ADMISSIONS INFO FOR STUDENTS WITH LEARNING DIFFERENCES

Phone: 801-422-2767 • Fax: 801-422-0174

SAT/ACT required: Yes
Interview required: No
Essay required: No
Additional application required: No
Documentation submitted to: University Accessibility Center

Special Ed. HS course work accepted: Yes
Separate application required for Programs/Services: No
Documentation required for:
- **LD:** Psychoeducational evaluation
- **ADHD:** Psychoeducational evaluation
- **ASD:** Psychoeducational evaluation

Brigham Young University (UT)

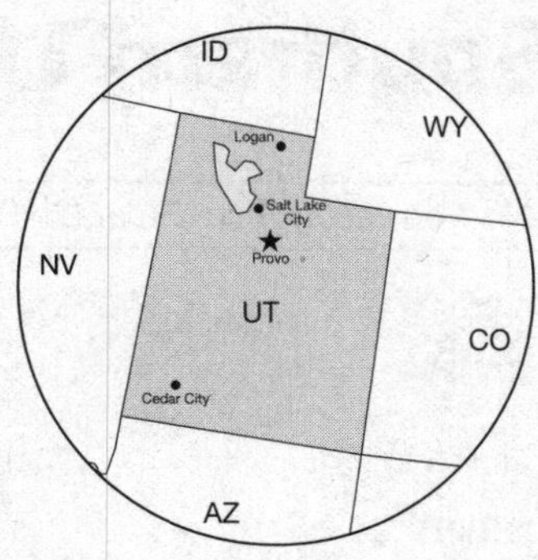

General Admissions

Very Important factors include: rigor of secondary school record, academic GPA, application essay, standardized test scores, recommendation(s), extracurricular activities, talent/ability, character/personal qualities, religious affiliation/commitment, volunteer work, work experience. *Important factors include:* first generation, racial/ethnic status. *Other factors include:* level of applicant's interest. *Freshman admission requirements:* High school diploma is required and GED is accepted. *Academic units recommended:* 4 English, 4 math, 3 science, 2 foreign language, 2 history.

Accommodations or Services

Accommodations are decided upon an individual basis after a thorough review of appropriate, current documentation. The accommodations requests must be supported through the documentation provided and must be logically linked to the current impact of the condition on academic functioning.

Financial Aid

Students should submit: FAFSA. *Need-based scholarships/grants offered:* College/university scholarship or grant aid from institutional funds; Federal Pell; Private scholarships; State scholarships/grants. *Loan aid offered:* Direct PLUS loans; Direct Subsidized Stafford Loans; Direct Unsubsidized Stafford Loans.

Campus Life

Activities: Choral groups; Concert band; Dance; Drama/theater; Jazz band; Literary magazine; Marching band; Music ensembles; Musical theater; Opera; Pep band; Radio station; Student government; Student newspaper; Student-run film society; Symphony orchestra; Television station. **Organizations:** 390 registered organizations, 22 honor societies, 25 religious organizations. **Athletics (Intercollegiate):** *Men:* baseball, basketball, cheerleading, cross-country, diving, football, golf, swimming, tennis, track/field (outdoor), track/field (indoor), volleyball. *Women:* basketball, cheerleading, cross-country, diving, golf, gymnastics, soccer, softball, swimming, tennis, track/field (outdoor), track/field (indoor), volleyball.

ACCOMMODATIONS

Allowed in exams:	
Calculators	Yes
Dictionary	Yes
Computer	Yes
Spell-checker	Yes
Extended test time	Yes
Scribe	Yes
Proctors	Yes
Oral exams	Yes
Note-takers	Yes
Support services for students with:	
LD	Yes
ADHD	Yes
ASD	Yes
Distraction-reduced environment	Yes
Recording of lecture alowed	Yes
Reading technology	Yes
Audio books	Yes
Other assistive technology	Yes
Priority registration	Yes
Added costs of services:	
For LD	No
For ADHD	No
For ASD	No
LD specialists	Yes
ADHD & ASD coaching	No
ASD specialists	No
Professional tutors	No
Peer tutors	Yes
Max. hours/week for services	Varies
How professors are notified of student approved accommodations	Student and director

COLLEGE GRADUATION REQUIREMENTS

Course waivers allowed	No
Course substitutions allowed	Yes
In what courses: Case by case basis	

Utah

Southern Utah University

351 W University Blvd, Cedar City, UT 84720 • Admissions: 435-586-7740 • Fax: 435-865-8223 **Support: S**

CAMPUS

Type of school	Public
Environment	Village

STUDENTS

Undergrad enrollment	10,274
% male/female	41/59
% from out of state	20
% frosh live on campus	34

FINANCIAL FACTS

Annual in-state tuition	$6,006
Annual out-of-state tuition	$19,822
Room and board	$7,349
Required fees	$764

GENERAL ADMISSIONS INFO

Application fee	$50
Regular application deadline	First day of semester
Nonfall registration	Yes

Admission may be deferred.

Range SAT EBRW	520–630
Range SAT Math	520–610
Range ACT Composite	20–27

ACADEMICS

Student/faculty ratio	20:1
% students returning for sophomore year	74

Most classes have 20–29 students.

Programs/Services for Students with Learning Differences

The Disability Resource Center at Southern Utah University continuously provides support and services to students with disabilities who are overcoming different educational difficulties because of their individual challenges. Reasonable accommodations are offered to participants in the program, giving them access to services requested by law. Cooperation between faculty, students, and community assures an atmosphere of understanding and acceptance.

Admissions

Students with learning disabilities submit the general application form. Students must have at least a 2.0 GPA and show competency in English, math, science, and social studies. The university uses an admissions index derived from the combination of the high school GPA and results of either the ACT or SAT. If students are not admissible through the regular process, special consideration by a committee review can be gained through reference letters and a personal letter. The university is allowed to admit 5% in "flex" admission. Students are encouraged to self-disclose their learning disability and submit documentation.

Additional Information

Students with disabilities are evaluated by the Disability Resource Center to determine accommodations or services. The following accommodations or services may be available on a case-by-case basis for students with appropriate documentation: the use of calculators, dictionary, computer or spell checker in exams, extended testing time, scribes, proctors, oral exams, notetakers, distraction-free testing environments, tape recorders in class, books on tape, assistive technology, and priority registration. Tutoring is available in small groups or one-on-one, free of charge. For-credit basic skills classes are offered in English, reading, math, math anxiety, language, and study skills.

ADMISSIONS INFO FOR STUDENTS WITH LEARNING DIFFERENCES

Phone: 435-865-8022 • Fax: 435-865-8235 • Email: alldredge@suu.edu

SAT/ACT required: Yes (Test optional through 2022)
Interview required: No
Essay required: No
Additional application required: No
Documentation submitted to: Disability Resource Center

Special Ed. HS course work accepted: Yes
Separate application required for Programs/Services: No
Documentation required for:
LD: Psychoeducational evaluation
ADHD: Psychoeducational evaluation
ASD: Psychoeducational evaluation

Southern Utah University

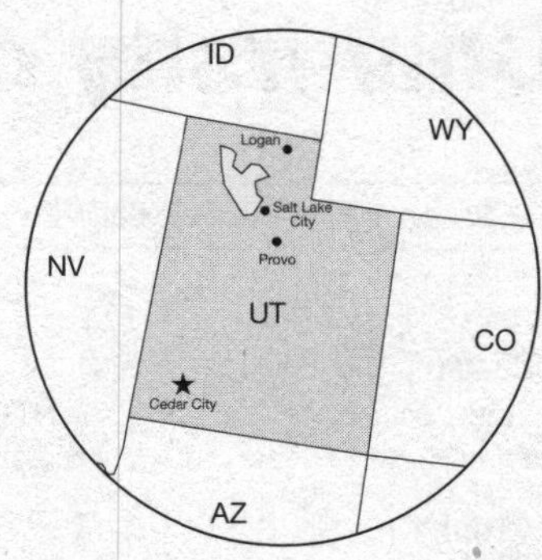

General Admissions

Very Important factors include: academic GPA, standardized test scores. *Important factors include:* level of applicant's interest. *Freshman admission requirements:* High school diploma is required and GED is accepted. *Academic units recommended:* 4 English, 3 math, 3 science, 1 science lab, 2 foreign language, 3 social studies.

Accommodations or Services

Accommodations are decided upon an individual basis after a thorough review of appropriate, current documentation. The accommodations requests must be supported through the documentation provided and must be logically linked to the current impact of the condition on academic functioning.

Financial Aid

Students should submit: FAFSA. Applicants will be notified of awards on a rolling basis beginning 3/15. *Need-based scholarships/grants offered:* College/university scholarship or grant aid from institutional funds; Federal Pell; Private scholarships; SEOG; State scholarships/grants. *Loan aid offered:* Direct PLUS loans; Direct Subsidized Stafford Loans; Direct Unsubsidized Stafford Loans. Federal Work-Study Program available. Institutional employment available.

Campus Life

Activities: Campus Ministries; Choral groups; Concert band; Dance; Drama/theater; International Student Organization; Jazz band; Literary magazine; Marching band; Music ensembles; Musical theater; Opera; Pep band; Radio station; Student government; Student newspaper; Student-run film society; Symphony orchestra; Television station. **Athletics (Intercollegiate):** *Men:* baseball, basketball, cross-country, football, golf, track/field (outdoor). *Women:* basketball, cross-country, gymnastics, softball, tennis, track/field (outdoor).

ACCOMMODATIONS

Allowed in exams:	
Calculators	No
Dictionary	Yes
Computer	Yes
Spell-checker	Yes
Extended test time	Yes
Scribe	Yes
Proctors	Yes
Oral exams	Yes
Note-takers	Yes
Support services for students with:	
LD	Yes
ADHD	Yes
ASD	Yes
Distraction-reduced environment	Yes
Recording of lecture allowed	Yes
Reading technology	Yes
Audio books	Yes
Other assistive technology	Yes
Priority registration	Yes
Added costs of services:	
For LD	No
For ADHD	No
For ASD	No
LD specialists	No
ADHD & ASD coaching	No
ASD specialists	No
Professional tutors	No
Peer tutors	No
Max. hours/week for services	Varies
How professors are notified of student approved accommodations	Student and letter

COLLEGE GRADUATION REQUIREMENTS

Course waivers allowed	No
Course substitutions allowed	No

Utah

University of Utah

201 South 1460 East, Salt Lake City, UT 84112 • Admissions: 801-581-8761 • Fax: 801-585-7864 **Support: S**

CAMPUS

Type of school	Public
Environment	Metropolis

STUDENTS

Undergrad enrollment	23,432
% male/female	53/47
% from out of state	22
% frosh live on campus	53

FINANCIAL FACTS

Annual in-state tuition	$9,286
Annual out-of-state tuition	$29,996
Room and board	$11,844

GENERAL ADMISSIONS INFO

Application fee	$55
Regular application deadline	4/1
Nonfall registration	Yes

Admission may be deferred.

Range SAT EBRW	573–680
Range SAT Math	570–700
Range ACT Composite	22–29

ACADEMICS

Student/faculty ratio	17:1
% students returning for sophomore year	89

Most classes have 20–29 students.

Programs/Services for Students with Learning Differences

The Center for Disability Services is dedicated to students with disabilities by providing the opportunity for success and equal access at the University of Utah. The Center for Disability Services is a designated which evaluates disability documentation, determines eligibility, and implements reasonable accommodations for enrolled students as guided by Section 504 of the Rehabilitation Act, the Americans with Disabilities Act, and University policy.

Admissions

There is no special application process for students with learning disabilities. All applicants to the university must meet the general admission requirements. Students who do not meet the admission requirements as a direct result of their disability may be admitted on the condition that course deficiencies are filled prior to earning 30 semester hours at the university. Conditional admission is determined by the Center for Disability and Access and the Admissions Office. Students must provide appropriate information regarding their disability and any services they received in high school due to their disability. Self-disclosure is recommended only if the student needs to inform the Admissions Office that they are working with the Center for Disability Services to consider conditional admission. Otherwise, disclosure is not recommended, but left to the student to make the decision.

Additional Information

The Center for Disability and Access provides services to students who provide documentation of a disability. Services include assistance with admissions, registration, and graduation, orientation to the campus, referrals to campus and community services, guidelines for obtaining services, general and academic advising, investigation of academic strengths and weaknesses, help with developing effective learning strategies, and coordination with academic and departmental advisors regarding program accommodations. The Center for Disability and Access has the right to set procedures to determine whether the student qualifies for services and how the services will be implemented.

ADMISSIONS INFO FOR STUDENTS WITH LEARNING DIFFERENCES

Phone: 801-581-5020 Fax: 801-581-5487 Email: smcaward@sa.utah.edu

SAT/ACT required: Yes (Test optional for 2021)
Interview required: No
Essay required: No
Additional application required: No
Documentation submitted to: Center for Disability and Access

Special Ed. HS course work accepted: Yes
Separate application required for Programs/Services: Yes
Documentation required for:
LD: Psychoeducational evaluation
ADHD: Psychoeducational evaluation
ASD: Psychoeducational evaluation

University of Utah

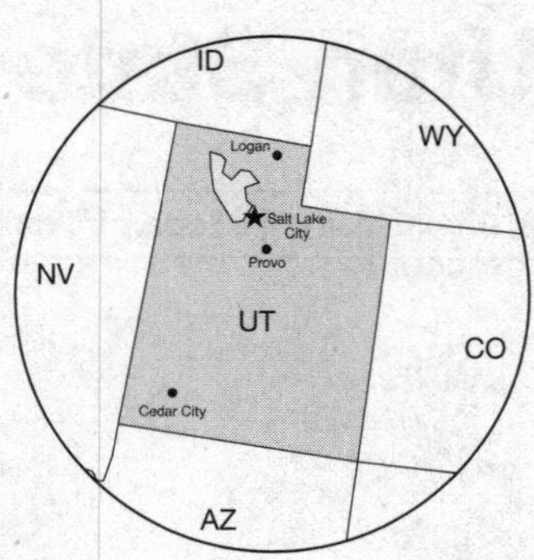

General Admissions

Very Important factors include: rigor of secondary school record, academic GPA. *Important factors include:* standardized test scores. *Other factors include:* class rank, interview, extracurricular activities, talent/ability, character/ personal qualities, first generation, alumni/ae relation, geographical residence, state residency, racial/ethnic status, volunteer work, work experience. *Freshman admission requirements:* High school diploma is required and GED is accepted. *Academic units required:* 4 English, 2 math, 3 science, 1 science lab, 2 foreign language, 1 history, and 4 academic electives.

Accommodations or Services

Accommodations are decided upon an individual basis after a thorough review of appropriate, current documentation. The accommodations requests must be supported through the documentation provided and must be logically linked to the current impact of the condition on academic functioning.

Financial Aid

Students should submit: FAFSA. *Need-based scholarships/grants offered:* College/university scholarship or grant aid from institutional funds; Federal Nursing Scholarships; Federal Pell; Private scholarships; SEOG; State scholarships/grants. *Loan aid offered:* Direct PLUS loans; Direct Subsidized Stafford Loans; Direct Unsubsidized Stafford Loans. Federal Work-Study Program available. Institutional employment available.

Campus Life

Activities: Campus Ministries; Choral groups; Concert band; Dance; Drama/ theater; International Student Organization; Jazz band; Literary magazine; Marching band; Model UN; Music ensembles; Musical theater; Opera; Pep band; Radio station; Student government; Student newspaper; Student-run film society; Symphony orchestra; Television station. **Organizations:** 513 registered organizations, 27 honor societies, 14 religious organizations, 11 fraternities, 7 sororities. **Athletics (Intercollegiate):** *Men:* baseball, basketball, cheerleading, diving, football, golf, skiing (downhill/alpine), skiing (Nordic/cross-country), swimming, tennis. *Women:* basketball, cheerleading, cross-country, diving, gymnastics, skiing (downhill/alpine), skiing (Nordic/cross-country), soccer, softball, swimming, tennis, track/field (outdoor), track/field (indoor), volleyball.

ACCOMMODATIONS

Allowed in exams:	
Calculators	Yes
Dictionary	Yes
Computer	Yes
Spell-checker	Yes
Extended test time	Yes
Scribe	Yes
Proctors	Yes
Oral exams	Yes
Note-takers	Yes
Support services for students with:	
LD	No
ADHD	No
ASD	No
Distraction-reduced environment	Yes
Recording of lecture alowed	Yes
Reading technology	Yes
Audio books	Yes
Other assistive technology	Yes
Priority registration	Yes
Added costs of services:	
For LD	No
For ADHD	No
For ASD	No
LD specialists	No
ADHD & ASD coaching	No
ASD specialists	No
Professional tutors	Yes
Peer tutors	Yes
Max. hours/week for services	Varies
How professors are notified of student approved accommodations	Student

COLLEGE GRADUATION REQUIREMENTS

Course waivers allowed	No
Course substitutions allowed	Yes
In what courses: Case by case basis	

Utah State University

0160 Old Main Hill, Logan, UT 84322-0160 • Admissions: 435-797-1079 • Fax: 435-797-3708 **Support: SP**

CAMPUS

Type of school	Public
Environment	Town

STUDENTS

Undergrad enrollment	20,913
% male/female	46/54
% from out of state	27

FINANCIAL FACTS

Annual in-state tuition	$6,549
Annual out-of-state tuition	$21,087
Room and board	$5,770
Required fees	$1,110

GENERAL ADMISSIONS INFO

Application fee	$50
Regular application deadline	Rolling
Nonfall registration	Yes

Admission may be deferred.

Range SAT EBRW	530–660
Range SAT Math	520–650
Range ACT Composite	21–28

ACADEMICS

Student/faculty ratio	20:1
% students returning for sophomore year	74

Most classes have 20–29 students.

Programs/Services for Students with Learning Differences

The mission of the Disability Resource Center (DRC) is to provide persons with disabilities equal access to university programs, services, and activities. This is accomplished by fostering an environment which supports the understanding and acceptance of persons with disabilities throughout the university community and the provision of reasonable and appropriate accommodations. The DRC affirms the right of persons with disabilities to obtain access in a manner promoting dignity and independence.

Admissions

Admission criteria for students with disabilities are the same as those for the general student body. A minimum 2.5 high school GPA and an ACT score of 17 are the minimum requirements for admission into a four-year bachelor degree program. Applicants with a least a 2.0 high school GPA, 14 ACT, and 85 index score may be admitted into a two-year associate degree program. In the two-year degree program, the student can either earn an AS degree or an AA degree, or change to a four-year bachelor degree after completing 24 credits with a minimum 2.5 GPA at USU. Applicants must apply at least two months prior to the beginning of classes to be considered for admission into the associate degree program, and students cannot begin this associate degree program in summer.

Additional Information

Aggies Elevated is a two-year certificate program for young adults with intellectual disabilities (ID) at Utah State University's main campus in Logan. Each student's progress in academics, independent living, social skills, and overall adjustment to college is continually evaluated. For some Aggie Elevated students, this two-year program may be their only college experience. For others, it is a starting point, a place to gain the skills necessary to go on to an associate's or bachelor's degree. It is a bridge between high school and a career. Coursework leading to the certificate includes foundation classes in reading and writing, career exploration, navigating adulthood, self-determination, and a wide variety of personal and vocational electives from the University's general education catalog. All coursework is credit-bearing, unless a student chooses to audit.

ADMISSIONS INFO FOR STUDENTS WITH LEARNING DIFFERENCES

Phone: 435-797-2444 • Fax: 435-797-0130 • Email: drc@usu.edu

SAT/ACT required: Yes (Test optional for 2021)
Interview required: No
Essay required: No
Additional application required: No
Documentation submitted to: Disability Resource Center

Special Ed. HS course work accepted: Yes
Separate application required for Programs/Services: No
Documentation required for:
LD: Psychoeducational evaluation
ADHD: Psychoeducational evaluation
ASD: Psychoeducational evaluation

Utah State University

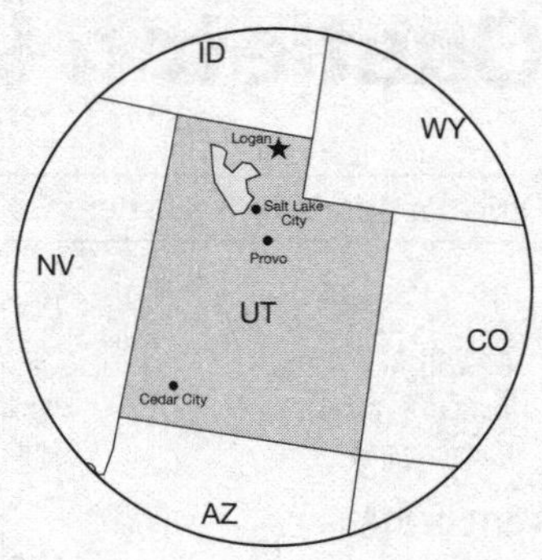

General Admissions

Very Important factors include: academic GPA, standardized test scores. *Other factors include:* rigor of secondary school record, class rank, recommendation(s). *Freshman admission requirements:* High school diploma is required and GED is accepted. *Academic units recommended:* 4 English, 4 math, 3 science, 3 science labs, 2 foreign language, 3.5 social studies.

Accommodations or Services

Accommodations are decided upon an individual basis after a thorough review of appropriate, current documentation. The accommodations requests must be supported through the documentation provided and must be logically linked to the current impact of the condition on academic functioning.

Financial Aid

Students should submit: FAFSA. Applicants will be notified of awards on a rolling basis beginning 4/1. *Need-based scholarships/grants offered:* College/university scholarship or grant aid from institutional funds; Federal Pell; Private scholarships; SEOG; State scholarships/grants. *Loan aid offered:* Direct PLUS loans; Direct Subsidized Stafford Loans; Direct Unsubsidized Stafford Loans. Federal Work-Study Program available. Institutional employment available.

Campus Life

Activities: Campus Ministries; Choral groups; Concert band; Dance; Drama/theater; International Student Organization; Jazz band; Marching band; Music ensembles; Musical theater; Opera; Pep band; Radio station; Student government; Student newspaper; Student-run film society; Symphony orchestra; Television station. **Organizations:** 32 honor societies, 8 religious organizations, 5 fraternities, 3 sororities. **Athletics (Intercollegiate):** *Men:* basketball, cross-country, football, golf, tennis, track/field (outdoor), track/field (indoor). *Women:* basketball, cross-country, gymnastics, soccer, softball, tennis, track/field (outdoor), track/field (indoor), volleyball.

ACCOMMODATIONS

Allowed in exams:	
Calculators	Yes
Dictionary	Yes
Computer	Yes
Spell-checker	Yes
Extended test time	Yes
Scribe	Yes
Proctors	Yes
Oral exams	Yes
Note-takers	Yes
Support services for students with:	
LD	Yes
ADHD	Yes
ASD	Yes
Distraction-reduced environment	Yes
Recording of lecture allowed	Yes
Reading technology	Yes
Audio books	Yes
Other assistive technology	Yes
Priority registration	Yes
Added costs of services:	
For LD	No
For ADHD	No
For ASD	No
LD specialists	Yes
ADHD & ASD coaching	No
ASD specialists	No
Professional tutors	Yes
Peer tutors	Yes
Max. hours/week for services	Varies
How professors are notified of student approved accommodations	Student and director

COLLEGE GRADUATION REQUIREMENTS

Course waivers allowed	Yes
In what courses: Under certain circumstances	
Course substitutions allowed	Yes
In what courses: Under certain circumstances	

Castleton University

Office of Admissions, Castleton, VT 05735 • Admissions: 802-468-1213 • Fax: 802-468-1476 **Support: SP**

CAMPUS	
Type of school	Public
Environment	Rural
STUDENTS	
Undergrad enrollment	1,988
% male/female	46/54
% from out of state	42
% frosh live on campus	49
FINANCIAL FACTS	
Annual in-state tuition	$11,832
Annual out-of-state tuition	$28,800
Room and board	$11,694
Required fees	$1,212
GENERAL ADMISSIONS INFO	
Application fee	$40
Regular application deadline	Rolling
Nonfall registration	Yes
Admission may be deferred.	
Range SAT EBRW	470–560
Range SAT Math	450–560
Range ACT Composite	18–22
ACADEMICS	
% students returning for sophomore year	64
Most classes have 10–19 students.	

Programs/Services for Students with Learning Differences

Services are provided through the Academic Support Center. Students should set up an evaluation with the Coordinator of Disability Services to review documentation, discuss requested accommodations, and secure approval for appropriate accommodations. Students must meet with the Coordinator of Disability Services *each semester* to secure accommodations.

Admissions

Castleton encourages students to apply early so that they have the best opportunity to make an informed decision and can be considered for financial aid. Applications for both fall and spring semesters are evaluated on a rolling basis. Castleton does not have an application deadline, and thus encourages careful attention to aid and scholarship deadlines. Students are required to complete 4 years of English, 3 years of mathematics, 2–3 years of laboratory science, 3–4 years of social studies, and 2 years of foreign language (recommended but not required). By special arrangement with the Vermont Department of Education and the local school district, Castleton will consider admitting as first-year Vermont students who have completed the eleventh grade.

Additional Information

The College STEPS Program partners with Castleton to support students of varying ability (e.g., Autism Spectrum Disorders, intellectual disabilities, and learning disabilities) between the ages 16 and 26. The primary goal is to prepare students for meaningful careers and autonomy after graduation. The program allows participants the opportunity to thrive within a college environment, while receiving the additional help and support needed.

ADMISSIONS INFO FOR STUDENTS WITH LEARNING DIFFERENCES

Phone: 802-468-1428 • Email:gerard.volpe@castleton.edu

SAT/ACT required: Yes (Test optional for 2021)
Interview required: No
Essay required: Yes
Additional application required: No
Documentation submitted to: Academic Support Center

Special Ed. HS course work accepted: Yes
Separate application required for Programs/Services: Yes
Documentation required for:
LD: Psychoeducational evaluation
ADHD: Psychoeducational evaluation
ASD: Psychoeducational evaluation

Castleton University

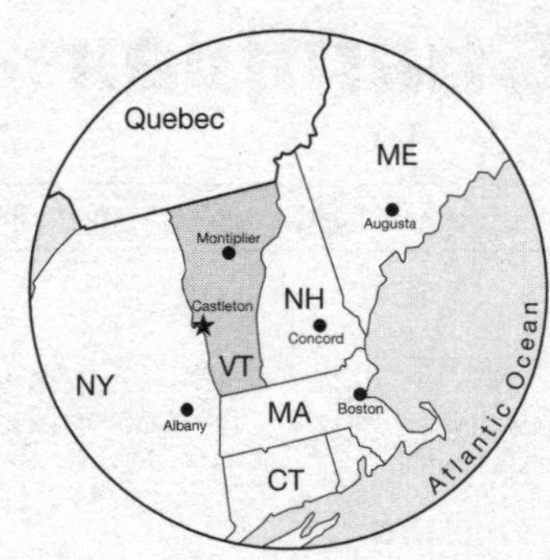

General Admissions

Very Important factors include: rigor of secondary school record, class rank, academic GPA, application essay, recommendation(s), character/personal qualities. *Other factors include:* standardized test scores, interview, extracurricular activities, volunteer work, level of applicant's interest. *Freshman admission requirements:* High school diploma is required and GED is accepted. *Academic units required:* 4 English, 3 math, 3 science, 2 science labs, 3 social studies, 3 history. *Academic units recommended:* 2 foreign language.

Accommodations or Services

Accommodations are decided upon an individual basis after a thorough review of appropriate, current documentation. The accommodations requests must be supported through the documentation provided and must be logically linked to the current impact of the condition on academic functioning.

Financial Aid

Students should submit: FAFSA. *Need-based scholarships/grants offered:* College/university scholarship or grant aid from institutional funds; Federal Pell; Private scholarships; SEOG; State scholarships/grants. *Loan aid offered:* Direct PLUS loans; Direct Subsidized Stafford Loans; Direct Unsubsidized Stafford Loans. Federal Work-Study Program available. Institutional employment available.

Campus Life

Activities: Campus Ministries; Choral groups; Concert band; Dance; Drama/theater; International Student Organization; Jazz band; Literary magazine; Marching band; Music ensembles; Musical theater; Pep band; Radio station; Student government; Student newspaper; Television station; Yearbook. **Organizations:** 40 registered organizations, 7 honor societies, 1 religious organization. **Athletics (Intercollegiate):** *Men:* baseball, basketball, cross-country, football, ice hockey, lacrosse, skiing (downhill/alpine), soccer, tennis. *Women:* basketball, cross-country, field hockey, ice hockey, lacrosse, skiing (downhill/alpine), soccer, softball, tennis.

ACCOMMODATIONS

Allowed in exams:	
Calculators	Yes
Dictionary	Yes
Computer	Yes
Spell-checker	Yes
Extended test time	Yes
Scribe	Yes
Proctors	Yes
Oral exams	Yes
Note-takers	Yes
Support services for students with:	
LD	Yes
ADHD	Yes
ASD	Yes
Distraction-reduced environment	Yes
Recording of lecture alowed	Yes
Reading technology	Yes
Audio books	Yes
Other assistive technology	No
Priority registration	No
Added costs of services:	
For LD	No
For ADHD	No
For ASD	No
LD specialists	No
ADHD & ASD coaching	Yes
ASD specialists	Yes
Professional tutors	Yes
Peer tutors	Yes
Max. hours/week for services	Varies
How professors are notified of student approved accommodations	Student

COLLEGE GRADUATION REQUIREMENTS

Course waivers allowed	No
Course substitutions allowed	No

Champlain College

163 South Willard Street Box 670, Burlington, VT 05402-0670 • Admissions: 802-860-2727 • Fax: 802-860-2767 **Support: S**

CAMPUS

Type of school	Private (nonprofit)
Environment	Town

STUDENTS

Undergrad enrollment	2,060
% male/female	64/36
% from out of state	78
% frosh live on campus	94

FINANCIAL FACTS

Annual tuition	$42,564
Room and board	$16,362
Required fees	$220

GENERAL ADMISSIONS INFO

Application fee	$0
Regular application deadline	1/15
Nonfall registration	Yes

Admission may be deferred.

Range SAT EBRW	570–670
Range SAT Math	540–650
Range ACT Composite	24–29

ACADEMICS

Student/faculty ratio	12:1
% students returning for sophomore year	83

Most classes have 10–19 students.

Programs/Services for Students with Learning Differences

Champlain College does not offer a special program for students with LD. Support services and academic accommodations are available when needed. Students with LD meet individually with a counselor at the start of the semester and are assisted in developing a plan of academic support. The counselor acts as liaison between the student and faculty. The college offers peer tutoring, writing assistance, accounting lab, math lab, and an oral communications lab. Mental health counseling and academic coaching are both offered. To obtain services, students must provide documentation of the disability to the Office of Accessibility, which should include the most recent educational evaluation performed by a qualified individual, and a letter from any educational support service provider who has recently worked with the student. The letter should include information about the nature of the disability, the support services, and/or program modifications provided.

Admissions

There is no special admissions procedure for students with LD. The admissions process is fairly competitive. The most important part of the application is the high school transcript. Upward grade trend and challenging course work are looked on favorably. Recommendations and college essay are required. All admission decisions are based on an assessment of the academic foundation needed for success in the required courses at the bachelor's degree level. Strong writing skills are important for all applicants. Minimum recommended preparation includes successful completion of a college preparatory curriculum. Students are expected to take a full course load of challenging academic subjects senior year. Applicants are evaluated based on the demands of their secondary school curriculum, grades earned, rank in class, standardized test scores, writing ability, teacher and counselor recommendations, and academic growth.

Additional Information

Students with learning disabilities who self-disclose receive a special needs form after they have enrolled. The coordinator meets with each student during the first week of school. The first appointment includes a discussion about the student's disability and the academic accommodations that will be needed. Accommodations could include, but are not limited to, tutoring, extended time for tests, readers for tests, use of computers during exams, peer notetakers, tape recording lectures, and books on tape. With

ADMISSIONS INFO FOR STUDENTS WITH LEARNING DIFFERENCES

Phone: 802-651-5961 • Email: sharris@champlain.edu

SAT/ACT required: No
Interview required: No
Essay required: Yes
Additional application required: No
Documentation submitted to: Accommodation Services

Special Ed. HS course work accepted: Yes
Separate application required for Programs/Services: No
Documentation required for:
LD: Psychoeducational evaluation
ADHD: Psychoeducational evaluation
ASD: Psychoeducational evaluation

Champlain College

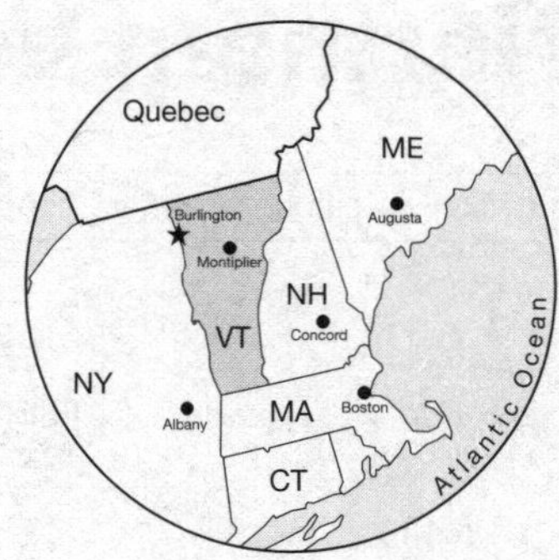

the student's permission, faculty members receive a letter discussing appropriate accommodations. The coordinators will continue to act as a liaison between students and faculty, consult with tutors, monitor the student's academic progress, and consult with faculty as needed.

General Admissions

Very Important factors include: rigor of secondary school record, academic GPA, talent/ability. *Important factors include:* application essay, recommendation(s), extracurricular activities, character/personal qualities, first generation, racial/ethnic status. *Other factors include:* class rank, standardized test scores, interview, alumni/ae relation, volunteer work, work experience. *Freshman admission requirements:* High school diploma is required and GED is accepted. *Academic units required:* 4 English, 3 math, 3 science, 2 science labs, 2 foreign language, 3 history, 5 academic electives. *Academic units recommended:* 4 math, 4 science, 4 foreign language, 4 history.

Accommodations or Services

Accommodations are decided upon an individual basis after a thorough review of appropriate, current documentation. The accommodations requests must be supported through the documentation provided and must be logically linked to the current impact of the condition on academic functioning.

Financial Aid

Students should submit: FAFSA. *Need-based scholarships/grants offered:* College/university scholarship or grant aid from institutional funds; Federal Pell; Private scholarships; SEOG; State scholarships/grants; United Negro College Fund. *Loan aid offered:* Direct PLUS loans; Direct Subsidized Stafford Loans; Direct Unsubsidized Stafford Loans. Federal Work-Study Program available. Institutional employment available.

Campus Life

Activities: Choral groups; Dance; Drama/theater; International Student Organization; Literary magazine; Musical theater; Radio station; Student government; Student newspaper. **Organizations:** 50 registered organizations.

ACCOMMODATIONS

Allowed in exams:	
Calculators	Yes
Dictionary	Yes
Computer	Yes
Spell-checker	Yes
Extended test time	Yes
Scribe	Yes
Proctors	Yes
Oral exams	Yes
Note-takers	Yes
Support services for students with:	
LD	Yes
ADHD	Yes
ASD	Yes
Distraction-reduced environment	Yes
Recording of lecture allowed	Yes
Reading technology	Yes
Audio books	Yes
Other assistive technology	Yes
Priority registration	Yes
Added costs of services:	
For LD	No
For ADHD	No
For ASD	No
LD specialists	No
ADHD & ASD coaching	No
ASD specialists	No
Professional tutors	Yes
Peer tutors	Yes
Max. hours/week for services	Varies
How professors are notified of student approved accommodations	Student with a letter from Office of Accessibility

COLLEGE GRADUATION REQUIREMENTS

Course waivers allowed	No
Course substitutions allowed	No

Vermont

Northern Vermont University

337 College Hill, Johnson, VT 05656-9408 • Admissions: 802-635-1219 • Fax: 802-635-1230 **Support: CS**

CAMPUS

Type of school	Public
Environment	Rural

STUDENTS

Undergrad enrollment	2,064
% male/female	41/59
% from out of state	36

FINANCIAL FACTS

Annual in-state tuition	$11,592
Annual out-of-state tuition	$25,680
Room and board	$11,694
Required fees	$13,012

GENERAL ADMISSIONS INFO

Application fee	$50
Regular application deadline	Rolling
Nonfall registration	Yes

Admission may be deferred.

ACADEMICS

% students returning for sophomore year	62

Most classes have 10–19 students.

Programs/Services for Students with Learning Differences

Northern Vermont University provides services to students with disabilities through a learning specialist at the Academic Support Service Program. The fundamental purpose of the program is to provide students with the appropriate services necessary to allow access to Northern Vermont University academic programs. Students with disabilities are integrated fully into the college community. In addition, students with disabilities may also be eligible for the TRiO program, which provides additional supports and services through the Learning Resource Center. The Learning Resource Center provides a friendly and supportive environment for any student who is academically struggling or underprepared to meet his or her educational goals. Services may include group and peer tutoring or professional tutoring in writing and math.

Admissions

Students with disabilities who demonstrate the academic ability to be successful at the post-secondary level are eligible for acceptance. Applicants with a disability are encouraged to contact the Admissions Office so that accommodations can be made available, where appropriate, throughout the admission process. Course requirements include 4 years of English, 2 years of college preparatory mathematics, 3 years of social sciences, and 2 years of science (one course with a lab).

Additional Information

The Summer Bridge Program offers workshops to help prepare for college including study skills, goal-setting, decision-making, and learning preferences. The program is open to low-income and first-generation students. It combines academic preparation and non-cognitive skills development with a sense of group identity and an early connection with the Academic Support Services staff that can make the difference between success and failure in the crucial first year of college. College Steps is a non-profit organization that partners with Northern Vermont University to support students ages 16–26 with social, communication, or learning challenges (including but not limited to students with significant learning disabilities, autism, developmental, or intellectual disabilities). College Steps expands support for young adults with functional skills sufficient to transition to a college environment, but who remain challenged without additional supports.

ADMISSIONS INFO FOR STUDENTS WITH LEARNING DIFFERENCES

Phone: 802-635-1259 • Fax: 802-635-1454

SAT/ACT required: No
Interview required: No
Essay required: Yes
Additional application required: No
Documentation submitted to: Academic Support Services

Special Ed. HS course work accepted: No
Separate application required for Programs/Services: No
Documentation required for:
LD: Psychoeducational evaluation
ADHD: Psychoeducational evaluation
ASD: Psychoeducational evaluation

Northern Vermont University

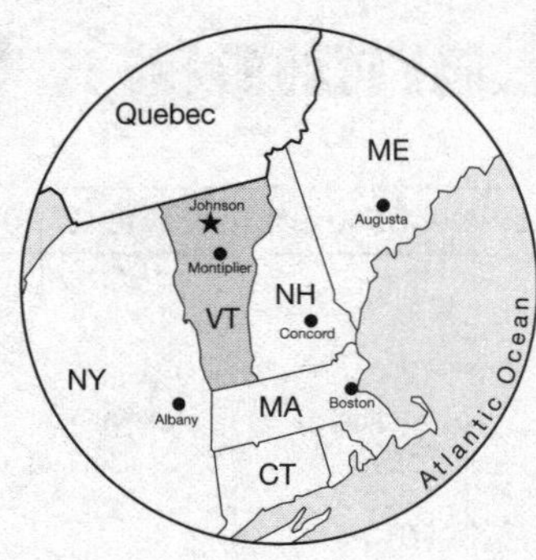

General Admissions

Very Important factors include: rigor of secondary school record, standardized test scores. *Important factors include:* class rank, academic GPA, application essay, recommendation(s), talent/ability, character/personal qualities. *Other factors include:* interview, extracurricular activities, volunteer work, work experience. *Freshman admission requirements:* High school diploma is required and GED is accepted. *Academic units required:* 4 English, 2 math, 2 science, 1 science lab, 3 social studies, 2 history. *Academic units recommended:* 4 English, 3 math, 3 science, 2 science labs, 1 foreign language, 3 social studies, 3 history.

Accommodations or Services

Accommodations are decided upon an individual basis after a thorough review of appropriate, current documentation. The accommodations requests must be supported through the documentation provided and must be logically linked to the current impact of the condition on academic functioning.

Financial Aid

Students should submit: FAFSA. Applicants will be notified of awards on or about 3/1. *Need-based scholarships/grants offered:* College/university scholarship or grant aid from institutional funds; Federal Pell; Private scholarships; SEOG; State scholarships/grants. *Loan aid offered:* Direct PLUS loans; Direct Subsidized Stafford Loans; Direct Unsubsidized Stafford Loans. Federal Work-Study Program available. Institutional employment available.

Campus Life

Activities: Choral groups; Concert band; Dance; Drama/theater; Jazz band; Literary magazine; Music ensembles; Musical theater; Radio station; Student government; Student newspaper; Yearbook. **Organizations:** 30 registered organizations, 1 honor society, 4 religious organizations. **Athletics (Intercollegiate):** *Men:* basketball, cross-country, golf, lacrosse, soccer, tennis. *Women:* basketball, cross-country, soccer, softball, tennis, volleyball.

ACCOMMODATIONS

Allowed in exams:	
Calculators	Yes
Dictionary	Yes
Computer	Yes
Spell-checker	Yes
Extended test time	Yes
Scribe	Yes
Proctors	Yes
Oral exams	No
Note-takers	Yes
Support services for students with:	
LD	Yes
ADHD	Yes
ASD	Yes
Distraction-reduced environment	Yes
Recording of lecture allowed	Yes
Reading technology	Yes
Audio books	Yes
Other assistive technology	Yes
Priority registration	No
Added costs of services:	
For LD	No
For ADHD	No
For ASD	No
LD specialists	Yes
ADHD & ASD coaching	No
ASD specialists	No
Professional tutors	Yes
Peer tutors	Yes
Max. hours/week for services	Unlimited
How professors are notified of student approved accommodations	Student

COLLEGE GRADUATION REQUIREMENTS

Course waivers allowed	No
Course substitutions allowed	Yes
In what courses: Case by case basis	

Vermont

Landmark College

19 River Road South, Putney, VT 05346-0820 • Admissions: 802-387-6718 **Support: SP**

CAMPUS

Type of school	Private (nonprofit)
Environment	Rural

STUDENTS

Undergrad enrollment	502
% male/female	66/34
% from out of state	90
% frosh live on campus	99

FINANCIAL FACTS

Annual tuition	$60,280
Room and board	$13,420

GENERAL ADMISSIONS INFO

Application fee	$75
Regular application deadline	5/1
Nonfall registration	Yes

Admission may be deferred.

ACADEMICS

Student/faculty ratio	6:1
% students returning for sophomore year	47

Most classes have 10–19 students.

Programs/Services for Students with Learning Differences

Landmark College is an accredited college designed exclusively for students of average to superior intellectual potential with Dyslexia, Attention Deficit Hyperactivity Disorder (ADHD), ASD, or specific learning disabilities. Life-changing experiences are commonplace at Landmark College. The college has invested substantially in technology and offers a wireless network in all of its classrooms, along with LAN, telephone, and cable connections in all the residence rooms. Entering students are expected to bring a notebook computer, as these are used in nearly every class session. The college's programs extensively integrate assistive technologies, such as Dragon Naturally Speaking and Kurzweil text-to-speech software. The college's 100+ full time faculty members are all highly experienced in serving students with learning disabilities, ASD, and attention deficit disorders. Over 100 staff members provide an array of support services that are unusually comprehensive for a student population of less than 450 students.

Admissions

Applicants to Landmark College must have a diagnosis of dyslexia, attention deficit disorder, ASD, or other specific learning disability. The college offers rolling admissions and enrolls academic semester students for fall and spring semesters. Enrolled students can earn up to 12 credits during the summer. A four-week skills development program is offered in the summer. A high school program for students aged 16–18 is also offered in the summer. Diagnostic testing within the last three years is required, along with a diagnosis of a learning disability or ADHD.

Additional Information

The Landmark College Transition Program is a two-week program for high school graduates and college students. Summer term includes pre-credit coursework to develop skills and strategies to be successful in college credit work. Students work with professional faculty to develop a writing process based on multi-modal writing techniques, learn, integrate, and practice study skills, and complete a communication or math course designed to integrate strategies and practice. The Landmark Study Abroad Program has developed programs with students' diverse learning styles in mind. Faculty design and teach experiential courses in their specific disciplines that fulfill Landmark core requirements while helping students gain confidence and independence in new academic structures. Faculty accompany students

ADMISSIONS INFO FOR STUDENTS WITH LEARNING DIFFERENCES

Phone: 802-387-4767 • Fax: 802-387-6868 • Email: mluciani@landmark.edu

SAT/ACT required: No
Interview required: Yes
Essay required: Yes
Additional application required: No
Documentation submitted to: Admissions

Special Ed. HS course work accepted: Yes
Separate application required for Programs/Services: No
Documentation required for:
LD: Psychoeducational evaluation
ADHD: Psychoeducational evaluation
ASD: Psychoeducational evaluation

Landmark College

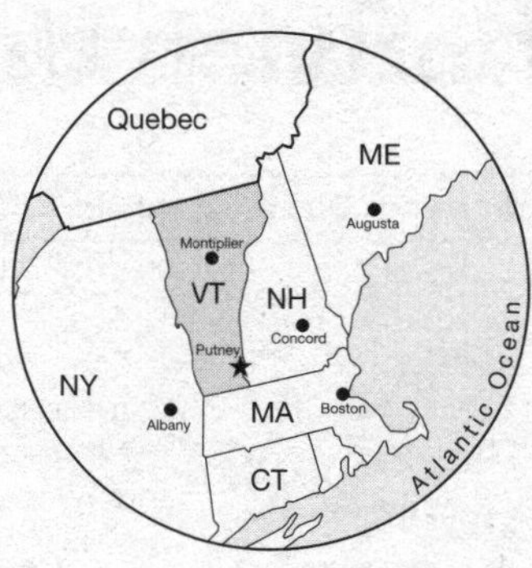

abroad, providing them with the Landmark College academic experience in an international setting. Landmark also offers a three-week summer session for high school students between the ages of 16 and 18, introducing students to the skills and strategies in reading and studying, including understanding and remembering readings and mastering the writing process. Landmark promotes self-advocacy, collaboration, and effective communication.

General Admissions

Very Important factors include: interview. *Important factors include:* rigor of secondary school record, recommendation(s), character/personal qualities. *Other factors include:* academic GPA, application essay, standardized test scores, extracurricular activities, talent/ability, alumni/ae relation, volunteer work, work experience. *Freshman admission requirements:* High school diploma is required and GED is accepted. *Academic units recommended:* 4 English, 3 math, 3 science, 3 science labs, 3 social studies, 3 history, 1 academic elective, 1 visual/performing arts.

Accommodations or Services

Accommodations are decided upon an individual basis after a thorough review of appropriate, current documentation. The accommodations requests must be supported through the documentation provided and must be logically linked to the current impact of the condition on academic functioning.

Financial Aid

Students should submit: FAFSA. *Need-based scholarships/grants offered:* College/university scholarship or grant aid from institutional funds; Federal Pell; Private scholarships; SEOG; State scholarships/grants. *Loan aid offered:* Direct PLUS loans; Direct Subsidized Stafford Loans; Direct Unsubsidized Stafford Loans. Federal Work-Study Program available. Institutional employment available.

Campus Life

Activities: Choral groups; Drama/theater; International Student Organization; Literary magazine; Music ensembles; Radio station; Student government; Student newspaper.

ACCOMMODATIONS

Allowed in exams:	
Calculators	Yes
Dictionary	Yes
Computer	Yes
Spell-checker	Yes
Extended test time	Yes
Scribe	Yes
Proctors	Yes
Oral exams	Yes
Note-takers	No
Support services for students with:	
LD	Yes
ADHD	Yes
ASD	Yes
Distraction-reduced environment	Yes
Recording of lecture alowed	Yes
Reading technology	Yes
Audio books	Yes
Other assistive technology	Yes
Priority registration	Yes
Added costs of services:	
For LD	No
For ADHD	No
For ASD	No
LD specialists	Yes
ADHD & ASD coaching	Yes
ASD specialists	Yes
Professional tutors	Yes
Peer tutors	No
Max. hours/week for services	Varies
How professors are notified of student approved accommodations	Director

COLLEGE GRADUATION REQUIREMENTS

Course waivers allowed	No
Course substitutions allowed	No

Vermont

Norwich University

Admissions Office, Northfield, VT 05663 • Admissions: 802-485-2001 • Fax: 802-485-2032 **Support: CS**

CAMPUS

Type of school	Private (nonprofit)
Environment	Rural

STUDENTS

Undergrad enrollment	3,266
% male/female	75/25
% from out of state	83
% frosh live on campus	97

FINANCIAL FACTS

Annual tuition	$40,608
Room and board	$14,854
Required fees	$2,342

GENERAL ADMISSIONS INFO

Application fee	$35
Regular application deadline	2/1
Nonfall registration	Yes

Admission may be deferred.

Range SAT EBRW	520–610
Range SAT Math	520–620
Range ACT Composite	21–26

ACADEMICS

Student/faculty ratio	15:1
% students returning for sophomore year	80

Most classes have 20–29 students.

Programs/Services for Students with Learning Differences

The Coordinator of Specialized Student Services provides services for students with suspected or documented disabilities. They assist with properly documenting the student's disabilities, understanding the student's Educational Profile and Academic Accommodations, providing training and information about assistive technology, facilitating communication with faculty, staff, and family members with the student's permission, offering academic coaching and counseling, and meeting with students on an as-needed or regular basis.

Admissions

Students with learning disabilities submit a general application. Admission criteria include high school GPA of a C or better, an SAT score of 850 or equivalent ACT, participation in activities, and strong college recommendations from teachers, counselors, or coaches. There are no course waivers for admission. The university is flexible on ACT/SAT test scores. If grades and other indicators are problematic, it is recommended that students provide detailed information to give a better understanding the disability. A complete psychodiagnostic evaluation is required. A small number of students who do not meet the general admission requirements may be admitted if they show promise. An interview is highly recommended. There are limited provisional admission slots.

Additional Information

All freshmen are assigned a student mentor, or CAM, for the fall semester. Mentors are academically successful sophomores who volunteer to meet with their mentees for 11–12 sessions throughout the fall term. Mentors are assigned by majors or schools, and they provide valuable information that is specific to all disciplines. The goals of the program include fine-tuning essential academic skills, working on time management, and helping freshmen navigate general school operations. The Academic Achievement Center (AAC) is available to provide peer tutoring. Staff assist with study, time management, organizational and learning skills, and provide academic coaching services. Comprehensive one-on-one and group tutoring across the curriculum is available.

ADMISSIONS INFO FOR STUDENTS WITH LEARNING DIFFERENCES

Phone: 802-485-2130 • Fax: 802-485-2684

SAT/ACT required: No
Interview required: Recommended
Essay required: No
Additional application required: No
Documentation submitted to: Academic Achievement Center (AAC)

Special Ed. HS course work accepted: Yes
Separate application required for Programs/Services: No
Documentation required for:
LD: Psychoeducational evaluation
ADHD: Psychoeducational evaluation
ASD: Psychoeducational evaluation

Norwich University

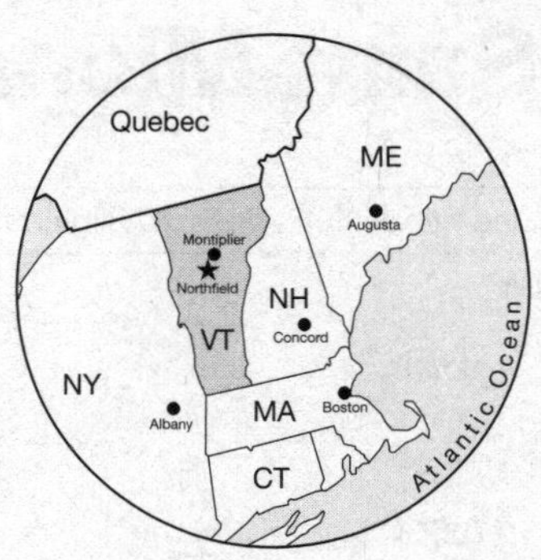

General Admissions

Very Important factors include: rigor of secondary school record, academic GPA, standardized test scores. *Other factors include:* class rank, application essay, recommendation(s), interview, extracurricular activities, talent/ability, character/personal qualities, alumni/ae relation, volunteer work, work experience. *Freshman admission requirements:* High school diploma is required and GED is accepted. *Academic units recommended:* 4 English, 4 math, 4 science, 3 science labs, 2 foreign language, 3 social studies, 3 history.

Accommodations or Services

Accommodations are decided upon an individual basis after a thorough review of appropriate, current documentation. The accommodations requests must be supported through the documentation provided and must be logically linked to the current impact of the condition on academic functioning.

Financial Aid

Students should submit: FAFSA. *Need-based scholarships/grants offered:* College/university scholarship or grant aid from institutional funds; Federal Pell; Private scholarships; SEOG; State scholarships/grants. *Loan aid offered:* Direct PLUS loans; Direct Subsidized Stafford Loans; Direct Unsubsidized Stafford Loans. Federal Work-Study Program available. Institutional employment available.

Campus Life

Activities: Campus Ministries; Dance; Drama/theater; International Student Organization; Jazz band; Marching band; Model UN; Radio station; Student government; Student newspaper; Yearbook. **Organizations:** 40 registered organizations, 8 honor societies, 4 religious organizations. **Athletics (Intercollegiate):** *Men:* baseball, basketball, cross-country, diving, football, ice hockey, lacrosse, riflery, rugby, soccer, swimming, track/field (outdoor), volleyball, wrestling. *Women:* basketball, cross-country, diving, riflery, rugby, soccer, softball, swimming, track/field (outdoor), volleyball.

ACCOMMODATIONS

Allowed in exams:	
Calculators	Yes
Dictionary	Yes
Computer	Yes
Spell-checker	Yes
Extended test time	Yes
Scribe	Yes
Proctors	Yes
Oral exams	Yes
Note-takers	No
Support services for students with:	
LD	Yes
ADHD	Yes
ASD	Yes
Distraction-reduced environment	Yes
Recording of lecture alowed	Yes
Reading technology	Yes
Audio books	Yes
Other assistive technology	Yes
Priority registration	Yes
Added costs of services:	
For LD	No
For ADHD	No
For ASD	No
LD specialists	Yes
ADHD & ASD coaching	No
ASD specialists	No
Professional tutors	Yes
Peer tutors	Yes
Max. hours/week for services	Varies
How professors are notified of student approved accommodations	Student and director

COLLEGE GRADUATION REQUIREMENTS

Course waivers allowed	No
Course substitutions allowed	Yes

In what courses: Case by case basis

Saint Michael's College

One Winooski Park, Box 7, Colchester, VT 05439 • Admissions: 802-654-3000 • Fax: 802-654-2906 **Support: CS**

CAMPUS

Type of school	Private (nonprofit)
Environment	City

STUDENTS

Undergrad enrollment	1,551
% male/female	46/54
% from out of state	85
% frosh live on campus	97

FINANCIAL FACTS

Annual tuition	$46,175
Room and board	$13,600
Required fees	$2,000

GENERAL ADMISSIONS INFO

Application fee	$50
Regular application deadline	2/1
Nonfall registration	Yes

Admission may be deferred.

Range SAT EBRW	585–660
Range SAT Math	570–650
Range ACT Composite	25–29

ACADEMICS

Student/faculty ratio	13:1
% students returning for sophomore year	83

Most classes have 10–19 students.

Programs/Services for Students with Learning Differences

Saint Michael's College is devoted to ensuring equal educational opportunities and a responsive campus environment for students with disabilities. Students wishing to disclose a learning disability or a disability that affects learning may receive additional support. A clear understanding of strengths and weaknesses in learning and the influence of the disability on current and past educational processes will afford a broader assessment of capabilities, challenges, and consonant needs. To ensure the provision of reasonable and appropriate accommodations for students with learning disabilities, students needing such accommodations must provide current and comprehensive documentation, including the diagnosis of the learning problem(s), a copy of the psychoeducational evaluation completed within the past 4–6 years that includes a measure of cognitive functioning, and current measures of reading, math, and written language achievement. Informational processing must also be assessed. The testing must be conducted by a certified professional, address the nature of the disability, and include the professional's assessment of how the learning difference will influence academic success. The report must also include recommendations for reasonable accommodations. The earlier the information is received, the better prepared we will be to address specific needs.

Admissions

Successful applicants for admission to Saint Michael's College are typically very strong students who are active learners prepared for a rigorous intellectual experience. Students should have a commitment to service, social justice, and community. St. Michael's College is devoted to ensuring equal educational opportunities and a responsive campus environment for students with disabilities. Support is provided through the Office of Accessibility Services located in the Academic Enrichment Commons. The director promotes self-awareness for students with disabilities by educating them about their rights so that they can independently advocate and make choices to meet or exceed the academic standards expected of them. To gain admittance, students are required to have completed 4 years of English, 2–3 years of modern language, 3–4 years of theoretical mathematics, 3–4 years of science (including at least 2 lab sciences), and 3–4 years of history and social sciences.

ADMISSIONS INFO FOR STUDENTS WITH LEARNING DIFFERENCES

Phone: 802-654-2000 • Fax: 802-387-6868 • Email: amessuri@smcvt.edu

SAT/ACT required: No
Interview required: No
Essay required: No
Additional application required: No
Documentation submitted to: Office of Accessibility Services

Special Ed. HS course work accepted: Yes
Separate application required for Programs/Services: No
Documentation required for:
LD: Psychoeducational evaluation
ADHD: Psychoeducational evaluation
ASD: Psychoeducational evaluation

Saint Michael's College

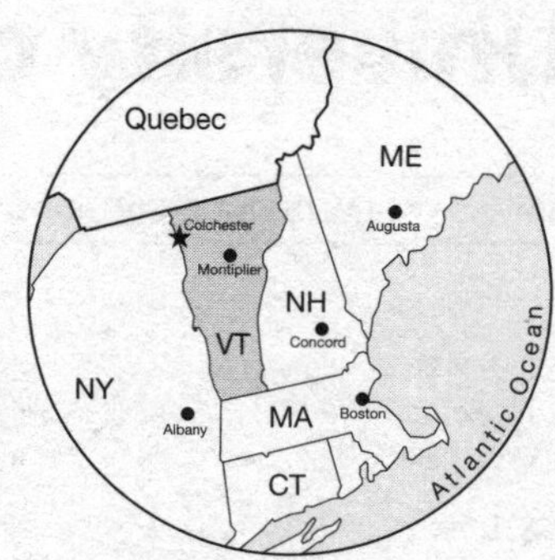

Additional Information
An academic support coach is available for students seeking assistance in personal choices, study skills, and time management in relation to academic performance. Collaborative Educational Consultant on staff are available on a fee-for-service basis. This service is a holistic, highly focused approach to helping students define and achieve academic goals. The one-to-one coaching model helps students identify their learning objectives, find their own solutions, and follow their plans through to completion. Students own their own learning when participating in Collaborative Educational Consulting. Students wanting individual tutors must first meet with their professors outside of class and attend at least one group or drop-in session.

General Admissions
Very Important factors include: rigor of secondary school record, class rank, academic GPA. *Important factors include:* application essay, standardized test scores, recommendation(s), talent/ability, character/personal qualities. *Other factors include:* interview, extracurricular activities, first generation, alumni/ae relation, geographical residence, state residency, racial/ethnic status, volunteer work, work experience, level of applicant's interest. *Freshman admission requirements:* High school diploma is required and GED is accepted. *Academic units required:* 4 English, 4 math, 3 science, 2 science labs, 2 foreign language, 3 social studies, 3 history. *Academic units recommended:* 4 English, 4 math, 4 science, 3 science labs, 4 foreign language, 4 social studies, 4 history.

Accommodations or Services
Accommodations are decided upon an individual basis after a thorough review of appropriate, current documentation. The accommodations requests must be supported through the documentation provided and must be logically linked to the current impact of the condition on academic functioning.

Financial Aid
Students should submit: FAFSA. *Need-based scholarships/grants offered:* Federal Pell; Private scholarships; SEOG; State scholarships/grants. *Loan aid offered:* Direct PLUS loans; Direct Subsidized Stafford Loans; Direct Unsubsidized Stafford Loans. Federal Work-Study Program available. Institutional employment available.

Campus Life
Activities: Campus Ministries; Choral groups; Concert band; Dance; Drama/theater; International Student Organization; Jazz band; Literary magazine; Music ensembles; Musical theater; Radio station; Student government; Student newspaper; Yearbook. **Organizations:** 40 registered organizations, 11 honor societies, 1 religious organization. **Athletics (Intercollegiate):** *Men:* baseball, basketball, cross-country, diving, golf, ice hockey, lacrosse, skiing (downhill/alpine), skiing (Nordic/cross-country), soccer, swimming, tennis. *Women:* basketball, cross-country, diving, field hockey, ice hockey, lacrosse, skiing (downhill/alpine), skiing (Nordic/cross-country), soccer, softball, swimming, tennis, volleyball.

ACCOMMODATIONS

Allowed in exams:	
Calculators	Yes
Dictionary	Yes
Computer	Yes
Spell-checker	Yes
Extended test time	Yes
Scribe	Yes
Proctors	Yes
Oral exams	No
Note-takers	Yes
Support services for students with:	
LD	Yes
ADHD	Yes
ASD	Yes
Distraction-reduced environment	Yes
Recording of lecture allowed	Yes
Reading technology	Yes
Audio books	Yes
Other assistive technology	Yes
Priority registration	No
Added costs of services:	
For LD	No
For ADHD	No
For ASD	No
LD specialists	Yes
ADHD & ASD coaching	Yes
ASD specialists	No
Professional tutors	Yes
Peer tutors	Yes
Max. hours/week for services	Varies
How professors are notified of student approved accommodations	Director

COLLEGE GRADUATION REQUIREMENTS

Course waivers allowed	No
Course substitutions allowed	No

University of Vermont

University of Vermont Admissions, Burlington, VT 05401-3596 • Admissions: 802-656-3370 **Support: SP**

CAMPUS	
Type of school	Public
Environment	Town
STUDENTS	
Undergrad enrollment	10,700
% male/female	41/59
% from out of state	72
% frosh live on campus	98
FINANCIAL FACTS	
Annual in-state tuition	$16,392
Annual out-of-state tuition	$41,280
Room and board	$12,916
Required fees	$2,410
GENERAL ADMISSIONS INFO	
Application fee	$55
Regular application deadline	1/15
Nonfall registration	Yes
Admission may be deferred.	
Range SAT EBRW	600–680
Range SAT Math	580–680
Range ACT Composite	26–31
ACADEMICS	
Student/faculty ratio	18:1
% students returning for sophomore year	87
Most classes have 10–19 students.	

Programs/Services for Students with Learning Differences

Student Accessibility Services (SAS) provides services and accommodations to all UVM students who have current documentation of a disability that substantially limits one or more major life activities, including but not limited to walking, talking, learning, hearing, or seeing.

Admissions

Students submit a common application to Admissions. Documentation of a student's disability is sent directly to SAS. Students are encouraged to voluntarily provide documentation of their disability. SAS reviews documentation and may consult with admissions if/when necessary as to how a student's disability has affected their academic record. Upon request, if time and resources allow, students may request a review of their documentation to assess eligibility and/or entrance requirements if they feel their disability has impacted them in such a way that they are missing a requirement such as foreign language. Students with LD or ADHD should submit a current educational evaluation that includes a comprehensive measure of both cognitive and achievement functioning. Course requirements include 4 years English, 3 years social science, 3 years math, 2 years physical sciences, and 2 years foreign language. Self-disclosing in the application is a matter of personal choice. At UVM, disclosing a disability will absolutely not have a negative impact on a student's admissibility.

Additional Information

Think College Vermont is an innovative, inclusive, academic, social, and vocational program for students with intellectual and developmental disabilities seeking a college experience and career path. Participants may earn a 12 credit-hour certificate of college studies for non-matriculated students designed to include studies in academic enrichment, socialization & recreation, independent living & self-advocacy skills, and integrated work experiences & career skills. Think College incorporates student-centered planning, academic advising, and peer mentors for an inclusive, supportive college experience. It is a two-year non-degree certificate program through the UVM Continuing and Distance Education and the UVM Center on Disability and Community Inclusion. SUCCEED also collaborates with the University of Vermont. Students have the opportunity to participate in four program areas: student housing/independent living, education, campus life, and career development. SUCCEED provides students with the tools to live more independently while actively participating in a true college experience. Students graduate

ADMISSIONS INFO FOR STUDENTS WITH LEARNING DIFFERENCES

Phone: 802-656-7753 • Fax: 802-656-0739 • Email: access@uvm.edu

SAT/ACT required: Yes (Test optional for 2021)
Interview required: No
Essay required: Yes
Additional application required: No
Documentation submitted to: Student Accessibility Services

Special Ed. HS course work accepted: No
Separate application required for Programs/Services: No
Documentation required for:
LD: Psychoeducational evaluation
ADHD: Psychoeducational evaluation
ASD: Psychoeducational evaluation

University of Vermont

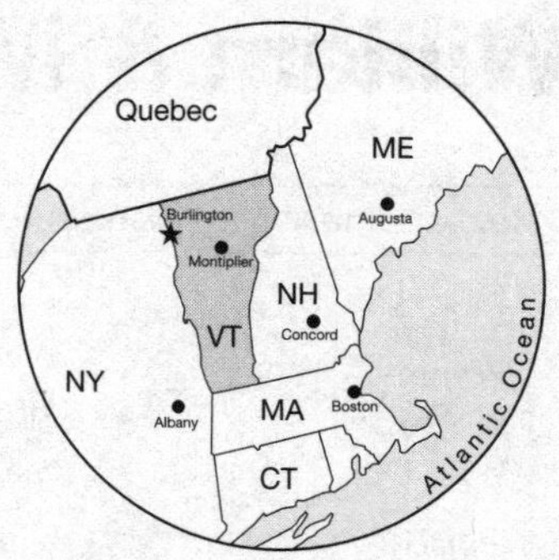

with the ability to live in their own apartment, develop meaningful friendships, obtain fulfilling employment, and establish social connections within their community.

General Admissions

Very Important factors include: rigor of secondary school record. *Important factors include:* class rank, academic GPA, application essay, standardized test scores, character/personal qualities, state residency. *Other factors include:* recommendation(s), extracurricular activities, talent/ability, first generation, alumni/ae relation, geographical residence, racial/ethnic status, volunteer work, work experience, level of applicant's interest. *Freshman admission requirements:* High school diploma is required and GED is accepted. *Academic units required:* 4 English, 3 math, 2 science, 1 science lab, 2 foreign language, 3 social studies.

Accommodations or Services

Accommodations are decided upon an individual basis after a thorough review of appropriate, current documentation. The accommodations requests must be supported through the documentation provided and must be logically linked to the current impact of the condition on academic functioning.

Financial Aid

Students should submit: FAFSA. *Need-based scholarships/grants offered:* College/university scholarship or grant aid from institutional funds; Federal Pell; Private scholarships; SEOG; State scholarships/grants. *Loan aid offered:* Direct PLUS loans; Direct Subsidized Stafford Loans; Direct Unsubsidized Stafford Loans. Federal Work-Study Program available. Institutional employment available.

Campus Life

Activities: Campus Ministries; Choral groups; Concert band; Dance; Drama/theater; International Student Organization; Jazz band; Literary magazine; Music ensembles; Musical theater; Pep band; Radio station; Student government; Student newspaper; Student-run film society; Symphony orchestra; Television station. **Organizations:** 214 registered organizations, 29 honor societies, 7 religious organizations, 8 fraternities, 6 sororities. **Athletics (Intercollegiate):** *Men:* basketball, cross-country, ice hockey, lacrosse, skiing (downhill/alpine), skiing (Nordic/cross-country), soccer, track/field (outdoor), track/field (indoor). *Women:* basketball, cross-country, diving, field hockey, ice hockey, lacrosse, skiing (downhill/alpine), skiing (Nordic/cross-country), soccer, swimming, track/field (outdoor), track/field (indoor).

ACCOMMODATIONS

Allowed in exams:	
Calculators	Yes
Dictionary	Yes
Computer	Yes
Spell-checker	Yes
Extended test time	Yes
Scribe	Yes
Proctors	Yes
Oral exams	Yes
Note-takers	Yes
Support services for students with:	
LD	Yes
ADHD	Yes
ASD	Yes
Distraction-reduced environment	Yes
Recording of lecture alowed	Yes
Reading technology	Yes
Audio books	Yes
Other assistive technology	Yes
Priority registration	Yes
Added costs of services:	
For LD	No
For ADHD	No
For ASD	No
LD specialists	Yes
ADHD & ASD coaching	Yes
ASD specialists	Yes
Professional tutors	Yes
Peer tutors	Yes
Max. hours/week for services	Varies
How professors are notified of student approved accommodations	Director

COLLEGE GRADUATION REQUIREMENTS

Course waivers allowed	No
Course substitutions allowed	No

William & Mary

Office of Admissions, Williamsburg, VA 23187-8795 • Admissions: 757-221-4223 • Fax: 757-221-1242 **Support: CS**

CAMPUS

Type of school	Public
Environment	Town

STUDENTS

Undergrad enrollment	6,256
% male/female	42/58
% from out of state	31
% frosh live on campus	99

FINANCIAL FACTS

Annual in-state tuition	$17,434
Annual out-of-state tuition	$40,089
Room and board	$12,926
Required fees	$6,194

GENERAL ADMISSIONS INFO

Application fee	$75
Regular application deadline	1/1
Nonfall registration	No

Admission may be deferred.

Range SAT EBRW	660–740
Range SAT Math	660–770
Range ACT Composite	30–34

ACADEMICS

Student/faculty ratio	11:1
% students returning for sophomore year	95

Most classes have 10–19 students.

Programs/Services for Students with Learning Differences

Student Accessibility Services fosters student independence, encourages self-determination, emphasizes empowerment and accommodation over limitation, and creates a comprehensive, accessible environment to ensure that individuals are viewed on the basis of their contributions. SAS strives to help students with disabilities to understand their strengths and challenges and the process in how to request accommodations.

Admissions

All applicants are expected to meet the same admission criteria. Students with disabilities may self-disclose their disability during the admission process to provide a better understanding of their challenges. The university is test optional, so neither the ACT or SAT is required for admission. For students who submit test scores, the mid 50% ACT score is 30–34 and SAT is 1320–1510. Interviews are available. An audition is not required for admission. However, students are encouraged to provide supplemental information about skills or talents in creative or performing arts if they plan to continue study in this area.

Additional Information

The staff of Student Accessibility Services (SAS) seeks to create a barrier-free environment for students with disabilities by considering reasonable accommodations upon request. The staff works closely with all college departments to identify appropriate options for accommodating students with disabilities. Additionally, they offer services when students need special housing accommodations. Peer tutors are available in the Tribe Tutor Zone and are available for individual sessions in Swem Library seven days per week to review material, answer questions, and help develop college-level study skills.

ADMISSIONS INFO FOR STUDENTS WITH LEARNING DIFFERENCES

Phone: 757-221-2510 • Fax: 757-221-2538 • Email: sas@wm.edu

SAT/ACT required: Yes (Test optional for 2021)
Interview required: No
Essay required: Yes
Additional application required: No
Documentation submitted to: Student Accessibility Services

Special Ed. HS course work accepted: Yes
Separate application required for Programs/Services: No
Documentation required for:
LD: Psychoeducational evaluation
ADHD: Psychoeducational evaluation
ASD: Psychoeducational evaluation

William & Mary

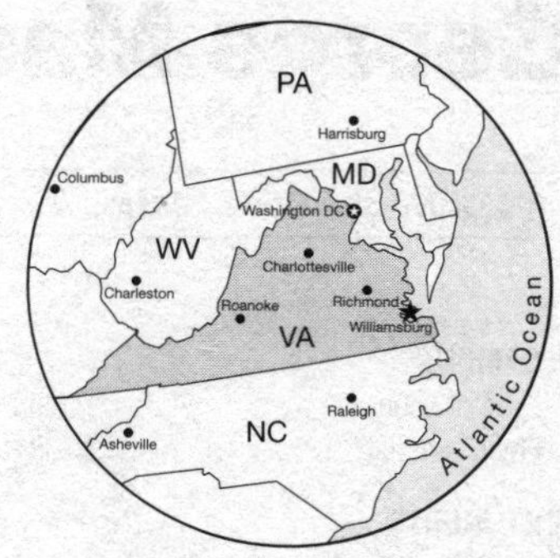

General Admissions

Very Important factors include: rigor of secondary school record, class rank, academic GPA, application essay, standardized test scores, recommendation(s), extracurricular activities, talent/ability, character/personal qualities, state residency, volunteer work, work experience. *Other factors include:* interview, first generation, alumni/ae relation, geographical residence, racial/ethnic status, level of applicant's interest. *Freshman admission requirements:* High school diploma or equivalent is not required. *Academic units recommended:* 4 English, 4 math, 4 science, 3 science labs, 4 foreign language, 4 social studies.

Accommodations or Services

Accommodations are decided upon an individual basis after a thorough review of appropriate, current documentation. The accommodations requests must be supported through the documentation provided and must be logically linked to the current impact of the condition on academic functioning.

Financial Aid

Students should submit: CSS/Financial Aid PROFILE; FAFSA. Applicants will be notified of awards on a rolling basis beginning 3/1. *Need-based scholarships/grants offered:* College/university scholarship or grant aid from institutional funds; Federal Pell; Private scholarships; SEOG; State scholarships/grants. *Loan aid offered:* Direct PLUS loans; Direct Subsidized Stafford Loans; Direct Unsubsidized Stafford Loans. Federal Work-Study Program available. Institutional employment available.

Campus Life

Activities: Campus Ministries; Choral groups; Concert band; Dance; Drama/theater; International Student Organization; Jazz band; Literary magazine; Model UN; Music ensembles; Musical theater; Opera; Pep band; Radio station; Student government; Student newspaper; Student-run film society; Symphony orchestra; Television station; Yearbook. **Organizations:** 475 registered organizations, 19 honor societies, 30 religious organizations, 19 fraternities, 14 sororities. **Athletics (Intercollegiate):** *Men:* baseball, basketball, cheerleading, cross-country, diving, football, golf, gymnastics, soccer, swimming, tennis, track/field (outdoor), track/field (indoor). *Women:* basketball, cheerleading, cross-country, diving, field hockey, golf, gymnastics, lacrosse, soccer, swimming, tennis, track/field (outdoor), track/field (indoor), volleyball.

ACCOMMODATIONS

Allowed in exams:	
Calculators	Yes
Dictionary	Yes
Computer	Yes
Spell-checker	Yes
Extended test time	Yes
Scribe	Yes
Proctors	Yes
Oral exams	Yes
Note-takers	Yes
Support services for students with:	
LD	Yes
ADHD	Yes
ASD	Yes
Distraction-reduced environment	Yes
Recording of lecture allowed	Yes
Reading technology	Yes
Audio books	Yes
Other assistive technology	Yes
Priority registration	Yes
Added costs of services:	
For LD	No
For ADHD	No
For ASD	No
LD specialists	No
ADHD & ASD coaching	Yes
ASD specialists	No
Professional tutors	Yes
Peer tutors	Yes
Max. hours/week for services	Varies
How professors are notified of student approved accommodations	Student and director

COLLEGE GRADUATION REQUIREMENTS

Course waivers allowed	No
Course substitutions allowed	Yes

In what courses: Foreign language course substitution, NOT a waiver

Virginia

George Mason University

4400 University Drive, Fairfax, VA 22030-4444 • Admissions: 703-993-2400 • Fax: 703-993-4622 **Support: SP**

CAMPUS

Type of school	Public
Environment	City

STUDENTS

Undergrad enrollment	26,013
% male/female	51/49
% from out of state	10
% frosh live on campus	62

FINANCIAL FACTS

Annual in-state tuition	$9,510
Annual out-of-state tuition	$32,970
Room and board	$12,090
Required fees	$3,504

GENERAL ADMISSIONS INFO

Application fee	$70
Regular application deadline	1/15
Nonfall registration	Yes

Admission may be deferred.

Range SAT EBRW	560–660
Range SAT Math	550–660
Range ACT Composite	24–30

ACADEMICS

Student/faculty ratio	17:1
% students returning for sophomore year	86

Most classes have 20–29 students.

Programs/Services for Students with Learning Differences

George Mason promotes equal access for students with disabilities in curricular and co-curricular activities. Under the administration of University Life, the center implements and coordinates reasonable accommodations and disability-related services that afford equal access to university programs and activities. Disability services are available to serve all students with disabilities, including those with cognitive, learning, psychological, sustained head injuries, sensory, mobility, and other physical impairments. The office welcomes and encourages all students with disabilities, whether registered with Disability Services or not, to identify themselves as members of the disability community and to engage in the diversity dialogue on campus by getting involved with Disability Services and other multicultural programs and activities.

Admissions

All applicants are expected to meet the same admission criteria. A personal statement is optional but highly recommended. In 250 words students should explain why they want to attend college. The Art and Visual Technology, Computer Game Design, Dance, Film and Video Studies, Music and Theater majors in the College of Visual and Performing Arts require an audition or portfolio review. The School of Nursing admission requires a second review of freshman applications for direct admission to the Bachelor of Science in Nursing (BSN) major. Applicants admitted to the university but not to the School of Nursing are considered as undeclared majors.

Additional Information

Enrolled students are paired with a peer mentor to help them socially acclimate. The Mason LIFE Program is an innovative post-secondary program for young adults with intellectual and developmental disabilities who desire a university experience in a supportive academic environment. The mission of the Mason LIFE Program is a dual purpose: the first is to provide a supportive academic environment for our students with intellectual and developmental disabilities; the second is to supply an apprenticeship for George Mason University students.

ADMISSIONS INFO FOR STUDENTS WITH LEARNING DIFFERENCES

Phone: 703-993-2474 • Fax: 703-993-4306 • Email: ods@gmu.edu

SAT/ACT required: No
Interview required: No
Essay required: Recommended
Additional application required: Yes
Documentation submitted to: Disability Services

Special Ed. HS course work accepted: Yes
Separate application required for Programs/Services: Yes
Documentation required for:
- **LD:** Psychoeducational evaluation
- **ADHD:** Psychoeducational evaluation
- **ASD:** Psychoeducational evaluation

George Mason University

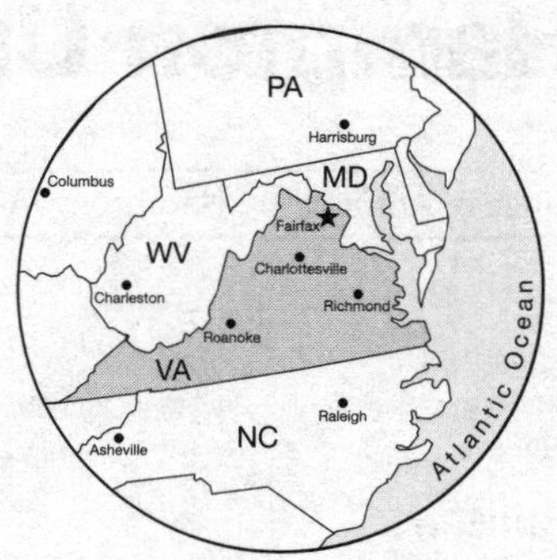

General Admissions

Very Important factors include: rigor of secondary school record, academic GPA. *Important factors include:* standardized test scores, talent/ability. *Other factors include:* class rank, application essay, recommendation(s), extracurricular activities, character/personal qualities, first generation, geographical residence, state residency, volunteer work, work experience, level of applicant's interest. *Freshman admission requirements:* High school diploma is required and GED is accepted. *Academic units required:* 4 English, 3 math, 2 science, 2 science labs, 2 foreign language, 3 social studies, 3 academic electives. *Academic units recommended:* 4 English, 4 math, 3 science, 3 science labs, 3 foreign language, 4 social studies, 5 academic electives.

Accommodations or Services

Accommodations are decided upon an individual basis after a thorough review of appropriate, current documentation. The accommodations requests must be supported through the documentation provided and must be logically linked to the current impact of the condition on academic functioning.

Financial Aid

Students should submit: FAFSA; Institution's own financial aid form. Applicants will be notified of awards on or about 3/1. *Need-based scholarships/grants offered:* College/university scholarship or grant aid from institutional funds; Federal Pell; Private scholarships; SEOG; State scholarships/grants. *Loan aid offered:* Direct PLUS loans; Direct Subsidized Stafford Loans; Direct Unsubsidized Stafford Loans. Federal Work-Study Program available. Institutional employment available.

Campus Life

Activities: Campus Ministries; Choral groups; Concert band; Dance; Drama/theater; International Student Organization; Jazz band; Literary magazine; Model UN; Music ensembles; Musical theater; Opera; Pep band; Radio station; Student government; Student newspaper; Student-run film society; Symphony orchestra; Television station; Yearbook. **Organizations:** 464 registered organizations, 15 honor societies, 46 religious organizations, 24 fraternities, 19 sororities. **Athletics (Intercollegiate):** *Men:* baseball, basketball, cheerleading, cross-country, diving, golf, soccer, swimming, tennis, track/field (outdoor), track/field (indoor), volleyball, wrestling. *Women:* basketball, cheerleading, crew/rowing, cross-country, diving, lacrosse, soccer, softball, swimming, tennis, track/field (outdoor), track/field (indoor), volleyball.

ACCOMMODATIONS

Allowed in exams:	
Calculators	Yes
Dictionary	Yes
Computer	Yes
Spell-checker	Yes
Extended test time	Yes
Scribe	Yes
Proctors	Yes
Oral exams	Yes
Note-takers	Yes
Support services for students with:	
LD	Yes
ADHD	Yes
ASD	Yes
Distraction-reduced environment	Yes
Recording of lecture alowed	Yes
Reading technology	Yes
Audio books	Yes
Other assistive technology	Yes
Priority registration	Yes
Added costs of services:	
For LD	No
For ADHD	No
For ASD	Yes
LD specialists	Yes
ADHD & ASD coaching	Yes
ASD specialists	Yes
Professional tutors	Yes
Peer tutors	Yes
Max. hours/week for services	Varies
How professors are notified of student approved accommodations	Student

COLLEGE GRADUATION REQUIREMENTS

Course waivers allowed	Yes
In what courses: Disability Services will evaluate all requests.	
Course substitutions allowed	Yes
In what courses: Disability Services will evaluate all requests.	

Virginia

Hampton University

Office of Admissions, Hampton, VA 23668 • Admissions: 757-727-5328 • Fax: 757-727-5095 **Support: S**

CAMPUS

Type of school	Private (nonprofit)
Environment	City

STUDENTS

Undergrad enrollment	3,714
% male/female	34/66
% from out of state	78
% frosh live on campus	82

FINANCIAL FACTS

Annual tuition	$ 26,198
Room and board	$12,986
Required fees	$2,964

GENERAL ADMISSIONS INFO

Application fee	$50
Regular application deadline	3/1
Nonfall registration	Yes

Admission may be deferred.

Range SAT EBRW	530–590
Range SAT Math	500–570
Range ACT Composite	20–26

ACADEMICS

Student/faculty ratio	14:1
% students returning for sophomore year	75

Programs/Services for Students with Learning Differences

The University is fully committed to complying with all requirements of the Americans with Disabilities Act of 1990 (ADA) and Section 504 of the Rehabilitation Act of 1973. In class, accommodations may be provided to students with a documented physical, mental, or learning disability. It is recommended to request accommodations within the first week of classes, understanding that accommodations are not retroactive. To obtain accommodations or to receive more information please contact the Office of the Director of Compliance and Disability Services or visit the office located in the Student Success Center.

Admissions

In reviewing applications for the right fit, the university takes a holistic approach, focusing on overall academic achievement, characteristics that demonstrate leadership potential, and personal qualities indicative of the highest ethical values. Students with a cumulative GPA of at least 3.3 or rank in the top 10% of their class have the option to choose whether or not to submit SAT or ACT. Applicants choosing not to submit standardized test scores are encouraged to submit at least one recommendation from a teacher in a core subject area. Homeschooled applicants, students attending schools outside the United States, and students wishing to be considered for merit-based scholarships must submit standardized test scores. High School students must complete at least 4 units of English, 3 units of college-preparatory mathematics, 2 units of foreign language, 2 units of social science, and 2 units in the natural sciences. The university recommends that candidates take the most rigorous academic program available in their schools, including at least five academic courses each year and AP, IB, and honors courses whenever possible.

Additional Information

The Office of Compliance and Disability Services provides and coordinates accommodations, support services, and auxiliary aids for qualified students with disabilities and qualified employees with disabilities.

ADMISSIONS INFO FOR STUDENTS WITH LEARNING DIFFERENCES

Phone: 757-727-5493 • Fax: 757-728-6973 • Email: denise.james@hamptonu.edu

SAT/ACT required: No
Interview required: No
Essay required: No
Additional application required: No
Documentation submitted to: University Testing, Office of Compliance and Disability Services

Special Ed. HS course work accepted: Yes
Separate application required for Programs/Services: No
Documentation required for:
LD: Psychoeducational evaluation
ADHD: Psychoeducational evaluation
ASD: Psychoeducational evaluation

Hampton University

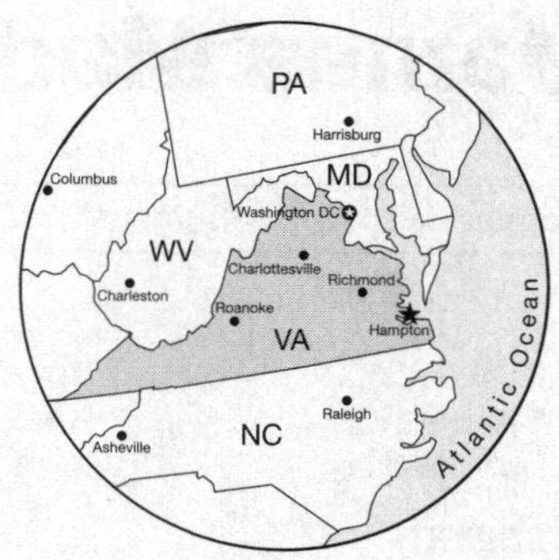

General Admissions

Very Important factors include: rigor of secondary school record, academic GPA, application essay, character/personal qualities. *Important factors include:* class rank, recommendation(s). *Other factors include:* interview, extracurricular activities, talent/ability, volunteer work, work experience, level of applicant's interest. *Freshman admission requirements:* High school diploma is required and GED is accepted. *Academic units required:* 4 English, 3 math, 2 science, 2 science labs, 2 social studies, 6 academic electives. *Academic units recommended:* 2 foreign language.

Accommodations or Services

Accommodations are decided upon an individual basis after a thorough review of appropriate, current documentation. The accommodations requests must be supported through the documentation provided and must be logically linked to the current impact of the condition on academic functioning.

Financial Aid

Students should submit: FAFSA. *Need-based scholarships/grants offered:* College/university scholarship or grant aid from institutional funds; Federal Nursing Scholarships; Federal Pell; Private scholarships; SEOG; State scholarships/grants. *Loan aid offered:* Direct PLUS loans; Direct Subsidized Stafford Loans; Direct Unsubsidized Stafford Loans. Federal Work-Study Program available.

Campus Life

Activities: Campus Ministries; Choral groups; Concert band; Dance; Drama/theater; International Student Organization; Jazz band; Literary magazine; Marching band; Music ensembles; Musical theater; Opera; Pep band; Radio station; Student government; Student newspaper; Symphony orchestra; Television station; Yearbook. **Organizations:** 85 registered organizations, 16 honor societies, 3 religious organizations, 5 fraternities, 4 sororities. **Athletics (Intercollegiate):** *Men:* basketball, cross-country, football, golf, sailing, tennis, track/field (outdoor), track/field (indoor). *Women:* basketball, bowling, cross-country, golf, sailing, softball, tennis, track/field (outdoor), track/field (indoor), volleyball.

ACCOMMODATIONS

Allowed in exams:	
Calculators	Yes
Dictionary	Yes
Computer	No
Spell-checker	No
Extended test time	Yes
Scribe	Yes
Proctors	Yes
Oral exams	Yes
Note-takers	Yes
Support services for students with:	
LD	Yes
ADHD	Yes
ASD	Yes
Distraction-reduced environment	Yes
Recording of lecture allowed	Yes
Reading technology	Yes
Audio books	Yes
Other assistive technology	Yes
Priority registration	Yes
Added costs of services:	
For LD	No
For ADHD	No
For ASD	No
LD specialists	Yes
ADHD & ASD coaching	Yes
ASD specialists	No
Professional tutors	Yes
Peer tutors	Yes
Max. hours/week for services	Varies
How professors are notified of student approved accommodations	Student and director

COLLEGE GRADUATION REQUIREMENTS

Course waivers allowed Yes
In what courses: Foreign language

Course substitutions allowed Yes
In what courses: Foreign language

Virginia

James Madison University

Sonner Hall, Harrisonburg, VA 22807 • Admissions: 540-568-5681 • Fax: 540-568-3332 **Support: CS**

CAMPUS	
Type of school	Public
Environment	Town
STUDENTS	
Undergrad enrollment	19,895
% male/female	42/58
% from out of state	22
% frosh live on campus	98
FINANCIAL FACTS	
Annual in-state tuition	$7,250
Annual out-of-state tuition	$24,150
Room and board	$11,588
Required fees	$5,080
GENERAL ADMISSIONS INFO	
Application fee	$70
Regular application deadline	2/1
Nonfall registration	No
Admission may be deferred.	
Range SAT EBRW	570–650
Range SAT Math	550–640
Range ACT Composite	23–28
ACADEMICS	
Student/faculty ratio	16:1
% students returning for sophomore year	89
Most classes have 20–29 students.	

Programs/Services for Students with Learning Differences

The Office of Disability Services (ODS) collaborates with the JMU community, providing programs and services that support the university in creating inclusive, equitable environments that value disability, diversity, and accessibility.

Admissions

There is no single academic program expected for all students to follow, however, the strongest applicants complete a rigorous secondary school curriculum. Competitive applicants challenge themselves beyond high school graduation requirements in the core academic areas of English, math, science, social science, and foreign language. During the admissions process, the admissions team at JMU is highly sensitive and knowledgeable concerning students with learning disabilities. Admission decisions are made without regard to disabilities, and all prospective students are expected to present academic credentials that are competitive. There are no specific courses required for admission into James Madison; however, students are expected to complete a solid college-prep curriculum. ODS is not involved in the JMU admission process unless contacted by the Office of Admissions.

Additional Information

The Office of Disability Services offers a number of services to students with disabilities, including classroom accommodations, such as extended time on tests, interpreters, and other classroom accommodations for deaf and hard of hearing students. Additional support includes assistive technology labs, test proctoring, alternative texts, and peer mentoring. Learning strategies instruction and screening & assessment services are available to all students, regardless of disability status. Additional on-campus services can be found at the Learning Resource Centers (LRC). LRC offers the following programs and services to all enrolled students: Communication Resource Center, Science & Math Learning Center, University Writing Center, supplemental instruction, Counseling and Student Development Center, and Career & Academic Planning.

ADMISSIONS INFO FOR STUDENTS WITH LEARNING DIFFERENCES

Phone: 540-568-6705 • Fax: 540-568-7099 • Email: schoolvl@jmu.edu

SAT/ACT required: No
Interview required: No
Essay required: No
Additional application required: Yes
Documentation submitted to: Support Program/Services

Special Ed. HS course work accepted: Yes
Separate application required for Programs/Services: Yes
Documentation required for:
LD: Psychoeducational evaluation
ADHD: Psychoeducational evaluation
ASD: Psychoeducational evaluation

James Madison University

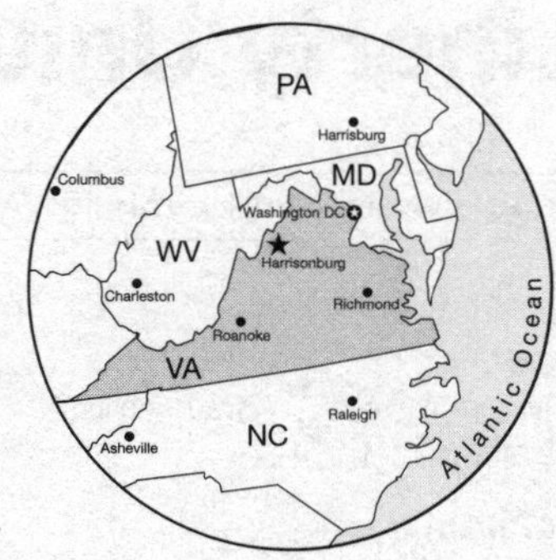

General Admissions

Very Important factors include: rigor of secondary school record, academic GPA. *Other factors include:* application essay, standardized test scores, recommendation(s), extracurricular activities, talent/ability, character/personal qualities, first generation, alumni/ae relation, geographical residence, state residency, racial/ethnic status, volunteer work, work experience. *Freshman admission requirements:* High school diploma is required and GED is accepted. *Academic units required:* 4 English, 4 math, 3 science, 3 foreign language, 2 social studies, 3 history. *Academic units recommended:* 4 English, 4 math, 3 science, 3 foreign language, 2 social studies, 3 history.

Accommodations or Services

Accommodations are decided upon an individual basis after a thorough review of appropriate, current documentation. The accommodations requests must be supported through the documentation provided and must be logically linked to the current impact of the condition on academic functioning.

Financial Aid

Students should submit: FAFSA. *Need-based scholarships/grants offered:* College/university scholarship or grant aid from institutional funds; Federal Pell; Private scholarships; SEOG; State scholarships/grants. *Loan aid offered:* Direct PLUS loans; Direct Subsidized Stafford Loans; Direct Unsubsidized Stafford Loans. Federal Work-Study Program available. Institutional employment available.

Campus Life

Activities: Campus Ministries; Choral groups; Concert band; Dance; Drama/theater; International Student Organization; Jazz band; Literary magazine; Marching band; Music ensembles; Musical theater; Opera; Pep band; Radio station; Student government; Student newspaper; Student-run film society; Symphony orchestra; Yearbook. **Organizations:** 353 registered organizations, 22 honor societies, 32 religious organizations, 15 fraternities, 13 sororities. **Athletics (Intercollegiate):** *Men:* baseball, basketball, cheerleading, football, golf, soccer, tennis. *Women:* basketball, cheerleading, cross-country, diving, field hockey, golf, lacrosse, soccer, softball, swimming, tennis, track/field (outdoor), volleyball.

ACCOMMODATIONS

Allowed in exams:	
Calculators	Yes
Dictionary	Yes
Computer	Yes
Spell-checker	Yes
Extended test time	Yes
Scribe	Yes
Proctors	Yes
Oral exams	Yes
Note-takers	Yes
Support services for students with:	
LD	Yes
ADHD	Yes
ASD	Yes
Distraction-reduced environment	Yes
Recording of lecture allowed	No
Reading technology	Yes
Audio books	Yes
Other assistive technology	Yes
Priority registration	Yes
Added costs of services:	
For LD	No
For ADHD	No
For ASD	No
LD specialists	No
ADHD & ASD coaching	Yes
ASD specialists	No
Professional tutors	No
Peer tutors	Yes
Max. hours/week for services	Varies
How professors are notified of student approved accommodations	Student

COLLEGE GRADUATION REQUIREMENTS

Course waivers allowed — Yes

In what courses: Generally, Math requirements cannot be waived.

Course substitutions allowed — Yes

In what courses: Foreign language

Virginia

Liberty University

1971 University Blvd, Lynchburg, VA 24515 • Admissions: 434-582-2000 • Fax: 800-628-7977 **Support: S**

CAMPUS

Type of school	Private (nonprofit)
Environment	Town

STUDENTS

Undergrad enrollment	12,984
% male/female	45/55
% from out of state	60
% frosh live on campus	93

FINANCIAL FACTS

Annual tuition	$23,800
Room and board	$10,478
Required fees	$1,476

GENERAL ADMISSIONS INFO

Application fee	$50
Regular application deadline	Rolling
Nonfall registration	Yes

Admission may be deferred.

Range SAT EBRW	530–640
Range SAT Math	510–620
Range ACT Composite	21–28

ACADEMICS

% students returning for sophomore year	85

Most classes have 20–29 students.

Programs/Services for Students with Learning Differences

The Office of Disability Academic Support, a component of the Center for Academic Support and Advising Services, was created to coordinate academic support services for Liberty University students who have documented disabilities. The Bruckner Learning Center helps students plan, develop, and maintain quality, university-wide academic support services.

Admissions

All applicants must submit an official transcript from an accredited high school and/or college, an official copy of a state high school equivalency diploma, or an official copy of the GED test results. The minimum acceptable unweighted GPA is 2.0. Applicants who fail to meet the minimum required GPA will be evaluated using other indicators of collegiate ability and may be admitted on academic warning. All applicants must submit ACT or SAT prior to admission. The minimum acceptable scores are SAT 800 or ACT 17.

Additional Information

If a student's entrance test scores indicate a deficiency in English or math, then the student will enroll in a basic composition class or fundamentals of math class. With the student's permission, instructors are provided with written communication providing information about the student's disability and suggestions of appropriate accommodations. The Academic Success Center offers support to students in the form of tutoring, faculty mentoring, writing assistance, and workshops. Peer tutors are also available for individual or group sessions.

ADMISSIONS INFO FOR STUDENTS WITH LEARNING DIFFERENCES

Phone: 434-592-4016 • Fax: 434-582-2297 • Email: odas@liberty.edu

SAT/ACT required: Yes (Test optional for 2021)
Interview required: No
Essay required: No
Additional application required: No
Documentation submitted to: Office of Disability Academic Support

Special Ed. HS course work accepted: Yes
Separate application required for Programs/Services: No
Documentation required for:
LD: Psychoeducational evaluation
ADHD: Psychoeducational evaluation
ASD: Psychoeducational evaluation

Liberty University

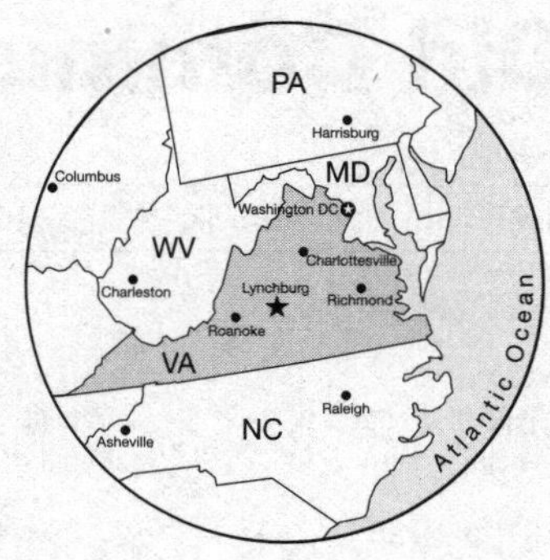

General Admissions

Very Important factors include: rigor of secondary school record, academic GPA. *Important factors include:* standardized test scores, character/personal qualities. *Other factors include:* class rank, application essay, recommendation(s), extracurricular activities, talent/ability, level of applicant's interest. *Freshman admission requirements:* High school diploma is required and GED is accepted. *Academic units recommended:* 4 English, 3 math, 2 science, 2 science labs, 2 foreign language, 2 social studies, 4 academic electives.

Accommodations or Services

Accommodations are decided upon an individual basis after a thorough review of appropriate, current documentation. The accommodations requests must be supported through the documentation provided and must be logically linked to the current impact of the condition on academic functioning.

Financial Aid

Students should submit: FAFSA. Applicants will be notified of awards on a rolling basis beginning 4/20. *Need-based scholarships/grants offered:* College/university scholarship or grant aid from institutional funds; Federal Pell; Private scholarships; SEOG; State scholarships/grants. *Loan aid offered:* Direct PLUS loans; Direct Subsidized Stafford Loans; Direct Unsubsidized Stafford Loans.

Campus Life

Activities: Campus Ministries; Choral groups; Concert band; Drama/theater; Literary magazine; Marching band; Music ensembles; Musical theater; Pep band; Radio station; Student government; Student newspaper; Symphony orchestra; Television station; Yearbook. **Organizations:** 25 registered organizations, 8 honor societies, 10 religious organizations. **Athletics (Intercollegiate):** *Men:* baseball, basketball, cheerleading, cross-country, football, golf, soccer, tennis, track/field (outdoor), track/field (indoor), wrestling. *Women:* basketball, cheerleading, cross-country, soccer, softball, tennis, track/field (outdoor), track/field (indoor), volleyball.

ACCOMMODATIONS

Allowed in exams:	
Calculators	Yes
Dictionary	Yes
Computer	Yes
Spell-checker	Yes
Extended test time	Yes
Scribe	Yes
Proctors	Yes
Oral exams	Yes
Note-takers	Yes
Support services for students with:	
LD	Yes
ADHD	Yes
ASD	Yes
Distraction-reduced environment	Yes
Recording of lecture alowed	Yes
Reading technology	Yes
Audio books	No
Other assistive technology	Yes
Priority registration	Yes
Added costs of services:	
For LD	No
For ADHD	No
For ASD	No
LD specialists	Yes
ADHD & ASD coaching	No
ASD specialists	No
Professional tutors	No
Peer tutors	Yes
Max. hours/week for services	Varies
How professors are notified of student approved accommodations	Director

COLLEGE GRADUATION REQUIREMENTS

Course waivers allowed	No
Course substitutions allowed	No

Old Dominion University

108 Rollins Hall, Norfolk, VA 23529-0050 • Admissions: 757-683-3685 • Fax: 757-683-3255 **Support: CS**

CAMPUS

Type of school	Public
Environment	Metropolis

STUDENTS

Undergrad enrollment	18,965
% male/female	45/55
% from out of state	8
% frosh live on campus	75

FINANCIAL FACTS

Annual in-state tuition	$11,020
Annual out-of-state tuition	$31,180
Room and board	$12,836
Required fees	$340

GENERAL ADMISSIONS INFO

Application fee	$50
Regular application deadline	2/1
Nonfall registration	Yes

Admission may be deferred.

Range SAT EBRW	500–600
Range SAT Math	480–580
Range ACT Composite	18–24

ACADEMICS

Student/faculty ratio	17:1
% students returning for sophomore year	80

Most classes have 10–19 students.

Programs/Services for Students with Learning Differences

The Office of Educational Accessibility is a welcoming, engaging, and supportive environment that offers dynamic educational support services for students who experience disabilities so they can be successfully accommodated and included in the rich diversity of university life. The office offers a wide variety of accommodations and support to students based on their individual needs and works collaboratively with partners across campus to ensure that all aspects of campus are inclusive in nature.

Admissions

Admission to Old Dominion University is based solely on the entrance requirements as described in the university catalog. Disclosure of a disability during the admissions process is not required or requested, and neither the nature nor the severity of an individual's disability is used as criteria for admission. The Office of Educational Accessibility does not participate in the admissions process. Preference is given to students enrolled in Advanced Placement (AP) or International Baccalaureate (IB), honors, and college-level dual enrollment courses. The most qualified applicants' high school curriculums include course work in the following areas: English (4 units), social sciences (3 units in world history, United States history, and United States government), mathematics (3 units in algebra, geometry, and algebra II), sciences (3 units of laboratory sciences), and foreign language (3 years of one foreign language or two years of two foreign languages).

Additional Information

Accommodations are based upon the documentation that the student presents and the discussion that the student has with the Office of Educational Accessibility. The accommodations may have to be adjusted during the course of the student's academic career at the university. Students are encouraged to reach out to the Office of Educational Accessibility each semester for any learning needs not being accommodated. Counseling and advising, study skills instruction, reading, writing, and math instruction, and tutorial assistance are available. Program staff design support services that focus on students' learning styles and special needs. There is a special section of Spanish for students with learning disabilities to meet the foreign language requirements, as well as developmental math, reading, spelling, and writing classes.

ADMISSIONS INFO FOR STUDENTS WITH LEARNING DIFFERENCES

Phone: 757-683-4655 • Fax: 757-683-5356 • Email: oea@odu.edu

SAT/ACT required: No
Interview required: No
Essay required: Yes
Additional application required: No
Documentation submitted to: Educational Accessibility

Special Ed. HS course work accepted: Yes
Separate application required for Programs/Services: No
Documentation required for:
LD: Psychoeducational evaluation
ADHD: Psychoeducational evaluation
ASD: Psychoeducational evaluation

Old Dominion University

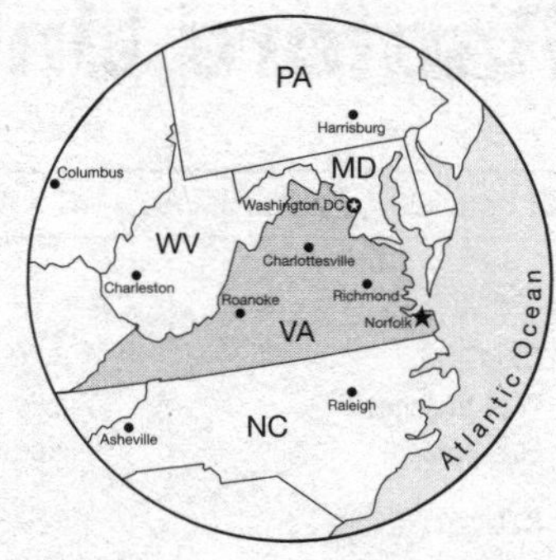

General Admissions

Very Important factors include: rigor of secondary school record, academic GPA, standardized test scores. *Important factors include:* application essay, recommendation(s), extracurricular activities, volunteer work. *Other factors include:* class rank, talent/ability, character/personal qualities, first generation, alumni/ae relation, level of applicant's interest. *Freshman admission requirements:* High school diploma is required and GED is accepted. *Academic units required:* 4 English, 3 math, 3 science, 3 foreign language, 3 social studies. *Academic units recommended:* 4 English, 4 math, 3 science, 3 foreign language, 3 social studies.

Accommodations or Services

Accommodations are decided upon an individual basis after a thorough review of appropriate, current documentation. The accommodations requests must be supported through the documentation provided and must be logically linked to the current impact of the condition on academic functioning.

Financial Aid

Students should submit: FAFSA. Applicants will be notified of awards on a rolling basis beginning 2/15. *Need-based scholarships/grants offered:* College/university scholarship or grant aid from institutional funds; Federal Nursing Scholarships; Federal Pell; Private scholarships; SEOG; State scholarships/grants; United Negro College Fund. *Loan aid offered:* Direct PLUS loans; Direct Subsidized Stafford Loans; Direct Unsubsidized Stafford Loans. Federal Work-Study Program available. Institutional employment available.

Campus Life

Activities: Campus Ministries; Choral groups; Concert band; Dance; Drama/theater; International Student Organization; Jazz band; Literary magazine; Marching band; Model UN; Music ensembles; Musical theater; Pep band; Radio station; Student government; Student newspaper; Student-run film society; Symphony orchestra. **Organizations:** 341 registered organizations, 18 honor societies, 25 religious organizations, 18 fraternities, 8 sororities. **Athletics (Intercollegiate):** *Men:* baseball, basketball, diving, football, golf, sailing, soccer, tennis, wrestling. *Women:* basketball, crew/rowing, diving, field hockey, golf, lacrosse, sailing, soccer, tennis.

ACCOMMODATIONS

Allowed in exams:	
Calculators	Yes
Dictionary	Yes
Computer	Yes
Spell-checker	Yes
Extended test time	Yes
Scribe	Yes
Proctors	Yes
Oral exams	Yes
Note-takers	Yes
Support services for students with:	
LD	Yes
ADHD	Yes
ASD	Yes
Distraction-reduced environment	Yes
Recording of lecture alowed	Yes
Reading technology	Yes
Audio books	Yes
Other assistive technology	Yes
Priority registration	Yes
Added costs of services:	
For LD	No
For ADHD	No
For ASD	No
LD specialists	No
ADHD & ASD coaching	Yes
ASD specialists	No
Professional tutors	No
Peer tutors	Yes
Max. hours/week for services	Varies
How professors are notified of student approved accommodations	Student

COLLEGE GRADUATION REQUIREMENTS

Course waivers allowed	No
Course substitutions allowed	Yes

Radford University

PO Box 6903, Radford, VA 24142 • Admissions: 540-831-5371 • Fax: 540-831-5038 **Support: CS**

CAMPUS

Type of school	Public
Environment	Village

STUDENTS

Undergrad enrollment	7,920
% male/female	39/61
% from out of state	7
% frosh live on campus	91

FINANCIAL FACTS

Annual in-state tuition	$7,922
Annual out-of-state tuition	$19,557
Room and board	$9,637
Required fees	$3,428

GENERAL ADMISSIONS INFO

Application fee	$0
Regular application deadline	2/1
Nonfall registration	Yes

Admission may be deferred.

Range SAT EBRW	480–570
Range SAT Math	460–540
Range ACT Composite	17–23

ACADEMICS

Student/faculty ratio	15:1
% students returning for sophomore year	71

Most classes have 10–19 students.

Programs/Services for Students with Learning Differences

The Center for Accessibility Services is committed to providing equal educational opportunities for individuals living with disabilities. The center serves and supports students, parents, and visitors seeking reasonable accommodations under the Americans with Disabilities Act and is dedicated to the ongoing goal of access and inclusion so that an individual may fully participate in the university experience.

Admissions

General admissions requirements must be met. Radford University views everything that an applicant submits in an effort to get to know that individual as well as possible. Applications are reviewed by members of the admissions committee to select potential Radford University students who will not only find academic success at Radford, but also become positive contributors to the community. Coursework required for admissions includes 4 years of English, 4 years of math, 4 years of science (one of the science courses must include a lab), 4 years of foreign language, 2 years of history, and 2 years of social studies.

Additional Information

The Learning Assistance and Resource Center helps student achieve academic success. In individual or group tutoring sessions, students acquire support from the College Reading and Learning Association certified trained tutors. Writing tutors aid students with writing assignments for any discipline. One-on-one consultations are available to students. With a learner-centered approach, the staff and tutors seek to meet each Radford University student's academic needs.

ADMISSIONS INFO FOR STUDENTS WITH LEARNING DIFFERENCES

Phone: 540-831-6350 • Fax: 540-831-6525 • Email: cas@radford.edu

SAT/ACT required: No
Interview required: No
Essay required: Yes
Additional application required: Yes
Documentation submitted to: Support Program/Services

Special Ed. HS course work accepted: Yes
Separate application required for Programs/Services: Yes
Documentation required for:
LD: Psychoeducational evaluation
ADHD: Psychoeducational evaluation
ASD: Psychoeducational evaluation

Radford University

General Admissions

Very Important factors include: rigor of secondary school record. *Important factors include:* academic GPA. *Other factors include:* class rank, application essay, standardized test scores, recommendation(s), interview, extracurricular activities, talent/ability, character/personal qualities, first generation, alumni/ae relation, volunteer work, work experience, level of applicant's interest. *Freshman admission requirements:* High school diploma is required and GED is accepted. *Academic units recommended:* 4 English, 4 math, 4 science, 4 science labs, 4 foreign language, 2 social studies, 2 history.

Accommodations or Services

Accommodations are decided upon an individual basis after a thorough review of appropriate, current documentation. The accommodations requests must be supported through the documentation provided and must be logically linked to the current impact of the condition on academic functioning.

Financial Aid

Students should submit: FAFSA. *Need-based scholarships/grants offered:* College/university scholarship or grant aid from institutional funds; Federal Pell; Private scholarships; SEOG; State scholarships/grants. *Loan aid offered:* Direct PLUS loans; Direct Subsidized Stafford Loans; Direct Unsubsidized Stafford Loans. Federal Work-Study Program available. Institutional employment available.

Campus Life

Activities: Campus Ministries; Choral groups; Concert band; Dance; Drama/theater; International Student Organization; Jazz band; Literary magazine; Model UN; Music ensembles; Musical theater; Opera; Pep band; Radio station; Student government; Student newspaper; Student-run film society; Yearbook. **Organizations:** 295 registered organizations, 16 honor societies, 14 religious organizations, 12 fraternities, 10 sororities. **Athletics (Intercollegiate):** *Men:* baseball, basketball, cheerleading, cross-country, golf, soccer, tennis, track/field (outdoor), track/field (indoor). *Women:* basketball, cheerleading, cross-country, diving, field hockey, golf, soccer, softball, swimming, tennis, track/field (outdoor), track/field (indoor), volleyball.

ACCOMMODATIONS

Allowed in exams:	
Calculators	Yes
Dictionary	Yes
Computer	Yes
Spell-checker	Yes
Extended test time	Yes
Scribe	Yes
Proctors	Yes
Oral exams	Yes
Note-takers	Yes
Support services for students with:	
LD	Yes
ADHD	Yes
ASD	Yes
Distraction-reduced environment	Yes
Recording of lecture allowed	Yes
Reading technology	Yes
Audio books	Yes
Other assistive technology	Yes
Priority registration	Yes
Added costs of services:	
For LD	No
For ADHD	No
For ASD	No
LD specialists	No
ADHD & ASD coaching	Yes
ASD specialists	No
Professional tutors	Yes
Peer tutors	Yes
Max. hours/week for services	Varies
How professors are notified of student approved accommodations	Student

COLLEGE GRADUATION REQUIREMENTS

Course waivers allowed	No
Course substitutions allowed	Yes
In what courses: Case by case basis	

Virginia

Roanoke College

221 College Lane, Salem, VA 24153-3794 • Admissions: 540-375-2270 • Fax: 540-375-2267 **Support: CS**

CAMPUS

Type of school	Private (nonprofit)
Environment	City

STUDENTS

Undergrad enrollment	1,953
% male/female	42/58
% from out of state	45
% frosh live on campus	91

FINANCIAL FACTS

Annual tuition	$45,200
Room and board	$14,580
Required fees	$1,820

GENERAL ADMISSIONS INFO

Application fee	$30
Regular application deadline	3/15
Nonfall registration	Yes

Admission may be deferred.

Range SAT EBRW	540–640
Range SAT Math	510–620
Range ACT Composite	21–27.5

ACADEMICS

Student/faculty ratio	11:1
% students returning for sophomore year	78

Most classes have 20–29 students.

Programs/Services for Students with Learning Differences

Accessible Education Services strives to meet the needs of students with documented disabilities in alignment with Roanoke College's commitment to providing equal access to educational opportunities for all students. Individuals with disabilities are encouraged to visit Roanoke College after their acceptance of admission. A personal visit enables the student and college representatives to meet and determine how the college can accommodate the student's physical and learning needs. All requests are handled on a case-by-case basis. Students are encouraged to submit their documentation shortly after being admitted to the college to ensure that their accommodations are in place prior to the beginning of their first term.

Admissions

Admission to Roanoke College is based on individual qualifications. No separate standards are used for students with documented disabilities. Admission is based on academic grades and courses, class rank, and standardized test scores. Roanoke College considers extracurricular activities, recommendations and other personal contacts beyond the paper application. Successful candidates complete a minimum of 18 academic courses in high school, including 4 in English, 2 in social studies, 2 in lab sciences, and at least 2 recommended foreign language courses. Additionally, there are 3 required courses in math. including geometry, algebra I, and algebra II. The middle 50% of students admitted have a GPA of 2.8–3.7 on a 4.0 scale, (equivalent to a low B to high A average), an SAT score of 1140–1270, and an ACT score of 22–28.

Additional Information

All services are accessed through the Disability Support Services office and the Goode-Pasfield Center for Learning & Teaching. Any special considerations or accommodations requested by the student will not be allowed until testing results have been received and reviewed by the Coordinator of Disability Support Services. All requests are handled on a case-by-case basis. Students are encouraged to submit their documentation shortly after being admitted to the college. The college does not permit substitutions for language, statistics, or mathematics requirements.

ADMISSIONS INFO FOR STUDENTS WITH LEARNING DIFFERENCES

Phone: 540-375-2247 • Fax: 540-375-2485 • Email: lleonard@roanoke.edu

SAT/ACT required: Yes
Interview required: Optional
Essay required: Yes
Additional application required: Yes
Documentation submitted to: Disability Support Services

Special Ed. HS course work accepted: Yes
Separate application required for Programs/Services: Yes
Documentation required for:
LD: Psychoeducational evaluation
ADHD: Psychoeducational evaluation
ASD: Psychoeducational evaluation

Roanoke College

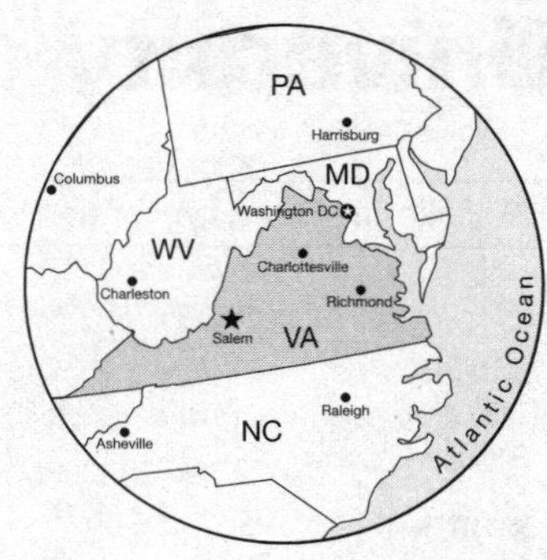

General Admissions

Very Important factors include: rigor of secondary school record, academic GPA, character/personal qualities. *Important factors include:* class rank, interview, extracurricular activities. *Other factors include:* application essay, standardized test scores, recommendation(s), talent/ability, alumni/ae relation, racial/ethnic status, volunteer work, work experience. *Freshman admission requirements:* High school diploma is required and GED is accepted. *Academic units required:* 4 English, 3 math, 2 science, 2 science labs, 2 foreign language, 2 social studies, 5 academic electives. *Academic units recommended:* 2 foreign language.

Accommodations or Services

Accommodations are decided upon an individual basis after a thorough review of appropriate, current documentation. The accommodations requests must be supported through the documentation provided and must be logically linked to the current impact of the condition on academic functioning.

Financial Aid

Students should submit: FAFSA; State aid form. *Need-based scholarships/grants offered:* College/university scholarship or grant aid from institutional funds; Federal Pell; Private scholarships; SEOG; State scholarships/grants. *Loan aid offered:* Direct PLUS loans; Direct Subsidized Stafford Loans; Direct Unsubsidized Stafford Loans. Federal Work-Study Program available. Institutional employment available.

Campus Life

Activities: Campus Ministries; Choral groups; Concert band; Dance; Drama/theater; International Student Organization; Jazz band; Literary magazine; Model UN; Music ensembles; Pep band; Radio station; Student government; Student newspaper; Student-run film society. **Organizations:** 100 registered organizations, 27 honor societies, 7 religious organizations, 5 fraternities, 4 sororities. **Athletics (Intercollegiate):** *Men:* baseball, basketball, cross-country, golf, lacrosse, soccer, tennis, track/field (outdoor), track/field (indoor). *Women:* basketball, cross-country, field hockey, lacrosse, soccer, softball, tennis, track/field (outdoor), track/field (indoor), volleyball.

ACCOMMODATIONS

Allowed in exams:	
Calculators	Yes
Dictionary	Yes
Computer	Yes
Spell-checker	Yes
Extended test time	Yes
Scribe	Yes
Proctors	Yes
Oral exams	Yes
Note-takers	Yes
Support services for students with:	
LD	No
ADHD	No
ASD	No
Distraction-reduced environment	Yes
Recording of lecture allowed	Yes
Reading technology	No
Audio books	Yes
Other assistive technology	Yes
Priority registration	No
Added costs of services:	
For LD	No
For ADHD	No
For ASD	No
LD specialists	No
ADHD & ASD coaching	Yes
ASD specialists	No
Professional tutors	No
Peer tutors	Yes
Max. hours/week for services	Varies
How professors are notified of student approved accommodations	Student

COLLEGE GRADUATION REQUIREMENTS

Course waivers allowed	No
Course substitutions allowed	No

University of Lynchburg

1501 Lakeside Drive, Lynchburg, VA 24501 • Admissions: 434-544-8300 • Fax: 434-544-8653 **Support: CS**

CAMPUS

Type of school	Private (nonprofit)
Environment	City

STUDENTS

Undergrad enrollment	1,935
% male/female	39/61
% from out of state	27
% frosh live on campus	83

FINANCIAL FACTS

Annual tuition	$40,910
Room and board	$12,138
Required fees	$970

GENERAL ADMISSIONS INFO

Application fee	$30
Regular application deadline	Rolling
Nonfall registration	Yes

Admission may be deferred.

Range SAT EBRW	500–600
Range SAT Math	470–570
Range ACT Composite	18–26

ACADEMICS

Student/faculty ratio	11:1
% students returning for sophomore year	75

Most classes have 10–19 students.

Programs/Services for Students with Learning Differences

The Center for Accessibility and Disability Resources works with students reasonable accommodations. University of Lynchburg does not offer programs and courses specifically designed for students with disabilities. Students with disabilities can benefit from reasonable accommodations approved on case by case basis. Approximately 10–12% of University of Lynchburg students are served through the Center for Accessibility and Disability Resources. The Accessibility and Disability Resources Coordinator offers additional support through Academic Success Mentoring and works with students to provide connections to other resources available on campus.

Admissions

Admission is based on individual qualifications. No separate standards are used for students with documented disabilities. Candidates for admission completed the following classes: English, social studies, math (including algebra I, algebra II, and geometry), science (including 2 lab sciences), and foreign language (minimum of two years of the same language—not including sign language). The average student profile consists of an average GPA of 3.2 on a 4.0 scale (B equivalent), an average SAT of 1120, and an average ACT of 23.

Additional Information

A College Success Strategies course is available and taught by a member of the academic and career services team and explores both the internal and external factors that contribute to college success. The course reinforces basic study habits, including time management, notetaking, active reading, and test preparation. Students learn academic vocabulary, how to set goals, and critical reading, writing, and thinking skills. The Get Organized (GO) Mentoring Program offers individual, short-term, targeted assistance to help students develop organizational skills, including improved organization of course materials and study habits, time management, priorities, connections to resources, and steps for completing tasks. Peer Assisted Supplemental Study (PASS) is utilized by many students.

ADMISSIONS INFO FOR STUDENTS WITH LEARNING DIFFERENCES

Phone: 434-544-8687 Fax: • Fax 434-544-8808 • Email: timmons.j@lynchburg.edu

SAT/ACT required: Yes (Test optional through 2022)
Interview required: No
Essay required: Yes
Additional application required: No
Documentation submitted to: Center for Accessibility and Disability Resources

Special Ed. HS course work accepted: Yes
Separate application required for Programs/Services: Yes
Documentation required for:
LD: Psychoeducational evaluation
ADHD: Psychoeducational evaluation
ASD: Psychoeducational evaluation

University of Lynchburg

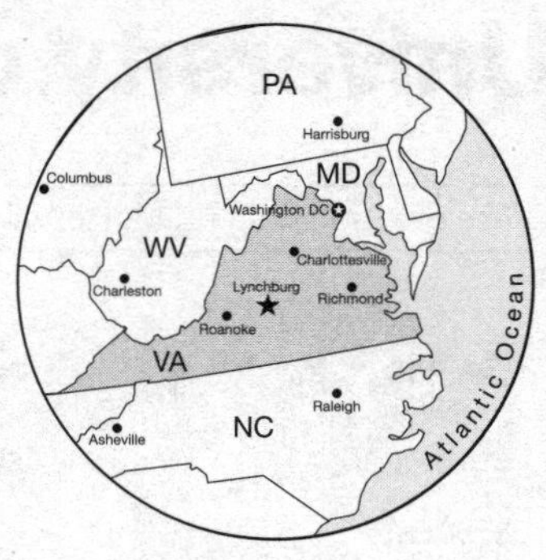

General Admissions

Very Important factors include: rigor of secondary school record, academic GPA, standardized test scores. *Important factors include:* interview. *Other factors include:* application essay, recommendation(s), extracurricular activities, talent/ability, character/personal qualities, volunteer work, work experience, level of applicant's interest. *Freshman admission requirements:* High school diploma is required and GED is accepted. *Academic units required:* 4 English, 3 math, 3 science, 2 science labs, 2 foreign language, 2 social studies, 2 history. *Academic units recommended:* 4 English, 4 math, 4 science, 2 science labs, 3 foreign language, 2 social studies, 2 history, 1 academic elective.

Accommodations or Services

Accommodations are decided upon an individual basis after a thorough review of appropriate, current documentation. The accommodations requests must be supported through the documentation provided and must be logically linked to the current impact of the condition on academic functioning.

Financial Aid

Students should submit: FAFSA; Institution's own financial aid form. Applicants will be notified of awards on a rolling basis beginning 3/15. *Need-based scholarships/grants offered:* College/university scholarship or grant aid from institutional funds; Federal Pell; SEOG. *Loan aid offered:* Direct PLUS loans; Direct Subsidized Stafford Loans; Direct Unsubsidized Stafford Loans. Federal Work-Study Program available. Institutional employment available.

Campus Life

Activities: Campus Ministries; Choral groups; Concert band; Dance; Drama/theater; International Student Organization; Jazz band; Literary magazine; Model UN; Music ensembles; Musical theater; Pep band; Student government; Student newspaper; Symphony orchestra. **Organizations:** 80 registered organizations, 14 honor societies, 10 religious organizations, 5 fraternities, 6 sororities. **Athletics (Intercollegiate):** *Men:* baseball, basketball, cheerleading, cross-country, golf, lacrosse, soccer, tennis, track/field (outdoor), track/field (indoor). *Women:* basketball, cheerleading, cross-country, equestrian sports, field hockey, lacrosse, soccer, softball, tennis, track/field (outdoor), track/field (indoor), volleyball.

ACCOMMODATIONS

Allowed in exams:	
Calculators	Yes
Dictionary	Yes
Computer	Yes
Spell-checker	Yes
Extended test time	Yes
Scribe	Yes
Proctors	Yes
Oral exams	Yes
Note-takers	Yes
Support services for students with:	
LD	No
ADHD	No
ASD	No
Distraction-reduced environment	Yes
Recording of lecture allowed	Yes
Reading technology	Yes
Audio books	Yes
Other assistive technology	Yes
Priority registration	No
Added costs of services:	
For LD	No
For ADHD	No
For ASD	No
LD specialists	No
ADHD & ASD coaching	Yes
ASD specialists	No
Professional tutors	No
Peer tutors	Yes
Max. hours/week for services	Varies
How professors are notified of student approved accommodations	Student

COLLEGE GRADUATION REQUIREMENTS

Course waivers allowed	No
Course substitutions allowed	No

University of Virginia

Office of Admission, Charlottesville, VA 22903 • Admissions: 434-982-3200 • Fax: 434-924-3587 **Support: CS**

CAMPUS

Type of school	Public
Environment	City

STUDENTS

Undergrad enrollment	16,593
% male/female	45/55
% from out of state	28
% frosh live on campus	100

FINANCIAL FACTS

Annual in-state tuition	$14,188
Annual out-of-state tuition	$48,036
Room and board	$12,350
Required fees	$3,116

GENERAL ADMISSIONS INFO

Application fee	$70
Regular application deadline	1/1
Nonfall registration	No

Admission may be deferred.

Range SAT EBRW	670–740
Range SAT Math	670–780
Range ACT Composite	30–34

ACADEMICS

Student/faculty ratio	14:1
% students returning for sophomore year	97

Most classes have 10–19 students.

Programs/Services for Students with Learning Differences

The Student Disability Access Center (SDAC) is the University of Virginia's designated access agency for students with disabilities. SDAC provides services to two groups of students: those who have been previously diagnosed with a disability, and those who have never been diagnosed but find themselves struggling academically and seek advice and support on their difficulties.

Admissions

The students with learning disabilities go through the same admissions procedure as all incoming applicants. After admission to the university, students must contact the SDAC to receive services. No criteria for admission are waived because of a disability. All applicants to UVA have outstanding grades, a high rank in their high school class, excellent performance in advanced placement and honor courses, extracurricular success, special talents, and interests and goals. Letters of recommendation are required.

Additional Information

Upon acceptance to the university, students are encouraged to apply for SDAC services online through the SDAC website, https://www.studenthealth.virginia.edu/sdac. Students are strongly encouraged to consult the Guidelines for Documentation of a Learning Disorder or ADHD available in the information section of the SDAC website. Services and accommodations are available for undergraduate and graduate students.

ADMISSIONS INFO FOR STUDENTS WITH LEARNING DIFFERENCES

Phone: 434-243-5180 • Fax: 434-243-5188 • Email: sdac@virginia.edu

SAT/ACT required: Yes (Test optional for 2021)
Interview required: No
Essay required: Yes
Additional application required: No
Documentation submitted to: SDAAC

Special Ed. HS course work accepted: Yes
Separate application required for Programs/Services: No
Documentation required for:
LD: Psychoeducational evaluation
ADHD: Psychoeducational evaluation
ASD: Psychoeducational evaluation

University of Virginia

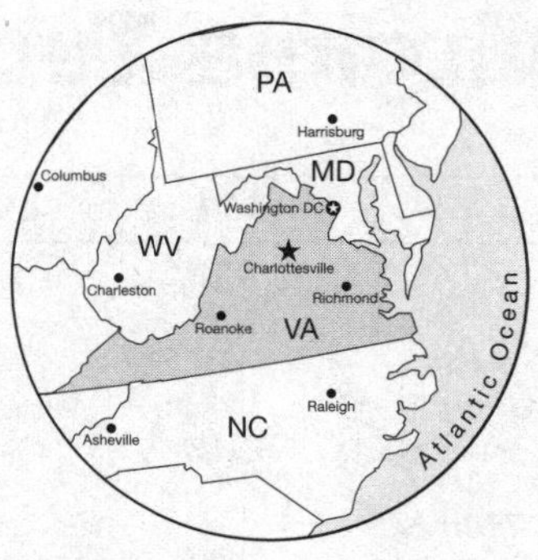

General Admissions

Very Important factors include: rigor of secondary school record, class rank, academic GPA, recommendation(s), character/personal qualities, state residency. *Important factors include:* application essay, standardized test scores, extracurricular activities, talent/ability. *Other factors include:* first generation, alumni/ae relation, geographical residence, racial/ethnic status, volunteer work, work experience. *Freshman admission requirements:* High school diploma is required and GED is accepted. *Academic units required:* 4 English, 4 math, 2 science, 2 foreign language, 1 social studies. *Academic units recommended:* 5 math, 5 science, 5 foreign language, 5 social studies.

Accommodations or Services

Accommodations are decided upon an individual basis after a thorough review of appropriate, current documentation. The accommodations requests must be supported through the documentation provided and must be logically linked to the current impact of the condition on academic functioning.

Financial Aid

Students should submit: CSS/Financial Aid PROFILE; FAFSA. *Need-based scholarships/grants offered:* College/university scholarship or grant aid from institutional funds; Federal Nursing Scholarships; Federal Pell; Private scholarships; SEOG; State scholarships/grants. *Loan aid offered:* Direct PLUS loans; Direct Subsidized Stafford Loans; Direct Unsubsidized Stafford Loans. Federal Work-Study Program available. Institutional employment available.

Campus Life

Activities: Choral groups; Concert band; Dance; Drama/theater; International Student Organization; Jazz band; Literary magazine; Marching band; Model UN; Music ensembles; Musical theater; Opera; Pep band; Radio station; Student government; Student newspaper; Student-run film society; Symphony orchestra; Television station; Yearbook. **Organizations:** 7 honor societies, 31 fraternities, 16 sororities. **Athletics (Intercollegiate):** *Men:* baseball, basketball, cross-country, diving, football, golf, lacrosse, soccer, swimming, tennis, track/field (outdoor), track/field (indoor), wrestling. *Women:* basketball, crew/rowing, cross-country, diving, field hockey, golf, lacrosse, soccer, softball, swimming, tennis, track/field (outdoor), track/field (indoor), volleyball.

ACCOMMODATIONS

Allowed in exams:	
Calculators	Yes
Dictionary	Yes
Computer	Yes
Spell-checker	Yes
Extended test time	Yes
Scribe	Yes
Proctors	Yes
Oral exams	Yes
Note-takers	Yes
Support services for students with:	
LD	Yes
ADHD	Yes
ASD	Yes
Distraction-reduced environment	Yes
Recording of lecture alowed	Yes
Reading technology	Yes
Audio books	Yes
Other assistive technology	Yes
Priority registration	Yes
Added costs of services:	
For LD	No
For ADHD	No
For ASD	No
LD specialists	Yes
ADHD & ASD coaching	Yes
ASD specialists	No
Professional tutors	No
Peer tutors	No
Max. hours/week for services	Varies
How professors are notified of student approved accommodations	Student and director

COLLEGE GRADUATION REQUIREMENTS

Course waivers allowed	No
Course substitutions allowed	Yes
In what courses: Cases by case basis	

Virginia

Virginia Tech

925 Prices Fork Road, Blacksburg, VA 24061 • Admissions: 540-231-6267 • Fax: 540-231-3242 **Support: CS**

CAMPUS

Type of school	Public
Environment	Town

STUDENTS

Undergrad enrollment	29,300
% male/female	57/43
% from out of state	23
% frosh live on campus	98

FINANCIAL FACTS

Annual in-state tuition	$11,420
Annual out-of-state tuition	$29,960
Room and board	$9,342
Required fees	$2,271

GENERAL ADMISSIONS INFO

Application fee	$60
Regular application deadline	1/15
Nonfall registration	Yes

Admission may be deferred.

Range SAT EBRW	590–680
Range SAT Math	590–710
Range ACT Composite	25–31

ACADEMICS

Student/faculty ratio	14:1
% students returning for sophomore year	93

Most classes have 20–29 students.

Programs/Services for Students with Learning Differences

Virginia Tech is committed to providing appropriate services and accommodations that allow identified students with disabilities access to academic programs. To achieve this goal, the university provides services through Services for Students with Disabilities (SSD). To be eligible for services, students must identify themselves to the SSD office. Students may be required to provide any available documentation of their disability. Academic coaching, assistive technology, classroom accommodations, outreach, education, advocacy, and consultations are available. Accommodations and services are determined on an individual basis. Students should contact the SSD office to schedule an appointment to discuss concerns and what information or documentation should be provided. After reviewing this documentation, the SSD staff will schedule a follow-up consultation to determine possible accommodations and next steps.

Admissions

The students with learning disabilities go through the same admissions procedure as all incoming applicants. Course requirements include 4 years English, 3 years math, 2 years science, 2 years social science, and 4 years electives. Some majors have other requirements, such as an additional year of advanced math or lab science. Most students who are selected for admission have completed more than the minimum requirements and have at least a B+ grade point average. The review is holistic and includes the rigor of the academic curriculum, grades, ethnicity, leadership and service, legacy, major, and personal statements.

Additional Information

Student Success Center staff members are available to meet with students individually to help design a plan for success and provide academic counseling that meets individual needs. These meetings occur on a weekly basis, but can be flexible depending on the student's needs. The Student Success Center offers free seminars on how to improve academic success in college and focus on applicable strategies and skill development in critical areas such as time management, study skills, and overcoming procrastination. The student PACs assist with these topics and more. Peer coaching is open to undergraduate students of any major.

ADMISSIONS INFO FOR STUDENTS WITH LEARNING DIFFERENCES

Phone: 540-231-3788 • Fax: 540-231-3232 • Email: ssd@vt.edu

SAT/ACT required: Yes (Test optional for 2021)
Interview required: No
Essay required: Yes
Additional application required: No
Documentation submitted to: Student Success Center

Special Ed. HS course work accepted: Yes
Separate application required for Programs/Services: No
Documentation required for:
LD: Psychoeducational evaluation
ADHD: Psychoeducational evaluation
ASD: Psychoeducational evaluation

Virginia Tech

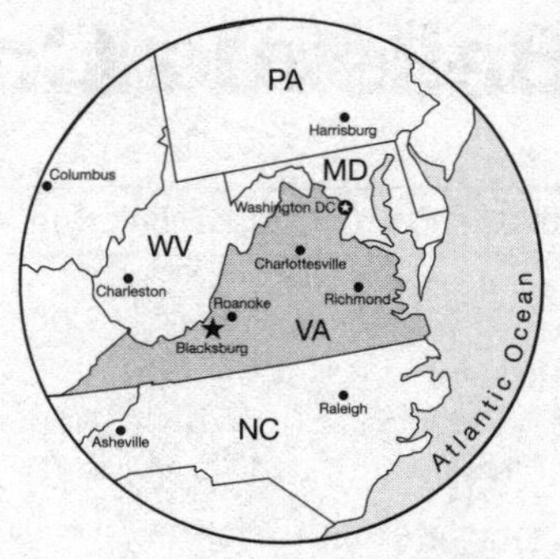

General Admissions

Very Important factors include: rigor of secondary school record, academic GPA, application essay, standardized test scores. *Other factors include:* extracurricular activities, talent/ability, character/personal qualities, first generation, alumni/ae relation, geographical residence, state residency, racial/ethnic status, volunteer work, work experience, level of applicant's interest. *Freshman admission requirements:* High school diploma is required and GED is accepted. *Academic units required:* 4 English, 3 math, 2 science, 2 science labs, 1 social studies, 1 history, 4 academic electives. *Academic units recommended:* 4 math, 3 science, 3 foreign language.

Accommodations or Services

Accommodations are decided upon an individual basis after a thorough review of appropriate, current documentation. The accommodations requests must be supported through the documentation provided and must be logically linked to the current impact of the condition on academic functioning.

Financial Aid

Students should submit: FAFSA. Applicants will be notified of awards on a rolling basis beginning 3/15. *Need-based scholarships/grants offered:* College/university scholarship or grant aid from institutional funds; Federal Pell; Private scholarships; SEOG; State scholarships/grants; United Negro College Fund. *Loan aid offered:* Direct PLUS loans; Direct Subsidized Stafford Loans; Direct Unsubsidized Stafford Loans. Federal Work-Study Program available. Institutional employment available.

Campus Life

Activities: Campus Ministries; Choral groups; Concert band; Dance; Drama/theater; International Student Organization; Jazz band; Literary magazine; Marching band; Model UN; Music ensembles; Musical theater; Opera; Pep band; Radio station; Student government; Student newspaper; Student-run film society; Television station; Yearbook. **Organizations:** 849 registered organizations, 13 honor societies, 90 religious organizations, 30 fraternities, 21 sororities. **Athletics (Intercollegiate):** *Men:* baseball, basketball, cheerleading, cross-country, diving, football, golf, soccer, swimming, tennis, track/field (outdoor), track/field (indoor), ultimate frisbee, water polo. *Women:* basketball, cheerleading, cross-country, diving, lacrosse, soccer, softball, swimming, tennis, track/field (outdoor), track/field (indoor), ultimate frisbee, volleyball, water polo.

ACCOMMODATIONS

Allowed in exams:	
Calculators	Yes
Dictionary	Yes
Computer	Yes
Spell-checker	Yes
Extended test time	Yes
Scribe	Yes
Proctors	Yes
Oral exams	Yes
Note-takers	Yes
Support services for students with:	
LD	No
ADHD	No
ASD	No
Distraction-reduced environment	Yes
Recording of lecture alowed	Yes
Reading technology	Yes
Audio books	Yes
Other assistive technology	Yes
Priority registration	No
Added costs of services:	
For LD	No
For ADHD	No
For ASD	No
LD specialists	No
ADHD & ASD coaching	No
ASD specialists	No
Professional tutors	Yes
Peer tutors	Yes
Max. hours/week for services	Varies
How professors are notified of student approved accommodations	Student

COLLEGE GRADUATION REQUIREMENTS

Course waivers allowed	No
Course substitutions allowed	No

Bellevue College

3000 Landerholm Cir SE, Bellevue, Washington 98007-6484 • Admissions: 425-564-1000 **Support: CS**

CAMPUS	
Type of school	Public
Environment	City
STUDENTS	
Undergrad enrollment	12,563
% male/female	45/55
% from out of state	3
FINANCIAL FACTS	
Annual in-state tuition	$4,461
Annual out-of-state tuition	$9,915
Room and board	$13,530
GENERAL ADMISSIONS INFO	
Application fee	$55
Regular application deadline	3/19
Nonfall registration	Yes

Programs/Services for Students with Learning Differences

Bellevue College supports students by offerring supports to meet each students' academic goals. Part of the college's vision as an institution is to provide access to learning support services. The Academic Success Center (ASC) offers drop-in tutoring, online tutoring, tutoring appointments, and specialized labs for math and writing, as well as reading instruction.

Admissions

Bellevue College Admits students who are high school graduates or have a GED. There is no special application process for students with learning differences. The college requires a student to have an average 3.2 GPA. Bellevue College is test-optional. High school students can also apply to Bellevue College through the Running Start Program.

Additional Information

The Disability Resource Center (DRC) is dedicated to helping students with requesting classroom accommodations, communicating with instructors, and identifying resources available within the community that can further support the student's academic needs. The Neurodiversity Navigators help neurodiverse students develop strong executive functioning skills, self-regulation skills, stronger social interactions, and self-advocacy skills. There is a regular meeting with trained peer mentors, career preparation, parent meetings, and more. The Basic and Transitional Studies Department provides students with high-quality basic and pre-college math and English literacy education while cultivating leadership potential.

ADMISSIONS INFO FOR STUDENTS WITH LEARNING DIFFERENCES

Phone: 425-564-2498 • Email: drc@bellevuecollege.edu

SAT/ACT required: No
Interview required: No
Essay required: No
Additional application required: No
Documentation submitted to: DRC

Special Ed. HS course work accepted: No
Separate application required for Programs/Services: No
Documentation required for:
LD: Psychoeducational evaluation
ADHD: Psychoeducational evaluation
ASD: Psychoeducational evaluation

Bellevue College

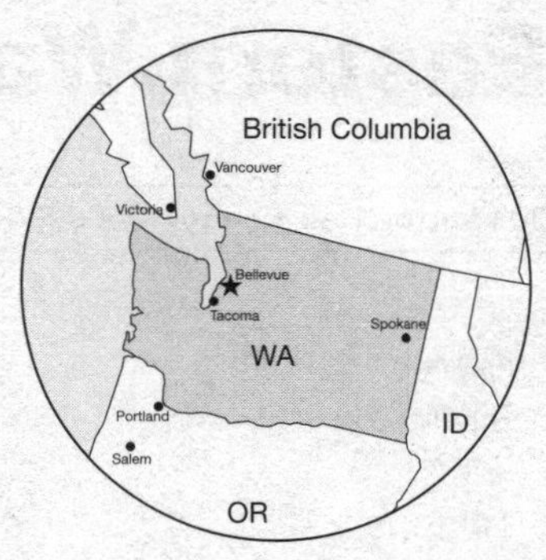

General Admissions

High school diploma is required and GED is accepted. **Note:** Bellevue College is a Washington State Community College. As such, the institution does not have nor provide the same requirements as the other programs reported in this book. There are a myriad of options for admissions. Please consult the Bellevue College website for more details.

Accommodations or Services

Accommodations are decided upon an individual basis after a thorough review of appropriate, current documentation. The accommodations requests must be supported through the documentation provided and must be logically linked to the current impact of the condition on academic functioning.

Financial Aid

Students should submit: FAFSA. *Need-based scholarships/grants offered:* College/university scholarship or grant aid from institutional funds; Federal Pell; Private scholarships; SEOG; State scholarships/grants. *Loan aid offered:* Direct PLUS loans; Direct Subsidized Stafford Loans; Direct Unsubsidized Stafford Loans. Federal Work-Study Program available. Institutional employment available.

Campus Life

Activities: Campus Ministries; Choral groups; Concert band; Dance; Drama/theater; International Student Organization; Jazz band; Literary magazine; Music ensembles; Musical theater; Radio station; Student government; Student newspaper; Symphony orchestra. **Organizations:** 104 registered organizations, 8 religious organizations. **Athletics (Intercollegiate):** *Men:* baseball, basketball, golf, soccer, tennis, volleyball. *Women:* basketball, golf, soccer, softball, tennis, volleyball.

ACCOMMODATIONS

Allowed in exams:	
Calculators	Yes
Dictionary	Yes
Computer	Yes
Spell-checker	Yes
Extended test time	Yes
Scribe	Yes
Proctors	Yes
Oral exams	Yes
Note-takers	Yes
Support services for students with:	
LD	Yes
ADHD	Yes
ASD	Yes
Distraction-reduced environment	Yes
Recording of lecture allowed	Yes
Reading technology:	Yes
Audio books	Yes
Other assistive technology	Yes
Priority registration	Yes
Added costs of services:	
For LD	No
For ADHD	No
For ASD	No
LD specialists	Yes
ADHD & ASD coaching	Yes
ASD specialists	Yes
Professional tutors	No
Peer tutors	Yes
Max. hours/week for services	Varies
How professors are notified of student approved accommodations	Student

COLLEGE GRADUATION REQUIREMENTS

Course waivers allowed	Yes
In what courses: Varies	
Course substitutions allowed	Yes
In what courses: Varies	

Eastern Washington University

304 Sutton Hall, Cheney, WA 99004 • Admissions: 509-359-6692 • Fax: 509-359-6692 **Support:**

CAMPUS

Type of school	Public
Environment	Town

STUDENTS

Undergrad enrollment	10,671
% male/female	45/55
% from out of state	6
% frosh live on campus	70

FINANCIAL FACTS

Annual in-state tuition:	$6,543
Annual out-of-state tuition:	$24,074
Room and board	$12,406
Required fees	$982

GENERAL ADMISSIONS INFO

Application fee	$60
Regular application deadline	9/1
Nonfall registration	Yes

Admission may be deferred.

Range SAT EBRW	460–570
Range SAT Math	420–530
Range ACT Composite	17–24

ACADEMICS

Student/faculty ratio	18:1
% students returning for sophomore year	70

Most classes have 10–19 students.

Programs/Services for Students with Learning Differences

The university does not offer a specialized curriculum for students with learning differences. Students must be enrolled at the university and are responsible for initiating contact with the (DSS). The staff work with students to modify programs to meet individual needs. Disability Support Services (DSS) helps coordinate appropriate and reasonable accommodations for students with disabilities. These accommodations are based on individual needs so that each student may receive an equal opportunity to learn. This is facilitated through support services, information sharing, advisement, and referral when requested. Students who require services and support need to contact DSS so that the disability can be verified, specific needs determined, and timely accommodations made. In most cases, documentation by a professional service provider will be necessary. Information is kept strictly confidential. It is important to share information that will enable DSS staff to provide appropriate, reasonable, and timely services tailored to individual needs.

Admissions

Individuals with disabilities are admitted via the standard admissions criteria that apply to all students. EWU is test optional. Applicants who do not submit a test score need to do one of the following in order to be evaluated by admissions: 1) submit a recommendation, 2) supply evidence of rigorous high school courses such as AP or IB, 3) provide evidence of success in the Running Start program, or 4) provide evidence of success in the College in the High School Program earning a 2.5 GPA for college-level English or math.

Additional Information

Examples of services for students with specific learning disabilities include alternative format textbooks; equipment loans; alternative testing arrangements such as oral exams, extended time on tests, relocation of testing site; note-takers; tutorial assistance (available to all students); referral to a Learning Skills Center, Writers' Center, and/or Mathematics Lab; accessible computer stations; and a Kurzweil Reader. Examples of services for students with ADHD are consultation regarding reasonable and effective accommodations with classroom professors; alternative testing; alternative format textbooks; note-takers; taped lectures; equipment loans; referrals to a Learning Skills Center, a Math Lab, a Writers' Center, and counseling and psychological services; information on ADHD; and informal counseling. First Year Experience (FYE) is a series of courses for first year students to

ADMISSIONS INFO FOR STUDENTS WITH LEARNING DIFFERENCES

Phone: 509-359-4796 • Fax: 509-359-7458 • Email: khills@ewu.edu

SAT/ACT required: No
Interview required: No
Essay required: Yes
Additional application required: No
Documentation submitted to: DSS

Special Ed. HS course work accepted: Yes
Separate application required for Programs/Services: No
Documentation required for:
LD: Psychoeducational evaluation
ADHD: Psychoeducational evaluation
ASD: Psychoeducational evaluation

Eastern Washington University

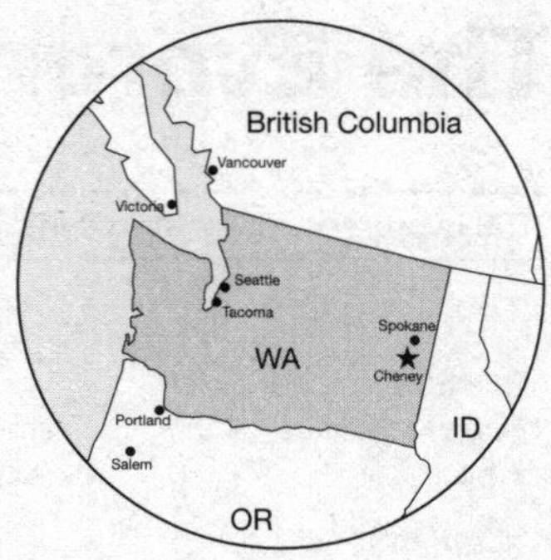

help with time management, goalsetting, academic planning, and more. The goal of this program is to help high school students transition to the university successfully.

General Admissions

Very important factors include: academic GPA, standardized test scores. *Important factors include:* rigor of secondary school record, application essay, *Other factors include:* recommendation(s), extracurricular activities, talent/ability, character/personal qualities, volunteer work, work experience. *Freshman admission requirements:* High school diploma or equivalent is not required. *Academic units required:* 4 English, 3 math, 2 science, 2 science labs, 2 foreign language, 3 social studies, 1 visual/performing arts, 1 unit from above areas or other academic areas.

Accommodations or Services

Accommodations are decided upon an individual basis after a thorough review of appropriate, current documentation. The accommodations requests must be supported through the documentation provided and must be logically linked to the current impact of the condition on academic functioning.

Financial Aid

Students should submit: FAFSA. Applicants will be notified of awards on a rolling basis beginning 3/1. *Need-based scholarships/grants offered:* College/university scholarship or grant aid from institutional funds; Federal Pell; Private scholarships; SEOG; State scholarships/grants. *Loan aid offered:* Direct PLUS loans; Direct Subsidized Stafford Loans; Direct Unsubsidized Stafford Loans. Federal Work-Study Program available. Institutional employment available.

Campus Life

Activities: Campus Ministries; Choral groups; Concert band; Dance; Drama/theater; International Student Organization; Jazz band; Literary magazine; Marching band; Model UN; Music ensembles; Musical theater; Pep band; Radio station; Student government; Student newspaper; Student-run film society; Symphony orchestra. **Organizations:** 99 registered organizations, 9 honor societies, 12 religious organizations, 9 fraternities, 11 sororities. **Athletics (Intercollegiate):** *Men:* basketball, cross-country, football, golf, tennis, track/field (outdoor), track/field (indoor). *Women:* basketball, cross-country, golf, soccer, tennis, track/field (outdoor), track/field (indoor), volleyball.

ACCOMMODATIONS

Allowed in exams:	
Calculators	Yes
Dictionary	Yes
Computer	Yes
Spell-checker	Yes
Extended test time	Yes
Scribe	Yes
Proctors	Yes
Oral exams	Yes
Note-takers	Yes
Support services for students with:	
LD	Yes
ADHD	Yes
ASD	Yes
Distraction-reduced environment	Yes
Recording of lecture allowed	Yes
Reading technology	Yes
Audio books	Yes
Other assistive technology	Yes
Priority registration	No
Added costs of services:	
For LD	No
For ADHD	No
For ASD	No
LD specialists	No
ADHD & ASD coaching	No
ASD specialists	No
Professional tutors	Yes
Peer tutors	Yes
Max. hours/week for services	Varies
How professors are notified of student approved accommodations	Student and Director

COLLEGE GRADUATION REQUIREMENTS

Course waivers allowed	No
Course substitutions allowed	No

The Evergreen State College

2700 Evergreen Pkwy NW, Olympia, WA 98505 • Admissions: 360-867-6170 • Fax: 360-867-5114 **Support: S**

CAMPUS	
Type of school	Public
Environment	City
STUDENTS	
Undergrad enrollment	2,527
% male/female	41/59
% from out of state	16
% frosh live on campus	72
FINANCIAL FACTS	
Annual in-state tuition	$7,005
Annual out-of-state tuition	$26,325
Room and board	$12,363
Required fees	$1,203
GENERAL ADMISSIONS INFO	
Application fee	$50
Regular application deadline	8/1
Nonfall registration	Yes
Admission may be deferred.	
Range SAT EBRW	530–640
Range SAT Math	470–580
Range ACT Composite	20–27
ACADEMICS	
Student/faculty ratio	21:1
% students returning for sophomore year	65
Most classes have 20–29 students.	

Programs/Services for Students with Learning Differences

Introduction: The Evergreen State College the Office of Access Services for Students with Disabilities is responsible for coordinating support services. Evergreen is committed to providing reasonable accommodations, including core services, to qualified students with disabilities. Evergreen will make modifications to its academic requirements that (1) are necessary to ensure that those requirements do not discriminate or have the effect of discriminating against a qualified student with a disability based on that disability, and (2) do not impose an undue hardship on the college or require significant alteration of essential program requirements. The college will provide an application for services. The director will meet with the student to review the application and discuss reasonable and appropriate accommodations. Guidelines for documentation requirements are available from Access Services and are noted here: http://www.evergreen.edu/access/eligibility.htm. Students should contact the Office of Access Services for Students with Disabilities Director with any questions.

Admissions

Students entering Evergreen directly from high school must complete a college-preparatory course load in high school. Students receive a decision two weeks after applying. Evergreen State is test optional, and the ACT and SAT are not required. No applicant is automatically denied. The Tacoma Program is a full-time course of study for students who have completed at least 90 transferable college credits. The Native Pathways Program (NPP) is a rigorous 12-credit program that provides opportunities to learn through western and indigenous pedagogy, while maintaining and promoting an indigenous worldview.

Additional Information

The Evergreen State College is committed to providing equal access, accommodations, and educational support for qualified students with disabilities. The college's approach is designed to be holistic and to empower students by promoting self-reliance, effective problem solving skills, enhanced academic and personal development, and equal access to college programs and activities for qualified students with disabilities.

ADMISSIONS INFO FOR STUDENTS WITH LEARNING DIFFERENCES

Phone: 360-867-6348 • Email: inocenc@evergreen.edu

SAT/ACT required: No
Interview required: No
Essay required: No
Additional application required: Yes
Documentation submitted to: Access Services

Special Ed. HS course work accepted: Yes
Separate application required for Programs/Services: Yes
Documentation required for:
- **LD:** Psychoeducational evaluation
- **ADHD:** Psychoeducational evaluation
- **ASD:** Psychoeducational evaluation

The Evergreen State College

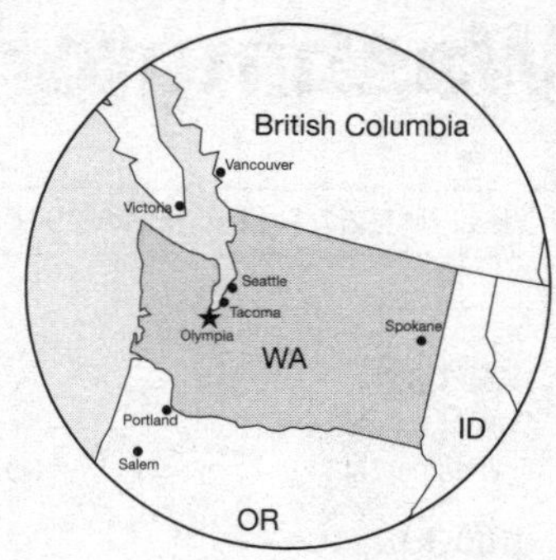

General Admissions

Very important factors include: rigor of secondary school record, academic GPA. *Important factors include:* standardized test scores, level of applicant's interest. *Other factors include:* application essay, recommendation(s), interview, extracurricular activities, volunteer work, work experience. *Freshman admission requirements:* High school diploma is required and GED is accepted. *Academic units required:* 4 English, 3 math, 2 science, 2 science labs, 2 foreign language, 3 social studies, 1 academic elective, 1 unit from above areas or other academic areas.

Accommodations or Services

Accommodations are decided upon an individual basis after a thorough review of appropriate, current documentation. The accommodations requests must be supported through the documentation provided and must be logically linked to the current impact of the condition on academic functioning.

Financial Aid

Students should submit: FAFSA. *Need-based scholarships/grants offered:* College/university scholarship or grant aid from institutional funds; Federal Pell; Private scholarships; SEOG; State scholarships/grants. *Loan aid offered:* Direct PLUS loans; Direct Subsidized Stafford Loans; Direct Unsubsidized Stafford Loans. Federal Work-Study Program available. Institutional employment available.

Campus Life

Activities: Campus Ministries; Choral groups; Dance; Drama/theater; Jazz band; Literary magazine; Music ensembles; Radio station; Student government; Student newspaper; Student-run film society; Television station. **Athletics (Intercollegiate):** *Men:* basketball, cross-country, soccer, track/field (outdoor), track/field (indoor). *Women:* basketball, cross-country, soccer, track/field (outdoor), track/field (indoor), volleyball.

ACCOMMODATIONS

Allowed in exams:	
Calculators	Yes
Dictionary	Yes
Computer	Yes
Spell-checker	Yes
Extended test time	Yes
Scribe	Yes
Proctors	Yes
Oral exams	Yes
Note-takers	Yes
Support services for students with:	
LD	Yes
ADHD	Yes
ASD	Yes
Distraction-reduced environment	Yes
Recording of lecture allowed	Yes
Reading technology	Yes
Audio books	Yes
Other assistive technology	Yes
Priority registration	Yes
Added costs of services:	
For LD	No
For ADHD	No
For ASD	No
LD specialists	No
ADHD & ASD coaching	Yes
ASD specialists	No
Professional tutors	No
Peer tutors	No
Max. hours/week for services	Varies
How professors are notified of student approved accommodations	Student and Director

COLLEGE GRADUATION REQUIREMENTS

Course waivers allowed	No
Course substitutions allowed	No

Washington

Washington State University

PO Box 641067, Pullman, WA 99164-1067 • Admissions: 509-335-5586 • Fax: 509-335-4902 **Support: S**

CAMPUS

Type of school	Public
Environment	Town

STUDENTS

Undergrad enrollment	25,562
% male/female	47/53
% from out of state	15
% frosh live on campus	84

FINANCIAL FACTS

Annual in-state tuition	$9,953
Annual out-of-state tuition	$24,531
Room and board	$11,648
Required fees	$1,888

GENERAL ADMISSIONS INFO

Application fee	$50
Regular application deadline	Rolling
Nonfall registration	Yes
Range SAT EBRW	510–620
Range SAT Math	510–610
Range ACT Composite	20–26

ACADEMICS

Student/faculty ratio	16:1
% students returning for sophomore year	79

Most classes have 20–29 students.

Programs/Services for Students with Learning Differences

The Access Center (AC) assists students who have a disability by providing academic accommodations. It is the student's responsibility to request accommodations if desired. The program may also refer students to other service programs that may assist them in achieving their academic goals. The new MYAccess (AIM) system enables students to request accommodations online. This will give the student direct access to a professor when requesting accommodations, such as extended time on tests. Through this service students can also request notetaking services. All academic adjustments are authorized on an individual basis. The program offers academic coaching. To be eligible for assistance, students must be currently enrolled at Washington State University and submit documentation of their disability. For a learning disability, the student must submit a written report that includes test scores and evaluation. AC works with students and instructors to determine and implement appropriate academic adjustments. Many adjustments are simple, creative alternatives for traditional ways of learning.

Admissions

All students must meet the general admission requirements. WSU is test optional for 2021 and will review the policy for future years. Students must have a 2.0 GPA and take 4 years English, 3 years math, 3 years social science, 2 years lab science, 2 years foreign language, and one year of fine or visual arts.

Additional Information

The Access Center Proctoring Office implements testing accommodations. Students need to reach out to the center to find out the procedure for this accommodation General assistance to students with learning disabilities can include pre-admission counseling, information about accommodations, information about the laws pertaining to individuals with disabilities, and self-advocacy. Typical academic adjustments for students with learning disabilities may include note-takers and/or audiotape class sessions, alternative testing arrangements, alternate print (mp3 files or text files), extended time for exams, essay exams taken on computer, and use of computers with voice output and spellcheckers. Services and accommodations are available for undergraduate and graduate students.

ADMISSIONS INFO FOR STUDENTS WITH LEARNING DIFFERENCES

Phone: 509-335-3417 • Email: access.center@wsu.edu

SAT/ACT required: Yes (Test blind for 2021)
Interview required: No
Essay required: No
Additional application required: No
Documentation submitted to: Access Center

Special Ed. HS course work accepted: No
Separate application required for Programs/Services: Yes MyAccess
Documentation required for:
LD: Psychoeducational evaluation
ADHD: Psychoeducational evaluation
ASD: Psychoeducational evaluation

Washington State University

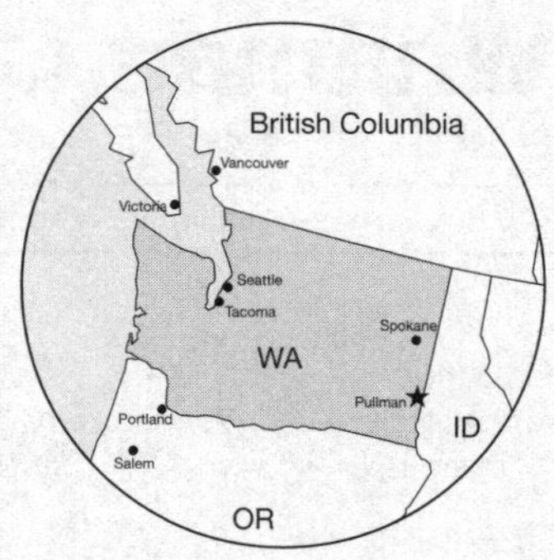

General Admissions

Very important factors include: academic GPA, standardized test scores. *Important factors include:* rigor of secondary school record, class rank. *Other factors include:* application essay, recommendation(s), extracurricular activities, talent/ability, character/personal qualities, volunteer work, work experience. *Freshman admission requirements:* High school diploma is required, and GED is accepted. *Academic units required:* 4 English, 3 math, 2 science, 2 foreign language, 3 social studies, 1 visual/performing arts, 1 unit from above areas or other academic areas. *Academic units recommended:* 4 English, 4 math, 2 science, 2 foreign language, 3 social studies, 1 visual/performing arts.

Accommodations or Services

Accommodations are decided upon an individual basis after a thorough review of appropriate, current documentation. The accommodations requests must be supported through the documentation provided and must be logically linked to the current impact of the condition on academic functioning.

Financial Aid

Students should submit: FAFSA. *Need-based scholarships/grants offered:* College/university scholarship or grant aid from institutional funds; Federal Nursing Scholarships; Federal Pell; Private scholarships; SEOG; State scholarships/grants. *Loan aid offered:* Direct PLUS loans; Direct Subsidized Stafford Loans; Direct Unsubsidized Stafford Loans. Federal Work-Study Program available. Institutional employment available.

Campus Life

Activities: Campus Ministries; Choral groups; Concert band; Dance; Drama/theater; International Student Organization; Jazz band; Literary magazine; Marching band; Model UN; Music ensembles; Musical theater; Opera; Pep band; Radio station; Student government; Student newspaper; Student-run film society; Symphony orchestra; Television station; Yearbook. **Organizations:** 456 registered organizations, 10 honor societies, 23 religious organizations, 27 fraternities, 14 sororities. **Athletics (Intercollegiate):** *Men:* baseball, basketball, cross-country, football, golf, track/field (outdoor). *Women:* basketball, crew/rowing, cross-country, golf, soccer, swimming, tennis, track/field (outdoor), volleyball.

ACCOMMODATIONS

Allowed in exams:	
Calculators	Yes
Dictionary	No
Computer	Yes
Spell-checker	Yes
Extended test time	Yes
Scribe	Yes
Proctors	Yes
Oral exams	Yes
Note-takers	Yes
Support services for students with:	
LD	Yes
ADHD	Yes
ASD	Yes
Distraction-reduced environment	Yes
Recording of lecture allowed	Yes
Reading technology	Yes
Audio books	Yes
Other assistive technology	Yes
Priority registration	Yes
Added costs of services:	
For LD	No
For ADHD	No
For ASD	No
LD specialists	No
ADHD & ASD coaching	No
ASD specialists	No
Professional tutors	No
Peer tutors	Yes
Max. hours/week for services	Varies
How professors are notified of student approved accommodations	Student

COLLEGE GRADUATION REQUIREMENTS

Course waivers allowed	No
Course substitutions allowed	No

Whitman College

345 Boyer Ave, Walla Walla, WA 99362 • Admissions: 509-527-5176 • Fax: 509-527-4967 **Support: CS**

CAMPUS

Type of school	Private (nonprofit)
Environment	Town

STUDENTS

Undergrad enrollment	1,579
% male/female	44/56
% from out of state	65
% frosh live on campus	100

FINANCIAL FACTS

Annual tuition	$55,560
Room and board	$13,800
Required fees	$408

GENERAL ADMISSIONS INFO

Application fee	$50
Regular application deadline	1/15
Nonfall registration	No

Admission may be deferred.

Range SAT EBRW	630–710
Range SAT Math	610–740
Range ACT Composite	28–33

ACADEMICS

Student/faculty ratio	9:1
% students returning for sophomore year	89

Most classes have 10–19 students.

Programs/Services for Students with Learning Differences

Whitman College is committed to the education of all qualified students, regardless of disability status. Students with disabilities must make a request for accommodations to the Assistant Director of Academic Resources. Students must disclose their disability, provide documentation, and reach out to the director. Academic Resource Center s(ARC)taff members work with staff and faculty colleagues to ensure that materials and instructions can be accessed and understood and that students are able to demonstrate their knowledge and interest appropriately as well. The Academic Resource Center offers academic coaching. One-on-one sessions are designed with particular goals in mind. Strategies and topics can include goal setting, time management, reading and study strategies, and overcoming procrastination

Admissions

Whitman is committed to the education of all qualified students, regardless of disability status. Whitman is test optional for most applicants. Homeschooled applicants and applicants from secondary schools that provide written evaluations rather than grades are strongly encouraged to submit ACT or SAT scores. International applicants are strongly encouraged to submit an ACT or SAT score when available. Whitman College requires international applicants whose first language is not English to submit an official score report for either the TOEFL or IELTS. For applicants who do submit a test score, Whitman will superscore test results from the ACT or the SAT.

Additional Information

Whitman College also offers individualized tutoring with ARC peer tutors. The Center fOr Writing and Speaking (COWS) is another support option. There are also skill building workshops and sessions that have common topics such as time management, note taking, critical reading skills, test-taking strategies, and managing test anxiety. Student Academic Advisers (SAs) are students who live in the first-year residence halls and provide guidance and support. The ARC offers many academic accommodations to students with an autism diagnosis to identify the best support methods for success.

ADMISSIONS INFO FOR STUDENTS WITH LEARNING DIFFERENCES

Phone: 509-527-5111 • Fax: 509-526-4701 • Email: keithaam@whitman.edu

SAT/ACT required: No
Interview required: No
Essay required: No
Additional application required: No
Documentation submitted to: Academic Resource Center

Special Ed. HS course work accepted: Yes
Separate application required for Programs/Services: No
Documentation required for:
LD: Psychoeducational evaluation
ADHD: Psychoeducational evaluation
ASD: Psychoeducational evaluation

Whitman College

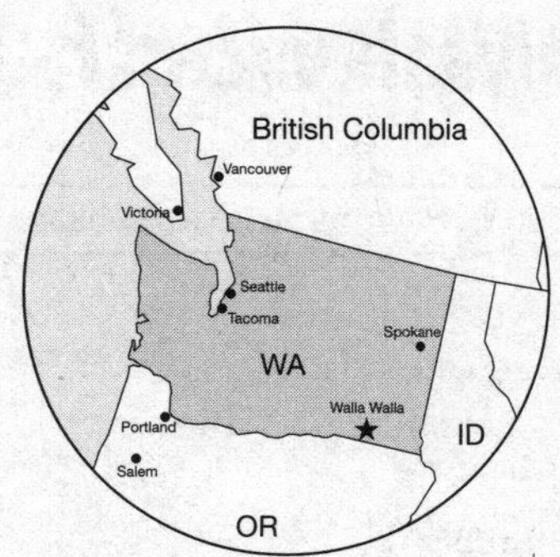

General Admissions

Very important factors include: rigor of secondary school record, academic GPA, application essay. *Important factors include:* recommendation(s), extracurricular activities, talent/ability, character/personal qualities. *Other factors include:* class rank, standardized test scores, interview, first generation, alumni/ae relation, geographical residence, state residency, religious affiliation/commitment, racial/ethnic status, volunteer work, work experience, level of applicant's interest. *Freshman admission requirements:* High school diploma is required, and GED is accepted. *Academic units recommended:* 4 English, 4 math, 3 science, 3 science labs, 2 foreign language, 2 social studies, 2 history.

Accommodations or Services

Accommodations are decided upon an individual basis after a thorough review of appropriate, current documentation. The accommodations requests must be supported through the documentation provided and must be logically linked to the current impact of the condition on academic functioning.

Financial Aid

Students should submit: CSS/Financial Aid PROFILE; FAFSA; Noncustodial PROFILE. *Need-based scholarships/grants offered:* College/university scholarship or grant aid from institutional funds; Federal Pell; Private scholarships; SEOG; State scholarships/grants. *Loan aid offered:* Direct PLUS loans; Direct Subsidized Stafford Loans; Direct Unsubsidized Stafford Loans. Federal Work-Study Program available. Institutional employment available.

Campus Life

Activities: Campus Ministries; Choral groups; Concert band; Dance; Drama/theater; International Student Organization; Jazz band; Literary magazine; Model UN; Music ensembles; Musical theater; Radio station; Student government; Student newspaper; Student-run film society; Symphony orchestra; Yearbook. **Organizations:** 86 registered organizations, 3 honor societies, 4 religious organizations, 4 fraternities, 4 sororities. **Athletics (Intercollegiate):** *Men:* baseball, basketball, cross-country, golf, soccer, swimming, tennis. *Women:* basketball, cross-country, golf, soccer, swimming, tennis, volleyball.

ACCOMMODATIONS

Allowed in exams:	
Calculators	Yes
Dictionary	Yes
Computer	Yes
Spell-checker	Yes
Extended test time	Yes
Scribe	Yes
Proctors	Yes
Oral exams	Yes
Note-takers	Yes
Support services for students with:	
LD	No
ADHD	No
ASD	No
Distraction-reduced environment	Yes
Recording of lecture allowed	Yes
Reading technology	Yes
Audio books	Yes
Other assistive technology	Yes
Priority registration	Yes
Added costs of services:	
For LD	No
For ADHD	No
For ASD	No
LD specialists	Yes
ADHD & ASD coaching	No
ASD specialists	No
Professional tutors	No
Peer tutors	Yes
Max. hours/week for services	Varies
How professors are notified of student approved accommodations	Director

COLLEGE GRADUATION REQUIREMENTS

Course waivers allowed	No
Course substitutions allowed	No

Whitworth University

300 W. Hawthorne Road, Spokane, WA 99251 • Admissions: 509-777-4786 • Fax: 509-777-3758 **Support: CS**

CAMPUS

Type of school	Private (nonprofit)
Environment	City

STUDENTS

Undergrad enrollment	2,387
% male/female	42/58
% from out of state	28
% frosh live on campus	92

FINANCIAL FACTS

Annual tuition	$45,050
Room and board	$12,000
Required fees	$1,200

GENERAL ADMISSIONS INFO

Application fee	$0
Regular application deadline	8/1
Nonfall registration	Yes

Admission may be deferred.

Range SAT EBRW	530–650
Range SAT Math	520–640
Range ACT Composite	21–29

ACADEMICS

Student/faculty ratio	12:1
% students returning for sophomore year	84

Most classes have 10–19 students.

Programs/Services for Students with Learning Differences

Whitworth University will not exclude otherwise qualified applicants or students with disabilities from participation in, or access to, its academic, housing, or extracurricular programs. Accessibility Services (AS) helps arrange accommodations for students seeking support. These services are determined on a case-by-case basis. Students interested in accommodations follow the accommodation process and meet with the AS each semester. These sessions are free of charge. There is an Academic Plan Advisor available through the Center for Academic Excellence.

Admissions

The goal of the university is for all students to succeed academically at Whitworth. In the case of students with documented learning disabilities, the university is careful to assess each student individually. It looks for the rigor of the academic record, the essay, the reputation of the high school, and participation in activities, service, or leadership. Applicants with a GPA of 3.0 or higher from an accredited high school or homeschool program may elect to exclude their test scores from consideration in the application process. Applicants who choose this option on their Whitworth application will have an interview with admissions. Whitworth applicants who choose this option usually have SAT scores below 1000, ACT scores below 19, or CLT scores below 64.

Additional Information

Whitworth University expects students to voluntarily disclose their disability, and request accommodations. Whitworth University will work to make adjustments to meet the specific needs of an individual and expects all students to play an active role in their education. It is a student's responsibility to familiarize himself or herself with the university's policies and specific course requirements. The Center for Academic Excellence (CAE) offers a variety of tutoring and advising services. The Peer tutoring services are free online for all students.

ADMISSIONS INFO FOR STUDENTS WITH LEARNING DIFFERENCES

Phone: 509-777-3380 • Fax: 509-777-3821 • Email: kmccray@whitworth.edu

SAT/ACT required: No
Interview required: No
Essay required: No
Additional application required: No
Documentation submitted to: Accessibility Services

Special Ed. HS course work accepted: Yes
Separate application required for Programs/Services: No
Documentation required for:
LD: Psychoeducational evaluation
ADHD: Psychoeducational evaluation
ASD: Psychoeducational evaluation

Whitworth University

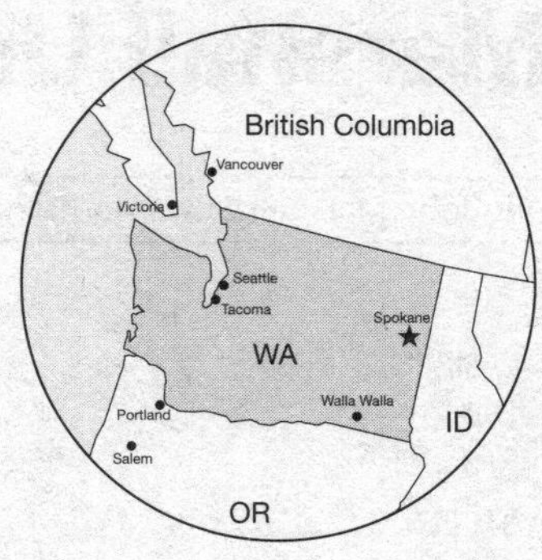

General Admissions

Very important factors include: academic GPA, application essay. *Important factors include:* rigor of secondary school record, standardized test scores, interview, extracurricular activities, character/personal qualities. *Other factors include:* recommendation(s), talent/ability, first generation, alumni/ae relation, geographical residence, state residency, racial/ethnic status, volunteer work, work experience, level of applicant's interest. *Freshman admission requirements:* High school diploma is required, and GED is accepted. *Academic units recommended:* 4 English, 3 math, 3 science, 2 science labs, 2 foreign language, 2 social studies, 2 history.

Accommodations or Services

Accommodations are decided upon an individual basis after a thorough review of appropriate, current documentation. The accommodations requests must be supported through the documentation provided and must be logically linked to the current impact of the condition on academic functioning.

Financial Aid

Students should submit: FAFSA. *Need-based scholarships/grants offered:* College/university scholarship or grant aid from institutional funds; Federal Pell; Private scholarships; SEOG; State scholarships/grants. *Loan aid offered:* Direct PLUS loans; Direct Subsidized Stafford Loans; Direct Unsubsidized Stafford Loans. Federal Work-Study Program available. Institutional employment available.

Campus Life

Activities: Campus Ministries; Choral groups; Concert band; Dance; Drama/theater; International Student Organization; Jazz band; Literary magazine; Music ensembles; Musical theater; Pep band; Radio station; Student government; Student newspaper; Symphony orchestra; Yearbook. **Athletics (Intercollegiate):** *Men:* baseball, basketball, cheerleading, cross-country, football, golf, soccer, swimming, tennis, track/field (outdoor). *Women:* basketball, cheerleading, cross-country, golf, soccer, softball, swimming, tennis, track/field (outdoor), volleyball.

ACCOMMODATIONS

Allowed in exams:	
Calculators	Yes
Dictionary	Yes
Computer	Yes
Spell-checker	Yes
Extended test time	Yes
Scribe	Yes
Proctors	Yes
Oral exams	Yes
Note-takers	Yes
Support services for students with:	
LD	Yes
ADHD	Yes
ASD	Yes
Distraction-reduced environment	Yes
Recording of lecture allowed	Yes
Reading technology	Yes
Audio books	Yes
Other assistive technology	Yes
Priority registration	No
Added costs of services:	
For LD	No
For ADHD	No
For ASD	No
LD specialists	No
ADHD & ASD coaching	Yes
ASD specialists	No
Professional tutors	No
Peer tutors	Yes
Max. hours/week for services	Varies
How professors are notified of student approved accommodations	Student and Director

COLLEGE GRADUATION REQUIREMENTS

Course waivers allowed	Yes
In what courses: Determined case by case.	
Course substitutions allowed	Yes
In what courses: Determined case by case.	

Marshall University

One John Marshall Drive, Huntington, WV 25755 • Admissions: 304-696-3160 • Fax: 304-696-3135 **Support: SP**

CAMPUS

Type of school	Public
Environment	Town

STUDENTS

Undergrad enrollment	9,414
% male/female	42/58
% from out of state	18

FINANCIAL FACTS

Annual in-state tuition	$7,190
Annual out-of-state tuition	$18,044
Room and board	$9,974
Required fees	$1,442

GENERAL ADMISSIONS INFO

Application fee	$40
Regular application deadline	2 weeks prior to term
Nonfall registration	Yes

Admission may be deferred.

Range SAT EBRW	480–590
Range SAT Math	460–560
Range ACT Composite	19–25

ACADEMICS

Student/faculty ratio	18:1
% students returning for sophomore year	72

Most classes have 20–29 students.

Programs/Services for Students with Learning Differences

Higher Education for Learning Problems (H.E.L.P.) is a comprehensive and structured tutoring support program for college students who have a diagnosed specific learning disability and/or attention-deficit disorder. It is a fee-based service where both academic and remedial tutoring is available, as well as support to develop skills around time management and more. There are seven divisions and programs providing academic assistance to a variety of learners within H.E.L.P. These divisions include College HELP, Medical Help for medical students, Community Help for children aged 6–18 with specific LD or ADHD, Skills Development providing remediation in academics skills and executive functioning, Summer Prep for new students, Diagnostic Services, and ACT test prep. LD specialists provide the tutoring and support.

Admissions

Students must apply to both Marshall University and to the H.E.L.P. Program. Students applying to H.E.L.P. must have a diagnosed Specific Learning Disability and/or Attention-deficit Disorder. General admissions requires a GPA of 2.0 and 19 ACT or SAT equivalent or 3.0 GPA and 16 ACT or SAT equivalent. A limited number of students not meeting these requirements may be admitted to University College through conditional admission and begin their studies on the Huntington campus. These students must complete 18 hours on the Huntington campus, take an academic support class, and, if ACT was below 18, take an English course. Some students may be offered provisional admission for one semester and can register for succeeding terms when all admission requirements have been met and all required materials have been received.

Additional Information

All newly admitted Marshall University summer students who have been admitted to the H.E.L.P. freshman program participate in the five week Summer Prep Learning Disabilities Program. Students take one Marshall University class in the morning for credit, and receive one hour of tutoring daily for that class. In the afternoons, the students attend three hours of College Prep. Students are assigned to three, one hour sessions based on their areas of greatest need. The areas covered are basic reading skills, reading comprehension, written expression, study skills, and math. The program is taught by Learning Disabilities Specialists. Students are taught

ADMISSIONS INFO FOR STUDENTS WITH LEARNING DIFFERENCES

Phone: 304-696-6252 • Email: help@marshall.edu

SAT/ACT required: Yes (Test optional for 2021)
Interview required: Yes
Essay required: Yes
Additional application required: Yes
Documentation submitted to: The College Program

Special Ed. HS course work accepted: Yes
Separate application required for Programs/Services: Yes
Documentation required for:
LD: Psychoeducational evaluation
ADHD: Psychoeducational evaluation
ASD: Psychoeducational evaluation

Marshall University

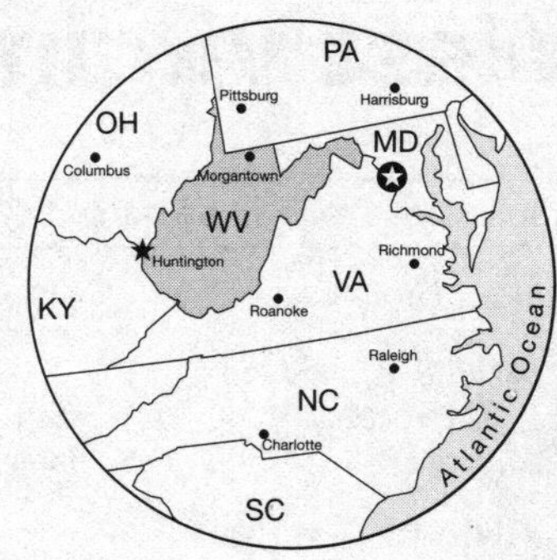

West Virginia

in small groups, generally with five to six students per group. In the College Program for Students with Autism Spectrum, students can participate in the program if they have met the acceptance criteria for Marshall University and also have been admitted to the College Program through a separate application process. The program uses a positive behavior support approach to assist participating students. Social, communication, academic, leisure, and personal living skills are assessed through person-centered planning. Personal goals are identified and strategies are developed based on the individual needs of each student.

General Admissions

Very important factors include: academic GPA, standardized test scores. *Other factors include:* rigor of secondary school record, recommendation(s). *Freshman admission requirements:* High school diploma is required, and GED is accepted. *Academic units recommended:* 4 English, 4 math, 3 science, 3 science labs, 2 foreign language, 3 social studies, 1 visual/performing arts.

Accommodations or Services

Accommodations are decided upon an individual basis after a thorough review of appropriate, current documentation. The accommodations requests must be supported through the documentation provided and must be logically linked to the current impact of the condition on academic functioning.

Financial Aid

Students should submit: FAFSA. Applicants will be notified of awards on a rolling basis beginning 3/1. *Need-based scholarships/grants offered:* College/university scholarship or grant aid from institutional funds; Federal Nursing Scholarships; Federal Pell; Private scholarships; SEOG; State scholarships/grants. *Loan aid offered:* Direct PLUS loans; Direct Subsidized Stafford Loans; Direct Unsubsidized Stafford Loans.

Campus Life

Activities: Campus Ministries; Choral groups; Concert band; Dance; Drama/theater; International Student Organization; Jazz band; Literary magazine; Marching band; Model UN; Music ensembles; Musical theater; Opera; Pep band; Radio station; Student government; Student newspaper; Symphony orchestra; Television station. **Organizations:** 100 registered organizations, 11 honor societies, 10 religious organizations, 12 fraternities, 7 sororities. **Athletics (Intercollegiate):** *Men:* baseball, basketball, cross-country, football, golf, soccer, track/field (outdoor). *Women:* basketball, cross-country, golf, soccer, softball, swimming, tennis, track/field (outdoor), volleyball.

ACCOMMODATIONS

Allowed in exams:	
Calculators	Yes
Dictionary	No
Computer	Yes
Spell-checker	Yes
Extended test time	Yes
Scribe	Yes
Proctors	Yes
Oral exams	Yes
Note-takers	Yes
Support services for students with:	
LD	Yes
ADHD	Yes
ASD	Yes
Distraction-reduced environment	Yes
Recording of lecture allowed	Yes
Reading technology	Yes
Audio books	Yes
Other assistive technology	Yes
Priority registration	Yes
Added costs of services:	
For LD	Yes
For ADHD	Yes
For ASD	Yes
LD specialists	Yes
ADHD & ASD coaching	Yes
ASD specialists	Yes
Professional tutors	Yes
Peer tutors	No
Max. hours/week for services	Varies
How professors are notified of student approved accommodations	Director

COLLEGE GRADUATION REQUIREMENTS

Course waivers allowed	No
Course substitutions allowed	Yes
In what courses: Case-by-case basis	

West Virginia University

Admissions Office, Morgantown, WV 26506-6009 • Admissions: 304-293-2121 • Fax: 304-293-3080 **Support: CS**

CAMPUS

Type of school	Public
Environment	Town

STUDENTS

Undergrad enrollment	21,086
% male/female	50/50
% from out of state	52
% frosh live on campus	92

FINANCIAL FACTS

Annual in-state tuition	$8,976
Annual out-of-state tuition	$25,320
Room and board	$10,902

GENERAL ADMISSIONS INFO

Application fee	$50
Regular application deadline	8/1
Nonfall registration	Yes

Admission may be deferred.

Range SAT EBRW	520–620
Range SAT Math	510–610
Range ACT Composite	21–27

ACADEMICS

% students returning for sophomore year	79

Most classes have 20–29 students.

Programs/Services for Students with Learning Differences

The Office of Accessibility Services (OAS) is dedicated to enhancing the educational opportunities for students with temporary or permanent disabilities at West Virginia University and all of its campuses. There is an application to complete and submit to the OAS. During the initial meeting (when students bring the application), students will be given information about how to access reasonable accommodations, which they must request each semester.

Admissions

There is no special admissions process for students with LD and ADHD. Students must meet admissions requirements. In-state students must have an average B+ GPA and out-of-state students must have a B+ GPA and either ACT of 21–27 or 510–600 SAT score to be considered for admission. Additionally, all applicants must have four years of English, three years of social studies, four years of math, three years of lab science, two years of same foreign language and one year of fine art. Students are not encouraged to self-disclose a disability in a personal statement during the application process. Appropriate services/accommodations will be determined after the student is admitted, and there is a separate application after general admissions.

Additional Information

To ensure access to university programs, specialists work individually with students to help them achieve academic success. There are no LD specialists on staff; however, counselors are available to provide services to all students. Some accommodations that are available with appropriate documentation include: priority registration, extended testing time, note-takers, distraction-free environments, books on tape, and assistive technology. MindFit is an additional program available to all students on campus for an additional fee. They offer an assessment service for students who have not had formal testing for LD or ADHD. The cost is $500. In additional to the academic support services, MindFit offers learning skills development. This is a short-term intervention with a professional academic coach. The staff meets one-on-one. It consists of three sessions, and the cost is $75. There is also academic enhancement options that provides academic support for students who learn differently. These tutors are trained to work with students with learning differences. There is a per semester cost depending on how many hours students need, at a rate of $1,550–$2,150/per semester.

ADMISSIONS INFO FOR STUDENTS WITH LEARNING DIFFERENCES

Phone: 304-293-6700 • Fax: 304-293-3861 • Email: Daniel.Long@mail.wvu.edu

SAT/ACT required: No
Interview required: No
Essay required: Not Applicable
Additional application required: No
Documentation submitted to: OAS

Special Ed. HS course work accepted: No
Separate application required for Programs/Services: Yes
Documentation required for:
LD: Comprehensive Psychoeducation report
ADHD: Comprehensive evaluation report
ASD: Comprehensive Psychoeducation evaluation report

West Virginia University

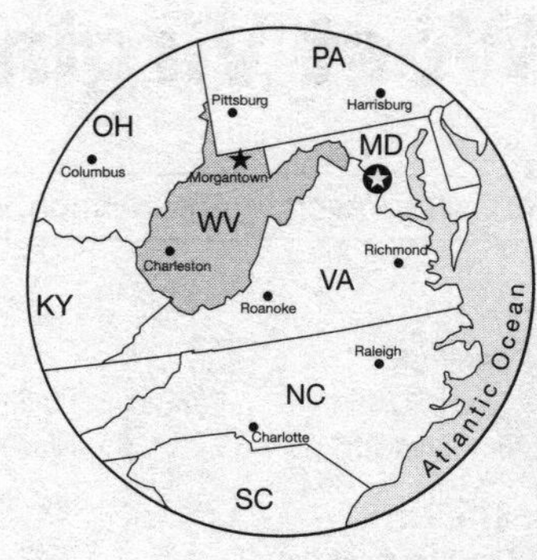

West Virginia

General Admissions

Very important factors include: academic GPA, standardized test scores. *Important factors include:* rigor of secondary school record, state residency. *Other factors include:* extracurricular activities, talent/ability. *Freshman admission requirements:* High school diploma is required, and GED is accepted. *Academic units required:* 4 English, 4 math, 3 science, 3 science labs, 2 foreign language, 3 social studies, 1 visual/performing arts.

Accommodations or Services

Accommodations are decided upon an individual basis after a thorough review of appropriate, current documentation. The accommodations requests must be supported through the documentation provided and must be logically linked to the current impact of the condition on academic functioning.

Financial Aid

Students should submit: FAFSA. *Need-based scholarships/grants offered:* College/university scholarship or grant aid from institutional funds; Federal Nursing Scholarships; Federal Pell; Private scholarships; SEOG. *Loan aid offered:* Direct PLUS loans; Direct Subsidized Stafford Loans; Direct Unsubsidized Stafford Loans. Federal Work-Study Program available. Institutional employment available.

Campus Life

Activities: Campus Ministries; Choral groups; Concert band; Dance; Drama/theater; International Student Organization; Jazz band; Literary magazine; Marching band; Model UN; Music ensembles; Musical theater; Pep band; Radio station; Student government; Student newspaper; Symphony orchestra. **Organizations:** 450 registered organizations, 26 honor societies, 26 religious organizations, 9 fraternities, 8 sororities. **Athletics (Intercollegiate):** *Men:* baseball, basketball, diving, football, riflery, soccer, swimming, wrestling. *Women:* basketball, crew/rowing, cross-country, diving, gymnastics, riflery, soccer, swimming, tennis, track/field (outdoor), track/field (indoor), volleyball.

ACCOMMODATIONS

Allowed in exams:	
Calculators	Yes
Dictionary	Yes
Computer	Yes
Spell-checker	Yes
Extended test time	Yes
Scribe	Yes
Proctors	Yes
Oral exams	Yes
Note-takers	Yes
Support services for students with:	
LD	Yes
ADHD	Yes
ASD	Yes
Distraction-reduced environment	Yes
Recording of lecture allowed	Yes
Reading technology:	Yes
Audio books	Yes
Other assistive technology	Yes
Priority registration	Yes
Added costs of services:	
For LD	Yes for Mindfit
For ADHD	Yes for Mindfit
For ASD	Yes for Mindfit
LD specialists	No
ADHD & ASD coaching	Yes
ASD specialists	No
Professional tutors	Yes
Peer tutors	Yes
Max. hours/week for services	Varies
How professors are notified of student approved accommodations	Student

COLLEGE GRADUATION REQUIREMENTS

Course waivers allowed	No
Course substitutions allowed	Yes
In what courses: Varies	

West Virginia Wesleyan College

59 College Avenue, Buckhannon, WV 26201 • Admissions: 304-473-8510 • Fax: 304-473-8108 **Support: SP**

CAMPUS

Type of school	Private (nonprofit)
Environment	Village

STUDENTS

Undergrad enrollment	1,131
% male/female	45/55
% from out of state	35
% frosh live on campus	89

FINANCIAL FACTS

Annual tuition	$31,074
Room and board	$9,415
Required fees	$1,178

GENERAL ADMISSIONS INFO

Application fee	$35
Regular application deadline	8/15
Nonfall registration	Yes

Admission may be deferred.

Range SAT EBRW	480–570
Range SAT Math	460–550
Range ACT Composite	18–24

ACADEMICS

Student/faculty ratio	14:1
% students returning for sophomore year	76

Most classes have 10–19 students.

Programs/Services for Students with Learning Differences

West Virginia Wesleyan College is strongly committed to providing excellent support to students with documented learning disabilities and attention difficulties. The Mentor Advantage Program provides an innovative, individualized support. It is designed to create a bridge to academic regulation in the college environment. The program is composed of several elements: one-on-one professional organizational mentoring, strategic academic content tutoring, weekly small group discussion, and an updated individualized accommodation plan. Students may enroll in the program as a package or sign up for various components separately, depending on the student need. In addition, Wesleyan offers an individualized clinical learning program that focuses on the improvement of reading skills and language comprehension. There is a professional tutor on duty to provide organizational and academic support 12.5 hours per day.

Admissions

The Director of the Learning Center reviews and decides the application outcome of students who disclose a disability. Applicants are encouraged to submit a psychoeducational evaluation if they believe it will help develop an accurate picture of student potential. For general admission West Virginia Wesleyan is test optional and does not require the submission of ACT or SAT. The office of admission will evaluate applications on many factors, including and most importantly, the high school record (course load and grades). They will also look at the student's character, leadership, and extracurricular activities. Interviews are encouraged. College prep courses required include 4 years English, 3+ years math, 3 years science, 3 years social studies, and recommend at least 2 years foreign language.

Additional Information

There are a number of programs available to students on campus through the Learning Center, including Foundational Program, Mentor Advantage Program, Day-time and Evening classes, and Lindamood-Bell Learning Techniques and Services for all Students. Students work with their comprehensive advisor on a weekly basis to cover the following areas: specialized academic advising, preferential preregistration for the first three semesters, implementation of accommodations to be used for college classes, development of academic, organizational, and self-monitoring strategies, discussion of priorities and motivational outlook, self-advocacy and social coaching as needed, and assistive technology lab with state-of-the-art software. A test-taking lab provides readers, scribes, note takers, and word-processing, as needed. Costs for the various services vary depending on the number of hours.

ADMISSIONS INFO FOR STUDENTS WITH LEARNING DIFFERENCES

Phone: 304-473-8563 • Fax: 304-473-8497 • Email: kuba_s@wvwc.edu

SAT/ACT required: Yes (Test optional for 2021)
Interview required: No
Essay required: Recommended
Additional application required: Yes
Documentation submitted to: The Learning Center

Special Ed. HS course work accepted: No
Separate application required for Programs/Services: No
Documentation required for:
- **LD:** Psychoeducational evaluation
- **ADHD:** Psychoeducational evaluation
- **ASD:** Psychoeducational evaluation

West Virginia Wesleyan College

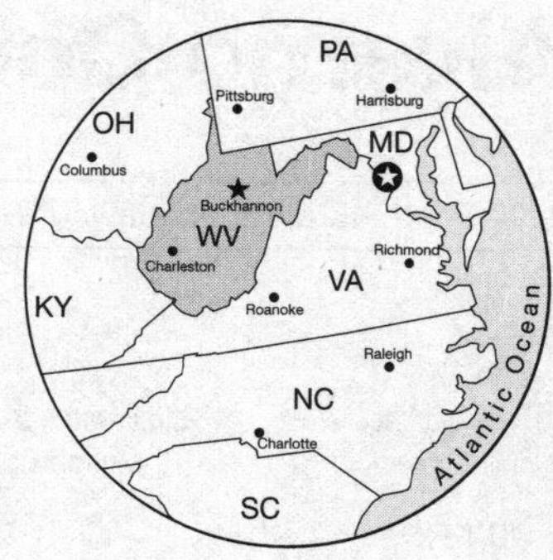

General Admissions

Very important factors include: rigor of secondary school record, academic GPA, talent/ability. *Important factors include:* class rank, standardized test scores, extracurricular activities, character/personal qualities, volunteer work, work experience, level of applicant's interest. *Other factors include:* application essay, recommendation(s), interview. *Freshman admission requirements:* High school diploma is required, and GED is accepted. *Academic units required:* 4 English, 3 math, 3 science, 1 science lab, 3 social studies. *Academic units recommended:* 2 foreign language.

Accommodations or Services

Accommodations are decided upon an individual basis after a thorough review of appropriate, current documentation. The accommodations requests must be supported through the documentation provided and must be logically linked to the current impact of the condition on academic functioning.

Financial Aid

Students should submit: FAFSA. *Need-based scholarships/grants offered:* College/university scholarship or grant aid from institutional funds; Federal Nursing Scholarships; Federal Pell; Private scholarships; SEOG; State scholarships/grants. *Loan aid offered:* Direct PLUS loans; Direct Subsidized Stafford Loans; Direct Unsubsidized Stafford Loans. Federal Work-Study Program available. Institutional employment available.

Campus Life

Activities: Campus Ministries; Choral groups; Concert band; Dance; Drama/theater; International Student Organization; Jazz band; Literary magazine; Marching band; Music ensembles; Musical theater; Opera; Pep band; Radio station; Student government; Student newspaper; Yearbook. **Organizations:** 75 registered organizations, 31 honor societies, 6 religious organizations, 6 fraternities, 5 sororities. **Athletics (Intercollegiate):** *Men:* baseball, basketball, cross-country, football, golf, soccer, softball, swimming, tennis, track/field (outdoor), track/field (indoor). *Women:* basketball, cross-country, golf, lacrosse, soccer, swimming, tennis, track/field (outdoor), track/field (indoor), volleyball.

ACCOMMODATIONS

Allowed in exams:	
Calculators	Yes
Dictionary	Yes
Computer	Yes
Spell-checker	Yes
Extended test time	Yes
Scribe	Yes
Proctors	Yes
Oral exams	Yes
Note-takers	Yes
Support services for students with:	
LD	Yes
ADHD	Yes
ASD	Yes
Distraction-reduced environment	Yes
Recording of lecture allowed	Yes
Reading technology	Yes
Audio books	Yes
Other assistive technology	Yes
Priority registration	Yes
Added costs of services:	
For LD	Yes
For ADHD	Yes
For ASD	Yes
LD specialists	Yes
ADHD & ASD coaching	Yes
ASD specialists	No
Professional tutors	Yes
Peer tutors	Yes
Max. hours/week for services	Varies
How professors are notified of student approved accommodations	Student

COLLEGE GRADUATION REQUIREMENTS

Course waivers allowed	No
Course substitutions allowed	No

Alverno College

3400 South 43rd Street, Milwaukee, WI 53234-3922 • Admissions: 414-382-6101 • Fax: 414-382-6055 **Support: S**

CAMPUS

Type of school	Private (nonprofit)
Environment	Metropolis

STUDENTS

Undergrad enrollment	1,090
% male/female	1/99
% from out of state	9
% frosh live on campus	40

FINANCIAL FACTS

Annual tuition	$29,808
Room and board	$8,620
Required fees	$900

GENERAL ADMISSIONS INFO

Application fee	$0
Regular application deadline	Rolling
Nonfall registration	Yes

Admission may be deferred.

Range ACT Composite	18–21

ACADEMICS

Student/faculty ratio	9:1
% students returning for sophomore year	71

Most classes have 10–19 students.

Programs/Services for Students with Learning Differences

The Office for Student Accessibility (OSA) supports students who have a physical, sensory, learning, and/or psychological disability that substantially limits a major life activity. The student has to provide appropriate documentation for the disability, and the Student Accessibility Coordinator reviews the documentation. The coordinator will identify the appropriate accommodations, and the student is in charge of sharing the information with their instructor. The student must also reach out to the instructor to ask someone in the class (for example) to be a notetaker for them.

Admissions

There is no special admissions for students with disabilities. Eligibility for admission is based on grades, courses, and test scores. Applicants need a high school diploma or equivalent with a 2.3 GPA. Applicants need 17 academic units including 4 years English, 3 years math, 3 years social sciences, 3 years science, and 2 years foreign language (recommended). Students must have a minimum 17 ACT or 920 SAT. Some applicants may be asked to take the Alverno Communication Placement Assessment. If GPA is between 2.0–2.3 or ACT between 17–21, the applicant may petition the admission office for an acceptance.

Additional Information

It's suggested that students contact the Coordinator for Student Accessibility at least one semester prior to admission; or immediately following diagnosis of a disability. Be prepared to provide written documentation to verify disability and to identify appropriate accommodations. Contact local Vocational Rehabilitation office (and the Social Security Administration as appropriate) to seek possible funding for educational costs and for other disability-related services. Remember to Identify and observe all deadlines (e.g., admissions, housing, financial aid, disability services) and keep a record of all correspondence and documents relevant to your education.

ADMISSIONS INFO FOR STUDENTS WITH LEARNING DIFFERENCES

Phone: 414-382-6026 • Fax: 414-382-6354 • Email: colleen.barnett@alverno.edu

SAT/ACT required: Yes (Test optional for 2021)
Interview required: No
Essay required: No
Additional application required: No
Documentation submitted to: OSA

Special Ed. HS course work accepted: No
Separate application required for Programs/Services: No
Documentation required for:
LD: Psychoeducational evaluation
ADHD: Psychoeducational evaluation
ASD: Psychoeducational evaluation

Alverno College

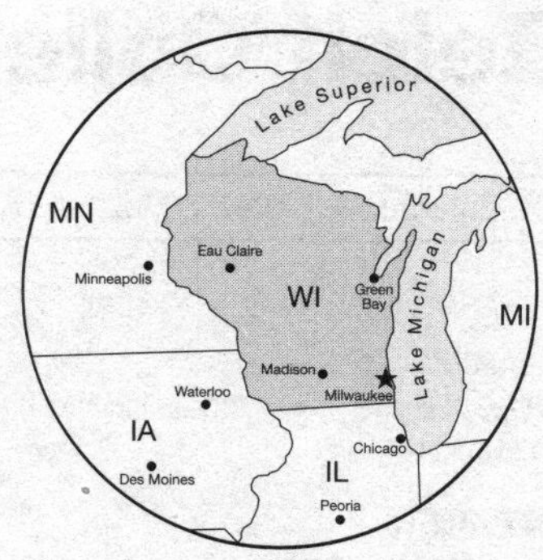

General Admissions

Very important factors include: academic GPA, standardized test scores. *Important factors include:* rigor of secondary school record. *Other factors include:* application essay, recommendation(s), interview, extracurricular activities, talent/ability, character/personal qualities, volunteer work, work experience, level of applicant's interest. *Freshman admission requirements:* High school diploma is required, and GED is accepted. *Academic units required:* 4 English, 3 math, 3 science, 3 social studies, 4 academic electives. *Academic units recommended:* 2 foreign language.

Accommodations or Services

Accommodations are decided upon an individual basis after a thorough review of appropriate, current documentation. The accommodations requests must be supported through the documentation provided and must be logically linked to the current impact of the condition on academic functioning.

Financial Aid

Students should submit: FAFSA. *Need-based scholarships/grants offered:* College/university scholarship or grant aid from institutional funds; Federal Pell; Private scholarships; SEOG; State scholarships/grants. *Loan aid offered:* Direct PLUS loans; Direct Subsidized Stafford Loans; Direct Unsubsidized Stafford Loans. Federal Work-Study Program available. Institutional employment available.

Campus Life

Activities: Campus Ministries; Choral groups; Dance; Drama/theater; International Student Organization; Literary magazine; Model UN; Music ensembles; Radio station; Student government; Student newspaper. **Organizations:** 36 registered organizations, 1 honor society, 2 religious organizations, 2 sororities. **Athletics (Intercollegiate):** *Women:* basketball, cross-country, soccer, softball, tennis, volleyball.

ACCOMMODATIONS

Allowed in exams:	
Calculators	Yes
Dictionary	Yes
Computer	Yes
Spell-checker	Yes
Extended test time	Yes
Scribe	Yes
Proctors	Yes
Oral exams	Yes
Note-takers	Yes
Support services for students with:	
LD	Yes
ADHD	Yes
ASD	Yes
Distraction-reduced environment	Yes
Recording of lecture allowed	Yes
Reading technology	Yes
Audio books	Yes
Other assistive technology	Yes
Priority registration	No
Added costs of services:	
For LD	No
For ADHD	No
For ASD	No
LD specialists	No
ADHD & ASD coaching	No
ASD specialists	No
Professional tutors	No
Peer tutors	Yes
Max. hours/week for services	Varies
How professors are notified of student approved accommodations	Student

COLLEGE GRADUATION REQUIREMENTS

Course waivers allowed	No
Course substitutions allowed	No

Wisconsin

Beloit College

700 College St., Beloit, WI 53511 • Admissions: 608-363-2500 • Fax: 608-363-2075 **Support: CS**

CAMPUS

Type of school	Private (nonprofit)
Environment	Town

STUDENTS

Undergrad enrollment	1,143
% male/female	45/55
% from out of state	82
% frosh live on campus	98

FINANCIAL FACTS

Annual tuition	$52,858
Room and board	$9,688
Required fees	$490

GENERAL ADMISSIONS INFO

Application fee	$0
Regular application deadline	7/1
Nonfall registration	Yes

Admission may be deferred.

Range SAT EBRW	550–680
Range SAT Math	530–700
Range ACT Composite	24–30

ACADEMICS

Student/faculty ratio	11:1
% students returning for sophomore year	79

Most classes have 10–19 students.

Programs/Services for Students with Learning Differences

The Learning Enrichment and Disability Services office provides academic opportunities (i.e., tutoring, one- on-one assistance) and support for all Beloit College students. The Disability Service works with students to find appropriate accommodations within the campus community. In addition, students with academic challenges and concerns (i.e., alert slips, academic probation) should reach out to Disability Services for assistance with implementing appropriate strategies to achieve personal and academic success. To accomplish these goals, the office will collaborate with faculty, staff, and students and help that student to self-advocate. Students are expected to obtain and use information and follow through with the appropriate resources.

Admissions

There is no special admissions procedure for students with learning differences. Each student is reviewed individually, and the final decision is made by the Office of Admissions. The college is competitive in admissions, but is test optional and has no absolute GPA or expected test scores. A minimum of 16 academic courses are required for admission. Courses recommended include 4 years of English, 3 years of math, 3 years of laboratory science, 2 years of a foreign language, and 3 years of social science or history. Applicants may ask to talk with an admission officer and can send additional recommendations and art portfolios.

Additional Information

Beloit College Learning Enrichment and Disability Services offers additional resources to all students in the areas of tutoring (most courses, including math and science), reading strategies, study strategies, time management, study groups, advising, mentoring, as well as assistance with computer usage and assistive technology. Improvement of writing and research skills as well as personal counseling, career guidance, and crisis intervention are also available at the college. There is free peer tutoring in a variety of subjects.

ADMISSIONS INFO FOR STUDENTS WITH LEARNING DIFFERENCES

Phone: 608-363-2572 • Fax: 608-363-7059 • Email: deleonj@beloit.edu

SAT/ACT required: No
Interview required: No
Essay required: No
Additional application required: No
Documentation submitted to: Learning Enrichment and Disability Services

Special Ed. HS course work accepted: Yes
Separate application required for Programs/Services: No
Documentation required for:
LD: Psychoeducational evaluation
ADHD: Psychoeducational evaluation
ASD: Psychoeducational evaluation

Beloit College

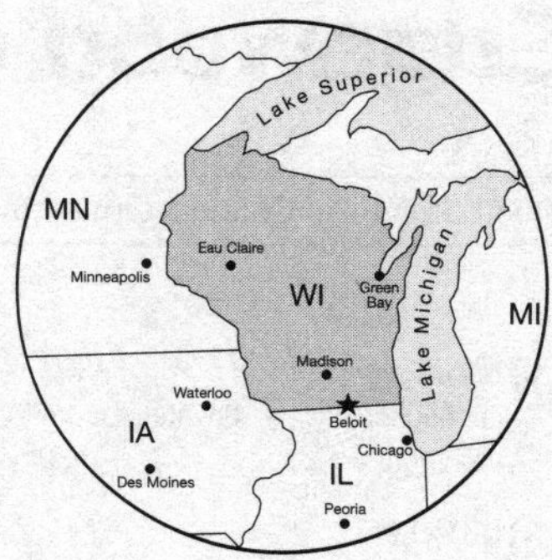

General Admissions

Very important factors include: rigor of secondary school record, academic GPA, application essay, recommendation(s). *Important factors include:* extracurricular activities, talent/ability. *Other factors include:* class rank, standardized test scores, interview, character/personal qualities, first generation, alumni/ae relation, racial/ethnic status, volunteer work, work experience, level of applicant's interest. *Freshman admission requirements:* High school diploma is required, and GED is accepted. *Academic units recommended:* 4 English, 3 math, 3 science, 3 science labs, 2 foreign language, 3 social studies.

Accommodations or Services

Accommodations are decided upon an individual basis after a thorough review of appropriate, current documentation. The accommodations requests must be supported through the documentation provided and must be logically linked to the current impact of the condition on academic functioning.

Financial Aid

Students should submit: FAFSA. Applicants will be notified of awards on a rolling basis beginning 2/22. *Need-based scholarships/grants offered:* College/university scholarship or grant aid from institutional funds; Federal Pell; Private scholarships; SEOG; State scholarships/grants. *Loan aid offered:* Direct PLUS loans; Direct Subsidized Stafford Loans; Direct Unsubsidized Stafford Loans. Federal Work-Study Program available. Institutional employment available.

Campus Life

Activities: Campus Ministries; Choral groups; Dance; Drama/theater; International Student Organization; Jazz band; Literary magazine; Model UN; Music ensembles; Musical theater; Radio station; Student government; Student newspaper; Television station. **Organizations:** 113 registered organizations, 6 honor societies, 3 religious organizations, 3 fraternities, 3 sororities. **Athletics (Intercollegiate):** *Men:* baseball, basketball, cross-country, football, golf, soccer, swimming, tennis, track/field (outdoor), track/field (indoor). *Women:* basketball, cross-country, soccer, softball, swimming, tennis, track/field (outdoor), track/field (indoor), volleyball.

ACCOMMODATIONS

Allowed in exams:	
Calculators	Yes
Dictionary	Yes
Computer	Yes
Spell-checker	Yes
Extended test time	Yes
Scribe	Yes
Proctors	Yes
Oral exams	Yes
Note-takers	Yes
Support services for students with:	
LD	Yes
ADHD	Yes
ASD	Yes
Distraction-reduced environment	Yes
Recording of lecture allowed	Yes
Reading technology	Yes
Audio books	Yes
Other assistive technology	Yes
Priority registration	Yes
Added costs of services:	
For LD	No
For ADHD	No
For ASD	No
LD specialists	No
ADHD & ASD coaching	No
ASD specialists	No
Professional tutors	No
Peer tutors	Yes
Max. hours/week for services	Varies
How professors are notified of student approved accommodations	Student

COLLEGE GRADUATION REQUIREMENTS

Course waivers allowed	No
Course substitutions allowed	Yes
In what courses: Case by case basis	

Edgewood College

1000 Edgewood College, Drive Madison, WI 53711-1997 • Admissions: 608-663-2294 • Fax: 608-663-2214 **Support: SP**

CAMPUS

Type of school	Private (nonprofit)
Environment	City

STUDENTS

Undergrad enrollment	1,330
% male/female	27/73
% from out of state	9
% frosh live on campus	81

FINANCIAL FACTS

Annual tuition	$32,620
Room and board	$12,050

GENERAL ADMISSIONS INFO

Application fee	$30
Regular application deadline	8/1
Nonfall registration	Yes

Admission may be deferred.

Range SAT EBRW	460–610
Range SAT Math	490–600
Range ACT Composite	20–25

ACADEMICS

Student/faculty ratio	10:1
% students returning for sophomore year	79

Most classes have 10–19 students.

Programs/Services for Students with Learning Differences

The Student Accessibility and Disability Services is open to supporting students who need to understand where to go to access accommodations. The Academic Success and Career Development Center (ASCDC) offers academic assistance and advising when a student is looking to develop a career choice and which major to choose. Students are offered free one-on-one math tutoring, peer tutors, and a writing center to help with assignments. Additional support is offered to assist in study skill development. The Cutting Edge Program is a program for students with intellectual developmental disabilities.

Admissions

The average GPA is 3.4 and 22 average ACT (or SAT equivalent). Admission to Edgewood College does not guarantee admission into individual schools or programs such as nursing and education. Candidates for the Cutting Edge program are encouraged to begin the admissions process a year in advance and submit all application materials by December prior to the year of entrance. Cutting Edge applicants must complete a separate application. Include a recent photo, school transcript, one letter of reference, an essay about "Why I Want to Go to College," and a current IEP or psychoeducational evaluation. Once these materials are received, a survey will be sent to be completed by a parent and a teacher.

Additional Information

The Cutting Edge Program accepts and supports 20 students per academic year. The individualized services support students in academics, student housing, and internships. There is a summer program for high school students with intellectual and developmental disabilities who are 16 to 21. Participants must be able to dress themselves, eat independently, and administer their own medications. During this week-long program, students attend classes, engage in campus life, explore the community, live in residence halls, and build connections with peers, staff, and faculty. This week-long program accepts up to 15 participants and is a "Parent-Free Zone."

ADMISSIONS INFO FOR STUDENTS WITH LEARNING DIFFERENCES

Phone: 608-663-8347 • Fax: 608-663-2278 • Email: cuttingedge@edgewood.edu

SAT/ACT required: Yes (Test optional through 2022)
Interview required: Yes
Essay required: Yes
Additional application required: Yes
Documentation submitted to: ASCDC or Cutting Edge

Special Ed. HS course work accepted: Yes
Separate application required for Programs/Services: Yes
Documentation required for:
- **LD:** Psychoeducational evaluation
- **ADHD:** Psychoeducational evaluation
- **ASD:** Psychoeducational evaluation

Edgewood College

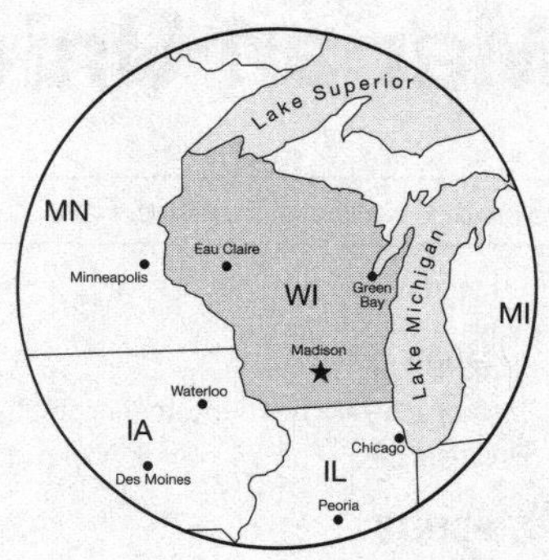

General Admissions

Very important factors include: class rank, academic GPA, standardized test scores. *Other factors include:* application essay, recommendation(s). *Freshman admission requirements:* High school diploma is required, and GED is accepted. *Academic units required:* 4 English, 2 math, 2 science, 1 science lab, 2 foreign language, 2 social studies, 1 history. *Academic units recommended:* 4 English, 2 math, 2 science, 1 science lab, 2 foreign language, 2 social studies, 1 history.

Accommodations or Services

Accommodations are decided upon an individual basis after a thorough review of appropriate, current documentation. The accommodations requests must be supported through the documentation provided and must be logically linked to the current impact of the condition on academic functioning.

Financial Aid

Students should submit: FAFSA. *Need-based scholarships/grants offered:* College/university scholarship or grant aid from institutional funds; Federal Pell; Private scholarships; SEOG; State scholarships/grants. *Loan aid offered:* Direct PLUS loans; Direct Subsidized Stafford Loans; Direct Unsubsidized Stafford Loans. Federal Work-Study Program available. Institutional employment available.

Campus Life

Activities: Campus Ministries; Drama/theater; International Student Organization; Music ensembles; Musical theater; Student government; Student newspaper; Symphony orchestra. **Organizations:** 48 registered organizations, 4 honor societies, 1 religious organization. **Athletics (Intercollegiate):** *Men:* baseball, basketball, cross-country, golf, soccer, tennis, track/field (outdoor), track/field (indoor). *Women:* basketball, cross-country, golf, soccer, softball, tennis, track/field (outdoor), track/field (indoor), volleyball.

ACCOMMODATIONS

Allowed in exams:	
Calculators	Yes
Dictionary	Yes
Computer	Yes
Spell-checker	Yes
Extended test time	Yes
Scribe	Yes
Proctors	Yes
Oral exams	Yes
Note-takers	Yes
Support services for students with:	
LD	Yes
ADHD	Yes
ASD	Yes
Distraction-reduced environment	Yes
Recording of lecture allowed	Yes
Reading technology	Yes
Audio books	Yes
Other assistive technology	Yes
Priority registration	Yes
Added costs of services:	
For LD	Yes
For ADHD	Yes
For ASD	Yes
LD specialists	Yes
ADHD & ASD coaching	Yes
ASD specialists	Yes
Professional tutors	Yes
Peer tutors	Yes
Max. hours/week for services	Varies
How professors are notified of student approved accommodations	Student and Director

COLLEGE GRADUATION REQUIREMENTS

Course waivers allowed	Yes
In what courses: Foreign Language	
Course substitutions allowed	No

Wisconsin

Marian University

45 South National Avenue, Fond du Lac, WI 54935 • Admissions: 920-923-7650 • Fax: 920-923-8755 **Support: CS**

CAMPUS

Type of school	Private (nonprofit)
Environment	Town

STUDENTS

Undergrad enrollment	1,327
% male/female	31/69
% from out of state	22

FINANCIAL FACTS

Annual tuition	$28,100
Room and board	$7,872
Required fees	$460

GENERAL ADMISSIONS INFO

Application fee	$0
Regular application deadline	Rolling
Nonfall registration	Yes

Admission may be deferred.

Range SAT EBRW	440–530
Range SAT Math	440–550
Range ACT Composite	17–22

ACADEMICS

Student/faculty ratio	13:1
% students returning for sophomore year	68

Most classes have 10–19 students.

Programs/Services for Students with Learning Differences

Marian University is committed to providing equal educational opportunities to students with learning disabilities and/or ADD/ADHD. In collaboration with the University's Center for Academic Success and Engagement, the Counseling and Consultation Services arranges accommodative services. Once the Director of Academic Support Services in the Office of Counseling and Consultation Services receives the self-disclosure form, a variety of accommodations can be provided.

Admissions

There is no special application or admissions procedure for students with learning disabilities. The admission committee looks for a minimum 2.0 GPA and 18 ACT or 940 SAT and rank in top 50% of class if rank is calculated. Applicants who do not meet this criteria but show potential for academic success may be admitted through our EXCEL Program on a provisional basis.

Additional Information

Disability Services offers the following services and accommodations to students who disclose a disability and submit appropriate documentation: notetakers, audio books, audio players, scan and read software, distraction free test environments, extended exam times, and test readers/scribes. The EXCEL Program provides students entering their first year of college with support and encouragement in their transition to college. EXCEL sets expectations for academic performance and offers smaller classes taught by EXCEL-prepared instructors, who provide individualized learning and promote the utilization of campus resources and services. Requirements of the EXCEL Program include achieving a minimum of 24 credits within the first two semesters, earning a 2.0 GPA within the first 2 semesters, attending the Excel Summer Bridge Program, enrolling in a maximum of 5 courses each semester, meeting with an academic advisor twice a week, and participating in academic services through meetings with instructors, tutors, learning specialists, and study groups.

ADMISSIONS INFO FOR STUDENTS WITH LEARNING DIFFERENCES

Phone: 920-923-8951 • Fax: 920-923-8135

SAT/ACT required: No
Interview required: No
Essay required: No
Additional application required: No
Documentation submitted to: Center for Academic Services

Special Ed. HS course work accepted: Yes
Separate application required for Programs/Services: No
Documentation required for:
LD: Psychoeducational evaluation
ADHD: Psychoeducational evaluation
ASD: Psychoeducational evaluation

Marian University

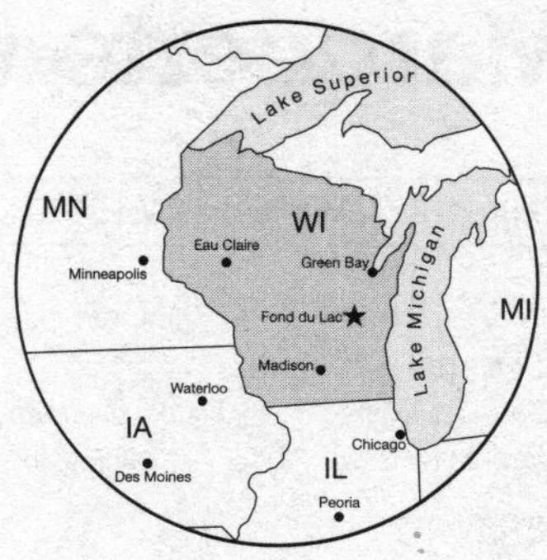

General Admissions

Very important factors include: rigor of secondary school record, class rank, academic GPA, standardized test scores. *Important factors include:* interview, character/personal qualities. *Other factors include:* application essay, recommendation(s), extracurricular activities, talent/ability, alumni/ae relation, volunteer work, work experience. *Freshman admission requirements:* High school diploma is required, and GED is accepted. *Academic units required:* 4 English, 2 math, 1 science, 1 science lab, 1 history. *Academic units recommended:* 3 math, 2 science, 2 foreign language.

Accommodations or Services

Accommodations are decided upon an individual basis after a thorough review of appropriate, current documentation. The accommodations requests must be supported through the documentation provided and must be logically linked to the current impact of the condition on academic functioning.

Financial Aid

Students should submit: Institution's own financial aid form. Applicants will be notified of awards on a rolling basis beginning 3/1. *Need-based scholarships/ grants offered:* College/university scholarship or grant aid from institutional funds; Federal Pell; Private scholarships; SEOG; State scholarships/grants. *Loan aid offered:* Direct PLUS loans; Direct Subsidized Stafford Loans; Direct Unsubsidized Stafford Loans. Federal Work-Study Program available. Institutional employment available.

Campus Life

Activities: Campus Ministries; Choral groups; Concert band; Dance; Drama/ theater; Jazz band; Literary magazine; Model UN; Music ensembles; Pep band; Student government; Student newspaper; Symphony orchestra. **Organizations:** 40 registered organizations, 6 honor societies, 1 religious organization, 1 fraternity, 1 sorority. **Athletics (Intercollegiate):** *Men:* baseball, basketball, cross-country, golf, ice hockey, soccer, tennis. *Women:* basketball, cross-country, golf, ice hockey, soccer, softball, tennis, volleyball.

ACCOMMODATIONS

Allowed in exams:	
Calculators	Yes
Dictionary	No
Computer	Yes
Spell-checker	Yes
Extended test time	Yes
Scribe	Yes
Proctors	Yes
Oral exams	Yes
Note-takers	Yes
Support services for students with:	
LD	Yes
ADHD	Yes
ASD	Yes
Distraction-reduced environment	Yes
Recording of lecture allowed	Yes
Reading technology	Yes
Audio books	Yes
Other assistive technology	Yes
Priority registration	Yes
Added costs of services:	
For LD	No
For ADHD	No
For ASD	No
LD specialists	Yes
ADHD & ASD coaching	Yes
ASD specialists	No
Professional tutors	Yes
Peer tutors	Yes
Max. hours/week for services	Varies
How professors are notified of student approved accommodations	Student

COLLEGE GRADUATION REQUIREMENTS

Course waivers allowed	No
Course substitutions allowed	Yes
In what courses: Varies	

Wisconsin

Marquette University

PO Box 1881, Milwaukee, WI 53201-1881 • Admissions: 414-288-7302 • Fax: 414-288-3764 **Support: CS**

CAMPUS

Type of school	Private (nonprofit)
Environment	Metropolis

STUDENTS

Undergrad enrollment	8,352
% male/female	46/54
% from out of state	70
% frosh live on campus	90

FINANCIAL FACTS

Annual tuition	$44,970
Room and board	$13,656
Required fees	$696

GENERAL ADMISSIONS INFO

Application fee	$0
Regular application deadline	12/1
Nonfall registration	Yes

Admission may be deferred.

Range SAT EBRW	560–650
Range SAT Math	560–670
Range ACT Composite	24–29

ACADEMICS

Student/faculty ratio	14:1
% students returning for sophomore year	90

Most classes have 10–19 students.

Programs/Services for Students with Learning Differences

The Office of Disability Services (ODS) is the designated office at Marquette University to coordinate accommodations for all students with identified and documented disabilities. The student and a staff member from ODS discuss the students disability, presenting documentation from a professional and how it will impact on the requirements of the student's courses. Based upon this evaluation, the ODS Staff provides a range of individualized accommodations. The student is responsible for delivering the letter provided by the ODS Representative to each instructor. Marquette University offers the College Success Program to assist students on the autism spectrum in navigating the university. College Success utilizes an interdisciplinary approach and works with the student to build the support team needed to thrive at Marquette. The team is trained on the best practices for working with people on the autism spectrum.

Admissions

There is no special admissions process for students with LD and ADD. All applicants for admission must meet the same admission criteria. Marquette requires applicants to have 4 years of English, 2–4 years of math and science, 2–3 years of social studies, and other additional subjects. Foreign language requirements for graduation vary by major and may be waived with appropriate documentation.

Additional Information

The College Success Program provides formal and informal support to help students academically, socially, and in independent living skills, including weekly seminars, one-to-one coaching, peer mentoring, and specific tutoring. The first two years focus on the transition to the rigors of academia. In the second two years of the program, the program works with students to identify strengths and skills to transfer to their career and life after college. There is a fee for the program per semester to cover individualized support, materials, and faculty training. The cost of this program is $3,000 per semester. ODS provides a number of accommodations for students with LD and AD/HD including texts in alternate formats and alternative testing arrangements. Tutoring is not provided through ODS.

ADMISSIONS INFO FOR STUDENTS WITH LEARNING DIFFERENCES

Phone: 414-288-1645 • Fax: 414-288-5799 • Email: jonathan.bartelt@marquette.edu

SAT/ACT required: No
Interview required: No
Essay required: Yes
Additional application required: No
Documentation submitted to: ODS

Special Ed. HS course work accepted: Yes
Separate application required for Programs/Services: No
Documentation required for:
LD: Psychoeducational evaluation
ADHD: Psychoeducational evaluation
ASD: Psychoeducational evaluation

Marquette University

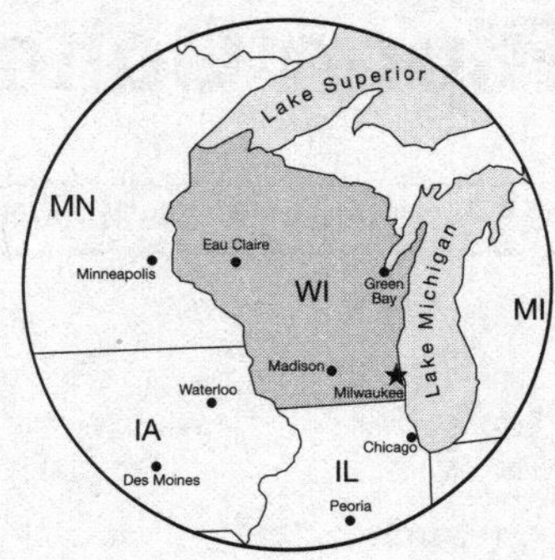

General Admissions

Very important factors include: rigor of secondary school record, academic GPA. *Important factors include:* application essay, standardized test scores, extracurricular activities, volunteer work. *Other factors include:* class rank, recommendation(s), talent/ability, character/personal qualities, first generation, alumni/ae relation, racial/ethnic status, work experience. *Freshman admission requirements:* High school diploma is required, and GED is accepted. *Academic units required:* 4 English, 2 math, 2 science, 2 science labs, 2 social studies, 2 academic electives. *Academic units recommended:* 4 English, 4 math, 4 science, 3 science labs, 2 foreign language, 3 social studies, 2 history, 5 academic electives.

Accommodations or Services

Accommodations are decided upon an individual basis after a thorough review of appropriate, current documentation. The accommodations requests must be supported through the documentation provided and must be logically linked to the current impact of the condition on academic functioning.

Financial Aid

Students should submit: FAFSA. Applicants will be notified of awards on or about 3/15. *Need-based scholarships/grants offered:* College/university scholarship or grant aid from institutional funds; Federal Pell; Private scholarships; SEOG; State scholarships/grants. *Loan aid offered:* Direct PLUS loans; Direct Subsidized Stafford Loans; Direct Unsubsidized Stafford Loans. Federal Work-Study Program available. Institutional employment available.

Campus Life

Activities: Campus Ministries; Choral groups; Concert band; Dance; Drama/theater; International Student Organization; Jazz band; Literary magazine; Model UN; Music ensembles; Musical theater; Pep band; Radio station; Student government; Student newspaper; Symphony orchestra; Television station; Yearbook. **Organizations:** 300 registered organizations, 16 honor societies, 14 religious organizations, 10 fraternities, 13 sororities. **Athletics (Intercollegiate):** *Men:* basketball, cheerleading, cross-country, golf, soccer, tennis, track/field (outdoor), track/field (indoor). *Women:* basketball, cheerleading, cross-country, soccer, tennis, track/field (outdoor), track/field (indoor), volleyball.

ACCOMMODATIONS

Allowed in exams:	
Calculators	Yes
Dictionary	Yes
Computer	Yes
Spell-checker	Yes
Extended test time	Yes
Scribe	Yes
Proctors	Yes
Oral exams	Yes
Note-takers	Yes
Support services for students with:	
LD	Yes
ADHD	Yes
ASD	Yes
Distraction-reduced environment	Yes
Recording of lecture allowed	Yes
Reading technology	Yes
Audio books	Yes
Other assistive technology	Yes
Priority registration	Yes
Added costs of services:	
For LD	No
For ADHD	No
For ASD	Yes
LD specialists	Yes
ADHD & ASD coaching	Yes
ASD specialists	Yes
Professional tutors	Yes
Peer tutors	Yes
Max. hours/week for services	Varies
How professors are notified of student approved accommodations	Student

COLLEGE GRADUATION REQUIREMENTS

Course waivers allowed	No
Course substitutions allowed	Yes
In what courses: Case-by-case basis	

Ripon College

PO Box 248, Ripon, WI 54971 • Admissions: 920-748-8337 • Fax: 920-748-8335 **Support: S**

CAMPUS	
Type of school	Private (nonprofit)
Environment	Village
STUDENTS	
Undergrad enrollment	787
% male/female	46/54
% from out of state	29
% frosh live on campus	97
FINANCIAL FACTS	
Annual tuition	$46,823
Room and board	$8,653
Required fees	$300
GENERAL ADMISSIONS INFO	
Application fee	$30
Regular application deadline	Rolling
Nonfall registration	Yes
Admission may be deferred.	
Range SAT EBRW	480–600
Range SAT Math	510–620
Range ACT Composite	19–25
ACADEMICS	
Student/faculty ratio	12:1
% students returning for sophomore year	78
Most classes have 10–19 students.	

Programs/Services for Students with Learning Differences

The Student Support Services (SSS) provides a wide variety of services on the campus, including academic and personal counseling, study skills information, and tutoring. Although the focus of the program is on first generation students, students of higher need, and students who are learning disabled, other students who feel they might qualify are encouraged to contact SSS. SSS offers free peer tutoring in specific subject areas. The aim of the tutoring program is to help students develop independent learning skills and improve their course grades.

Admissions

Students with learning disabilities are screened by admissions and must meet the same admission criteria as all other applicants. There is no set GPA required; courses required include four years English, algebra and geometry, two years natural science, two years social studies, and seven additional units. Ripon is test optional, and no ACT or SAT scores are required for admission.

Additional Information

SSS provides tutoring in subject areas; skills classes for no credit in time management, note-taking, test-taking strategies, reading college texts, writing papers, studying for and taking exams, and setting goals; and counseling/guidance. Student Support Services provides intensive study groups, LD support and internships. SSS provides students with peer contacts who provide students with one-on-one support and is useful in helping students adjust to college life, to provide a contact for the student to go to with problems or issues, organize group tutoring, and to help students open their minds and see hope in their future.

ADMISSIONS INFO FOR STUDENTS WITH LEARNING DIFFERENCES

Phone: 920-748-8107 • Fax: 920-748-8382

SAT/ACT required: No
Interview required: Yes
Essay required: Yes
Additional application required: No
Documentation submitted to: Student Support Services

Special Ed. HS course work accepted: Yes
Separate application required for Programs/Services: No
Documentation required for:
- **LD:** Psychoeducational evaluation
- **ADHD:** Psychoeducational evaluation
- **ASD:** Psychoeducational evaluation

Ripon College

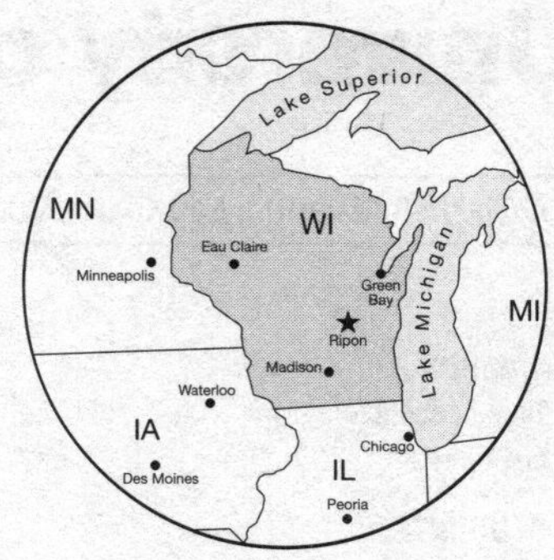

General Admissions

Very important factors include: rigor of secondary school record, interview. *Important factors include:* class rank, academic GPA, extracurricular activities, character/personal qualities. *Other factors include:* application essay, standardized test scores, recommendation(s), talent/ability, volunteer work. *Freshman admission requirements:* High school diploma is required, and GED is accepted. *Academic units required:* 4 English, 2 math, 2 science, 2 social studies. *Academic units recommended:* 4 math, 4 science, 2 foreign language, 4 social studies.

Accommodations or Services

Accommodations are decided upon an individual basis after a thorough review of appropriate, current documentation. The accommodations requests must be supported through the documentation provided and must be logically linked to the current impact of the condition on academic functioning.

Financial Aid

Students should submit: FAFSA. *Need-based scholarships/grants offered:* College/university scholarship or grant aid from institutional funds; Federal Pell; Private scholarships; SEOG; State scholarships/grants. *Loan aid offered:* Direct PLUS loans; Direct Subsidized Stafford Loans; Direct Unsubsidized Stafford Loans. Federal Work-Study Program available. Institutional employment available.

Campus Life

Activities: Campus Ministries; Choral groups; Concert band; Dance; Drama/theater; International Student Organization; Jazz band; Literary magazine; Music ensembles; Musical theater; Pep band; Radio station; Student government; Student newspaper; Student-run film society; Symphony orchestra; Television station; Yearbook. **Organizations:** 45 registered organizations, 13 honor societies, 4 religious organizations, 5 fraternities, 3 sororities. **Athletics (Intercollegiate):** *Men:* baseball, basketball, cross-country, cycling, football, golf, soccer, swimming, tennis, track/field (outdoor), track/field (indoor). *Women:* basketball, cross-country, cycling, golf, soccer, softball, swimming, tennis, track/field (outdoor), track/field (indoor), volleyball.

ACCOMMODATIONS

Allowed in exams:	
Calculators	Yes
Dictionary	Yes
Computer	Yes
Spell-checker	Yes
Extended test time	Yes
Scribe	Yes
Proctors	Yes
Oral exams	Yes
Note-takers	Yes
Support services for students with:	
LD	Yes
ADHD	Yes
ASD	Yes
Distraction-reduced environment	Yes
Recording of lecture allowed	Yes
Reading technology	Yes
Audio books	Yes
Other assistive technology	Yes
Priority registration	No
Added costs of services:	
For LD	No
For ADHD	No
For ASD	No
LD specialists	No
ADHD & ASD coaching	No
ASD specialists	No
Professional tutors	No
Peer tutors	Yes
Max. hours/week for services	3hrs/week/class
How professors are notified of student approved accommodations	Student and Director

COLLEGE GRADUATION REQUIREMENTS

Course waivers allowed	No
Course substitutions allowed	No

University of Wisconsin—Eau Claire

105 Garfield Avenue, Eau Claire, WI 54701 • Admissions: 715-836-5415 • Fax: 715-831-4799 **Support: CS**

CAMPUS	
Type of school	Public
Environment	City
STUDENTS	
Undergrad enrollment	9,993
% male/female	38/62
% from out of state	31
% frosh live on campus	94
FINANCIAL FACTS	
Annual in-state tuition	$7,361
Annual out-of-state tuition	$15,637
Room and board	$8,216
Required fees	$1,479
GENERAL ADMISSIONS INFO	
Application fee	$50
Regular application deadline	8/2
Nonfall registration	Yes
Range SAT EBRW	510–650
Range SAT Math	540–660
Range ACT Composite	21–26
ACADEMICS	
Student/faculty ratio	22:1
% students returning for sophomore year	82
Most classes have 20–29 students.	

Programs/Services for Students with Learning Differences

The University offers a number of avenues to receive support. There is an Academic Skill Center through which students can receive supplemental instructions and tutoring. The Student Success Program, for example, is an academic program that provides small classes to first year students. These students entered the university because they demonstrated potential for learning and need extra support to transition. This program also offers a course in study skills strategies, course tutoring, as needed, through the first two years, and an academic coach for one-on-one guidance throughout the year.

Admissions

There is no alternative admissions for students with learning differences unless they request an exception to the admission requirements. Students applying with exception must submit a letter and application to the Services for Students with Disabilities office. They must include all updated documentation establishing both the existence of a disability and a resulting need for the exception being requested. The average GPA is 3.4, middle 50% ACT is 22–27 (SAT equivalent) and average class rank is 74% if reported. Course requirements include 4 year English, 3 years math, 3 years social science, 3 years natural science, 4 years additional college prep courses or art, music, speech, or computer science. Grade trend is considered as well as rigor in courses and senior year courses.

Additional Information

The writing workshop provides a place for reflective writing and how to use it to explore thoughts, feelings, and experiences. Common accommodations include extended time, readers, and scribes for testing, plus note takers, assistive technology, and tutoring. Students also have access to a wide variety of student service centers and units across campus.

ADMISSIONS INFO FOR STUDENTS WITH LEARNING DIFFERENCES

Phone: 715-836-5800 • Fax: 715-831-2651 • Email: ssd@uwec.edu

SAT/ACT required: No
Interview required: No
Essay required: No
Additional application required: Yes
Documentation submitted to: SSD

Special Ed. HS course work accepted: Yes
Separate application required for Programs/Services: Yes
Documentation required for:
LD: Psychoeducational evaluation
ADHD: Psychoeducational evaluation
ASD: Psychoeducational evaluation

University of Wisconsin— Eau Claire

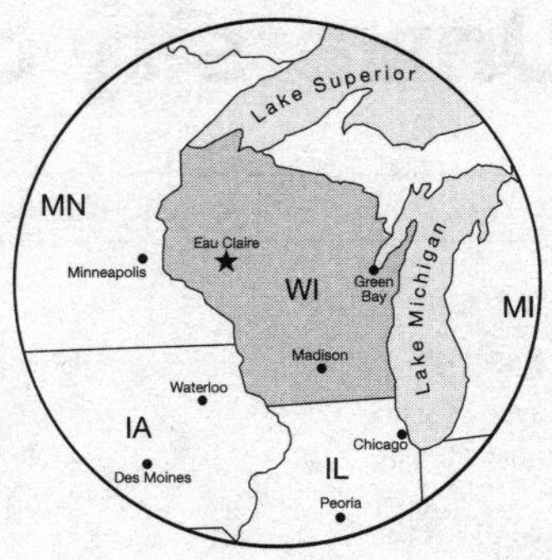

General Admissions

Very important factors include: rigor of secondary school record, class rank, academic GPA, standardized test scores. *Important factors include:* application essay, *Other factors include:* recommendation(s), interview, extracurricular activities, talent/ability, character/personal qualities, first generation, geographical residence, state residency, racial/ethnic status, volunteer work, work experience, level of applicant's interest. *Freshman admission requirements:* High school diploma is required, and GED is accepted. *Academic units required:* 4 English, 3 math, 3 science, 3 social studies, 4 academic electives. *Academic units recommended:* 4 English, 4 math, 4 science, 4 social studies.

Accommodations or Services

Accommodations are decided upon an individual basis after a thorough review of appropriate, current documentation. The accommodations requests, provided to the Services for Students with Disabilities program, must be supported through the documentation provided and must be logically linked to the current impact of the condition on academic functioning.

Financial Aid

Students should submit: FAFSA. *Need-based scholarships/grants offered:* College/university scholarship or grant aid from institutional funds; Federal Pell; Private scholarships; SEOG; State scholarships/grants. *Loan aid offered:* Direct PLUS loans; Direct Subsidized Stafford Loans; Direct Unsubsidized Stafford Loans. Federal Work-Study Program available. Institutional employment available.

Campus Life

Activities: Campus Ministries; Choral groups; Concert band; Dance; Drama/theater; International Student Organization; Jazz band; Literary magazine; Marching band; Model UN; Music ensembles; Musical theater; Opera; Pep band; Radio station; Student government; Student newspaper; Student-run film society; Symphony orchestra; Television station. **Organizations:** 230 registered organizations, 17 honor societies, 10 religious organizations, 3 fraternities, 3 sororities. **Athletics (Intercollegiate):** *Men:* basketball, cross-country, diving, football, golf, ice hockey, swimming, tennis, track/field (outdoor), track/field (indoor), wrestling. *Women:* basketball, cross-country, diving, golf, gymnastics, ice hockey, soccer, softball, swimming, tennis, track/field (outdoor), track/field (indoor), volleyball.

ACCOMMODATIONS

Allowed in exams:	
Calculators	Yes
Dictionary	Yes
Computer	Yes
Spell-checker	Yes
Extended test time	Yes
Scribe	Yes
Proctors	Yes
Oral exams	Yes
Note-takers	Yes
Support services for students with:	
LD	Yes
ADHD	Yes
ASD	Yes
Distraction-reduced environment	Yes
Recording of lecture allowed	Yes
Reading technology	Yes
Audio books	Yes
Other assistive technology	Yes
Priority registration	Yes
Added costs of services:	
For LD	No
For ADHD	No
For ASD	No
LD specialists	Yes
ADHD & ASD coaching	Yes
ASD specialists	Yes
Professional tutors	Yes
Peer tutors	Yes
Max. hours/week for services	Varies
How professors are notified of student approved accommodations	Student

COLLEGE GRADUATION REQUIREMENTS

Course waivers allowed	No
Course substitutions allowed	Yes
In what courses: Case by case basis	

University of Wisconsin—Madison

702 West Johnson Street, Suite 101, Madison, WI 53715–1007 • Admissions: 608-262-3961 • Fax: 608-262-7706 **Support: CS**

CAMPUS

Type of school	Public
Environment	City

STUDENTS

Undergrad enrollment	31,185
% male/female	48/52
% from out of state	38
% frosh live on campus	92

FINANCIAL FACTS

Annual in-state tuition	$10,746
Annual out-of-state tuition	$38,634
Room and board	$12,200

GENERAL ADMISSIONS INFO

Application fee	$60
Regular application deadline	2/1
Nonfall registration	Yes

Admission may be deferred.

Range SAT EBRW	630–710
Range SAT Math	680–780
Range ACT Composite	27–32

ACADEMICS

Student/faculty ratio	17:1
% students returning for sophomore year	95

Most classes have 10–19 students.

Programs/Services for Students with Learning Differences

The McBurney Disability Resource Center provides students with disabilities equal access to the programs and activities of the University. Students with disabilities who tend to do well have graduated from competitive high school or college programs and are reasonably independent, proactive in seeking assistance, and use accommodations similar to those offered here. Students are provided support in a variety of areas depending on their documentation. The center works collaboratively with students and instructors to support necessary accommodations.

Admissions

The admission review process is the same for all applicants. Factors in the review process may include self-disclosed disability information in the written statement, grades, rank, test scores, course requirements completed, and potential for success. Disclosure of disability will not have a negative effect on a student's admission application. If a student wishes to disclose a disability they may do so in the "additional statement" on the application. Suggested information to include is the date of diagnosis or the onset of the disability, and the ramifications of the disability on course requirements, attendance, and academic performance. This information will be considered during the admission review by trained admission counselors. Any documentation about the disability should be submitted to the McBurney Disability Resource Center.

Additional Information

The McBurney Orientation and Service Training (MOST) Program helps new freshmen and their parents get the MOST out of their transition to UW—Madison. Topics covered in the MOST program include how to use approved classroom accommodations, understanding faculty expectations and perspectives, navigating campus resources, and implementing accommodations. Alternative testing accommodations provide access to course tests, mid-terms, quizzes, final exams, and other assessments. Most common alternative testing accommodations are provided within the departments. Students should discuss and arrange their test accommodations with faculty as early as possible.

ADMISSIONS INFO FOR STUDENTS WITH LEARNING DIFFERENCES

Phone: 608-263-2741 • Fax: 608-265-2998 • Email: mcburney@studentlife.wisc.edu

SAT/ACT required: Yes (Test optional through 2023)
Interview required: No
Essay required: Yes
Additional application required: No
Documentation submitted to: McBurney Disability Resource Center

Special Ed. HS course work accepted: No
Separate application required for Programs/Services: No
Documentation required for:
LD: Psychoeducational evaluation
ADHD: Psychoeducational evaluation
ASD: Psychoeducational evaluation

University of Wisconsin—Madison

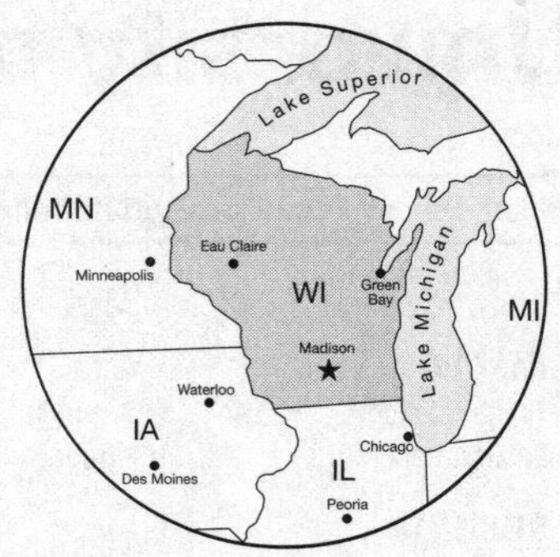

General Admissions

Very important factors include: rigor of secondary school record, application essay. *Important factors include:* academic GPA, standardized test scores, state residency. *Other factors include:* class rank, recommendation(s), extracurricular activities, talent/ability, character/personal qualities, first generation, racial/ethnic status, volunteer work, work experience, level of applicant's interest. *Freshman admission requirements:* High school diploma is required, and GED is accepted. *Academic units required:* 4 English, 4 math, 3 science, 3 foreign language, 3 social studies, 2 unit from above areas or other academic areas. *Academic units recommended:* 4 English, 4 math, 4 science, 2 science labs, 4 foreign language, 4 social studies, 2 unit from above areas or other academic areas.

Accommodations or Services

Accommodations are decided upon an individual basis after a thorough review of appropriate, current documentation. The accommodations requests must be supported through the documentation provided and must be logically linked to the current impact of the condition on academic functioning.

Financial Aid

Students should submit: FAFSA. Applicants will be notified of awards on a rolling basis beginning 1/30. *Need-based scholarships/grants offered:* College/university scholarship or grant aid from institutional funds; Federal Pell; Private scholarships; SEOG; State scholarships/grants. *Loan aid offered:* Direct PLUS loans; Direct Subsidized Stafford Loans; Direct Unsubsidized Stafford Loans. Federal Work-Study Program available. Institutional employment available.

Campus Life

Activities: Choral groups; Concert band; Dance; Drama/theater; International Student Organization; Jazz band; Literary magazine; Marching band; Music ensembles; Musical theater; Opera; Pep band; Radio station; Student government; Student newspaper; Student-run film society; Symphony orchestra; Television station; Yearbook. **Organizations:** 986 registered organizations, 27 honor societies, 26 fraternities, 11 sororities. **Athletics (Intercollegiate):** *Men:* basketball, cheerleading, crew/rowing, cross-country, football, golf, ice hockey, soccer, swimming, tennis, track/field (outdoor), wrestling. *Women:* basketball, cheerleading, crew/rowing, cross-country, golf, ice hockey, soccer, softball, swimming, tennis, track/field (outdoor), volleyball.

ACCOMMODATIONS

Allowed in exams:	
Calculators	Yes
Dictionary	Yes
Computer	Yes
Spell-checker	Yes
Extended test time	Yes
Scribe	Yes
Proctors	No
Oral exams	Yes
Note-takers	Yes
Support services for students with:	
LD	Yes
ADHD	Yes
ASD	Yes
Distraction-reduced environment	Yes
Recording of lecture allowed	Yes
Reading technology	Yes
Audio books	Yes
Other assistive technology	Yes
Priority registration	Yes
Added costs of services:	
For LD	No
For ADHD	No
For ASD	No
LD specialists	Yes
ADHD & ASD coaching	No
ASD specialists	Yes
Professional tutors	No
Peer tutors	Yes
Max. hours/week for services	5
How professors are notified of student approved accommodations	Student

COLLEGE GRADUATION REQUIREMENTS

Course waivers allowed	No
Course substitutions allowed	No

Wisconsin

University of Wisconsin—Milwaukee

Department of Admissions and Recruitment, Milwaukee, WI 53211 • Admissions: 414-229-2222 • Fax: 414-229-6940 **Support: CS**

CAMPUS

Type of school	Public
Environment	Metropolis

STUDENTS

Undergrad enrollment	21,107
% male/female	47/53
% from out of state	12
% frosh live on campus	60

FINANCIAL FACTS

Annual in-state tuition	$9,598
Annual out-of-state tuition	$21,168
Room and board	$10,635

GENERAL ADMISSIONS INFO

Application fee	$50
Regular application deadline	Rolling
Nonfall registration	Yes

Admission may be deferred.

Range ACT Composite	19–24

ACADEMICS

Student/faculty ratio	19:1
% students returning for sophomore year	76

Most classes have 20–29 students.

Programs/Services for Students with Learning Differences

The Accessibility Resource Center (ARC) offers a wide range of academic support services to students with learning disabilities, attention deficit hyperactivity disorders, Autism Spectrum Disorder and traumatic brain injuries. There is no waiting list or caps on participation. This program is well suited for students who are fairly independent and willing to seek the support services they need. Recommended academic accommodations are based on documentation of disability and disability-related needs. The accommodations may include but are not limited to: note-taking assistance, exam accommodations, alternate format textbooks, and priority registration. In addition to academic accommodations, staff is available to meet individually with students to work on study strategies, time-management issues, and organization.

Admissions

Admission into UWM is necessary for participation. The Accessibility Resource Center does not make admission decisions. Although most admitted students have an extremely strong academic record, the university also admits students with a wide range of academic preparation. The admission committee considers academic preparation, evidenced by the pattern and rigor high school coursework, class rank (if available), overall GPA, and grades in specific courses related to an intended major at UWM. Courses required include 4 years English, 3 years math, 3 natural science, 3 social science/history, 2 electives in college prep courses, and 2 electives. Foreign language is not required for admission to UWM but taking at least two years of a foreign language in high school will speed the path to graduation. To graduate from UWM, a student must complete a foreign language requirement that differs depending on the degree. UWM is test optional and does not require the ACT or SAT for admissions.

Additional Information

Students who meet eligibility criteria receive individual counseling and guidance. In addition, students may be eligible for academic accommodations based upon specific disability-related needs. There is a social group for students on the autism spectrum called Autism Group, in which students meet twice a month and have the opportunity to engage in informal conversations, activities, and events decided on by the members. Additionally, there is a Computer & Assistive Technology Lab where students who have had an initial screening for the need for assistive technology

ADMISSIONS INFO FOR STUDENTS WITH LEARNING DIFFERENCES

Phone: 414-229-6287 • Fax: 414 229-2237 • Email: archelp@uwm.edu

SAT/ACT required: Yes (Test optional for 2021)
Interview required: No
Essay required: No
Additional application required: No
Documentation submitted to: Accessibility Resource Center

Special Ed. HS course work accepted: No
Separate application required for Programs/Services: Yes
Documentation required for:
LD: Psychoeducational evaluation
ADHD: Psychoeducational evaluation
ASD: Psychoeducational evaluation

University of Wisconsin—Milwaukee

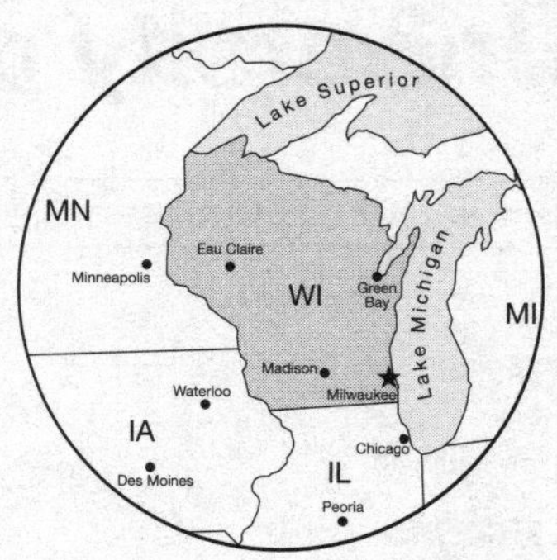

are able to access resources as needed. Specific, individualized recommendations for each student are evaluated. Eligible students will have portable, flexible access to technology. Assistive Technology is based on student need and there is training in the use of Assistive Technology.

General Admissions

Very important factors include: rigor of secondary school record, academic GPA, standardized test scores. *Important factors include:* application essay, *Other factors include:* class rank, recommendation(s), interview, extracurricular activities, talent/ability, character/personal qualities, first generation, racial/ethnic status, volunteer work, work experience. *Freshman admission requirements:* High school diploma is required, and GED is accepted. *Academic units required:* 4 English, 3 math, 3 science, 1 science lab, 3 social studies, 4 academic electives. *Academic units recommended:* 4 English, 4 math, 4 science, 1 science lab, 2 foreign language, 4 social studies, 4 academic electives.

Accommodations or Services

Accommodations are decided upon an individual basis after a thorough review of appropriate, current documentation. The accommodations requests must be supported through the documentation provided and must be logically linked to the current impact of the condition on academic functioning.

Financial Aid

Students should submit: FAFSA. *Need-based scholarships/grants offered:* College/university scholarship or grant aid from institutional funds; Federal Pell; Private scholarships; SEOG; State scholarships/grants. *Loan aid offered:* Direct PLUS loans; Direct Subsidized Stafford Loans; Direct Unsubsidized Stafford Loans. Federal Work-Study Program available. Institutional employment available.

Campus Life

Activities: Campus Ministries; Choral groups; Concert band; Dance; Drama/theater; International Student Organization; Jazz band; Literary magazine; Model UN; Music ensembles; Musical theater; Opera; Pep band; Radio station; Student government; Student newspaper; Student-run film society; Symphony orchestra. **Organizations:** 296 registered organizations, 4 honor societies, 18 religious organizations, 10 fraternities, 7 sororities. **Athletics (Intercollegiate):** *Men:* baseball, basketball, cross-country, diving, soccer, swimming, track/field (outdoor). *Women:* basketball, cross-country, soccer, swimming, tennis, track/field (outdoor), volleyball.

ACCOMMODATIONS

Allowed in exams:	
Calculators	No
Dictionary	Yes
Computer	Yes
Spell-checker	Yes
Extended test time	Yes
Scribe	Yes
Proctors	Yes
Oral exams	Yes
Note-takers	Yes
Support services for students with:	
LD	Yes
ADHD	Yes
ASD	Yes
Distraction-reduced environment	Yes
Recording of lecture allowed	Yes
Reading technology	Yes
Audio books	Yes
Other assistive technology	Yes
Priority registration	Yes
Added costs of services:	
For LD	No
For ADHD	No
For ASD	No
LD specialists	Yes
ADHD & ASD coaching	No
ASD specialists	No
Professional tutors	No
Peer tutors	Yes
Max. hours/week for services	3
How professors are notified of student approved accommodations	Student

COLLEGE GRADUATION REQUIREMENTS

Course waivers allowed	No
Course substitutions allowed	Yes
In what courses: Case by case basis	

Wisconsin

University of Wisconsin—Oshkosh

Dempsey Hall 135, Oshkosh, WI 54901 • Admissions: 920-424-0202 • Fax: 920-424-1098 **Support: SP**

CAMPUS

Type of school	Public
Environment	City

STUDENTS

Undergrad enrollment	12,540
% male/female	39/61
% from out of state	9
% frosh live on campus	83

FINANCIAL FACTS

Annual in-state tuition	$6,298
Annual out-of-state tuition	$13,872
Room and board	$8,506
Required fees	$1,396

GENERAL ADMISSIONS INFO

Application fee	$50
Regular application deadline	Rolling
Nonfall registration	Yes

Admission may be deferred.

Range ACT Composite	19–24

ACADEMICS

Student/faculty ratio	22:1
% students returning for sophomore year	73

Most classes have 20–29 students.

Programs/Services for Students with Learning Differences

Project Success is a language remediation project that is based on mastering the entire sound structure of the English language. These students are academically able and determined to succeed, in spite of a pronounced problem in a number of areas. Help is offered in the following ways: direct remediation of deficiencies through the Orton-Gillingham Technique, one-on-one tutoring assistance, math and writing labs, guidance and counseling with scheduling course work and interpersonal relations, extended time, and by providing an atmosphere that is supportive. The goal is for students to become language independent in and across all of these major educational areas: math, spelling, reading, writing, comprehension, and study skills. Students are assigned a case manager, also called an organizational tutor, who meets with the student on a weekly basis or more often if deemed necessary.

Admissions

Students may apply to Project Success in their junior year of high school. Applicants apply by writing a letter, in their own handwriting, indicating interest in the program and why they are interested. Applications are processed on a first-come, first-served basis. Those interested should apply at least 1 to 2 years prior to the student's desired entrance semester. Students and parents will be invited to interview. The interview is used to assess family dynamics in terms of support for the student and reasons for wanting to attend college. The director is looking for motivation, stability, and the ability of the students to describe the disability. Acceptance into Project Success does not grant acceptance into the university. Admission to the university and acceptance into Project Success is a joint decision, but a separate process is required for each. General admissions procedures must be followed before acceptance into Project Success can be offered.

Additional Information

Incoming freshmen to Project Success must participate in an 6-week summer school program consisting of simultaneous multisensory instructional procedures (SMSIP). This is considered a transitional opportunity to gradually support the new student entering college, and is mandatory for students who are not in "full standing." This summer option includes college credit in general education requirements. The Project Success program offers the following remedial and support services for all students enrolled in its program: organizational tutors, mathematics courses/tutoring,

ADMISSIONS INFO FOR STUDENTS WITH LEARNING DIFFERENCES

Phone: 920-424-3100 • Fax: 920-424-0858 • Email: projectsuccess@uwosh.edu

SAT/ACT required: Yes (Test optional for 2021)
Interview required: No
Essay required: No
Additional application required: Yes
Documentation submitted to: Project Success

Special Ed. HS course work accepted: Yes
Separate application required for Programs/Services: No
Documentation required for:
LD: Psychoeducational evaluation
ADHD: Psychoeducational evaluation
ASD: Psychoeducational evaluation

University of Wisconsin—Oshkosh

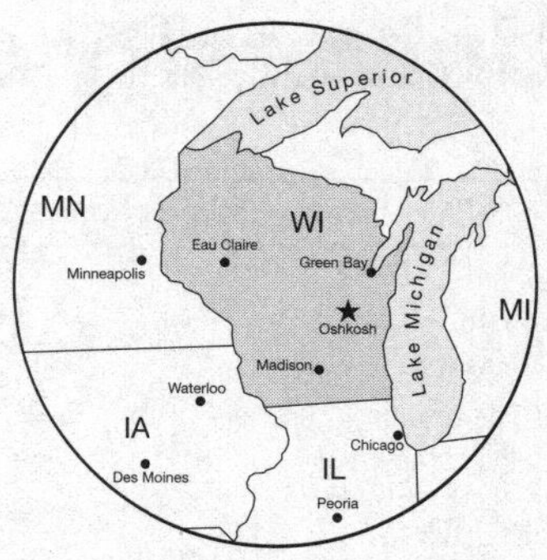

remedial reading and spelling courses, English/written expression courses/tutoring, and content area tutoring. Additionally, students are eligible for extended-time testing opportunities. Services and accommodations are available for undergraduate and graduate students.

General Admissions

Very important factors include: rigor of secondary school record, class rank, academic GPA, standardized test scores. *Important factors include:* application essay, recommendation(s), first generation. *Other factors include:* interview, extracurricular activities, talent/ability, character/personal qualities, alumni/ae relation, volunteer work, work experience. *Freshman admission requirements:* High school diploma is required, and GED is accepted. *Academic units required:* 4 English, 3 math, 3 science, 3 science labs, 3 social studies, 2 history, 4 academic electives. *Academic units recommended:* 4 math, 4 science, 4 science labs, 2 foreign language, 4 social studies, 1 history, 1 visual/performing arts.

Accommodations or Services

Accommodations are decided upon an individual basis after a thorough review of appropriate, current documentation. The accommodations requests must be supported through the documentation provided and must be logically linked to the current impact of the condition on academic functioning.

Financial Aid

Students should submit: FAFSA; State aid form. *Need-based scholarships/grants offered:* College/university scholarship or grant aid from institutional funds; Federal Nursing Scholarships; Federal Pell; Private scholarships; SEOG; State scholarships/grants; United Negro College Fund. *Loan aid offered:* Direct PLUS loans; Direct Subsidized Stafford Loans; Direct Unsubsidized Stafford Loans. Federal Work-Study Program available. Institutional employment available.

Campus Life

Activities: Campus Ministries; Choral groups; Concert band; Dance; Drama/theater; International Student Organization; Jazz band; Literary magazine; Model UN; Music ensembles; Musical theater; Pep band; Radio station; Student government; Student newspaper; Student-run film society; Television station. **Organizations:** 175 registered organizations, 15 honor societies, 6 religious organizations, 8 fraternities, 5 sororities. **Athletics (Intercollegiate):** *Men:* baseball, basketball, cross-country, diving, football, soccer, swimming, tennis, track/field (outdoor), track/field (indoor), wrestling. *Women:* basketball, cross-country, diving, golf, gymnastics, soccer, softball, swimming, tennis, track/field (outdoor), track/field (indoor), volleyball.

ACCOMMODATIONS

Allowed in exams:	
Calculators	Yes
Dictionary	Yes
Computer	Yes
Spell-checker	No
Extended test time	Yes
Scribe	No
Proctors	Yes
Oral exams	No
Note-takers	Yes
Support services for students with:	
LD	Yes
ADHD	Yes
ASD	Yes
Distraction-reduced environment	Yes
Recording of lecture allowed	Yes
Reading technology	Yes
Audio books	Yes
Other assistive technology	Yes
Priority registration	Yes
Added costs of services:	
For LD	No
For ADHD	No
For ASD	No
LD specialists	Yes
ADHD & ASD coaching	No
ASD specialists	No
Professional tutors	Yes
Peer tutors	Yes
Max. hours/week for services	Varies
How professors are notified of student approved accommodations	Student and director

COLLEGE GRADUATION REQUIREMENTS

Course waivers allowed: Yes
In what courses: UW—Oshkosh has special accommodations in place relating to the foreign language requirement.

Course substitutions allowed: Yes
In what courses: UW—Oshkosh has special accommodations in place relating to the foreign language requirement.

University of Wisconsin—Stevens Point

1108 Fremont St., Stevens Point, WI 54481 • Admissions: 715-346-2441 • Fax: 715-346-3296 **Support: S**

CAMPUS

Type of school	Public
Environment	Town

STUDENTS

Undergrad enrollment	7,763
% male/female	45/55
% from out of state	11
% frosh live on campus	72

FINANCIAL FACTS

Annual in-state tuition	$6,698
Annual out-of-state tuition	$15,402
Room and board	$7,630
Required fees	$1,603

GENERAL ADMISSIONS INFO

Application fee	$25
Regular application deadline	9/1
Nonfall registration	Yes

Admission may be deferred.

Range SAT EBRW	500–600
Range SAT Math	540–640
Range ACT Composite	19–24

ACADEMICS

Student/faculty ratio	19:1
% students returning for sophomore year	73

Most classes have 20–29 students.

Programs/Services for Students with Learning Differences

The Disability & Assistive Technology Center (DATC) at the University of Wisconsin-Stevens Point is comprised of the Disability Services and Assistive Technology programs. The DATC provides accessibility, accommodation, and assistive technology services to students with disabilities, working individually with qualified students to identify, design, and implement an accommodation plan that will aid them in acquiring equal access to their education. The DATC aims to create a learning environment that will help maximize opportunities for our students to succeed. Students develop a good rapport with staff.

Admissions

There is no separate admission procedure for students with learning disabilities. However, students are encouraged to make a pre-admission inquiry and talk to the director of DATC. The university does not require letters of recommendation. However, if an academic record is not strong or has extenuating circumstances that should be considered, applicants are welcome to submit letters of recommendation for review. Students interested in the BA Dance, BA Drama, BFA Musical Theatre, BFA Acting, and BFA Design Technology programs and Music are required to complete an on-campus performance audition and/or interview. The university is test optional, so ACT or SAT scores are not required to be admitted.

Additional Information

Through DATC students can access classroom accommodations including recorded lectures, copies of PowerPoint slides, proctored exams, extended time, a reader, scribe, and a computer for test taking. Leading Edge is an opportunity for new freshmen and transfer students with disabilities to learn about accommodations and academic support services at UWSP. The program provides students with a smoother transition to college by having accommodations in place prior to the start of classes. Leading Edge students can move into the residence hall in advance and get an opportunity to have an individual intake meeting or documentation review with a DATC advisor. They also have access to assistive technology demonstrations and instruction on how to use the portal to request accommodations and exams.

ADMISSIONS INFO FOR STUDENTS WITH LEARNING DIFFERENCES

Phone: 715 346-3365 • Fax: 715-346-4143 • Email: datctr@uwsp.edu

SAT/ACT required: No
Interview required: No
Essay required: No
Additional application required: No
Documentation submitted to: DATC

Special Ed. HS course work accepted: No
Separate application required for Programs/Services: Yes
Documentation required for:
LD: Psychoeducational evaluation
ADHD: Psychoeducational evaluation
ASD: Psychoeducational evaluation

University of Wisconsin—Stevens Point

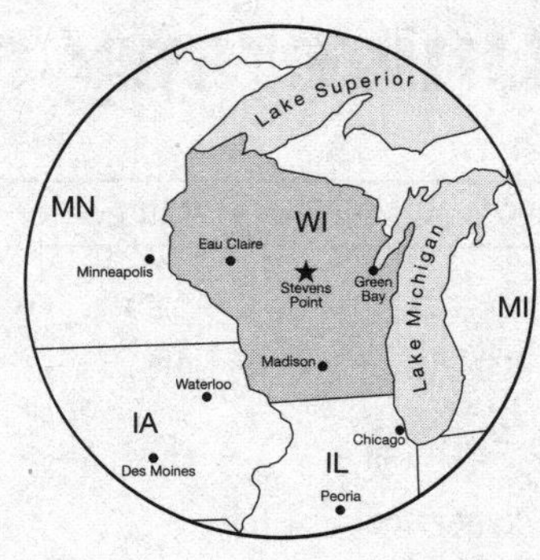

General Admissions

Very important factors include: rigor of secondary school record, class rank, academic GPA, standardized test scores. *Important factors include:* application essay, recommendation(s), talent/ability, first generation. *Other factors include:* interview, extracurricular activities, character/personal qualities, alumni/ae relation, geographical residence, state residency, racial/ethnic status, volunteer work, work experience. *Freshman admission requirements:* High school diploma is required, and GED is accepted. *Academic units required:* 4 English, 3 math, 3 science, 3 social studies, 4 academic electives. *Academic units recommended:* 4 English, 4 math, 4 science, 4 social studies, 4 academic electives.

Accommodations or Services

Accommodations are decided upon an individual basis after a thorough review of appropriate, current documentation. The accommodations requests must be supported through the documentation provided and must be logically linked to the current impact of the condition on academic functioning.

Financial Aid

Students should submit: FAFSA. *Need-based scholarships/grants offered:* College/university scholarship or grant aid from institutional funds; Federal Pell; Private scholarships; SEOG; State scholarships/grants. *Loan aid offered:* Direct PLUS loans; Direct Subsidized Stafford Loans; Direct Unsubsidized Stafford Loans. Federal Work-Study Program available. Institutional employment available.

Campus Life

Activities: Campus Ministries; Choral groups; Dance; Drama/theater; International Student Organization; Jazz band; Model UN; Music ensembles; Musical theater; Opera; Pep band; Radio station; Student government; Student newspaper; Student-run film society; Symphony orchestra; Television station. **Organizations:** 185 registered organizations, 11 honor societies, 10 religious organizations, 5 fraternities, 3 sororities. **Athletics (Intercollegiate):** *Men:* baseball, basketball, cross-country, diving, football, ice hockey, swimming, track/field (outdoor), wrestling. *Women:* basketball, cross-country, diving, golf, ice hockey, soccer, softball, swimming, tennis, track/field (outdoor), volleyball.

ACCOMMODATIONS

Allowed in exams:	
Calculators	Yes
Dictionary	No
Computer	Yes
Spell-checker	Yes
Extended test time	Yes
Scribe	Yes
Proctors	Yes
Oral exams	No
Note-takers	Yes
Support services for students with:	
LD	Yes
ADHD	Yes
ASD	Yes
Distraction-reduced environment	Yes
Recording of lecture allowed	Yes
Reading technology	Yes
Audio books	Yes
Other assistive technology	Yes
Priority registration	Yes
Added costs of services:	
For LD	No
For ADHD	No
For ASD	No
LD specialists	No
ADHD & ASD coaching	No
ASD specialists	No
Professional tutors	No
Peer tutors	Yes
Max. hours/week for services	Varies
How professors are notified of student approved accommodations	Student

COLLEGE GRADUATION REQUIREMENTS

Course waivers allowed	No
Course substitutions allowed	Yes
In what courses: Case by case basis	

Wisconsin

University of Wisconsin—Whitewater

800 West Main Street, Whitewater, WI 53190-1791 • Admissions: 262-472-1440 • Fax: 262-472-1515 **Support: SP**

CAMPUS

Type of school	Public
Environment	Village

STUDENTS

Undergrad enrollment	11,020
% male/female	51/49
% from out of state	16
% frosh live on campus	97

FINANCIAL FACTS

Annual in-state tuition	$7,726
Annual out-of-state tuition	$16,536
Room and board	$7,650

GENERAL ADMISSIONS INFO

Application fee	$50
Regular application deadline	8/1
Nonfall registration	Yes

Admission may be deferred.

Range SAT EBRW	490–600
Range SAT Math	490–590
Range ACT Composite	19–24

ACADEMICS

Student/faculty ratio	19:1
% students returning for sophomore year	80

Most classes have 30–39 students.

Programs/Services for Students with Learning Differences

The University of Wisconsin—Whitewater Center for Students with Disabilities, Project ASSIST program offers support services for students with learning disabilities and ADD/ADHD. This Program is fee-based depending on the level of support required for tutoring and other accommodations. This is an academic driven program with the goal to strengthen students time management, organization, and problem solving skills. The student requests the support each semester. The Project ASSIST Summer Transition Program is a four-week program in which students enroll in a three-credit study skills class, one credit New Student Seminar and non-credit Project ASSIST class. Areas addressed include learning strategies, comprehension concerns, written language skills, study habits, time management, and self-advocacy skills. The philosophy of the program is that students with learning disabilities can learn strategies to become independent learners.

Admissions

All applicants must meet the same criteria for general admission. Students should apply to both the university and Project Assist in the Center for Students with Disabilities. Program staff review the documentation and application regarding eligibility for academic accommodations and Project ASSIST. Programs of Opportunity and Conditional Admissions offers admission to a limited number of students depending on review of documentation and reason for admission denial. Students applying to the LIFE program will complete an application. Applications will be screened than the prospective student will be contacted by the program staff with an invitation for a face to face interview or notice that the student is not being considered for admission.

Additional Information

Tutoring services provided by undergraduate and graduate students take place in a one-to-one setting, where students work with tutors on study, math, and written language strategies in the context of specific course work. Computer lab with assistive technology, small group support and academic advising available. In addition, drop-in tutoring is available each weekday and early evening. The University of Wisconsin-Whitewater also offers the LIFE (Learning is for Everyone) program, which provides a complete college experience for young adults between the ages of 18–25 who have an intellectual disability. With ample support, specialized instruction, on-campus residential living, and community integration, the program serves

ADMISSIONS INFO FOR STUDENTS WITH LEARNING DIFFERENCES

Phone: 262-472-4711 Fax: 262-472-4865 Email: csdat@uww.edu

SAT/ACT required: No
Interview required: No
Essay required: Yes
Additional application required: Yes
Documentation submitted to: Center for Students with Disabilities

Special Ed. HS course work accepted: Yes
Separate application required for Programs/Services: No
Documentation required for:
LD: Psychoeducational evaluation
ADHD: Psychoeducational evaluation
ASD: Psychoeducational evaluation

University of Wisconsin—Whitewater

a critical need in the region and community. The program has two components, a Basic Program (2 years) and an Advanced Program (2 years), both of which are designed to facilitate independent living and employment success for persons with significant cognitive limitations.

General Admissions

Very important factors include: rigor of secondary school record, class rank, standardized test scores. *Other factors include:* academic GPA, application essay, recommendation(s), interview, extracurricular activities, talent/ability, character/personal qualities, first generation, geographical residence, state residency, racial/ethnic status, volunteer work, work experience, level of applicant's interest. *Freshman admission requirements:* High school diploma is required, and GED is accepted. *Academic units required:* 4 English, 3 math, 3 science, 1 science lab, 3 social studies, 4 academic electives. *Academic units recommended:* 4 math, 4 science, 2 foreign language, 4 social studies.

Accommodations or Services

Accommodations are decided upon an individual basis after a thorough review of appropriate, current documentation. The accommodations requests must be supported through the documentation provided and must be logically linked to the current impact of the condition on academic functioning.

Financial Aid

Students should submit: FAFSA; Institution's own financial aid form; State aid form. Applicants will be notified of awards on or about 4/15. *Need-based scholarships/grants offered:* College/university scholarship or grant aid from institutional funds; Federal Pell; Private scholarships; SEOG; State scholarships/grants. *Loan aid offered:* Direct PLUS loans; Direct Subsidized Stafford Loans; Direct Unsubsidized Stafford Loans.

Campus Life

Activities: Choral groups; Concert band; Dance; Drama/theater; Jazz band; Literary magazine; Marching band; Music ensembles; Musical theater; Opera; Radio station; Student government; Student newspaper; Symphony orchestra; Television station. **Organizations:** 130 registered organizations, 4 honor societies, 8 religious organizations, 9 fraternities, 8 sororities. **Athletics (Intercollegiate):** *Men:* baseball, basketball, cross-country, diving, football, soccer, swimming, tennis, track/field (outdoor), track/field (indoor), wrestling. *Women:* basketball, bowling, cross-country, diving, golf, gymnastics, soccer, softball, swimming, tennis, track/field (outdoor), track/field (indoor), volleyball.

ACCOMMODATIONS

Allowed in exams:	
Calculators	Yes
Dictionary	Yes
Computer	Yes
Spell-checker	Yes
Extended test time	Yes
Scribe	Yes
Proctors	Yes
Oral exams	Yes
Note-takers	Yes
Support services for students with:	
LD	Yes
ADHD	Yes
ASD	Yes
Distraction-reduced environment	Yes
Recording of lecture allowed	Yes
Reading technology	Yes
Audio books	Yes
Other assistive technology	Yes
Priority registration	Yes
Added costs of services:	
For LD	No
For ADHD	No
For ASD	No
LD specialists	Yes
ADHD & ASD coaching	No
ASD specialists	No
Professional tutors	Yes
Peer tutors	Yes
Max. hours/week for services	Varies
How professors are notified of student approved accommodations	Student

COLLEGE GRADUATION REQUIREMENTS

Course waivers allowed	No
Course substitutions allowed	Yes
In what courses: Case by case basis	

Wisconsin

University of Wyoming

Dept 3435, Laramie, WY 82071 • Admissions: 307-766-5160 • Fax: 307-766-4042 **Support: CS**

CAMPUS

Type of school	Public
Environment	Town

STUDENTS

Undergrad enrollment	9,807
% male/female	49/51
% from out of state	35
% frosh live on campus	87

FINANCIAL FACTS

Annual in-state tuition	$4,350
Annual out-of-state tuition	$18,090
Room and board	$10,615
Required fees	$1,441

GENERAL ADMISSIONS INFO

Application fee	$40
Regular application deadline	8/10
Nonfall registration	Yes

Admission may be deferred.

Range SAT EBRW	540–640
Range SAT Math	520–640
Range ACT Composite	22–28

ACADEMICS

Student/faculty ratio	15:1
% students returning for sophomore year	76

Most classes have 20–29 students.

Programs/Services for Students with Learning Differences

The University Disability Support Services (UDSS) offers a variety of supports. This Program is within Student Educational Opportunity and the Division of Student Affairs Accommodations are not automatically initiated: they must be requested for each course and each semester for which they are needed. Faculty are not required to provide accommodations without notification from the DSS. Students must self-identify and request accommodations.

Admissions

Students with learning disabilities or ADHD must meet the same admission criteria as other applicants, which include a 3.0 GPA, 21 ACT or 1060 SAT. The Curriculum for Success includes 4 years English, 4 years math, 3 years social science, 4 years science, and 4 years of foreign language courses (one of which must be taken in grades 9–12), -or- fine and performing arts or career vocational education or combinations of these three disciplines (2 years must be in sequenced in the same discipline). However, the University of Wyoming will review applications from students who do not meet the general admission criteria. Admission with Support applicants have a GPA of 2.5–2.9, a minimum ACT 17 or SAT of 920 or have a GPA of 2.3–2.4 and a minimum ACT of 20 or SAT or 1030. Students admitted with support may be asked to participate in UW's Bridge program or other academic transition programs.

Additional Information

The Wyoming Institute for Disabilities (WIND) is an academic unit in the College of Health Sciences and a University Centers for Excellence in Developmental Disabilities (UCEDD). WIND works to assist individuals with developmental disabilities, their families, professionals, and University of Wyoming students through education, training, community services, and early intervention. Note-taking accommodations may include: Sonocent or other lecture recording devices, volunteer note-takers, and access to course materials. Accommodations are similar to those provided students on the Laramie campus, but may be coordinated in a different fashion due to distance factors. Students anticipating the need for disability-related accommodations for online courses should contact and provide documentation of their disability to DSS as early as possible.

ADMISSIONS INFO FOR STUDENTS WITH LEARNING DIFFERENCES

Phone: 307-766-6189 • Fax: 307-766-4010 • Email: obriaman@uwyo.edu

SAT/ACT required: Yes (Test optional for 2021)
Interview required: No
Essay required: No
Additional application required: No
Documentation submitted to: UDS

Special Ed. HS course work accepted: Yes
Separate application required for Programs/Services: No
Documentation required for:
LD: Psychoeducational evaluation
ADHD: Psychoeducational evaluation
ASD: Psychoeducational evaluation

University of Wyoming

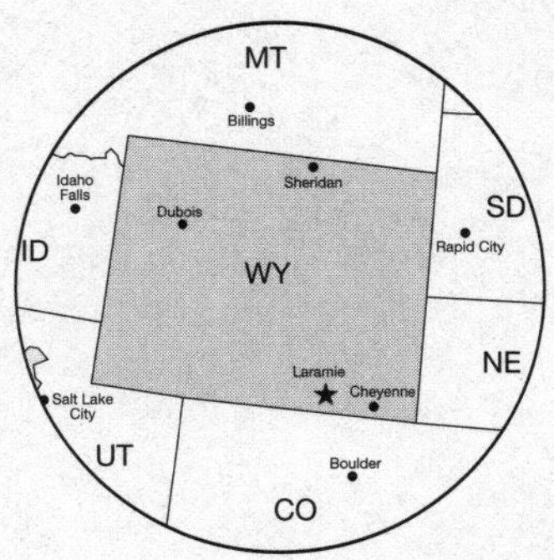

General Admissions

Very important factors include: rigor of secondary school record, academic GPA, standardized test scores. *Other factors include:* application essay. *Freshman admission requirements:* High school diploma is required, and GED is accepted. *Academic units required:* 4 English, 4 math, 4 science, 3 science labs, 2 foreign language, 3 social studies, 2 academic electives, 2 unit from above areas or other academic areas. *Academic units recommended:* 4 English, 4 math, 4 science, 3 science labs, 2 foreign language, 3 social studies, 2 academic electives.

Accommodations or Services

Accommodations are decided upon an individual basis after a thorough review of appropriate, current documentation. The accommodations requests must be supported through the documentation provided and must be logically linked to the current impact of the condition on academic functioning.

Financial Aid

Students should submit: FAFSA. *Need-based scholarships/grants offered:* College/university scholarship or grant aid from institutional funds; Federal Pell; Private scholarships; SEOG; State scholarships/grants. *Loan aid offered:* Direct PLUS loans; Direct Subsidized Stafford Loans; Direct Unsubsidized Stafford Loans. Federal Work-Study Program available. Institutional employment available.

Campus Life

Activities: Campus Ministries; Choral groups; Concert band; Dance; Drama/theater; International Student Organization; Jazz band; Literary magazine; Marching band; Model UN; Music ensembles; Musical theater; Opera; Pep band; Radio station; Student government; Student newspaper; Student-run film society; Symphony orchestra; Television station. **Organizations:** 195 registered organizations, 41 honor societies, 11 religious organizations, 9 fraternities, 5 sororities. **Athletics (Intercollegiate):** *Men:* basketball, cheerleading, cross-country, diving, football, golf, swimming, track/field (outdoor), track/field (indoor), wrestling. *Women:* basketball, cheerleading, cross-country, diving, golf, soccer, swimming, tennis, track/field (outdoor), track/field (indoor), volleyball.

ACCOMMODATIONS

Allowed in exams:	
Calculators	Yes
Dictionary	No
Computer	Yes
Spell-checker	Yes
Extended test time	Yes
Scribe	Yes
Proctors	Yes
Oral exams	No
Note-takers	Yes
Support services for students with:	
LD	Yes
ADHD	Yes
ASD	Yes
Distraction-reduced environment	Yes
Recording of lecture allowed	Yes
Reading technology	Yes
Audio books	Yes
Other assistive technology	Yes
Priority registration	Yes
Added costs of services:	
For LD	No
For ADHD	No
For ASD	No
LD specialists	Yes
ADHD & ASD coaching	No
ASD specialists	No
Professional tutors	No
Peer tutors	Yes
Max. hours/week for services	Varies
How professors are notified of student approved accommodations	Student and Director

COLLEGE GRADUATION REQUIREMENTS

Course waivers allowed	No
Course substitutions allowed	No

Wyoming

Alternative Post-Secondary Options

Program	Overview	Contact Information
Anchor to Windward, Inc.	Structured living experience	Anchor to Windward, Inc. Marblehead, MA Phone: 978-740-0013
The Autism Program at Ancilla College (APAC)	To support highly capable college students on the autism spectrum and to give faculty and staff the resources for providing a supportive campus community. APAC will enhance the quality of campus life and increase the potential for career and/or future academic success.	https://www.ancilla.edu/autism/
Bancroft NeuroHealth	Various therapeutic services for children and adults with autism, and other neurological impairments.	Bancroft Admissions Office Haddonfield, NJ Phone: 856-429-0010
Bellevue College Neurodiversity Navigators	To provide educational opportunities that lead to successful academic outcomes in the areas of executive functioning, self-regulation, social interaction, self-advocacy, and career preparation. The program also offers advocacy and access services for neurodivergent students and actively promotes a campus and community environment of inclusion.	Sara Sanders Gardner Program Director, Adjunct Faculty Phone: 425-564-2172 Email: sara.gardner@bellevuecollege.edu
Berkshire Hills Music Academy	Post-secondary school in which young adults with learning and developmental disabilities live in a college setting while developing musical potential. Two-year certificate program.	Berkshire Hills Music Academy South Hadley, MA Phone: 413-540-9720
Berkshire Center	Two independent living experiences are offered via the College Internship Program and the Aspire Program. Aspire is for those with Asperger's and non-verbal learning differences.	Admissions Director Lee, MA Phone: (877) Know-CIP
Bethesda College program at Concordia in WI program	A two-year program designed to meet the higher education needs of students with intellectual, developmental, and other complex disabilities. These students experience the full range of college learning and life with a blended model of instruction centered on intellectual, vocational, social, personal, and spiritual growth.	Concordia Wisconsin Campus Mequon, WI Phone: 262-243-2183
Casa de Amma	Lifelong residential community for young adults who function independently but require assistance and structure in daily living.	Casa de Amma San Juan Capistrano, CA Phone: 949-496-9901
Castleton University College Steps	College Steps is a nonprofit that provides customized college support for students with learning and social challenges such as learning disabilities, autism, and executive functioning deficits. College Steps supports students to achieve success in post-secondary education, work, and life.	https://www.castleton.edu/academics/college-steps/
Center for Adaptive Learning	A supportive living program for those 18+ with a neurological disability.	Center for Adaptive Learning Concord, CA Phone: 925-827-3863
Chapel Haven	Residential program teaching independent living to young adults.	New Haven, CT Phone: 203-397-1714 Ext 113 or 148
Chapel Haven West	Residential program teaching independent living to young adults.	University of Arizona Tucson, Arizona Phone: 877-824-9378

Program	Overview	Contact Information
College of Charleston REACH Program	A four-year, fully inclusive certificate program for students with mild intellectual and/or developmental disabilities. The program works toward the advancement of knowledge and skill in Academics, Socialization, Independent Living and Career Development.	College of Charleston Charleston, SC 29424 Phone: 843-953-4849
College Excel	Support programs for young adults 18–27 years of age who are ready to begin or continue in college. Program provides college-accredited courses, skill development classes, tutoring, life skills education, and life coaching.	College Excel Bend, OR Phone: 541-388-3043
College Internship Programs	Post-secondary academic, internship and independent living experiences for those ages 18–25 with Asperger's and non-verbal learning differences. Students participate in the College Internship Programs and can also attend classes at local colleges or community colleges.	CIP National Admissions Office Lee, MA admissions@cipworldwide.org Additional branches in Berkley, CA; Long Beach, CA; Melbourne, FL; Bloomington, IA; Lee, MA; and Amherst, NY.
College Living Experience	College program for students with autism spectrum disorders, Asperger's nonverbal learning disorder, ADD/ADHD, and other learning disabilities	National Admissions Columbia MD Phone: 800-486-5058 Additional branches in Costa Mesa, CA; Monterey, CA; Denver, CO; Washington, DC; Fort Lauderdale, FL; Columbia, MD; and Austin, TX.
Drexel Academic and Career Program	Two-year non-degree postsecondary experience for young adults with autism spectrum disorder (ASD). Students will receive a Certificate of Achievement upon program completion from the A.J. Drexel Autism Institute.	A.J. Drexel Autism Institute Philadelphia, PA Phone: 215-571-3401
Edgewood College	Individualized education program that offers inclusion for students with intellectual developmental disabilities.	Edgewood College Madison, WI 53717 Phone: 608-663-2340
Elmhurst Life Skills Academy ELSA	Assistance for students with special needs in completing college and transitioning into independent adults. Locations in Florida, Colorado and Texas.	Elmhurst Life Skills Academy Elmhurst, Illinois Phone: 630-617-3752
Evaluation & Development Center	Center provides services to anyone 16+ who is vocationally handicapped to attain greater productivity and self-sufficiency.	Evaluation & Development Center Carbondale, IL Phone: 618-453-2331
George Mason University Mason Learning into Future Environments (LIFE) Program	A supportive academic university experience that offers a four-year postsecondary curriculum of study to students with intellectual and developmental disabilities (IDD) who begin the program between 18–23 years of age.	Jorgenson, Linn Academic Program Coordinator Phone: 703-993-4171 Fax: 703-993-3681
Gersh College Experience at Daemen College	Post-secondary, undergraduate program for students with neurobiological disorders like Asperger's ADHD, OCD, Tourette's Syndrome, Anxiety or Depression, Autism Spectrum, and Nonverbal Learning disorders.	Mellville NY Phone: 631-385-3342
The Horizons School	Non-degree program focused on life and social skills and career development for young adults with learning disabilities.	The Horizons School Birmingham, AL Phone: 800-822- 6242
Independence Center	Transitional residential program for young adults 18–30.	Independence Center Los Angeles, CA Phone: 310-202-7102

Program	Overview	Contact Information
Kent State University Career and Community Studies	A program that creates meaningful experiences for students with intellectual and developmental disabilities by maximizing their opportunities to become self-determined and autonomous adults.	Career & Community Studies, Phone: 330-672-0725
Lesley University	A comprehensive two year non-degree, campus-based program for highly motivated young adults with diverse learning disabilities and other special needs.	Lesley University Cambridge, MA Phone: 617-868-9600
Life Development Institute	High school and post-secondary programs teaching independence.	Life Development Institute Glendale, AZ Phone: 623-773-2774
LIFE Skills, Inc.	Services to enhance higher levels of independence for young adults 18+ with developmental disabilities, brain injury, or mental illness.	LIFE Skills, Inc. Iowa City, Iowa Phone: 319-354-2121
Maplebrook School	Residential and day school consisting of vocational and college programs for those 11–21.	Maplebrook School Amenia, NY Phone: 845-373-9511
Marquette University On Your Marq	Academic, social, and independent living support provided for students on the autism spectrum who are working towards a bachelor's degree.	Emily Raclaw, MS, LPC Director of On Your Marq Phone: 414-288-0203 Email: emily.raclaw@marquette.edu
Minnesota Life College	Apartment-living instructional program for young adults whose learning disabilities pose serious challenges to their independence. Must be 18+ and have completed K–12 education. Vocational skills and workforce readiness.	Minnesota Life College Richfield, MN Phone: 612-869-4008
New York Institute of Technology Vocational Independence Program	3 year certificate program for vocational major or degree program for those 18+ with significant learning disabilities and who have received special education services during high school years.	VIP Program NY Institute of Technology Central Islip, NY Phone: 631-348-3354
OPTIONS at Brehm	2 year and 4 year degree programs for young adults with complex learning disabilities.	OPTIONS at Brehm Carbondale, IL Phone: 618-457-0371
PACE Program at National Louis University	Provides integrated services to empower students aged 18–30 to become independent adults within the community.	PACE National Louis University Skokie, IL 60077 Phone: 224-233-2670 http://www.nl.edu/pace/
Pathway at UCLA	Two-year certificate program for students with developmental disabilities providing a blend of educational, social, and vocational experiences.	Pathway UCLA Extension Los Angeles, CA Phone: 310-794-1235
Riverview School	Ages 12–20 in secondary program, 19–23 in post secondary program (GROW). Co-ed residential school for students with complex language, learning, and cognitive disabilities.	Riverview School East Sandwich, MA Phone: 508-888-0489
Shepherds College	Three-year post-secondary program for students with intellectual disabilities.	Union Grove, WI Phone: 262-878-5620
Syracuse University Inclusive U	Students complete individualized coursework with mentors and Peer2Peer support, and attend weekly seminars on topics like health and wellbeing, budgeting, dating and relationships, and conflict resolution. Semester-long internships, social and extracurricular activities, and on-campus jobs help them to explore their career options and gain marketable job skills.	taishoffcenter@syr.edu Phone: 315-443-4058

Program	Overview	Contact Information
Taft College The Transition to Independent Living Program	A post-secondary educational experience for adults having developmental/intellectual disabilities. The comprehensive program provides instruction, training, and support on a community college campus. Students acquire the functional, social, and career skills necessary to live a productive and normalized lifestyle.	Aaron Markovits Program Director Phone: 661-763-7773
Texas A & M University Aggie ACHIEVE (Academic Courses in Higher Inclusive Education and Vocational Experiences)	A four-year inclusive program at Texas A & M University created to equip young adults with intellectual and developmental disabilities for future employment. ACHIEVE students live in on-campus residence halls and have access to all campus-related activities and events.	Dr. Carly Gilson FOUNDER & FACULTY DIRECTOR https://aggieachieve.tamu.edu/about/
University of Georgia Destination Dawgs	A mix of foundational courses alongside directed studies tailored to each students' interests and career goals.	Lisa Ulmer | Program Associate Director and Director of Academic Development Phone: 706-542-3457
University of Iowa R.E.A.C.H. (Realizing Educational and Career Hopes)	A 2-year certificate for students with multiple learning and cognitive disabilities.	The University of Iowa Iowa City, IA Phone: 319-384-2127
University of West Florida Argos for Autism Program (AAP)	A Beyond Access service offered by Student Accessibility Resources that provides academic, social, life skills, and career planning support to students with autism who attend the University of West Florida. The goal of the AAP is to enhance their college experience by providing assistance with navigating the college experience.	SAR at 850-474-2387 or sar@uwf.edu
University of Wisconsin-Whitewater LIFE (Learning is for Everyone) Program	A complete college experience for young adults between the ages of 18–25 who have an intellectual disability. Provides ample supports, specialized instruction, on-campus residential living, and community integration.	College of Education & Professional Studies Whitewater, WI Phone: 262-472-1905
Vista Vocational & Life Skills Center	Three year post-secondary training program for 18+ with neurological disabilities.	Vista Vocational & Life Skills Center Westbrook, CT Phone: 800-399-8080
The Washington State University College of Education ROAR (Responsibility, Opportunity, Advocacy, and Respect) Program	Two-year secondary program that provides educational opportunities and a college experience to young adults from around the country with intellectual or developmental disabilities. It closely follows WSU's land-grant mission of access, engagement, and service to the community.	Pullman, WA Phone: 509-335-2525
Wellspring Foundation	Intensive residential treatment for various populations including girls 13–18 and adults. Highly structured programs designed to treat a wide range of emotional and behavioral problems including affective, personality, attachment, eating, and traumatic stress disorders.	The Wellspring Foundation, Inc. Bethlehem, CT Phone: 203-266-8000

Recommended Websites

Independent Educational Consultants Association
www.IECAonline.com

LDA of America
www.ldanatl.org

Council for Exceptional Children
www.cec.sped.org

Council for Learning Disabilities
www.cldinternational.org

Alphabetical Index

H

I

J

K

L

M

N

O

V

W

X

The Princeton Review®

FIND AND AFFORD THE RIGHT COLLEGE FOR YOU!

From acing tests to picking the perfect school, The Princeton Review has proven resources to help students like you navigate the college admissions process.

Visit PrincetonReviewBooks.com to browse all of our products!

The Princeton Review is not affiliated with Princeton University. Test names are the registered trademarks of their respective owners, who are not affiliated with The Princeton Review.

About the Authors

Marybeth Kravets, MA, is the President of Marybeth Kravets & Associates LLC providing educational and college consulting to students with and without learning differences and is also the Director of College Counseling at Wolcott College Prep High School, Chicago, Illinois. She received her BA in Education from the University of Michigan in Ann Arbor, and her MA in Counseling from Wayne State University in Detroit, Michigan. She is a Past President of the National Association for College Admission Counseling (NACAC) and also served as the President of the Illinois Association for College Admission Counseling. Marybeth Kravets is a recipient of the Harvard University Club of Chicago Community Service Award for her lifelong dedication to serving students who are economically challenged or challenged with learning differences. Marybeth serves on the Board of Trustees for the United World College-USA and the Board of Trustees for College Bound Opportunities, Highland Park, Illinois. For additional information or to contact Marybeth Kravets for consultation email or call:

Marybeth Kravets
847-212-3687 (cell)
Marybeth@kravets.net

Imy Wax is a Psychotherapist, Licensed Clinical Professional Counselor (LCPC), National Board Certified Counselor (NBCC), Certified Educational Planner (CEP), and a Therapeutic and Educational Consultant. As a consultant, Imy travels 100,000 miles a year visiting programs, schools, colleges and post-secondary options for children, adolescents and young adults throughout the U.S. and Internationally, often as a guest speaker.

Imy is a frequent presenter at professional and parental conferences. She has authored and been quoted in numerous journal articles and conducts workshops for parents and school districts. She is also a wife, mother to four, and grandmother to seven. Her daughter was the inspiration for this book.

Imy is often called upon by mental health professionals and attorneys to assist them in identifying appropriate education and program alternatives for their students and clients. She is the founder and President of The Aspire Group (www.theaspiregroup.com). For over 30 years, Imy and her team continue to be that "objective voice," guiding, supporting, and empowering families in making an informed decision that will secure and enhance their child's future. Imy believes that there should never be a "closed door" to one's Hopes and Dreams and that today is but a stepping stone to a better tomorrow; and that each child's journey is unique to them.

For additional information or to contact Imy Wax for consultation, email or phone:

Imy Wax
847-945-0913 (office)
844-945-0913 (toll free)
+1 224-619-3558 (Skype # -International)
Imy@TheAspireGroup.com